April 18–23, 2015
Seoul, Republic of Korea

Association for Computing Machinery

Advancing Computing as a Science & Profession

SIGCHI

CHI 2015
CROSSINGS

CHI 2015

Proceedings of the

33rd Annual CHI Conference on Human Factors in Computing Systems

Sponsored by:

ACM SIGCHI

Supported by:

Samsung, Golfzon, Google, Microsoft, NAVER, SK Planet, AutoDesk, Daumkakao, Disney Research, FuturePlay, Hyundai Motor Group, Language Grid, LG, NSF, Adobe Systems, H9Works, Yonsei University, KIPFA, and Samsung Art & Design Institute

Association for
Computing Machinery

Advancing Computing as a Science & Profession

The Association for Computing Machinery
2 Penn Plaza, Suite 701
New York, New York 10121-0701

ISBN: 978-1-4503-3145-6 (Digital)

ISBN: 978-1-4503-3776-2 (Print)

Additional copies may be ordered prepaid from:

ACM Order Department
PO Box 30777
New York, NY 10087-0777, USA

Phone: 1-800-342-6626 (USA and Canada)
+1-212-626-0500 (Global)
Fax: +1-212-944-1318
E-mail: acmhelp@acm.org
Hours of Operation: 8:30 am – 4:30 pm ET

Printed in the USA

From the General and Technical Program Chairs

Welcome to CHI 2015, the premier international forum for human-computer interaction (HCI). In its early days, HCI focused on optimizing interactions between a user and a computer. Today, computers pervade our world, impacting our lives in varied and subtle ways. By never focusing solely on technology itself but always on innovations and their effects throughout human lives, HCI has increasingly come to mean *human-centered innovation.*

The theme for the conference this year is *CROSSINGS* which represents our excitement about crossing into Asia and also reflects CHI's core principle of crossing disciplines, crossing people and technology, crossing research and business, crossing physical and digital, … crossing you and me.

This year's conference brings CHI to Asia for the first time in its 33-year history, continuing the SIGCHI commitment to making CHI a truly international community. The city of Seoul represents one of many innovation centers in Asia and provides a fantastic opportunity to showcase groundbreaking content from across the region. In addition to an exciting technical program, we are holding four special symposia devoted to breakthrough insights and innovations from the Chinese, Japanese and ASEAN research communities.

The exciting keynote program features speakers who will bring fresh perspectives to CHI including Dean ***Lou Yongqi*** of Tongji University, China, a prominent global thinker on social and sustainable design; Executive VP ***Donghoon Chang***, MFA, head of Samsung Electronic's design strategy; Senior Research Fellow ***David Min***, PhD, head of the Software Center at LG Electronics; and ***PSY***, the media record breaker and innovator discussing creative methods and the impact of social media on to cross cultural boundaries.

CHI is honored this year to be the forum chosen by the recipient of one of ACM's top awards, the Athena Lecturer Award, ***Susan T. Dumais*** who developed novel algorithms and interfaces for interactive retrieval that have made it easier for people to find, use and make sense of information. She will present insights from her experiences at a special keynote session at the conference.

CHI 2015 includes two days of focused workshops and four days of technical content, including CHI's prestigious technical program, with 16 parallel sessions of rigorously reviewed research Papers, engaging Panels, Case Studies and Special Interest Groups (SIGs), an extensive Course program and invited talks from SIGCHI's award winners: Leysia Palen, Jean Scholtz, Michel Beaudouin-Lafon, Jim Hollan, Susan Dray and the new inductees to the CHI Academy.

We also host student research, design, and game competitions, and last-minute SIGs for discussing current topics. The popular alt.chi forum entered its tenth year of provocation to the HCI community. Interactivity's hands-on demonstrations showcase the best of interactive technology and innovation. The program also highlights more than 200 Work-In-Progress posters. Evening events include the CHI 2015 conference reception, Sponsors and University events, local performances and the Job Fair. Across all tracks, CHI received over 2800 submissions and accepted nearly 1000 that will appear in the ACM Digital Library.

We are deeply indebted to an enormous number of volunteers, without whom CHI 2015 would not be possible, including over 3800 reviewers, over 200 senior members of the program committee, nearly 100 members of the CHI 2015 conference organization committee and, of course, the more than 180 student volunteers. We are also deeply grateful to the ongoing support of the Korean HCI society who demonstrated incredible hospitality by moving their own conference's time and location to make room for

CHI in Seoul and who provided tremendous resources from their membership to support CHI logistically and in attracting novel content from around Asia.

We hope you will see fresh insights, strengthen connections and find new collaborators in Asia. *Above all, we hope you enjoy this unique experience of CHI 2015!*

General Conference Chairs

Bo Begole
Huawei, USA

Jinwoo Kim
Yonsei University, Korea

Technical Program Chairs

Kori Inkpen
Microsoft Research, USA

Woontack Woo
KAIST, Korea

From ACM SIGCHI's President and Vice President for Conferences

SIGCHI is proud to sponsor the premier annual conference in the field of human-computer interaction. We are extremely grateful to the CHI 2015 Conference Chairs Jinwoo Kim and Bo Begole, to Technical Program Chairs Woontack Woo and Kori Inkpen, and to their wonderful crew, who succeeded to build an impressive program and experience.

CHI 2015 is in Seoul, Korea, the first CHI ever in Asia. CHI started in Gaithersburg, MD, USA, in March 1982. That first conference in Gaithersburg drew over 900 attendees, and since then CHI, with the official name: "ACM Conference on Human Factors in Computing Systems" moved to annual, originally moving between the USA and Canada. Starting with 1993 CHI traveled between locations in Europe and North America. This year is another big step forward, made possible thanks to the Korean HCI Society that helped understand and navigate the local context, that moved its annual conference 3 months earlier to December 2014, and at the same time supported CHI's Technical Program meeting.

CHI has continued to grow and broaden its range of topics and contributing disciplines: the founding psychologists and software engineers began to meet new visions from ethnography, sociology, communication sciences and arts, among others. Relevant industries, as well as research institutes and academia, showed an increasing — and often long-lasting — interest and involvement (through volunteers and through sponsorship for conference expenses). This year's Conference Committee truly succeeded in crossing borders of all kind, providing new and unique opportunities for all participants to meet something entirely different.

CHI is an ideal forum for people to meet formally as well as informally, to exchange knowledge and views, to share experiences, and to learn. The CHI conference brings together professionals from research and practice; people from industry, academia, and from government; long-term veterans of HCI, young professionals and students; all in an environment designed to encourage interaction. We invite you to actively participate in that interaction: introduce yourself to people, interact with presenters and speakers, renew old friendships and make new ones

CHI is organized on behalf of ACM's Special Interest Group on Computer-Human Interaction (SIGCHI), an international community of professionals who share an interest in the many diverse facets of HCI. SIGCHI is committed both to advancing the field of HCI, to facilitate exchange of information within the SIGCHI community, and to support students to enter the domain.

The CHI conference is arguably the single most visible activity of SIGCHI, but we also sponsor and support a wide range of specialized conferences and workshops in areas ranging from interactive systems design to user interface technology to computer-supported cooperative work to "intelligent" user interfaces. Visit the SIGCHI website at **http://www.sigchi.org** to find our conference schedule, listing upcoming as well as past conferences.

SIGCHI and ACM produce some of the most respected publications in the field. All members receive interactions, a highly-acclaimed magazine covering the broad field of HCI and user interface design. ACM Transactions on Computer-Human Interactions (ToCHI), now in its 21st year, is our flagship journal – a quarterly publication with the top-quality archival research aimed at researchers and those translating research into practice.

SIGCHI is truly an international organization, with around 40 local chapters and 3 student chapters in 25 countries on 6 continents. We encourage all SIGCHI members to join their local chapter — or if there isn't one in your area, we would love to help you create one. And don't forget virtual communities! SIGCHI hosts dozens of electronic mailing lists on topics ranging from HCI and the Web, to HCI educations, to public policy and beyond. Those lists range from dozens of subscribers to thousands, and are an excellent way to keep up with the field and with friends and colleagues.

Finally, on behalf of ACM SGICHI, we again want to thank the conference committee and all of the hundreds of volunteers who make this conference possible. Their work makes this a rewarding experience for all of us.

Gerrit C. van der Veer
SIGCHI President

John "Scooter" Morris
SIGCHI Vice-President for Conferences

About SIGCHI

CHI 2015 is sponsored by ACM's Special Interest Group on Computer-Human Interaction (ACM SIGCHI). ACM, the Association for Computing Machinery, is an educational and scientific society uniting the world's computing educators, researchers, and professionals to inspire dialogue, share resources, and address the field's challenges. ACM strengthens the profession's collective voice through strong leadership, promotion of the highest standards, and recognition of technical excellence. ACM supports the professional growth of its members by providing opportunities for life-long learning, career development, and professional networking. ACM offers its more than 100,000 worldwide members cutting edge technical information through world class journals and magazines, dynamic special interest groups, and globally recognized conferences.

Visit www.acm.org for more information about the ACM.

SIGCHI is the premier international society for professionals, academics, and students who are interested in human-computer interaction (HCI). We provide a forum for the discussion of all aspects of HCI through our conferences, including our flagship CHI conference, publications, web sites, email discussion groups, and other services. We advance education in HCI through courses, workshops, and outreach, and we promote informal access to a wide range of individuals and organizations involved in HCI. Members can be involved in HCI-related activities with others in their region through local SIGCHI chapters. Come to the SIGCHI Town Hall meeting on Wednesday, April 22, at 12:50 to 14:30 in Room 308 or visit www.sigchi.org to learn more about SIGCHI.

Membership Information

Please contact ACM's Member Services Dept.
Online: www.acm.org
Tel: +1-800-342-6626 (USA/Canada)
+1-212-626-0500 (International)
Fax: +1-212-944-1318
Email: acmhelp@acm.org

Write:

Association for Computing Machinery, Inc.
General Post Office
P.O. Box 30777
New York, NY 10087-0777, USA

CHI 2015 Papers and Notes Chairs' Welcome

The CHI Papers and Notes programme is continuing to grow and this year! We are pleased that CHI continues to be the leading conference for research in human-computer interaction.

This year we considered more than 2120 submissions, ~600 of which were notes. This represents a continuation of ~4% annual growth in submissions. We accepted 486 submissions (~23%): 379 papers and 107 notes.

The CHI review process demands a tremendous amount of work from all areas of the human-computer interaction community. As co-chairs of the process, we are amazed at the ability of the community to organize itself to accomplish this task. We would like to thank the 2809 individual reviewers for their careful consideration of these papers. Every submission received at least three external reviews.

We also deeply appreciate the huge amount of time donated to this process by the 225-member program committee, who paid their own way to attend the face-to-face program committee meeting, an event larger than most ACM conferences.

We are proud of the work of the CHI 2015 program committee and hope that you enjoy these papers and notes, which represent the best research in human-computer interaction.

CHI 2015 Paper and Notes Chairs

Andy Cockburn
University of Canterbury

Janna McGrenere
University of British Columbia

Table of Contents

Supporting Change in Developing Countries

Privacy, Security & Interruptions

Making & Sharing Assistive Technologies

Matching & Facilitating Social Interactions

Family Communication

Session Chair: Siân Lindley, *Microsoft Research, UK*

Crowdsourcing Fans & Friends

Session Chair: Shaun Lawson, *University of Lincoln, UK*

Managing Personal Privacy

Session Chair: Sameer Patil, *Yahoo Labs, USA*

Health Sensors & Monitoring

Session Chair: Regan Mandryk, *University of Saskatchewan, Canada*

Kids Haptic, Wearable, Tangible Learning

Session Chair: Shuli Gilutz, *Interdisciplinary Center (IDC) Herzliya, Israel*

Motivation & Participation

Session Chair: Meredith Morris, *Microsoft Research, USA*

Sustainability & Recycling

Session Chair: Adrian Clear, *Lancaster University, UK*

Tangible Interactions

Session Chair: Otmar Hilliges, *ETH Zurich, Switzerland*

New Evaluation Approaches

Session Chair: David England, *Liverpool John Moores University, UK*

Evaluating Crowdsourcing

Session Chair: Bongwon Suh, *Seoul National University, Republic of Korea*

Smart Smartphone Authentication

Session Chair: Andrea Bianchi, *Sungkyunkwan University, Republic of Korea*

DIY Healthcare: Apps & Wearables

Session Chair: David Coyle, *University College Dublin*

Social Embodied Interaction

Session Chair: Gina Venolia, *Microsoft Research, USA*

Innovation in Theories & Products

Session Chair: Volker Wulf, *University of Siegen, Germany*

Design and 3D Object Fabrication

Session Chair: David Kim, *Microsoft Research, UK*

Understanding & Extending Touch Interfaces

Session Chair: Theophanis Tsandilas, *INRIA, France*

Sharing & Collaboration @ Work

Session Chair: Steven Drucker, *Microsoft Research, USA*

Families and Their Use of Technology

Session Chair: Jennifer Marlow, *Carnegie Mellon University, USA*

Understanding Crowdwork in Many Domains

Session Chair: Uichin Lee, *Korea Advanced Institute of Science and Technology, South Korea*

Player Performance & Experience in Games

Session Chair: Jan Smeddinck, *University of Bremen, Germany*

Neighborhoods & Disadvantaged Communities

Session Chair: Katharina Reinecke, *University of Michigan, USA*

Enhanced Security with Passwords & CAPTCHAs

Session Chair: Serge Egelman, *University of California, Berkeley, USA*

Accessibility at Home & on The Go

Session Chair: Hironobu Takagi, *IBM Research, Japan*

Telepresence Video, Robots, and Walls

Experience Design for Games

Digital & Materials Fabrication

Tactile Notifications for Phones & Wearables

Visualizing Statistics & Graphs

Session Chair: Benjamin Bach, *INRIA, France*

Understanding Everyday Use of Mobile Phones

Session Chair: Matt Jones, *Swansea University, UK*

GUI Size, Resolution & Layout

Session Chair: Enrico Rukzio, *Institute of Media Informatics, Germany*

Kids Social, Emotional & Special Needs

Session Chair: Konstantinos Kazakos, *Newcastle University, UK*

HCI for Civic Engagement

Security Feedback & Warnings

Wellness & Wearables

Task Interruption & Resumption

Using Random Body Parts for Input

Session Chair: Patrick Baudisch, *Hasso Plattner Institute, Germany*

Brain & Physiological Data use for HCI

Session Chair: Jacob Robert, *Tufts University, USA*

Software Engineering Tools

Session Chair: Feng Tian, *Chinese Academy of Sciences, China*

HCI at Home

Session Chair: David Geerts, *Social Spaces, Belgium*

UX Methods 4

Session Chair: Benjamin Hanrahan, *Xerox Research Center Europe, France*

Augmented & Virtual Reality in the Real World

Session Chair: Morten Fjeld, *Chalmers University of Technology, Sweden*

Gesture Elicitation & Recognition

Session Chair: Niels Henze, *University of Stuttgart, Germany*

Programming Environments

Session Chair: Joonhwan Lee, *Seoul National University, Republic of Korea*

Digital Collections, Practice & Legacy

Session Chair: Will Odom, *Simon Fraser University, Canada*

Multilingual Communication

Session Chair: Hao-Chuan Wang, *National Tsing Hua University, Taiwan*

Empowering Users

Session Chair: Maarten Thissen, *The Hague University of Applied Sciences, The Netherlands*

Accessibility for Vision Impaired Users

Session Chair: Xiaojuan Ma, *Huawei Technologies, Hong Kong*

Understanding Gamers

Session Chair: Toni-Jan Keith Monserrat, *National University of Singapore, Singapore*

Bridging Communities

Session Chair: Edward Cutrell, *Microsoft Research India, India*

Gender & Technology

Session Chair: Antonella De Angeli, *University of Trento, Italy*

Email & Social Media at Work

Session Chair: Pernille Bjorn, *IT University of Copenhagen, Denmark*

Understanding & Protecting Kids Tech Use

Session Chair: Svetlana Yarosh, *University of Minnesota, USA*

Social Media & Citizen Science

Session Chair: Elena Glassman, *Massachusetts Institute of Technology, USA*

Disasters & Humanitarian Events

Session Chair: Tawanna Dillahunt, *University of Michigan, USA*

Home Physiotherapy & Rehabilitation

Session Chair: Yi-Ping Hung, *National Taiwan University, Taiwan*

Interaction Techniques for Tables & Walls

Session Chair: Tom Bartindale, *Newcastle University, UK*

Interacting with GUIs

Session Chair: David Flatla, *University of Dundee, UK*

CHI 2015 Organization

General Conference Chairs
Jinwoo Kim, *Yonsei University, Korea*
Bo Begole, *Huawei, USA*

Technical Program

Technical Program Chairs
Woontack Woo, *KAIST, Korea*
Kori Inkpen, *Microsoft Research, USA*

Papers
Andy Cockburn, *University of Canterbury, New Zealand*
Joanna McGrenere, *University of British Columbia, Canada*
Jun Rekimoto, *University of Toyko, Japan*

Case Studies
Danielle Cooley, *DGCooley Consulting, USA*
Joonhwan Lee, *Seoul National University, Korea*

Courses
Regina Bernhaupt, *ICS-IRIT, France*
Matt Jones, *Swansea University, UK*

Interactivity
Julie Rico Williamson, *University of Glasgow, UK*
Juhyun Eune, *Seoul National University, Korea*

Video Showcase
Jinwook Seo, *Seoul National University, Korea*
Rodrigo de Oliveira, *Google, USA*

SIGs
Enrico Rukzio, *Ulm University, Germany*
Simone Barbosa, *PUC-Rio, Brazil*

Doctoral Consortium
Si-Jung "Jun" Kim, *University of Central Florida, USA*
Jaime Teevan, *Microsoft Research, USA*
Sue Fussell, *Cornell University, USA*

Workshops
Juergen Steimle, *Max Planck Institute for Informatics, Germany*
Bongshin Lee, *Microsoft Research, USA*

Works in Progress
Shamsi Iqbal, *Microsoft Research, USA*
Shaun Lawson, *University of Lincoln, UK*
Shendong Zhao, *National University of Singapore, Singapore*

Student Research Competition
Seungyon "Claire" Lee, *Google, USA*
Geehyuk Lee, *KAIST, Korea*

Student Design Competition
Youn-Kyung Lim, *KAIST, Korea*
Anirudha Joshi, *ITT Bombay, India*

Student Game Competition
Floyd Muller, *RMIT University, Australia*
Alessandro Canossa, *Northeastern University, USA*
Soojin Jun, *Yonsei University, Korea*

alt.chi
Silvia Lindtner, *University of California, Irvine, USA*
Morgan Ames, *Intel, USA*
Henry Duh, *University of Tasmania, Australia*

TOCHI Papers
Jeffrey Nichols, *IBM Research, USA*

Best of CHI Awards
Mark Billinghurst, *University of Canterbury, New Zealand*

Panels
Khai Truong, *University of North Carolina, Charlotte, USA*
Elaine M. Huang, *University of Zurich, Switzerland*

Conference Theme Chair
Kyle Hyunsuk Kim, *Hongik University, Korea*

Industry Liaison
Garett Dworman, *TecEd, USA*

Operations

Chair's Assistant
Yoojin Lee, *Yonsei University, Korea*

Chair's Assistant
Nik Martelaro, *Stanford University, USA*

Student Volunteer
Jon Haber, *University of Calgary, Canada*
Siroberto Scerbo, *Virginia Tech, USA*
Jieun Wee, *Seoul National University, Korea*

Technology Liaisons
Sara Drenner, *University of Minnesota-Twin Cities, USA*
Scooter Morris, *University of California, San Francisco, USA*

Webmaster
Juho Kim, *MIT, USA*
TJ Monserrat, *National University of Singapore, Singapore*

Social Media
Max Wilson, *Nottingham University, UK*
Kwangsu Cho, *Sungkyunkwan University, Korea*

Data Managerment
Max Van Kleek, *University of Southampton, UK*
BoYu Gao, *Konkuk University, Korea*

Proceedings
Deana Brown, *Georgia Tech, USA*
Jaejeung Kim, *KAIST, Korea*

Infrastructure Accessibility Chair
Jongbae Kim, *Yonsei University, Korea*

Digital Accessibility Chair
Jeff Bigham, *University of Rochester, USA*

Scheduling
Christophe Hurter, *ENAC, France*
Juho Kim, *MIT, USA*

Mobile Apps
Stephen Oney, *Carnegie Mellon University, USA*
Eiji Hayashi, *Carnegie Mellon University, USA*
Jason Wiese, *Carnegie Mellon University, USA*
Célia Martinie, *Université Paul Sabatier, France*

Video Previews
Fanny Chevalier, *INRIA, France*
Stéphane Huo, *Université Paris-Sud, France*

Posters
Hyun Joo Song, *Seoul National University, Korea*

Translations
Sue Fussell, *Cornell University, USA*
Naomi Yamashita, *NTT, Japan*

Local Hospitality
Junho Choi, *Yonsei University, Korea*

Sponsors, Exhibits & Recruitment
Carol Klyver, *Foundations of Excellence, USA*

Registration
Yvonne Lopez, *Executive Events, Inc. USA*
Brooke Daley, *Executive Events, Inc. USA*

PCS Liaisons
Max van Kleek, *University of Southampton, UK*
Carol Klyver, *Foundations of Excellence, USA*
Scooter Morris, *University of California, San Francisco, USA*

Demand in My Pocket: Mobile Devices and the Data Connectivity Marshalled in Support of Everyday Practice

Carolynne Lord, Mike Hazas, Adrian K. Clear, Oliver Bates, Rosalind Whittam, Janine Morley, and Adrian Friday
Lancaster University, UK
{c.lord, m.hazas, a.clear, o.bates, r.whittam, j.morley, a.friday}@lancaster.ac.uk

ABSTRACT
This paper empirically explores the role that mobile devices have come to play in everyday practice, and how this links to demand for network connectivity and online services. After a preliminary device-logging period, thirteen participants were interviewed about how they use their iPhones or iPads. Our findings build a picture of how, through use of such devices, a variety of daily practices have come to depend upon a working data connection, which sometimes surges, but is at least always a trickle. This aims to inform the sustainable design of applications, services and infrastructures for smartphones and tablets. By focusing our analysis in this way, we highlight a little-explored challenge for sustainable HCI and discuss ideas for (re)designing around the principle of 'light-weight' data 'needs'.

Author Keywords
Sustainability; mobile devices; practices; energy; network demand

ACM Classification Keywords
H.5.2 Information Interfaces and Presentation: Miscellaneous

INTRODUCTION
"You have the power to create, shape, and share your life. It's right there in your hand. Or bag. Or pocket."

– iPhone 5S advert

There can be little doubt that the development, adoption and use of mobile computing technologies changes experiences of daily life, if only in subtle ways. A defining aspect is the 'connectivity', both social and network, that such mobile, ready-to-hand devices facilitate. Whilst there is a rich literature exploring consequences of social ('always on') connectivity for family life and wellbeing [29], there is little consideration of the environmental consequences of the increasingly intensive and extensive forms of mobile network connectivity that appear to be developing. In general, network traffic is significant from an energy perspective. By proportion, the energy required to operate the network and data centres is estimated to be about half that used to power domestic ICT goods [4, 30]. Some predict that this proportion will further increase as 'thinner' more efficient consumer devices become standard and as processing and storage functions are increasingly carried out 'in the cloud': from an estimated 25% of the total energy consumption associated with the production, network operation and in-home use of ICT and entertainment devices in 2012, to 50% by 2017 [4]. As this prediction indicates, the network aspects of ICT-related practices are changing. Expectations of what forms of content can be accessed, and when, are increasing, as pervasive high-bandwidth connectivity (e.g. public Wi-Fi, LTE) and services that make use of it, are instigated, marketed and used.

In this paper, we investigate the data demand associated with smartphones and tablets, as opposed to other computing technologies such as laptops, given that (1) these small, battery-powered devices allow data to be consumed at many places in and outside the home, alongside more conventional computing; (2) they require that modern mobile data networks (3G/LTE) be provisioned and able to handle demand at peak times; and (3) the energy demand arising from data associated with mobile devices is high, relative to the energy it takes to charge them.

Based on the assumption that energy and data are used primarily in the accomplishment of social practices (e.g. [20, 27]) we aim to develop a better understanding of the sources and patterns of demand through a practice-based analysis of mobile device use, supplemented with fine grained measures of network and application use. This frames critical challenges for the (re)design of mobile applications and services to foreground sustainability, specifically lighter-weight forms of network connectivity. We offer some suggestions of how this might be achieved.

RELATED WORK
Research into the environmental consequences of the growth of Internet traffic and 'cloud-based' services has

CHI 2015, April 18 - 23 2015, Seoul, Republic of Korea
Copyright 2015 ACM 978-1-4503-3145-6/15/04...$15.00
http://dx.doi.org/10.1145/2702123.2702162

largely focused on the challenge of quantifying the energy used (e.g. [5, 6, 22-24]) and exploring possible future trends (e.g. [4, 18]). However, much uncertainly remains: Coroama and Hilty [5] show four orders of magnitude (1000 times) difference among estimates of Internet-related energy demand, expressed in kilowatt-hours per gigabyte. More recent estimates focus on particular components of the Internet and the delivery of specific services, and tend to be more modest (e.g. 0.052kWh/GB in 2014 for core networks [22] compared with 7kWh/GB in 2008 for core, access and business servers [30]).

Yet, even modest estimates of the electricity intensity of Internet traffic reveal its significance. This is especially so for mobile devices, where the energy used by core networks, access networks and consumer routers to deliver digital content outweighs that used directly to charge the devices [22, 24]. In fact, mobile networks can be especially energy intensive when delivering video content [24]. Whilst there has been some discussion of how to manage and reduce the volumes of data more generally – including user feedback, reducing video resolution depending on context, improving web design and caching [18, 24] – this has not so far considered mobile devices in particular and how they are used.

One consideration for reducing data flows is the distinction between overall and peak demand [18]. The latter is growing for both mobile (cellular) and home (broadband) services as it co-evolves with service provisioning [21]. Because social networking and real-time ("on demand") streaming of content is rising, the largest peaks are becoming more pronounced. The most recent estimates have suggested that streaming makes up about 40% of the prime time traffic in Europe (home and mobile), and in the US (mobile); on US home networks, it is about 60% of the prime time traffic. "This continuing phenomena means network operators need to be doing their capacity planning around peak growth rates", instead of aggregate monthly consumption [21, p. 28].

Kawsar and Brush studied the use of mobile devices in 86 homes using aggregate router logs of networked applications, supplemented with surveys and interviews in a subset of the homes [11]. They explored how different factors (such as screen size) affect which device is chosen to perform a specific activity; and also where (living room, kitchen) and what time of day these activities tended to be performed. Whilst there was no report of the data demand associated with particular applications, they did show higher occurrences of most networked applications in the late afternoon and evening [11, fig.4].

Numerous studies have looked at particular aspects of smartphone usage, for example measuring and improving battery life by altering people's awareness and management of apps [1]; creating understandings of how mobiles and their apps have changed webpage visits [28]; how this might relate to social and economic status [19]; what time of day apps are typically opened and for how long [2]; and how smartphone usage differs in those who might be considered "at risk" to technological addiction [12]. These analyses have been presented in a primarily quantitative way, with implications pointing to ways to further enhance smartphone interaction, or otherwise to help manage it.

In contrast to previous discussions of reducing the environmental impacts of 'consumer' IT use (e.g. [20]) this paper focuses specifically on the impacts of, and demand for, data connectivity. It seeks to explore the basis of data demand in everyday life and hence offer new insights. This follows in the footsteps of practice-based studies in other areas (e.g. [3, 27]).

METHODS AND PARTICIPANTS

We recruited thirteen participants to take part in a mobile device-use study. The study focused on smartphone (Apple iPhone) use for six of them, and tablet (Apple iPad) use for the other seven. No participants were studied for both. Flyers were distributed throughout the university and then further participants were recruited through the researchers' social networks. Participants consisted of students, university administration staff, a teacher and a stay at home mother. There was no financial incentive for taking part in the study. Pseudonyms are used throughout.

The study consisted of two parts. In the first, a software logger was installed on each participant's device, which recorded minutely traces of the power state of the device, battery levels, mobile and Wi-Fi data usage, the foreground app, and the state of the screen. These were recorded locally on the device and transferred from it before the second study part. For each of the participants, the logger ran on their device, collecting data for at least two weeks (11 days for Sarah). Whilst this data allowed us to understand the types of activities that the participants carried out on their devices, it was not possible to explicitly link app use to specific practices and, as such, interviews were necessary to uncover how app use was situated in everyday life.

A semi-structured interview was carried out with each participant covering a number of topics related to mobile device usage, including: typical practices that included mobile device use, mobile and Wi-Fi connectivity management and use, power management and charging practices, and times of uses. The interview questions were tailored to account for differences between phone and tablet devices. Graphs of app use, charging times and connectivity were prepared and introduced towards the end to encourage further elicitation. These ranged from under twenty minutes to one hour. They were fully transcribed, and then independently open-coded by two researchers. These were then consolidated and re-coded for emerging themes.

Name	Device	Top 3 Apps by Foreground time (% network use)	Other significant network users (%)	Notable areas of practice (from interviews)	Wi-Fi (mobile) daily demand in megabytes	
					Median	Max
Joel	iPhone 4	Text Messaging (5.2%) Safari (5.1%), Twitter (2.6%)	Remote speaker (37.2%), NoApp (29.5%)	Social networking, boredom, email, news, shopping, cycling	76 (10)	445 (71)
Colin	iPhone 5	Orchestra (Todo's, 17.6%), Safari (7.9%), Phone (5.8%)	Own App (38.5%), NoApp (18.1%)	Work, communication, relaxing	32 (45)	299 (100)
Ben	iPhone 4	Email (6.6%), Phone (5.2%), Facebook (5.1%)	NoApp (58.2%)	Boredom, work, social networking	44 (12)	599 (32)
Martin	iPhone 4	Text Messaging (1.2%), Tumblr (73.5%), Safari (1.7%)		Communication, blogging, socialising	355 (0)	1592 (4)
Daniel	iPhone 4	Alarm (4%), Text Messaging (4%), Safari (9.1%)	Youtube (28.2%)	Social networking, browsing, online shopping	86 (6)	330 (21)
Sarah	iPhone 4	Text Messaging (7.8%), Phone (0.6%), Email (2.3%)	NoApp (46.6%)	Exercise, work, communication, email, killing time	25 (5)	97 (19)
Kathryn	iPad 3 (3G)	BBC News (4.8%), Alarm (0.3%), Gmail (4.2%)	NoApp (25%), Skype (40.5%)	Work, home, media, communication, gaming, email	95 (0)	1182 (32)
Pete	iPad 2	iBooks (6.4%), Dictaphone (6.4%) Safari (77.1%)		Table-top games, university	6 (0)	61 (0)
Mandy	iPad 2	Facebook (7.7%), Safari (13.8%), Youtube (38.3%)		Cooking, socializing, work	518	4388
Rebecca	iPad Mini 1	Amazon Player (8%), Safari (9.8%), Facebook (43.8%)	NoApp (23.1%)	Socialising, organisation, work,	95	460
Jenni	iPad Mini 1	Safari (15.5%), Words w/ Friends (0.3%), Email (4.9%)	Preferences (58.4%), NoApp (19.2%)	Home, Reading, Browsing	15	285
Bill	iPad 1	Imo (messaging, 9.2%), Safari (66%), NY Times (20.3%)		Work, research, browsing	33	952
Erica	iPad Mini 2	Safari (30%), YouTube (39.5%), Pinterest (0.7%)	NoApp (3.1%)	Communication, research, work, gaming, TV, browsing	130	1252

Table 1: Description of participants' uses of their devices

OVERVIEW OF DATA DEMAND AND DEVICE USE

The participants' uses of their devices has been summarised in Table 1. The top three apps were devised based on their time in the foreground; 'other' network uses relate to data needed for processes running in the background. 'NoApp' refers to the demand associated with in-app, and device updates which the user did not directly request.

Medians typically ranged from the tens to hundreds of megabytes; and daily maximums stretched from hundreds of megabytes, to over four gigabytes. On average, these levels of data flow seem to be within typical bounds for European users at the time of the research (2014): reported as 13.3 MB per day on mobile networks and 705.7 MB per day on fixed networks (which includes other domestic Internet access) [21].

Our participants' devices had daily direct energy demand due to charging from around 1.8Wh (Sarah) to 4.2Wh (Ben) for phones, and 2.5Wh (Rebecca) to 25.8Wh (Kathryn) for tablets, due to their larger screens and batteries.

To put these data demands into an energy context, we apply a modest estimate of electricity intensity for accessing these services via the Internet. In the absence of a current and general purpose estimate, we use a figure of 0.2 kWh/GB (a composite from [22, 23, 24] which reflects data centre, access and core networks, and assumes a mix of text and video traffic). A daily use of 100MB might equate to 20Wh via Wi-Fi (approximately double that, 35Wh, over 3G/LTE). For phones and small tablet in particular, this is an order of magnitude greater than the typical daily charging energy we observed.

Yet, if the energy per GB estimate is realistic, it might take several years for data connectivity to exceed the impacts of manufacturing and transporting the mobile devices. These range from 29 (iPhone 4)[1] to 60 kgCO2e (iPhone 5) for phones, and from 75 (iPad 2 and iPad Mini 1) to 135 kgCO2e (iPad 3 and Mini 2) for tablets. To put that in energy terms, equivalent emissions from the UK electricity

[1] Apple. 2010-2014. iPhone and iPad Environmental Reports, https://www.apple.com/uk/environment/reports/, last accessed 15th January 2015.

grid correspond to 50–200 kWh (depending on device model).

FINDINGS: DATA DEMAND IN CONTEXT

The findings are structured as follows, (1) most dominant use of the mobile device, practices of non-traditional communication – or filling time; (2) the supporting of other non-IT related practices; (3) an investigation of those practices where the mobile device was unable to stabilize as a material element of that practice; (4) more traditional practices associated with that device and (5) other, non-practice data demand findings.

Keeping up with the world ...or filling time?

The logging data and supplementary interviews revealed the wide variety of platforms and techniques to stay in contact with social networks. The discussion of more 'traditional' communication (i.e. phone calls and SMS messages) will be dealt with later.

Whilst iPad participants – Mandy, Erica and Rebecca – all reported an increase in the number of platforms used for social networking or email; they had all originally used at least one of these platforms before acquiring the device. Mandy, Rebecca, Kathryn and Erica noted that their use of these had increased since acquiring their iPads. Whilst for Kathryn this meant that her device had led her to develop an '*auto email-checking reflex*', others discussed the way in which their devices allowed them to easily and quickly access and use their social media platforms, which had then impacted on the frequency of their use.

"sometimes I'll get bored, and say that I'm going on my iPad for 10 minutes to check something and I'll be there 45 minutes, because something's led me to something else, and something else and something else" (Mandy, iPad)

The combination of notifications and ease of access to these platforms meant that for these participants, it had become easier and quicker to check these accounts; to satisfy the expectation of knowing what was happening online. This has paradoxically been said to be the result of too much frequent checking; which forms a habit [28].

Investigation into those participants that owned an iPhone, however, revealed that whilst there was certainly evidence to suggest that non-traditional communication was carried out through these devices, it was with a different motivation to that which was evident with the iPad users. Here, participants noted the way in which social media and email notifications were dealt with; activating what would otherwise be 'dead time'. Dead time has been defined as the "small pockets of time not focused on one specific activity and often perceived as 'unproductive time', like waiting for the bus or commuting" [20]. Whilst this 'dead' time has always existed, it is the increased possibility of being able to use this time 'productively' which has repainted it as dead; as it is in moments where we are unable to use time 'effectively' in which they are perceived as dead, or empty.

Smart mobile devices are hugely powerful information and entertainment devices, placing the World Wide Web, social networks, media and games in the user's pocket. They are designed and marketed to be always to hand, and quickly and easily drawn upon. Given that smartphones are designed to be carried around it is no surprise then that one of their most prevalent places in everyday life has come to be one of filling this otherwise 'dead' time.

"Uh I suppose when I'm out and about I probably use my social networks more, 'cause I'm bored" (Colin, iPhone)

They are frequently unsheathed in life's periods of transition; while waiting, bored, or travelling. It is because of their multifaceted nature, however, that the use of dead time was not restricted to non-traditional communication and some participants such as Daniel noted the use of other apps, like YouTube for the filling of this dead time.

The use of the device to fill dead time was not limited to the iPhone, and similarities were seen in those participants who owned an iPad. Despite this, the scales of time that our participants reported to fill with mobile device usage differed, and ranged from a few minutes to an hour. This led to variation in the activity carried out. iPad participants could be seen to speak of filling larger chunks of time (up to an hour), and this practice was quite structured and routine: in Pete's case, it involved filling time between scheduled university lectures:

"I do that if I've got an hour free... I mean not now, I'm doing coursework, but usually I'd have, say an hour between lectures, I'd get my iPad out, go on Wikipedia, Or TV Tropes, perhaps, as that's my weakness (laughs). Erm, and... just sort of peruse that for a while." (Pete, iPad)

In contrast, the iPhone participants spoke about using their mobile devices to stimulate themselves for a few spare minutes when periods of free time or boredom arose. Some examples of such periods that participants listed are: times when they are waiting, coffee breaks, and social situations that were not stimulating enough.

As this indicates, dead time can occur during the enactment of existing practices, like travelling or cooking. Both Joel and Pete used their mobile devices during bus journeys to browse the Internet or check for updates. In Pete's case, this practice was enabled by the availability of Wi-Fi on the bus. For many participants, the mobile device had come to play an important bedtime role, being called upon last thing before sleeping and first thing in the morning. And, for Joel, mobile device use made the mundane activity of cooking more bearable:

"But then sometimes... especially when I'm in my kitchen, cooking and I'm waiting for something to cook, I'll be constantly refreshing it because I'm bored and I want some... stimulation." (Joel, iPhone)

From our participants' accounts, it is clear that, aside from the affordances of the mobile device itself, the design of mobile applications and models for presenting and accessing content play a major role in data demand for filling time. Certain applications are conducive to a quick distraction. For example, the abundance of free games in the App Store that can be easily browsed, installed, played once, and forgotten about thereafter. Social networking applications like Twitter and Facebook can be relied upon for almost constant updates of content that can be quickly and easily accessed. Not only do such applications promise immediate relief from boredom, but also they are conducive to feelings of needing to stay in touch and updated. Without regular attention, content builds up, becomes unmanageable, potentially missed, and dated.

Supporting practices in new ways

In this section we shall explore those practices which were previously non-IT related, to demonstrate – as others have done [20] – how the integration of mobile devices can be seen to increase the energy, or data intensity, of that practice. Various participants discussed the way they had incorporated their devices into practices that they previously enacted without the use of a technology. Sarah reported her use of the Strava app to log her running times and distances, which then allowed her to share this data with her friends – something which she felt was an important motivating factor for the enactment of this practice.

"yeah the social side of it really helps because you're kind of held a bit more accountable because your friends can see whether you've been or not, and they comment on the fact that you've not been in a while or they can help you motivate yourself, saying 'You did really well', or 'You did it really quickly.'" (Sarah, iPhone)

From this, we can see that not only has the iPhone been successfully incorporated into the practice of running for Sarah, but this was a conscious desire on her part; trying out various apps to enable this incorporation. Pete, on the other hand, had incorporated his iPad into his learning practices by audio recording his lectures, which in turn allowed him to revise by listening back over these lectures. Whilst this integration could not be said to transform the practice beyond recognition, new features had been added to Pete's enactment of this. The iPad – and the functionalities it provides – had enabled a new way of working and Pete talked of its uses in understanding notes he had made earlier in the year, which could otherwise be confusing.

"It's why I have them on there really. It's so, when I look back at my notes I've got stuff that I've got written down at the time...which doesn't always makes sense [...] whatever I've actually got there, can then be delivered in context to how it was given." (Pete, iPad)

Others, however, could be seen to use their devices in a more supportive role. Joel used his phone to navigate and track his cycling routes, and to stream music from a music library server during the cycling practice. This supportive role was more prevalent in the discussions with iPad users who noted the importance of its screen size and the convenience it offered to this type of use. One such usage was that of background noise. Mandy, who described herself as a sociable person, recounted the way in which she had begun to use her iPad as a source of background noise to support domestic practices, like cooking, eating, studying, and sleeping, in an otherwise quiet home. This was mostly with YouTube, the total demand for which was 10GB over 5 weeks. This use of the iPad had extended to support her working practices, increasing the sense of comfort and convenience.

"[...] I'll be writing an essay on my laptop and have a film or something on my iPad playing, so I don't have to switch tabs so I can constantly be on my laptop." (Mandy, iPad)

Other examples, where the practice itself was transformed by the integration of the device, included Mandy's use of her iPad as a second screen for lecture slides when she was working on essays on her laptop; or Rebecca's use of her iPad for additional entertainment when watching TV she did not enjoy with her parents.

Migrated practices

So far we have seen how the new ubiquitous functionalities provided by mobile devices have increased data demand by extending or supporting existing practices to enable new forms of these. There are, however, practices which would have previously have been carried out through other IT means, and had now migrated over to mobile devices, such as video calling (i.e. Skype) and media watching. Colin, who could be seen to have a 24-hour connection to his work life, discussed the way in which his iPhone had allowed him to use Skype on the go. Further investigation revealed that use of this particular app, however, was restricted to the instant messaging abilities, and any video calls were carried out through what he felt was a suitable device, a PC. For Kathryn, however, her iPad and its mobile data connection had allowed her to use Skype outside of Wi-Fi areas. This, however, was limited to special occasions.

"That would have been when I Skyped my dad form the hospital, 'cause he couldn't make it over to see the baby. So everyone was there, and I sent to my Mam 'Get Dad on Skype', and I put him on so that he could see a video of the baby" (Kathryn, iPad)

On this occasion almost 800MB of mobile data was consumed, in making the half-an-hour Skype video call.

Given the way in which mobile devices have been positioned by their manufacturers, and the surrounding advertising campaigns and discourses, as ideal devices for media watching and listening, it was surprising that the participants reported only using their devices for these, under specific conditions. Whilst those iPhone participants only reported the use of their devices for media when they were out and about, to fill dead time, the iPad participants found that their devices were only used when convenience was necessitated over comfort. When there was a more 'suitable' device available, these resources were usually drawn upon. For example, Kathryn – who worked away from home for long periods of time – found that her iPad was ideal to stream media from online services, rather than taking her heavier laptop away with her too.

By contrast, Bill reported the most use of his iPad's media capabilities; employing its use mostly as a music player. This, however, was again in those times where his more suitable, and specific music devices, were unavailable or unsuitable i.e. when his iPod ran out of battery or when he wanted to play music through speakers. This type of use was also seen to be employed by Rebecca:

"Sometimes I'll listen to it on the bus too, like for music, but that's only if my iPod has ran out of battery or, I have something on my iPad which isn't on my iPod like I have Amazon Music on my iPad. I've been using that quite a lot recently, which is not what I'd normally use, because I've just bought an album and it's taking ages to send to me – in the post– so I have it on Amazon Music and was just accessing it through that." (Rebecca, iPad)

Here, data demand can be seen to be increased by the availability of online services such as Amazon Cloud Player which now offer the possibility of listening to music which has been ordered in a physical form from the online marketplace, whilst the customer waits for the order to be delivered. Although the total demand for this app was relatively small at 88MB, it must be considered that this was in addition to energy arising from manufacture and transport of the physical CD, and simply supported listening to the music while waiting for the CD to arrive.

Enduring practices

Interestingly, by contrast, we also saw practices that did not comfortably extend to the mobile environment in spite of functionality being available to support them. Almost all participants related a practice that their mobile device was capable of playing a part in, but the device was deemed inadequate in some way. Internet browsing was one of the most common examples across smartphone participants. There were various reasons for this, and they were always linked to the availability (close proximity in time and space) of a more suitable laptop or PC. Sarah found connection speeds to be too slow on her phone and the screen size too small for comfortable browsing. Joel had a similar opinion but spoke of particular content (e.g. for comparison purposes) that was unsuitable for phone browsing.

One particular form of browsing that usually did not take place on iPhone devices was online shopping. Again, constraints of the device were linked to the amount of content from various sources that was being consumed, and also the amount of clicks that this process usually involved. Online shopping on eBay was an exception to this. This is partly due to the app being considered well-designed for mobile use, but also because the auctioning model of shopping that it supports – where auctions could end at any time of the day and where the end point required, or attracted, the most attention, i.e. raising bids – was more suited to mobile use and sporadic interaction. Whilst the iPad participants did not discuss this particular problem, possibly due to the bigger screen size; they did note another limitation which had impacted on the devices incorporation into practices. Whilst seven of the participants owned iPads, only one had a mobile data enabled tablet; the others only supported a Wi-Fi connection and, as such, were spatially bound to areas that had a connection. This can be seen to not only affect the use of the device, but the expectations of its user. Rebecca could be seen to be frustrated at its inability to allow her to make use of the dead time, on her commute. Meanwhile Kathryn – whose iPad was mobile enabled – discussed the way in which it allowed for more 'flexibility'. This flexibility, however, was not understood to be the same as a phone and the management of data connection was stricter here, to avoid incurring additional charges. The others – when questioned about their lack of a mobile data plan – cited economic factors as a reason for their avoidance of these particular models and it could be said that given the ubiquity of smartphones – and the cost of a data plan – an additional data plan for their iPad was not perceived to be a necessity.

Many of participants – iPhone and iPad – considered their mobile devices to be unsuitable for lengthy textual correspondence. While text messages and social network chatter were comfortably received and responded to on the go using mobile devices, email was done single-facedly: incoming emails were read, often in response to push notifications, but replies were usually composed on a more suitable typing device. Although the iPad's onscreen keyboard is larger than the iPhone's, this was echoed by Kathryn, who – dependent on time – would answer her emails on her laptop.

"So I guess I'd probably also switch to the laptop if I didn't have a lot of time, or I wanted to do some emails quickly or something. Quite often I'll read the emails on the iPad, and then I'll unread them, so it highlights, and [I'll] answer [them] on the laptop." (Kathryn, iPad)

More 'traditional' uses of the device

The interview data revealed that despite the many ways in which the participants had incorporated their iPhones into their previously established configurations of practices, they were still highly valued for their ability to send and receive traditional phone calls and SMS messages. For example, Sarah, who had been seen to incorporate her iPhone into the practice of running – in what could be described as a data-intensive way – reported phone calls and texts to be the *'thing [she'd] miss the most'*, if she lost her phone, given that her other technologies did not allow this.

Given that the discussion of the findings has revealed that iPads are not similar to iPhones; in either their use, or meaning, we are positioning the traditional use of this as an eBook Reader. This is the consequence of most of the iPad participants noting this particular use, and the form of the device itself lending it to direct comparisons to e-Readers. Pete used his device the most in this way, having downloaded rule books for tabletop games, which allowed him and his friends to refer to these during gameplay.

"For gaming, you tend to have just a whole selection of source books on there which just... so maybe just to share around the group, "This is what you've got," "this is what you're trying to do," etc. I'll hand it over to them because someone in my group, has a character that does various things, they don't exactly know the wording of it [...] and we've got this tablet to share so everyone's got what they need, all the time." (Pete, iPad)

Similarly, Kathryn discussed her use of the iPad for this. Although again, the use here could be described as somewhat of a portal to resources. Her work in an archive meant that she was unable to physically move the documents outside of her place of work and the iPad allowed her access to these, through the use of the online service Dropbox.

App and device maintenance

Having discussed the everyday practices into which mobile devices were (un)successfully incorporated, or used to support, we will now move on to discuss other data demand findings related to the management of these devices, i.e. their apps and data use. There were various participants, such as Martin, Ben and Colin, who exhibited an awareness of the data demand associated with app updates and notifications, although they noted this in terms of constraints associated with their data allowance plans. Whilst some actively managed their connectivity to avoid exceeding their allowances – which will be discussed in more detail in the following section – there was evidence to suggest that others enabled automatic updates and notifications for the added functionality that it brought to the app. For example, Sarah discussed the way in which her Strava app updated to sync her running data to her profile, which was enabled by her mobile data plan.

"It tends to happen while I'm out, because I hit stop on the app and then it sends it straight away so it syncs." (Sarah, iPhone)

Although it is difficult to compare, given that no iPhone participant left their device unpowered for more than a night, participants who left their iPads off for more than a few hours were seen to incur data demand peaks after having recharged, and powered them up. For example, having left her device unpowered for eight consecutive days, the logs demonstrated that upon powering up and staying on the Home screen (no foreground app), Erica's iPad consumed 800MB of Wi-Fi data.

Whilst the data demand associated with updating an app and its notifications is relatively small, when these have accumulated after a period of a few days; over many apps, they amass to a small peak in data demand.

Connectivity management

Management of data usage and connectivity varied across participants. Generally, smartphone participants always had at least Wi-Fi or mobile data switched on, and sometimes both. The actual data configuration employed was linked to convenience or cost. Three participants (Sarah, Ben, and Daniel) left both their mobile and Wi-Fi data switched on all the time so that they automatically connect as required. Martin switched Wi-Fi off when his battery is low, but otherwise left it constantly always on, whereas mobile data was on infrequently to ensure that he did not get charged. By contrast, Joel regularly switched Wi-Fi off to avoid being automatically connected to public hotspots that required him to enable connectivity through a log in screen. He preferred to use mobile data as an alternative, finding this more convenient.

Out of the seven participants who owned an iPad, only Kathryn had a mobile data contract associated with her device. This allowed her to avoid the strict pre-planning of downloads for their use on the go. Most iPad participants were Wi-Fi only and did not see the value in managing this connection; leaving it on and ready to use, for those times where they found themselves in an area which was Wi-Fi enabled. None of these participants turned their devices off, when not in use and left them in standby, citing good battery life and convenience as their reasoning behind this.

IMPLICATIONS FOR DESIGN

Our findings point to a number of ways that interaction designers might shift or reduce data demand associated with smartphones and tablets, without targeting the way these devices are currently configured within practice, nor raising questions about whether it should be this way.

Low-bandwidth options for background noise

Some participants used video streaming to provide background noise (Mandy) or to listen to the music associated with video (Pete). We might envision an audio-only option for streamed video content. Apps might locally cache a selection of previously streamed media, and offer it as an "instant" option for listening only. As others have suggested [18], such caching might also help to 'time shift' downloads to non-peak times.

Smaller and more strategic app updates

Recently in the news, the release of iOS 8 caused a 10% rise in traffic creating a record high for Virgin Media in the UK.[2] And in the cases of our tablet participants that

[2] http://www.engadget.com/2014/09/19/ios-8-virgin-media-record/, last accessed 15th January 2015.

switched off the tablet for a few days at a time, we observed spikes in throughput, as the device powered up and began downloading app updates. This points to a need for a more directed strategy in handling how and when apps are updated. App deployers might stagger update downloads across times of low network traffic. Before broadband Internet became widely available in homes, applications developers prioritised smaller patches which would take little bandwidth, yet would still apply the changes required to that application. We might return to such patches, far reducing app updates from the tens or hundreds of megabytes that are common now.

Additionally, many of our participants (Joel, Ben, Kathryn, Mandy, Erica) had more than twenty apps installed, yet from their interviews and device logs, only a small amount of these were used regularly. Devices might offer to update only the apps that have been used recently, instead of auto-downloading or offering to update everything installed on the device (e.g. "Update All" in the App Store).

Screen off, Network off

With each participant, we observed a significant amount (typically hundreds of megabytes per week) of demand during times that no app was in the foreground, and the screen was switched off (i.e. the device was not in active use). In these cases, the data demand generated was certainly not timed with practice, and in fact may not have been necessary at all (e.g. for push notifications later picked up on another device).

Such cases can be easily detected by a device operating system, which could suppress Wi-Fi and mobile data when the device is not being used. For iOS in particular, the "Background App Refresh" option might default to "off", or ask for permission to conduct network activity while in the background, much as prompts for location services do. For those truly concerned about getting timely push notifications during instances when they do not want to be interrupted, the "ringer off" or "Do not disturb" modes for notifications might instead switch off Wi-Fi/data.

IMPLICATIONS FOR UNDESIGN

These findings show that addressing data demand is not just a question of encouraging certain behavioral changes from users [18] but of how 'always-on' connectivity and data intensive transfers are designed into services, applications and even devices. So while the strategies outlined above might lead to measurable reductions, we view the data demand of mobile devices as part of a wider assumption (shared by users, designers and providers) that devices have access to certain intensities and continuities of network service. Data to the home and over cellular networks has been rising for years [21]. For specific areas one might make arguments, for example about whether it is more sustainable to stream content over a network, or distribute through physical transport networks on DVD or CD [30]. When it comes down to it, streamed media and mobile devices have resulted in more diverse forms of watching, and more watching overall. Social networks and photo sharing have created demand where there was little demand before. And the constantly changing requirements for apps, and expectations that they stay current to the changing designs of hardware, operating system and UIs, have increased the amount of network needed to maintain the functionality and usability of the device and the apps that run on it.

"Concerns with environmental sustainability in HCI exemplify a design imperative for undesigning" [17]. What would be ways of undesigning the data demand of mobile devices? Our findings lend some specific insights.

Social networks stay local

The social networking apps used by participants, and the fitness apps used by Sarah and Ben, relied on relatively local connectivity – most often to communicate with others in UK. And yet, these apps connected to data centres. We might envision social networking, social fitness training, and social gaming which are peer-to-peer by design. The meanings and competencies derived from this kind sharing could still go on, but without relying on big data centres and traversing many hops over edge and metro networks. The peer-to-peer networking and security technologies to make such things feasible already exist; but a challenge would be to shift ideas of what normal social networking is.

Already, those with mobile devices experience disruption: batteries run out, and network connectivity is lost. If social networking were peer-to-peer, outages in communication would become more common, occurring whenever either peer lost power or network. But, from what our participant accounts indicate it is the daily or weekly contact with others that is important, not that such contact is guaranteed to be instant, reliable or constant. If such expectations were to change, then this would also allow social network apps to time-shift their traffic to times of low network load. Push notifications, no longer explicitly *instant*, could be batched together and delivered during network troughs. In many cases it was the *textual* communication which was important; short messages could be sent via the traditional channel of SMS.[3]

Tune in to broadcast media

Radios have historically supported music listening and "background noise" (Mandy) very well; and analogue and digital radios remain easy to come by. We could certainly envision mobile devices with radio tuners implemented alongside the more complex Bluetooth, Wi-Fi and GSM protocols. As above, the challenge to overcome would be to shift expectations away from "on demand" songs and the

[3] SMS delivery is not guaranteed, nor is necessarily timely. Moreover, in areas where mobile data-driven social networking has risen, SMS is now underutilised.

type of playlists created by services such as Spotify. And yet, listening to live broadcast radio remains well within many people's experience. It is still relied upon in many homes worldwide, and where data connectivity is patchy (e.g. long car journeys).

Similarly, a built-in TV tuner might also support video watching on mobile devices. Or a local network connection to smart TVs or a set-top box could be used. These would no longer rely on network connectivity far afield, nor data centres and content distribution networks. As a result, such video would no longer be "on demand" in the sense that it is now, but rather locally stored for time-shifted watching similar to VCRs and PVRs. As with modern PVRs, there could still always be "something to watch", but it wouldn't necessarily support watching multiple episodes from the same TV series in a row (Mandy). Rather, forms of watching might return to those of the pre-streaming era.

Emphasise dead time as slow time

All of our participants discussed using their mobile devices during short windows of 'dead time' [20], waiting for something else to happen, or moments of boredom. These networked interactions were rarely characterised as particularly meaningful; at times they seemed simply compulsive (Kathryn) or stressful (Ben, Colin). Instead of pushing the latest news articles or social network chatter, we might work towards apps that are 'counterfunctional' [16] to this trend, making for more meaningful and data-free short periods of time as has been called for, elsewhere [13]. This could be through the promotion of 'ludic activities' [7], e.g. e-reader apps that provide compilations of short pieces of text (short stories, poems); or "slow" apps designed for anticipation of content [14] or that "promote moments of reflection and mental rest" [8] by guiding short meditation or relaxation exercises.

Reflecting on practice, as a practice

During the interviews, some of our participants expressed doubt or frustration about the way that their time-use of mobile devices had developed. This manifested in a number of ways: checking the device too often (Ben, Kathryn, Daniel); wasted time playing games (Jenny, Pete); the "buildup" of social networking and news updates (Mandy, Colin, Kathryn); all the new social networks and other services one signed up for after first getting a smartphone or tablet (Kathryn, Mandy, Rebecca, Erica); apps downloaded once and then never used again (Erica, Mandy).

In the spirit of 'reflective design' [23], we might envision apps which actually help us reflect on how we spend time with our mobile device: which apps are used at particular times of day, how much time we spend with each app, and which apps seem to be sitting around, unused. Whilst there are currently commercial options available, there has been some research which has examined the effects of different functionalities on the user. Like the Affective Diary [10], the reflection app might include a diary functionality to allow the person to annotate what took place in each session, identifying its relevance to everyday life. Annotations might be provided for periodic review, to help a person reflect on the persistence in ways of digital doing, and changes over time.

Preist and Shabajee [18] also suggest that data-based feedback could help to raise awareness and promote greater care over media consumption amongst those who are already environmentally focused. Indeed, amongst our interviewees there were a few concerns about battery life and data quota (Kathryn, Martin) but none made the connection between data and energy. This could be another goal for a diary app for mobile devices: it could provide tallies of the aggregate amounts and burst data rates for each app. Alongside, setting limits on time-use and times-of-use of certain apps (like plugins available for some browsers), the app could apply limits to data use. Primarily, however, we envisage that it is not data intensity but time-use that will engage users.

CONCLUSION

Mobile data demand is the product of an interconnected system that extends far beyond a practitioner and their mobile device. The functionality that defines these devices as 'smart' requires data connectivity. And, hence, the supporting mobile data and Wi-Fi infrastructures, with provision ranging through large multinational telephone companies to local coffee shops and transport companies. Interaction designers creating mobile apps draw on this infrastructure to promote novel and attractive uses of these devices; these in turn rely on publishers of digital data feeds and content generated by end-users. In this paper, we have described the product of this system in terms of its impact on (disrupted, enhanced, occasioned) everyday practices of end-users, and we have drawn attention to the increasingly intensive data demands of these.

There is a pressing need to foreground sustainability in mobile computing, and to start considering "undesign" as the most promising route to this. Mobile devices and their data connectivity have brought about new ways of being and doing, and images evoking these have made their way out of developed nations (where their use is most intense) across the world [9]. At each turn, HCI researchers and practitioners would do well to consider how we might move away from escalating data connectivity, and what genuine advantages this might also afford for quality of life [26].

ACKNOWLEDGEMENTS

This work has been funded by the UK research councils and supported by a PhD CASE studentship funded by the EPSRC and Microsoft Research. We would like to thank our participants and our CHI reviewers, the quality of whose feedback was exemplary.

REFERENCES

1. Athukorala, K., Lagerspetz, E., von Kügelgen, M., Jylhä, A., Oliner, A., Tarkoma, S., and Jacucci, G. 2014. How carat affects user behavior: implications for mobile battery awareness applications. *Proc. CHI.* 1029-1038.
2. Böhmer, M., Hecht, B., Schöning, J., Krüger, A., & Bauer, G. 2011. Falling asleep with Angry Birds, Facebook and Kindle: a large scale study on mobile application usage. *Proc. CHI.* 47- 56.
3. Clear, A., Morley, J., Hazas, M., Friday, A., and Bates, O. 2013. Understanding Thermal Comfort: New Directions for Ubicomp. *Proc. UbiComp,* 113–122.
4. Corcoran, P., & Andrae, A. 2013. Emerging trends in electricity consumption for consumer ICT. http://vmserver14.nuigalway.ie/xmlui/handle/10379/3563. Accessed September 2014.
5. Coroama, V. and Hilty, L. 2014. Assessing Internet energy intensity: A review of methods and results, *Environmental Impact Assessment Review* 45, 63–68.
6. Coroama, V., Schien, D., Preist, C., and Hilty, L. 2014. The Energy Intensity of the Internet: Home and Access Networks. In *ICT Innovations for Sustainability*, Aebischer and Hilty (eds.), Springer. 137–155.
7. Gaver, W.W., Bowers, J., Boucher, A., et al. 2004. The Drift Table: Designing for Ludic Engagement. *CHI EA '04*. 885–900.
8. Hallnäs, L. and Redström, J. 2001. Slow Technology – Designing for Reflection. *Personal Ubiquitous Comput.* 5, 3. 201–212.
9. Harmon, E. and Mazmanian, M. 2013. Stories of the smartphone in everyday discourse: Conflict, tension and instability. *Proc. CHI.* 1051–1060.
10. Höök, K., Ståhl, A., Sundström, P., and Laaksolaahti, J. 2008. Interactional Empowerment. *Proc. CHI*. 647–656.
11. Kawsar, F. and Brush, A.J. 2013. Home computing unplugged: Why, where and when people use different connected devices at home. *Proc. UbiComp*. 627–636.
12. Lee, U., Lee, J., Ko, M., et al. 2014. Hooked on smartphones: an exploratory study on smartphone overuse among college students. *Proc. CHI.* 2327–2336.
13. Leshed, G. and Sengers, P. 2011. I lie to myself about the freedom in my own schedule: productivity tools and the experiences of busyness. *Proc. CHI.* 905 – 914.
14. Odom, W.T., Sellen, A.J., Banks, R., et al. 2014. Designing for Slowness, Anticipation and Re-visitation: A Long Term Field Study of the Photobox. *Pro. CHI*. 1961–1970.
15. Oulasvirta, A., Rattenbury, T., Ma, L., Raita, E. 2012. Habits make smartphone use more pervasive. *Pervasive and Ubiquitous Computing.* 16. 105–114.
16. Pierce, J. and Paulos, E. 2014. Counterfunctional Things: Exploring Possibilities in Designing Digital Limitations. *Proc. DIS*. 375–384.
17. Pierce, J. 2014. Undesigning interaction. *Interactions* 21, 4. 36–39.
18. Preist, C. and Shabajee, P. 2010. Energy Use in the Media Cloud: Behaviour Change, or Technofix? *Proc. CloudCom*. 581–586.
19. Rahmati, A., Tossell, C., Shepard, C., Kortum, P., and Zhong, L. 2012. Exploring iPhone usage: the influence of socioeconomic differences on smartphone adoption, usage and usability. *Proc MobileHCI.* 11–20.
20. Røpke, I., and Christensen, T. H. 2012. Energy impacts of ICT – insights from an everyday life perspective. *Telematics and Informatics* 29, 4. 348–361.
21. Sandvine. 1h 2014. *Global internet phenomenon report.* Sandvine Incorporated ULC.
22. Schien, D., Shabajee, P., Yearworth, M. and Preist, C. 2013. Modeling and assessing variability in energy consumption during the use stage of online multimedia services. *Journal of Industrial Ecology*, 17, 6. 800–813.
23. Schien, D. and Preist, C. 2014. A review of top-down models of internet network energy intensity. *ICT4S.* 87 – 94.
24. Schien, D., Coroama, V. C., Hilty, L. M. and Preist, C. 2015. The energy intensity of the Internet: edge and core networks. In: *ICT Innovations for Sustainability.* Springer. 157 –170.
25. Sengers, P., Boehner, K., David, S., and Kaye, J. 2005. Reflective Design. *Pro. CC*. 49–58.
26. Sengers, P. 2011. What I learned on Change Islands: reflections on IT and pace of life. *Interactions* 18, 2. 40–48.
27. Strengers, Y. 2011. Designing Eco-feedback Systems for Everyday Life. *Proc. CHI.* 2135–2144.
28. Tossell, C., Kortum, P., Rahmati, A., Shepard, C., & Zhong, L. 2012. Characterizing web use on smartphones. *Proc. CHI*. 2769–2778.
29. Turkle, S. 2011. *Alone Together: Why do we expect more from technology and less from each other?* New York: Basic Books.
30. Weber, C. L., Koomey, J. G. and Matthews, H. S. 2010. The energy and climate change implications of different music delivery methods. *Journal of Industrial Ecology*, 14, 5. 754–769.
31. Willum, O., 2008. Residential ICT related energy consumption which is not registered at the electric meters in the residences. *Willum Consult and DTU Management Engineering*. Copenhagen.

An In-Situ Study of Mobile App & Mobile Search Interactions

Juan Pablo Carrascal
Pompeu Fabra University
jp.carrascal@upf.edu

Karen Church
Yahoo Labs
kchurch@yahoo-inc.com

ABSTRACT
When trying to satisfy an information need, smartphone users frequently transition from mobile search engines to mobile apps and vice versa. However, little is known about the nature of these transitions nor how mobile search and mobile apps interact. We report on a 2-week, mixed-method study involving 18 Android users, where we collected real-world mobile search and mobile app usage data alongside subjective insights on why certain interactions between apps and mobile search occur. Our results show that when people engage with mobile search they tend to interact with more mobile apps and for longer durations. We found that certain categories of apps are used more intensely alongside mobile search. Furthermore we found differences in app usage before and after mobile search and show how mobile app interactions can both prompt mobile search and enable users to take action. We conclude with a discussion on what these patterns mean for mobile search and how we might design mobile search experiences that take these app interactions into account.

Author Keywords
Mobile Search; Mobile Apps; User Study

General Terms
Human Factors

ACM Classification Keywords
H.5.2 Information interfaces and presentation: Miscellaneous

INTRODUCTION
People adopt a range of ingenious methods when trying to satisfy their daily information needs but the Internet has become the dominant means of finding information for smartphone users in particular [6]. A recent comScore report[1] shows that mobile devices accounted for 55% of Internet usage in the United States in January 2014. Native mobile apps made up the majority of that traffic (85%), while the remaining 15% came from mobile browsers. With a wealth of information seeking apps at their fingertips, mobile users can now issue queries directly from within these apps. For example, Yelp can be used to search for local businesses, Google Maps can be used to find directions, while IMDB can be used to look for movie reviews. Thus the boundaries between mobile search engines and mobile apps have become blurred.

Smartphone users sometimes switch between mobile search and other mobile apps to satisfy their information needs. Brown et al. [4] describes one such switching interaction in which mobile search and mobile maps are used interchangeably — with search being used to find information about certain places and maps being used to get directions to those places. It's likely that such switching interactions occur across a diverse range of everyday apps, i.e. beyond just maps applications. One of the goals of this work is to understand such switching behaviors.

Past research has also shown that mobile search can be triggered by our conversations and our surroundings [1, 7, 9, 24]. Furthermore, the results of mobile search can feed into next actions and plans [4]. Thus it's likely that some of these mobile search *triggers* and *actions* may relate to or be supported by interactions with mobile apps. For example, a text message from a friend may prompt a search or after searching for a local restaurant, a person may call to make a dinner reservation. The goal of this paper is to explore these interactions and to investigate if and how mobile search and app usage relates to mobile search triggers and actions.

While patterns of mobile app usage and mobile search have been studied separately [3, 18, 11, 2, 8, 13, 14, 26, 27, 22], the relationships between them have not been examined in-depth. A detailed study of in-situ app and search engine use will provide insights into how we can support more enriching cross app and search engine experiences, and assist mobile users in completing their daily information seeking tasks. To shed light on these interactions we conducted a 2-week mixed-method study involving 18 Android users. We combined interviews, a daily online diary and real-world mobile usage data to gather rich insights into mobile information seeking behaviors. Over the 2-week period we collected approximately 54,000 mobile app launches, over 840 mobile search sessions and over 500 diary entries. Our results highlight that when users engage in mobile search activity, they interact more with other mobile apps and for longer durations. Furthermore certain categories of mobile apps are more prevalent in sessions involving search, compared to sessions with no search activity. Our core contributions are:

- We define and introduce cross app and search interactions as an important and challenging research opportunity in the field of mobile HCI and mobile information retrieval.

[1]Mobile apps overtake PC Internet usage in U.S., See: cnnmon.ie/1cfHe0Z

- We analyze and characterize app and search interactions from a unique perspective, combining real-world in-situ search and app usage with qualitative insights.
- We discuss what our findings mean for future mobile information seeking services.

RELATED WORK

Significant effort has been placed on understanding people's daily information needs and how those needs are addressed [10, 6]. Studies focused on mobile information needs highlight that 72% of mobile needs are influenced by explicit contextual factors including activity, location, time and conversation [21]. The act of fulfilling information needs is also affected by contexts [5], with location being particularly influential [15]. Furthermore, the internet is a prominent means of addressing mobile information needs [21] in particular among experienced mobile Internet users [12].

As mobile device use has become more prominent, there has been a growing interest in understanding how and why people access and consume online content via their mobile phones. Some of this research focuses on behaviors of early-stage smartphone devices, e.g. [16, 9], while other work attempts to shed light on modern device use [4]. Qualitative studies have highlighted that the majority of mobile Web access occurs in stationary, familiar environments like home and work [20, 7]. The main motivations for general mobile Web usage are awareness and staying up-to-date [23], while mobile search motivations are more inclined to relate to curiosity [7]. Mobile search has been shown to be a social act, often sparked by conversations [9] and conducted in the presence of others [7]. Similar social influences have been found for local mobile search [1, 24]. While these qualitative studies have revealed interesting aspects of mobile search behavior, their reliance on interviews, diaries and survey data mean they lack details on actual search interactions.

Other research focused on analyzing actual Web usage patterns of real mobile phone users using datasets from commercial search engines like Google as well as operator-specific search services [2, 8, 13, 14, 26, 27, 22]. Overall these studies highlight that mobile queries tend to be shorter than their desktop counterparts, users tend to submit fewer queries per session compared to desktop users and that adult related content is very popular. Recent studies show signs of evolving patterns, highlighting that the increased popularity of modern smartphones is having an impact on search behavior. For example, mobile queries are becoming less homogenous, mobile query length is steadily increasing and interest in local content is rising. These studies have helped shape our understanding about how mobile users seek online information, however their focus on logs-based analysis means they lack insights about why certain behaviors have emerged.

As the adoption of smartphones has increased dramatically in the last few years, the number and diversity of native mobile applications — so called *apps* — have also risen. This has given rise to a number of studies aimed at understanding how people engage with native mobile apps. Böhmer et al. [3] studied app use among over 4,100 Android phone users and highlighted the prevalence of communications related apps throughout the day, with certain categories of apps being used more often at certain times, e.g. Clock in the morning. Tossell et al. [25] looked at Web use on smartphones and found that native internet applications like Mail, Facebook, Maps and Weather are visited twice as much as browsers. These studies provide us with a concrete understanding on the types of mobile app interactions among modern smartphone users, however they suffer from a lack of understanding on the specifics of what's being done within the applications themselves.

There are of course a few exceptions. For example, McGregor et al. [18] use a video-data collection method to record 100 days of iPhone use and highlight 3 distinct usage patterns: *micro-breaks*, *digital knitting* and *reading*. Lee et al. [17] explored if and how app usage relates to smartphone overuse and addiction in college studies. And most recently Ferreria et al. [11] looked at app micro-usage and found that 40% of all app launches last less than 15 seconds and such short interaction happen mostly when a person is at home and alone.

Work by Brown et al. [4] is particularly relevant. Using innovative video data collection of everyday smartphone use, they focus on what prompts the use of particular applications at specific times or in specific situations, focusing on web search and maps use. They highlight 'occasioned search', that is search triggered by the environment or local events. Our goal is to expand upon these insights to explore the unique interaction between mobile search and general mobile app usage, specifically how search is influenced by app usage and how app interactions influence mobile search actions. Brown et al. also highlight the use of the mobile Web and mobile maps interchangeably in information searches. In this paper we examine such interactions but explore switching between search and a range of mobile apps that smartphones users engage with daily, i.e. beyond just maps applications.

In summary, past work has explored mobile search and mobile app usage primarily in isolation. Thus questions about how mobile search and app usage is interlinked remain largely unanswered. In this paper we present an in-depth investigation on the relationship between mobile apps and mobile search, exploring the triggers, actions and app interactions in and around mobile search. Furthermore, we study this behavior from a unique perspective, combining both real-world in-situ search and app usage with qualitative insights.

STUDY METHOD

We conducted a 2-week in-situ field study in June and July 2014 where we collected both objective and subjective data. Objective data was collected via two apps installed on participant's smartphones, which tracked their actual mobile app and mobile search usage. Subjective data was gathered at the start and end of the study in initial and final in-person interviews as well as daily via an online diary where participants reviewed and described specifics of their mobile searches.

Participants

We recruited 18 participants (10 male; 8 female) from 8 different cities in the Greater San Francisco Bay Area using a professional recruiting agency. Participants ranged in age between 18-48, with an mean age of 32.7 (sd: 9.8) and had a diverse set of occupations including students, administrative assistants, social workers, managers, chemists, homemakers and construction workers. Their education levels ranged from high school to college degree. All participants were active users of mobile search engines like Google and Yahoo. All of them owned Android smartphones as their main communication device, the majority of which were Samsung Galaxy phones (N=14). Participants were compensated for the time.

Procedure

The study was conducted between June and July 2014 and was comprised of three stages:

1. Initial interview and app installation

The initial interview was semi-structured and lasted from 30 minutes to 1 hour, depending on the scope and diversity of participant's mobile search and app usage. The interviews covered (a) their daily mobile device habits; (b) their general mobile search engine use; (c) concrete examples of their most recent mobile search, focusing on aspects such as what triggered the search in the first place and any actions that took place as a result of the search; and (d) apps they use for searching and situations in which they choose an app over a search engine for satisfying their needs. To conclude the interviews, we installed two custom apps on their smartphones:

AppLogger: a logging app that ran as an android service in the background of the participants' phone and kept track of all device *usage events* including app launches, turning the screen on and off, unlocking the phone, and accessing the home screen. Each logged usage event includes an app or event name, a timestamp, and the duration of the event.

MSearch: a mobile search app which embedded the search functionality of a well known commercial search engine. This app collected time stamped search data including search queries and search interactions (i.e. clicks). Participants moved the app icon to their homescreen during the initial interview to ensure the search app was easily accessible.

2. Two-week mobile search and online diary study

Participants were asked to use the MSearch app for all their mobile search needs over the 2-week study period and to review their mobile searches in a Web-based online diary tool. All queries and clicks generated through our search app were sent to a server for processing. Queries and clicks were grouped into sessions using a session delta of 5 minutes and these search sessions formed the basis of the participants' diary. The online diary was designed to capture the motivations, triggers and actions surrounding their mobile searches. To minimize the time burden on participants, the diary presented participants with a maximum of 3 of their mobile search sessions per day, which were selected at random. Below is a list of the 9 questions we asked for each of the 3 daily search sessions. In parenthesis we indicate if a question was multiple choice (closed), or freeform text (open):

1. What information were you looking for? (open)
2. What were you doing at the time of the search? (open)
3. Where were you at the time and did your location influence the search? If so, how? (closed/open)
4. Who were you with at the time and did the people around you influence the search? If so, how? (closed/open)
5. Did you share the information you found with other people? If so, how? (closed/open)
6. How important was it to find the information you searched for? (closed, 5-point Likert scale)
7. How urgent was it to find the information you searched for? (closed, 5-point Likert scale)
8. Could you find the information? If not, what alternative approaches did you try to find the information? (closed)
9. What did you do with the information you found during the search? Did you take any additional actions? (open)

Note that participants were encouraged to access and fill their online diary each evening, a task which took approx. 5-10 mins to complete. Participants were also sent a daily email for the duration of the study to remind them about the study.

3. Final interview and app removal

At the end of the 2-week study, participants attended a final in-person interview. Prior to the interview, we reviewed their mobile search and mobile app log data as well as their diary entries to extract specific usage behaviors we wanted to follow up on. We probed participants about two or three of their reported mobile searches and asked them more details regarding the triggers, actions and associated app interactions in and around those searches. To conclude, both the AppLogger and MSearch apps were uninstalled from the participants phone. All in-person interviews were audio recorded and transcribed.

RESULTS

Quantitative data from both mobile search and mobile app usage was analyzed per-session and in aggregate to understand the types and nature of mobile search interactions; the nature and duration of mobile app use; and the interaction between mobile app and mobile search. *Qualitative data* from the transcribed interviews and the diary responses were analyzed using grounded theory-based affinity analysis, an approach commonly used to organize and group large quantities of subjective data into a logical set of themes or categories. We extracted over 3,000 individual quotes from the qualitative data, which made up individual data items in our analysis. These data items were iteratively reviewed and grouped by the authors to find repeating themes across participants.

Basic Descriptive Statistics

The results reported here are based on the mobile app and search logs gathered between 23rd June and 13th July 2014. Although the mobile search part of the study lasted 14 days, the *AppLogger* ran for an average of 16 days (sd : 2.57) due to scheduling final participant interviews. Before exploring the interactions between mobile apps and mobile search, we much first analyze app usage and mobile search separately.

Mobile App Usage

Over 189K mobile phone usage events were logged over the entire study duration with an average of 10,515.3 events per

Table 1. App usage summary showing number of unique apps, app launches and average usage time of apps grouped by app category

Category	# Launches	% Launches	# Unique Apps	Avg Dur(secs)	App Examples
Social networking	9714	17.98	17	107.6	Facebook, Twitter, Instagram, OkCupid
Browser & Search	7727	14.30	10	112.9	Chrome, Google Search, Firefox
SMS/Texting	5964	11.04	2	63.6	Build in Messaging
Phone & Audio	5456	10.10	10	25.8	Dialer, Google Voice, Skype, Voxer
Email	3928	7.27	4	54.0	Gmail, Yahoo mail, SolMail
Games	2780	5.15	73	264.1	Slotmania, CandyCrush, Words
Contact	2574	4.76	4	53.0	Contacts, Mr. Number
Music & Audio	2468	4.57	16	74.0	Pandora, iHeartRadio, SoundCloud
Photography	2172	4.02	19	36.4	Shutterfly, Gallery, Camera, PicCollage
System & Settings	1904	3.52	12	29.5	Software updates, Android Settings
Tools & Utilities	1777	3.29	45	30.8	Calculator, Clean Master, Media Storage
Instant Messaging	1831	3.39	10	79.6	Snapchat, ChatOn, Kik, Trillian
Media & Video	1338	2.48	10	275.8	YouTbe, Netflix, BitTorrent
Productivity	1169	2.16	24	61.4	Calendar, Quickoffice, LastPass, Gnotes
Travel & Local	1035	1.92	13	111.6	Maps, Muni Alerts, Yelp
Entertainment	370	0.68	19	239.7	Meme Generator, Series Guide, IMDB
Unknown	346	0.64	23	142.5	*Not applicable*
Shopping & Retail	254	0.47	12	138.3	eBay, Groupon, Macy's, LivingSocial
Finance	252	0.47	15	58.1	Wells Fargo, Chase, PayPal, Mint
Health & Fitness	228	0.42	10	156.7	S Health, Fitit, Push Ups, My Diet Coach
Education	181	0.34	1	22.2	SMCC
Lifestyle	169	0.31	12	65.8	dscout, 7-Eleven, AIDS Walk
Weather	146	0.27	5	19.2	The Weather Channel, Weather Widget
News & Magazines	124	0.23	7	73.0	Flipboard, yahoo, Glamlife
Business	71	0.13	7	112.5	VPN Client, CamCard, Job Search
Personalization	28	0.05	7	129.9	Zedge, Live wallpaper, travel wallpaper
Sports	9	0.02	1	47.8	theSocre
Books & Reference	7	0.01	6	49.4	Dictionary, Wikipedia, Audible

participant (Mdn : 11165.5, sd : 6124.7). Of these, 54,022 corresponded to app launches, with an average of 3,001.2 app launches per participant (Mdn : 2867.5, sd : 2003.9). The remaining events were device events such as turning the display on/off, unlocking the phone and accessing the homescreen. A total of 394 unique mobile apps were launched across our 18 participants during the study, with an average of 53.6 unique mobile apps launched per participant (Mdn : 52, sd : 20.6).

While prior work shows that users spend an average of 1 hour using mobile apps [3, 19], our participants spent significantly more time. The average time our participants spent interacting with mobile apps is $>$ 4.5 hours per day (Mdn : 248.2 mins, sd : 173.3 mins). In contrast, Table 1 highlights that individual mobile app usage is often short, lasting an average of just 90 seconds (Mdn : 17, sd : 241.5), slightly longer than Böhmer et al.'s 71 second average. Overall we found that 73.5% of app uses were one minute or less in duration and approx. 40% of uses are 15 seconds or less which is in line with findings by Ferreria et al. [11].

To get a better sense of the types of apps used, we manually classified the 394 unique apps into corresponding Google Play categories. We did this mapping by searching the Play store based on app name. Similar to the Böhmer et al. study we made some minor changes to the Google Play categorization. Specifically, we opted for one high-level games category instead of multiple micro-categories of Games (e.g. arcade, brain & puzzle, etc.). We opted to have a separate Browsers & Search category and a separate Systems & Settings category for handling the default Android settings apps. Finally we opted to break-out communications-related categories such as Contacts, SMS/Texting and Instant Messaging. Table 1 highlights that the top 3 categories are *Social networking*, *Browsers & Search Engines* and *SMS*, while almost 55% of app usage in our study relates to *Communications*.

Table 2. Distribution of search topics across all 882 unique queries

Topic	# Queries	% Queries
Entertainment	144	16.3
Trivia	144	16.3
Local	133	15.1
Shopping & Coupons	106	12.0
Travel & Commuting	84	9.5
Technology	49	5.6
Health & Fitness	45	5.1
General Information	42	4.8
Cooking, recipes & ingredients	28	3.2
Sport	24	2.7
Auto	24	2.7
Misc	17	1.9
Search & Navigational	12	1.4
Stocks & Finance	12	1.4
News & Weather	10	1.1
Employment	6	0.7
Education	1	0.1

Mobile Search Usage

Participants issued 882 unique queries through the *MSearch* app resulting in 2794 webpage visits. These webpage visits include both click-throughs and follow-on links. This corresponds to an average of 50.1 unique mobile search queries (Mdn : 47.5, sd : 23.9) and 158 webpage visits (Mdn : 112, sd : 122.4) per participant over the 2 week study period.

A mobile search session is a sequence of queries and search interactions (i.e. clicking on the next page of results or on an individual search result) issued by a single user within a small time period. Using a standard mobile search session delimiter of 5 minutes [13], we identified a total of 843 search sessions. We found an average of 1.6 unique queries per session

($Mdn: 1$, $sd: 1.2$). Approximately 78% of sessions resulted in at least one click-through (647 sessions) while the average number of webpage visits (click-throughs and follow-ons) per session is 4.9 ($Mdn: 3$, $sd: 5.7$).

Compared to previous studies of mobile search patterns we observe that our participants issued longer search queries. The average number of words per query is 3.55 ($Mdn: 3$, $sd: 2.1$), compared to 3.05 reported in a 2013 Bing study [22]. Finally to get a better sense of the types of queries our participants issued, we manually classified all 882 unique search queries into a set of search categories. Cohen's kappa was used to measure intercoder reliability. After two iterations of independently coding 200 unique search queries and discussing any conflicts, a Cohen's Kappa value of 0.74 was reached. The remaining dataset was then divided, and each author independently coded his or her part of the dataset. The resulting classification is shown in Table 2. We found that our participants predominately issued mobile search queries related to *Entertainment, Trivia, Local, Shopping & Coupons* as well as *Travel & Commuting*.

The Online Diary

Participants contributed a total of 535 diary entries describing details of specific mobile searches. This equates to 29.7 entries per user over the course of the study. According to their answers, most of the searches were conducted at home (70.1%), followed by work/school (7.7%) or commuting (7.7%). Other locations mentioned included bars, cafes or restaurants, someone else's home, the gym, shopping and running errands. In 26% of the cases, participants stated that their location at the time influenced their search.

In contrast to past research on mobile search, we found that participants reported that they were mostly alone when searching (51.2%). The rest of the time they were with their partner or spouse (22.4%), relatives (12.9%), friends (7.3%), work colleagues or school mates (3.9%) or others (2.2%). In 15.5% of the time, the person accompanying the participant had an influence on searching.

Most of the time the information sought was found (80.6%). In 17.4% of cases the participants considered the information to be partially found. When participants couldn't find the information, they either did nothing (29.4%) or relied on alternative methods including: asking somebody (23.5%), using other search engines (23.5%), reading the information somewhere—in a map, etc.—(2.9%), or something else (20.6%). In 17.4% of cases, the information found was shared with somebody else. In the following section we being our investigation of cross app and mobile search interactions.

Cross App and Mobile Search

To explore the relationship between mobile search and mobile app usage we must first define cross app and search interactions. Figure 1 presents the sequence of actual mobile app and search interactions for a 1 hour period (12-1pm) on a single day for a real participant in our study. It shows that a user's day is typically comprised of a number of *"Sessions"*. Similar to Böhmer's definition of an app chain [3], we define a session as *a sequence of interactions that occur without the device being in standby mode, i.e. the display switching off, for longer than 30 seconds*. In other words, if the phones display is off for more than 30 seconds, all following app interactions belong to the next session. While if the phones display is off for 30 seconds or less, the following app interactions belong to the preceding session.

Some of these sessions involve the user turning their display on without actually launching any apps. For example to check the time or to check for any missed notifications, both of which would be visible on their lock screen and/or homescreen of the phone. In other sessions, the user launches and interacts with specific mobile apps. Sometimes this may be a single app launch, while in other cases this can involve opening a chain of apps. The diagram highlights that this particular user interacts with her device regularly throughout the hour but more intensely in the first 30 minutes. She primarily uses SMS but also plays a number of games (e.g. Pet Rescue Saga), browses the Internet and interacts with Facebook. Thus we define sessions in which at least one mobile app was launched as *"App Sessions"*.

Aside from mobile app interactions, the figure also highlights that the participant engaged with mobile search on two occasions. First submitting the query 'advance screenings san francisco' and visiting a website advancescreenings.com. Minutes later she submits the query 'rotten tomatoes' and visits another website. These queries (Q) and search clicks (C) are identified in bold in the figure. Thus some *"App Sessions"* involve the user engaging with mobile search, while other app sessions do not. We define these as $AppSessions_{search}$ and $AppSessions_{nonsearch}$ respectively.

Note that this particular user interacts with SMS before, during and soon after her mobile searches. This implies that her overarching task — deciding on a movie — involved cross app and search interaction. Note that final interviews with the participant confirmed she went to a movie as a result of this search. It appears that the participant switched between mobile search and other mobile apps. Likewise given most of this switching occurs with SMS, it appears as though she was communicating with someone at the time. Thus it's likely that the conversations within these interactions with SMS may have prompted the mobile search and in turn influenced the resulting action (e.g. making plans to go to the movies). The goal of this work is to understand more about the nuances of these cross app and search interactions. In the following section we dive into our analysis.

Are Search and Non-Search Sessions Different?

To investigate the mutual influence and interaction between mobile search and mobile app usage, we explore differences between $AppSessions_{search}$ and $AppSessions_{nonsearch}$ in terms of app launches, unique apps used and session duration. To do this we extracted a list of all *App Sessions* in our dataset, that is sessions that include at least one launch of at least one mobile app. We excluded the first app session of every participant from all subsequent analyses since it corresponds to the installation of the *MSearch* app which was done during the initial interview. We found a total of 12,307 app sessions in our dataset. Our *MSearch* app was used in 913

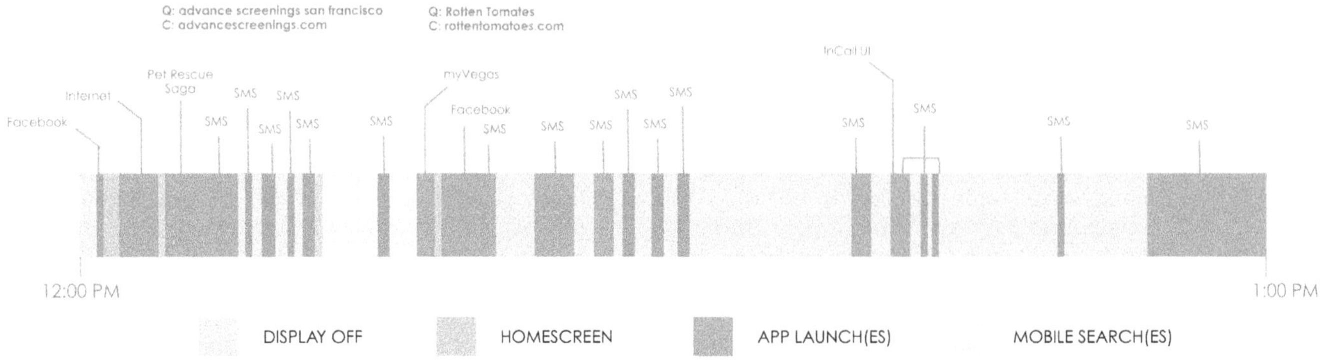

Figure 1. Participant timeline for a 1 hour period of a single day showing sequences of mobile device interactions in the form of mobile app launches, home screen interactions and mobile searches.

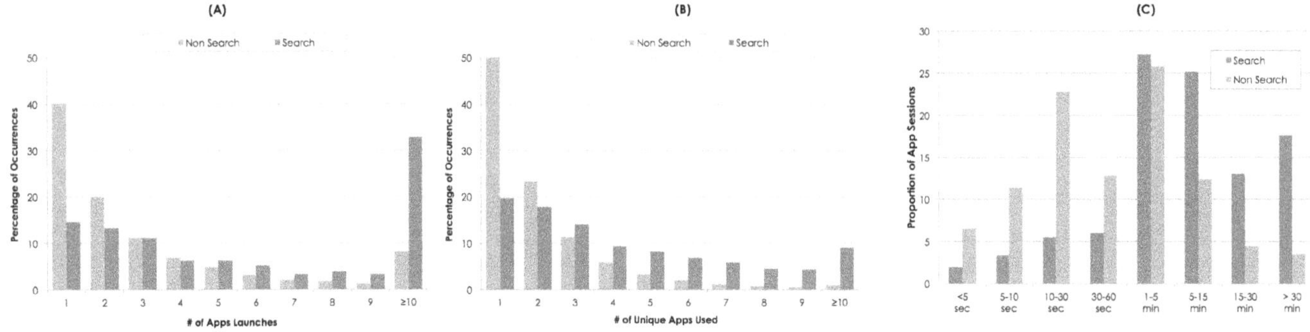

Figure 2. (A) Number of app launches in $AppSessions_{search}$ vs. $AppSessions_{nonsearch}$; (B) Number of unique apps used in $AppSessions_{search}$ vs. $AppSessions_{nonsearch}$; (C) Session duration of $AppSessions_{search}$ vs. $AppSessions_{nonsearch}$

sessions, and in remaining $11,394$ it was not. We therefore split the dataset in two: 913 $AppSessions_{search}$ and 11,394 $AppSessions_{nonsearch}$ for comparison purposes.

Figure 2(A) shows the distribution of $AppSessions_{search}$ (red) and $AppSessions_{nonsearch}$ (blue) grouped by the total number of app launches. The figure suggests that app sessions involving mobile search include a higher number of app usages compared to non-search sessions. We found that $AppSessions_{nonsearch}$ include an average of 3.9 app launches (Mdn : 2, sd : 6.9), while $AppSessions_{search}$ involve an average of 10.8 app launches (Mdn : 5, sd : 25.7). A non-paired Welch's t-test confirmed that there is a significant difference between the groups ($t = 8.14, p < 0.01$, Cohen's $d = 0.72$). Note that Cohen's d here measures the magnitude of the difference. Thus when mobile users engage with search, the intensity of their app interactions (i.e. app laucnhes) increases. Figure 2(B) shows a similar pattern for the number of unique apps used in search *vs.* non-search app sessions. That is when users engage in $AppSessions_{search}$, they interact with a higher number of unique mobile apps. We found that $AppSessions_{nonsearch}$ include an average of 2.2 distinct mobile apps (Mdn : 1, sd : 2.2), while $AppSessions_{search}$ involve using an average of 4.6 unique apps (Mdn : 3, sd : 3.9). This implies there is greater diversity in their behaviors during search sessions, that is when users engage with search, they interact with a higher number of different apps compared to when users are not engaged in search. We tested this and again found this difference to be significant ($t = 18.68, p < 0.01$, Cohen's $d = 1.18$).

Finally we explored temporal differences in the form of overall session duration. Figure 2(C) highlights that app sessions involving search typically last longer than app sessions with no search. The average duration of $AppSessions_{search}$ is 1377 seconds (Mdn : 372, sd : 4940.9) compared to 348.2 seconds (Mdn : 52, sd : 1275.6) for $AppSessions_{nonsearch}$. This difference was also found to be significant ($t = 6.28, p < 0.01$, Cohen's $d = 0.57$) between the $AppSessions_{search}$ or $AppSessions_{nonsearch}$ datasets. These results indicate that when users engage with search, they engage for longer periods than when they are not engaged with search. All in all these results indicate that $AppSessions_{search}$ tend to be more app-intensive than $AppSessions_{nonsearch}$ on a number of levels. To investigate why these differences occur, we turn our analysis to app interactions within these sessions to see if certain apps or certain categories of apps tend to be used more intensively in and around mobile search activity.

How are Search and Non-Search Sessions Different?

In this section we investigate differences in usage of different categories of apps between $AppSessions_{search}$ and $AppSessions_{nonsearch}$. We opted to make these comparisons at a category level as opposed to single app level for two reasons: (1) because of individual preferences, different participants used different apps from the same category

Table 3. T-test (non-paired) results for comparing launch frequency and usage time of app categories between search and non-search sessions. These categories displayed significantly higher launch frequency and significantly longer usage time in search sessions compared to non-search sessions.

	Launch frequency		Usage duration	
Category	t*	Cohen's d	t*	Cohen's d
Browsers	15.10	1.29	23.19	1.60
Email	3.80	0.16	8.80	0.57
Entertainment	2.62	0.23	4.12	0.35
Finance	1.98	0.10	2.02	0.10
Games	5.15	0.42	6.06	0.44
Media & Video	1.98	0.15	3.02	0.21
Photography	2.22	0.10	2.84	0.14
Shopping & Retail	2.60	0.20	3.90	0.23
SMS/Texting	3.07	0.23	4.14	0.24
Social networking	3.81	0.29	3.87	0.26
Tools & Utilities	2.80	0.30	4.94	0.33
Unknown	2.91	0.16	2.93	0.21
Weather	2.87	0.13	3.39	0.17

*All coefficients are significant at $p < .05$.

(*e.g.* Gmail and the Android email client, the native Internet browser and Google Chrome); and (2) we wanted to limit the influence of apps that are only used by single participants.

To perform the comparisons, we extracted the frequency of app launches and the usage time of every category of app on a per-session basis. Then we compared the frequency and duration of categories of apps in $AppSessions_{search}$ and $AppSessions_{nonsearch}$. Comparisons were assessed with a non-paired Welch's t-test. Table 3 highlights that we found a significantly higher launch frequency and significantly longer usage time in $AppSessions_{search}$ compared to $AppSessions_{nonsearch}$, for certain app categories. Categories including Browsers, Email, SMS, Social Networking, Shopping & Retail and Entertainment were all used more intensively when people engaged with mobile search, both in terms of app launches and duration of app usage. This implies that when users are in *information seeking* mode, they engage more heavily with certain types of apps. To investigate further, we turn our analysis to the triggers of mobile search to see if certain app interactions prompt users to search.

Triggers & App Interactions

Through qualitative analysis of diary and interview data, we identified 6 key triggers of mobile search. While understanding the prompts of mobile search is not new, our goal here is to shed light on the relationship between triggers and app interactions. The 6 triggers we identified were either external or internal. External triggers are sensory stimuli, that is things you can see, touch or hear. In contrast internal triggers are connected with our thoughts, emotions, body, or pre-existing habits. External triggers included (1) media, e.g. watching tv, listening to music, reading a newspaper; (2) conversations, face to face as well as conversations across messaging, email and social networking app; (3) Tangible external triggers, that is noticing something material in their physical surroundings; (4) Activities & Events; (5) Physiological signals like hungry and stress and finally (6) State of Mind, e.g. random thoughts.

While some of the so-called triggers are unlikely related to app usage, **Media** and **Conversations** are the exception. Given prevalence of entertainment and media related apps as well as messaging apps, it's likely that some of these app interactions prompted mobile searches. P11 for example discussed this situation: *"I was listening to the music in there and I remember that I think that particular person was supposed to be on this podcast"*; he then did a search for the podcast in question. He was listening to music on his phone at the time. Similarly P15 described a situation in which she was texting a friend about flights which prompted a search, *"Our conversation about her wanting to fly. She had looked up some prices and I said 'that seems really high!'. I was like 'let me check'"*.

To understand more about how app interactions might trigger mobile searches we extracted the first apps launched within a search session (excluding our search app) and found that Facebook (8.3%), VEVO (4.8%), Calendar (3.2%), Messaging (3.1%) and Gmail (3%) were the top apps launched first within search sessions. We decided to take a manual look at the data to see if we could make any connections between the first app launched in a session and the query (mobile search) immediately succeeding that app interaction. P5, for example uses SeriesGuide which helps people manage (re)watching their favorite TV shows. Looking at the data we found that P5 issued a query 'Friday night dinner tv wiki' immediately after an interaction with SeriesGuide. The topic of P5's query after interacting with SeriesGuide, an entertainment app, was also entertainment related. P1 issued two media & music related queries 'video2mp3' and 'worldstar hiphop' immediately after launching his music player. P18 for example, issued the query 'closer Hollywood sign' while vacationing in Los Angeles immediately after interacting with Google Maps. That is she issued a query with local intent (i.e. tied to a physical location) after interacting with a location-based maps application. P8 interacted with Yelp and immediately afterwards searched for 'ca dmv wait time'. Again this highlights a connection between an app that enables people to search for local businesses and services and a query for information tied to a local business. Finally P4 queried for 'bcbg generation jelly thong sandals' a type of footwear after using the Macy's department store app. Again her interaction with a shopping app appears to have sparked a search for a specific product.

While these interactions are not generalizable across all our users, nor are they indicative of the interactions of all smartphone users, they do provide anecdotal evidence of real connections between apps and mobile search and help shape our understanding of specific app-to-search use cases. Overall these insights demonstrate that interactions with apps can in fact prompt mobile searches.

Apps Before & After Search

Next we dig deeper into mobile search sessions and explore differences in app usage *before* and *after* mobile search. We find 8391 app launches within $AppSessions_{search}$, 2715 (32%) happen *before* the first launch of our app within sessions, and 4746 (57%) occur after the first launch of our app within sessions. The remaining 11% relate to launches of the *MSearch* app. Additionally, we found that out of the 913 $AppSessions_{search}$, 338 (36.3%) sessions *began* with a launch of the *MSearch* app. This indicates that for $AppSessions_{search}$, there is frequently more app activity after mobile search than before.

To explore differences in pre and post search interactions, we extracted the frequency of app launches per app category before the first appearance of the *MSearch* app and after the last appearance of the *MSearch* app, on a per-session basis. This allowed us to obtain additional insights about how certain categories of apps might be related to mobile search triggers and actions. We assessed this by a paired t-test comparing the launch frequency of every app category before and after the search activity. We found significant differences for some categories, in particular *after* mobile search activity (Table 4). These differences indicate that within search sessions, certain app categories tend to be launched more frequently *after* mobile search has taken place. Overall we found the use of browsers is more frequent after mobile search. Likewise communications apps like Email, SMS and Phone & Audio are used more often after mobile search than before.

Table 4. T-test (paired) results from comparing launch frequency of app categories before and after the search activity. These categories displayed significantly more launches after searching.

Category	t*	Cohen's d
Browsers	6.63	0.31
Email	4.38	0.20
Games	2.74	0.13
Phone & Audio Communication	2.35	0.11
Photography	3.65	0.17
SMS/Texting	2.60	0.11
Social networking	2.06	0.10
System & Settings	2.25	0.11
Tools & Utilities	3.57	0.17
Unknown	2.49	0.11

*All coefficients are significant at $p < .05$.

We were interested in exploring if these post-search app interactions relate in anyway to mobile search actions. Based again on data from interviews and diary responses we identified 9 key mobile search actions among our participants, namely: (1) consuming content, i.e. watching, reading, listening; (2) sharing information; (3) keeping information which involved saving it digitally or taking down notes as well as making mental notes; (4) buying goods/services; (5) booking something; (6) planning something; (7) visiting somewhere; (8) contacting a person, business or place; (9) making/doing, e.g. cooking a recipe. Again drawing from the qualitative data, we find that some of these actions indeed map directly to app usage. For example:

- *P4 "Downloaded new music to my phone before proceeding to the gym"*
- *P2 "Called the store and confirmed they have what I'm looking for and will stop by after work Tuesday to buy..."*
- *P1 "Posted the picture of a Mohawk warrior on Facebook."*
- *P6 "Sent information back and forth to sister by Voxer."*

We find that *sharing* actions in particular were done directly from the mobile device. This involved emailing links to websites, sharing details in threads of conversations in messaging apps in particular, as well as taking and sending screenshots of interesting content. This taking and sending of screenshots likely relates to the prevalence of *Photography* apps after search compared to before search. Note that this category of app includes the phones in-built photo gallery app which is the primary source for sharing screenshots on smartphones.

Overall our results highlight differences in app interactions before and after search, and once again anecdotal evidence suggests that app interactions are used to support certain mobile search actions. In the following section we turn our attention to switching between search and other apps.

Switching between Apps in Search

We found that 337 out of the 913 total $AppSessions_{search}$ involved 2 or more launches of the $MSearch$ app. This may be down to participants using mobile search twice within a single session or it may be because participants switched to/from other mobile apps in between their mobile searches. The later appears more likely. To investigate we extract the top 10 apps (in terms of app launches), within these 337 sessions. Table 5 shows that most of these top apps relate to communications, primarily email, texting and social networking.

Table 5. Top 10 apps (in terms of launch frequency) in sessions that involve 2 or more launches of the $MSearch$ app

No	App	Freq	Perc
1	Msearch	1001	18.0
2	Facebook	572	10.3
3	Internet	306	5.5
4	Email	266	4.8
5	Messaging	196	3.5
6	GO SMS Pro	174	3.1
7	Chrome	174	3.1
8	Messages	165	3.0
9	Gmail	164	3.0
10	System	136	2.4

In the interviews, participants shed light on their sometimes very complex switching between apps and services to either address their information needs or to share their findings. P8 for example is an avid coupon user and actively uses apps like Groupon and LivingSocial to find discounts and deals. He explained an interesting example of how he uses both mobile search and other apps when looking for concert tickets: *"I will actually go to Ticketmaster, see the price and then open up another window or another Groupon like that and then if I get one [groupon code], I'll copy it. Get out of there and go back to Ticketmaster to where it usually has a little icon where it says you can enter a coupon code, so paste it."*. At times when he cannot find tickets, he will also visit sites like craigslist. This highlights the disjoint and fragmented sequences of interactions involved. Groupon gives him discount codes, Ticket Master enables the purchase, while search engines allow him to find upcoming concerts in the first place.

P6 described similar sequences of interactions this time using Voxer with her sister *"She had me sign up for Voxer so that she can communicate with me, which is actually kind of cool because while I'm searching for stuff, we can talk back and forth or we could text or we can send pictures between us"*. In an attempt to find information about a local beach she explained how her searching the Web and communicating with Voxer were interlinked, *"I will give her the information and she'll look at it, and then she'll text me something back and then we'll both look at it, so we were just going back and forth with ideas"*.

To shed light on reasons for such switching behaviors, in the interviews we asked participants if and why they use and switch to other apps like Yelp, Maps and IMDB, etc. for searching. It appears that search engines are used for broad information needs, while apps are used for more specific questions. One participant likened the interaction to starting with search and drilling down with apps. Search engines were also seen as offering more options, enabling participants to cast a wide net. This was particularly useful for shopping related needs where options and prices are important, e.g. *P4 "I would look at the search first because then it gives me an idea because sometimes there are some things that talk about prices, like what range and where you would find that price from what app or what location"*. Heimonen [12] found a similar trend comparing search to known websites.

DISCUSSION

In this paper we have taken a first in-depth look at the complex cross app and search interactions surrounding mobile information seeking. Our results indicate that users who engage in search activity, i.e. search sessions, interact more with other mobile apps and for longer durations within those sessions. We found significant differences in the categories of apps used within search sessions compared to non search sessions. Specifically, browsers, email, SMS, social networking, shopping & retail and entertainment related apps are used more intensively when people engage with mobile search.

Using both qualitative insights and quantitative analysis we highlight that some app interactions lead to searches, while other app interactions are used by participants to take action after a search. Anecdotal evidence highlights that categories of app usage and search topics are linked, e.g. an interaction with Yelp leads to additional local search queries issued via a search engine. Our results also show that there is more app activity *after* mobile search than *before*, suggesting that participants tend to start their app sessions with the *intention* of searching. In line with related work [4], this implies that interactions with the material world tend to create more information needs and information seeking behaviors than virtual interactions.

Our insights into the categories of apps used before and after mobile search, as well as complex switching between apps and search, point to an overarching theme of *task completion*. In our earlier examples, we find that for one participant the task was going to a concert with his girlfriend. For another participant it was going to a beach with her family. What was common across a number of these tasks was that our participants used multiple information sources and often shared the information found with others to make joint decisions on day to day things. This involves using a range of apps both for the *finding* and *sharing* phases of these tasks. This highlights not only that tasks are more important than individual mobile app usage, but that tasks are often collaborative or social in nature. Future mobile search experiences should take such social interactions into account.

While beyond the scope of this research, it would be interesting to gather similar data for a longer time period and with more users to determine if such patterns could be mined to provide *predictive* mobile search capabilities. For example, perhaps the probability of issuing certain queries is higher after using certain types of apps. And likewise the probably of using certain apps is higher after engaging with different types of mobile search interactions. If such probabilities can be detected, future mobile search could pre-empt these behaviors and offer more proactive search experiences. Essentially supporting users in task continuation and task completion.

While many of these insights would not have been possible without a detailed analysis of both the quantitative and qualitative data from our study, there are of course some limitations to our approach. We built a custom mobile search app for the purpose of the study, thus we were only aware of searches conducted within our $MSearch$ app. This means we may be missing searches conducted in other search engines and other apps. Likewise the fact that participants behaviors were tracked may have resulted in some deviation from the participants' normal behavior. That said our analysis does shed significant light on the nuances of search and app interactions. Albeit challenging, we would encourage future work to extend upon this study and perhaps incorporate searches across apps.

It's also important to highlight that we have explored mobile search and mobile app interactions within *sessions*, using a 30 second display-off window as a delimiter. Based on interviews with our participants we found that people also conduct searches that span multiple sessions to address a given need, and these sessions can span differing hours, days, weeks, even months. Particularly when searches were related to bigger things like buying a car or planning a vacation. We would encourage future research to consider search and app interactions across multiple sessions and multiple timeframes to see if other interesting patterns emerge.

Finally we should mention our participants who all live in the Greater San Francisco Bay area. While we made every effort to recruit a diverse sample of participants, we are aware that mobile search and app usage patterns may differ in other parts of the world. Thus we would encourage future work in this space in other cities and other countries around the world. Similarly our sample size was small — 18 Android users — thus we cannot claim that our pool of participants is large enough to be representative of the entire population of Android users. However we are confident that they were diverse enough to provide us with rich insights and to offer concrete hypotheses that could be used in future larger-scale studies.

CONCLUSIONS

In this paper we build upon and extend past research on mobile search and mobile app usage, focusing on the complex interactions and relationships between native apps and mobile search engines. By taking a step back from search and exploring the interactions in and around search, we have explored mobile information seeking in a new light. We provide a detailed understanding of cross app and search use and discuss what these findings mean for mobile information seeking and for improving future search experiences. As the landscape of smartphones continues to evolve and the lines between apps and search engines continue to blur, we would argue that more studies of this nature will be needed.

REFERENCES

1. Amin, A., Townsend, S., Ossenbruggen, J., and Hardman, L. Fancy a drink in canary wharf?: A user study on location-based mobile search. In *Proceedings of INTERACT '09:*, Springer-Verlag (2009), 736–749.
2. Baeza-Yates, R., and Velasco, J. A study of mobile search queries in japan. In *Query Log Analysis: Social and Technological Challenges, WWW Workshop* (2007).
3. Böhmer, M., Hecht, B., Schöning, J., Krüger, A., and Bauer, G. Falling asleep with angry birds, facebook and kindle: a large scale study on mobile application usage. In *Proceedings of Mobile HCI'11*, ACM (2011), 47–56.
4. Brown, B., McGregor, M., and Laurier, E. iphone in vivo: Video analysis of mobile device use. In *Proceedings of CHI'13*, ACM (2013), 1031–1040.
5. Chua, A. Y. K., Balkunje, R. S., and Goh, D. H.-L. Fulfilling mobile information needs: a study on the use of mobile phones. In *Proceedings of ICUIMC '11*, ACM (2011), 92:1–92:7.
6. Church, K., Cherubini, M., and Oliver, N. A large-scale study of daily information needs captured in situ. *In TOCHI 21*, 2 (2014), 10.
7. Church, K., and Oliver, N. Understanding mobile web and mobile search use in today's dynamic mobile landscape. In *Proceedings of MobileHCI'11*, ACM (2011), 67–76.
8. Church, K., Smyth, B., Cotter, P., and Bradley, K. Mobile information access: A study of emerging search behavior on the mobile internet. *In TWEB 1*, 1 (2007), 4.
9. Cui, Y., and Roto, V. How people use the web on mobile devices. In *Proceeding of WWW '08*, ACM (2008), 905–914.
10. Dearman, D., Kellar, M., and Truong, K. N. An examination of daily information needs and sharing opportunities. In *Proceedings of CSCW'08*, ACM (2008), 679–688.
11. Ferreira, D., Gonçalves, J., Kostakos, V., Barkhuus, L., and Dey, A. K. Contextual experience sampling of mobile application micro-usage. In *Proceedings of MobileHCI'14*, ACM (2014).
12. Heimonen, T. Information needs and practices of active mobile internet users. In *Proceedings of Mobility '09*, ACM (2009), 1–8.
13. Kamvar, M., and Baluja, S. A large scale study of wireless search behavior: Google mobile search. In *Proceedings of CHI'06*, ACM (2006), 701–709.
14. Kamvar, M., Kellar, M., Patel, R., and Xu, Y. Computers and iphones and mobile phones, oh my!: a logs-based comparison of search users on different devices. In *Proceedings of WWW'09*, ACM (2009), 801–810.
15. Komaki, D., Hara, T., and Nishio, S. How does mobile context affect people's web search behavior?: A diary study of mobile information needs and search behaviors. In *Proceedings of AINA*, IEEE (2012), 245–252.
16. Lee, I., Kim, J., and Kim, J. Use contexts for the mobile internet: A longitudinal study monitoring actual use of mobile internet services. *International Journal of Human-Computer Interaction 18*, 3 (2005), 269–292.
17. Lee, U., Lee, J., Ko, M., Lee, C., Kim, Y., Yang, S., Yatani, K., Gweon, G., Chung, K.-M., and Song, J. Hooked on smartphones: an exploratory study on smartphone overuse among college students. In *Proceedings of CHI'14*, ACM (2014), 2327–2336.
18. McGregor, M., Brown, B., and McMillan, D. 100 days of iphone use: Mobile recording in the wild. In *Proceedings of CHI '14 EA*, ACM (2014), 2335–2340.
19. Nielsen. An era of growth: The cross-platform report. http://bit.ly/1pcoQFU, March 2014.
20. Nylander, S., Lundquist, T., and Brännström, A. At home and with computer access: why and where people use cell phones to access the internet. In *Proceedings of CHI'09*, ACM (2009), 1639–1642.
21. Sohn, T., Li, K. A., Griswold, W. G., and Hollan, J. D. A diary study of mobile information needs. In *Proceedings of CHI'08*, ACM (2008), 433–442.
22. Song, Y., Ma, H., Wang, H., and Wang, K. Exploring and exploiting user search behavior on mobile and tablet devices to improve search relevance. In *Proceedings of WWW'13*, ACM (2013), 1201–1212.
23. Taylor, C. A., Anicello, O., Somohano, S., Samuels, N., Whitaker, L., and Ramey, J. A. A framework for understanding mobile internet motivations and behaviors. In *Proceedings of CHI'08 EA*, ACM (2008), 2679–2684.
24. Teevan, J., Karlson, A., Amini, S., Brush, A. B., and Krumm, J. Understanding the importance of location, time, and people in mobile local search behavior. In *Proceedings of MobileHCI'11* (2011).
25. Tossell, C., Kortum, P., Rahmati, A., Shepard, C., and Zhong, L. Characterizing web use on smartphones. In *Proceedings of CHI '12*, ACM (2012), 2769–2778.
26. Vojnovic, M. On mobile user behaviour patterns. In *International Zurich Seminar on Communications*, IEEE Communications Society (2008).
27. Yi, J., Maghoul, F., and Pedersen, J. Deciphering mobile search patterns: a study of yahoo! mobile search queries. In *Proceedings of WWW'08*, ACM (2008), 257–266.

The Composition and Use of Modern Mobile Phonebooks

Frank Bentley and Ying-Yu Chen
Yahoo Labs
San Francisco, CA USA
{fbentley, yyc}@yahoo-inc.com

ABSTRACT
Over the past decade, the mobile phonebook has evolved from a relatively short list of people that one calls and texts to a many-hundred person list of aggregated contacts from around the web. This is happening at a time when an increasing number of mobile applications are relying on the mobile phonebook to create one's social network in their services. Through a large-scale study of the phonebooks of 200 diverse participants, containing 65,940 contacts, we set out to understand today's mobile contact lists. Our participants reported that they did not recognize the names of 29% of their contacts and we found that the most frequently contacted five contacts represent greater than 80% of all calls and text messages with phonebook contacts. We conclude with implications for the design of mobile applications that rely on phonebook data.

Author Keywords
Mobile; Phonebook; Communication.

ACM Classification Keywords
H.5.m. Information interfaces and presentation (e.g., HCI): Miscellaneous.

INTRODUCTION
Mobile phones are becoming the main tool for daily communication needs. Recent research has shown that people are actively using their phones for hours per day and spending the majority of their time in communications-related applications [5]. An increasing number of these applications are relying on the mobile phonebook to create one's social network in their services. For some apps, phonebook entries are seen as "trusted" contacts who all get to automatically know if you're using the same app. In some cases, apps automatically share various rich presence information related to a contact's context.

In parallel, since the introduction of MotoBlur in 2009 [2], mobile phonebooks are now aggregators across many networks (calling, multiple email providers, Facebook, LinkedIn, Twitter, etc.) making them much more than just lists of people that you call on the phone. However, there has not been a systematic study investigating these new social phonebooks since they were first launched publicly five years ago. This is despite over one billion active Android users[1] having access to a variety of different forms of aggregated phonebooks and major applications with hundreds of millions of users accessing these lists. Who is really in your socially-connected phonebook? And what can this say about the suitability of this list for various services (location sharing, auto-friending, etc.)?

We set out to explore these questions for the purposes of improving the design of mobile phonebooks and providing implications for the design of new communications applications that take advantage of mobile phonebook data. Through a study of 200 diverse participants from across the United States, we analyzed phonebook entries and call log data for their 65,940 contacts. Participants reported that they had "no idea" who 29% of their contacts were and we found that the most frequently contacted five contacts represent greater than 80% of all calls and text messages with people in the phonebook. This has strong implications for current phonebooks that attempt to treat an average of 308 contacts equally, and for new communications systems which need to make sense of contact data to onboard users into their services.

RESEARCH QUESTIONS
We began this work with a series of research questions related to understanding the composition of current smartphone contact lists, current communication practices on mobile devices, and how contacts might be used in a variety of applications. With respect to the phonebooks, we wanted to know: How many contacts do people have? Which services are linked? Who are these contacts? Are they current friends/colleagues? Former contacts?

With respect to communication history, we were interested in exploring: What percentage of contacts do people actually communicate with? How often? What percentage of communication goes to the top five or ten contacts? When was last time of communication to specific types contacts in any form?

CHI 2015, April 18 - 23 2015, Seoul, Republic of Korea
Copyright 2015 ACM 978-1-4503-3145-6/15/04···$15.00
http://dx.doi.org/10.1145/2702123.2702182

[1] http://www.engadget.com/2014/06/25/google-io-2014-by-the-numbers/

Finally, we were interested in exploring how contacts might be used in applications that integrate with mobile phonebooks. Particularly, we wanted to understand: How comfortable would people be in sharing various aspects of their lives (location, TV viewing, photostream, calendar, etc.) with these contacts? Are there differences between contacts that users call or text regularly and other contacts? How comfortable would people be with automatically adding specific contacts in particular kinds of applications (e.g. chat, location sharing, etc.)?

In order to explore these questions, we designed an online survey that integrated with participants' mobile phonebooks to collect data. We will describe the survey and methods below after introducing some background and related work.

RELATED WORK

Research into mobile phonebooks and communication patterns has been explored since the early 2000s. This research has included developing new phonebooks with a variety of features, studying their use, and studying call logs to understand fundamental qualities of daily life such as commute patterns. However, we could not find an example of a paper that deeply explored the use of the new, socially-aggregated contact lists that are common on over a billion of today's smart phones. Nor could we find a study of current mobile communication practices to phone contacts. This type of information is essential to build new communications systems as well as to understand how communication has changed in the era of the smartphone.

Early work in the field of Mobile HCI explored augmented phonebooks. Context Phonebook [22] was an example of this work that augmented phonebooks with rich presence information about contacts, such as their location or current ringer profile. ContextPhone [20] was a later example of this type of system. Motion Presence from Motorola Labs [4] took another spin on this idea, and provided a more privacy-preserving, binary "in-motion" indicator next to the names of close friends and family in the phonebook to help moderate availability and support micro-coordination [16]. These projects all explored what it would mean to have rich, real-time social information about contacts visible in the phonebook and how people would engage with such systems.

This early research led to commercial phonebooks that aggregated data from social networks. The MotoBlur service [2] became the first commercial social phonebook, aggregating contacts from Facebook, MySpace, Twitter, and other social networks into the phonebook. This necessitated a matching process that would link together contacts from multiple services. It also led to contact lists that ballooned from the small number of people one actually calls and texts to lists of potentially thousands of contacts aggregated from one's "friends" across social networks. This type of phonebook is now the default on Android and Windows Phone and has been largely unstudied since its introduction over five years ago.

A number of researchers have recently explored using call data records (CDRs) from mobile operators to understand patterns of human mobility. Eagle [9] set out a wide-ranging research area to use mobile phone logs to explore large populations and minimize the errors of data that is collected using self-reports. He explored the possibility of using large-scale CDRs for understanding human mobility patterns, social network structure, and the ability to confirm theories such as Milgram's social distance experiment. Furletti *et al.* [10] explored using CDRs to estimate mobility flow in and out of a city. We were inspired by this area of work and explicitly chose to base our communications findings on real call and SMS logs uploaded from phones, instead of relying on self-reported communication frequency.

Several researchers have studied SMS usage patterns in smaller-scale studies. Battestini *et al.* [1] explored SMS behaviors with 70 university students, finding that on average they texted 47 contacts. Grinter and Eldridge [11] studied ten British teenagers and found they they texted between 10-15 other people. Ito [14] studied the phonebooks of Japanese teenagers, finding that while they had many contacts, they only communicated with a few people. We were curious to see what communications practices looked like for a broader audience and with modern smartphones, a combination that we have not seen studied in detail.

Other researchers have explored tie strength with regards to the contacts in mobile phone books. In perhaps the closest study to our work, Min *et al.* [19] explored the contacts in mobile phonebooks and asked 40 participants to rate the tie strength to a curated selection of contacts. However, in their focus on tie strength, the authors did not explore the contact list more fully. In particular, none of our research questions above to understand the larger phonebook and communication patterns can be answered with the data in their paper. Because they did not choose random contacts from the phonebook, the overall makeup of the phonebook cannot be determined. Wiese *et al.* [24] extended this work to show that contacts who are contacted frequently are often high tie-strength, but contacts that are not frequently contacted on the telephone are not necessarily weak ties.

In addition to the academic literature, there are now a large number of commercial mobile applications that upload contact data or otherwise attempt to integrate with the phonebook. Wildly popular applications such as WhatsApp, Facebook, LinkedIn, Twitter, Instagram, Yelp, Path Talk and Foursquare all either automatically, or with user consent, access the mobile phonebook and use the contacts that are stored there to set up lists of potential communication partners [23]. Other smart mobile phonebooks, such as the current Android and Windows Phone contact lists also provide some level of social integration. The design of these default phonebooks can be enhanced with deeper knowledge of how people communicate and the types of contacts that are stored.

The literature contains gaps in understanding the content of socially-connected mobile phonebooks and current mobile communication patterns. To this end, we created our study to quantify who is in current mobile phonebooks, communication patterns with these people, and the suitability of automatically sharing information with these contacts or adding them in a variety of mobile services. This knowledge will help anyone designing new mobile communication applications or any services that wish to integrate with the mobile phonebook. In addition, we provide an understanding of current communication practices that is interesting from a sociological viewpoint. We will return to this topic in the discussion.

METHOD

In order to answer our research questions, we conducted an online survey in the summer of 2014. We chose to create an Android application that participants could install to collect metadata about their phonebooks and call histories. Android currently has a global market share of 80% of all smartphones [18] and is interesting as it enables complete access to the phonebook from any application with no further user consent than approving the installation of the app. Android phonebooks also merge their contacts from several services into the global contact list (e.g. Gmail, Facebook, LinkedIn). This merging of a variety of different types of contacts into the phonebook has the potential to include a wide set of people, changing the contact list from its traditional role of a relatively short list of people that a person actually calls or text messages. This change has deep implications for the design of mobile applications that rely on phonebook data as discussed above.

Survey

The study was conducted as an online survey, with 200 diverse participants from around the United States. Participants downloaded a small Android application to their phone which retrieved phonebook metadata from the device. We did not collect any information that could be used to contact the people from the phonebook, such as phone numbers or email addresses. Instead, we uploaded the "Name" field (for identification during the survey) as well as boolean values indicating if a phone number or email address was present for each contact. We also uploaded metadata about call and SMS history (timestamp and duration/length only, not actual message content). All information was sent via HTTPS to our server, and each participant was given a code when this upload completed that they could enter into the web-based survey to continue. Participants were shown sample data and had to explicitly agree to the collection of their data before installing the mobile application.

Upon entering the code, we selected 25 random contacts from their uploaded phonebooks and asked participants several questions about these people. They were asked to identify the type of relation that they had with the person (e.g. friend, family, colleague, business, unknown, etc.), the last time they communicated with that person in any way, questions on how comfortable they would feel automatically sharing various types of information with each contact, as well as four questions to assess their tie strength with each contact. For tie strength, we used the questions and scales presented in [24]. These include: "How close do you feel to this person?" "I talk with this person about important matters," "I would be willing to ask this person for a loan of $100 or more," and "I enjoy interacting with this person socially."

Following the questions relating to their 25 randomly selected contacts, we asked for general information about their phonebooks (e.g. which services they synced to their phonebook) as well as general demographic information. The survey took an average of 17 minutes to complete, and participants were compensated for their time.

Participants Demographics

Our 200 participants comprised a very representative sample of the adult American population. They ranged in age from 18-64 (mean = 30, $\sigma = 8$), 51% were female, and 34% had completed college (compared to a US average of 33.5% [21]). They resided in 35 different states, including all regions of the country, and 80% lived in urban areas (compared to a US average of 81% [15]). All had owned their smartphone for at least 6 months. We chose to conclude the study upon reaching 200 participants as the data was not significantly changing after the addition of the final 50 participants. For example, the mean length of the contact lists changed by fewer than 10 contacts (3%).

RESULTS

From our 200 participants, we collected information about 65,940 total contacts. We also received detailed survey responses relating to 4,975 contacts (the random 25 chosen for each participant). A total of 25 contacts (0.5%) were skipped by participants while completing the survey. We also received call logs for 74,493 calls and SMS metadata about 306,228 messages totaling 14,711,628 characters.

In addition, we collected qualitative responses from two open ended questions: one asking participants if anything had surprised them after participating in the study and another asking if they planned on changing anything in their phonebooks after participating. All together, we captured 227 responses that were longer than a single word and analyzed them for themes in an affinity analysis. Themes from these notes will be discussed in parallel with the quantitative data to enhance the presentation of the statistics with explanations from our participants.

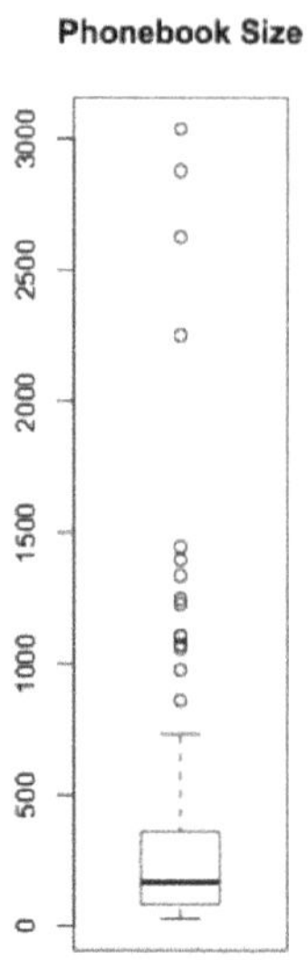

Figure 1: The number of contacts in an Android phonebook. Note that while the mean was 308, there were fourteen participants (7%) with more than 1000 contacts.

In the following subsections, we will describe the composition of today's mobile phone books, explore current mobile communications patterns, and discuss the desirability of sharing various information with particular types of contacts.

Phonebook Composition

Figure 1 shows the distribution of the number of contacts in an Android phonebook. The mean size was 308 contacts with 25% of participants having contact lists with greater than 360 contacts. Phonebooks ranged in size from 26 to 3,038 contacts.

Where did these contacts come from? As expected on a Google Android phone, 84% of participants reported connecting their Google/Gmail accounts to their phonebook. 70% of participants reported connecting their Facebook accounts, while 17% connected their Yahoo accounts. As 71% of American adults use Facebook [7] and Yahoo's mobile email market share is currently 19%, this shows that a high percentage of people choose to sync these services to their phonebook (which is the default behavior on Android for these applications). Eleven percent of participants did not sync their phonebook with any of these services.

Who were these contacts? We asked participants to categorize each of their 25 randomly selected contacts into the categories shown in Figure 2. Most strikingly, over 29% of contact names could not be recognized by the participants (the survey response was phrased "I have no idea"). This is likely due to the fact that a variety of services were linked to their account, including Facebook or LinkedIn where they are likely to have contacts that they have never met in person. This is validated by the open ended responses that were placed at the end of the survey.

Participants were surprised by how many people in the phone book they didn't know or that they didn't communicate with. In the open-ended responses, they shared that they did not previously realize who was in their phonebooks: "I have a lot more people in there that I have no idea who they are than I thought." Another told us: "I realized I have no clue who most people in my contacts are, and yes, it has been VERY surprising!" Several participants even thanked us for showing them how many people they did not know and said that they planned to clean out their phonebooks after participating.

Many participants did not know how contacts got in their phonebook. For example, one participant expressed his/her confusion: "I'm surprised that there are as many people in there that I don't remember adding or calling or texting." Some participants expressed concern as they had no idea how the contacts got in: "I had no idea I had so many contacts!!! I am shocked and a little concerned."

Some participants were surprised that Gmail contacts were in their phonebooks, and reported not liking this. These were often called "junk contacts" or "random contacts," especially those that came from services such as Craigslist. This confused some participants: "I'm confused all the contacts came from. I assume the app used my email too? Because wow, that's a lot of contacts." Some responses

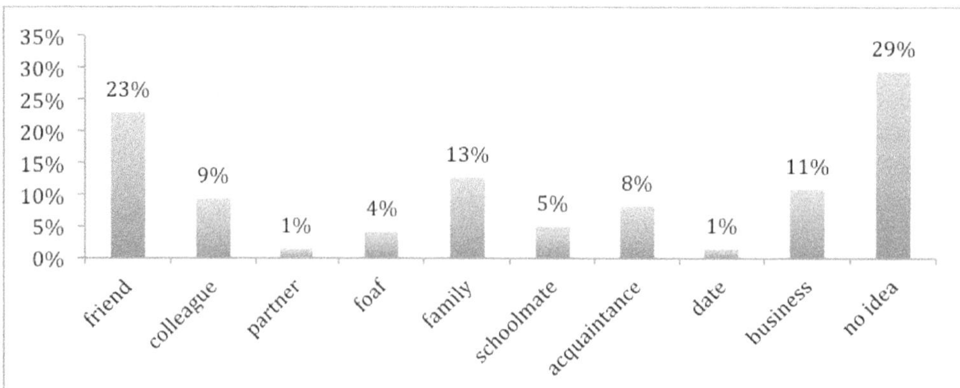

Figure 2: Percentages of contacts by category. There are more contacts that the participants could not identify than friends.

indicated that they did not like this feature of Android. One participant told us, "I really hate how Google automatically adds anyone I ever received email from."

Similar responses came with regards to contacts from other services: "There's lot's of junk there, including Skype contacts," or, "People I follow on twitter are there for some reason." Completing the survey helped them realize that there were contacts in their phonebooks from social networking apps: "I never knew that contacts from social applications (Tango, Viber, Skype, etc.) are included as part of the contacts."

As to the other contacts that participants did recognize, 23% were Friends, 13% were Family, and 9% were Colleagues. We find it interesting that 11% of the contacts were Businesses (such as restaurants, repairmen, etc.). Figure 2 contains more detail on the other categories. Note that a single contact can be in multiple categories.

Turning to tie-strength as a different measure of closeness, 46% of all contacts were rated with a tie-strength of 0 (the lowest possible score on all four questions), as shown in Figure 3. Interestingly, the remainder of the contacts fell fairly evenly between 1-6% for each remaining value of tie strength. We find this encouraging as participants clearly thought about their responses and did not simply answer all four tie-strength questions the same way. It is interesting to note that 6% of contacts were rated as the highest level on all four questions relating to tie strength, representing 10 contacts in the median sized phonebook.

Investigating the contact fields that are populated for each contact, we observed that 55% of phonebook entries have a phone number populated, while 45% have an email address. 5% of contacts have both an email address and a phone number, while another 5% do not have any phone number

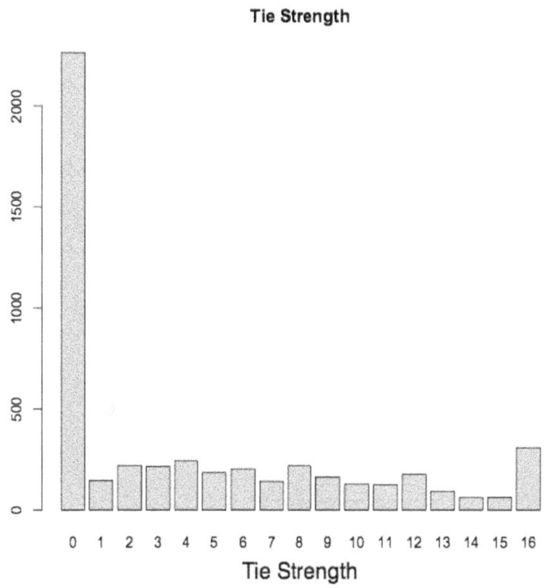

Figure 3: The number of contacts of varying tie strengths. Note that 46% of all contacts have a tie-strength of 0 while 6% have the maximum possible tie strength of 16.

or email address populated. These contacts without contact information can appear from linked sources such as Facebook, LinkedIn, or Twitter where the connected user does not share their phone or email contact information with the participant.

Most contacts conformed to a "FirstName LastName" pattern, however 26% of contact names did not contain a space and are presumed to be first names or nicknames only. A look through these contact names shows examples

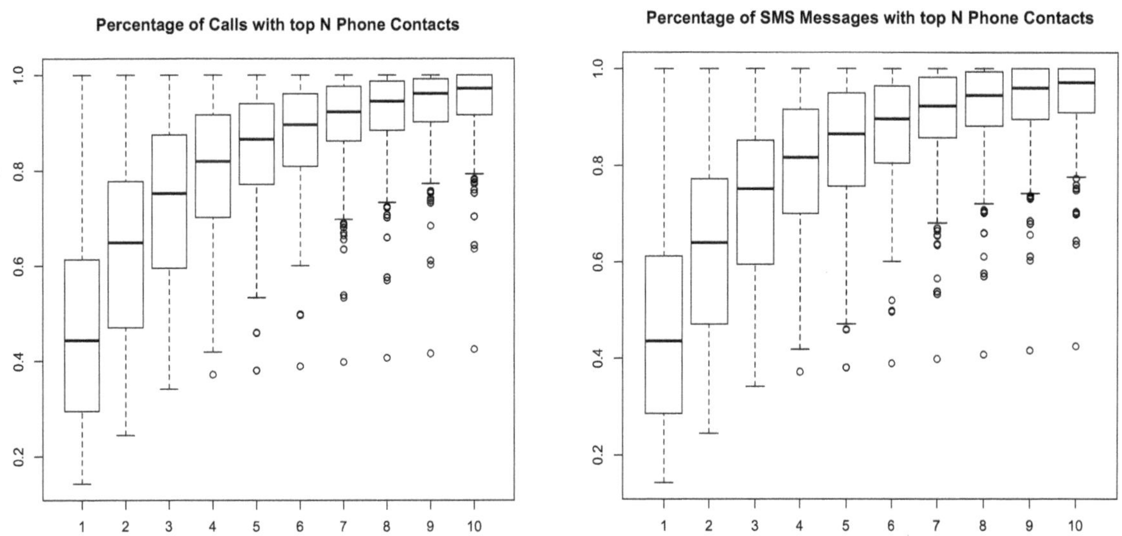

Figure 4: The percentage of calls (left) and SMS messages (right) for the top N most frequently contacted users from the contact list. On average, over 80 percents of all calls and SMS messages are with the top 5 contacts.

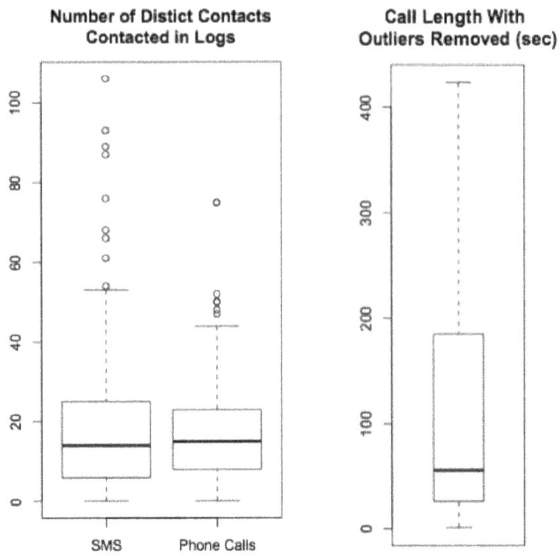

Figure 5: Left: Number of distinct contacts that were contacted via SMS (since phone was purchased) or via phone calls (in the past 500 calls). Right: The length of calls, in seconds. Note that outliers are removed and there were some very long calls (some up to 10 hours) in the dataset.

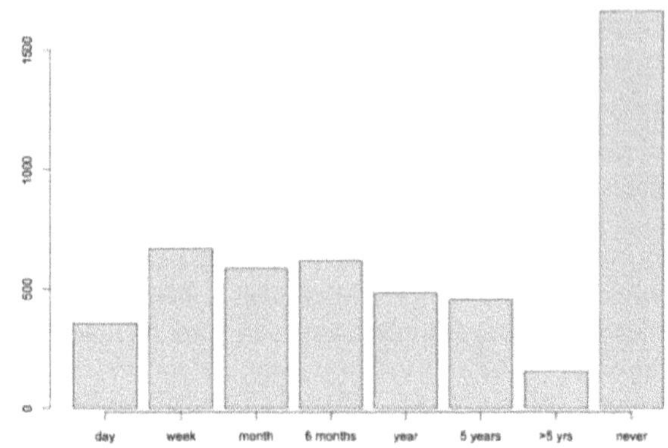

Figure 6: Last time of contact across any medium (including social networking and face to face) for the contacts shown to our participants.

such as "Work," "Bank," "School," "Stinky," and "Roomie." However, even contacts with spaces do not necessarily represent proper names. We saw entries such as "My Wife," "Lover Boy," "Handsome Husband," and "Mom and Dad" in the name fields. This is important for services that attempt to merge contacts with online profiles as name matches are not possible for these types of contacts. It is also important for services that expect to use the contact's name for creating profiles or sending out invitations to join a service. Getting an invite addressed to "Stinky" might not be what that contact would expect or appreciate.

The most common names in the phonebooks were "Mom" (10% of participants), "Dad" (9% of participants), and "Home" (6% of participants). Overall, we can see that mobile phonebooks today contain a wide array of contacts from many broad contexts of a person's life, many of whom are not even recognized by name.

Contact Patterns

After investigating the call logs, we have found that 84% of all calls and 81% of SMS messages with people in the phonebook are to the five most frequently contacted people. Looking at the ten most frequently contacted people yields 94% of phone calls and 92% of all SMS messages that are made with people in the phonebook (see Figure 4).

As the average phonebook size was over 300 entries, we wanted to investigate what percentage of these contacts were ever contacted through phone calls or SMS. Most Android phones limit the call log length to the past 500 calls. Of these 500 calls, an average of only 17 distinct contacts (6% of all contacts) were represented. SMS logs trace back much farther on average to include anyone messaged since the phone was first used. Our participants had an average of 19 distinct contacts (also 6% of all contacts) in the SMS logs. A surprisingly few number of contacts make up the total of all phone or SMS communications, as can be seen in Figure 5. An interesting population to consider is the 25% of participants who had called fewer than eight contacts or messaged fewer than six.

These numbers are similar to the 10-15 contacts that were text messaged in Grinter and Eldridge's study of British teens [11], and much lower than the 47 contacts found in Battestini *et al.*'s college student population [1].

It is also interesting to explore recency of contact. Of contacts that were text messaged, the median length of time since last contact was 26 days with 25% of text messaged contacts having been contacted in the past 8 days. For contacts that were called, the median length since last contact was slightly longer at 36 days with 25% of called contacts being called in the past 17 days.

Digging deeper into the call logs, 27% of all calls were incoming and answered, 19% were incoming and unanswered, and 54% of calls were outgoing calls placed by the participant. We find the high number of missed calls quite interesting, and have not previously seen this reported in the literature. It is also interesting to note that 31% of all calls were with people who were not stored in the phonebook at all. This number was slightly higher for outgoing calls which represented 55% of calls with participants not in the phonebook. It is notable that 65% of all incoming calls from unknown numbers (not stored in the phonebook) were not answered, representing a large majority of all unanswered calls.

If we investigate the self-reported time of last contact in Figure 6, we can see that 33% of all contacts have never been contacted at all. In total, participants reported that 55% of contacts had not been contacted in any way in over 6 months (including face to face or through social media). This compares to 80% of contacts that had not been contacted in the past six months as seen through the "last contacted" field in the phone logs (which can include services other than calling or messaging). Clearly, these logs are not enough to fully capture the people that one communicates with, since much communication occurs in other applications or face to face and is thus not visible from the phonebook metadata.

As for the communications themselves, phone calls averaged 271 seconds in length. The median call length was 56 seconds, with 75% of calls being shorter than 185 seconds. However, there are some very long multi-hour calls in the logs. Because of these, the call lengths shown in Figure 5 have outliers removed to enhance readability. Just under 1% of calls lasted over one hour and just over 2% of calls lasted between 30-60 minutes. For SMS messages, the average message length was 48 characters and the average message history with an individual contact totaled 75 messages (ranging from 1 to 6645 messages).

Since most mobile phonebooks contain a "recent calls" list, we were interested in investigating how well the recent calls list represented the contacts that are most likely to be contacted. We looked at the most recent N calls for N up to 10 in order to investigate what percentage of the most frequently contacted N contacts are represented in a recent contacts list of length N. The results can be seen in Figure 7. Note that for ten contacts, only a median of six of the most frequently contacted ten contacts appear in this list of the ten most recent calls. While a recents list might be great to contact "temporary" contacts that might be relevant over the course of a day or weekend, it does not provide easy access to the most frequently contacted people.

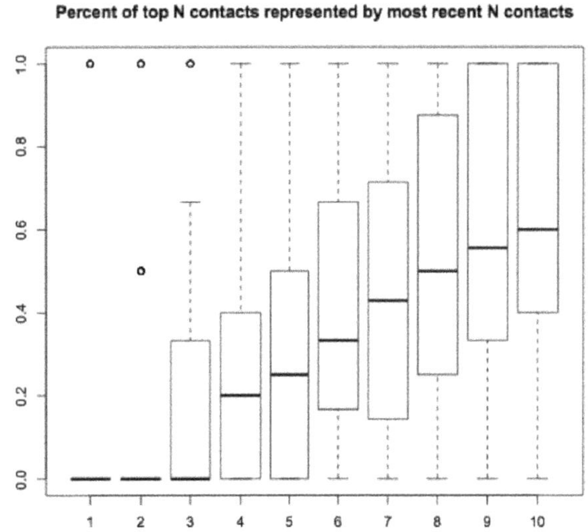

Figure 7: An investigation into the suitability of the "recent calls" list to represent the most contacted contacts. A contact list of the ten most recent calls only captures a median of 6 of the most frequently contacted contacts.

Desirability of Sharing

As the mobile phonebook is now being used by a wide variety of mobile apps to auto-populate contact lists or to determine people to automatically share information with, we were interested in exploring how users felt about sharing a variety of information with their 25 randomly selected contacts. While we recognize that the CHI literature points to complex contextual factors in the decision to share rich presence [6], since many applications with hundreds of millions of users ask each user to choose friends and sharing preferences upon installation, we found these to be relatively important questions to ask.

Table 1 highlights sharing preferences for a variety of different presence information. These types of information

	Friend	Colleague	Partner	FOAF	Family	Schoolmate	Acquaintance	Date	Business
Location	41	16	79	20	46	33	16	31	5
TV Shows	36	13	67	21	40	35	14	28	3
Calendar	32	14	70	16	38	37	11	15	4
Transportation	31	12	71	13	37	30	15	22	4

Table 1: The percentage of contacts from different categories that participants feel comfortable always seeing their location, TV shows they are watching, calendar free/busy times, or mode of transportation.

	Friend	Colleague	Partner	FOAF	Family	Schoolmate	Acquaintance	Date	Business
Chat App	53	22	71	22	51	48	21	34	4
Music App	42	17	64	19	42	41	15	26	3
Location App	31	12	60	10	36	27	9	16	2

Table 2: The percentage of participants who felt comfortable automatically adding a contact as a 'buddy' in a variety of apps.

have been explored in previous research (e.g. Consolvo *et al.* [6], Bentley *et al.* [3], Harboe *et al.* [12]) and are along the lines of information currently being shared in commercial products, for example Facebook's recent addition of TV and Location sharing to its mobile application and Path Talk's sharing of location, music, and mode of transport.

Unsurprisingly, participants felt most comfortable sharing rich presence information with their partner, with 79% willing to share location, and 70% willing to share their calendar. Family, friends, and schoolmates clustered at similar percentages in the 33-45% range while colleagues, acquaintances, and businesses ranked lowest. The differences between the three groups mentioned above are all statistically significant with X^2 between 25-276 and $p<10^{-8}$ for each pairwise comparison between groups. Tie-strength was positively correlated with all aspects of sharing rich presence information and for friending in mobile applications, with $r>0.5$ and $p<10^{-16}$ for all comparisons between overall tie strength and each type of rich presence data.

We find it interesting that our participants did not indicate a significant difference in willingness to share different types of information. The type of person mattered far more than the type of information shared.

We found similar differences when participants were asked if they were willing to let a new application directly connect them to their contacts. Here we also see that participants are more willing to automatically connect to their partners, followed by the set of friends, family and schoolmates, followed everyone else (see Table 2). We will return to the implications of these findings in the discussion.

Actions to Clean Up Their Phonebooks

In the open-ended responses at the end of the survey, many participants indicated that they planned on cleaning up their phonebooks in some way. Some participants decided to unsync specific services. People said that they would "disconnect my Facebook friends from my phone" or "unsync contacts from Google."

Aside from unsyncing entire applications, many participants said that they would remove specific contacts from their phone books. They said that they would "clear out," "delete," or "weed out" people they didn't know or the "unnecessary" contacts. Our participants specifically pointed out "old contacts" as people that they would like to delete. One participant told us: "I will be deleting contacts I no longer talk to because I know for a fact I do not talk to over 200 people. I feel that it is cluttering my phone." Another person told us that they will "remove contacts I no longer utilize on a regular basis (i.e. people I don't call at least once in a year)." Some of these contacts were "one off" contacts such as "people I had classes with at college" and were no longer relevant to the participant.

This idea of "temporary contacts" was interesting to us. For example, many participants had contact information for people that they bought or sold something with on Craigslist. After the transaction was completed, these people were no longer needed, yet almost always remained in the phonebook due to the effort required to find and then delete a specific contact.

Some participants said that they would like to delete some contacts, but that they are too lazy and it takes effort. One participant said that "it's probably going to take more than an hour to do." Another said that they had "a long trip as a passenger tomorrow and will spend some of the time deleting [contacts]." Yet, for others it was just too much effort. They told us: "I don't know if I care to go through that trouble [to clean up the contact list]" or "I'm lazy and it doesn't hurt anything to have them in there." And some participants liked having every contact always available: "I'm not sure I will delete any since I like to keep numbers handy should I ever need them for any reason."

Overall, most users wanted to remove some contacts, but realized that the effort required and the sheer number of contacts that they would have to look through meant that this would be a large task.

DISCUSSION

A thorough analysis of the contents of modern Android phonebooks, which make up 80% of the smartphone market, enables us to explore the implications of this work on the design of new mobile social applications. Particularly, the design of applications that import contact data or new phonebook interactions can benefit from our findings. In addition, our analysis of mobile communication patterns is interesting from a sociological point of view.

Usage Based Favorites

A major finding was that despite having an average of 308 contacts in the phonebook, over 80% of calls and messages were to just five people, and over 92% of communications occurred with just ten people. Despite this, most mobile phonebooks still provide the A-Z list as the most common selection mechanism. Some have the ability to "favorite" a contact, but this feature seems rarely used and is not always very visible for users. Even if contacts are favorited, launching the Contacts app on most Android phones still defaults to the A-Z list.

To better align with user behavior, contact lists (and applications that import these lists) should help users easily find their top ten contacts based on available communication history. All of this can be done on-device without the need to upload contact data to a server and can provide the user with the person they are looking for over 92% of the time without the need to scroll through hundreds or even thousands of names.

"Trusted" Contacts

Applications should not assume that just because a person is present in a mobile phonebook, that they are a trusted contact. Over 29% of all contacts in our participants' phone books were completely unknown to them, and only 6% scored the highest in perceived tie-strength. Applications should see the phonebook as a very extended social graph, including many friends of friends or former acquaintances. While there might be some services where it is appropriate to include all of these people as contacts, our research shows that people are highly uncomfortable automatically sharing location or calendar data with over 80% of the people in their phonebooks. Applications should be careful to allow users to select the specific contacts that will be able to see a particular aspect of their context.

Aggregated Lists

Back when MotoBlur was first designed [2], it was assumed that people would want all of their contacts accessible on their mobile device. However, as the number of social networks that a user belongs to has increased and friend counts on these networks have also increased, it has become clear that for some users there are just too many contacts in their phonebooks. Our qualitative data, showing that many users planned to prune their lists after participating in the study, shows that there needs to be a way to control who gets added to the phonebook, or at least who is visible. Making it clearly visible which services are linked, how to unlink them, or providing controls to filter out specific contacts are all desired features.

Transient Contacts

An interesting finding was around the use of transient contacts: people who are only in your life for a very short amount of time. Perhaps this is someone you're buying a couch from off of Craigslist or the email of a teaching assistant for a class that will last 12 weeks. Having an easy way to add a contact for a set duration is important and will lessen the current "clutter" of large contact lists full of contacts that have not been contacted in years and were only relevant for a very short time.

Implications for Theory

Over the years, many theories relating to communication patterns have been created. In this section, we will discuss our findings with respect to other work that has addressed the size of social networks. For example, Dunbar's Number [8] states that humans can have approximately 100-200 stable social relationships. While we saw a mean of over 300 contacts, the median was 164, very close to this number. In later work, Hill and Dunbar [13] found that family represented 21% of those in one's social network. We found this percentage to be only 13%. This could be due to a larger number of "friends" and colleagues being imported through services such as Facebook or LinkedIn and can more accurately describe today's broader social connections where it is easier to minimally stay in touch with large numbers of more distant friends.

We can also look at theories related to close contacts, such as Marsden's Discussion Contacts [17]. In this work, he found that Americans typically have three contacts with which they discuss "important matters." We asked this question in our survey as well, and we found a higher number of "Discussion Contacts." For the median phonebook size, there were 10 contacts in the highest tie strength bucket, which included the question on discussing "important matters." Interestingly, despite there being more Discussion Contacts in our data, we found almost exactly the same percentage of family versus friends that were discussion contacts as compared to Marsden's research. Marsden found 1.5 kin and 1.4 non-kin (a ratio of 1.07) while we found a ratio of 1.05 despite having a higher percentage of friends in the phonebook as discussed above. Further research along these lines would be required to make strong claims here.

LIMITATIONS

While we believe that the scale of our analysis and the strong diversity of our participants enables us to make the strong quantitative claims above, there are a few limitations to our method.

First, only participants who had access to the web from a computer, and could install our application onto their smartphone could participate. However, as we saw an education distribution and urban/rural split that were almost identical to the US population, this does not seem to have affected recruitment.

Second, our study only contains participants from the United States. While many participants self-identified as immigrating from other countries, and we covered over 30 states with our participants, communication patterns in other parts of the world are likely different and would need to be studied independently.

Finally, this study only represents a snapshot of the phonebook as of Summer 2014. As mobile phonebooks change and as more services add integration to the phonebook and insert contacts from their services, the makeup of the phonebook will likely change. Also, the rise of services such as WhatsApp (which is still not extremely popular in America due to a lesser need to send international messages) likely will limit the usefulness of SMS logs for analysis over time and in other regions. Currently, the SMS app is the most used app of any category on Android in the US.

CONCLUSION

We have described a study investigating the composition of Android phonebooks and communication history with a variety of contacts. Through collecting data from 200 participants about their 65,940 contacts as well as metadata for 74,493 calls and 306,228 SMS messages we have shown that mobile phonebooks are far more than a list of trusted contacts who are called and massaged frequently.

Since 29% of contacts are completely unknown and more than 80% of communication is to five people, this work has strong implications on the design of applications that use the phonebook to import contacts and for the design of mobile phonebooks that currently make it hard to access the most frequently contacted people in one's life.

Although Android is the dominant smartphone OS, it would be interesting to conduct this study on other phone platforms. Windows Phone has a very similar mechanism for applications to integrate with the phonebook and understanding differences in use for certain design differences between the platforms would be interesting. Overall, we expect the findings of our research to be useful for those designing new phonebooks as well as those creating new communications applications that take advantage of the contact list available on mobile platforms.

REFERENCES

1. Agathe Battestini, Vidya Setlur, and Timothy Sohn. 2010. A large scale study of text-messaging use. In Proceedings of MobileHCI 2010.
2. Frank R. Bentley, JoEllen Kames, Rafiq Ahmed, Rhiannon Sterling Zivin, and Lauren Schwendimann. 2010. Contacts 3.0: bringing together research and design teams to reinvent the phonebook. In CHI '10 Extended Abstracts.
3. Bentley, Frank, and Crysta J. Metcalf. "The Use of Mobile Social Presence." IEEE Pervasive Computing 8.4 (2009): 35-41.
4. Frank R. Bentley and Crysta J. Metcalf. 2007. Sharing motion information with close family and friends. In Proc. CHI '07. ACM, New York, NY, USA, 1361-1370.
5. Böhmer, Matthias, Brent Hecht, Johannes Schöning, Antonio Krüger, and Gernot Bauer. "Falling asleep with Angry Birds, Facebook and Kindle: a large scale study on mobile application usage." In Proc. Mobile HCI '11.
6. Consolvo, Sunny, et al. "Location disclosure to social relations: why, when, & what people want to share." In Proc. CHI 2005.
7. Maeve Duggan and Aaron Smith Social Media Update 2013. 2013. http://www.pewinternet.org/fact-sheets/social-networking-fact-sheet/
8. R.I.M Dunbar. 1998. The Social Brain Hypothesis. Evo. Anthro., 6:178.
9. Eagle, Nathan. "Mobile phones as sensors for social research." Emergent technologies in social research. Oxford University Press, New York (2011): 492-521.
10. Furletti, Barbara, et al. 2014. "Use of mobile phone data to estimate mobility flows. Measuring urban population and inter-city mobility using big data in an integrated approach." In Proceedings of the 47th Meeting of the Italian Statistical Society.
11. Rebecca Grinter and Margery Eldridge. 2003. Wan2tlk?: everyday text messaging. In Proc. CHI 2003.
12. Harboe, Gunnar, et al. "Ambient social tv: drawing people into a shared experience." In Proc. CHI 2008.
13. Hill, Russell A., and Robin IM Dunbar. "Social network size in humans." Human nature 14.1 (2003): 53-72.
14. Ito, M., Mobile Phones, Japanese Youth, and the Re-Placement of Social Contact. In Proceedings of Annual Meeting for the Society for the Social Studies of Science, (Cambridge, MA, 2001).
15. Lisa Lambert. More Americans move to cities in past decade-Census. Reuters. Mar 26, 2012. http://www.reuters.com/article/2012/03/26/usa-cities-population-idUSL2E8EQ5AJ20120326
16. Ling, Rich, and Birgitte Yttri. "Nobody sits at home and waits for the telephone to ring: Micro and hyper-coordination through the use of the mobile telephone." Telenor Forskning og Utvikling, FoU Rapport 30 (1999): 99.
17. Marsden PV. 1987. Core discussion networks of Americans. Am. Sociol. Rev. 52:122-313
18. Natasha Lomas. 2014. Android Still Growing Market Share By Winning First Time Smartphone Users. Techcrunch. http://techcrunch.com/2014/05/06/android-still-growing-market-share-by-winning-first-time-smartphone-users/
19. Jun-Ki Min, Jason Wiese, Jason I. Hong, and John Zimmerman. 2013. Mining smartphone data to classify life-facets of social relationships. In Proc. CSCW '13. ACM, New York, NY, USA, 285-294.
20. Raento, Mika, Antti Oulasvirta, Renaud Petit, and Hannu Toivonen. "ContextPhone: A prototyping platform for context-aware mobile applications." Pervasive Computing, IEEE 4, no. 2 (2005): 51-59.
21. Catherine Rampell, Data Reveal a Rise in College Degrees Among Americans. New York Times. June 13, 2013. http://www.nytimes.com/2013/06/13/education/a-sharp-rise-in-americans-with-college-degrees.html
22. A. Schmidt, T, Stuhr, and H.W. Gellersen. 2001. Context-Phonebook - Extending Mobile Phone Applications with Context. In Proc. Mobile HCI 2001.
23. Jennifer VanGrove. 2012. Your address book is mine: Many iPhone apps take your data. Venture Beat. http://venturebeat.com/2012/02/14/iphone-address-book/
24. Jason Wiese, Jun-Ki Min, Jason I. Hong, and John Zimmerman. 2015. "You Never Call, You Never Write": Call and SMS Logs Do Not Always Indicate Tie Strength. In Proc. CSCW '15.

Effects of Display Size and Resolution on User Behavior and Insight Acquisition in Visual Exploration

Khairi Reda[1,2], Andrew E. Johnson[3], Michael E. Papka[1,4], Jason Leigh[2]
[1]Argonne National Laboratory, [2]University of Hawai'i at Mānoa, [3]University of Illinois at Chicago,
[4]Northern Illinois University
{kreda, papka}@anl.gov, ajohnson@uic.edu, leighj@hawaii.edu

ABSTRACT

Large high-resolution displays are becoming increasingly common in research settings, providing data scientists with visual interfaces for the analysis of large datasets. Numerous studies have demonstrated unique perceptual and cognitive benefits afforded by these displays in visual analytics and information visualization tasks. However, the effects of these displays on knowledge discovery in exploratory visual analysis are still poorly understood. We present the results of a small-scale study to better understand how display size and resolution affect insight. Analyzing participants' verbal statements, we find preliminary evidence that larger displays with more pixels can significantly increase the number of discoveries reported during visual exploration, while yielding broader, more integrative insights. Furthermore, we find important differences in how participants performed the same visual exploration task using displays of varying sizes. We tie these results to extant work and propose explanations by considering the cognitive and interaction costs associated with visual exploration.

Author Keywords

Large high-resolution displays; visualization; exploratory visual analysis; cognitive biases.

ACM Classification Keywords

H.5.m. Information Interfaces and Presentation (e.g., HCI): Miscellaneous

INTRODUCTION

Exploratory analysis represents one of the main use cases for visualizations. Often, the primary reason for employing visualization is to enable users to broadly explore their data, acquire new insights, and ask new meaningful questions [29]. Interactive visualization tools foster exploration by affording interactions that enable one to navigate large information spaces and perceive new relationships [6]. However, as datasets grow in size and complexity, visual exploration becomes a more difficult and straining process, requiring users to virtually navigate increasingly large information spaces (by panning and zooming or switching between windows, for instance). Such actions come at significant cognitive costs as they force users to switch between different projections of the data and integrate visual features across *temporally-separated* views. Conventional displays tend to perpetuate this behavior [3], for they typically provide limited resolution and can only show a small fraction of the data at a time. Faced with this overhead, a user's natural response would be to reduce virtual navigation and potentially ignore parts of the information space [16]. Such accommodating behavior could negatively impact the quantity and breadth of discoveries.

CHI 2015, April 18–23 2015, Seoul, Republic of Korea

ACM 978-1-4503-3145-6/15/04...$15.00
http://dx.doi.org/10.1145/2702123.2702406

Large high-resolution displays (LHDs) are increasingly being used as visual interfaces for the exploration of large datasets [21]. Compared to traditional displays, LHDs enable one to view a larger portion of the data space at once, reducing the need for virtual navigation [3]. Numerous studies have demonstrated the cognitive and perceptual benefits of LHDs [1, 2, 3, 4, 8, 13, 31]. However, the majority of these studies comprised relatively simple or abstract tasks under controlled conditions. The larger effects of adopting LHDs in exploratory visual analysis remain unclear.

In this paper, we report on a study examining the benefits of LHDs in *multiple-view* visualizations. We employ an insight-based methodology within the context of a realistic, open-ended visual exploration scenario. Analyzing participants' verbal statements, we measure the quantity and breadth of insights they acquire under two experimental conditions (*small* vs. *large* display), and ask the following question: What are the effects of increasing the size and resolution of the display on knowledge discovery in exploratory visual analysis?

We review extant research and contribute a theoretical discussion of how interaction costs might affect user behavior in visual exploration, and how LHDs can potentially alleviate some of those costs. Following that, we elaborate on the methodology we used to quantify participants' insight acquisition and exploratory behavior, and report on our results. These results provide preliminary evidence that larger displays with more pixels can significantly increase the number of discoveries reported by users during visual exploration, while yielding broader, more integrative insights. We propose explanations for these results and discuss the limitations of our study.

BACKGROUND AND RELATED RESEARCH

Visual exploration is a process of broadly surveying data from a flexible point of view to identify salient patterns and formulate preliminary hypotheses and narratives to account for observations. In contrast to confirmatory analysis, which is typically aimed at answering specific questions, visual exploration is intended to lead to new meaningful questions [29] and broaden one's understanding of their data. Hence, a crucial challenge for interactive visualizations lies in the design of usable interfaces that minimize the cognitive workload on users, and thus invite rather than hinder exploration.

Coordinated multiple views and virtual navigation

A useful paradigms for designing effective visualization interfaces is to distribute information along multiple coordinated views and juxtapose them. The main premise here is that "users understand their data better if they interact with the presented information and view it through different representations" [25]. Multiple-view visualizations have been proven effective in a variety of applications, ultimately becoming a standard technique in visual analytics. Yet, the scalability of this technique is arguably limited by display size and resolution, as adding additional views would require the sacrifice of precious pixels. Consequently, visualizations incorporate a limited number of views (typically 2–6). When the amount of information is too large to fit, views are presented in sequence using virtual navigation techniques, such as panning and zooming, overview+detail, and window switching [7]. Virtual navigation thus involves the *temporal* separation of views, requiring users to switch between different projections of the data. Conversely, juxtaposition entails the *spatial* separation of views, enabling more coherent access to information at the cost of complicating the interface. Visualization designers therefore need to balance a trade-off between separating views temporally and adding additional views to the interface. Wang Baldonado et al. suggest that extra views should be added parsimoniously to highlight diversity, correlations, and disparities within the data [30]. However, these design heuristics were primarily driven by the desire to minimize the pixel 'footprint' of the visualization at a time when display pixels where far more expensive. Here we examine an alternative perspective that considers the cognitive costs associated with visual exploration.

The costs of visual exploration

One useful model for understanding the cost structure of visual exploration is Lam's framework of interaction costs [11]. Similar in spirit to the *seven stages of actions* [15], the framework articulates the cognitive costs incurred at each of the seven stages involved in using interactive visualization tools (see Figure 1). Taken collectively, these costs also imply a form of 'cognitive resistance' that users must overcome in order to form and set new exploratory goals for themselves. Since users tend to minimize the cost of acquiring information [18], a bias to the path of least resistance may cause them to (unknowingly) steer their strategy to exploit isolated subsets of data, which could negatively impact the discovery process.

Reducing visual context-switching by incorporating more views and using larger displays with more pixels could dramatically alter the cost structure of visual exploration. Specifically, we would expect a decrease in *view-change* costs

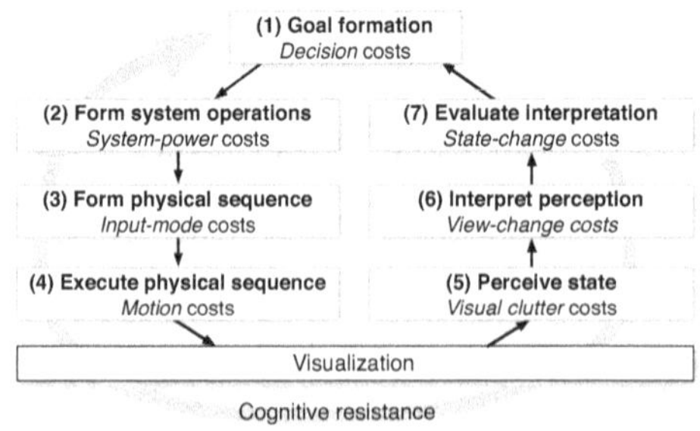

Figure 1. The sequence of stages users take when interacting with a visualization (in bold) along with the associated costs (in *italics*) [11]. Users may experience 'cognitive resistance' that could dissuade them from forming new exploratory goals in response to high interaction costs.

(stage 6) as there would be fewer disruptions from virtual navigation [3], and users would need to rebuild their 'mental map' less frequently [20]. Additionally, we would expect a reduction in the costs of integrating information across multiple views (stage 7) as users would be able to physically switch between views with embodied actions [1] and access them in a non-sequential fashion. Experimental work also seems to support this conjecture. For instance, for visual comparison tasks, Plumlee and Ware found pan and zoom interfaces to be slower than interfaces with multiple views due to the increased workload on visual working memory imposed by the former [19]. Adding extra views, however, is likely to impose a different type of overhead, which manifests in rising *physical motion* costs (stage 4) from having to execute more strenuous physical actions (e.g., more frequent head turns). Furthermore, we would expect increasing *visual clutter* costs (stage 5) from having to operate on a more cluttered visualization and having to manage one's attention in a larger spatial environment.

Evidence for benefits of large high-resolution displays

As display technology improves and its cost decline, the use of LHDs for data analysis is becoming more prevalent. There is a large body of HCI research on the benefits of using LHDs in general knowledge work [8]. In visualization, LHDs have been shown to improve user performance in tasks such as target search [4], spatial judgment [28], pattern perception [31], and object classification and manipulation [13]. These benefits are partly conferred by the reduction in the frequency of virtual navigation when users are given the the opportunity to physically navigate the data space with eye movements and head turns [3]. However, most of these benefits pertain to low-level outcomes (i.e., performance time and accuracy) in basic tasks and static visualizations. In interactive visualization, results were largely dependent on the interaction method employed, with some standard techniques (e.g., context+focus lenses) resulting in poor performance [10]. In higher-order visual analytic tasks, LHDs provided considerable cognitive benefits to intelligence analysts working with large quantities of text documents [1]. Memory externalization and enabling the creation of semantically-rich spatial representations were two of the main affordances conferred [2].

Summary

Although several studies have considered the cognitive affordances of LHDs in complex sense-making activities, these studies adopted the analysis of text documents as a model task. Interestingly, users did not perform any better or worse in these studies when given a larger display with more pixels [1, 2]. Given the differences in how people process textual and visual representations [12], we would expect different outcomes in analytical tasks involving predominantly visual contents. Researchers have begun to study how interface characteristics (e.g., latency [14]) affect the exploratory behavior of users. However, the effects of display size on exploratory visual analysis remain poorly understood.

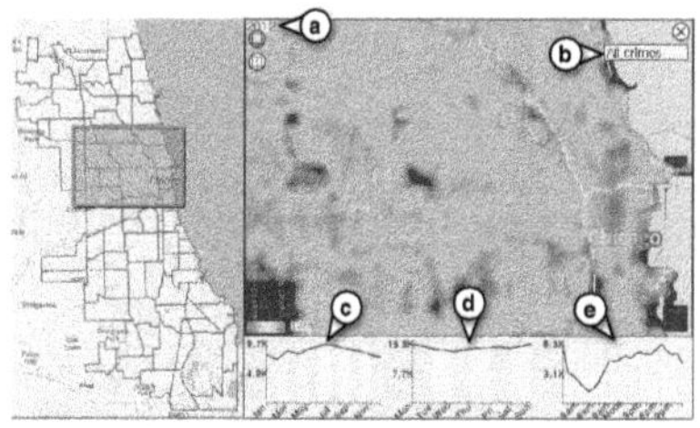

Figure 2. An overview map (left) and a compound view showing one year's worth of criminal activity (a) for a particular type of crime (b). The heatmap shows the aggregate spatial distribution of crime over the year. Three line charts show crime trends within the map at three temporal scales: monthly (c), daily (d), and hourly (e).

METHODOLOGY

Our first goal in this study is to understand the effects of increasing the physical size and resolution of the display on the quantity and breadth of insights acquired by users during visual exploration. Our second goal is to understand potential variations in user behavior as a result of adopting physically larger displays with more pixels. We investigate these effects in a realistic setting by employing an open-ended visual exploration task situated in a real-world scenario and dataset. To that end, we employ two experimental conditions: a *small* and a *large* display. While the two conditions provide an identical visualization tool, they afford distinct experiences. The *large display* allows for the juxtaposition of a larger number of views at the potential risk of overloading the visualization with too much information. The *small display* provides a simpler visualization with less information, requiring users to frequently switch between views.

Scenario and dataset

To induce a realistic exploratory behavior, we selected a scenario that revolved around the analysis of crime activity in the city of Chicago. The city has made available a dataset containing the majority of crimes that have occurred between 2001 and present[1]. Crime records contain location (down to a city block), date and time, and the type of crime. For our experiment, we used a subset comprising crimes committed between 2006 and 2012, inclusive. This resulted in approximately 2.8 million crime records, which we then categorized into 8 distinct crime types.

This dataset furnishes a suitable example to study the analytical behavior of users within the context of a visual exploration task. The scenario provides a semantically rich task for participants to try to find spatio-temporal patterns that govern criminal activity and to explore cause and effect narratives. We also consider the domain to be appropriate for a participant pool drawn from the general population.

Visualization

One of the challenges of conducting user studies on LHDs is that there are very few standard tools that can take advantage of the platform. For this study, we designed a custom visualization tool based on the coordinated multiple views model [25] with an overview+detail navigation technique [7]. We employed two types of visual representations: heatmaps to show aggregate crime density in a particular geographic area, and line charts to illustrate crime trends at three time scales: monthly, daily, and hourly. The two representations were integrated in compound views with the three line charts showing the aggregate number of crimes occurring within the extents of the geographic map (see Figure 2). Each compound view shows crime data according to crime type (e.g. narcotics-related, serious, or all) for a single year. The view can be panned using familiar mouse-drag operations, which also refreshes the line charts to reflect crime trends within the updated geographic extents.

We made a design decision to limit the compound views to a single scale (i.e., zooming was not supported). This eliminates a confounding factor introduced when participants are allowed to 'read' the visualization at multiple scales. However, we provided a slider to adjust the level of aggregation in the heatmaps.

View creation and coordination

Additional compound views can be created from the overview map, or by extending an existing view. Views created directly from the overview map are not coordinated, whereas views extended from existing ones are 'chained' together and coordinated to respond to interactions. Chained views share the same geographic extents and brushing-and-linking state, but can be set to show different crime types or different years. Additionally, panning the map in one view updates all chained views. The visualization also shows a visual link between the left/right-most view in a chain to the corresponding focal rectangle in the overview map, giving participants a visual cue to identify chained from non-chained views. To help users organize the views on the display, we provided two layout modes: a free form layout enabled users to position and resize views freely using a familiar window-based metaphor, and a structured layout which spreads the chained views around the center of the display and aligns them with the bezels.

The rationale behind the notion of view chaining was to give users some flexibility in specifying which views should be coordinated. In conventional visualization interfaces, all views are typically coordinated to collectively respond to all actions. On LHDs, however, there are advantages to employing

[1]The dataset is available from https://data.cityofchicago.org/Public-Safety/Crimes-2001-to-present/ijzp-q8t2

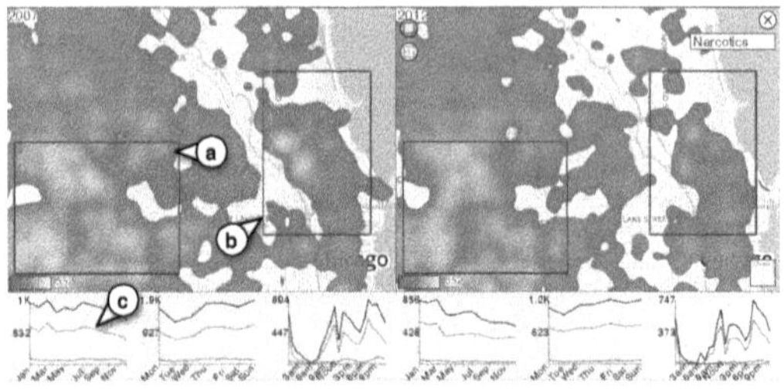

Figure 3. Two chained views comparing narcotics-related crimes in 2007 (left) and 2012 (right). Two bounding boxes highlight crime patterns in the two neighborhoods (a and b). Bounding boxes are synchronized across all chained views. They also cause additional trend lines to be drawn to illustrate crime patterns within subregions (c).

a *loose coordination* model in which a subset of the views are coordinated. For instance, non-coordinated views can function as independent magic lenses to view disparate parts of a large geographic map. Non-coordinated views can also serve to scaffold multiple exploratory branches, enabling a user to simultaneously pursue several lines of inquiry.

Brushing-and-linking

Rectangular bounding boxes can be created and moved within the heatmap, which are updated accordingly across all chained views. In addition to highlighting subregions of interest, bounding boxes cause additional trend lines to be visualized in the chart area reflecting crime patterns in the selected subregions within the context of the broader trend (see Figure 3). Moreover, line charts can be brushed to display the spatial distribution of crimes within a particular time window.

Apparatus

We used the *CAVE2* environment as our LHD apparatus [21]. CAVE2 is a cylindrical system measuring 7.3 meters in diameter and 2.4 meters in height. The environment consists of 72 thin-bezel LCD panels arranged in 18 columns and 4 rows, creating an approximately 320-degree panoramic environment at a total resolution of 74 Megapixels. We choose CAVE2 because the cylindrical configuration of the environment allows users to view the displays at similar distances and visual angles form the center, which reduces geometric distortion in the periphery compared to flat wall displays [5].

Participants

Ten volunteer participants, mostly computer science graduate students, were recruited from our laboratory. The participants, 4 females and 6 males, ranged in age from 25 to 54 years (*mean* = 31.3, *SD* = 8.3). Participants reported their familiarity with interactive visualizations on a 5-points Likert scale, with 1 being "not at all familiar" and 5 being "very familiar" (*mean* = 4.2, *SD* = 0.7). Participants also reported how often they perform data analysis tasks as part of their work on a 5-points Likert scale, with 1 being "never" and 5 being "a great deal" (*mean* = 3.4, *SD* = 0.9). To reduce the chance of inducing an interface novelty effect, we recruited participants who had prior experience using LHDs (primarily for collaborative group meetings). Additionally, all participants resided in the Chicago metropolitan area, and thus were familiar with the city. While it is likely that participants brought their existing perceptions of crime prevalence throughout the city, we consider this to be an acceptable compromise as our goal was not to measure the accuracy of participants' findings, but rather to understand their strategy and the nature of insights they acquire.

Procedure

Participants were seated in the center of the environment on a swivel, height-adjustable chair at a distance of approximately 4 meters from the displays, and interacted with the visualization using a standard mouse and keyboard setup. Participants were also provided with a notepad and a pen to use during the activity, if desired. We provided the participants with a description of the dataset and a list of questions as a starting point into the analysis. However, participants were told and encouraged to freely explore the dataset and to follow up on questions that interested them. Examples of the questions provided include:

- Identify crime 'hotspots' throughout the city. Are there distinct hotspots for specific types of crime?
- How does crime in the city vary with time of day, day of the week, and season?
- Are there correlations between different types of crimes?

The experiment began with a 15 minutes training session with the experimenter demonstrating the visualization environment and its various interactive features. Participants were then given 150 minutes (2.5 hours) to explore the Chicago crime dataset, and instructed to think aloud during the activity. Participants were informed that they could end the experiment when they felt that they have exhaustively explored the dataset. Otherwise, the experiment was terminated when the 150 minutes of allotted exploration time has elapsed. The session was video and audio recorded.

Study design

We used a between-subjects design with a single dependent variable: The display size (*small*, *large*). Half of the participants undertook the study using a small display while the other half experienced the visualization on a large display. Because large displays have been known to provide gender-specific benefits in some cases [27], we balanced the gender ratio in the two conditions. We also attempted to balance the average self-reported data analysis experience as much as possible across the two conditions. The mean reported data analysis experience for the small display condition was 3.6 compared to 3.2 for the large display.

Figure 4. Comparison between the two experimental conditions.

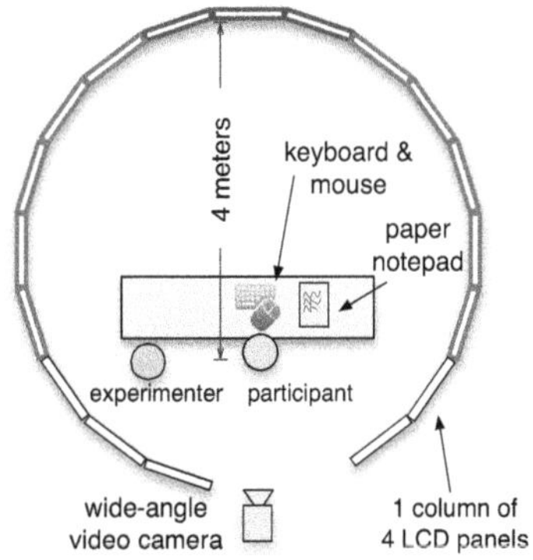

Figure 5. A top down view of the experimental setup in CAVE2. The small display condition utilized 3 of the 18 columns (shown in blue). The large display condition utilized 13 columns (red and blue).

The small display condition utilized 3 of the 18 columns available in the CAVE2 environment, giving participants a resolution of 4,098 x 3,072 (12.5 Megapixels) and approximately a 40-degree field-of-view. The large display condition utilized 13 columns giving participants a resolution of 17,758 x 3,072 (54.5 Megapixels) and approximately a 190-degree field-of-view. The visualization interface was identical in both conditions, but the display size implicitly modulated the number of views that could be seen at a time. Figure 4 illustrates the two conditions. An overview of the experimental setup is shown in Figure 5.

Analysis

We focused our analysis on the video and audio data, which contained a record of the participant's verbal protocol as well as the state of the visualization at the time. Due to the close correspondence between the verbal protocol and the state of the visualization, we decided to encode the verbalizations directly from the video.

Verbal protocol encoding

We developed a coding scheme inspired by insight-based evaluation methods [26, 14]. As our goal was to understand the effects of increasing the display size on insight acquisition and exploratory behavior, we focused on two themes: *insights* (observations and hypotheses) and *exploratory goals*. Coding was performed by a single coder using the following process: Data from two representative participants was coded in three passes to develop the final set of codes. In the first pass, the coder tagged discoveries, hypotheses, decision making, inquiries, deductions, and general comments. These were further aggregated in the second coding pass. In the third pass, the coder developed a criteria for measuring the *breadth* of insights. The final coding scheme comprised the following categories (see Table 1 for examples):

- *Observation:* A unit of knowledge acquired from looking at and interacting with the visualization.
- *Hypothesis:* A conjuncture made by the participant, usually as a result of making a series of observations.
- *Question:* A statement reflecting an inquiry about the data.
- *Goal:* A statement reflecting the formation of an exploratory objective. Questions and goals are functionally similar in the sense that they both serve to orient the exploration process. However, we found that objectives, when articulated, were more indicative of forthcoming exploratory actions, and thus were coded separately.
- *Comment:* Represents a generic verbal statement made by the participant, usually about some aspect of the visualization environment or the user interface.

Table 1. Examples of coded statements from the verbal protocol.

Code	Example statement
Observation	"In the Loop, the crime pattern is high on Monday, high on Sunday, low through the week... There's a dip from Tuesday, Wednesday, Thursday, Friday, Saturday, but it's high on Sunday and Monday."
Hypothesis	"Maybe there was a drop in supply [in reference to a noticeable dip in narcotics-related crimes in 2012]. Because... there's a lot of things that go into the narcotics trade; it's not just a local phenomenon, it's like a global thing."
Question	"Why has the peak crime time at night changed [to an earlier hour] across all crimes?"
Goal	"So I'm gonna go and investigate why is it that, in the earlier years, there were more crimes at one point in time happening in the afternoon."

Breadth of insights

In addition to the above codes, we assigned a score to each observation or hypothesis based on its "broadness" (or "narrowness"), on a scale of 1 to 5. In this scheme, higher scores reflect broader insights that join multiple dimensions of the information space, where as lower scores imply relatively isolated findings. The scoring criteria is outlined in Table 2.

Hypotheses

Our hypotheses for this experiment were:

H1—We hypothesize that the cumulative number of observations would be higher with the large display, driven by the ability to see more views simultaneously. We also expect the rate of observations (defined as the number of observations reported during a minute of analysis) to increase with the large display.

H2—We predict a higher number of hypotheses with the large display, Similarly, we also expect an increase in the rate of hypothesis formulation.

H3—Lastly, we expect participants to acquire more integrative insights with higher breath score on the large display.

These predictions are based on a case study we undertook to evaluate the use of LHDs for the visual analysis of ensemble data [22, 24]. They also represent our extrapolation of results from earlier large display studies, which indicate improved performance time in basic information visualization tasks [3, 31]. We predict that these low-level productivity gains would encourage participants to dedicate more effort to the analytical task and ultimately improve the discovery process. A counter argument is that participants may not be able to incorporate the additional views afforded by the large display into their analysis, which would lead to comparable outcomes in both conditions.

Table 2. Criteria for scoring insights based on their breadth along with example statements.

Score	Criterion	Example statement
1	Isolated features in one view.	"I can see that there are a lot of non-serious crimes, which is kind of expected, for downtown Chicago."
2	Comparative insights involving two level-1 features.	"In this time period [2012], [there are] more weapon violations near the lake [compared to inland areas]."
3	Temporal trends (over several years) or spatial patterns (involving multiple neighborhoods).	"Across all years it's the same seasonal trends [in narcotics-related crimes] of peaking in the summer and then dropping off in the fall."
4	Temporal or spatial trends combining an additional dimension (e.g., crime category).	"The spikes [in burglaries] seem to be consistent [across the years]... It looked like there's a pattern... If you compare this [burglaries in the northside], with this [burglaries in the southside], same thing."
5	Integrated spatio-temporal patterns with observed variations or correlations between multiple crime types.	"A lot of people in this region [near north-side] are buying drugs, but they're not fighting. There's no gang activity. There are much fewer deaths resulting from the narcotics trade. Whereas, disproportionately, in the southern regions there are more narcotics related homicides."

RESULTS

We first look at the length of the exploratory activity, and report on the quantity and the rate of insight acquisition. We then examine the temporal distribution of insights and describe variations in the behavior of participants between the two conditions.

Exploration time

The length of the exploratory activity comprises the time period spent by the participants actively exploring the dataset. Recall that the maximum time for exploration was 150 minutes. However, participants were free to end the experiment when they felt they were finished, with most participants choosing to terminate the activity earlier. Figure 6 illustrates average exploration times under the two display conditions. We found a significant effect for display size on exploration time (*two-sample* $t(8) = 3.697, p < .01$). Participants with the large display spent an additional 40 minutes on average on the activity (*mean* = 126.4, *SD* = 17.0) compared to their counterparts with the small display (*mean* = 86.4, *SD* = 17.2).

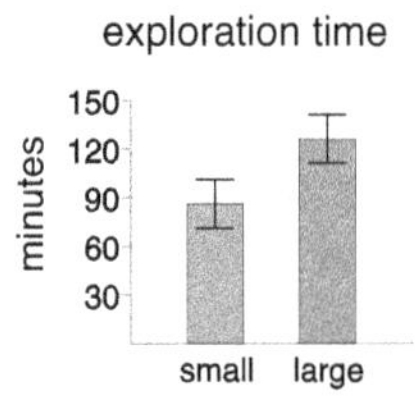

Figure 6. Average length of the exploration activity under the two display conditions. Error bars are 95% CIs.

Reported observations

We analyzed the number of observations reported by participants during the exploratory activity, and also looked at the distribution of scores assigned under our breadth metric. Figure 7 (left chart) illustrates the average number of reported observations for each score-level in addition to the combined total. There was a significant effect for display size on the number of observations ($t(8) = 3.23, p < .05$), with the large display eliciting approximately 74% more observations on average. We performed chi-squared test with Yates' correction to examine the relation between the display size and the breadth of observations. The display size had a significant effect on the distribution of scores ($\chi^2(4, N = 1327) = 263.37, p < .001$), with the large display inducing broader insights in general.

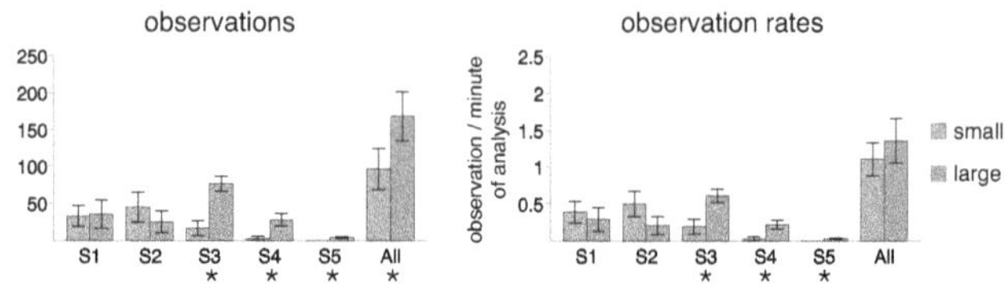

Figure 7. Average number of observations reported by participants (left chart) and observation rates (right). We report the distribution of *breadth* scores (S1–S5) as well as the combined average/rate (right most column in either chart). Error bars are 95% CIs. Stars denote significant differences between the two display conditions ($p < .05$, Bonferroni corrected for 5 tests).

We performed post-hoc analysis to further investigate the effects of display size on observations for each score level individually. Bonferroni correction was applied to maintain a significance level of $p < .05$ to each of the five comparison tests. There was a significant effect for display size on level-3 observations corresponding to temporal and/or spatial trends, with the large display eliciting approximately three times more observations on average ($t(8) = 8.161, p < .001$). Similarly, there were significantly more level 4 and 5 observations reported with the large display ($t(8) = 5.475, p < .001$ and $t(8) = 6.324, p < .001$ respectively). The numbers of observations scored at 1 and 2 were not significantly affected ($t(8) = .217, p = .83$ and $t(8) = 1.552, p = .15$ respectively). Interestingly, none of the small display participants reported observations that garnered a breadth score of 5.

Observation rates

While the number of observations reported by the large display participants is higher, this result does not factor in the longer exploration time exhibited by this group. Thus, we calculated a rate of observation which normalizes the number of observations for each participant by the time it took him/her to complete the activity. Figure 7 (right chart) illustrates these rates (in units of *observation per minute of analysis*). After normalization, we find no significant difference in the combined rates ($t(8) = 1.294, p = .23$). However, post-hoc analysis with Bonferroni correction finds the following significant differences: The rates of level 3 and 4 insights were significantly higher with the large display ($t(8) = 5.96, p < .001$ and $t(8) = 5.597, p < .001$, respectively). Level-5 observations were acquired at a rate of 0.3 compared to *nil* on the small display ($t(8) = 7.466, p < .0001$).

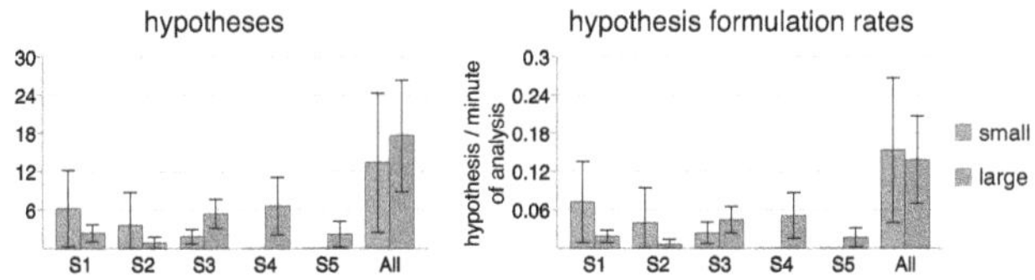

Figure 8. Average number of hypotheses formulated by participants (left chart) and hypothesis formulation rates (right). Error bars are 95% CIs.

Hypothesis formulation

Figure 8 (left chart) illustrate the average number of hypotheses as well as their breadth distribution. In contrast to reported observations, we do not find a significant effect for display size on the combined number of hypotheses ($t(8) = .587, p = .57$). A chi-squared test with Yates' correction, however, indicates a significant effect on the distribution of breadth scores ($\chi^2(4, N = 145) = 67.38, p < .001$). Again, the large display appeared to skew the distribution towards higher breadth scores with the distribution seemingly centered at level-4. Interestingly, none of the small display participants formulated hypotheses that were scored at 4 or 5. Post-hoc analysis with Bonferroni correction finds no further significant differences.

Hypothesis formulation rates

We calculated the rates of hypothesis formulation by normalizing the number hypotheses by the duration of exploration for each participant. Figure 8 (right) illustrates these rates (in units of *hypothesis per minute of analysis*). The combined rate was not affected by the display size ($t(8) = .215, p = .83$). Post-hoc analysis finds no further significant effects for the display size.

There was no significant effect for display size on the number of goals ($t(8) = 1.529, p = .16$) and questions ($t(8) = 0.985, p = .35$) articulated by participants.

Temporal distribution of insights

Lastly, due to the observed variation in the time that participants chose to allocate to the activity under the two display conditions, we looked at the temporal distribution of insights. Figure 9 illustrate the aggregate distribution of insights (including observations and hypotheses). Remarkably, the trend curves are quite similar in both conditions, although the peaks are approximately 25% higher and the curve is 33% wider in the large display. The first insight was acquired approximately 3 minutes into the activity with the small display compared to 6 minutes with the large display, which suggests a higher learning curve in the latter condition. Insight acquisition peaks halfway through the activity in both conditions (at 60 minutes in the small display vs. 75 minutes in the large display), after which the number of insights reported appear to decline steadily. Notably, we see an earlier peak in both conditions around the 30-minute mark, followed by a dip, then a second seemingly-higher peak. This suggests a strategy recalibration by participants after an initial exploration attempt. The distribution also indicates that insight acquisition was not temporally concentrated around a few points in time, but rather spread throughout the different phases of the activity.

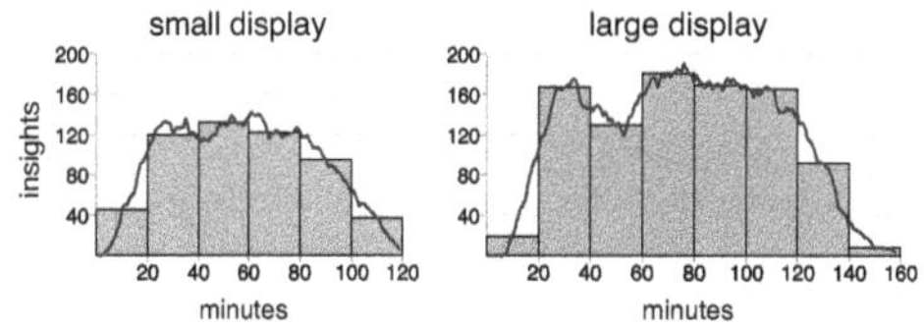

Figure 9. Temporal distribution of insights in the small (left) and large display (right). The trend lines illustrate fine-grained temporal changes in the number of insights acquired within a 20-minute window.

Participants' behavior and strategy

To understand potential effects for display size and resolution on user behavior, we looked for patterns in participants' transitions between 'mental' and 'interaction' events [23]. That is, moments when the participant is performing mental computation in his/her head, and moments when he/she is interacting with the visualization, hence offloading some of the information processing onto the visualization tool. We calculate transition probabilities between these two classes of events, and compare them across the two display conditions. Since we are interested primarily in insight acquisition, we focused on three primary mental events: *Making observations*, *Hypothesis formulation*, and *Goal formation.* As for interactions, we were interested in two general categories of interactions:

- *Layout-preserving interaction:* Includes actions that do not result in major changes to the state and layout of the visualization. For our visualization, these actions comprised brushing-and-linking and map panning operations.
- *Layout-changing interaction:* Comprises action that result in major changes to the visualization state, potentially requiring the participant to rebuild his/her 'mental map' [20]. This category comprised the following interactions: Creating, closing, and positioning views as well as changing the year or the crime type in one or more views.

These two categories of interactions are likely to incur varying costs as the latter induce a temporal separation of views, whereas the former preserve the existing layout.

Event transition diagrams

For each participant, we combine the mental events from the coded verbal protocols with interaction events (which we manually coded from the video recording) into a single sequence sorted by timestamp. This sequence can be thought of as an 'extended log file' that captures both mental and computational processes within the combined human-computer cognitive system. We then visualize these transitions in a state transition diagram. To reveal systematic variations in user behavior, we averaged transition frequencies for participants under the same condition, giving us two 'average diagrams' corresponding to the small and the large displays. Figure 10 shows the two average diagrams side-by-side (top) as well as a difference diagram and adjacency matrix (bottom).

There are important differences between the two conditions; the large display diagram exhibits decreased transitions to the *Modify layout* state (column 1 of the adjacency matrix), indicating that participants were less likely to initiate layout-disruptive actions. Participants were also less likely

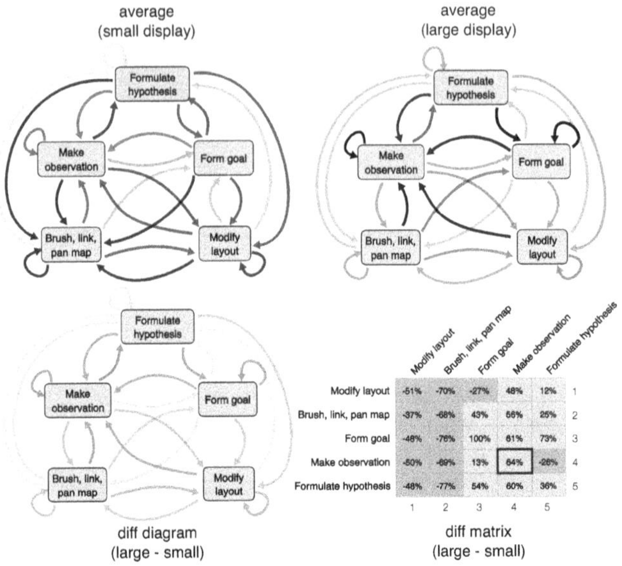

Figure 10. Top: two transition diagrams comparing average transition probabilities under the small and large displays. Edge weights represent transition probability between two states (with log transformation applied); darker arrows represent more likely transitions. Bottom: a *difference* diagram illustrating the effect of increasing the display size on transition probabilities. Edges that have been strengthened are color coded with orange whereas weakened edges are color coded with purple. The adjacency matrix shows percentage changes for each edge, with outlined cells indicating significant differences between the two display conditions ($p < .05$, Bonferroni corrected for 25 tests).

to perform brushing-and-linking and map panning operations. More importantly, however, we generally see an increased tendency for participants to transition from interaction states to insight-generating mental states with the large display (columns 4 and 5) in the large display. We also see increased likelihood for participants to form goals, suggesting that their activity was often driven by deliberate exploratory goals. Furthermore, we see an increased likelihood for participants to remain in insight-generating states (elements (4,4), and (5,5) in the adjacency matrix). Post-hoc analysis indicates a significant increase in the probability of remaining in the *Make observation* state ($t(8) = 4.995, p < .001$).

DISCUSSION

Our results suggest important consequences for increasing the physical size and resolution of the display on the quantity and breadth of insights acquired, and on user engagement.

Insight acquisition

Our results show a significant increase in the quantity of observations reported by participants during visual exploration, given a larger display with more pixels. Participants generated 74% more observations on average with the large display, partially confirming our first hypothesis (H1). One possible explanation is that the larger display enabled participants to see more interesting features, by enabling them to perform the bulk of their analysis using mental map-preserving interactions (e.g. brushing-and-linking) and physical embodied actions (eye movements and head turns). These participants were also able to simultaneously see more views, representing crime patterns in different years, in multiple areas of the city, and/or distinct types of crime. Participants who used the smaller display, on the other hand, had to perform a greater amount of virtual navigation to cover the same breadth. The (hypothetically) lower cognitive cost of physical navigation may have induced participants to revisit information more frequently and ultimately acquire more insights, given a display that can accommodate more views.

However, and contrary to our prediction, we do not find significant differences in the *rates* of observation between the two conditions (H1). One at first may be inclined to conclude that the increase in the number of observations was simply due to participants spending more time on the activity with the large display (recall that participants spent an additional 40 minutes on average on the task with the large display). However, comparing the temporal distribution of insights in Figure 9, one can see that the large display generally induces more insights in the same time ranges compared to the small display. In retrospect, our limited sample set combined with individual variations between participants may have overwhelmed differences in insight acquisition rates, which are nevertheless visible at the aggregate level.

As for our second hypothesis, which predicts an increase in the number of hypotheses formulated by participants when given a larger display (H2), we do not find evidence to support it. Although there is a slight trend suggesting an increase in the cumulative number of hypotheses in the large display (see Figure 8), these differences are not significant. Furthermore, the aggregate rate of hypothesis formulation is quite similar for all participants, regardless of the display size.

Breadth of insight

A key difference between the large and small display lies in the distribution of breadth scores. On the large display, most observations garnered a score of 3. Conversely, the majority of observations on the small display were scored at 1 or 2. This is consistent with our prediction that the large display would afford the acquisition of more complex and integrative insights (H3). We see a similar trend in the distribution of hypotheses, though the differences were not significant.

This result can be explained by taking into account changes to the cost structure of visual exploration wrought by the increase in the size and resolution of the display. The large display, by encouraging the *spatial separation* of views, affords the cognitive integration of features and patterns found in multiple views. We see evidence of this form of integration in our analysis of participants' behavior. For example, Figure 10 shows a tendency for participants to remain in insight-generating mental states (e.g., *Making observation*), where they are likely to integrate their findings and potentially develop more complex insights. In this sense, a larger display is likely to keep participants in a more fruitful 'cognitive zone' by reducing interruptions due to virtual navigation [9]. Conversely, the small display participants, having had to frequently switch between temporally-separated views, where less likely to retain relevant information in their working memories, which would have decreased their chance of integrating individual observations.

From a top-down perspective, participants with the large display may have had more opportunity to form ambitious exploratory goals. Such goals could have been perceived as too costly on the small display. We find some evidence for this in Figure 10, which suggests a tendency for the large display participants to transition more often to *Form goal*. Anecdotal evidence from participants' comments also supports this conjecture. For instance, when participant S3, who undertook the experiment with the small display, was asked why he had focused his analysis on crimes in 2012 (the most recent year), the participant responded: "I only bothered to look at the years when I knew something about an area– like *Cabrini Green* and the *Taylor* area". This comment suggests that the cost of exploring temporal trends in this case was inhibitory that the participant generally avoided it unless he knew a priori what to focus on. In other words, in circumstances of weak information scent [18], a small display may skew the exploratory goals of users toward the acquisition of relatively isolated insights which represent a 'low-hanging fruit'. This phenomenon is somewhat similar to the 'narrowing in' behavior observed by Patterson et al. [16], which caused intelligence analysts to inadvertently miss highly-profitable information that were beyond their self-set search scope. A larger display may afford a wider 'spotlight', enabling users to incorporate a richer variety of information in their analysis.

Cognitive engagement

Our study also raises the question of why participants chose to devote significantly more time to the task, given a larger display with more pixels. One possible explanation is that participants were simply more 'engaged' with the analytical task, with the large display serving to sustain their attention for longer durations. The notion of engagement is widely cited in the HCI literature as a positive quality that is often correlated with effective designs. In visual analytics, we can speak of *cognitive engagement* as the tendency of being invested in the analytical process beyond superficial interest [17].

A spatially larger visualization environment may provide users with more compelling and interesting visual stimuli by affording physical navigation as a data exploration modality. Alternatively, engagement may arises through a self-sustaining process where gaining insights is likely to drive users' curiosity, prompting them to seek further discoveries. The usability of the visualization interface plays a crucial role here; by eliminating unnecessary cognitive costs, the visualization becomes more usable and feel more inviting to exploration. In this sense, LHD-based visualizations could engender more engagement by reducing the costs associated with visual context switching. Ultimately, increased cognitive engagement could improve the overall discovery process as suggested by our study.

STUDY LIMITATIONS

Our between-subjects study is based on a relatively modest number of participants. Therefore, we consider the results to be preliminary. Additional studies are thus needed to confirm and clarify some of the trends we observed.

Although participants in our study were occasional users of LHDs (primarily in collaborative group meeting settings), they did not have prior experience in the analytical scenario posed by the study. This may have impacted their level of motivation, selection of strategy, and their understanding of phenomena depicted in the visualization. A domain expert might be able to override some of the heuristic biases faced by participants, and potentially overcome some of the constraints experienced by participants in the small display condition.

Another limitation stems from the visualization environment we employed in the study. To make the experiment more manageable we opted for a minimalistic visualization, employing only two types of representations (heatmaps and line charts) in a small-multiples layout. Additionally, to reduce the learning curve, we utilized standard input devices (keyboard and mouse). One should therefore be careful when extrapolating our results to visualizations that employ more diverse representations and/or different interaction methods.

Lastly, owing to the lack of guidelines on designing visualizations for LHD environments, we had to make some unusual design decisions. For instance, we introduced a notion of *loose coordination* in which some views are coordinated and others are not. While we do believe these decisions are justified, we acknowledge the need for a more systematic investigation culminating in the articulation of a design space for LHD-based multiple-view visualizations.

CONCLUSIONS

Thanks to advances in display technology, large high-resolution displays (LHDs) are being increasingly seen as cost-effective instruments for the visual analysis of large datasets. Compared to conventional displays, LHDs enable greater quantities of information be visualized at once, potentially alleviating the 'tunnel vision' phenomenon experienced by data analysts. We have conducted a small-scale, between-subjects study to investigate the effects of adopting LHDs on exploratory visual analysis. We find that increasing the physical size and resolution of the display can significantly improve the quantity and breadth of insights acquired by users. Moreover, we find that a spatially larger visualization interface can improve user engagement and engender more effective exploratory behavior. These results provide preliminary evidence that the adoption of LHDs as a visualization instrument may positively impact the discovery process in data science applications. The aforementioned benefits may be attributed to a reduction in the cognitive costs of visual exploration wrought by LHDs, which promote the spatial separation of information and lessen the need for visual context switching.

ACKNOWLEDGMENTS

This paper has benefited tremendously from the feedback of anonymous CHI reviewers. We are very appreciative of their volunteer efforts. This work was supported in part by the Office of Science of the U.S. Department of Energy under contract DE-AC02-06CH11357. Equipment used in this study was funded by National Science Foundation award CNS-0959053 and Department of Energy contract DE-SC005067.

REFERENCES

1. Andrews, C., Endert, A., and North, C. Space to think: large high-resolution displays for sensemaking. In *Proc. of CHI'10*, ACM (2010), 55–64.
2. Andrews, C., and North, C. The impact of physical navigation on spatial organization for sensemaking. *Visualization and Computer Graphics, IEEE Trans. on 19*, 12 (2013), 2207–2216.
3. Ball, R., and North, C. Analysis of user behavior on high-resolution tiled displays. *Human-Computer Interaction-INTERACT 2005* (2005), 350–363.
4. Ball, R., North, C., and Bowman, D. Move to improve: promoting physical navigation to increase user performance with large displays. In *Proc. CHI'07*, ACM (2007), 191–200.
5. Bezerianos, A., and Isenberg, P. Perception of visual variables on tiled wall-sized displays for information visualization applications. *Visualization and Computer Graphics, IEEE Trans. on 18*, 12 (2012), 2516–2525.
6. Card, S., Mackinlay, J., and Shneiderman, B. *Readings in information visualization: using vision to think.* Morgan Kaufmann, 1999.
7. Cockburn, A., Karlson, A., and Bederson, B. B. A review of overview+detail, zooming, and focus+context interfaces. *ACM Computing Surveys 41*, 1 (2008), 2.
8. Czerwinski, M., Smith, G., Regan, T., Meyers, B., Robertson, G., and Starkweather, G. Toward characterizing the productivity benefits of very large displays. In *Proc. Interact 2003*, vol. 3 (2003), 9–16.
9. Green, T., Ribarsky, W., and Fisher, B. Building and applying a human cognition model for visual analytics. *Information Visualization 8*, 1 (2009), 1–13.
10. Jakobsen, M. R., and Hornbæk, K. Interactive visualizations on large and small displays: the interrelation of display size, information space, and scale. *Visualization and Computer Graphics, IEEE Trans. on 19*, 12 (2013), 2336–2345.
11. Lam, H. A framework of interaction costs in information visualization. *Visualization and Computer Graphics, IEEE Trans. on 14*, 6 (2008), 1149–1156.
12. Larkin, J. H., and Simon, H. A. Why a diagram is (sometimes) worth ten thousand words. *Cognitive Science 11*, 1 (1987), 65–100.
13. Liu, C., Chapuis, O., Beaudouin-Lafon, M., Lecolinet, E., and Mackay, W. E. Effects of display size and navigation type on a classification task. In *Proc. CHI'14*, ACM (2014), 4147–4156.
14. Liu, Z., and Heer, J. The effects of interactive latency on exploratory visual analysis. *Visualization and Computer Graphics, IEEE Trans. on 20*, 12 (2014), 2122–2131.
15. Norman, D. A. *The Design of Everyday Things*. Basic Books, 2002.
16. Patterson, E. S., Roth, E. M., and Woods, D. D. Predicting vulnerabilities in computer-supported inferential analysis under data overload. *Cognition, Technology & Work 3*, 4 (2001), 224–237.
17. Peters, C., Castellano, G., and de Freitas, S. An exploration of user engagement in hci. In *Proceedings of the International Workshop on Affective-Aware Virtual Agents and Social Robots*, no. 9, ACM (2009), 1–3.
18. Pirolli, P. L. *Information foraging theory: Adaptive interaction with information*. Oxford Univ. Press, 2007.
19. Plumlee, M. D., and Ware, C. Zooming versus multiple window interfaces: Cognitive costs of visual comparisons. *ACM Transactions on Computer-Human Interaction (TOCHI) 13*, 2 (2006), 179–209.
20. Purchase, H. C., Hoggan, E., and Görg, C. How important is the "mental map"?–an empirical investigation of a dynamic graph layout algorithm. In *Graph Drawing*, Springer (2007), 184–195.
21. Reda, K., Febretti, A., Knoll, A., Aurisano, J., Leigh, J., Johnson, A., Papka, M., and Hereld, M. Visualizing large, heterogeneous data in hybrid-reality environments. *Computer Graphics and Applications 33*, 4 (2013), 38–48.
22. Reda, K., Johnson, A., Mateevitsi, V., Offord, C., and Leigh, J. Scalable visual queries for data exploration on large, high-resolution 3d displays. In *Proc. SC Companion*, IEEE (2012), 196–205.
23. Reda, K., Johnson, A. E., Leigh, J., and Papka, M. E. Evaluating user behavior and strategy during visual exploration. In *Proceedings of the Fifth Workshop on Beyond Time and Errors: Novel Evaluation Methods for Visualization*, ACM (2014), 41–45.
24. Reda, K., Offord, C., Johnson, A., and Leigh, J. Expanding the porthole: leveraging large, high-resolution displays in exploratory visual analysis. In *CHI'14 EA*, ACM (2014), 2047–2052.
25. Roberts, J. C. State of the art: Coordinated & multiple views in exploratory visualization. In *Coordinated and Multiple Views in Exploratory Visualization, Fifth International Conference on*, IEEE (2007), 61–71.
26. Saraiya, P., North, C., and Duca, K. An insight-based methodology for evaluating bioinformatics visualizations. *Visualization and Computer Graphics, IEEE Trans. on 11*, 4 (2005), 443–456.
27. Tan, D. S., Czerwinski, M., and Robertson, G. Women go with the (optical) flow. In *Proc. CHI'03*, ACM (2003), 209–215.
28. Tan, D. S., Gergle, D., Scupelli, P., and Pausch, R. With similar visual angles, larger displays improve spatial performance. In *Proc. CHI'03*, ACM (2003), 217–224.
29. Tukey, J. W. We need both exploratory and confirmatory. *The American Statistician 34*, 1 (1980), 23–25.
30. Wang Baldonado, M. Q., Woodruff, A., and Kuchinsky, A. Guidelines for using multiple views in information visualization. In *Proc. AVI'00*, ACM (2000), 110–119.
31. Yost, B., Haciahmetoglu, Y., and North, C. Beyond visual acuity: the perceptual scalability of information visualizations for large displays. In *Proc. CHI'07*, ACM (2007), 101–110.

Subjective and Objective Effects of Tablet's Pixel Density

Lars Lischke, Sven Mayer, Katrin Wolf, Alireza Sahami Shirazi, Niels Henze
VIS, University of Stuttgart
Stuttgart, Germany
{firstname.lastname}@vis.uni-stuttgart.de

ABSTRACT
Pixel densities are increasing rapidly. We can observe this trend in particular for mobile devices like smartphones and tablets. Previous work revealed an effect of pixel density on subjective feedback and objective performance only for low resolution cathode ray tube screens. It is unclear if this effect persists for the four times higher pixel densities of current mobile devices. Therefore, we conducted a study to compare four pixel densities with 359, 180, 120, and 90 pixels per inch. While participants performed three tasks involving images, text and videos on a tablet, we measured perceived effort, perceived visual quality, task completion time, error rate, and body pose. Our results show that the effect of the pixel density highly depends on the content. We found that only for text, the four pixel densities have clearly different perceived media qualities. Pixel density seems to have a smaller effect on perceived media quality for images and videos and we found no effect on objective measures. Results show that text should be displayed in high resolution, while this is less important for images and videos.

Author Keywords
Pixel density; Resolution; Tablet;

ACM Classification Keywords
H.5.m. Information Interfaces and Presentation (e.g. HCI): Miscellaneous

INTRODUCTION & BACKGROUND
The resolution of computer displays constantly increased over the last decades. While the highest resolution of the first IBM PC introduced in 1981 was 640 × 200 pixels, current desktop screens have often a full high definition resolutions of 1980 × 1080 pixels or higher. Similar trends can be observed in other domains. In particular, the screen resolution of mobile devices increased. While the first Apple iPhone, introduced in 2007, and the first Android device, introduced in 2008, had a resolution of 320 × 480 pixels, recent devices, such as the Samsung Galaxy S5 come with 1920 × 1080 pixels. Although the screen size has been increased at the same time, the resolution has grown faster. This results in an increase of the typical pixel density, measured in pixels per inch (PPI), from 170 PPI in 2007 up to 432 PPI in 2014.

Previous research investigated the effect of visual displays. In particular, researchers looked at the difference between reading on papers and on computer screens. In contrast to earlier work [4], results by Ball and Hourcade show that comprehension and reading speed is similar using paper and computer displays [2]. The authors explain the contradiction of previous work with participants' increased familiarity but also through the improvement of technology. Thus, the work suggests that the characteristics of the computer screen have an effect on real world tasks. Menozzi et al. compared different display technologies using a visual search task [6]. While the results show that improved output devices can increase users' performance they also suggest that even clear differences do not necessarily result in a measurable effect.

Surprisingly only few researchers investigated the effect of resolution or pixel density. Ziefle examined the effect of cathode ray tube (CRT) screens' pixel density (60 PPI and 120 PPI) in comparison to text printed with 255 dots per inch (DPI) [10]. For a proof-reading task, she found that paper significantly outperformed the other conditions but observed no significant difference between the two screen conditions. In a complementing study, however, Ziefle compared three pixel densities (62 PPI, 69 PPI, and 89 PPI) and found a difference between the two lower densities and the higher one in terms of subjective feedback and objective performance when searching for characters. When liquid-crystal displays (LCDs) replaced CRTs, studying the effect of pixel density became challenging as one LCD cannot display different densities. Therefore, studies that aimed to compare different densities have been conducted using different displays (e.g. [5, 9]) or with one display by changing the size of the visual output [3]. In both cases, one cannot differentiate between the effect of the display or its size and the effect of the pixel density.

Overall, previous work showed that an increase of pixel density from 69 to 89 PPI can improve participants' subjective ratings and objective performance for one specific task [10]. The pixel density of current devices is, however, much higher than what could be considered by Ziefle at that time. In particular, mobile devices have a pixel density that is almost five times higher than 89 PPI. It remained unclear if further increasing the pixel density from 89 PPI will sustain the positive effect. Furthermore, previous work only found an effect for search tasks using texts. While current mobile devices are

CHI 2015, April 18–23, 2015, Seoul, Republic of Korea.

ACM 978-1-4503-3145-6/15/04 ...$15.00.
http://dx.doi.org/10.1145/2702123.2702390

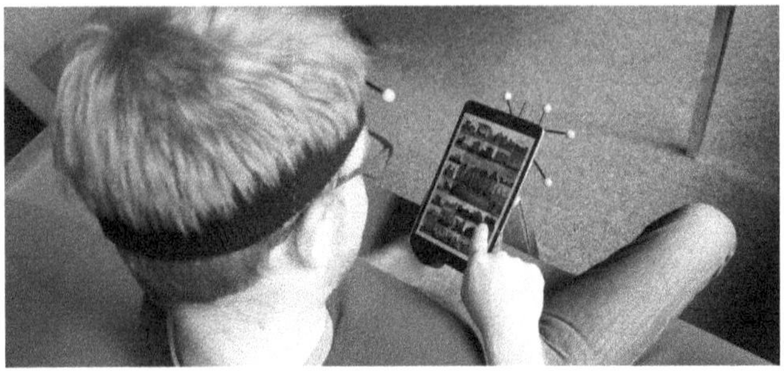

Figure 1. A participant performing the image task.

certainly used for reading, they are also used for a wide range of multimedia tasks involving images and videos [7].

As previous work does not provide insights about the effect of even moderately high pixel densities, it remains unclear if the ongoing increase of density provides an advantage for users. Therefore, we investigate the effect of pixel densities for three tasks using texts, images, and videos. Using a high resolution tablet device with a pixel density of 359 PPI we simulate four lower pixel densities and can thereby investigate different densities using a one device. In the conducted study we assess the effect of the four pixel densities on subjective measures, objective measures, and the participants' pose.

EXPERIMENT

In this study we used three tasks to assess the effect of pixel density on tablets. We used a tablet device with a resolution of 2560 × 1600 pixels and a density of 359 PPI. We combine groups of 4, 9, and 16 pixels resulting in additional pixel densities of 179.5, 119.7, and 89.8 PPI. In the following we use 180, 120 and 90 PPI to describe the densities we used. These three lower pixel densities and the native pixel density result in four conditions. Using a repeated measures design, every participant performed all three tasks with all four conditions. The order of the conditions was balanced using Latin square. We recruited 16 participants (5 female) with an age between 21 and 43 ($M = 26.7$, $SD = 5.2$) through our university's mailing list. All of them had normal or corrected to normal vision.

Tasks

We designed three tasks which represent actions commonly performed on tablets. Messaging, information look-up and browsing social media are key activities performed on tablets [7]. On a more abstract level looking at and comparing images, reading texts, and watching videos are sub-tasks of these tasks.

In the image comparison task we presented five sets of 32 images. Every image set contained images of persons or objects. All images were collected by searching for keywords on Flickr. As categories we used portraits of women and men, landscape photos of castles, cars, and coins. All images in one set were comparable in terms of color and perspective. Thereby we tried to minimize color-based search strategies. The images were arranged in a grid with five columns and eight rows. All images had a size of 21.2 mm × 21.2 mm (300 × 300 pixels on the highest density). In the upper center we placed one image which was three times lager (63.8 mm × 63.8 mm). One of the smaller images showed the same person or object as the larger one but from a different perspective. Participants' task was to compare the small images to the larger image and to select the matching image as fast as possible. Figure 1 shows the task with a participant searching the correct image. Every participant performed the task using each of the five categories and each of the four pixel density. We ensured that every image was only shown once to an individual participant. Furthermore the positions of the small images were randomized. We will call this "image task".

The second task was to count how often a specific word appears in a given text. Before one text was shown to the user we displayed a message that specified the word that should be counted. To support the participant the target word was displayed in in the upper left corner while the text was shown. We selected 12 text sequences with a length of 300 words from different fairy tales in English language. All words which should be counted were common English words, like "she", "with" or "into" with a length of three or four characters. The target word was included in the text between one and eight times. As font we used a regular font (Sans) without serif with a font size of 45 pixels at full resolution. This equals a height of 3.2 mm. The font style and size is comparable to the standard font on the used tablet. We placed the text in the center of the screen. On the bottom of the screen we placed ten buttons to enter how often the target word was counted in the text. For every condition we repeated this task three times. In the following we call this task "text task".

In the last task the participant watched three videos with a length of 10 seconds that showed five people standing in a circle and passing three balls around. The position of the camera was fixed and showed the whole group all the time. The task for the participants was to count the total number of throws in the video. We decided to use videos in which people are passing balls around, because the action happening in all videos are comparable. Each video was played once with a frame rate of 20 fps. Participants could not pause or replay the video. After watching a video, participants were asked to enter the number of throws. We call this "video task".

Procedure

To measure the distance between the tablet and the eyes of the participant while he or she was performing the task, we used a motion capture system. Therefore we mounted optical markers on the tablet and asked the participants to wear a headband with optical markers. While the participant was performing the tasks he or she was sitting on a chair without using a table. Every participant performed 33 trails which results from four pixel densities times the five sets of images, the three sets of texts and the three sets of videos. After performing one task on one density, we asked to answer two questions. First, to rate perceived mental effort (PE) on SMEQ scale [11]. This scale goes from 0 (no effort) to 150 (high effort) and is known to be very sensitive with small sample sizes [8]. Second, to rate perceived media quality (PMQ) on ITU-T P.910 ques-

		90 PPI		120 PPI		180 PPI		359 PPI	
		M	SD	M	SD	M	SD	M	SD
Task	Image	4.01	2.40	4.78	2.39	6.71	1.97	7.36	1.44
	Text*	2.15	1.58	3.95	1.71	6.03	2.00	8.05	1.40
	Video	3.72	1.86	5.16	1.56	6.59	1.57	6.14	1.80

Table 1. Perceived mental effort PE to perform the task per screen resolution.
*** denotes significant effects at the .05 level.**

		90 PPI		120 PPI		180 PPI		359 PPI	
		M	SD	M	SD	M	SD	M	SD
Task	Image*	37.38	21.69	55.94	27.98	42.25	35.82	39.50	27.91
	Text*	52.50	30.69	43.06	22.79	30.31	20.88	32.13	25.32
	Video*	41.88	31.02	35.56	23.41	31.81	24.71	28.13	22.01

Table 2. Perceived media quality PMQ per screen resolution.
*** denotes significant effects at the .05 level.**

tionnaire, which goes from 0 (bad) to 10 (excellent) [1]. The study tool automatically logged task completion time (TCT) and error rate (ER).

Apparatus
Differing characteristics of even similar displays, such as contrast, brightness or response time might influence the results of the study. Therefore, we decided to use only one device to minimize the number of uncontrolled variables. In the study we used a regular Android tablet, namely a Samsung Galaxy Tab Pro 8.4[1]. The tablet has a 8.4 inches large display with WQXGA (2560 × 1600) screen resolution. To lower the perceived pixel density we scaled down the material used in the study to the respective density. We scaled the content up again using nearest-neighbor interpolation. Thereby, groups of pixels are combined without any smoothing. With the use of a motion capture system and the attached markers we measured the distance between the eyes of the participant and the tablet, while he or she was performing the tasks.

RESULTS
For each task, we compared PE, PMQ, TCT, and ER between the four different pixel densities by conducting one-way ANOVAs. Degrees of freedom have been corrected using Greenhouse-Geisser estimation of sphericity if necessary.

As post-hoc tests, we conducted t-tests with Bonferroni correction. Table 2 shows the resulting values for PMQ per pixel density and task and Table 1 shows the resulting values for PE per pixel density and task. Overall, we found no significant effects on distance between tablet and head and on error rate.

Image Task
We could not show a significant effect of pixel density on PE ($F_{1.63,24.39} = 3.35, p = .061, \eta^2 = .182$). However, the analysis revealed a significant effect of pixel density on PMQ ($F_{3,45} = 12.6, p < .001, \eta^2 = .456$). Post-hoc tests revealed that PMQ for 359 PPI was significantly higher than for 120 PPI ($p < .001$) as well as than for 90 PPI ($p < .001$). Furthermore, we found a significant difference on PMQ between 180 PPI and 90 PPI ($p < .015$). Post-hoc tests revealed no significant difference for all other pairwise comparisons. The analysis revealed significant differences for TCT ($F_{3,36} = 6.625, p < .003, \eta^2 = .356$). Post-hoc test revealed significant effects for TCT while performing the task with the highest pixel density (359 PPI) vs. 120 PPI ($p < .045$). Furthermore, the differences between 120 PPI and 90 PPI were significant ($p < .005$). However, the analysis could not reveal significant differences between the other pixel densities.

Text task
Significant effects for PE were found ($F_{3,45} = 13.13, p < .001, \eta^2 = .467$). Post-hoc test showed that PE for performing the task at 359 PPI was significantly lower than at 90 PPI ($p < .009$). Furthermore, the analysis reveals significant differences between 180 PPI and 120 PPI ($p < .018$) and between 180 PPI and 90 PPI ($p < .002$). However the analysis revealed no significant effect between all other resolutions. The analysis revealed significant differences on PMQ ($F_{3,45} = 48.52, p < .001, \eta^2 = .764$). Post-hoc tests showed that all used pixel densities were perceived significantly different (359 PPI vs. 180 PPI: $p < .027$; 180 PPI vs. 120 PPI: $p < .003$, and all other pairs: $p < .001$. The analysis of TCT revealed no significant differences ($F_{3,36} = 1.728, p = .179, \eta^2 = .126$).

Video task
The analysis revealed no significant effects on PE ($F_{3,45} = 3.82, p = .016, \eta^2 = .203$). However, the analysis revealed significant differences for PMQ ($F_{3,45} = 18.38, p < .001, \eta^2 = .551$). Post-hoc tests showed that PMQ differs significantly between the highest (359 PPI) and the lowest (90 PPI) pixel density ($p < .003$). Furthermore, the three lower pixel densities were perceived significantly different (180 PPI vs. 120 PPI: $p < .009$; 180 PPI vs. 90 PPI: $p < .001$; 120 PPI vs. 90 PPI: $p < .008$). The analysis of TCT revealed no significant differences ($F_{3,36} = 1.012, p = .399, \eta^2 = .078$).

DISCUSSION & CONCLUSION
The results of our study show that the influence of pixel density depends on the performed task. Perceived media quality differs for all three tasks. The results suggest that pixel density is particularly important for text related tasks. Only for the text task, participants rated all four presented pixel densities significantly different. In addition, perceived mental effort while performing the text related task differs significantly between the different pixel densities. This indicates that a higher pixel density and thereby a clearer font makes reading easier. In contrast, not all densities in the image task were rated significantly different. We found no differences between 359 PPI and 180 PPI, 180 PPI and 120 PPI, and between 120 PPI and 90 PPI. This indicates that the perceived differences of the visual quality for images did not vary as

[1] `www.samsung.com/us/mobile/galaxy-tab/SM-T320NZKAXAR` (last access 09-19-2014)

much as for text. Perceived video quality differs between pixel densities of 180 PPI, 120 PPI, and 90 PPI. However, perceived quality of the highest pixel density is only different compared to the lowest quality. This indicates that for video watching a higher quality might not be necessary. Overall, we could not show that a higher pixel density is beneficial in terms of task completion time or error rate. Also the results demonstrate that the distance between users' head and device does not change depending on the pixel density of the screen.

In contrast to previous work [10] that investigated the effect of pixel density, our work focuses on mobile devices which today have screens with a much higher pixel density. Moreover, we use additional types of content, which are today commonly used on smartphones or tablets. As Ziefle's work [10] indicates, the effect of pixel density is task dependent. In contrast to Ziefle's work on lower pixel densities [10], our results do not show a continuously increasing positive effect of the display's pixel density on TCT and ER. This might have different reasons. First, low visual quality might be compensated by the human vision. Second, Menozzi et al. [6] indicate that obvious differences in the visual quality do not necessarily haven an objective effect.

Our results suggest that pixel densities, used for modern smartphones and tablets, have little positive effect on objective measurable variables. However, pixel density has a clear effect on perceived visual quality which is leveling off for high densities. Hence the results rise the question, if a further increase of screen resolution is necessary. In particular for price sensitive and emerging markets economically priced hardware with an screen resolution of 180 PPI could be sufficient. The results indicate that reading on a screen with a resolution of 180 PPI has the lowest PE. If we consider only measurable performance as important, even cheaper hardware is suitable. Additionally the perceived visual quality depends on the media type. While visual text quality is very distinguishable, the pixel density is less important for videos. This shows even more potential for using economically priced hardware. The visual quality of videos seems to be less important. This allow to deploy less computational power to display videos in devices for emerging markets. This affects also the needed quality of network connections, because it might be not necessary to send large amount of data to display high resolution videos. The perceivable differences in the media quality allow in contrast also to argue for costly high quality displays. This discussion is in particular important, if we transfer our results from tablets to other mobile devices, like smartwatches. Smartwatches are designed to provide fast access to bits of information. Our results show that this is still possible without measurable disadvantages on displays with very low resolution. The screen resolution has the largest perceivable effect on reading. However, smartwatches are not designed to read longer text. Hence, we could argue that lower screen resolutions are reasonable for smartwatches. This could allow to use less computational power and thereby save battery life.

Our work raises different related research questions. The influence of the screen size is strongly connected to effects we analyzed. The screen size can influence the pixel density and the amount of content which can be displayed at once. In this study we compared only different screen resolutions on the same screen size. Furthermore the size of the content, e.g. the size of the text font, might interfere with the pixel density and thereby effect user's performance and the task load. In this initial study we used content size which is typical for this tablet. The question about influence of the screen size, calls for analyzing same variables in other settings. So it would be interesting to proof our assumption that high display resolutions are not necessary on smartwatches. To analyze the effect of display resolution in a desktop settings would be interesting, because the user is using the screen often a longer time.

Acknowledgments: This work is partly financial supported by German Research Foundation (DFG) within Cluster of Excellence in Simulation Technology (EXC 310/2) at the University of Stuttgart.

REFERENCES

1. Recommendation ITU-T P.910 Subjective video quality assessment methods for multimedia applications. Telecom. Standard. Sector of ITU (2008).
2. Ball, R., and Hourcade, J. P. Rethinking reading for age from paper and computers. *IJHCI 27*, 11 (2011).
3. Chen, C.-H., and Chiang, S.-Y. Effects of screen resolution and column ratio on search performance and subjective preferences. *Displays 33*, 1 (2012).
4. Dillon, A. Reading from paper versus screens: A critical review of the empirical literature. *Ergonomics 35*, 10 (1992).
5. Huang, D.-L., Patrick Rau, P.-L., and Liu, Y. Effects of font size, display resolution and task type on reading chinese fonts from mobile devices. *International Journal of Industrial Ergonomics 39*, 1 (2009).
6. Menozzi, M., Lang, F., Naepflin, U., Zeller, C., and Krueger, H. Crt versus lcd: Effects of refresh rate, display technology and background luminance in visual performance. *Displays 22*, 3 (2001).
7. Müller, H., Gove, J., and Webb, J. Understanding tablet use. In *Proceedings of MobileHCI* (2012).
8. Sauro, J., and Dumas, J. S. Comparison of three one-question, post-task usability questionnaires. In *Proceedings of CHI* (2009).
9. Yang, S.-N., Tai, Y.-C., Hayes, J. R., and Sheedy, J. Superior smartphone display quality enhances viewing performance and comfort. *Faculty Scholarship* (2011).
10. Ziefle, M. Effects of display resolution on visual performance. *Journal of the Human Factors and Ergonomics Society 40*, 4 (1998).
11. Zijlstra, F., and Doorn, L. v. The construction of a scale to measure subjective effort. *Tech. Rep. Delft University of Technology* (1985).

Push-Edge and Slide-Edge: Scrolling by Pushing Against the Viewport Edge

Sylvain Malacria[1,2], Jonathan Aceituno[2,3], Philip Quinn[4], Géry Casiez[2,3], Andy Cockburn[4], Nicolas Roussel[2]

[1]University College London, United Kingdom, [2]Inria Lille, France
[3]University of Lille, France, [4]University of Canterbury, New Zealand

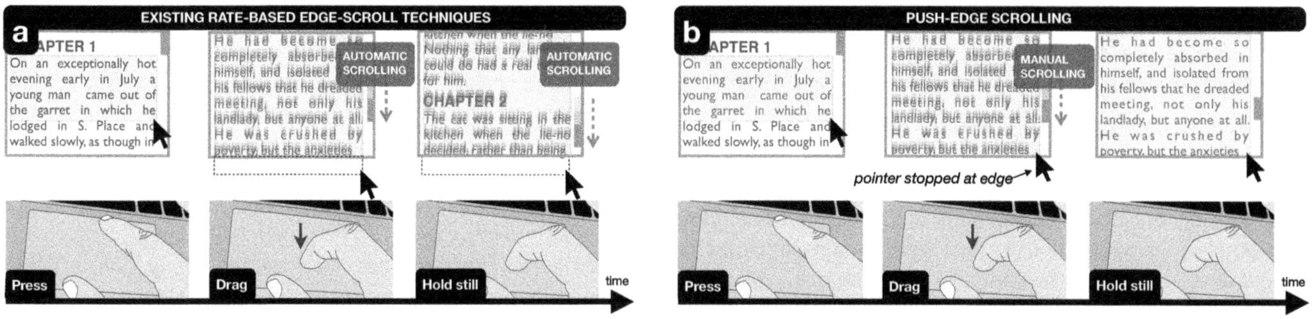

Figure 1. When selecting text with a touchpad, downward movements after crossing the viewport edge will (a) change the rate of automatic scrolling with existing techniques (rate control); or (b) manually scroll the document, stopping the pointer at the edge with *push-edge scrolling* (position control).

ABSTRACT

Edge-scrolling allows users to scroll a viewport while simultaneously dragging near or beyond a window's edge. Common implementations rely on rate control, mapping the distance between the pointer and the edge of the viewport to the scrolling velocity. While ubiquitous in operating systems, edge-scrolling has received little attention, even though previous works suggest that (1) rate control may be suboptimal for isotonic pointing devices like mice and trackpads and (2) space beyond the window's edge might be scarce, limiting scrolling control. To address these problems, we developed Push-edge scrolling (and Slide-edge scrolling, its inertial variant), two novel position-based techniques that allow scrolling by 'pushing' against the viewport edge. A controlled experiment shows that our techniques reduce overshoots and offer performance improvements by up to 13% over traditional edge-scrolling.

Author Keywords

Edge-scroll; rate control; position control; inertia; autoscroll.

ACM Classification

H.5.2 [**User Interfaces**] Interaction styles.

INTRODUCTION

Scrolling while dragging an object is a common interaction problem when working within the confines of a viewport. Dragging is achieved by moving an input device in a special state (e.g., holding down a mouse button) – which allows actions such as moving file icons and selecting regions of text. Dragging tasks are straightforward when the start and end locations are both contained within the viewport, but many activities require scrolling to bring the end location into view – for example, selecting several paragraphs of text, or manipulating data in a large spreadsheet. The dragging state precludes using scrollbars or other on-screen navigation tools, and device-specific mechanisms, like the mouse wheel, are not always responsive during dragging.

To allow scrolling while dragging, interfaces support *edge-scroll* (also called *autoscroll*) that triggers a scrolling motion when a dragged pointer enters a *control area* near the edge of the viewport. For example, in Figure 1a the user first presses the trackpad button with the thumb, then uses another finger to drag the pointer downwards and select a text region. When the pointer enters the control area (typically the region between the window border and the screen edge), the document starts scrolling until the pointer leaves this area or the user exits the dragging mode. The most common approach to control edge scroll is rate-based: inside the control area, scrolling velocity is based on the pointer's distance from the viewport edge [2].

While edge-scroll is commonplace and designs have been disclosed [7, 8], we are unaware of any empirical work, which is surprising because current techniques suffer from two major limitations. First, prior research on pointing and scrolling suggests that rate control may be inappropriate for edge-scrolling [11, 12]. Second, the size of the control area is inconsistent and possibly limited, for instance when the window is maximised or with small displays, offering suboptimal control.

Based on these limitations, we introduce *push-edge scrolling* (Figure 1b) and its inertial variant, *slide-edge scrolling*. These

CHI 2015, April 18 - 23 2015, Seoul, Republic of Korea

ACM 978-1-4503-3145-6/15/04...$15.00
http://dx.doi.org/10.1145/2702123.2702132

novel *position*-based techniques block the pointer as it reaches the edge of the viewport, and transform subsequent pointing device movements that would otherwise move the pointer into scrolling displacements. Experimental results demonstrate that *push-edge* and *slide-edge scrolling* outperform rate-based techniques in a text selection task.

LIMITATIONS IN CURRENT EDGE-SCROLL TECHNIQUES

Edge-scrolling should allow users to quickly scroll to close or distant target locations, but there are two main reasons to question the adequacy of current designs with respect to these goals: rate control may not be superior to position control with common input devices, and window placement can limit scrolling control because it constrains the control area.

Mouse and Trackpad Rate Control

Prior research suggests that rate-based methods for scrolling control are most desirable when the user's primary task is reading because they facilitate a smooth and continuous scrolling speed [12], or when input is provided through an isometric input device such as a trackpoint [11]. In contrast, isotonic devices, such as mouse or trackpads, are less suited to rate control because they lack a self-centring effect, requiring fine coordination to control movement and to explicitly get back to zero point to stop it [6]. In summary, there is support for exploring position-based alternatives to rate-based edge-scroll. Such a mechanism for normal scrolling was patented [4], scrolling a view depending on the distance between the cursor and an activation point. However, the distance-based nature of its transfer function makes it hard to precisely control scrolling velocity. Moreover, scrolling has to be explicitly activated by pressing a button, unlike edge-scrolling which is as a direct extension of the dragging action.

Control Area Size and Location

Current edge-scroll methods rely on the availability of a control area outside the viewport. Scrolling begins when a dragged pointer enters this area, and the scroll velocity increases as the pointer moves away from the viewport's edge. Therefore, the actual size of the control area limits the maximum scrolling velocity in rate control. If the control area lies inside the viewport, it has to be small enough to avoid unintended scrolling, at the expense of the granularity of control. A common alternative is to expand the control area from the viewport edge so that it takes up the whole display space beyond. However, available screen space is likely scarce when maximised windows or small displays, making the control area smaller. Either way, a small control area is likely to make rate-based edge scrolling hard to control for the user.

When using position control, it is possible to overcome this problem by blocking the pointer when it crosses the edge [1] so that every subsequent movement will scroll the view instead of moving the pointer, effectively having a zero-sized control area that does not impede scrolling control.

PUSH-EDGE AND SLIDE-EDGE SCROLLING

Push-edge scrolling is designed to overcome the above limitations and permit rapid and accurate scrolling while a dragging state is maintained. It operates by 'capturing' the cursor at the viewport edge, and mapping subsequent device signals that would otherwise move the cursor as input to a scrolling transfer function (Figure 1b) – further movement away from the viewport results in scrolling displacements of the view, while the cursor remains captured in a fixed position at the edge. The captured cursor is released either by moving it back towards the viewport, by releasing the dragging state, or when scrolling reached the end of the document.

However, the range of a pointing movement – from a pixel to a screen – is much narrower than the range of a scrolling movement – from a few lines to hundreds of pages [3, 5]. Thus, using raw pointing device displacements only might not scale to long distance scrolling. Consequently, *push-edge scrolling* converts motor-space device displacements d (in metres) into display-space scrolling displacements D (in pixels) by multiplying d with a unitless gain produced by a *sigmoid* transfer function [10] and converting the result in pixels using the pixel density of the display. The transfer function transforms the device velocity v (in metres per second) using a linear interpolation between constants g_{min} and g_{max} in the interval (v_1, v_2), and is clamped elsewhere.

Since the physical range of motion is different between devices, we used the results of a pilot study to calibrate the transfer function differently for a trackpad ($g_{min} = 1$, $g_{max} = 15$, $v_1 = 0.2$ m/s, $v_2 = 0.5$ m/s) and mouse ($g_{min} = 1$, $g_{max} = 10$, $v_1 = 0.1$ m/s, $v_2 = 0.5$ m/s).

Because the transfer function is not rate-based, it requires repeatedly lifting and repositioning the mouse or finger (*clutching*) to scroll very long distances. To reduce clutching-induced effort, we also designed *slide-edge scrolling*, a variant of push-edge that applies inertia to continue scrolling after the user stops operating the pointing device based on a simulation of residual momentum [9]. When the raw device velocity at liftoff v_l exceeds 0.15 m/s, friction progressively decreases velocity V over time according to the function $V(t) = V_l \times e^{-4t}$ – where t is the time elapsed since liftoff, in seconds.

EXPERIMENT

We conducted an experiment to compare performance, amount of control, and perceived workload between push-edge (Push), slide-edge (Slide), and a traditional rate-based edge-scroll (Rate) using a mouse and a trackpad in a one-dimensional text selection task. The primary hypothesis (**H1**) was that selection time would be lower for Push and Slide than for Rate; secondary hypotheses are: (**H2**) inertia (Slide) reduces selection time, (**H3**) Push and Slide offer better control and result in less overshoots than *Rate*, and (**H4**) inertia (Slide) reduces physical effort in long selections.

Method

The experiment was conducted on a 13″ Apple MacBook Pro Retina running OS X 10.9.4, with display resolution set to *Best* (1280×800 px, 116 ppi). Input was provided through the laptop's trackpad and a Logitech M90 optical mouse on a plywood desk. The pointing transfer function was set to the fourth tick of the *Tracking Speed* slider in the respective touchpad and mouse preference panels. Raw device input was used for Push and Slide. Experimental software was written in Objective-C with the Cocoa API. Raw device input was monitored using the I/O Kit and Apple's private multitouch API. The Quartz Event Services API was used to lock the pointer. The software implemented push-edge and slide-edge scrolling, and it used Apple's default rate-based edge-scroll method for the *Rate* condition. It is defined in the `autoscroll:` method of the `NSClipView` class – which scrolls the viewport *p* pixels every 100 ms, where *p* is the pointer-to-edge distance.

Procedure, task, and design

Participants were instructed to perform a sequence of top-to-bottom text selections as quickly and accurately as possible. The window was displayed at the centre of the screen, 400 pixels tall, containing 21,480 lines of text typeset with *Ubuntu Mono Regular* 13px (Figure 2). For each trial, participants had to select a section of text framed and coloured blue – starting eight lines from the bottom of the viewport, and varying in size. Supposing that edge-scroll is mainly target-directed, we overlaid a gradient on the scrollbar as a hint of the number of lines participants had to select. As the task was one-dimensional, selecting anywhere on a line selected the entire line. Every selection required concurrently dragging and scrolling using the requested device and edge-scroll technique. Other scrolling methods and devices were disabled.

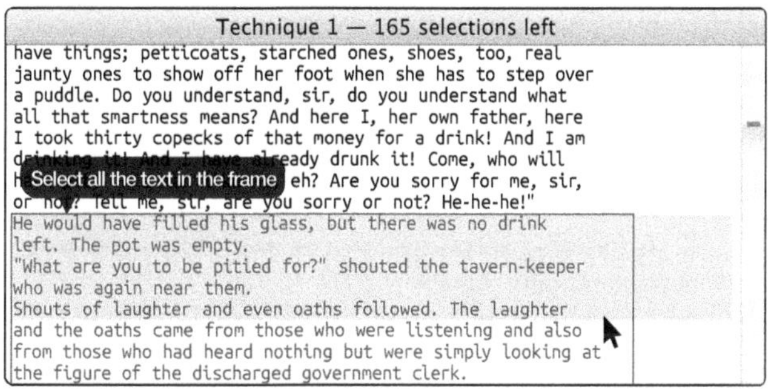

Figure 2. Experimental software for the text selection task.

To perform a selection, participants had to move the pointer to the top of the blue text, press the pointing device button to start the selection (and enter a dragging mode), and scroll downwards until they reached the bottom of the blue text. Once the pointer was positioned over the last line, they could release the button to complete the selection. If their selection did not exactly capture the blue text, an error was recorded, and the trial was repeated.

The experiment used a $2 \times 3 \times 3 \times 4$ within-subjects design for the factors: *device* (mouse and trackpad), *technique* (Push, Slide, and Rate), *block* (1-3, with the first block serving as opportunity for learning the new methods), and *size* (shortest: 15; short: 45; long: 135; longest: 405 lines of text to be selected). The order of *technique* and *device* was counterbalanced. *Sizes* were presented from the shortest to the longest, one for each *block*, with 5 consecutive repetitions for a given size within a block – for a total of 360 trials per participant. Participants completed NASA-TLX worksheets after each technique. The experiment lasted ~45 minutes.

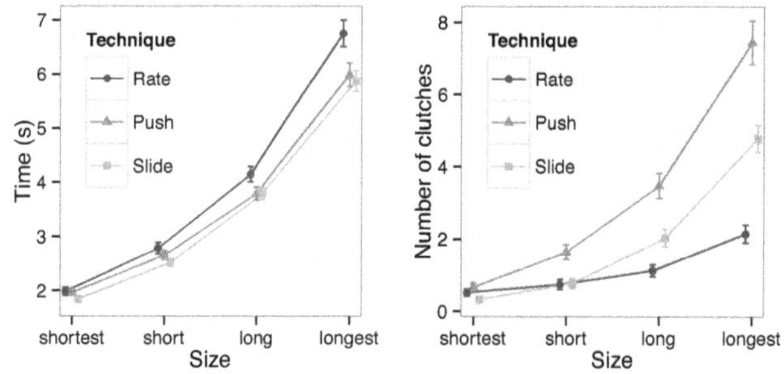

Figure 3. Mean trial time (left) and number of trackpad clutches (right) by size and technique (error bars denote 95% CI).

Participants

Twenty-four university staff and students (five female) participated in the experiment (mean age 30.4, $\sigma = 7.0$). Most used a trackpad as their primary pointing device (58%).

Results

Results for each of the dependent variables (*trial time*, *overshoot distance*, and *number of clutches*) are presented below. Error rate was not significantly different (p=.313) between Push (6.0%), Slide (5.7%), and Rate (6.9%). We excluded error trials from analyses. We also excluded the first repetition of each size, as changes were not immediately noticed.

Trial time

Trial time is the total text selection time, from the first mouse movement after the button was pressed, to the button release.

Repeated-measures ANOVA[1] revealed a significant effect of *block* on trial time ($F_{2,46} = 28.0$, $p < .001$, $\eta_p^2 = .55$; block 1: 4.0s, 2: 3.7s, 3: 3.6s), with a significant *technique*×*block* interaction ($F_{4,92} = 3.0$, p=.023, $\eta_p^2 = .11$) due to a learning of the new technique behaviour during the first block. As we are concerned with user performance after familiarization, the remaining analysis discards the first block.

There were significant main effects of *device* ($F_{1,23} = 28.7$, $p < .001$, $\eta_p^2 = .56$), *technique* ($F_{2,46} = 6.9$, p=.002, $\eta_p^2 = .23$), and *size* ($F_{1.1,25.6} = 360.8$, $p < .001$, $\eta_p^2 = .94$), and a significant *technique*×*size* interaction ($F_{2.4,55.3} = 4.2$, p=.014, $\eta_p^2 = .16$) on trial time. Post-hoc tests revealed that trial time was significantly lower for Slide than for Push (p=.009) or Rate (p=.006) with the shortest size, and than for Rate with the short size ($p < .004$). Trial time was also found significantly higher with Rate than with both Push and Slide for the long (respectively, p=.014 and p=.004) and longest (respectively, p=.029 and p=.003) sizes.

Importantly, Push and Slide consistently outperformed Rate by up to 13% in the longest size (Figure 3, left), supporting **H1**. There was no significant *device*×*technique* interaction (p=.405), suggesting that the benefits of Push are consistent across devices. Finally, inertia had no effect on performance as post-hoc tests revealed no significant difference between Push and Slide (p=.405), leading to rejection of **H2**.

[1]Greenhouse-Geisser corrections to the degrees of freedom were applied when sphericity was violated. Pairwise comparisons used Bonferroni correction.

Overshoot distance

Overshoot distance was measured as the maximum scroll distance beyond the target bounds that was reached during the trial. As expected, ANOVA confirmed that overshoot distance increases with *size* ($F_{1.4,31.0} = 106.1$, $p < .001$, $\eta_p^2 = .82$). There was also a significant effect of *Technique* ($F_{2,46} = 66.7$, $p < .001$, $\eta_p^2 = .74$), with Rate having the largest overshoot distance (369 px) and Push the least (262 px; Slide: 279 px); supporting **H3**. The increased overshooting with Rate likely stems from the need for the user to return the cursor to a location inside the window before scrolling stops after they notice the target has come into view.

Physical effort: clutching and perceived workload

We analysed the number of clutches used on the trackpad, assuming that frequent clutching indicates high physical workload. ANOVA showed significant main effects of *technique* ($F_{2,46} = 47.3$, $p < .001$, $\eta_p^2 = .67$) and *size* ($F_{1.3,30.7} = 172.4$, $p < .001$, $\eta_p^2 = .88$), as well as a significant *technique*×*size* interaction ($F_{2.2,50.2} = 28.2$, $p < .001$, $\eta_p^2 = .55$). As Rate allows continuous scrolling to be maintained without movement, it is unsurprising that it has significantly less clutching than Push. Pairwise comparisons between Slide and Push confirmed that the addition of inertia decreases clutching (Figure 3, right).

NASA-TLX responses showed *physical demand* to be lower with Rate than Push or Slide, for both the mouse (Friedman $\chi^2(2) = 17.2$, $p < .001$) and trackpad ($\chi^2(2) = 11.9$, p=.003). We also found that for the mouse, Slide had significantly higher perceived *effort* than Rate ($\chi^2(2) = 7.7$, p=.022), which probably stems from the difficulty of lifting the mouse while maintaining a high tangential velocity. Therefore, clutching and subjective data only partially support **H4**.

DISCUSSION

Our key finding is that push-edge and slide-edge scrolling both improved text selection time over a rate-based edge-scroll technique. The performance benefits were consistent for both trackpad and mouse pointing devices. Workload measures suggest that push-edge scrolling is best combined with mouse input, and slide-edge scrolling best with a trackpad.

It is likely that the actual performance benefits for push-edge and slide-edge scrolling over rate-based methods are understated with our results. Our experiment intentionally used a relatively small window centered on the screen, which is a 'best case' scenario for traditional techniques because of the large control area outside the window. When a window extends to the edge of the display (e.g., when maximised) the control area is compromised or unavailable, substantially impairing traditional methods – but there is no reason to anticipate any performance detriment in this case with our techniques.

The target of an edge-scrolling action while selecting text is consequently located in the scrolled viewport. However, there are situations where the scope of a dragging action may span multiple viewports (e.g. dragging a file between two windows) where moving the pointer beyond the viewport edge could be interpreted either as the continuation of the dragging action or as a request to activate edge-scroll. Current systems use various methods to distinguish these actions, such as waiting for a pointer to dwell over an interior control area in order to start scrolling. The relative merits of each approach, as well as their applicability to our techniques are left for future work.

Finally, one potential usability issue of our techniques is that they temporarily remove the user's direct control of the cursor as it is 'captured' by the window edge. The immediate feedback of seeing the viewport scroll should mitigate the user's surprise, but not if it reaches its terminus. To help visually communicate the captured cursor state, the techniques could apply a visual resistance effect to the viewport.

CONCLUSION

Edge-scroll is extensively used to enable scrolling while a concurrent dragging state is maintained. Most existing designs use rate control, where cursor position into a control area around the window edge controls scrolling velocity. We showed the potential performance limitations of current techniques and designed push-edge and slide-edge scrolling to work around them by allowing to scroll by "pushing against the viewport edge". Experimental results demonstrate that push-edge and slide-edge scrolling significantly improve performance.

ACKNOWLEDGMENTS

This work was supported by ANR (TurboTouch, ANR-14-CE24-0009). Thanks to UCLIC members, F. Chevalier, G. Bailly, T. Pietrzak and A. Goguey for their helpful comments.

REFERENCES

1. Accot, J., and Zhai, S. More than dotting the i's — foundations for crossing-based interfaces. In *Proc. CHI '02*.
2. Apple Computer Inc. *Macintosh human interface guidelines*. Addison-Wesley Publishing, nov 1992.
3. Cockburn, A., Quinn, P., Gutwin, C., and Fitchett, S. Improving scrolling devices with document length dependent gain. In *Proc. CHI'12*.
4. Hinckley, K., and Bathiche, S. Positional scrolling, 2006. US Patent 7,071,919.
5. Hinckley, K., Cutrell, E., Bathiche, S., and Muss, T. Quantitative analysis of scrolling techniques. In *Proc. CHI'02*.
6. Kim, W., Tendick, F., Ellis, S., and Stark, L. A comparison of position and rate control for telemanipulations with consideration of manipulator system dynamics. *IEEE Journal of Robotics and Automation 3*, 5 (1987).
7. Kwatinetz, A. Scrolling contents of a window, US. Patent 5495566 (1996).
8. Li, S., and Shrader, T. Scrolling a target window during a drag and drop operation, US. Patent 5740389 (1998).
9. Quinn, P., Malacria, S., and Cockburn, A. Touch scrolling transfer functions. In *Proc. of UIST '13*.
10. Roussel, N., Casiez, G., Aceituno, J., and Vogel, D. Giving a hand to the eyes: Leveraging input accuracy for subpixel interaction. In *Proc. of UIST '12*.
11. Zhai, S. *Human performance in six degree of freedom input control*. PhD thesis, University of Toronto, 1995.
12. Zhai, S., Smith, B. A., and Selker, T. Improving browsing performance: A study of four input devices for scrolling and pointing tasks. In *Proc. INTERACT'97*.

Investigating Visual Feedforward for Target Expansion Techniques

Maxime Guillon[1,2], François Leitner[2], Laurence Nigay[1]

[1]Univ. Grenoble Alpes, LIG, CNRS
F-38000 Grenoble, France
{maxime.guillon, laurence.nigay}@imag.fr

[2]Aesculap SAS
F-38130 Échirolles, France
{maxime.guillon, francois.leitner}@bbraun.com

ABSTRACT

Target expansion techniques facilitate the pointing task by enlarging the effective sizes of targets. When the target expansion is applied to both the motor and visual spaces, the visual feedforward mechanism is key: Indeed it provides a visual aid to the user on the effective expanded targets prior to the execution or completion of the pointing task, enabling the user to take full advantage of the target expansion technique. Focusing on feedforward mechanisms, we introduce a design space that allows us to describe, classify and design target expansion techniques. To do so we first introduce and characterize the concept of *atomic feedforward mechanism* along three design axes. We then describe a target expansion technique as a combination of atomic feedforward mechanisms using a matrix-based notation. We provide an analytical exploration of the design space by classifying existing techniques and by designing six new techniques. We also provide a first experimental exploration of the design space in the context of distant pointing. The experimental protocol includes an innovative target layout for handling non-centroidal target expansion. The results show that feedforward dynamicity increases movement time and decreases subjective usability, while explicit expansion observability efficiently supports error prevention for distant pointing.

Author Keywords

Target expansion; feedforward; pointing; distant pointing.

ACM Classification Keywords

H.5.2. Information interfaces and presentation: User Interfaces

INTRODUCTION

Pointing to targets is an elementary task universally present in graphical user interfaces (GUI). Thus researchers have proposed many targeting assistance techniques [1, 3, 4, 6, 8, 10, 11, 12, 15, 16, 17, 18] to optimize pointing. Pointing can be accurately modeled using Fitts' law [4, 9, 13]. Fitts' law states that two non-exclusive ways to reduce the difficulty of a pointing task are by reducing the distance from the starting point (A-Amplitude) to the target and/or by enlarging the target (W-Width). We focus on targeting assistance techniques that enlarge the effective sizes of targets (W) both in the motor and visual spaces. Such target expansion techniques rely on a partitioning of the space. An example of space decomposition is the Voronoi tessellation [3, 7, 8, 10, 11] that maximizes the use of empty space and is unambiguous since only one target is contained in each Voronoi cell. Several target expansion techniques implement a target expansion algorithm based on the Voronoi tessellation [3, 6, 8, 10, 11, 15]: The expanded targets then correspond to the Voronoi cells and the user can point anywhere inside the target Voronoi cell instead of pointing at the target. For target expansion both in the motor and visual spaces, the design challenge of target expansion techniques is to make the motor target expansion visually observable through a feedforward mechanism. The visual feedforward mechanism is key since it provides a visual aid to the user on the effective expanded targets prior to the execution or completion of the pointing task, enabling the user to take full advantage of the target expansion technique. Recent studies [10, 16] confirm the key role that the feedforward mechanism plays in the performance of a target expansion technique.

Focusing on feedforward mechanisms for target expansion, this paper proposes a design space for describing, classifying and designing target expansion techniques. Three design axes characterize the concept of *atomic feedforward mechanism*, an elementary unit that can be combined for designing a target expansion technique. We present a matrix-based notation for describing target expansion techniques as a combination of *atomic feedforward mechanisms*. We provide an analytical exploration of the design space by classifying existing target expansion techniques and by designing six new target expansion techniques that involve *atomic and combined feedforward mechanisms*. We also provide a first experimental exploration of the design space. To do so the experimental protocol includes an innovative target layout that can handle non-centroidal target expansion for controlling various shifts between a target's centroid and its expanded target's centroid.

CHI 2015, April 18 - 23 2015, Seoul, Republic of Korea
Copyright 2015 ACM 978-1-4503-3145-6/15/04...$15.00
http://dx.doi.org/10.1145/2702123.2702375

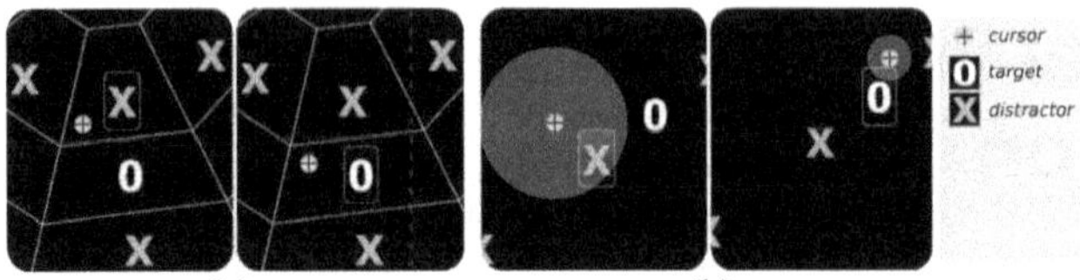

Figure 1. (a) VTE: The visual feedforward is the display of all the Voronoi cells. The goal target ("0") can be selected when the cursor is within the Voronoi cell of the "0" target. (b) Bubble Cursor: The visual feedforward is a bubble with the cursor at the center. The goal target ("0") can be selected when the bubble reaches the "0" target.

We note that the experimental exploration of the design space is conducted in the context of distant pointing because: (1) Techniques enhancing target selection by expanding the targets demonstrated their efficiency in distant pointing for various contexts, including virtual 3D environments [18], large displays [17] and operating rooms [10]. (2) Our application domain is augmented surgery, where efficient distant pointing techniques are important when considering the cognitive workload of the surgeons. Moreover the GUIs involved in augmented surgery are particularly suited to target expansion techniques. Indeed, for target enlargement, dividing the motor space into areas is beneficial only if the motor space contains empty space not used for interaction (the effective sizes of the targets being extended into the adjacent empty space). In the augmented surgery GUIs that we study, classical desktop-based functions (e.g., selection of a group of items, of an empty space) are not supported so that, the entire motor space can be altered without any functionality loss.

MOTIVATION: VARIETY OF FEEDFORWARD MECHANISMS FOR TARGET EXPANSION TECHNIQUES

Existing target expansion techniques exhibit different characteristics of visual feedforward that motivated us to establish a design space. For illustrating this variety, we consider two radically different target expansion techniques that employ the same target expansion algorithm, based on a Voronoi tessellation for partitioning the space into Voronoi cells (i.e. the expanded targets). First the Voronoi-based Target Expansion (VTE) technique [10] provides an explicit static feedforward mechanism by displaying the entire space partitioning (i.e. the Voronoi tessellation) before and during the pointing task (Figure 1-a). Second, Bubble Cursor [8] provides a dynamic feedforward by visually augmenting the cursor: a round bubble that expands to constantly reach the closest target (Figure 1-b). The bubble feedforward implicitly conveys the target expansion algorithm to the user, since the target's expanded shape (i.e. the target's Voronoi cell) is not displayed.

DESIGN SPACE

Since a target expansion technique can implement several visual feedforward mechanisms, we introduce the concept of *atomic feedforward mechanism* to designate an elementary mechanism that can be combined within a technique.

Augmented Element \ Expansion Observability / Dynamicity	implicit: static	implicit: discrete	implicit: continuous	explicit: static	explicit: discrete	explicit: continuous
cursor(s)	Impossible		Bubble Cursor [10], Lazy Bubble [14], Rope Cursor, Bubble Lens [17], Dynaspot [7]	Impossible		
space			Ghost-hunting [13]	VTE [12], MTE, Starburst [3], Bubble Lens [17]		eVTE
target(s)		Target Highlight, IFC [18], Dynaspot [7]		Bubble Lens [17]	Cell Painting	

Figure 2. Atomic feedforward mechanisms characterized along three axes. Target expansion techniques are located within the design space. Empty squares in the design space highlight unexplored design possibilities.

This section first examines design axes for characterizing an atomic feedforward mechanism, independently from its visual form (e.g., color, shape) and from the underlying expansion algorithm. We then describe an entire target expansion technique using a matrix notation by considering the combination of atomic feedforward mechanisms provided during a pointing movement.

Atomic Feedforward Mechanisms: Three Axes

Figure 2 presents three axes for an atomic feedforward mechanism.

Axis Dynamicity: As defined in [2, 10, 19], a feedforward mechanism can be static or dynamic. Some of the dynamic feedforward mechanisms are discrete, while others are continuous [2, 19]. While continuous feedforward mechanisms constantly change when the cursor moves, discrete ones intermittently change at discrete points in time (e.g., when the hovered target changes). For example Bubble Cursor [8] is a case of continuous feedforward, the bubble being updated continuously. VTE [10] is static, permanently displaying the complete Voronoi tessellation.

Axis Expansion Observability: The *Expansion Observability* axis characterizes the visual observability of the motor target expansion. A feedforward mechanism makes observable the current target cell, the cells of several targets (for instance the ones close to the cursor) or the space partitioning (i.e. all the cells). Existing mechanisms provide spatial information. No symbolic approach (e.g., letters) has been studied for target expansion feedforward since the pointing task is spatial. We further describe an atomic feedforward mechanism by distinguishing explicit or implicit expansion observability.

- Explicit feedforward: When the cell of a target or the cells of several targets are directly observable (with different visual clues including lines or colors), the feedforward mechanism is explicit: This is a spatial information that informs the user where to click. By showing one screenshot of the technique, an observer can directly observe the target's cell (Figure 1-a: VTE).

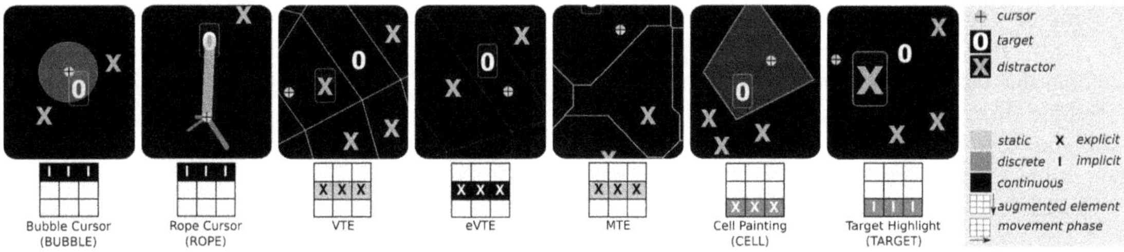

Figure 3. Developed and experimentally compared target expansion techniques involving one type of atomic feedforward mechanism (for each technique: a screenshot and its matrix-based representation).

- Implicit feedforward: If the user has to use indirect means (e.g., cursor responses to various positions) in order to estimate the target's cell, then the feedforward is implicit. An implicit feedforward mechanism provides spatial clues relative to its previous state: The mechanism is therefore dynamic (discrete or continuous) and informs the user when to click. For example Bubble Cursor is implicit since the targets' cells are not displayed: When the dynamic visual bubble reaches the target, the user can select it by clicking (Figure 1-b: Bubble Cursor).

Axis Augmented Element: Various visual clues (e.g., color, shape, size) characterize the feedforward visual form. In addition for target expansion, a discriminating characteristic of the visual form is the *element* of the pointing task that is visually *augmented*: the cursor, the space and the target. Since the cursor is moving, cursor-based feedforward is by definition dynamic. A space-based visual feedfoward, partly or fully, modifies the available empty space while a target-based feedforward modifies the visual appearance of a target. For instance with VTE, the visual appearance of the targets is not modified: It is a space-based feedforward mechanism, as opposed to a target-based mechanism that doubles the size of the current selected target.

The resulting three-axes design space (Figure 2) defines 16 types of atomic visual feedforward mechanisms that serve as a basis for the design of target expansion techniques.

Combined Atomic Feedforward Mechanisms

Target expansion techniques combine different types of atomic feedforward mechanisms. To characterize the combination of feedforward mechanisms, we consider *when* the mechanisms are used according to the three phases of the pointing movements that the Optimized Initial Impulse Model defined [14]: (1) The preliminary phase precedes any pointing movement. It includes the time of target spotting and anticipation and neuromotor programming of the movement. (2) The ballistic phase designates the first reaching movement which is fast and imprecise. (3) The corrective phase only happens if the ballistic movement does not land on the target. Indeed because of neuromotor noise, corrective small and precise submovements are often needed for performing difficult pointing tasks.

If a technique uses several atomic feedforward mechanisms simultaneously (i.e. during the same phase), the mechanisms are combined in a *parallel* way. *Sequential* combination then describes feedforward mechanisms used during consecutive phases. Atomic feedforward mechanisms are therefore described at the granularity of the movement phase [14].

Matrix-based Notation for Describing a Technique

An atomic mechanism corresponds to one and only one square within the classification scheme of Figure 2. Contrastingly, a target expansion technique combining different feedforward mechanisms corresponds to different types (and therefore squares) in the classification scheme of Figure 2 (e.g., Dynaspot and Bubble Lens described in the following section). The comparison of techniques is then not straightforward. We therefore define a compact visual notation for describing an entire target expansion technique based on the characteristics of the involved feedforward mechanisms and their combination scheme (matrices of Figures 3 and 4). A 3x3 matrix represents a target expansion technique. Columns represent the 3 movement phases along a horizontal time axis, in chronological order from left to right. Lines correspond to the *augmented element* axis of Figure 2: from the *cursor* (top) to the *target* (bottom) through the *space* (middle). Each cell of the matrix then represents one type of augmented element during one movement phase. A blackness code represents the *dynamicity* axis: light gray for *static*, dark gray for dynamic *discrete* and black for dynamic *continuous*. Finally, a "X" in the cell is used for an *explicit* feedforward along the *expansion observability* axis (e.g., VTE matrix in Figure 3) and a "I" for an *implicit* one (e.g., BUBBLE matrix in Figure 3).

ANALYTICAL EXPLORATION OF THE DESIGN SPACE: EXISTING TARGET EXPANSION TECHNIQUES

Figure 2 classifies target expansion techniques from the literature according to their underlying feedforward mechanisms. Figures 3 and 4 represent the described target expansion techniques using our matrix-based notation.

Cursor-Based Mechanisms: Bubble Cursor, Lazy Bubble and Cone Cursor

The Bubble Cursor [8] feedforward mechanism illustrates well the intensively studied type of *implicit continuous* augmentation of the *cursor* (BUBBLE matrix in Figure 3). By limiting its size to reach only one target [8], the bubble potentially shows which target is on the point of being designated: This de facto constitutes an error prevention mechanism. Lazy Bubble and Cone Cursor [12] are variations along the continuum from a traditional point cursor to Bubble Cursor. These techniques implement *implicit continuous* feedforward by visually augmenting the *cursor*: Their users know when to click to select a target rather than where to click.

Space-Based Mechanisms: Voronoi-based Target Expansion (VTE), Starburst and Ghost-hunting

As previously described, VTE [10] displays the entire Voronoi diagram once, before the movement begins. VTE illustrates a type of feedforward that make the target expansion mechanism explicitly observable (VTE matrix in Figure 3). Starburst [3] proposes a new partitioning of the space, especially suited to clusters of targets. Like VTE, its feedforward mechanism is an *explicit static* augmentation of the *space*. Ghost-hunting [11] creates an avatar for each target (a *ghost*) which constantly indicates the optimal trajectory to reach the target depending on the cursor's position. Its expansion algorithm is also based on a Voronoi tessellation. This technique uses an *implicit continuous* augmentation of the *space* (Ghost-hunting matrix in Figure 4), even if the avatars could also modify the targets' appearance by intersecting them.

Target-Based Mechanisms: Visual Target Expansions and Implicit Fan Cursor (IFC)

Feedforward mechanisms that highlight the target have been intensively studied [13, 20]. Amongst them, Cell Painting (Figure 3) expands the target to its cell by painting the full expanded target shape with a semi-transparent color. The feedforward mechanism is therefore an *explicit discrete* augmentation of the *target* (CELL matrix in Figure 3). When the target is scaled, namely TARGET in Figure 3, or highlighted by changing its color [13, 20], the feedforward mechanism becomes an *implicit discrete target* augmentation (TARGET matrix in Figure 3). In terms of *expansion observability*, it only makes observable the current target and not the cell (in contrast to Cell Painting).

Implicit Fan Cursor (IFC) [16] was originally designed as a *continuous cursor*-based feedforward mechanism. With this first design, namely the Fan Cursor technique, a fan-shaped cursor's activation area dynamically adjusts its spanning angle and orientation to minimize the cursor's movements. In [16] Fan Cursor is compared with a design alternative, namely Implicit Fan Cursor (IFC), based on highlighting the target: Instead of the cursor fan-shaped activation area, the current target is highlighted and slightly expanded. Results show that the *discrete* augmentation of the *target* (IFC) (IFC matrix in Figure 4) is more efficient than the initial Fan Cursor technique.

Combined Mechanisms: Dynaspot and Bubble Lens

Dynaspot [6] extends Bubble Cursor [8] with an implicit mode-switching enabling desktop-based interaction. Above a cursor speed threshold of 150 pixels/s, targets are

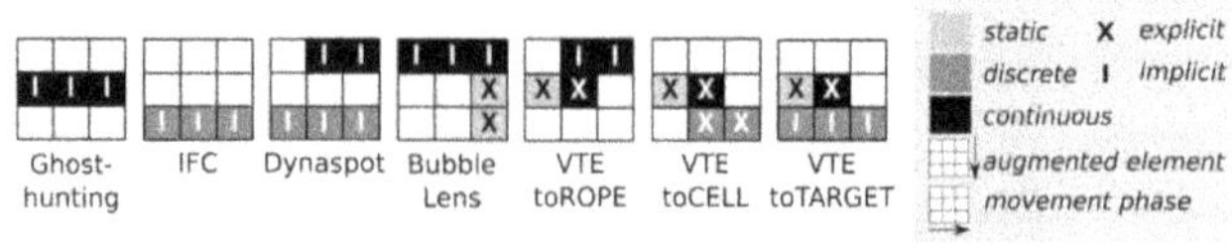

Figure 4. Matrix-based representation of existing target expansion techniques and of designed techniques combining different types of atomic feedforward.

expanded according to a Voronoi tessellation. The bubble, contrary to Bubble Cursor, grows to a predefined maximum width and shrinks back when the cursor slows down under the threshold. The expansion phase nevertheless lasts for about 300 ms after the cursor speed falls under the threshold. During the expansion phase, the closest target is highlighted. Thus this technique combines two complementary feedforward mechanisms. First, the bubble, an *implicit continuous cursor*-based feedforward mechanism, informs about the target expansion activation state. Second the target highlight is an *implicit discrete target*-based feedforward mechanism that indicates the designated target (Dynaspot matrix in Figure 4).

Bubble Lens [15] behaves like Bubble Cursor [8], with the addition of a local magnification when the targets are small and dense. Thanks to kinematic triggering, magnification is triggered on the downward slope of the first corrective submovement [14, 15] in a smoothed velocity profile. Thus, the magnification happens only during the corrective phase of a pointing movement [14]. During the magnification phase, the targets and the space are expanded in a round area of interest (a different expansion algorithm than the one based on a Voronoi diagram). Since the targets and the space are represented in their expanded forms, independently from the cursor's movements, the magnification combines two *explicit static* feedforward mechanisms: a visual *space* expansion and a visual *target* expansion. To sum up, since Bubble Cursor is still active during the magnification, two expansion algorithms and three feedforward mechanisms are therefore active simultaneously (Bubble Lens matrix in Figure 4). A matrix having several filled cells in a column (Figure 4) represents the parallel combination of atomic feedforward mechanisms supported by Dynaspot and Bubble Lens. We note that the matrix-based notation allows us to describe the parallel combinations of mechanisms based on different *augmented elements* only.

ANALYTICAL EXPLORATION OF THE DESIGN SPACE: DESIGNING NEW TARGET EXPANSION TECHNIQUES

Exploiting the design space, we designed six new target expansion techniques. While BUBBLE is well established, VTE outperformed it [11]. So we started from these two techniques whose characteristics are different along the design axes. Based on BUBBLE and the *expansion observability* axis we designed ROPE. Based on VTE and the *dynamicity* axis we designed eVTE and MTE. Finally studying feedforward for each movement phase prompted us to combine them.

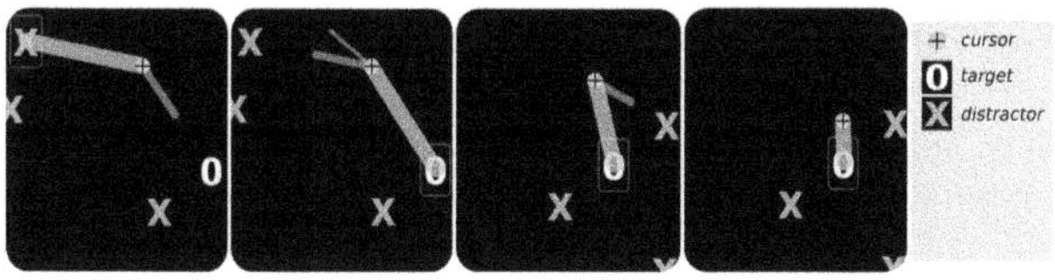

Figure 5. Rope Cursor: Dynamic main/mini ropes indicating the current target and the neighboring targets.

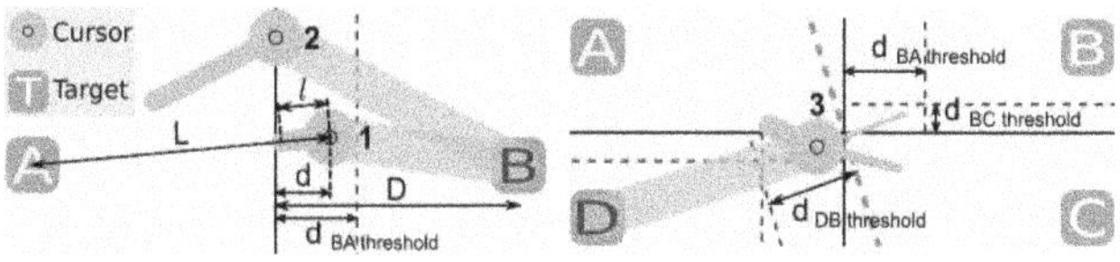

Figure 6. Rope Cursor: Parameters for computing the length and width of the main/mini ropes.

Technique 1: Rope Cursor

Our design goal was to increase the *expansion observability* of Bubble Cursor while minimizing the visual disturbance of the *dynamicity* of the bubble area. To do so we use lines instead of a bubble area as shown in Figure 5: A main line (i.e. the rope) joins the cursor to the closest target and supplementary smaller lines (i.e. the mini-ropes) dynamically indicate the proximity of neighboring targets.

When the cursor is closer to a border of the hovered Voronoi cell than a distance threshold (Figure 6: cases 1 and 2, where $d < d_{BA\ threshold}$), a mini rope appears on the cursor. We arbitrarily define this distance threshold at one third of the distance from the designated target to the corresponding border (Figure 6: $d_{BA\ threshold} = D/3$). Thus, distance thresholds can be different in a cell, as shown in Figure 6 ($d_{BA\ threshold} \neq d_{BC\ threshold}$). When a target shares only one corner with the hovered cell (Figure 6: case 3, targets D and B), we define a distance threshold equal to one third of the distance from the designated target to the corresponding corner (Figure 6: the widest dashed line represents the bisection of a segment DB). The mini-rope is oriented towards the direction of the target whose cell's border is close (distance threshold) to the cursor. Thus, the mini-ropes directly designate the approaching neighboring targets. For instance in Figure 6 cases 1 and 2, the mini-rope indicates target A. While the cursor is approaching the border, the mini rope linearly grows within a range of *0* to *L/2* in Figure 6. Thus, when the cursor is about to cross the border (Figure 6: case 2), the mini-rope is as long as half the distance separating the cursor from the designated neighboring target, making the border crossing transition smooth. This mini-rope behavior represents the remaining distance to the neighboring cell (Figure 6: *d*). Indeed, at any time the ratio between *l* and *L/2* is equal to the ratio of $d_{BA\ threshold} - d$ and $d_{BA\ threshold}$. Complementary to its length, the mini-rope's width indicates the proximity order of neighboring targets: The wider the mini-rope is, the closer the cursor is to the target. Each mini-rope's width is equal to the immediately wider (mini-)rope's width divided by 2 (Figure 3, 5 and 6). Rope Cursor is a new technique based on the *cursor* that is *implicit* and *continuous* (ROPE matrix in Figure 3). Rope Cursor provides a better *expansion observability* than Bubble Cursor, while still being *implicit*. Indeed the 3 mini-ropes (but more is possible) show the proximity of 3 neighboring targets simultaneously (Figure 3 and 6), while the bubble is constrained to adjust its round geometry to only two closest targets [8] (Figure 1-b: Bubble Cursor).

Technique 2: Erasable Voronoi-based Target Expansion (eVTE)

The *static* display of the Voronoi diagram provided by VTE may disturb the visual perception of the underlying GUI and hide useful information. To address this issue, we explored the *dynamicity* axis. To make VTE *dynamic*, the transparency of the Voronoi diagram is coupled to the cursor's speed. The diagram's transparency follows a sigmoidal function of the cursor's speed. Thus, at high speed the Voronoi diagram disappears in a continuous and progressive way to reveal the GUI. The technique, namely Erasable VTE (eVTE), also supports the possibility of temporarily erasing the diagram by shaking the cursor. eVTE is a new technique that is (*explicit*, *continuous*, *space*-based) (eVTE matrix in Figure 3). eVTE then fills an empty square in Figure 2: a design possibility so far unexplored.

Technique 3: Manhattan Target Expansion (MTE)

MTE is based on a partitioning of the space among the targets according to a Voronoi diagram computed in Manhattan distance (Figure 7). Contrary to the Euclidean distance (e.g., VTE), the Manhattan distance between two points (also called rectilinear distance) is the sum of the absolute differences of the Cartesian coordinates of the two points. Voronoi diagrams in such a geometry include only vertical, horizontal and 45°-oriented lines (MTE in Figure 3 and Figure 7). The resulting partitioning on screen could then be more aesthetic and consistent with GUI. In using this innovative space partitioning, we propose a technique with the same characteristics as VTE according to our design axes (*explicit*, *static*, *space*-based) (MTE matrix in Figure 3) but with a different expansion algorithm.

Techniques 4-5-6: Combined Feedforward Mechanisms

Our design goal for these three techniques addressed the same issue as for eVTE: the VTE's Voronoi diagram permanent display visual overload. As opposed to the design of eVTE, this time we explored the *combination* of feedforward mechanisms. Since VTE enhances the movement anticipation [10], we kept VTE during the preliminary phase. We then explored the combinations of VTE with three different feedforward mechanisms for the ballistic and corrective phases: ROPE (*implicit*, *continuous*, *cursor*-based), CELL (*explicit*, *discrete*, *target*-based) and TARGET (*implicit*, *discrete*, *target*-based) (Figure 3). The resulting techniques are respectively called VTEtoROPE, VTEtoCELL and VTEtoTARGET and are represented using our matrix-based notation in Figure 4. First, like Dynaspot

[6], the feedforward mechanism switching occurs at the early ballistic phase, as soon as the anticipation time is over: The VTE's Voronoi diagram progressively disappears with a visual fade-out effect, its transparency quadratically increasing from full opacity to full transparency in 300 ms. Thus a dynamic continuous version of VTE is still present during the ballistic phase for 300 ms (as represented by the black cell in the matrices of Figure 4), in parallel with another feedforward mechanism (ROPE, CELL or TARGET). Second, while TARGET is active during the entire movement (three phases) in VTEtoTARGET, we explored another type of combination with VTEtoROPE and VTEtoCELL. Indeed ROPE and CELL start to be active at the early ballistic phase and remain active until the end of the movement (two phases only).

Summary: As illustrated by the three techniques, VTEtoROPE, VTEtoCELL and VTEtoTARGET, the combination of feedforward mechanisms defines numerous possibilities. The resulting design space defined by the three axes of an atomic feedforward mechanism and by the combination of atomic mechanisms therefore opens a vast set of design possibilities. We started the analytical exploration of the design space by classifying existing target expansion techniques and by designing six new ones. In the rest of the paper we embark on its experimental exploration.

EXPERIMENTAL EXPLORATION OF THE DESIGN SPACE

The goals of the experiment were to lead a first experimental exploration of the design space and to evaluate the 6 new techniques. In the experiment, in addition to comparing the 6 above techniques, we included Bubble Cursor and VTE as baselines. We also included TARGET as an atomic *target*-based feedforward. To sum up, we have therefore compared the following 9 techniques: VTE, BUBBLE, ROPE, eVTE, MTE, VTEtoROPE, VTEtoCELL, VTEtoTARGET and TARGET. We thus compared at least one technique per line of the design space (Figure 2) and one technique per column (except the column *implicit-static*). Our hypotheses are as follows:

- (H1) Within a cell, continuously changing feedforward produces noise and redundancy (Shannon's information theory) while the selected target does not change. We expect these ineffective stimuli to slow down the selection task.
- (H2) The atomic and combined techniques with explicit feedforward at movement start will be faster than the others. Users will optimize their ballistic gesture [14] according to a larger target size (Fitts' law).
- (H3) The atomic and combined techniques with explicit feedforward at movement end will be more precise. Users will obtain more powerful error anticipation means by evaluating the distance between the cursor and the target boundaries.

New Target Layout for Non-Centroidal Tessellations

This section presents the new target layout that we propose to be able to measure the shifting of the pointing movement endpoints induced by the visual feedforward mechanism.

Shifting of the pointing movement endpoints

The users optimize their pointing gestures depending on the perceived size of the target they are aiming at [14]. As a consequence, the target's centroid (its center of mass) is a good predictor of the movement endpoint, as demonstrated in [9] with targets of arbitrary shapes. By comparing the mean distance from the movement endpoints to the targets' centroids ($d_{toTarget}$) with the mean distance from the movement endpoints to the target cells' centroids (i.e. expanded targets' centroids) (d_{toCell}), we identify three cases for a feedforward mechanism:

- If $d_{toCell} < d_{toTarget}$, "cell-centered mechanism".
- If $d_{toCell} > d_{toTarget}$, "target-centered mechanism".
- If $d_{toCell} \approx d_{toTarget}$, "mixed-centered mechanism", as the pointing movement endpoints have no clear tendency.

The fact that a feedforward mechanism is cell-centered is experimental proof that the expanded target's shape has been taken into account by the users during the pointing movement. While we can expect that an explicit feedforward mechanism will provoke such a shifting from the target's centroid to the cell's centroid, the timing of such an explicit feedforward is of importance. Indeed, it determines the moment the users will perceive the expanded targets and therefore the remaining time for the optimization of the pointing movements.

For the case of Voronoi target expansion, existing target layouts make it difficult to observe the endpoints according to our three cases (i.e. cell, target and mixed). Indeed as in [6, 8, 15, 16, 17], a square Voronoi cell has a centroid matching that of the target: This is mathematically called a centroidal Voronoi tessellation [7]. The geometric layout described in [4] and used in [10] creates a pseudo-hexagonal Voronoi cell, whose centroid is very close to the corresponding target's centroid. In [1], cells' centroids are shifted from targets' centroids along a unique radial direction.

New target layout

We therefore propose a new target layout that shifts Voronoi cells' centroids from the targets' centroids along different controllable directions (Figure 7). The layout is fully reproducible and based on an ISO 9241-9 task [1]. The ISO task places a set of goal targets [1, 16] on a virtual circle. We add one distractor target at the center of this circle. We further define three constraints for the other distractors: (1) Distractors are placed on concentric circles. (2) Each concentric circle contains the same number of distractors. (3) The distractors of distinct circles are aligned along the radii. These constraints define trapezoidal Voronoi cells (Figure 7).

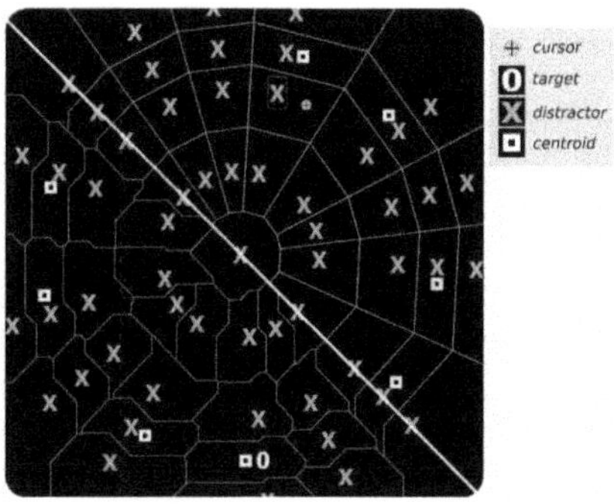

Figure 7. New target layout for non-centroidal Voronoi cells along with VTE (top) and MTE (bottom). The outlined squares are the centroids of the targets' cells (targets from the ISO 9241-9 task). The goal target (i.e. the white zero) is shifted from its Voronoi cell centroid in an anti-clockwise direction.

In order to create non-centroidal trapezoidal Voronoi cells, we then place the distractors (1) on circles with aperiodic diameters or (2) along radii in aperiodic directions (Figure 7). The cells' centroids are therefore shifted from the targets' centroids, respectively along (1) a radial direction or (2) a tangential direction (the outlined squares in Figure 7). In the context of an ISO 9241-9 task, targets are placed along periodic directions. To obtain distractors along radii in aperiodic directions, the distractors are added on the bisector of every two slices (i.e. angle between two radii) (Figure 7).

Apparatus and Participants

Our application domain is intra-operative distant interaction for computer-assisted surgery. By using orthopedic hardware and software certified material, we reproduced in part surgical conditions. Eighteen unpaid volunteers (6 women and 12 men) were all right-handed, ranging in age from 22 to 51 years. They stood in front of a table, 1.8 m away from the screen. They selected the target with a foot-switch three button medical pedal and controlled a cursor with an Aesculap virtual pointer. This ray-casting system [1] projects on the screen the axis of a metallic pointer on which an IR reflective rigid-body is clipped. An NDI Polaris IR tracker provides pointer positions and orientations. The software application was running on a 2.3 GHz Quadcore PC with Windows 7. We used a 24" LCD display at 1920 x 1200 resolution.

Implemented Techniques

Figure 3 gives screenshots of all the atomic feedforward mechanisms we implemented. The behavior of Bubble Cursor was the same as in [8, 10, 16]. The Rope Cursor main rope's and mini-ropes' widths were respectively 24, 12, 6 and 3 pixels. The transparency of the eVTE's diagram varied from full opacity to full transparency when the cursor speed varied from 0 to 1500 pixels/s, according to a sigmoid function. These values were fixed during pre-tests by conducting an analysis of pointing movements that were performed with the Aesculap's pointing system. With TARGET, the target was scaled by 1.618.

For the three combined techniques, we detected the ballistic phase using a cursor speed threshold, which we determined to be 500 pixels/s. This speed threshold was evaluated at around 150 pixels/s in [6, 18], but the settings were different than ours. For applying the threshold of 500 pixels/s we filtered the cursor's speed by computing the mean of the 4 last instant speeds. Thus, we excluded the speed peaks induced by the pedal presses and the noise induced by the hand jitters amplified by the distance between the users and the screen. This method clearly revealed one ballistic phase per pointing movement on smoothed velocity profiles.

Task and Procedure

Participants achieved ISO 9241-9 pointing tasks with 9 targets, the first one being the start target and 8 target selections being then recorded (Figure 7). The Aesculap's C++ software platform provided the workflow management functions, as well as the application *black-cockpit* look and feel (Figures 1, 3, 5 and 7). The targets included a white "0" for goal-targets and a gray "X" for distractor targets. A thin border highlighted the designated target. This target highlight corresponds to a minimal feedforward mechanism (*implicit*, *discrete*, *target*-based), present in all the techniques. A short sound confirmed successful selections. When participants selected a distractor target, we displayed the current error number during 100 ms in place of the "X" of the corresponding distractor. Mistaken trials were removed from selection time measures. We collected selection times, cursor trajectories, velocity profiles, errors and movement endpoints.

The participants were instructed to be as fast and as accurate as possible. They answered a System Usability Scale (SUS) [5] on the technique they just experienced before starting the next one. To do so, we provided an imaginary concrete context of distant interaction with a TV. Finally, the participants were asked to rank the 3 techniques they appreciated the most, having access to visual recall on paper sheet, similar to the screenshots of Figure 3. The techniques were counter-balanced across participants using a Latin square. The experiment lasted approximately 40 minutes and started with a 5-minute training session.

Design

The experiment used a 9 techniques x (2 x 2 x 2) target layouts within-participant design. We used the above described target layout including two distractor circles with the diameters of 400 and 1200 pixels. We varied the goal target circle diameters (600 or 1000 pixels). For each of these two movement amplitude conditions, we also considered the presence or not of an additional circle of distractors with a diameter of 800 pixels. The last condition is related to the shift of the centroids along the tangential direction: Distractors are either added to the bisector of every two slices or are not added. We therefore obtained 2 x 2 x 2 target layouts, randomly ordered for each participant.

Technique	Representation	Classification	Selection Time	Error Rate
MTE		Cell-centered ***	1308 ms	5.13 %
VTE		Cell-centered ***	1310 ms	6.34 %
TARGET		Target-centered ***	1394 ms	8.09 %
ROPE		Mixed-centered	1424 ms	6.03 %
VTEtoTARGET		Cell-centered ***	1431 ms	6.78 %
BUBBLE		Target-centered **	1440 ms	7.41 %
VTEtoCELL		Cell-centered ***	1456 ms	5.93 %
eVTE		Cell-centered ***	1477 ms	5.40 %
VTEtoROPE		Cell-centered **	1527 ms	7.61 %

x explicit static augmented element
I implicit discrete movement phase
continuous

Table 1. For each technique: (1) its matrix-based representation (2) its classification based on movement endpoints (3) its mean selection time (4) its mean error rate.

64 selections (8 layouts x 8 selections) per technique and per participant were recorded. A total of 10368 selections (9 techniques x 18 participants x 64 selections) were recorded.

Results

In this section, we use the following code for test significance: * denotes $p < .05$; ** denotes $p < .01$; *** denotes $p < .0001$. We removed 149 outliers (1,44 % of the data) due to double clicks or tracking freeze. For studying the movement endpoints, we computed $d_{toTarget}$ and d_{toCell} for each technique: We then compared them using pairwise Wilcoxon tests. One-way Repeated-Measures ANOVA revealed a significant effect of techniques on selection time ($F_{8,9496} = 36.8$ ***). We ran pairwise t tests using the Holm-Bonferroni method to compare selection time between techniques. For error rate, we performed a Pearson's Chi-squared independence test between success of target selection and the 9 techniques.

Table 1 shows the classification of the techniques based on movement endpoints. MTE, VTE, VTEtoTARGET, VTEtoCELL, eVTE and VTEtoROPE were measured cell-centered. BUBBLE and TARGET were target-centered, while ROPE was mixed-centered. The techniques are ordered in increasing order of mean selection time: in Table 1 from the top to the bottom and in Figure 8-left from the left to the right. MTE was the best performing technique, faster than the other techniques (*** with all, except VTE no significant difference). In second position, VTE was faster than every other technique (*** with all). In third position, TARGET was faster than VTEtoCELL**, eVTE*** and VTEtoROPE***. The difference with BUBBLE was not significant (p = .08). ROPE was faster than eVTE*. VTEtoROPE was by far the slowest technique (* with eVTE, ** with VTEtoCELL, *** with all the other techniques).

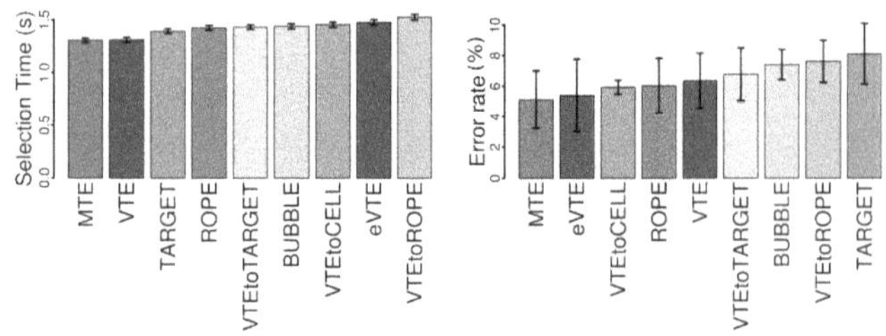

Figure 8. (left) Mean selection time, (right) Error rate per technique, with 95% confidence intervals.

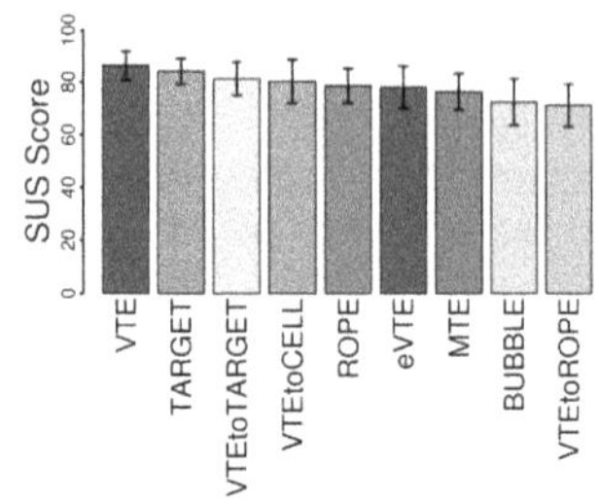

Technique	Preference Ranking Score	#1	#2	#3
VTEtoCELL	36	5	3	2
TARGET	28	4	2	2
VTEtoTARGET	27	3	3	3
MTE	18	1	4	1
VTEtoRope	15	2	1	2
ROPE	14	1	2	3
VTE	10	0	3	1
BUBBLE	8	1	0	3
eVTE	6	1	0	1

Figure 9. (left) Mean SUS scores with 95% confidence intervals. (right) Preference ranking scores and the number of times the techniques were ranked 1st, 2d or 3rd.

In Figure 8-right, the techniques are ordered from the left to the right with increasing order of error rate. MTE, contrary to VTE, was significantly less error-prone than BUBBLE*, VTEtoROPE* and TARGET**. eVTE was less error-prone than VTEtoROPE* and TARGET*.

SUS Scores and Qualitative Results

In Figure 9-left, the techniques are ordered from the left to the right with decreasing order of mean SUS score. VTE and TARGET were perceived the most usable, with a mean SUS score above 84. BUBBLE and VTEtoROPE were perceived the less usable techniques with a mean SUS score of about 72.

Based on the qualitative data we collected, we computed a preference ranking score for each technique. The table of Figure 9-right shows them from the top to the bottom in decreasing order. We computed the preference ranking score (S) of a technique using the formula: $S = 5 \times 1^{st} + 3 \times 2^{d} + 3^{rd}$, where 1st, 2^{d} and 3rd were its rankings at the corresponding place. We checked that with lower coefficients (respectively 3, 2 and 1), the results remained similar. Participants preferred VTEtoCELL, then TARGET and VTEtoTARGET. VTE, BUBBLE and eVTE obtained the lowest preference ranking scores.

Discussion

In terms of target expansion algorithm, the Voronoi tessellation in Manhattan distance is promising. Indeed, MTE is significantly the fastest and the less error-prone technique. In Manhattan distances, Voronoi diagram lines are oriented along only 3 different directions: This implies more symmetrical and periodic patterns. This visual characteristic (related to human cognition) explains this good performance of MTE. MTE however suffered a lack of learning effects (being the only technique based on Manhattan distances) as compared to the other techniques: This explains its bad mean SUS score. We discuss the other significant observed results in light of the design axes.

Dynamicity to Be Mininized

Selection time: The experiment shows that *the selection time increases with the dynamicity of the feedforward mechanisms* (H1). First, the three less dynamic techniques are the fastest ones. MTE and VTE, the two static techniques, are significantly the two fastest techniques. TARGET, an implicit dynamic-discrete technique, is faster than all the techniques involving a dynamic-continuous feedforward mechanism including those using implicit feedforward. However the differences between TARGET and ROPE, VTEtoTARGET and BUBBLE are not significant. Second, eVTE and VTEtoCELL, the two explicit dynamic techniques, are significantly slower than VTE and MTE, the two explicit static techniques.

Error rate: Contrary to VTE, eVTE is significantly less error-prone than TARGET and VTEtoROPE. One explanation is that continuous feedforward mechanisms constantly provide new information and attract the user's gaze. On the one hand, the resulting extra cognitive load makes the technique slower. On the other hand, *driving the user's attention can make the technique more accurate when useful information is provided at the right time of the pointing movement* (i.e. corrective phase for eVTE).

Subjective usability: Going one step further than static versus dynamic, we define the degree of dynamicity of a visual feedforward mechanism as the quantity of pixels that the mechanism modifies (or as the flow of modified pixels, which is the temporal derivative of the quantity of pixels the mechanism modifies). Based on this measure we classify the techniques in increasing degree of dynamicity as follows: VTE, MTE, TARGET, VTEtoTARGET, VTEtoCELL, then the techniques involving only dynamic-continuous mechanisms. Thus except for the special case of MTE explained above, there is a direct mapping between the mean SUS score and the degree of dynamicity. One explanation is that *dynamicity of visual feedforward increases user's cognitive workload and therefore decreases the perceived usability*. Such an additional cognitive workload is notable when using ray-casting pointing (with 5 degrees of freedom) that already causes a significant cognitive workload.

User preference: The users have a clear preference for discrete feedforward mechanisms. VTEtoCELL, VTEtoTARGET and TARGET, the only three techniques involving discrete feedforward, obtained the three best preference scores. This is consistent with previous work [16, 18], where a discrete target highlight mechanism was reported to perform better than a continuous cursor-based mechanism. We therefore confirmed these time performance results for the case of distant pointing and reinforced them with qualitative results as well as subjective usability results.

Explicit Expansion Observability

Shifting of the pointing movement endpoints: The results show a direct mapping between the explicit/implicit nature of the feedforward mechanisms and the shift of observed movement endpoints (Table 1). Indeed, the techniques involving explicit feedforward mechanisms (i.e. all except TARGET, BUBBLE and ROPE) are cell-centered techniques. The implicit techniques, TARGET and BUBBLE, are target-centered, while ROPE is mixed-centered, because the mini-ropes increase the observability of the cell boundaries without explicitly presenting them. If the users have no information on target expanded shapes, they rely on the target shapes. When providing explicit information, we allow the users to aim at the expanded target shape (cell-centered): This is fully consistent with the Optimized Initial Impulse Model [14]. *Explicit feedforward mechanisms thus have a direct impact on the optimization of the pointing task* (H2). As a consequence, the two fastest techniques (MTE and VTE) are cell-centered.

Error rate: When focusing on the movement landing phase (the ballistic phase ending and the potential corrective phase), the techniques providing explicit feedforward are the less error-prone ones (even if the differences are not significant) along with Rope Cursor. *An explicit feedforward allows the users to directly know the remaining distance to the cells' borders by providing a spatial information* and therefore to anticipate potential errors (H3). For the case of Rope Cursor, the mini-ropes' length also provides this information by an implicit continuous feedforward mechanism. Indeed Rope Cursor displays the distance of the cursor to the borders of the expanded cells but not the expanded cells themselves.

Compatibility of Augmented Elements for Combination of Feedforward Mechanisms

The quantitative results indicate that the combination of a space-based feedforward mechanism with a cursor-based feedforward mechanism of VTEtoROPE is not suitable. VTEtoROPE involves a too cognitively demanding switching between augmented elements. Contrastingly, *the combination of a space-based mechanism with a space-based or target-based mechanism is promising* and requires further studies. Moreover it is important to test these combined mechanisms as well as eVTE in the context of a GUI since their goal is to reduce the visual overload of a Voronoi diagram displayed on top of a GUI.

CONCLUSION

The key concept we introduce for the design of target expansion techniques is the atomic feedforward mechanism. The concept is key because it provides a visual feedforward aid to the user by employing a target expansion algorithm. The atomic feedforward mechanism has three design axes, namely dynamicity, expansion observability and augmented element. These design axes allow us now to classify existing target expansion techniques by studying the combination of atomic mechanisms according to the phases of the pointing movement. We further define a matrix-based notation for concisely representing a target expansion technique as a combination of atomic feedforward mechanisms. The design space directs us to design six novel target expansion techniques with atomic/combined feedforward, thus demonstrating the generative power of this design space.

As a first experimental exploration of the design space we ran a controlled comparative experiment. To do so we define a new target layout that can handle non-centroidal target expansion. The experimental results show that: (1) The dynamicity of the feedforward mechanism increases the selection time and reduces user acceptance; (2) Explicit feedforward increases subjective usability and reduces the error rate. Moreover, in terms of our new techniques, MTE performs better than techniques in euclidean distance. Amongst the implicit feedforward techniques including Bubble Cursor, Rope Cursor supports an efficient error prevention mechanism, with an error rate comparable to the one of the explicit feedforward techniques.

Our analytical and experimental exploration of the design space was broad, considering all three axes. This exploration allowed us to identify specific areas in the design space that must be further explored in a systematic way (by varying parameters along one axis only) as part of laboratory and field experiments. Our long-term goal is to define a predictive model of the performance of a target expansion technique by modeling the factors related to the visual feedforward mechanisms.

ACKNOWLEDGEMENTS

We would like to thank Gilles Bailly, Marcos Serrano and the CHI reviewers for their insightful comments. Special thanks to George Serghiou for proof-reading the final version. This work has been partially supported by the LabEx PERSYVAL-Lab (ANR-11-LABX-0025-01).

REFERENCES

1. Bateman, S., Mandryk, R. L., Gutwin, C. and Xiao, R. Analysis and comparison of target assistance techniques for relative ray-cast pointing. *IJHCS 71*, 5 (2013), 511-532.
2. Bau, O. and Mackay, W. OctoPocus: a dynamic guide for learning gesture-based command sets. In *Proc. UIST 2008*, (2008), 37-46.
3. Baudisch, P., Zotov, A., Cutrell, E. and Hinckley, K. Starburst: a target expansion algorithm for non-uniform target distributions. In *Proc. AVI 2008*, (2008), 129-137.
4. Blanch, R. and Ortega, M. Benchmarking pointing techniques with distractors: adding a density factor to Fitts' pointing paradigm. In *Proc. CHI 2011*, (2011), 1629-1638.
5. Brooke, J. SUS: A Quick and Dirty Usability Scale. *Usability Evaluation in Industry* (1996), 189-194.
6. Chapuis, O., Labrune, J. and Pietriga, E. DynaSpot: speed-dependent area cursor. In *Proc. CHI 2009*, (2009), 1391-1400.
7. Du, Q., Faber, V. and Gunzburger, M. Centroidal Voronoi tessellations: Applications and algorithms. *SIAM Review 41,* 4 (1999), 637-676.
8. Grossman, T. and Balakrishnan, R. The bubble cursor: enhancing target acquisition by dynamic resizing of the cursor's activation area. In *Proc. CHI 2005*, (2005), 281-290.
9. Grossman, T., Kong, N. and Balakrishnan, R. Modeling pointing at targets of arbitrary shapes. In *Proc. CHI 2007*, (2007), 463-472.
10. Guillon, M., Leitner, F. and Nigay, L. Static Voronoi-Based Target Expansion Technique for Distant Pointing. In *Proc. AVI 2014*, (2014), 41-48.
11. Kuwabara, C., Yamamoto, K., Kuramoto, I., Tsujino, Y. and Minakuchi, M. Ghost-hunting: a cursor-based pointing technique with picture guide indication of the shortest path. In *Proc. IUI 2013*, (2013), 85-86.
12. Laukkanen, J., Isokoski, P. and Räihä, K. The cone and the lazy bubble: two efficient alternatives between the point cursor and the bubble cursor. In *Proc. CHI 2008*, (2008), 309-312.
13. McGuffin, M. and Balakrishnan, R. Fitts' law and expanding targets: Experimental studies and designs for user interfaces. *ACM TOCHI 12,* 4 (2005), 388-422.
14. Meyer, D. E., Abrams, R. A., Kornblum, S., Wright, C. E. and Smith, J. E. Optimality in human motor performance: ideal control of rapid aimed movements. *Psychological Review 95*, 3 (1988), 340-70.
15. Mott, M. and Wobbrock, J. Beating the bubble: using kinematic triggering in the bubble lens for acquiring small, dense targets. In *Proc. CHI 2014*, (2014), 733-742.
16. Su, X., Au, O. and Lau, R. The Implicit Fan Cursor: A Velocity Dependent Area Cursor. In *Proc. CHI 2014*, (2014), 753-762.
17. Tse, E., Hancock, M. and Greenberg, S. Speech-filtered bubble ray: improving target acquisition on display walls. In *Proc. ICMI 2007*, (2007), 307-314.
18. Vanacken, L., Grossman, T. and Coninx, K. Multimodal selection techniques for dense and occluded 3D virtual environments. *IJHCS 67*, 3 (2009), 237-255.
19. Vermeulen, J., Luyten, K., Van den Hoven, E. and Coninx, K. Crossing the bridge over Norman's gulf of execution: revealing feedforward's true identity. In *Proc. CHI 2013*, (2013), 1931-1940.
20. Zhai, S., Conversy, S., Beaudouin-Lafon, M. and Guiard, Y. Human on-line response to target expansion. In *Proc. CHI 2003*, (2003), 177-184.

GACA: Group-Aware Command-based Arrangement of Graphic Elements

Pengfei Xu[1] Hongbo Fu[2] Chiew-Lan Tai[1] Takeo Igarashi[3]
[1]HKUST [2]City University of Hong Kong [3]The University of Tokyo

ABSTRACT

Many graphic applications rely on command-based arrangement tools to achieve precise layouts. Traditional tools are designed to operate on a single group of elements that are distributed consistently with the arrangement axis implied by a command. This often demands a process with repeated element selections and arrangement commands to achieve 2D layouts involving multiple rows and/or columns of well aligned and/or distributed elements. Our work aims to reduce the numbers of selection operation and command invocation, since such reductions are particularly beneficial to professional designers who design lots of layouts. Our key idea is that an issued arrangement command is in fact very informative, instructing how to automatically decompose a 2D layout into multiple 1D groups, each of which is compatible with the command. We present a parameter-free, command-driven grouping approach so that users can easily predict our grouping results. We also design a simple user interface with pushpins to enable explicit control of grouping and arrangement. Our user study confirms the intuitiveness of our technique and its performance improvement over traditional command-based arrangement tools.

Author Keywords

Layout editing; alignment; arrangement commands; group-aware

ACM Classification Keywords

H.5.2. Information Interfaces and Presentation (e.g. HCI): User Interfaces – Graphical user interfaces (GUI)

INTRODUCTION

Creating accurate layouts of graphic elements is vital for many graphic applications. Almost all modern graphic editors such as Adobe Illustrator and Microsoft PowerPoint support command-based arrangement operations for precise alignment and/or equal spacing of graphic elements. An arrangement command is essentially a 1D operation associated with an arrangement axis and applied to a set of user-selected elements. For example, the command "align top" is associated with a horizontal arrangement axis and changes only the vertical coordinates of the selected elements.

CHI 2015, April 18 - 23 2015, Seoul, Republic of Korea.

http://dx.doi.org/10.1145/2702123.2702198

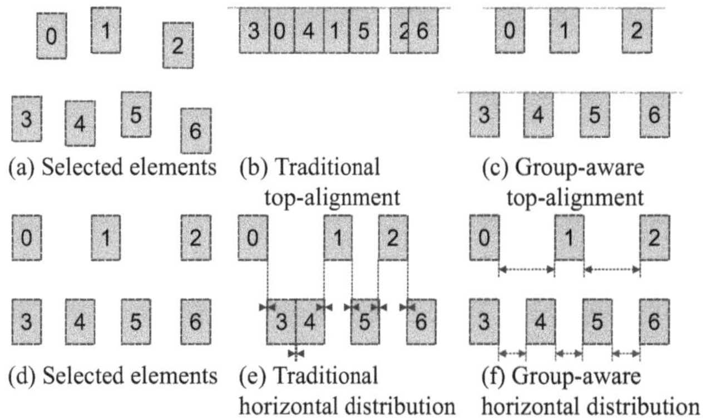

Figure 1. When applied to the same sets of selected elements, our group-aware technique, GACA, achieves more desired results (right) than traditional command-based arrangement (middle).

We observe that an arrangement command works well for a group of elements that are distributed along the corresponding axis, but might cause unexpected results when the selected elements exhibit a 2D pattern instead, i.e., there are multiple element groups distributed perpendicular to the arrangement axis. Figure 1 (a) shows a simple top alignment example. It is easy to see that there are two vertically distributed groups of elements: one containing elements $\{e_0, e_1, e_2\}$ and the other containing elements $\{e_3, e_4, e_5, e_6\}$. A simple top-alignment of all elements $\{e_0, ..., e_6\}$ thus would cause a typically undesired result in Figure 1 (b) instead of a more desired one in Figure 1 (c). To circumvent this problem, the user has to select each group of elements and apply the command to individual groups. Similarly, a *group-oblivious* horizontal distribution of all elements $\{e_0, ..., e_6\}$ in Figure 1 (d) causes an undesired result in Figure 1 (e). In short, 2D layout editing through traditional arrangement commands often involves many steps of element selection and command invocation, which could be very tedious and error-prone [17].

We aim to improve the performance of command-based arrangement tools for achieving 2D layouts, involving multiple rows and/or columns of well aligned and/or distributed elements. Motivated by the above observation, we intend to automatically derive desired groups present in the selected elements, when an arrangement command is issued. The issued command suggests the search for such groups perpendicular to the arrangement axis, reducing to a one-dimensional grouping problem. We present a parameter-free grouping approach to produce easily predictable results. We also introduce a simple but effective user interface with pushpins to enable explicit user control (Figure 5).

Our technique, which we call GACA, is able to significantly reduce the number of selection operations and arrangement commands for achieving 2D layouts, which are commonplace in desktop publishing, graphic design and preparation of presentations. For instance, to turn the layout in Figure 1 (d) into the one in Figure 1 (f), two selection operations and two group-oblivious horizontal distribution commands are reduced to a single selection operation and a single group-aware horizontal distribution command. The intuitiveness of GACA and its performance improvement over traditional command-based arrangement tools are confirmed by our user study. We expected our tool to be particularly useful for professional designers who often need to design lots of layouts.

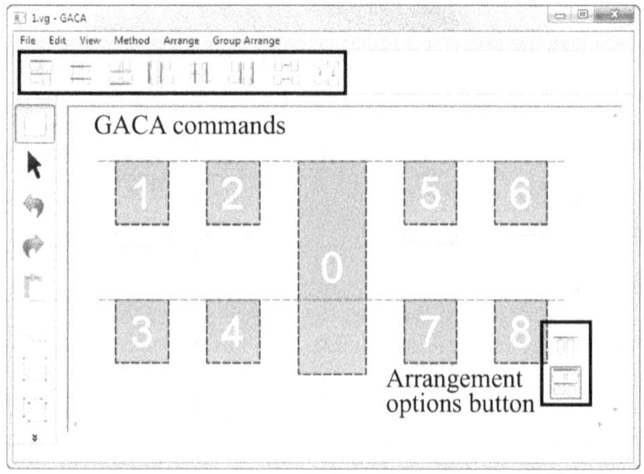

Figure 2. Main user interface of our system. Our current system supports 8 group-aware arrangement commands.

RELATED WORK

Various layout editing techniques like constraint-based techniques [3, 11, 15] have been proposed and even integrated into commercial graphic editors like OmniGraffle, Visio, and InDesign. Since our goal is to improve arrangement commands, which are fundamental in these editors and can coexist with their other arrangement tools, below we focus on reviewing those existing tools that are closely relevant to arrangement commands only.

It is hard to track down the history of command-based arrangement tools [13, 4]. Although the underlying technology of such tools has advanced very little since day one, due to their simplicity and power they are still being offered by almost all modern graphic editors. Such commands are very useful for improving geometric relationships between selected elements in terms of both alignment and distribution. However, as discussed previously, due to the 1D nature, an arrangement command often gets confused by the existence of multiple elements groups distributed perpendicular to the arrangement axis.

Unlike arrangement commands, which achieve alignment tasks in an indirect way, snapping techniques [2, 1, 5, 7] allow precise positioning in a more direct way. They are more suitable for aligning individual elements one by one but provide little control over precise spacing of elements. Thus snapping and command-based arrangement complement each other, and they are often used together for complex layout editing tasks. We expect that GACA can and should be used together with snapping and other arrangement techniques in practical applications. Therefore, our evaluation focused on the performance of GACA compared to traditional arrangement commands.

There are several attempts to beautify rough layouts of elements either locally [9] or globally [12, 6]. Like snapping, which can be considered as the simplest local beautifier, the local beautifiers [9] are often direct and more suitable for alignment but not distribution tasks. In contrast, the global beautifiers [20] are essentially indirect, often invoked by a single "beautification" command, and thus akin to command-based arrangement. However, unlike traditional command-based arrangement, global beautification requires an input layout to be very close to a desired layout in a user's mind. For example, given a layout in Figure 3 (a), it is very likely that beautification solutions would automatically decide to bottom-align all the elements, rather than the result in Figure 3 (b). In contrast, our goal is to enhance the arrangement commands while still allowing the user to explicitly control the layout by manually issuing proper commands.

On the other hand, GACA is inspired by such layout beautification techniques by inferring relationships among selected elements, and thus requires these elements to roughly form rows or columns. However, while the global beautifiers have a higher degree of intelligence, they can easily cause unwanted results because of ambiguity in the input layout [9]. In contrast, our technique inherits the explicit control feature of command-based arrangement tools and exploits the information carried in the commands, which greatly reduces the level of ambiguity.

There exist many advanced graph layout algorithms (e.g., [18, 14]), which typically take a large set of graphic elements and turn them into visually or artistically pleasing layouts, either automatically or with little intervention. They have very different goals from ours. For example, the technique proposed by Reinert et al. [14] evenly distributes graphical primitives to reflect the artistic goals inferred from several interactively placed primitives. In other words, their focus is to let the computers design layouts for the users, with no or little user intervention. In contrast, we aim at designing a better tool to help users design layouts themselves. With our tool, the user explicitly edits the layout by a series of manual selection operation and command invocation.

Our work is also related to perceptual grouping of elements, which aims to group elements with certain common characteristics. For instance, Nan et al. [10] integrate the well-known Gestalt principles, including similarity, proximity, continuity, closure, and regularity, to detect groups of objects in architectural drawings. Xu et al. [19] identify groups of elements covered by a user-specified scribble using proximity, similarity, and common region in visual perception. It is possible to adapt these techniques for our 1D grouping problem. However, these algorithms are often sensitive to the choice of parameters, possibly causing unpredictable results, as illustrated in Figure 6. Instead, we take a more partitioning-based solution and introduce a parameter-free approach.

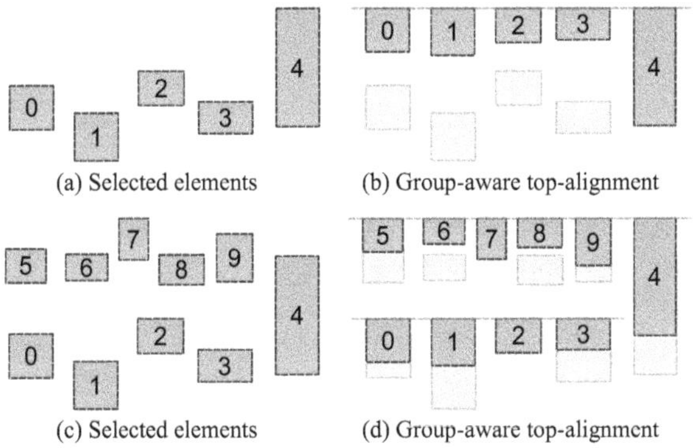

Figure 3. Group-aware top-alignment. (b) and (d) are group-aware alignment results of (a) and (c), respectively.

USER INTERFACE

As shown in Figure 2, our current system supports commonly used commands for vertical alignment ("align left", "align center", "align right"), horizontal alignment ("align top", "align middle", "align bottom"), horizontal distribution ("distribute horizontally") and vertical distribution ("distribute vertically"). Each command is associated with either a horizontal or a vertical arrangement axis. In our prototype, we simply use rectangles to represent elements, since their arrangement is often operated at the bounding-box level.

We will describe our main user interface using top-alignment as an example. The idea can be easily generalized to other arrangement commands. Since the top-alignment command has a horizontal arrangement axis, to get desired results the user needs to roughly place elements of interest to form a pattern consisting of one (Figure 3 (a)) or multiple (Figure 1 (a)) horizontal rows of elements. It is possible to have elements (e.g., element e_4 in Figure 3 (c)) spanning multiple rows. To top-align the elements of interest, the user first selects them and then issues the "align top" command from a toolbar (in our current implementation) or menu to the selected elements.

If there is only a single row of elements to be top-aligned, our group-aware top-alignment produces the same result (Figure 3 (b)) as group-oblivious top-alignment. For simplicity, our tool aligns the top edges of the selected elements with the top edge of the topmost element (i.e., element e_4 in this example). In case there are multiple rows of elements, our tool automatically identifies such rows and then applies the top-alignment command to the individual rows of elements, often leading to more desired results (Figure 1 (c) and Figure 3 (d)).

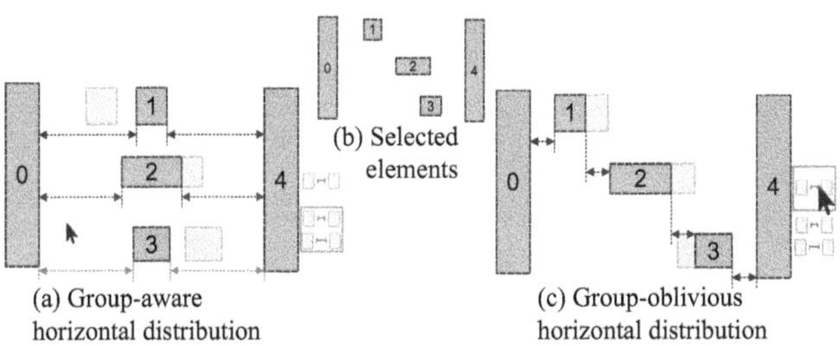

Figure 4. The user may easily switch between the results of group-aware (a) and group-oblivious (c) arrangement (horizontal distribution in this example) using the "Arrangement Options" button. The input selected elements are shown in (b).

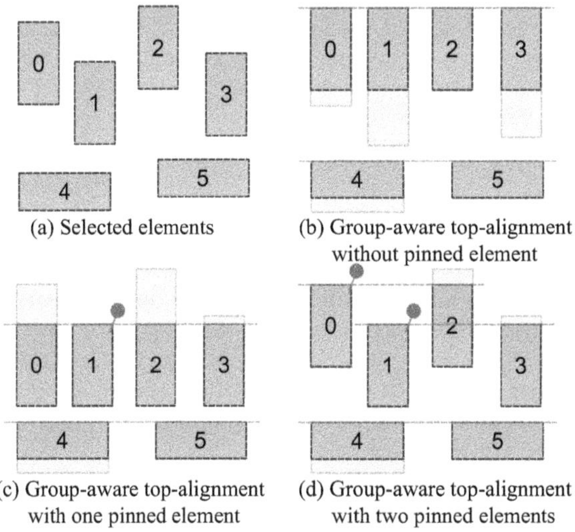

Figure 5. The user may use pushpins to specify reference elements (c) and additional arrangement groups (d). (a) is the input selected elements and (b) is the default result by group-aware top-alignment.

The user may use the provided visual cues (Figure 4 (a)) to better understand how the selected elements are moved by a certain command. First, after issuing a command, the elements before movement are displayed semi-transparently. This visual effect disappears if the user deselects the elements or issues another arrangement command. Second, to emphasize the achieved arrangement result, the alignment line(s) or the equal-spacing arrow(s) appears after the user issues an alignment or distribution command, respectively. Such lines or arrows fade away within seconds to avoid visual clutter. Please see the accompanying video for live demos.

It is not always the case that group-aware arrangement produces more user-desired results than group-oblivious arrangement. The user may easily switch between the results by group-aware and group-oblivious arrangement using a simple "Arrangement Options" button (Figures 2 and 4(b)), which is similar to the "Paste Options" button in Microsoft Office products. This button appears next to the selected elements and does not show up when group-aware and group-oblivious results are the same. It disappears after a deselection operation.

The user may use the pushpin tool to explicitly specify reference elements or determine arrangement groups. *A single pushpin* can be employed to indicate the reference element for alignment. The user can place a virtual pushpin at a selected element by right-click to fix its position during subsequent arrangement. A second right-click on the same element removes the associated pushpin. As shown in Figure 5, without such a pushpin the top-alignment command uses the topmost element, i.e., element e_2, as the reference element to align elements $\{e_0, e_1, e_2, e_3\}$ (Figure 5 (b)). If e_1 is pinned, it becomes the reference element, leading to a different alignment result (Figure 5 (c)). The user may use *multiple pushpins* to control the determination of arrangement groups. For example, by default, elements $\{e_0, e_1, e_2, e_3\}$ are considered within a single arrangement group. A single pushpin does not change the grouping behavior. But if pins are placed on both e_0 and e_1, this group breaks into two groups (e_0 and e_2; e_1 and e_3), producing the alignment result as shown in Figure 5 (d).

METHODOLOGY

Our core problem is how to automatically identify the arrangement groups distributed along the direction perpendicular to a given arrangement axis. The design of our solution is driven by a key guideline: the technique should be very intuitive to use. In other words, after getting familiar with GACA, the user should be able to completely predict the result of a given arrangement task. This motivates us to design a *parameter-free* approach.

Group-Aware Alignment

Straightforward Approach. Our first attempt was to adopt a perception-based clustering approach, similar to Nan et al. [10]. Given an arrangement axis, the problem here is reduced to a 1D clustering problem, e.g., by clustering the top edges of the selected elements by proximity in the case of top-alignment. This approach is sensitive to the choice of parameters. For example, to turn the layout in Figure 3 (a) into the one in Figure 3 (b), a large threshold is needed to cluster all elements into a single group. However, the same threshold may undesirably group all elements in Figure 3 (c) into a single group. A small clustering threshold would require the input layout to be very close to the desired layout, and thus result in a beautification-like arrangement scheme, whose behavior is different from that of command-based arrangement (see the discussion in related work). Moreover, such a beautification-based approach is still parameter-sensitive. For example in Figure 6 (a), it is unclear which group element e_4 belongs to. Hence such a clustering approach easily leads to multiple possible results (Figure 6 (b)–(d)), which are unpredictable to the user. A suggestion-based interface (e.g., [9, 8]) might be adapted for ambiguity resolution. However, combinations of local ambiguous relationships may easily lead to a large set of global suggestions. How to effectively present such suggestions to the user is not obvious.

Our Approach. We aim to retain the power of traditional arrangement commands but avoid their undesired results of overlaps after alignment (Figure 1 (b)). This motivates us to design a two-step approach: first group elements in a relaxed setting (similar to perception-based clustering, using a large clustering threshold) and then refine the groups by examining undesired overlaps between elements if they get aligned in the same group. The two steps can be achieved by *graph construction* and *graph partitioning*, respectively.

First, our approach *dynamically* constructs an undirected graph (Figure 7) after an alignment command is issued. Each node in the graph represents an element in the selection. An edge is added to connect a pair of nodes if their corresponding elements *potentially* belong to the same group. Each connected component of the graph thus corresponds to a potential alignment group.

The key to graph construction is to determine if an edge is needed between a pair of nodes. Again we use top-alignment to illustrate the idea. We assume that the selected elements are defined in a 2D Cartesian coordinate system, with the x-axis pointing rightward and the y-axis downward. We project the vertical edges of their bounding boxes to the y-axis. If these edges overlap, we consider the corresponding elements as in a single row. This is largely consistent with perception-based clustering, but does not involve any parameter. For example, the projected vertical edges of elements $\{e_0, e_1\}$ in Figure 7 (a) overlap and form a group, and similarly, elements $\{e_2, e_3, e_4\}$ form another group. Requiring all pairs of elements to overlap each other at the y-axis is too stringent a requirement, making it difficult to handle, for example, the selected elements in Figure 7 (b), where the projected vertical edges of elements e_1 and e_2 do not overlap. Our relaxed requirement thus only requires the projected vertical edge of an element to overlap that of at least one of the elements in the same group. This implies that the presence of an element of large height (e.g., element e_3 in Figure 7 (c)) would allow a large height deviation of elements in the same group. However this rule alone would misidentify elements $\{e_0, ..., e_5\}$ in Figure 7 (c) as a single group. This happens when an element spans across multiple desired rows of elements. Fortunately, this problem can be easily solved by our next graph partitioning step.

Second, we perform a simple graph partitioning procedure on each connected graph component *if necessary* (to avoid serious overlaps between alignment elements). We check if any pair of elements have their projected horizontal edges to the

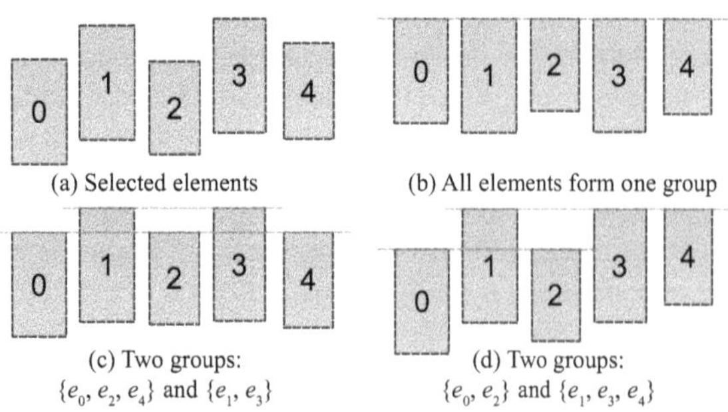

Figure 6. A clustering-based approach may lead to multiple possible results, highly dependent on the clustering threshold.

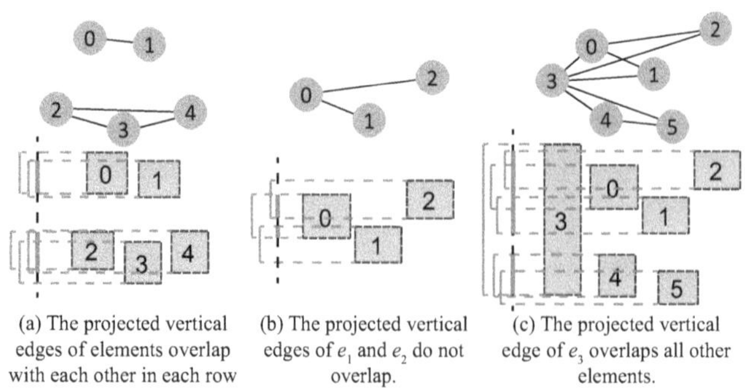

Figure 7. Illustration of graph construction for top-alignment.

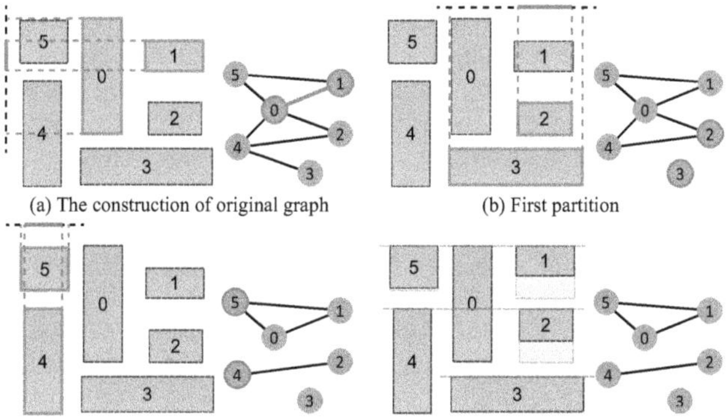

(a) The construction of original graph (b) First partition

(c) Second partition (d) Final graph and arrangement result

Figure 8. Illustration of graph partitioning for top-alignment.

Algorithm 1 Graph Partitioning

Find partition pairs set $\mathcal{P}$
while $\mathcal{P}$ is not empty **do**
  Find partition pair $p = (e_i, e_j)$ with smallest error
  if e_i and e_j belong to the same component $\mathcal{G}$ **then**
    for all $e \in \mathcal{G}$ **do**
      if $d(e, e_i) < d(e, e_j)$ **then**
        Assign e to e_i
      else
        Assign e to e_j
      end if
    end for
    Update graph
  end if
  Remove p from $\mathcal{P}$
end while

x-axis (the arrangement axis) overlapped (e.g., elements e_2 and e_3 in Figure 8 (b)). Such a pair of elements (e_i, e_j) may not exist. If it exists, the two elements e_i and e_j are not supposed to be in the same arrangement group and thus induce a graph partitioning on the graph component. The partitioning is done by assigning each of the rest of the elements, denoted as e, to e_i or e_j depending on whether the top edge of e is closer to that of e_i or e_j. For example, element e_4 in Figure 8 (b) is assigned to the group containing element e_2. The edges crossing the resulting two groups are removed (making element e_4 belong to the row of element e_2). We use all the identified element pairs to partition the graph incrementally. The order is according to the error of a pair of elements (e_i, e_j), denoted $d(e_i, e_j)$, defined as the distance between the alignment edges of e_i and e_j (e.g., the top edges for top-alignment). Pairs with smaller errors have higher priority of being used to partition the graph. In Figure 8, the pair (e_2, e_3) has a smaller error compared with (e_4, e_5), so it is used to partition the graph first. Algorithm 1 gives the detail of the partition process. Every pair of user-specified pushpins in the same connected component will also trigger the same graph partitioning step performed on the component.

Group-Aware Distribution

We use a slightly different way to construct the graph for distributing a set of selected elements in a group-aware manner.

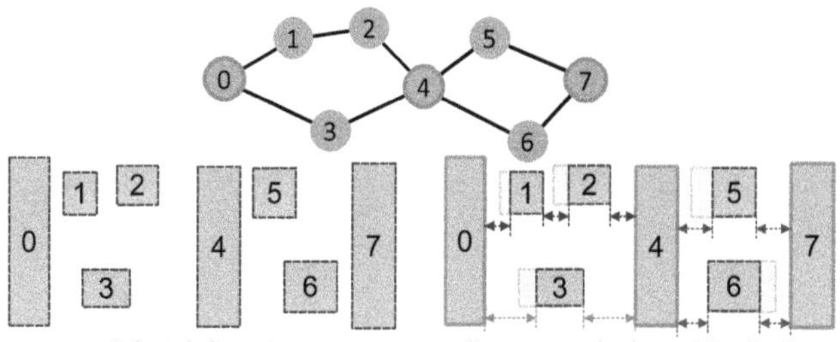

Figure 9. An example of group-aware horizontal distribution. Automatically fixed elements are highlighted in red.

Let us take horizontal distribution as an example. An edge is established between a pair of elements if and only if their projected vertical edges overlap each other *and* they are horizontally adjacent (i.e., no other element in-between them). For example, in Figure 4 (b), elements e_0 and e_2 are connected by an edge, but elements e_0 and e_4 are not. We enforce such a neighborhood condition since equal spacing aims to equalize the spacings between neighboring elements.

Next we identify the horizontal distribution groups in the constructed graph. First, we identify the horizontally outermost elements (e.g., elements e_0 and e_7 in Figure 9) in each connected component and fix their positions. Second, we fix the nodes whose degrees are greater than two. Such nodes correspond to elements that might be shared by multiple distribution groups (e.g., element e_4 in Figure 9). Without fixing those nodes, their positions after distribution would highly depend on the order of applying the distribution command to individual groups, making the distribution results hard to predict. Third, the user-pinned elements, if any, are also fixed as well. Finally, we identify a path starting from one fixed element to another fixed element as a distribution group. For instance, the example in Figure 9 results in four distribution groups (elements $\{e_0, e_1, e_2, e_3\}$; elements $\{e_0, e_3, e_4\}$; elements $\{e_4, e_5, e_7\}$; elements $\{e_4, e_6, e_7\}$).

USER STUDY

To evaluate the effectiveness of GACA we conducted a user study, which consisted of two parts. In Study I we examined the intuitiveness of GACA and in Study II we compared GACA to traditional command-based arrangement tools. The same group of participants helped in both studies.

Study I: Evaluation of Intuitiveness

We recruited twelve university students to help with our study. All of them were familiar with the behavior of traditional command-based arrangement tools. Three participants even considered themselves as experts in using these tools.

There were in total three sessions: tutorial session, practice session and questionnaire session. In the tutorial session, each participant was briefed on how to use GACA by showing them eight simple static examples, with pairs of layouts before and after issuing a certain command. Please refer to the supplementary material for the tutorial examples. In the practice session, we first demonstrated the user interface of GACA, including the use of pushpins and the "Arrangement

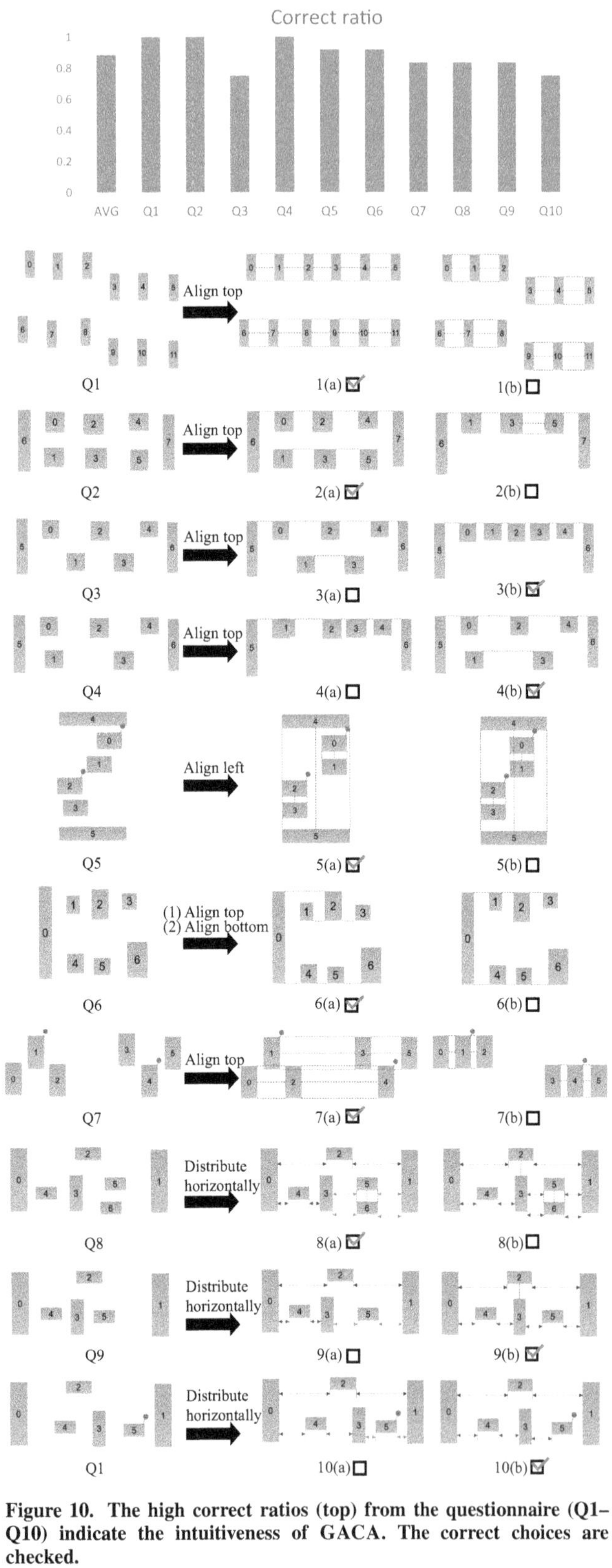

Figure 10. The high correct ratios (top) from the questionnaire (Q1–Q10) indicate the intuitiveness of GACA. The correct choices are checked.

Options" button. The participants then tried GACA. They could try the tutorial examples, or apply different commands to layouts created by themselves. When the participants were first introduced to the pushpin tool, some of them were curious about the results with multiple pushpins. They noticed that conflicts may arise if multiple pinned elements were in a single group. After they were told about another function of the pushpin tool, i.e., forming different groups, they felt comfortable and agreed that the results were logical. When they tried the tool, they quickly understood how it worked and conveyed that the visual feedback helped them to perceive the arrangement results.

After they felt confident with the use of GACA, they were asked to complete a ten-question form (Figure 10). In each question, the participants were given a layout of elements and asked to predict the result of applying a given command of GACA. Four choices were given: two possible arrangement results (Figure 10), "neither", and "not sure". After the questionnaire session, we briefly explained the answer to each question. It took about 30 minutes on average for each participant to complete Study I.

Figure 10 plots the average score of each question over the participants. It shows that the arrangement results were highly predictable to the participants, indicating the intuitiveness of GACA. The performance for Q3, the question we predicted to be the most difficult, was the lowest. This is possibly because some participants might get confused by the existence of the perceptually salient groups (elements e_0, e_2, and e_4; elements e_1 and e_3), which, however, were grouped into a single row by GACA (see more discussion in the "Discussion" section). From the algorithmic point of view, the layouts in Q3 and Figure 3 (a) were treated in a very similar way.

Study II: Comparison with Traditional Tools

To better test the performance of traditional and group-aware arrangement commands, no other arrangement tools including snapping were provided in the study. Traditional arrangement commands were integrated into our software and could be invoked from the toolbar (see the accompanying video). Specifically, we provided six traditional alignment commands (align top/middle/bottom/left/center/right) and two traditional distribution commands (distribute horizontally/vertically), whose implementation was similar to the ones in MS PowerPoint 2013.

Tasks and apparatus. There were in total 7 tasks (Figure 11). The tasks were designed to simulate a layout creation process. In each task, the participants were asked to create a target layout by moving a grid of numbered elements from an input zone to a target zone (see the accompanying video). The general operations supported in the study included selection (by single click or rectangle selection), move, grouping and ungrouping. Element creating, resizing and removal were disabled.

The study was conducted on an ordinary PC (DELL OptiPlex 960), with 3.00 GHz Intel Core 2 Duo CPU and 4.00 GB RAM. The target layout of each task was displayed on a sep-

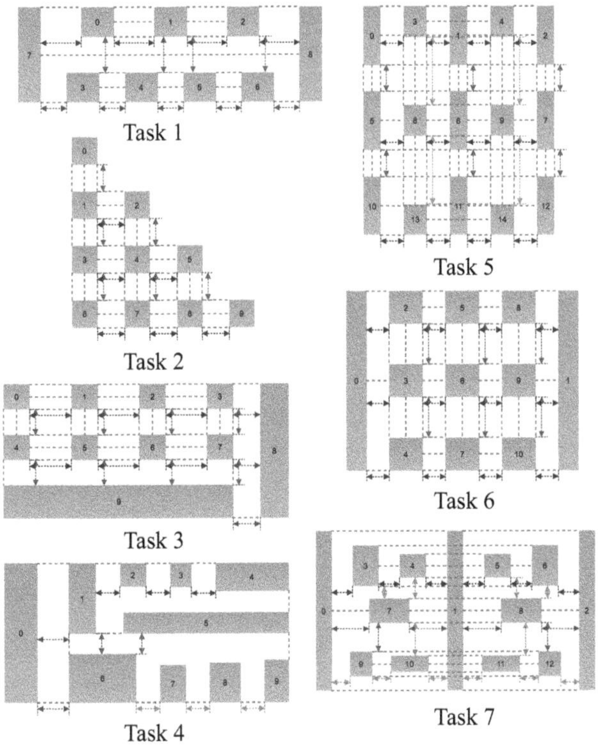

Figure 11. The tasks in Study II. They were designed to simulate a layout creation process.

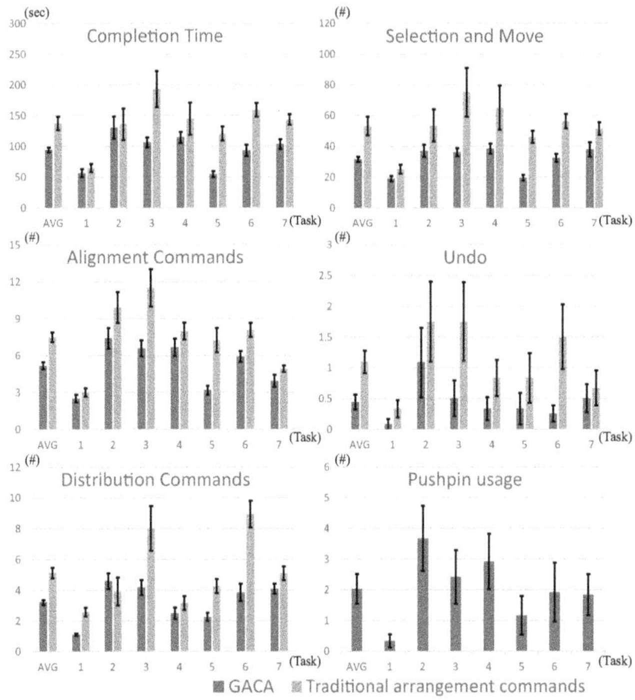

Figure 13. The statistics of Study II. On average GACA needed significantly less completion time, fewer operations of selection and move, fewer undo operations, and fewer arrangement commands per task. The usage of pushpin varied with tasks. Error bars represent the standard error of mean.

arate monitor, with clearly visualized alignment and equal-spacing relationships. The same group of 12 participants from Study I helped with Study II. Each participant was asked to complete each task twice, with our technique and traditional command-based arrangement tools, respectively. The order of the techniques was counter-balanced across participants. In total there were 7 (tasks) $\times$ 2 (techniques) $\times$ 12 (participants) = 168 trials.

Performance measures. During the study, the following information was recorded: the completion time of individual trials, the numbers of general operations (move, undo, grouping, ungrouping), the number of alignment commands, the number of distribution commands. For GACA, two pieces of additional information were recorded: the numbers of pushpin operation and "Arrangement Options" button click.

Results. Figure 13 plots the statistics of the core information. The average completion time per task among the participants was significantly less with GACA (93.9 seconds) than the traditional tools (137.2 seconds). A 2 (TECH) $\times$ 7 (TASK) ANOVA confirmed that there was significant difference in completion time between our technique and traditional tools ($F(1, 154) = 28.025$, $p < 5 \times 10^{-7}$). No significant interaction TECH $\times$ TASK was found ($F(6, 154) = 2.053$, $p = 0.062$), which indicated that the performance improvement of our technique over traditional tools was not affected much by the tasks. However, we noticed that the degree of performance improvement still varied with the tasks. For Task 1, due to its simplicity the performance improvement of our technique was not significant ($p = 0.38$, measured by paired t-test), as expected. For Task 2, the improvement was not significant either ($p = 0.88$). We observed that for this task our group-aware distribution commands might violate the existing alignment relations when the elements distributed diagonally were not equally spaced (see Figure 12). To deal with this problem, the participants either issued extra alignment commands or equally distributed individual rows or columns of elements separately. Some participants also performed pushpin operations to fix the already aligned elements. Since Task 4 contained only few multi-row or multi-column patterns, no significant improvement was found ($p = 0.29$). However, our technique was still slightly better, mainly because the participants took the advantage of the pushpin tool to fix already-aligned elements. For the remaining tasks our technique was significantly faster ($p < 0.05$ for Tasks 3, 5, 6 and 7). This is largely because the participants often issued a single command to multiple groups of elements in these tasks, implying that they were aware of the advantages of our technique and willing to use it when possible.

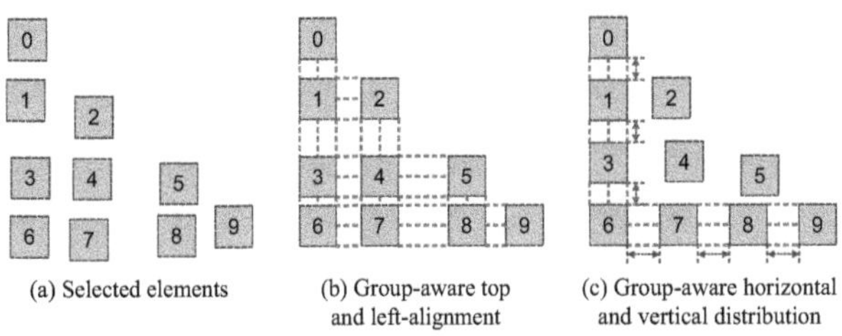

Figure 12. Our group-aware distribution commands might violate the existing alignment relations when the elements distributed diagonally are not equally spaced.

On average, fewer alignment (5.17 vs. 7.52) and distribution (3.21 vs. 5.13) commands per task were issued with GACA. The ANOVA also confirmed that there was statistically significant difference between GACA and traditional tools ($F(1, 154) = 33.430$, $p < 4 \times 10^{-8}$ for alignment commands; $F(1, 154) = 32.331$, $p < 7 \times 10^{-8}$ for distribution commands). The ANOVA also found significant interactions between techniques and tasks for alignment ($F(6, 154) = 2.282$, $p = 0.039$) and distribution ($F(6, 154) = 4.811$, $p = 0.0002$) commands, indicating that the degree in which GACA reduced the number of command invocation depended on tasks. It was found that selection and move were the most commonly used general operations. Confirmed by ANOVA, on average our technique needed significantly fewer selection and move operations per task, (31.45 vs. 53.14, $F(1, 154) = 32.744$, $p < 6 \times 10^{-8}$), indicating that our technique was less tedious. No significant interaction ($F(6, 154) = 1.133$, $p = 0.35$) between techniques and tasks was found for selection and move operations.

The participants understood the pushpin tool quickly and tended to use it when necessary. The usage of pushpin tool depended on the tasks (see Figure 13). For Task 1, most participants did not use the pushpin tool. On average 0.33 pushpin operations were performed for this task. The usage of the pushpin tool was the highest for Task 2: 3.67 pushpin operations on average. This is mainly because of the failure of our group-aware distribution when diagonal elements are not equally spaced (Figure 12). For Task 4, most participants used the traditional tools and ours in a similar way. Our tool was still slightly better, mainly due to the use of the pushpin tool. Although most participants knew how to take advantage of the pushpin tool, some users used pushpins for extra assurances.

During the use of GACA, the "Arrangement Options" button was almost never clicked: only one participant decided to switch to the group-oblivious result only once. This suggests that the results by GACA were almost never worse than those by group-oblivious arrangement. We thus believe that GACA could be used as a better replacement of the traditional command-based arrangement tools. The participants performed undo operations when they were not satisfied with the current results of either group-oblivious or group-aware arrangement tools. On average significantly fewer undo operations were used with GACA (0.44 vs. 1.10, $F(1, 154) = 10.210$, $p < 0.002$, confirmed by ANOVA). This reflects that the results by GACA were often expected and desired. However, a significant difference in the number of undo operations was not found for any of the individual tasks.

After completing all the tasks, each participant was asked to rate the two techniques. Ten of them were in favor of GACA, including the three participants who reported themselves as expert users of traditional command-based arrangement tools. However, two participants preferred the traditional tools since they felt more familiar and thus comfortable with them. Most of the participants expressed that at the beginning of Study II they felt a bit unsure of the behavior of GACA. This was not unexpected since after all the logic behind GACA was a bit more complicated than the traditional tools. After completing Study II most of them felt very confident of GACA.

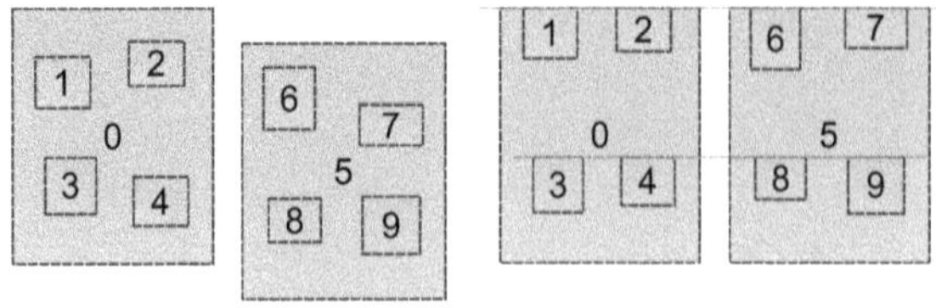

(a) Selected overlapping elements (b) Group-aware top-alignment

Figure 14. Applying GACA to overlapping elements.

DISCUSSION

As described in the "Group-Aware Alignment" section, each pair of elements that would cause overlap between each other after alignment induces a graph partitioning. This rule, however, does not apply to pairs of elements that already intersect with each other before alignment. Figure 14 shows such an example of applying GACA to a set of overlapping elements. A more desired result might be achieved by forming elements e_0 and e_5 as a group and elements e_1, e_2, e_6, and e_7 as another group, since the enclosing relation here implies a two-level organization of elements. This problem is interesting to explore further in the future.

Our grouping strategy is not completely compatible with perceptual grouping, which refers to the human visual ability to extract a meaningful higher-level structure from low-level primitive features [10, 16]. For cases where our approach and perceptual grouping lead to the same grouping results (e.g., Figures 1 (a) and 3 (c)), the user may employ GACA with little thinking. However, when the grouping result by our approach is different from the one in the user's mind (e.g., the input layout in Q3 of Study I), the user might get confused by her perception. Whether the user is still able to predict the result of our approach is highly dependent on her familiarity with GACA. This was confirmed by our user study: although a user could quickly understand how GACA works, it still took time to get used to it. Therefore for novice users, the advantage of our grouping strategy might not be apparent. While for users who are familiar with GACA, it is expected that the performance of our tool would increase. It would be interesting to study the learning process of the users for different grouping strategies.

It is possible to incorporate more perceptual rules for the determination of arrangement groups. However, we have to address two major problems. First, perceptual grouping results can be hierarchical and might not be unique. How to effectively determine the most user-desired result is a challenging problem. Second, perceptual grouping is sensitive to the choice of parameters. Adaptive determination of parameter setting, e.g., to handle the input layouts in Figures 1 (a) and 3 (c), could be intractable. Solving these two problems would further improve the predictability of grouping.

CONCLUSION AND FUTURE WORK

We presented a novel group-aware command-based arrangement technique called GACA. It helps to achieve layouts involving multiple rows and/or columns of well aligned and/or distributed elements. Our user studies confirmed that our technique is intuitive and outperforms the traditional command-based arrangement tools, even for novice users. Still, the user's familiarity with GACA may affect its performance. Therefore, GACA would be particularly useful to professional designers who do lots of layout creating or editing tasks.

Our GACA tool aims to improve the traditional arrangement commands, which arrange the elements defined in a 2D Cartesian coordinate. With coordinate transformation, our algorithm can achieve more complex arrangement tasks, for example, fan-stack arrangements by replacing the Cartesian coordinates with polar coordinates. How to define an intuitive and efficient tool to perform the coordinate transformation would be an interesting problem. Similar to traditional arrangement commands, GACA does not support numeric specification of the arrangement results. It would be useful to provide such a numeric entry after the user issues an arrangement command so that more desired arrangement results can be obtained. To achieve this, it would be necessary to perform a more sophisticated analysis after command invocation. This would be an interesting future direction.

Acknowledgements

We thank the reviewers for their insightful and constructive comments. We also appreciate the user study participants for their time. This work was partially supported by grants from the Research Grants Council of HKSAR, China (Project No. 16209514, 16201315, 113513, 11204014) and JSPS KAKENHI (Grant No. 26240027).

REFERENCES

1. Baudisch, P., Cutrell, E., Hinckley, K., and Eversole, A. Snap-and-go: helping users align objects without the modality of traditional snapping. In *CHI '05* (2005), 301–310.
2. Bier, E. A., and Stone, M. C. Snap-dragging. In *ACM SIGGRAPH Computer Graphics*, vol. 20 (1986), 233–240.
3. Dwyer, T., Marriott, K., and Wybrow, M. Dunnart: A constraint-based network diagram authoring tool. In *Graph Drawing* (2009), 420–431.
4. Frisch, M., Kleinau, S., Langner, R., and Dachselt, R. Grids & guides: multi-touch layout and alignment tools. In *CHI '11* (2011), 1615–1618.
5. Frisch, M., Langner, R., and Dachselt, R. Neat: a set of flexible tools and gestures for layout tasks on interactive displays. In *ITS '11* (2011), 1–10.
6. Galindo, D., and Faure, C. Perceptually-based representation of network diagrams. In *ICDAR '97*, vol. 1 (1997), 352–356.
7. Heo, S., Lee, Y.-K., Yeom, J., and Lee, G. Design of a shape dependent snapping algorithm. In *CHI EA '12* (2012), 2207–2212.
8. Igarashi, T., and Hughes, J. F. A suggestive interface for 3D drawing. In *UIST '01* (2001), 173–181.
9. Igarashi, T., Matsuoka, S., Kawachiya, S., and Tanaka, H. Interactive beautification: a technique for rapid geometric design. In *UIST* (1997), 105–114.
10. Nan, L., Sharf, A., Xie, K., Wong, T.-T., Deussen, O., Cohen-Or, D., and Chen, B. Conjoining gestalt rules for abstraction of architectural drawings. *ACM Trans. Graph. 30*, 6 (2011), 185:1-185:10.
11. Nelson, G. Juno, a constraint-based graphics system. In *ACM SIGGRAPH Computer Graphics*, vol. 19 (1985), 235–243.
12. Pavlidis, T., and Van Wyk, C. J. An automatic beautifier for drawings and illustrations. In *ACM SIGGRAPH Computer Graphics*, vol. 19 (1985), 225–234.
13. Raisamo, R., and Raiha, K.-J. A new direct manipulation technique for aligning objects in drawing programs. In *UIST* (1996), 157–164.
14. Reinert, B., Ritschel, T., and Seidel, H.-P. Interactive by-example design of artistic packing layouts. *ACM Trans. Graph. 31*, 6 (2013), Article No. 218.
15. Ryall, K., Marks, J., and Shieber, S. An interactive constraint-based system for drawing graphs. In *UIST '97* (1997), 97–104.
16. Saund, E., Fleet, D., Larner, D., and Mahoney, J. Perceptually-supported image editing of text and graphics. In *UIST '03* (2003), 183–192.
17. Scarr, J., Cockburn, A., Gutwin, C., and Bunt, A. Improving command selection with commandmaps. In *CHI '12* (2012), 257–266.
18. Tollis, I., Eades, P., Di Battista, G., and Tollis, L. *Graph drawing: algorithms for the visualization of graphs*, vol. 1. Prentice Hall New York, 1998.
19. Xu, P., Fu, H., Au, O. K.-C., and Tai, C.-L. Lazy selection: a scribble-based tool for smart shape elements selection. *ACM Transactions on Graphics 31*, 6 (2012), Article No. 142.
20. Xu, P., Fu, H., Igarashi, T., and Tai, C.-L. Global beautification of layouts with interactive ambiguity resolution. In *UIST 14* (2014), 243–252.

Designing Social and Emotional Skills Training: The Challenges and Opportunities for Technology Support

Petr Slovák[1,2], Ran Gilad-Bahrach[2], Geraldine Fitzpatrick[1]
[1]Human Computer Interaction Group, Vienna University of Technology, Austria
[2]Microsoft Research, Seattle, USA

ABSTRACT
Social and emotional skills are crucial for all aspects of our everyday life. However, understanding how digital technology can facilitate the development and learning of such skills is yet an under-researched area in HCI. To start addressing this gap, this paper reports on a series of interviews and design workshops with the leading researchers and developers of 'Social and Emotional Learning' (SEL) curricula. SEL is a subfield of educational psychology with a long history of teaching such skills, and a range of evidence based curricula that are widely deployed in primary and secondary schools. We identify the shared challenges across existing curricula that digital technology might help address: the support for out-of-session learning, scaffolding for parental engagement, and feedback for the curricula developers. We argue how this presents an opportunity for mutually beneficial collaborations, with the potential for significant real-world impact of novel HCI systems, and can inform HCI work on supporting social and emotional skills development in other domains.

AUTHOR KEYWORDS
Social and Emotional Skills, SEL, Education.

ACM CLASSIFICATION KEYWORDS
H.5.m. Information interfaces and presentation

INTRODUCTION
The importance of social and emotional skills in our everyday life is widely acknowledged [11, 15]. Such skills predict success at work and academic accomplishments [5, 6], as well as personal well-being and sustained close relationships [7]. Recent HCI work strongly suggests the potential for technology to play a key role in supporting the development of such interpersonal and self-regulation skills (e.g., [8, 12]), and a number of systems have been developed in support of specific disadvantaged populations, such as people with autism spectrum disorders [11], or those in cognitive behavioral therapy [4]. However, understanding how such skills are taught and learned by the general population, and how technology can play a role in this, is yet an under-researched area in HCI.

CHI 2015, April 18–23, 2015, Seoul, Republic of Korea.

ACM 978-1-4503-3145-6/15/04 ...$15.00.
http://dx.doi.org/10.1145/2702123.2702385

To start addressing this gap, this paper presents findings from interviews and participatory workshops with key researchers and developers of 'Social and Emotional Learning' (SEL) curricula in educational psychology — a field that has now more than 25 years of history in developing SEL curricula as part of prevention programs for general and at-risk student populations in primary and secondary schools [6, 7]; and a wide range of curricula deployed across US and elsewhere [5, 15]. Through these engagements, we identify what the SEL experts consider to be the key challenges and opportunities where technology could be of use, setting up an initial agenda for future HCI work in this space (cf. also [14]).

In the rest of this paper, we begin with an overview of how technology has been previously used to support emotional and interpersonal skills as part of HCI research, and then outline the goals, methods and real-world impact of existing SEL curricula. Following our recruitment and methodology process, we present the three key challenges identified from the interview and workshop data: the *need to facilitate practice and learning out-of-the-classroom*, *scaffold parental support and engagement with SEL curricula*, and *provide feedback on use for curricula developers*. Each of these challenges is also complemented with an example of a prospective HCI project that was identified and elaborated on together with our workshops participants.

Overall, this paper contributes the first empirical discussion of the challenges and opportunities for technology support of social and emotional learning in the setting of SEL curricula. This highlights the importance of social and emotional skills learning for non-disadvantaged populations, and identifies SEL as an area with complementary interests and challenges to HCI. We also emphasize how the SEL contexts can provide an excellent test-bed for emerging HCI technologies.

RELATED WORK

Technology and interpersonal training in other settings
While existing work suggests the potential of technology support for developing social and emotional skills, the research is still in its beginning. A growing body of work has recently focused on technology support for social skills training for disadvantaged populations. Most of this work supported people with autism spectrum disorders (see review [11]), or those undergoing talk-based therapy (e.g., [4]). In contrast, design and research around supporting the development of social and emotional skills for non-challenged populations has so far received only limited attention within HCI. Existing work includes early explorations in a diverse set of topics such as

using mobile sensing to emotional regulation for parents of ADHD children [12], and exploring the opportunities offered by virtual agents to augment the training of communication skills for medical students [9], US Army soldiers [3], or during work interviews [8]. However, all of these systems embrace only single, isolated aspects rather than the full complexity of social and emotional skills that are needed and developed within the SEL curricula (cf. [14]).

SEL curricula - history, goals, and methods

Social and emotional learning in education is a mature field, with 25+ years' history of peer-reviewed curricula that have already been deployed to millions of pupils. This suggests the potential for considerable real-world impact for any HCI technology deployed in support of a SEL program. Moreover, hundreds of randomized control trial studies find measurable and significant positive effects of SEL curricula, such as the improvements in academic performance [5, 7], or mental health and violence prevention [15].

The skills taught in SEL curricula are those that have been identified by psychologists and educators as crucial not only to development in childhood and teenage years, but more importantly as key skills for adult life, such as self-awareness, self-management, social awareness, relationship skills, and responsible decision making [7]. The core of most curricula is a set of SEL focused, structured classroom lessons [10], usually 25-40 minutes long and administered once a week throughout the whole school year (or multiple years). The lessons use predominantly experiential, active approaches, such as role-play and modeling, to support learning. Such an experiential approach is key as social and emotional skills integrate both cognitive and non-cognitive aspects. The learners thus need extensive examples and opportunities for personal experience and practice, complemented by feedback and opportunities for self-reflection on progress. All curricula aim to develop skills that 'transfer' to situations out of the lesson, i.e., that the learners are able to apply and use the new skills in their everyday life.

As outlined in the Findings section, curricula still face significant challenges (e.g., effectively supporting out-of-classroom learning and reinforcement), and there is no work so far that would explore how incorporating digital technology may address these. Moreover, the sustained reliance on experiential, often non-cognitive learning is what sets SEL apart from learning of traditional academic subjects such as math or literature, and brings unique challenges to supporting learning of social and emotional skills with technology. These issues raise different requirements, needs, and challenges for designing technology in support of SEL training that go beyond the existing work on academic learning within HCI.

METHODOLOGY

The present study builds on a literature review [14] that drew on a wide sample of SEL literature including 5 books, 66 academic articles, and 34 SEL programs. One gap identified in existing work was little or no discussion of the opportunities for technology support of SEL programs. Our aim was thus to identify the areas of SEL training that are challenging and for which HCI technologies are likely to have high impact.

Participants: We recruited SEL curricula developers and their key trainer(s) from seven established SEL curricula. This allowed us to tap into their unique overview of the challenges 'on-the-ground', gained from directly supporting and training the school personnel implementing their curricula in real-world settings. Both developers and trainers also possess the analytical skills and experience to identify the areas they perceive as most challenging for teachers or students. Overall, we interviewed 14 SEL experts – 9 developers, 5 trainers, with SEL experience of median 18 and average 20.8 years. Participants were reimbursed $100 for their time.

Interview topics and analysis: The semi-structured interview aimed to identify the participants' understanding of the challenges the learners, parents, teachers and curricula developers face as of now. We also inquired about what they perceive as the key components of the program, and which aspects are most difficult to learn or teach. The recorded interviews (53-75 min long) were conducted in person or over phone. Each interview was audio recorded, annotated in the software package InqScribe, partially transcribed, and thematically analyzed as per the 6 steps process outlined in [2].

Workshops: Two groups of SEL experts (2 and 4 people) also took part in a series of two workshops each (four workshops altogether). The first workshop was four hours long. We started by presenting four areas of possible technology support (reminders and data collection on-the-go; sensing and feedback of nonverbal emotional cues; supporting communities; games and augmented reality), selected on the basis of the literature review [14] and the interviews. We followed with an extended discussion on how these or similar systems might be relevant to SEL. We aimed to inspire the SEL experts to think about new possibilities, and open up the design space. We then asked the SEL experts to identify 8-10 challenges they perceive as most important for their curriculum. These challenges served as input into the second workshop conducted several days later, where we discussed technology support for two selected challenges in more detail.

IDENTIFIED CHALLENGES AND OPPORTUNITIES

A number of challenges appeared consistently across different curricula and were prioritized by developers and trainers alike. We highlight three areas that our interviewees perceived as most promising for technology support, and complement each with a short description of a possible HCI project, identified as part of the workshops. We end with a list of the other challenges emphasized by our interviewees.

Facilitate practice and learning beyond SEL lesson

Generalization of taught skills to situations beyond the SEL lesson is the core objective of all SEL programs, and a key recurring challenge appearing across all interviews. The social and emotional situations in which students are expected to apply the learnt skills cannot be fully replicated in class. The skills are thus practised in situations that progressively resemble real-world setting, but then need to be reinforced in actual, out-of-class situations (on the playground, at home, in other lessons etc.). Curricula however face several challenges in this regard, as the learners generally find it very difficult to practice skills without external support. As such, out-of-lesson learning is still strongly dependent on coaching by an adult (teacher, school staff or parent), who provides the on-going cues, prompts and reminders needed by learners. This limits the effectiveness of the training, and does not empower the learners to depend on their own resources or to practise/learn independently. Our participants highlighted the potential of wearable and mobile technology to support out-of-lesson learning, both in terms of providing the in-situ, just-in-time coaching support (as per, e.g., [12]), or in facilitating novel training situations that could reinforce and support the generalization of skills.

Exemplary project: Emotional regulation, e.g., the ability to calm down when stressed or angry, was highlighted by the majority of developers and trainers as the key skill that is required for any other learning to take place. It is however also one of the most difficult skills for the learners to learn and transfer. As one opportunity, the participants in both workshops envisioned how combining a computer game (which can be used to elicit strong emotions) with bio-feedback of bodily stress (providing the just-in-time cues and prompts to trigger the calming down strategies taught by SEL courses) could provide the learners with valuable novel opportunities for practice. Previous work in other settings, e.g., [1], suggests that such systems could also be effective in SEL. As the strong emotions elicited by a game are naturally felt (as opposed to role-played interactions), the curricula developers hypothesized that such practice would be more likely transfer to other settings.

Provide tools to scaffold parents engagement with SEL

Parents are overwhelmingly understood as the one of the key agents of change by all SEL curricula, especially given the importance that adult modeling of skills plays for young learners. While most curricula have a wealth of content to support the parental role (e.g., in the form of workshops, or paper documents sent home with children), they lack the tools to distribute it effectively and struggle to engage parents to support SEL at home. For example, the workshops are costly for schools, parental turn-out is often low, and the materials sent home are rarely read or acted on. This is a serious problem, especially as many parents could themselves benefit from SEL concepts (e.g., anger management, or emotional self-awareness), and might be reinforcing unhelpful habits otherwise. As exemplified in the project suggestion below, our interviewees were optimistic about the opportunities for mobile technology to support parents' engagement with SEL learning and to scaffold reinforcement of crucial SEL concepts through playful interactions with their children.

Exemplary project: The workshop participants discussed how digital technology could help infuse SEL concepts into everyday parent-child interactions, such as bed-time reading for pre-K to K2 learners, effectively scaffolding reinforcement of SEL curricula in engaging and playful ways. Building on the existing HCI research on facilitating parent-child interaction with technology, such as Family Story Play [13], an interesting design challenge for HCI is exploring the potential that digital technology may offer beyond what can be accomplished with a non-digital book. Our participants were particularly excited about the opportunities of infusing the stories with interactive prompts, cues, and activities that would better scaffold discussions around key SEL concepts for both parent and child. Examples might be a focus on problem solving (e.g., show different story outcomes based on the child's choice), or perspective taking and awareness of emotions (e.g., 'what might Mary feel now?'). Moreover, the curricula developers envisioned that such scaffolded interactions can also be designed to promote the parents coaching abilities around SEL concepts. For example, being able to formulate how one feels is an important aspect of many curricula, but something that parents often struggle to support. The scaffolding designed into the interactive book might make such interaction more accessible even for parents who would otherwise find such topics uncomfortable.

Feedback for curricula developers

While all curricula undergo extensive piloting and rigorous randomized controlled trials to gauge their outcome, they are still mostly distributed in printed form. Once sent out, the curricula developers then do not necessarily get feedback from teachers or parents to provide support for fidelity of deployment, identify aspects of curricula (e.g., specific activities) that are in need of further improvements, or allow for rapid innovation and change (e.g., A/B testing of new activities across schools). Incorporating digital technology could help address all these challenges as well as promote a sense of ownership for the teachers, parents, and learners.

Exemplary project: Although most curricula have documents and activities that are sent to support parent involvement, curricula designers receive very little feedback about whether and how these are used by parents. Our participants were excited about providing the family with a physical object that serves as a portal to an underlying digital content, e.g., a QR link on a fridge magnet or a digital frame. Such an object could then be incorporated into homework exercises, serve as an ambient reminder of SEL concepts (e.g., constantly visible on the fridge door), and also facilitate collecting the needed feedback from the parents and children, or even empowering the users to create and share new content. Moreover, curricula designers could work with dynamic content updates (e.g., a machine learning based tailoring), as well as large scale comparisons of effectiveness of different activities across broad populations.

Additional challenges

Our participants mentioned a number of additional challenges that were shared across the curricula. These included support for online, but still experiential training (to lower costs for participating schools' budgets), as well as the lack of tools to create, support and maintain supportive peer networks for parents and staff taking part in SEL programs. A prevalent issue is also the lack of time on the part of the teachers, further encumbered by their wish to, understandably, co-create and own the lessons they teach, despite having little time to do so. Finally, most of the existing curricula focus mainly on elementary and early middle-school, as engaging older students brings different dynamics and developmental challenges. Our interviewees were however optimistic about the potential of mobile technology (widely used in this population) to promote novel curricula design and ways of learning.

DISCUSSION

The interviews and workshops with SEL experts helped us identify some of the key SEL challenges that digital technology is likely to be well-suited to address, pointing toward plausible agenda for future work. As supporting SEL in education has not been addressed in HCI so far, this study provides the first step into this significant but under-researched area; and orients HCI research to the importance of social and emotional skills learning for non-disadvantaged populations.

We argue that HCI involvement with SEL has the potential to not only address some of the key SEL challenges, but can also advance HCI research beyond the focus on HCI in education (see also [14]). SEL brings the knowledge of techniques and methods to teach and support interpersonal aspects that are then likely to translate to other HCI contexts such as workplace or everyday life. In particular, each of the exemplary projects show-cases such possibility of extending the HCI research, which provides new tools and opportunities for the learners, with the SEL domain knowledge on how the development of skills can be scaffolded.

Moreover, SEL in education provides an excellent context for exploring applications of emerging HCI technologies, such as social signals processing or affective computing systems. In particular, the existing curricular structure provides the detailed content and learning context (e.g., weekly lessons) in which novel HCI systems can be embedded, thus offloading a crucial aspect that can otherwise make or break the system and/or limit the uptake. SEL curricula also provide well motivated challenges for technology that, together with the long history of SEL learning, can guide HCI community to focus on most beneficial social and emotional aspects to detect and support. Finally, designing to support SEL curricula offers the opportunity of large impact and scale, allowing successful technologies to build on such existing distribution channels, as well as the large-scale evaluation practices common in SEL community.

CONCLUSIONS

This paper points to the complementary interests of SEL and HCI fields, highlighting the potential for mutually beneficial collaborations. As the first step, we draw on interviews and participatory workshops with leading curricula designers, identify the opportunity to address some of the key challenges in SEL curricula with digital technology, and illustrate these with three exemplary projects. We hope this paper can inspire future work in this complex and intriguing research space.

ACKNOWLEDGEMENTS

We are grateful to the SEL experts for their time and deep engagement with the interviews; and to Mary Czerwinski for her guidance and support in this work.

REFERENCES

1. S. Bouchard, F. Bernier, E. Boivin, B. Morin, and G. Robillard. Using biofeedback while immersed in a stressful videogame increases the effectiveness of stress management skills in soldiers. *PloS one*, 7(4):e36169, Jan. 2012.
2. V. Braun and V. Clarke. Using thematic analysis in psychology. *Qualitative research in psychology*, (February 2013):37–41, 2006.
3. M. Core, D. Traum, H. C. Lane, W. Swartout, J. Gratch, M. van Lent, and S. Marsella. Teaching Negotiation Skills through Practice and Reflection with Virtual Humans. *SIMULATION*, 82(11):685–701, Nov. 2006.
4. D. Coyle, G. Doherty, M. Matthews, and J. Sharry. Computers in talk-based mental health interventions. *Interacting with Computers*, 19(4):545–562, July 2007.
5. J. A. Durlak, R. P. Weissberg, A. B. Dymnicki, R. D. Taylor, and K. B. Schellinger. The impact of enhancing students' social and emotional learning: a meta-analysis of school-based universal interventions. *Child development*, 82(1):405–32, 2011.
6. M. J. Elias. *Promoting social and emotional learning: Guidelines for educators*. ASCD, 1997.
7. M. T. Greenberg. Schoolbased prevention: current status and future challenges. *Effective Education*, 2(1):27–52, Mar. 2010.
8. M. E. Hoque, M. Courgeon, J.-C. Martin, B. Mutlu, and R. W. Picard. MACH: My Automatic Conversation Coach. In *UbiComp '13*, page 697, New York, New York, USA, Sept. 2013. ACM Press.
9. K. Johnsen, A. Raij, A. Stevens, D. S. Lind, and B. Lok. The validity of a virtual human experience for interpersonal skills education. In *CHI '07*, page 1049, New York, USA, Apr. 2007. ACM Press.
10. S. M. Jones and S. M. Bouffard. Social and Emotional Learning in Schools: From Programs to Strategies. Social Policy Report. Volume 26, Number 4. *Society for Research in Child Development*, 2012.
11. J. A. Kientz, M. S. Goodwin, G. R. Hayes, and G. D. Abowd. Interactive Technologies for Autism. *Synthesis Lectures on Assistive, Rehabilitative, and Health-Preserving Technologies*, 2(2):1–177, 2013.
12. L. Pina, K. Rowan, A. Roseway, P. Johns, G. R. Hayes, and M. Czerwinski. In Situ Cues for ADHD Parenting Strategies Using Mobile Technology. In *Pervasive Health '14*, 2014.
13. H. Raffle, M. Spasojevic, R. Ballagas, G. Revelle, H. Horii, S. Follmer, J. Go, E. Reardon, K. Mori, and J. Kaye. Family story play: reading with young children (and elmo) over a distance. In *CHI '10*, page 1583, New York, New York, USA, 2010. ACM Press.
14. P. Slovak and G. Fitzpatrick. Teaching and developing social and emotional skills with technology. *TOCHI (in minor revision)*.
15. K. Weare and M. Nind. Mental health promotion and problem prevention in schools: what does the evidence say? *Health Promotion International*, 26(S1):i29–i69, Nov. 2011.

Designing Autism Research for Maximum Impact

Elizabeth J. Carter
Carnegie Mellon University
Pittsburgh, PA
ejcarter@cs.cmu.edu

Jennifer Hyde
Carnegie Mellon University
Pittsburgh, PA
jdtam@cs.cmu.edu

ABSTRACT

In recent decades, rates of autism spectrum disorder (ASD) have risen dramatically, and research into assistive technologies for this population has similarly escalated. For technology to be adopted, technologists need to communicate with practitioners across fields and match methodological and evaluation standards. We provide a set of recommendations for researchers to bridge the gap between fields and maximize the impact of their research, including instructions on how to identify and describe research participants and how to avoid research confounds and challenges specific to this population. We also advocate that researchers in ASD maintain a nimble, adaptable approach when performing experiments.

Author Keywords

ASD; Autism; User Studies; Methodology.

ACM Classification Keywords

H.5.m. Information Interfaces and Presentation (e.g., HCI): Miscellaneous

INTRODUCTION

In recent years, there has been a boom in technology designed for individuals with autism spectrum disorder (ASD), particularly children. There are thousands of desktop and mobile applications, toys, and robots that advertise their use for ASD[1]. Scholarly publications on computer-based ASD therapy have increased more than 18-fold since 1998 (Figure 1). The human-computer and human-robot interaction (HCI and HRI) communities have developed technologies to improve specific skills. However, the majority are not widely adopted. Often, they do not make it beyond prototypes or are never fully developed and tested. Practitioners remain unaware or unsure of promising technologies because of a lack of interdisciplinary interaction. These communities must interlace if new technologies for individuals with ASD are to have maximal impact. Therefore, we believe that the HCI and HRI communities need a specific agenda to produce high-quality ASD research, which we briefly introduce.

[1]E.g., the Apple App Store listed 1,600+ apps for ASD as of Sept. 2014.

CHI'15, April 18 - 23 2015, Seoul, Republic of Korea

ACM 978-1-4503-3145-6/15/04... $15.00
http://dx.doi.org/10.1145/2702123.2702471

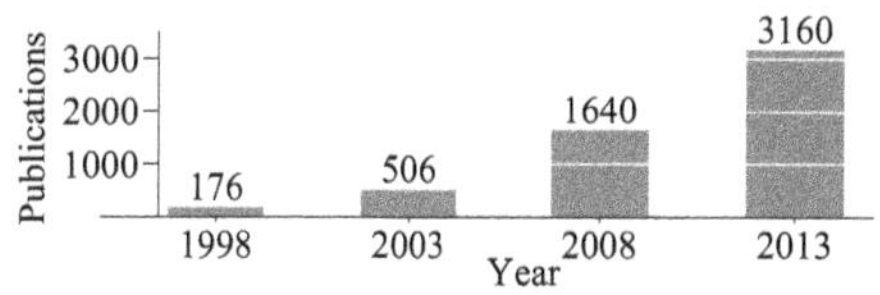

Figure 1. Number of papers per year regarding software for ASD based on a Google Scholar search for "autism therapy computer software".

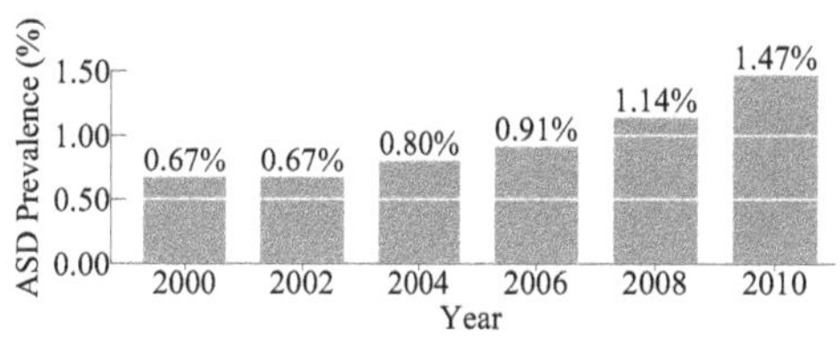

Figure 2. Increasing prevalence rates of ASD in the US from 2000-2010.

Prior work mainly addressed specific concerns or features that should be considered when designing and evaluating technologies for ASD (e.g., [9]), though a recent book provides comprehensive practical considerations for ASD research [13]. Based on our own experience and expertise, we have developed a brief set of recommendations to bridge the gap between fields, provide basic information, and inspire new researchers to delve into the detailed literature. Our suggestions fall into three categories: (1) provide detailed participant characterization to communicate across fields and increase impact; (2) consider potential confounds in experiment design that arise from the unique characteristics of ASD; and (3) be "nimble" and adaptable during experimentation.

BACKGROUND: AUTISM SPECTRUM DISORDER

ASD is characterized by early-onset, persistent deficits in social interaction and communication, restricted interests, and repetitive behavior patterns [2]. It is a lifelong disorder that impacts education, health care, and employment opportunities. Additionally, because it is a spectrum disorder, individuals vary greatly in their symptoms. Notably, the prevalence rates of ASD have risen dramatically, doubling in the US to 1 in 68 children and 1 in 42 boys since 2000 (Figure 2) [7]. Up to $262b is spent in the US annually for support [5].

Intervention during childhood can impact lifelong severity of ASD (e.g., [10]), providing an important research target. Historically, adult therapists implemented interventions, which limits their duration, is expensive, and requires more therapists to match diagnosis rates. Technology-based therapies are often more accessible in terms of time, convenience, and cost and can supplement traditional therapy.

IDENTIFYING AND DESCRIBING PARTICIPANTS

The use of standardized measures for identifying research participants with ASD is of paramount importance. These measures were introduced to ensure that the population of individuals used in autism research were specifically and consistently described with a common vocabulary [14].

Researchers in various disciplines currently recruit, identify, and describe participants with ASD differently. We compared how HCI/HRI and other fields perform autism research. First, we selected three prominent journals with a focus on ASD and include publications from researchers in psychology, speech-language pathology, genetics, education, and neuroscience: *Journal of Autism and Developmental Disorders* (impact factor: 3.384), *Autism Research* (IF: 4.532), and *Research in Autism Spectrum Disorders* (IF: 2.378). We found the 20 most recent articles in each journal[2] that fit these criteria: (1) all participants were under age 18 years and had ASD; (2) studies had 5 to 200 participants; and (3) studies were not developing or assessing a standardized measure. All 60 articles were published in 2014. Next, we characterized the participant identification and description methods (Table 1). Fifty-six articles included clear descriptions of assessments. Forty-six papers included clinical diagnosis using DSM-IV [1], DSM-V [2], and/or ICD [20] criteria, 35 used the Autism Diagnostic Observation Schedule–Generic (ADOS, [15]), 23 used the Autism Diagnostic Interview–Revised (ADI, [14]), and 22 papers used other standardized measures. On average, each paper used 2.18 methods of identification.

To examine HCI and HRI research, we searched the ACM Digital Library, IEEE Xplore, and Springer for papers from 2011-2014[3]. We examined each paper to determine whether it (1) contained the term "autism" or "autistic"; and (2) had significant ASD content. From the remaining 63 papers, we noted (1) whether participants included children with ASD[4]; (2) how many children with ASD participated; and (3) what diagnoses and diagnostic measures were described. Only fifteen papers clearly described their ASD diagnosis method (Table 1). Other papers varied widely, ranging from having a mixed group of children and failing to disclose how many had ASD, including children recruited from schools or treatment centers without describing placement requirements, and failing to describe recruitment and identification.

The ADI [14] and the ADOS [15] are the most commonly used measures in autism journals. They were developed over decades of research, determine whether an individual meets DSM and ICD criteria for ASD, and must be administered by a trained tester. While these are considered the "gold standard" tests, other standardized measures have been created that can be administered quickly by a non-expert (e.g., questionnaires that caregivers complete [8, 17, 18]).

[2]Beginning with the most recent issue: *JADD* Vol. 44, Iss. 9; *AR* Vol. 7, Iss. 4; *RASD* Vol. 8, Iss. 10.

[3]We searched the ACM and IEEE libraries for full papers from proceedings that contained the word "autism." We also searched Springer for computer science, HCI, and HRI papers that contained the word "autism."

[4]A number of papers with "autism" in the title or as a keyword did not perform any testing with individuals with ASD.

Table 1. Comparison of participants and assessments across disciplines.

	Psychology	HCI and HRI
Participants		
Mean	48	11†
Median	30	8†
Range	12-164	1-71†
ASD Assessment		
Clinical Diagnosis		
ADOS	35 (58%)	6 (10%)
ADI	23 (38%)	3 (5%)
ADOS+ADI	21 (35%)	2 (3%)
Other	18 (30%)	10 (16%)
Total‡	*46 (77%)*	*14 (22%)*
Other		
SCQ [17]	9 (15%)	2 (3%)
CARS [18]	5 (8%)	3 (5%)
SRS [8]	4 (7%)	1 (2%)
Other	5 (8%)	0 (0%)
Total‡	*22 (36%)*	*4 (6%)*
Total‡	*56/60 (93%)*	*15/63 (24%)*

† Excludes data from papers that did not report number of ASD participants.
‡ Some studies used multiple methods of assessment.

It is important to note whether the participants have a clinical diagnosis of autism because other forms of diagnosis, such as those provided by schools, might place children in the most appropriate therapeutic environment using a functional diagnosis without needing precision. Additionally, clinical diagnoses generally rely on DSM or ICD criteria and provide for differential diagnosis. Standardized measures also give more specific information about an individual's characteristics, providing researchers with the capability to correlate outcomes (e.g., a child with greater social deficits might show higher amounts of improvement over time with a particular therapy than a child with fewer social deficits). This is critical for intervention research [19].

It may be impossible or impractical to obtain clinical diagnoses for all participants, particularly for a large study. However, while standardization of measures with other fields does require investment, such as finding a collaborator who can administer an ADOS or using a combination of other diagnostic instruments, we think that the resulting greater returns in impact will create more value for the invested research dollars spent than that which is currently achieved. For example, a clinician is more likely to perform an expanded test of an intervention if it was described clearly, piloted on a known number of individuals with precise diagnoses, and has quantifiable results. At minimum, we recommend that researchers include at least one reliable, specific measure for accurate participant identification and description. Standardized and detailed assessment allows readers to know more about a necessarily small sample and predict generalization.

AVOIDING CONFOUNDS

In all areas of research, experimenters must carefully control and balance differences across conditions to eliminate potential confounds. In ASD research, the nature of what constitutes a confound can differ because of cognitive characteristics and personal intervention histories.

Individuals with ASD have a detail-focused cognitive style with a bias towards processing local information [11]. In practical terms, children with ASD often attend to small details more than do typically developing (TD) children, potentially affecting experiment participation and performance. For example, one study examined how children with ASD interacted with an avatar versus people [6]. The researchers controlled for cartoon appearance, use of a projection screen, confederates' training with ASD, vocabulary, speaking style, and speech speed. Had the authors not controlled for the confederates' experience and behaviors, they would not have observed equivalent responses to the avatar and an untrained adult. Even with TD children, issues such as what shirt color a character wears can affect assessments of character preference [3]. To avoid this specific confound, we designed a study where a character wore the same shirt in various conditions. One child with ASD spoke extensively about the topic, asking why the character had no shirts in different colors. From our experience, seemingly minor details do not go unnoticed.

Another consideration when creating technology-based interventions for ASD is the children's previous intervention and technology experience. For example, children who attend speech therapy may respond differently to a speech-related intervention or speech-language pathologist than children who have not had this experience [6]. Additionally, children who have tablets at home are likely to perform better and feel more comfortable with a tablet-based application than children who do not have experience with tablets and may show a longer learning curve [16]. It is important to assess prior experiences that may affect results, particularly when they differ from those of TD individuals.

NIMBLENESS IN RESEARCH

Children with ASD exhibit behaviors that can affect study procedures and results. Therefore, it is important to be prepared, and it is even more important to adapt to unexpected situations. "Nimbleness" has saved us from canceling experiment sessions or eliminating participants' data. Additionally, nimbleness of thought allows our experimenters to notice design and performance issues and adapt procedures. While research procedures cannot be fully personalized, a little flexibility can increase participant comfort while maintaining research integrity. This also helps researchers ensure that these participants, who are difficult to recruit, have the best experiences possible and are likely to participate in future research.

One characteristic of ASD is inflexible behavior, such as "insistence on sameness, inflexible adherence to routines, or ritualized patterns... (e.g., extreme distress at small changes, difficulties with transitions, rigid thinking patterns...)" [2]. For researchers, this signifies that many children with ASD will have difficulty immediately adapting to an unfamiliar environment. A number of tactics can increase the probability of success. For example, many laboratories send families materials such as stories, photographs, and even movies to demonstrate what will happen at the research lab and prepare participants (e.g., [12]). Additionally, extra care can be taken in the lab to ensure that the children enjoy experiences. In our lab, the experimenter chats for a few minutes with each child to make him or her feel comfortable, verify comprehension of the activities that will occur, and attain his or her assent to the procedure. When possible, we present task instructions as stories to provide a coherent narrative and an enjoyable co-reading experience. This procedure also provides multiple checkpoints for comprehension. For complex tasks and unusual experiences, other laboratories include habituation procedures prior to the actual experiment, such as having children with ASD use pretend ("mock") scanners that are as similar to magnetic resonance imaging scanners as possible in appearance and noise prior to a scan [12]. Participant dropout rates can indicate whether a procedure includes methods to manage common complications, making it important to report these rates in publications.

Another aspect of inflexible behavior is an adherence to rigid thinking patterns. In one of our experiments, an experimenter followed a script to converse with children with ASD about creating ice cream sundaes. Occasionally, a participant could not eat ice cream. When this situation occurred with a TD child, the child continued with the task because he knew the flavors generally. However, for a child with ASD, the experimenter had to be flexible and change the topic to sorbet so that the child was not stymied by this detail and did not extensively discuss allergies. This alteration had no qualitative impact on experiment administration consistency for our dependent measures and preserved conversation flow. In another study, we discovered that, unlike TD children, a number of children with ASD would not comply with task instructions to identify an animated character's emotional state as happy, angry, or sad. Multiple children with ASD were unwilling to use a negative label. One child stated that he wanted everyone to "be happy all of the time", only selecting that response. Another individual admitted that he was "tricking" the experimenter by answering incorrectly for angry stimuli because he did not want the character to be angry. The experimenter was nimble enough to notice that the children were producing unusual, restricted patterns of response and ended the task.

ASD is also characterized by communication deficits, including echolalia and incorrect conversational turn-taking [2]. In our experience, this has resulted in adjustments in task administration and outcome measures. For example, a child with echolalia will repeat previously heard speech. This presents an issue when a child repeats the last selection from a multiple choice list, a potentially inaccurate indication of preference. If experimenters notice echolalia, they can ask the same question multiple times, randomizing choice order. Some children stop echoing when asked the same question multiple times. Additionally, including multiple question types (open vs. closed) enables researchers to obtain converging responses. Therefore, verifying responses and randomizing choice order are especially important. Another challenge in the ASD population is inappropriately regulated conversational turn-taking. Researchers often use mean length of utterance (MLU) as an indicator of conversation quality. In TD children, higher MLUs may indicate more engagement in the conversation. However, because children with ASD often monologue about their own interests, higher MLU values are not an accurate indicator of conversation quality. We developed a new measure classifying utterances as on- or off-topic to assess reciprocal conversation.

Another consideration in designing ASD research is motivation. Because children with ASD have social abnormalities [2], they may lack intrinsic social motivation to complete a task. Moreover, common reinforcement techniques for TD children may need to be adapted for ASD children to suit their interests (for review, see [9]). Additionally, there has been an assumption in technology research that children with ASD prefer interacting with technology over humans (e.g., [4]). However, recent research suggests that this is not necessarily the case [6], so care must be taken not to assume that children with ASD will be willing participants in a technology study simply because of the use of technology. Taken together, all of these individual considerations can be addressed by researcher flexibility when studying this population.

CONCLUSION AND RECOMMENDATIONS

We noted important differences in reporting and research styles between fields and detailed lessons that we learned from designing studies involving children with ASD. To improve technology research, we suggest that researchers adhere to the following recommendations:

1. Select/evaluate participants using standardized, validated ASD assessment methods and clinical diagnosis, when available. Include a detailed description of participants with their dropout rate.
2. Limit potential confounds in comparison tasks to avoid fixation on minute differences.
3. Be prepared to adapt research protocols and measures based on participants' individual characteristics.

With these recommendations in mind, we believe that HCI and HRI research on ASD can achieve a greater impact and improve interdisciplinary communication.

ACKNOWLEDGMENTS

We thank D. Williams, J. Forlizzi, M. Vazquez, J. Hodgins, and our research participants.

REFERENCES

1. American Psychiatric Association. *DSM-IV-TR: Diagnostic and statistical manual of mental disorders, text revision*. American Psychiatric Association, 2000.
2. American Psychiatric Association. *DSM-V: Diagnostic and statistical manual of mental disorders, 5th Edition*. American Psychiatric Publishing, 2013. Section 299.00.
3. Andrist, S., Leite, I., and Lehman, J. Fun and fair: influencing turn-taking in a multi-party game with a virtual agent. In *Proc. IDC* (2013), 352–355.
4. Baron-Cohen, S., Golan, O., and Ashwin, E. Can emotion recognition be taught to children with autism spectrum conditions? *Phil Trans Royal Soc B 364*, 1535 (2009), 3567–3574.
5. Buescher, A., Cidav, Z., Knapp, M., and Mandell, D. Costs of autism spectrum disorders in the united kingdom and the united states. *JAMA Pediatrics 168*, 8 (2014), 721–728.
6. Carter, E., Williams, D., Hodgins, J., and Lehman, J. Are children with autism more responsive to animated characters? A study of interactions with humans and human-controlled avatars. *J Autism Dev Disord 44*, 10 (2014), 2475–2485.
7. Centers for Disease Control and Prevention. Prevalence of autism spectrum disorder among children aged 8 years – Autism and developmental disabilities monitoring network, 11 sites, United States, 2010. *MMWR 63*, SS02 (2014), 1–21.
8. Constantino, J. *Social Responsiveness Scale*. WPS Torrance, CA, 2005.
9. Fletcher-Watson, S. A targeted review of computer-assisted learning for people with autism spectrum disorder: Towards a consistent methodology. *J Autism Dev Disord 1*, 2 (2014), 87–100.
10. Granpeesheh, D., Dixon, D., Tarbox, J., Kaplan, A., et al. The effects of age and treatment intensity on behavioral intervention outcomes for children with autism spectrum disorders. *Res Autism Spect Dis 3*, 4 (2009), 1014–1022.
11. Happé, F., and Frith, U. The weak coherence account: detail-focused cognitive style in autism spectrum disorders. *J Autism Dev Disord 36*, 1 (2006), 5–25.
12. Kana, R., Murdaugh, D., Libero, L., Pennick, M., et al. Probing the brain in autism using fMRI and diffusion tensor imaging. *J Visual Exp*, 55 (2011).
13. Kientz, J. A., Goodwin, M. S., Hayes, G. R., and Abowd, G. D. Interactive technologies for autism. *Synthesis Lectures on Assistive, Rehabilitative, and Health-Preserving Technologies 2*, 2 (2013), 1–177.
14. Lord, C., Rutter, M., and Le Couteur, A. Autism diagnostic interview-revised: a revised version of a diagnostic interview for caregivers of individuals with possible pervasive developmental disorders. *J Autism Dev Disord 24*, 5 (1994), 659–685.
15. Lord, C., Risi, S., Lambrecht, L., Cook, E., et al. The autism diagnostic observation schedule-generic: A standard measure of social and communication deficits associated with the spectrum of autism. *J Autism Dev Disord 30*, 3 (2000), 205–223.
16. O'Malley, P., Lewis, M., Donehower, C., and Stone, D. Effectiveness of using iPads to increase academic task completion by students with autism. *Univer J of Ed Res 2*, 1 (2014), 90–97.
17. Rutter, M., Bailey, A., and Lord, C. *Social Communication Questionnaire*. WPS Torrance, CA, 2003.
18. Schopler, E., Reichler, R., and Renner, B. R. *The Childhood Autism Rating Scale*. Irvington NY, 1986.
19. Warren, Z., McPheeters, M., Sathe, N., Foss-Feig, J., et al. A systematic review of early intensive intervention for autism spectrum disorders. *Pediatrics 127*, 5 (2011), e1303–e1311.
20. World Health Organization. *International Statistical Classification of Diseases and Related Health Problems, tenth revision (ICD-10)*. WHO, 2008.

Networked Empowerment on Facebook among Parents of Children with Special Needs

Tawfiq Ammari, Sarita Schoenebeck
School of Information
University of Michigan
{tawfiqam,yardi}@umich.edu

ABSTRACT
Theories of empowerment explain how people gain personal and political control to take action to improve their lives. However, empowerment theories were developed prior to the Internet and fail to account for the speed and scale that people can find one another online. One domain where empowerment is critical is caring for children with special needs, in which parents are required to navigate a complex maze of services and processes to access care for their child. We conducted 43 interviews with parents of children with special needs to investigate whether using social media sites helps them to perform this caregiving work. Critically, parents are able to do this through almost real-time access to other parents on Facebook. This work introduces the concept of *networked empowerment*, that describes how parents find other parents, access resources, and explore new ways for promoting health advocacy among caregivers at a local and national level. We conclude with design implications for facilitating faster and better access to information and support for caregivers.

Author Keywords
Parents, special needs, disabilities, social media, empowerment, children.

ACM Classification Keywords
H.5.m. Information interfaces and presentation (e.g., HCI): Miscellaneous.

INTRODUCTION
Accessing support services can be time consuming and emotionally exhausting for parents of children with special needs [45]. Often newly diagnosed and in unfamiliar territory, parents are expected to fight for their children's needs amid a complex network of local, state, and federal requirements [30]. Furthermore, information tends to be distributed across multiple websites and contain unfamiliar acronyms, rules, and hierarchies. Parents have to navigate medical and educational services that are splintered across organizations and hierarchies [31,50] while simultaneously coping with and adapting to their new identity as a parent of a child with special needs [18].

Not surprisingly, parents turn to the Internet to seek information and access social support related to raising their child [5,21,27]. Prior work suggests that parents find support in online groups (e.g., Facebook Groups, Yahoo Groups) where they can access geographic-based parents (e.g., to discuss local school services) or cased-based parents (e.g., to discuss autism) [5]. Promisingly, parents feel less judged online in these contexts than they do offline among family and members of their community [5]. However, it is not known whether social media supports parents in learning how to negotiate for services for their child—a complex and demanding activity that requires intensive and ongoing effort [17]. This is vitally important for understanding how to support the millions of children who are diagnosed with special needs each year in the U.S. and many more worldwide [9].

We conducted 43 semi-structured interviews with parents of children with special needs about their use of social media related to their children's needs. Results show that as parents need to access health and education services for their children, they turn to social media sites—primarily Facebook groups—to learn from other parents about how to access these services. We draw from empowerment theories to show how parents cope with and respond to receiving a diagnosis of a child with special needs [51]. We present a new concept of *networked empowerment* that describes how parents whose children have received a special needs diagnosis find other parents, mobilize resources, and become advocates. This work introduces new insights into the networked properties of social media sites for empowering parents of children with special needs. HCI researchers can leverage this information to design more supportive platforms for special needs families and to explore new ways of promoting health advocacy among caregivers at a local and national level. We conclude with design approaches for supporting faster and better support for caregivers on social media sites.

CHI 2015, April 18 – 23, 2015, Seoul, Republic of Korea.

ACM 978-1-4503-3145-6/15/04…$15.00 .
http://dx.doi.org/10.1145/2702123.2702324

RELATED WORK

Empowerment Theory

Empowerment describes a process in which people gain understanding and control over personal, social, economic, or political forces in order to take action to better their lives [51]. When people face difficult situations, marginalized identities, or new environments where personal roles change, they can feel disempowered, no longer able to control their own outcomes [36]. Living in a cycle of disempowerment can lead to learned helplessness, where future outcomes continue to suffer because individuals no longer believe they can control and change their future and thus, stop trying [1]. In contrast, empowerment allows people to face challenges and adapt to new roles [36].

Zimmerman's model of psychological empowerment identifies three components: intrapersonal component, interactional component, and behavioral component [51]. The intrapersonal component describes "how people think about themselves" which includes self-efficacy, perceived competence, and mastery. Self-efficacy refers to the perception of a person's own ability to do the actions required to achieve a goal [6]. Greater feelings of competency correspond with the belief that other people have less control over oneself [44]. The interactional component describes people's awareness of social and political issues in their contexts, and how they can act on choices available to them to achieve their goals. Finally, the behavioral component describes "actions taken to directly influence outcomes" [51]. This includes behaviors to manage stress and adapt to change, and taking action to acquire help and resources. Together the interpersonal, interactional, and behavioral components come together to show how a person who believes that she can influence a given context (intrapersonal component) understands systems and processes located within that context (interactional component) and engages in behaviors to exert control in the context (behavioral component).

Formal Empowerment

Proactive empowerment refers to the pursuit of chosen and desired activities (e.g., environmental concerns) [24,49] whereas *reactive empowerment*—the focus of this work—refers to capacity acquired in response to a threat (e.g., disaster relief, health diagnosis) [24,49]. Reactive empowerment can be brought about in two ways: *formal empowerment* is brought forth by political decision-making systems when they allow some measure of meaningful citizen participation in policy making [37]. *Instrumental empowerment* is defined as the ability of an individual to affect the decision-making process outside of legal or policy infrastructures. Formal empowerment is usually enacted through laws mandating citizen participation, such as the Individualized Education Plan for special education, in which schools are legally mandated to take into consideration feedback from parents [45]. Though formal empowerment is designed to support citizens, Rich et al., note that "formal empowerment, by itself, is neither sufficient nor necessary to give citizens the capacity to control their situation with respect to specific issues" [37]. They describe how "trappings of formal empowerment" could be employed by public officials to frustrate citizen engagement by using "pro forma hearings to consume the energies of the citizens" [37].

Empowerment in HCI

Empowerment is a core concept in many areas of HCI research. In 1990, Shneiderman penned a "Declaration of Empowerment" to incorporate social good into technology design and to attend to users' needs in the design process [38]. He proposed that HCI researchers and developers commit ourselves to "studying ways to enable users to accomplish their personal and organization goals while pursuing higher societal goals and serving human needs" [38]. Ladner emphasized user empowerment, especially in the context of empowering people with disabilities, to create or configure technologies on their own [22]. He presents the example of text-to-speech techniques that are used in screen readers that are optimized for blind users [22]. Malinverni, et al. have considered empowerment dimensions of participatory design as a means for improving the design results and for children with special needs [26]. Hook et al. extend these ideas to consider "interactional empowerment" that can help users to make sense of their emotions and make meaning through their use of a system.

Empowerment has also been incorporated into the "do-it-yourself" movement that suggests passive consumers can become active producers, though researchers question whether this is actually the case [4]. Empowerment is especially critical in marginalized communities; Shroff and Kam put forth a design model for empowering low-income women in India [39]. They propose aligning the technology design process with particular stages of women's lives. These prior studies place the user and user experience as central to the empowerment process; however, none of these have investigated social media use nor drawn from empowerment theory literature, an important gap we address in this work.

Accessing Care for Children with Special Needs

Approximately 1 in 6 children are diagnosed with a special need in the United States today [9]. Special needs is used as a diagnostic term to indicate a requirement of assistance; however, the severity of needs ranges widely, from mild cases of attention deficit disorder to severe cases of cerebral palsy. The special needs label tends to be inclusive, an approach we adopt in our work, and can refer to a range of needs including autism, down syndrome, visual disabilities, hearing disabilities, dyslexia, cystic fibrosis, cleft lips, learning disabilities, etc. When receiving diagnoses, the families of special needs children require new and often greater kinds of social, emotional, and instrumental support than they previously required [17,25]. Families also have more information needs related to specialized educational and health resources [18].

Education Services for Children with Special Needs

About 6.4 million (13% of all public school) students receive special education services each year. Students with a special need are entitled to an Individualized Education Plan (IEP) [3], a document that ensures each student receive adequate and personalized services depending on her needs. However, many parents consider the IEP process to be a difficult process to engage with [3]. Although children are guaranteed provision of services by law [26], proving that they need such services is not easy. Parents experience a power imbalance with the school district, entering the negotiation process with little knowledge about organizational, legal, and disability issues [23]. Parents cannot typically determine when a proposed service is adequate or not, lacking what professionals call "judgmental knowledge" [42]. Finally, special needs laws are legislated on a federal level but enacted on a state and local district level, making it difficult for parents to know what to expect of their own district [42].

Health Support Online

Some of parents' information and social support needs are met by offline support groups [2,7,40], a movement which grew in the 1980s with greater acceptance of special needs in American culture [40]. Caregivers also use online health communities and social media sites for information and social support [5,11,21,27,47]. Participation in health-related online support groups and communities can be empowering for patients, especially those who suffer from poorly-understood medical conditions [14] or lack of offline support [11]. They also provide support for caregivers [19], an increasingly important consideration as care, especially for chronic health problems, becomes part of the domestic home environment [16]. Online health communities also provide a platform for political activism relevant to participants' conditions [43].

The anonymity afforded by some online communities related to health provides participants an opportunity to share their experiences without fearing concern about stigmatizing effects [47]. However, relationships formed in anonymous environments are usually short-lived [11] and might be impersonal [47]. In contrast, social media sites typically require the use of real names or identifications that are linked to a user profile [8]. Newman et al. [34] suggest that online health communities fall short of providing the support and accountability needed by participants to change their health behavior. Building on this prior work, our research explores the ways that parents learn how to access services and resources through social media sites.

Parent Gender, Education*			Child Gender, Age, Diagnosis†			**
P1	F	GD	M	4	Down Syndrome	f2f
P2	F	CD	M	6	Heart Condition	S
P3	M	CD	M	21	Head Trauma	f2f
P4	F	GD	M,F	4,4	Autism	f2f
P5	F	NA	M	18	Brain Condition	S
P6	F	HS	F	2	Spina Bifida	S
P7	F	HS	M,M ,M	14,11, 5	Celiac, Asperger's, ADHD, Autism	S
P8	F	GD	M	13	Mental Illness, undetermined	S
P9	F	HS	M	4	Mitochondrial Disease, Cerebral Palsy	S
P10	M	HS	M	7	Noonan Syndrome	S
P11	M/F	HS/ HS	F	18	Learning Disorder, Fatty Oxidation Disorder	f2f
P12	F	CD	F	18	Brain Tumor	f2f
P13	F	GD	F	5	Down Syndrome	f2f
P14	F	GD	F	7	Cerebral Palsy	f2f
P15	F	HS	M	3	Cerebral Palsy	f2f
P16	F	GD	F	2	Abnormal Brain Development	S
P17	F	GD	M	6	Down Syndrome	S
P18	F	NA	M	6	Down Syndrome	S
P19	M	GD	M	6	Prune Belly Syndrome	S
P20	M	CD	M	6	ADHD	f2f
P21	M	CD	M	8	Smith-Magenis Syndrome	S
P22	M	GD	F	6	Autism	P
P23	M	CD	F	9	Down's	P
P24	M	GD	F	9	Smith-Magenis Syndrome	P
P25	M	CD	M	10	Autism	P
P26	M	HS	M,M F,F	14,12, 9,9	Autism, ADHD	P
P27	M	CD	M	5	Autism	P
P28	M	GD	M,M	5,3	Autism, Fetal Alcohol Syndrome	P
P29	M	HS	M	6	Autism	f2f
P30	M	GD	M	5	Down Syndrome	S
P31	M	CD	M	21	Autism	P
P32	M	GD	F	9	Deaf, Blind	P
P33	M	GD	M	7	CHARGE Syndrome	P
P34	M	GD	M	6	Autism	P
P35	M	CD	M	9	Wilson's Disease	S
P36	M	CD	F	7	Down Syndrome	P
P37	M/F	CD GD	F	6	Sjogren-Larsson Syndrome	S
P38	M	CD	F	5	Micro deletions	S
P39	M	GD	M	12	Autism	P
P40	M	CD	F	10	Marfan Syndrome	P
P41	M	GD	M	5	Autism	P
P42	M	GD	F	15	Cerebral Palsy	P
P43	M	HS	F	6	Sturge-Weber	P

Table 1: *GD: Graduate Degree; CD: College Degree; HS: High School. M: Married, D: Divorced, W: Widowed. **f2f=face to face; P=Phone; S=Skype.

METHODS

We conducted 43 interviews with a parent of a child with special needs in the United States. Our recruitment process embraced a broad definition of special needs. Thus, if parents responded to our recruitment messages and considered themselves parents of children with special needs, we invited them to participate in our interview. We recruited participants through hospital systems, community organizations, Facebook groups, and snowball sampling. For Facebook groups, we asked permission of the group administrators before posting a recruitment message to the group. We conducted interviews until we reached data saturation, hearing consistent themes from participants. However, our first phase of interviews oversampled mothers, a phenomenon that has been frequently observed in research studies of parents. To address this imbalance, we recruited fathers in a second phase. We again conducted interviews until we reached data saturation, hearing consistent themes from fathers. The interview protocol with fathers was similar to the protocol in the first phase, with additional questions specific to fatherhood.

In total, we conducted 43 interviews with 17 mothers and 28 fathers (two interviews were with husband and wife pairs for a total of 45 participants). Nineteen participants' highest level of education was graduate degrees, 15 had college degrees, and 11 had high school diplomas (see Table 1 for participant demographics). Of the participants, 38 were married, 6 had been previously married but were now separated or divorced, and one was widowed. Participants had between one to four children, 18 of whom were female and 32 of whom were male, a distribution that reflects the more frequent rate of special needs among boys. Autism was the most common diagnosis (n=12); others ranged from relatively common conditions like Down Syndrome to rare conditions like Smith-Magenis Syndrome and Noonan Syndrome.

Interviews were conducted in-person, over the phone, or on Skype. In-person interviews were conducted in local coffee shops or the participants' workplace in a U.S. city. We conducted interviews in 11 states, including in the West, Midwest, South, and Northeast. In-person participants completed a paper consent form, and telephone and Skype participants completed a web-based consent form. The interviews ranged in length from 40 minutes to 2.5 hours (due to interruptions) and the median length was 53 minutes. We used a semi-structured interview protocol. We began with warm-up questions about the participant's family and daily life. The focus of the interview was split into two sections: the child's special needs and the parent's social media use. The first section asked about the child's needs, when she was diagnosed, and how the family's life was impacted after the diagnosis.

The second section focused on how parents used social media sites to learn about caring for their children's needs. We asked parents about what sites they visited, what recent interactions they had on the site, where they felt comfortable sharing information about their children online or not, and who they trusted on these sites. The interviews were transcribed and coded using NVivo. We coded each of the interview transcripts from the first phase using an inductive approach [12]. The research team discussed the codes then conducted a second pass of coding. After conducting the second phase of interviews, we conducted a final pass of coding across all of the interviews. Discussing the themes iteratively resulted in 17 main themes. Table 2 depicts five of the main themes derived throughout the theme description process. Most respondents (n=38) described their use of Facebook; all of them discussed the use of social media.

Limitations

Participants in this study identified as heterosexual and were currently married or had been married. This research oversampled participants with graduate degrees. Because we recruited parents through special needs organizations offline and online, we interviewed parents who were by definition engaged in empowerment processes. This is particularly important to note because studies suggest that low income families and single-mother families have higher rates of special needs children [33].

Theme	# interviews	# instances
Social media used by parents	43	448
Interacting with service organizations	32	112
Information seeking	36	95
Social support	32	95
Privacy and disclosure management	27	63

Table 2. Subset of key themes from interviews.

RESULTS

Results are organized around three major stages observed in parents' stories raising a child with special needs: going online after receiving a diagnosis, learning about services from other parents, and becoming advocates for the child's needs. For each, we draw on empowerment theory to describe the challenges parents experience and the process of becoming empowered that they go through.

Going Online after Receiving a Diagnosis

As they adjusted to their new roles, participants felt overwhelmed by the amount of information they received after their child's diagnosis. They went home and searched keywords provided to them by their health care provider to better grasp their child's diagnosis.

> There's a lot of medical terms that are thrown at us all the time… we just have to Google. Google these terms and what they mean and what things that it comes up with just to get an idea, because we don't always know and the doctor sometimes just throw it all on us. -P15

Some participants tried to educate themselves about their child's condition, oftentimes developing an understanding that helped them to steer their health care providers to a more specific diagnosis. P20's primary care physician had diagnosed their child with sensory processing disorder but his wife believed it was attention deficit hyperactivity disorder and was eventually shown to be right. Similarly, P24's wife found out about a genetic test "by doing research online" which they requested, and which led to their child's diagnosis. However, online information-seeking had downsides. Participants felt that the prognoses they received through doing online research themselves was too negative. Searching online often returned the worst possible outcome, leaving participants feeling "anxious" and "depressed" after viewing negative prognoses online.

> Google is the worst for giving you like worst case scenario. So, I always talk to families, I'm like, "Don't Google stuff. Just don't do that." That's what I used to kind of at the beginning of our journey with William [pseudonym] and it was just... You'll just read bad stuff and kind of the bad side to it about life expectancy and stuff like that. So, I always try and turn families away from going to Google. -P08

Turning to Social Media Sites to Overcome Anxiety

To help overcome feelings of anxiousness and depression resulting from these prognoses, participants sought out information from other parents on Facebook groups about topics like medications, hospital services, specially designed clothes, and special education services. Participants also valued the experiential information they could gather on Facebook:

> You can search a website, you can Google things, you can glean or gather information on the web in millions of sites but to talk to someone that does it day-in-day-out, I think that probably the most informative and helpful way. And that's what I found on Facebook... If I needed a question answered, I have a couple of friends that I know I'd be able to just type in their name, ask a question and be able to get a response in a pretty timely manner. -P16

Such stories revealed other children's ages, severity of condition, and other details, enabling participants to believe that children could achieve the same outcomes.

> [Facebook] is a great avenue to bring people together, you know, worldwide. And just say, "Wow, there's Janie. Her daughter did that? You know she didn't walk until 4? Mine didn't walk until 4." You know, we feel better about it because we're not alone... And learning information takes that fear away because of the medical side doesn't always... They don't know how to connect with families. -P10

On Facebook groups participants followed other parents' stories about their children's progress, especially when their children were undergoing an operation, starting new medications, moving to a new school, or experiencing other transitions.

> I've read [about] other kids... having a similar surgery to what we had... I read their day-to-day update, then I see what happens so that when my kid's in the hospital having surgery, I can [be prepared].... stuff like that, that I wouldn't have known if I hadn't read about other people's stories. -P02

Parents reported lurking online before posting, allowing them to identify individuals and communities with children with similar conditions. For participants whose children experienced sensory challenges, narratives about navigating daily life were valuable. For example, some children with autism had negative reactions when sitting in a chair at the dentist office or the barber shop, and relied on local information about dentists and barbers who had more experience working with children with special needs. Parents also relied on local Facebook groups to access local services like accessible playgrounds (e.g., for children with Cerebral Palsy) and other appropriate activities.

Role Changing and Coping Behaviors

Diagnosis of a special need occurred at three different stages: 1) neonatal diagnosis, before the child was born (e.g., Down Syndrome, Spina Bifida); 2) diagnosis at birth (e.g., Cerebral Palsy); and 3) diagnosis when developmental milestones were not met (e.g., Autism Spectrum Disorder, Attention Deficit Hyperactivity Disorder). Each of these kinds of diagnosis introduced unique challenges and opportunities for participants. When participants first learned of a diagnosis, they recalled being in a state of shock and told us could not remember most of what their primary health provider said during the appointment where they received their child's diagnosis. Many participants indicated that their friends, colleagues, neighbors and at times, even family members, could not understand the conditions they were experiencing. During the early post-diagnosis stages, participants struggled to cope with the diagnosis and the impact it would have on the rest of their life. As one participant explained:

> When [my son] was first born, I was extremely angry with how he was, and I didn't want to be around a lot of my friends that had perfectly normal children. Because all I heard was "oh, you know, little Johnny did this and did that" and my kid can't even eat. So it was extremely difficult the first couple of years. -P19

Participants noted that they experienced a role change from identifying as a parent to identifying as a parent of a child with special needs. Through this identification process, they started to comprehend that their children might not live a typical childhood and they began to go on social media as part of the coping process. Accessing other families of children with special needs helped them to learn how to cope with and adapt to their new roles and identities.

Learning about Services from other Parents Online

Participants told us that finding social workers and care providers who could help them find the resources and services they needed was an ongoing struggle and often a stressful and emotional one. Health and education systems were difficult to navigate and required learning how to manage multiple people, stakeholders, and obstacles. As one parent said:

> The whole art of handling kids is learning how to navigate hundreds of people in your life. So you have a social worker from the school who ends up being useless. You have a social worker from the ventilation clinic. You have a social worker from the ICU. You

> have a social worker from the Cardiac unit. You have the local county's social worker. And then you have a social worker from hospice. They were all from different organizations, but they're all trying to help give you resources. -P10

Most parents echoed this observation, lamenting that social workers did not have adequate or accurate information. One participant whose child has cerebral palsy said that most families were served by a children's services department for the state she lived in, but felt that this service was "clueless" when she tried to call them or go to their website for help. Participants emphasized that experiential information from families online helped them to overcome gaps in their knowledge about navigating health and medical care. Providers often did not have the time or ability to form strong social connections with a family and address all of their needs. One parent shared:

> Our daughter, she's 15, it becomes a hard job to bathe her because she's so big and she's very clumsy. Physically, I can do it. My wife can't do it anymore. Through these discussions in this [Facebook] group, I discovered that there was a service that you can use, and it's actually free of charge, where twice a week somebody comes and bathes her. -P42

While parents had to deal with varying health resources depending on type and severity of their children's special need, almost all of them had to negotiate for special education services with government agencies.

Learning about School Services

Participants told us the school IEP was one of the most difficult and demanding processes they had to manage. They reported that school administration and specialists who took part in the IEP evaluation process acted as gatekeepers, limiting their children's access to resources. Each school district maintained different processes and requirements for serving special needs children and websites were under-maintained, if they existed at all. As a result, parents received little information about how to discover what services were available and what services their child was entitled to. Further, the cycle of requesting a service and being denied was an emotionally draining process that left them exhausted and angry.

Participants turned to social media sites to learn more about these services. In particular, they relied heavily on Facebook Groups to learn how they should advocate for needed services. Within these groups they could read other parents' stories about negotiating IEP processes in a particular school district. Drawing on these stories, participants were able to discover what services their particular school district typically provided, what services would be best suited for their children, and whether service providers were known to withhold mandated services.

> Because my wife and I work in a tandem on a lot of stuff, she asked a lot of questions from the folks here locally and I did a lot of research online, talking to some of the families that I noticed were sharing a lot [about] their IEP programs, the challenges... some of the tips to help improve in those areas. And my wife and I would share notes of how to approach IEPs more effectively. -P25

In cases in which other parents reported that they had experienced difficulty accessing services through the school, participants became aware that they might have to negotiate more forcefully for their own children's needs. Accessing other parents online prepared parents for a battle they might have to fight, mitigating the power imbalance parents experience when they face special needs providers by arming them with knowledge and insight about how the process will play out.

Becoming Advocates for a Cause

The process of trying to access services for their child with the support of other parents online pushed participants to embrace advocacy beyond the needs of their own child. Participants typically posted on their Twitter or Facebook timelines about legal, policy, and budgetary issues related to their children's condition. P01 used Twitter, saying that being an advocate was "part of [her] Twitter identity". P08 similarly said she preferred to use her Twitter for advocacy purposes, keeping it "pretty clean" while her Facebook feed was more personal and "quite a bit livelier and funnier." Other participants preferred Facebook over Twitter's character limit. P23 and his wife used their Facebook timeline to "out" the diagnosis of their child, saying:

> I guess the biggest event for us was that we actually outed my daughter about a year and a half ago. So a lot of people in our network, even cousins and uncles and aunts, actually didn't know her diagnosis because we didn't want to use that to define who she was… [But] we really, really wanted to boost fundraising [for] this non-profit that we're organized with. -P23

Facebook Groups for Advocacy

Participants who had become advocates or had participated in the process of advocacy described two kinds of Facebook Groups: more private groups to organize and strategize and more public groups to advocate for policy change. Participants circulated online petitions in both of these platforms, especially when seeking change within local or national organizations or legal processes. Some participants also advocated in-person either in their local cities or by traveling to their local state capitols. P12 had traveled to Washington, D.C. to advocate in person and now used Facebook to recruit other parents to send letters to their congressmen. Participants such as P12, whose child was now 18 and had moved through the childcare system, not only had become advocates for the cause but also began to offer themselves as resources to help new parents. These "veteran" participants identified themselves as people who knew the system, and could help newly diagnosed parents who would be following in their footsteps. They took on the responsibility of providing resources and practical advice for parents coping with a new diagnosis. P21 shared about the Smith-Magenis group he created:

> It's mostly newly diagnosed people saying, "Hey, I just got this diagnosis and here's a picture of my kid and I'm glad that I know that we're not alone." Fifty people say, "Welcome to the group. Welcome to the journey. Here's some resources for you." It's a lot of that stuff. But also fundraising updates, research updates, conference updates, stuff like that. -P21

Addressing Rare Conditions

Participants whose children had rare conditions were especially likely to embrace and give back to their online communities. Because they typically could not find extensive resources online or in bookstores (and often, their healthcare providers knew less about the condition), they shared experiential information online with other parents worldwide. For example, P37's daughter was diagnosed with Sjögren-Larsson Syndrome (SLS), a rare syndrome, the symptoms of which intersect with other syndromes, making it hard to diagnosis and treat. P37 could not find offline support groups or organizations and there was no SLS Facebook Group so P37 created it himself:

> So, right away, I just was thinking, "Well, this is rare. I've come to this growing huge social media site [Facebook] looking for information, and there is none. That means somebody else is somewhere doing the same thing, or will do, or has done the same thing I'm doing. So, I should create just some page with the name of that syndrome on it." -P37

At the time of the interview, the SLS Facebook page had 141 likes and had connected SLS families in the U.S., Jordan, Iran, France, and Sweden, among other countries. Participants also described interacting directly with families with rare conditions. When P40's daughter was diagnosed with Marfan Syndrome, they learned of another family who had this condition, contacted them through email and began Skyping with them. P21, whose son was diagnosed with Smith-Maginis Syndrome described "emergency Skyping sessions" that mothers organized on their Facebook groups if they had had a particularly difficult day. Though participants with less rare, high prevalent, conditions also engaged in these behaviors, they did not report having to work as hard to find online support groups for their children's condition.

Participants in densely populated urban areas could typically find local organizations and other parents to meet in person (e.g., through a hospital). However, participants in rural areas often did not have access to local organizations and thus, created and relied on Facebook Groups and other channels like Listservs that offered coordinating mechanisms. In some cases, these Facebook groups evolved into 501(c)(3) non-profits and other "real, formalized groups" as P19 termed them.

> We've created a Facebook page for our group. It's a [state] non-profit, working on federal non-profit status. So, with other, a couple of other parents.... We all wanted to create something that was missing up in the [rural region], so we developed it sort of grass roots, so we're very much a grass roots organization. -P09

Creating an online identity and brand helped legitimize a particular cause or need, which was especially important among geographically isolated parents who might otherwise feel unable to access the support they needed.

DISCUSSION

Towards a Model of Networked Empowerment

Through their process of adjusting to their child's diagnosis, parents work to overcome the anxiety and uncertainty that follows a diagnosis, navigate the complex process of accessing services, and become advocates for their child's needs as well as for the special needs cause more generally. Results reveal categories of social media behaviors that map to components of psychological empowerment from prior work [51] (see Figure 1). Specifically, the intrapersonal component (how people think about themselves) involves reading other parents' stories, posting questions to other parents, developing cognitive models of how to care for one's own child, and developing the belief that one can care for their own child. The interactional component (people's awareness and ability to act towards goals) involves learning about health and education services, developing an understanding of these services, and learning how to access resources within them. Finally, the behavioral component (taking action to achieve broader outcomes) involves answering other parents' questions, welcoming newly diagnosed parents, creating groups for sharing information or advocacy, and campaigning and fundraising on social media sites.

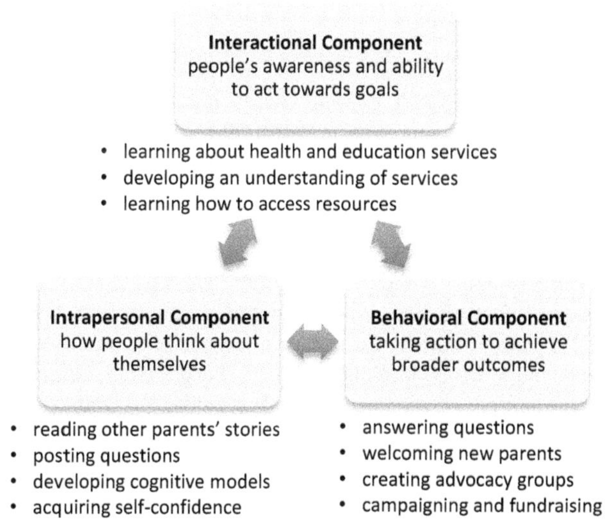

Figure 1. Model of networked empowerment on social media sites that builds on psychological empowerment theory [51].

Drawing on these social media behaviors and empowerment components we introduce the concept of *networked empowerment* that describes how social media sites help parents to find other parents, overcome power imbalances between parents and service providers, and mobilize resources to support the special needs cause. Unlike with offline groups, parents are now able to do this through almost real-time access to other parents on Facebook. boyd and Ellison describe social networking sites as public or semi-public profiles, with articulated lists of users, and an ability to traverse profiles and content [8,15]. Similarly, Wellman and Rainie [46] describe the web as a networked social operating system in which the "boundaries between producers and consumers are becoming blurred", and "the boundaries that used to exist between public realms and private havens are no longer as rigid." Prior empowerment theories insufficiently account for parents' ability to find and "traverse" other parents' profiles and/or content and access knowledge and resources to overcome health and education structures.

We find that parents engage in what Huh and Ackerman [20] referred to as "illness trajectory alignment" as they looked for parents whose children suffered from similar conditions and who maintained similar illness "medical models" [28]. Parents collectively engage in collaborative sensemaking [35] of their children's medical conditions. When they found such parents, they might communicate with them in other means (e.g. form a closed Facebook group, communicate through Skype, or meet in person). Specifically, when advocating for change through, parents often use Twitter and public Facebook Groups while opting to use closed or secret Facebook groups when discussing potentially stigmatizing conditions related to their children's needs. The next section presents design recommendations for supporting networked empowerment for families online.

Design Approaches for Networked Empowerment

Needs-Based Search: Finding Other Parents

Parents feel anxious after looking up a diagnosis online, a phenomenon described as "cyberchondria" by White and Horvitz which they define as unfounded escalations of concerns about symptom [48]. After this point, parents turn to social media sites, where they can access information, resources, and advice from other parents. Prior work suggests that chronic disease patients reverted to online health communities for support, especially family and friend support is lacking, [28,41]. Participants described health and education special needs services as complex and confusing, a sentiment documented in prior literature (e.g., [45]). Echoing Davis et al. [13], participants reported that they relied heavily on veteran parents on social media sites to learn about IEPs and to prepare for their IEP meeting.

Though Facebook groups for special needs are pervasive (searching for "[city name] + autism" typically returns a variety of results), searching Facebook groups for a particular condition returns a list of groups that has little apparent structure or order. As a result, parents may join groups that are not the best fit for their needs, and may miss groups that are relevant. Prior work suggests that parents of children with special needs use groups either based on location or on diagnosis [5]. One design solution is for sites like Facebook to index groups by diagnosis and region, allowing parents to more quickly find relevant groups to them.

An additional challenge facing online platforms is how to provide summaries and visualizations of content to a newcomer. This need is especially pressing in the context of health concerns (and indeed, researchers are looking to address this problem [32]). Integrating join dates, profile information, and content shared could provide a unique kind of profile that allows parents to find other parents in similar stages of a diagnosis. However, a challenge would be balancing privacy considerations for parents who may not want their families' healthcare needs indexed online (though, it is worth noting that participation in any of these groups makes this information already stored in Facebook's servers). In addition, parents may eagerly welcome new parents who fit the demographics of the group, but may want the content (and perhaps even existence) of the group to remain private to everyone else, making findability of such groups for newly diagnosed parents an important challenge for social media designers.

Network Structure for Resource Mobilization and Advocacy

Empowerment models have typically described community involvement in organizations and neighborhoods [51]. This research extends that work into online spaces, highlighting community involvement on social media sites, primarily Facebook. Extensive prior work has shown how information spreads through social networks (e.g., [10]). Our work explores how parents access information in the context of special needs care. Parents learn to navigate service providers and negotiate for services with these providers, transforming what might be an isolated, stigmatized process of seeking access to services to a networked process. Indeed, veteran parents also began to advocate on a broader level than their child's own needs, educating other parents, community members, and sometimes lawmakers in both their online and offline environments. By tapping into online groups and gaining critical awareness, participants learned how to mobilize resources to negotiate for their children's needs, a process that requires bringing together a collective group of people and organizations [29]. However, translating networked activity among parents to collective movements that impact policy at a local and national level is more challenging. One approach is to use automated techniques to understand what policy challenges are expressed by parents, which kinds of services and organizations are over- or under-delivering necessary services, and how services and parents might work together in collaboration rather than opposition towards shared goals. While we find that parents turn to social media sites for mobilization and advocacy, there is little evidence that such efforts have resulted in change on a local or global scale. Future work in HCI should investigate the effects of mobilization for accessing health services and should explore ways of designing social media sites that better support parents and caregivers to perform this advocacy work.

CONCLUSION

We introduce a new model of networked empowerment that highlights how social media facilitates the process of empowerment through access to other parents at various stages of the special needs trajectory. These results can be translated to other contexts where individuals need to overcome structural boundaries to access services, especially related to health and education needs. Future research should investigate the experiences of parents who do not learn how to access care for their child and how they might be better supported to do so. Future work should also explore crowdsourcing techniques for collecting and aggregating information about how to navigate and access education and health services.

ACKNOWLEDGEMENTS

We thank Facebook for their support of this work. Any opinion, findings, and conclusions or recommendations expressed in this material are those of the authors and do not necessarily reflect the views of Facebook.

REFERENCES

1. Abramson, L.Y., Seligman, M.E., and Teasdale, J.D. Learned helplessness in humans: critique and reformulation. *J. of Abn. Psych.87*, 1 (1978), 49.
2. Ainbinder, J.G., Blanchard, L.W., Singer, G.H., et al. A qualitative study of parent to parent support for parents of children with special needs. *Journal of Pediatric Psychology 23*, 2 (1998), 99–109.
3. Altshuler, S.J. and Kopels, S. Advocating in schools for children with disabilities: What's new with IDEA? *Social Work 48*, 3 (2003), 320–329.
4. Ames, M., Bardzell, J., Bardzell, S., Lindtner, S., Mellis, D., and Rosner, D. Making Cultures: Empowerment, Participation, and Democracy – or Not? In *Ext Abst CHI 2014*, 1087-1092.
5. Ammari, T., Morris, M.R., and Schoenebeck, S.Y. Accessing Social Support and Overcoming Judgment on Social Media among Parents of Children with Special Needs. In *Proc. ICWSM*, (2014).
6. Bandura, A. *Social Learning Theory*. General Learning Press, New York, 1977.
7. Bennett, T., DeLuca, D.A., and Allen, R.W. Families of children with disabilities: Positive adaptation across the life cycle. *Children & Schools 18*, 1 (1996), 31–44.
8. boyd, danah and Ellison, N. Social network sites: Definition, history, and scholarship. *13*, 1 (2007), 11.
9. Boyle, C.A., Boulet, S., Schieve, L.A., et al. Trends in the prevalence of developmental disabilities in US children, 1997–2008. *Ped. 127*, 6 (2011), 1034–1042.
10. Centola, D. The spread of behavior in an online social network experiment. *Science 329*, 5996 (2010), 1194–1197.
11. Chung, J.E. Social interaction in online support groups: Preference for online social interaction over offline social interaction. *Computers in Human Behavior 29*, 4 (2013), 1408–1414.
12. Corbin, J. and Strauss, A. *Basics of Qualitative Research: Techniques and Procedures for Developing Grounded Theory*. SAGE, 2008.
13. Davis, T.S., Gavazzi, S.M., Scheer, S.D., and Uppal, R. Measuring individualized parent advocate services in children's mental health: A contextualized theoretical application. *Journal of Child and Family Studies 20*, 5 (2011), 669–684.
14. Davison, K.P., Pennebaker, J.W., and Dickerson, S.S. Who talks? The social psychology of illness support groups. *American Psychologist 55*, 2 (2000), 205.
15. Ellison, N.B. and boyd, D. Sociality through social network sites. *The Oxford handbook of internet studies*, (2013), 151.
16. Fitzpatrick, G. and Ellingsen, G. A review of 25 years of CSCW research in healthcare: contributions, challenges and future agendas. *Computer Supported Cooperative Work (CSCW) 22*, 4-6 (2013), 609–665.
17. Floyd, F.J. and Gallagher, E.M. Parental stress, care demands, and use of support services for school-age children with disabilities and behavior problems. *Family Relations*, (1997), 359–371.
18. Gowen, J.W., Christy, D.S., and Sparling, J. Informational needs of parents of young children with special needs. *J. of Early Int. 17*, 2 (1993), 194–210.
19. Hu, C., Kung, S., Rummans, T.A., Clark, M.M., and Lapid, M.I. Reducing caregiver stress with internet-based interventions: a systematic review of open-label and randomized controlled trials. *JAMIA*, (2014), amiajnl–2014.
20. Huh, J. and Ackerman, M.S. Collaborative help in chronic disease management: supporting individualized problems. In *Proc. CSCW '12, ACM* (2012), 853–862.
21. Huws, J., Jones, R., and Ingledew, D. Parents of Children with Autism using an Email Group: A Grounded Theory Study. *Journal of Health Psychology 6*, 5 (2001), 569–584.
22. Ladner, R.E. Access and Empowerment: Commentary on "Computers and People with Disabilities." *ACM Trans. Access. Comput. 1*, 2 (2008), 11:1–11:5.
23. Lake, J. and Billingsley, B. An Analysis of Factors That Contribute to Parent-School Conflict in Special Education. *Rem. & Spec. Ed. 21*, 4 (2000), 240–251.

24. Lindell, M.K. and Perry, R.W. *Behavioral foundations of community emergency planning.* Hemisphere Publishing Corp, 1992.
25. Ludlow, A., Skelly, C., and Rohleder, P. (2011). Challenges faced by parents of children diagnosed with autism spectrum disorder. *Journal of health psychology, 17*(5), 702-711.
26. Malinverni, L., MoraGuiard, J., Padillo, V., Mairena, M., Hervás, A., and Pares, N. Participatory Design Strategies to Enhance the Creative Contribution of Children with Special Needs. In *Proc. IDC '14.*
27. Mandell, D.S. and Salzer, M.S. Who joins support groups among parents of children with autism? *Autism 11*, 2 (2007), 111–122.
28. Mankoff, J., Kuksenok, K., Kiesler, S., Rode, J.A., and Waldman, K. Competing online viewpoints and models of chronic illness. In *Proc. CHI '11, ACM* (2011), 589–598.
29. McCarthy, J.D. and Zald, M.N. The enduring vitality of the resource mobilization theory of social movements. In *Handbook of sociological theory.* Springer, 2001, 533–565.
30. McPherson, M., Arango, P., Fox, H., et al. A new definition of children with special health care needs. *Pediatrics 102*, 1 Pt 1 (1998), 137–140.
31. Meyer, J., Scott, W.R., and Strang, D. Centralization, fragmentation, and school district complexity. *Administrative Science Quarterly*, (1987), 186–201.
32. Miller, K. Care Coordination Impacts on Access to Care for Children with Special Health Care Needs Enrolled in Medicaid and CHIP. *Maternal and child health journal*, (2013), 1–9.
33. Newacheck, P.W., Strickland, B., Shonkoff, J.P., et al. An epidemiologic profile of children with special health care needs. *Pediatrics 102*, 1 (1998), 117–123.
34. Newman, M.W., Lauterbach, D., Munson, S.A., Resnick, P., and Morris, M.E. It's not that I don't have problems, I'm just not putting them on Facebook: challenges and opportunities in using online social networks for health. In *Proc. CSCW '11*, ACM (2011), 341–350.
35. Paul, S.A. and Reddy, M.C. Understanding together: sensemaking in collaborative information seeking. In *Proc. CSCW '10*, ACM (2010), 321–330.
36. Rappaport, J. Empowerment meets narrative: Listening to stories and creating settings. *American Journal of community psychology 23*, 5 (1995), 795–807.
37. Rich, R.C., Edelstein, M., Hallman, W.K., and Wandersman, A.H. Citizen participation and empowerment: The case of local environmental hazards. *American Journal of Community Psychology 23*, 5 (1995), 657–676.
38. Shneiderman, B. Human Values and the Future of Technology: A Declaration of Empowerment. In *Proc. of the Conference on Computers and the Quality of Life, ACM* (1990), 1-6.
39. Shroff, G. and Kam, M. Towards a Design Model for Women's Empowerment in the Developing World. *In Proc. CHI 2011, ACM* (2011), 2867-2876.
40. Singer, G.H., Marquis, J., Powers, L.K., et al. A multi-site evaluation of parent to parent programs for parents of children with disabilities. *Journal of Early Intervention 22*, 3 (1999), 217–229.
41. Skeels, M.M., Unruh, K.T., Powell, C., and Pratt, W. Catalyzing social support for breast cancer patients. In *Proc. CHI '10, ACM* (2010), 173–182.
42. Trainor, A.A. Reexamining the promise of parent participation in special education: An analysis of cultural and social capital. *Anthropology & Education Quarterly 41*, 3 (2010), 245–263.
43. Van Uden-Kraan, C.F., Drossaert, C.H., Taal, E., Shaw, B.R., Seydel, E.R., and van de Laar, M.A. Empowering processes and outcomes of participation in online support groups for patients with breast cancer, arthritis, or fibromyalgia. *Qualitative Health Research 18*, 3 (2008), 405–417.
44. Wallston, K.A. Perceived control and health behaviour. *Cambridge handbook of psychology, health and medicine 1*, (1997).
45. Wang, M., Mannan, H., Poston, D., Turnbull, A.P., and Summers, J.A. Parents' perceptions of advocacy activities and their impact on family quality of life. *Research & Practice for Persons with Severe Disabilities 29*, 2 (2004).
46. Wellman, B. and Rainie, L. *Networked: The new social operating system.* Cambridge, The MIT Press, 2012.
47. White, M. and Dorman, S.M. Receiving social support online: implications for health education. *Health education research 16*, 6 (2001), 693–707
48. White, R.W. and Horvitz, E. Cyberchondria: studies of the escalation of medical concerns in web search. *ACM TOIS 27*, 4 (2009), 23.
49. Wise, M. and Kenworthy, L. *Preventing industrial toxic hazards: A guide for communities.* Inform, 1990.
50. Wyngaarden Krauss, M., Wells, N., Gulley, S., and Anderson, B. Navigating systems of care: Results from a national survey of families of children with special health care needs. *Children's Services: Social Policy, Research, and Practice 4*, 4 (2001), 165–187.
51. Zimmerman, M.A. Psychological empowerment: Issues and illustrations. *American journal of community psychology 23*, 5 (1995), 581–599.

Toward 3D-Printed Movable Tactile Pictures for Children with Visual Impairments

Jeeeun Kim
University of Colorado Boulder
430 UCB
Boulder, Colorado 80309 USA
jeeeun.kim@colorado.edu

Tom Yeh
University of Colorado Boulder
430 UCB
Boulder, Colorado 80309 USA
tom.yeh@colorado.edu

ABSTRACT
Many children's books contain movable pictures with elements that can be physically opened, closed, pushed, pulled, spun, flipped, or swung. But these tangible, interactive reading experiences are inaccessible to children with visual impairments. This paper presents a set of 3D-printable models designed as building blocks for creating movable tactile pictures that can be touched, moved, and understood by children with visual impairments. Examples of these models are canvases, connectors, hinges, spinners, sliders, lifts, walls, and cutouts. They can be used to compose movable tactile pictures to convey a range of spatial concepts, such as in/out, up/down, and high/low. The design and development of these models were informed by three formative studies including 1) a survey on popular moving mechanisms in children's books and 3D-printed parts to implement them, 2) two workshops on the process creating movable tactile pictures by hand (e.g., Lego, Play-Doh), and 3) creation of wood-based prototypes and an informal testing on sighted preschoolers. Also, we propose a design language based on XML and CSS for specifying the content and structure of a movable tactile picture. Given a specification, our system can generate a 3D-printable model. We evaluate our approach by 1) transcribing six children's books, and 2) conducting six interviews on domain experts including five teachers for the visually impaired, one blind adult, two publishers at the National Braille Press, a renowned tactile artist, and a librarian.

Author Keywords
Tactile Pictures; 3D Printing; Movables; 3D Modeling;

ACM Classification Keywords
H.5.m. Information interfaces and presentation

INTRODUCTION
Movable pictures, such as those found in lift-the-flap books, are popular in children's books. They are beneficial for the development of emergent literacy in young children. These pictures are movable in that the paper on which the pictures are printed has non-stationary parts that children can move with their hands by lifting, pulling, and spinning these parts. These movements then cause the visual content of the pictures to change. For example, when the child lifts a flap, another object that was previously hidden underneath the flap appears, as shown in Figure 1. These types of tangible interactions with movable pictures are mostly paper-based with no electronics involved. Through such interactions, children are able to connect kinetic experiences (flipping) with visual experiences (something appears).

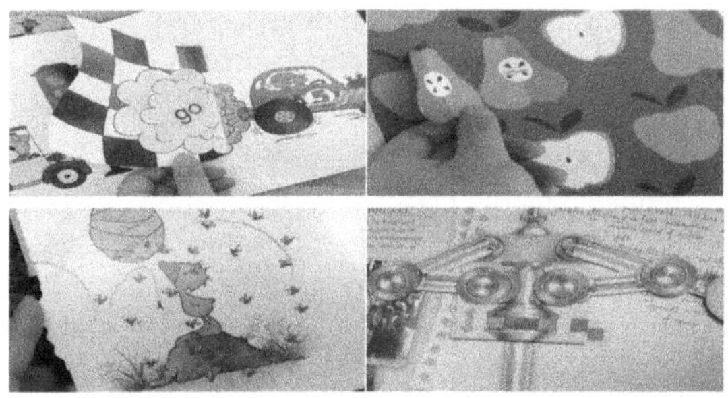

Figure 1. Current children's books with movable parts, flipping paper flap to uncover hid pictures(top), roll spinner seeing iterative hid pictures(bottom left), or slide up to trigger other parts' movement(bottom right).

For children who are visually impaired (VI), however, the benefits of movable pictures are limited. VI children can still obtain the kinetic experiences as they flip, pull, and spin. But they are unable to relate these kinetic experiences to corresponding visual experiences. They are unable to see that a flap is a part of an object or that there is another object underneath. When the visual experiences are inaccessible, the kinetic experiences offer limited benefits.

Figure 2. 3D-printed stationary tactile pictures from Goodnight Moon (top), Harold and Purple Crayon (bottom).

CHI 2015, April 18 - 23 2015, Seoul, Republic of Korea
Copyright 2015 ACM 978-1-4503-3145-6/15/04...$15.00
http://dx.doi.org/10.1145/2702123.2702144

3D printing has been shown to be a promising method to interpolate pictures in regular children's books accessible to VI children [13, 19]. A picture can be 3D modeled and printed to be touched, felt, and understood by a VI child. Figure 2 includes some examples of 3D-printed tactile pictures based on *Goodnight Moon* and *Harold and the Purple Crayon*, two children's book classics. However, thus far, 3D printing has been limited to static images.

Figure 3. 3D-printed *movable* tactile pictures (our work).

In this paper, we present a set of 3D structures designed as building blocks for creating *movable* tactile pictures that can be 3D printed (see Figure 3). We further present a design language for specifying the content and the structure of a movable tactile picture based on XML and CSS (analogous to Web design). We evaluate this approach first by transcribing six existing children's books and next by reporting our interviews with domain experts.

RELATED WORK

3D printing has emerged as a promising method for helping parents replicate tactile books [13]. In addition, 3D printing has been used for tactile visualization for people who are visually limited [7]. 3D printing affords ease in replicating and customizing book images, which are key challenges in creating tactile graphics [14], while helping children with visual impairments develop emergent literacy [19].

For parents interested in creating tactile graphics, there are resources and guidelines [18, 20] that introduce essential elements of good tactile pictures. For example, these guidelines emphasize the importance of interaction and mobility. The majority of tactile books have mobility features that guide children's interactions. Figure 1 shows how current tactile books incorporate mobility interactions. A bunny is moving through the book page by page, from the room to the bed, saying goodnight to everything. If tangible interaction provides nonvisual access to the pictures [6, 17], how can we incorporate interaction features into 3D-printed books?

Books that incorporate tangible interactions encouraged children's interests into the content, opening up perceptual motor skill that evolves to linguistic skills [12]. Holding children's attention is the key to develop emergent literacy in association with books [5]. Therefore, books combining various tangible techniques with 3D printing can play a huge role in promoting children's active participation [8, 16]. Because interaction engages disabled children in an inclusive learning process and encourages development of early narratives [4], tangible interaction would be an essential component of 3D-printed tactile books.

The majority of parents and teachers of VI children do not have a clear understanding of 3D printing, even though this emerging technology helps them create unique educational materials for their children [20]. Online 3D design warehouses [11, 15] have provided the easy opportunity for them to print a pre well-made 3D design. For example, it is not necessary to have a refined skillset to design a fine giraffe in 3D; even blind children can print a giraffe via voice command and then touch it to get a notion of what it looks like [21]. 3D warehouses also enable reuse of 3D tactile models for novice designers. But if parents want to customize a premade model by integrating mobility to create a tactile book, how does the technology support their needs is another area uncovered.

FORMATIVE STUDIES

Moving Primitives

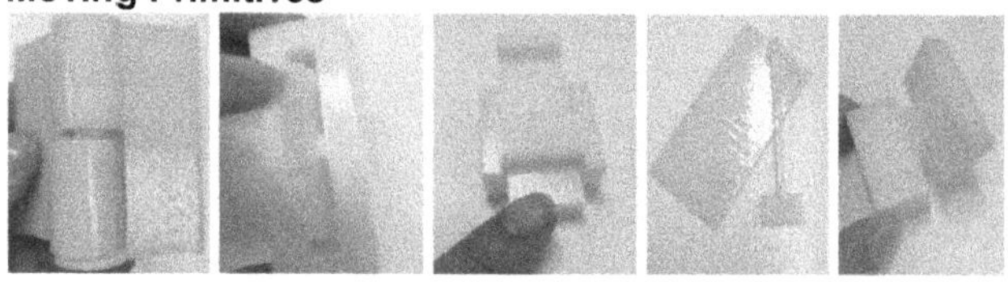

Figure 4. 3D-printed moving primitives, hinge, spinner with holder, pulley, swing, and opener (from left to right).

We undertook first formative study to understand the range and rate of paper-based moving mechanisms appear in today's children's books and to determine whether 3D-printed models can be created to emulate these moving mechanisms. We surveyed many children's books (n > 70), and focused 32 children's books that incorporate movable pictures and identified several common moving structures, such as hinge, pulley, and spinner. Mostly, out of 10 regular books for age 0-3 children who develop very early stage of literacy, 1 book had movable parts, such as lifted flap, and some really popular books were recreated as interactive books. We experimented with different methods that came up from theses books into 3D-equivalents (Figure 4).

Design Workshops

Figure 5. Two design workshops. Participants freely utilize Lego bricks, Play-doh, and other craft materials to design movable tactile pictures from children's book.

Our second formative study was designed to help us understand how individuals would approach the design of movable tactile pictures. We were particularly interested in individuals with high motivation but little or no prior experience with 3D printing. We invited local middle and high school students to participate in two design workshops (n = 6, n = 18, respectively). They came to our workshops as they were self-motivated to learn about a new technology, 3D printing. Figure 5 shows design process from workshops. They were given a task of creating a 3D model based on a movable picture in a children's book. They were free to choose their favorite books to model (more motivation). Instead of using 3D modeling software, students were given a set of physical materials since those are more accessible for novice designer (e.g., Lego bricks, Play-Doh).

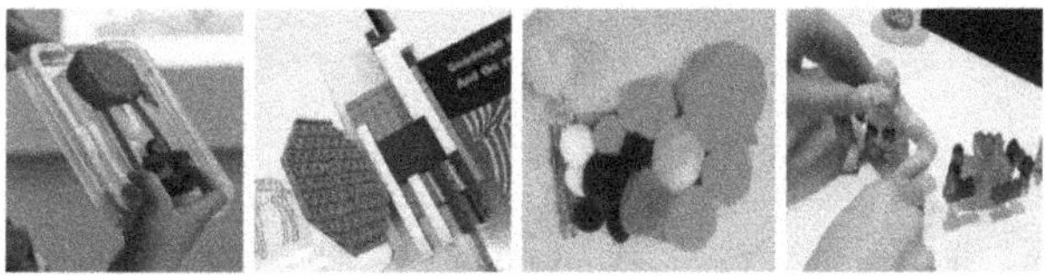

Figure 6. Students' hand-made movable tactile pictures.

Overall, students maintained a high interest throughout the design activity. They created many interesting tactile models (Figure 6), such as a hot-air balloon carrying a boy (*Harold and the Purple Crayon*), a giraffe behind a door that opens (*Dear Zoo*), a butterfly with wings that bend (The Very Hungry Caterpillar) and a gorilla with rotating arms hitting its chest (*From Head to Toe*). They liked to relate familiar experiences with mobile objects, such as flapping wings and swinging doors.

Wood Prototypes

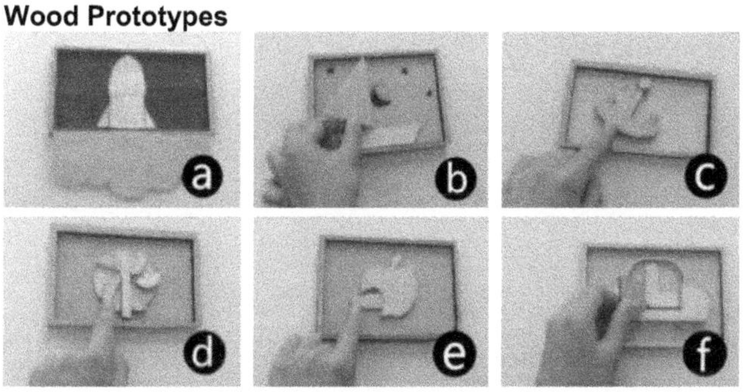

Figure 7. Wooden prototypes of movable tactile pictures. A rocket hidden by cloud (a), the moon uncovered by the waving sail (b), swinging biking (c), a spinning giant wheel with falpping carts (d), a warm passing through the apple (e), and a car with opening door and two spining wheels (f)

The aim of our third formative study was to create initial prototypes of movable tactile pictures and gather preliminary data on how young children may react to these pictures. We used wood as the material and a laser cutter as the fabrication technique to create a series of prototypes to illustrate selected scenes in children's books.

Figure 7 shows some of the prototypes. The rocket covered by a cloud (a) is an example of a hinge, as is the moon behind the sail (b) of a boat. The biking roller coaster (c) is an example of a swing, and the giant wheel is an application of a spinner (d). The spinner is easily applied to any kind of wheel, such as the tire, which is combined with another hinge for the car door, which uncovers a chair and handle inside the car (f). If the rotating angle is limited, it will be also used to represent seesaw, etc. To present a caterpillar that eats through the apple, a pulley is a trigger that enables children to move a part of picture (e).

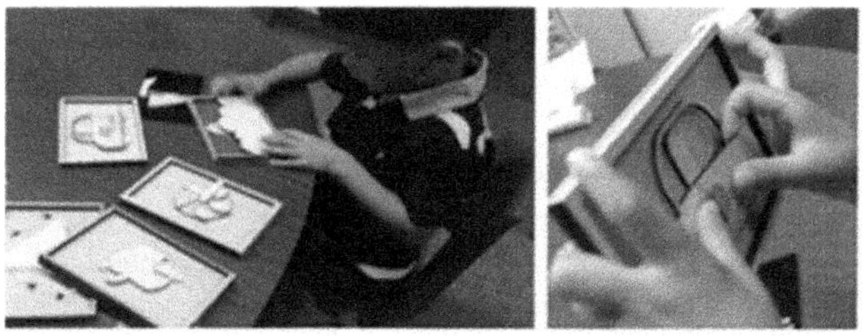

Figure 8. A sighted child plays with a movable tactile picture, playing and interacting like handling toys

We brought our prototypes to a local preschool to observe how sighted preschoolers interacted with these movable pictures. Figure 8 shows how kid plays with tactile pictures. At this early stage of our research, sighted children were good proxies for gathering initial feedback. We were interested in (1) how much they are involved in interaction with pictures, (2) how much they intuitively interact with moving parts, and (3) how they play with moving tactile pictures. Sighted children naturally opened the door of the car, waved the sail of a boat, touched behind the flag, spun the wheel, and pushed and pulled the caterpillar. One child made his own narrative with the rocket while playing, saying, "Ready, 5, 4, 3, 2, 1, blaster!" Another asked what was behind the apple. The sighted preschoolers dealt with the tactile pictures as toys; they had a lot of curiosity, and tinkered with movable part of each picture despite the lack of context.

MOVABLE TACTILE PICTURES

The goal of this research is to enable the creation of 3D printed tactile picture books that a VI child can touch and move. Here, we present a suite of reusable 3D components we developed for the purpose of creating movable tactile pictures.

Design Goals

During our formative studies, we identified a number of design requirements that have influenced many of our design choices as we were developing these 3D components.

- **Easy to move and touch:** This design element supports the goal of the project, i.e., making tactile pictures movable and touchable for VI children.
- **Easy to print:** A model can look nice in a design environment yet not be easy to print with a low-cost 3D printer. The model may have invalid geometry. It may require support material. It may be necessary to break a model into parts that can be separately printed.

• **Easy to assemble:** When the pieces are printed separately, the process of assembling them must be easy.
• **Easy to customize:** It should be possible to customize various aspects of a component.
• **Easy to reuse:** The parts should be easy for people to reuse to make new tactile pictures.
• **Hard to break:** Young children are often *destructive*. Parts should be sufficiently sturdy to allow repeated uses.

There are additional factors worth considering but not as pressing as those above: Are models mass producible? How can we incorporate multiple materials and colors?

Page and Canvas

We modeled a book as a series of tile-like pages. Each page is composed of three types of components: canvases, tactile objects, and connectors. A canvas acts as a container for one or more tactile objects. Each tactile object is physically joined to a canvas by a connector. The most basic page has one canvas, one object, and a connector joining the two. A more complex page may have multiple canvases of different sizes and different heights, all joined together. We model a canvas as a flat, rectangular solid. The attributes are sizes and positions. A canvas can have a frame and rounded corners.

Tactile Objects

Relief

Relief is the most common form of tactile graphics apper in today's children's books for VI children. A tactile artist creates a master mold using clay or equivalent materials. Then a specialized printer is used to press paper against the mold to re/produce the image in relief. Two methods can be used to bring relief patterns into 3D. One way is through the use of a 3D scanner. Another way is to use computer vision to extract salient features and map them to different heights. Then a terrain map type of structure can be generated as shown in Figure 9.

Figure 9. Relif patterns in 3D-printed tactile pictures. Additive method that brings volumes up (left), and subtractive method that line of areas put back from canvas base (right)

3D "Things"

Many premade, ready-to-print objects are now available on sharing sites such as Thingiverse. We used two methods to incorporate premade "things" into a model. The first method involves choosing a prominent side or viewing perspective, for example, the profile view of a cow or a top view of a bucket. This method is preferred when the story needs to emphasize a particular attribute of an object, for instance, how tall a cow is. Given an imported model, the process of obtaining a perspective 3D model is as follows: First, we define a plane cutting through the imported object. Next, we define a large cube on one side of the plane. Finally, we take the difference between the object and the cube to obtain a perspective representation of an object. This process results in a flat surface of 3D tactile picture to be attached flat canvas, being cutt out the part of 3D object with a sharp surface.

The second method involves representing an object as the whole, for example, the entire cow or the entire bucket. This method is preferred when the story emphasizes free exploration of an object from multiple viewing perspectives; for instance, what does a cow look like?, and how thin its legs are? at a different page. Given an imported object, we may keep it as is, scale it to convey its relative size in comparison with another object, or flatten it a bit to reduce the overall thickness of the page, as shown in Figure 10.

Figure 10. A pre-made cow model in various perspectives, split in half x-, y-, z-axis. So that a butt and tail, a head, side view, four legs, top view, and the entire appearance (from left to right) can be represented as series.

Movables

We defined a *movable* as a set of structure components that can be added to, or integrated with canvases and tactile objects to make them movable by a VI child.

Hinge

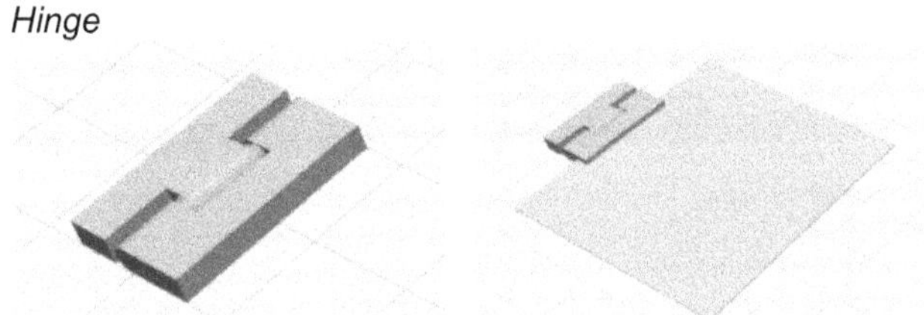

Figure 11. A hinge movable (left), added to a canvas (right).

A hinge movable is designed to provide a tangible experience equivalent to that of opening a door or flipping a lid. Many hinge models can be found on Thingiverse. We tested several and decided to settle down to one, [Thing No. :436737] because (1) it is printable without scaffolding, so even low-end printer can print, (2) it fits our canvas models quite well by combining it through as shown the right of Figure 11, (3) it does not need additional fabrication because printed at once, and (4) it is parametric so that we can customize size, length, volume of nubs, and so forth. Several attributes, such as radius and height of nubs, gap between slot and cone head are adjustable. We made enhancements to the model to make a print-and-assemble design possible. First, we added a clamp-like structure to make it easy to attach an existing tactile picture page to it. Second, we created a trough-like component that can be glued to a canvas as a holder of the hinge, when those parts were printed separately with mid-end 3D printers.

Track

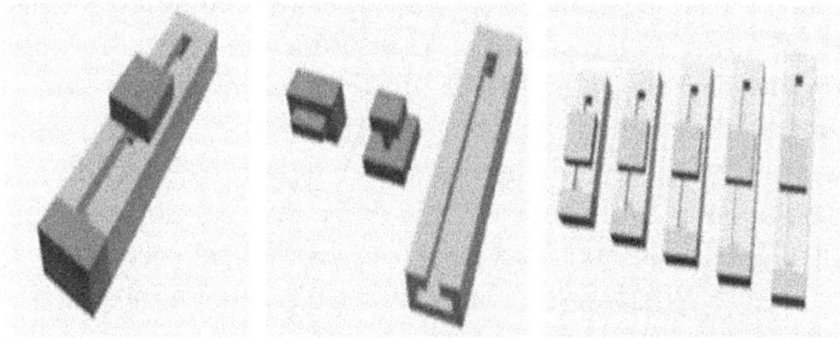

Figure 12. A track movavle (left), in parts of cover, placeholder of tactile picture, and pathholder (middle), with varying heights (right)

A track movable is designed to enable a tactile object to be moved by a VI child along the direction of the track, for instance, dragging a rocket from down side of a picture to the upper side, and towing a bumper car from the left side to the right. We model the track after a typical drapery track, which consists of a long horizontal track in an upside-down T shape, so that an arbitrary tactile object can be attached to a moving platform. (Figure 12).

Spinner

Figure 13. A spinner movable combined (left), in parts of pivot and rolling disc (right).

A spinner movable enables a tactile object to be spun, turned, or rotated by a child, for instance, turning a wheel of a vehicle. For VI children, there are plenty of physical analogies to the real world in toys such as cars and trains. We model the spinner using two components. One component is a base with a pivot. The other is a wheel with a flat top disc that connects to a tactile picture. The components can be printed separately and then put together. A rolling tactile object can be placed on top (Figure 13).

Slider

Figure 14. A slider movable carrying a cloud. A tactile cloud picture is placed on top of base that slides through side path.

A slider movable enables a child to slide a canvas to the side, for instance, to reveal the content underneath the upper canvas. In comparison, a track movable is mainly used for moving a single object. The physical analogy a child can relate to would be a French door. A slider has two tracks along the two sides parallel to the direction of movement (Figure 14).

Lift

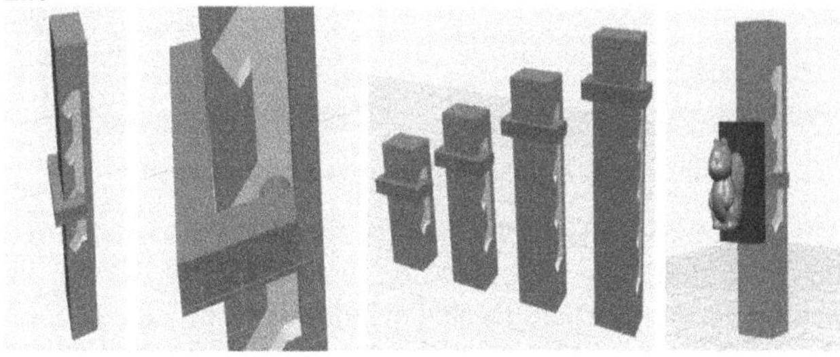

Figure 15. A lift movable to raise or lower an object. According to the the number of slots, a squirrel tactile picture is carried in different height, being combined to the holder.

A lift movable enables a child to raise or lower a tactile object. It is modeled as a vertical stack with a track on each side (Figure 15).

CONCEPTS

Our goal in terms of promoting emergent literacy for young children is to enable the creation of a new class of tactile pictures that are *movable* so that they can convey mobility concepts that would be hard to do using traditional static tactile pictures.

Linear Movement

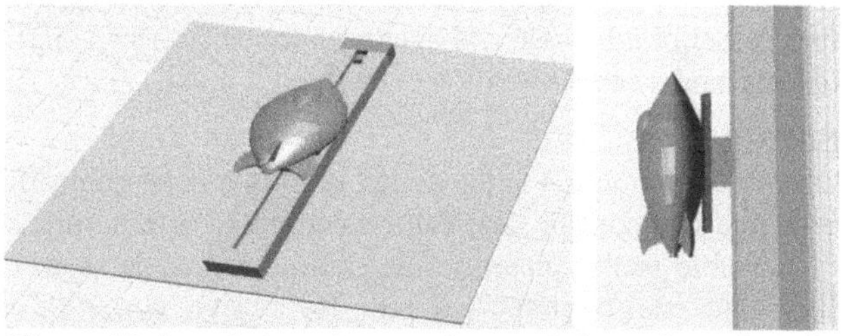

Figure 16. A rocket can be moved up and down through path.

This example conveys the concept that a rocket can move along a straight line. It is achieved using a tactile object (rocket), a canvas, and a track (Figure 16).

Further/Higher Vs. Nearer/Lower

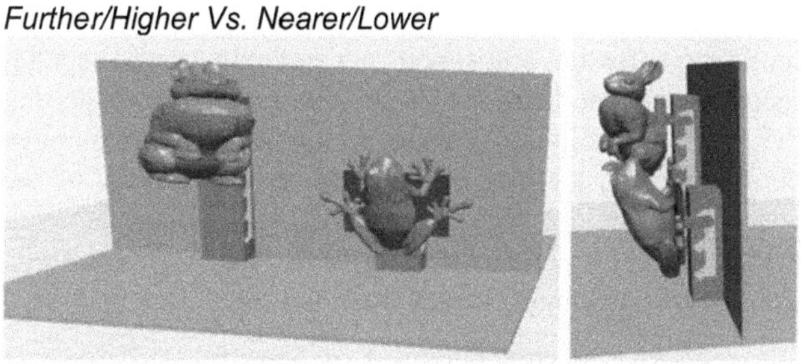

Figure 17. A rabbit can "jump" highter than a frog.

This example conveys the concept that a rabbit jumps further than a frog. A child can pull a rabbit and a frog up from the ground and discover that the rabbit can be pulled higher. It is achieved using two lift movables, each of which holds an object, at different heights (Figure 17).

Front/Behind

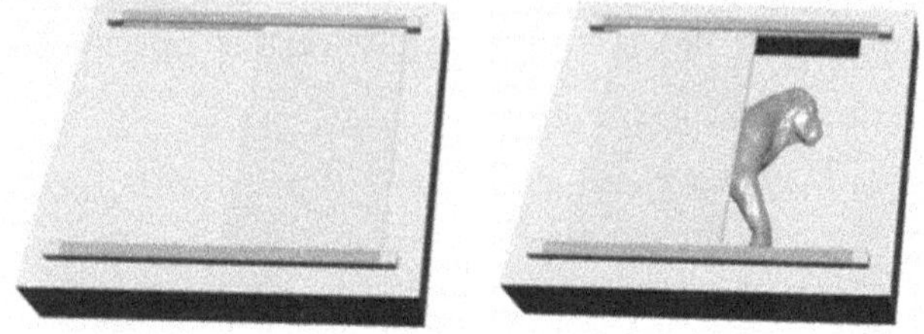

Figure 18. A gorrila is behind a sliding door.

This example conveys the concept that a gorilla is behind a door. A child can slide the door and discover the gorilla behind it. Also, a handle and window can be added upon the door to represent details, as it is another individual canvas. This effect is achieved using a slider movable, two canvases, and several tactile objects (Figure 18).

Motion

Figure 19. Wheels of a tricycle and a trailer spin.

The example conveys the concept that the wheels of a cart spin. It is achieved using multiple spinner movables, a tactile object of a wheel attached to each spinner, a raised-line model of a bicycle and a cart, imported tire-shaped 3D objects, and a canvas holding everything (Figure 19).

DESIGN LANGUAGE

Our first contribution is the design of a suite of reusable 3D printable components that can be composed into a variety of movable tactile pictures. We share our models as STL files that can be imported into the design space of a currently available 3D modeling software application. The designer can use a mouse and a keyboard to move, scale, pan, and rotate these models to form a coherent picture. However, two issues must be considered. First, the composition process is manual and laborious. Second, considerable skill is required to operate the GUI of the 3D modeling software, and serious understanding on 3D spatial recognition to perform the composition task. We argue that the task of designing a page of movable tactile pictures could be made simpler by drawing on the analogy of the task of designing Web pages. The two pillars of Web design are HTML for content/structure and CSS for style. We can take inspiration from these concepts.

We propose a design language for specifying a movable tactile picture based on XML and CSS. We chose XML since it is the most popular MarkUp language specifying "contents", out of other programming option. Similarly, CSS was chosen due to its popularity on specifying "styles", that can be applied to unify design on a "set" of pages. A designer can define the content and structure of a tactile picture in an XML file and can also specify the style attributes of each element in a style sheet (CSS) to uniformly apply on related files. Combined XML/CSS will reach out to the entire web development community, which is far larger than that of the 3D printing and design. Another important benefit is that XML/CSS is text-based and is accessible to blind users via a screen reader, which means even sharing task is simply copying text based code and pasting into the web browser. Note that we do not claim that XML/CSS is at a level of abstraction accessible to everyone. What we do claim is that this level of abstraction would empower a much larger user population than skilled 3D modelers to contribute to the 3D movable picture design. Moreover, our system can pave the way for others to build a WYSIWYG editor to further lower the barrier.

Hello Squirrel Example

This most basic example puts a squirrel tactile object (imported from an STL file) onto a blank canvas.

```
<canvas>
    <object src="squirrel.stl">
</canvas>
```

Complex Example

```
<canvas>
  <track length="30" direction="north" slope="20">
    <spinner>
       <object src="rocket.stl" x="10" y="10"/>
    </spinner>
  </track>
  <door orientation=south y="50%" height="50%">
    <canvas width="100%" height="100%">
       <object src="cloud.stl"/>
    </canvas>
  </door>
</canvas>
```

We present a complex example to highlight the key features of our design language. This example defines a rocket situated above a spinner, which is situated beneath a track. This rocket can be rotated and moved up and down. A door is added to cover the lower half of the canvas (y = 50%, height = 50%). A cloud is added on the door. This door can be opened along the south direction, as an equivalent of wood prototype in Figure 7a.

Implementation

To implement the functionality to generate a model from a specification, we need to redesign all our models as programs that we can invoke with different parameters. Our initial choice was OpenSCAD; however, we found a better solution in OpenJSCAD [1] not only because the former lacked the crucial features of a real programming language,

[1] http://openjscad.org

but also because it provides modeling capabilities equivalent to OpenSCAD as well as supports Javascript, allowing us to use both object-oriented and functional programming. For instance, we are able to represent each component as an object with easy to customize attributes and combined with other objects programmatically. Also, we could use existing Javascript libraries to parse the XML and style sheet in the design specification. We plan to open our source to compile the design into 3D models.

APPLICATIONS

The goal of our research was to make more children's books with movable pictures accessible to VI children. Therefore, we applied our approach to the task of transcribing regular children's books into movable pictures.

Dear Zoo

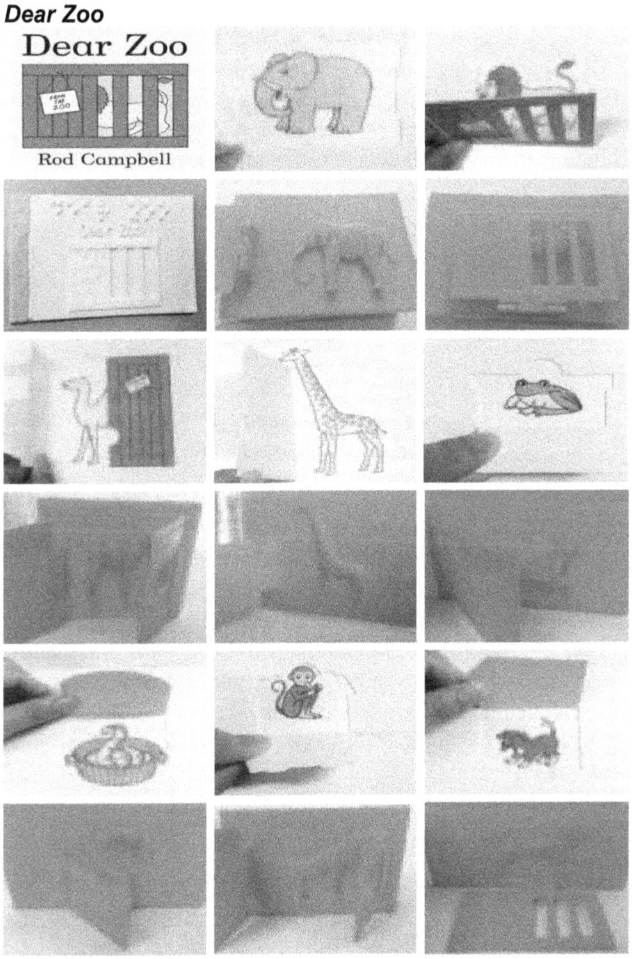

Figure 20. All pages in *Dear Zoo* with braill printed cover.

We modeled all eight pages in this book as shown in Figure 20. This book was a good test bed for our proposed design language because all the pages share a common moving mechanism (i.e., hinge) but vary in details, such as the tactile object, the orientation of the hinge (horizontal vs. vertical), coverage (half vs. full), and configuration (one side vs. split). We used the same template and customize certain aspects of this template to generate these models.

Figure 21. Doors with various tactile patterns and cutouts.

We used four different types of doors to enhance the variety in the touch experiences (Figure 21). These differences allow children to evolve from thinking about the simple shape of the door to experiencing various moving directions shapes, and unique attributes.

Figure 22. Dear Zoo as two volumes of binder.

Real book spine like format is still important feature to be given for *book reading* experience, so we bound pages as book format with the title printed cover page (Figure 22).

All the Fun of the Fair

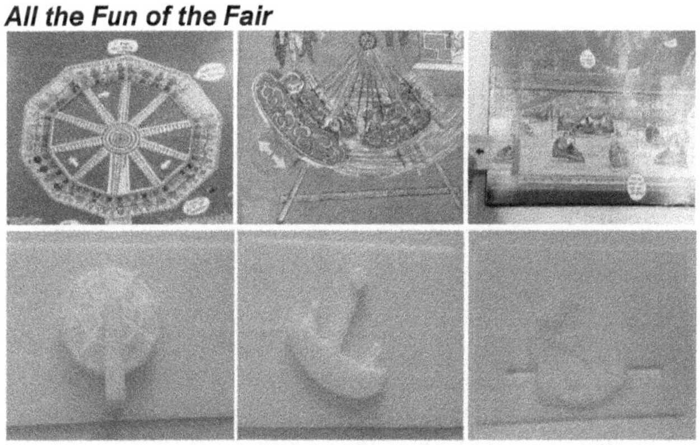

Figure 23. Selected pages in *All the Fun of the Fair*. A spinning giant wheel (left), swinging biking roller coster (middle), and sliding bumper car(right).

The second book we chose was *All the Fun of the Fair* by Robert Crowther. This book employs a rich set of moving mechanisms. Figure 23 shows the three scenes using variety of movements. A rolling wheel is represented by a spinner, which is combined with the wheel frame as a tactile picture. A biking roller coaster is turned into a swing with shapes of human passengers. The horizontal track is used to represent a bumper car in a playground. Children can move the picture of a boy riding a bumper car to the left and right.

When I'm Big

Figure 24. Selected pages in *When I'm Big*. A lift lofts the rocket (top), and a slider carries a fire fighter riding an automatic ladder to reach the roof (bottom) .

The third book we transcribed was *When I'm Big* by Paula Hannigan. We chose this book because it delivers spatial concept of linear up/down very well with iterative interaction in different pages within various situations. We were interested in scenes that include elements that go up and down. We used lift movables and slider movables to achieve this effect, attaching relative tactile pictures on top (Figure 24).

Hop, Skip, and Jump, Maisy

Figure 25. Selected pages in *Hop, Skip, and Jump, Maisy*. Maisy's riding automobile(left) and bike (middle), with spinner, and drikning juice slided by track (right).

The fourth book we transcribed was *Hop, Skip, and Jump, Maisy* by Lucy Cousins. This book illustrates the daily life of Maisy mouse. It includes many kinds of interactive mobility. For example, wheels of a car and a bike are modeled using a spinner movable with a wheel object attached to it. The picture of Maisy drinking juice represents the remaining amount of juice in the glass, held upon a track movable. VI children can pull down the track through the path, touching the top of "juice" with their other hand, and feel how the relative height of the juice decreases, understanding a virtual concept they will never be able to see directly in real life (Figure 25).

What's the Opposite?

Figure 26. Selected pages in *What's the Opposite*. A rocket behind the cloud flap(left), a car behind a flag flap(middle), and a door flap opening (right).

The fifth book we transcribed was *What's the Opposite?* by Eric Hill (Figure 26). This book introduces spatial concepts in contrast, as children lift the flap and uncover something behind it: a rocket under the cloud, a moving car behind the flag, etc. Flapping parts of each page are combined with a hinge that enables readers to turn over objects.

Gossie Plays Hide and Seek

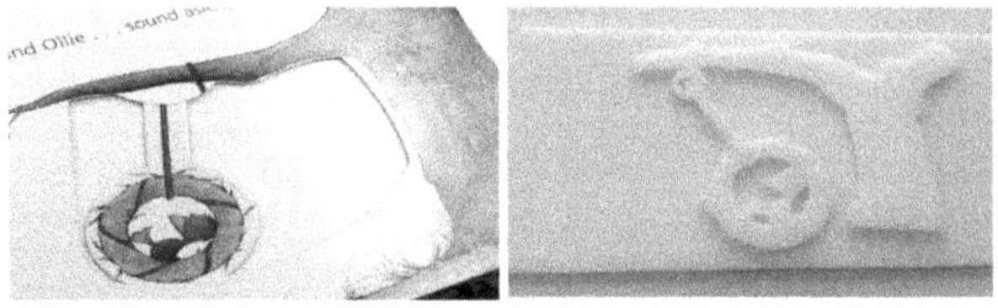

Figure 27. A page in *Gossie Plays Hide and Seek*. A tree swing is defined by spinner movable.

The sixth book we transcribed was *Gossie Plays Hide and Seek* by Olivier Dunrea. This book includes a set of examples of spinners by which children uncover hidden objects (Figure 1, bottom left). One interesting feature is that Gossie bird is getting on the swing that hangs over the tree (Figure 27). Connected with tactile pictures of tree and bird, this feature will more specifically introduce the concept of a tree swing to blind children. Our design language was able to specify the tree and the spinner movable in limited angle. The swing has to be separately modeled, printed, and added to the small flat disc top.

EVALUATION BY DOMAIN EXPERTS

We presented our prototypes to various domain experts to receive feedback and to understand the potential benefits and limitations of the prototypes from diverse perspectives. Six interviews were conducted including 10 participants. The experts participating in these interviews were 1) a blind adult with congenital blindness, 2) four teachers of preschool-age blind children, 3) two publishers who run the Children's Braille Book Club at the National Braille Press (NBP), 4) a renowned tactile graphic artist with more than 30 years of experience, 5) a teacher at a school for deaf children, and 6) a librarian who runs a children's maker space. Each interview ran for about an hour. During an interview, we demonstrated a series of 3D-printed tactile pictures and asked the expert(s) to give us feedback.

Motivator for Active Reading

Compared to stationary tactile pictures, all experts agreed that movable pieces help children learn mobility and spatial concepts by being actively engaged in the book reading. Usually, VI children are in a passive reading situation; they listen to parents and teachers reading. Giving control to children with movable pictures encourages them to dive deeply into the story. The Teacher of blind and deaf students said that having an opportunity to manipulate parts of pictures is a huge motivator. Even for sighted kids, tinkering with pictures allows them to pay attention to what they are doing and helps them retain a focus on mobility.

Literacy Evolution through Variations of Interaction

All teachers and the artist liked the four variations of doors of *Dear Zoo*, because they believed this teaches distinct concepts by same iteration. Children will learn what the cage looks like on the first page, and then concentrate on the smaller door to feel how it is different from the previous plain shape. Children finalize this development in their emergent literacy as they open a pair of doors in two directions, or a flap door down. This process presents the versatility of door shapes and opening actions. Not only that; by touching part of animal inside via the ribs of the cage and through the window, children can try to guess the salient feature of the animal, such as monkey's tail and bumps on a camel's back. This activity can be the trigger for remembering the specific animals.

Post-assembly as a Fun Activity

Our movable pictures are often broken down into separate flat pieces in order to print faster and more reliably (e.g., avoid scaffolding). Post-assembly is necessary but we were concerned about the burden it may put on users. The librarian and the teachers of VI children commented that doing special tasks makes the educational material unique for their children. They suggested the process of putting individual pieces together *"could add more fun"* to the overall reading experience and would *"make the book even more meaningful to an individual child."*

Design Considerations

From the discussions with experts, we have identified several important design considerations for further improvements to our approach in creating 3D-printed movable tactile pictures.

How should a series of concept be presented?

As the door example from *Dear Zoo* illustrates, iterating a simple interaction with various types helps children to build a firm concept of literacy. Tactile book publishers from National Braille Press recommended that we transcribe *Noah's Ark* for our next creation. That book introduces a pair of animals on each page, using different postures and perspectives. At the end of the book, a composite of all the animals reveals different perspectives, their relative size differences, and presents the spatial concept by relying on the animals' relative positions, such as in the sky where birds *fly*, and on the ground where the snake *crawls*.

What is the age of the child?

A child's developmental level of literacy depends greatly on the age of the child. For older kids who already know what a mouse looks like, the tactile picture needs to present very detailed appearance of a mouse, e.g., including four legs and a relatively fat thigh. However, for children ages 0–2, who have never heard of or touched a mouse, it is more important to emphasize its long, curvy tail and big round ears, even if exaggerated beyond those of a mouse.

What is the key intended message to convey?

The relative size of objects in one page and the simplicity of the abstraction are controversial points, so we need to be careful in considering these design factors. When the book is targeting young children and we want to introduce the shape of an animal, experts say we do not need to consider the size at that page. For example, an elephant on the first page of *Noah's Ark* can be the same size as a duck on the second page, because the two pages are intended to convey the concept of shape not relative sizes of each animal.

How should a picture be simplified?

The level of simplicity follows two previous design considerations: age and key idea. A good tactile picture highlights only one concept per object at one page. If too much detail is incorporated, it causes distraction. To keep children's attention on the picture, it needs to focus on the noticeable feature of object interpreted in a tactile picture.

How can co-reading be supported?

Sighted children hear countless other relevant words as well as a story when their parents co-read children's books, thus enhancing book-reading experiences [1, 2]. Transcribing an exact picture is an important task, but providing context by formatting the page to encourage questioning and answering will induce strong intellectual curiosity in children. For example, a window in a door at *Dear Zoo*, leads children to touch inside the window first, can foster interaction between children and parents, asking and answering to guess what that is, and building substantial bonds that help co-readers understand children's interests.

How can textures and colors be incorporated?

Most of our prototypes were uniform in color, and their textures were based on a single material. Several experts commented that high-contrast colors could be attractive to children with residual vision. They advised against precise colors, which is almost impossible for current 3D printing without painting. For example, a giraffe's body does not necessarily need to be ocher in color with brown spots. One suggestion was to use one solid color for the background, another solid color for an animal's body, and yet another color for doors in *Dear Zoo*. In addition, polygonal textures, such as raised dots, could be used to represent the brown spots on the giraffe's body without coloring them.

Other Suggestions and Comments

Experts also had a few comments on our next iteration. They suggested that the book be printed as same as original book published. Grabbing too small pieces makes the page more fragile, but larger 3D-printed objects are more legible. All of the experts recommended soft textures, e.g., using fabrics and yarn. It was commented that smoothing the surfaces would enhance the tactile experience and make it more attractive. Synthesizing several printing techniques or even hands-on fabrication of various materials will enrich children's understanding of natural attributes of real-life objects. In addition, pictures always support children's development of literacy; tactile pictures will provide children an excellent opportunity to learn braille inversely. By putting simple words in braille beside the tactile pictures and movables, VI children will remember braille efficiently with the memory of touch experience.

LIMITATION AND FUTURE WORKS

In this work, we elected to focus on domain experts who are advocates for VI children as user test subjects. It is a sensitive matter to conduct "study" on young children with visual impairments. Treating VI children as subjects in controlled experiments in this phase should be extremely cautious. We rather want them to receive quality models that have been iteratively designed and validated by domain experts. Rather, we delivered our physically printed tactile picture books to the community has VI children, such as family, school, and the public library for people with visual impairments, Colorado Talking Book Library (CTBL) for circulation. Also, we shared the printable file online, recording more than 100 downloads per books, and we have started collecting feedback from users. We will focus our research efforts into see the effectiveness of 3D printed movable tactile pictures as educational materials, by observing differences on literacy development level given regular children's books and our model. We would love to report our findings as design probe to define more moving primitives, and improve the proposed system in near future.

CONCLUSION

We present an approach to creating 3D-printed *movable* tactile pictures for making children's books' interactive contents accessible to VI children. We defined five 3D movable structures that can be used to transcribe mobility features from pictures, demonstrated how our approach could be applied to the transcription of six children's books. Findings from six interviews with domain experts revealed that movable tactile pictures would be desirable for VI children. Several ideas for improvements and refinements to our technique are highlighted.

REFERENCES

1. Alborzi, H., et al. Designing StoryRooms: Interactive Storytelling Spaces for Children. In *Proc*. DIS '00, ACM Press, 95-104
2. Beukelman, D., & Mirenda, P., (2005) Augmentative and alternative communication: Supporting children and adults with complex communication needs. Paul H.Brookes.
3. Brown, C., Hurst, A., VizTouch: Automatically Generated Tactile Visualizations of Coordinate Spaces. In *Proc*. TEI'12, ACM Press, 131-138
4. Budd J., Madej K., Stephens-WellsJ., Jong , J., Katzur E., Mulligan L. PageCraft: learning in context a tangible interactive storytelling platform to support early narrative development for young children. In *Proc*. IDC '07, ACM Press, 97-100
5. Bus, A. G., (2003). Joint Caregiver-Child Storybook Reading: A Route to Literacy Development, Handbook of Early Literacy Research., Vol.1, The Guilford Press
6. Cassell J, Ryokai K., (2001). Making Space for Voice: Technologies to Support Children's Fantasy and Storytelling, Personal and Ubiquitous Computing, Vol.5, Issue 3, Springer, 169-190
7. Craig, J C, and Sherrick, C E (1982). Dynamic Tactile Displays in Tactual Perception, Ed Schiff, W and Foulke, E, Cambridge: University Press.
8. Fontijn, W., and Mendels, P. StoryToy the Interactive Storytelling Toy. In *Proc*. Pervasive Computing'05
9. Garzotto, f., Bordogna, M., Paper-based Multimedia Interaction as Learning Tool for Disabled Children. In *Proc*. IDC '10, ACM Press, 79-88
10. Garzotto, F. Broadening children's involvement as design partners: from technology to "experience", In *Proc*. IDC '08. ACM Press, 186-194
11. Google SketchUp 3D warehouse https://3dwarehouse.sketchup.com
12. Hengeveld B., Hummels C., Overbeeke K. Tangibles for Toddlers Learning Language. In *Proc*. TEI'09, ACM Press, 161-168
13. Kim, J., Stangl, A., Eisenberg, A., & Yeh, T. Tactile Picture Books for Young Children with Visual Impairment, Works-in-Progress, TEI'14
14. Lipson, H. & Kurman, M., (2013). Fabricated: The New World of 3D Printing, Wisely
15. MakerBot Thingiverse http://thingiverse.com
16. Marshall P., Do tangible interfaces enhance learning?, In *Proc*. TEI '07, ACM Press, 163-170
17. McGookin, D., Robertson, E., and Brewster, S.A., Clutching at straws: using tangible interaction to provide non-visual access to graphs, In *Proc*. CHI'10, ACM Press, 10-15
18. Philippe C., (2009). The Typhlo & Tactus Guide to Children's Book with tactile illustrations, Les Doigts Qui Revent
19. Stangl, A., Kim, J., Yeh, T., 3D Printed Tactile Picture Books for Children with Visual Impairments: A Design Probe, In *Proc*. IDC '14, ACM Press, 321-324
20. Suzette, W., (2013). Guide to Designing Tactile Illustrations for Children's Books, the American Printing House for the Blind
21. Yahoo japan Hands On Search, http://sawareru.jp/en/

Multimodal Analysis in Participatory Design with Children: A Primary School Case Study

Jan Derboven[1], Maarten Van Mechelen[1], Karin Slegers
CUO | Social Spaces, iMinds-KU Leuven
Parkstraat 45 bus 3605, 3000 Leuven
firstname.lastname@soc.kuleuven.be

ABSTRACT
We describe a multimodal method for the analysis of co-design outcomes in participatory design (PD) with children. The multimodal approach we take allows researchers to treat both verbal (notes, writings) and tangible material outcomes as complementary ways of communicating design ideas. We argue that an integrated approach in which both PD outcomes are compared and contrasted can result in a richer analysis, in which underlying values can be identified more clearly. To illustrate the method, we describe a PD process with primary school children.

Author Keywords
Participatory Design; Values; Multimodality.

ACM Classification Keywords
H.5.m. Information interfaces and presentation (e.g., HCI): Miscellaneous.

INTRODUCTION

Participatory design with children

Participatory Design (PD) is often defined as *"a set of theories, practices, and studies related to end-users as full participants in activities leading to software and hardware computer products and computer-based activities"* [12]. Future users are at the core of the methodology: in PD, these users are considered co-designers of their technology, and of the practices that are reified in that technology [2]. Participatory designers, in turn, are seen as 'facilitators' who try to empower users in making design decisions together [14]. Generative techniques such as 'co-design' are often used in PD. The basic principle behind co-design is to let people make designerly artifacts and tell a story about what they have made. These stories are then used to inform and inspire the design process [13].

CHI 2015, April 18–23, 2015, Seoul, Republic of Korea.
Copyright is held by the owner/author(s). Publication rights licensed to ACM.
ACM 978-1-4503-3145-6/15/04…$15.00.
http://dx.doi.org/10.1145/2702123.2702475

Within the area of Child Computer Interaction (CCI), children have participated in the design of technology for over two decades, using a variety of established methods (e.g. [4,10,16]). Nevertheless, it has been acknowledged that it is not easy to involve children as design partners in open-ended, future directed work. Scaife and Rogers [10] for instance, say that: *"On the one hand, the kids come up with many wonderful suggestions [...], on the other hand, many of their ideas are unworkable in computing terms"*. This statement is exemplary for a tendency to analyze co-design artifacts solely in 'computing terms', that is, on a functional or attribute level (e.g. [4,16]). However, the values that are embedded in co-design artifacts are often more interesting than the ideas or functionalities per se [5]. Unfortunately, these values (things a person or a group considers important in life [9]) are rarely expressed explicitly. Shifting the focus from functionalities and attributes to the underlying motives behind design choices made during co-design can reveal why specific design attributes are important and how they serve children's values. This is in line with recent work by Iversen et al [6] who have attempted to rekindle values in a more 'authentic' approach to PD by focusing on the values that emerge and develop in the course of the design process.

Besides this tendency to focus on concrete design ideas or a set of functionalities when co-designing technology with children, PD researchers often limit themselves to a descriptive analysis of co-design artifacts or rely exclusively on what children say or write about their creations (e.g. [4,13]). However, co-design artifacts should not be regarded as neutral means of accessing children's perspectives. They are always 'constructed' and therefore do not give access to the participants' personal values in a direct and unmediated way. Buckingham [3] refers to this approach as 'naïve empiricism', arguing that data from creative research cannot be taken at face value: *"these data need to be analyzed with special attention for its visual dimensions"*. Both 'textual outcomes' (i.e., written ideas and what children say about their creation) and 'tangible outcomes' (i.e., the co-design artifact) should be analyzed and interpreted in relation to each other. Nevertheless, the current literature on PD offers little guidance on how to do this in a structured way.

The contribution of this paper lies in offering a method that will enable PD researchers to analyze co-design outcomes by identifying the dominant themes and underlying values,

[1] Both authors contributed equally to this paper.

and to integrate both textual and tangible co-design outcomes in a structured analysis. This method is based on multimodal social semiotics [7,8]. Multimodality provides an interesting perspective on the analysis of co-design outcomes, as it provides an integrated framework for analyzing various ways of communicating, including spoken and written language, but also visual and other modes of communication. As such, it allows for an integration of both textual and tangible co-design outcomes, treating them as different modes used to communicate the same ideas and values.

Case Study: (Cyber) Bullying in Primary School

In this paper, we describe the analysis of a series co-design sessions with children, focusing on the dominant themes and underlying values. We focus on a case study in which 49 primary school children aged 9 to 10 were involved in two co-design sessions. These sessions aimed at designing tangible, digital tools to make primary school children more self-regulatory in combating traditional bullying and cyberbullying. This goal was translated into an understandable design challenge for children: what tools do they need to improve the class atmosphere and prevent bullying? To make it more tangible, we used a fictional story of a class with a negative atmosphere as a starting point for co-design.

METHOD

Participatory Design Process

The co-design sessions took place in two schools. In total, 49 children aged 9 to 10 participated and the sessions resulted in 11 co-design artifacts created by an equal number of groups of 4 to 5 children (see [15] for an in-depth description of the method used). One researcher was involved in each co-design session facilitating two to three groups of children at the same time without intervening in the creation process. The co-design sessions resulted in various outcomes. For each group, we analyzed:

1. a collage of two problematic class situations defined by the children (e.g. children excluding each other from playing games, bullying,...);
2. verbal descriptions on post-its of how a super hero would solve these problems (e.g. Spiderman capturing 'bad' children in a web). From these solutions, the children picked two for further elaboration;
3. an artifact designed by the children that embodies the super heroes' solutions chosen in 2;
4. transcripts of verbal presentations of the artifact.

Multimodal Analysis

Multimodality, an interdisciplinary approach based on social semiotics, considers communication and representation to be *"more than language, and attends systematically to the social interpretation of a range of forms of making meaning"* [7]. While this type of analysis has been used for researching e.g. games and social networking [7], we argue this approach is useful in PD for analyzing both textual and tangible co-design outcomes. Text and tangible artifacts, as different modes, have different affordances: each have specific characteristics that make it suitable for communicating specific information. For instance, while speech is more suitable for narratives, material objects can be easier to communicate moods and emotion. While one specific mode might communicate more information than another, the multimodal approach integrates all modes in the analysis. Through this integration, the analysis becomes a holistic study of the central message that all modes contribute to.

Visual and material objects can, however, be interpreted in different ways, and it can be difficult to make interpretations that are valid in the context of the PD process. Through a comparative analysis between the original ideas and the results, we were able to trace how ideas emerged and evolved throughout the PD process, from initial ideas to results. As such, we were able to interpret the ideas in the co-design artifacts in the light of their origins in the super hero solutions (2) and the description of class situations (1). Tracing this evolution was crucial, as it allowed us to 'ground' the analyses of artifacts (3) and presentations (4) and, as such, add validity to the interpretations. Besides grounding the analyses in the evolution from original ideas to co-design outcomes, we used a hermeneutic approach [11] in order to strengthen the validity: we checked the analysis of the artifact against the verbal transcription, and vice versa. Considering the material artifact and the verbal transcripts as different forms of the same idea, it is the coherence between text and artifact that validates the analysis.

This hermeneutic approach was applied in a 'close reading' [1]: this is an analytic method originating in the humanities that examines formal and thematic elements in texts and artifacts. It consisted of two main steps:

1. Two researchers independently identify recurring themes and underlying values through a detailed analysis of the data. This step comprises several activities:
    - Tracing the evolution from the children's problem definition (1) and original ideas (2) to the eventual results (3 & 4).
    - Performing a low-level analysis of functionality and attributes of co-design artifacts (3) and verbal presentations (4). Special attention is given to elements highlighted in and across modes.
    - Performing a high-level analysis of recurring themes by identifying the discourses (i.e., children's view on social reality) that underly the artifacts and presentations (3 & 4).
    - Performing a meta-analysis of values underpinning tangible (3) and textual outcomes (4); these are seldom explicitly expressed.
2. Both researchers collaboratively refine recurring themes and underlying values to arrive at a common understanding of the data. This is an iterative process of going back and forth between the different steps.

RESULTS

In this section, we describe the analysis of both textual and tangible co-design outcomes. We highlight our main findings, illustrating the use of multimodality to analyze the values underpinning these outcomes. While the PD sessions resulted in four outcomes, the collage and post-its served as intermediate stages and have been used to validate the analysis. We focus on the final artifacts and their presentation.

From Attributes to Underlying Themes

Friendly Authority: Transduction from Artifact to Presentation

Groups 3, 7 and 10 created artifacts with human-shaped figures, and groups 4, 5, 6 and 8 all created 'robots'. These groups associated all kinds of functionality with their figures, ranging from ringing a bell when things threaten to go wrong (group 3), to a DJ robot for a class party (group 4 – figure 1, right). Beyond these specific functionalities, these anthropomorphic figures all represented some type of authority, influencing the children's behavior. Generally, the robots did not look sterile, but had some kind of personality that was implicitly described in the participants' presentations (e.g. *"he tells very good jokes")*, and more explicitly visualized in the artifacts. While all robots had some kind of regulatory function, most robots looked funny or friendly in some way. For instance, group 3 made a kind-looking figure with a big red heart. The DJ robot by group 4 created a fun atmosphere, and would *"eat all bad ideas"*.

Only group 6 created a rather severe-looking robot (figure 1, left), with a clearly regulating, authoritative function (visualized in a traffic light on his body). However, while the severe component was present in the visual appearance of the robot and mentioned in the children's presentation, it was not present in the further material elaboration. Whereas the robot did contain games to reward well-behaved children, the punishing aspect was not elaborated: the artifact only 'highlighted' (gave special weight to [8]) the rewards. This observation suggests that disciplinary punishment was not central to the children's understanding of a tool to prevent and combat (cyber-)bullying in a class context. While many artifacts took the shape of an authoritative figure, the 'transduction' (i.e., the translation from one mode to another [8]) from the textual to the tangible added an important nuance. The objects showed that the authority is always friendly, focused on rewarding rather than on punishment.

Good and Bad Children: Agency and Group Processes

Although the children were asked to invent objects that would improve the classroom atmosphere, none of the PD groups made representations of the class, the teacher, or other actors in their artifacts. Therefore, it was important to analyze the children's presentations to determine whether or not the artifacts themselves had *agency*, and to determine their *orientation* [8]: whether the artifacts are oriented at specific bullies, victims, or the class group as a whole.

In analyzing artifact orientation, three dominant artifact categories emerged. The first category consisted of artifacts with agency that concentrated on the class group as a whole (3 out of 11 artifacts). Children explained their function without referring to 'good' or 'bad' children. For example, the DJ robot (figure 1, right) improved the class atmosphere by telling jokes and by 'eating all bad ideas', while another robot gave children a magic potion to make them friendly.

The remaining 8 artifacts were clearly targeted at either bullies or 'bad' children and victims or 'good' children. We distinguish two further categories. Artifacts in the second category (5 artifacts out of 11) distinguish between 'bad' and 'good' but were not targeted at punishing bad children. Two artifacts with agency focused on mediation instead of punishment, and three tools without agency made children forget their bad behavior, or resolved tensions through play. A third category (3 artifacts without agency) mentioned both rewarding and punishment, but focused on the rewards (e.g. allowing good children to play games). In these artifacts, punishment was not elaborated, or only minimally.

The analysis above shows that not only the artifact itself and its attributes are important, but also the way it mediates between other actors on a more abstract level. On the one hand, the first two categories (8 out of 11 artifacts) either made no reference to bullies and victims, or concentrated on resolving tensions between bullies and victims while also avoiding punishment. On the other hand, the remaining artifacts (3 out of 11) more clearly encouraged good children and punished bad children. In these artifacts, however, the punishing was understated: the focus was on rewarding.

Figure 1: Goofy DJ robot (right) vs. severe-looking robot (left), groups 4 and 6.

From Themes to Values

From the themes emerging from the analysis above, information on the children's values can be deduced. The artifacts in the first two categories, focusing on the class atmosphere as a whole or on mediation and play, fit in a 'no-blame' discourse. In this discourse, it is important not to single out the bad children to punish them, but to take a preventive attitude by defusing tensions in the classroom. On the other hand, the artifacts in the third category did use a discourse focused on rewards and punishment; still, these artifacts highlighted the positive aspect of rewarding.

In general, however, both the 'no-blame' artifacts and the artifacts differentiating between good and bad children pointed towards an emphasis on values of soft authority and positivity in various ways. The 'no-blame' artifacts did this by focusing on the class group as a whole or used strategies such as mediation or play. The artifacts with agency had a friendly type of authority, rather than a strict, punishing one. Even the artifacts centered around good and bad behavior had a heavy focus on rewarding good behavior, understating the punishment aspect. Going beyond specific functionalities, these emerging values of 'soft' authority and positivity provide designers with a well-grounded starting point for designing tangible, digital anti-bullying tools.

ANALYZING PARTICIPATORY DESIGN VALUES

When analyzing the outcomes of co-design sessions, it is essential to pay attention to both textual and tangible outcomes. As textual and tangible co-design outcomes are different ways of communicating the same ideas, it is important to analyze which aspects have been *transduced* [8] from the textual to the tangible and vice versa, and which have not. This way, it becomes clear how different modes complement each other in communicating a message.

The multimodal analysis allowed us to create rich analyses of both textual and tangible outcomes. The analysis teased out dominant themes and values, going beyond the surface of functionalities and attributes. For instance, the appearance of the anthropomorphic figures added important nuances to their interpretation. The analysis did not focus only on the functionalities of the figures, but on their 'personality', implicitly present in the verbal presentations of the artifacts, and more explicitly in their tangible form. As these personalities can be linked to underlying values concerning the prevention and reconciliation of conflicts, the artifact analysis was important to arrive at a nuanced interpretation.

While the current PD literature offers little guidance on the analysis of material outcomes, multimodality offers a structured framework to analyze both textual and material outcomes, and the transduction between the two. The case study above focuses on tangible and verbal modes, but multimodality can be useful in the analysis of other modes as well [7]. As such, we believe that the approach is applicable in various PD situations, with different design challenges and materials. Especially analytic concepts (e.g. highlighting, agency, orientation) are instrumental in analyzing discourse and values underpinning co-design outcomes.

In the case study presented above, multimodality provided a framework to identify the values underlying the children's design choices within and across co-design teams. Using the framework, designers can go beyond the surface level of cherry-picking participants' ideas. In future work, we will further tailor the multimodal framework to the analysis of co-design outcomes, and apply it to various case studies.

ACKNOWLEDGMENTS

This study is part of the EMSOC project, funded by IWT (Agency for Innovation by Science and Technology), and two PhD projects funded by UHasselt and iMinds.

REFERENCES

1. Bardzell, J. (2011). Interaction criticism: An introduction to the practice. *Interact. Comput.* 23(6), 604-621.
2. Bjerknes, G. Ehn, P., and Kyng, M. (1987) . *Computers and democracy: A Scandinavian challenge.* Brookfield.
3. Buckingham, D. (2009). 'Creative' visual methods in media research: possibilities, problems and proposals. *Media, Culture and Society*, 31, 633-652.
4. Guha, M.L., Druin, A. & Fails, J.A. (2013). Cooperative Inquiry revisited: Reflections of the past and guidelines for the future of intergenerational co-design. *Int. J. of Child-Computer Interaction*, 1(1), 14-23.
5. Halloran, J., Hornecker, E., & Stringer, M. (2009). The value of values: Resourcing co-design of ubiquitous computing. *CoDesign* 4 (5), 245-273.
6. Iversen, O.S., Halskov, K., & Leong, T.W. (2010). Rekindling values in participatory design. *In Proc. PDC '10*, p. 92-100. ACM Press.
7. Jewitt, C. (2013) Multimodal Methods for Researching Digital Technologies. In: Price, S., Jewitt, C., Brown, B. (Eds.) *The SAGE Handbook of Digital Technology Research*, pp. 250-265. Sage.
8. Kress, G. (2010) *Multimodality. A Social Semiotic Approach to Contemporary Communication.* Routledge.
9. Rokeach, M. (1973). *The Nature of Human Values.* Free Press.
10. Scaife, M. and Rogers, Y. (1999). Kids as informants: Telling us what we didn't know or confirming what we knew already, in A. Druin (Ed.), *The design of children's technology*, pp.29-50. Morgan Kaufmann.
11. Schön, D. (1984). *The Reflective Practitioner: How Professionals Think In Action.* Basic Books.
12. Schuler, D. and Namioka, A. (1993). *Participatory Design: Principles and Practices.* L. Erlbaum Assoc. Inc.
13. Sleeswijk Visser, F., Stappers, P.J., van der Lugt, R., Sanders, E.B.N. (2005). Contextmapping: Experiences from practice. *CoDesign* 1(2), 119-149.
14. Spinuzzi C., 2005, The Methodology of Participatory Design. In: *Technical Communication.* 52 (2), 163-175.
15. Van Mechelen, M., Gielen, M., Vanden Abeele, V., Laenen, A. and Zaman, B. (2014). Exploring challenging group dynamics in participatory design with children. In *Proc. IDC '14* , 269-272. ACM Press.
16. Walsh, G., Druin, A., Guha, M.L., Foss, E., Golub, E., Hatley, L., Bonsignore, E. and Franckel, S. (2010) Layered elaboration: a new technique for co-design with children. In *Proc. CHI 2010*, 1237-1240. ACM Press.

The Fun-Serious Ambiguity in Educational Games

Jan Derboven, Bieke Zaman, Jorick Vissers, David Geerts, Dirk De Grooff
CUO | Social Spaces, iMinds – KU Leuven
Parkstraat 45 bus 3605 - Leuven (B)
Firstname.lastname@soc.kuleuven.be

ABSTRACT
We describe a study of Monkey Tales, an educational game targeted at primary school children. Starting from the assumption that all meaning is socially constructed, we focus our attention on the way an educational game, and its balance between fun and serious aspects, is constructed in public texts (game manufacturer's communication and game reviews) and in individual use (the way players and their parents talk about the game). Through an analysis of public texts and individual use, we show how the balance between the fun and the serious in Monkey Tales is constructed in different ways.

Author Keywords
Educational games; fun-serious balance; discourse.

ACM Classification Keywords
H.5.m. Information interfaces and presentation (e.g., HCI): Miscellaneous.

INTRODUCTION
The tension between the fun and the serious in educational games is an important aspect in educational game research. This tension, it has been argued, stems from a deeply rooted 'cultural (op)positioning of play and education' [6]. Although researchers increasingly acknowledge the potential of learning through play (e.g., [8]), finding a good combination of the fun and the serious is still very challenging for most educational games.

Educational gaming researchers make efforts to find this optimal fun-serious balance. The focus on work and education-oriented values needs to go hand in hand with a focus on playful user experiences, entertainment, and fun. Traditionally, many educational gaming models separate the 'serious' and the 'fun' as "formal and informal processes of learning", treating them as being incompatible [13]. However, research has looked into this incompatibility, and existing educational game evaluation frameworks include guidelines on how to embed learning content in a game (e.g. [13]), trying to overcome the inherent tension between transferring 'serious' content and the fun factor inherent in enjoyable games. In this work, and in empirical studies of educational games, researchers generally agree that instead of merely 'sugarcoating' the educational content, a tight integration between learning content and game elements is desirable (e.g., [4,9,13,14]).

We approach the fun-serious relation in educational games from an alternative angle: we do not look at the relation between the fun and the serious from the designer's point of view (focusing on designers' intentions such as incorporating learning goals, aiming for maximal effectivity, etc.). Instead, we assume the meaning of a game is not entirely predefined, but constructed through discourse and use. We focus on how the fun-serious balance is socially constructed [2] by analyzing the way it surfaces in public texts (the game manufacturer's promotional material and game reviews) and in individual use (the game as seen by players and their parents). As such, we contribute to educational game research by showing that apart from the design and implementation of educational games, their reception and use warrants further research. Where different perceptions of the fun-serious balance co-exist, they might not always align with the desigers' educational intentions.

MONKEY TALES
The educational game we use as a case study is *Monkey Tales*, an educational math game series for children in primary school. The game exists in different versions, targeting children of different age groups, with different math proficiencies. The game we used was targeted at children in the 5th and 6th grades of primary school (age 10-11), and developed specifically for playing at home.

The game is structured in several layers (see Figure 1). The game levels are conceived of as rooms in a 3D world the player has to pass through. In every room, the player has to solve a 3D logic puzzle while also avoiding traps and adversaries – no math is involved here. In every 3D world level, players encounter an arcade game machine: players have to play and win a mini game on this machine in order to move to the next level. The game layer with the logic puzzles does not involve math – the 'serious' elements in the game are only to be found in the mini game layer. This

CHI 2015, April 18–23, 2015, Seoul, Republic of Korea.

ACM 978-1-4503-3145-6/15/04...$15.00.
http://dx.doi.org/10.1145/2702123.2702519

layer concentrates on the math, combining 'serious' math exercises with 'fun' arcade game-style game play.

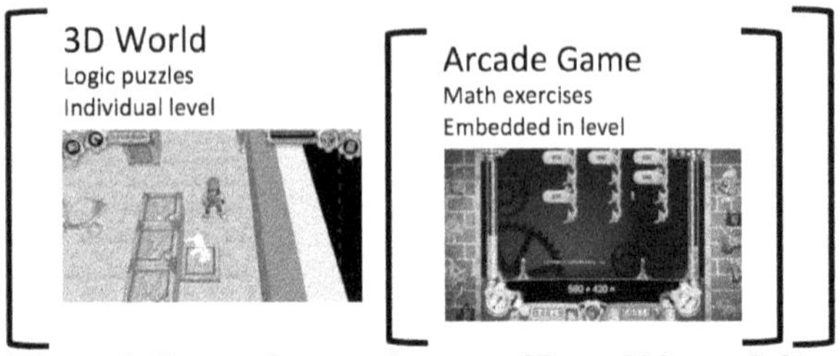

Figure 1. Two main game layers: a 3D world layer (left), with an arcade game layer embedded in it (right).

METHOD

We use discourse analysis [2,7] to analyze how people talk about educational games, and how they use and interpret them. The discourse surrounding educational games can be seen as a part of what Gee ([8], p. 143) calls 'cultural models'- "images, story lines, principles or metaphors that capture what a particular group finds "normal" or "typical" in regard to a given phenomenon." This discourse is considered "normal" in daily interaction, and therefore often remains implicit. Investigating discourse has proven useful in HCI to investigate how a specific discourse instructs users on how a specific technology can be used [10]: discourse can provide a 'way in' to understand how people think about the technology. Here, we investigate the discourse surrounding *Monkey Tales* to find out how the game manufacturer and reviewers position the game, and how players and their parents talk about it, and integrate the game in their daily life.

Data Collection and Analysis

The data collected in this study consisted of three types: marketing material from the game developer (the website and the leaflet included with the game), online game reviews (six reviews from websites dedicated to e.g. game reviews [5,16] and game-based learning [1]), and observations from a user study. This user study was performed in 8 families (3 girls and 5 boys, aged 10 or 11, and their parents) for 6 months. It included a diary study and interviews, complemented by a long-term user experience study [15] in which 6 families participated.

The marketing material and the reviews have been incorporated in this study, as they represent public discourses that, at least to some extent, regulate the way educational games are perceived. The family perspective, on the other hand, shows how the educational game is used and perceived in daily life. All data have been analysed using discourse analysis, focusing on the fun-serious balance. We specifically investigated whether the fun-serious balance is a fixed design characteristic, or whether this characteristic varied across sources, determined by the discourse surrounding the game, and individual players' interpretation and use.

RESULTS

In the analysis presented below, the promotional material and the reviews are considered public texts that shape the educational gaming discourse. They play a role in shaping and representing the dominant cultural model [8] concerning educational games. The children's use of the game, and the discourse between parents and children is considered private discourse. Below, we discuss the theme of the game's fun-serious balance as it emerges in both public and private discourse.

Promotional Material: Shifting the Fun-Serious Balance

On the Monkey Tales web site [12], the game company stresses the seamless combination of gaming and didactics: they claim 'story and the challenges in the game motivate your child effortlessly' to practice 'drill exercises' at home. The relation between skill development and motivation is foregrounded: '*Monkey Tales* combines the motivational strength of a game with a professional, didactic concept to practice the elementary math of primary school'. This text wants to convince parents that *Monkey Tales* motivates children to practice math while having fun: the emphasis of the text is on training skills.

While this text is targeted at parents, the website also offers a video for children using a short narrative about the central game character, showing a lot of in-game action. This trailer *reverses* the focus described above: it is not on skill development, but on fun. The video follows a typical before-and-after pattern, in which the main character struggles with math before playing the game. Initially, he closes his homework book in frustration, but after having played the game, he effortlessly solves his homework exercises. The main part of the video, however, shows fast-action gaming in the 3D gaming world. While the genre is different, the before-and-after pattern discusses the skill-training theme, similar to the game description on the website. The emphasis is reversed, though: in the video, the focus is on gaming, not the math skills. In this sense, the promotional point of view stricly separates the parents' view (emphasizing the serious) and the children's view (emphasizing the fun).

Game Reviews: the Elusive Fun-Serious Balance

The motivational fun factor is a dominant theme in the reviews. They stress the difficulty of finding the ideal fun-serious balance: an educational game needs to be fun so children want to play it. The Wired review states that "it's an incredibly difficult thing to create a[n educational] game that both entertains and teaches" [16]. The reviewer's children agree that most educational games focus too much on education, and are "not fun, but silly and boring and lame". Brutalgamer.com has the same opinion: "*[...] It's more elusive than that ever cited needle in a haystack. An educational game....that's actually fun? [...] I'll believe *that* when I see it, my friend.*" [5]

All reviews in the corpus agreed to a large extent on the fact that *Monkey Tales* does a rather good job at finding an appropriate fun-serious balance. The Avatargeneration review [1] even cites academic research into the effects of *Monkey Tales*, stating that "*the students who played the game have significantly better answers to an arithmetic test [...] and reported higher motivation and learning efficiency.*" Test results, learning efficiency and higher motivation are again juxtaposed as two aspects the game handles well: on the one hand, the fun aspect of the game motivates the children, and on the other, the educational content results in better test results.

Concerning the fun aspect of *Monkey Tales*, Brutalgamer.com makes the critical side note that playing Monkey Tales was fun for a young test player, but it can be too overtly educational for older kids, even if the exercises are more difficult: "*The sixth grader said 'I know it's math, and that's why I don't like it.' [...] The fact that it was so overtly educational in those portions turned him off a bit.*"

While the promotional point of view strictly separated the parents' view (emphasizing the serious) and the children's view (emphasizing the fun), the reviews show a more negotiated position. The separate goals of parents and children are still prominent (parents want education, but children want a fun game). However, the reviews also discuss the trade-off between the fun and the serious in a more nuanced way: the same game can be fun for one player, but too educational for another.

Daily Use: Negotiating the Fun and the Serious

When educational games and other media are introduced into the home, the nature of the media and the rules surrounding it need to be communicated. Due to their dual nature combining fun and education, educational games can be expected to be the subject of complex interactions when they are introduced: the 'accepted' view on educational games needs to be negotiated between parents and their children. In that way, the game becomes the subject of a negotiation of game values [3], and, especially, which of those game values (play or education) is dominant. This was also the case in our six-month study of the game.

Most parents in our study did not like their children playing computer games very much: parents kept an eye on their children's computer use, and limited that time if necessary: 6 out of 8 parents or children confirmed this in the diaries or interviews. However, parents expressed a rather positive relationship towards educational games, considering them useful, to some extent: if parents cannot stop their children from playing video games anyway, educational games at least have the benefit that they might teach their children some useful skills. *Monkey Tales* was considered to have a good balance between fun and educational content:

Mother of respondent 2: *Yes, I think they* [educational games] *are useful, because he likes playing games, and in that way, they can learn something. They have to be playful, so I think this...* [Monkey Tales] *was a good combination.*

This 'good balance' echoes the cultural model found especially in the game reviews. However, the interviews with the children showed that they use this discourse, and especially the elusiveness of the fun-serious balance to their own benefit. Some children shifted the focus from the educational to the fun depending on whom they were talking to. In this way, the fun-serious balance proved to be the subject of ongoing negotiations. Several parents allowed their children some more freedom because of the educational nature of the game, allowing children to play *Monkey Tales* longer than 'regular' games. As a result of this freedom, children tried to convince their parents further that Monkey Tales is a 'good' game worth playing. They emphasized the educational content, stressing the difficulty of the exercises. For instance, when the mother of respondent 8 claimed that some exercises were too easy, he was quick to defend the game by stressing its difficulty:

Mom: *Actually, he only counted the thousands, or something like that. The consequence is that you can start estimating – those numbers* [to choose the right answer from], *they were really like 6000 or 5000, or,... So you can immediately see...*
R8: *But no!*
Mom: ... *So I think if the numbers would have been closer together...*
R8: *But no, mom, sometimes you had to choose between 4,23; 4,24 and 4,25. (indignant) Hey, that's really difficult!*

While the respondents explicitly stressed the educational content towards their parents, they reported liking the game especially because the math was *limited*: "*because it's a game, and it's one math game per game [level], and it's not math exercises the entire time*" (resp. 8). Moreover, several respondents developed strategies to limit the math-solving effort as much as possible, with respondent 8 using the most inventive math-avoiding tactics. Rather than shooting the *right answers to math problems* to earn points in the math games, the player ended up shooting *any answer* randomly, assuming (or hoping) that the right answers shot 'by accident' would earn enough points to pass the game.

Respondent 8: *With the cannon, I always win, but I just keep the space bar pressed, and I move from right to left, and it's over.*

While parents tended to reproduce promotional view (their own educational agenda vs. the children's focus on play) or the negotiated view (the 'good balance between fun and serious' found in the game reviews), players like respondent 8 were skilled at shifting the fun-serious focus, very much as in the game's promotional material. Depending on the 'target group', these children shifted from a focus on the math (when talking to their parents) to a focus on the game elements (when playing, and talking to the researchers).

DISCUSSION AND CONCLUSION

Although promotional material, reviews and user discourse are quite different resources in terms of function and availability (public vs. private), they initially start from one commonly held view. In this view, educational games unite education and fun, potentially resulting in a tension in the game. This is apparent in the promotional material ('seamlessly combining' education and play), the reviews ('needle in a haystack'), and the interviews with parents (the game as 'a good combination').

While the problem of marrying fun and serious is an agreed-upon challenge, determining the right fun-serious balance is another matter. Concerning this balance, all resources investigated showed some form of ambiguity or conflict. The three resources represent different points on a continuum, making the fun-serious balance is an emergent characteristic which might tip over from one side to the other. The promotional point of view stricly separated the parents' view and the children's view, and determined its focus depending on the target group. The reviewers' point of view presented a more 'negotiated' position: the fun-serious balance is a trade-off, and a good balance for one player, might prove too educational for another.

This ambiguity is found even stronger in daily interactions. The family observations show that within one family, the focus can change from one situation to the next. The fun-serious ambiguity becomes a negotiation space between parents and children. In discussions with their parents about *Monkey Tales*, some children explicitly highlighted the math, while they focused on the fun aspects during actual play. Discussions about the game became struggles in which the accepted view on *Monkey Tales* was at stake: 'merely a game', or a useful educational tool.

Users creatively re-imagine what a specific technology means, based on their interests in a particular situation. These interpretations can be based on a dominant cultural model, or be entirely personal. The case study shows that interpretations are not static: users switch between interpretations, depending on which position is most interesting in a given situation. Technology appropriation does not necessarily lead to a stable interpretation, but can become a switching between different meanings, depending on the context. Based on this interpretive flexibility, we believe that more research into the effectivity of educational games is needed, as the *Monkey Tales* case shows that context and personal interpretation potentially have a significant impact on the fun-serious balance. However, even if this variability has far-reaching consequences, it does not necessarily need to be a threat: it can also be an opportunity for game designers to conciously allow players some choice to focus on either the fun or on the serious.

ACKNOWLEDGEMENTS

This research is part of G@S, a project cofunded by iMinds (Interdisciplinary institute for Technology), a research institute founded by the Flemish Government. Companies and organizations in the project are CUO|Social Spaces, ICRI and ITEC (KU Leuven), SMIT (VUB), MICT and MMLab (UGent), Belgacom, Larian Studios, Grin Multimedia, Die Keure, with project support of IWT.

REFERENCES

1. Avatargeneration (2014) *Chimply Marvellous Monkey Tales Educational Games.* http://www.avatargeneration.com/2014/01/chimplymarvellous-monkey-tales-educational-games/ Accessed 09-10-2014.
2. Barker, C. (2000). *Cultural Studies. Theory and Practice*. The Alden Press.
3. Barr, P., Noble, J., & Biddle, R. (2007). Video Game Values: Human-Computer Interaction and Games. *Interact. Comput.* 19(2), 180-195.
4. Bellotti, F., Berta, R., De Gloria, A. (2010). Designing Effective Serious Games: Opportunities and Challenges for Research. *iJET* 5(SI3), 22-35.
5. Brutalgamer.com (2011) *Monkey Tales Games (PC) Review*. brutalgamer.com, Accessed 12-09-2013.
6. De Castell, S., Jenson, J. (2003). OP-ED. Serious Play. *Journal of Curriculum Studies* 35(6), 649-665.
7. Fairclough, N. (2013) *Critical Discourse Analysis. The Critical Study of Language. 2nd Edition*. Routledge.
8. Gee, J.P. (2007). *What Video Games have to Teach Us about Learning and Literacy*. Palgrave Macmillan.
9. Habgood, M.P.J. (2007). *The Effective Integration of Digital Games and Learning Content*. Unpublished doctoral dissertation, University of Nottingham.
10. Harmon, E. & Mazmanian, M. (2013). Stories of the Smartphone in everyday discourse: conflict, tension & instability. In *Proc. CHI '13*, 1051-1060. ACM.
11. Isbister, Flanagan, & Hash, 2010 Designing Games for Learning: Insights form Conversations with Developers. *Proc. CHI '10*, 2041-2044. New York: ACM.
12. Larian Studios (2010). *monkeytalesgames.com.* Accessed 07-18-2013.
13. Meyer, B. & Sorensen, B.H. (2009). Designing Serious Games for Computer Assisted Language Learning – a Framework for Development and Analysis. In: Kankaanranta, M., & Neittaanmäki, P. (Eds.), *Design and Use of Serious Games* (pp. 69–82). Springer.
14. Mitgutsch, K., & Alvarado, N. (2012). Purposeful by design? A Serious Game Design Assessment Framework. In: *Proc. FDG '12*, 121-128. ACM.
15. Vissers, J., De Bot, L., & Zaman, B. (2013). MemoLine: evaluating long-term UX with children. In *Proc. IDC '13*, 285-288. New York: ACM.
16. Wakelin, N. (2011) Review: Monkey Tales PC Games Combine Math, Mazes and Fun! *Wired Geekmom* www.wired.com/geekmom/ Accessed 12-09-2013.

HCI, Civic Engagement & Trust

Mike Harding, Bran Knowles, Nigel Davies, Mark Rouncefield
Lancaster University
Lancaster, Lancashire, UK
hardingm@comp.lancs.ac.uk, branknowles9@gmail.com, nigel@comp.lancs.ac.uk,
m.rouncefield@lancaster.ac.uk

ABSTRACT
There is a widespread belief that pervasive technologies will encourage and facilitate partnerships between citizens and civic authorities, enabling individuals to play a greater role in civic planning, service delivery and infrastructure management. However, at present sustained use and perceived value of civic engagement technologies remains low because the design space is poorly understood by system developers who focus almost exclusively on empowering citizens rather than adopting an informed, inclusive approach that addresses the needs of both citizens and civic authorities, and helps establish trusted relationships between these different stakeholders. We report on an extensive study of civic engagement in the domain of public infrastructure maintenance and provide insights into the civic management processes to support future design of trusted civic engagement interactions.

Author Keywords
Civic Engagement; citizen participation; crowdsourcing; trust;

ACM Classification Keywords
H.4.m Information Systems Applications: Miscellaneous

INTRODUCTION
This paper is concerned with understanding and encouraging citizen engagement in civic life, and, consequently, in the design of trusted interactions with civic authorities. Growing populations and increasing demands on ageing civic infrastructure [9] make this a timely topic to explore. Two largely independent streams of research have begun to focus on these issues: (i) smart city programs that attempt to use pervasive sensing to monitor and understand the behaviour of cities as complex systems and (ii) civic engagement tools that provide citizens with technologies that enable them to play a greater role in the management and maintenance of their city.

CHI 2015, April 18 - 23, 2015, Seoul, Republic of Korea
Copyright 2015 ACM 978-1-4503-3145-6/15/04 $15.00
http://dx.doi.org/10.1145/2702123.2702255

Civic crowdsourcing tools have demonstrated the potential to integrate the collective knowledge of citizens [1], empowering users to take an active role in civic decision-making, urban management and service delivery. Maintenance of urban infrastructure [17], monitoring of environmental noise pollution and water management highlight areas of public concern where citizens have been able to collaborate with civic workers. However, interest in long-term civic engagement and use; and the perceived value of civic crowdsourcing applications has remained low, so any vision of civic authorities and citizens acting as partners appears a considerable distance from being realised.

Here, we consider opportunities, challenges and considerations for the HCI community in developing technologies that facilitate more effective civic engagement by addressing two contributory factors, that we argue represent important issues currently limiting the uptake of civic technology. Firstly, the current focus on a single stakeholder group (i.e. citizens) rather than the adoption of an inclusive design process that addresses the complex inter-relational concerns of both citizens and civic authority stakeholders, and secondly, a lack of appreciation of the high levels of mistrust that exist between citizens and their civic authorities. Why engage with a civic process if you believe nothing is likely to happen as a consequence? Most civic engagement tools tend to be implemented on mobile devices such as smartphones making them relatively easy to prototype. However, and in contrast, designing applications for civic authorities is complex and time-consuming. Civic systems tend to need to integrate with large, bespoke software platforms used to manage city infrastructure and hence are not typically amenable to the type of rapid prototyping and experimental approaches that have proved successful in the domain of the citizen. Such factors also lead to a lack of appreciation of the importance of trusted working relationships between citizens and civic authorities, and that understanding these relationships requires significant effort to involve each stakeholder group in the design process.

In this paper we investigate two different, but clearly and essentially related, issues: how to design for civic engagement and how to think about trust in ICT design in the domain of civic urban maintenance. We report on an extensive participatory design and iterative prototyping approach involving civic authorities, private contractors and the public. Through a series of formative ethnographic studies (including workshops & in-field observation) we firstly, contribute an in-depth understanding of urban maintenance processes, stakeholder relationships and perspectives on trust. Secondly, from this formative analysis of stakeholder perspectives and the domain we identify design considerations to inform the secondary phase of our research, the development and evaluation of a civic engagement prototype system. Finally we provide an analysis of stakeholder experiences with the deployed system prototype, and conclude by discussing future opportunities, challenges and design considerations that we have learnt from this (generally failed) deployment.

BACKGROUND AND METHODS

Our goal in this study was to understand the complex landscape of public infrastructure maintenance from multiple stakeholder perspectives to identify opportunities, challenges and considerations for pervasive technologies that facilitate 'trusted' civic engagement by design. Through our work we consider two main questions:

1. How do stakeholders rationalise their relationships? and, relatedly, exactly how is trust manifested in civic relationships and operationalised by stakeholders?

2. How might proposed civic engagement interactions through ICT facilitate trusted relationships? and, relatedly, how might they be integrated and experienced by public individuals, local authorities and private contractor workers?

We contribute an extensive study of the complexities and inter-dependencies that impact on stakeholder relationships in the public infrastructure maintenance domain and identify pragmatic considerations for researchers developing civic engagement technologies applicable beyond infrastructure maintenance.

Related Work

Civic engagement refers to an individual or collective action designed to identify or address a particular public concern such as urban maintenance that includes activities from refuse collection, upkeep of social housing, flood risk management through to highway repair. To most citizens (and indeed researchers) urban maintenance appears as a 'black box', with civic authorities seeming to make arbitrary decisions concerning which activities to undertake and when. It is probably unreasonable to expect citizens to know or care too much about the fine details of urban maintenance, but this lack of appreciation of a complex culture (where mistrust is commonplace) makes it challenging for citizens to understand or appreciate the activities of civic authorities, and difficult for citizens to form trusted partnerships with government authorities where mistrust and suspicion is the social norm.

Current efforts to empower citizens in civic life and local authority decision-making have led to a growing number of pervasive technologies that aim to encourage citizen engagement. We believe that current state-of-the-art civic engagement technologies fall short in motivating citizens to effectively contribute information that civic authorities are willing to trust and act upon, and will continue to remain unpopular unless inherent aspects of mistrust that exist are addressed in the design process. This requires considering both citizen and civic authority perspectives.

Citizen engagement technologies [18][24][16] in the domain of urban maintenance such as FixMyStreet [17], an established commercial civic crowdsourcing mobile application that enables users to exchange non-emergency, street-level issue reports (e.g. potholes, flooded highways), demonstrate a lack of understanding of the domain and interactions they aim to support. King et al.'s analysis of FixMyStreet from the perspective of platform developers, citizens and civic workers highlights that, in the majority of cases the system's design placed expectations on citizens themselves (typically the originator of the report) to update the status after observing that the problem had been resolved in-situ. Overall, citizens positively indicated a preference to using such a pervasive civic reporting application in comparison to traditional reporting channels (e.g. telephone, authority website), citing ease of use and time saving as key benefits. However, civic officials interviewed demonstrated scepticism, highlighting a badly executed design with concerns over accountability (i.e. citizens can post anonymously) and negative impact on existing channels for citizen engagement. Civic customer service workers noted further concern about the impact FixMyStreet could have on public perception of service reliability, citing reported issues that potentially go unresolved for extended periods of time that may have been fixed or are scheduled for completion. Critically for our research, King et al. highlighted a need to further explore requirements across all civic stakeholders in order to better inform the design to support more effective two-way citizen-civic relationships and address underlying institutional and citizen mistrust. Consequently, through an empirical participatory design process, we undergo this exploration and provide insights in the domain from multiple perspectives, whilst providing pragmatic considerations for addressing the inherency of mistrust in citizen and civic authority relationships in the public maintenance domain.

We have identified few related works in the literature that have attempted to undertake an empirical, participatory design process to understand the complexities of citizen-civic engagement in this domain; or that have taken a nuanced approach in considering trust in the design of ICT; or have been motivated by a need to address issues of trust. Aoki et al. [5] investigated the use of participatory sensing technologies to influence environmental authority decision-making through citizen involvement by examining key stakeholder perspectives, but this understanding was not applied to inform the design or develop implications for design. In our own previous work we have followed an empirical approach to understand the design of a civic system that supports the capture of accurate, 'trusted data' to address domain process inefficiencies. Our work in this paper focuses specifically on facilitating cooperative working relationships between civic authorities and the public, and considers how a broad understanding of citizen and civic relationships can inform the design of ICT to support trusted citizen-civic relationships. Exploring trust relationships between organisations, workers and public individuals through our investigation here has highlighted a need to consider our own perspective on trust in this domain. Moreover, in this work we particularly focus on aspects of human vulnerability, fear and harm as more applicable measures of trust (Rousseau et al. [22] and Baier [7]) and provide empirical examples (specifically in relation to knowledge sharing) where levels of trust manifest across both civic workers and citizens rooted predominantly in the acceptability of being vulnerable to another person or organisation's expected positive behaviours (or ill will).

Parker et al. examined [19] models for developing citizen trust in local civic services and argue that a focus on improving service performance does not necessarily correlate to increased levels of civic trust, referred to as the "performance paradox". They propose a model where trust can be developed in three key areas of interaction with the citizens (i) personal, on-going two-way interaction with civic worker individuals (ii) civic service delivery, and (iii) open and transparent decision-making. Through 'unwrapping' the 'black box' of urban maintenance we demonstrate how considerations for the design of civic engagement technologies can be realised to support similar models of interaction to potentially formulate trust, particularly approaches for supporting sustainable, two-way bidirectional interaction between citizen and civic worker individuals, a requirement highlighted by King et al.

Studies of trust in the context of mobile crowdsourcing systems have focused primarily on approaches to quantify trust metrics and mechanisms for supporting trust management across distributed devices [8]. A number of studies have investigated methods for quantifying trust (e.g. reputation) [25] to support optimised decision-making in pervasive crowdsourcing systems such as Amazon Mechanical Turk [4] and GeoTruCrowd [13]. While a common feature of systems that aim to provide visualise representations of trust between people, through our investigations we demonstrate findings that highlight concern where such digital representations can act to counterintuitively erode trust in citizen-civic relationships.

Civic Infrastructure Maintenance

In this section we provide a brief context of urban maintenance describing the complex processes and stakeholder relationships involved. Civic authorities invest significant sums of money in managing the maintenance of our urban areas [3]. But to most citizens, urban maintenance appears as a 'black box' with civic authorities seeming to make arbitrary sets of decisions about which activities to undertake leading to difficulties in establishing trusted partnerships. For example, consider the apparently simple case of a citizen reporting a problem with a street light in their neighbourhood. While the citizen may feel that they have performed their civic duty and submitted a reasonable report of the fault, in reality a detailed inspection would be needed to comply with the relevant standards (which currently runs to several hundred pages for the UK). As a result, the civic authority will typically send out a trained inspector which for the average citizen appears to indicate that the authority didn't believe their report. Examples of this kind of disconnect are prominent in highways maintenance, particularly in road resurfacing and road-side drainage management activities. Maintenance activities related to flood risk management such as gully cleansing regimes involve maintenance crews periodically cleaning silt and debris from road-side drains. Over time gullies can become overrun with silt and other environmental waste causing blockages in the drainage network. If left untreated prior to a weather event, blocked gullies can contribute significantly to the development of flooding in urban areas. Therefore, private contractors (common in the UK) are employed by civic authorities to cleanse an agreed number of gullies throughout the year. However, residents often perceive that the civic authority have not performed the necessary maintenance of gullies to mitigate the flood risk prior to a flood event taking place. In earlier work [14] we identified the complex hierarchy of organisation and intra-organisational stakeholders involved in the process of civic highways maintenance. Indeed, citizens are often mistaken in their assumption that their local civic authorities both manage and execute repairs. More commonly, private companies are employed to perform tasks in the field while civic personnel manage requests from citizens and internal inspectors, schedule defects to be fixed and inspect the quality of the repair work once completed.

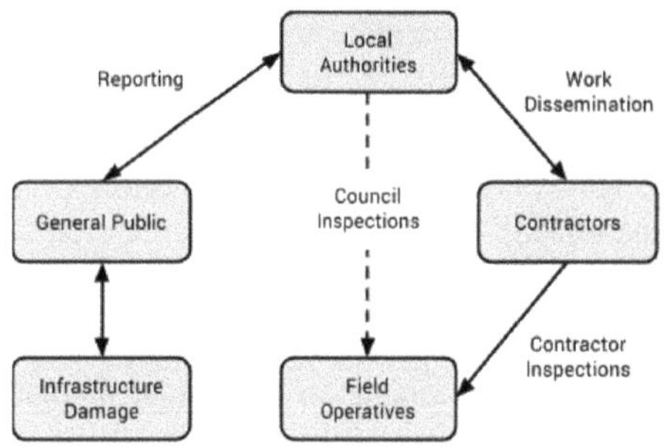

Figure 1. Highways maintenance actors and process

Areas such as highways maintenance have traditionally suffered from high levels of mistrust both externally from citizens dissatisfied with the quality of service, and internally amongst civic authorities and private contractors [11]. Mistrust is demonstrated in civic working practices through extensive inspections and monitoring of workers and contractors.

Method

In order to undertake an inclusive investigation of the problem domain we adopted a participatory design and iterative prototyping approach, engaging firstly in prior fieldwork with stakeholders through a series of formative ethnographic studies (including stakeholder workshops & one-to-one semi-structured interviews), and a subsequent iterative design process of civic engagement technology probes and prototypes that were evaluated through three focus groups and an in-situ user trial over an 8 month period involving local residents, civic authority and private contract workers operating in an urban area of the UK. Our formative work to understand highways maintenance processes, stakeholder relationships and perspectives on trust spanned a one year period involving 70 interviews with over three months of observing and shadowing stakeholders.

Through a formative analysis of stakeholder perspectives and the domain we identified design considerations to inform the secondary phase of our research, the development and evaluation of a civic engagement prototype system. Analysis of stakeholder experiences with the technologies deployed have allowed us to perform a thematic analysis and provide an insightful discussion around key opportunities, challenges and implications for researchers investigating the design of future civic engagement technologies.

UNDERSTANDING STAKEHOLDER PERSPECTIVES

Civic Authorities & Contractors

Our fieldwork with civic authorities and contractors involved informal, semi-structured interviewing (asking about work and trust incidents) and periods of observation (shadowing highways inspectors or highways maintenance gangs as they went about their everyday work). The fieldwork reported here was carried out by two ethnographers at seven different sites in the UK. Our fieldwork reveals instances of how trust is achieved in everyday work; and what sort of things produce trust and trustability or distrust and suspicion. Of particular interest was the detailed explication of the work of council inspectors and road maintenance gangs and their perception of and by the public.

The fieldwork provided numerous instances of trust in action, in particular of how trust is part of a developing organisational relationship that needs to be maintained as organisations change, acquire new staff or implement new procedures. However we found tremendous variation, and much suspicion, in the relationships between councils, contractors and the public. There was particular concern shown about how to effectively manage information flow between officials and the public, and how public individuals would perceive feedback (or lack of) from local authorities. One council official when asked about trust in the council amongst the public responded:

"If asked, most of them would say we don't fully trust the council. The problem is we don't get back to the public, that's changing this year. Or another response from a council official: *Ideally Mrs Smith can come into [the council] walk-in centre and ask what's happening on her street."*

When we look for trust in the fieldwork we find it manifested in various ways, some of which may be more consequential for design than others. We find aspects of trust in people; in their interpersonal interactions; shared histories and so on. We find trust too in particular processes: in systems, data, routines and various forms of technology, paperwork and computer work, through which processes are accomplished. To gain a greater understanding of stakeholder perspectives in this domain we conducted a two-day workshop with 25 participants from the highways maintenance sector including civic authority, private contractor and industry ICT providers. From this session participants identified a model and visualisation of trust that emphasised the difficulty in gaining trust and the speed and ease with which it can be lost, raising important design challenges for citizen-civic engagement that mediates bidirectional interaction, such as, the challenge of mitigating negative experiences to avoid catastrophic impacts on trust. Overwhelmingly participants agreed openness, and methods to support detection and early warning were essential for maintaining trust relationships to soften the impact and loss of trust if expectations were not met. In terms of factors that decrease trust the group highlighted the issue of inaccurate out-of-date or missing data. In particular, participants felt it was important to have transparency and awareness of the source and ownership of the data.

Citizens' & Local Communities

Our understanding of citizen perspectives were shaped by a number of interview and focus group studies which report on in this section.

National Highways Transport Survey

Our first study featured semi-structured interviews with 31 citizens who had originally taken part in the UK National Highways Transport survey [11]. The goal of the survey was to understand whether public individuals felt they could trust their local authority, and whether they trusted that services where reliable. Telephone discussions last between 15 and 35 minutes and were framed around the following questions: (i) can you remember any specific incidents that may have caused you to trust or distrust your civic authority?, (ii) is there anything more generally you'd like to say about the highways in your area and how they are maintained, and (iii) can you think of anything your civic authority actively does to make you trust them more?

Respondents to the first two questions focused primarily on the negative experiences where mistrust in their civic authority was compounded: *"Yes, basically [the problem is] potholes around the village where I live. There are hundreds of them but they [the civic authority] don't seem to bother to repair them. I've contacted the council and neighbours have on several occasions. They took the details but did nothing."*

Further respondents highlighted issues around highways maintenance tasks such as salting and gritting roads during adverse weather to address safety concerns. Supporting civic service awareness poses a particular challenge in the design of civic crowdsourcing applications that typically support a unidirectional flow of information from citizens to civic authorities. Traditional crowdsourcing approaches provide means for a requester (i.e. civic authority) to utilise the crowd to perform a task (e.g. report an issue). For civic authorities crowdsourcing can provide a heightened awareness of urban areas they would not typically gain through their internal workforce. However, it is important to consider the reverse whereby citizens are often unable to be in locations where civic authorities are actively performing work. Public awareness of council activities and understanding of civic authority constraints can help mitigate mistrust by managing citizen expectations. Responses to the final question focused around offline 'push' interaction from civic authorities, and the use of promotional news-sheets to help inform the public about civic services. When discussed many respondents either did not read them or believed the information to be inaccurate.

Focus Groups & Workshop

We further explored citizen perspectives of trust through two focus groups and a one day workshop following a similar structure to the civic authority 2-day workshop where we asked about the extent to which they trusted either their local council or contractors; their opinion of the information they were given and whether they were provided sufficient information about the activities of their local council. The results were not inspiring, suggesting a general level of distrust, both for politicians in general and for the ways in which information was presented:

"the information is too generalised ... its not always easy to find information in detail ... its all manipulated information ... it doesn't mean anything to me ... They give you information that they want you to see and think that's great"

During the workshop in particular we found the public were much better at generating visions of distrust rather than trust. This focus on the negative somewhat reflects Parker et al. findings [19] that demonstrate the public are more motivated to engage with civic authorities when there is a problem or issue to address. The group discussed the negative impacts of formalising trust in a digitally measurable manner. In particular, participants felt moving away from offline social contracts, which require trust to work, to formal indicators, which require authority and punishment erodes trust and that trust is very hard to gain but very easy to lose. The group also discussed the importance of personalisation and personal interaction when considering factors that impacted on their trust in organisations. Indeed, they highlighted examples of interacting with their council only to be met by an automated process (e.g. telephone IVR systems) or a human following a script. Participations felt less scripted, personal interaction would lead to greater empathy and capabilities to form affective bonds allowing parties to better formulate relational trust.

TRUSTED CIVIC ENGAGEMENT THROUGH ICT

Following our formative analysis of stakeholder perspectives and domain processes in this section we identify key design considerations and describe the implementation of a civic engagement platform.

Design Considerations

Identification, Capture and Persistence of Evidence

A common theme identified through our formative studies is a need to provide accurate, attributable evidence of activities. At present such evidence is typically created through a mix of electronic workflow systems, paper inspection trails and citizen reports. A shared, trusted repository of evidence that could be accessed by all stakeholders has the potential to significantly improve trust relationships.

Individual and Institutional Entity Representation

Closely related to the need for evidence is the requirement to be able to accurately attribute the source of evidence. For citizens and institutions accountability is critical to ensure stakeholders act responsibly when performing public activities, accountability also provides a means for stakeholders to assess the reliability of actions by being able to associate the action with the user entity who performed it. Without appropriate representation of real-world entities such as physical objects, citizens, road workers or civic institutions in the digital space, delivering technological capabilities to support attribution, and to allow users to build trust relationships becomes difficult. Indeed, the optional registration of citizen and civic users in engagement tools such as FixMyStreet highlight this problem where information is published through anonymous identities. For civic stakeholders, this limits opportunities to form relationships with citizen contributors and restricts capabilities to validate the reliability of the issues reported.

Explicit Support for Transparency and Trust Management

Much of our early findings indicate that supporting end-to-end bidirectional flow of information between citizen and civic stakeholders is essential in order to mitigate against civic mistrust. The highways maintenance stakeholder workshop further highlighted a need for intelligence in civic engagement platforms that can assess and provide early warning to a trusting entity of potential problems, including features to monitor citizen-civic dialogue exchanges to mediate automated triggering of system-generated information (e.g. detecting a citizen has not received feedback regarding a reported issue and sending reminders to civic stakeholders to provide a response).

Social Communication Channels

Offline opportunities for explicit social interaction and shared experiences facilitates individuals to form trustworthy relationships. However, traditional online interfaces for citizens to engage with civic authorities often act to depersonalise civic engagement (e.g. digital web forms for reporting problems) and promote relationship formulation with the authority rather than individuals within the civic authority. By allowing citizens and civic individuals to communicate in more freeform social ways increases the opportunity to understand one another, to become familiar with one another, and develop more effective trusted relationships when addressing a particular civic concern. Analysis of the citizen workshop also suggested that a reliance on formalised digital representations of stakeholder trustworthiness has the potential to erode trust (citizens reacted negatively to heavily scripted interactions with authorities).

System Prototype Overview

Our system probe comprised three core elements (1) a civic engagement platform providing functionality to support the integration and coordination of 3rd party front-end mobile citizen reporting and back-end civic management tools, (2) a mobile issue reporting application for citizens, and (3) a web based interface for civic authorities to enable civic workers to provide real-time correspondence on citizen reports.

Public Mobile Application

An initial public mobile application probe was developed to allow participants involved in our early public focus groups to (1) gain an awareness of the types of civic authority information that could be shared and visualised, (2) provide a tangible demonstration of how the public could interact with such information to support further engagement with managing civic authorities, and (3) discuss the interaction design to elicit further user requirements prior to an in-field deployment. The main screen of the prototype (Figure 2 left) provided a visualisation of real-time highways maintenance activities plotted on a map. Users of the prototype could view detailed information about the status of an on-going maintenance activity including start times and estimated completion times. Selecting a map icon provided information on specific workers (e.g. council, private contractor workers) involved in the coordination and completion of the work, providing personalised information that is not readily available to the public.

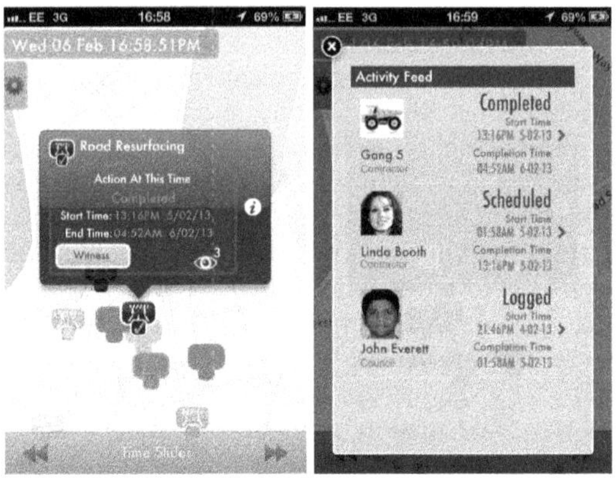

Figure 2. Initial prototype design

Following on from our initial probe we updated the design and implemented a functional prototype named 'Flooder' that supported the reporting of events related to flooding, allowing users to receive & report context-sensitive real-time updates about local flood issues. The public mobile application enabled users to view real-time flood data, including forecasted rainfall and gully silt level data integrated from a gully collection system [14] used by the council overlaid on a map and list view. Accessing information via the map allowed citizens to view flood information near to their current location. Users also had the capability to define areas of interest by providing a location that could be applied to filter the citizen reports they received. This second iteration of the application integrated with the civic engagement platform, leveraging enhanced features to represent public user entities (i.e.

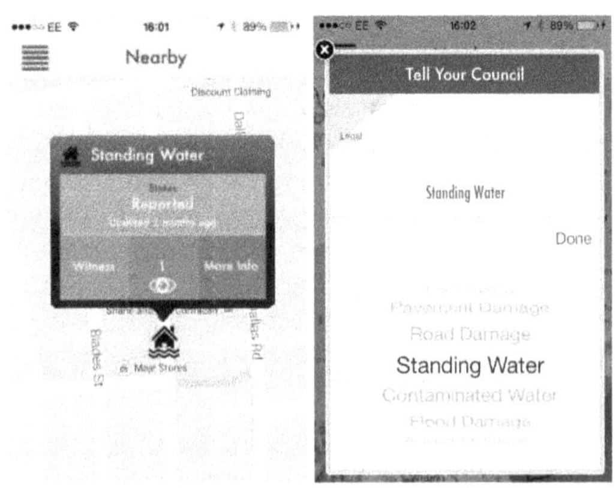

Figure 3. Flooder/SmartStreet application

local residents) and store public report information in the platform's open data repository, enabling 3rd party applications (i.e. web interface for civic authorities) to access report information and provide mechanisms to communicate directly with users of the Flooder application. Furthermore, this version of the mobile application included an interaction mechanism to 'witness' problems that had already been reported by other members of the public. This provided a metric civic authorities could use to prioritise issues that impacted on the greatest number of residences but also provided a means for residents to validate information reported by the civic authority to strengthen its trustworthiness. The constraint of only allowing the reporting of flood events and the impact on the perceived usability of the application from users (highlighted in our analysis) led to a 3rd evolution of the public application that enabled users to report about general issues such as potholes and street trash (Figure 3).

Civic Authority Report Management Interface

A report management web interface component was developed to provide civic operators involved in the management of public complaints and issue reporting with capabilities to view reports and communicate directly with public individuals using the Flooder/StreetSmart mobile application. Our early investigation into existing information workflows and management of public reporting highlighted a reliance on email systems to manage communications between civic operators and public individuals. Indeed, upon receiving a report, typically through telephone communication, contact details and the nature of the report are forwarded onto an operator given the role of handling specific types of report (e.g. street damage, waste management). Depending on the nature of the report it is then scheduled (typically after a physical assessment by a council inspector) as a works order by the managing civic authority. Based on our insights into the reporting process we designed a web interface that could be easily accessed by multiple workers from a computer with a web browser. In particular, the web interface included capabilities to view a list of Flooder/StreetSmart reports updated in real-time, and controls in the interface to allow civic operators to update the status of reports as new information regarding a particular report became available.

Each report was shown in a list view that included specific details about the report including, the issue description, cause, visual evidence, number of witnesses, the time the report was submitted, status of the report and the location of the issue reported. On receiving a report the civic operator could update the status of a particular report to one of work 'scheduled', 'started' or 'completed'. On a status change instigated by the civic operator the civic interface generated a request to the civic engagement platform to notify citizen users of changes related to reports they were interested in. In addition to a notification on the mobile application, the civic interface generated a personalised message (including the name of the civic operator) that gave more detailed information about the status change.

TRIALS & EVALUATION

In order to validate our civic engagement platform design and provide additional insight into the application domain we deployed the system in an area of the UK that commonly experience annual issues related to flooding and highways degradation. In particular we wanted to investigate the ways in which members of the public encounter issues such as damaged pavements, broken streetlights or roads that have become blocked with floodwater. Indeed, it is often assumed that citizens choose not to report such problems - either through a lack of time or because they believe their civic authority is already dealing with the problem. Over time as issues remain unresolved members of the public may begin to question the competency of their civic authority in dealing with issues, and begin to lose trust in their ability to deliver services. In contrast, civic authorities may be unaware of particular issues or are already in the process of scheduling workers to fix reported problems unbeknown to the public. Therefore, through a series of system user focus groups we aimed to gain a deeper understanding of such behaviours in reporting and sharing information through the system. The civic and citizen facing components were trialled over an 8-month period with a 12 participant opportunity sample.

Qualitative user feedback was gathered throughout using three participant focus groups and an online social networking group. The first focus group took place prior to the application being deployed in order to understand existing attitudes to civic reporting. Subsequently we deployed the application, provided participants with application training and then conducted a further focus group. Based on the feedback from this second focus group, and in response to a change to the needs of the users, we created a new version of the application that we then obtained feedback on from a final focus group. This second version of the application, called StreetSmart included other forms of data than those on the Flooder application such as roadworks and a facility for our user group to post reports. Prior to the deployment of the system, participants were given a demonstration of the application to help inform the design prior to a full user deployment. Participants were asked to consider a range of questions related to information sharing with local authorities and personal opinions about the initial system designs.

Stakeholder Experiences & Analysis

In general, participants favoured an application that was multi-functional and offered a range of information sources and functions that could be customised to their own preferences. In particular, participants showed a strong will to become active contributors: *"I think you would do. If there was a pot-hole on the road that you kept hitting ... and all you had to do was click on an app and go pothole down our road."* However, there was some concern about the consequences of witnessing, especially being labelled a "nosey neighbour".

We next considered the question of anonymity and asked participants if this was important to them when reporting and witnessing faults. *"It would be to a lot of people ... Depends on what it is, if it is related to a person, you wouldn't want that person to know ... But if it is something happening then you wouldn't mind, and if someone knows you are a trusted person, like maybe they see your name they are going to trust it. The council would trust you so they broadcast it. If you attach your name to it then they wont think it was a bogus report. So long as they don't send it out with your name."*

Since the mobile applications depended upon people's willingness to report and witness events we enquired into our participants experiences in this regard – had they ever reported anything to the council: *"some yes ... [Interviewer "such as"] ... lights out, pot holes. Online you can report ... I put a request in to look into speed bumps where cars were speeding ... I called the number on the website ... they told me to get other people in the community to make the same request to give it more weighting ... but nothing has been done ... I could call up and follow it up, but I haven't had any letter of why or why they haven't done anything. There is no indication that it is being looked into."*

The issue of feedback seemed important to our focus group and we asked when they would expect feedback: *"Within 6 months you would expect some feedback to say what conclusion they had come to (speed bumps), but it would be good to know before ... so there could be some kind of appeal etc. I don't like automated responses, only as some proof to say I did send the email but you didn't reply."*

During deployment, unusually for England, we were blessed with several months of drought. In consequence, most of the social networking group discussions concerned some of the technical and administrative details of the loaned phone and application. For example, there was some concern about the maps on the application, how much information they displayed and how up-to-date they were.

There was also some concern expressed (repeated in later focus groups) about the sheer practical difficulties of posting or witnessing, in particular the need to accompany a post with a photo, given that our participants were likely to be engaged in driving a car at the time they saw a reportable incident. There were also some issues connected to the amount of information appearing on screen, how useful such information was and the extent to which this merely contributed to an overall sense of clutter. After the trial had run for a couple of months without any significant amount of rain, we held a focus group to share and discuss participant experiences. Unfortunately, and despite our participants enthusiasm for the trial, no flooding had been witnessed.

Another particularly significant factor that impacted strongly on the trial was the difficulty in recruiting champions within the civic authorities. Despite significant enthusiasm, a series of personnel changes and operational challenges meant that even when our participants witnessed events there was no-one in the council to respond. It is clear that this impacted on our participants and the trial, diminishing, to an extent, some of the strong initial enthusiasm. That said there remained a significant level of support for the study and many of the comments at the focus group concerned ways in which particular features of the application could be improved. Although the application was considered easy to use and very user friendly there were some suggestions for improvements:

"its quite hard if you want to be quick ... to put an exact location ... By the time you press it you could be 3-4 miles away, you want to do it, especially if you have to stop your car or something like that, it could be a bit away ... so you want a couple of ways of notifying of when there is a flood ... One where you can just press on the location and then write a report and another one where you can't do that because your driving at the time but when you stop further up the road you want to pin point it more accurately"

"... or just use ... my location and have a drop down of reports instead of filling it in yourself have an automatic one that is already filled in so you just then go back and edit it later on ... So you could do that and go ... oh theres flooding here with a drain ... and then give a description of what it is when you've stopped the car"

Reflecting earlier comments on their distrust of politicians in general there was also some discussion concerning the whole subject of trust and whether and how it might be impacted by using the application and the response of the council.

" ... Im not very political, but if you don't trust the council, just because they're posting on the app it doesn't mean they're trustworthy. The app doesn't make any difference."

The second half of the trial involved the StreetSmart application. We held a final focus group with our participants who generally considered the application a good idea and an easy method of communicating problems to the council and making the public aware of problems. In particular the variety of topics that were reportable using StreetSmart were considered an advantage over the more limited reporting options of Flooder. Users reported a broad range of issues from the usual flooding, blocked drains and standing water to fly tipping and public disorder. However, much of the focus group discussion was dominated by reports of technical issues such as difficulties of reporting whilst travelling (so that occasionally people would make a report, of standing water or a blocked drain for example, and accompany it with a picture of something entirely unrelated).

Other technical issues raised by our participants included occasional poor signal issues; that the map would not always provide an accurate indication of their location since it was not always up-to-date with regard to street names (this was explained as an issue with Apple maps) and unnecessarily cluttering the map. Finally, and perhaps most significantly, one persistent and de-motivating gripe from our participants was the lack of any feedback from the council via the system. There was little feedback noted, or indication that issues had been scheduled to reassure participants that someone was listening, and that their efforts were not entirely fruitless.

DISCUSSION

Patrick et al. in 'Designing systems that people will trust' [20] argue that *'online users have to develop the knowledge needed to make good trust decisions, and developers must support them by making trustable designs'* and give some specific advice, six lessons, to developers who want to build a trusted service. We have considered their advice and the extent to which it might be applicable to citizen engagement services as revealed in our research. Some, such as ease of use characteristics and reducing uncertainty seem important to almost any design; others seem especially relevant to our experiences and interest in 'trust', most obviously that *'external factors or context that may seem to be unrelated to the situation can affect trust'* and, most importantly that, *'trust probably develops in stages. In the first stage, superficial interface properties, such as colours and designs, can have a large effect on initial trust decisions. Later, users may make trust decisions based on more reasoned analysis of information'* suggesting that our application may ultimately prove successful. In these final sections, we use our broad understanding of stakeholder experiences both within the domain and with our prototype technologies to formulate a number of common themes around key opportunities, challenges and implications for researchers investigating the design of future civic engagement technologies.

Understanding both citizens and civic authorities fears & vulnerabilities

While there are a number of current commercial civic engagement applications available [17] [6] [16], we would argue that in most cases such systems do not prioritise trust relationship formulation as a key requirement during design; or evaluate empirically the impact of such technologies on stakeholder perspectives towards trust. What emerged in both our initial field studies and in the evaluation of our prototype engagement technology was the extent of longstanding mistrust, even cynicism, between the stakeholders, with the civic authority fearing litigation and the public anticipating disinterest and inaction from the authorities; and how quickly and easily trust and eager anticipation could change to mistrust and suspicion. As researchers we needed to both understand and manage this difficult situation, hence our emphasis on a holistic approach. Interviews with both citizens and civic workers evinced a general under-current of fear and vulnerability in the sharing of information and knowledge in a civic context. Commonly, civic workers expressed concerns of publicising internal activities because of fear of litigation, while public individuals worried over how their information would be used both by their civic authority and other members of the public. Clearly, understanding such vulnerabilities is essential to ensure stakeholders can reasonably begin to trust each other (Baier [7]).

Integrating with corporate I.T solutions

While citizen applications may be effectively deployed as small mobile applications, systems designed for civic authorities require integration with much larger corporate I.T systems and workflows, and this represents a significant obstacle to innovation. Indeed our integration with two civic platforms (including a works orders platform) was constrained to a unidirectional flow of information from the civic platforms to our civic engagement platform. Clearly, to support greater integration between public facing and civic solutions - civic authorities must consider how such systems are opened to enable the utilisation of new forms of information gathered and shared through public civic engagement tools that deliver more effective civic engagement experiences.

Supporting feedback, transparency & activity awareness

All of our stakeholder engagement exercises highlighted the frustration that the different stakeholders felt with the lack of feedback and transparency in most maintenance systems. In our case, even though we recognised its importance in developing and maintaining trusted relationships, the lack of feedback and transparency was largely unrelated to the technology but instead a product of political and organisational factors over which we had no control. A recurring observation from our fieldwork and evaluation study was the lack of appreciation amongst the different stakeholders of the challenges each faces. For example in most cases it was a surprise to several participants that their local civic authority did not actually perform work in the field but outsourced work to several contractors, and therefore their suspicion of 'the council' was often entirely misplaced.

New working practices & civic decision strategies

Previous work [14] has demonstrated the impact of new technology on working practices in urban maintenance. Our deployment of technology highlighted the challenges civic authorities face in adapting to new levels of citizen interaction with civic processes and suggested the need for a change in working practices - to support such applications. This is not just a concern for the contractor and authority stakeholders since citizens would also need to accustom themselves to changes in everyday working practices. A related common theme through our analysis with citizens is a perceived disconnect between work activities observed in the field (e.g. returning to a particular area multiple times to repair potholes) and a general lack of understanding of internal organisational decision strategies, processes and contractual constraints.

To date these points have not been considered during the development of civic engagement tools and yet our research suggests that all of these are crucial to the creation of successful systems. Understanding and then operationalising trust in systems or trust in applications is difficult, as Thatcher et al [23] indicate. Unlike Goncalves et al [10] we were not especially motivated to explore psychological aspects of citizen engagement or disengagement but note their comment that *'a successful system should allow citizens to easily express the details of the service changes they desire, this is not enough on its own, and citizens require additional motivation to actively participate'*.

In evaluating our civic engagement application, and its relative failure, aspects of Grudin's [12] classic analyses of why applications fail seem appropriate. With the loss of our 'champion' the council's priorities were attuned to more obvious 'political' considerations. As one of our contractors said in regard to 'smart gully services' (where only selected gullies are cleaned) *"the problem with the council is that the guy who was most interested has left ... the drainage engineer said, no, we're cleaning them all ... I can understand why ... autumn comes, the leaves fall and we get blocked gullies ... if a gully sucker pulled up in a street and only cleaned one they'd (the public) all be on the phone"*

Success might have been more likely had we recruited a greater number of users - what Grudin terms 'critical mass' - and we could have thought more carefully about the adoption and deployment process, (although nobody could have predicted the drought). Certainly it could be suggested that our civic engagement application was a technical success but an organisational failure, that is, there was a need for a clearer understanding of the necessary support within the council for implementing and managing change. As Akamavi et al [2] suggest, civic engagement presents both organisations and individuals with opportunities for sharing knowledge but any success is dependent on an organisational culture and trust that supports knowledge sharing. The relative failure of civic authorities to actively engage with the system underlines our much broader argument that designing for civic engagement requires a much more complex view of trust, including how it is manifested in everyday interaction and relationships within and between the different stakeholders as well as 'through' the technology.

CONCLUSION

This paper considers two different, but clearly and essentially related, issues: how to design for civic engagement and how to think about trust in IT design. There is a clear thread in research and analysis that points to technology as fostering and encouraging social detachment and disengagement, as in Putnam's famous concerns about "bowling alone" [21]. This paper has pursued a rather different research agenda to consider the ways in which technology might contribute to increasing citizen engagement. This is based on a reasonable belief that we are heading towards a future that will increasingly involve partnerships between citizens and civic authorities to enable individuals to become more engaged in civic planning, service delivery and infrastructure management. But this application domain is poorly understood by most system designers who focus almost exclusively on empowering citizens rather than considering the needs of both citizens and civic authorities and establishing trusted relationships between these stakeholders. Our analysis of the trust relationship between the different stakeholders highlights issues that appear crucial to fostering civic engagement, issues that are integral to but go well beyond the initial design of the technology to include its deployment and evaluation.

In this paper we have provided detailed insights into civic management processes that we believe will benefit developers of future civic engagement systems. Based on these insights we have described the design, implementation and evaluation of an open engagement platform to support experiments with two-way dialogues across mobile citizen and back-end civic technologies used to support a civic-engagement tool that has provided further insights into the domain of citizen-civic engagement. Olphert et al. suggest that e-government development is typically *'characterised by a techno-centric approach with minimal engagement of citizens'* and consequently advocate a participatory approach *'providing citizens with the necessary skills and capabilities to engage effectively offers the key to the successful development of systems such as e-government which impact our lives in the 21st century Information Society'* [15].

Our research suggests that part of that participatory approach involves understanding user notions of trust, as part of the design, co-design and re-design of trusted technologies to support civic engagement. This paper has been concerned with exactly this issue of how technology can be designed, developed and utilised to encourage and facilitate active citizen involvement, and how this both impacts on and is impacted by different stakeholders and different manifestations of trust.

REFERENCES

1. *The Wisdom of Crowds: Why the Many Are Smarter Than the Few*. James Surowiecki, 2005.
2. Akamavi, N., and Kimble, C. Knowledge sharing and computer supported collaborative work: the role of organisational culture and trust. In *Proceedings of the 10th Conference of the United Kingdom Academy of Information Systems*, Citeseer (2005), 22.
3. Alliance, A. I. Annual local authority road maintenance (alarm) survey 2014. `http://www.asphaltindustryalliance.com/images/library/files/ALARM_Survey_2014.pdf`.
4. Amazon. Amazon mechanical turk website. `https://www.mturk.com/`.
5. Aoki, P. M., Honicky, R. J., Mainwaring, A., Myers, C., Paulos, E., Subramanian, S., and Woodruff, A. A vehicle for research: Using street sweepers to explore the landscape of environmental community action. In *Proceedings of the SIGCHI Conference on Human Factors in Computing Systems*, CHI '09, ACM (New York, NY, USA, 2009), 375–384.
6. Association, A. P. Nyc 311 - issue reporting mobile application. `http://www1.nyc.gov/connect/applications.page`. Accessed: 2014-07-26.
7. Baier, A. Trust and antitrust. *Ethics 96*, 2 (1986), 231–260.
8. El Husseini, A., M'hamed, A., El Hassan, B., and Mokhtari, M. Trust-based authentication scheme with user rating for low-resource devices in smart environments. *Personal Ubiquitous Comput. 17*, 5 (June 2013), 1013–1023.
9. for an Urban Future, C. Caution ahead: Overdue nvestments for new york's aging infrastructure. `http://nhtsurvey2013.econtrack.co.uk`, March 2014.
10. Gonçalves, J., Kostakos, V., Karapanos, E., Barreto, M., Camacho, T., Tomasic, A., and Zimmerman, J. Citizen motivation on the go: The role of psychological empowerment. *Interacting with Computers* (2013), iwt035.
11. Group, N. S. S. National highways public satisfaction survey. `http://nhtsurvey2013.econtrack.co.uk`.
12. Grudin, J. Why cscw applications fail: problems in the design and evaluationof organizational interfaces. In *Proceedings of the 1988 ACM conference on Computer-supported cooperative work*, ACM (1988).
13. Kazemi, L., Shahabi, C., and Chen, L. Geotrucrowd: Trustworthy query answering with spatial crowdsourcing. In *Proceedings of the 21st ACM SIGSPATIAL International Conference on Advances in Geographic Information Systems*, SIGSPATIAL'13, ACM (New York, NY, USA, 2013), 314–323.
14. Knowles, B., Harding, M., Blair, L., Davies, N., Hannon, J., Rouncefield, M., and Walden, J. Trustworthy by design. In *Proceedings of the 17th ACM Conference on Computer Supported Cooperative Work Social Computing*, CSCW '14, ACM (New York, NY, USA, 2014), 1060–1071.
15. Olphert, C. W., and Damodaran, L. Citizen participation and engagement in the design of e-government services: The missing link in effective ict design and delivery. *J. AIS 8*, 9 (2007).
16. openPlans Organisation. Open311 civic issue tracking specification. `http://open311.org/`.
17. openSociety. Fix my street website. `http://www.fixmystreet.com/`.
18. Org., N. Neat streets website. `www.neatstreets.com.au`.
19. Parker, S., Spires, P., Farook, F., and Mean, M. *State of Trust - How to Build Better Relationships Between Councils and the Public*. Demos, 2008.
20. Patrick, A., Marsh, S., Briggs, P., et al. Designing systems that people will trust.
21. Putnam, R. D. *Bowling Alone: The Collapse and Revival of American Community*. Simon & Schuster, New York, 2000.
22. Rousseau, D. M., Sitkin, S. B., Burt, R. S., and Camerer, C. Not so different after all: A cross-discipline view of trust. *Academy of Management Review 23* (1998).
23. Thatcher, J. B., Carter, M., Li, X., and Rong, G. A classification and investigation of trustees in b-to-c e-commerce: General vs. specific trust. *Communications of the Association for Information Systems 32* (2013).
24. Tsampoulatidis, I., Ververidis, D., Tsarchopoulos, P., Nikolopoulos, S., Kompatsiaris, I., and Komninos, N. Improvemycity: An open source platform for direct citizen-government communication. In *Proceedings of the 21st ACM International Conference on Multimedia*, MM '13, ACM (New York, NY, USA, 2013), 839–842.
25. Yu, H., Shen, Z., Miao, C., and An, B. A reputation-aware decision-making approach for improving the efficiency of crowdsourcing systems. In *Proceedings of the 2013 International Conference on Autonomous Agents and Multi-agent Systems*, AAMAS '13 (Richland, SC, 2013), 1315–1316.

Factful: Engaging Taxpayers in the Public Discussion of a Government Budget

Juho Kim[1] **Eun-Young Ko**[2] **Jonghyuk Jung**[2] **Chang Won Lee**[2] **Nam Wook Kim**[3] **Jihee Kim**[2]
[1] MIT CSAIL, Cambridge, MA USA
[2] KAIST, Daejeon, Republic of Korea
[3] Harvard SEAS, Cambridge, MA USA
juhokim@mit.edu {key44, heretor92, chiyah, jiheekim}@kaist.ac.kr namwkim@seas.harvard.edu

ABSTRACT

While a government budget determines how taxpayers' money is allocated to various programs and stakeholders that compete for limited resources, the extensiveness and complexity of the budget and its process hinder taxpayers from understanding the budget information and participating in the public discussion. To engage taxpayers in the public discussion around budgetary issues, we leverage news articles containing budgetary information for design opportunities. We present Factful, a web-based annotative article reading interface that enhances the article with fact-checking support and contextual budgetary information by processing open government data. In our lab study, participants using Factful discussed more critically with more fact-based supporting statements. They built a rich context surrounding the relevant budget facts beyond what was presented in the article. Factful presents a simple yet powerful model for supporting fact-oriented budgetary discussions online by leveraging open government data.

Author Keywords

Budget; Discussion support; Open government data; Annotation tool; Fact-checking; Deliberative democracy.

ACM Classification Keywords

H.5.2. Information Interfaces and Presentation

INTRODUCTION

The idea of "deliberative democracy" emphasizes that citizens should actively participate in decision making and related discussions [6]. Open and public discussions are essential to realize its ideal, whose characteristics include informed (i.e., arguments should be presented with accurate and relevant information), balanced (i.e., conflicting views need to be considered), and substantive (i.e., arguments should be judged by evidence and not by other external factors), among others [8]. As more and more public discourses take place online via social media, news outlets, and discussion forums, there is a growing attention to support a deliberative democracy in online discussion environments. The HCI community has actively analyzed existing online discourses and designed systems to promote informed and balanced discussions [4, 18, 19, 21, 25]. On the other hand, with more governments engaging in open data policies, there are opportunities in using data to better inform online deliberation. In this work, we specifically focus on supporting **budget-related discussions online** by leveraging open budget data.

A government budget is a layout of the government's financial plans on how to spend its revenues (e.g., tax), which is its answer to how to best allocate limited resources. It contains an immense amount of information divided into a large number of programs and services, as everyone's life in a constituency is involved. Moreover, the budget and its processes are complex and multidimensional. There are numerous decisions to make in budget procedures, which determine how budgets are prepared, approved, and carried out. In making the decisions, various interests and tradeoffs must be considered. Although such complex and subtle nature of budget lends itself to public discussions [11], most taxpayers do not actively engage in them. Firstly, the extensiveness and complexity of the budget and its processes hinder taxpayers from understanding how their tax money is spent and which government programs they can benefit from. Secondly, not many interactive channels exist for taxpayers to participate in discussions, as well as stay informed and engaged.

This research addresses the question of how to engage taxpayers in the public discussion of a government budget online. To identify the challenges taxpayers face in accessing and understanding budgetary information and participating in budgetary discussions, we conducted a) 182-person online survey on budget awareness, b) interviews with three experts in a government budget sector, and c) interviews with five taxpayers. Findings reveal that the budget is extremely complex and extensive, making it difficult for taxpayers to understand it with a balanced view. Discussions around budgetary issues are often intertwined with objective facts (e.g., amounts allocated to programs) and subjective opinions (e.g., stakeholders competing against each other for more resources). Such complexity makes it difficult to engage in more meaningful discussions for experts and taxpayers alike.

For many taxpayers, media outlets were the primary channel through which they learned about the budget-related issues.

CHI 2015, April 18–23 2015, Seoul, Republic of Korea

ACM 978-1-4503-3145-6/15/04$15.00
http://dx.doi.org/10.1145/2702123.2702352

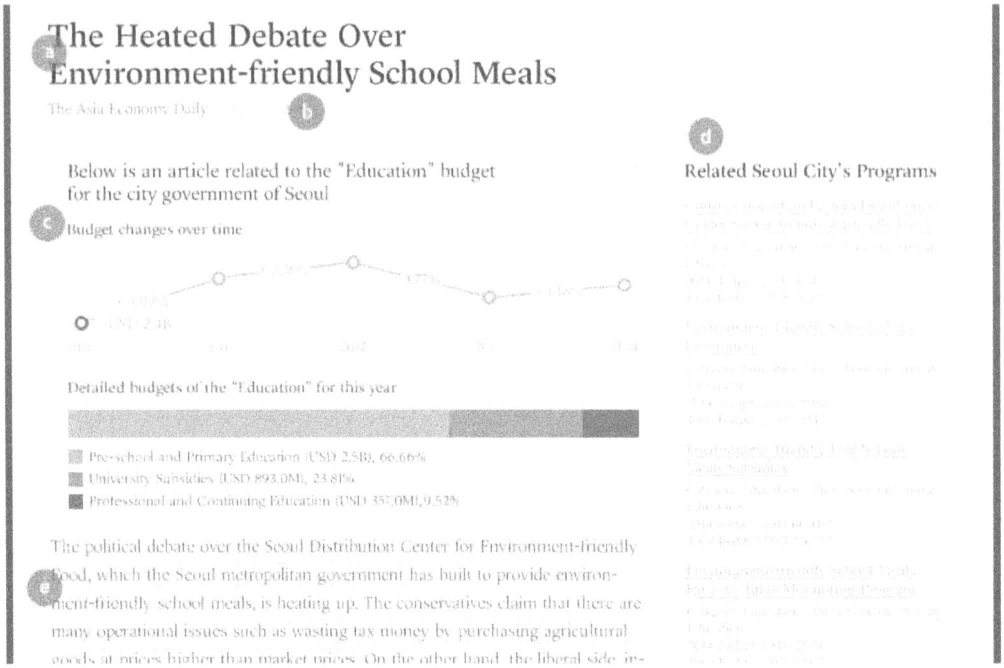

Figure 1. Overview of Factful powered by open budgetary data from the Seoul metropolitan government: (a) title of the article, (b) posted date and news outlet, (c) contextual budget category panel (education), (d) individual budget programs relevant to the article, (e) article content.

We also noted that taxpayers are conscious of how fact-based and balanced the article is, and that they often rely on social channels such as reader comments, social media, and discussion forums to get additional information. We conclude that there are unique opportunities to raise public awareness and support discussions on budgetary issues by leveraging the article reading experience, which is already familiar and social to many taxpayers. Specifically, we explore two ideas: 1) provide customized support for **fact-checking** and 2) embed **contextual budget information** related to an article.

To support fact-oriented discussions around budgetary issues, we built Factful, a web-based interface for reading articles (Figure 1). A reader can request fact-checking on any part of the article through in-place annotations. Other readers reading the same article can respond to the request by adding relevant references and scoring their confidence in the references. Factful also automatically analyzes the article text and inserts related budget information, including semantically matching programs, temporal changes in budget size, and programs of similar budget sizes. Factful also supports annotation-based threaded comments for general discussion.

To evaluate the effect of fact-checking support and contextual information in promoting budgetary discussions, we conducted a laboratory study where participants read budget-related articles with discussion only, discussion + fact-checking, and discussion + fact-checking + contextual information. In our lab study, participants using Factful discussed more critically with fact-based statements. They built a rich context surrounding the relevant budget facts, beyond the article content. With a more critical view and richer context around the budget-related articles, they engaged in fact-oriented discussions more actively.

The contributions of the paper are as follows:

- A survey and interviews with budget experts and taxpayers that revealed design challenges for improving public awareness on budgetary issues.
- Factful, a web-based article reading application with annotation support for fact-checking and automated support for contextual budget information.
- Results from a laboratory study showing that participants using Factful showed more critical view on the article and discussed with richer context.

RELATED WORK

We discuss previous work on supporting political discussions online, with specific focus on fact-checking and reading support with contextual information.

Political Fact-checking

Fact-checking normally refers to the act of verifying the truth of public facts and claims. Political fact-checking is most common, which is normally done by journalists who specialize in assessing political claims by reviewing large amounts of documents [13]. Media companies or non-government organizations publicly share their fact-checking results online, from websites such as `factcheck.org` and `politifact.org`. To overcome the labor-intensive and costly nature of expert-driven approaches, automated or community-driven solutions to detect and even fix misinformation have been introduced. Computational fact-checking [29] models claims into parameterized queries to fight vague or questionable statements. Finder [7] combines user-reported and automatically mined disputable claims to highlight disputable claims on any web page. Reddit had a successful experiment in community-powered political fact-checking during the U.S. presidential debate [1], in which anyone could submit a political claim for the community to verify. On-demand fact-checking has been explored in the crowdsourced voters' guide [17]. Maater [22] attempts to tap into the wisdom of the crowd for fact-checking, which lets readers contribute information sources and improved assessments. Our work extends these crowd-moderated approaches to provide fact-checking specifically for the domain of government budgets.

Involving taxpayers in the fact-checking process may also align with how people accept new facts. Previous research argues that learning a new political fact and correcting misinformation is not a simplistic process [10], which involves people to internally assess new information against their current beliefs [30]. Accepting this view, fact-checking should be seen a persuasive process rather than a point solution of showing or checking facts. Meola et al. [23] and Metzger [24] argue that fact-checking approaches should be catered to the ability and motivation of users, and advocate for techniques that allow responding to tasks that are most needed, comparing multiple references, and considering peer or editorial review. Garrett and Weeks [10] argue that real-time corrections to political misperceptions can raise resistance, and suggest socially recommended corrective messages as a potential solution to avoid biases. Factful attempts to enable social interactions around facts with annotation-based fact-checking requests and responses.

Supporting Political Discussions Online

Online news services and discussion forums, while they lower the barriers to participation for anyone interested, also face challenges in monitoring the quality of comments. Discussion forums implement different moderation mechanisms, such as community guidelines with dedicated moderators or aggregated crowd ratings [20, 26]. Research has shown that individual motivation in reading and writing online comments affects perceptions of quality [5].

While the web hosts diverse perspectives and information, selective exposure [9] prevents people from accessing them because individuals favor information that confirms and reinforces their current views, resulting in polarization. Previous research has introduced social mechanisms and interfaces to promote listening, balanced perspectives, and exploration of diverse opinions. Examples include visualizing the political lean in the reading behaviors [25] and source expertise indicators [21]. ConsiderIt [18] facilitates a fact-grounded political discourse with personal pro/con lists for an issue. Added social layers help users browse others' lists. Reflect [19] encourages active listening and deliberation in online comments. It adds a listening box to the comment section, asking users to summarize the points made in the original comment. Inspired by these systems, we innovate on budgetary discussion support that little previous research has focused on.

[1] `http://www.reddit.com/r/politicalfactchecking/comments/10w86s/official_politicalfactchecking_thread_for_the_9pm/`

Reading Enhancements

Enhancing the news reading experience with additional information is another method for promoting a healthier discussion. Anchored discussion is an alternative form of commenting that allows readers to directly annotate on specific parts of text (e.g., `medium.com`). The Reader's Helper [12] detects the reader's topics of interest and automatically annotate phrases containing these topics to help readers quickly locate items of interest. Tell Me More [15] automatically fetches stories that provide additional yet relevant quotes, actors, figures, and information and presents snippets in the sidebar of the screen. Videolyzer [4] supports credibility evaluation of claims via video and text annotations. Contextifier [14] augments articles about a company with annotated stock visualizations. Kong et al. [16] applied crowdsourcing to extract references between text and charts to maximize the effect of visual reinforcements in charts. In an educational setting, an interface supporting anchored annotation led to more frequent and specific comments than a discussion board [1]. Factful takes a similar approach to these systems by analyzing the article text and inserting contextual information to relevant parts.

SURVEY & INTERVIEWS: KEY OBSERVATIONS

To better understand the current challenges taxpayers face in accessing, processing, and discussing with budgetary information, we conducted a web-based survey as well as a series of interviews with both taxpayers and experts.

Taxpayer Survey & Interviews

We designed a web-based survey to gauge taxpayers' budgetary awareness in South Korea. The survey asked respondents about their perception of the government budget, followed by quiz questions that asked to estimate the size of various budget programs. We also inserted a simple A/B test for a question that asked people's opinions about whether to increase or decrease the roadwork budget. In one condition, we displayed detailed contextual information about related programs and their relative sizes against the roadwork program. The other programs were sibling programs in the transportation and logistics category, which is the parent category of the roadwork program. The goal of this setup was to see if presenting contextual information affects people's opinions.

Responses were collected by an external commercial survey agency that controlled for the age, income level, and political affiliations of the respondents. Total of 182 people responded (82 female), with our target age (20 - 59) reflecting the age distribution of the Korean population as of 2013: 20s (21%), 30s (25%), 40s (31%), and 50s (23%). 82% had college or higher education. Self-reported annual income ranges showed 10% with no income, 66% below USD 46K, and 24% higher than USD 46K (Korea's GDP per capita in 2013: USD 26K). Self-reported political affiliations showed 41% liberal, 30% conservative, 18% neither, and 11% not specified.

To complement the survey data with a qualitative understanding of taxpayers' awareness and challenges, we conducted semi-structured interviews with five taxpayers: three college students with ages 20, 22, and 23 each, and two income-taxpayers, one in the top 20% income percentile and the other in the top 1%. Each interview session took about 30 mins. The interviewees were guided to articulate their knowledge and experiences on a government budget. Here we summarize main findings from both the survey and the interviews.

1. Low awareness and interest in budgetary issues. In 7-point Likert scale questions (1-negative, 7-positive), survey respondents showed moderate interest in knowing about the government budget (4.6) and believed knowing about it is useful to them (4.5), but indicated they were not quite knowledgeable (3.1) and didn't actively search for budgetary information (3.2). On a question about estimating the relative proportion of the military budget within the entire government budget (10.2% as of 2013), respondents' estimates were almost twice higher (20.26%, median=20, SD=14.05). When we asked survey respondents to select a budgetary program larger in size between two options (e.g., welfare vs military), only 39% of the answers were correct, averaged over four such comparison questions per session. While incorrectly guessing simple numbers may not directly correspond to lack of awareness, many respondents expressed interest in improving their budgetary knowledge.

Interviewees felt disconnected from budgetary information, as an interviewee said, *"I feel distant from all the big numbers that don't really mean anything to me."* They also expressed frustration that there is no channel to make their voices heard in the process of writing a budget proposal, executing the budget, or settling the budget. Echoing the survey results, interviewees commented that they didn't have enough budgetary knowledge, which in turn made them reluctant to participate in online discussions. As an individual's influence is rather insignificant, taxpayers responded that their interest and awareness on budget-related issues are short-lived and volatile, unless anything directly concerns their daily lives.

2. Contextual information matters in opinion formation. In forming opinions about budgetary issues, access to relevant and contextual information may matter. In the A/B test setting that asked survey respondents to indicate their opinion on the change of the roadwork budget, the group with no contextual information replied that it should increase by 22.6% on average, while the group with contextual information only desired a 9.2% increase ($p = 0.01$ with Mann-Whitney's test, $z = -2.5$). No significant differences were found between different age, income, or political affiliation groups. Where does this difference come from? A possible explanation is that by seeing other programs in the same category, respondents might have realized the tradeoff involved in raising the roadwork budget and compared the relative importance against other programs that were displayed. This can be especially true for a majority of taxpayers with limited awareness and understanding of the budget, who are less likely to hold a strong current view that may add resistance. While this simple intervention is not meant to conclusively demonstrate the value of contextual information, it provides an insight that contextual information may affect how people form opinions about budgetary issues.

3. News media are the familiar and preferred way to learn about budgetary issues. A majority of our survey respondents said they regularly read articles online (74%), with 7% via social networks. This is comparable to the U.S. data, which shows 50% of population reading online news and 10% on social networks in 2012 [2]. Interviewees also confirmed that news outlets were their primary source of information to learn about budgetary issues. None had attempted to read government reports, and they found official reports to be hard to access and interpret when shown by the researchers. The interviewees mentioned that information presented in news articles is more accessible because they are written in a comprehensible, engaging manner. They were also well-aware of the fact that information presented by media is potentially biased. They also pointed out that other people's comments help them recognize the potential subjectivity, bias, or error in an article. Comment sections to news articles serve as an alternative source of learning through a means of social interaction. A U.S. survey aligns with this observation, with 37% of users finding commenting on news stories as an important feature to have, and 25% have a commenting experience [27].

Expert Interviews

We further conducted semi-structured interviews with three experts in the government budget domain: a former congressman, a current staff member to a congressman, and a current government official in the Ministry of Strategy and Finance in South Korea. By interviewing domain experts, we hoped to understand why channels for accessing and discussing government budgets are not very public-facing, and what challenges existing resources and media face in raising taxpayers' budgetary awareness. Each interview session took about 1-2 hours. The interviewees were asked to walk through the budget processes they had worked on, and to elaborate on how they made budget-related decisions and handled the complexity of the budget. Here we summarize key findings drawn from the interviews.

1. Budget-related issues are multifaceted. All three interviewees emphasized that the budget entails various goals such as economic growth, job creation, and solid social safety net, so that careful decision making and discussions with multiple interest groups and government ministries are needed.

2. Budget is too extensive for a small group of experts. We observed that the budget procedures cover extensive information to be handled by a small number of experts in the executive and the legislature. Therefore, fact-checking itself can become a big challenge and sometimes important matters can be missed in the process even among experts. An interviewee said, *"The system is short-staffed ... it's impossible to check every detail of a government budget in a review process."*

3. Budget-related processes are black boxes to taxpayers. We observed that budget-related facts and processes are often obscure and not accessible to taxpayers. An interviewee said, *"(Taxpayers) sometimes only see their own interests and fail to realize that compromises need to be made. Therefore, it is challenging for us to accommodate what taxpayers want."* Moreover, we observed that publicly available resources are often presented poorly for taxpayers to develop the necessary perspectives. Budget reports are often dispersed across multiple websites of ministries and agencies, leaving the public in disarray when they try to gather information.

DESIGN GOALS

Our findings from the survey and interviews imply that budgets are complex, contextual, and extensive, and that taxpayers commonly rely on news articles to access budget-related information. To addresses these challenges and promote open budgetary discussions, we decided to augment the article reading experience already common to many, rather than design a completely new channel. We have identified design goals for a **budgetary discussion support tool** below. The individual design goals provide concrete guidelines to encourage public participation in budgetary discussions while reading news articles.

Present rich, contextual budgetary facts while reading. The taxpayers in our interviews listed the lack of relevant knowledge as one of major factors which discourage them to engage in a discussion of a government budget. Accessing relevant facts and supporting evidence can help construct a richer context, potentially leading taxpayers to construct more informed opinions. A reading interface can fetch relevant facts for easier access, thus reducing the need to search for external data. As a result, discussions can also be more fact-oriented and focused on budgetary issues.

Provide built-in methods for evaluating the credibility of facts and claims. The taxpayers in our interviews raised questions on the objectivity of news media. They expressed concerns around lack of diversity in the political spectrum certain media cover and potential biases in information sources and interpretations. Social- or crowd-based moderation can be a potential solution, as interviewees suggested that they rely on other's comments and statements to complement their understanding. Interface support can be designed to rate the credibility of information sources, compare multiple possible sources for a fact, and vote on other's facts and claims. Embedding the fact-checking process and discussion into an article itself can potentially lower the barrier to participation.

Add structured, lightweight, and multiple ways to participate. According to our survey and interviews, a common challenge taxpayers faced in joining budgetary discussions was lack of confidence in their ability to contribute. Therefore, it would make sense to design multiple ways to participate, especially lightweight and structured methods that require little effort and domain understanding, to motivate users who are not knowledgeable about the matter. We explore raising annotated questions and requesting fact-checking as lightweight methods. Having multiple ways to contribute allows users to engage at different depths, depending on personal interests or level of commitment.

Let readers initiate discussion with meaningful chunks of information. Due to the complexity of budget discussions, users can benefit from being able to scope and initiate discussion with any level of information they are interested in. Supporting annotative discussion can give users more control in what the discussion should be about. In most cases, budget-related conversions pertain to a specific topic, while official documents tend to hold more information than the topic covers. The implications are that the information needs to be refined and broken down into digestible units for readers to encourage participation. Annotations at a finer-grain level can reduce the cognitive load for readers and promote a clearly scoped discussion.

FACTFUL: BUDGET-AWARE READING INTERFACE

This section introduces **Factful** (Figure 1), a system for supporting budgetary discussions online by enhancing the article reading experience. Factful analyzes an article, queries the budget database to fetch relevant budgetary facts, and adds the fact-checking and contextual budget information layers to the article reading UI. While the **contextual budget information** layer presents automated, ambient information that helps readers learn about relevant facts, the **fact-checking** layer supports active, social discussions that are fact-driven. We expect the two layers to complement each other in serving the goal of improving budgetary awareness and discussion.

Processing Budget Data

To serve snippets of budgetary facts at various granularities (e.g., article-, number-, and word-level), Factful maintains a database of budgetary information per each budget program, indexed by its name, hierarchical category structure, and temporal changes in the amount. Our current database is built with budget data from the Seoul metropolitan government in South Korea. The original interface was designed in Korean and was translated to English for the screenshots in this paper. With the recent commitment to open government data, the Seoul metropolitan government was the first in the world to publicly release their internal official documents in April, 2014. They publish 75.9% of their internally communicated documents since 2013. Related to the budget, the published documents contain detailed information about daily budget transactions of each program and of each department.

To meet our specific needs to construct per-program references, we merged two datasets from the city's open government project [`opengov.seoul.go.kr`]. First, Factful processes and indexes these internal documents to construct a database for enhancing the reading interface. The second source is *Clean Budget*, which has the general budget information of each program, including this year's assigned budget, total budget, executed budget, etc. Our data processing module retrieves the budget category information of each program by mining the city's open government gateway website and processing the city's official documents. Our current dataset covers the city's programs in full, from 2010 to 2014. For 2014, the city government assigned approximately USD 24 billion, with its structure containing 13 first-level categories and 4629 individual programs (as of September 2014, continuously growing over time). The database construction needs to be performed once initially, although incremental program updates to the database can be made anytime.

Displaying Contextual Budgetary Information

When a user opens an article using Factful, Factful analyzes the article text, issues a set of queries to the database for relevant facts, and displays the retrieved contextual snippets in the UI. We explore three types of contextual budget information, which we describe below.

1. Annual budget changes and article-level category: Factful presents the reader with an overview of a high-level budget that's most relevant to the current article (e.g., education, welfare, environment), as can be seen in Figure 1c. The idea is to equip the reader with high-level budgetary information before reading the article. Upon detecting the closest budget category, Factful generates a graph of annual budget changes for the selected category with the amount and a percentage of difference against the previous year. Factful also shows a list of third-level categories (e.g., pre-school education, general management of university from Figure 1c), which belong to the root-level category (e.g., education). The budget amount for the current year and the relative proportion within the category are displayed.

Our category detection algorithm works as follows: 1) all the budget program names are parsed and stored in a bag-of-words model; 2) frequent words within each category (above a pre-configured threshold), stop words, and short words (shorter than two characters, may be specific to the Korean language) are removed; 3) keep a tally of how many hits each category finds by going through each word from the article; 4) assign a "fit" score for the current category by summing all hits; and 5) pick the category with the highest score.

2. List of most relevant programs: When only presented with high-level budget category information, our pilot users complained that they would benefit more from concrete programs they could intuitively understand the purpose of. We decided to display a list of most relevant individual programs to the article (Figure 1d). Located in the sidebar, each entry displays the name, amount, higher-level categories it belongs to, and a URL that links to a government-maintained webpage with more information.

Our program suggestion algorithm picks top five programs for the current article, by using a customized TF-IDF algorithm [28]. Factful considers all program names as a corpus, and each program as a document. For each non-stop word in the article, the TF-IDF score is computed against each program. After all words are processed, the highest scoring N programs are presented. This simple TF-IDF method returned relevant programs for a number of articles spanning various domains in our internal tests. This may be the case because most budget-related articles focus on a specific topic and include many official budgetary terms. Some practical notes are that language-specific customization and weight adjustment with respect to word length (the longer the more weight, may be specific to Korean) affect results.

3. Automatic annotations with amount matching: Our interviews with taxpayers showed that they were turned away from a large amount of budget units that don't provide enough context in everyday lives. When monetary values are present in an article, Factful automatically highlights these values and annotates with budget programs that are of similar amounts (Figure 5b). The idea is to give readers comparison points, leading them to consider alternative options that the given

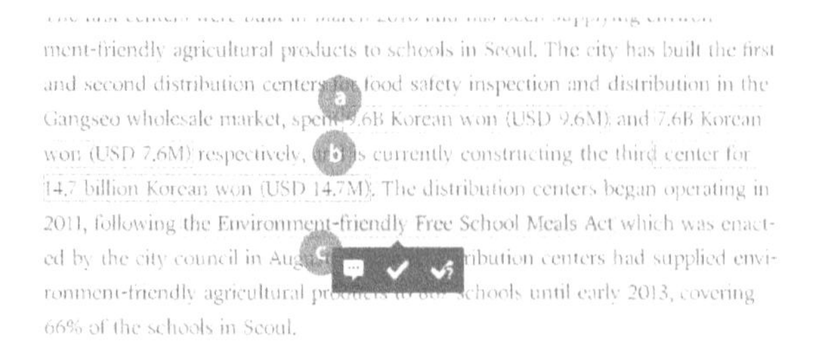

Figure 2. Dashed boxes indicate annotative regions for commenting, fact-checking and fact-check requesting: (a) a blue box indicates that Factful automatically annotated money amounts with budgetary information, (b) a gray box indicates there exists either users' comments, fact-checks, or fact-checking requests in the covered text, (c) a orange-highlighted indicates a current selection, which opens a popup menu with options for commenting, fact-checking, and fact-check requesting (from left to right). The menu opens when the user selects a dashed box or highlights content by mouse-dragging.

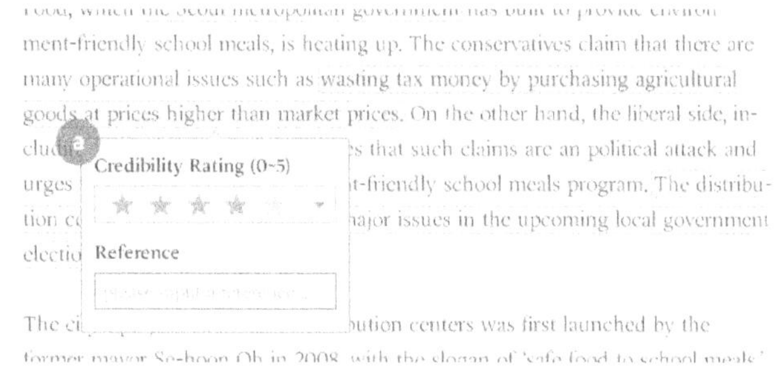

Figure 3. Annotative fact-checking interactions: clicking on the fact-check button opens a popup (a), so that a user can evaluate the credibility of the highlighted phrase in a 5-point scale, and add a URL reference that verifies the phrase.

amount in the article can achieve. Our amount-matching algorithm simply identifies all monetary values from an article with a rule-based detector, queries the database with items of similar amounts and categories, and displays top matches in the sidebar.

Annotative Fact-Checking

The fact-checking layer supports crowd-moderated, annotative fact-checking activities to encourage fact-driven discussions. Upon highlighting a phrase in an article, users can fact-check by adding a reference and assigning a credibility score, request a fact-check to make an open call, and start a threaded discussion with comments (Figure 2c).

Fact-checking: Factful has built-in support for fact-checking activities. Readers can initiate a new fact-checking activity by selecting a questionable phrase, or respond to a fact-checking request submitted by others. Fact-checking involves 1) providing an external reference to a statement made in the selected part of the article, and 2) evaluating how credible the statement is in a 5-point scale (Figure 3a). A fact-checked item provides a list of references and a brief summary of credibility ratings of the highlighted section (Figure 4a).

Fact-checking requests: Fact-checking requests are the most lightweight way to participate in the Factful-supported discussion. When a reader encounters a questionable statement, but does not have enough knowledge or feel committed to

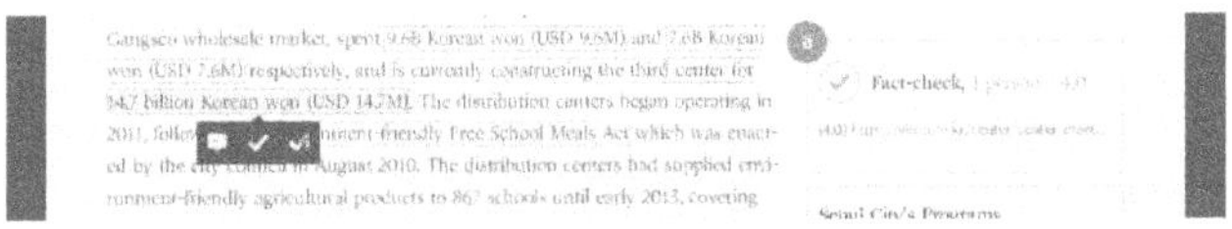

Figure 4. Fulfilling a fact-check request changes the sidebar display: (a) the number of completed fact-checks for the phrase, with a list of URLs entered and average credibility score.

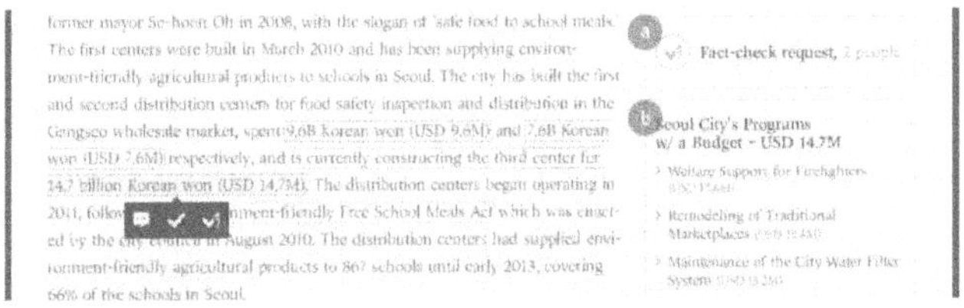

Figure 5. Budgetary fact enhancements for the selected phrase (orange-highlighted): (a) the number of fact-check requests for the phrase, (b) a list of Seoul city's programs most relevant and closest to the amount included in the phrase

actively engaging in the verification process, he can simply click the fact-checking request button. By separating the request and verification processes, tasks are smaller in size with low entry barriers. (Figure 5a). Despite the simplicity, fact-checking requests are still valuable because they initiate budgetary fact research and open discussions by leaving visual anchors for future readers.

Threaded discussion support: Factful supports threaded discussions based on annotations, as can be seen in other online venues like Medium [`medium.com`] (Figure 6). It is designed to serve as a place for open-ended discussions, complementing fact-checking activities and contextual budgetary information. Readers may leave a comment by highlighting a phrase and clicking the comment button (Figure 2c).

EVALUATION

To assess the effects of Factful on taxpayers as news consumers, we conducted a lab study that asked participants to read news articles on a government budget and discuss with others. We compared the baseline (annotative commenting only), Fact-checking (annotative commenting with the fact-checking layer), and Factful (fact-checking and contextual budgetary information) conditions. We hypothesized that reading news articles on budgetary issues with Factful leads to richer discussions. Specifically:

- H1. Readers will hold a more critical view on the article with Factful.
- H2. Readers will discuss with more fact-based statements with Factful.
- H3. Readers will build a rich context surrounding the relevant budget facts using Factful.
- H4. Readers will initiate and engage in the discussion with more existing discussion activities.

Participants

We recruited 38 participants from a behavioral study participant pool at a university. We divided them into three groups of 12, 13, and 13: the baseline, Fact-checking, and Factful groups, respectively.

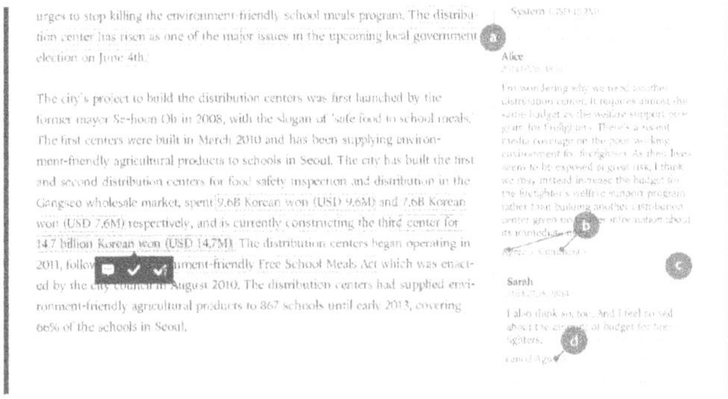

Figure 6. Threaded discussion support: (a) annotative discussion thread, (b) readers can agree (analogous to "like") or reply to an existing comment, (c) a threaded comment, (d) the cancel button for "agree".

Tasks and Procedures

Our lab study used a between-subject design (baseline, Fact-checking, and Factful), where the interfaces progressively included the additional fact-checking and contextual budgetary information support. The baseline condition supported threaded discussions, the Fact-checking condition supported fact-checking in addition to the baseline condition, and the Factful condition had contextual budget information in addition to the Fact-checking condition. In an hour-long session, each participant read three articles and engaged in unstructured discussions with a given interface, for seven minutes each. They were paid $10 for their participation and time.

We selected three articles that directly covered Seoul's budget and policies: 1) a political dispute regarding eco-friendly school meals, 2) a critical view on the Seoul metropolitan government for wasting its budget on advertising its tap water 'Arisu', and 3) a grand-scale waterway construction project. Participants could see activities of others who used the same interface as they did, and engage in discussions with them. We ensured that each participant read articles in a randomized order, meaning that they will see different levels of activity (i.e., the first article they read is likely to have much less discussion than the third one).

For each article, participants answered questionnaires before and after reading an article. The pre-reading survey asked about self-evaluated interest and informedness on the subject matter of the article in 7-point Likert scale (1-low, 7-high), while the post-reading survey included the questions about their interest and informedness again, and how credible and fact-based the article was. In addition to reading articles and filling out surveys, participants were allowed to search any relevant information on the web. The session ended with a final survey about the experience of each conditions' features and their usability.

Methods for Analyzing Discussion

To compare the quality of discussion we conducted a discourse analysis and quality assessment. To understand the characteristics of each comment, we coded the comments based on two dimensions: the topic that a comment addresses (related to budget, policy, or else), and the intention of a comment (express an opinion, provide information, or ask a ques-

1. Topic: Budget, Policy, Others

2. Intention

Opinion	w/ objective basis
	w/ subjective basis
	w/ no basis
Information	new & verifiable
	confirming existing
	unverifiable
Question /Info request	objective
	subjective
Simple statement	

Table 1. Discussion coding categories: each comment is coded with one of the 25 categories.

tion). Chen et al. [3] have explored similar fact attributes and comment categorization. The intention category was further segmented as shown in Table 1. This coding scheme led to total 25 exclusive categories (3x8 = 24 + simple statement such as "nice"). Two researchers extensively discussed the coding scheme with a few examples to arrive at the presented scheme. They then independently classified each comment into the 25 categories in a blind condition. Note that comments containing several sentences with different intentions were separated into multiple comments as they were heterogeneous in nature. For the total of 404 comments from all study sessions, inter-rater reliability was 0.613 (unweighted Cohen's Kappa). The two researchers discussed in person to reach agreement and finalize the labels.

Additionally, we asked five external raters to rate the quality of discussions using dimensions derived from Fishkin's work on deliberation [8]: informed, balanced, conscientious, substantive, and comprehensive. We turned these dimensions into statements and presented as 10-point scale (1-low quality, 10-high quality) questions for external raters. We also asked the raters to score the overall discussion quality from each interface condition. For a consistent evaluation environment, all interface enhancements were removed to only display the comments.

Results

Overall, participants reported limited interest in and knowledge of topics covered in articles. For 7-point scale questions, the mean self-reported interest levels were 4.03 (SD=1.48), 3.92 (SD=1.74), and 3.13 (SD=1.61), and knowledge levels were 2.47 (SD=1.52), 2.62 (SD=1.76), and 2.28 (SD=1.19) for baseline, fact-checking, and Factful groups, respectively.

We now present a summary of participants' discussion activities from the study. Table 2 shows per person activity counts. While the total number of comments is not significantly different across interface conditions, fact-checking requests and fact-checking were used more frequently in the Factful group than the fact-checking group. Note that fact-checking requests are a lighter form of contribution than comments, and fact-checking requires much more effort.

activities/person	Baseline	Fact-checking	Factful
Comments	10.5	10.85	10.54
Fact-checks	-	0.58	0.83
Fact-check requests	-	2.75	3.25
Comment "likes"	5.67	6.83	4.58
Total activities	16.17	21.92	20.08
Thread length in words	13.04	10.18	14.37

Table 2. Summary of discussion-related activities during the lab study

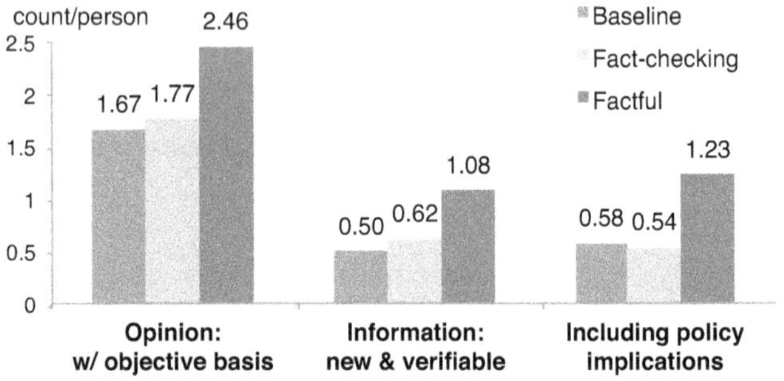

Figure 7. Summary of discourse analysis, showing per-interface comparisons for certain comment types.

The amount of activity is probably not informative enough because people were in a lab study with time limits and external incentives, not completely voluntarily participating. We instead focus on the differences between activity types and discussion quality, which we expect will depict the differences between the conditions more accurately.

Results of our discourse analysis are presented in Figure 7. Of the three labels presented, opinions with objective basis and new and verifiable information are derived from Table 1. We additionally counted comments that included policy implications. Factful users made more comments in all three labels presented, although the differences were not statistically significant (Kruskal-Wallis Test, $p > 0.2$).

The distribution of comment types in each condition is presented in Table 3. The Factful group created more questions and less simple statements than the other groups.

H1 (Readers will hold a more critical view on the article with Factful.) We asked a 7-point Likert-scale question (1-not at all, 7-very much) on how much they trust the article after each session. Average score was lower in Factful (4.03) than in baseline (5.08) and fact-checking (4.77) (Mann-Whitney Test, $p < 0.01$, $z = 2.19$ for baseline and $p < 0.05$, $z = 3.29$ for Fact-checking). Also, external raters' discussion quality score for the Factful group was higher (6.6) than baseline (4.93) and fact-checking (5.67) groups ($p < 0.05$, χ^2=6.97).

While the number of critical opinions per person was not significantly different between three groups (5.14, 4.15, 5.54 per person), the subjects of critic were different between groups. While Factful participants left 10 (0.77 per person) critics about articles, no baseline participant cast doubt on the ar-

count/person	Baseline	Fact-checking	Factful
Opinion	6.25	5.23	6.23
Information	0.83	1.00	1.08
Question	2.00	2.23	3.08
Simple statement	1.42	1.85	0.69

Table 3. The number of comments per each participant, for each comment type and interface condition.

ticles. Instead of criticizing the articles, baseline participants criticized each other (1.25 per person) more than the other two groups did (0.31 for fact-checking and 0.46 for Factful).

H2 (Readers will discuss with more fact-based statements with Factful.) Factful participants discussed with more objective supporting arguments (2.46 per person) than the other two groups (1.67 for baseline, 1.77 for fact-checking). Additionally, they raised more questions asking for objective information (2.54 questions per person) than the other two groups (1.75 for baseline, 1.77 for fact-checking). In addition to simply reading or asking for facts, Factful participants introduced out-of-article information by extending what was available in the article. Although they wrote information-providing comments (1.08 per person) only slightly more than the two other groups (0.83 for baseline and 1.00 for fact-checking), almost half of those were objective information from external sources. Comments from the other two groups were more focused on existing information and unverifiable information.

H3 (Readers will build a rich context surrounding the relevant budget facts using Factful.) The Factful group engaged in discussions with more policy implications than the other two groups. More than just criticizing the government policies and budget spendings, Factful participants came up with new ideas that would be helpful for policy makers. They suggested more opinions with policy implications (1.23 per person) than the other two groups (0.58 for baseline, 0.54 for fact-checking), although the difference was not statistically significant. External raters gave a significantly higher score (6.93) to discussions in Factful for the criterion 'they discussed with various perspectives and supporting grounds' (Kruskal-Wallis Test, $p < 0.05$, χ^2=7.71).

H4 (Readers will initiate and engage in the discussion with more existing discussion activities.) For all participants in all groups, the self-reported interest level increased more after the third session (4.76) than after the first (4.07), although the difference was only marginally statistically significant (Mann-Whitney Test, p=0.06, z=-1.91). If the trend continues with more users, the exposure to other users' accumulated activities may affect the commenting behavior. Being able to initiate discussions not only from the article but also from other users' comments or fact-checking requests can also lead to more active discussions.

DISCUSSION

The role of contextual information: Eight of 13 participants using Factful said that the similar budget-sized program information from automated annotations served as a basis of evaluating government spending. Factful users commented that *"Without such information, it would be hard to determine if the given government spending is worth or not."* [Factful group, p07], and *"By seeing that information, I was able to critically evaluate the government spending with relevant budgetary issues, not blindly agreeing with the article."* [Factful group, p02] Six participants said that the sectoral budget information gave them a basic idea of the article topic and related budgets. One participant noted that the sectoral budget information in Factful made reading through the article easier, because he felt the budget terms and numbers in the article were less obscure.

Expertise in fact-checking: Our study results suggest that participants with low awareness still participated in fact-checking (0.83 times per article per person with Factful). While some fact-checking activities would require domain expertise and reviewing multiple sources, we observed many simple activities such as adding missing references and verifying factual information from a single source. Also, readers not knowledgeable about budgets may still be domain experts related to certain budget programs and do fact-checking.

Generalization to other datasets and countries: In this paper we used news articles and budget structure of South Korea, and a question remains – how the findings might generalize to different cultures. As previous research shows that we can identify common generic budget processes regardless of the legal structure [11], we believe many countries share similar issues in their budget and related processes.

Limitations

Our study mainly focused on understanding the feasibility of our ideas in the context of Factful. The lab study had several limitations. First, study participants were mostly students at a university. Further study is needed to see if the study findings can generalize to taxpayers of varying political standpoints and socio-economic status. Also, the lab setting may have biased the types of social interactions that took place. As more taxpayers engage in open online discussions, quality control and information overload can be issues. When applied to opinionated claims, social voting and the wisdom of the crowd may have a limited effect for quality control [13]. We will consider novel quality control mechanisms and ways to simplify the view.

CONCLUSION AND FUTURE WORK

Despite the importance of a government budget for taxpayers, they have low interest and awareness in budgetary issues and discussions. This paper explored the idea of embedding the contextual budget information and fact-checking layer into news article reading, with the goal of engaging taxpayers in the budgetary discussions online. We implemented this idea with Factful, a web-based newsreading interface powered by the budgetary facts of the Seoul metropolitan government.

For future work, we plan to deploy Factful as a live system and study how taxpayers' budgetary awareness and discussion behaviors change. We will also consider a publisher's and journalist's perspective, as Factful may be useful in data journalism and internal fact-checking for newsrooms. For generalization, we will explore other civic domains that are rich in factual, structured data such as budgeting process and auditing, as well as healthcare (e.g., disease and nutritional facts). With scalable UIs and techniques to present budgetary facts to more taxpayers, Factful presents a simple yet powerful model for leveraging open government data to support a deliberative democracy online.

ACKNOWLEDGMENTS

This research is supported by the Undergraduate Research Program and High-Risk High-Return Program at KAIST. Juho Kim is partly supported by the Samsung Fellowship.

REFERENCES

1. Brush, A. J. B., Bargeron, D., Grudin, J., Borning, A., and Gupta, A. Supporting interaction outside of class: Anchored discussions vs. discussion boards. In *CSCL'02* (2002), 425–434.
2. Caumont, A. 12 trends shaping digital news, 2013. Pew Research Center. [Online; posted 16-October-2013].
3. Chen, Y., Yang, J., and Ribarsky, W. Toward effective insight management in visual analytics systems. In *IEEE PACIFICVIS '09* (2009), 49–56.
4. Diakopoulos, N., Goldenberg, S., and Essa, I. Videolyzer: Quality analysis of online informational video for bloggers and journalists. In *CHI '09*, ACM (2009), 799–808.
5. Diakopoulos, N., and Naaman, M. Towards quality discourse in online news comments. In *CSCW'11*, ACM (2011), 133–142.
6. Elster, J. *Deliberative democracy*, vol. 1. Cambridge University Press, 1998.
7. Ennals, R., Trushkowsky, B., and Agosta, J. M. Highlighting disputed claims on the web. In *WWW'10*, ACM (2010), 341–350.
8. Fishkin, J. S., and Luskin, R. C. Experimenting with a democratic ideal: Deliberative polling and public opinion. *Acta Politica 40*, 3 (2005), 284–298.
9. Frey, D. Recent research on selective exposure to information. *Advances in experimental social psychology 19*, 1 (1986), 41–80.
10. Garrett, R. K., and Weeks, B. E. The promise and peril of real-time corrections to political misperceptions. In *CSCW '13*, ACM (2013), 1047–1058.
11. Gomez, P., Friedman, J., and Shapiro, I. Opening budgets to public understanding and debate: Results from 36 countries. *OECD Journal on Budgeting 5*, 1 (2005).
12. Graham, J. The reader's helper: A personalized document reading environment. In *CHI'99*, ACM (1999), 481–488.
13. Graves, L. *Deciding What's True: Fact-Checking Journalism and the New Ecology of News*. PhD thesis, Columbia University, 2013.
14. Hullman, J., Diakopoulos, N., and Adar, E. Contextifier: Automatic generation of annotated stock visualizations. In *CHI'13*, ACM (2013), 2707–2716.
15. Iacobelli, F., Birnbaum, L., and Hammond, K. J. Tell me more, not just "more of the same". In *IUI'10*, ACM (2010), 81–90.
16. Kong, N., Hearst, M. A., and Agrawala, M. Extracting references between text and charts via crowdsourcing. In *CHI'14*, ACM (2014), 31–40.
17. Kriplean, T., Bonnar, C., Borning, A., Kinney, B., and Gill, B. Integrating on-demand fact-checking with public dialogue. In *CSCW'14*, ACM (2014), 1188–1199.
18. Kriplean, T., Morgan, J., Freelon, D., Borning, A., and Bennett, L. Supporting reflective public thought with considerit. In *CSCW '12*, ACM (2012), 265–274.
19. Kriplean, T., Toomim, M., Morgan, J., Borning, A., and Ko, A. Is this what you meant?: Promoting listening on the web with reflect. In *CHI '12*, ACM (2012), 1559–1568.
20. Lampe, C., and Resnick, P. Slash(dot) and burn: Distributed moderation in a large online conversation space. In *CHI'04*, ACM (2004), 543–550.
21. Liao, Q. V., and Fu, W.-T. Expert voices in echo chambers: effects of source expertise indicators on exposure to diverse opinions. In *CHI'14*, ACM (2014), 2745–2754.
22. Liaw, R., Zilnik, A., Baldwin, M., and Butler, S. Maater: Crowdsourcing to improve online journalism. In *CHI EA'13*, ACM (2013), 2549–2554.
23. Meola, M. Chucking the checklist: A contextual approach to teaching undergraduates web-site evaluation. *portal: Libraries and the Academy 4*, 3 (2004), 331–344.
24. Metzger, M. J. Making sense of credibility on the web: Models for evaluating online information and recommendations for future research. *Journal of the American Society for Information Science and Technology 58*, 13 (2007), 2078–2091.
25. Munson, S. A., Lee, S. Y., and Resnick, P. Encouraging reading of diverse political viewpoints with a browser widget. In *ICWSM* (2013).
26. Otterbacher, J. 'helpfulness' in online communities: A measure of message quality. In *CHI'09*, ACM (2009), 955–964.
27. Purcell, K., Rainie, L., Mitchell, A., Rosenstiel, T., and Olmstead, K. Understanding the participatory news consumer. *Pew Internet and American Life Project 1* (2010), 19–21.
28. Salton, G., and McGill, M. J. *Introduction to modern information retrieval*. McGraw-Hill, 1983.
29. Wu, Y., Agarwal, P. K., Li, C., Yang, J., and Yu, C. Toward computational fact-checking. *Proc. of the VLDB Endowment 7*, 7 (2014).
30. Zaller, J. *The nature and origins of mass opinion*. Cambridge university press, 1992.

Contesting the City: Enacting the Political Through Digitally Supported Urban Walks

Clara Crivellaro[1], Rob Comber[1], Martyn Dade-Robertson[2], Simon J. Bowen[1], Peter Wright[1], Patrick Olivier[1]

[1]Culture Lab, School of Computing Science
Newcastle University, UK

[2]School of Architecture Planning and Landscape
Newcastle University, UK

{c.crivellaro/rob.comber/martyn.dade-robertson/s.bowen/p.c.wright/p.olivier}@ncl.ac.uk

ABSTRACT

We present a method for the situated discovery and articulation of issues at the intersection between the politics of place making and city planning. We describe the construction and use of designed tools, such as historical political archives; counterfactual maps; and cards to invite situated dialogue between the social and institutional practices and mechanisms that produce our cities. Grounded in an account of the political as vernacular and embodied, our analysis advance understandings on the politics of design, and on the complex interrelationship between places and political spaces. We outline how HCI can adopt methods and develop sensitivities to support democratic practices and publics envisioning their urban futures.

Author Keywords

Walking, digital media, place, politics.

ACM Classification Keywords

H.5.m. Information interfaces and presentation (e.g., HCI): Miscellaneous.

INTRODUCTION

The role of design and technologies to support socio-political action and publics affecting change in their everyday lives is an area of growing interest in HCI [7, 32, 34]. This area is characterized by a political activist agenda [9, 26, 36] where methods and approaches are developed to support publics participating in the creation of their socio-material futures [23, 39], prompt reflection [30], debates and contestations [3, 8, 27] and action [29, 32]. With the recent turn in HCI research engaging with matters of concern and to support democratic practices [13, 1, 8], the HCI community is just beginning to understand how methods to engage with public issues, and imagined futures can impact on people's everyday lives [18, 39]. In this paper, we explore a method (City Walks) for the situated discovery of issues connecting city residents with the processes and mechanism at play in the construction of their cities. The method involves a two-part socio-material design of digitally supported walks that situates vernacular debate about the city, in the city itself and puts historical and institutional perspectives into play with the lived and felt experiences of local people [42]. We contribute 1) a theoretical framework positioned in vernacular political discourse [18]; 2) a detailed description of how the framework informed our City Walks method and the design of digitally supported tools; 3) a deployment of the method, which combined digital archive material and newly generated content on the walks. We provide an analysis of the data collected through the walks and post-walk interviews to illuminate the method's political work [8], design in use [41] and guide future research on HCI's role as initiator of political spaces for action and change.

CHI 2015, April 18 - 23, 2015, Seoul, Republic of Korea

ACM 978-1-4503-3145-6/15/04...$15.00.
{HYPERLINK "http://dx.doi.org/10.1145/2702123.2702176"}

BACKGROUND

HCI researchers have advanced critical debates and insights on the value and diversity of design activities [39] exploring the relationship between design, technology and the political [1, 10, 31]. Political consciousness has been conceptualized in HCI as a process along and across time in which people come to define what matters to them and directions for change [2, 7, 13]. This perspective entails the potential for HCI to facilitate opinion formation and connect those affiliating to particular values and beliefs with each other [13, 7]. For example, [25] highlight how resources, experiences and technologies play a central role in the development of affiliations. Further [1] advised the need to provide social mapping and collaborative tools for advocacy groups to connect and work together.

The focus on relationality in HCI is convoyed by an acknowledgement of the socio-material structure of human activities [3, 35, 25] when designing with and for communities and environments. For instance, [11] define the work of design as the creation of a socio-technical situation focusing on the people and the environment in which technology is used to serve social ends. Similarly, [3] explore how technology and participatory design processes create "socio-material" relations to open agonistic spaces where poly-vocal debates can engender innovative solutions. Other practices such as adversarial [8] and speculative design [28] explore the potential for design to tackle public concerns. In the first instance, [8] suggests that political design involves the initiation of spaces to contest matters of concern rather than improving "mechanisms and procedures to governance" [8[p.9]]. Likewise, speculative design, comprising cross-disciplinary practices, aims at instigating debates by highlighting uncomfortable or unintended consequences of issues [28]. While in these works HCI design is positioned as initiator of inquiries around public issues, [31] questioned how political artifacts might actually enter real-life human actions, and urged design to intervene in the urban space.

In this regard researchers have stressed the need to investigate further situated, embodied everyday practices and the interrelationship between space, place and technology [17, 22]. For example, [2, 35] highlight how political notions of sustainability must be understood in connection to the felt experiences and social practices in physical environments. Similarly, [37] suggest bridging the interface and embodiments in order to develop critical approaches to the study of space and place of political actions and its implication for democracy.

With politically engaged research entering the CHI community's discourse, we not only need to further understand how HCI design might *"do"* the work of politics [10], but also how it can contribute to civic life and democratic practices in significant ways. With this paper we apply a methodological perspective based on vernacular politics [18] to the design of a method for the situated and co-located discovery and articulation of issues and debates in and about the city. Utilising the city's material fabric and situated media, we aim at opening political spaces and dialogue between the concerns of everyday life and the politics of city planning.

METHODOLOGICAL FRAMEWORK

Our City Walks method is inspired by Hauser's analysis of the politics of everyday talk (vernacular rhetoric) in social movements, defined as collective challenges associated with people's sustained interaction with authorities [18]. Hauser's perspective locates the possibilities for social action in and through everyday talk – seen as site for the expression of values that is inherently subversive precisely because it is spoken by those who are not in power [18]. In Hauser's model everyday talk is characterized by *'polyvocality'*, reflecting a variety of 'voices' entering a discourse in which everyday objects, acts and expressions are seen as symbolic re-presentations of a social reality whose meanings are contingent and socially constitutive. In Hauser's account, everyday talk associated with social movements comprises three further defining features. Firstly, it can contain *'negative bonding with the opposition'* to define values and aims. For instance, *'negative bonding'* might involve building a connection with opposing authorities or perspectives in order to ascertain needs, values and wishes. A second characteristic feature is that it entails the exposure of *'markers of positionality'*, signifying affiliation or disassociation with particular beliefs or norms. Such markers might be performed in codes of language, dress or public behavior for instance. Lastly, everyday talk builds social movements through *'expressions of solidarity'* – 'ways of doing and saying' that supports the movement's aims and values [18].

Drawing from this model, our method explores how everyday actions, including designed objects, their uses and interactions, can entail opportunities to turn the mundane into interrogations of the status quo. Our methodological framework also recognizes that HCI researchers are necessarily implicated as political voices in the process of participation by bringing people's perceptions into the service of a particular organizational effort [41]. Thus, we considered our involvement in the production of the method and of the city through our study and interventions [15].

RESEARCH CONTEXT AND PROCESS

Our method was developed in Newcastle upon Tyne, a city of 279,100 inhabitants, located in the North East of England. The research involved the collaboration with Amber - a local Film and Photography Collective; Northern Architecture - a local charity championing architecture and place making; and Amblr - a multi-media company. Amber's collective artistic agenda, dedicated to documenting urban regeneration in Northern England, has been regarded as oppositional due to their aspiration to produce alternative representations of working class communities through photography and filmmaking [20].

At the center of our City Walk method is an historical archive, here a 1960s film archive provided by Amber, comprising local politicians' interviews revealing controversies and anecdotes about major redesign and infrastructural developments aimed at turning Newcastle upon Tyne into the modern city of the 21st century. The political archive provided a rich resource to engage with the political processes that led to the city's present socio-material constitution and elicit reflection and discussions around the city's possible futures. The research developed over a period of eight months. From an initial examination of Amber's archive coupled with situated inquiry, a walk and co-design workshops with study partners, the research involved the socio-material design of the City Walks method and the recruitment and delivery of the walks. A total of 30 participants engaged in the walks, recruited by one of our study partners, and through a social media site. Participants were diverse in background, nationality, occupation and gender and ranged from 21 to 65 years of age. In the next section we describe the initial research leading to the method's socio-material design.

Scoping design opportunities

Firstly we conducted research within the city's urban core in order to develop sensitivities and understanding on the relationship between the issues raised in the archive, the visible material traces of the past and practices in the contemporary city. In line with [33], we utilized photography, diaries, interviews and situated engagements with people met in these locations. We also sought to explore the contemporary significance of the archive with research partners and to this end, we invited them to co-design a walk through the city and narrate compelling aspects of the archive from their perspectives. The walk raised questions around our relationships with civic space, authority and planning practices and the way individual and collective values are reflected in the material fabric of the city. Following the walk, research partners convened to co-design the City Walk method.

THE CITY WALK METHOD

City Walk was co-designed as a two-part method, exploring Hauser's everyday talk and its features: *negative bonding*, *markers of positionality* and *polyvocality*. In part one, the archive material was used to construct tools to elicit participants' expression of issues and positions and provoke discussion. Data generated in part one informed the design of tools used in the second part of City Walks, where participants' voices were integrated with the archival material (figure 1). In the next sections we illustrate the socio-material design rationale of the digital elements and tools in the first and second parts of the method.

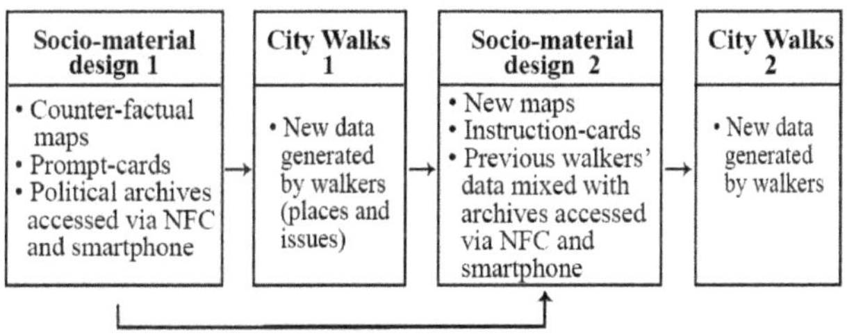

Figure 1. The City Walks two parts method design process

Socio-material design 1

Urban walking as an everyday act of resistance. We chose to employ walking as an occasion for dialogue and a potential mundane expression of resistance. Walking has long been considered a practice of cultural, ecological and political significance. For instance, [12] regarded walking a tactic of resistance, entailing enactments that either uphold or disregard the status quo. Further, [38, 40] explored walking in cities as a democratizing force seeking equality of access, freedom of movement and the dissolution of state control. In recent years walking has also been utilized in the social sciences as method to engage with our identities as reflected in our surroundings. For instance [6] proposed an understanding of places as experiential 'gathering' processes, constitutive of one sense of self and [21] demonstrated how walking with people allows us to gain a better understanding of different ways of 'being in the world'. Rather than an individual activity, we looked at group walks as *collective, relational* and *dynamic* endeavors [41], aiming at creating collective experiences and opportunities for dialogue.

The city map as a rhetorical artifact. In order to initiate inquiry, we chose to design a counterfactual map of the city as a way to problematize the 'real'. In this respect, [24] highlighted the latent politics embedded in maps effected through the revelation or disguise of textual/visual information. Further, [19] noted maps' power of naming as strongly connected with the power to individuate, reinforce or create identities. The design of a counterfactual map was intended to stimulate reflection and new relationships between what is there and what could be there. The counterfactual map's design was informed by historically unrealised plans, a subjective interpretation of political visions as described in the political archives, and the initial situated research and walk with research partners. The map featured counterfactual streets and fictional buildings, highlighted unofficial histories and practices in the city (graffiti, skateboarding, etc.), and assigned existing buildings and areas with different purposes (eg. university as a hub of free education, shopping center as the city parliament, etc.). The counterfactual map (figure 2, bottom-left) also intended to scaffold the negotiation of the walk among participants through collaborative sense making.

The political archive as a resource for negative bonding. We used the archive as a way to engage participants with institutional processes. In so doing our aim was to stimulate connections to current mechanisms of city planning and participants' expression of personal stances, opinions and values. We selected audio material from the film archive according to the following categories: excerpts exposing political mechanism underpinning planning projects, particular regeneration efforts in the city and visions of democracy. Inspired by these archival extracts we designed 12 prompts cards featuring open-ended statements and questions inviting personal responses (figure 2, top-left). NFC technology embedded in each card gave access to archival excerpts held on mobile phones. Extracts ranged from 30 seconds to 2.5 minutes in length and were listened to via a Bluetooth portable speaker, inviting participants to gather around it (figure 2, bottom-right).

Prompt cards as markers of positionality in place and space. Each group member was given two prompt cards, which they were invited to associate with particular sites of their choice *along* the walk. Having identified a site, participants were asked to stop the group, explain their choice and then listen to the archival content embedded in the card. Talking time was set to two minutes per participant at a time and participants were also given the tasks to audio-record and photo-document group members' opinions and site choices. In this way, through their card 'placement' participants would enact a *'marker of positionality'* in both place and space: the situated place in the city and the discursive space in which meaning is constructed and exposed (figure 2, top-left and right).

In summary, the socio-material design (figure 2) intended to invite negotiation and implicate participants in shaping the walk by associating their cards to sites they found significant along the way. Groups were given routes based on the counter-factual map to provide a loose structure and ensure groups would do their walk within the time limit.

Figure 2. Socio-material design – 1

City Walks 1

19 participants took part in walks during the first part of our method. Each walk involved small groups (4 to 6 participants) to ensure each member equal opportunities to have input in the walk within time constraints. Each walk lasted between 2.5 and 3.5 hours.

During walks, participants spent time examining the map, discussing possible interpretations and navigational choices, which involved many playful moments that helped them socialise. Decoding the map, given its ambiguous design, was a slow, discursive and ongoing process unfolding with the act of walking, and comparing the counterfactual map with the city. Participants generated stops at sites and topics for discussion by associating their cards to particular sites of choice. Personal associations between the counterfactual map, cards and the city influenced choices. While for most participants these were serendipitous, others reserved their cards for particular sites on their routes. For instance a participant placed his card *'capitalism – making the rules and living within them'* at the University site, marked in the map as 'Hub of Free Education'. This prompted a discussion around the capitalization of education and the role of universities in forging new urban developments. Another participant placed her card *'revolutionary perspective – what do you think would be beneficial in the city'* in a private car park where she had organized a public cultural event in the past. This was followed by a debate about the loss and re-appropriation of public places. Another participant placed his card *'owning the future – properties snapped up by builders and developers'* at the site of a building used by local skateboarders that was recently demolished, and marked on the map as 'old town'. In this way, the participant highlighted how new developments and policies dictate the exclusion of particular cultural practices in the city. Listening to the archive material in the walks sparked further questions, and was used to exemplify or extend discussions in other directions. Participants having to take photos of each other produced playful moments, and also provided opportunities to consider what aspects of the location highlighted particular issues that participants wanted to communicate.

Socio-material design 2

The walks comprising the first part of our method as described above, provided new content (places and opinions) that was used for the construction of socio-material design in the second part of our method (figure 3).

Polyvocality - cumulating diverging voices. Content generated in City Walks 1 informed a new counterfactual map and the participants' voices were put into dialogue with the voices of the archive. Participants' new audio material were mixed with short archival extracts. Each new mix of recordings featured diverging opinions and contradictory histories and was assigned to the particular locations pinpointed in previous walks by participants. In this way, the *'polyvocality'* of multiple perspectives would be exposed at each location.

Figure 3. Socio-material design - 2

Hence, we made booklets corresponding in the new map to particular locations whose names were inspired by the new audio materials. For instance, a construction site was renamed as 'Owning the Future Square' where a previous walker had talked about the loss of a culturally important place; an incomplete walkway was renamed 'Monument to People's Power', referring to a campaign that stopped a planning development, and so on. Each booklet included instructions encouraging site exploration, NFC tags triggering related audio material and a question for groups to collectively consider at each place. Lastly a brochure was designed to contain booklets and map (figure 3, top-left).

City Walks 2

11 new participants took part in walks during the second part of our method. Each walker/participant was given a brochure and each group the following instructions: collectively decide locations to visit from the ones presented in the brochure; collectively work out a route to get to those locations; at each locations open the booklet relating to it and follow the instructions. Participants were also given a camera, smart phone and Bluetooth portable speaker. A time limit for talking was not set for these walks

leaving their unfolding purposely open to internal group dynamics.

As in previous walks, examining the map and negotiating ways to reach each location produced a playful atmosphere and helped participants socialise. Following the instructions at each location produced excitement and curiosity. The mix of audio materials presenting divergent opinions and the 'questions' provoked notably different interpretations that led to animated discussions. Participants engaged in debates around issues of land ownerships in the city, new and old planning rules, the uncertain future of particular areas and possible alternative uses of specific places.

ANALYSIS

The data set, including field notes, audio and photographic documentation of the walks taken by researchers and participants and follow up interviews were analysed using a thematic analysis approach [5]. Findings are presented under the following themes: *re-discovering the city and revealing issues, instigating situated debates, and sources and validations of imagining.*

Re-discovering the city and revealing issues

The walks invited each group to *organize* themselves in order to perform their walk. For some participants the lack of a leader was *"challenging"*, entailing a realization that *"working in small groups can be hard work"*. Yet the walks were also a creative process of discovering and questioning *"real things that you don't normally talk about with other people"*. This is reflected in the words of a participant who felt, that it "*seemed to be more about the process of travelling rather than reaching a destination"*. In this respect the tools provided were important in shaping group dynamics and the way walks and discussions unfolded. For instance, walks' long duration and participants' negotiation of the counterfactual map were significant aspects that allowed personal contemplation of the map and developed participants' confidence in sharing their thoughts. Furthermore, for walkers *"having to physically come back together to listen closely to one sound output"* added to the social experience.

The cards in walks comprising part one of our method provided walkers with a focus to pinpoint and articulate significant aspects of individual and collective identities expressed through everyday practices, (hi)stories and memories - exposing affiliations to particular values and social practices as reflected in chosen places. Personal anecdotes, discussions, and reflections took place both whilst walking along and standing face-to-face. At times, participants detoured from the suggested route in order to take the group to particular places they wanted to talk about. The exposure of personally meaningful stories, ideas and issues as reflected in the material city assembled walkers around specific urban situations and matters of concerns – e.g. the city football stadium as symbol of local identity; a cycle route traversed by a participant everyday under a road bypass; the proposal for a new public square; the capitalization of education reflected in new developments; preclusion of cultural practices such as graffiti in public spaces; etc. In this way, places came to re-present personal concerns while uncovering tensions between city planning and people's lived experiences, values and cultural practices in the city. Below, two participants draw a distinction between places driven by market imperatives and what people value doing in places.

"I used to hang around here a lot when I was a kid and it used to have a different atmosphere round here than it does now, now they've opened it out and made it quite corporate [...] There used to be little lovely dark cubby holes and stuff, where as a kid, when you wanted to get away from adult control or whatever, was good to hang around. Now there's a Wagamama. It just doesn't feel right, you know? It just doesn't know what it is anymore" (Kay)

"it is like a public square, but what is surrounding it is actually commercialised so it's all driving towards actual profit rather than community interaction. It's just a bit of a threat that more public squares will becoming sterilised" (Drew)

Kay's sketch of her activities as a youngster in the square, highlight her embodied connections to the place. The square's loss of identity due to new developments is re-contextualized in other locations and near-future prospects by Drew. The market driven values reflected in the square are illustrated as '*sterile*' and presented in conflict to an idea of 'public-ness' and '*community interaction'* associated instead with idiosyncrasies and diversity. Another participant further emphasised such contrast, reflecting on young people's practices in the city.

"Some of that is about that kind of grass roots thing. It's not about public consultation, but about the public doing things and then being recognised, which that kind of visionary, top down development doesn't really allow" (Tom)

In this excerpt, Tom contributes a consideration of the tense relationship between place making and the bureaucratic and formal procedure of town planning, highlighting a central aspect of such tension: the necessity to acknowledge social production processes by local authorities.

While participants in part one of our method were given individual cards, in part two groups were given tasks inviting site exploration and questions to collectively consider alongside the audio material. The paths walkers traversed and places they dwelled in engendered contingent associations, interpretations and feelings, entailing an aspect of 'extra-ordinariness' within the ordinary.

"you would never walk around spaces like that because you don't make time in your day to do things like that [...] and you get the feeling, the atmosphere by being there" (Tina)

Tina refers here to walking across a site of a demolished building and climbing the roof of a car park – highlighting the embodied nature of her experiences. Maps and instructions prompted the discovery of issues, but also the revealing of *dis/associations* with particular places/practices in the city. For example, a group collectively identified a pub as the 'City Parliament' marked on the map. The booklet suggested entering the 'Parliament' and listening to the conversations for a few minutes. However the group jointly decided to abstain from it, labeling the place as *"not the kind of place where people like me go to"*. Yet being there challenged participants' own judgments. Here Joy reflects on a particular encounter.

"We sort of said we are not going in there, it looks really horrible, but then someone really nice came out and started to chat on with us" (Joy).

After spending time there, participants revisited their own assumptions. For some participants, standing in that particular place and the topic at hand ('your own parliaments') assumed symbolic meaning, reflected in the influences that *being there* had on their discussion. In this way, re-discovering places and issues, through the audio materials gathered in previous walks and from the archive, turned locations in the city into public matters. Below, a participant reconsiders city planning as a matter of collective participation.

"You just take it for granted [...] as we are about as involved now as in the 60ies that is we are not involved at all – somebody else is doing it all" (Joan)

Joan draws a connection between past and contemporary socio-political dynamics in city planning – making the past relevant to her perceived present state of affairs.

Instigating situated debates

The groups engaged discursively in the walks, examining the causal nexus of the specific concerns at hand. Issues generated by participants and topics heard in related audio materials engendered challenging discussions. In this respect, holding a recording device while talking was significant in pacing and drawing attention to talking and listening times. Differences in individual and collective visions relating to social needs, urban developments and technologies were exposed also in respect to the tensions of past visions (heard in the archival material) and near-future developments. For instance, a group standing in the construction site of a new development (marked in the map as 'Citizens Lab') endeavored in a discussion around technological advance expressed in the new construction of a center for scientific excellence. Yet, the group' discourse was challenged by one of the participants.

"I think that his [politician] *analysis of computing trips lots of people up - that is the infrastructure that we need to make things happen doesn't rely on bricks and mortar. In many respects this is a very regressive development, precisely because of that [...] All of this stuff about big data, it's all disappearing into air" (Andy)*

Andy's vision for a better communication infrastructure is contrasted with the near-future development, first proposed in the 1960s, highlighting how in his view interventions should adapt to collective needs. In this way, audio excerpts evoked in participants' different interpretations and opinions reflecting individual worldviews. Walkers engaged in debates assembling 'knowledges' and life experiences tied to particular notions of belonging, historical and socio-political circumstances. For example, in walks comprising part two of our method, audio extracts around the distribution of decisional power regionally or nationally evoked different memories in participants: of a time of political turmoil in a participants' youth; experiences participating in regional assemblies; cultural experiences in a participants' native country.

"Up till I came to England I didn't know I was working class I had no idea. I had no idea about that kind of politics you know the North East went through miners strike and some really hard times [...] I didn't have to live through that so I can see why is a row thing probably in a lot of people's minds [...] you know politics in Ireland is religion while here is a class thing" (Joy)

Recollecting aspects of sensitive lived experiences of power (and powerlessness) in a time of political struggle engendered emotional reactions in some of the participants. Joy hints at the ways socio-political histories of place infer particular identities, also reflected in her understandings of what might constitute politics and the political. Joy here displays empathic engagement towards experiences and associated emotions evoked in walkers-others, but also reflects on the difficulty to fully comprehend them. In this regard, differences among walkers' life experiences were framed with an impossibility to agree on certain matters.

"I am from the North East [...] Lou *is a lovely woman but she is not from the North East and she will never know what it was like to grow up in the North East under Thatcher regime [...] Its stuff that I am passionate about and my passion comes from a different way of thinking and growing up in a different way" (Vera)*

Vera exposes boundaries of membership defined around her sense of belonging to a particular (hi)story and personal investment excluding those who don't shared her same experiences. Boundaries of membership came to the fore also in other instances. For example in the following excerpts, two participants expressed disengagement and uneasiness towards other member's modalities of debating.

"I always have been taught to be polite to let other people have their say. Unfortunately other people aren't quite as polite in that respect [...] and sometimes its pointless to argue with someone when you know that the argument can't be won" (Tim)

"I don't feel like I belong to a party because I still feel new to the area [...] You could see that people are really passionate [...] it goes to lots of arguments because lots of people don't know how to express themselves calmly or speak up their mind clearly" (Ella)

Participants illustrate debating as a civil, thoughtful, composed endeavor rather than a passionate one. Also, while Tim equates debating to a competition to be *'won'*, Ella detached from debates relating to party politics due to a lack of affiliation. Yet for most participants the confrontation with different worldviews played a crucial part of the experience. In the following extract Eve explains how these engendered reflections in regards to her values and how these are mirrored in her daily actions.

"it was very honest that she was saying those things like I don't bother getting interested and I thought well yes there are things that are happening that interest me or that I get concerned about but I don't necessarily act on them [...] it actually had an impact. You know calling the council asking what's going on, I don't think I would have thought in that way before this [walk]*" (Eve)*

Eve refers to phoning the council the day after the walk to inquire about a new development in her neighborhood. Her action here is presented as a result of the walk experience and reflections around her role in respect to her concerns.

Sources and validation of imagining

For participants as well as for researchers, the walks were learning experiences - an opportunity to listen to different perspectives, learn from others and reflect on institutional and social roles and practices that produce the city. They were occasions to reconsider the city. Walkers' accounts, such as the re-appropriation of a private car park for public events, and anecdotes from the archive opened prospects to re-consider places in the city in new ways.

"it does change things for how I perceive those parts of the city because it makes you think about other possibilities. I won't be able to visit those places again without remembering reflections of things that happened, 'cos they sit in my memory" (Lou)

The walks produced new 'memories' in the participants' life repertoire, but also opened up new ways of thinking. The experience is formulated below as having a situational, but also ongoing effect beyond the walk itself.

"I came home and I researched a lot of things that we did on the walk [...] so I looked at the maps and what used to be there [...] also what could it be used for in the future like straight away I went and checked if there were any news about the site" (Tim)

The ambiguity of the counterfactual map opened avenues for further inquiries and readings. While walking, participants appropriated it confronting it with the city, making conjectures, becoming its *'creative actor'*. Some participants projected a strong sense of locality in the map.

"I found the map really interesting, the fact that it seems a lot more socialist than we actually are at the minute, or that we've come to be in Newcastle because obviously, that's our heritage, it's very socialist and very much about the workingman." (Kay)

Kay presents a particular characterisation of history and politics – a collective historical past at odds with the present state of affair. In this respect, the archives, histories and personal stories were used as resources, evidence and exemplars to hinder or validate the envisioning of other possibilities. For instance, in the following excerpt, Lou refers to the possibility of proposing new rules in the city.

"you couldn't really do, how would you do that but then when we heard that bit of the archive I thought 'oh! They did do it so it's not impossible and they just decided [...] and they did it." (Lou)

In this way, the archive provided a resource to validate and open up alternatives in respect to the way rules and political decisions are made. On the other hand, uncertainty around the future of particular places, audio material with diverging opinions and situated explorations of places worked together affectively to entrust walkers with choices between alternatives and imminence on the matter.

"We were a bit concerned that it was going to be another shopping mall [...] so it got us thinking about what it could be and something that hopefully would be free for people to use." (Ella)

"I just thought leave it green [...] You live in the city and you pay all the taxes and nobody ask you [...] it could be my fault cause I don't keep up on what's on the website but they don't tell you because they don't want people to know because they already have plans [...] but if there we were more of [...] we could have a bit more control if the people had to listen to us " (Fay)

In these excerpts, walkers reflect on the tensions between institutional and civic roles, rights and responsibilities. Monetary-based (*'taxes'*) relations to governance that presents ready-made solutions are contrasted with opportunities for publics to propose their own. Conceiving a different prospect for the place is coupled with a call for publics to 'voice' and institutions to 'listen', both necessary to achieve change. In Fay's vision, the institutions-people relationship is characterized by mutual promises and dependency. Matters of mutual reliance and expectations around the action of others were also reflected in the visions afforded by technologies. For instance, in part two City Walks, a group was confronted with envisaging 'citizen's advertisements' as opposed to commercially led ones. A participant proposed a public LED displays for tweets in the public square where they were standing, and the group engaged in a discussion around its practicalities considering issues of censorship.

"you don't really have a stand on either way [...] it wouldn't be possible, one people would abuse it, if it wasn't policed and if it was policed then the police would abuse it " (Dom)

Dom suggests the impossibility of reaching freedom of expression in public places. His expectations around other people's behavior display a polarization limiting the possibility of conceiving alternatives. Here, potentials afforded by technology are critically positioned in regard to issues of surveillance and authority. Furthermore, the use of a particular technology in the walks (smart phone and NFC tags) sparked concerns around its potential to support civic action and democratic processes.

"It's not just about Wi-Fi richness though it's about what you carry in your pocket. Some people won't have a device. It's like that from now on you have to pay a license to be able to comment on a planning application. It puts limitation on the right to comment for instance [...] so it's a question of democracy and the landscape of access of connectivity" (Les)

Les exposes critical tensions in socio-technical prospects, which while serving a re-distribution of power, may actually contribute to widening the gap of inequality and exclusion. Yet, for other participants, the particular use of technology stimulated reflections not simply in terms of what technology might afford, but also around citizens' own conduct in relation to governance.

"I don't know the city well enough [...] I just stick to my own little place [...] but if you complain about something you are not really having a say as about what it becomes [...] We are the people who live here and we should say what we want [...] unless people went out and left messages, have a say you know – you might start and see things changing a bit for the better" (Joy)

Joy envisages people going for walks in the city and leaving messages about their concerns in places as a way to actively contribute to the making of places ('*what it becomes*'). It is notable here, how Joy's everyday practice ('sticking to her own little place') is contrasted by a formulation of her own sense of (future oriented) 'civic' agency.

DISCUSSION AND FUTURE WORK

Our method and analysis of deployments show how HCI can initiate situated dialogue between the politics of city planning and practices and concerns of everyday life through design and technologies. It also reveals how envisioning alternative possibilities is entangled with lived experiences, historical memory and expectations towards ourselves, others and authorities. In the next section, we discuss the benefits and tensions afforded by our City Walks method, how situated media and design can construct political spaces to impact the making of places and HCI research' challenges as initiator of political processes to support democratic practice.

Places and political spaces

The tools in our two-part method implicated participants in the construction of situated political spaces inviting the expression of cultural identities, values and concerns as reflected in the material fabric of the city. Previous research argued that designing for place requires the provision of structures for place making through participation, appropriation and adaptation [17]. The maps, cards association to places and unveiling of audio material opened spaces for alternative relationships to form, conveying rich implications for the layering of meaning and the re-appropriation of places through discursive spaces [18]. Our method provides a framework for the revealing of 'positionings' within the production of the city, connecting cultural processes of place making and the political sphere.

Research has long stressed the centrality of physicality and the need for HCI design to adopt methods [35] and approaches [14] to engage with embodied practices [2] and sensorial aspects of places [22]. Further [14, 41] argued for the importance to engage with places' socio-political, economic and historical contexts HCI designs for. The use of a our socio-technical tools including the political archive and data gathered across the walks, configured the city as material evidence for public discourse [8], as something to inquire into through situated cross-examination, open to potential subversions and imaginations [14, 15]. In this sense, our method, involving the situated connection of causal nexuses and institutional processes with the material city and the lived experience of people through technologies and mapping tools, has political rather than ethnographic purpose.

Previous work highlighted the extent to which design and interfaces can be political [8, 24]. This method adopts this problem/design space alongside situated media by exploiting its potential to prompt embodied connections and different approaches by which the city can be understood, interpreted and re-imagined [14]. Future work might investigate how this method can be used to produce multiple maps and experience the city from different perspectives for an embodied engagement with concerns towards the development of political spaces, place meaning and the constitution of publics [10, 26] to affect change.

Debates and dialogue

Previous research called for HCI to engage with the design of politics and the negotiation of meaning as an important site of political activity [13]. This method provides an instantiation in which HCI design and situated media can shape social activities for political ends. Based on our methodological perspective, the design of tools and media content with diverging perspectives set the walkers in shared circumstances inviting collaborative sense-making while prompting critical engagement and debates.

The use of cards in the first part of our method assured a 'safe' space for the individual expression of concerns, affording moments for self-reflection also when listening to others. Audio content in walks of the second part of the method provoked discussion that despite pointing to an impossibility of agreement, provided an opportunity for walkers to connect to each other's across lines of difference and re-discover or remember what mattered to them. Also, the audio material provoked at times emotionally charged debates and challenging accounts of lived experiences, which had an impact on both participants and researchers. Previous work urged the need to engage with controversies among people with opposing concerns [3, 8], but highlighted that constructive debates require the ability to accepts others' views as legitimate [3].

Yet, our findings highlight that such abilities can be assumed, showing tensions around rules of engagement, equality in walkers' modalities of expression and notions of contestation as something to be won. Future research might engage with nuanced approaches to disputes, where con-testing - from its etymological root '*bearing witness together*' – might entail the provision of encounters between institutions and individuals and among city residents in which we can expose *together* and testify to one another (rather than against one another). However, while these political processes are critical to advance public understanding (dialogue) and opinion formation, they can also entail unintended consequences. Future work might explore further the provision of participatory 'safe spaces' to do so, while bringing to the fore the '*polyvocality*' of people's views side by side.

Methods for democratic practices

Previous work urged methods to build technical and social capacity [26] to increase people's sense of agency in shaping future uses of technology [23]. Our method offered opportunities to articulate, imagine, but also contest uses and consequences of technologies to facilitate current and near-future productions of the city. Building on previous work that reconfigured the design process as initiator of publics [26], and concerned with the construction of material environments [8], our method explores how HCI design can be used to build social capacity through situated examinations of the past, present and future making of our socio-material environment. Most critically it provided opportunities to articulate how political processes of city planning and the city '*should be*' [27] while reflecting on individual and collective roles and agency in this regard.

In line with previous work that stressed how the awareness of ourselves as agents of change is entwined with the institutional organisation and regulation that produce cities [13] - a central aspect of our method is that it afforded encounters and explorations of our relationship with current and historical authority, while constituting new experiences in the life repertoire of walkers. As civic action stems from past experiences, where experience is set against aspirations for a different imagined situation judged in terms of practicalities and opportunity for realization [16] - we argue that such explorations are a crucial step towards sustainable ways to support publics defining for themselves what might constitute their sense of agency and the 'common good'. Entailing the engagement with others self-interests and authorities, our method is a step towards the building of collective capacities that are in dialogue with the institutions that can actualize civic will [4].

Previous work called for an investigation of how the practices of design contribute to public discourse and civic life [8, 31]. By working in public, with and for publics, we attempted to make HCI research accountable and open to public inspection. Our methodological perspective, concerned with vernacular politics as a site for the expression of values and of social action, provides a way in which HCI can support everyday politics, and begin to explore the consequences of our work in this realm. The challenge for HCI design supporting democratic practice requires that we also understand how democracy is lived [18]. As civic communications contain empirical evidence of a political learning process, we call future work to further investigate how communication practices in their multiple forms (technologies, designed objects, everyday debates, mobilities, media spaces, the material city, etc.) shape public understanding and choice to guide the re-making of our socio-material futures.

CONCLUSION

We presented the design of a two-part method, City Walks, informed by a rhetorical model of everyday talk in social movements. In the construction of our method, we positioned HCI research as initiator of political spaces exploring everyday concerns in dialogue with the mechanisms and practices of city planning through the use of a historical archive, counterfactual maps and participants newly generated content. Our method offers a way in which HCI research can contribute to civic life and public discourse. We argue that if HCI design wants to engage with the concerns of everyday life (everyday politics) it needs to develop methods and understanding on the consequences of the tools it uses to forge discussions and debates, which are at the heart of opinion formation.

ACKNOWLEDGMENTS

We thank research participants and partners, Amber, Amblr and Northern Architecture. This research was funded by the AHRC Creative Exchange Knowledge Exchange Hub (AH/J005150/1) and the EPSRC Digital Economy Theme Social Inclusion through the Digital Economy Research Hub (EP/G066019/1).

REFERENCES

1. Aoki, P.M., Honicky, R.J., Mainwaring, A., et al. A Vehicle for Research : Using Street Sweepers to Explore the Landscape of Environmental Community Action. In *Proc. of CHI '09*, ACM (2009), 375-384.
2. Bidwell, N., Syia, M., Marsden, G., et al. Walking and the social life of solar charging in rural africa. ACM *TOCHI,* (2008), 20, 4, 22.
3. Björgvinsson, E., Ehn, P., and Hillgren, P.A. Participatory design and "democratizing innovation". In *Proc. PDC 2010*, ACM (2010), 41-50.
4. Boyte, H.,C., *Everyday Politics: Reconnecting Citizens and Public Life*, University of Pennsylvania Press, 2005.
5. Braun, V., Clarke, V., Using thematic analysis in reaserch, Qualitative Research in Psychology, 2006, 3(2), 77-101.
6. Casey, E.,S., How to get from space to place in a farily short stretch of time, in *Senses of Place*, Santa FE:School of American Research Press, 1997.
7. Crivellaro, C., Comber, R., Bowers, J., Wright,P., Olivier,P., A Pool of Dreams: Facebook, Politics and the Emergence of a Social Movement, In *Proc.CHI'14*, ACM Press (2014), 3573-3582.
8. DiSalvo, C. *Adversarial Design (Design Thinking, Design Theory)*. The MIT Press, 2012.
9. Di Salvo, C., Nourbakhsh,I., Holstius, D., Neighborhood Network Project: A case Study of Critical Engagement and Creative Expression Through Participatory Design. In *Proc. of CHI'10*, ACM Press (2010), 41-50.
10. Di Salvo, C, Lukens, J., Lodato, T., Jenkins, T., Kim, T., Making Public Things: How HCI Design Can

Express Matters of Concern. In *Proc. CHI'14*, ACM Press (2014), 2397-2406.

11. Dearden, A. and Light, A. Designing for e-Social Action An Application Taxonomy. In *Proc. Design Reaserch Society Conference 2008*, Sheffield Hallam University (2008).
12. De Certeau, M., *The practice of everyday life*, Berkeley University of California Press, 2011.
13. Dourish, P. HCI and environmental sustainability: the politics of design and the design of politics, In *Proc. DIS 2010*, ACM(2010), 1-10.
14. Dourish, P., Mainwaring, D, S., Ubicomp's Colonial Impulse, In *Proc.Ubicomp'12*, ACM (2012), 133-144
15. Farias, I., The Politics of Urban Assemblages, *City*, 2011, 15(3), 365-374
16. Fowler, A. Biekart, K., (eds) *Civic Driven Change: Civic Imagination in Action*, The Hague Institute of Social Studies, 2008.
17. Harrison, S., Dourish, P., Re-place-ing space: The Role of Place and Space in Collaborative Systems, In *Proc. CSCW '96*, ACM Press (1996), 67-76.
18. Hauser, G., McClellan, E., D., Vernacular Rhetoric and Social Movements: performances of resistance in the rhetoric of the everyday, in McKenzie Stevens, S., Malesh, P., *Active Voices: Composing a Rhetoric of Social Movements*, Suny Press, 2009.
19. Harvey, D., The Condition of Postmodernity, Wiley-Blackwell, 1999.
20. Holland, R., Vail, J., The art of social movement: cultural opportunity, mobilisation and framing in the early formation of the Amber Collectives, *Poetics*, 2012, 40, 22-43.
21. Lee, J., Ingold, T., Fieldwork on Foot: Perceiving, Perceiving, Routing, Socializing, in Collins, P., Coleman, S., (eds) *Locating the Field, Space, Place and Context in Anthropology*, Oxford: Berg, 2006.
22. Lentini, L., Decortis, F., Space and Places: When Interacting with and in Physical Space Becomes a meaningful Experience, *Personal Ubiquitous Comput,* 2010, 14, 407-415.
23. Light, A., Democratizing Technology: Making Transformations using designing, Performance and Props, In *Proc. CHI'11*, ACM Press, (2011), 2239-2242.
24. Light, A., The Politics of Representing Culture in Ubiquitous Media: Challenging National Cultural Norms by Studying a Map with Indian and British Users, *Personal Ubiquitous Comput*, 2011, 15:585-596
25. Le Dantec, C., Di Salvo, K., Infrastructing and the formation of publics in participatory Design, *Social Studies of Science*, 2013, 43(2), 241-264
26. Le Dantec, C., Participation and Publics: Supporting Community Engagement. *In Proc. CHI'12*, ACM Press (2012), 1351-1360.
27. Le Dantec, C., The Right Way to Make Smart City, http://goo.gl/Y9tNDr, retrieved on 05.22.14
28. Lukens, J., Di Salvo, C., Speculative Design and Technological Fluency, MIT Press, 2012, 3(4), 23-40.
29. Kuznetsov, S., Odom, W., Moulder, V., et al. HCI , Politics and the city : engaging with urban grassroots movements for reflection and action. *Ext. Abtracts CHI 2011*, ACM (2011), 2409-2412.
30. Kuznetsov, S., Paulos, E., and Gross, M. WallBots: interactive wall-crawling robots in the hands of public artists and political activists. *In Proc. DIS 2010*, ACM Press (2010), 208–217
31. Markussen, T., The Disruptive Aesthetic of Design Activism: Enacting Design between Arts and Politics, *DesignIssue*, 2013, 29, 1.
32. Olander, S., Lenskjold,T.,U., Yndigegn, Foverskov,M., Mobilising for Community Building and Everyday Innovation, *Interactions*, 2011, 18(4), 28-32.
33. Paulos,E., Jenkins, T., Urban Probes: Encountering our Emergent Urban Athmosphere. In *Proc. CHI'05,* ACM Press (2005), 341-350.
34. Paulos, E., Citizen Science: Enabling Participatory Urbanism, in Foth, M., *Handbook of Research on Urban Informatics: The Practice and Promise of The Real Time City*, IGI Global, 2009.
35. Pink, S., Mackley, L.,K., Mitchell, V., et al. Applying the lens of sensory ethnography to sustainable HCI, *ACM TOCHI*, 2008, 20, 4, 25.
36. Ratto, M., Boler, M., *DIY Citizenship: Critical Making and Social Media*, The MIT Press, 2014.
37. Rodriguez-Amat, R.J., Brantner, C., Space and Place matters: a tool for the analysis of geolocated and mapped protests, *New Media and Society*, 2014, 1-20.
38. Sadler S., *The Situationist City*, MIT Press, 1999.
39. Sanders, E., B., N., Stappers, P.J., Probes, Toolkits and Prototypes: Three Approaches to Making in Co-Design, *CoDesign*, 2014, 10(1), 5-14.
40. Self, W., Walking is Political, The Guardian, retrieved on 03.14, http://goo.gl/X44Fbb
41. Suchman, L., *Human Machine Reconfigurations Plans and Situated Actions*, Cambridge University Press, 2000
42. Wright, P., McCarthy, J., *Experience-Centered Design: Designers, Users and Communities in Dialogue*, Morgan and Claypool, 2010.

Data-in-Place: Thinking through the Relations Between Data and Community

Alex S. Taylor[1], Siân Lindley[1], Tim Regan[1], David Sweeney[1]
Vasilis Vlachokyriakos[3], Lillie Grainger[4], Jessa Lingel[2]

Microsoft Research
Cambridge, UK[1]/MA, USA[2]
{ast, sianl, timregan, dsweeney, jlingel}@microsoft.com

Culture Lab[3]
School of Computer Science
Newcastle Univ., UK
v.vlachokyriakos@newcastle.ac.uk

School of Geography[4]
Univ. of Nottingham
Nottingham, UK
lillie.grainger@hotmail.co.uk

ABSTRACT
We present findings from a year-long engagement with a street and its community. The work explores how the production and use of data is bound up with place, both in terms of physical and social geography. We detail three strands of the project. First, we consider how residents have sought to curate existing data about the street in the form of an archive with physical and digital components. Second, we report endeavours to capture data about the street's environment, especially of vehicle traffic. Third, we draw on the possibilities afforded by technologies for polling opinion. We reflect on how these engagements have: materialised distinctive relations between the community and their data; surfaced flows and contours of data, and spatial, temporal and social boundaries; and enacted a multiplicity of 'small worlds'. We consider how such a conceptualisation of *data-in-place* is relevant to the design of technology.

Author Keywords
Data; data-in-place; digital civics; community; place.

INTRODUCTION
Data—as it is being articulated in the rubrics of big data, data science, business intelligence, etc.—has been attributed a very special status. It has come to be seen as a proxy for the facts [7, 13, 28]. Yes, it needs to be collected and analysed, and in some cases highly technical and specialised tools and knowhow are required to do so. Yet wrapped up in the hubris, it is seen as a raw, exhaustive resource to be mined and, once in hand, used with authority. With data's collection and specialised analysis, controversies can be settled [2, 21].

CHI 2015, April 18 - 23 2015, Seoul, Republic of Korea

ACM 978-1-4503-3145-6/15/04...$15.00
http://dx.doi.org/10.1145/2702123.2702558

Of course, this surprisingly popular idea grossly oversimplifies the kind of outcomes that can be gleaned using data and how data is used in practice. Data scientists are well aware of the pitfalls of reading too much into their data and drawing out factitious results. Their work is replete with inferences and informed judgements, refuting data's immediate equivalency with the facts and suggesting a good deal of interpretive skill is required to get data to do work. Numerous commentators in HCI [e.g., 24, 29] and from the social sciences [*cf.* 15 for comprehensive review] have demonstrated as much and made convincing arguments that spell out the limitations of (big) data and data analytics. Broadly, the critiques target the imagined objectivity of data and data processing, and point out the intrinsic biases that become visible when data is, in practice, amassed and subject to analysis. A reoccurring theme is that the objective stance is seen to deny the politics and ethical questions bound up in using data. The assumption is that the presumed rawness of the data and its sheer scale (alongside the automation of the analysis), obviate any kind of perspectivism.

Also raised in these arguments are questions about the situated nature of data and its analysis. Seen as anything but raw, data is understood to be produced or enacted through on-going circulations and relations. Data, from this viewpoint, doesn't by itself assert things in the world; rather, it helps to surface, assemble, cement and (at times) unravel forms of knowing, ideas, controversies, and so on. Also, it combines with and is entangled in wider forms of life, not always simplifying and narrowing in on the facts, but often further complicating what is at stake and introducing new and different forms of trouble.

What these developing ideas are beginning to point to then is the need for a reconceptualisation of data, one that accounts for the ways in which it is contingent on very particular circumstances. The call is for a data that doesn't presume an intrinsic generality, but that acknowledges precisely its place in and amongst other worldly things. It is this invitation to think differently about data that we respond to in this paper. As a preliminary exercise, we explore the possibilities of addressing the recognised challenges by using the concept of *data-in-place*. We introduce this term not to merely situate data in particular physical spaces or within particular activities, but rather to think of it in terms of a *social geography* in which data, people, and things intermingle to continuously enact place.

The impetus here is a theorising in urban sociology and geography in which the reductionist tendencies of seeing "the social" as ultimately quantifiable are being countered "by rethinking sociality as a spatial complex of uneven and constantly evolving human and nonhuman forces..." [26, p.3]. This opens up a way of seeing data as threading into "spatially variable surfaces" [26, p.11] that materialise specific configurations of people, things and places, and give form to the very particular kinds of worlds we live in. As we'll go on to show, this conceptualisation doesn't lessen the importance of data, but orients the possibilities in different ways—shifting the emphasis away from data reconciling facts and oversimplifying what people want and how they behave, to ways of enabling rich and heterogeneous human and nonhuman assemblages to coexist and emerge.

Data in Place

Below, we describe how we've begun to think about data-in-place through a project being conducted on Tenison Road, a single, mostly residential road in Cambridge (UK). The details of this now year-long project will follow. First though, it is worth giving some explanation to why we've come to conjoin data and communal life and, through that, started to think about data-in-place as a productive concept.

Community has drawn increasing attention in HCI over recent years. Communities have been seen as a convenient resource for 'in the wild' trials [8, 25], while a range of projects have sought to introduce technologies and services into neighbourhoods [25, 19, 3, 4, 14]. For ourselves, most salient amongst these have been projects that consider how technology (infra)structures underlay and enmesh with communities and their geography. This presents a compelling position from which to understand technology's ubiquitous presence in the everyday. Dourish and Bell [12] write of the shaping forces such infrastructures exert in communities (and elsewhere), demonstrating just how instrumental they are to human and collective experiences.

Data has a relevance here, as it too weaves into these infrastructures, with its dependence on the networks of ubiquitous computing to be sensed and routed. What studies in HCI are beginning to demonstrate is, again, how closely intertwined communities, place and data come to be in this web of the sociotechnical. Projects such as the Tidy Street project [5] and Visualising Mill Road [17] show the speed with which data finds its way into a community's social geography (even with relatively simple data infrastructures), highlighting the particular socio-spatial configurations and also the possibilities for intervening in and disrupting them [also see 11, 12].

Alongside this research, there has been a growing concern for data as it pertains to civic and communal life. Whether we like it or not, it is becoming increasingly clear that this is an arena in which data will have a significant and meaningful impact on our lives [30, 9]. With issues of engagement, participation and public welfare paramount in public discourses and policy making, civic and communal life is increasingly being subject to what is being referred to as "datafication" [18]. Metrics are being collected to gauge everything from the state of citizens' eating habits to their happiness, and in turn these 'assets' are being used to determine public initiatives and policies. Ostensibly, data is operating as a stand in for collectives, citizens and publics, and decisions are being made on the basis of data about how society should be organised and run.

This loose grouping of work and thinking around data, community and place highlight, as the geographer Wilson phrases it, a particular "imbrication of the urban and the digital, the techno and the cultural" [31, p. 859]. In different but connected ways, they indicate a growing intensity of action at the nexus of data (infra)structures and the ways we live together. Furthermore, they foreground the very material ways in which data—commonly perceived as remote, neutral and general—makes its presence felt when situated in real-world places and, simultaneously, the tensions that can arise when we inhabit those places together.

This, then, is what has led our sights to converge on data and communal life, and directed our attention towards data-in-place. Our extended engagement with Tenison Road is born out of the sense that there is a need to understand not only how to generate, analyse and use data, but how, over time, it comes to entangle and settle in a place. The work we present thus aims to thicken the understandings we have of data in the places we live, on roads, in communities, and in neighbourhoods. By working through data-in-place, our hope is to develop a way to express how such places intermingle with data. In short, we want to provide a conceptualisation of data directed at how data comes to matter.

In what follows, we'll first describe how we've engaged with Tenison Road through a diverse set of activities and interventions. We aim, here, to explain why we chose Tenison Road, and to illustrate our commitment to engaging deeply and over an extended period with a community in order to study data-in-place. Next, we'll review three ways that we've been working with residents, each presenting insights into how they are making sense of data and putting it to use. This will lead into a breakdown of how the research has helped to conceptualise data-in-place. We'll introduce four approaches to thinking about the concept that are helping us to make sense of the project's results. We'll conclude by reflecting on how this thinking might shape the design of interactive data systems and infrastructures.

ENGAGEMENTS

Why Tenison Road then? From the outset we were motivated to understand experiences with data from the inside, not abstracting away from the difficulties and quandaries thrown up by examining real people and their understandings and uses of data. Thus, we started the project by surveying the data we could find about our own local communities, the places where each of the project team live. The results varied enormously, showing the differing concerns of city and rural communities, and the uneven nature of data such as national statistics and geo-located social media. This led us to thinking about how a single community might understand the heterogeneous forms of data that it could amass about itself. Through a meandering decision-making process, we pondered on the road our research lab had recently moved onto, Tenison Road. We appreciated the varied demographic on the road, but we were also drawn to how our own presence was likely to further complicate the question of how data comes to matter in a place. Our hearts, then, settled on studying Tenison Road.

Tenison Road is a street in Cambridge that runs for roughly half a mile from Station Road (leading to the railway station) to Mill Road (one of the more cosmopolitan and diverse Cambridge areas; Fig. 1). The variety of residents include students and tenants who live near Mill Road, family housing around the Green at the centre, and tourists who stay in bed and breakfast lodgings nearer the railway station. The smattering of 'commercial' enterprises include a lighting shop, pub, language school, YMCA, charity, solicitors' office, and our lab. Notably, the road is also part of the site of a major redevelopment program around the station. Our lab represents an early stage of the development, which is otherwise manifest in considerable building works surrounding the southern end of Tenison Road. Needless to say, both the works and final development are having and will have serious implications for Tenison Road itself.

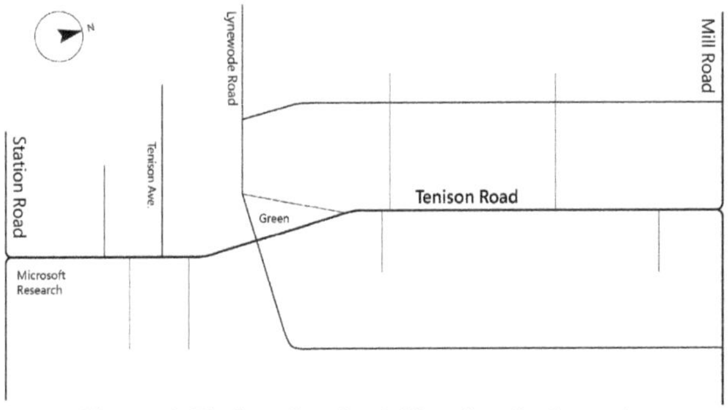

Figure 1. Tenison Road neighbourhood schematic.

In October 2013, we delivered about one hundred invitations to the properties on Tenison Road for a project launch hosted at our lab. Since then, the backbone of our engagement has been a series of topically-driven, evening community meetings, which occur approximately every month. These are organised via email (about 60 residents have signed up to our email list) and are usually attended by 20-30 residents plus members of the project team. Over 12 months, we've also sought to encourage other data-related engagements with the residents, including asking them to complete data notebooks, occasional data surveys (on local plant and wild life), installing and managing different 'data technologies' (see below), and on-going impromptu interactions in person and electronically. More formally, we've also conducted, with residents and proprietors, ten in-depth interviews concerning the geography of the road. The first five of these focused on the social geography of the street, while the latter five focused on the ways in which data and information flows through it. In both cases, participants used printed maps to illustrate their thoughts. In all, the project has consisted of a diverse set of engagements aimed at building a trusted relationship with the community and insights into their evolving views of data.

As well as empirical insights, a range of ideas for what we've called 'data technologies' have emerged through these different engagements. To date, our activities have given rise to: the deployment of five off-the-shelf Air Quality Eggs [1] in residents' homes; the building and deployment of a system for monitoring vehicle traffic and noise levels; the production of a paper-based archive of the street's history and a complementary online databank; and the deployment of an existing system, PosterVote (Fig. 2a) [30], which supports push-button voting using augmented posters installed on the street. The research team are also in the midst of deploying over thirty bespoke voting devices, named Bullfrogs (Fig. 2c), that allow residents to participate in hyper-local polling and voting from their homes.

Data from these technologies are being collated on the project website, and were also showcased at a street party held in August 2014 (an event run with the local community to celebrate the street's 125th anniversary). The street party was an opportunity to engage residents who were not already involved in our project, and enabled the material archive and traffic data to be displayed—the latter was visualised on bespoke physical charts (Fig. 2b). We also ran a number of data exercises at this event; for example, households were invited to design bunting flags to show the number of years they'd lived on the street (Fig. 2d).

Figure 2. PosterVote installed on Tenison Road (a), and the physical charts (b) BullFrogs (c) and custom bunting (d) at street party.

THINKING THROUGH THE DATA

It's not possible, within the scope of this paper, to cover all of the data exercises and related discussions undertaken in the past year. We limit ourselves here to three major strands of the project that have played a significant part in our engagements. These address social heritage through the curation of existing data; traffic through the capture of vehicle and environmental data; and the complexities associated with polling residents for their opinions on local issues. We consider approaches to dealing with existing data first.

Archiving: Dealing with Existing Data

A theme identified early on as being of significance to the residents was that of community: how can a sense of community be collectively fostered, and can data have a role in this? These questions led to, amongst other things, the creation of two archives of Tenison Road's history, one physical and one digital. In this section, we consider the ways that the archives bring data together to produce a historical narrative. In particular, we attend to the role that certain individuals on the road have played in developing this narrative, and how their activities appear to have been bound up with particular temporal, spatial and social factors.

The two archives, although both about the road, are produced in quite different ways. The physical archive is being curated by one of the residents, a trained archivist and former librarian, who has volunteered as part of the project to collate content from sources including census data, newspaper clippings, information from fellow residents and the occasional found object. Building this archive is a serious endeavour; at the time of writing it takes the form of three large ring-bound folders, two of which form the main archive and one that is a loan copy available to others. In contrast, the digital archive, or 'databank', was built by the research team, and residents can upload their own content to it via a website. The different formats obviously have implications for access: the physical archive is stored at the archivist's home, and can only be viewed with her consent, whereas the databank can be seen and contributed to by anyone with access to the web. This leads to its own issues; for example, some residents are uncertain of the ethics of publishing details online about the people who used to live in their houses, a factor that is not queried when it comes to the physical archive. Yet a broader problem is the rather diffuse responsibility for updating the databank, in contrast to the clear role the archivist has taken on with its physical counterpart. While the databank is somewhat sparse, the physical archive is substantial, and continues to grow.

The archivist has fully embraced the task of producing the ring-bound archive, and is able to articulate a clear motivation for doing so: "I want to see certain improvements are made in planning and safeguarding our heritage". Documenting local places with "heritage assets" that are of "local interest" could, in her view, be brought to bear on any future discussions about proposals to renovate the street, and may be of special value where buildings have no formal protections against redevelopment. This endeavour entails creating a holistic but unique document, one which extends existing records that can be obtained from the library and online sources. Accordingly, she seeks to engage other residents in its production, drawing in content that they have about their own houses (such as house deeds and photos), to enrich the archive further. She has organised it to make it easy to find content about each house, to support the personal interests of different individuals. However, engaging others in a way that might encourage them to dig out any relevant content that they have is not straightforward:

"I try but it's quite hard because if you think about it people are at work... What I'm trying to do by presenting the archive at these public occasions [e.g. the street party and community meetings] and answering questions... I am then hoping if you cast your bread upon the waters it might come back fruitcake."

The archivist points out the value of the street party and community meetings, as in the ordinary course of events little happens that might give her the opportunity to publicly share the archive and even less occurs that might engage others in the process of its production.

Indeed, interviews with other residents resonate with the view that there are few places on the street that serve as hubs for the exchange of information or data [cf. 20]; instead, people are more likely to encounter others while *moving* through the street. Yet, while the street is described by residents as a thoroughfare, they rarely move along its full length, often walking or cycling along the streets that run off it to reach the town centre or the north of Cambridge. Thus, the people they encounter tend to be those who use the same routes, at the same times. These spatial and temporal qualities to the road give rise to fluid networks of information exchange, motivated by common interests and needs. For instance, one resident described how he knows "a lot of people from dog walking", and that this gives rise to "a lot of exchange around general dog chat" but also to "social manoeuvring". He gives an example of how a proposal from the council to require dogs be kept on their leads in the local cemetery was retracted, due to "people saying they would write to their MP [Member of Parliament], and they did, so it escalated very quickly and was a word of mouth thing". Networks can thus be responsive to triggers, but they are dependent on common concerns.

The archivist too is connected to other residents of Tenison Road through the location of her home, her daily routines, and her own concerns with local issues. Indeed, her presence on the street is felt; she keeps her neighbours' keys, accepts deliveries on their behalf, and was described as an "expert" by others through her role in producing the physical archive. But this does not, it seems, make it easy for her to gather archival data. Consequently, and despite her efforts to engage others, the archive is largely made up of her own research, found objects (including a letter from a former UK Prime Minister, which was found amongst a neighbour's recycling in a shared alleyway), and content from a few people who attend the meetings and attended the street party. Also worth noting, in a minority of cases her role is a barrier to the inclusion of content. On one occasion a resident preferred to give a set of photos, found during home renovations, to the research team. She viewed these as depicting content that the archivist might be too close to, having been resident on the street when the people who these items had belonged to had lived there. Thus, the production of the archive is directly influenced by spatial factors (e.g. the location of the archivist's home), temporal factors (e.g. her ability to connect with people who work to different temporalities) and social factors (e.g. the privacy implications bound up with her role as archivist).

Traffic and Local Redevelopment: Capturing Data

The second strand of the project we wish to highlight is one that involves residents more broadly, and has implications for not only those who live on the street but also for those who pass through it. Below, we reflect on our efforts to capture data about the street's environment, an effort that was, unsurprisingly, precipitated by residents' concerns over the local redevelopment plans and their impact on traffic on the street. The findings show again that data collection is most impassioned when it is driven by matters that are clearly meaningful to a place. At the same time they extend this, showing more clearly the competing interests of different parties.

Residents were keen from the outset of the project to capture data about Tenison Road's traffic. The deployment of a thermal camera (mounted on our building) and Air Quality Eggs is being done in part out of curiosity (some residents wondered whether their back gardens would have better air quality than their front gardens, for example) but principally to amass data as "evidence" and even as "ammunition" in dialogues with the council. Traffic calming plans put forward by the council, through a public consultation, have raised concerns and residents have seen the data as a way to prioritise the issues and put forward their case. The collection of data about air quality in particular was seen to be a means of effecting change, having been cited by one of the residents (also secretary of the local residents' association, and considered to be someone who "knows everything") as being used by another nearby street to demand the implementation of traffic calming measures. In one meeting, this resident heralded: "The purpose of data is action."

Notably, the council does already collect local air quality data. There is an air quality station visible from the street, but residents have no straightforward means of accessing the data that it produces. Speaking at a meeting, one said, "The information is there, but it's buried." However, there is a further reason as to why residents wish to collect their own data. The council and especially the developers are seen as having an agenda that is at odds with that of the residents, and this is believed to be reflected in the data that they collect. At interview, one resident commented:

"The council writes to us a lot about planning applications, we get quite a lot of junk mail from the council. They've sent us recently a survey about our views of the street and sent it online which I think is pretty terrible, I think if you looked at it, it has one of those questions where it says 'Do you really agree, do you strongly agree, do you agree a bit or don't you care' and it always tips to the answer and they make it so long that you get half way down and give up."

This view that data is non-representative or biased extends to measures of speed taken by the police force (who have reportedly done so wearing high-visibility jackets, which cause the traffic to slow down) and estimates of volume presented by the developers (which simply haven't been accepted as having face validity). Thus, one resident highlighted at a meeting the distinction between data "coming from us" and "being done to us". Importantly, this view extends to the researchers' role in the project as well; her desire is to be directly involved in the production of data.

The above demonstrates a certain unity amongst the residents in terms of their aspiration to use data to negotiate with the council. However, discussions at community meetings also reveal divergent voices in terms of how traffic calming might be accomplished in practice. Concerns in relation to this include parking, noise pollution, air pollution, speed, volume of traffic, implication for safety, and implication for community and the sense that one can connect with neighbours living across the road. Traffic calming measures that might, for example, reduce speed (e.g. 'speed bumps') could also increase noise (due to the need to brake and change gear on approach) and reduce the number of parking spaces on the street. One resident has described how he wouldn't mind speed, so long as it was "silent speed", but this opinion has been contested by others. The multiplicity of viewpoints that surfaces is difficult to reconcile with the process of collecting data for 'the street', which implies a collective goal. Next, we consider what data could potentially bring to a situation like this, where there is a recognition of multiple viewpoints and different stakeholders.

Voting and Polling: Making Data

In this last of three sections, then, we begin to consider how technologies for voting on local issues and polling residents from the street might have a role to play in acknowledging and addressing multiplicities. We will see how data is seen as having a capacity to draw people together, but also how the perceived ability to deal with multiple viewpoints is bound up with stakeholders that are thought of as neutral.

At the time of writing, one voting technology (PosterVote) has been deployed on the street—mainly in relation to recently proposed traffic calming measures—and another (Bullfrog) has been demonstrated at the street party and is midway through a field trial. The use of these technologies on Tenison Road are still, therefore, in their nascent stages, but they have nevertheless been utilized in grounding discussions at community meetings about what questions might be asked of the street, and the challenges bound up with framing these. At the heart of these discussions is a recognition that Tenison Road is fairly heterogeneous, encompassing areas that are "wholly privately owned, quite big houses, people that are more established in life versus… student, buy to let areas". The people who attend the community meetings tend to be owner-occupiers, who are part of the community around and near to the green. They themselves recognise, "Our group is interesting, committed, but it's a particular demographic of Tenison Road."

Residents also understand that polling technologies such as PosterVote, that can be installed on the street itself, may offer a means to gather data from people who do not attend the meetings, including those who pass through rather than live on Tenison Road (e.g., pedestrian commuters who use it to access the railway station). However, they note issues around "who frames the questions" and people's "agendas". Indeed, in discussions about the possibility of using PosterVote to canvas opinion about whether a new local history board should be installed on the Green, one resident suggests a positive community sentiment: "yes, because I think you'll find support". Yet, at the same time, there is dissent. At least one resident (through correspondence with both the resident association's secretary and the council) has vigorously protested yet more "clutter" on the road.

The community meetings held in our offices have been identified as one avenue where such dissent can be acknowledged: "you guys are obviously aliens, you're above and beyond Tenison Road […] trying not to be dictatorial […] makes you not of Tenison Road". As people with no stated agenda, who do not live on the street, we have been described as bringing an impartiality to the project that is expressed through the provision of "a neutral space" to meet in and a stability in initiating meetings that are separate to those run by the residents' association (who are seen as having a particular set of concerns). The resident quoted above expands: "I see you guys as people who don't have an axe to grind about the data, you just want it to flow".

This neutrality has been deemed important also in the ways data is produced. In the context of the project, data is seen as a potential "catalyst to try and build some kind of cohesive community". But the issue of collecting data is not straightforward, either because it necessitates directly asking for information from neighbours, or because it means dealing with conflicting voices that may be expressed through anonymous polls. In relation to the former, some residents have expressed the need for someone outside of the street to take the "patriarchal" role of collecting data. We have noted the archivist's tactic of sparking people's interest in the archive rather than explicitly asking them to contribute content to it, and reticence to ask for information was also quite visible when a resident initially volunteered for the role of producing the bunting for the party, but then withdrew with the explanation that it would be inappropriate for her to ask questions of people living on the street (eventually we engaged a local artist to undertake this role). In relation to the latter, the problem of managing differences of opinion has been raised explicitly in discussions about what should happen when the project ends.

Thus, while data is seen as potentially drawing community together, the problem of framing questions and dealing with differences of opinion mean that generating data is a potentially divisive endeavour for communities to engage in.

THINKING THROUGH DATA-IN-PLACE

Broadly, then, over the last twelve months, what's come to be apparent in working with the residents of Tenison Road is how they've been able to grasp the value of data and its relevance to local concerns. Much of the above is an indication, it seems fair to say, of the well-rounded ideas residents have developed about data and what it can do for them. Despite protestations from many—voicing their ineptitude with technology—it's clear the data we've been collecting is coming to be a viable way for residents to think about and act on local matters. In this light, the data seems not a portentous technology set to dramatically transform daily life or decisively determine facts and outcomes, but more a substance being drawn into (and sometimes rubbing up against) the everyday business of living on a road.

As a concept, data-in-place thus helps to draw out ideas of data coming into being through growing and shifting relations with a street, its residents and the environment. For HCI, what though can we learn by seeing things in terms of this gradual and on occasion capricious emergence of situated and contingent data, what conclusions might we draw that have relevance to the design of interactive technology?

Accessible and Sustainable Data Systems

A straightforward implication points to the design of data systems that should be either more accessible for non-technical users or that incorporate some sustained technical support. Strikingly, it has not been a lack of understanding of the relevance or importance of data that has hindered people's imaginations on Tenison Road. Rather, residents have, quite reasonably, voiced worries about their lack of know-how and confidence to install and run data based technologies. On numerous occasions and in various contexts, we've been told the data-related activities we've been collectively involved in would have been impossible without us. To put it bluntly, putting data into a place is, we've found, an active venture and, unsurprisingly, demands a specialist knowledge and commitment to keep it going.

This raises a number of issues echoed in a relevant paper by Taylor et al. [25] that discusses withdrawing from community engagements. The paper's authors highlight the heavy reliance on researchers to keep deployed systems working and the challenges involved in building solutions that can be sustained once projects have been completed and researchers leave. This will no doubt be a persistent problem in, as Taylor et al. refer to it, "experimental technology" research. However, it's also the case, we imagine, that a range of services now openly available and appearing to garner a user base will provide viable solutions for communities wanting to collect and exploit data (e.g. *Netatamo* and *Withings Home*, and services like *Neighborland*).

Beyond these practical concerns, what we want to develop here are implications that account for the more nuanced relations between place, community and data that have surfaced in our research. Broadly, we see our emerging results giving rise to a conceptualisation of data that remains, as it were, on the ground. This isn't to repudiate the value of (big) data, but to recognise that the situated qualities of data—of data in place—open up a new set of possibilities for designing data orientated tools and systems. We see this data-in-place having implications for a design approach that accommodates the always emerging assemblies of place, community and data, and at the same time one that enables specific and unique configurations to flourish. Below we elaborate on four strands of thinking that we hope help to orient design in this way. Through ideas of *mattering*, *contours*, *structures and boundaries*, and *multiples*, our aim is to suggest that data technologies might be conceived of as an ecosystem of devices and services. Here, the provenance of data across networks of people, places and technologies would be treated as something continually enacted in-place, and the data would purposefully be enriched and thickened based on the always emergent relations.

Mattering

Key to making sense of data in this way then is understanding how it materialises in place. Counter to the common view of data as abstract and general—figuratively in the clouds—we've come to understand it as something that is always, in some form, bound up with what matters. This is meant in both senses of the word, in that we see data coming into being in material ways, and also in ways that are meaningful—that matter—to people. This point is well-developed by Wilson [31], so we'll not dwell on it here. Let us briefly though illustrate it through the voting and polling systems we've been working on with the community.

In line with similar concerns for the hyper-local [3, 14, 30], our exercises in engaging the community in local forms of participation have purposefully sought to link locally formed opinions to place. For example, in using PosterVote to let people express their degree of support for the council's proposed traffic calming measures, posters were located where those changes would be made, materialising votes on specific devices and in very specific locations. With Bullfrog, our aim is to do the same, but provide the community with a mechanism that produces a denser map of the things people want to ask, their responses, and how these are located and perhaps distributed along the road.

What residents' reflections on these aims show, so far, is how the data—in this case the results of local votes and polls—is meaningful precisely for how it comes into being, materially. As we've seen, the material configurations of posters along Tenison Road matter to residents because they do more than simply record counts of votes—they seek to address the uneven demographic distribution along the road and different degrees of involvement both in our research project and the council's attempt at a democratic process. The very existence of posters with particular questions and in certain places is recognised to embody impartial agendas, reflecting intensities of feeling and the differing notions of a collective good on the road.

We find much is lost, then, if data is abstracted away from place, not understood as coming to matter in place. Furthermore, this understanding of data shows how it privileges some readings, and discounts or deters others. In short, the mattering of data, how it materialises and comes to be meaningful in place, presents a way of enriching its value. What we begin to tackle here is how we might come to conceptualise this in a productive way.

Contours

Residents' mapping exercises have etched out fluid movements and transient encounters with data across and along Tenison Road; news on the street is most remarkable for how it travels, not how it stays fixed in particular sites. Passing people on a dog walk, the chat over the garden fence or the chance encounter on the way to the shops are the forms of transmission. These are temporally sensitive and opportunistic, threaded into small geo-temporal moments in which residents interact and share news with those they already know through common interests.

Seeing data in place (and mapped), these read as contours that data both follows and etches out. On maps, they read like a networked tapestry, one knitted into and inexorably interwoven with the road's physical and social geography. Our data-in-place helps to tease out the ways these contours are performed, how they are embroidered (to continue the analogy) into the places people inhabit.

Take our role in collecting and managing data on Tenison Road. As we've recounted, we hold a peculiar position in the eyes of the residents. Our perceived role as an "outsider", somehow "alien" to the community, positions us as "neutral". We've been described as simply interested in the "flow" of data. This neutral status as overseer of data flows—of installing and maintaining devices for voting and polling for instance—is understood not just to be technical, but also a facilitator of 'community'.

Flows materialise data in particular ways, forming contours between and around how it is generated and maintained. By sensing and managing the data to ease these flows, we build surfaces and structures that shape the capacities for data's movement into and along the road. boyd and Crawford [6] begin their article '*Critical questions for big data*' by citing Kranzberg's famous quote: "Technology is neither good nor bad, nor is it neutral". So it is here. We intensify the collection of data at points on Tension Road with our traffic and air quality monitoring, and build data structures on our servers that place these readings along an incrementally growing timeline (in human readable increments). This figures Tenison Road in particular spatiotemporal terms, foregrounding discrete regions of space-time to be preserved and, in some cases, used (i.e., in conversations with local government). Interjecting data into Tenison Road is then grafting and knitting data into a geography of the neighbourhood; despite our perceived neutrality, our work with the data gives shape to a new and emerging kind of place.

Structures and Boundaries

Positioning data in place like this, rather than in the abstract, also requires a different consideration of how it is produced and shared. In place, this is circumscribed by local temporalities, spatiality and sociality—by residents having their distinctive rhythms; traveling by different routes and using different modes: walking, cycling and driving; and having friendships and acquaintanceships built around common interests. So for example, the archive includes found objects, which were discovered in the alleyway next to the archivist's street, while the Air Quality Eggs are located on the houses of residents who come to the community meetings, and who live towards the centre of the road. The community meetings are organised around the nine-to-five working day, a temporality that cannot suit everyone [23], and the proposition of attending them may in any case be of greater interest to people who consider themselves to have a vested interest in the street (e.g., owner-occupiers) than those passing through (e.g., students and tenants, not to mention commuters and tourists).

The temporalities, spatiality and sociality thus give shape to contours through which data 'flows' on Tenison Road. They also structure the data itself. For example, a new formal network may be precipitated by nearby development plans to build new homes behind a row of existing homes, while dog walkers might form a more fluid network that may nevertheless quickly react against a proposed requirement for dogs to be put on leads. In either case, the data coalesces and spreads across the road at/between different regions and in distinct rhythms, building uneven networks of data nodes and classifications purposefully assembled for a common use. Far from generic or arbitrary, these 'data structures' are consequently deeply entwined with place, caught up in the geospatial and temporal rhythms of what matters on the road and to its residents.

Boundaries are a feature of these structures too. Not necessarily connected in time or space, the structures keep data separate. Residents can, of course, intersect with different structures and thus move and share data. However, generally, a lack of common concerns inhibits the flow. Even though the data might be useful to both parties, we're unlikely to see those protesting the development share data with the dog walkers, simply by dint of the different motives. Boundaries to data are, then, a product of the road's social geography. Indeed, some boundaries are upheld deliberately, with a view to protecting privacy. It is difficult to abstract away, anonymise, and decontextualize data in small communities; prior work by Cross has highlighted the ways that members of a small, rural community might object to the sharing of data even within that community [10]. On Tenison Road, too, we see residents reticent to engage in data collection when this means directly soliciting it.

Data-in-place, then, is not simply an aggregation across individuals living on a street, but a reflection of a community with its own spatial, temporal and social structures and boundaries. In some cases, efforts are made to overcome these boundaries, while in others, work is done to ensure they are upheld. But ultimately, structures and boundaries shape production and carve out certain paths for sharing.

Multiples

The shifting positions people can inhabit, and the different places they can be in the flows of data suggest what might be thought of as a multiplicity of 'small worlds' [27, 22]. The contours and boundaries performed as data suffuses Tenison Road mark out realms with distinctive relations between people, things, places, etc., each with an internal logic accounting for the flows and connections.

Such worlds are in the making on Tenison Road, forming perhaps most visibly around the major development plans and local government initiatives, which aim to appease local residents through 'traffic calming'. The County Council, through a traffic survey, circumscribes and marks out a territory by counting vehicle turns at each junction along the road. The map of numbers produced from this operates in a comparative logic; data counts for how it can establish particular categories of road and expected traffic flows. On Tenison Road, the council wants to determine whether there is in fact a traffic problem to be answered by comparing this data to surveys on similarly categorised roads, and, if they can afford it, further surveys at the same junctions.

On the road, the rationale is different. The same data is an impetus for residents to ask questions that they tell us are more relevant to life on Tenison Road. It's the speed between the junctions they say that matters, and the noise and pollution. The neighbourhood is described as literally and figuratively divided by the fast moving and high volumes of traffic. Yes, the residents have different motives here (some wanting slower and less cars, and some wanting quiet), but the data counts for what we are told emphatically is a "quality of life" for the neighbourhood, a push for a common good through collective action. It's this that has driven, above all else, the installation of the sensors that monitor sound levels, traffic speed and air quality.

Seeing data find its place in these ways shows multiple worlds of relations and logics if not yet formed, then in the making. Critically, though, these worlds aren't easily differentiated. The traffic monitoring matters are of course much more complicated, with actors and relations flowing across both these worlds and the numerous others that have a stake in who will and won't travel along Tenison Road. Let us make a last point to illustrate how the multiples work into and through one another.

As part of the project's collective deliberations over traffic, one discussion has developed into the possibility of tracking residents' changing movements and travel routines over the course of the year, aiming to reflect the changes afoot to the built environment. To this end, two residents have volunteered to wear location-tracking devices and feed their geo-temporal data into the larger corpus of traffic data. An email received from a father and his two children (who all regularly attend community meetings), responding to this location-tracking, asks how the data might be understood in terms of another of the project's data exercises, the archive:

"*... I appreciate traffic is a major theme but we all think we don't want to end up being the city council traffic department. Traffic is about people moving and people moving in the wider aspect is hugely interesting- moving for work, moving for school, moving for fun. we'd all be very up for tracking ourselves and seeing how our movement phenotypes differ.*

I think the ideas of archive and record are more interesting and potentially engaging in wider sphere and would be very interested how we could use the tools of today to record life and movement. combining the movement record within the sociological record might be able to make traffic just that little more permanent than the more short term but ever present gripes of urban traffic."

This message situates location data in terms of quite a different sense of movement along Tenison Road. The data is seen as constitutive of a "movement record" that locates the to-ings and fro-ings on the road in wider trajectories of time and social life. The data is not so clearly judged in terms of collective action and communal good, but rather in how a community hopes to learn about itself and represent itself, historically. Movement data, but also "the tools of today", become entangled in particular moments and these are located in extended lines of changing human, machine and social relations. Through data-in-place, we see then a multiplicity of worlds being brought into being. These worlds are small, and spatially and temporarily bounded, but the point is data weaves its way into them, as a shaping force.

CONCLUSIONS

This paper represents an effort to think through data and how it comes to be actively entangled in social and communal life. Through *data-in-place*, we've presented a conceptualisation that aims to thicken and deepen what we've observed to be the tight-knit and always emerging relations between people, places and data. Our data-related activities and engagements with a road's community have been interpreted in terms of *mattering*, *contours*, *structures and boundaries*, and *multiples*, each of which seek to capture the experiences of using and being exposed to data.

In this, our broad aim has been to show how data-in-place might open up ways of thinking about our interactions with data. We've foregrounded the unevenly distributed and heterogeneous nature of data when it is encountered in place. We've seen too how data materialises in distinct ways and ways that matter, differently, to people and places. Our own interventions on Tenison Road draw on these ideas, experimenting with a diverse range of ways to generate and experience data. PosterVote, the Bullfrogs, the physical charts, and a variety of on and offline surveys and data representations have been designed to be sensitive to the distinctive qualities of data each engenders when put in place.

In these terms, we suggest it may be helpful to approach design in terms of an ecosystem of data forms for generating, viewing and possibly analysing data. Of course, ideas of device ecosystems have been around for some time, and it's fair to say that the growing and evolving range of services and apps available online and on mobile devices will meet this need. We thus see the value here being in how we consider extending the ecosystem analogy to include our situated interactions with data, and how we build a rich variety of data-driven systems and services to accommodate the materially and spatially bound ways we live with data.

The notions of contours, and the changing structures and boundaries seen through data-in-place direct attention to the ways we structure data and, in turn, enable access to it. At a high level, this implies that we need to think of structures that support some kind of representation of data's active presence in place. These might express how data travels geographically and between people, and when, where and with whom it gathers significance (traversing through the contours and across the boundaries of a social geography). They may represent the different ways these parties invest in and (re-)inscribe data with particular understandings, across time and space. Productive here, would be a structure representing the rich geo-temporal tapestry data is entangled in. It would show it not to be a singular set of static facts, but part of the continuous and processual circulation of things, people, places, motives, ideas, and so on.

Further, this suggests the need to treat data as something that multiple parties have a stake in, perhaps even jointly own. Current data services do not deal with the distinction between personal and collective ownership well, failing to capture how a group in the workplace differs from a family, interest group, resident association, or neighbourhood. Proposals for rethinking what community ownership of data might look like include the notion of data co-ops, storage services set up to be of benefit to a community rather than of value to shareholders [16]. As we have seen, communities raise a particular set of issues when it comes to stewardship and privacy, issues that could be explicitly acknowledged through design. This might take the form of encrypting parts of a dataset, making data available for limited, or even future periods of time, and linking it to a specific agenda that the data is associated with. Perhaps, as motives shift or the role of stewarding changes hands, access to data would need to be renegotiated.

These modest ideas are offered as illustrations in our thinking through of the relations between data and communal life. As we extend our work with Tenison Road and develop similar programs elsewhere, our aim is to further examine data's presence in place and see whether as a conceptualisation of data, data-in-place can come to help people and communities live productive and meaningful lives. In doing so, we seek to build on what we have expressed here: that the ways in which data is produced are shaped by the social and material qualities of place, qualities that, if recognised in the design of data technologies, might underpin a very different understanding of the uses data might be put to.

REFERENCES

1. Air Quality Eggs. http://airqualityegg.com. Accessed September 9 2014.
2. Anderson, C. The end of theory. *Wired magazine.* (2008), 16-07.
3. Aoki, P.M., Honicky, R.J., Mainwaring, A., Myers, C., Paulos, E., Subramanian, S. and Woodruff, A. A vehicle for research: using street sweepers to explore the landscape of environmental community action. In *Proc. CHI 2009*, ACM Press (2009), 375-384.
4. Bellotti, V., Cambridge, S., Hoy, K., Shih, P. C., Renery Handalian, L., Han, K. and Carroll, J. M. Towards community-centred support for peer-to-peer service exchange: rethinking the timebanking metaphor. In *Proc. CHI 2014*, ACM Press (2014), 2975-2984.
5. Bird, J. and Rogers, Y. The pulse of Tidy Street: measuring and publicly displaying domestic electricity consumption. *Pervasive 2010 Workshop on Energy Awareness and Conservation through Pervasive Applications.*
6. boyd, d. and Crawford, K. Critical questions for big data: provocations for a cultural, technological, and scholarly phenomenon. *Info Com Soc 15*, 5 (2012), 662-679.
7. Bowker, G.C. The Theory/Data Thing. *IJOC 8*, (2014), 1795–1799.
8. Carroll, J. and Rosson. M.B. Wild at home: the neighborhood as a living laboratory for hci. *ACM Trans. Comput.-Hum. Interact. 20*, 3 (July 2013), Article 16.
9. Crawford, K., Faleiros, G., Luers, A., Meier, P., Perlich, C. and Thorp, J. Big data, communities and ethical resilience, a framework for action." *Bellagio/PopTech Fellows White paper* (2013). http://www. rockefeller-foundation.org/blog/big-data-communities-ethical.
10. Cross, J. Life off the grid. Presented at the *Symposium on Producing Data: Practices, Materialities, Values.* September 3 2014, Edinburgh, UK.
11. Dourish, P. Re-space-ing place: "place" and "space" ten years on. In *Proc.* CSCW '06, ACM Press (2006), 299-308.
12. Dourish, P. and Bell, G. The infrastructure of experience and the experience of infrastructure: meaning and structure in everyday encounters with space. *Environ Plann B 34*, 3 (2007), 414–430.
13. Gitelman, L, ed. *Raw Data is an Oxymoron.* MIT Press, 2013.
14. Hu, Y., Farnham, S.D. and Monroy-Hernández, A. Whoo.ly: facilitating information seeking for hyperlocal communities using social media. In *Proc. CHI 2013*, ACM Press (2013), 3481-3490
15. Kitchin, R. (2014). Big Data, new epistemologies and paradigm shifts. *Big Data & Society 1*, (1).
16. Klein, E. Who owns our data? *Presented at the Symposium on Producing Data: Practices, Materialities, Values*. September 4 2014, Edinburgh, UK.
17. Koeman, L., Kalnikaitė, V., Rogers, Y. and Bird, J. What chalk and tape can tell us: lessons learnt for next generation urban displays. In *Proc. PerDis 2014*, ACM Press (2014), 130-135.
18. Mayer-Schonberger, V. and Cukier, K. *Big Data: A Revolution that will Change How We Live, Work and Think.* London: John Murray, 2013.
19. McGookin, D., Brewster, S.A. and Christov, G. Studying digital graffiti as a location-based social network. In *Proc. CHI 2014*, ACM Press (2014), 3269-3278.
20. Pettigrew, K. Waiting for chiropody: Contextual results from an ethnographic study of the information behaviour among attendees at community clinics. *Info Process Manag 35*, 6 (1999), 801-817.
21. Prensky, M. H. sapiens digital: from digital immigrants and digital natives to digital wisdom. *Innovate 5* (3, 2009).
22. Savolainen, R. Small world and information grounds as contexts of information seeking and sharing. *Libr Inform Sci Res 31*, 1 (2009), 38-45.
23. Sharma, S. *In the Meantime: Temporality and Cultural Politics*. Duke University Press, 2014.
24. Strengers, Y. Smart energy in everyday life: are you designing for resource man? *Interactions 21*, 4 (July 2014), 24-31.
25. Taylor, N., Cheverst, K., Wright, P. and Olivier, P. Leaving the wild: lessons from community technology handovers. In *Proc. CHI 2013*, ACM Press (2013), 1549-1558.
26. Thrift, N. (2014). The "sentient" city and what it may portend. *Big Data & Society 1* (1).
27. Urry, J. Small worlds and the new 'social physics'. *Global networks* 4, 2 (2004), 109-130.
28. van Dijck, J. Datafication, dataism and dataveillance:. *Surveillance and Society 12*, (2014), 197–208.
29. Vertesi, J. and Dourish, P. The value of data: considering the context of production in data economies. In *Proc. CSCW 2011*, ACM Press (2011), 533-542.
30. Vlachokyriakos, V., Comber, R., Ladha, K., Taylor, N., Dunphy, P., McCorry, P. and Olivier, P. PosterVote: expanding the action repertoire for local political activism. In *Proc. DIS 2014*, ACM Press (2014), 795-804.
31. Wilson, M.W. Data matter(s): legitimacy, coding, and qualifications-of-life. *Environ Plan D 29*, 5 (2011), 857–872.

Scaling the Security Wall

Developing a Security Behavior Intentions Scale (SeBIS)

Serge Egelman
International Computer Science Institute
Berkeley, CA, USA
egelman@cs.berkeley.edu

Eyal Peer
Bar-Ilan University
Ramat Gan, Israel
eyal.peer@biu.ac.il

ABSTRACT

Despite the plethora of security advice and online education materials offered to end-users, there exists no standard measurement tool for end-user security behaviors. We present the creation of such a tool. We surveyed the most common computer security advice that experts offer to end-users in order to construct a set of Likert scale questions to probe the extent to which respondents claim to follow this advice. Using these questions, we iteratively surveyed a pool of 3,619 computer users to refine our question set such that each question was applicable to a large percentage of the population, exhibited adequate variance between respondents, and had high reliability (i.e., desirable psychometric properties). After performing both exploratory and confirmatory factor analysis, we identified a 16-item scale consisting of four sub-scales that measures attitudes towards choosing passwords, device securement, staying up-to-date, and proactive awareness.

Author Keywords

Psychometrics; Individual differences; Security behavior

ACM Classification Keywords

H.1.2. Models and Principles: User/Machine Systems; K.6.5. Management of Computing and Information Systems: Security and Protection; J.4. Social and Behavioral Sciences: Psychology

INTRODUCTION

Each year, billions of dollars are spent on computer security education programs. Many employers require employees to undergo training regimens, prior to granting network or computer access, or on an ongoing basis. The U.S. National Institute of Standards and Technology (NIST) offers guidelines for these programs [46], and even the U.S. Department of Homeland Security has a "National Cyber Security Awareness Month" [42]. The NIST guidelines state that "formal evaluation and feedback mechanisms are critical components of any security awareness, training, and education program" [46], yet provide no evaluation metrics. Measuring attack rates is a suboptimal strategy: fewer successful attacks may simply be due to fewer attempts; increased attack success may be due to new vulnerabilities, increased sophistication, or other factors that are independent of user behavior.

In addition to training and education programs, a plethora of organizations offer tips and advice to end-users on how they can stay safe online. However, due to the wide range in specific actionable items offered, most end-users are likely to be confused about which advice to follow and which to ignore. For example, the U.S. Computer Emergency Readiness Team (US-CERT) offers over 500 actionable items [41], whereas Verizon, a large U.S. cellular phone provider and ISP, offers only 4 items [43]. If there are a core set of general behaviors underlying most of this computer security advice, the actionable items offered to end-users can be drastically reduced to be made more memorable. Similarly, in certain cases, reliable self-reporting of these behaviors could replace the need to perform costly and time-consuming observational studies.

When studying human behavior, researchers across many different fields will often use scales as proxies for observation. Scales "are intended to measure elusive phenomena that cannot be observed directly" [11]. Scales are therefore highly useful when behavioral or observational experiments are either too costly, complex, or simply not possible. A scale can also measure how attitudes or behaviors change over time. For instance, the Westin privacy index is used to segment the population based on attitudes towards online privacy, and while there is substantial debate about whether it is predictive of actual privacy behaviors [48], it is still a useful tool that researchers use to examine how privacy attitudes evolve over time [22]. While carefully constructed scales are a core tool when studying human behavior in other domains, they have yet to be applied to the study of computer security behaviors.

We developed a new scale for assessing the computer security behaviors of end-users: the Security Behavior Intentions Scale (SeBIS). In short, our scale measures users' self-reported adherence to computer security advice. We employed the 4-step scale development procedure offered by Netemeyer *et al.* [29], wherein we used common security advice offered to end-users as our content domain, generated and refined the individual questions, performed Exploratory Factor Analysis (EFA) to explore underlying constructs and develop sub-scales, and then performed Confirmatory Factor Analysis (CFA) to finalize our scale and measure its reliability. Our resulting security behaviors scale was evaluated on 3,619 respondents, and consists of 16 items that measure 4 underlying constructs: device securement, password generation, proactive awareness, and updating behaviors.

CHI 2015, April 18 - 23 2015, Seoul, Republic of Korea.

ACM 978-1-4503-3145-6/15/04...$15.00.
http://dx.doi.org/10.1145/2702123.2702249

RELATED WORK

Several models have been created to analyze how humans make security decisions (e.g., [47, 9, 30]), which researchers have used to offer recommendations. For instance, Egelman *et al.* showed that when less-frequent high-risk warnings appear similar to frequent low-risk security warnings, users ignore both [12]. Felt *et al.* showed that smartphone permission warnings are overlooked because they occur too frequently and with poor timing [16]. In this vein, usable security research has greatly improved the security interventions to which users are exposed. We posit that further gains can be made by differentiating users according to individual traits and offering different intervention designs based on those traits. However, for this to be possible, we first need a reliable tool for measuring users' traits, such as their adherence to common computer security practices.

Scales are most often used in psychology, as a means of measuring underlying psychological constructs. One scale that might be relevant to our work is the Domain-Specific Risk-Taking (DoSpeRT) scale, which measures a person's self-reported propensity to engage in risky behaviors across four dimensions: ethical, financial, health/safety, recreational, and social [4]. We hypothesize that an individual's propensity to take safety risks may predict their computer security behaviors. Other psychometrics may also apply: for instance, high impulsivity (e.g., [31]) may predict an individual's willingness to visit questionable URLs, low concern for future consequences (e.g., [21]) may predict an individual's disinclination for running security software, and so forth.

While we are not aware of any studies to develop a scale to measure end-user security behaviors, researchers have raised questions about the psychological underpinnings of computer crime for over three decades. Copes *et al.* created a survey instrument to examine correlations between victimization and demographic factors [8]. Sherizen suggested that there may exist certain "markers" that could be used to detect the propensity for committing online crimes [38]. Only recently have others started to explore this concept. For instance, self-control is a psychological construct with corresponding scales that can be used to measure its prevalence in people. Researchers have administered these scales to see if they correlate with either committing online crimes [27], or being the victim of online crimes [5, 26].

Measuring more general types of computer security behaviors has been limited to within organizations. Stanton *et al.* created a taxonomy of workplace computer security behaviors, and showed that they could be grouped by two dimensions: intentions and expertise [39]. Ng *et al.* [30] used factor analysis to create and evaluate a model of end-user security behavior. Their goal was to use this model to predict email security behaviors, whereas our goal is the development of a composite measurement scale.

Privacy is related to security and has several of its own scales that have been developed over the years and are actively used by researchers to better understand people's attitudes and intentions. The most well known privacy scale is the Westin index, which is used to classify consumers into three groups based on their privacy attitudes: fundamentalists, pragmatists, and the unconcerned [22]. While the Westin index is well-cited and frequently used by privacy researchers, it has been shown to be a poor predictor of privacy-preserving behavior (e.g., [48, 16]). The scale is therefore used to illustrate the gap between stated preferences (as measured by the Westin index) and observed behaviors (as measured through empirical studies)—the so-called "privacy paradox." Thus, the self-reported data may not be "wrong," but instead there may be many other factors at play that influence behavior [1, 2].

The Westin index is unidimensional and therefore only measures one aspect of privacy, whereas other scales measure privacy attitudes and behaviors across multiple dimensions. Malhotra *et al.* developed the Internet Users' Information Privacy Concerns (IUIPC) scale by performing careful factor analysis, and showed that privacy concerns can be measured across three dimensions: control over information, awareness of privacy practices, and attitudes about information collection [23]. Buchanan *et al.* developed three different unidimensional privacy scales, which together measure concerns, general behaviors, and use of technical solutions [6].

The Security Behavior Intentions Scale (SeBIS) is a new scale to measure end-users' intentions to comply with computer security advice. We followed the scale development procedure outlined by Netemeyer *et al.* [29]:

1. **Construct Definition and Content Domain:** Clearly defining the construct that the scale intends to measure.
2. **Generating and Judging Measurement Items:** Creating a pool of candidate questions and then evaluating the questions to remove ones that are invalid.
3. **Designing and Conducting Studies to Develop and Refine Scale:** Performing EFA to reduce the set of questions and explore latent constructs to build a model.
4. **Finalizing the Scale:** Performing CFA to confirm that the scale fits the intended model, as well as reliability analysis.

In the remainder of this paper, we describe how we applied each of these steps and their results. We then describe how we used our scale to explore correlations between self-reported security behaviors and existing psychometrics.

CONSTRUCT DEFINITION AND INITIAL ITEMS

The goal of our scale is to measure end-users' intentions to comply with common security advice. This created two constraints: limiting our metric to security behaviors applicable to most end-users (*vis-à-vis* advice for corporate users, etc.), and only consisting of "widely accepted" security behaviors. We examined the advice offered to end-users by nationwide U.S. ISPs, US-CERT, and industry consortia. Based on this advice, we enumerated a preliminary set of computer security behaviors, omitting advice that was too technical.

Our initial list consisted of 26 behaviors. Next, we met with a group of six computer security experts who offered additional items, increasing our set to 30 behaviors. We transformed these 30 behaviors into personal statements that could be answered based on degree of agreement (i.e., "strongly agree" to "strongly disagree"). To minimize acquiescence bias (i.e., the

#	Question	N/A		μ	σ
A1	*I apply software updates as soon as my computer prompts me.*	5	(1.0%)	3.20	1.221
A2	*I am happy to use an older version of a program, as long as it meets my needs.*	5	(1.0%)	^{r}1.99	1.000
A3	*Whenever I step away from my computer, I lock the screen.*	5	(1.0%)	2.50	1.306
A4	*Others can access my smartphone or tablet without needing a PIN or passcode.*	21	(4.4%)	^{r}3.34	1.545
A5	*When I discover a computer security problem at work, I'm likely to promptly report it to my employer.*	64	(13.4%)	4.08	0.995
A6	*It's important to use a WiFi password to prevent unauthorized people from using my home network.*	11	(2.3%)	4.66	0.690
A7	*I frequently click links in email messages to see what they are, regardless of who sent the message.*	5	(1.0%)	^{r}4.51	0.922
A8	*It's important to run anti-virus software on my computer.*	7	(1.5%)	4.35	0.941
A9	*When browsing websites, I frequently mouseover links to see where they go, before clicking them.*	4	(0.8%)	4.13	0.977
A10	*When using public WiFi, I visit the same websites that I would visit when using the Internet at home.*	20	(4.2%)	^{r}2.93	1.266
A11	*I usually do not pay attention to where I'm downloading software from.*	2	(0.4%)	^{r}4.38	0.900
A12	*I frequently backup my computer.*	5	(1.0%)	3.07	1.165
A13	*I frequently visit websites even when my web browser warns me against it.*	8	(1.7%)	^{r}3.98	1.028
A14	*I circumvent my employer's computer usage policies when they prevent me from completing a task.*	86	(18.0%)	^{r}3.54	1.184
A15	*I am careful to never share confidential documents stored on my home or work computers.*	15	(3.1%)	4.36	0.757
A16	*Frequently checking the access control settings on social networking websites isn't worth the time it takes.*	18	(3.8%)	^{r}3.56	1.165
A17	*I always write down my passwords to help me remember them.*	6	(1.3%)	^{r}3.60	1.313
A18	*Creating strong passwords is not usually worth the effort.*	6	(1.3%)	^{r}4.05	1.047
A19	*I frequently check my financial accounts for fraudulent charges.*	10	(2.1%)	4.11	0.914
A20	*If I receive a suspicious email from a company that I do business with, I'll phone the company to make sure the email is accurate.*	22	(4.8%)	3.52	1.236
A21	*I never give out passwords over the phone.*	7	(1.5%)	4.53	0.787
A22	*I frequently purchase things that I see advertised in unsolicited emails.*	4	(8.8%)	^{r}4.51	0.840
A23	*I tend to ignore computer security stories in the news because they don't impact me.*	4	(8.8%)	^{r}3.83	1.050
A24	*I use encryption software to secure files or email messages.*	10	(2.1%)	2.74	1.225
A25	*Once I create a password, I tend to never change it.*	5	(1.0%)	^{r}3.30	1.182
A26	*I try to create a unique password for every account I have.*	5	(1.0%)	3.21	1.284
A27	*Rather than logging out of websites, I usually just navigate elsewhere or close the window when I'm done.*	7	(1.5%)	^{r}3.06	1.299
A28	*I always make sure that I'm at a secure website (e.g., SSL, "https://", a lock icon) when transmitting information online.*	4	(0.8%)	3.80	1.173
A29	*I frequently use privacy software, "private browsing" or "incognito" mode when I'm online.*	6	(1.3%)	3.17	1.247
A30	*I frequently let others use my computing devices (e.g., smartphone, tablet, laptop).*	3	(0.7%)	^{r}3.79	1.172

Table 1. Initial set of security questions evaluated on a 5-point Likert scale (from "strongly disagree" to "strongly agree") by 479 participants. Depicted are the questions, the rate of "N/A" responses, and the average responses and standard deviations after recoding negatively-phrased questions (^{r}).

propensity for respondents to agree with every question) [34], we reworded half the questions to be negatively phrased (i.e., agreement with the statement indicates *not* following common security advice). Thus, our initial question pool consisted of the 30 questions listed in Table 1.

Method and Demographics

In August of 2014, we performed an initial evaluation of our questions. We recruited participants from Amazon's Mechanical Turk, restricting the survey to participants based in the U.S. who had an approval rate of 95% or greater. We paid each participant $1.00 to complete our survey, which consisted of the 30 aforementioned statements evaluated on a Likert scale ("strongly disagree (1)," "disagree (2)," "neither agree nor disagree (3)," "agree (4)," and "strongly agree (5)"). We gave participants a "N/A" option and the ability to simply not answer questions so that we could determine whether any questions were not applicable to our audience.

We were concerned that social desirability bias may have an impact on participants' responses [10]. That is, some participants may misreport their behaviors in order to make it appear as though they engage in more socially acceptable behaviors (e.g., participants may be ashamed to admit engaging in ill-advised behaviors). We took two steps to mitigate this concern. First, we advertised the experiment as a "computer behavior survey," so as to not specifically mention security during recruitment (thereby minimizing a potential selection bias). Second, we asked all participants to complete the 10-item Strahan-Gerbasi version of the Marlowe-Crowne Social Desirability Scale [40], which we then correlated with participants' responses to the security behavior questions.

As with all surveys, we were concerned with being able to deter and detect careless responses. Based on Meade and Craig's recommendation [25], we included two separate "instructed response items" in our survey. On the first page of the survey after the consent form, we included the following:

> *This study requires you to voice your opinion using the scales below. It is important that you take the time to read all instructions and that you read questions carefully before you answer them. Previous research on preferences has found that some people do not take the time to read everything that is displayed in the questionnaire. The questions below serve to test whether you actually take the time to do so. Therefore, if you read this, please answer 'three' on the first question, add three to that number and use the result as the answer on the second question. Thank you for participating and taking the time to read all instructions.*
>
> *I would prefer to live in a large city rather than a small city.* [Strongly disagree (1), (2), (3), (4), (5), (6), Strongly agree (7)]
>
> *I would prefer to live in a city with many cultural opportunities, even if the cost of living was higher.* [Strongly disagree (1), (2), (3), (4), (5), (6), Strongly agree (7)]

If participants failed to select 3 and 6, respectively, they were given a second opportunity featuring bolded instructions. If they failed a second time, they were prevented from completing the survey. In addition to this attention check task, we included a second question hidden amongst the true/false Strahan-Gerbasi social desirability statements: *I do not read the questions in surveys.* We excluded participants who answered "true" for this question from our analysis.

We received a total of 503 responses, though removed 24 (4.8%) who did not answer the second attention check question correctly. Our resulting sample of 479 participants consisted of 273 males (57.0%) and ages ranged from 18 to 69 (μ = 33.2, σ = 10.5). Thirty-six percent of our participants (173 of 479) held bachelor's degrees, while an additional 12.9% had completed some graduate school, and median household income was between $35,000 and $50,000. We therefore consider our sample to be representative of the U.S. online population, albeit with a slight male skew.

Results

We observed that the internal reliability of our initial question set was quite high (Cronbach's $\alpha = 0.83$). We performed Pearson correlations between the Strahan-Gerbasi social desirability scale and each question, and only observed one to be statistically significant: A28 ($r = 0.160$, $p < 0.0005$). However, given the small effect size (i.e., 2.6% of variance is shared between this question and the social desirability scale), we chose to retain the question. This suggests that participants answered truthfully and consistently. At the same time, we discovered several issues with our items, which highlighted the need for question refinement: non-applicability, poor item-total correlation, and ceiling effects.

Non-Applicability

We measured how many participants skipped items or responded with a "N/A" option. Two questions stood out, *A5* and *A14*, which both had to do with workplace computer usage. Participants did not respond to these questions 13.4% and 18.0% of the time, respectively. In hindsight, possible confounds are obvious: for instance, not having a job involving computer use. Thus, we decided to remove the question about circumventing policies (*A14*) and reworded *A5* to focus on promptly fixing/reporting security problems in general.

Additionally, questions *A22* and *A23* were not answered by 8.8% of participants. The former concerned buying items advertised via unsolicited emails, which we decided is not a security concern *per se*. The latter had to do with ignoring computer security stories in the news, which we felt was ambiguous: it did not describe a specific behavior, and a negative response could indicate either not following the news or disagreeing with the impact of computer security stories. Instead, we reworded it to be about proactively changing passwords after publicized data breaches.

We also realized that file sharing (*A15*) and social networking (*A16*) might not be widely applicable. We removed *A17* because there is no longer a clear consensus that writing down passwords is a poor practice (especially if it leads to creating stronger passwords). Similarly, we removed *A30*, which concerned sharing devices with others, because research suggests that this behavior is quite nuanced [13], and therefore this question may have been ambiguous.

Poor Item-Total Correlation

Item-total correlation measures how well the responses to one item correlate with the other items in the scale (i.e., homogeneity). Questions are deemed to not represent the rest of the scale when their item-total correlations are below 0.2 [14]. This occurred in four questions: *A2* (0.117), *A3* (0.147), *A17* (0.113), and *A29* (0.196). We observed that these questions all used qualifiers (e.g., "I *frequently*..." or "I *always*..."). Given that the purpose of the scale was for participants to report how frequently they engaged in each activity, we realized that we needed to remove the qualifiers from each statement and change the response format so that, instead of measuring agreement with a certain behavior, our scale would measure the frequency of engaging in that behavior using the options of, "always," "often," "sometimes," "rarely," and "never."

Ceiling Effects

Because a scale is designed to quantify one respondent's response relative to others, it is important that individual questions exhibit adequate variance; if everyone responds in the same manner, the scale is of little utility. Ceiling and floor effects occur when questions fail to capture sufficient variance; responses lie at one end of the spectrum because the provided responses did not adequately capture the true range of opinions. We observed that this was the case with questions *A6*, *A7*, *A8*, *A11*, *A15*, *A21*, and *A22*. The average responses to these questions were close to the maximum (i.e., $4.0 < \mu < 5.0$), and had relatively low standard deviations (i.e., $\sigma < 1.0$). As a result, we explored alternate wordings.

Additional Testing

We evaluated the impact of wording changes on responses, both with regard to variance and applicability. These iterations involved 2,184 additional participants, who we recruited in the same manner as our initial sample. Additionally, we also screened out participants who had completed a previous iteration of the survey. We produced a refined set of 24 questions that exhibited adequate variance, were applicable to almost all participants, were free from ceiling effects, and showed high item-total correlations.

REFINING THE SCALE

We recruited an additional cohort of participants so that we could perform Exploratory Factor Analysis (EFA) on the resulting 24 items. We describe our methodology and results.

Methodology

We recruited 500 new participants to respond to a set of 24 security questions (Table 2). Additionally, we randomly assigned a fifth of our sample to complete the 16-item Privacy Concerns Scale [6]. We did this to assess the discriminant validity of our scale: whether it was measuring a new construct or something already captured by existing privacy scales (PCS correlates significantly with other established privacy scales, the Westin Index [22], and the IUIPC [23]). (We piloted established psychometric tests on the participants who did not receive PCS, which we describe later in this paper.)

#	Question	N/A		μ	σ
B1	*When I'm prompted about a software update, I install it right away.*	1	(0.2%)	3.23	0.993
B2	*When my computer wants me to reboot after applying an update or installing software, I put it off.*	0	(0.0%)	^{r}3.08	1.116
B3	*I try to make sure that the programs I use are up-to-date.*	1	(0.2%)	3.89	0.914
B4	*I manually lock my computer screen when I step away from it.*	5	(1.1%)	2.58	1.386
B5	*I set my computer screen to automatically lock if I don't use it for a prolonged period of time.*	3	(0.7%)	3.47	1.552
B6	*I log out of my computer, turn it off, put it to sleep, or lock the screen when I'm done using it.*	1	(0.2%)	3.87	1.283
B7	*I use a PIN or passcode to unlock my mobile phone.*	18	(3.9%)	3.27	1.798
B8	*I use a password/passcode to unlock my laptop or tablet.*	22	(4.8%)	3.99	1.525
B9	*If I discover a security problem, I continue what I was doing because I assume someone else will fix it.*	15	(3.3%)	^{r}3.98	0.972
B10	*When someone sends me a link, I open it without first verifying where it goes.*	0	(0.0%)	^{r}3.85	1.068
B11	*I verify that my anti-virus software has been regularly updating itself.*	9	(2.0%)	3.59	1.215
B12	*When browsing websites, I mouseover links to see where they go, before clicking them.*	0	(0.0%)	3.48	1.115
B13	*I know what website I'm visiting based on its look and feel, rather than by looking at the URL bar.*	3	(0.7%)	^{r}2.92	1.107
B14	*I backup my computer.*	2	(0.4%)	2.97	1.216
B15	*When I hear about websites that have been hacked, I wait to change my passwords until I have been personally notified.*	16	(3.5%)	^{r}3.41	1.232
B16	*I use some kind of encryption software to secure sensitive files or personal information.*	20	(4.4%)	2.56	1.401
B17	*I do not change my passwords, unless I have to.*	0	(0.0%)	^{r}2.40	1.103
B18	*I use different passwords for different accounts that I have.*	1	(0.2%)	3.59	1.084
B19	*I do not include special characters in my password if it's not required.*	2	(0.4%)	^{r}2.95	1.349
B20	*When I create a new online account, I try to use a password that goes beyond the site's minimum requirements.*	2	(0.4%)	3.37	1.193
B21	*When I'm done using a website that I'm logged into, I manually log out of it.*	0	(0.0%)	3.64	1.125
B22	*I submit information to websites without first verifying that it will be sent securely (e.g., SSL, "https://", a lock icon).*	1	(0.2%)	^{r}3.65	1.103
B23	*I use privacy software, "private browsing," or "incognito" mode when I'm browsing online.*	3	(0.7%)	2.55	1.119
B24	*I clear my web browsing history.*	0	(0.0%)	3.31	1.114

Table 2. Revised set of security questions evaluated on a 5-point Likert scale (from "never" to "always") by 456 participants. Depicted are the questions, the rate of "N/A" responses, and the average responses and standard deviations after recoding negatively-phrased questions (^{r}).

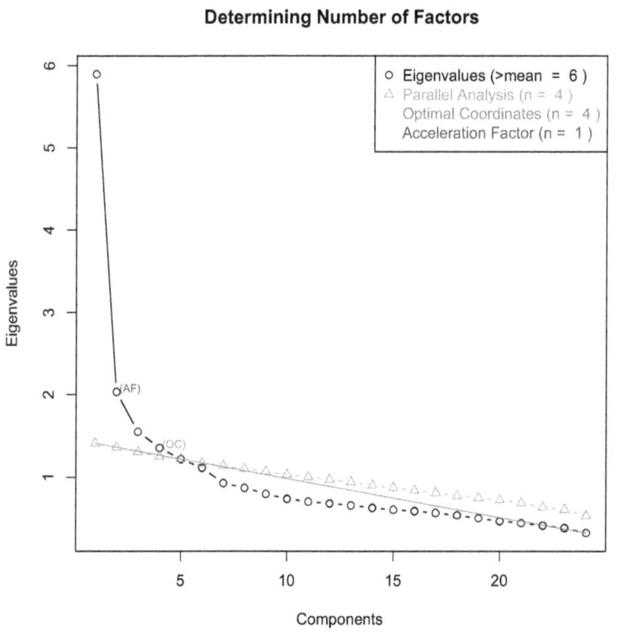

Figure 1. Scree plot showing eigenvalues from EFA, acceleration factor, optimal coordinates, and parallel analysis. We extracted 4 components.

Since we found that responses to the security questions did not correlate with social desirability, we removed the Strahan-Gerbasi scale, which also removed our second attention check (i.e., *I do not read the questions in surveys*). To compensate for this, we followed Meade and Craig's recommendation to screen out careless responses based on completion times [25]. Because reading speed is so varied and because there was no obvious threshold in our data, we removed participants whose completion times were in the top 10% (i.e., those finishing the survey in under $227s$), which left us with 456 valid responses.

Results

We examined individual questions in terms of means, standard deviations, and applicability. Table 2 shows that the ceiling effects in our initial experiments disappeared: all means were below 4.0 and standard deviations exceeded 0.9. Similarly, each question was applicable to over 95% of our participants. Thus, we proceeded to factor analysis and measured reliability. While we allowed participants to omit specific questions so that we could measure applicability, factor analysis and reliability metrics (e.g., Cronbach's alpha) require all scale items. As a result, we removed 80 participants who omitted responses to any questions, leaving us with a sample size of 376 for the remainder of our analysis. This sample size still exceeds the recommendation of Hair *et al.* to use a minimum of 5 participants per item [18].

Factor Analysis

Bartlett's test of sphericity ($\chi^2(276) = 2037.7, p < 0.0005$) and the Measure of Sampling Adequacy (0.869) showed that our data were correlated and measured common factors. We performed an exploratory Principal Component Analysis (PCA) and extracted six components based on the Kaiser criterion (i.e., retaining all components with eigenvalues > 1.0). Since the Kaiser criterion is considered to be overly inclusive [15], we also determined the optimal coordinates and performed parallel analysis (Figure 1). Determining optimal coordinates involves linear regression to fit a line to the smallest eigenvalues and then determining the point at which an eigenvalue diverges [33]. As can be seen in Figure 1, this test indicated that we should retain four components.

	Passwords	Securement	Awareness	Updating	
α	0.764	0.728	0.668	0.719	
IIC	0.449	0.407	0.288	0.469	ITC
B18	.742				0.512
B20	.742				0.629
B19	.735				0.580
B17	.692				0.543
B5		.760			0.526
B8		.724			0.513
B7		.720			0.502
B4		.714			0.547
B22			.727		0.496
B10			.697		0.488
B9			.628		0.402
B13			.552		0.326
B12			.540		0.403
B1				.797	0.474
B3				.773	0.589
B11				.726	0.580

Table 3. Factor loadings (PCA with Varimax rotation; loadings < 0.25 removed) from EFA. The first two rows depict reliability measures: Cronbach's α and average inter-item correlation. The last column depicts each item-total correlations.

Parallel analysis involves extracting eigenvalues from random data [19]. Any retained eigenvalues should be greater than those extracted due entirely to random sampling error. Thus, the eigenvalues generated by parallel analysis are compared to those generated by EFA, and when the ith eigenvalue of the former is greater than the ith eigenvalue of the latter, it is concluded that there are $i - 1$ underlying components. This corroborated our decision to extract four components.

We applied a Varimax rotation and considered an item to be loaded on a factor if its loading exceeded 0.5. We also applied Saucier's criterion of only considering an item to be loaded on a component if its loading on that component was more than twice as high as its loading on other components [36]. Based on these requirements, we removed the following seven items: *B6*, *B14*, *B15*, *B16*, *B21*, *B23*, and *B24*. Finally, we observed that removing *B2* increased Cronbach's alpha of its associated sub-scale from 0.707 to 0.719. Thus, we retained the remaining 16 items and reran PCA. The rotated factor loadings are depicted in Table 3.

The four components that we extracted predicted over 55.6% of variance. Based on each component's items, four distinct themes emerged: password generation (e.g., creating strong passwords, changing passwords), device securement (e.g., using a PIN on a smartphone, locking a desktop screen when stepping away), proactive awareness (e.g., checking links before clicking them), and updating (e.g., applying software updates in a timely manner). Each of these components accounted for 26.7%, 11.6%, 9.0%, and 8.3% of variance, respectively. Our scale thus consists of four sub-scales.

Reliability

We examined scale reliability in three parts. First we computed Cronbach's alpha for the full scale ($\alpha = 0.801$) and its sub-scales (see Table 3). We observed that our data complied with the metric used by McKinley *et al.* [24]: a multi-component scale is reliable if $\alpha > 0.6$ for all sub-scales and $\alpha > 0.7$ for a majority of sub-scales.

Next, we calculated the item-total correlation of each item, which is the Pearson correlation between the item and the average of all other items in its sub-scale. Everitt recommends a threshold of 0.2 [14], which our items all exceeded. Finally, we calculated the average inter-item correlation; Robinson *et al.* classify average inter-item correlations between 0.20 and 0.29 as "extensive" and above 0.30 as "exemplary" [35]. The lowest average inter-item correlation was found in the "awareness" component, though it was still 0.288 (i.e., "extensive"), whereas the reliability of the other three components was consistently above 0.4. Thus, by all three measures, we concluded that our sub-scales each had high reliability.

Discriminant Validity: Correlation with Privacy Concerns

We randomly selected one fifth of our participants[1] to complete an additional question set: the 16-item Privacy Concern Scale developed by Buchanan *et al.* [6]. The reason for using this scale in particular was that it is unidimensional and has high internal reliability; across the 68 participants (18% of 376) who completed it, $\alpha = 0.935$. We performed Pearson correlations between participants' average privacy concern score, and the average scores for each of our new scale's four sub-scales: *passwords* ($r = 0.151$, $p < 0.219$), *securement* ($r = 0.153$, $p < 0.213$), *awareness* ($r = 0.251$, $p < 0.039$),[2] and *updating* ($r = 0.164$, $p < 0.183$). The lack of significant correlations suggests that security behaviors are orthogonal to privacy concerns, and therefore our new scale is measuring something different.

FINALIZING THE SCALE

Based on the previous EFA, we created a final survey instrument that included only the 16 final questions (Table 4), in random order, with the N/A option removed (i.e., all questions were now required). We included additional questions from several well-studied psychometric tests in an attempt to correlate the self-reported security behaviors measured by our instrument with existing psychometrics. In this section we describe the Confirmatory Factor Analysis (CFA) that we performed and how it showed reasonable goodness of fit between our questions and the hypothesized latent factors. We show how the scale also has good reliability and how its underlying constructs relate to well-established psychometrics.

Factor Analysis

We recruited an additional cohort of 500 participants from Mechanical Turk to participate in a final experiment. We followed the recommendation of Peer *et al.* [32], who showed that restricting tasks to workers who have completed over 500 previous tasks and at least 95% approval rates negates the need for attention check questions. In addition to these two requirements, we restricted participation to those 18 or over in the U.S. who had not been exposed to one of our previous question sets. We included the initial instructed response question, but did not do any post hoc screening.

[1] As we noted earlier, the remaining participants completed other psychometrics, which we piloted prior to our CFA experiment, discussed in the next section.

[2] Upon applying the Bonferroni correction to account for multiple testing, we do not consider this to be statistically significant.

#	*Device Securement* (28.47% of variance explained; $\lambda = 4.555$)	μ	σ
F4	I set my computer screen to automatically lock if I don't use it for a prolonged period of time.	3.20	1.559
F6	I use a password/passcode to unlock my laptop or tablet.	3.78	1.525
F3	I manually lock my computer screen when I step away from it.	2.63	1.343
F5	I use a PIN or passcode to unlock my mobile phone.	3.21	1.733
#	*Password Generation* (12.95% of variance explained; $\lambda = 2.071$)	μ	σ
F12	I do not change my passwords, unless I have to.^{r}	2.65	1.091
F13	I use different passwords for different accounts that I have.	3.75	1.037
F15	When I create a new online account, I try to use a password that goes beyond the site's minimum requirements.	3.31	1.096
F14	I do not include special characters in my password if it's not required.^{r}	3.30	1.292
#	*Proactive Awareness* (8.36% of variance explained; $\lambda = 1.337$)	μ	σ
F8	When someone sends me a link, I open it without first verifying where it goes.^{r}	4.01	1.014
F11	I know what website I'm visiting based on its look and feel, rather than by looking at the URL bar.^{r}	3.17	1.077
F16	I submit information to websites without first verifying that it will be sent securely (e.g., SSL, "https://", a lock icon).^{r}	3.69	1.102
F10	When browsing websites, I mouseover links to see where they go, before clicking them.	3.69	1.027
F7	If I discover a security problem, I continue what I was doing because I assume someone else will fix it.^{r}	4.08	0.976
#	*Updating* (6.77% of variance explained; $\lambda = 1.082$)	μ	σ
F1	When I'm prompted about a software update, I install it right away.	3.07	1.035
F2	I try to make sure that the programs I use are up-to-date.	3.78	0.890
F9	I verify that my anti-virus software has been regularly updating itself.	3.55	1.228

Table 4. The final questions for the Security Behavior Intentions Scale and associated sub-scales. The means of reverse-scored questions (denoted by ^{r}) have been recoded. The final question numbers have been enumerated from F1-F16 in order to differentiate them from prior exploratory questions. Responses were reported on the following scale: *Never (1)*, *Rarely (2)*, *Sometimes (3)*, *Often (4)*, **and** *Always (5)*.

Participants' genders were split fairly evenly: 46.8% were female, 52.8% were male, and two declined to specify. Participants' ages ranged from 19 to 71 ($\mu = 34.3$, $\sigma = 10.78$), median income was between $35,000 and $50,000, and 37.8% of participants held bachelor's degrees (an additional 14% had completed some or more graduate school). We therefore believe our sample is comparable to our previous samples and is also representative of the U.S. online population.

We performed PCA using a Varimax rotation, extracted four components, and observed that all items were loaded on the same unique component that they were in the previous experiment. These four components predicted 56.6% of variance, and are shown in Table 4 along with the mean responses.

Next, we performed CFA by examining the goodness-of-fit of our data to the latent variable model. Multiple metrics showed that our data adhered to the model. We did not rely on the chi-square goodness-of-fit test, because of our large sample size [44]. Instead, we examined the relative chi-square [28], the Root Mean Square Error of Approximation (RMSEA), the Standardized Root Mean Square Residual (SRMR), the Comparative Fit Index (CFI), and the Tucker-Lewis Index (TLI).

Our relative chi-square statistic, χ^2/df, was approximately 2.71. While there is no firm consensus on the exact cutoff value to indicate a "good" fit, our statistic is below 3, which is the more stringent requirement recommended by Hair *et al.* [18]. Our analysis yielded a RMSEA of 0.058 and a SRMR of 0.050, which are both below recommended cutoff points; Hu and Bentler recommend a cutoff of 0.06 for RMSEA and 0.08 for SRMR [20]. Finally, our CFI and TLI were 0.920 and 0.902, respectively, which are above the 0.90 cutoff recommended by Netemeyer *et al.* [29].

Reliability

We calculated the composite reliability of the four sub-scales (Table 5) [17]. Since these values are all above the threshold of 0.6 recommended by Bagozzi and Yi [3]. Additionally,

	Securement	Passwords	Awareness	Updating
CR	0.78	0.78	0.64	0.69
ICC	0.89	0.86	0.81	0.81

Table 5. Each sub-scale's composite reliability (CR) and average measures intraclass correlation coefficient (ICC) during test-retest.

we conducted a test-retest procedure to make sure responses were stable over time. Eleven days after our 500 participants had completed our survey, we invited them to participate in a followup survey for an additional $1 payment. Of the 500 invited, 354 participated. We calculated the average measures intraclass correlation coefficient between their sub-scale average scores (Table 5), and found that all of them were above the 0.6 threshold recommended by Weir [45].

Relation to Psychological Constructs

We explored whether certain psychological constructs may be correlated with an individual's security behaviors. Thus, participants completed several additional scales:

- **Domain-Specific Risk-Taking Scale (DoSpeRT)** [4], which measures propensity for risk-taking across five dimensions: ethical (1), financial (2), health/safety (3), recreational (4), and social (5).
- **General Decision-Making Style (GDMS)** [37], which measures how people approach decision-making with regard to five dimensions: rational (1), avoidant (2), dependent (3), intuitive (4), and spontaneous (5).
- **Need for Cognition (NFC)** [7], which is a unidimensional scale that measures the propensity to engage in "cognitive endeavors."
- **Barratt Impulsiveness Scale (BIS)** [31], which measures impulsivity across three dimensions: attention (1), motor (2), and non-planning (3).
- **Consideration for Future Consequences (CFC)** [21], which is a unidimensional scale measuring how much attention people pay to long-term consequences.

	Securement	Passwords	Awareness	Updating
$DoSpeRT_1$		**-.201	**-.226	**-.201
$DoSpeRT_2$				
$DoSpeRT_3$			**-.204	**-.164
$DoSpeRT_4$				
$DoSpeRT_5$		*.141		
$GDMS_1$		**.145	**.224	**.229
$GDMS_2$	*-.133	**-.220	**-.230	**-.247
$GDMS_3$			**-.157	
$GDMS_4$				
$GDMS_5$				*-.129
NFC	**.164	**.290	**.231	**.253
BIS_1		**-.243	*-.140	**-.218
BIS_2			**-.147	**-.145
BIS_3		**-.235	**-.171	**-.247
CFC	**.184	**.317	**.307	**.303

Table 6. Correlations between sub-scales and various psychometrics. $^*p < 0.005$, $^{**}p < 0.001$.

Because this work is exploratory, we performed Pearson correlations rather than building a regression model (Table 6). To counteract effects from repeated testing, we only report correlations significant at the $p < 0.005$ level. Across all four sub-scales, participants who were more inquisitive (as determined by the NFC scale) were more likely to report engaging in better security practices. We also noted that the highest correlation across all four sub-scales was with consideration for future consequences (CFC), suggesting that good security behaviors are tied to long-term thinking.

Our initial hypothesis was that willingness to take risks involving health or safety would be inversely correlated with computer security behaviors; we observed this was true, but only for behaviors involving proactive awareness and keeping software updated. Similarly, across all four sub-scales, people who engaged in "better" security behaviors were less likely to procrastinate (as determined by the GDMS avoidant sub-scale). People scoring low on GDMS dependence scored high on SeBIS awareness; being proactive about computer security means *not* relying on other people. Many of the security behaviors also correlated inversely with impulsivity: this suggests that adhering to security advice involves foresight.

DISCUSSION

The final Security Behavior Intentions Scale (SeBIS) consists of 16 items, which map uniquely onto four factors: device securement (locking devices using passwords, PINs, etc.), password generation (creating and using passwords), proactive awareness (noticing and taking into account environmental security cues), and updating (ensuring software is up-to-date). The scale showed high psychometric properties: all subscales were internally consistent, all items loaded highly on their respective component and did not load highly on other components, correlations between sub-scales were low, two administrations of the same test to the same sample showed high correlations, and some of the sub-scales were correlated with some other, well-established, psychological constructs.

Both researchers and practitioners can use this new scale for various ends. Researchers may use it to measure intended security behaviors and examine how these change between different populations, over time, or following educational interventions. They may also use the scale to determine users' involvement in security-related situations, which could mediate how users may respond to different security mitigations. For example, researchers who are interested in compliance with security warnings may use the scale to explore whether some types of warnings are more effective for one type of user or another. The scale may also be used to explore its predictive ability of real world behaviors (e.g., falling for phishing attacks) and estimate the effectiveness of various interventions (e.g., security education) by measuring changes in the scale following the interventions, and over time.

Practitioners may use this scale in various organizational settings. First, they may use it to estimate the security behaviors among their employees and to identify prevalent weaknesses which could then be remedied using targeted interventions. This may help reduce the cost, and increase the effectiveness, of organizational training aimed at improving end-user security behavior. Second, they may use the scale to examine the common behaviors among their employees in order to try to match the organization's security policy with employees' natural behavior. For example, if an organization realizes that many of its employees do not lock their computers when stepping away, the organization may instigate a policy of forcing all computers to be locked after a short period of idle time. Lastly, managers may use the scale to identify "extreme" individuals (both on the high and low ends of the scale) and take targeted actions toward these individuals (e.g., reward the highly secure ones and educate the lowly secure ones).

Another potential implication of this scale could be for public policy. As described in the beginning, current computer security recommendations targeted at end-users are highly scattered, inconclusive and inconsistent. This could be very confusing to end-users who are not highly educated on this topic. Instead, a different type of policy, or set of policies, could be formed if policy makers knew the current prevalent attitudes and behaviors of the general public. The scale we developed can help assess these attitudes and behaviors on a large scale, and inform policy makers on the specific domains and situations that pose a potentially higher risk due to users' lower adherence to security standards.

Future Work

While we established the reliability and content validity of SeBIS in this paper, there is still much work to be done. We showed that it correlates with several well-studied psychometrics. However, it is unclear how they interact with each other and how they could be used to predict security behaviors. In future work, we expect to perform studies to examine other psychometrics and build a predictive model. One of our ultimate goals is to be able to use existing psychometrics to infer a user's computer security attitudes and behaviors so that adequate mitigations can be tailored to their needs and abilities based on observations of other behaviors.

Some may be concerned that SeBIS targets both personal and business contexts at the same time. While the final scale contains questions that are likely to be *impacted* by workplace policies (e.g., screen locking, software updates), we believe this is a minor concern: like the vast majority of psychometric tests, responses are self-reported, and self-reports are impacted by exogenous factors (i.e., not just personal factors). We do not presume to explain *why* people report behaving the way they do, just how secure they report behaving. In fact, if our measure is impacted by policies, it actually makes it more relevant for organizational experiments: it can show how a change in workplace policy affected (or failed to affect) employee behaviors. Still, we agree that this issue does need to be addressed empirically, which is why studies are needed to compare SeBIS results between corporate and home users.

Similarly, while SeBIS is reliable and stable over time, it is not clear how well it correlates with actual security behaviors, since it only measures intentions. We plan to perform experiments to examine how each of its component sub-scales correlate with behaviors, as well as how other psychometrics could be used to predict computer security behaviors. Given its demonstrated reliability and discriminant validity, our results show that SeBIS is still a useful tool for measuring *intentions* and how they might change over time or vary between individuals. However, if construct validity is also strong, then in many cases SeBIS may be a reasonable substitute for performing costly and time-consuming laboratory experiments.

ACKNOWLEDGMENTS

This work was supported by NSF under award CNS-1343433. We would also like to thank Alessandro Acquisti, Chris Hoofnagle, Diogo Marques, David Wagner, members of the Berkeley Laboratory for Usable and Experimental Security (BLUES), and Refjohürs Lykkewe.

REFERENCES

1. Acquisti, A., and Grossklags, J. Losses, gains, and hyperbolic discounting: An experimental approach to information security attitudes and behavior. In *Proceedings of The 2nd Annual Workshop on Economics and Information Security (WEIS '03)* (2003).
2. Acquisti, A., and Grossklags, J. Privacy and rationality in individual decision making. *IEEE Security & Privacy* (January/February 2005), 24–30.
3. Bagozzi, R. P., and Yi, Y. On the evaluation of structural equation models. *Journal of the academy of marketing science 16*, 1 (1988), 74–94.
4. Blais, A.-R., and Weber, E. U. A domain-specific risk-taking (dospert) scale for adult populations. *Judgment and Decision Making 1*, 1 (2006), 33–47.
5. Bossler, A. M., and Holt, T. J. The effect of self-control on victimization in the cyberworld. *Journal of Criminal Justice 38*, 3 (2010), 227–236.
6. Buchanan, T., Paine, C., Joinson, A. N., and Reips, U.-D. Development of measures of online privacy concern and protection for use on the internet. *Journal of the American Society for Information Science and Technology 58*, 2 (2007), 157–165.
7. Cacioppo, J. T., Petty, R. E., and Feng Kao, C. The efficient assessment of need for cognition. *Journal of personality assessment 48*, 3 (1984), 306–307.
8. Copes, H., Kerley, K. R., Huff, R., and Kane, J. Differentiating identity theft: An exploratory study of victims using a national victimization survey. *Journal of Criminal Justice 38*, 5 (2010), 1045–1052.
9. Cranor, L. F. A framework for reasoning about the human in the loop. In *Proceedings of the 1st Conference on Usability, Psychology, and Security*, USENIX Association (Berkeley, CA, 2008).
10. Crowne, D. P., and Marlowe, D. A new scale of social desirability independent of psychopathology. *Journal of consulting psychology 24*, 4 (1960), 349.
11. DeVellis, R. F. *Scale Development: Theory and Applications*, 2nd ed., vol. 26 of *Applied Social Research Methods Series*. Sage Publications, 2003.
12. Egelman, S., Cranor, L. F., and Hong, J. You've been warned: An empirical study of the effectiveness of web browser phishing warnings. In *Proceeding of The 26th SIGCHI Conference on Human Factors in Computing Systems*, CHI '08, ACM (New York, NY, USA, 2008), 1065–1074.
13. Egelman, S., Jain, S., Portnoff, R. S., Liao, K., Consolvo, S., and Wagner, D. Are you ready to lock? understanding user motivations for smartphone locking behaviors. In *Proceedings of the 2014 ACM SIGSAC Conference on Computer & Communications Security*, CCS '14, ACM (New York, NY, USA, 2014).
14. Everitt, B. S. *The Cambridge Dictionary of Statistics*. Cambridge University Press, Cambridge, UK, 2002.
15. Fabrigar, L. R., Wegener, D. T., MacCallum, R. C., and Strahan, E. J. Evaluating the use of exploratory factor analysis in psychological research. *Psychological methods 4*, 3 (1999), 272.
16. Felt, A. P., Ha, E., Egelman, S., Haney, A., Chin, E., and Wagner, D. Android permissions: user attention, comprehension, and behavior. In *Proceedings of the Eighth Symposium on Usable Privacy and Security*, SOUPS '12, ACM (New York, NY, USA, 2012).
17. Fornell, C., and Larcker, D. F. Evaluating structural equation models with unobservable variables and measurement error. *Journal of Marketing Research 18*, 1 (1981), pp. 39–50.
18. Hair, J. F., Tatham, R. L., Anderson, R. E., and Black, W. *Multivariate Data Analysis*, 6 ed. Prentice Hall, 2006.
19. Horn, J. L. A rationale and test for the number of factors in factor analysis. *Psychometrika 30*, 2 (1965), 179–185.
20. Hu, L.-t., and Bentler, P. M. Cutoff criteria for fit indexes in covariance structure analysis: Conventional criteria versus new alternatives. *Structural Equation Modeling: A Multidisciplinary Journal 6*, 1 (1999), 1–55.
21. Joireman, J., Shaffer, M. J., Balliet, D., and Strathman, A. Promotion orientation explains why future-oriented people exercise and eat healthy evidence from the two-factor consideration of future consequences-14

scale. *Personality and Social Psychology Bulletin 38*, 10 (2012), 1272–1287.

22. Kumaraguru, P., and Cranor, L. F. Privacy Indexes: A Survey of Westin's Studies. Tech. Rep. CMU-ISRI-5-138, Carnegie Mellon University, December, 2005. `http://reports-archive.adm.cs.cmu.edu/anon/isri2005/abstracts/05-138.html`.
23. Malhotra, N. K., Kim, S. S., and Agarwal, J. Internet users' information privacy concerns (iuipc): The construct, the scale, and a causal model. *Information Systems Research 15*, 4 (December 2004), 336–355.
24. McKinley, R. K., Manku-Scott, T., Hastings, A. M., French, D. P., and Baker, R. Reliability and validity of a new measure of patient satisfaction with out of hours primary medical care in the united kingdom: development of a patient questionnaire. *British Medical Journal 314*, 7075 (1997), 193.
25. Meade, A. W., and Craig, S. B. Identifying careless responses in survey data. *Psychological methods 17*, 3 (2012), 437.
26. Modic, D., and Lea, S. E. G. How neurotic are scam victims, really? the big five and internet scams. `http://ssrn.com/abstract=2448130`, September 2012.
27. Moon, B., McCluskey, J. D., and McCluskey, C. P. A general theory of crime and computer crime: An empirical test. *Journal of Criminal Justice 38*, 4 (2010), 767–772.
28. Mueller, R. O. *Basic principles of structural equation modeling: An introduction to LISREL and EQS*. Springer, 1996.
29. Netemeyer, R. G., Bearden, W. O., and Sharma, S. *Scaling Procedures: Issues and Applications*. SAGE Publications, 2003.
30. Ng, B.-Y., Kankanhalli, A., and Xu, Y. C. Studying users' computer security behavior: A health belief perspective. *Dec. Sup. Systems 46*, 4 (2009), 815–825.
31. Patton, J. H., Stanford, M. S., et al. Factor structure of the barratt impulsiveness scale. *Journal of clinical psychology 51*, 6 (1995), 768–774.
32. Peer, E., Vosgerau, J., and Acquisti, A. Reputation as a sufficient condition for data quality on amazon mechanical turk. *Behavior Research Methods 45*, 4 (December 2013).
33. Raîche, G., Walls, T. A., Magis, D., Riopel, M., and Blais, J.-G. Non-graphical solutions for cattell's scree test. *Methodology: European Journal of Research Methods for the Behavioral and Social Sciences 9*, 1 (2013), 23.
34. Ray, J. J. Reviving the problem of acquiescent response bias. *The J. of Social Psychology 121*, 1 (1983), 81–96.
35. Robinson, J. P., Shaver, P. R., and Wrightsman, L. S. Criteria for scale selection and evaluation. In *Measures of personality and social psychological attitudes*. Academic Press, 1991, ch. 1, 1–16.
36. Saucier, G. Mini-markers: A brief version of goldberg's unipolar big-five markers. *Journal of Personality Assessment 63*, 3 (1994), 506–516.
37. Scott, S. G., and Bruce, R. A. Decision-making style: The development and assessment of a new measure. *Educational and psychological measurement 55*, 5 (1995), 818–831.
38. Sherizen, S. Criminological concepts and research findings relevant for improving computer crime control. *Computers & Security 9*, 3 (1990), 215–222.
39. Stanton, J. M., Stam, K. R., Mastrangelo, P., and Jolton, J. Analysis of end user security behaviors. *Computers & Security 24*, 2 (2005), 124–133.
40. Strahan, R., and Gerbasi, K. C. Short, homogeneous versions of the marlowe-crowne social desirability scale. *Journal of clinical psychology* (1972).
41. United States Computer Emergency Readiness Team. Tips. `https://www.us-cert.gov/ncas/tips`. Accessed: September 12, 2014.
42. United States Department of Homeland Security. National Cyber Security Awareness Month 2014. `http://www.dhs.gov/national-cyber-security-awareness-month-2014`, September 8 2014. Accessed: September 12, 2014.
43. Verizon. Security. `http://www.verizon.com/Support/Residential/Internet/FiosInternet/General+Support/Security/Security.htm`, 2014. Accessed: September 12, 2014.
44. Wang, L., Fan, X., and Willson, V. L. Effects of nonnormal data on parameter estimates and fit indices for a model with latent and manifest variables: An empirical study. *Structural Equation Modeling: A Multidisciplinary Journal 3*, 3 (1996), 228–247.
45. Weir, J. P. Quantifying test-retest reliability using the intraclass correlation coefficient and the sem. *The Journal of Strength & Conditioning Research 19*, 1 (2005), 231–240.
46. Wilson, M., and Hash, J. Building an Information Technology Security Awareness and Training Program. Special Publication 800-50, National Institute of Standards and Technology, Gaithersburg, MD, US, October 2003. `http://csrc.nist.gov/publications/nistpubs/800-50/NIST-SP800-50.pdf`.
47. Wogalter, M. S. Communication-Human Information Processing (C-HIP) Model. In *Handbook of Warnings*, M. S. Wogalter, Ed. Lawrence Erlbaum Associates, 2006, 51–61.
48. Woodruff, A., Pihur, V., Consolvo, S., Brandimarte, L., and Acquisti, A. Would a privacy fundamentalist sell their dna for $1000...if nothing bad happened as a result? the westin categories, behavioral intentions, and consequences. In *Proceedings of the 2014 Symposium on Usable Privacy and Security*, USENIX Association (2014), 1–18.

How Polymorphic Warnings Reduce Habituation in the Brain—Insights from an fMRI Study

Bonnie Brinton Anderson,* C. Brock Kirwan,* Jeffrey L. Jenkins,* David Eargle,† Seth Howard,‡ Anthony Vance*

*Brigham Young University
{bonnie_anderson, jeffrey_jenkins, kirwan, anthony.vance}@byu.edu

†University of Pittsburgh
dave@daveeargle.com

‡Google Inc.
sethhoward@google.com

ABSTRACT
Research on security warnings consistently points to habituation as a key reason why users ignore security warnings. However, because habituation as a mental state is difficult to observe, previous research has examined habituation indirectly by observing its influence on security behaviors. This study addresses this gap by using functional magnetic resonance imaging (fMRI) to open the "black box" of the brain to observe habituation as it develops in response to security warnings. Our results show a dramatic drop in the visual processing centers of the brain after only the second exposure to a warning, with further decreases with subsequent exposures. To combat the problem of habituation, we designed a polymorphic warning that changes its appearance. We show in two separate experiments using fMRI and mouse cursor tracking that our polymorphic warning is substantially more resistant to habituation than conventional warnings. Together, our neurophysiological findings illustrate the considerable influence of human biology on users' habituation to security warnings.

Author Keywords
Security warnings; habituation; functional magnetic resonance imaging (fMRI); mouse cursor tracking.

ACM Classification Keywords
H.5.2. Information interfaces and presentation: User Interfaces; J.4. Social and Behavioral Sciences.

INTRODUCTION
Warning messages are one of the last lines of defense in computer security and are fundamental to users' security interactions with technology. Consequently, researchers have actively sought to understand how users interact with security warnings and why warnings are so pervasively ignored [3]. A key contributor to the disregard of security warnings is *habituation*—i.e., the diminishing of attention because of frequent exposure to warnings [16]. Although habituation has been inferred as a factor in many security-warning studies [e.g., 23], little research has examined habituation in the context of security directly because habituation as a mental state is difficult to observe using conventional methods. Therefore, there is a gap in our understanding regarding how habituation to security warnings occurs in the brain, limiting researchers' efforts to design warnings that can mitigate its effects.

This study addresses this gap by using functional magnetic resonance imaging (fMRI) to open the "black box" of the brain to observe habituation to security warnings. Specifically, we point to the *repetition suppression* (RS) effect, the reduction of neural responses to stimuli that are repeatedly viewed, as the neurological manifestation of habituation. By investigating how RS occurs in the brain, we can take a more precise approach to the design of security warnings that are resistant to the effects of habituation. Accordingly, the research objectives of this paper are: to (1) investigate how and where in the brain habituation develops in response to security warnings and (2) design a security warning that is substantially more resistant to habituation than the status quo.

We investigate these research objectives in two experiments. In Study 1, we designed a polymorphic warning that demonstrated substantially more resistance to habituation as compared to conventional warnings in the relevant brain regions. In Study 2, we use mouse tracking as a surrogate for attention to cross-validate that the polymorphic warning is more resistant to habituation in a more ecologically valid scenario.

BACKGROUND INFORMATION
Research frequently points to the role of habituation in the failure of warnings [e.g., 22]. For example, users click through 50% of SSL warnings in 1.7 seconds, a finding that "is consistent with the theory of warning fatigue" [1]. In another study, habituation was proposed to explain why only 14% of participants recognize changes in the content of confirmation dialogs [4]. These studies and others, however, do not directly measure habituation as a mental

CHI 2015, Apr 18-23, 2015, Seoul, Republic of Korea
ACM 978-1-4503-3145-6/15/04.
http://dx.doi.org/10.1145/2702123.2702322

state; rather, they indirectly measure habituation by observing users' responses to warnings. Therefore, measuring the occurrence of habituation in the brain through neuroscience instruments (e.g., fMRI) presents an opportunity to quantify the antecedents, onset, and impacts of habituation on security-warning behavior.

Neuroscience allows researchers to open the "black box" of cognition by directly observing the brain. Using neuroscience methodologies holds promise for "providing a richer account of user cognition than that which is obtained from any other source, including the user himself" [20]. We define *neurosecurity* as applying neuroscience to behavioral information security to better understand and improve users' security behaviors. One ultimate goal of neurosecurity is to design more effective user interfaces (UIs) that can help users make informed decisions [25].

fMRI is a method of choice in neuroscience because of its superior ability to identify areas of the brain that are activated during decision making. fMRI measures neural activity by tracking changes in the level of blood oxygenation, which are driven by changes in the metabolic demands of active neural populations. This phenomenon is known as the *blood oxygen level dependent* (or BOLD) effect. By measuring changes in blood flow to different brain regions, researchers can identify distinct brain regions where activity is correlated with specific cognitive processes. Thus, fMRI is well suited to investigate how habituation to security warnings occurs in the brain.

Repetition Suppression: A Neuroscience View of Habituation

The neural underpinnings of habituation have been well studied in the context of simple behavior in model organisms. For example, a series of now-classic studies using sea slugs demonstrated that neural responses to a given stimulus decrease with repeated exposures to that stimulus [17]. This kind of RS to repeated stimuli has also been observed in humans across a variety of brain regions and experimental situations [for review, see 13].

The exact cause and purpose of RS may vary according to brain region. In the visual processing system, RS appears to be related to repetition priming and may reflect the facilitation of stimulus processing with repeated exposures [9]. This type of response is highly influenced by the similarity of the repeated stimuli, where a more robust RS is associated with more similar stimuli [18].

Moreover, research has found that neural measures can be more sensitive than behavioral measures to RS effects [21]. Therefore, the RS effect is an effective way to assess the underlying neural computational processes of behavior. In this study, we utilized the differential RS effect in various brain regions to map the sensitivity of those regions to stimulus repetition of security warnings.

Our objective is to design a security warning implementation that is substantially more resistant to habituation than the status quo. Several approaches have been suggested to increase attention to security warnings and thus reduce habituation. For example, following design guidelines found in the warning literature, researchers have designed and tested a variety of warning attractors [e.g., 2]. These studies demonstrated that habituation can be reduced through UI design.

Wogalter states, "habituation can occur even with well-designed warnings, but better designed warnings with salient features can slow the habituation process. Where feasible, changing the warning's appearance may be useful in reinvigorating attention switch previously lost because of habituation" [27]. In line with this reasoning, polymorphic warnings—i.e., warnings that change their appearance to reduce habituation—have been suggested as a way to reduce habituation. For example, [5] found that study participants who received software warning dialogs with randomized options opened risky e-mail attachments significantly less than those who received conventional warnings.

Despite this finding, it is not clear whether polymorphic warnings actually mitigate habituation, as past studies have not measured habituation directly. Furthermore, research has only tested polymorphic warnings that randomize options in dialog boxes, acknowledging that "the design space for polymorphic dialogs is vast" [5]. It is therefore unknown which types of polymorphic warnings are most effective at reducing the effects of habituation. Thus, our research objectives are to (1) use fMRI to determine whether a polymorphic warning design is able to reduce RS in the brain in response to repeated exposure to security warnings and (2) identify the polymorphic variations that are most effective in reducing the RS effect.

Hypothesis

Polymorphic warnings garner more attention over time due to the novelty of their changing appearance. Changing appearance of the warning reinvigorates attention [27], especially in brain regions that have been shown to demonstrate RS to exact repetitions of visual stimuli [e.g., ventral visual processing stream; 26]. For this reason, polymorphic warnings that continually change their appearance will slow the rate of habituation. Accordingly, we hypothesize

For polymorphic warnings, brain regions associated with visual processing, such as the occipital lobe, will have a higher BOLD response upon successive viewings as compared with static warnings.

STUDY 1: FMRI

We conducted an fMRI laboratory experiment to test our hypothesis following the guidelines of Dimoka [10]. fMRI was selected because of its high spatial resolution, which makes it an ideal choice for determining brain regions involved in specific cognitive functions. fMRI uses the same equipment as clinical MRIs and is equally noninvasive; it also measures activity in the whole brain in a grid comprised of three-dimensional pixels (or *voxels*) that are 3 mm to a side, approximately every 2 seconds.

In order to test our hypothesis, we first developed a polymorphic warning implementation. To do so, we relied on the warning science literature [e.g., 27] to develop 12 graphical variations to a warning dialog expected to capture attention. Our polymorphic warning artifact rotated through the graphical variations on each subsequent exposure. The variations are displayed in Figure 3.

fMRI Procedures

Participants were given a verbal briefing about the MRI procedures and the task. Participants laid down on their backs on the fMRI table and had a volume coil placed over their heads to allow imaging of the entire brain (see Figure 1). They were then moved via the fMRI table into the MRI scanner. Participants viewed the experimental images on a large monitor at the opening of the MRI scanner by use of a mirror placed over their face. The monitor was configured to display images in reverse so that they appeared normal when viewed through the mirror. The technical details of the fMRI scans, experimental procedures, and data analyses are documented in the appendix.

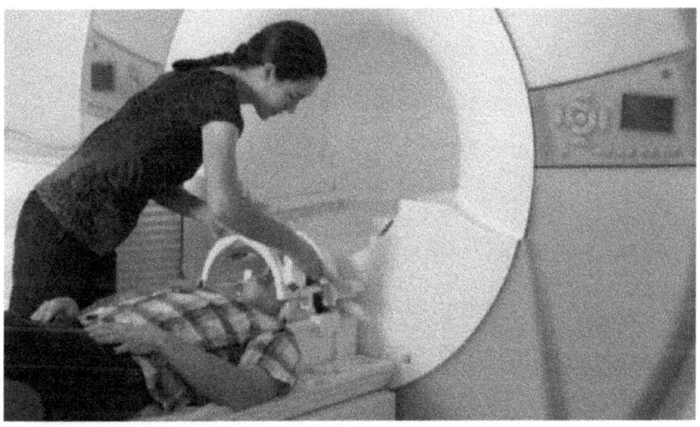

Figure 1. The fMRI scanner. A volume coil (with mirror to view the computer monitor) is placed over the participant's head.

Experimental Design

We created a unique set of 560 images for each participant. Forty images of general software applications (such as Microsoft Word or Mozilla Firefox) were displayed one time each. These images created a baseline of unique presentations throughout the task that served as our fMRI contrast. Of a pool of 40 warning images, 20 were selected randomly by computer algorithm to receive the polymorphic treatment and the other 20 were given the static treatment. The polymorphic warnings were shown one time each per variation (for a total of 13 unique images per warning), and the same static warnings were shown 13 times. The 560 images were randomized for each participant across five blocks of 6.5 minutes each (with a 2-minute break in between) in order to relieve participants' fatigue during the task. Participants were shown images for 3 seconds each with a 0.5-second inter-stimulus interval.

Experimental Task

Before being placed inside the fMRI scanner, participants were given an fMRI button box (see Figure 2) to indicate if each image shown was (1) identical to one seen before the task, (2) similar yet different from one seen previously in the task, or (3) new, never seen before in the task.

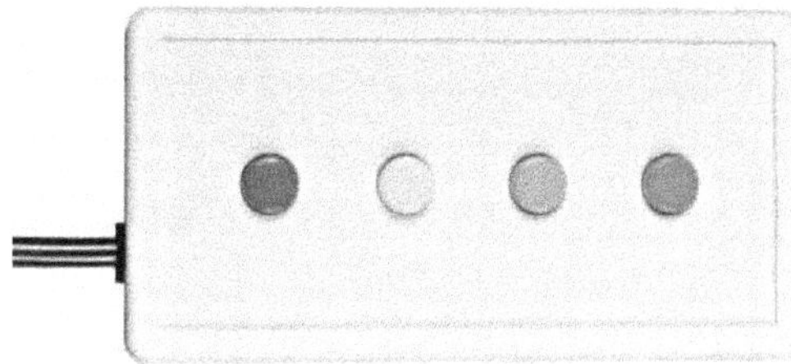

Figure 2. fMRI button box.

This process was used to provide behavioral performance data that ensured that participants were appropriately engaged in the task. Our subsequent analysis of the responses ("old", "similar", and "new") to each stimulus type (novel, static, polymorphic manipulations) revealed that participants performed the task as expected. At the conclusion of the fMRI scan, participants were led to an adjoining room to complete a brief posttest survey. To ensure manipulation validity, the posttest survey included a manipulation check asking if the participants noticed the variations in the images. All but one of the participants reported that they noticed the experimental treatment, indicating that they were on the whole successfully manipulated.

Participants

Twenty-five participants were recruited from the university community. We screened participants to require MRI compatibility, native English speakers, corrected-normal visual acuity, and right-handedness and excluded those with color-blindness or who were taking psychotropic medications. All participants were given an informed consent form to sign in accordance with the university's institutional review board (IRB) protocol. Of the 25 participants, 21 were male and 4 were female. Participant age ranged from 20–27 years of age with a mean age of 23.68 years. Participants were paid $25 for approximately 1 hour in the scanner.

Data Analysis

We first performed an ANOVA on the fMRI data with stimulus type (polymorphic, static) and repetition number as factors. We found four regions where there was a stimulus type × repetition number interaction, indicating that these regions reacted differently to repeated exposures to static and polymorphic warnings. Two regions, the left and right superior parietal cortex (Figure 4, upper panels) have been implicated in attentional processing [7]. In these regions, activation was higher for polymorphic than for static warnings, consistent with sustained attention and reduced repetition suppression for the polymorphic warnings. The other two regions, bilateral medial prefrontal cortex and the left retrosplenial cortex (Figure 4, lower

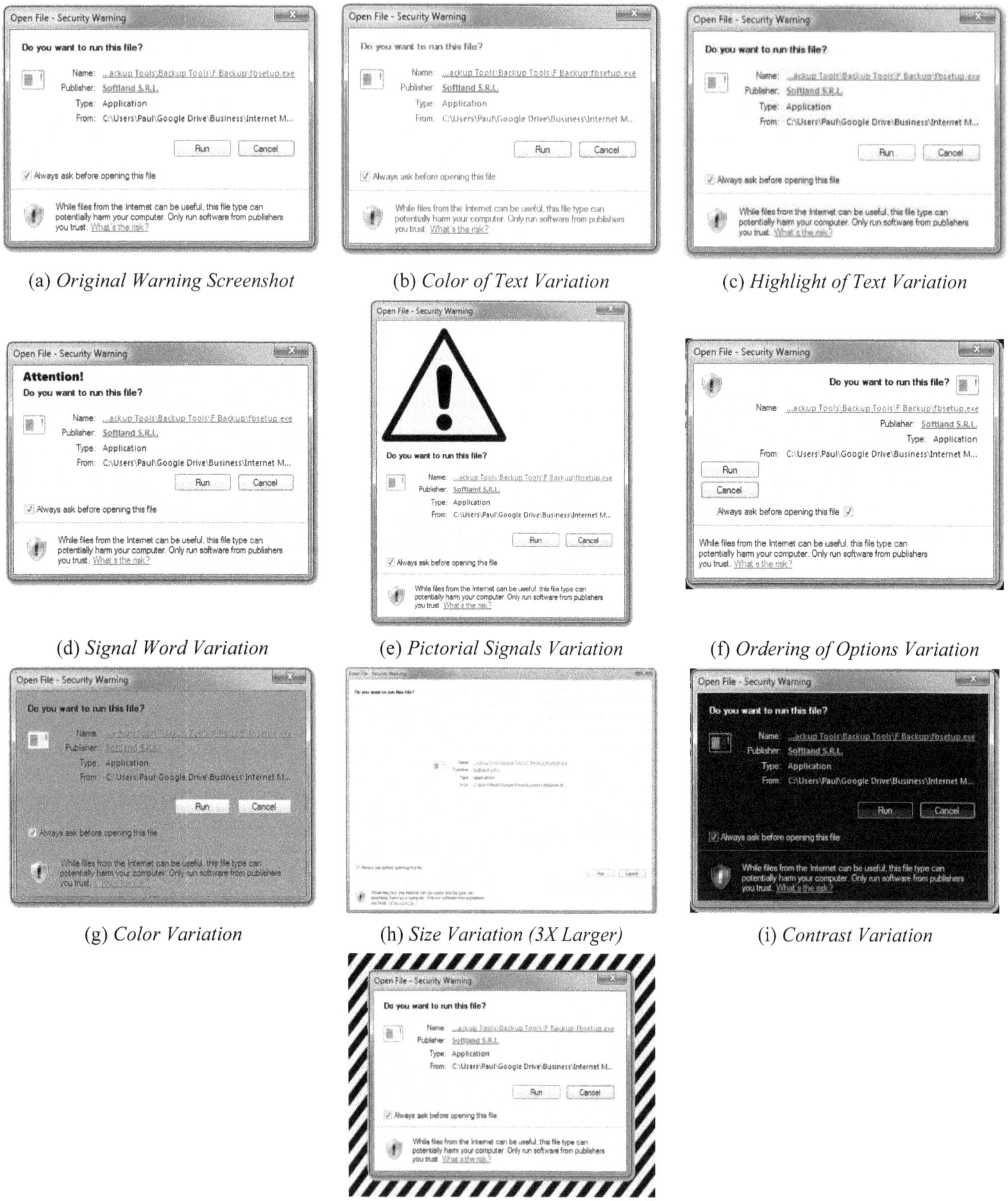

(a) *Original Warning Screenshot* (b) *Color of Text Variation* (c) *Highlight of Text Variation*

(d) *Signal Word Variation* (e) *Pictorial Signals Variation* (f) *Ordering of Options Variation*

(g) *Color Variation* (h) *Size Variation (3X Larger)* (i) *Contrast Variation*

(j) *Border Variation*

Figure 3. Polymorphic warning design variants.

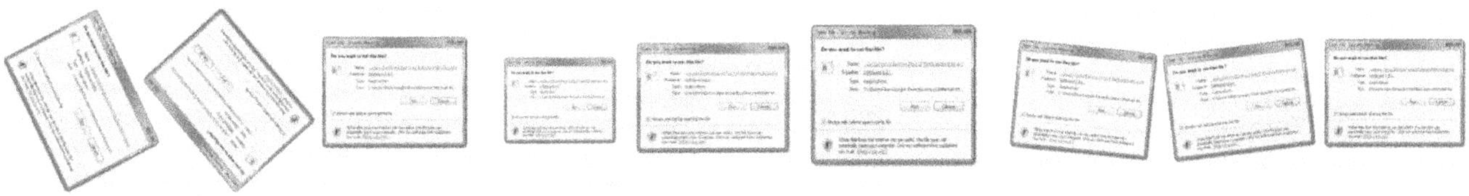

(k) *Twirl Animation Variation* (l) *Scale/Zoom Animation Variation* (m) *Jiggle Animation Variation*

Figure 3 (continued). Polymorphic warning design variants.

panels), have both been implicated in memory retrieval processes and as nodes in the default mode network (DMN) [6].In both regions, activation was higher for static than for polymorphic images for later presentations, consistent with either increased recognition memory processes or increased default mode activation for static but not for polymorphic warning images. Thus, our hypothesis was supported.

We also examined the specific polymorphic warnings collapsing across presentation order to determine which polymorphic variations were the most resistant to the RS effect. Accordingly, we examined the specific polymorphic warnings collapsing across presentation order to determine which polymorphic variations were most resistant to the RS effect. To quantify the most resistant variations for use in Study 2, we performed a *t*-test contrasting polymorphic and static warning images. Resulting statistical parameter maps were thresholded using a false-discovery rate of .05 and a spatial extent threshold of 1,080 mm^3. The largest cluster of activation comprised bilateral visual processing streams (including occipital, dorsal parietal, and inferior temporal lobes). Mean fMRI activations in this cluster for each polymorphic variation were then compared against the mean activation for static images (collapsed across repetitions) and ranked. Figure 5 depicts the mean beta fMRI activation for each polymorphic variation. Each manipulation had significantly greater fMRI activation than static images (Bonferroni-corrected *p*-value = .0038) with the exception of the "border" manipulation (p=.009). The highest scoring variations ("jiggle", "scale", "window color", and "symbol") were selected for Study 2.

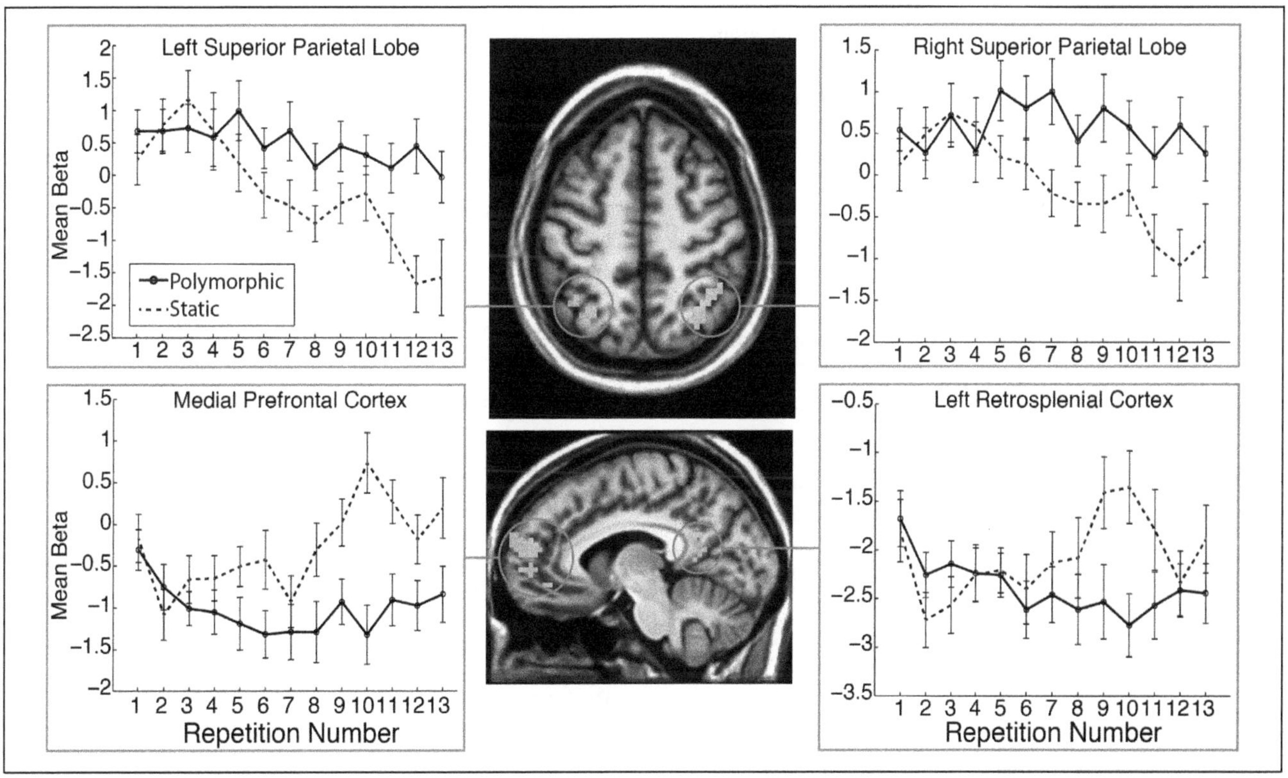

Figure 4. Brain regions that had a significant stimulus type × repetition number interaction. In the upper panels, the superior parietal lobes had elevated levels of activation for the polymorphic warnings, consistent with sustained attention. In the lower panels, the medial prefrontal cortex and the retrosplenial cortex had greater activation for static than for polymorphic images, consistent with memory retrieval.

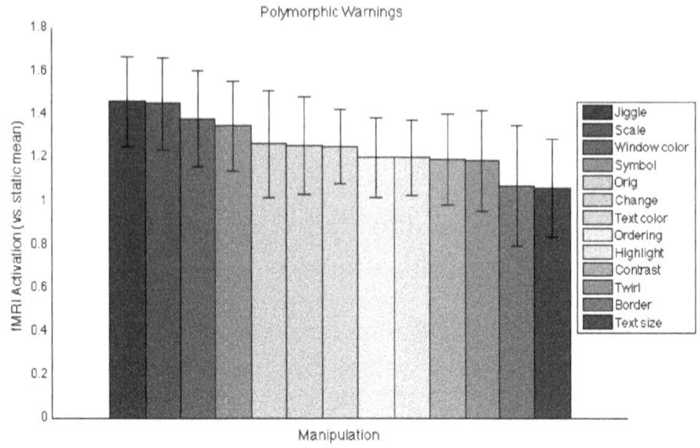

Figure 5. Mean fMRI activation for each polymorphic warning variation. Zero on the Y-axis indicates mean activation for static images (collapsed across repetitions). Error bars represent standard error of the mean.

STUDY 2: MOUSE CURSOR TRACKING

The results of Study 1 demonstrated that polymorphic warnings substantially reduced the occurrence of RS compared with conventional static warnings. However, constraints inherent in the fMRI method necessarily introduced artificiality into Study 1 that limited its ecological validity (e.g., participants must lie still in a supine position, view images rather than naturally interact with a computer). To address this limitation, we designed a behavioral laboratory experiment in which participants responded to security warnings in the natural course of completing a task on their personal laptops. To measure attention given to the warning, we analyzed users' mouse cursor movement (i.e., how a person responded using the laptop touchpad) through an embedded JavaScript library, which collected the x, y coordinates and timestamp of each movement at a millisecond precision rate and sent them to a web service for post hoc analysis. Although there is no causal link between the neural activation in Study 1 and the mouse tracking behavior in Study 2, both neurophysiological methods serve to corroborate each other.

We selected Google Chrome extension permission warnings as the warning type. During the course of the experiment, participants were required to search for, install, and evaluate 20 weather extensions for usability and aesthetics. Because a permission warning is displayed whenever a Google extension is installed, participants also received 20 permission warnings. In this way, they were naturally habituated while completing the task.

Experimental Design

Two experimental manipulations were included in the experiment. First, participants were randomly assigned the polymorphic warning treatment or the static warning treatment (a between-subject manipulation). The polymorphic treatment group randomly utilized the four most effective variations identified in Study 1 (Figure 5). The control group received conventional warnings that did not change their appearance. Second, the content of the warnings was randomly manipulated between reasonable and unreasonable permission requests (a within-subject manipulation) to motivate participants to read the warnings.

Ethics

The university IRB approved a deception protocol in which we led participants to believe that their objective was to evaluate Google Chrome extensions. Additionally, we received permission to perform a man-in-the-middle attack to spoof Google.com search results in order to ensure that only our experimental Chrome extensions were installed. After the experiment, participants were debriefed and told the true purpose of the experiment and assured that the extensions did not gather any personal information.

Experimental Task

To heighten perceived risk, participants were asked to use their personal laptop and were required to read the following disclaimer: "The researchers have not tested all possible weather extensions that you may encounter. The university is not responsible for any potential malicious software that may be installed as a result of this study. Each participant has the responsibility to use good judgment in deciding which extensions to install and evaluate."

Next, participants were asked to use Chrome and search Google.com to find 20 different weather extensions and evaluate them usability and aesthetics. However, as previously stated, we performed a man-in-the-middle attack to manipulate the Google search results. If a query related to Chrome weather extensions was shown, the search returned our spoofed results. Each of the links in the spoofed results pointed to sites under our control with legitimate URLs. Our Chrome extension transparently redirected HTTPS traffic to HTTP to avoid SSL certificate errors. Finally, we caused traffic to the Chrome Web Store to redirect to a "down for maintenance" page. Consequently, participants were required to use the in-line Chrome extension installation process on individual web sites.

The manipulated Google search results included more than 40 different weather extensions. Participants were only required to evaluate 20 of these, and only 3 of these at random presented an unreasonable permission warning. If a participant received a permission warning requesting unreasonable permissions, the participant was free to not install the extension. Participants had ample time to go back to the Google search results to find an alternative extension.

Participants

Eighty students from the university community participated in the study. Technical limitations on a few participants' laptops inhibited data collection of the mousing data. As a result, we had analyzable data from 76 participants across 1,466 warnings (40 in the treatment group and 36 in the control group). Approximately 63% of the participants were male, and the average age was 22.35 years. The participants were paid $7.50 for the 45-minute task.

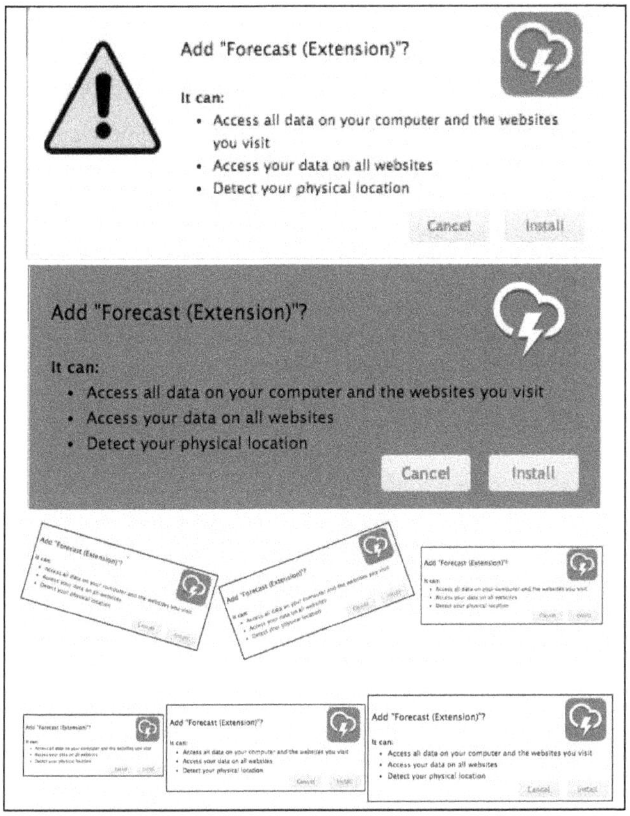

Figure 6. Pictorial, red, jiggle, and zoom variations.

Data Analysis

We analyzed users' mouse cursor movements to measure attention given to the warning, and thereby habituation. Research has repeatedly shown that the mouse cursor denotes where users' devote their attention, following the eye when navigating a webpage [14]. Attention given to information (e.g., warning information) can be inferred through a collection of mouse cursor movement statistics. For example, area-under-the-curve (AUC) is often used to denote attention [12]. AUC is the geometric area between a user's movement trajectory and a straight line connecting the user's starting point when a warning is shown and the final destination point (e.g., the button the user clicks to dismiss the warning) [see 12 for calculations]. When information from a warning catches users' attention, it causes them to deviate from this straight line as the cursor moves toward the warning information. AUC is a measure of total deviation from the idealized response trajectory or, in other words, total attention given to other information [12]. Other indicators of attention include people moving greater distance as they explore the warning, initially accelerating more slowly as they process information, changing directions more often while exploring a warning, moving more slowly indicating increased cognitive processing, and having greater click latency indicating increased cognitive processing. Although inferring attention through one statistic alone can be challenging, interpreting all the statistics together provides strong support of attentional changes.

To explore the influence of polymorphic warnings on mouse cursor movement indicators of attention and thereby habituation, we constructed a linear mixed-effects model, accounting for the repeated nature of the data nested within each participant. To model habituation across multiple warning exposures, we included a fixed effect of the warning order number in the model. The participant identifier was included as a random effect to allow variability across participants. The model included a fixed effect for whether participants were in the treatment group. In addition, the model contained a fixed effect for whether the warning cautioned that the add-on was requesting reasonable information or unreasonable information (coded as isMalicious). As participants were allowed to naturally complete the task for ecological validity, they could potentially revisit websites, reinstall extensions, and see the warning for those extensions again. Hence, a fixed effect was also included regarding whether the warning was being reinstalled. The model included interaction terms for treatment × Order and isMalicious × Order. AUC, initial acceleration, direction changes, movement speed, and click latency were included as dependent variables.

The results are shown in Table 1 and support the results of the fMRI study. The warning order number was significantly correlated with all of the mousing statistics in the predicted directions, suggesting that habituation increased with subsequent exposures (i.e., with warning order number). The use of polymorphic warnings was also significantly correlated with all of the mousing statistics in the predicted directions, suggesting that people habituate less when polymorphic warnings are shown.

Mousing Statistic	treatment	isMalicious	order	isReinstalled	treatment ×order	isMalicious ×order
AUC	60.53 ***	0.87 ns	902.71 ***	71.68 ***	156.81 ***	0.71 ns
Initial Acc.	9.81 ***	0.26 ns	110.26 ***	42.53 ***	12.46 ***	0.48 ns
Direction Changes	112.50 ***	0.20 ns	10.90 ***	15.08 ***	0.04 ns	8.55 **
Speed	16.06 ***	0.47 ns	155.58 ***	23.55 ***	8.62 **	0.31 ns
Distance	21.70 ***	1.15 ns	17.45 ***	118.83 ***	3.94 *	0.88 ns
Click Latency	85.26 ***	1.29 ns	8.26 **	35.84 ***	0.21 ns	0.89 ns

Chi-squared shown in cells, df = 1 for all tests
* $p < .05$, ** $p < .01$, ***$p < .001$, ns = not significant

Table 1: Study 2 Chi-Squared Test Results

In addition, the results suggest that people habituate more slowly when polymorphic warnings were shown (the interaction between treatment and order was significantly correlated with all of the statistics except for click latency).

Three additional variables were included in the model. First, we explored whether the content of the warning influenced habituation (isMalicious). Interestingly, the content of the warning did not influence habituation for any of the statistics. This finding suggests that changing the content of a warning may not be enough to deter the influence of habituation. Likewise, the interaction between isMalicious and Order of the warning did not significantly influence any of the statistics, suggesting that the content of the message may not decrease habituation even during early encounters. Finally, if an extension was being reinstalled, it influenced all of the statistics.

To further elaborate on how polymorphic warnings influence attention in terms of users' mouse cursor movements, Table 2 displays the population means, standard deviations, and effect sizes of each mousing statistic for the static warning treatment group and the polymorphic warning treatment group.

GENERAL DISCUSSION

This paper makes several contributions. First, in Study 1, we extended previous research on habituation by using neuroscience to observe habituation as it occurs in the context of human-computer interaction (HCI). Additionally, this study demonstrated how the RS effect can be directly measured in the brain using fMRI. Whereas previous HCI research measured habituation indirectly by observing its effects, such as inattentive behaviors [4], this study measured habituation directly as it occurs in the brain. Specifically, we showed how using a simple, repeated exposure, experimental design can permit researchers to detect the existence and size of the RS effect using the BOLD response. Using this method, we illustrated the precipitous drop in visual processing after only one repeated exposure and a large overall drop after 13 exposures. These results can provide researchers with a useful baseline of the RS effect in response to security warnings for future research.

Second, we demonstrated in Study 1 that polymorphic warnings are more resistant to RS than static warnings. Although polymorphic warnings have been proposed before [5], previous polymorphic variations were limited to the repositioning of options on the warning dialog. In contrast, this study utilized warning science literature to derive 12 polymorphic variations that can be generically applied to a wide variety of security warnings (see Figure 3).

Additionally, past research has not examined the influence of polymorphic warnings on habituation (either directly or indirectly) but rather measured frequency of risk-taking behavior. Therefore, it was previously unknown whether polymorphic warnings could indeed reduce habituation. We addressed this research gap by establishing that polymorphic warnings reduce the occurrence of RS to be significantly below that of conventional static warnings.

Third, we analyzed the fMRI data to select the polymorphic variations that were most effective in reducing RS. In this way we were able to identify the four most effective variations (see Figure 5) from our set.

Fourth, the results of the mouse cursor tracking experiment corroborated our fMRI findings. Specifically, we found that that polymorphic warnings resulted in both *reduced* habituation (as evidenced by the main effect) and *slower* habituation (as indicated by the interaction effect of the polymorphic treatment and the warning display order) compared with static warnings. According to Dimoka et al., "no single neurophysiological measure is usually sufficient on its own, and it is advisable to use many data sources to triangulate across measures" [11]. Using two complimentary neurophysiological measures allowed us to compensate for weaknesses inherent in each method. For example, the mouse cursor tracking method allowed us to implement the polymorphic warning UI artifact and test it within a natural task on participants' own personal computers, significantly enhancing the ecological validity of this research.

Mousing Statistic	Static Warnings mean (sd)	Polymorphic Warnings mean (sd)	Difference Effect Size Cohen's D
AUC	0.09 (0.63)	1.03 (0.65)	1.47***
Initial Acc.	10.10 (1.06)	9.31 (1.33)	0.66**
Direction Changes	4.52 (4.48)	5.29 (8.18)	0.17*
Speed	3.19 (0.79)	2.65 (0.73)	0.71**
Distance	0.40 (0.51)	0.66 (0.82)	0.37*
Click Latency	124.90 (73.50)	152.71 (239.19)	0.16*
* Small effect size <.5, ** Medium effect size < .8, *** Large effect size > .8			

Table 2: Population descriptive statistics and effect sizes of polymorphic treatment

Finally our methodology is itself a contribution in that it illustrates the usefulness of applying neuroscience to the domain of security and HCI generally. Because automatic or unconscious mental processes underlie much of human cognition and decision making, they likely play an important role in a number of other security behaviors, such as security education, training, and awareness (SETA) programs, password use, and information security policy compliance. Additionally, neuroscience methods have the potential to lead to the development of more complete behavioral security theories and guide the design of more effective security interventions.

LIMITATIONS AND FUTURE RESEARCH

This research is subject to a number of limitations. First, both studies used laboratory experiments that necessarily introduced artificiality into their respective tasks. In particular, the current technology of fMRI limits the flexibility and realism of experimental tasks. Fortunately, these problems in the fMRI study were at least partially compensated for by the mouse cursor tracking study in which participants conducted a much more ecologically valid task. However, we leave to future research the application of field methodologies that can achieve greater levels of external validity.

Second, although we presented strong evidence that the polymorphic warning reduces habituation behavior, we did not demonstrate that it leads to lower click-through behavior [25]. This was due to our chosen context of permission warnings and our associated experimental design. For some security warnings, inappropriate click-through behavior can be determined objectively. For example, in the case of web browser malware warnings, the false positive rate is extremely low [1]. Thus, users' choice to ignore these warnings can be objectively labeled as inappropriate. In contrast, in the context of privacy permission warnings, labeling inappropriate click-through behavior is difficult because privacy concerns vary by individual and are subjective [19]. Therefore, clicking through a permission warning for one person may be due to carelessness, whereas for another the same choice may be the result of considered deliberation. For this reason, we selected the mouse cursor tracking measures as our dependent variables in Study 2 because they directly and objectively measure habituation—the focus of this study. We leave to future research to investigate whether polymorphic warnings reduce click-through behavior in other contexts.

CONCLUSION

Users' habituation to security warnings is pervasive, and is often attributed to users' carelessness and inattention [15]. However, we demonstrate that habituation is largely obligatory as a result of how the brain processes familiar visual stimuli. A chief implication of our results is that because habituation occurs unconsciously at the neurobiological level, interventions designed to encourage greater attention and vigilance on the part of users—such as SETA programs—are incomplete on their own. Our findings suggest that a complimentary solution is to develop UI designs that are less susceptible to habituation. We show that the polymorphic warning artifact developed in this study is one such effective design. Our results point to future research opportunities for security interventions that take into account the biology of the user.

ACKNOWLEDGMENTS

We thank Lorrie Faith Cranor for her constructive comments on this manuscript. This work was supported by the National Science Foundation under Grants CNS-1422831 and DGE-1247842; the Rollins Center for Entrepreneurship and Technology at Brigham Young University; and the Berg Center for Ethics and Leadership at the University of Pittsburgh.

APPENDIX: FMRI TECHNICAL DETAILS

Equipment: MRI scanning took place at a university MRI research facility with the use of a Siemens 3T Tim-Trio scanner. For each scanned participant, we collected a high-resolution structural MRI scan for functional localization in addition to a series of functional scans to track brain activity during the performance of the various tasks. Structural images were acquired with a T1-weighted magnetization-prepared rapid acquisition including a gradient-echo (MP-RAGE) sequence with the following parameters: TE = 2.26 ms, flip angle = 9°, slices = 176, slice thickness = 1.0 mm, matrix size = 256 × 215, and voxel size = 1 mm × 0.98 mm × 0.98 mm. Functional scans were acquired with a gradient-echo, echo-planar, T2*-weighted pulse sequence with the following parameters: TR = 2000 ms, TE = 28 ms, flip angle = 90°, slices = 40, slice thickness = 4.0 mm (no skip), matrix size = 64 × 64, and voxel size = 3.44 mm × 3.44 mm × 3 mm.

Protocol: We first performed a 10-second localizer scan, followed by a 7-minute structural scan. Following these, we started the experimental task. We used E-Prime software to display the stimuli and synchronize the display events and scanner software. Total time in the scanner was 55 minutes.

Analysis: MRI data were analyzed with the Analysis of Functional Images (AFNI) suite of programs [8]. Briefly, functional data were slice-time corrected to account for differences in acquisition time for different slices of each volume; then, each volume was registered with the middle volume of each run to account for low-frequency motion. Data from each run were aligned to the run nearest in time to the acquisition of the structural scan. The structural scan was then co-registered to the functional scans. As in previous studies [e.g., 21], spatial normalization was accomplished by first warping the structural scan to the Talairach atlas [24] followed by warping to a template brain with Advanced Neuroimaging Tools (ANTs). Behavioral vectors were created that coded for stimulus type (e.g., security warnings, general software application screenshots) and repetition number. These were then entered into single-participant regression analyses. Stimulus events were modeled using a stick function convolved with the canonical hemodynamic response. Regressors coding for motion and scanner drift were also entered into the model as nuisance variables. Resulting beta values were blurred with a 5-mm FWHM Gaussian kernel. Beta values for the conditions of interest were then entered into group-level analyses, such as ANOVAs or *t*-tests, which were used to determine functional ROIs. All tests were corrected for multiple comparisons using a false-discovery rate of 0.05 and a spatial extent threshold of 20 contiguous voxels (540 mm^3). Finally, the single-presentation general computing screenshots served as the implicit baselines.

REFERENCES

1. Akhawe, D. and Felt, A.P. Alice in warningland: A large-scale field study of browser security warning effectiveness. Proc. USENIX Security '13, USENIX Association (2013), 257-272.
2. Bravo-Lillo, C., Cranor, L., Komanduri, S., Schechter, S., and Sleeper, M. Harder to ignore? Revisiting pop-up fatigue and approaches to prevent it. In Proc. SOUPS 2014, USENIX Association (2014), 105-111.
3. Bravo-Lillo, C., Cranor, L.F., Downs, J., Komanduri, S., and Sleeper, M. Improving computer security dialogs. Proc. INTERACT 2011, Springer-Verlag (2011), 18-35.
4. Bravo-Lillo, C., Komanduri, S., Cranor, L.F., Reeder, R.W., Sleeper, M., Downs, J., and Schechter, S. Your attention please: Designing security-decision UIs to make genuine risks harder to ignore. In Proc. SOUPS 2013, ACM (2013), 1-12.
5. Brustoloni, J.C. and Villamarín-Salomón, R. Improving security decisions with polymorphic and audited dialogs. In Proc. SOUPS '07, ACM (2007), 76-85.
6. Buckner, R.L., Andrews-Hanna, J.R., and Schacter, D.L. The brain's default network. Ann. N. Y. Acad. Sci. 1124, 1 (2008), 1-38.
7. Buschman, T.J. and Miller, E.K. Top-down versus bottom-up control of attention in the prefrontal and posterior parietal cortices. Science 315, 5820 (2007), 1860-1862.
8. Cox, R.W. Afni: Software for analysis and visualization of functional magnetic resonance neuroimages. Comput. Biomed. Res. 29, 3 (1996), 162-173.
9. Desimone, R. Neural mechanisms for visual memory and their role in attention. Proc. Natl. Acad. Sci. 93, 24 (1996), 13494-13499.
10. Dimoka, A. How to conduct a functional magnetic resonance (fMRI) study in social science research. MIS Quart. 36, 3 (2012), 811-840.
11. Dimoka, A., Banker, R.D., Benbasat, I., Davis, F.D., Dennis, A.R., Gefen, D., Gupta, A., Lschebeck, A., Kenning, P.H., Pavlou, P.A., Muller-Putz, G., Riedl, R., Vom Brocke, J., and Weber, B. On the use of neurophysiological tools in IS research: Developing a research agenda for NeuroIS. MIS Quart. 36, 3 (2012), 679-702.
12. Freeman, J.B. and Ambady, N. Mousetracker: Software for studying real-time mental processing using a computer mouse-tracking method. Behav. Res. Methods 42, 1 (2010), 226-241.
13. Grill-Spector, K., Henson, R., and Martin, A. Repetition and the brain: Neural models of stimulus-specific effects. Trends Cogn. Sci. 10, 1 (2006), 14-23.
14. Guo, Q. and Agichtein, E. Towards predicting web searcher gaze position from mouse movements. In Proc. CHI'10, ACM (2010), 3601-3606.
15. Herley, C. So long, and no thanks for the externalities: The rational rejection of security advice by users. In Proc. NSPW 2009, ACM (2009), 133-144.
16. Kalsher, M. and Williams, K. Behavioral compliance: Theory, methodology, and result. In Handbook of warnings Lawrence Erlbaum Associates, Mahwah NJ (2006), 313-331, 2006.
17. Kandel, E.R. The molecular biology of memory storage: A dialogue between genes and synapses. Science 294, 5544 (2001), 1030-1038.
18. Lueschow, A., Miller, E.K., and Desimone, R. Inferior temporal mechanisms for invariant object recognition. Cereb. Cortex 4, 5 (1994), 523-531.
19. Malhotra, N.K., Kim, S.S., and Agarwal, J. Internet users' information privacy concerns (IUIPC): The construct, the scale, and a causal model. Inf. Syst. Res. 15, 4 (2004), 336-355.
20. Minnery, B.S. and Fine, M.S. Neuroscience and the future of human-computer interaction. Interactions 16, 2 (2009), 70-75.
21. Motley, S.E. and Kirwan, C.B. A parametric investigation of pattern separation processes in the medial temporal lobe. J. Neurosci. 32, 38 (2012), 13076-13084.
22. Schechter, S.E., Dhamija, R., Ozment, A., and Fischer, I. The emperor's new security indicators. In Proc. SP'07, IEEE (2007), 51-65.
23. Sunshine, J., Egelman, S., Almuhimedi, H., Atri, N., and Cranor, L.F. Crying wolf: An empirical study of SSL warning effectiveness. In Proc. SSYM'09, (2009), 399-416.
24. Talairach, J. and Tournoux, P. Co-planar stereotaxic atlas of the human brain: 3-dimensional proportional system: An approach to cerebral imaging. Thieme, Stuttgart, 1988.
25. Vance, A., Anderson, B.B., Kirwan, C.B., and Eargle, D. Using measures of risk perception to predict information security behavior: Insights from electroencephalography (EEG). J. Assoc. Inf. Syst. 15, 10 (2014), 679-722.
26. Vuilleumier, P., Henson, R., Driver, J., and Dolan, R. Multiple levels of visual object constancy revealed by event-related fMRI of repetition priming. Nat. Neurosci. 5, 5 (2002), 491-499.
27. Wogalter, M.S. Communication-human information processing (C-HIP) model. In Handbook of warnings, M.S. WOGALTER Ed. Lawrence Erlbaum Associates, Mahwah, NJ (2006), 51-61, 2006.

Improving SSL Warnings: Comprehension and Adherence

Adrienne Porter Felt[1], Alex Ainslie[1], Robert W. Reeder[1], Sunny Consolvo[1], Somas Thyagaraja[1], Alan Bettes[1], Helen Harris[1], Jeff Grimes[2]
[1]Google, [2]University of Pennsylvania
[1]{felt, ainslie, rreeder, sconsolvo, somast, bettes, helenharris}@google.com, [2]jeffgrimes@chromium.org

ABSTRACT
Browsers warn users when the privacy of an SSL/TLS connection might be at risk. An ideal SSL warning would empower users to make informed decisions and, failing that, guide confused users to safety. Unfortunately, users struggle to understand and often disregard real SSL warnings. We report on the task of designing a new SSL warning, with the goal of improving comprehension and adherence.

We designed a new SSL warning based on recommendations from warning literature and tested our proposal with microsurveys and a field experiment. We ultimately failed at our goal of a well-understood warning. However, nearly 30% more total users chose to remain safe after seeing our warning. We attribute this success to opinionated design, which promotes safety with visual cues. Subsequently, our proposal was released as the new Google Chrome SSL warning. We raise questions about warning comprehension advice and recommend that other warning designers use opinionated design.

INTRODUCTION
Dissidents, drug dealers, and diplomats have one thing in common: they rely on SSL to help keep their online communication private. SSL protects their e-mails, tweets, and bank statements from eavesdropping or tampering in transit. When something goes wrong with a supposedly secure connection, most browsers alert the user with a warning. The user must then decide whether to adhere to or ignore the warning.

An ineffective SSL warning can cost users. For some, deciding to proceed under adverse conditions can lead to physical harm or imprisonment. For others, an attack in an urban coffee shop might lead to unauthorized credit card charges. We argue that an effective SSL warning ought to accomplish:

1. *Comprehension.* The user should be able to make an informed decision after seeing an SSL warning. He or she should understand the source of the threat, the data that is at risk, and the likelihood of a false positive warning.
2. *Adherence.* The warning should encourage users to act in a conservatively safe manner by not proceeding.

Comprehension is our preferred goal, but adherence is an alternative if and when we cannot achieve comprehension.

CHI 2015, April 18–23, 2015, Seoul, Republic of Korea
ACM 978-1-4503-3145-6/15/04.
http://dx.doi.org/10.1145/2702123.2702442

The literature cautions that SSL warnings may currently fail at one or both of these goals. Study participants mistake SSL warnings for messages about security updates, cookies, or malware [2, 10, 14, 16, 38]. This confusion leads to potentially harmful myths. For example, some people believe that their anti-virus software or operating system will protect them (it won't) [10, 38]. Furthermore, Google Chrome users adhered to only a third of SSL warnings [1].

We set out to design a new SSL warning that informs (or, failing that, convinces) users. We based our proposal on best practices drawn from warning literature. For comprehension, researchers advise that text should be simple, non-technical, brief, and specific (e.g., [6, 23, 24, 26, 38]). For adherence, the literature recommends promoting a clear course of action (e.g., [20, 38, 40]). Our proposal attempts to incorporate these suggestions. We hypothesized that the resulting proposal would improve comprehension and adherence.

We tested our proposal against three survey-based comprehension metrics, using 7,537 microsurvey responses. For comparison, we also tested SSL warning text from four browsers. Our proposed text slightly improved one aspect of comprehension (the threat source), but overall comprehension rates remained low for all warning texts. Why do all warnings — including ours — fail? Although we tried to follow best practices, we faced tradeoffs between contradictory advice. Our choices may not have been optimal. This suggests a need for more research into the relative importance of brevity, specificity, and non-technicality in security warnings.

Turning to our secondary goal of adherence, we ran a field experiment to measure how opinionated design affects adherence rates. *Opinionated design* is the use of visual design cues to promote a recommended course of action. Our proposal substantially increased adherence rates — by nearly 30 percentage points. This demonstrates that opinionated design can have a large impact on user safety and decision making. Following this experiment, our proposed SSL warning was released as the new Google Chrome 37 SSL warning. Adherence in the field subsequently increased from 37% to 62%, meaning that millions of additional users a month choose to act safely due to our warning design changes.

MOTIVATION: SSL WARNINGS

What Is SSL?
When a user visits a website over HTTPS, the browser tries to establish an SSL/TLS[1] connection to the website's server. SSL is supposed to ensure two properties: secrecy and authentication. *Secrecy* means that an eavesdropper should not

[1]We henceforth say "SSL" for consistency with older literature.

be able to see or modify the e-mails and Tweets that a user sends over SSL. To this end, the browser encrypts the data that flows between the browser and a website's server. The browser also *authenticates* the server to make sure the server is not lying about its identity. Without authentication, a network attacker could pretend to be the server and thereby access the data. Authentication is needed to ensure secrecy.

Browsers display SSL warnings when the encryption is too weak or the server could not be authenticated. The connection is immediately halted, pending the user's decision about the warning. In some cases, the problem indicates a real attack. Syrian Internet users saw SSL warnings when the Syrian Telecom Ministry allegedly attacked Facebook users.[2] Similarly, SSL warnings alerted Chinese Internet users to attacks on Google[3] and GitHub[4]. However, in other cases, misconfigured servers or firewalls cause spurious warnings.

Our Definition of Comprehension

To achieve our goal of comprehension, an ideal SSL warning would convey the following:

- *Threat source.* SSL warnings are about network attacks, not malicious or compromised servers. This means that the supposed attacker is at some point between the user's computer and the website's server. The threat does not stem from the website itself. An informed user might consider how much she trusts her local network connection and ISP. For example, a user might reasonably mistrust a WiFi connection at LaGuardia Airport — or any Internet connection in Syria. An informed user would not evaluate how benign or malicious the destination website is.
- *Data risk.* The user's data on the destination website is at risk of eavesdropping or tampering. Furthermore, this applies to all data already on the website, not just new data that the user enters after clicking through the warning. The user's local data and data on unrelated HTTPS websites are not at stake. For example, a user who faces a warning on a banking website should know that her banking statements might be read by someone else if she clicks through the warning. An informed user would therefore consider the sensitivity of her data on the destination website.
- *False positives.* Misconfigured websites and WiFi log-in screens cause spurious warnings in the absence of an attack. Websites with good security practices (such as e-mail providers and banks) are unlikely to be misconfigured. When weighing the likelihood of a false positive, an informed user would consider the website's reputation and whether the website normally works correctly.

Motivating Literature

Prior studies have shown that confusion about SSL warnings is widespread, and users overwhelmingly ignore some SSL warnings. However, experiments have shown that warning design changes can potentially help adherence.

[2] https://www.eff.org/deeplinks/2011/05/syrian-man-middle-against-facebook

[3] http://www.netresec.com/?page=Blog&month=2014-09&post=Analysis-of-Chinese-MITM-on-Google

[4] http://www.netresec.com/?page=Blog&month=2013-02&post=Forensics-of-Chinese-MITM-on-GitHub

Comprehension

SSL is a nuanced, technical topic that touches on other technical topics like network connections and authentication. Although people might understand that SSL relates to or provides security, they might not understand how.

Several studies have demonstrated that people conflate SSL warnings with other security topics. Interviewees told Bravo-Lillo et al. [10] that SSL warnings are about anti-virus software, security updates, or certifications for exemplary security practices. One interviewee described an SSL certificate as, *"...like a credential or like a plug-in that allows you to use software, and it means your security is up to date on your computer."* Dhamija et al. [14] asked participants to describe an SSL warning shortly after seeing it; participants said things like, *"I accepted the use of cookies,"* and *"It was a message from the website about spyware."* Sunshine et al. [38] tested SSL warning comprehension with a survey, and some respondents said that SSL warnings are about viruses or worms. (Fewer than half of their respondents could accurately explain an SSL warning in their own words.) Researchers have also reported that their participants confused malware and phishing warnings with SSL warnings [2, 16].

This confusion leads some people to believe potentially harmful myths. As an example, one respondent told Sunshine et al. [38], *"I use a Mac so nothing bad would happen"* — perhaps true if the threat were malware, but incorrect and potentially dangerous for a network attack on SSL.

People who can reason about SSL false positives should be alarmed by SSL warnings on banking websites. However, Bravo-Lillo et al. [10] reported that six of their non-expert interviewees believe the opposite to be true: they said that SSL warnings could be ignored on banking websites because banks have good security practices. Some study participants similarly told Sunshine et al. [38] that they thought real attacks were less likely to occur on banking websites, although they were slightly more likely to heed warnings for banking websites than library websites in an experiment.

However, SSL is not impossible to understand. Biddle et al. [7] improved comprehension of Internet Explorer 7's certificate dialog boxes. They attributed their success to removing technical language and separating the concepts of secrecy and authentication. Although they did not study warnings, we hope the same success can be translated to warnings.

Adherence

Laboratory studies have consistently shown that participants ignore a majority of SSL warnings. In a laboratory phishing experiment, 68% of participants (15 of 22) clicked through an old Firefox SSL warning without stopping to read it [14]. (A click-through rate is the inverse of the adherence rate.) In another experiment, a third to half of participants clicked through Internet Explorer 7's SSL warning and entered credentials into a banking website [34]. Sunshine et al. exposed 100 study participants to SSL warnings during information lookup tasks; most participants (55% to 100%, depending on the warning and website) ignored the warnings [38]. Their study also showed that warning design could change click-

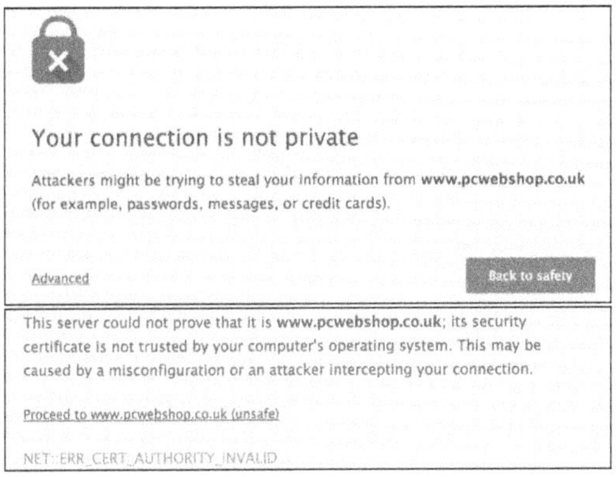

Figure 1. Our proposed warning. Default view on top, with the expanded "Advanced" section shown below.

through rates. Sotirakopoulos et al. replicated the Sunshine study with similar results, but 40% of their participants said during an exit survey that the laboratory environment had influenced their decision [37].

Field data is more optimistic about the ability of warnings to promote adherence. Large-scale field data from Mozilla Firefox showed that Firefox users adhered to nearly 70% of SSL warning impressions, which is a fairly good adherence rate [1]. Unfortunately, users adhered to only 30% of Google Chrome SSL warnings [1]. In a subsequent field experiment, Felt et al. found that differences in warning design accounted for a third to a half of the difference in behavior between browsers [18]. We briefly ran a version of the Firefox SSL warning in Google Chrome, and Google Chrome SSL warning adherence rates increased to 44%.

DESIGNING A NEW WARNING

Based on best practices from the warning literature, we proposed a new warning for Google Chrome. Our text is supposed to be simple, non-technical, brief, and specific, and the design is opinionated. Figure 1 shows our proposal. In this section, we describe how we arrived at the proposal.

Communicating the Threat

Technical Jargon

Warning researchers recommend using simple, non-technical language for warnings that are intended for a broad user base [6, 23]. People are more likely to read beyond the first sentence of a warning if it uses simple language [36]. Advertisements and warnings that contain technical language hold less interest and are less likely to be remembered or obeyed [3, 22]. For example, people are more likely to follow the simple instruction "open a window" than the more complex instruction "use in a well-ventilated room" [20].

SSL warnings have traditionally used technical terms such as "certificate" and "security credentials." Both advanced and novice users find these terms confusing, and researchers recommend removing them [6, 7, 10, 38]. For example, a participant told Biddle et al. that *"I don't know if my information is safe, because I don't know what 'encrypted' means"* after seeing Internet Explorer 7's certificate dialog box [7].

Warning	SMOG grade
Proposal	6.6
Google Chrome 36	11.0
Internet Explorer 11	10.5
Mozilla Firefox 31	8.7
Safari 7	8.0

Table 1. SMOG readability grades for different SSL warning texts.

Mozilla has removed more technical terms with each revision of the Firefox warning. In contrast, Google Chrome 36 and Internet Explorer 11 use many technical terms, respectively:

> *"...the server presented a certificate issued by an entity that is not trusted by your computer's operating system."*

> *"The security certificate presented by this website was not issued by a trusted certificate authority."*

We removed all technical terms from the primary text of our proposal. Our decision to adhere to simple, non-technical language means that our proposed text is more general and less educational than other warnings. However, we hoped that the warning would be more accessible to a broad audience.

For curious or expert users, a more technical explanation can be read by clicking on "Advanced." There, a secondary paragraph explains the cause of the error. Other SSL warnings similarly make use of secondary text. We do not expect many users to read the secondary text.

Reading Level

Following the recommendation to use simple language, we targeted a low reading level. Browsers are used by a broad audience. Newspaper articles — which have a similar audience — are typically written at a sixth grade reading level. While working on the text of our proposal, we tested it using the SMOG formula [30]. Table 1 shows the SMOG grades of our proposal and alternative warnings, using the title and primary text of each warning (see Table 2).

Brevity

Large quantities of text look like they will take effort to read, so people often read none of it [24]. Consequently, warnings should be as brief as possible [6, 7]. However, this presented a challenge: it is not possible to explain all aspects of the threat model in a single short paragraph. We therefore faced a tradeoff between brevity and comprehensiveness. We chose brevity, as we felt that conveying some of the topic was preferable to a user reading none of the text.

Specific Risk Description

People are more likely to comprehend and comply with a warning if it describes the risks explicitly and unambiguously [19, 26, 27, 40]. Warning researchers recommend providing specific, explicit, and comprehensive details about the consequences of ignoring a security warning [6, 10, 17].

This advice is at odds with the other recommendations for simplicity, non-technicality, and brevity. However, prior research demonstrates that all are important. We tried to accomplish both specificity and simplicity by providing a short list of example data types that could be stolen ("for example, passwords, messages, or credit cards"). This is more concrete than simply saying "information" or "data," and we hoped it

Browser	Title	Primary text
Google Chrome 36	The site's security certificate is not trusted!	You attempted to reach example.com, but the server presented a certificate issued by an entity that is not trusted by your computer's operating system. This may mean that the server has generated its own security credentials, which Chrome cannot rely on for identity information, or an attacker may be trying to intercept your communications. You should not proceed, especially if you have never seen this warning before for this site.
Proposal (Chrome 37)	Your connection is not private	Attackers might be trying to steal your information from example.com (for example, passwords, messages, or credit cards).
Internet Explorer 11	There is a problem with this website's security certificate	The security certificate presented by this website was not issued by a trusted certificate authority. Security certificate problems may indicate an attempt to fool you or intercept any data you send to the server. We recommend that you close this webpage and do not continue to this website.
Mozilla Firefox 31	This Connection is Untrusted	You have asked to connect securely to example.com, but we can't confirm that your connection is secure. Normally, when you try to connect securely, sites will present trusted identification to prove that you are going to the right place. However, this site's identity can't be verified.
Safari 7	Safari can't verify the identity of the website "example.com"	The certificate for this website is invalid. You might be connecting to a website that is pretending to be "example.com", which could put your confidential information at risk. Would you like to connect to the website anyway?

Table 2. The text from different SSL warnings, for self-signed certificate errors.

would help users understand the data at risk. However, our text is less specific than warnings with technical terms.

Illustration

Illustrations can improve warning comprehension. Adding an illustrative symbol to a medical warning reduces the amount of time it takes to learn the information in the warning [31]. Furthermore, illustrations make warnings more attention-grabbing and memorable [13, 25, 28].

Existing SSL warnings use abstract illustrations that imply danger. Examples include a security guard (Mozilla Firefox 31) or a red shield (Internet Explorer 11). We followed suit and included an illustration of a red lock. Although this is abstract, it matches the security indicators used in the URL bar. Unfortunately, abstract symbols are more difficult to understand than concrete symbols [15, 21].

Risk Level

To gain user attention, warnings must stand out from the surrounding environment. Red warnings yield higher adherence rates and lower detection times than warnings printed in black or green [8, 28]. Sunshine et al. suggest that SSL warnings should be red to make them "scary" [38].

On the other hand, warnings need to communicate an appropriate level of risk. Several research studies have found that users confuse SSL warnings with phishing and malware warnings [2, 16, 38]. Since SSL warnings have much higher false positive rates, this confusion can harm the reputation of the more accurate phishing and malware warnings. ANSI recommends the use of signal words (e.g., "Danger," "Warning,") with associated colors (red, orange, yellow) for decreasing levels of risk [4]. Since we cannot determine the risk of physical harm for a particular user, none of the signal words are appropriate per ANSI standards.

We decided that color would still be appropriate for indicating risk levels without tying the warnings to physical risks. We therefore reserved a red background for malware and phishing warnings, which we consider higher-risk than SSL warnings. The SSL warning could have an orange or yellow background because it is lower risk but still a significant security threat. However, this presented a challenge: orange and yellow come close to failing our accessibility guidelines for contrast on a computer screen. At suitable levels of vibrancy, yellow and orange lack sufficient contrast with either white or black text. We therefore prepared an SSL warning proposal with a gray background and red lock; although red is present, it is limited to an accent color.

Opinionated Design

We used visual design techniques to promote the safe choice as the preferred option. We call this *opinionated design*. Even without reading, the user should understand the instruction.

Clear instructions improve both comprehension and adherence rates [20, 40]. Simply providing information without a clear instruction does not necessarily influence behavior. For example, people don't always choose healthier products after reading nutritional labels [5]. Sunshine et al. recommend emphasizing a clear course of action in SSL warnings [38], and Microsoft's NEAT guidelines say that warnings should be clearly explained and actionable [32].

Choice Attractiveness

We wanted adherence to be a more visually attractive choice than non-adherence. The safe button is therefore a bright blue color that stands out against the background. Other Google properties use the same blue button style for primary actions, so people should associate the button style with a default choice. In contrast, the unsafe choice is a dark gray text link.

Choice Visibility

Several warnings hide the unsafe choice. The Google Chrome malware warning hides the "proceed" button behind an "Advanced" link, and users must click four times to proceed through the Mozilla Firefox SSL warning. These hurdles improve the adherence rate by 2–15%, depending on the complexity of each additional step [1, 18]. Similarly, Bravo-Lillo et al. found that adding small hurdles to installation dialogs improved participants' installation decisions [9, 11].

We hypothesize that the increase in adherence occurs due to a mix of factors. Finding the hidden choice requires effort, which can serve as a deterrent, and we believe that users view a hidden choice as not recommended by the browser. Furthermore, the additional click slightly increases the amount of time that users must spend looking at (and, ostensibly, thinking about) the warning [9, 11]. We view these mechanisms positively because they serve convince undecided users.

However, hiding the link to proceed can have side effects. It increases the amount of effort to ignore a false positive, and some users might not realize that the hidden choice is available. For example, some participants asked Sunshine et al. to switch browsers because they found the Mozilla Firefox SSL warning too complex to proceed through [38].

We ultimately hid the link to proceed, but we tried to make its presence obvious. Figure 1 shows the default warning state; the user must click "Advanced" to reveal the link to proceed. Since "Advanced" is one of only two actions in the warning, we hope that users will try it and find the link to proceed before becoming frustrated.

COMPREHENSION

We tested whether the text of our proposed warning helps microsurvey respondents understand the threat model. We compared our proposed text to the SSL warning text from other major browsers (see Table 2).

Methodology

We created three survey-based comprehension metrics. Each survey consisted of a single comprehension question accompanied by a mock warning image. We collected a total of 7,537 Google Consumer Survey (GCS) responses.

Survey Questions

We tested each aspect of comprehension separately:

1. *Threat source.* The warning text should convey that a network attacker is the source of the threat. To measure this aspect of comprehension, we asked:

   What might happen if you ignored this error while checking your email?
   - Your computer might get malware
   - A hacker might read your email

   If respondents understood the warning text, they should have selected the e-mail answer choice. The answer order was randomized for display.

2. *Data risk.* The warning text should convey that a specific website's data is at risk. We asked two versions of the following question:

   If you ignored this error on {facebook.com, bankofamerica.com}, what information might a hacker be able to see?
   - Photos my friends have posted
   - Movies I have watched
   - Bank statements I have received
   - Documents on my computer
   - All of the above

   Respondents should have been able to match the website to the data type: photos if asked about "facebook.com," and bank statements for "bankofamerica.com." The answer order was randomized, except for "All of the above."

3. *False positives.* We also want users to believe that an SSL warning on a website with above-average website security practices is more — not less — likely to be a real attack. We asked two versions of the same question:

Figure 2. Mock warning images (our proposal and Google Chrome 36). We changed the URL appropriately for each question.

   If you ignored this error while paying bills online, how likely is it that a hacker could see your bank account balance?

   If you ignored this error while watching movies, how likely is it that a hacker could see what movies you have watched?

   Each was accompanied by a five-point Likert-style scale, ranging from "Not at all likely" (left) to "Extremely likely" (right). Only the endpoints were labelled.

   If respondents understood how false positives occur, they should have assigned a higher score to the question about banking than the question about movies.

Mock Warning Images

The survey questions were accompanied by mock warning images. We matched the URL in each image to the URL in the question it accompanied. Since we wanted to compare the text of multiple warnings, the images needed to clearly display the warning text without any distractions or confounds. To do this, we created a neutral, unbranded warning layout. We used the same layout with text from: our proposal, Google Chrome 36, Internet Explorer 11, Mozilla Firefox 31, and Safari 7. Figure 2 shows two examples of mock warning images.

The mock warning images contained the title and primary body text from each respective warning (Table 2). For all browsers, we chose the text that corresponds to a self-signed certificate error because it is the most common cause of SSL warnings [1]. Instead of varying the button text, each image had a blue "Ignore error" link to match the language used in our questions ("If you ignored this error..."). Wherever the warning texts included a specific browser name (e.g., "Safari"), we substituted the phrase "your browser."

Incentives

Our GCS respondents answered these questions in lieu of a paywall. Each respondent had to answer a single question to proceed to the website. We chose to use GCS because they interrupt respondents on their way to websites, much like SSL warnings. GCSs are displayed on a variety of non-Google websites (e.g., news websites). We did not pay respondents, but they were able to gain free access to websites that normally cost money.

Sample Size

We requested a sample size of 300 for each of 5 variants and 5 conditions, although we occasionally received a few extra responses. We ended with a total of 7,537 survey responses.

Demographics

The GCS platform performs stratified sampling using inferred demographic and location information [29]. Their stratified sampling targets the most recent Current Population Survey (CPS) of Internet users [29]. Pew Research studied the GCS respondent population in 2012 and concluded that GCS respondents *"conform closely to the demographic composition of the overall internet population"* [33]. Sosik et al. found slight demographic differences but concluded that that technology usage and adoption was similar across GCS, Survey Sampling International (SSI), Knowledge Networks (KN), and Pew respondents [35].

We did not screen respondents for the threat source and data risk questions. However, we wanted to ensure that respondents for the false positive questions were familiar with online financial transactions. We screened respondents to the false positive questions with the same preliminary question: *"Have you ever checked your bank account balance online?"*

Limitations

Our respondents did not face any real danger. It is possible that people facing real warnings are more motivated to think about a warning, out of concern for his or her online safety. However, Google Chrome users decide within 2.1 seconds for half of SSL warning impressions in the field [1]. We therefore don't believe that the lack of danger invalidates our findings.

Our samples per condition might not be completely independent. It is possible — albeit unlikely — that some respondents might have answered multiple questions. For example, a person might see multiple questions from the same set if (s)he answers surveys on multiple computers. Unfortunately, we can neither prevent nor identify this situation due to the platform's anonymity. Given the low probability and our large sample size (at least 300 per condition), we treat our samples as independent when performing statistical testing.

We focused on comprehension amongst English-speaking U.S. Internet users. Our results may not translate to other cultures or languages. Once we achieve high comprehension rates in a single language, future work should investigate how to best translate that success to other countries.

Study Ethics

Our survey questions did not ask about sensitive topics, and we did not collect any personally identifiable information. The GCS platform anonymizes survey responses. The survey questions were reviewed by multiple researchers who have completed privacy and ethics training.

Results

Comprehension rates were low for the threat source and data risk metric for all warning versions. Our proposal improved the threat source metric, but we made no progress in conveying the data risk. However, respondents in aggregate were able to reason about false positives for all warning versions.

Threat Source

Our proposed warning text improved respondents' understanding of the threat source. Table 3 shows how many respondents answered correctly per warning. Our proposal increased the chances of a correct response from 37.7% (Chrome 36) to 49.2% (proposal). Responses varied significantly across the warning versions ($\chi^2 = 13.43, p = 0.0093$).

Condition	"A hacker might read your email"	N
Proposal	49.2%	301
Chrome 36	37.7%	300
Safari	35.9%	304
Firefox	39.3%	300
Internet Explorer	39.3%	300

Table 3. Rate of correct responses to the threat source question. ("What might happen if you ignored this error while checking your email?")

facebook.com						
Condition	**Photos**	**Movies**	**Docs**	**Bank**	**All**	**N**
Proposal	**12%**	6%	5%	2%	75%	302
Chrome 36	**14%**	7%	4%	2%	73%	303
IE 11	**10%**	7%	7%	3%	73%	302
Safari 7	**13%**	5%	5%	4%	73%	304
Firefox 31	**11%**	7%	6%	2%	74%	302
bankofamerica.com						
Condition	**Photos**	**Movies**	**Docs**	**Bank**	**All**	**N**
Proposal	3%	7%	8%	**18%**	65%	303
Chrome 36	6%	6%	9%	**18%**	62%	302
IE 11	4%	8%	8%	**19%**	51%	301
Safari 7	5%	8%	7%	**14%**	67%	301
Firefox 31	3%	5%	3%	**20%**	69%	302

Table 4. Responses to the data risk question. ("If you ignored this error on [website], what information might a hacker be able to see?")

Participants performed *worse than random chance* for all of the warnings except for our proposal. This suggests that the warning texts are counterproductive when describing the threat source. Although our proposal performed better than the alternatives, we still only achieved the same rate as random guessing. Substantial room for improvement remains.

Data Risk

Ideally, users should know specifically what data is at risk when they encounter an SSL warning. We provided a list of example data types ("passwords, messages, or credit cards") in the hopes that it would help respondents draw this inference. However, respondents overwhelmingly overestimated the scope of the risk.

We asked respondents what type of data would be at risk on facebook.com or bankofamerica.com. As Table 4 shows, a majority of respondents selected "All of the above" instead of the more specific responses. The intended responses — photos for facebook.com, bank statements for bankofamerica.com — were a distant second in popularity. The warning text did not significantly affect participants' ability to answer these questions precisely ($\chi^2 = 7.79, p = 0.955$; $\chi^2 = 22.72, p = 0.121$).

Some participants may have reasonably selected "All of the above" for the Facebook question because Facebook users can post movies in addition to photos. However, we do not believe that is why a majority of participants overestimated the risk. Participants could not reasonably make the same inference for Bank of America, yet participants responded similarly to that question.

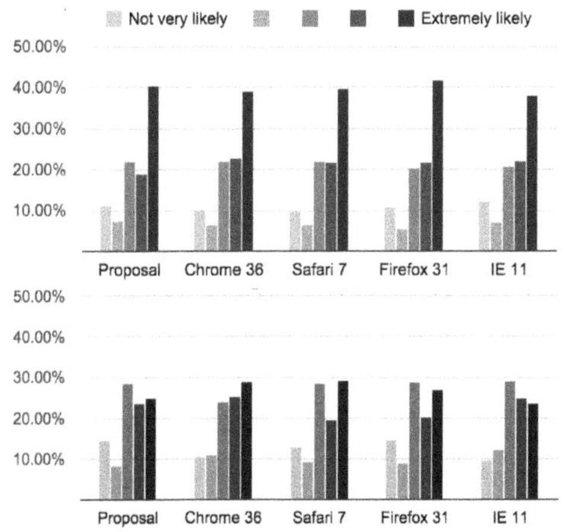

Figure 3. Responses to the false positive questions. Banking (top) and watching movies (bottom). ("If you ignored this error..., how likely is it that a hacker could...?")

False Positives

In prior work, interviewees told researchers that they thought SSL warnings were more likely to be false positives on banking websites [10, 38]. Although some individuals may hold this belief, our respondents in aggregate do not seem to. As Figure 3 shows, respondents rated an attack as more likely for a banking website than for a movie website. This relationship held true for all warning versions. We view this result with optimism, as it shows that participants have some ability to estimate the likelihood of a false positive.

Our proposal did not stand out from the alternatives. The warning version did not significantly affect responses to the banking question ($\chi^2 = 4.306, p = 0.9983$).

Discussion

None of the warning text that we tested — including our proposal — succeeded at our primary goal of comprehension for all three metrics. This suggests a need for future work on improving SSL warning comprehension.

We had hoped that following best practices would yield a dramatic improvement in comprehension. This did not happen, apart from a modest increase on the threat source metric. Why didn't we see more of an improvement?

Not all best practices can be simultaneously satisfied, which meant that we had to make tradeoffs. In particular, it is challenging to design text that is brief, simple, and non-technical while also specific and comprehensive. We chose to emphasize brevity and simplicity, but the optimal warning text for comprehension might be longer or more technical. In future work, researchers could explore different points in this space (e.g., technical and brief vs. non-technical and long).

There are other recommendations that we did not pursue but might prove fruitful. One avenue is a more concrete illustration that explains an SSL warning. For example, one could illustrate an eavesdropper listening to a connection between a client and server. Another option is to make the warning highly specific to the situation, for example by displaying the user's Facebook credentials in the warning if the error is for facebook.com.

ADHERENCE

Since we could not achieve high comprehension rates, we hoped to at least accomplish our secondary goal: guide users to act in a conservatively safe manner. We ran a large-scale, controlled field experiment in Google Chrome to measure how warning design affects adherence rates. Following this experiment, one of our proposals was released as the new SSL warning for Google Chrome.

Methodology

We deployed experimental SSL warnings on pre-release versions of Google Chrome and observed how they affected adherence. Figure 4 shows the experimental conditions.

Hypotheses

Our proposal is designed to promote the safe choice. In contrast, the Google Chrome 36 warning presents the safe and unsafe choices as visual equals. We hypothesized that the Google Chrome 36 warning ($Cond_A$) would have lower adherence rates than our proposal ($Cond_C$).

We wanted to test the influence of opinionated design, but we were faced with a confound: $Cond_C$ has both new text and a more opinionated design. To address this, we created $Cond_B$: our proposed new text, in the less opinionated Chrome 36 design. By comparing $Cond_A$ to $Cond_B$, we could see how much of the difference was due to the text.

We also experimented with the warning's background color. Following ANSI standards, we initially planned to associate the SSL warning with a bright yellow color. However, this came close to failing accessibility guidelines for contrast on computer screens. We tested both yellow and gray backgrounds. If the yellow background ($Cond_D$) resulted in a higher adherence rate in the pre-release experiment, we would have adjusted the design to improve the contrast.

Experimental Platform

We pseudorandomly assigned a small fraction of pre-release Google Chrome users (Canary and Dev channels) to receive the experimental warnings. By default, pre-release users participate in a statistical reporting program to help identify regressions and test new features in Chrome. Their clients periodically send pseudonymous statistical reports to Google Chrome servers, including information such as whether the user clicked through any SSL warnings. Chrome tags the reports by experimental condition, allowing us to measure the adherence rate per condition. All of the conditions ran at the same time from June 24 – July 24, 2014. We limited the experiment to English.

Some release users also choose to opt in to statistical reporting. Once Google Chrome adopted $Cond_C$ as its new SSL warning, we used the statistical reports to measure how release users responded to the new warning. We measured adherence rates for the new SSL warning twice: from August 26 – September 20, 2014 (right after the release of Chrome 37), and from December 7, 2014 – January 4, 2015.

Study Ethics

A change to a warning carries a risk that the new warning might be less effective. However, users experience this same

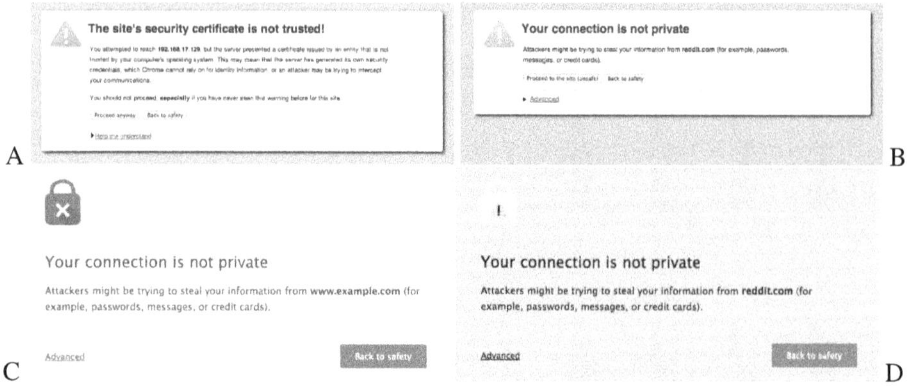

Figure 4. Conditions for our field experiment. *A* is the Chrome 36 warning, and *C* is the Chrome 37 warning.

risk every time the Chrome team modifies a warning. We included only conditions that we thought would improve adherence, and we monitored the experiment closely to ensure it did not decrease adherence. If any of the conditions had decreased adherence, we would have halted the experiment.

Chrome's statistical reports are pseudonymous, and our experiment did not involve any personally identifiable information. The reports did *not* include any information about what websites triggered the SSL warnings. Users can opt out of statistical reporting at any time in Chrome settings.

Our experiment went through an internal experimental review process before it launched.

Limitations

We do not know whether the warning impressions were due to real attacks or false positives. Our overall goal is adherence, but we cannot calculate whether adherence is higher or lower during real attacks.

One possible experimental confound is the effect of novelty. Over time, users become accustomed to seeing — and disregarding — the same warning [12, 39]. Consequently, they may no longer pay much attention to it. A new warning can interrupt this rote behavior and gain user attention. It is therefore possible that our new warnings have a higher adherence rate simply because they are novel. However, SSL warnings are relatively rare events for most users; our statistical reports suggest that most users see one or fewer SSL warnings a month. Furthermore, we monitored the warning on release channels from August 2014 to January 2015. We did not see any change in adherence over time. This suggests that the improvement in adherence is not due solely to novelty.

Another consideration is the bias introduced by demographics. The release and pre-release versions of Google Chrome have different demographics. Early adopters seek out the pre-release versions of Chrome for early access to bleeding-edge features. As such, it is possible that they react differently to warnings than the general population. However, the adherence rates for $Cond_C$ were similar across pre-release and release versions. This suggests that the two populations might also react similarly to the other warning conditions, although we cannot be sure. We do not wish to test the other conditions on release users now that we believe the other conditions are more likely to result in users becoming the victims of attacks.

	Text	Design	Adherence	N
A	Original	Original	30.9%	4,551
B	Proposed	Original	32.1%	4,075
C	Proposed	Proposed (gray)	58.3%	4,633
D	Proposed	Proposed (yellow)	53.3%	4,528

Table 5. Adherence rates from the field experiment.

Results

Opinionated Design

Opinionated design substantially improved adherence. As Table 5 shows, our opinionated proposal ($Cond_C$) yielded a higher adherence rate than the older warning ($Cond_A$): 58.3% vs. 30.9%. This is a substantial increase of nearly 30 percentage points. On some days, that could amount to more than a million Google Chrome warning impressions. We attribute this improvement to the change in design and not to the change in text. The proposed text in the old design ($Cond_B$) increased the adherence rate by only 1.2%, which is a very small change.[5]

Following the experiment, $Cond_C$ was adopted as the new warning for Google Chrome. We monitored the adherence rate as the new warning rolled out, to ensure that release users also responded favorably. Indeed, the new warning improved adherence rates among release users who participate in statistical reporting. During the last month of Google Chrome 36, the adherence rate was 37% for 24,747,395 impressions. After the release of Google Chrome 37 in August 2014, the adherence rate increased to 62% for 20,214,251 impressions. Several months later, the adherence rate remained high at 61% for an additional 26,529,405 impressions.

Color Scheme

Contrary to our expectations, the yellow version of our proposal ($Cond_D$) performed worse than the gray version ($Cond_C$) by five percentage points (53.3% vs. 58.3%). We did not pursue the yellow background color further.

[5] A careful reader may note that the unsafe button is slightly larger in $Cond_B$ than $Cond_A$, due to differences in string lengths. This presents us with two possibilities: the text did not influence decision making, or did influence their decision making but the larger button size counteracted the effect. Either possibility supports the finding that opinionated design (using button appearance and visibility) increases adherence.

Discussion

We dramatically improved adherence rates with design cues that (a) promote the safe choice and (b) demote the unsafe choice. This demonstrates that opinionated design can substantially change how users react to browser security warnings. Our results therefore support prior researchers' recommendations [20, 38, 40]. Other warning designers may wish to adopt opinionated designs, if they have not already.

One remaining concern pertains to button visibility. Some users might miss the "Advanced" link and think it is impossible to click through the new warning. Some might switch browsers to proceed. We want to improve adherence rates by convincing users — not by confusing, frustrating, or tricking them. Unfortunately, we have no way to directly measure how many users grow frustrated or switch browsers. Instead, we have been monitoring the Google Chrome help center for complaints about the new design. Thus far, we have not seen complaints from users who could not find the link to proceed. However, warning designers should remain vigilant that excessively complex warnings might have this side effect. Other warning designers may want to consider less aggressive forms of opinionated design that do not completely hide the option to proceed.

To our surprise, our proposed text did not affect adherence rates even though it moderately improved threat source comprehension. We hope that future work will explore this topic further: how are comprehension and adherence related for SSL warnings? Within the same population, will improving comprehension increase (or decrease) adherence? Studying this question for the general population is different from separating users into expert and non-expert populations, as prior researchers have done [1, 10].

CONCLUSION

We proposed and evaluated a new SSL warning, which was released for Google Chrome 37. Our proposal dramatically improved adherence rates: from 31% to 58% in a controlled field experiment, and from 37% to 62% in the field following the release of the new warning. The increased adherence rate has held for more than four months after the release. Based on the results of our controlled field experiment, we attribute the improvement to our use of opinionated design. This demonstrates the potential power of opinionated design in helping users make safe security decisions.

Unfortunately, comprehension rates remain lower than desired for all of the SSL warning texts that we tested. This is disappointing, as we view comprehension as more important than adherence. We attempted to follow best practices for both adherence and comprehension, and we were surprised that this strategy yielded success for adherence but not comprehension. We attribute the low comprehension rates to the difficulty of creating an SSL warning that is simultaneously brief, non-technical, simple, and specific. Future work might improve comprehension by determining which pieces of advice are the most important. We urge readers to further pursue this line of research and develop understandable warnings.

GREETZ TO:

Chris Palmer, Glen Murphy, Ryan Sleevi, and Pariza Tabriz for their dedication to making security more usable; and to Ed Chi and Ulfar Erlingsson for their feedback on this project.

REFERENCES

1. Akhawe, D., and Felt, A. P. Alice in Warningland: A Large-Scale Field Study of Browser Security Warning Effectiveness. In *USENIX Security Symposium* (2013).
2. Almuhimedi, H., Felt, A. P., Reeder, R. W., and Consolvo, S. Your Reputation Precedes You: History, Reputation, and the Chrome Malware Warning. In *SOUPS* (2014).
3. Anderson, R. E., and Jolson, M. A. Technical wording in advertising: implications for market segmentation. *Journal of Marketing 44* (1980).
4. ANSI. Product safety signs and labels: Z535.4.
5. Arron, J., Egans, R., and Mela, D. Paradoxical Effect of a Nutrition Labeling Scheme in a Student Cafeteria. *Nutritional Research 15* (September 1995).
6. Bauer, L., Bravo-Lillo, C., Cranor, L. F., and Fragkaki, E. Warning design guidelines (cmu-cylab-13-002).
7. Biddle, R., van Oorschot, P., Patrick, A. S., Sobey, J., and Whalen, T. Browser interfaces and extended validation ssl certificates: an empirical study. In *ACM Workshop on Cloud Computing Security* (2009).
8. Braun, C. C., Greeno, B., and Silter, N. C. Differences in behavioral compliance as a function of warning color. In *Human Factors and Ergonomics Society Annual Meeting* (1998).
9. Bravo-Lillo, C., Cranor, L., Komanduri, S., Schechter, S., and Sleeper, M. Harder to ignore?: Revisiting pop-up fatigue and approaches to prevent it. In *SOUPS* (2014).
10. Bravo-Lillo, C., Cranor, L. F., Downs, J., and Komanduri, S. Bridging the gap in computer security warnings: A mental model approach. *IEEE Security and Privacy 9*, 2 (2011).
11. Bravo-Lillo, C., Cranor, L. F., Downs, J., Komanduri, S., Reeder, R. W., Schechter, S., and Sleeper, M. Your attention please: Designing security-decision uis to make genuine risks harder to ignore. In *SOUPS* (2013).
12. Breznitz, S. Cry Wolf: The Psychology of False Alarms.
13. Bzostek, J. A., and Wogalter, M. S. Measuring visual search time for a product warning label as a function of icon, color, column, and vertical placement. In *Human Factors and Ergonomics Society Annual Meeting* (1999).
14. Dhamija, R., Tygar, J. D., and Hearst, M. A. Why phishing works. In *CHI* (2006).
15. Edworthy, J., and Adams, A. *Warning design: a research perspective*. Taylor and Francis, 1996.
16. Egelman, S., Cranor, L. F., and Hong, J. You've been warned: an empirical study of the effectiveness of web browser phishing warnings. In *CHI* (2008).

17. Egelman, S., and Schechter, S. The importance of being earnest [in security warnings]. In *Financial Cryptography and Data Security*, Lecture Notes in Computer Science. Springer Berlin Heidelberg, 2013.
18. Felt, A. P., Reeder, R. W., Almuhimedi, H., and Consolvo, S. Experimenting At Scale With Google Chrome's SSL Warning. In *CHI* (2014).
19. Fischhoff, B., Riley, D., Kovacs, D. C., and Small, M. What information belongs in a warning? *Psychology Marketing 15*, 7 (1998).
20. Frantz, J. P. Effect of location and procedural explicitness on user process of and compliance with product warnings. *Human Factors 36* (1994).
21. Frutiger, A. *Signs and symbols: their design and meaning*. Von Nostrand Reinhold, 1989.
22. Glover, B. L., and Wogalter, M. S. Using a computer simulated world to study behavior compliance with warnings: effect of salience and gender. In *Human Factors Society Annual Meeting* (1997).
23. Hancock, H., Bowles, C. T., Rogers, W. A., and Fisk, A. D. Comprehension and retention of warning information. *Handbook of warnings* (2006).
24. Hartley, J. *Designing instructional text*, 3 ed. Kagan Page and Nichols, 1994.
25. Kalsher, M. J., Wogalter, M. S., and Racicot, B. M. Pharmaceutical container labels and warnings: preference and perceived readability of alternative designs and pictorials. *International Journal of Industrial Ergonomics 18* (1996).
26. Laughery, K. R., and Stanush, J. A. Effects of warning explicitness on product perceptions. In *Human Factors Society* (1989).
27. Laughery, K. R., and Vaubel, K. P. Explicitness in consequence information in warnings. *Safety Science 16* (1993).
28. Laughery, K. R., Young, S. L., Vaubel, K. P., and Brelsford, J. W. The noticeability of warnings on alcoholic beverage containers. *Journal of Public Policy and Marketing 12* (1993).
29. McDonald, P., Mohebbi, M., and Slatkin, B. Comparing Google Consumer Surveys to Existing Probability and Non-Probability Based Internet Survey. In *Google Whitepaper* (2012).
30. McLaughlin, G. H. Smog grading — a new readability formula. *Journal of Reading* (1969).
31. Morrow, D. G., Hier, C. M., Mendard, W. E., and Leirer, V. O. Icons improve older and younger adults' comprehension of medication information. *Journal of Gerontology: Psychological Sciences 53B* (1998).
32. Reeder, R., Kowalczyk, E. C., and Shostack, A. Poster: Helping engineers design NEAT security warnings. In *SOUPS* (2011).
33. Research, P. A Comparison of Results from Surveys by the Pew Research Center and Google Consumer Surveys.
34. Schechter, S. E., Dhamija, R., Ozment, A., and Fischer, I. The emperor's new security indicators. In *IEEE Symposium on Security and Privacy* (2007).
35. Schwanda-Sosik, V., Bursztein, E., , Consolvo, S., Huffaker, D. A., Kossinets, G., Liao, K., McDonald, P., and Sedley, A. Online Microsurveys for User Experience Research. In *CHI (Extended Abstracts)* (2014).
36. Silver, N., Leonard, D. C., Ponsi, K. A., and Wogalter, M. S. Warnings and purchase intentions for pest-control products. *Forensic Reports 4* (1991).
37. Sotirakopoulos, A., Hawkey, K., and Beznosov, K. On the Challenges in Usable Security Lab Studies: Lessons Learned from Replicating a Study on SSL Warnings. In *SOUPS* (2011).
38. Sunshine, J., Egelman, S., Almuhimedi, H., Atri, N., and Cranor, L. F. Crying Wolf: An Empirical Study of SSL Warning Effectiveness. In *USENIX Security Symposium* (2009).
39. Thorley, P., Hellier, E., and Edworthy, J. Habituation effects in visual warnings. *Contemporary ergonomics* (2001).
40. Trommelen, M. Effectiveness of explicit warnings. *Safety Science 25* (1997).

A Spoonful of Sugar? The Impact of Guidance and Feedback on Password-Creation Behavior

Richard Shay, Lujo Bauer, Nicolas Christin, Lorrie Faith Cranor, Alain Forget, Saranga Komanduri, Michelle L. Mazurek*, William Melicher, Sean M. Segreti, Blase Ur

Carnegie Mellon University
Pittsburgh, PA
{rshay, lbauer, nicolasc, lorrie, aforget, sarangak, billy, ssegreti, bur}@cmu.edu

*University of Maryland
College Park, MD
mmazurek@cs.umd.edu

ABSTRACT
Users often struggle to create passwords under strict requirements. To make this process easier, some providers present real-time feedback during password creation, indicating which requirements are not yet met. Other providers guide users through a multi-step password-creation process. Our 6,435-participant online study examines how feedback and guidance affect password security and usability. We find that real-time password-creation feedback can help users create strong passwords with fewer errors. We also find that although guiding participants through a three-step password-creation process can make creation easier, it may result in weaker passwords. Our results suggest that service providers should present password requirements with feedback to increase usability. However, the presentation of feedback and guidance must be carefully considered, since identical requirements can have different security and usability effects depending on presentation.

Author Keywords
Passwords; Password-composition policies; Security policy; Usable security; Authentication

ACM Classification Keywords
D.4.6 Management Of Computing and Information Systems: Security and Protection—*Authentication*

INTRODUCTION
Service providers ask for complex passwords. For example, Yahoo requires passwords with at least eight characters and multiple character classes.[1] Users often have difficulty meeting complex password requirements and resort to predictable and insecure choices, such as appending digits or symbols, or including common substrings or keyboard patterns [15, 16, 19]. Some service providers now offer *requirements feedback*: real-time password-creation feedback telling users whether they have met the requirements, such as green check marks indicating satisfied requirements (Figure 1). Other service providers offer *guidance*: walking users through a multi-step password-creation process (Figure 2).

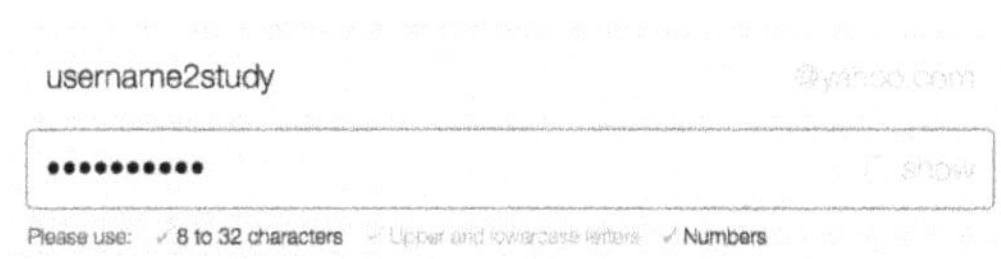

Figure 1: Yahoo's real-time password-creation feedback.

In this paper, we present the first analysis of the usability of requirements feedback and guidance mechanisms. Prior work has considered the security and usability effects of complex password-composition requirements [9] and examined feedback specifically in the context of password meters that provide estimates of password strength [3, 17]. We studied techniques intended to help users successfully navigate difficult requirements. Using a 6,435-participant, between-subjects online study, we considered real-time requirements feedback for three strict composition policies. For one policy, we examined two approaches to multi-step password-creation. In *guidance*, we guided participants to enhance a simple password by adding components until it met all requirements. In *insertion*, inspired by Forget et al. [5], participants created a simple password and the system inserted random characters. We tested how these approaches affect users' ability to create conforming passwords quickly and correctly, users' perceptions of these approaches, and how the approaches impact the security and memorability of the resulting passwords.

We found that requirements feedback helped participants create passwords meeting strict requirements without making errors, and in some cases gave participants more confidence in the strength of their passwords. Passwords created with requirements feedback were as strong as those without. Thus, requirements feedback may help make complex password-composition requirements more palatable to users.

Compared to having participants create a password under a strict policy in a single step, both the guidance and inser-

[1] `https://edit.yahoo.com/registration`

CHI 2015, Apr 18-23 2015, Seoul, Republic of Korea
ACM 978-1-4503-3145-6/15/04.
`http://dx.doi.org/10.1145/2702123.2702586`

Figure 2: Dashlane's multi-step password-creation process.

tion techniques led to a reduction in password security. While user sentiment toward the process of creating passwords with guidance was more positive than creating a password without guidance, the resulting passwords were less likely to exceed the stated requirements and more likely to be cracked after a large number of guesses. Likewise, randomly inserting a few characters into passwords leaves them vulnerable to having those characters brute-forced. Overall, our results demonstrate that looking only at password requirements is insufficient. The presentation of those requirements can affect usability and security.

Next, we present related work and then our research questions and methodology. Then, we discuss our results and their practical implications.

RELATED WORK

Password-composition policies often include requirements on character length and content. Furnell found that the password restrictions of 10 popular websites were highly variable and sometimes conflicted [6, 7]. Recent studies compared the usability and security of passwords adhering to various policies. Many such studies collect passwords from the crowdsourcing service Amazon Mechanical Turk (MTurk). In one of our previous studies, we compared the security and usability of various password policies that required more characters than is typical in practice. We found that some policies requiring longer passwords led to more usable and secure passwords than a more typical policy that required fewer characters but had other more complex requirements. However, security suffered when participants placed required uppercase letters, digits, and symbols at the start and end of their passwords, and included common substrings and keyboard patterns [15]. Our current research builds on this work by examining mechanisms intended to make password requirements that prevent such predictable behavior easier for users to handle.

Several studies explored how to encourage users to choose more secure passwords. Furnell and Bär found that users chose more secure passwords when presented with text advice or a password-strength meter [8]. We found that more stringent-scoring meters effectively led to stronger passwords, but at the cost of usability [17]. Egelman et al. found that the mere presence of a password meter led to more secure passwords, but only for valued accounts [3]. Rather than providing feedback in the form of a password-strength meter, our research evaluates the impact of providing real-time feedback on compliance with requirements.

Forget et al. explored persuading users to create more secure passwords by adding random characters to user-created passwords. Users could *shuffle* to have a different set of random characters placed at different locations. The authors found that inserting two characters increased password security without perceptibly affecting usability. Adding more than two characters resulted in decreased usability but no more security, since users would select weaker pre-improvement passwords to compensate for the increased memory load of additional characters [5]. Our research builds on this with a condition that also inserts random characters into participants' passwords. We use a much larger sample size, and test recall after a few days as well as a few minutes.

Moshfeghian and Ryu found that many popular websites poorly present password restrictions. The authors suggest best practices for password-creation design. Their advice includes placing password guidance and feedback in clear and concise language in close proximity to password fields, providing real-time feedback to reduce failed attempts, using red-colored feedback for unfulfilled requirements, and using globally recognizable visual elements (e.g., green check marks) to communicate feedback [12]. Our study's presentation of password requirements follows these best practices and provides empirical evidence of their effectiveness.

RESEARCH QUESTIONS

Our four research questions examine how strict password requirements can be made more usable through visual elements, requirements feedback, guidance, and automatic insertion of random characters. Our *base* set of strict requirements requires that passwords contain at least 12 characters and three character classes (three of either lowercase letters, uppercase letters, digits, or symbols).

Question Q_1**:** *How do the blacklist and pattern requirements affect password security and usability when applied to strict requirements?* The *blacklist* requirement prohibits passwords from containing any substring in a blacklist. *Pattern* requires that passwords begin and end with a lowercase letter. These requirements are grounded in prior work that has found users often include common substrings in passwords, and often begin and end them with required non-lowercase character classes [15]. Based on previous findings [9, 15], we expected adding either requirement to the base requirement would increase strength and decrease usability.

Question Q_2**:** *Does an organization-branded look-and-feel help users create or recall passwords with strict requirements?* We collected data in two conditions that displayed the same information and had the same requirements, but differed in their branding and text color. Our base condition took its look-and-feel from Carnegie Mellon University, including its wordmark and red-and-white color scheme, while the base-plain condition used default black-and-white HTML rendering without a logo or wordmark. We wondered whether the distinct visuals of the former may help participants recall their passwords, perhaps by acting as a memory cue. This has real-world implications because users often create and subsequently recall passwords on websites with distinct branding, and select predictable passwords based on visual cues [2].

Question Q_3**:** *How does requirements feedback affect password creation, recall, and strength when applied to strict password requirements?* We compared sets of conditions that differed only in whether participants received real-time requirements-compliance feedback during password creation. We examined the effects of this requirements feedback on password security and usability.

Question Q_4**:** *Does a three-step password-creation process, using either guidance or insertion, make it easier to create passwords that have strict requirements?* We compared three conditions with the base and pattern requirements that included requirements feedback. One condition asked participants to create passwords in a single step, while two conditions used three steps. In one of the three-step conditions, we guided participants through a password-creation process (guidance) such that they created a simple password and then were asked to add more characters. In the other three-step condition, participants created a simple password and then we randomly inserted two more characters (insertion).

METHODOLOGY

In this section, we discuss our data collection and analysis procedures, which were approved by our institutional review board. Our experimental protocol is based on a protocol used successfully to contrast password-composition policies in prior research [9, 15].

We conducted an online between-subjects study on Amazon's Mechanical Turk crowdsourcing service (MTurk) in two parts. Participants were informed that this would be a two-part study with additional compensation for completing both parts. We paid participants 55 cents for completing *Part One* and 70 cents for completing *Part Two*. In Part One, we asked participants to imagine they were creating a new password for their email account. The requirements and feedback varied by condition. Participants then completed a short survey before we asked them to recall their password. In Part Two, we emailed participants two days later and invited them to recall their password and complete a second survey.

Except when looking at dropout rates, our analysis includes only participants who completed Part One. For metrics specific to Part Two, we consider only participants who returned

Condition	Pattern	Blacklist	Feedback	Brand	Three-step
Base				University	
$Base_{rt}$			✓	University	
Blacklist		✓		University	
$Blacklist_{rt}$		✓	✓	University	
Base-plain				Plain	
Pattern	✓			University	
$Pattern_{rt}$	✓		✓	University	
Guide	✓		✓	University	Participant adds
Insert	✓		✓	University	System adds

Table 1: Requirements of each condition. All require at least 12 characters and three character classes. Pattern requires starting and ending with lowercase letters. The blacklist requirement prohibits certain substrings in passwords. Three-step uses a multiple-step process to create the password.

and completed Part Two within three days of being sent the follow-up invitation. Thus, all Part Two participants had created their passwords two to five days earlier. Our usability metrics included self-reported sentiment and how many attempts participants needed to create and recall their password. We also measured password strength using a state-of-the-art password cracker, as described below.

Conditions

Conditions, listed in Table 1, were assigned round-robin. They share the *base* requirements – that passwords have at least 12 characters and three character classes. Prior work suggests these are usable yet strong requirements [15].

Password Creation in One Step

Base used the base requirements. ***Pattern*** required passwords to begin and end with lowercase letters, as shown in Figure 3. ***Blacklist*** required that passwords not contain substrings from a 41,329-string blacklist. This blacklist was based on common substrings in cracked passwords in a prior study [15] and substrings we thought would be easily guessed. The blacklist prohibited:

- 123!, amazon, character, monkey
- number, survey, this, turk
- Any year between 1950 and 2049
- The same character four or more times in a row
- Any four consecutive characters from password
- Any four sequential digits
- Any four sequential letters in the alphabet
- Any four consecutive characters on the keyboard

$\boldsymbol{Base_{rt}}$, $\boldsymbol{Blacklist_{rt}}$, and $\boldsymbol{Pattern_{rt}}$ are analogues of the above conditions, except they employ requirements feedback. As participants entered their passwords, listed requirements were accompanied with either a green check mark (for a fulfilled requirement) or a red message indicating why the requirement is not fulfilled. Figure 4 shows $Pattern_{rt}$. To keep these conditions similar to their analogous conditions without requirements feedback, participants were permitted to submit non-compliant passwords (and then were told that they would have to try again to create a compliant password).

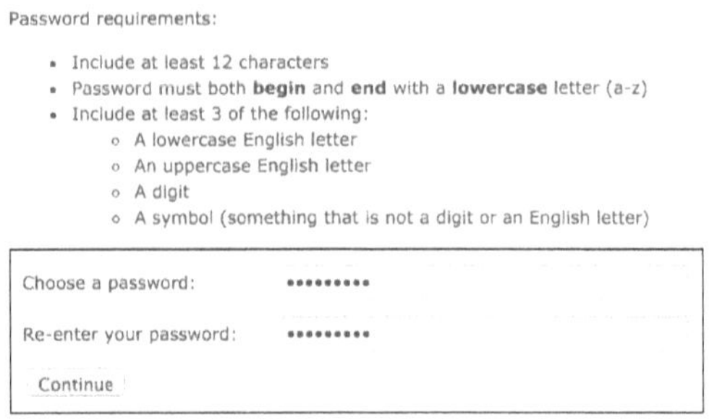

Figure 3: Password-requirements presentation for *Pattern* as "password!" is entered.

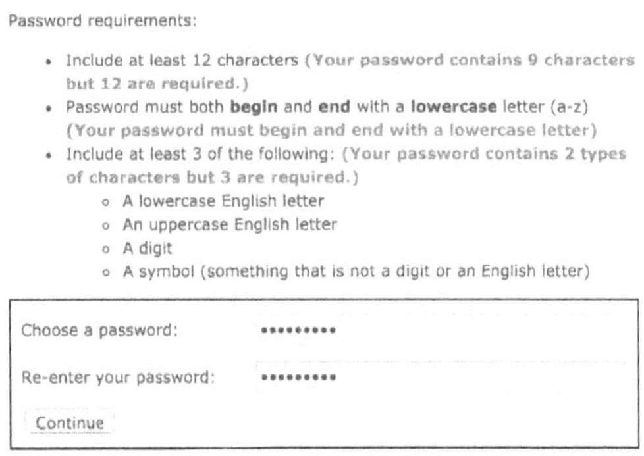

Figure 4: Password-requirements presentation for $Pattern_{rt}$ as "password!" is entered.

All conditions except ***Base-plain*** were displayed with Carnegie Mellon University's branding (colors, fonts, and wordmark). *Base-plain* is identical to *Base*, except it employs no branding, instead using default black-and-white HTML rendering, in order to address Q_2.

Password Creation in Three Steps

Two conditions – ***Guide*** and ***Insert*** – employed a three-step password-creation process. Both used requirements feedback and led to passwords meeting the same requirements as $Pattern_{rt}$. Figures 5 and 6 show the first two steps of *Guide* and *Insert*. The main difference between them is that *Insert* has a step in which the system randomly inserts characters into the password, while *Guide* instructs participants to insert additional characters.

In *Step 1*, we asked participants, "To start, please enter a password with at least 10 characters. It can be a word, and it needs to start and end with a lowercase letter." In *Step 2*, passwords were enhanced to meet the requirements of *Pattern*. In *Guide*, participants were shown their password in an editable text field and asked to enhance the password until meeting the requirements. In the second step for *Insert*, participants were shown their system-enhanced password, with the two newly added characters in green text. Below, participants were shown a text box with their non-enhanced password in plaintext, and were asked to modify it to match what was above. Finally, in *Step 3*, we asked participants to confirm their passwords in a blank password text field.

Figure 5: The first two steps of password creation in *Guide*.

Figure 6: The first two steps of password creation in *Insert*.

To insert two random characters in *Insert*, we first selected two characters of two different character classes, chosen from nine symbols $@!\$ * \#. - \&\_$, eight digits, and 24 uppercase letters (removing *O*, *0*, *I*, and *1*, since they may be confused with each other). We then inserted these characters between the first ten characters of the initial password. There are 960 different ways to choose characters of two different character classes from these three sets (with order mattering). There are 45 different ways to select two spaces between the first ten characters. Thus, there are $960 \times 45 = 43,200$ different ways of inserting characters.

Statistical Testing

We perform omnibus tests to detect whether our conditions differ from one another. When they do, we perform a set of corrected pairwise tests. Rather than testing each pair of conditions, we test selected pairs to help answer our research questions. The pairwise comparisons are as follows.

Q_1: *Base–Blacklist*; *Base–Pattern*; *Blacklist–Pattern*
Q_2: *Base–Base-plain*

Q_3: *Base–Base*$_{rt}$; *Blacklist–Blacklist*$_{rt}$; *Pattern–Pattern*$_{rt}$
Q_4: *Pattern*$_{rt}$*–Guide*; *Pattern*$_{rt}$*–Insert*

We use a significance level $\alpha = .05$. Quantitative tests use Kruskal-Wallis (KW) for omnibus testing and Holm-Bonferroni-corrected (HC) Mann-Whitney U (MW) for pairwise testing. For their effect size, we used the "common language effect size" [10]. This is the probability that a random participant from one condition has a more favorable value than a random participant from the other condition. If they have the same value, a coin flip determines the winner. Categorical comparisons use the Chi Square test for omnibus comparisons and Holm-Bonferroni-corrected Fisher's Exact Test (FET) for pairwise comparisons. For effect size, we calculate the odds ratio for each significant pairwise comparison.

Measuring Password Strength

To measure password strength, we calculated *guess numbers* [9] for each password. A guess number is an estimate of the number of guesses that an attacker would require to guess successfully a participant's study password. This simulates an offline attack, in which an attacker has stolen a hashed password file and can make a number of guesses bounded only by computation speed and hardware availability. A sophisticated attacker will start by guessing the most likely passwords and proceed in order of decreasing probability. To generate guess numbers, we used the probabilistic context-free grammar (PCFG) password-cracking technique introduced by Weir et al. [20] and updated in subsequent work [9, 15]. The PCFG algorithm trains on structures and character strings from existing password corpora, creating a lookup table up to a certain given number of guesses. We trained the cracker on public data including words from the Google corpus [1], the Openwall cracking dictionary,[2] and the leaked MySpace [13] and RockYou [18] datasets. We also trained our strings on passwords collected during previous passwords-research studies.

We used the PCFG algorithm to make guesses with at least twelve characters and three character classes, as required by all of our conditions. Some of our conditions required passwords to begin and end with a lowercase letter; these were trained as a separate group and only made guesses starting and ending with a lowercase letter. We divided each group of passwords into two subsets and used one as training data to crack the other (two *folds*). This simulated an attacker with access to passwords created under similar requirements. We generated at least 2×10^{13} guesses per condition.

Insert asked participants to create a password of at least ten characters that started and ended with a lowercase letter. The system then added random characters of 43,200 different possible combinations. The traditional PCFG approach was ineffective against *Insert*, cracking only one password after 10^{12} guesses. We then used a better-targeted approach for our security results. We used the PCFG algorithm to crack the pre-enhancement passwords, and then multiplied the number of guesses by 43,200. This simulated an attacker who knows the random-character insertion algorithm and brute-forces through all possible permutations.

[2] `openwall.org`

Limitations

Limitations of our method of studying password-composition policies have been discussed in prior papers employing a similar approach [9,15]. As with any MTurk study, there is a concern about external validity, since participants created passwords for use only within the context of the study, and thus the passwords held little value to participants. However, two recent studies suggest that experimental studies may be a reasonable way to examine actual password behavior. Mazurek et al. contrasted characteristics of MTurk studies with genuine university passwords. They found that study passwords were very similar to university passwords across a number of metrics, suggesting that MTurk passwords were viable for learning about actual user behavior [11]. Fahl et al. also compared genuine university passwords with study passwords and found that the password sets resembled each other [4].

Our methodology is also temporally limited. We looked at password recall after a few minutes and after a few days. Actual password usage can involve using a password long after its creation, which we did not examine. We did not test every possible permutation of password requirements, guidance, and feedback. It is possible that other feedback formats would interact differently with other sets of requirements. In addition, we only tested one example of guidance and one of insertion. Our branding only included plain branding and that of a university. It is possible that some more dramatic branding scheme would have made a bigger difference.

RESULTS

This section presents our findings. We discuss our participants, followed by password strength, and then usability results for password creation and recall. Table 2 summarizes results for password creation, Table 3 summarizes password characteristics, and Table 4 presents other study metrics.

Participants

We collected data in May and June 2014; 7,262 participants began our study and 6,435 finished Part One. We invited those who finished Part One to return for Part Two. 3,934 total participants finished Part Two within three days of being invited.

Among our 6,435 Part One participants, the median age was 28 years. 99.2% of participants disclosed their gender; 46.7% were male and 52.5% female. 95.7% stated their highest degree; 45.9% held a Bachelor's degree or higher.

Participants in *Pattern*$_{rt}$ (84.7%) were less likely to finish Part One than those in *Guide* (90.8%) or *Insert* (93.8%) (HC FET, p=.001). The higher dropout rates may suggest greater user difficulty and frustration. 64.1% of participants who completed Part One returned for Part Two within five days and this did not vary by condition (χ^2_8=2.77, p=0.948). 95.3% of participants who started Part Two within five days finished, and this too did not vary by condition (χ^2_8=4.64, p=0.795).

	Creation errors			Creation time			Creation difficult			Creation annoying		
condition pairs	mean	p-val	effect	med (sec)	p-val	effect	% agree	p-val	effect	% agree	p-val	effect
Q1: Impact of blacklist and pattern requirements												
Base – Blacklist	0.7 – 0.8	.152	–	**61** – 88	<.001	0.665	**24** – 32	.002	1.536	55 – 61	.212	–
Base – Pattern	**0.7** – 1.5	<.001	0.651	**61** – 122	<.001	0.802	**24** – 50	<.001	3.17	**55** – 77	<.001	2.643
Blacklist – Pattern	**0.8** – 1.5	<.001	0.628	**88** – 122	<.001	0.655	**32** – 50	<.001	2.065	**61** – 77	<.001	2.115
Q2: Impact of branded look-and-feel												
Base – Base-plain	0.7 – **0.6**	.039	0.534	61 – 60	1	–	24 – 23	1	–	55 – 57	1	–
Q3: Impact of password-creation feedback												
Base – Base$_{rt}$	0.7 – **0.3**	<.001	0.635	61 – 60	1	–	24 – 22	1	–	55 – 55	1	–
Blacklist – Blacklist$_{rt}$	0.8 – **0.4**	<.001	0.632	88 – 86	.621	–	32 – 29	.618	–	61 – 56	.281	–
Pattern – Pattern$_{rt}$	1.5 – **0.6**	<.001	0.701	122 – **109**	.019	0.546	50 – 49	1	–	77 – 77	1	–
Q4: Impact of guiding and insertion through creation												
Guide – Pattern$_{rt}$	0.8 – 0.6	.114	–	116 – **109**	.036	0.54	**29** – 49	<.001	2.35	**67** – 77	<.001	1.622
Insert – Pattern$_{rt}$	0.7 – **0.6**	.023	0.537	**101** – 109	.019	0.545	**17** – 49	<.001	4.684	**45** – 77	<.001	3.912

Table 2: Password-creation metrics and comparisons. For each metric, we provide an average value, the result of a significance test, and the effect size (as described in the Methodology). For significant comparisons, the significantly better value is in bold.

	Exceed min class			Password length			Cracked after 2×10^{13} guesses			Storage		
condition pairs	%	p-val	effect	mean (char)	p-val	effect	%	p-val	effect	%	p-val	effect
Q1: Impact of blacklist and pattern requirements												
Base – Blacklist	71 – 67	.176	–	13.6 – 13.8	.285	–	28 – **21**	.012	1.474	49 – 57	.091	–
Base – Pattern	**71** – 57	<.001	1.844	13.6 – **14.1**	<.001	0.58	28 – **8**	<.001	4.323	**49** – 69	<.001	2.308
Blacklist – Pattern	**67** – 57	<.001	1.508	13.8 – **14.1**	.003	0.553	21 – **8**	<.001	2.933	**57** – 69	.003	1.649
Q2: Impact of branded look-and-feel												
Base – Base-plain	71 – 73	.449	–	13.6 – 13.5	1	–	28 – 30	.835	–	49 – 52	1	–
Q3: Impact of password-creation feedback												
Base – Base$_{rt}$	**71** – 53	<.001	2.174	13.6 – 13.6	1	–	28 – 30	.835	–	49 – 50	1	–
Blacklist – Blacklist$_{rt}$	**67** – 51	<.001	1.898	13.8 – 13.6	.285	–	21 – 24	.525	–	57 – 55	1	–
Pattern – Pattern$_{rt}$	**57** – 39	<.001	2.06	14.1 – 14.2	1	–	8 – 10	.525	–	69 – 61	.154	–
Q4: Impact of guiding and insertion through creation												
Guide – Pattern$_{rt}$	22 – **39**	<.001	2.267	13.8 – **14.2**	.008	0.547	16 – **10**	.02	1.582	62 – 61	1	–
Insert – Pattern$_{rt}$	15 – **39**	<.001	3.684	13.7 – **14.2**	<.001	0.562	29 – **10**	<.001	3.416	76 – **61**	<.001	1.962

Table 3: Password characteristics and comparisons. *Exceed min class* is exceeding the minimum number of character classes.

Password Strength

We observe an overall cracking rate of 21.7% after 2×10^{13} guesses, varying significantly by condition, as shown in Table 3. The percentage of passwords cracked after each guess is shown in Figure 7. As observed in Table 3, we found no effect of real-time requirements-compliance feedback on password strength (see Q_3). On the other hand, both *Pattern* and *Blacklist* performed better than *Base*, and *Pattern* performed better than *Blacklist* (see Q_1).

Passwords created under *Pattern*$_{rt}$ were significantly less likely to be cracked than those created under *Guide* or *Insert*. Thus our three-step password creation processes both decreased password strength compared to creating a password with the same requirements in a single step (see Q_4).

While *Insert* was vulnerable to the partial-brute-force approach described in the Methodology, it did perform well against a more traditional PCFG attack. Using a traditional PCFG approach, after 10^{12} guesses (we did not continue to 10^{13}), over 5% of each other condition had been cracked, compared to 0.1% of *Insert*. However, *Insert* appeared much weaker once we instead applied PCFG to its pre-splice passwords and multiplied the resulting guess numbers by the total number of splicings, 43,200, to simulate brute-forcing the possible splicings. We see that using a relatively small amount of random text to increase password strength is vulnerable to being brute-forced.

We used nine symbols, chosen to be distinct and easy to recognize. While increasing the number of symbols would have increased security, it would not have been substantial. Using 19 symbols rather than nine would have resulted in 72,000 insertion configurations instead of 43,200. Using 32 symbols would have led to 109,440 configurations. Using the same cracking technique, using 32 symbols would lead to a cracking rate of 26.1%, compared to the current 28.6%.

Exceeding Minimum Requirements

In addition to looking at results of the PCFG cracker, we looked at the structural components of passwords. While all passwords required 12 characters and three characters classes, participants were free to exceed either requirement.

Table 3 shows percentages of participants who exceeded the minimum three-character-class requirement. *Pattern*$_{rt}$ par-

	Finished Part One			Part One recall time			Part two recall attempts			Part two recall difficult		
condition pairs	%	p-val	effect	med (sec)	p-val	effect	mean	p-val	effect	% agree	p-val	effect
Q1: Impact of blacklist and pattern requirements												
Base – Blacklist	88 – 88	1	–	10 – 10	1	–	1.9 – 1.9	1	–	36 – 43	.368	–
Base – Pattern	88 – 84	.131	–	**10** – 11	<.001	0.568	1.9 – 1.7	.244	–	**36** – 54	<.001	2.087
Blacklist – Pattern	88 – 84	.131	–	**10** – 11	.004	0.554	1.9 – 1.7	.83	–	**43** – 54	.004	1.616
Q2: Impact of branded look-and-feel												
Base – Base-plain	88 – 91	.384	–	10 – 9	1	–	1.9 – 1.9	1	–	36 – 32	.944	–
Q3: Impact of password-creation feedback												
Base – Base$_{rt}$	88 – 89	1	–	10 – 10	1	–	1.9 – 1.9	1	–	36 – 35	.983	–
Blacklist – Blacklist$_{rt}$	88 – 89	1	–	10 – 10	1	–	1.9 – 2.0	1	–	43 – 40	.983	–
Pattern – Pattern$_{rt}$	84 – 85	1	–	11 – 11	1	–	1.7 – 1.7	1	–	54 – 46	.094	–
Q4: Impact of guiding and insertion through creation												
Guide – Pattern$_{rt}$	**91** – 85	.001	1.781	10 – 11	.181	–	2.0 – 1.7	.088	–	42 – 46	.944	–
Insert – Pattern$_{rt}$	**94** – 85	<.001	2.718	12 – 11	1	–	2.0 – 1.7	.146	–	53 – 46	.26	–

Table 4: User-behavior metrics and comparisons.

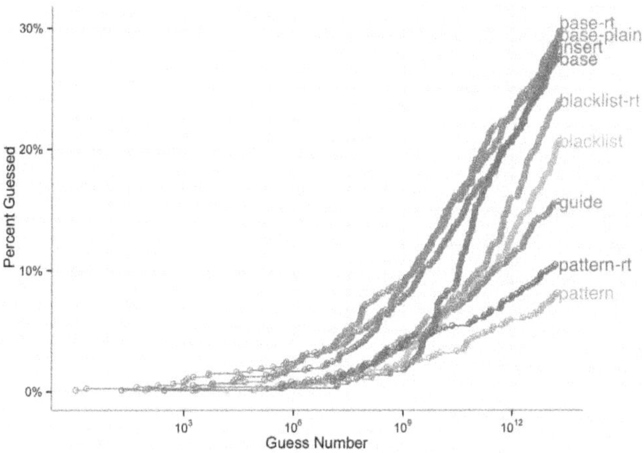

Figure 7: The percentage of passwords cracked in each condition by the number of guesses made in log scale. Our cutoff for guess numbers is 2×10^{13}. Table 3 shows comparisons.

ticipants were more likely to exceed the minimum than those in *Guide* or *Insert*. In addition, participants in all three real-time-feedback conditions were less likely to use four character classes than those in the same conditions without real-time feedback. This may be due to participants with real-time feedback feeling that they are "done" once they see the green check mark beside the requirement (see Q_3).

Although all conditions required a minimum of 12 characters, 59.1% of participants created longer passwords, with a mean password length of 13.8 characters. Length by condition and significant differences are shown in Table 3. While both *Guide* and *Insert* had shorter passwords than *Pattern$_{rt}$* (see Q_4), we did not see significant length differences between conditions with and without real-time feedback.

Previous work found that increasing password length by one lowercase letter makes a password 70% as likely to be guessed [11]. Thus, the length difference between *Pattern$_{rt}$* and the three-step conditions may contribute substantially to the security differences between these conditions.

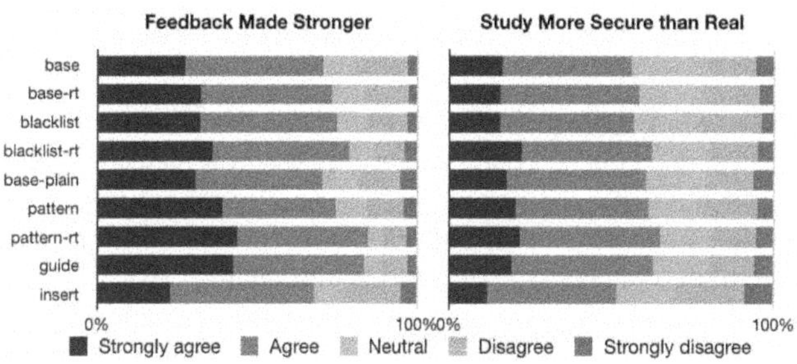

Figure 8: Participant agreement with "The feedback and instructions I saw while creating my password led me to create a stronger password than I would have otherwise." and "If my main email provider had the same password requirements as used in this study, my email account would be more secure."

User Perception of Password Strength

To measure perception of how feedback affected password security, we asked our participants whether they agreed with the statement, "The feedback and instructions I saw while creating my password led me to create a stronger password than I would have otherwise." Figure 8 shows the responses. The only significant pairwise differences were that *Pattern$_{rt}$* participants (84.3%) were more likely to agree than those in either *Pattern* (74.2%) or *Insert* (67.4%) (HC FET, p<.001). A possible explanation for the low agreement from *Insert* participants is that they anticipated creating a weaker initial password, because they expected to have its strength increased. Alternatively, they may not have perceived much security in adding two random characters (see Q_4).

We asked participants whether they agreed with, "If my main email provider had the same password requirements as used in this study, my email account would be more secure." Figure 8 shows responses. *Pattern$_{rt}$* participants (64.9%) were more likely to agree than *Insert* participants (51.2%) (HC FET, p<.001). 79.6% of participants indicated that their primary email account was from a web email provider. The low agreement is surprising because the study requirements are much more demanding than most web email providers.

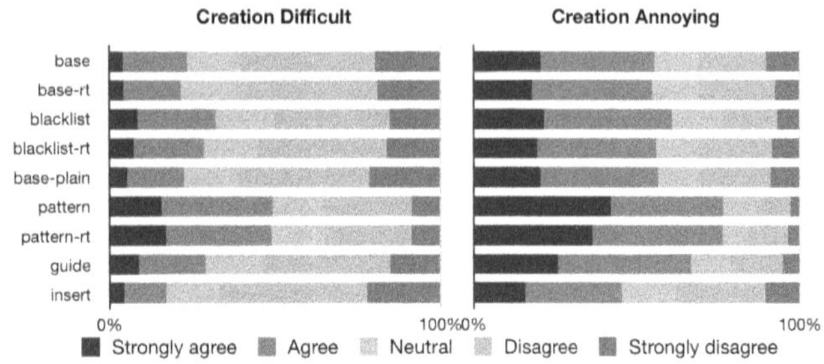

Figure 9: Participant agreement with "Creating a password that meets the requirements given in this study was difficult/annoying."

Usability

This section presents results for usability metrics and self-reported sentiment. We begin by focusing on the password-creation process, and then Part One and Part Two recall.

Password Creation

To understand password creation, we look at self-reported user sentiment, password-creation time, and how participants failed to create a password meeting their requirements. Then, we look at the effects of web-page branding.

Password-Creation Sentiment

Figure 9 illustrates participants' agreement with password creation being difficult and annoying respectively, with pairwise differences in agreement shown in Table 2. We did not detect any significant difference in perceived password-creation difficulty or annoyance between a condition and its real-time-feedback counterpart. Thus, our real-time feedback did not cause participants to perceive password creation as any more or less difficult or annoying (see Q_3). Creating a password under $Pattern_{rt}$ was both more difficult and more annoying than doing so under either *Guide* or *Insert*. This suggests that our three-step conditions reduced the difficulty and annoyance of the *pattern* requirement (see Q_4).

Password-Creation Time

Table 2 shows significant differences in how long participants took creating their passwords. $Pattern_{rt}$ took significantly less time than *Guide* but significantly more time than *Insert*. This may be due to the fact that *Insert* participants did not have to decide which special characters to include (see Q_4). Requirements feedback helped participants create passwords in $Pattern_{rt}$ more quickly than in *Pattern* (see Q_3).

Password-Creation Errors

Table 2 compares how many errors participants made while creating a password in each condition. We consider creation errors a metric of password-creation difficulty. We observe that requirements feedback helps participants successfully create a password with fewer errors for all three pairs of conditions with requirements feedback. This suggests that real-time requirements-compliance feedback helps participants to adhere to strict password requirements (see Q_3).

To understand the impact of guiding and insertion (see Q_4), we examined the errors participants made when creating passwords in each of our four conditions with the pattern requirement. *Pattern* had the highest error rate, with an average of 1.5 creation errors per participant. The most common error was failure to meet the pattern requirement, with an average of 1.1 such errors per participant. With the addition of real-time feedback, $Pattern_{rt}$ participants made significantly fewer errors: .6 overall errors and .3 pattern errors each. While *Guide* participants had a significantly lower dropout rate and reported finding password creation easier and less annoying than $Pattern_{rt}$ participants, they did not make significantly fewer errors or create their passwords more quickly. We saw similar sentiment improvements for *Insert* participants, and significant improvement in password-creation time, without a reduction in overall error rate. *Insert* participants averaged .7 errors and .07 pattern errors. This suggests that requirements feedback reduces the high error rate associated with the pattern requirement, but our three-step approaches did not result in further error-rate reductions.

Effects of Branding

We did not observe any significant effects of the university branding (see Q_2). To understand the impact of branding, we looked for the presence of context-related keywords in *Base* and *Base-plain*. *Base* was more likely to contain keywords related to the university (1.3% to 0.7%),[3] but the difference was not significant (χ^2_1=0.73, p=0.393). On the other hand, *Base-plain* passwords were more likely to contain generic study-related keywords,[4] (2.3% to 1.0%) but this was also not significant (χ^2_1=3.198, p=0.074).

Part One Recall

Participants were asked to recall their passwords in Part One after completing a brief survey. 92.9% of participants did so correctly on the first try, taking 1.1 attempts on average, with significant pairwise differences between conditions. The median time for Part One recall was 11 seconds, and significant differences are shown in Table 4. Passwords in *Pattern* took significantly more time to enter than those in either *Base* or *Blacklist*. This may indicate participants struggling more to remember or type passwords created under these conditions.

Part Two Recall

This section looks at data from the 3,934 participants who returned for Part Two within three days of being invited. 59.9% of participants successfully entered their password on the first attempt, and this did not vary significantly by condition (χ^2_8 =13.844, p=.086), as shown in Table 4.

Participants who mentioned storing their passwords in the surveys, or whom we detected pasting or autofilling during password recall, are considered *storage* participants. Others are *no-storage* participants. 58.5% of returned participants are storage participants, with significant differences shown in Table 3. *Insert* participants were more likely to be storage participants than those in $Pattern_{rt}$. Those in *Pattern* were more likely to do so than participants in *Base* or *Blacklist*.

[3]"cmu," "carnegie," "mellon," or "university"

[4]"turk," "amazon," "mechanical," "survey," "study," or "research"

It appears that the pattern requirement, and the insertion of random characters, cause participants to be less able to memorize their passwords, or at least anticipate being less able and therefore write them down. 57.1% of no-storage participants entered their passwords successfully in one attempt, and this did not vary by condition (χ^2_8=12.189, p=0.143).

We asked whether participants had already used their study passwords. 74.1% indicated creating a new one, and 23.0% indicated using a similar password. Few (4.4%) reused a password exactly, likely because our requirements differ from most service providers. *Pattern* participants were more likely to create a brand new password (84.0%) than *Base* (76.7%) or *Blacklist* (79.2%). This may help explain why *Pattern* participants were more likely to store their passwords.

We asked participants whether they agreed with the statement, "Remembering the password I used for this study was difficult." Table 4 shows significant differences. *Pattern* was more difficult to recall than either *Base* or *Blacklist*.

DISCUSSION

We address our research questions in light of our findings.

Q1: Impact of blacklist and pattern requirements

As expected, the blacklist and pattern requirements increase password strength but decrease usability. Furthermore, the pattern requirement leads to more security but less usability than the blacklist requirement. As shown in Table 3, *Base* passwords were significantly more likely to be cracked after 2×10^{13} guesses than *Blacklist*, which in turn were significantly more likely to be cracked than *Pattern*.

Among these conditions, *Pattern* proved least usable: participants had more difficulty both creating and recalling their passwords. *Pattern* participants were error-prone in password creation, and they reported finding password creation both difficult and annoying at significantly higher rates (Table 2). Participants in this condition also spent more time recalling their passwords in Part One and were more likely to store their passwords (Table 3). While error rates during Part Two recall did not differ significantly, *Pattern* participants were more likely to report difficulty in Part Two recall (Table 4).

Usability differences between *Blacklist* and *Base* were less pronounced and generally limited to password creation. Adding a blacklist requirement may increase security without making password recall significantly more difficult.

Q2: Impact of branded look-and-feel

We originally thought that branding would help users to remember their password (among the many other passwords people must routinely manage), although security could suffer if users created passwords that included words related to a brand. However, we found no evidence for a difference between branded and plain presentation in any of our analyses.

While we found no difference with the branding we used, a different visual presentation might have had more impact. Our branded design contained no images other than a university wordmark. Branding that included images, or a brand that was more familiar to participants, may have had a different effect. Further investigation into the effects of stronger branding on password behavior could prove interesting.

Q3: Impact of password-creation feedback

Our findings show some upside and limited downside to giving participants requirements feedback. We found that requirements feedback made password creation less error-prone for all three pairs of conditions we compared.

As shown in Table 3, requirements feedback participants were less likely to use a fourth character class. This may be due to the feedback giving users the feeling of being "done." In conditions without requirements feedback, participants may not have realized when the requirements were met and so added additional character classes to be sure. While this trend could potentially have some adverse effect on security, we found no significant difference in guessability after 2×10^{13} guesses.

Requirements feedback seems reduce user error, an increase in perception of strength, and little to no impact on password security. Thus, requirements feedback seems to be a useful feature to add to password-creation interfaces.

Q4: Impact of guiding and insertion

We tested the impact of our three-step conditions by comparing $Pattern_{rt}$ with both *Guide* and *Insert*. All three conditions had the same requirements. The latter two used an interactive three-step process to create the password over several steps.

Participants in *Guide* and *Insert* both found password creation less annoying and difficult than $Pattern_{rt}$, as seen in Table 2. They were also more likely to complete Part One of the study. Despite all three conditions enforcing the same requirements, passwords in *Guide* and *Insert* were significantly more likely to be cracked than those in $Pattern_{rt}$ — over twice as likely in the case of *Insert* (Table 3). This demonstrates that looking only at password-composition requirements is insufficient to paint an accurate picture of resulting security.

Participants in the three-step conditions made shorter passwords with fewer character classes (Table 3), resulting in more easily cracked passwords. One possible explanation is that participants did not feel a sense of ownership over their passwords. Prior research suggests that passwords are a way that users feel personal responsibility for computer security [14]. Perhaps this sense of ownership and responsibility was diminished because the system was more of an active participant in the process. Another explanation is that users may have trusted that the system was helping them create a strong password, and focused on following the instructions rather than on trying to increase password security.

Further research might explore whether other ways of guiding participants through password-creation can retain usability gains without sacrificing security. For example, a variation on *Guide* might ask participants to create a simple password with at least 11 characters, rather than 10, to account for the fact that participants following a traditional one-step password-creation process are more likely to exceed minimum length requirements. Alternatively, the guidance might encourage participants to exceed minimum requirements by telling them that this is a good way to increase the security of their password. *Guide* specifically told participants to add "two more characters to the middle of your password" and did not suggest that they could add more. Overall, we observe that the details associated with password-creation instructions matter and that instructions and procedures should be tested to determine their impact on both usability and security.

CONCLUSION

We evaluated three approaches to help users cope with strict password-composition policies: requirements feedback, guidance, and insertion. We found that requirements feedback helps prevent user errors while creating strong passwords. Our multi-step password-creation processes – guidance and insertion – made password-creation easier, but resulted in weaker passwords. While prior passwords research often focused on which sets of requirements lead to strong passwords, most past research has not looked at the impact of presentation and instructions (beyond password meters), or at ways to help users cope with strict requirements. We believe these findings will be valuable to service providers who wish to make their increasingly strict password-composition requirements easier for users to swallow.

ACKNOWLEDGMENTS

This research was supported in part by NSF grants DGE-0903659 and CNS-1116776, and by a gift from Microsoft Research.

REFERENCES

1. Brantz, T., and Franz, A. The Google Web 1T 5-gram corpus. Tech. Rep. LDC2006T13, Linguistic Data Consortium, 2006.
2. Chiasson, S., Forget, A., Stobert, E., Biddle, R., and P.C. van Oorschot. Multiple password interference in text and click-based graphical passwords. In *CCS* (2009).
3. Egelman, S., Sotirakopoulos, A., Muslukhov, I., Beznosov, K., and Herley, C. Does my password go up to eleven?: The impact of password meters on password selection. In *CHI* (2013).
4. Fahl, S., Harbach, M., Acar, Y., and Smith, M. On the ecological validity of a password study. In *SOUPS* (2013).
5. Forget, A., Chiasson, S., van Oorschot, P. C., and Biddle, R. Improving text passwords through persuasion. In *SOUPS* (2008).
6. Furnell, S. An assessment of website password practices. *Computers & Security 26*, 7 (2007), 445–451.
7. Furnell, S. Assessing password guidance and enforcement on leading websites. *Computer Fraud & Security 2011*, 12 (2011), 10 – 18.
8. Furnell, S., and Bär, N. Essential lessons still not learned? Examining the password practices of end-users and service providers. In *Human Aspects of Information Security, Privacy, and Trust* (2013), 217–225.
9. Kelley, P. G., Komanduri, S., Mazurek, M. L., Shay, R., Vidas, T., Bauer, L., Christin, N., Cranor, L. F., and Lopez, J. Guess again (and again and again): Measuring password strength by simulating password-cracking algorithms. In *IEEE SP* (2012).
10. Kerby, D. S. The simple difference formula: An approach to teaching nonparametric correlation. In *Innovative Teaching*. 2014.
11. Mazurek, M. L., Komanduri, S., Vidas, T., Bauer, L., Christin, N., Cranor, L. F., Kelley, P. G., Shay, R., and Ur, B. Measuring password guessability for an entire university. In *CCS* (2013).
12. Moshfeghian, S., and Ryu, Y. S. A passport to password best practices. *Ergonomics in Design: The Quarterly of Human Factors Applications 20*, 2 (2012), 23–29.
13. Schneier, B. Myspace passwords aren't so dumb. `http://www.wired.com/politics/security/commentary/securitymatters/2006/12/72300`, 2006.
14. Shay, R., Ion, I., Reeder, R. W., and Consolvo, S. "My religious aunt asked why I was trying to sell her viagra": Experiences with account hijacking. In *CHI* (2014).
15. Shay, R., Komanduri, S., Durity, A. L., Huh, P. S., Mazurek, M. L., Segreti, S. M., Ur, B., Bauer, L., Christin, N., and Cranor, L. F. Can long passwords be secure and usable? In *CHI* (2014).
16. Shay, R., Komanduri, S., Kelley, P. G., Leon, P. G., Mazurek, M. L., Bauer, L., Christin, N., and Cranor, L. F. Encountering stronger password requirements: user attitudes and behaviors. In *SOUPS* (2010).
17. Ur, B., Kelley, P. G., Komanduri, S., Lee, J., Maass, M., Mazurek, M., Passaro, T., Shay, R., Vidas, T., Bauer, L., Christin, N., and Cranor, L. F. How does your password measure up? The effect of strength meters on password creation. In *USENIX Security* (2012).
18. Vance, A. If your password is 123456, just make it HackMe. The New York Times, `http://www.nytimes.com/2010/01/21/technology/21password.html`, January 2010.
19. Weir, M., Aggarwal, S., Collins, M., and Stern, H. Testing metrics for password creation policies by attacking large sets of revealed passwords. In *CCS* (2010).
20. Weir, M., Aggarwal, S., de Medeiros, B., and Glodek, B. Password cracking using probabilistic context-free grammars. In *IEEE SP* (2009).

Snot, Sweat, Pain, Mud, and Snow — Performance and Experience in the Use of Sports Watches

Jakob Tholander
Mobile Life@Stockholm university
Postbox 7003, 16407, Kista, Sweden
jakobth@dsv.su.se

Stina Nylander
Mobile Life@SICS
Box 1263, 16429, Kista, Sweden
stny@sics.se

ABSTRACT
We have conducted interviews with ten elite and recreational athletes to understand their experiences and engagement with endurance sport and personal and wearable sports technology. The athletes emphasized the experiential aspects of doing sports and the notion of feeling was repeatedly used to talk about their activities. Technology played both an instrumental role in measuring performance and feeding bio-data back to them, and an experiential role in supporting and enhancing the sport experience. To guide further interaction design research in the sports domain, we suggest two interrelated ways of looking at sports performances and experiences, firstly through the notion of *a measured sense of performance*, and secondly as *a lived-sense of performance.*

Author Keywords
Sports; experience; heart rate monitors; performance; feeling.

ACM Classification Keywords
H.5.m. Information interfaces and presentation (e.g., HCI): Miscellaneous.

INTRODUCTION
Measuring results as accurately as possible is the primary way of assessing sports performance. Consequently, performance metrics have been a strong driving force in the development of sports technology for heart rate monitors, GPSs, motion-capture, and video analysis. Of the limited work in sports in HCI, the majority has taken an experiential perspective manifested as exertion games, social support, and gamification. This has created a view on people's engagement in sports as being either about improving results or about enjoying the experience. We attempt to expand what sports performance means in HCI by proposing two interrelated notions of a *measured sense of performance*, and *a lived-sense of performance*, put them in relation to themes in experience-oriented HCI, and discuss their implications for interaction design research. Similar points to our distinction have been made in experience oriented HCI research, design [17], and aesthetics [35]. We argue that HCI has not sufficiently explored the connection between experience and athletic performance, but has in most cases been limited to either viewpoint. Our paper is an attempt to engage with this connection. To design technologies for sports, we argue that these experience-focused perspectives need to be put in relation to sports performance to support a richer range of sports experiences.

CHI 2015, April 18 - 23 2015, Seoul, Republic of Korea
Copyright 2015 ACM 978-1-4503-3145-6/15/04…$15.00
http://dx.doi.org/10.1145/2702123.2702482

Endurance sports such as running, cycling, triathlon, and cross-country skiing is currently growing remarkably. This is seen in increasing participation in races and organized training groups, and the development of new forms of mass races such as ultra-marathons, swim-run races over large distances, and trail running. Hand in hand with this, a proliferation of mobile technologies dedicated to sports and exercise has emerged, such as watches, sensors, and apps. This technical and commercial development has brought increased attention of HCI to the domain of sports and novel ways of using technology in sports activities, examples include social sharing of heart-rate during cycling [34], interactive shirts for sharing running data [33], and novel feedback mechanisms for golfers [28], skiers [21], and runners [27]. So far, a significant part of the research in interactive sports technologies has been concerned with socio-motivational technologies [2, 23, 24], new forms of play [12, 15], gamification [5], bodily interaction [36], and explorations of technical challenges for wearable sports technologies [3, 4, 21, 39]. Social and playful experiences are indeed important for many people's engagement in sports, however, our study shows that there are users that desire technology that stay within the boundaries of the sport as such and the sports performance it involves - without transforming it into play or games. When it comes to supporting, enhancing or augmenting the sporting activities through deep engagement with the details of their execution, it turns out that less work has been reported. Counter-examples include [11, 19] which led to an innovative training device for advanced psychomotor skills in handball, Stienstra et al.'s. [34] work on sonification of speed skating motion; and Spelmezan's [33] vibrational feedback for snowboarding instruction.

By drawing on a set of "in-depth interviews" with elite and recreational athletes, we map out key characteristics of athletes' experiences and engagement in endurance sports, and technologies that support this in various ways such as sports watches and heart-rate monitors. For a large group of engaged athletes, there is a close connection between the experience of the sport and how it is performed, and sports is valued for a lot more than pure measurable performance. Moreover, it is not only goals and results that motivate athletes, but many additional factors such as the reward from meeting various challenges, the ability to manage exertion and fatigue, and the sheer fun and enjoyment of running, skiing, and cycling. Reoccurring in our material was the notion of *feeling*, and the various roles it played in building instrumental and experiential aspects of the athletes' performances. As put by one of our participants:

".. *and then you run ten kilometers and it feels like... well, did I run or am I going to run? I don't feel the difference in my legs. That feeling is priceless in a way.*" Karl (recreational athlete)

We believe that our proposed notions of *measured sense of performance* and *lived-sense of performance* effectively characterize the experiences of doing sports in relation to sensor-based performance technologies, such as heart-rate monitors, GPS:es and sports watches.

BACKGROUND

Health and wellness has been an important trend in CHI research, as well as in the domain of consumer electronics during the last decade. Many commercial and research-oriented sports technologies such as sports watches, heart-rate monitors and exercise apps are designed to automatically gather and present data with the purpose of generating a log of performed activities. The focus of these logs is on devising interactions for improved practice and racing. Rewards for improvements and goal achievements are common mechanisms used in such designs. Successful examples from research include the Ubifit project which worked on automatic recognition of activity to relieve users from data input, and combined it with visual feedback to motivate users [5], whereas Ahtinen et al. restricted their application to the activity of walking but offered goal setting and the ability to represent the goal as a journey to support motivation [1]. Many commercially developed apps such as Runkeeper, Endomondo and Run Zombie, run! also use rewards of various kinds to increase motivations.

Social mechanisms such as opportunities for sharing data is commonly used in commercial products and in research. Research systems have also explored a wider range of social mechanisms such as displaying heart-rate data to other athletes [20, 38], the ability to watch live video of others practicing [24], setting up competitions between friends [37], or interacting with others working out in remote locations [23]. These attempts have made substantial and important contributions to the field, especially when it comes to exploring how to engage people in sports and exercise.

When looking closer at the specific domain of sports, there are several bodies of research within the CHI community. Primarily the following approaches can be identified: *technical explorations* aiming at new technology for existing sports, for example wearable sensors [4, 19], *new forms of play or sports*, such as PingPongPlus [15], and various exertion games e.g. [22], *instructional technology*, aiming to improve the skills of athletes by providing instructions through various modalities such as vibration [3, 33] or sound [34].

Research has also been inspired to use sports technology in new settings. The availability of robust and accurate heart-rate monitors for sports use has made it possible to create new types of social awareness systems based on heart-rate data. Several systems have been developed around heart-rate data, such as allowing family members to see each other's' heart-rate as a way of indicating mood, activity, and emotional state [6, 32]. Heart rate monitors have also been used to select music in manner that support mood and exercise [39], and to control game features [25].

More recent research on sports and HCI has started to pick up on experiential dimensions of sports, striving to design aspects beyond the immediately instructional and result oriented. Notable examples are Pijnapple & Mueller's work on skateboarding [30], Nylander et al.'s work on golf [28], and Stienstra et al. on speed skating [34]. In line with this recent trend, we argue that the experiential aspect of sports holds a potential ground for unexplored forms of interactions [29] which has received little attention in the performance-oriented, motivational, and gamification approaches.

We argue that a key element for future research is to understand the motivations and experiences around people's engagement in sports and exercise. Much research in this area is based on the underlying assumptions that people engage in sports and exercise for result oriented and goal-directed purposes, such as running faster, finishing a race, or losing weight [3, 7, 8]. Consequently, the primary role of any kind of sports technology would then be to support or simplify for athletes in achieving these goals, supposedly by making it more fun, more social or more personally rewarding. In contrast to this, and in line with sports psychology [10], our work shows that many athletes are driven by a broader set of experiences of sports. We argue that interaction design research in this area needs to broaden what it means to engage in sports and exercise, and the underlying reasons as to why people do this, in order to find novel design directions. Another important element in furthering the research around interactive technologies for sports is to understand people's real-life practices in sports and their technology use. A number of studies have investigated various logging [31] and bio-sensing technologies from a broader lifestyle and health point of view [32]. Contrary to those, the goal of our work has been to put sports experiences at center stage in order to draw out the elements that are characteristic to technology and interaction targeted for sports. Given the large amount of users in this area, we argue that that this is an underexplored domain.

METHOD

We conducted 10 in-depth interviews with elite (3) and recreational (7) athletes. Participants were recruited using email in the authors' extended personal network and through the Swedish Federation of Orienteering. We selected endurance athletes who practiced at least three times a week, but did not pose any requirements on their main sport, their technology use, or their level of fitness. We recruited both elite and recreational athletes, since the practices and requirements of the elite have a strong influence on what recreational athletes do or want in terms of practice schedules and choice of technology. Our elite participants spent 15-20 hours a week practicing, normally distributed on 9-13 sessions, while the recreational athletes reported 3-7 sessions a week. The recreational athletes were interviewed in locations they chose themselves, most commonly at work, and elite athletes were interviewed in conjunction to a test session of the Swedish National Orienteering team's study on running biomechanics. The interviews were semi-structured and focused on aspects such as: schedule, goals, technology used, performance, experience and motivation, social sharing, learning, and identity management. They lasted 45-70 minutes and were recorded, transcribed, and analyzed by the authors through open coding in a collaborative fashion.

Nine of the participants owned GPS equipped heart-rate monitors, and seven used them regularly during practice. One of the participants was recovering from injury and found the heart-rate monitor stressful during the rehabilitation phase, and one only used the GPS functionality in the watch. Our three elite athletes were members of the Swedish national team of orienteerers and diligent users of GPS using special purpose tools to analyze their data and evaluating their orienteering skills. Several participants also used various apps such as Runkeeper or Funbeat, as well as the online forums that heart-rate monitor suppliers provide for storing and analyzing data.

RESULTS

The participants in our interviews were happy to talk about their practice and openly shared stories of successes as well as failures. Some of them had brought the technology they used and showed us their training plans. Technology has shaped and reshaped the practice of training of several of the participants. Heart-rate monitoring has changed the aims of various workouts and to some extent created new forms of practice. Certainly they talked a lot about becoming better runners and cross-country skiers and how the technology played a part in that. However, they repeatedly came back to the importance of the subjective experiences of running or skiing both for the sake of improvement, and just as importantly, for the experience itself. We will go into detail on the three main themes from the interviews: feeling and experience; goals and rewards; and collecting, perceiving and sharing data.

FEELING AND EXPERIENCE

A theme that kept coming back in our interviews regarded the notion of feeling. We will unpack some ways that the notion of feeling were used, and how we can understand that in relation to interaction design research in sports. Technology served both the purpose of improving performance and enhancing experiences, and played a role in the participants' getting to know their bodies better. The relationships between the technology and the various ways that the participants expressed themselves around the notion of feeling served a variety of purposes. We have organised these into three main themes: technologies and feeling for a) enhancing experiences, b) improving sports performance, c) learning about effort and performance.

Enhancing experiences

A first observation is that the word 'feeling' was used to describe a variety of aspects of their practice, racing and overall experiences of their sport. Feeling was used to describe the role of the technology they used, what they were striving to achieve, and to talk about the role of speed, distance and exertion during practice. Feeling thus had a number of different meanings to our participants, but in overall it points to the centrality of the felt dimensions of their experiences of training and racing. When talking about practice, they kept coming back to the importance of having a good feeling, and the necessity of developing a sense of a number of factors such as exertion, speed, and heart-rate level. These were considered critical to learn to know their bodies. They considered all this as essential both for improving performance and having a desired experience.

Let us illustrate this broad usage of the word feeling by a quote from one of our participants. In the following, he discusses how he looks at his training and the use of heart-rate monitors.

"*on some routes I check how it feels, because that is what I use my heart-rate monitor for, it is to describe the embodied feeling in relation to the perceived effort, so it is a lot of feedback, that is what I use it for. That is what I say to a lot of people who start using a heart-rate monitor is that they should learn about their bodies via their watch, how it feels and so that you know how it is to breathe at a certain heart-rate level ... but then you have to know your maximum heart-rate, you have to know a little more about how recovery works. If I do interval training, I check the span a lot, from going towards maximum, and the recovery job. When doing hills for instance, I check when I start again, so I don't check the time that much, I go more on heart-rate and feeling ... like now it is the right time to go for another one.*" Paul (recreational athlete).

Throughout this quote Paul repeatedly uses the notion of "feeling" and "feel" when talking about his practice. For instance, to calibrate his feeling for various exertion levels to his actual heart-rate levels during practice and racing, learn about how his body feels and responds to various forms of practice. Breathing and feeling and exertion relates to various heart-rate levels, and guide him during interval sessions regarding how fast to run, how long to rest between repetitions. The heart-rate monitor is thus used as a support for looking inwards towards his subjective experiences of how his body feels, as well as for looking outwards towards objective measures about his performance. These processes are interrelated and plays a dual role in creating his experience of practice.

Let us further analyze the experiential dimensions of how the participants talked about the notion of feeling and their experiences of endurance training and sports watches. Paul used the notion of feeling to emphasize a variety of felt dimensions of his practice in relation to his body, and particularly the role of heart-rate data in building these. Examples include sense of speed, sense of exertion, runners high, being one with nature. Paul, who had used heart-rate based training for more than ten years, described the process of adjusting his level of exertion during a workout in the following way:

"[it's] *like a mirroring of the feeling I am aiming for, that is why I use a heart-rate monitor. Like a confirmation about how it feels when I breathe*" Paul (recreational athlete).

This stands in contrast to some of our other participants who had racing performance in focus. Paul focused on the experiences he got from his practice saying things like that he strove to "find the right feeling", to "get to know your body", and "it must be fun". His attention always first went to himself and his body, and secondly to the watch and the heart-rate data to nuance or confirm the feeling.

Improving the performance

Another common way that the participants talked about feeling was as a tool or instrument that they 'used' during their practice sessions. For instance, Peter, an experienced runner, skier and coach of runners and swimmers, talked about how a workout feels in a similar way to how he talked about heart-rate data from his watch. Feeling was treated an additional data source comparable to speed, time, distance, and heart-rate. According to him, the feeling during a workout should match data from the watch, and especially the heart-rate. He argued that during practice, heart-rate data was the most important data from the watch since cardio vascular capacity is what in the end determines someone's performance.

"*Well, what you want to see is, I mean, exertion in relation to your speed is where you strive for an improvement ... either make your running more efficient so that you can run faster with less exertion, or improve your 'engine' so that you can run faster at lower heart-rate.* "Peter (recreational athlete).

Contrary to some of the other participants, this instrumental view is illustrated in his emphasis that his goal was not to achieve a good feeling for the sake of itself. The goal is to be able to run faster, and feeling is an important tool in the process of improvement. A nuanced sense for your heart-rate allows athletes to control the level of exertion that is required to carry out various workouts for improving the factors that build cardio vascular capacity. At the end of the day, for Peter, it is how fast one can run that counts, so the final evaluation is still based on time and distance.

Heart-rate data was claimed by the participants to support them in following their plan for a particular workout. Several participants had defined the heart-rate zones that they should stay within during a particular work out. For instance, Mark discussed the difficulties he had in staying within the so-called A1-zone, the zone defined for plus two-hour workouts. On several occasions, he had tested his heart-rate thresholds at a professional testing facility and had his upper A1-threshold defined at 125. However, he often ended up above this which could cause the workout to not have the intended effect:

"*so it it is so easy for me to end up at a heart-rate of 135 even though I want to stay below 125, but then I let the heart-rate control, so that is what keeps the speed down. Because if I rely on speed and feeling, I go too fast*" Mark (recreational athlete).

Learning about effort and performance

For Mark, relying on feeling is not sufficient to allow him to efficiently follow his workout plan. He has a solid background in long-distance running at national elite level, however, compared to some of our other participants he was rather unexperienced in heart-rate based training (about 18 months). His subjective sense for his level of exertion was not fine-grained enough to stay in the A1 zone without relying on his watch. Based on his heart-rate readings he adjusted the speed, and thereby the exertion level to follow his workout plan. Ultimately, through further interaction he might learn to calibrate his speed and exertion to appropriate heart-rate levels without relying on his watch.

The way the heart-rate monitor help to support the learning about one's body was brought up by Max who had experiences similar to Mark. When talking about how he used his watch, he said that by looking at the heart-rate data in real-time, he learned about the relation between his perceived exertion levels and his heart-rate:

"*if you are not in good shape it always feels like you are going really hard, but the more you run you the better you become at knowing your level of exertion. In the beginning, it could feel hard even though my heart-rate was low so then the watch helped me increase the speed. That I don't have to do that much anymore.*" Max (recreational athlete)

Firstly, quite similar to Mark's experiences this points to how the heart-rate data helped him realize that often when he felt that he was going as hard as he could, he was actually not close to maximum heart-rate. Secondly, through his interaction with the watch he has built up a more nuanced feeling of his level of exertion. An exertion level that he previously experienced as really hard, was now understood as not being at his maximum. Thus, he had learnt to reinterpret how to relate such a feeling of exertion to a particular heart-rate level, and adjust how to carry out his workout. This shows how an improvement of physical capacity together with interaction with heart-rate data not only provided instrumental information about his workouts, but also transformed his subjective experiences of running.

Interacting with the heart-rate monitor is a learning process in which athletes build a more nuanced picture of their bodies. In such a process, the heart-rate monitor works as an instrument to help athletes to build such knowledge and how they react to various forms of practice. In the long run they might develop a sense for their bodies that does not require relying on the heart-rate monitor in their practice.

GOALS AND REWARDS

The majority of our participants were not primarily goal-driven in terms of measurable results. Given the significant amount and time and effort that that such keen athletes put in, elite as well as amateurs, we had expected this to be more prominent. Quite the contrary though, several of them primarily brought more 'soft' benefits as key goals that they strived for. These aspects included a mix of social motivations, aspects of well-being, lifestyle, and identity. While most of them did have performance goals such as running a marathon under three hours or winning medals at international championships, these were always interwoven with other "softer" rewards. When asking the elite athletes that were part of the national team in orienteering what motivated them to put in all the hours, sometimes during the most unpleasant conditions, apart from mentioning the dream of becoming world number one, they all emphasized less measurable factors such as the social aspects of practice and competing, their social life together with the team, and the rewards from challenging oneself.

In a similar fashion, most of the amateurs presented well-defined goals when specifically being asked for it. These goals ranged from running an ultra marathon, running a 45 minutes 10k, or a sub 5 hour Vasaloppet a (Swedish ski race). However, for several of them, achievements in the form of reaching measurable goals were much less important than training as part of a lifestyle and the role of their sport in building their identities.

Paul for instance said that his goal was that it should feel good when practicing. He wanted it to "feel good" in the Vasaloppet. He did not have a specific time goal even though he would appreciate a good result. Similarly, Karl talked about goals as

"if you do not have any goals that are really important to you, then it is the everyday practice that are the actual goals. They are kind of the product,that is what you do. Karl (recreational athlete)

The participants brought up a variety of rewards that they got from their training. These ranged from appreciating the feeling of exhaustion after having completed a really tough workout, making a plan and following it over a long period of time, as well as to beating your personal record in a race. Thus, in addition to being rewarded by the measurable results and improvements, the experiential aspects of practice including planning, execution, and reflection, was described as important goals and rewards.

Rewards were not necessarily formulated as being about performing well and feeling strong, but often linked to the satisfaction of achieving what they had set out to do, in a specific way. Sometimes this was to push themselves really hard and thus the rewarding feeling would be about a combination of exhaustion and sense of achievement.

"*It felt really tough, and I knew that my legs would be completely dead for the coming two days, and the other day I walked like ... I could hardly walk in the hallway, it was ridiculous.* " Paul.

This is an example of how participants appreciatively talked about aspects that in other circumstances would not necessarily be categorized as rewards, such as pain and exhaustion. Other forms of rewarding feelings were connected to the experience of the results of the practice in terms of performing better and thus feeling a clear improvement in following workouts. For Paul, the reward is a combination of feeling and result, he manages something that he did not before while feeling stronger. He connects his story of the reward with the preparations, the preceding heavy gym work which made him feel anything but good:

"*sometimes when I have done a leg workout at the gym, and then two days later get on the bike. Then you notice the effect of the workout and the rest, in certain stretches uphill you notice that you can push a lot harder than usual without the heart-rate rising very much ...* " Paul.

The fact that he managed to push himself hard enough during the gym workout adds value since it shows him that he could put in the effort needed to achieve the result.

Rewards were sometimes not related to a specific workout or even participants' exercise plans or goals. Karl's feeling cited above about having completed his practice without effort, is both a sense of being a really strong and fit runner and a deep sense of happiness in being able to run without even getting tired. In line with this, several of the other participants brought up that short-cuts in the training are not interesting, rather, rewards come in relation to the effort you put in. One of them said that the optimal reward did not necessarily increase with an improved time in race, but came that he throughout the race had the sense that he had done everything right, that his body felt really good, no matter if he beat his personal best in the race or not.

"*Downhill from Evertsberg, that is so damn great, you just wow ... that feeling is really hard to beat, if you have done it right up to the top, and then you get the downhill, I mean, that!*" Paul.

One participant formulated this as finding the "right equation"; figuring out everything that needed to be done, and then being able do it. He emphasized that the reward of practice cannot simply be measured from how well you performed in the final race, but rather in the experience of completing the whole process from start to end. The motivation came from range of factors such as performing the sports itself, challenge oneself, and following a plan. This created long-term motivation for engaging in these activities for substantial periods of time.

COLLECTING, PERCEIVING, AND SHARING DATA

Most commercial applications for endurance sports focus on automated data collection and documentation of your practice, thus providing a training log based on data, such as time distance, speed, and heart- rate, and various sharing opportunities through social media. However, the participants in our study manipulated their data in a number of ways since they found that the basic measures provided were not sufficient.

Precision of data

Our participants critically examined data in relation to how they perceived their practice. One common way was to analyze the reliability of the data. Peter, e.g., emphasized that the he always strove for the most accurate data.

"*Well, what you want to see is the exertion in relation to your speed, that is where you strive for an improvement ... either make your running more efficient so that you can run faster with less exertion, or improve your 'engine' so that you can run faster at lower heart-rate.* Peter

For him it was of key importance to have the most accurate measurement of speed since he found speed to be the most accurate measure of improvement and wanted to put it in exact relation to heart-rate. He found that the GPS-based speed calculation was too coarse. Therefore, he used an additional foot sensor to measure speed and calibrated his foot sensor each time he bought a new pair of shoes.

A related aspect of the precision of data reported by our participant regarded the accuracy of GPS data. Especially interesting was how the elite orienteers reviewed their GPS logs after workouts and races in order to analyze their route choices and orienteering technique, for improvement of speed and map reading, and managing difficult passages such as going in and out from check-points.

I overlay data on the map, often it's quite quick to get it to fit, but it depends... I mean, the GPS is probably right but not the map, which is an interpretation of the reality. Then I can adjust the GPS trail to the map. It's simple, I just drag it. Susan (elite athlete).

This process of correcting the GPS track according to the correct track points to the importance of acknowledging that GPS data in combination with maps has error sources, not only because of the off-drift of the GPS but also because of limits of cartography, (rocks can only be of two sizes on the map). Orienteers could in some detail remember the exact route choices they had made based on the GPS data. Similarly, Paul had quite exact recollections of his heart-rate and breathing at various points in the terrain. The sense for his body and the heart-rate data played a role in how he experienced and remembered the physical environment. Based on this he could remember a workout in detail, as well as adapt and combine the various trails he ran, biked, and skied. The sense of his body, such as heart-rate and breathing, was a way of remembering that was tightly coupled with his experience of the local geography and the parts of nature he used.

Using heart-rate data in practice

One central aspect that we explored in the interviews concerned how the participants used and interpreted the data from their heart-rate monitors. The most important use of the data was when participants looked at, and reflected on, their data during workouts. The purpose was to quickly verify that their heart rate were at the level they wanted it and to make sure they could complete the session the way they wanted to.

"*It can be super quick, just like, how does it feel when I breathe...like the general feeling and the level of exertion.*" Paul.

The participants often had specific goals for a workout, for example, reaching a certain heart-rate threshold, or staying within a certain heart-rate zone. To make sure that the workout would have the desired effect they calibrated their pace by checking their heart-rate so that they worked hard enough, or not too hard.

"*When I felt like, this is really tough, I can't keep the pressure up, I checked the watch and saw I had a heart-rate of 153 and realized I needed to slow down to be able to keep on going the last 90 seconds. So the combination of how it feels and the watch makes me slow down*" Mark

The only case of looking at the data in any detail were Karl who had seen that some of his readings were really off for a long period. In combination with unusual tiredness and difficulties of sleeping after workouts he made an EKG and it turned out that he had a heart condition that required two operations. This is an interesting case of how sports technology potentially can interact with health care, even though it was quite unusual.

Post-practice analysis was reported as being less frequent. It was done both on separate sessions and for longer periods of time. Post-analysis of specific workouts mostly concerned the specific goals set for a certain workout, and served as input for learning how to perform similar workouts in the future.

"*I check that the level of the heart-rate is where I want it to be, for example for 800 meter intervals, I want around 92, 93, 95, well at least above 92% of my max heart-rate. If it's lower I didn't push hard enough, and will try to push harder next time.* " Peter

When analyzing longer periods of time, as well as long-term goals, participants looked at high level information rather than data from specific workouts, or even aggregated data from series of workouts such hours and kilometers during a given time period.

Often, the subjective comments that athletes made after each practice session were the parts of their data that was given most weight in the analysis. In a way, how athletes experienced the different components and sessions in their practice was used as a coarse tool for evaluation. Negative comments, or a sequence of negative comments, indicated that a closer analysis of the exercise plan was needed.

"*well, if you evaluate continuously, you often start from my comments. And if that is, like, if it felt bad several days in a row, well, then you might need to look at heart-rate data, speed data, or everything to find out what is wrong.*" Lisa (elite athlete)

In summary, analysis of collected data rarely occurred at the level of detail that sports watches and exercise apps provide. However, subjective aspects of practice and racing plays in important role both during practice and in post activity analysis of short as well as the long term perspectives. Therefore, we argue that given the fact that participant spent little time on post analysis, we argue that next generation sports technology should support users by aggregating data and representing data in novel ways, supporting users in real-time and post-activity reflection and analysis of their practice, and more importantly designing ways of meaningfully integrating the subjective experiences of their practice with the collected data.

Sharing of data

Our participants only shared data through online tools to a limited extent. Neither did they look at the data of others in any significant way. All of them used various online forums for uploading and saving data, and they did store it publically. Some of them had a few friends in their forum, like 'my wife', or 'one of my running buddies', but the interaction was limited to occasional brief comments. When we probed them about their use of sharing features they had difficulties seeing any personal value or purpose, beyond basic awareness of the number of workouts their friends did. Since social features are some of the most appreciated aspects of endurance sports applications and online training forum are highly used, we had expected this to be the case also among our participants. For instance, Anna who had several running friends and belonged to a running club said:

"*Why should I want to share and why would anyone want to look*" Anna (recreational athlete)

Anna's quite absolute denial of any value for her in sharing data illustrate the position of most of our participants on this matter, namely that their reasons for the significant time put into practice and racing was primarily personal. They did not actively share information about their activities or their data, neither did they look at the data of others. This does not mean that they were asocial in any way, or found no value in learning and socialising with others around their sport. Most of them practiced together with friends and in training groups to various extents. However, the social values of their practice were not found through online sports forums or social media.

The clearest case of interest in what others shared was by Mark who regularly checked the workouts of those his training friends that used the same watch brand, which gave suggested recovery time after each workout.

"*... he is always at 90 hours of rest, and it's like, it's a bit prestigious ...*" Mark.

This was interpreted primarily in a 'macho' way as a measure of how hard you practiced, and not of any significant value that they would use to adapt their practice.

Given the strong interest in heart-rate based training it could be expected that the participants would also show interest in sharing and looking at others heart-rate data to learn more. We believe that one important reason for this is due to the physiological differences between individuals which cause heart-rate data to differ extensively between individuals. This makes it difficult, or even meaningless, to compare and interpret someone else's heart-rate data without knowing at least their maximum and minimum heart-rate, their various thresholds and preferably also a number other aspects of their practice.

The heart-rate diagrams that most systems generate are quite detailed, based on moment-to-moment readings. Most users claimed that this level of granularity was too detailed in order to conduct post-workout analysis of any significance. Most participants based any post-workout analysis on fairly basic measures such as average and maximum heart-rate of a workout. Not even the elite runners claimed that their coaches analysed the heart-rate diagrams for each workout, or over longer periods of time.

DISCUSSION

What we first would like to highlight from our study is how our participants emphasized the felt dimensions and experiences of doing sports, and in particular, the lived-sense of being an athlete. One of them aptly labeled the deep engagement in the sports that he loved to perform under the notion of "snotsport". To him, such a notion included a deep appreciation of the sport as such, the pain, lactic acid, exertion, exhaustion, snot, sweat, and the rewards that he experienced from taking these on as they are. He loved endurance practice and the ability to manage the effort and the exertion that followed. He even claimed that it put him in closer connection to his body during exertion. Important about the characteristics of 'snotsport' is that athletes of our study did not want distractions from them while performing their sport, rather these were core elements as to why many of them loved their sport and continued to engage in it. Hence, sports should be challenging and one does not need distractions from that.

Furthermore, our results point to a number of tensions in the relationship between subjective experiences and instrumental purposes of sports performance. This could be seen in (i) how technology was used both for looking 'inwards' towards their felt bodies, and looking 'outwards' towards objective measures of the performance, (ii) how technology and feeling worked as complementary sources in analysing workouts and learning about their bodies reactions to various experiences, (iii) how subjective memories were put in relation to external data, such as GPS and heart rate, in order to interpret the outcome of workouts and filling gaps in accuracy of the data. From a interaction design point of view this suggest that technologies for sports performance need to be understood as serving dual purposes that live between the athletes' experiences and objective measure of their performance. This duality will be further conceptualized below.

A lived and a measured sense of performance

A key finding regards the centrality of the *notion of feeling* to the users' experiences of their sport. The notion of feeling played a number of roles in participants' practice, such as being a tool for interpreting signals from their bodies, developing a sense of speed in relation to intensity of breathing, and learning about their bodies' reactions at various perceived exertion levels. Subjective experiences played a similar role as data received from sports watches, as well as being goals to strive for in themselves.

The notion of feeling can be understood in two main ways in relation to endurance training and the use of heart-rate monitoring, *instrumentally and experientially*. These two ways can be illustrated by the perspectives on practice of two of our participants. Firstly, Peter who had a strong focus on improving his performance and used his watch and heart-rate monitor primarily as a tool to improve his practice, and thereby in the end reaching his over-arching goal of racing faster. Secondly, Paul who had a strong focus on the experiential and felt dimensions of his practice and used his watch to enhance its experiential aspects.

Thus, to our participants *performance* came to mean more than measurable effects or results achieved in races. We argue that a design oriented understanding of sports performance needs to capture instrumental as well as experiential dimensions. To conceptualize the use of sports technologies, we argue that it requires an understanding of the relationship between the technologies and the experiences people have. This relationship is necessarily of an interrelated character. Such a dual appreciation of instrumental and experiential aspects of sports and exercise can be distinguished through what we call a *lived sense of performance* and *a measured sense of performance.*

- A *measured sense of performance* captures the instrumental purposes of the use of sports technologies. External data sources and information about users' practice and bodies provide possibilities for an outside perspective of their performance and how that contributes to efficiently carry out workouts and races. Examples of this is how they pace themselves, balance their various thresholds, and evaluate performances.
- A *lived sense of performance* captures the subjective and experiential purposes of sport technology use and how it enriches the various experiences that users get engaged in during practice. Memories, experiences, and technology also provide users with opportunities to look inward. Examples of this include performing workouts in a way that puts them in closer connection to the bodily experiences or their strive for runners' high. This notion contributes to pin-pointing the felt-life and lived-dimensions of performing in sports.

Similar to ideas proposed in other domains such as that of celebratory technologies in food experiences [9], these two notions of performance suggests that experiences of sports and sports technology arises in an interplay between instrumental and measureable on the one hand, and subjective and felt aspects of performing in sports on the other. We argue that sports provide a rich, and currently largely unexplored area for the design of technologies for such experiences, even though other domains of HCI, such as embodied and affective interaction have addressed such non-functional and non-instrumental aspects of bodily experiences in various design projects [13, 18, 36].

The notions of *a measured and lived-sense of performance* connect to current conceptualizations of interaction design research that brings in ideas from STS theory relating notions of performativity and material agency [16]. The distinction between *representational and performative technologies* proposed by [26] suggest that technology plays dual roles in the users' experiences, both as ways of portraying real-life events, and as agents that interfere in users' activities. From such a viewpoint, sports technologies not only measure and represent data from users' activities and bodies, they reflexively act as agents that do things in and affects these experiences, thus performing aspects of the experience together with the users. Technologies provide representations of established facts as well as dynamically intervene in user's felt lives during, before and after practice.

Toward novel representations of sports experiences

The deep appreciation of the *sport* including all elements that come with it, painful as well as enjoyable, is what the participants found rewarding and motivating and the reasons for putting in the time and efforts that they did. Participants came back to how painful elements such as fatigue and lactic acid gave them a sense of achievement that were central to their enjoyment of the sport. Hence, this was not parts of the experience that they would like to get rid of, or something that technology in any sense should 'design away'. This would provide a new starting point for technologies design for such a practice. Key elements of the activity should not be transformed into something playful or game-like. Thus, from this perspective, interaction design research need to reflect on the ways in which technology transforms the key elements of the sport.

This perspective resembles what Grimes & Harper [9] call celebratory technologies. Such technologies would draw on what athletes claim to be the central elements of their experiences to design engaging sports experiences. One way of realizing this could be through Interactional Empowerment [14], which advocates designs that empower and support users in creating their own meaning from biodata, not designing systems which create the meaning for the users. Thereby such design would put users in an even stronger connection to their sport. Such explorations should build on the core elements of people's experiences of sports, as properties to highlight, emphasize and support rather than to conceal and diminish.

Novel measures and representations of sports data

We argue that there is a need for novel kinds of representations and "measuring sticks" of sports performances. This is especially relevant for data such as heart-rate data which is highly individual. The fact that two individuals with equal physical capacity in most cases has different maximum heart-rate and different heart-rate thresholds means that there is a *lack of common reference points* that allow for straightforward understanding, interpretation, and comparison between individuals. This requires a partially different set of aggregations than the current ones, in order to bridge individual variations. By developing a richer set of measures that connects to heart-rate rather than to speed and distance, it could be easier for athletes to perform workouts the way they had intended.

The fact that people are not only driven by 'hard' goals in their training, but largely emphasized the "soft" elements, often without connecting them to the measurable goals, has consequences for what we put in focus in the design of technologies for these users. Given that it was primarily the bodily experiences and the joy they got from a really good workout or race that motivated several of our participants, we should explore ways of designing sports technologies that better match those drivers. This leads to the question of what kinds of measures and perspectives current systems provide. Should data by necessity be considered as true or should it rather be one of many elements the build user experience. What new measures can we design that suites the variety of goals athletes have for their practice, such as getting to the perfect feeling in training and following their workout regimen. We argue for the importance of showing users that sports data have sources of error relevant to deal with. Data of this kind should not be treated in a black-box fashion but looked upon as opening up interesting opportunities for interaction. Current systems gather data that are seen as objective, such as distance, speed, time and heart-rate, and are consequently presented as such to the user. However, as our study shows, athletes have a variety of subjective ways of valuing their performance, which cannot straightforwardly be connected to the data in its current form. Thus, we need representations that relate to users' individual and subjective measures for their performances.

FINAL REMARKS

While the field of sports and sports technology is rapidly growing with the possibility of light-weight sensors our results point to that these should not only be designed with exact measurements of technique and performance in mind, but also as a way to connect to and enrich users lived-sense and experiences of performing their sports. We propose that the notions of measured sense of performance and lived sense of performance push us to think about what kind of technologies we design in health, exercise and sports. These technologies should not only provide sports performance data, but should aim at opening up possibilities for interactions that connect to the lived, and felt-life of doing various physical activities.

ACKNOWLEDGMENTS

We would like to thank our participants and Vinnova, the Swedish Governmental Agency for Innovation Systems.

REFERENCES

1. Ahtinen, A., Huuskonen, P. and Häkkilä, J., Let's All Get Up and Walk to the North Pole: Design and Evaluation of a Mobile Wellness Application. In proceedings of *NordiCHI*, (2010).
2. Ahtinen, A., Isomursu, M., Mukhtar, M., Mäntyjärvi, J., Häkkilä, J. and Blom, J., Designing Social Features for Mobile and Ubiquitous Wellness Applications. In proceedings of *MUM*, (2009), ACM Press.
3. Bial, D., Appelmann, T., Rukzio, E. and Schmidt, A., Improving Cyclists Training with Tactile Feedback on Feet. In proceedings of *HAID*, (2012), 41-50.
4. Chi, E.H., Song, J. and Corbin, G., "Killer App" of Wearable Computing: Wireless Force Sensing Body Protectors for Martial Arts. In proceedings of *UIST*, (Santa Fe, NM, 2004), 277-285.
5. Consolvo, S., McDonald, D.W., Toscos, T., Chen, M.Y., Froehlich, D., Harrison, B., Klasnja, P., LaMarca, A., LeGrand, L., Libby, R., Smith, I. and Landay, J.A., Activity sensing in the wild: a field trial of ubifit garden. In proceedings of *CHI*, (2008), 1797-1806

6. Curmi, F., Ferrario, M.A., Southern, J. and Whittle, J., HeartLink: Open Broadcast of Live Biometric Data to Social Networks. In proc of *CHI*, (2013), 1749-1758.
7. de Oliveira, R. and Oliver, N., TripleBeat: Enhancing Exercise performance with Persuasion. In proceedings of *MobileHCI*, (2008), 255-264.
8. Eriksson, M. and Bresin, R., Improving Running Mechanics by Use of Interactive Sonification. In proceedings of *Interactive Sonification Workshop*, (Stockholm, Sweden, 2010), 95-98.
9. Grimes, A. and Harper, R., Celebratory Technology: New Directions for Food Research in HCI. In proceedings of *CHI*, (2008), 467-476.
10. Hassmén, P., Hassmén, N. and Plate, J. *Idrottspsykologi*. Natur & Kultur, 2003.
11. Hillerup Fogtmann, M., Grönbaek, K. and Kofod Ludvigsen, M., Interaction Technology for Collective and Psychomotor Training in Sports. In proc *ACE*, (2011).
12. Hämäläinen, P., Ilmonen, T., Höysniemi, J., Lindholm, M. and Nykänen, A., Martial Arts in Artificial Reality. In proceedings of *CHI*, (Portland, OR, 2005), 781-790.
13. Höök, K., Transferring qualities from horseback riding to design. In proceedings of *NordiCHI*, (2010), 226-235.
14. Höök, K., Ståhl, A., Sundström, P. and Laaksolahti, J., Interactional Empowerment. In proceedings of *CHI*, (2008), ACM Press, 647-656.
15. Ishii, H., Wisneski, C., Orbanes, J., Chun, B. and Paradios, J., PingPongPlus: design of an athletic-tangible interface for computer-supported cooperative play. In proceedings of *CHI*, (1999), 394-401.
16. Leahu, L. and Sengers, P., Freaky: performing hybrid human-machine emotion. In proc *DIS*, (2014), 607-616.
17. Lim, Y.-K., Stolterman, E., Jung, H. and Donaldson, J., Interaction gestalt and the design of aesthetic interactions. In proceedings of *CHI*, (2007), 239-254
18. Loke, L. and Robertson, T. Studies of Dancers: Moving from Experience to Interaction Design. *International Journal of Design*, *4* (2). 39-54.
19. Ludvigsen, M., Hillerup Fogtmann, M. and Grönbaek, K., TacTowers: An Interactive Training Equipment for Elite Athletes. In proceedings of *DIS*, (2010), 412-415.
20. Mauriello, S., Gubbels, M. and Froehlich, J., Social fabric fitness: the design and evaluation of wearable E-textile displays to support group running. In proceedings of *CHI*, (Toronto, CA, 2014), ACM Press, 2833-2842.
21. Michahelles, F. and Schiele, B. Sensing and Monitoring Professional Skiers. *IEEE Pervasive Comp*, *2005* (july-sept). 40-46.
22. Mueller, F., Agamanolis, S. and Picard, R.W., Exertion Interfaces: Sports over a Distance for Social Bonding and Fun. In proceedings of *CHI*, (2003), 561-568.
23. Mueller, F., Vetere, F., Gibbs, M.R., Edge, D., Agamanolis, S. and Sheridan, J.G., Jogging over a distance between Europe and Australia. In proceedings of *UIST*, (New York, NY, 2010), 189-198.
24. Nagargoje, A., Maybach, K. and Sokoler, T., Social Yoga Mats: Designing for Exercising / Socializing Synergy. In proceedings of *TEI*, (2012), 87-90.
25. Nenonen, V., Lindblad, A., Häkkinän, V., Laitinen, T., Jouhtio, M. and Hämäläinen, P., Using Heart Rate to Control an Interactive Game. In proceedings of *CHI*, (San Jose, CA, 2007), 853-856.
26. Normark, M. and Tholander, J., Performativity in Sustainable Interaction: The Case of Seasonal Grocery Shopping in EcoFriends. In proc *CHI*, (2014), 271-280.
27. Nylander, S., Jacobsson, M. and Tholander, J., RunRight; Real-time Visual and Audio Feedback on Running. In proceedings of *CHI EA,* (2014), 583-586.
28. Nylander, S., Kent, A. and Tholander, J., SwingSound - Experiencing the Golf Swing through Sound. In proceedings of *CHI EA,* (2014), 443-446.
29. Nylander, S. and Tholander, J., Designing for movement - the case of sports. In proceedings of *International workshop on Movement and Computing (MOCO)*, (2014), ACM Press, 130-135.
30. Pijnappel, S. and Mueller, F., 4 design themes for skateboarding. In proceedings *CHI*, (2013), 1271-1274
31. Rooksby, J., Rost, M., Morrison, A. and Chalmers, M., Personal Tracking as Lived Informatics. In proceedings of *CHI*, (Toronto, CA, 2014), ACM Press, 1163-1172.
32. Slovák, P., Janssen, J.H. and Fitzpatrick, G., Understanding Heart Rate Sharing: Towards Unpacking Physiosocial Space. In proc of *CHI*, (2012), 859-868.
33. Spelmezan, D., An Investigation into the Use of Tactile Instructions in Snowboarding. In proceedings of *MobileHCI*, (2012), 417-426.
34. Stienstra, J., Bruns Alonso, M., Wensveen, S. and Kuenen, S., How to Design for Transformation of Behavior through Interactive Materiality. In proceedings of *NordiCHI*, (2012), ACM Press, 21-30.
35. Ståhl, A., Löwgren, J. and Höök, K. Evocative Balance: Designing for Interactional Empowerment. *International Journal of Design*, *8* (1). 43-57.
36. Tholander, J. and Johansson, C., Design qualities for Whole Body Interaction - Learning from Golf, Skateboarding and BodyBugging. In proc of *NordiCHI*, (2010), 493-502.
37. Toscos, T., Faber, A., An, S. and Praful Gandhi, M., Chick Clique: Persuasive Technology to Motivate Teenage Girls to Exercise. In proc of *CHI EA*, (2006), 1873-1878.
38. Walmink, W., Wilde, D. and Mueller, F., Displaying heart rate data on a bicycle helmet to support social exertion experiences. In proc of *TEI*, (2014), 97-104
39. Wijnalda, G., Pauws, S., Vignoli, F. and Stuckenschmidt, H. A Personalized Music System for Motivation in Sport Performance. *IEEE Pervasive Computing*, *2005* (july-september). 26-32.

Contextual Influences on the Use and Non-Use of Digital Technology While Exercising at the Gym

Misha Patel
Foolproof and University College London
London, United Kingdom
misha.patel@foolproof.co.uk

Aisling Ann O'Kane
University College London
London, United Kingdom
a.okane@cs.ucl.ac.uk

ABSTRACT
The use of wearable technology will become significantly more prevalent in the coming years, with major companies releasing devices such as the Samsung Gear Fit. With sensors, such as pedometers and heart rate monitors, embedded in these devices it is possible to use them for fitness purposes. However, little is known about how wearable adopters actually use wearable and existing technologies during exercise. In an exploratory situated study of technology use and non-use in the context of the gym, fitness informatics adopters showed varied practices related to distraction, appropriating technology into their routines, and information needs. We discuss this variance in relation to individual differences and the impact of the physical nature of the gym. Although further research might show other influencing factors such as the social context, we make a case for the use of situated studies to uncover tensions that lead to use and non-use of technology that arise in the different unfolding situations of using wearables in everyday life, including at the gym, which is a surprisingly complex context.

INTRODUCTION
There has been an increase in the popularity and availability of personal informatics tools. This includes the growth of fitness mobile applications being developed for smartphone use, but also standalone wearable devices. The popularity of these technologies will continue to grow with large companies releasing smartwatches with embedded activity-tracking functionality, such as the Samsung Gear Fit. This trend has led the domains of exercise, fitness and wellbeing to be of increasing interest to the HCI community (e.g. [29]).

There has been significant emphasis on designing technology to encourage people to engage in physical activity. This includes the design of ubiquitous computing tools [4], the development of fitness device infrastructures [23], virtual trainers [12] and interactive social computer games [27]. These HCI studies have been concerned with the user evaluation of bespoke persuasive fitness technologies. However, people who adopt personal informatics typically do not use just one type of technology; for instance, Rooksby and colleagues discovered that some people interweave their use of different activity trackers [36]. There is a dearth of exploratory research that has investigated how and why different people use and do not use various technologies during physical activity, including at the gym: a popular place for regular exercise.

Regular physical activity is essential for good health and wellbeing, bringing about a range of physical, social and mental health benefits that are important for both the individual and for society [4]. As people become more aware of these rewards, the prevalence of people who go to the gym (also known as fitness centres or health clubs) is rising, with over a hundred new facilities opening in the UK in 2013 alone, and with memberships rising to 12.6% of the UK population [20]. Although users' behaviours and needs regarding mobile fitness technology have been investigated, there is little research on technology use at the gym and many studies use self-reported and retrospective data independent of the context of use (e.g. [19, 36]. As behavioural insights are typically obtained after the interactions occur and independent of their context, it is argued that such methods do not elicit comprehensive information about behaviour as it really happens in the world [11].

Examining interactions with technology within the context of use is crucial, as user actions are fundamentally embedded within a particular situation [39] and context is an ever-changing unfolding notion [18]. There have been exploratory situated studies investigating general technology use within contexts including the workplace [7] and the home [9]; however there has been little exploratory investigation into the use of technology in gyms. An 'in the wild' approach [35] is particularly appropriate for research into the use of fitness mobile applications and wearable devices, as they are designed to be used in an diversity of uncontrollable settings [28]. As fitness informatics adopters are inherently interested in the use of new technology, we

CHI 2015, April 18 - 23, 2015, Seoul, Republic of Korea

ACM 978-1-4503-3145-6/15/04...$15.00
http://dx.doi.org/10.1145/2702123.2702384

explored how the gym context influenced their adoption, use and non-use of digital technologies for purposes ranging from tracking to entertainment during individual physical activity.

BACKGROUND AND RELATED RESEARCH

Physical Activity and Fitness Research

Exercise is well studied in the domains of sports psychology and behaviour change. The concepts behind some persuasive technologies to support physical activity are loosely based on health behaviour change theories, featuring elements of social support, motivation and self-efficacy.

Motivation is a key feature of exercise and can account for individual differences in behaviours, inspiring people to engage in exercise. Intrinsic motivation is described as performing a behaviour for its own sake [40]; exercising for the enjoyment of the experience. It has been shown that performance feedback and having a personal choice of the type of music to listen to influences situational motivation [40]. On the other hand, extrinsic motivation is doing something as a means to an end as opposed to for its own sake, for instance exercising for the purpose of a reward such as achieving a weight loss target [40].

It has been found that tracking one's activity is beneficial for fitness behaviour change [38]. Setting goals for oneself is also a well-known strategy that has been shown to contribute towards behaviour change for fitness activity [13]. The design of many mobile fitness applications revolves around activity tracking and goal setting with the aim of increasing user's physical activity [14].

As well as the influence of individual personal goals on motivation, research has also demonstrated the motivational effects of external stimulation during physical activity. Engaging in technology for entertainment such as watching TV and listening to music has been discovered to have positive psychological and physiological effects on exercise performance [5]. In a review, Karagoris and Priest [26] summarised that during repetitive, endurance-related anaerobic activities, listening to self-selected motivational music demonstrated performance enhancing effects (e.g. an increase in stamina). Music was found to reduce perceptions of exertion; it is hypothesized that this may be due to a 'dissociation' effect through which music distracts attention away from the pain associated with the exercise [34]. Another way in which music has been shown to increase performance is through the characteristics of synchronous music, whereby the rhythm moderates movement patterns [6].

Another theoretical concept that relates to the individual's experience during exercise is 'flow' [33]. 'Flow' is a positive state of mind characterised by complete immersion and absorption in an activity [17]. Research has mentioned the positive effects of 'flow' on physical activity adherence [33].

Interactive Technology to Aid Physical Activity

The availability of health and fitness tracking capabilities is growing with the release of new commercially available technologies [21]. In light of this, fitness tracking sensors, such as heart rate monitors, accelerometers, pedometers and GPS (to track outdoor running and cycling) are being added to mobile and wearable devices such as smartphones and smartwatches. For instance, the Samsung Gear Fit tracks everyday activity such as the number of steps, presenting values to the user such as calories burnt and distance achieved, and it interfaces with Samsung phones for GPS and to provide notifications (e.g. text messages) through the watch.

There has been some research investigating behaviour relating to the use of personal informatics technology for general health and wellbeing. Ahtinen and colleagues [2] conducted a cross-cultural field study involving a technology probe where participants recorded subjective experiences about their use of a wellness mobile app for two weeks. Findings showed that cultural and environmental factors influenced user needs and usage of the application.

Similarly, Rooksby et al. [36] explored the area of 'lived informatics' in terms of the ways in which people use health and wellbeing activity tracking devices they have already adopted. The self-reported study revealed several categories of tracking behaviour, including documentary tracking (where participants track their activity for reasons such as facilitating understanding of their activity or sharing their stories with others) and directive tracking (where participants track their activity in order to reach a goal).

Approaches to Studying Fitness Technology

The majority of HCI research that investigates fitness technology use is for the purpose of evaluating specific fitness technologies. The Sports Tracker, a mobile outdoor sports tracking application [1], was evaluated through examining usage habits and user experience data for existing users of the application, which were collected through one-off phone interviews and text-message questionnaires lasting two weeks. Consolvo et al. [14] conducted a field evaluation of Houston, a mobile application that enables step-count tracking to enhance users' physical activity levels. A three-week in-situ evaluation study was implemented where participants used the application, were interviewed about their experiences, and completed questionnaires and daily records of step counts. Another system that was evaluated 'in the wild' was the UbiFit Garden system [15]; a mobile application along with a fitness device which displays a visualisation of the user's physical activity. The evaluation of the system was run on mobile phones that participants used and they were interviewed to examine user experiences. These studies have focused on investigating the use of specific technology, rather than looking at the range of technologies that can be and are used for personal fitness.

Other than Rooksby and colleagues [36] who used interviews and on-going self-reports on the use of personal informatics discussed above, there are only a limited number of studies within the HCI literature that take a more open, exploratory approach in examining general user behaviour in the domain of health. Fritz et al. [19] investigated the behaviour of long-term users of activity monitoring devices to find out how they use their devices; however they only used retrospective interview data to do so. On the other hand, Goodman [22] used more extensive methods (blog readings, interviews, diary reports for activity logging, and pedometer data) to explore people's health issues and behaviours in their daily lives, but only as a work in progress in order to discover ways in which health technology could be designed to support behaviour change. However, there have been few exploratory studies into technology use in the context of the gym.

Other than a few studies of specific technologies, many investigations looking at technology use in this review did not carry out situated research. The methods that were primarily used consisted of post-hoc interviews, diaries, experience sampling methods and logging devices [1,36]. The use of these methods undermines the pertinent role of the environment and situation of the activity in influencing interactions with technology [35]. As Brown et al. [11] argue, subtle but meaningful interactions with technology may be lost if the data is based on retrospective and self-reported information rather than the actual behaviour as it happens in the real world, during real time. Additionally, retrospective reports lack detail and may not capture every occurrence of use as they are susceptible to report bias, where recall is dependent on what the participant remembers and considers relevant [3]. Logging devices can obtain data at the point of use, but they only provide a conceptual outline of device usage and produces descriptions of only general use rather than understanding particular accounts of use [11]. Based on Brown and colleagues' rich findings on mobile phone use using situated methods, the current exploratory research warrants a situated approach to investigate technology use in the context where fitness informatics may be used: the gym.

METHODOLOGY

Context of the Study

The study took place in a busy London university gym, which is also open to the general public. Permission was gained from the gym to recruit members for the study. It is a relatively basic gym with regards to the facilities and technology available, in comparison to other more expensive gyms nearby. Other than a separate floor for group classes, it comprises four main areas with: machines for aerobic exercises (e.g. treadmills, cross trainers and exercise bikes), resistance machines, free weights and a mat area for stretching or floor exercises (see Figure 2, left). Aerobic exercises are activities that involve constant repetitive movements of the arms and legs, heightening

Figure 1: Samsung Gear Fit worn on the wrist at the gym

heart rate and respiration (e.g. running), and it can involve interval training consisting of systematic fluctuation of speed. Anaerobic exercises comprise short bursts of intense exertion (e.g. weightlifting) where recovery breaks ('deadtime') are usually taken in between exercises or 'reps'. On the wall in front of the aerobic machines are a set of mirrors and five television screens displaying various subtitled programs while loud, popular music plays through speakers around the whole gym area.

Autoethnography

The initial phase in this research was a four-week autoethnography study by the first author with the Samsung Gear Fit (see Figure 1), as described above. The purpose of this autoethnography was to obtain an in-depth understanding of the various contexts of everyday use [30] of a fitness related wearable device. Her experiences relating to its use were documented in textual diary entries at the end of every day. The insights influenced the structure and format of the user study, and the diary entries were analysed as part of the findings.

In-Situ User Study

Participants

Recruitment posters were put up in the gym and around the university campus. Participants were only recruited if they were members of the gym and currently used or had used wearable technology or fitness applications. This ensured that participants had at least some prior experience with using tracking technology and the facilities in the gym to prevent the additional extrinsic motivation of making them exercise or adding technology only for the purpose of the study [32]. Participants gave informed consent as stipulated by UCL ethical procedures and were financially compensated with £10 cash on completion of the session.

The study involved 11 participants: four females and seven males between the ages of 21 and 35 years (mean age of 26 years). Nine participants were students and two were professionals, all living in London. Eight participants currently owned or had used a wearable device including: Fitbit3, Nike Fuelband4, Sony Smartband5, heart rate monitor and pedometer. Five participants occasionally used a smartphone application for tracking running or diet. Eight participants brought in their smartphones to the gym to listen to music, watch TV, use messaging and social media,

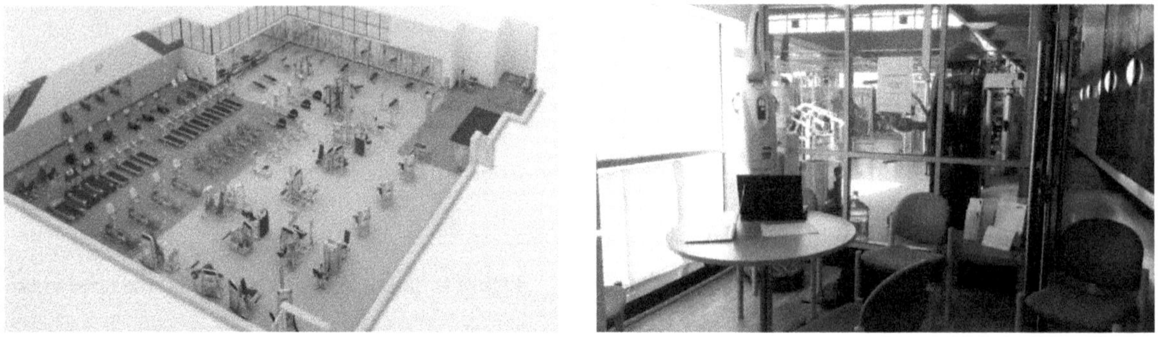

Figure 2: The layout of the gym (left), and the location of the contextual interviews and in-situ coding meetings (right)

or as a tool to record their exercise. Pseudonyms are used in the findings to preserve anonymity.

User Study Procedure

To test and refine the chosen methodology, two participants who fulfilled the recruitment criteria took part in pilot studies. Data from pilot study was not directly included in the results of the main user study as the participant observation changed significantly after their participation, but the findings did contribute to the overall analysis.

The main user study involved three different data collection phases for each of the 11 participants, conducted by the first author: entry briefing and contextual interview, participant observations and dialogue during exercise, and exit contextual interview and debrief.

The semi-structured contextual entry interviews lasted between 30 and 45 minutes and were conducted in the gym reception area next to a big window with a view of the context of use (see Figure 2, right), which can give a richer account than other types of interviews [25]. Interviews were semi-structured with the aim of developing rapport with participants and for them to feel comfortable to talk about their experiences. The purpose of the interview was to gain understanding of how they currently perceive their use of technology during exercise. An initial interview script for the first interview was generated as a product of the autoethnography and pilot interviews, and was used to guide the interview. Questions involved asking about their exercise routines (e.g. *What are your motivations for exercise; why do you attend the gym?*), participants' experience of various technologies during exercise (e.g. *What type of wearable technology or fitness applications do you use or have you used in the past?*) and how they use technology when exercising (e.g. *Do you think the use of this technology impacts on your exercise behaviour?*). Using an exploratory approach, the interview questions were adapted as relevant themes emerged from the data. The interviewer would sometimes prompt the participant to keep focus on relevant conversation. Interviews were audio recorded to facilitate transcription.

Immediately after the interview, the first author carried out participant observation whilst they performed their usual exercise regime in the gym to capture technology interaction. Participants were asked to engage in dialogue where they verbalised their thoughts and feelings to capture their experience and motivations underlying certain actions. Observations lasted for the duration of the participant's exercise routine, but no longer than one hour. The first author was dressed in workout clothing and was situated near the participant on an exercise machine in order to blend in. Observation notes were written on a smartphone, as the gym did not allow video capture.

Post-interviews were conducted immediately after the participant observations and lasted for about ten minutes, taking place in context (Figure 2, right). The researcher clarified any questions about the participant's observed behaviour, and then summarised the information gathered from the interview and observation.

Data Analysis

Iterative data gathering and analysis proceeded with the interviews being immediately transcribed and the textual observations written out in full, and then both coded for salient themes by the first author. Throughout the analysis process, emerging themes and insights were discussed between the authors in the context of the gym [31] during in-situ coding meetings (see Figure 2, right), which helped to adapt the focus of questions asked in subsequent interviews [16]. The data analysis process took part in four stages, loosely following the phases of thematic analysis [10]: immediately transcribing the data, becoming familiar with it; open coding of the data between each interview looking for salient themes from the interviews, observations, and autoethnography; and axial coding to categorise them systematically using an affinity diagram [24]. Finally, three rounds of categorisation were performed to drill down from issues with adoption, carrying and using technology, focusing on fitness and non-fitness technology, uncovering tensions leading to use and non-use that are presented in the findings. Data were also analysed through the links to previous literature [10].

FINDINGS

The findings are arranged in three separate themes that arose from the data, but there is much overlap between topics. The themes are presented as the following use and non-use tensions: technology used for distraction vs. technology causing disruption; information needs met by technology vs. avoiding information provided by technology; and exercise influencing technology use vs. technology use influencing exercise.

Distraction vs. Disruption

There were many cases where participants used technology to distract themselves from the task at hand: exercising. On the other hand, there were situations where technology used for non-fitness reasons caused disruption to exercise, so participants actively avoided it.

Technology Used for Distraction

Six participants were observed using technology as a source of distraction: they got immersed in watching videos, listening to music or audio books, or looking at the machine display. This diverted their attention away from thinking about the exercise towards the distraction technology. Participants suggested that they required distraction from concentrating on performing certain exercises in the gym as this reduced the intensity of their perception of the pain, effort and tiredness experienced during exercise (cf. [34]).

(Referring to the machine display and music) "*Having something else to concentrate on takes my mind away from pain and tiredness*" (Andy, interview)

"*I try not to think about what I am doing so I watch TV on my phone. Distraction is my key. When I cannot use my phone I have to concentrate on it and I feel every second of it*" (Juliette, observation and dialogue)

The need to divert attention meant that some participants used any technology they could to distract them. One participant watched TV to distract her from her cross trainer exercise, regardless of the value of entertainment it provided.

"*I would watch TV just to take my mind off what I'm doing, even though I don't really like what's on*" (Helen, observation and dialogue)

This need to use technology for distraction was mainly observed for participants performing aerobic exercises that did not necessarily require attention on the activity or the machine display in order to achieve performance, such as running at a steady pace on the treadmill. This type of exercise allowed participants to disengage their attention from the exercise and to direct it towards something else. However, when participants performed interval training or weight training, many did not use technology for the purpose of distraction.

"*I only watch TV on my phone when I'm doing aerobic exercises like on the elliptical machine, but I don't on the resistance machines*" (Juliette, observation and dialogue)

Technology Use Causing Disruption

One of the reasons that participants didn't make as much use of technology during anaerobic exercises as they did for aerobic exercises was because many preferred to mentally count the number of repetitions they were performing to keep track of their exercise progress and therefore needed to direct their attention towards the task.

"*I would stop listening to music and focus on counting the reps in my head instead, so I know how many I can manage to do today*" (Sammy, observation and dialogue)

Unlike aerobic machines, the resistance machines did not provide automatic activity tracking functionality and so participants were required to manually count their repetitions. This need for concentration on counting repetitions inhibited the use of any technology that might disrupt this, even when participants would have preferred to use it for distraction purposes. Three participants would have still preferred to use their phones to watch TV and listen to music during weight training, but they did not, because it conflicted with their need to count their repetitions.

"*It would be great if the machine or my [wrist] Fitbit could automatically count my reps so I could listen to my music properly*" (Sammy, observation and dialogue)

Even for aerobic exercise, disruption could be unwelcome and technology could be avoided to minimise it. When the smartphone notification feature was active on the Samsung Gear Fit during the first author's activity on the cross trainer, it disrupted her concentration. She found this constant disruption frustrating and eventually disabled that feature for the rest of the duration of her exercise sessions.

"*The notifications made me lose concentration of what I was doing and I had to slow down just to read the message which was annoying, so I turned it off*" (autoethnography diary)

Another reason why people avoided disruption stems from their beliefs about the relationship between exercise and technology use. Some participants believed that exercise is an opportunity to focus on the mind and body: to be immersed in the experience of exercise. The deep concentration may be related to a sense of 'flow'; a state characterised by complete immersion and absorption in an activity [17].

"*I think exercise should be a time to get away from unnecessary technology and distractions and just focus on exercising and being in the zone, that's why I don't even bring my phone with me*" (Kevin, interview)

Summary of the Distraction/Disruption Tension

The findings show that unintentional disruption to concentration can consequently impact performance, enjoyment, or even the ability to exercise, which can be viewed negatively and lead to disengagement. For the design of technology that might be used in the gym, this must be balanced with people's desire to dissociate from the exercise through distraction, as entertainment can motivate people to exercise more often and for longer.

Information Needs vs. Avoiding Information

Many participants wanted to use technology to monitor their practices and to motivate themselves by reviewing their fitness information. Unfortunately, these information needs sometimes conflicted with their need to avoid demotivating information, both in the gym and outside it.

Information Needs Met by Technology

Nine participants primarily used the measures of time, distance, calories and heart rate on the fitness tracking displays on aerobic machines. Using these measurements, participants monitored their current progress, set themselves goals and moderated their level of exertion to reach their goal. This goal directed tracking behaviour relates to the 'directive tracking' style [36]. For example, two participants were concerned with maintaining their heart rate within a certain range and therefore during aerobic exercises they constantly focused their attention on the heart rate display, moderating their exertion level to achieve their target heart rate.

"*I look at the heart rate monitor, if it is lower than my target then I speed up to try and reach it*" (Kevin, observation and dialogue)

It was observed that participants used different aspects of performance feedback values to motivate their activity, and this was dependent on the exercise as well as what part of the exercise they were at. For instance, four participants found seeing that there was little time remaining of their workout motivated them to increase exertion.

"*When I see there is only 40 secs left I think to myself, "come on you can do it!"*" (Marie, observation and dialogue)

As well as for motivational purposes, activity monitoring is sometimes required for particular exercises. The three participants who performed interval training exercises used the information on the machine display as a way to structure their workout. They explained that they used the time display as an indicator for when they needed to adjust their speed control.

"*I'm looking at the time so I know that every two minutes I need to change my speed*" (Marie, observation and dialogue)

In contrast, some participants chose to focus on less reliable information; two participants focused on the calorie counter on the machine display as an aid for exercise motivation. Although they knew this was an inaccurate measure, it was satisfying for them just to know that calories were being burned as their exercise goals were related to weight loss and body shape. This was also observed for the Nike Fuelband where there was satisfaction gained by reaching the 'next full number' on a constantly ascending or descending value, such as aiming to achieve 3000 Fuelpoints rather than stopping at 2800.

"*I would never stop before I reach a full number, even though I don't really know what the Fuelpoints are based on*" (Harry, observation and dialogue)

Participants reviewed performance data logged by the activity tracking technology after they had exercised at the gym. Eight participants described that they enjoyed looking at their performance data from wearable devices to facilitate a better understanding of their fitness behaviour ('documentary tracking' [36]).

"*Data is knowledge when you look at it in the right way*" (Nigel, interview)

One reason why participants used fitness technology outside of the gym was to motivate exercise behaviour in the gym. Martin claimed the Fuelband data motivated him to exercise in order to not break the streak of goal achievement he had developed; the motivation stemmed from the disappointment of the thought of not meeting the goal. This shows the powerful motivational effect that tracking fitness and goals setting can have on the participant's behaviour.

"*I was addicted to meeting my daily goals; once you develop streaks, you don't want to break it.*" (Martin, interview)

Avoiding Information Provided by Technology

Conversely, some participants suggested that they avoided information to evade the feelings of shame and disappointment of not being able to meet a goal. Harry explained that he avoided wearing his Nike Fuelband device on certain days where he knew that he would not go to the gym in order to avoid the negative affect associated with seeing an unmet goal. This may relate to the participant self-identity as "*somebody who always reaches his goal*" and so he avoids behaviour that would violate that perception.

"*When I am too busy to exercise as much, I don't wear the Fuelband. I don't like to see that I have not reached my goal so would rather not wear it at all on some days*" (Harry, interview)

Avoiding looking at certain measures of fitness tracking was observed and some participants explained that they found it demotivating during their exercise. For constant aerobic fast paced, high intensity exercises (e.g. running on the treadmill), six participants consciously avoided looking at the time on the machine display.

Juliette placed her phone on the display pad, deliberately covering the time during use of the elliptical machine (Juliette, observation notes)

"*I avoid looking at the time when I'm running, it makes my goal seem further away*" (Nigel, observation and dialogue)

A reason for this was because participants believed that watching the clock increases their perception of their effort and tiredness, and reduces the perceived speed of time. This distortion of perception of time could have a negative effect on some participants' motivation and consequently affect their performance.

"*When I am tired I avoid constantly looking at the time, it makes it feel like more effort and time seems to go slower!*" (Marie, observation and dialogue)

As well as the time measure, participants avoided looking at other values that also indicated low performance progress. Two participants did not look at the progress display near the beginning of their workout when progress was low because they found it de-motivating. This highlights that the use of technology is influenced by certain temporal stages within a workout.

"*I don't want to look at calories at the beginning because it is low and I think I am not doing well*" (Sammy, observation and dialogue)

Similarly, it was observed that some participants avoided viewing their performance data until after their workout session as opposed to during. One reason for this is because seeing a larger achievement at the end provided a greater sense of accomplishment and surprise rather than viewing smaller increments of progress.

"*I prefer to see my data after exercise because I feel good when I have seen that I have burnt 500 calories in one go, it is a nice surprise when I see I have done well*" (Juliette, interview)

Summary of the Information Needs Tension

Our findings suggest that that there is a fine line to be walked with regards to fitness information presented to people at the gym. Information at the time of exercise helped participants to monitor and adjust performance, but it could also be demotivating if it showed low progress. Even arbitrary data points can motivate people if they are shown positive results, but people can also avoid the use of fitness technology altogether if they expect there to be negative results.

Exercise Shaping Tech Use vs. Tech Use Shaping Exercise

Another tension that arose from the data was caused by the physical nature of the context: the exercises influenced the use of digital technology, but the technology could also influence people's exercise at the gym.

Exercise Influencing Technology Use

One factor that influenced the use of technology was the restrictions imposed by physical characteristics of the exercise. Exercise involves dynamic body movements, which then limit the types of digital technology that can be used. An example of this was the impracticality of using technology that required sustained visual attention, such as reading when running. Harry stated that he would have liked to use his mobile phone but the physicality of running does not make this possible, forcing him to not use the technology as desired.

"*I would like to read from my phone when I'm running, but it's difficult when I'm moving around so I have to wait until the breaks*" (Harry, observation and dialogue)

Additionally, the specific aspects of exercising in the gym limited the functionality that was useful on wearables. The Samsung Gear Fit was unable to track the first author's use of the bicycle machine in the gym because the smartphone was required for the GPS distance tracking function, which went against her expectations of just using a wearable device during exercise without the need of a phone.

"*I was excited to be able to use the 'cycle' tracking function at spin class. However I discovered that this feature only works when the phone is nearby for GPS detection. I felt disappointed*" (autoethnography diary)

The physical set up of the equipment also restricted the participants being able to use technology in their desired way. For example, Juliette usually prefers to watch TV on her phone and the elliptical trainer allows her to do this because the machine also provided a shelf to place her phone. In contrast, the resistance machines did not afford a physical space to place a phone and so she was unable to watch TV during that exercise. She described that this limitation consequently affected her experience of the exercise as she was forced to focus on her performance, thus increasing her awareness on the feelings of pain. Having this repeated experience contributed to her losing motivation for this exercise and she stopped using resistance machines altogether.

Technology Use Influencing Exercise

The desire to use some technology during exercise proved to be strong enough to actually impact the way participants exercised in the gym. Juliette adapted the way she used the elliptical trainer in a way to minimize interaction with the display: she exercised at a constant speed and set the time to the maximum workout length to watch a TV program on her tablet.

"*I guess I want to keep at a steady pace so I can concentrate on watching TV and not have to think about changing my speed or playing with the display [...] I don't really want to be distracted from my distraction!*" (Juliette, observation and dialogue).

There were some situations where participants wanted to use technology for performance tracking but the functionality of technology led to a change in the physical activity. Juliette wanted to monitor her performance on the elliptical trainer but her Fitbit did not capture her strides when she held onto the handlebars, so she chose not to hold on to the handlebars as a way of gaining stride information.

"*It's annoying that the Fitbit doesn't count my gym activity [...] I don't hold onto the handlebars so my strides can count towards my daily step count. It looks stupid and makes the exercise harder*" (Juliette, observation and dialogue)

It was uncovered that this same participant had a strategy of avoiding the use of non-fitness related technology outside of the gym in order to motivate her to exercise: Juliette refrains from watching TV and films on Netflix at home and sets herself a rule that she can only watch TV at the gym. This motivates her to go to the gym to exercise as it allows the opportunity to watch her favourite programs.

"*I feel less guilty when I'm bingeing on Netflix at the gym. I promised myself I would only watch them here [in the gym] and not at home*" (Juliette, observation and dialogue)

Summary of the Exercise/Technology Tension

The findings indicate that the physicality of the gym impacted the ways people were able to use technology, leading to issues of frustration. The need to use technology impacted exercise negatively in some cases, but its active avoidance could also motivate exercise. Technology impacting exercise and exercise impacting technology use led to disengagement and engagement with both the technologies and the exercises.

DISCUSSION

'Going to the gym' can be perceived as a singular activity in a box; people going in, exercising and coming out. However, the findings of this situated exploratory study show that this is not the case; the gym is a complex and dynamic environment. This includes variety in the physicality of exercises, the physical design, and the facilities as well as how an exercise changes over its course. The most dominant factor is the difference in types of exercise performed in the gym influencing the use and non-use of digital technology: exercises are inherently different in the way that they are performed and what they demand from the individual. For example, the physicality of the context of exercising at the gym meant a participant was looking for distraction on their smartphones during the 'deadtime' between reps or when they were bored on the treadmill, but were very frustrated by any disruption when they were concentrating on form or particularly when counting reps on non-digital resistance machines. Across the data set, exercise was found to influence the occupation of physical space, the physical equipment and how people were feeling in the moment, and therefore influenced the technologies available and participants' use and non-use of technology.

Beyond the complexity of the environment, we found that the people who go to the gym can have very different technology needs. There are many available technology choices in the gym and participants used and adopted them in different ways. This variety in use was related to participants' motivations for exercise, their health goals, how they valued exercise, their individual preferences towards certain technologies, and simply their personal taste. For example, intrinsic motivation to exercise meant that participants monitored in-the-moment heart rate information or avoided technology altogether to achieve a sense of 'flow', but extrinsic motivation meant that other participants actively avoided low performance values on a Fuelband or prioritized watching TV on their phone for distraction and therefore did not use resistance machines. With regards to fitness technologies, we found there were differences in the way that individuals used the activity tracking technology, in line with Rooksby et al. [36].

Rather than independently determining behaviour, the complexity of the environment and the complexity of individual differences are intertwined in how they influence the use and non-use of technology in the gym. Non-use has been gaining attention in the HCI domain in recent years (e.g. [8]). Satchell and Dourish [37] talk about different types of non-use of technology such as active resistance, disenchantment, and disinterest, but these categories do not cover the non-use that we found among the fitness informatics adopting participants. Our participants opted in and opted out of using technology based on the type of exercise they were doing, the physical space afforded near that exercise, and the point they were at in a particular exercise. This opting in and opting out of technology use was also closely linked to people's individual differences, particularly their values, motivations, and preferences.

This study took a step towards expanding our understanding of the influence that context of use can have on the rhythms/routines of the gym visit and rhythms/routines of technology use. However, even with this targeted scope, it did not access the complete complexity of the gym context. This study involved a limited amount of participants, focused on working out alone at the gym and participants may have been influenced by the presence of a researcher observing them, which influence its representativeness. If the study involved the recruitment of participants who come to the gym to exercise with a partner (or 'gym buddy') or observed people in group classes, it might have uncovered factors relating to how the social context influences fitness technology use.

Features such as sensors and pedometers are being added to smartwatches under the assumption that this is what people want and are able to use throughout different settings, including during exercise. In reality, a large number of people choose the gym as their regular source of physical activity, and this context influences what people want to use and what they can actually use. We found that if participants want to use some of these features, they choose to alter the way they exercise, for example where a participant with a wrist FitBit did not use the handlebars on the elliptical and felt unbalanced while gaining pedometer information. Similarly, people can opt out of features of the technology entirely if it does not fit into their exercise preferences, as was the case where text notifications were disabled on the Samsung Gear Fit to prevent disruption.

This research has particular relevance to the growing trend for wearable technologies, especially those geared towards fitness, such as the Samsung Gear Fit or Apple Watch. The use of these increasingly popular technologies has not been comprehensively explored in the context of everyday life, and much work still needs to be completed focusing on how different aspects of people's lives influence use and non-use, and how the use of the technology in turn influences people's lives. By using a situated approach, the current study reveals use and non-use tensions that arise for fitness technologies that may be used in the gym, as it is a complex space and individual differences are wide-ranging. We should be wary of context-independent design and research of wearable technologies that are meant to be useful in all environments, including in and outside of the gym and in conjunction with the use of a variety of other technology. Wearable technology is inherently mobile and therefore its use is influenced by the unfolding and dynamic context in which it is used, as well as the individual using it. As such, a situated approach to design and 'in the wild' evaluation would allow for the investigation of contextual factors that influence the various uses and non-uses of these emerging technologies.

CONCLUSION

The aim of this study was to investigate the use and non-use of technology during exercise in the gym. Through taking a situated exploratory approach to this research, it was revealed that the gym context is complex and dynamic, and the complexities of the context influence the use and non-use of technology. Use and non-use tensions became evident with regards to distraction vs. disruption, information needs vs. information avoidance, and technology influencing exercise vs. exercise influencing technology. People's choices to opt in or opt out of using technology were dependent on context and situation, influenced by individual differences as well as the physicality of the gym. Values, motivations, and preferences influenced use and non-use of technology. On the other hand, even if the design of the technology caters for the variance in users, it cannot be assumed that the technology will be used in the in the same way throughout the exercise, for all exercises, and in the same places. This is because context is dynamic and people react in accordance to their environment at that particular moment in time [18,39]. These findings point to the importance for future work to take a situated approach to understand, design and evaluate technology to be used in a variety of contexts by a variety of individuals, such as wearable devices for fitness.

ACKNOWLEDGEMENTS

This research has been funded in part by the UK Engineering and Physical Sciences Research Council CHI+MED project [EP/G059063/1] with support from the Samsung Research and Development Institute UK.

REFERENCES

1. Ahtinen, A., Isomursu, M., Huhtala, Y., and Kaasinen, J. Tracking Outdoor Sports – User Experience Perspective. *Ambient Intelligence,* (2008), 192–209.

2. Ahtinen, A., Ramiah, S., Blom, J., and Isomursu, M. Design of Mobile Wellness Applications : Identifying Cross-Cultural Factors. In *Proc. OzCHI,* ACM Press (2008), 164–171.

3. Ainsworth, B.E., Sternfeld, B., Slattery, M.L., Daguisé, V., and Zahm, S.H. Physical activity and breast cancer: evaluation of physical activity assessment methods. *Cancer 83*, 3 Suppl (1998), 611–20.

4. Albinali, F., Intille, S., Haskell, W., and Rosenberger, M. Using wearable activity type detection to improve physical activity energy expenditure estimation. In *Proc. UbiComp 2010*, ACM Press (2010), 311.

5. Annesi, J.J. Effects of music, television, and a combination entertainment system on distraction, exercise adherence, and physical output in adults. *Can. J. of Behavioural Science 33,* 3 (2001) 193.

6. Anshel, M.H. and Marisi, D.Q. Effect of Music and Rhythm on Physical Performance. *Res. Quart. Am. All. for Health, Phys. Ed. and Rec. 49*, 2 (1978), 109–113.

7. Bardram, J.E. Plans as Situated Action : An Activity Theory Approach to Workflow Systems. In *Proc. ECSCW 1997,* Springer (1997), 17-32.

8. Baumer, E.P.S., Ames, M.G., Brubaker, J.R., Burrell, J., and Dourish, P. Refusing, Limiting, Departing: Why We Should Study Technology Non-use. In *Proc. CHI EA 2014*, ACM Press (2014), 65–68.

9. Blythe, M. and Monk, A. Notes towards an ethnography of domestic technology. In *Proc. DIS 2002*, ACM Press (2002), 277.

10. Braun, V. and Clarke, V. Using thematic analysis in psychology. *Qualitative research in psychology 3*, 2 (2006), 77–101.

11. Brown, B., McGregor, M., and Laurier, E. iPhone in Vivo: Video Analysis of Mobile Device Use. In *Proc. CHI 2013*, ACM (2013), 1031–1040.

12. Buttussi, F., Chittaro, L., and Nadalutti, D. Bringing mobile guides and fitness activities together : a solution based on an embodied virtual trainer. In *Proc. Mobile HCI 2006*, ACM. (2006), 29-36.

13. Cobb, L.E., Stone, W.J., Anonsen, L.J., and Klein, D. a. The Influence of Goal Setting on Exercise Adherence. *J. of Health Ed. 31*, 5 (2000), 277–281.

14. Consolvo, S., Harrison, B., Smith, I., et al. Conducting In Situ Evaluations for and With Ubiquitous Computing Technologies. *IJHCI 22*, 1-2 (2007), 103–118.

15. Consolvo, S., Libby, R., Smith, I., et al. Activity sensing in the wild. In *Proc. CHI 2008*, ACM Press (2008), 1797.

16. Corbin, J.M. and Strauss, A. Grounded theory research: Procedures, canons, and evaluative criteria. *Qual. Soc. 13*, 1 (1990), 3–21.

17. Csikszentmihalyi, M. and Csikszentmihalyi, S. *Optimal Experience: Psychological Studies of Flow in Consciousness*. Cambridge University Press, 1992.

18. Dourish, P. What we talk about when we talk about context. *Per. and Ubiq. Comput. 8*, 1 (2004), 19–30.

19. Fritz, T., Huang, E.M., Murphy, G.C., and Zimmermann, T. Persuasive Technology in the Real World : A Study of Long-Term Use of Activity Sensing Devices for Fitness. In *Proc. CHI 2014,* ACM (2014), 487–496.

20. Future Fit Training. The UK Fitness Industry Report - commentary. 2013. http://www.futurefit.co.uk/personal-training/news-and-views/2013/10/02/uk-fitness-industry-report/.

21. Gittleson, K. BBC News - Can Nike's Fuelband really motivate you to exercise? 2013. http://www.bbc.co.uk/news/technology-24543910

22. Goodman, E. Seeing fit : Visualizing physical activity in context. In *Proc. CHI EA 2006,* ACM (2006), 797–802.

23. Gupta, N. and Jilla, S. Digital Fitness Connector: Smart Wearable System. In *Proc. ICI 2011*, IEEE (2011), 118–121.

24. Hartson, H.R. and Pyla, P.S. *The UX Book: process and guidelines for ensuring a quality user experience*. Elsevier, Amsterdam ; Boston, 2012.

25. Holtzblatt, K. and Jones, S. Contextual inquiry: A participatory technique for system design. *Participatory design*, (1993), 180–193.

26. Karageorghis, C.I. and Priest, D.-L. Music in the exercise domain: a review and synthesis (Part I). *Int. Review of sport and exercise psych. 5*, 1 (2012), 44–66.

27. Lin, J.J., Mamykina, L., Lindtner, S., Delajoux, G., and Strub, H.B. Fish ' n ' Steps : Encouraging Physical Activity with an Interactive Computer Game. UbiComp (2006), 261–278.

28. Moran, T.P. and Dourish, P. Introduction to this special issue on context-aware computing. *HCI 16*, 2-4 (2001), 87–95.

29. Nylander, S., Tholander, J., Mueller, F., and Marshall, J. HCI and sports. In *Proc. CHI EA 2014*, ACM Press (2014), 115–118.

30. O'Kane, A.A., Rogers, Y., and Blandford, A.E. Gaining empathy for non-routine mobile device use through autoethnography. In *Proc. CHI 2014*, ACM Press (2014), 987–990.

31. Oulasvirta, A., Kurvinen, E., and Kankainen, T. Understanding Contexts by Being There: Case Studies in Bodystorming. *Per. Ubiq. Comput. 7*, 2 (2003), 125–134.

32. Pelletier, Luc G., Michelle S. Fortier, Robert J. Vallerand, Kim M. Tuson, Nathalie M. Briere, M.R.B. Toward a new measure of intrinsic motivation, extrinsic motivation, and amotivation in sports: The Sport Motivation Scale (SMS). *J. Sport & Exercise Psych. 17*, 35–53.

33. Petosa, R.L. and Holtz, B. Flow for Exercise Adherence: Testing an Intrinsic Model of Health Behavior. *Amer. J. Health Edu. 44*, 5 (2013), 273–277.

34. Potteiger, J.A., Schroeder, J.M., and Goff, K.L. Influence of music on ratings of perceived exertion during 20 minutes of moderate intensity exercise. *Perceptual and motor skills 91*, 3 Pt 1 (2000), 848–54.

35. Rogers, Y. Interaction design gone wild: striving for wild theory. *Interactions 18*, 4 (2011), 58.

36. Rooksby, J., Rost, M., Morrison, A., and Chalmers, M.C. Personal tracking as lived informatics. In *Proc. CHI 2014*, (2014), 1163–1172.

37. Satchell, C. and Dourish, P. Beyond the User: Use and Non-use in HCI. In *Proc. OZCHI 2009*, ACM (2009), 9–16.

38. Speck, B.J. and Looney, S.W. Effects of a minimal intervention to increase physical activity in women: daily activity records. *Nursing Research 50*, 6 (2001), 374–8.

39. Suchman, L. *Plans and Situated Actions*. Cambridge University Press, 1987.

40. Vallerand, R.J. and Losier, G.F. An integrative analysis of intrinsic and extrinsic motivation in sport. *J. Applied Sport Psych. 11*, 1 (1999), 142–169.

TastyBeats: Designing Palatable Representations of Physical Activity

Rohit Ashok Khot[1], Jeewon Lee[1], Deepti Aggarwal[2], Larissa Hjorth[3], Florian 'Floyd' Mueller[1]
[1]Exertion Games Lab, RMIT University, Australia, { rohit, jeewon, floyd }@exertiongameslab.org
[2]Microsoft Centre for Social NUI, University of Melbourne, Australia, daggarwal@student.unimelb.edu.au
[3]RMIT University, Australia, larissa.hjorth@rmit.edu.au

Figure 1: TastyBeats is a fountain-based interactive system that creates a fluidic spectacle of mixing sport drinks based on heart rate data of physical activity.

ABSTRACT
In this paper, we introduce palatable representations that besides improving the understanding of physical activity through abstract visualization also provide an appetizing drink to celebrate the experience of being physically active. By designing such palatable representations, our aim is to offer novel opportunities for reflection on one's physical activities. We present TastyBeats, a fountain-based interactive system that creates a fluidic spectacle of mixing sport drinks based on heart rate data of physical activity, which the user can later consume to replenish the loss of body fluids due to the physical activity. We articulate our experiences in designing the system as well as learning gained through field deployments of the system in participants' homes for a period of two weeks. We found that our system increased participants' awareness of physical activity and facilitated a shared social experience, while the prepared drink was treated as a hedonic reward that motivated participants to exercise more. Ultimately, with this work, we aim to inspire and guide design thinking on palatable representations, which we believe opens up new interaction possibilities to support physical activity experience.

CHI 2015, April 18 - 23 2015, Seoul, Republic of Korea.

ACM 978-1-4503-3145-6/15/04...$15.00.
http://dx.doi.org/10.1145/2702123.2702197

Author Keywords
Palatable representation; fluidic interfaces; physical activity; quantified self; personal informatics; Human-Food Interaction (HFI).

ACM Classification Keywords
H.5.m. Information interfaces and presentation (e.g., HCI): Miscellaneous.

INTRODUCTION
Activity trackers like pedometers and heart rate monitors are becoming increasingly popular to support physical activity experiences [41]. These devices collect personally relevant data such as bodily responses to physical activity and provide opportunities to reflect on the collected data through self-monitoring [22]. For example, pedometers count the number of steps taken in a day, while heart rate monitors inform about exercise intensity. Research suggests that regular use of these devices can increase user motivation for physical activity [35, 43].

One key aspect of tracking physical activity is visualization, which improves understanding of the data [22, 35]. "Seeing" makes knowledge credible [4] and "*greater visibility of information puts an added responsibility to act on*" as pointed out by Viseu and Suchman [45]. For example, by visualizing physical activity data, users can gain a better understanding of their physical activity levels and can make this gained knowledge actionable towards their health and fitness related aims [22]. However, physical activity data such as heart rate is abstract in nature and does not have a "*natural counterpart that can be graphically reproduced*", as noted by Vande Moere [44]; thus highlighting the role of designers for creating meaningful mappings to communicate this information to the user. In response, previous works in the field of HCI have looked at different on-screen visualization methods [1, 7, 8, 12, 23]. A screen, on one hand, offers the capacity to stimulate visual senses, but on other hand, often reduces the user interaction to just the reading of information due to its flat display surface. We think that there is an opportunity to explore new ways of engaging with physical activity data that should go beyond visualizing data on screens. We believe that physical activity data is not just a number, but rather a unique and personal outcome that reflects the amount of energy expended and efforts invested by the user; which we think needs to be emphasized and celebrated.

We, therefore, introduce *palatable representations* that besides improving the understanding of physical activity through fluidic visualization also provide an appetizing drink to celebrate the experience of being physically active. Palatable representation for us involves the use of drinkable fluids such as sports drinks to represent physical activity data. As a proof of concept, we present *TastyBeats*, an interactive system that utilizes heart rate data of physical activity to create a personalized sports drink. *TastyBeats* employs a fountain-based interaction to fashion a fluidic spectacle that can also be tasted, thus offering vivid ways of engagement with the data. Additionally, the prepared drink serves as a refreshment to replenish body fluids that were lost during physical activity. As such, palatable representations contribute to the human energy cycle, where the energy, which is lost during the physical activity, is given back to the body in the form of a drink.

In order to understand how palatable representations can support the everyday physical activity experience, we conducted "in the wild" [34] field deployments of the *TastyBeats* system. We deployed *TastyBeats* in three households for a period of two weeks where six participants, two from each house, interacted with the system on a daily basis. Participants were asked to measure their heart rate data for the entire day and then prepare a drink in the evening. We found that our system increased awareness about physical activity and the experience was rewarding and motivating for the participants. We utilize these findings as well as our experiences of designing the system to articulate interesting aspects of palatable representations, which we believe opens up new interaction possibilities to support the human energy-cycle.

RELATED WORK

Commercial physical activity sensor systems often support visualizations of physical activity data through an accompanying website or a smartphone app, where physical activity data is analyzed through numbers, bar charts and graphs. Studies, however, show that many people have low graph literacy skills and, therefore, do not easily grasp statistical data [15]. As a result, much of the health and physical activity related smartphone apps could fall short in engaging people. In response, prior works have looked at other ways of representing physical activity data.

Visualization through digital metaphors

Consolvo et al. [7] redesigned mobile phone screens in the form of a virtual garden where the flowers grow in size as the user performs physical activity; This method of visualization motivated participants in maintaining their physical activity as participants wanted to make the virtual flowers grow. In another system called Fish'n'Steps [23], user's step count was mapped to an animated fish, which became happy or sad based upon how many steps the user had taken in a day. However, authors found that participants were not interested to look at the fish when they were inactive because they knew that their sedentary activity would make the fish sad [23]. In other works, Anderson et al. [1] developed a system called Shakra where physical activity of the user was monitored using mobile cell signal information; they found that increasing awareness about physical activity encouraged reflection upon one's physical activity. These works suggest that digital metaphors to visualize physical activity data have the potential to motivate users to achieve health goals.

Visualization through physical metaphors

Along with digital metaphors, researchers have also explored physical metaphors for representing physical activity data. For example, Jafarinaimi et al. [18] created a physical sculpture that provides feedback on sitting in a proper posture. Recently, Khot et al. [19] and Stusak et al. [40] designed 3D printed physical metaphors to represent physical activity data in a material form; their accompanying studies reveal that user relationship with physical activity gets positively influenced with physical metaphors. These works suggest that physical medium has great potential to support the physical activity experience.

Visualization through informative art

Fan et al. [12] explored the feasibility of informative art by designing and studying various abstract visualizations of physical activity. They found that people have different tastes when it comes to appreciating and relating to abstract visualizations of their physical activity data. This work suggests us to consider varied preferences of the users, while designing visualization schemes.

Visualization through playful systems

Prior works have also utilized physical activity data to enhance gameplay experiences and thereby, creating opportunities for physical activities around playful systems. For example, the Run Zombie Run [36] mobile app harnesses an engaging game-based narrative to make users jog more. Berkovsky et al. [3] have looked at virtual game rewards in exchange of physical activity while Nenonen et al. [28] utilized heart rate data as a game input. In other works, TripleBeat system [29] allows runners to stay in their target heart rate zones through virtual competition. These works suggest the potential of a playful interface to support the physical activity experience.

Rethinking physical activity representation

Review of the existing literature suggests that there is an emphasis on using the digital medium to represent physical activity, which not only limits the interaction opportunities to visualization but also overlooks the multi-sensory aspect of experiencing the physical activity data. Since physical activity data can approximately reflect the amount of energy invested by the user in a physical activity, we believe there is an opportunity to harness this information to contribute to the human energy cycle by "*giving back to the body what it has lost during physical activity*".

Supporting this, we introduce palatable representations that turn physical activity data into an appetizing sports drink. Since intense physical activity sessions can cause loss of body fluids; sports drinks can help in the recovery of such body fluids [37]. However, we are also aware that the human energy-cycle is much more complex as the literature on exercise and nutrition suggests [37]: We, therefore, do not portray that a created sports drink exactly matches with an hourly exercise, for instance. However, considering the trends in quantified self [41] and food printing [38, 47], we see an opportunity to combine the two. For example, quantified self focuses on sensing energy expenditure, whereas food printing focuses on new ways of producing energy that can be consumed. We find this an intriguing combination that we believe holds an exciting premise for HCI.

To the best of our knowledge, there has not been any exploration on using fluids to represent physical activity. However, past works in HCI have explored fluids for creating novel interactive experiences. For example, the Currency Fountain [9] shows the currency rates using a water fountain based display while Geurts et al. [17] designed a Splash Controller for interactive play experiences with water. Similarly, Steve Mann designed various fluidic musical instruments such as the Water Hammer Piano [25]. The Student Innovation Contest at UIST 2013 featured various fluidic interaction possibilities developed using the PumpSpark water fountain kit [11]. A few other works explored the use of soap bubbles [42] as well as water jets [33] for tangible interactions with computer systems. These works illustrate the potential of fluids in representing information and creating engaging experiences. However, there has not been much exploration on drinkable fluids except a system by Daisuke that transforms backend web processing data into a drink [10]. In response, we propose *TastyBeats* as the first exploration of using drinkable fluids to represent physical activity data.

WHAT IS TASTYBEATS?

TastyBeats is an interactive system that transforms heart rate data of a physical activity into a personalized drink. We employ a fountain-based interaction in the preparation of the drink, which not only provides visualization of the performed physical activity but also turns this event into a spectacular and celebratory event.

The *TastyBeats* setup includes a central glass and four containers as shown in Figure 1. Each container has a food graded water pump [14] fitted at the bottom. These pumps shoot drinks from the containers into the central glass (Refer Figure 2) and are driven by Arduino [2]. Working of the system is explained below.

Figure 2: TastyBeats in action.

Mapping heart rate data to different drinks

TastyBeats divides heart rate values into four zones following Fletcher's classification of physical activity levels based on heart rate [13], however, the range of values were slightly adjusted to suit the current interaction. Each zone has a characteristic drink as explained below. In the current prototype, we have used Mio liquid enhancers [26] for preparing the drinks because they came in a variety of flavors and they had zero sugar and zero calories. We want to highlight that the use of sports drinks was mainly driven from the interaction angle; we did not intend to advocate sports drinks or the usefulness of them in relation to physical activity.

1) Low activity zone: Water

The first zone is a low activity zone where the user is mostly sedentary or doing light physical activities such as standing and walking. This zone corresponds to a range of heart rate values varying from 60 to 95 beats per minute (bpm). Since there is not much physical activity happening in this zone, we choose water to represent this zone.

2) Moderate activity zone: Light flavored water

The second zone describes aerobic activities corresponding to a range of heart rate values from 96 to 130 bpm. We choose light flavored water such as mango-peach flavor of Mio liquid water enhancers to represent this zone.

3) High activity zone: Electrolytes

Third zone describes aerobic activities with high intensity and corresponds to a range of heart rate values lying in between 131 to 165 bpm. Such activities if done for a longer duration may require electrolyte supplements [37]. We therefore choose Mio liquid enhancer containing electrolytes to represent this zone.

4) Intense activity zone: Rich flavored water

The fourth zone corresponds to intense physical activities with heart rate values between 166 to 195 bpm that usually do not last more than 10 minutes [37]. We choose a dark red and rich flavored (Mio fruit punch flavor) drink to describe its occurrence in a physical activity session.

Dynamics of the fluid spectacle

We use Polar H7 heart rate monitor [30] and its accompanying smartphone app, Polar Beat to record the heart rate data of a physical activity session. The Polar Beat app saves the heart rate data on Polar website, from where we download the heart rate data in XML format. *TastyBeats* application written in Processing [31] then identifies the pattern of heart rate zones from the XML file and sends this pattern to the *TastyBeats* system via serial communication. This pattern enumerates identified heart rate zones along with their frequency. For example, for a set of heart rate values: (69,75,83,102,150), the heart rate pattern would be [(zone: 1, freq.: 3), (zone: 2, freq.: 1), (zone: 3, freq.: 1)].

The *TastyBeats* system reads the pattern sequentially and accordingly drives the pumps from the corresponding containers. The pumps shoot the drink into the central glass for 2 seconds, so that the central glass can accommodate multiple shoots from every container. The central glass gets full by 30 shoots with 400ml of drinks. Now, for a longer physical activity session, 7-8 hours in our case, we optimized our system so that it shoots drink only when the pattern moves to a different zone. For example, if the heart rate data stayed in the same zone, shooting happens only once. The system stops when the pattern gets finished or the glass gets filled with 30 shoots.

Design process and considerations

We have taken an incremental and exploratory approach for designing the TastyBeats system where the data gathered from one trial informed the system design for the next trial. As such the design inquiry for TastyBeats was carried out in three phases as explained below.

In the first phase, regular focus group discussions were held with participants from the community surrounding our research lab. The participants came from varied academic backgrounds such as industrial design, computer science, and HCI, which helped us to draw from their experience and discuss advanced topics such as engaging aspects of a palatable interface. Several design ideas were proposed for the possible interface demonstrating the diversity in user expectations as well as choices for an interactive setup (Figure 3). Below we mention the key topics we discussed and how we came up with the final design of the system.

Figure 3: Other design options for TastyBeats were discussed but not considered due to a) less interaction possibility with equidistant pumps, b) self-priming issue with the pumps.

Arranging the containers (setup)

Initially, there were ideas about keeping all four containers at equal distance from the central glass such as in a semi-circular or square fashion (Figure 3a). However, we decided to put the containers in a straight line around the central glass (as shown in Figure 1) that offered us more interaction flexibility. For example, containers that are further apart from the central glass give higher elevation for the water shoot than the ones that are closer to the central glass; making it easier to see the differences in the heart rate while witnessing the system interaction.

Choosing the physical activity data

We chose heart rate as opposed to other physiological measures such as METs and steps because heart rate is more personal as well as dynamic. As a result, the chances that the system would produce distinctly flavored drinks are high. For example, an activity comprising of transitions between low and moderate activity zones will add water and light flavored water respectively into the central glass, while an activity causing rapid transitions between different zones will add more flavors as well as electrolytes to the drink. From our study, we also found that using heart rate enabled tracking of other psychological factors such as stress, which we believe are also essential while considering the overall well being of a person.

Creating the personalized drink

To create a personalized drink, different parameters such as smell, texture, viscosity, and flavor were considered. However, our design choices were limited due to the hardware (pumps) available with us. As a result, we had to discard some of the drink parameters. For example, the pumps did not work with carbonated water, thus giving texture to the drink was not feasible; Additionally, since the pumps were not self-primed, they needed to be immersed in liquid for pumping (Figure 3b). As a result, we looked only at such parameters with which the pumps could work successfully. We therefore utilized three parameters: flavor, volume and color of the drink to create a meaningful mapping between the physical activity data and created drink. Flavor of the drink is based on the identified heart rate zones in the data, while the recurring occurrence of these zones within the data contributes to the volume of the drink (which increases with the activity duration) thus describing both quality as well as the quantity of the activity. Finally, color is used to signify the highest reached heart rate zone in the data, besides it also creates a visual appeal to understand the data even from a distance.

In the second phase, we exhibited early versions of the TastyBeats systems at three different academic venues where more than 400 participants interacted with the system. Each of these exhibitions helped us to refine our design further by resolving issues such as food safety (using materials that are food safe). Other findings from the exhibitions are explained in [20]. In the final phase, we field deployed the system in various houses to study its use in everyday context, which we discuss in the next section.

TASTYBEATS IN ACTION (FIELD STUDY)

We conducted an exploratory "in the wild" study [34] to understand how *TastyBeats* will integrate into everyday physical activity experiences and what effect it can have on everyday physical activity. Given the exploratory nature of this work, we focused on gathering a rich set of opinions that illustrate reflective thinking about a system rather than a majority.

Recruitment

The study took place in three households across a large metropolitan city for a period of two weeks. In total, we had six participants: 1 couple in mid thirties (Chad: 37 yrs., Male; Sarah: 34 yrs., Female), 1 couple in mid twenties (Dave: 28 yrs., Male; Sarah: 26 yrs.) and two housemates (Adam: 26 yrs. Male; Rahim: 29 yrs., Male). Our intention behind using more than one participant from the same house was to investigate the affect of palatable representations on social dynamics as explored in previous works on material representations [19, 40]. Figure 4 provides demographic details of the participants along with their level of physical activity every week (low: 1-2 days, moderate: 3-4 days, high: more than 4 days). All participants had tried electrolytes-based sports drinks before, but their main source of rehydration was water.

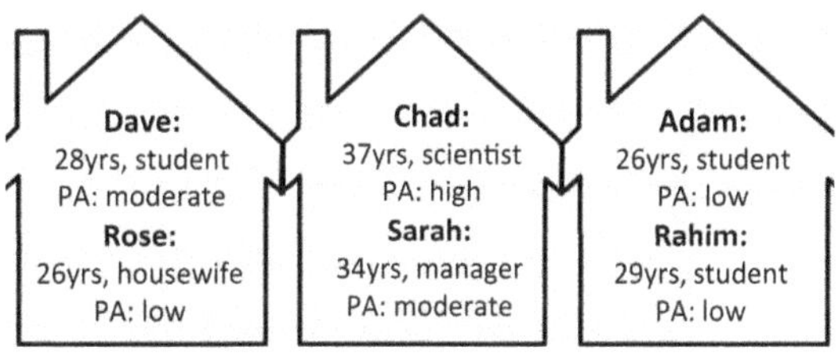

Figure 4: Demographic details of our study participants along with their level of physical activity (PA).

Setup

Each house received a kit containing the TastyBeats system, two Polar H7 heart rate monitors, two iPods and a poster explaining the study's procedure (Figure 5). We also provided sanitizers and napkins to clean the glasses and accidental spilling of drinks. We also provided users with a MacBook Air to run the *TastyBeats* system. Participants were not compensated to participate and the system was taken back at the end of the study. Following the cultural probing practice [16], we also supplied diaries and asked participants to reflect upon their experiences with the system.

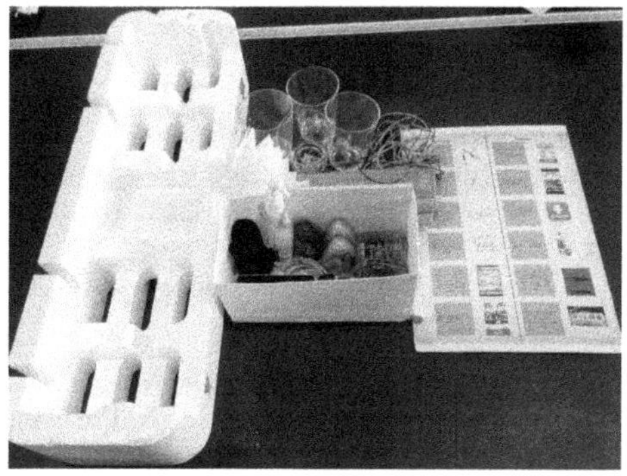

Figure 5: Each house received a kit containing the TastyBeats system and a poster explaining the study's procedure.

Procedure

We installed the *TastyBeats* system in every household at a location of the participants' choice (which we noted). We first gave a demo on how the system works with dummy data and explained the study procedure. We also printed an A3 poster detailing the study steps (Figure 5), asking the participants to perform the following tasks:

Tasks in the morning:

We asked the participants to wear the heart rate monitor and start the recording of the heart rate data through the Polar Beat application installed on the iPod. Usually the recording started around 7-8 am when participants began their day. We asked participants to continue their day as usual which may or may not involve physical activity.

Tasks in the evening:

In the evening, usually around 5-6 pm, when participants returned home from work, we told them to stop the Polar Beat application on the iPod and take off the heart rate monitor. Once the recording was stopped, the heart rate data from the day was synced to the Polar website. Participants then prepared the *TastyBeats* setup, which involved pouring water into the four containers and adding the liquid enhancers (two pinches) into three of them. We then asked the participants to press a button that downloaded the data and started the *TastyBeats* program on the provided laptop. The program then started the *TastyBeats* interaction, which involved shooting drinks into the central glass based on the heart rate data. The interaction lasted around 3-4 minutes. Finally, the participant was free to taste the prepared drink.

Data source

The main source of data was the interview conducted at the end of the study in participants' home, which went for about 45 to 60 minutes per participant. The post interviews focused on participants' experiences with the *TastyBeats* system. We also utilized the diaries given to the participants as well as photos and videos taken by the participants to further support the interviews. We visited each household two times (first and last day) and spent around 4 hours in total with participants at each house. We also maintained contact with everyone through emails and phone calls in case they needed any technical support. We took notes and recorded interviews, which were later coded and analyzed for common themes using a grounded theory approach.

FINDINGS

Given the long time frame necessary to achieving health benefits as a result of physical activity, it is often difficult to judge the efficacy of short design-led study interventions [5, 21]. Instead, it has been suggested that such interventions should be judged based on their impact on practices [5] and how they brought about changes in people's attitudes (rather than behaviors), fostering mindfulness and leaving room for stories [32]. We describe below key insights gained from the deployments.

Accommodating TastyBeats

All participants welcomed the system with curiosity and considered it a part of their kitchen ambience. The system occupied a space on the kitchen slab in both couples' home (Figure 6). Adam and Rahim, however, placed the system in a private room as one of their other roommates had a cat and they thought she might mess with the system.

Figure 6: The TastyBeats system was placed on the kitchen slab in Dave and Rose's house.

Experiencing TastyBeats

All participants tracked their data for around 7-8 hours every day. The couples preferred to have their drink after dinner usually around 9 pm. Dave mentioned that the drink was like a personalized dessert or pleasurable treat for the tiring day activity, while referring to the sweet taste of the drink, Sarah said: "*it is like having a grape juice before going to bed*". Adam and Rahim did not have a preferred time for the drink; sometimes they had it just after coming back from work and some other times a little later.

Enjoying the interaction

All participants actively took part in making the drink everyday and keenly observed how the drink was being made through the fountain-based interaction. As such, the system became a part of their daily routine. According to Adam, the system was "*something you always want to see, once you come home*", to which Rose added, "*its nice to see the machine making a drink and the taste of the drink is also very good, but it is also very healthy, that way you feel good about it.*" Along with the drink, the participants also appreciated the interactive quality of the system: "*the best part of it is watching the interaction, shooting into the cup*", Dave commented. Rose was delighted to see her heart rate transformed into a drink, she mentioned, "*compared to regular apps with only show the data, this prepares the drink, and that way its kind of special, it feels that you are getting energy back.*"

Taste as a surprise

Sarah mentioned, "*Seeing the drink is one thing, but if it's the same color everyday, then there is no surprise. Surprise is the taste, which is different on daily basis.*"

Taste as a satisfaction

Chad also commented, "*Tasting it [drink] adds an element of satisfaction. It would have been less engaging if I was not allowed to drink it.*" Adam felt, "*it is like drinking your own progress, literally.*"

Witnessing the interaction

Chad mentioned, "*This (TastyBeats) is kind of neat where I can see the different levels mixing in. You actually get to interpret how active your day was based upon the drink being mixed. So, I think its more of incentive to see it mixed because you get a better understanding of why the drink is the way it is.*"

Relating TastyBeats to physical activity

Participants mentioned that the presented data in its fluid form offered new insights into their physical activity routines. As a result, they became more attentive to their bodily responses and everyday activities.

Correlating activities to drink

Participants were able to correlate different days' activities with the drink that was created in the evening, which in turn encourage them to try new physical activities. Rose tried different physical activities such as running, cycling and household cleaning on different days. She was able to differentiate how her heart rate data in these activities was reflected in the drink. Rahim confirmed this by saying: "*I did see the differences [in the drink], when I had a more active day, there were subtle changes in the taste.*"

Identifying bodily warning signals

The dark rich flavored drink that Sarah received on three consecutive sedentary days made her realize that she had very high heart rates. She told her husband about it and consequently they looked up the Internet to learn about "normal" heart rate values and possible reasons for higher values. They then tried to swap around the heart rate monitors on the next day to see if there was a fault with it. Sarah said: "*What it [TastyBeats] made me aware of was my heart rate. It is not something that I think of. When I saw my high heart rate [through the dark red colored drink], I felt my pulse for the first time. It made me think about the reasons and found that medication is one of the factors [she was on a medication for a while during the study period].*"

Motivating to exercise

A recurrent theme was the motivating quality of the system, linking to the theme of fulfilling the energy-cycle. Participants reported that the system encouraged them to not miss their daily workouts. Rose said: "*Just to see what drinks you get and how much, you feel like going out and running, sometimes it's like an inspiration.*" Adam responded similarly, "*it motivated me to exercise more*".

On a sedentary day, Chad received a drink containing mostly water, to which he replied, "*It was little bit frustrating to get watery drink, but it was not unexpected. That kind of motivated me for more physical exercise the next day to get drinks from level 3 and 4.*"

Taking health more seriously

Dave spoke extensively about how *TastyBeats* made him be more serious about his as well as his wife's health. He said, "*I will continue cycling to work from now onwards*". Other participants also reported that the system encouraged them to not miss their daily workouts. Dave, Rose and Chad started walking or cycling to the work instead of driving.

Social dynamics around TastyBeats

Participants said that they often prepared their drinks together, laughing and discussing their activities with each other. Usually participants saw each other only in the evening. As such they did not know precisely how active the other person was during the day: The understanding came by watching the interaction when other person's drink was being made. Chad said in the interview, "*it's good that me and Sarah doing it [the study] together, as we get to see each other's heart rate from the drinks being made*" [with a smile], "*in that way, Sarah now knows much more about me and my activities.*"

Facilitating competition

Adam felt the system was highly competitive: he competed with Rahim in terms of who will burn more calories and get a better drink. He narrated to us a funny incident that happened during the study. "*On Saturday, I stayed at home reading and watching TV, I did not go anywhere, but my friend Rahim went and played some sport [football with friends] and did some jogging and stuff like that, so it was physically very active day for him and for me it was very very inactive, just the opposite. When he came back, we did our drinks [together]. We started with him and his drink was pretty amazing and very concentrated, using lot of drink from [container] 3 and 4 and almost nothing from 1. After that it was my turn, since there was no activity by me, I did not get anything, just a little bit of water [from container 1] and nothing from the other. It was just funny. It was so obvious that he did lot of activities and I got what I deserved. So we started laughing, it was so fun!*"

Cheating felt bad (tasteless)

Adam further added, "*later on the same day, when we were having dinner, I felt like having a drink. So what I did, I cheated the system. I uploaded Rahim's data and got the same drink that he got. Kind of funny that he did the activities and I got the drink. But actually to be honest, it didn't feel good at all, I felt that what I told Rahim too, you know what, this drink is personal, I feel like it is yours and I am drinking it. It feels like drinking something that does not belong to me. So it did not taste good, really honestly.*"

Creating personal affection with drinks

Participants from the other houses also felt that the drink was personal to them and is not something to be shared: Rose said, "*sharing my drink with others is a bit weird, I will tell others about it [my drink], but I will not share the drink, definitely.*" Additionally, Chad was interested to store the drink from his intense workouts so that he can cherish those activities for a longer time.

Appreciating TastyBeats

Most participants spoke enthusiastically about the system as well as about their participation in the study with their friends. To our surprise, Adam maintained voice memos to log his as well as Rahim's interactions with the system.

Appreciating the palatability

During the follow-up interviews, we discussed various possible scenarios in which part of the interaction was missing. We asked what if we take away the palatable aspect by just mixing colorful water based on heart rate data. To which, all participants responded negatively. Chad said, "*It would probably be less of incentive especially when you are wearing the heart rate monitor for exercise and at last you can't drink it. It is like producing something but you won't get a reward out of it, other than some water which you can't keep with you*" Dave worried that, "*Having a drink is something like a reward for what you have done. But if it was just water, which you have to throw away, the beauty of interaction would have disappeared.*"

Waiting for the rewards

Rahim narrated us the following story, "*one day I came home running from my office, I was exhausted and needed something to drink, I could have picked something from the fridge, but instead I poured the drink into the glasses and then drank it once the interaction was over, that way I knew what my heart rate was.*" Chad further added, "*If I was thirsty, it's a little bit frustrating that you have to set it up and then you have to wait. But seeing the interaction is also rewarding.*"

Welcoming the abstract visualizations

Dave appreciated the abstract nature of *TastyBeats* and mentioned, "*for a non athlete like me, detailed data does not make much sense, once in a while you may want to know what your heart rate details are, but on a daily basis abstract interpretation of data is good enough*".

Issues with TastyBeats

Along with the positives, participants also mentioned a few issues with the system that needs to be addressed.

Cumbersome heart rate monitoring

Rose and Sarah found wearing the heart rate monitor for the whole day as cumbersome. Sarah said, "*You need a little bit of discipline for putting it on everyday during the rush hours in the morning.*" To which, Adam proposed a solution: "*Eventually I will come to know what drink I get for what activity. So next time when I had a similar activity, I can just look back in history and plug in the data to get a similar drink, that way I do not need to wear the heart rate monitor or the similar activities.*"

Irregular size drinks

In our system, volume of the drink was based on the duration of physical activity and its type. As participants' activities varied during the study period, they received drinks of different volume. However, Dave did not like getting drinks of different volumes, and wished for a standard size drink irrespective of the duration of his physical activity.

The leftovers

Participants did not like the fact that containers were open from the top, which led to the wastage of the leftover drinks. Dave and Adam asked if the system could be sealed from the top so that they can reuse the remaining drinks rather than throwing them out.

The spilling

The system occasionally spilled drink on nearby surfaces, which was not appreciated by participants, as it required cleaning and led to wasting of food. Rose said, "*Little droplets are okay. But not too much.*"

DISCUSSIONS

We discuss below the experiences that the palatable representations of physical activity elicited for our participants.

Rewarding aspects of palatable representations

According to the Goal Setting Theory [24], incentives are important to sustain a user's interest in an activity. Previous works in HCI have looked on virtual rewards and incentives to support physical activity among people [3]. However, according to the study by Munson and Consolvo [27], virtual points and rewards do not have a lasting impact because system assigned rewards are found to support motivation only in the early stages of usage. Therefore, it may be worthwhile to consider a greater scope of reward types. Possibly, rewards that change over time can be a valuable benefit for physical activity.

In this work, we explore this dimension through an appetizing drink and a visceral spectacle of creating the drink, both of which participants found equally rewarding. In case of Chad, even though he was dehydrated due of cycling, he waited for the interaction to end to get a deserving drink. Participants find watching the interaction as the best part of *TastyBeats*, and were very keen to witness the interaction not only for their own but also for their partner's everyday activity. Furthermore, participants also developed a personal affection with their drink mainly because the drink embodied their personal data. Rose was motivated to perform different physical activities to see how it would reflect in the drink and what it taste like. One participant, Adam, even tried to cheat the system by creating drink from his friend's data, but that drink did not taste good for him. Lastly, there was always a surprise element associated with how the drink will taste. We therefore encourage designers to equally focus on the interaction aspects as well as the palatability of the resultant drink while designing palatable representation.

Shared spectacle of personal data triggers discussions and playful interactions

Most of the existing works in visualizing physical activity is geared towards individual use [41]. Physical activity data is often collected and shown on a private computer or smartphone screen. In this work, we explored public display of data in a private setting like home through a shared system of creating a drink. Often the drink was made together and participants keenly observed the process of making the drink. In that process, they became more aware of each other's physiological state, which in turn triggered discussions and playful social interactions. Participants often competed to get a bigger drink and shared moments of laughter when the prepared drinks were drastically different from each other. Recently, a few other works have also started to explore public consumption of heart rate data. For example, Walmink et al. [46] created an augmented helmet that project heart rate data of the wearer in real time to fellow cyclists while Curmi et al. [8] allowed public display of heart rate data on social networks. These works illustrate potential for social interaction in public sharing of data but with a risk of privacy. However, in our study, participants did not raise privacy concern, as the data was presented in an abstract form. Therefore, one way to address privacy related issues could be to use such abstract forms of visualizations that provides basic information about the physical activity, but hides intrinsic details from the user.

Finally, making data public with fluids means that there are chances of spillage, which can be fun, but we found that participants did not like wasting food (drinks in our case). Therefore, there is a tradeoff in terms of the spectacle and the palatable quality of the drink.

STUDY LIMITATIONS

Here, we mention the two main limitations of this work. Firstly, *TastyBeats* creates a drink only at the end of the day. There are situations when such a drink might be needed right after a physical activity, which was not supported by the current version of *TastyBeats*. Secondly, our study reports results from a 2 weeks intervention. Longitudinal studies might be needed before drawing conclusions on the motivational aspects of the system. Despite these limitations, we believe our work offers first insights into a palatable representation that could inform the design of future systems aiming to support human energy cycle through palatable representation.

CONCLUSION

Main contribution of this work is the first conceptual understanding of the design of palatable representations. We presented results from an "in the wild" field deployments of the *TastyBeats* system that offers insights into how people understand and react to personal data when presented in a palatable form. *TastyBeats* served as a mediator for reflective thoughts and discussions besides offering a public and vibrant vista of their heart rate.

Recent advancements in food printing have opened up new possibilities for creating engaging interactions and experiences around food [6, 38, 39, 47]. However, existing explorations mainly utilize mechanical and time-consuming techniques to produce food. Through this work, we explore another dimension of producing personalized food using a vibrant, attractive and familiar setting of water fountains, which we think would guide designers towards thinking differently about food printing methods.

Our work also intertwines the two growing fields in HCI, namely, quantified self and food printing, thus it might raise issues on their relationship and relevance. Our work also informs the design of food printing machines, highlighting an opportunity to print things "*we do not currently have*", like heart rate. Our work brings to the fore the idea that one can eat one's own data such as heart rate. This might inspire a discussion of the role of HCI in the human-energy cycle. In future, it would also be interesting to see how *TastyBeats* is applicable in other settings such as in gymnasiums or public events like marathons. Finally, our work has scratched only the surface of palatable representation, and we encourage designers to consider new possibilities afforded by such representations to support user's experience with physical activity.

REFERENCES

1. Anderson, I., Maitland, J., Sherwood, S. Shakra: Tracking and Sharing Daily Activity Levels with Unaugmented Mobile Phones. *Mobile Networks and Applications* 12, (2007), 185-199.
2. Arduino, http://www.arduino.cc/.
3. Berkovsky, S., Coombe, M., Freyne, J., Bhandari, D., and Baghaei, N. Physical activity motivating games: virtual rewards for real activity. In *Proc. CHI'10*, ACM (2010), 243-252.
4. Bloch, M. Truth and sight: Generalizing without universalizing. *J. Roy. Anthropol. Inst, 14*, 2008, 22-32.
5. Brynarsdttir, H., Håkansson, M., Pierce, J., Baumer, E. P. S., Disalvo, C. and Sengers, P. Sustainably unpersuaded: how persuasion narrows our vision of sustainability. In *Proc. CHI'12*, ACM (2012), 947-956.
6. Comber R., Choi, J.H., Hoonhout J. and O'hara, K. Editorial: Designing for human-food interaction: An introduction to the special issue on 'food and interaction design', *IJHCS,* 2014, 72(2), 181-184.
7. Consolvo, S., McDonald, D.W. and Landay, J. Theory-driven design strategies for technologies that support behavior change in everyday life. In *Proc. CHI'09*, ACM (2009), 405-414.
8. Curmi, F., Ferrario, M.A., Southern, J., and Whittle, J. HeartLink: open broadcast of live biometric data to social networks. In *Proc. CHI'13,* ACM (2013), 1749-1758.
9. Currency fountain. http://www.koert.com/work/datafountain/.
10. Daisuke, A. Weburette. In *Proc. SA'12*, ACM (2012).
11. Dietz, P., Reyes, G., and Kim, D. The PumpSpark fountain development kit. In *Proc. DIS'14*, ACM (2014), 259-266.
12. Fan, C., Forlizzi, J. and Dey, A. A Spark Of Activity: Exploring Information Art As Visualization For Physical Activity. In *Proc. Ubicomp '12*, ACM (2012), 81-84.
13. Fletcher G., Balady G., Amsterdam E., et al. Exercise standards for testing and training: a statement for healthcare professionals from the American Heart Association. *Circulation*. 2001, 1694-1740.
14. Food grade mini water pump. http://www.lightobject.com/High-temperature100-39C-DC-12V-185LMin-29GPH-mini-Water-Pump-Food-grade-P711.aspx.
15. Galesic, M., and Garcia-Retamero, R. Graph literacy: A crosscultural comparison. *Medical Decision Making,* 2011, 31, 444-457.

16. Gaver, W., Dunne, A., and Pacenti, E. Cultural Probes. *Interactions*, 1999, 21-29.

17. Geurts, L., and Vanden Abeele, V. Splash controllers: game controllers involving the uncareful manipulation of water. In *Proc. TEI'12*, ACM (2012), 183-186.

18. Jafarinaimi, N., Forlizzi, J., Hurst, A. and Zimmerman, J. Breakaway: an ambient display designed to change human behavior, In *Proc. CHI EA'05*, ACM (2005), 1945-1948.

19. Khot, R., Hjorth, L., and Mueller, F. Understanding physical activity through 3D printed material artifacts. In *Proc. CHI'14*, ACM (2014), 3835-3844.

20. Khot, R., Lee, J., Hjorth, L. and Mueller, F. TastyBeats: Celebrating Heart Rate Data with a Drinkable Spectacle. In *Proc. TEI'15,* ACM (2015), 229-232.

21. Klasnja, P., Consolvo, S., and Pratt, W. How to evaluate technologies for health behavior change in HCI research. In *Proc. CHI'11*, ACM (2011), 3063-3072.

22. Li, I., Dey, A. and Forlizzi, J. Understanding my data, myself: supporting self-reflection with ubicomp technologies. In *Proc. UbiComp '11*, ACM (2011), 405-414.

23. Lin, J.L., Mamykina, L., Lindtner, S., Delajoux, G. and Strub, H.B. Fish'n'Steps: Encouraging physical activity with an interactive computer game. In *Proc. Ubicomp'06*, Springer (2006), 261-278.

24. Locke, E., and Latham, G. *A theory of goal setting and task performance*, Prentice Hall, 1990.

25. Mann, S., Janzen, R., Huang, J., Kelly, M., Ba, L. J., and Chen, A. User-interfaces Based on the Water-hammer Effect: Water-hammer Piano As an Interactive Percussion Surface. In *Proc. TEI '11*, ACM (2011), 1-8.

26. Mio liquid water enhancers, http://www.makeitmio.com/.

27. Munson, S. and Consolvo, S. Exploring Goal-setting, Rewards, Self-monitoring, and Sharing to Motivate Physical Activity, *Pervasive Health* (2012), 25-32.

28. Nenonen, V., Lindblad, A., Häkkinen, V., Laitinen, T., Jouhtio, M., and Hämäläinen, P. Using heart rate to control an interactive game. In *Proc. CHI'07*, ACM (2007), 853-856.

29. Oliveira, R., and Oliver, N. TripleBeat: enhancing exercise performance with persuasion. In *Proc. MobileHCI '08*, ACM (2008), 255-264.

30. Polar heart rate monitors, http://www.polar.com/en/products.

31. Processing, https://processing.org.

32. Purpura, S., Schwanda, V., Williams, K., Stubler, W., and Sengers, P. Fit4life: the design of a persuasive technology promoting healthy behavior and ideal weight. In *Proc. CHI'11*, ACM (2011), 423–432.

33. Richter, H., Manke, F., and Seror, M. LiquiTouch: liquid as a medium for versatile tactile feedback on touch surfaces. In *Proc. TEI'13*, ACM (2013), 315-318.

34. Rogers, Y. Interaction Design Gone Wild: Striving for Wild Theory. *Interactions* 18, 4, 2011, 58-62.

35. Ruckenstein, M. Visualized and Interacted Life: Personal Analytics and Engagements with Data Doubles. *Societies*, (2014), 4, 68–84.

36. Run zombie run, https://www.zombiesrungame.com/.

37. Sawka M., Burke L., Eichner E., Maughan R., Montain S., and Stachenfeld N. American College of Sports Medicine position stand. Exercise and fluid replacement. *Med Sci Sports Exerc*. (2007), 39, 377-90.

38. Schoning, J., Rogers, Y., and Kruger, A. Digitally Enhanced Food. *IEEE Pervasive Computing*, 2012, 11(3), 4-6.

39. Spence, C. and Piqueras-Fiszman, B. Technology at the dining table. *Flavour*, 2013, 2 (1), 16.

40. Stusak, S., Tabard, A., Sauka, F., Khot, R., Butz, A. Activity Sculptures: Exploring the Impact of Physical Visualizations on Running Activity. *Visualization and Computer Graphics*, IEEE, 99 (1), 2014.

41. Swan, M. Sensor mania! The Internet of things, wearable computing, objective metrics, and the Quantified Self 2.0. *J. Sens. Actuator Netw*. 2012, 1, 217–253.

42. Sylvester, A., Döring, T., and Schmidt, A. Liquids, Smoke, and Soap Bubbles - Reflections on Materials for Ephemeral User Interfaces. In *Proc. TEI'10*, ACM (2010), 269-270.

43. Tudor-Locke, C., Bassett, B.R., and Swartz, A.M. A preliminary study of one year of pedometer self-monitoring. *Annals of Behavioral Medicine*, 2004, 158-162.

44. Vande Moere, A. Beyond the tyranny of the pixel: Exploring the physicality of information visualization. In *Proc. IV'08*, IEEE (2008), 469-474.

45. Viseu, A., and Suchman, L. Wearable Augmentations: Imaginaries of the Informed Body. In *Technologized Images, Technologized Bodies*, Berghahn Books, 2010, 161–184.

46. Walmink, W., Wilde, D., and Mueller, F. Displaying heart rate data on a bicycle helmet to support social exertion experiences. In *Proc. TEI'14*, ACM (2014), 97-104.

47. Wei, J., Ma, X., and Zhao, S. Food Messaging: Using an Edible Medium for Social Messaging. In *Proc. CHI'14*, ACM (2014), 2873-2882.

As Light as your Footsteps: Altering Walking Sounds to Change Perceived Body Weight, Emotional State and Gait

Ana Tajadura-Jiménez[1], Maria Basia[1], Ophelia Deroy[2], Merle Fairhurst[2], Nicolai Marquardt[1], Nadia Bianchi-Berthouze[1]

[1]UCL UCL Interaction Centre
UCL, London, UK
[a.tajadura, maria.basia.13, n.marquardt, n.berthouze]@ucl.ac.uk

[2]Centre for the Study of the Senses, University of London, London, UK
[ophelia.deroy, merle.fairhurst]@sas.ac.uk

ABSTRACT
An ever more sedentary lifestyle is a serious problem in our society. Enhancing people's exercise adherence through technology remains an important research challenge. We propose a novel approach for a system supporting walking that draws from basic findings in neuroscience research. Our shoe-based prototype senses a person's footsteps and alters in real-time the frequency spectra of the sound they produce while walking. The resulting sounds are consistent with those produced by either a lighter or heavier body. Our user study showed that modified walking sounds change one's own perceived body weight and lead to a related gait pattern. In particular, augmenting the high frequencies of the sound leads to the perception of having a thinner body and enhances the motivation for physical activity inducing a more dynamic swing and a shorter heel strike. We here discuss the opportunities and the questions our findings open.

Author Keywords
Auditory body perception; multimodal interfaces; sonification; interaction styles; emotion; evaluation method

ACM Classification Keywords
H.5.2. User Interfaces: Auditory (non-speech) feedback; interaction styles.

INTRODUCTION
Our societies are seeing an increase in inactive and sedentary lifestyles that causes 6% of deaths each year and is a risk factor for many chronic diseases [36,61]. Further, concern about general body appearance reflects in the growth of the fitness industry and of surgery procedures to change one's appearance [32]. This has led to a raising awareness of the need to make people feel good about their bodies and motivate them toward physical activity so that they stay physically and mentally healthy and independent [33].

CHI 2015, Apr 18-23 2015, Seoul, Republic of Korea
ACM 978-1-4503-3145-6/15/04.
http://dx.doi.org/10.1145/2702123.2702374

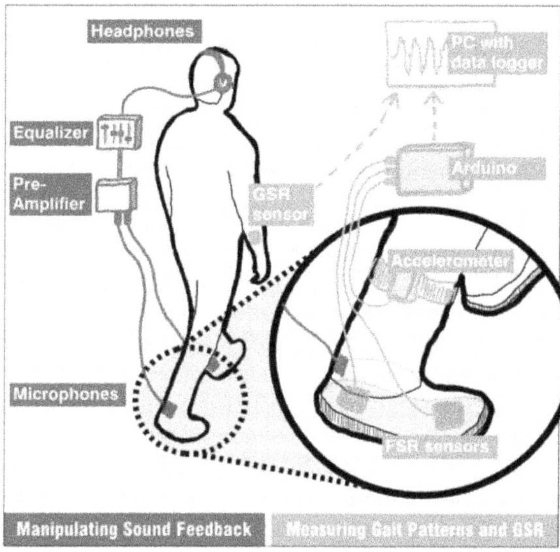

Figure 1. Overview of the experimental setup: (left) manipulating sound feedback; (right) sensing gait and galvanic skin sensor (GSR).

To tackle the problem, various activity tracking devices and applications are appearing on the market, such as *Fitbit* or *Nike Fuelband*. To increase exercise adherence, these technologies typically exploit cognitive behavioral strategies based on setting goals and providing rewards [21]. Here we take a very different and complementary approach that alters the perception of one's own body in order to enhance self-esteem, body feelings and the motivation for and quality of physical activity. Specifically, we propose to exploit the multisensory nature of body perception [55] and induce changes in perceived body weight by manipulating the sound feedback received while walking (Figure 1).

Our physical body is our means of perceiving the world but also our means of expression, of acting and interacting [2, 16,45]. How we perceive our body in terms of its appearance and its action capabilities is thus vital for self-esteem and for engaging in physical activity and social interaction. Interestingly, recent neuroscience research has shown that, rather than being fixed, the perception of our body (mental body model) is continuously updated by the body-related multisensory experiences that accompany our interactions with the environment [3,51,55]. Theories of 'forward internal models' of motor-to-sensory transformations [60] suggest that we predict the sensory feedback (e.g., the sound of our steps) we should receive from our actions by considering, among other factors, the mental model of one's body dimensions and configuration. When the received sensory feedback does not match these predictions an update of our internal body model may occur.

The possibility of altering the perceived physical appearance and the physical capabilities of one's own body through sensory feedback derived from one's actions may offer a practical way to make people feel good about their bodies [9,41], thus facilitating healthy changes in self-esteem and motor behavior. In our paper, we explore how sound feedback received while walking may be altered to induce changes in body perception and related emotion and behavior. Walking was chosen as it is an everyday gentle and easy form of physical activity, fit for people of all ages and most abilities, and with many associated health benefits such as a risk reduction in many chronic diseases [34].

Sound feedback was chosen for three reasons further developed in the background section. First, sound offers an excellent potential for consumer applications used during walking, when headphones and portable sound devices are often used. Second, the link between walking sounds and the perceived walker's weight is known. Heavier bodies produce lower spectral mode sounds than lighter bodies and listeners pick up on these cues when estimating properties of the heard walker [17,29]. While prior studies explored the effects of passive listening to walking sounds in the perceived body of an unknown walker, our study focuses on changes in the perception of *one's own body* due to altering self-produced walking sounds. Finally, sound has shown to have positive effects in sport, dance and motor rehabilitation [11,19,42,46,58], such as enhancing body awareness and movement coordination. Sensory feedback has shown for example, to ease motor learning by enhancing body-related information, such as the distance to a target posture [30,48], and to improve self-efficacy [49]. Yet, none of these studies has explored the possibility of altering one's own body size perception with sound, to enhance physical performance, self-esteem and positive attention to one's body. Such feedback could be integrated in applications such as *Fitbit* to complement its strategies to increase exercise adherence. Our paper aims to make both a theoretical and technological contribution in this direction by proposing and evaluating a system that effectively uses bodily-related sound feedback to evoke changes in the perceived body and measure changes in behavior and emotion.

BACKGROUND AND RELATED WORK

Walking Patterns (Gait) and Acoustic Signals

Gait is a periodic movement of each of the lower limbs from one position of support to the subsequent one [56]. It highly varies across individuals, due to age, gender or weight. Troje et al. [54] explored the link between gait and these various factors. They developed an application[1], based on motion data captured from eighty walkers, which displays an animated point-light walker whose gait changes according to various settings. In particular, the light-heavy setting appears to change the acceleration of the limbs and the straightness of the walker's posture. Other work showed that obese, as compared to normal weight walkers, display longer heel strike and reduced ankle mechanical joint power that relates to lower acceleration for the forward progression [25].

When walking, the force exerted by the foot against the ground can be represented as a time varying spectrum [57]. The low frequency components (under 300 Hz) are responsible for the displacement of the walker's center of mass. They depend on the walker's weight and walking rate and are essentially independent of footgear or walking surface [15], unlike the high frequency components, which can depend on the footgear and ground material [57]. The impact of the foot on the ground gives rise to acoustic signals, which frequency spectra shares properties with the ground force spectra. For instance, walking sounds produced by heavier bodies contain more energy in the low frequency components than those sounds produced by lighter bodies.

Information Conveyed by Walking Sounds

Listeners can extract various sorts of information from walking sounds (for a review see [57]). For instance, they can discriminate between solid and aggregate ground materials based solely on walking sounds [18]. They can also extract properties of a walker's body from the acoustic features of the walking sounds, including the gender, the emotional state and the size/hardness of the shoe soles of the heard walker [17]. Judgments of gender and shoe characteristics depend on the sound spectral characteristics and judgments of emotional state depend on the sound intensity and temporal features (average pace, pace irregularity). Listeners also rely on the sound spectra when asked to judge the posture of a heard walker (upright, stooped) [37]. Li et al. [29] found that the acoustic features from which listeners deduct the gender of a heard walker, including spectral peak and high frequency components, change with the weight and height of the walker. In fact, these authors demonstrated that shifting the spectral mode of the walking sounds to lower frequencies (at least to 125 Hz) increased the 'male' reports, while shifting it to higher frequencies (1000 Hz) increased the 'female' reports.

Hearing One's Footsteps Changes Gait and Emotion

While several studies have investigated the effects of vibrotactile patterns [59], musical temporal patterns [50] and musically induced arousal [28] on human gait, as well as the effects of a broad range of sounds in emotion [5], few studies have focused on the specific effect of self-produced walking sounds. Some of these studies have suggested that

[1] biomotionlab.ca/Demos/BMLwalker.html

the use of sounds, including footsteps and other sounds, synthesized in real-time from users' gait pattern improves navigation and interaction with a virtual reality (VR) environment [35]. Sound also enhances robot-assisted lower extremity motor adaptation during physical rehabilitation [62]. Another study [31] showed that delaying the provision of self-produced footstep sounds altered the gait period without the walkers being aware of the change. This study also showed that the delays in sound feedback reduced agency, i.e, the feeling of having produced the sounds.

Two recent studies have looked at how changing the perceived ground or shoe material by altering self-produced walking sounds can affect a walker's emotional state and motor behavior. Listening to pre-recorded footstep sounds produced by high heels of different materials and different types of ground affects women's emotional state when these sounds are presented in synchrony with their own footsteps [53]. Similarly, Bresin et al. [7] showed that hearing self-produced footsteps sounds as if they were produced on different ground surfaces seems to influence both walkers' emotion and their walking speed. However, the behavioral results did not reach significance, perhaps due to participants being over-conscious about their movement, as they were asked to walk in a specific emotion-related style.

Using Walking Sounds to Change the Perceived Body

Most of neuroscience studies on the plasticity of our mental body model have focused on visual and tactile feedback to alter people's perception of their body (e.g., perceiving and acting as if one's arm was longer). Recently, a few studies have shown that sound can also be used for this purpose. For example, sounds generated by tapping one's hand on a surface inform us of how long our tapping arm is [51] as well as the strength applied when tapping [14]: altering these sounds results in changes in arm extent and strength, as well as in movements and emotional state [14]. Sound may also change the perceived body material properties. For example, one's hand feels stiffer and heavier when altering the sound received when an object hits the hand so that it resembles the sound produced when the object hits marble [47]; or one's body feels as composed of metallic parts or 'robotized' if, when moving it, one receives sound and vibro-tactile feedback constructed from recordings of a real robot actuation [26]. The variation of sound spectra and amplitude also alters the perceived body material properties. Increasing both the high frequency components and the overall amplitude of the sound elicited when rubbing two hands together increases the perceived smoothness and the perceived dryness of the skin [20,24].

The studies discussed above suggest we use the sounds derived from bodily movements to build a model of our body appearance and of its capabilities for interaction, and that these sounds influence behavior and emotion. Here we explore for the first time how these sounds can alter the perception of one's own body weight, and look at how these changes may impact on emotion and gait behavior.

METHOD

Motivation and Hypothesis

The aim of the study is to investigate the effects of walking sounds on one's body perception to inform the design of ubiquitous technology for behavioral changes and wellbeing. Given the previous work showing how shifting the frequency mode of walking sounds influences the perceived weight of the heard walker (i.e., another person's body [29]), we posited that altering self-produced footstep sounds may likewise result in changes in the perceived weight of one's own body. We hypothesized that shifting the spectral mode of self-produced footstep sounds to lower frequencies may result in a perceived heavier body, while shifting it to higher frequencies may result in a perceived lighter body.

We further posit that these changes in perceived body weight may come together with behavioral and emotional changes given the tight links between these three dimensions: by perceiving one's body as lighter, one may feel more positive about this body and behave as if it were lighter. For instance, this perception may accelerate movements of the lower limbs [25,54] or induce an upright posture, which in turn may affect emotional arousal and dominance (i.e., feeling in control, stronger). Indeed, upright posture and dominance are known to relate to each other [8,37,54]. On the contrary, feeling heavier may result in a longer heel strike [25] or/and a larger exerted force of the feet against the ground [15,57]. Feeling lighter may also reflect in other experiential aspects, like for instance, one may feel faster or stronger, with this new body.

Participants

Twenty-two paid participants (age=18-35, four male and eighteen female, normal hearing) naïve to the study aim took part in the experiment. Their mean body weight and height (SD) was 59.25(10.55) Kg and 164.82(6.91) cm.

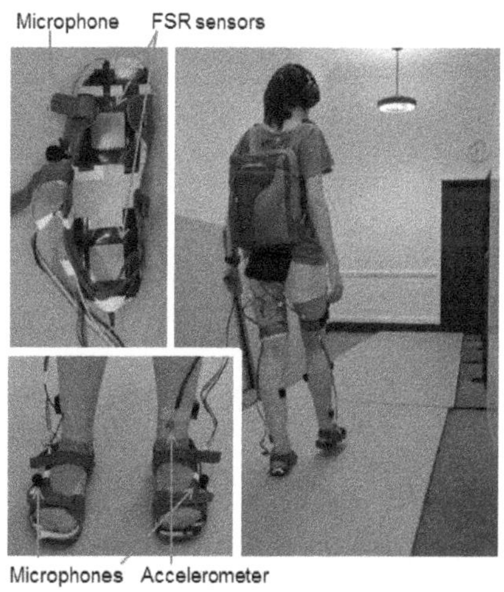

Figure 2. (left) Sandals with microphones, FSRs and accelerometer; (right) a participant during one condition[2].

[2] Ten additional EMG/accelerometer sensors were attached to walker's body for further analyses (not presented here).

Materials

Our prototype allows the dynamic modification of footstep sounds, as people walk, and measurement of walking behavior changes. We used strap sandals (EU size 42) that are easy to wear, fit a wide range of foot sizes, and have hard rubber sole, so that they elicited clear and distinctive footstep sounds. As shown in Figures 1 and 2, each sandal was equipped with a microphone (Core Sound, frequency response 20 Hz-20 kHz) that captured the walking sounds and two force-sensitive resistors (FSR; 1.75x1.5" sensing area) attached to the front and the rear part of the sandal insole that detected the exerted force by feet against the ground (as in [7]). A triple axis accelerometer (Sparkfun) was attached to the walker's left ankle. FSRs and an accelerometer were connected to an Arduino Uno microcontroller board linked via Bluetooth (Arduino XBee) to a computer that acquired their data (Arduino 1.0.5, Processing 2).

As shown in Figure 1, the microphones connected to a small stereo pre-amplifier (SP-24B) and this connected to a stereo 9-band graphic equalizer (Behringer FBQ800) that changed the sound spectra. The resulting sound was fed back via closed headphones (Sennheiser HDA 300) with high passive ambient noise attenuation (>30 dBA) that muffled the actual sound of footsteps. The analogue sound loop had minimal latency (<1 ms). Arduino board, pre-amp and equalizer were fitted into a small backpack the walker could carry (~2 Kg, 35x29x10 cm). The cables from sandals to backpack were attached with Velcro straps to the walker's legs. Finally, a GSR sensor (Affectiva Q Sensor; 32 Hz) in the walker's wrist measured emotional arousal [4].

The experiment was conducted in a quiet and dimly lit room, with an 8.5x1.22 m corridor created by using wooden boards (medium-density fiber, 2.5 cm thick; Figure 2). The ground and footwear materials are relevant as they affect the resulting sounds [29]. The hard rubber soles in contact with the wooden board produce clear sounds. We placed vertical panels on the corridor side to occlude objects in the lab that could distract people's attention or could have served as a reference when judging one's body dimensions.

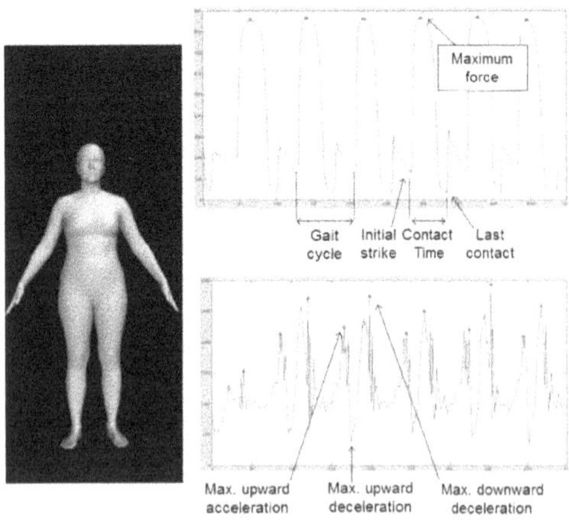

Figure 3. (left) Body visualization tool; (right-top) examples of FSR and (right-bottom) and accelerometer data.

Experimental Design

Sound Feedback Conditions

Three sound feedback conditions were designed based on [29]: a 'Control' condition in which participants were provided with their natural footsteps sounds equally amplified across frequency bands; a 'High frequency' condition in which the frequency components of the footsteps sounds in the range 1–4 kHz were further amplified by 12 dB and those in the range 83–250 Hz were attenuated by 12 dB; and a 'Low Frequency' condition in which the frequency components in the range 83–250 Hz were further amplified by 12 dB and those above 1 kHz were attenuated by 12 dB.

Multi-Measurement Approach

The user experience was evaluated by combining self-reporting, physiological and objective behavioral measures:

Perceived Body Weight: To measure perceived body weight, we used a body visualization tool (bodyvisualizer.com; see Figure 3) adopted by other studies for the same purpose [39]. People adjusted the weight related dimension of the body of a 3D avatar displayed on the screen to correspond to their perceived body size [10,27,39].

Behavioral Changes (Gait Patterns): The 'stance' and the 'swing' of the two phases of a gait cycle (i.e., the time between two successive steps made by one foot [12]) were analysed. The stance phase starts with the strike of the heel on the ground and ends when the toes lose contact with the ground. The FSR data of the left foot was used to quantify the exerted force (peak and mean values) of the heel and toes against the ground and their contact times, as well as the stance and the gait cycle times (see Figure 3). We focused on data from the left foot since we did not have any specific hypothesis on left/right asymmetries (additionally, data from one right sensor seemed abnormal). The swing phase starts with the foot lifting, first accelerating and then decelerating (midswing) while preparing for the next heel strike and while the other foot is on the ground. The foot accelerates again when the flexor muscles are activated to move the foot forward and downwards [56]. The accelerometer data was used to quantify the foot lifting acceleration and deceleration, as well as the downward acceleration.

Emotional Responses: Emotional valence, dominance, and arousal felt by participants were quantified by using the 9-item graphic scales of the self-assessment manikin questionnaire [6]. Arousal was also quantified based on physiological changes recorded by the GSR biosensor [4].

Perceived Body Behavior: We quantified other aspects of the experience by asking participants to rate their level of agreement with some statements (7-point Likert-type response items, from strongly disagree to strongly agree). We checked whether participants felt as if they were the agents of the sounds (agency [31]), as many studies have shown that large discrepancies between modalities and delays between actions and sensory feedback disrupt agency and diminish the sensory-induced bodily illusions [31,51]. The questionnaire included statements assessing whether participants had a vivid feeling (vividness [51]) or had unexpected feelings about their body (surprise). We also looked at feet localization as sound may interact with proprioception [51], and used 7-point Likert-type response items to assess the perceived walking speed (slow vs. quick), body weight (light vs. heavy), body strength (weak vs. strong) and body straightness (stooped/hunched vs. straight).

Experimental Procedure

A within-subjects design was preferred given the greater variability of body size perception between subjects [22] due to psychological condition, thoughts about ideal body size, media exposure or body dissatisfaction [39]. As in other studies assessing perceived body size [10,27,39] we adopted various strategies to compensate for practice /habituation bias. First, condition randomization served to discard differences due to practice. Second, while the avatar's parameters were set to match the participant's gender and height, the initial avatar's weight varied across trials to avoid anchor effects of the initial value [10,27,39]. This was set to match the participant's weight ± 25% (whether it was + or - was counterbalanced across the two repetitions). Participants changed the avatar's weight by pressing two keys. Finally, to distract participants from the manipulation of one's body weight, we mixed the avatar's task with two other 'fake' tasks related to objects weight: a 'spanner task' and a 'lifting weights task'. For the 'spanner task' we showed participants three metal spanners (13, 15, 17 mm) and told them that in each trial they would have to carry one of them and later provide assessments of its length and weight. In fact, in order to keep weight constant we always gave participants the 15 mm spanner, though this was not made clear to them. For the 'lifting weights task' we used a self-efficacy scale assessing the perceived ability to lift various weights [1]. Participants were fully debriefed as to the purpose of the study after the experiment ended.

After participants had been equipped with all the sensors and had been provided with task instructions, they performed two initial practice blocks (one without and one with the equipment on) in order to familiarize themselves with the task. Next, they completed a set of three experimental blocks differing in the sound feedback condition (Low frequency, High frequency and Control) presented in a randomized order. Then, the full set of three conditions, in another randomized order was repeated, in order to collect more data points. In each block, participants were given the 15 mm spanner and, while holding it in their hand, they walked in place for 10 s (marching phase). After a go-ahead signal they walked along the 8.5 m wooden-floor corridor (walking phase). Note that the marching phase was introduced to increase sound exposure but that the analyses of gait patterns focused on the walking phase. Participants were asked to walk at a self-paced, comfortable speed. At the end of the corridor, participants placed the spanner on a black cloth bag and adjusted the avatar on the body visualization tool so that it matched their own perceived body dimensions (see Figure 3 – left).

After this body visualization task, participants were asked to complete the questionnaire that assessed, in this order, (1) the perceived spanner length and weight; (2) self-efficacy regarding lifting different weight objects; (3) body feelings (speed, weight, strength, straightness, agency over footstep sounds, vividness, surprise, feet localization); and (4) emotional feelings (valence, arousal, dominance).

RESULTS

First of all, we confirm that all participants attributed the sounds to themselves, as a product of walking. As shown in Table 1, participants agreed that the sounds they heard were produced by their own body (agency scale), and did not find the experience more or less vivid or surprising than normal (non-significant differences between conditions). Given the confirmation of perceived agency, we proceeded with the analysis of the other collected data.

For the gait analyses (FSR and accelerometer), for each trial and for each extracted parameter (see Methods) we calculated the average of all steps in the walking phase. Then, for all physiological data (FSR, accelerometer and GSR), individual z-scores were calculated to reduce intra-subject variability [4]. We analyzed normal data (normality tested with Shaphiro-Wilk) with two-way repeated measures analyses of variance (ANOVA), with 3x2 within-subject factors sound condition and repetition. Significant effects were followed by paired samples one-tailed t-tests, with the significance alpha level adjusted to multiple comparisons. If the ANOVA did not show an effect of repetition, we averaged the data across repetitions and used t-tests to compare the three sound conditions[3]. In case of non-normal data, we attempted normalization by LOG-transformation. If normalization was not achieved (i.e., GSR and questionnaire data) we analyzed the data with non-parametric Wilcoxon tests. Results of these analyses are presented in the next sections.

Perceived Body Weight (Body Visualization)

As shown in Figure 4, the sound condition affected perceived body weight, as measured by the body visualization tool. The ANOVA on the LOG-transformed data showed significant differences between sound conditions ($F(2,42)=4.02$, $p=0.026$, $\eta^2=0.16$). T-tests comparing the three sound conditions revealed that the High frequency feedback was associated with a significantly lighter body than the Control feedback ($t(21)=2.73$; $p=0.006$). The High vs. Low frequency comparison indicated a trend towards statistical significance ($p=0.04$), but the Control vs. Low frequency comparison was far from significance ($p>0.2$). *These results indicate that the High frequency condition caused participants to feel as having a thinner body.*

[3] A p-value equal to 0.017 corresponds to a significance level of alpha=0.05 when Bonferroni correction for 3 levels is applied.

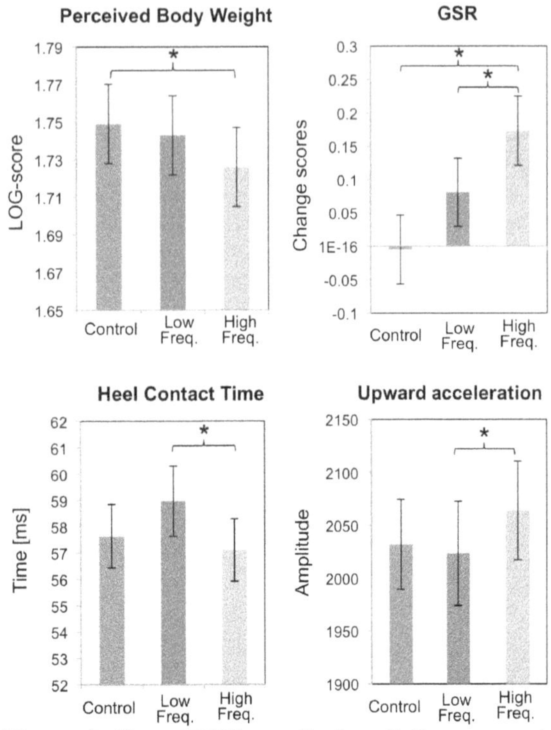

Figure 4. Mean (±SE) results for all three sound conditions. * marks significant differences between means.

Foot Pressure (FSR Sensor Data)

The pressure data for one participant and for one trial for two participants were lost. For the remaining 21 participants, data showed an average of 5.34 (SD=0.64) steps in each walking phase. Of all parameters, only the heel contact time with the ground revealed a significant effect of sound condition ($F(2,36)=6.38$, $p=0.004$, $\eta^2=0.26$; Figure 4). T-tests on the z-scored data revealed that the heel remained in longer contact with the ground in the Low than in the High frequency condition ($t(20)=2.79$, $p=0.006$). The Low frequency vs. Control comparison indicated a trend towards statistical significance ($p=0.039$). No other differences were found. *These results suggest an increase in body weight perception in the Low frequency condition.*

Foot Acceleration (Accelerometer Data)

Acceleration data for one participant and for one trial for another participant were lost. For the remaining 21 participants, the net acceleration was calculated as the square root of the sum of the squares of the three acceleration components. Of all parameters, only the upward foot acceleration revealed significant effects of sound condition ($F(2,38)=3.94$, $p=0.028$, $\eta^2=0.17$; Figure 4). T-tests on the z-scored data revealed larger acceleration during the foot upward movement in the High than in the Low frequency condition ($t(20)=2.62$; $p=0.008$). The High frequency vs. Control comparison indicated a trend towards statistical significance ($p=0.029$), but no other differences were identified. *These results suggest a decrease in body weight perception in the High frequency condition.*

Scales	Control	High freq	Low freq
Emotional valence*	5.5(2.5-7.5)	6(5-8.5)	5.25(3-8)
Arousal	4.5(2-7.5)	5(2.5-7.5)	4.5(2-7.5)
Dominance	5(2.5-8.5)	5.5(4-8.5)	5(2.5-8)
Speed*	4(2-6.5)	5(3-6.5)	4 (1.5-6)
Weight	4(2-6.5)	4(1.5-5.5)	4.25(2-6.5)
Strength	4(2.5-6)	4.5(3.5-6)	4(2.5-5.5)
Straightness	5.25(2.5-7)	5.25(2.5-7)	5(2-7)
Agency	6(1-7)	6.5(1-7)	6.5(2-7)
Vividness	3(1-6)	2.75(1-6.5)	3.5(1-6)
Surprise	4(1-6.5)	4.25(1-7)	4(1-7)
Feet localization*	5.25(3-7)	6(4-7)	5.5(2-7)

Table 1. Median(Range) for questionnaire data (7-level Likert items except for 9-level valence, arousal and dominance scales). * marks significant mean differences.

Emotional Response (GSR, Self-assessment Manikin)

GSR data from three participants were lost due to technical problems. For the remaining 19 participants, GSR change scores were calculated for each condition by subtracting the minimum from the maximum response during each condition (from the beginning of the marching phase to the end of the walking phase). Wilcoxon paired comparisons on the z-scored data did not reveal an effect of repetition; thus we averaged the data across repetitions and used further Wilcoxon tests to compare the three sound conditions[3]. As shown in Figure 4, the sound condition affected the GSR scores. Higher changes were elicited by the High than the Low frequency ($T=39$, $p=0.011$) and the Control condition ($T=28$, $p=0.003$), while the Low frequency vs. Control comparison did not achieve statistical significance.

The questionnaire data provided further insight into participants' emotional feelings. As shown in Table 1, they felt more positive in the High than in the Low frequency condition ($T=22$, $p=0.008$). A trend towards statistical significance was observed for the High frequency vs. Control comparison ($p=0.037$). No significant main effects of sound condition on arousal and dominance were found, but results indicate a trend in the direction of greater feelings of arousal in the High frequency than in the Control condition ($p=0.029$). There was also a trend towards greater feelings of dominance in the High frequency than in the Low frequency ($p=0.022$) and the Control conditions ($p=0.041$). *In brief, our results indicate that the High frequency condition caused participants to feel more aroused and positive.*

Perceived Body Behavior

For the questionnaire items on perceived body behavior, Wilcoxon paired comparisons did not reveal a repetition effect; thus we used further Wilcoxon tests to compare the three sound conditions (mean across repetitions). We report the comparisons that reached significance ($p<0.017$) or that showed a trend towards significance ($p<0.05$).

The sound condition affected perceived speed. As shown in Table 1, participants felt quicker in the High than in the Low frequency condition (T=23, p=0.005), and they tended to feel quicker in the High frequency than in the Control condition (p=0.022). Although no significant effects of sound condition were found for perceived body weight, strength and straightness of the body the statistical comparisons revealed trends towards a significant lighter (p=0.024), stronger (p=0.037) and straighter (p=0.029) body in the High than in the Low frequency condition.

Attention to one's body

Finally, it was found that participants were more confident in localizing their feet in the High frequency than in the Control condition (T=100, p=0.011); moreover they tended to feel more confident in the High than in the Low frequency condition (p=0.020). *These results and the more positive emotion reported suggest that the High frequency condition may have enhanced the proprioceptive feedback or possibly even generated a more positive attention to one's body.*

DISCUSSION

We investigated the alteration of one's footsteps sounds to modulate the perception of one's body and enhance self-esteem, body feelings and the quality of walking. We found that shifting the frequency of self-produced footstep sounds alters the perceived body weight, emotional state, perceived physical abilities and gait. This modulation process could be used to improve the efficacy of technology for wellbeing and for motivating physical activity. The next sections discuss the specific effects and their implications and possible applications, and perspectives for further work.

Body dimensions

We had hypothesized that shifting the spectral mode of self-produced footstep sounds to lower frequencies may result in a perceived heavier body, while shifting it to higher frequencies may result in a perceived lighter body. The second part of this hypothesis was confirmed by our results in the body visualization task as, after the High frequency feedback, participants set the dimensions of the avatar that represented their body to correspond to a lighter body. We also observed that participants tended to feel lighter in the High than in the Low frequency condition (questionnaire data).

Our approach exploits the multisensory nature of body perception and builds on previous neuroscience research showing that how people perceive their body can be changed by altering body-related multisensory cues [3,13,38,51,55]. Our findings constitute a novel contribution to this research in which the majority of works have focused on visual, tactile and proprioceptive cues. Although walkers receive information about their body from vision, sound, touch (via the tactile sensory receptors in the skin of the feet) and proprioception [57], we show that altering sound cues alone can change perceived body weight and other related body percepts. In this way we contribute to the growing interest in HCI on the possibilities offered by multisensory integration mechanisms for enhancing the user experience.

Moreover, our findings advance current research looking specifically at walking sounds as a source of information about events. While previous research has explored how material identity in VR can be conveyed even when some modalities are absent [14], we focused on walking sounds as a way of altering body perception. A few studies have looked at walking sounds as information on the appearance of an unknown walker's body during passive listening [17,29,37]. However, to the best of our knowledge, this is the first study looking at walking sounds as a source of real-time information as to the appearance of one's own body.

Emotional State and Physical Abilities

We further hypothesized that changes in perceived body weight would come together with emotional changes, given the tight links between body perception and self-esteem [9,41]. We showed that listening to walking sounds with higher frequencies resulted in people reporting feeling more positive. People were also more physiologically aroused during this sound feedback condition, as evidenced by the GSR recordings. In addition, we observed trends towards an increase in participants' perceived abilities, as they reported feeling more in control (dominance ratings) when listening to the high frequency version of their footsteps.

There were further changes in participants' perception of their physical capabilities as they felt quicker and more confident in localizing their feet (i.e., better proprioception) after this condition. They also tended to feel stronger. The enhancement in perceived strength and proprioception caused by changes in self-produced footstep sounds relates to previous findings showing similar effects of self-produced tapping sounds [14]. Finally, we observed that participants tended to feel as if they were walking with a straighter posture when listening to higher than lower frequency versions of their footsteps. This adds to previous findings on the links between the perceived posture of the heard walker and the spectral frequency of walking sounds [37] and between body posture and emotional state [8].

The possibility of operating at the level of the perception of one's own body using sound feedback can apply to the design of systems aimed to enhance wellbeing. In fact, feeling more positive and energized, quicker and in better control of one's body relates to enhanced self-esteem and a better predisposition for physical activity. These systems could benefit the increasing number of people who are concerned with the appearance of their bodies [32] and about what their body can do. There are a number of clinical cases of body- and action-distortions leading to body-impairments [9] and to deficits in emotional states, such as some cases of chronic pain [49] or anorexia nervosa [41]. Apart from these cases, many young people in their teen years, older adults, and a significant proportion of the remaining population often have these concerns to the detriment of their emotional state and motor performance. Altered feedback on walking sounds might help to recalibrate distorted feelings of one's own body weight and capabilities, and to feel more positive and in control of one's body. Our findings can inform the design of more effective therapies using VR and serious gaming technologies to enhance wellbeing. Sound feedback in these applications can optimize user's embodiment in a virtual character that may have different anthropomorphic characteristics than the user [44,57].

Gait

We further posited a link between changes in perceived body weight and gait. Based on prior research we hypothesized that a condition eliciting a lighter perceived body would result in a larger acceleration of lower limbs [25,54], while a condition eliciting a heavier perceived body would result in longer duration of the heel strike [25] and a larger exerted force by the feet against the ground [15].

Our results provide support for these hypotheses. First, a higher frequency mode resulted in larger acceleration of the upward movement of the lower limbs during walking, which is consistent with previously observed gait patterns of lighter walkers [25,54]. This result is interesting from the point of view of increase in physical activity. Second, a lower frequency mode resulted in an increase in the time participants kept their heel in contact with the ground, as measured by the force sensitive resistors, which is consistent with walking with "heavier" steps [25]. It should be noted that, although most of the self-reported changes seem to derive from shifting the spectral mode to higher but not to lower frequencies, we were able to observe behavioral changes for the low frequency mode. Thus, these changes seem to occur without users being aware of them [51].

Our study provides more insight into the updating of 'forward internal models' of motor-to-sensory transformations [60], as sound has rarely been investigated as feedback to body models. We suggest that the observed gait changes may result from an attempt to reduce the sensory discrepancies that our feedback introduces. Gait changes may have contributed to maintain the sound-induced bodily illusion. In fact, all observed changes in body perception, emotion and gait may reinforce each other during the process [43].

Sound feedback is currently used in many HCI applications aimed at increasing exercise adherence, facilitating movement and enhancing positive emotions, including applications used in sport and motor rehabilitation contexts [11,19,42,45,46,58]. Here we show that operating at the level of the perception of one's body by using sound feedback can also enhance physical performance (reflected in the acceleration of lower limbs), self-esteem and positive attention to one's body. While we show the short-term effect of brief exposure to manipulated walking sounds, it remains to be tested whether the effects may differ after longer exposure due to habituation [40], or generalize to other environments with different lighting, environmental noise or ground/footgear materials [29,53], as well as the longer term effects. Moreover, while our subject sample does not allow testing gender differences, it is possible they exist given the media pressure on women on body size [52]. Further, as alteration in the sound can lead to different perception of shoe material and style (e.g., high heel vs. heavier shoes), the subject's gender may have inhibitory or enhancing effects on the experience. Research has indeed shown that different sounds are preferred for walkers of different genders [57]. We observed that when removing the four males in the current sample, the data show even stronger effects in perceived body weight (sound condition: $p=0.021$), heel contact time (sound condition: $p=0.001$), perceived speed (High vs. Low: $p=0.003$) and emotional arousal (High vs. Control: $p=0.016$), thus suggesting gender differences and the need for further investigation.

Implications Beyond Walking

In this study, we focused on walking but future research should explore a similar approach of using sound feedback to enhance other types of physical activity. It should be noted that we used shifts in frequency mode due to their relation to body weight [17,29] but that different sound manipulations might be needed to induce similar effects during physical activities other than walking. Our study highlights the importance of a careful selection of sounds in order to optimize the desired effects. Prior research has shown the importance of keeping sensorimotor discrepancies under a certain threshold to maintain the feeling of agency and enhance the multisensory-induced effects [31,51]. Furthermore, we suggest that the relative contributions of shifts in frequency spectra and in loudness to our observed effects need to be considered. We were surprised to see that the perceived body weight, as quantified in the body visualization task, was slightly (but not significantly) higher in the Control than in the Low frequency condition. While the self-reported weight in the questionnaire was not higher for the Control condition, it is possible that the muffling of the high frequencies in the Low frequency condition was not completely achieved or that our results might depend on an interaction between spectral mode and loudness, rather than spectral mode alone. We opted for manipulating frequency spectra based on prior research findings [29], but this resulted in the three sounds conditions differing also in loudness [23]. Past studies have demonstrated that overall sound amplification of body-related sounds (e.g., rubbing hands) may lead to changes in perceived sound source characteristics [20,24]. Future research may also test the optimum magnitude of frequency shifts.

Finally, while we presented results from a lab study, our prototype could be further developed to allow running studies in the open. A more refined and compact version of our system could be comprised of wireless headphones and microphones connected to a smartphone in which sound equalization takes place and in which the integrated accelerometer/gyroscopes are used to record the body activity. This system could be used for walking, running or physical rehabilitation applications that could increase the users' performance, creating a more pleasurable experience of physical activity and providing motivation for it [49].

CONCLUSIONS

Our results broaden the understanding of how auditory sensory feedback can be used to design technology that changes the perceived physical appearance and physical capabilities of one's body. We make a theoretical contribution to HCI, by bridging psychological research on multisensory stimuli updating one's body model and HCI research on the design of sensory-augmentation technologies supporting wellbeing. This study therefore forms the basis of a larger effort to design sound and motion technology that triggers changes in how we perceive and use our bodies. Technologies integrating our proposed feedback may become an extension of the users themselves, providing a different experience of their bodies and impacting their self-esteem and motivation to perform physical activity.

ACKNOWLEDGMENT

Supported by and ESRC ES/K001477/1 grant 'The Hearing Body' and partially by AHRC AH/L007053/1 'Rethinking the Senses' and EPSRC EP/H016988/1 'Emo&Pain' grants. We also thank Dr Torsten Marquardt for his advice.

REFERENCES

1. Bandura, A. Guide for constructing self-efficacy scales. *Self-efficacy beliefs of adolescents* 5 (2006), 307-337.
2. Bianchi-Berthouze, N. Understanding the role of body movement in player engagement. *Human Computer Interaction 28*(2013), 42-75.
3. Botvinick, M., and Cohen, J. Rubber hands 'feel' touch that eyes see. *Nature 391* (1998), 756.
4. Boucsein, W. *Electrodermal activity*. New York: Plenum press, 1992.
5. Bradley M.M., and Lang, P.J. Affective reactions to acoustic stimuli. *Psychophysiology 37*(2000), 204-215.
6. Bradley M.M., and Lang, P.J. Measuring emotion: the self-assessment manikin and the semantic differential. *Journal of behavior therapy and experimental psychiatry 25*, 1(1994), 49-59.
7. Bresin, R., de Witt, A., Papetti, S., Civolani, M., and Fontana, F. Expressive sonification of footstep sounds. *Proc. ISON* (2010), 51-54.
8. Carney, D.R., Cuddy, A.J., and Yap, A.J. Power posing brief nonverbal displays affect neuroendocrine levels and risk tolerance. *Psychological Science 21*(2010), 1363-1368.
9. Carruthers, G. Types of body representation and the sense of embodiment. *Consciousness and Cognition 17*(2008), 1302-1316
10. Cazzato, V., Mian, E., Serino, A., Mele, S., and Urgesi, C. Distinct contributions of extrastriate body area and temporoparietal junction in perceiving one's own and others' body. Cognitive, Affective, & Behavioral Neuroscience (2014), 1-18.
11. Cesarini, D., Hermann, T., and Ungerechts, B. A real-time auditory biofeedback system for sports swimming. *Proc. ICAD* (2014).
12. Cunado, D., Nixon, M. S., and Carter, J.N. Automatic extraction and description of human gait models for recognition purposes. *Computer Vision and Image Understanding 90*, 1(2003), 1-41.
13. de Vignemont, F., Ehrsson, H.H., and Haggard, P. Bodily illusions modulate tactile perception. *Current Biology 15*, 14(2005), 1286-1290.
14. Furfaro, E., Bianchi-Berthouze, N., Bevilacqua, F., and Tajadura-Jiménez, A. Sonification of surface tapping: Influences on behaviour, emotion and surface perception. *Proc. ISON* (2013), 21-18.
15. Galbraith F., and Barton M. Ground loading from footsteps. *JASA 48*, 5B (1970).
16. Gallagher, S. *How the body shapes the mind*. Clarendon Press, Oxford; New York, 2005.
17. Giordano, B.L., and Bresin, R. Walking and playing: what's the origin of emotional expressiveness in music? *Proc. ICMPC9* (2006), 149.
18. Giordano, B.L., Visell, Y., Yao, H.Y., Hayward, V., Cooperstock, J.R., and McAdams, S. Identification of walked-upon materials in auditory, kinesthetic, haptic, and audio-haptic conditions. *JASA 131*(2012), 4002-12.
19. Großhauser, T., Bläsing, B., Spieth, C., Hermann, T. Wearable sensor-based real-time sonification of motion and foot pressure in dance teaching and training. *J. of the Audio Engineering Society* 60, 7/8(2012),580–589.
20. Guest S., Catmur C., Lloyd D., and Spence C. Audiotactile interactions in roughness perception. *Experimental Brain Research 146* (2002), 161-171.
21. Harrisson, D., Marshall, P., Bianchi-Berthouze, N., and Bird, J. Tracking physical activity: Problems related to running longitudinal studies with commercial devices. *Proc. Ubicomp & ISWC,* ACM Press (2014), 699-702.
22. Hennighausen, K., Enkelmann, D., Wewetzer, C., and Remschmidt, H. Body image distortion in Anorexia Nervosa--is there really a perceptual deficit? *European Child &Adolescent Psychiatry, 8* (1999), 200-206.
23. ISO 226:2003. Acoustics -- Normal equal-loudness-level contours.
24. Jousmäki, V., and Hari, R. Parchment-skin illusion: sound-biased touch. *Current Biology 8*(1998), R190-191.
25. Ko, S.-u., Stenholm, S., and Ferrucci, L. Characteristic gait patterns in older adults with obesity—Results from the Baltimore Longitudinal Study of Aging. *Journal of Biomechanics, 43*(2010), 1104-1110.
26. Kurihara, Y., Hachisu, T., Kuchenbecker, K.J., Kajimoto, H. Jointonation: robotization of the human body by vibrotactile feedback. *Proc. SIGGRAPH,* ACM Press (2013).
27. Legenbauer, T., Vocks, S., Betz, S., Baguena Puigcerver, M.J., Benecke, A., Troje, N.F., and Ruddel, H. Differences in the nature of body image disturbances between female obese individuals with versus without a comorbid binge eating disorder: an exploratory study including static and dynamic aspects of body image. *Behavior Modification, 35, 2* (2011), 162-186.
28. Leman, M., Moelants, D., Varewyck, M., Styns, F., van Noorden, L., and Martens, J.P. Activating and relaxing

music entrains the speed of beat synchronized walking. *PloS one 8,* 7(2013), e67932.
29. Li, X.F., Logan, R.J., and Pastore, R.E. Perception of acoustic source characteristics: walking sounds. *JASA 90*, 6(1991), 3036-3049.
30. Magill, R.A., and Anderson, D.I. The roles and uses of augmented feedback in motor skill acquisition. *Skill Acquisition in Sport: Research, Theory and Practice*. N. Hodges, A.M. Williams, eds. Routledge, 2012.
31. Menzer, F., Brooks, A., Halje, P., Faller, C., Vetterli, M., and Blanke, O. Feeling in control of your footsteps: Conscious gait monitoring and the auditory consequences of footsteps. *Cognitive Neuroscience 1*(2010), 184-192.
32. NHS, *Cosmetic surgery.* www.nhs.uk/conditions/Cosmetic-surgery
33. NHS, *Health and fitness.* www.nhs.uk/livewell/fitness
34. NHS, *Walking for Health*. www.nhs.uk/Livewell
35. Nordahl, R. Increasing the motion of users in photorealistic virtual environments by utilising auditory rendering of the environment and ego-motion. *Proc. Presence* (2006), 57-63.
36. OECD. *Health at a Glance 2013: OECD Indicators*. OECD Publishing, 2013.
37. Pastore, R.E., Flint, J.D., Gaston, J.R., and Solomon, M.J. Auditory event perception: the source—perception loop for posture in human gait. *Perception & psychophysics 70*(2008), 13-29.
38. Petkova, V.I. and Ehrsson, H.H. If I were you: Perceptual illusion of body swapping. *PLoS ONE 3*, 12(2008).
39. Piryankova, I.V., Stefanucci, J.K., Romero, J., Rosa, S. D.L., Black, M.J., and Mohler, B.J. Can I recognize my body's weight? The influence of shape and texture on the perception of self. *ACM Trans. Appl. Percept. 11*(2014), 1-18.
40. Polich, J. Habituation of P300 from auditory stimuli. *Psychobiology 17*, 1 (1989), 19-28.
41. Pollatos, O., Kurz, A.-L., Albrecht, J., Schreder, T., et al. Reduced perception of bodily signals in anorexia nervosa. *Eating Behaviours 9*, 4(2008), 381-388.
42. Rosati, G., Rodà, A., Avanzini, F., and Masiero, S. On the role of auditory feedback in robotic-assisted movement training after stroke. *Computational Intelligence and Neuroscience,* (2013), ID586138.
43. Sakurai, S., Katsumura, T., Narumi, T., Tanikawa, T., Hirose, M. Interactonia balloon. *SIGGRAPH* (2012).
44. Sanchez-Vives, M.V., and Slater, M. From presence to consciousness through virtual reality. *Nature Reviews Neuroscience 6*, 4(2005), 332-339.
45. Savva, N., Scarinzi, A., and Bianchi-Berthouze, N. Continuous recognition of player's affective body expression as dynamic quality of aesthetic experience. *IEEE IEEE Transactions on Computational Intelligence and AI in Games 4*(2012), 199-212
46. Schaffert, N., Mattes, K., and Effenberg, A.O. Listen to the boat motion: acoustic information for elite rowers. *Proc. ISON* (2010), 31-38.
47. Senna, I., Maravita, A., Bolognini, N., and Parise, C.V. The Marble-Hand Illusion. *PloS one 9*, 3 (2014).
48. Sigrist, R., Rauter, G., Riener, R., Wolf, P. Augmented visual, auditory, haptic, and multimodal feedback in motor learning: A review. *Psychonomic Bulletin & Review 20*, 1 (2013), 21–53.
49. Singh, A., Klapper, A., Jia, J., Fidalgo, A., Tajadura-Jimenez, A., Kanakam, N., Bianchi-Berthouze, N., and CdeC Williams, A. Motivating people with chronic pain to do physical activity: opportunities for technology design. *Proc. CHI'14,* ACM Press (2014), 2803-2812.
50. Styns, F., van Noorden, L., Moelants, D., and Leman, M. Walking on music. *Human movement science 26*, 5(2007), 769-785.
51. Tajadura-Jiménez, A., Väljamäe, A., Toshima, I., Kimura, T., Tsakiris, M., and Kitagawa, N. Action sounds recalibrate perceived tactile distance. *Current Biology 22*, 13(2012), R516-R517.
52. Tiggemann, M. Gender differences in the interrelationships between weight dissatisfaction, restraint, and self-esteem. *Sex Roles 30* (1994), 319-330.
53. Tonetto, P.L.M., Klanovicz, C.P., Spence, C. Modifying action sounds influences people's emotional responses and bodily sensations. *i-Perception*, *5*(2014), 153-163.
54. Troje, N.F. Retrieving information from human movement patterns. In *Understanding Events: How Humans See, Represent, and Act on Events* (pp. 308-334). Oxford University Press, 2008.
55. Tsakiris, M. My body in the brain: a neurocognitive model of body ownership. *Neuropsychologia 48,* 3(2010), 703-712.
56. Vaughan, C.L., Davis, B.L., and O'connor, J.C. *Dynamics of human gait*. Champaign, Illinois: Human Kinetics Publishers, 1992.
57. Visell, Y., Fontana, F., Giordano, B. L., Nordahl, R., Serafin, S., and Bresin, R. Sound design and perception in walking interactions. *International Journal of Human-Computer Studies 67*, 11(2009), 947-959.
58. Vogt, K., Pirro, D., Kobenz, I., Holdrich, R., and Eckel, G. PhysioSonic: evaluated movement sonification as auditory feedback in physiotherapy. *Proc. CMMR/ICAD*, (2009), 103-120.
59. Watanabe, J., and Hideyuki, A. Pace-sync shoes: intuitive walking-pace guidance based on cyclic vibro-tactile stimulation for the foot. *Virtual Reality 14*(2010), 213-9.
60. Wolpert, D.M., and Ghahramani, Z. Computational principles of movement neuroscience. *Nature Neuroscience 3*(2000), 1212-1217.
61. World Health Organization. *Global health risks: mortality and burden of disease attributable to selected major risks*. Geneva, 2009.
62. Zanotto, D., Rosati, G., Spagnol, S., Stegall, P., and Agrawal, S.K. Effects of complementary auditory feedback in robot-assisted lower extremity motor adaptation. *IEEE Transactions on Neural Systems and Rehabilitation Engineering, 21*, 5(2013), 775-786.

SwitchBack: Using Focus and Saccade Tracking to Guide Users' Attention for Mobile Task Resumption

Alex Mariakakis[1], Mayank Goel[1], Md. Tanvir Islam Aumi[1], Shwetak N. Patel[1], Jacob O. Wobbrock[2]

[1]Computer Science & Engineering | DUB Group
University of Washington
Seattle, WA 98195 USA
{atm15, mayank, tanvir, shwetak}@cs.washington.edu

[2]The Information School | DUB Group
University of Washington
Seattle, WA 98195 USA
wobbrock@uw.edu

ABSTRACT
Smartphones and tablets are often used in dynamic environments that force users to break focus and attend to their surroundings, creating a form of "situational impairment." Current mobile devices have no ability to sense when users divert or restore their attention, let alone provide support for resuming tasks. We therefore introduce *SwitchBack*, a system that allows mobile device users to resume tasks more efficiently. SwitchBack is built upon *Focus and Saccade Tracking (FAST)*, which uses the front-facing camera to determine when the user is looking and how their eyes are moving across the screen. In a controlled study, we found that FAST can identify how many lines the user has read in a body of text within a mean absolute percent error of just 3.9%. We then tested SwitchBack in a dual focus-of-attention task, finding that SwitchBack improved average reading speed by 7.7% in the presence of distractions.

Author Keywords
Situational impairments; mobile; gaze-tracking; reading.

ACM Classification Keywords
H.5.2. Information interfaces and presentation: User Interfaces – *input devices and strategies.*

INTRODUCTION
Mobile computing devices such as smartphones and tablets are now some of the most common devices in our environment. The ubiquity of mobile devices allows users to consume information everywhere. Although these devices are being used in a variety of environments, they do not have any significant awareness of the differences among environments or how these differences affect their users' behaviors. When users are negatively impacted in their ability to interact with technology by environmental conditions, they can be said to be *situationally impaired* [31]. Situational impairments may be caused by a number of factors, such as motion, temperature, ambient noise, *etc.*

CHI 2015, April 18 - 23 2015, Seoul, Republic of Korea

http://dx.doi.org/10.1145/2702123.2702539

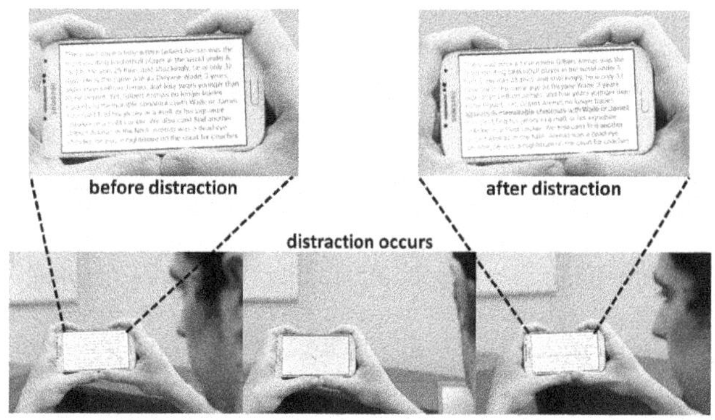

Figure 1. SwitchBack highlights where the user was last looking in a body of text before he or she turned away to handle a distraction.

One of the most significant contextual factors that affects people's mobile device usage is divided attention. For example, if pedestrians are checking email on their smartphones while walking across the street, they must break their attention from their devices to maintain awareness of their surroundings, or else they put themselves at risk of physical injury. Studies have shown that mobile phone related injuries among pedestrians doubled between 2005 and 2010, reaching almost 4% of all pedestrian accidents [27]. Some cities have even begun issuing tickets to pedestrians who are caught texting while walking [28]. Although safety is of the utmost concern when it comes to situational impairments, damage to users' productivity is also a concern. In the aforementioned scenario, it is likely that when pedestrians return their attention to their mobile devices, they will have lost track of their progress. Context-switching incurs a startup cost that can accumulate to the point where users' comprehension is negatively affected [25].

To address these concerns, we present *SwitchBack* (Figure 1), a system that uses the camera on a mobile device to determine when the user is unable to pay visual attention to the device, pause the task (if applicable), and then help the user to efficiently resume the task when the user returns his or her gaze to the device. SwitchBack is built upon our underlying camera-based attention-tracking algorithm called *Focus and Saccade Tracking (FAST)*, which, through the front-facing camera, approximates when and how the user is looking at the screen, even if users are wearing corrective lenses or glasses.

A high-level description of FAST is as follows. FAST first determines whether or not the user is looking at the screen. If the user is looking, FAST measures the movement of the user's pupil relative to the rest of the eye to track where the user is looking on the screen. In cases when the screen is displaying text (*e.g.*, emails or web articles), FAST detects quick, horizontal jumps. These gaze jumps, or *saccades*, are used as a proxy to determine when the user moves to a new line and to estimate where the user is in a body of text. FAST continually audits its estimate by checking whether the user's observed reading speed is within the expected range (200 – 400 wpm [16]).

Once SwitchBack detects that the user has returned from a distraction by looking back at the screen, it guides the user back to where he or she last left off by highlighting the appropriate region of text. FAST can also be used to enable automatic scrolling when the user reaches the end of the text visible on the screen. This capability can prove very helpful in a number of situations, for example, when a user has gloves on and the capacitive touchscreen will not work.

We evaluated FAST to quantify its performance for attention and saccade tracking, and for supporting reading task resumption. By incorporating information about the user's reading speed, FAST is able to estimate how many lines the user has read in a body of text within a mean absolute percent error of just 3.9%. We evaluated the effectiveness of SwitchBack in helping the user complete their mobile tasks in the presence of external distractions. In a controlled user study, participants, while experiencing distractions, improved their average reading speed during a reading task by 7.7% (roughly 19 words per minute) when using SwitchBack compared to the control condition.

The main contribution of this paper is to demonstrate that SwitchBack can be used in reading applications to facilitate the user resuming the reading of a body of text after attending to an outside distraction. This contribution comes in three parts: (1) the FAST algorithm for detecting when and where the user is looking at the screen using the camera found on commodity mobile phones and without the need for any additional illumination hardware; (2) the ability of FAST to track a user's reading pattern and guide them to the most recently read line of text when they return from another task; and (3) an evaluation of SwitchBack showing that it improves reading speed in situations of divided attention.

RELATED WORK

SwitchBack uses FAST to detect when and how the user is looking at the screen. FAST is related to, and can leverage, any sort of gaze tracking technique. Since SwitchBack is intended to help users with their mobile devices, we also discuss prior research regarding attention tracking for interface interactions.

Gaze-Tracking Technologies and Techniques

The most similar work to SwitchBack is EyePhone [24], a hands-free interfacing system intended for mobile applications that are used while the user is driving a vehicle. EyePhone uses the front-facing camera of a smartphone to monitor the user's gaze on the screen. Rather than tracking relative changes in the user's gaze, however, EyePhone monitors the absolute position of the user's gaze to make selections on the screen. While absolute position provides more information about the user's attention, gaze-tracking accuracy quickly degrades as the phone moves further away from the user's face (<20% accuracy for button selection at ~45 cm). By comparison, our use of relative changes can be easily extracted from the noisy eye-tracking signal, particularly the large ones that occur as the user's eyes travel from one side of the screen to the other. We will demonstrate how relative tracking results in a robust system suitable to use in motion.

Thorough reviews of gaze-tracking have been written by Hansen and Ji [12] and Morimoto and Mimica [26]. We briefly highlight a few innovations and direct readers to their surveys for more detail. Active gaze-tracking systems typically use infrared (IR) light because of the glint that appears when IR light is reflected off of the boundary of the lens and the cornea. Off-the-shelf devices[1,2] and wearable sensors integrated with eyeglasses [35] are normally used to shine IR light onto the user's face. From there, either Pupil Center Corneal Reflection [11] or machine learning [2] is used to learn resulting gaze coordinates. Passive gaze-tracking systems do not rely on any extra hardware, but rather process video and images from the camera using computer vision techniques. Machine learning methods like neural networks [33] have been used to develop a mapping from high dimensional image data in pixel space to low dimensional data in gaze-coordinate space.

Beyond EyePhone, gaze-tracking has not been heavily investigated in mobile computing. Drewes *et al.* [6] devised gaze-based gestures for a mobile device, but utilized an external IR tracker. Commercial entities have perhaps advanced development most. Companies like the Eye Tribe[2] sell active IR-based eye-trackers that are small enough to be mobile device accessories. Samsung gives the appearance of gaze-tracking through their Smart Scroll and Smart Pause features, but these systems actually monitor the orientation of the user's face. Recently, Qualcomm[3] has integrated a passive method of gaze-tracking in the facial processing SDK included on their Snapdragon processor.

[1] http://www.tobii.com/

[2] https://theeyetribe.com/

[3] https://developer.qualcomm.com/mobile-development/add-advanced-features/snapdragon-sdk-android

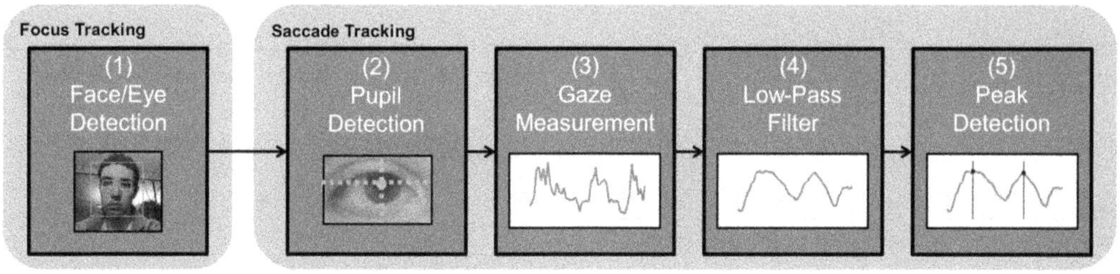

Figure 2. The FAST algorithm. **(1)** The user's face and eyes are detected in order to establish whether the user is focused on the screen or not. If the user is facing the screen, **(2)** the pupils are identified and compared relative to the bounding box of the eye to **(3)** identify the user's gaze in the horizontal and vertical directions. **(4)** These measurements are applied through low-pass filtering and **(5)** peak detection to identify saccades.

FAST uses this Qualcomm library for gaze feature extraction.

Attention and Interface Interaction

The design of SwitchBack's task-resumption feedback draws inspiration from Phosphor [4], a system that modified user interfaces on desktops to highlight changes in widget settings that users may otherwise miss. Similar techniques have been used to draw attention [23] and migrate users between different interface layouts [3]. SwitchBack shows similar transitions when users resume tasks on their mobile devices. Unlike SwitchBack, none of these techniques is aware of users' attention.

Visual fixations have been interpreted as both a measurement of interest and uncertainty [15,16]. Saccades have been used to reveal marked shifts in behavior [9,10]. Scanpaths, or sequences of saccades and fixations, describe how a user searches through an interface [1,10]. Goldberg and Kotval [9] showed that deviation from a normal scanning behavior indicates poor user training or bad layout design. Blink rate [5] and pupil size [22,29] have been used as an indexes of cognitive workload, but may be affected by outside factors like ambient light.

Just and Carpenter [16] monitored the eye fixations of users as they read scientific passages. Their main discovery was that readers make longer pauses when processing loads are greater (*e.g.*, longer words, confusing phrases). They also showed that people read in a saccadic, sequential manner. We use this latter fact to design the reading algorithm underlying our system.

The motivation behind SwitchBack follows closely with that of the work demonstrated in Gazemarks. Kern *et al.* [18] observed that people manage multitasking search situations by using placeholders like fingers or pens. Gazemarks tracks the user's gaze using an off-the-shelf gaze-tracker and provides digital placeholders, in the form of shadowed circles, to guide the user's attention when they switch tasks. We differ from Gazemarks in two ways: (1) We observe that relative gaze changes (*i.e.*, saccades) are better suited for monitoring attention on mobile devices than absolute gaze coordinates. Gazemarks was developed for desktops, which presume a stable environment with large screens and off-the-shelf eye-trackers, thus allowing them to use absolute gaze coordinates to track attention. (2) To motivate our FAST technique, we designed the SwitchBack application. While our interface modification is similar to the one applied in Gazemarks, reading is a use case that Kern *et al.* only briefly mention, but never develop.

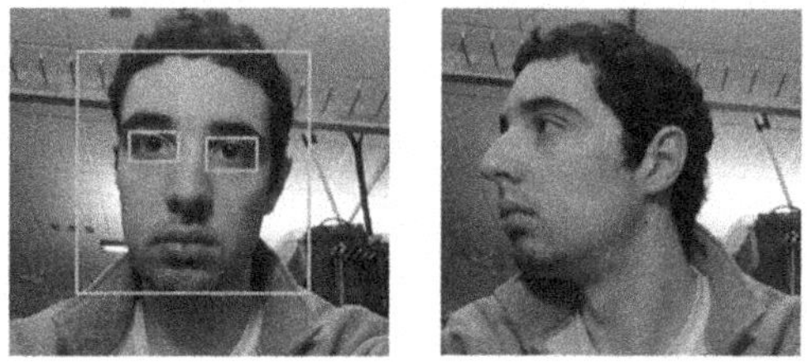

Figure 3. (a) If the user is looking at the screen, his face and eyes are detected. **(b)** When the user begins to look away, his face is either no longer detected or has turned too much for him to be focused on the screen.

THE DESIGN OF *SWITCHBACK*

SwitchBack is built upon our FAST algorithm (Figure 2), which has two major components. The first is *focus tracking*, which determines whether or not the user is facing the screen. The second is *saccade tracking*, which observes the position of the user's pupil relative to the rest of their eye to determine how the user's gaze changes over time. We combine these components within SwitchBack and apply highlighting to aid task resumption.

Focus and Saccade Tracking (FAST)

Focus Tracking

FAST takes frames from the front-facing camera and passes them through the Qualcomm Snapdragon SDK for processing. The SDK detects faces and the orientation of those faces. Both face detection and face orientation are useful for focus tracking. If a face is not detected on the screen, there is no way for the user's eyes to be tracked and the user is probably not attending to the screen (Figure 3b). Even if the user's face is in the view of the camera, the user may not be attending to the screen. In this case, we set bounds on the yaw (*i.e.*, side-to-side angle) of the face according to the typical angle formed between the distance from the user's face to the center of the screen and the

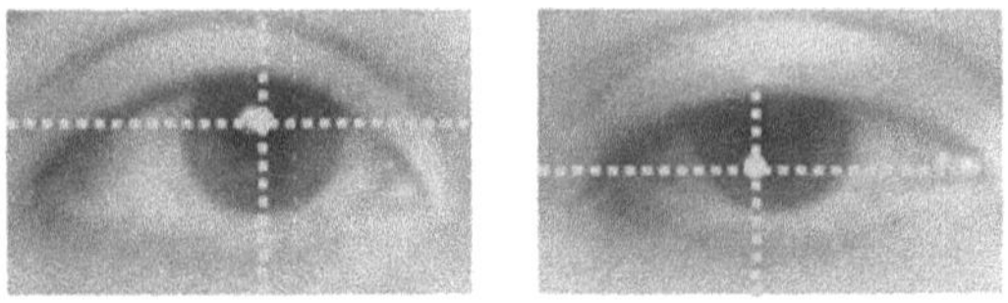

Figure 4. The position of the pupil relative to the rest of the eye changes as the user looks from (a) the top left to (b) the bottom.

distance from the user's face to the outside edge of the screen. If the user turns his face past these bounds, we infer that the user's attention is directed elsewhere.

Even when the user is facing the screen, face detection may briefly fail due to transient lighting conditions or occlusion by hands. To prevent false triggers indicating that the user has turned away, FAST maintains a sliding window of 2 seconds (overlap of 1/16 fps = 62.5 ms). It only infers that the user's attention has left the screen when the face is not detected for a window's duration. Any distractions shorter than that duration are so brief that the user likely will have not lost their focus from their previous task. As soon as the user is facing the screen again, FAST infers that his attention is back on the screen.

Saccade Tracking

Once SwitchBack detects that the user is looking at the screen, the system tries to detect saccades, or fast eye movements. In cases where the user is reading something on their screen, saccades can be used to estimate the number of lines that the user has read. To detect saccades, SwitchBack tries to detect the user's pupil by finding the darkest portion of his eye.

With the face, eyes, and pupil detected, gaze direction can be quantified using the same geometrical observations that have inspired gaze tracking technology in the past [6,12,26]. Figure 4 shows that the center of the pupil shifts depending on where the user is looking at the screen; we use this fact to form horizontal and vertical features that encode the position of each pupil within their respective eyes. Feature values range from 0 to 1, with 0.5 meaning that the eye is in the exact center along a specific dimension. The features are passed through a first-order infinite impulse response (IIR) filter with a cutoff frequency of roughly 2.5 Hz; this is a low-complexity low-pass filter that suppresses high-frequency noise in time series measurements.

Gaze coordinates on the screen can be inferred either through calibration or knowing the position of the user's head in the camera's field of view. EyePhone [24] divides the bounding box around the user's eye and the screen into a grid and uses a one-to-one grid cell mapping to associate pupil locations to targets on the phone. For our purposes, we do not need to know exactly where the user is looking on the screen. Instead, we are only interested in drastic gaze changes, implying that a saccade has occurred.

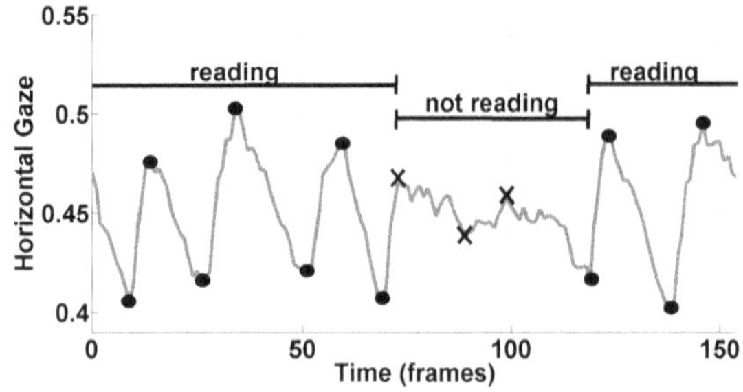

Figure 5. Peaks and troughs are detected throughout the signal, but only indicate saccades when the amplitude of the signal is large. Low magnitude values correspond to when the user is looking to the right, whereas higher magnitude values correspond to looking left.

Figure 5 plots the estimated horizontal location of a user's pupil with respect to time as the user moves their eyes, pauses for a few seconds, and then continues to move their eyes. Low magnitude values correspond to when the user is looking to the right, whereas higher magnitude values correspond to looking left. The signal jumps whenever the user's gaze changes drastically and a saccade occurs. FAST detects these movements in real-time by looking for local optima within a window. Note that saccade detection is agnostic to the amplitude of the signal, so such a system can be prone to noise appearing in flat signals. To prevent this from affecting FAST's line prediction, a detected optimum is only counted as a saccade if the gaze location changes significantly afterwards. The threshold for determining significant changes was determined empirically by iterating through different values and optimizing the results from the data collected in our technology evaluation. In Figure 5, the local optima marked with circles are considered saccades by the algorithm, while the crosses mark some of the local optima that are rejected by the algorithm because the signal exhibits less deviation during those times.

FAST in the Context of Reading

While reading English prose, right-to-left saccades indicate when users begin to read a new line (Figure 5). Between saccades, users' gaze exhibits sawtooth-like behavior as their gaze gradually sweeps across the screen.

Despite the filtering described earlier, there are still cases where noise in the signal and sporadic glances may be inferred as saccades but not necessarily correspond to actual saccades when the user looks at a new line. False positives like these would advance the estimate of the user's most recently read line too far. If face and eye detection fail for a brief period of time, it is also possible that saccades will be missed. False negatives cause the estimate of the user's reading position to lag behind. If there is no mechanism for correction, the errors can accumulate over time and cause frustrating results for the user.

To remedy this issue, we take advantage of the fact that we know the arrangement of the text within the application. In other words, we know how many words[4] appear in each line. Combining this with knowledge about typical human reading speeds (200-400 words per minute [16]), FAST can predict how long it expects a user to read the next line of text, comparing that expected range, $<t_{min}, t_{max}>$ with the measured interval between saccades, $t_{measured}$. There are three possibilities:

1. $t_{min} < t_{measured} < t_{max}$: The measured interval falls within the expected range, so we accept the saccade as a proxy for a new line and increment the line estimate accordingly.
2. $t_{measured} < t_{min}$: The measured interval falls short of the expected range, so we infer that not enough time has passed between line breaks, label that saccade as a false positive, and do nothing to the line estimate.
3. $t_{measured} > t_{max}$: The measured interval was longer than expected, so at least one saccade was likely missed. This means that the user read more text than what appears on the current line. We look ahead in the text, increment the line count, and update t_{min} and t_{max} until the expected range surrounds $t_{measured}$.

If the user looks away, pauses, or backtracks slightly while reading a line, $t_{measured}$ will overestimate the time it takes for the user to read the line. These moments can be segmented out of the time-varying signal, as shown in Figure 5, because they do not share the same sawtooth-like behavior as the reading moments. Therefore, $t_{measured}$ is only calculated using segments when the signal has the sawtooth-like behavior and the user is reading.

There are a couple of further considerations that should be taken into account when incrementing the line count. First, the current line for the user must lie within the screen; *e.g.*, if the first five lines of an article appear on a page, there is no way that the user is reading the sixth line. We use this fact to correct SwitchBack's estimate when the error becomes very large. Another important consideration to make about the text is line length. In Figure 6, for example, a user was able to jump directly to the third line after she read the first. This is caused by the fact that the user was able to read the second line during the right-to-left saccade (marked by the red arrow in Figure 6). We handle cases like this by ignoring lines that span less than a third of the screen (including line breaks) in the aforementioned calculations.

Technology Evaluation of FAST

Prior to conducting our primary user evaluation of SwitchBack, we conducted a technology evaluation to inform our design and quantify the accuracy of FAST. We

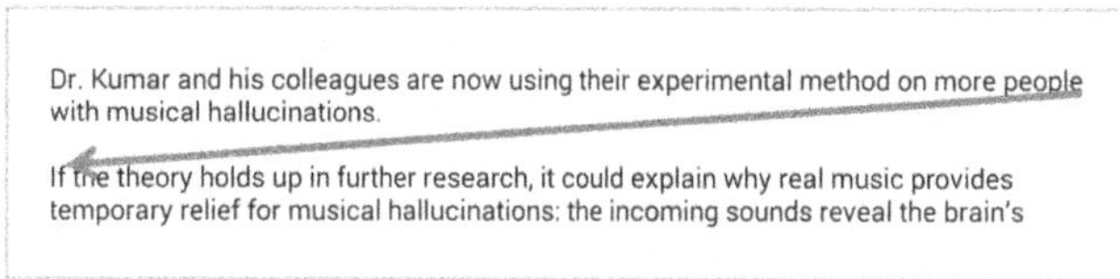

Figure 6. When there is spacing between lines, the user's eyes can follow the arrow and still read the second line.

collected reading data from 8 participants (5 males, 3 females), each of whom volunteered for a 20-minute session. Two of the participants wore glasses during the experiment.

We collected data using our custom reading application (Figure 1) on a Sony Xperia Z smartphone, which has a 5-inch screen, 1080×1920 pixel display, and 2.3 MP front-facing camera. Participants were asked to hold the smartphone in landscape mode while reading 6 different excerpts of text from the New York Times with size 15 font (roughly 1.8 mm in height) and presented as a single contiguous paragraph. Each article was clipped to 20 lines in length so the user did not have to scroll. We chose to use contiguous text in this experiment to gather sufficient data to estimate the time it takes for the typical user's eyes to travel across the width of the screen. The text was displayed on the screen with black text on a white background. Participants were asked to read 3 articles while standing and 3 articles while walking on a treadmill at a comfortable pace. The study was counterbalanced across conditions. The walking condition was added to evaluate how FAST performs in the presence of extraneous vibrations due to walking. Horizontal and vertical gaze angle were recorded by the application and processed offline using MATLAB.

Line prediction error is defined as the difference between the number of lines in the excerpt and FAST's line prediction. Our results show that FAST achieves a mean absolute prediction error of 0.8 (SD = 1.1) out of the 20 lines of text per trial, translating to 3.9% error. We also found that most of the errors tended to be positive, indicating that FAST overestimated the user's reading position slightly.

To delve deeper into our results, a mixed-effects model analysis of variance was used to analyze the data, with fixed effects for *Walking*, *Glasses*, and *Gender*, and a random effect for *Subject*. (Random effects are appropriate when levels of a factor are not of specific interest, but represent a larger population about which inferences are meant to be drawn [7]. Mixed-effects models are also appropriate for handling repeated measures over the same subjects due to their ability to model covariance in the data [21].)

We expected FAST to be more accurate while participants were standing than walking. Although FAST looks at relative, and not absolute, pupil position, we believed that the shaking of the front-facing camera caused by walking would still affect our performance. However, the average

[4] We use "word" to mean a group of five characters, consistent with terminology used in text analysis.

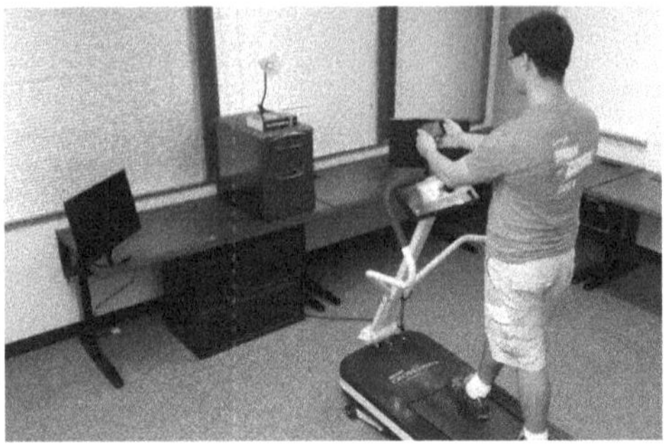

Figure 7. To support the different conditions, the experimental setup included a treadmill for walking, a lamp for consistent lighting, and a monitor on either side for distractions.

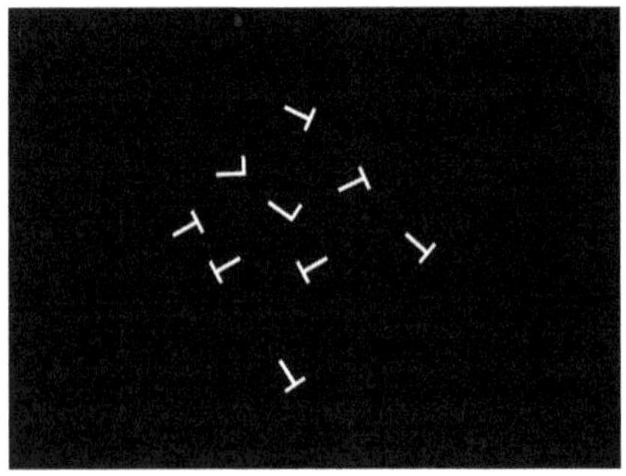

Figure 8. The distraction task required participants to distinguish between rotated T's and L's within a fixed amount of time.

lines-of-error while walking was 0.30 (*SD* = 0.92), and while standing was 0.29 (*SD* = 1.42), so there was no detectable difference ($F_{(1,29.9)} = 0.00$, *n.s.*).

We also expected FAST to perform worse for users who wore glasses because we believed that the computer vision component within FAST might perform poorly. The average error for people wearing glasses was 0.50 (*SD* = 1.83), and the error for those not wearing glasses was 0.21 (*SD* = 0.82), but that difference was also not statistically significant ($F_{(1,4.1)} = 0.52$, *n.s.*).

We did not expect any difference in performance across gender. The average error for males was 0.36 (*SD* = 1.32) and for females was 0.19 (*SD* = 0.98). This difference was not statistically significant ($F_{(1,4.7)} = 0.18$, *n.s.*).

SwitchBack Reading Application

We developed a reading application to guide the user's attention back to where they were last looking in a body of text after attending to an outside distraction (Figure 1). While users are reading, FAST keeps track of where they are looking using saccade tracking corrected with information about the text. FAST detects when users look away from the screen and saves the estimated line a user was last reading. Once a user turns her attention back to the screen, SwitchBack highlights the line that was saved, aiding task resumption.

USER EVALUATION OF SWITCHBACK

We conducted a user study for our SwitchBack reading application with the intent of demonstrating that SwitchBack allows users to more easily resume reading on mobile devices after looking away due to distraction.

Participants

Seventeen participants (9 male, 8 female) ranging from 19 to 52 years old (*M* = 26.7, *SD* = 7.2) were recruited for our study. The participants were evenly distributed between Caucasian, Asian, and South-Asian races. Five participants wore glasses during the study, and all but two of the participants owned and used a smartphone on a daily basis.

Apparatus

Participants used our custom application on a Sony Xperia Z smartphone with a 5-inch capacitive touch screen, 1080×1920 pixel display, and 2.3 MP front-facing camera. The reading application was the same as the one developed for the FAST evaluation study. The only difference was that SwitchBack would be enabled in one condition. When active, SwitchBack guided the user's focus of attention by highlighting a line of text, as shown on the right side of Figure 1. The text was highlighted whenever the user turned away from the screen and then disappeared 5 seconds after they returned to the application. Eight New York Times articles between 500 and 600 words (*M* = 522, *SD* = 18) were chosen for the study; their average readability score was 46.3 according to the Flesch Reading Ease test [19]. A diffused light source subtly illuminated the experiment area, ensuring consistent lighting conditions for all participants; special care was exercised to ensure that the lighting would not affect participants' reading ability.

To study the effect of SwitchBack in the presence of distractions, we devised a secondary distraction task and introduced it as a condition. The task was adapted from an attentionally-demanding task used by Yokoyama et al. [36]. The software for the task was written in C++ and ran on a Windows desktop with two monitors placed on either side of the user (Figure 7). Both screens began completely black. Every 25-40 seconds, one of the two screens played a tone to direct the user's attention away from the phone. The screen then displayed a combination of T's and L's (always 9 in total) with white text and at different orientations (Figure 8). Time intervals, screen selection, letter rotations, and letter selections were all randomized to simulate unexpected distractions and prevent anticipation.

To simulate a natural setting where users might face distractions, participants were asked to walk on a treadmill (Figure 7) for a portion of the experiments. The treadmill was set to a speed of about 1.4 m/s.

Procedure

The procedure was designed to fit in a single 45-minute session. Each session began with a pre-study questionnaire about the participant's mobile device experience and habits. Once completed, participants were introduced to the experimental setup and asked to familiarize themselves with the application. We also informed participants that they would be tested for reading comprehension through a four question multiple choice test at the end of each trial. Participants read a different article per trial to avoid familiarization with the text or encouraging them to skim. The order of the articles was randomized using Latin Squares to ensure that specific articles did not impose a bias on a particular set of conditions.

At the beginning of each trial, the experimenter ensured that the participant began reading with their face within the front-facing camera's field of view when the phone was held in landscape mode. Participants were asked to read each article in its entirety and to scroll whenever they desired. When the distraction task was active, participants were asked to verbally report either the number of T's or L's to the experimenter whenever letters appeared on one of the two outside monitors before returning to the reading; since the number of letters on the screen remained constant, we allowed participants to report the number of either letter. On average, participants experienced 4.4 distractions per trial (SD = 1.7) when the distraction task was active.

At the end of each trial, participants were asked to complete a short multiple choice test of reading comprehension and a NASA Task Load Index (TLX) questionnaire [13] to provide feedback concerning their experience.

Design & Analysis

The study was a within-subjects 2×2×2 factorial design. The factors and levels were:

- ***Posture***: *Sitting* and *Walking*.
- ***Distraction***: *Distraction* and *No Distraction*.
- ***Interface***: *SwitchBack* and *Control*.

Posture was the first factor that was counterbalanced. Within each posture, *Distraction* was counterbalanced, followed by *Interface*. Each participant completed every unique combination of conditions, leading to 17×2×2×2 = 136 total trials for the study.

Average reading speed, measured in words per minute (WPM), was the main measure for assessing SwitchBack's performance. To calculate reading speed, we divided the total number of characters in the text read by the time the user spent reading and divide that by 5, the standard for characters per word used in text analysis. Our calculation excludes the time spent completing the distraction task, when applicable.

A mixed-effects model analysis of variance was used to analyze our data, with fixed effects for *Distraction*, *Posture*, and *Interface*, and random effects for *Article* and *Subject* [7,21]. Overall, reading speed was normally distributed according to a nonsignificant Shapiro-Wilk W-test (W = 0.989, p = .383) [32].

Being ordinal in nature, Likert ratings (1-20) for the NASA TLX instrument were analyzed using the nonparametric Aligned Rank Transform procedure [14,30]. This procedure allows for an analysis of variance (ANOVA) to be used to

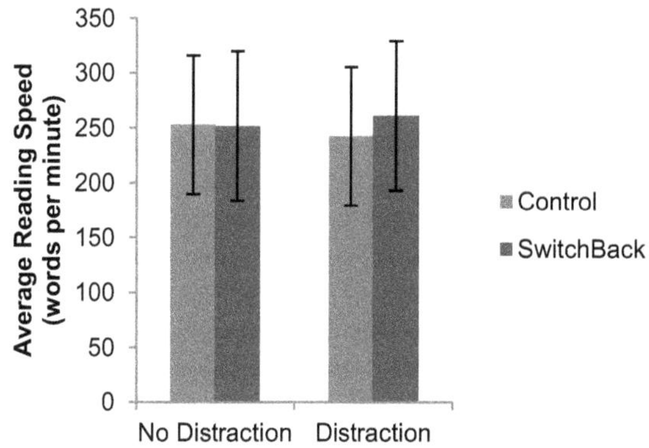

Figure 9. SwitchBack resulted in 19.0 WPM (7.7%) faster reading speeds than the control condition in the presence of distractions. Error bars show standard deviations.

test for main and interaction effects after aligning and ranking the data separately for each effect. Despite using analysis of variance, the procedure is considered nonparametric due to its ranking preprocessing step. The ARTool by Wobbrock *et al.* [34] was used to prepare the data for analysis using the Aligned Rank Transform procedure. Each of the 17 subjects filled out the 6 NASA TLX workload scales (1-20) after each of 8 articles, resulting in 17×6×8 = 816 individual ratings.

RESULTS

Reading Speed

Reading speed results are shown in Figure 9. Across all trials, the average reading speed was 252.0 WPM. This rate is near the lowest quarter of the expected range for typical reading rates, 200 – 400 WPM [16], which we believe can be attributed to the fact that users were asked to read for comprehension, rather than speed.

We looked at the *Interface* × *Distraction* interaction to evaluate the performance of our system. We found this interaction to have only a marginal effect on reading speed ($F_{(1,105)}$ = 2.93, p = .09). Without our distraction task, SwitchBack never has to modify the interface, so we dug deeper into this trend by looking at the effect of SwitchBack just in the presence of distractions. As we expected, a pairwise comparison shows that SwitchBack significantly increased reading speeds ($F_{(1,107.8)}$ = 4.61, $p <$ .05) in those cases. This translated to an extra +19.0 WPM increase in users' reading speed when SwitchBack was used in the presence of distractions, a +7.7% increase from the average reading speed across all users. Although the interaction was only a trend, prior work has convincingly argued for the appropriateness of doing *post hoc* comparisons on trend-level interactions [8].

We also gathered findings that confirmed that our experimental treatments did indeed increase workload, as intended. The *Distraction* × *Posture* interaction had a marginal effect on reading speed ($F_{(1,110.6)}$ = 2.83, p = .09), and in the presence of distractions, walking lowered reading speeds ($F_{(1,111.7)} = 4.01, p < .05$).

NASA TLX Questionnaire

It was our hope that through our NASA TLX questionnaires, we would demonstrate that SwitchBack generally decreased perceived workload. While we were not able to detect any significant differences, we found that SwitchBack marginally lessened the mental demand experienced by our users ($F_{(1,112)} = 3.25, p = .07$). This finding corroborates the findings concerning improvement in average reading speed; that is, reading speed should increase if mental demand decreases since the user is allowed to focus more on reading.

The NASA TLX questionnaires were more revealing about the effects of our dual focus-of-attention study design. For example, both walking ($F_{(1,112)} = 21.56, p < .0001$) and the distraction tasks ($F_{(1,112)} = 21.09, p < .0001$) significantly increased frustration for users. Similar trends can be observed across all the other aspects of the survey: mental demand, physical demand, temporal demand, success/failure, and effort.

DISCUSSION

Our goal was to develop a system that eases the user back into a task on their mobile device. To demonstrate this, we developed a SwitchBack reading application that identifies the user's reading pattern through gaze tracking and guides the user back to the proper location in the text after turning away. SwitchBack's FAST algorithm was able to identify the appropriate line to highlight with a mean absolute percent error of 3.9%. In an evaluation of SwitchBack's effect on performance during a reading task with distractions, SwitchBack improved average reading speeds by 7.7% in the presence of distractions.

We focused on smartphones for our user study because smartphones are currently one of the most pervasive devices in the world and we wanted to explore the constraints of working with small screens. SwitchBack is even better suited for devices like the Amazon Kindle, which are made specifically for long-form reading. In fact, we are confident that FAST would have higher accuracy with such devices because larger screens create more smooth and noticeable saccades. By tackling the hardest set of conditions for validating FAST (*i.e.,* a small screen and walking), we informally demonstrated that FAST would work on larger devices; doing the converse would not have been possible.

While evaluating the performance of the FAST algorithm alone, we found that it performed sub-optimally in roughly 15% of the trials. These can be attributed to two causes. The first cause was occlusion when the user unknowingly covered the camera with their thumb. We conducted our experiments in the device's landscape orientation because the Snapdragon SDK did not have the accuracy to support the narrower portrait news article width. Future mobile devices with multiple front-facing cameras, like the Amazon Fire, may alleviate such issues. The second cause relates to situations when participants were unable to tell if their face was within the camera's field of view while reading. We considered adding visual feedback to remedy this issue, similar to the approach taken by Samsung for their Smart Scroll feature [17]; however, we found this to be a distraction in itself that led to extraneous saccades. A wide-angle camera lens would alleviate the issue of the user's face moving out of the camera frame in most cases.

While testing SwitchBack's reading application, we found that some of our users had already developed their own way to keep track of where they were in a large body of text. For instance, one participant told us that she scrolled so that the line she was reading was always at the top of the screen; of course, she could not rely on this once she had scrolled to the bottom of the page. Other participants stated that they kept track of where they were by remembering a key phrase in the article as a "mental bookmark," despite our complicated distraction task. While such bookmarks should impose more cognitive load on the user and impair their ability to complete other tasks, a field study with ecologically valid distractions would be insightful towards examining more realistic cognitive load tradeoffs.

Our use of FAST in the SwitchBack application ignores gaze position in the vertical direction because of its poor accuracy, which may be partially attributed to the short height of the smartphone screen while it is the landscape orientation. In ignoring the vertical gaze position, we were forced to concede a few assumptions involving the advancement of the line count. First, we assume that the user begins reading from the first line of text. We believe this is fair for new bodies of text that the user has not seen previously, but there is a solution for accommodating other starting locations without vertical gaze position. Since SwitchBack is implemented on devices with touchscreens, the user can double tap a word to simultaneously activate the gaze-tracking and notify the system of their starting point. The second assumption we concede in SwitchBack is that the user reads each line in sequential order. This assumption is confirmed by research in psychology that focuses on reading analysis [16], but the possibility still remains that users will go back and reread missed portions of their text. If the saccade is small and occurs quickly after the user reaches a new line, FAST will treat it as a false positive and continue tracking as normal; however, our algorithm does not address jumps when the user goes back *multiple* lines.

Currently, SwitchBack is a one-size-fits-all system (*i.e.*, no training or customization for each user); however, one could imagine a system that learns the device owner's reading habits over time. SwitchBack could begin by checking if the user's reading speed falls within the wide range of typical human speeds, as in our implementation, but then narrow that window to the particular user's reading speed to ensure more reliable line prediction. The performance of SwitchBack could also be improved by taking into account the text being read. Currently, SwitchBack uses word count to estimate the amount of time it expects the user will take to read a line. Lines with larger words and more complicated content require a heavier cognitive load [20], causing the user to spend more time reading them. We examined articles from The New York Times that were of medium cognitive load according to the Flesch Reading Ease test [19]. Accounting for the content of the text on a deeper level would improve SwitchBack's estimation of the user's reading speed and allow our system to scale to text of varying cognitive load (*e.g.,* scientific articles and children's stories) and different reading behaviors (*e.g.*, skimming). Even further, techniques like Kalman filtering could account for the content of the text and personalize predictions.

FUTURE WORK

The SwitchBack reading application modifies a user interface by highlighting where the user was last reading after he or she attends to an outside distraction. There are other reading application modifications that can be applied using FAST. One that was explored, but not tested in our user study, was automatic scrolling once the user reaches the bottom of the text, similar to Samsung's Smart Scroll [17]. Currently, Smart Scroll and Smart Pause only use face detection and orientation to control the screen, but incorporating information about the user's eyes could provide a better experience. Another possible modification, geared primarily towards users with poor eyesight, could be a magnifying glass-like feature that enlarges the current line of text for the user.

Testing the SwitchBack outside of a laboratory setting would validate the application's robustness. We did not evaluate SwitchBack outdoors because of the lack of control over conditions like the number of distractions encountered. We simulated walking with the treadmill to introduce some of the factors that would be met outdoors, but we have yet to test SwitchBack in different lighting conditions. We are confident that applications involving relative gaze changes are more robust to such conditions than applications involving absolute gaze position since saccades may be inferred with missing or incorrect data.

We have used FAST in the context of reading, but we believe that it enables a broader range of applications. For instance, SwitchBack could be used by advertising companies to gauge whether or not their advertisements are engaging to users. FAST can be applied to any combination of text and images so long as the layout of the content on the screen is known.

CONCLUSION

As people become more attached to their mobile devices, the ability to balance attention towards their devices and awareness of their surroundings deteriorates. We have presented SwitchBack, a generalizable system for easing the user's focus-of-attention back into a mobile device task after attending to an outside distraction. To evaluate SwitchBack, we focused on reading applications. We performed a technology evaluation to determine the performance of our Focus and Saccade Tracking (FAST) algorithm and found that we were able to estimate how many lines participants had read in a body of text to within a mean absolute percent error of just 3.9%. We then conducted a user study on our custom SwitchBack reading application. SwitchBack increased participants' reading speeds by 7.7% in the presence of distractions. It is our hope that SwitchBack and FAST will prove useful towards realizing more situationally-aware mobile devices in the future.

ACKNOWLEDGEMENTS

This work was supported in part by the National Science Foundation under grant IIS-1217627. Any opinions, findings, conclusions or recommendations expressed in this work are those of the authors and do not necessarily reflect those of the National Science Foundation.

REFERENCES

1. Aaltonen, A., Hyrskykari, A., and Räihä, K. 101 spots, or how do users read menus? *Proc. CHI '98*, (1998), 132–139.
2. Baluja, S. and Pomerleau, D. *Non-intrusive gaze tracking using artificial neural networks.* 1994.
3. Bartram, L. Can motion increase user interface bandwidth in complex systems? *Proc. Systems, Man, and Cybernetics '97.*, (1997), 1686–1692.
4. Baudisch, P., Tan, D., and Collomb, M. Phosphor: explaining transitions in the user interface using afterglow effects. *Proc. UIST '06*, (2006), 169–178.
5. Brookings, J., Wilson, G., and Swain, C. Psychophysiological responses to changes in workload during simulated air traffic control. *Biological psychology 42*, 3 (1996), 361–377.
6. Drewes, H., Luca, A. De, and Schmidt, A. Eye-gaze interaction for mobile phones. *Proc. Mobility '07*, (2007), 364–371.
7. Frederick, B. Fixed-, Random-, and Mixed-Effects ANOVA Models: A User-Friendly Guide for Increasing the Generalizability of ANOVA Results. *Advances in Social Science Methodology*, (1999), 111–122.
8. Games, P. Multiple comparisons of means. *American Educational Research Journal 2*, 8 (1971), 531–565.
9. Goldberg, J. and Kotval, X. Computer interface evaluation using eye movements: methods and constructs. *International Journal of Industrial Ergonomics 24*, 6 (1999), 631–645.
10. Goldberg, J. and Stimson, M. Eye tracking in web search tasks: design implications. *Proc. Symposium on*

Eye Tracking Research and Applicaitons '02, (2002), 51–58.

11. Goldberg, J. and Wichansky, A. Eye tracking in usability evaluation: A practitioner's guide. *The mind's eye: cognitive and applied aspects of eye movement research*, (2003), 537–605.
12. Hansen, D. and Ji, Q. In the eye of the beholder: A survey of models for eyes and gaze. *IEEE Transactions on Pattern Analysis and Machine Intelligence 32*, 3 (2010), 478–500.
13. Hart, S. and Staveland, L. Development of NASA-TLX (Task Load Index): Results of empirical and theoretical research. *Advances in psychology 52*, (1988), 139–183.
14. Higgins, J. and Tastoush, S. An aligned rank transform test for interaction. *Nonlinear World 1*, 2 (1994), 201–211.
15. Jacob, R. and Karn, K. Eye tracking in human-computer interaction and usability research: Ready to deliver the promises. *Mind*, (2003).
16. Just, M. and Carpenter, P. A theory of reading: From eye fixations to comprehension. *Psychological review 87*, 4 (1980), 329.
17. Kang, D., Ryoo, S., Kim, J., Kim, C., and Seo, Y. Apparatus and method for detecting speaking person's eyes and face. *US Patent 6,611,613*, 2003. http://www.google.com/patents/US6611613.
18. Kern, D., Marshall, P., and Schmidt, A. Gazemarks: gaze-based visual placeholders to ease attention switching. *Proc. CHI '10*, (2010), 2093–2102.
19. Kincaid, J.P., Fishburne Jr, R.P., Rogers, R.L., and Chissom, B.S. *Derivation of new readability formulas (automated readability index, fog count and flesch reading ease formula) for navy enlisted personnel.* 1975.
20. Kintsch, W. and Keenan, J. Reading rate and retention as a function of the number of propositions in the base structure of sentences. *Cognitive Psychology 5*, 3 (1973), 257–274.
21. Littell, R.C., Henry, P.R., and Ammerman, C.B. Statistical analysis of repeated measures data using SAS procedures. *Journal of Animal Science 4*, 76 (1998), 1216–1231.
22. Marshall, S.P. Method and apparatus for eye tracking and monitoring pupil dilation to evaluate cognitive activity. *US Patent 6,090,051*, 2000. http://www.google.com/patents/US6090051.
23. McCrickard, D.S., Catrambone, R., and Stasko, J.T. Evaluating animation in the periphery as a mechanism for maintaining awareness. *Proc. IFIP '01*, (2001), 148–156.
24. Miluzzo, E., Wang, T., and Campbell, A.T. EyePhone: activating mobile phones with your eyes. *Proc. SIGCOMM '10*, (2010), 15–20.
25. Monsell, S. Task switching. *Trends in Cognitive Sciences 7*, 3 (2003), 134–140.
26. Morimoto, C.H. and Mimica, M.R. Eye gaze tracking techniques for interactive applications. *Computer Vision and Image Understanding 98*, 1 (2005), 4–24.
27. Nasar, J.L. and Troyer, D. Pedestrian injuries due to mobile phone use in public places. *Accident Analysis & Prevention 57*, (2013), 91–95.
28. Newcomb, A. Texting While Walking Banned in New Jersey Town - ABC News. 2012. http://abcnews.go.com/blogs/headlines/2012/05/texting-while-walking-banned-in-new-jersey-town/.
29. Pomplun, M. and Sunkara, S. Pupil dilation as an indicator of cognitive workload in human-computer interaction. *Proc. International Conference on HCI '03*, (2003).
30. Salter, K. and Fawcett, R. The ART test of interaction: A robust and powerful rank test of interaction in factorial models. *Communications in Statistics: Simulation and Computation 22*, 1 (1993), 137–153.
31. Sears, A., Lin, M., Jacko, J., and Xiao, Y. When computers fade: Pervasive computing and situationally-induced impairments and disabilities. *Proc. HCI International '03*, (2003), 1298–1302.
32. Shapiro, S. and Wilk, M. An analysis of variance test for normality (complete samples). *Biometrika 52*, 3,4 (1965), 591–611.
33. Stiefelhagen, R., Yang, J., and Waibel, A. Tracking eyes and monitoring eye gaze. *Proc. Workshop on Perceptual User Interfaces*, (1997), 98–100.
34. Wobbrock, J.O., Findlater, L., Gergle, D., and Higgins, J.J. The Aligned Rank Transform for nonparametric factorial analyses using only ANOVA procedures. *Proc. CHI '11*, (2011), 143–146.
35. Ye, Z., Li, Y., Fathi, A., et al. Detecting eye contact using wearable eye-tracking glasses. *Proc. UbiComp '12*, (2012), 699–704.
36. Yokoyama, T., Sakai, H., Noguchi, Y., and Kita, S. Perception of direct gaze does not require focus of attention. *Scientific reports 4*, (2014), 3858.

EyeBookmark: Assisting Recovery from Interruption during Reading

Jaemin Jo[1] Bohyoung Kim[2] Jinwook Seo[1]
[1]Human-Computer Interaction Laboratory, Department of Computer Science and Engineering, Seoul National University, 1 Gwanak-ro, Gwanak-gu, Seoul 151-744, Korea
[2]Department of Radiology, Seoul National University Bundang Hospital, 82 Gumi-ro, 173 Beon-gil, Budang-gu, Seongnam-si, Gyeonggi-do 463-707, Korea
jmjo@hcil.snu.ac.kr, bhkim@snubh.org, jseo@snu.ac.kr

ABSTRACT
In this paper, we present gaze-based bookmarking, EyeBookmark, to mitigate the deleterious effect of interruption during reading. The key idea of EyeBookmark is to provide a visual cue to help people decide where to resume reading. We design four highlighting methods and conduct a controlled user study with a proof-of-concept design to verify the usefulness of EyeBookmark. The user study demonstrates not only that participants preferred our highlighting methods but also that such highlighting methods significantly reduced the time taken to resume reading after interruption regardless of the difficulty of text.

Author Keywords
Interruption; Eye-tracking; Reading.

ACM Classification Keywords
H.5.2. Information interfaces and presentation (e.g., HCI): User Interfaces.

INTRODUCTION
Reading is an everyday activity to gather and extract information from text. Reading requires continuous visual attention. However, during reading, we are often distracted by various interrupting sources such as smartphones' alarm or engaging conversation with other people. Such unexpected distractions lead us to suspend reading until the distractions are dealt with. When we return to the text, we cannot resume reading immediately; for example, it takes a while to restore the context of the text and scan where to initiate rereading. As a result, interruption during reading induces resumption lag—the time taken to restart reading after interruption—and finally hinders reading performance.

As a remedy for such overheads of reading resumption, we present gaze-based bookmarking, or EyeBookmark, which helps people to restart reading promptly after interruption. The key idea of EyeBookmark is to highlight the last reading position in several ways when people attempt to resume reading. We design four highlighting methods (Figure 1) and conduct a controlled user study to verify the usefulness of EyeBookmark.

For ease of explanation, we adopt two terms, pre- and post-interruption periods, to represent periods before and after an interruption, respectively. In a similar way, we divide text into pre- and post-interruption texts which refer to the texts located before and after the word that one was reading when the interruption occurred.

CHI 2015, April 18–23, 2015, Seoul, Republic of Korea.

ACM 978-1-4503-3145-6/15/04…$15.00.
http://dx.doi.org/10.1145/2702123.2702340

RELATED WORK
Interruption has been extensively investigated not only in HCI but also in other fields such as psychology. We review previous research in following three thematic areas.

Theoretical Bases Latorella [5] proposed the interruption management stage model (IMSM) to explicate how interruption affects performance of tasks. In that work, Latorella emphasized the notion of *interruption resilient interfaces* which are interfaces that aid task resumption after interruption. EyeBookmark achieves interruption resiliency by providing a visual cue for reading. McFarlane and Latorella [6] suggested prospective UI support examples for each phase of interruption: before, during, and after interruption. In that sense, EyeBookmark is a practical example of the after interruption UI support.

Spatial Memory during Reading EyeBookmark complements the use of spatial memory for recovery from interruption. Inhoff and Weger [4] found that memory for word location during reading is not precise, which implies there may be cost for searching the last read position after interruption. Cane et al. [2] suggested highlighting the last seen word for efficient recovery from interruption. Also, they verified such highlighting reduces the reading time of the pre-interruption text in the post-interruption period. However, such reading time can be inappropriate to represent the exact resumption lag because people can seek the word within the post-interruption text. Therefore, we manually inspected fixation patterns to obtain the accurate resumption lag. Also, in addition to marking only one word, we design and compare four different highlighting methods.

Reading and Eye-tracking in HCI Exploiting eye-tracking technology, several HCI studies clarified people's reading behavior and attempted to improve reading performance. Buscher et al. [1] modeled preferred reading regions using normal distributions. Using this model, Sharmin et al. [8] proposed gaze-based auto-scrolling when reading text. Text 2.0 [9] assisted reading by superimposing additional information on text depending on the context of reading. Duggan and Payne [3] presented design guidelines based on their findings on people's reading behavior—*satisficing*. A patent (US7429108) presented methods to provide a reading place-marker using gaze-tracking but has not been evaluated yet through controlled experiments.

EYEBOOKMARK

As mentioned above, the main idea of EyeBookmark is to highlight the last reading position. To achieve this, an eye tracker keeps track of gazes when reading text. Once an interruption occurs, the position of the last fixation is identified. When getting back into reading after interruption, the last reading position is highlighted on text to present a restarting point. We believe such highlighting reduces unnecessary visual search through the text and assists the continuation of reading.

Highlighting Methods We design four highlighting methods as shown in Figure 1. *Point* method is the simplest but intuitive. It shows the position of the last fixation using a circle-shaped marker. It attracts attention to a resuming point but hardly conveys the context of the last reading.

Sentence method and *previous sentence* method indicate the context of the last reading in addition to the last fixation position. The *sentence* method highlights the sentence that they did not finish due to the interruption, whereas the previous sentence method marks the previous sentence of the unfinished sentence. We observed that people usually search for the beginning of the interrupted sentence to reread the whole sentence when getting back into reading after interruption. The sentence and previous sentence methods can reduce such visual search time.

In the sentence and previous sentence methods, the area of the highlighted region varies depending on the length of a sentence. If the sentence is too long or short, those methods can accentuate excessive or insufficient context for recovery from interruption. To mitigate this problem, the *block* method highlights a fixed number of lines including and preceding the last fixated word. The major strength of the block method is to provide a consistent amount of visual cue regardless of the length of a sentence.

PILOT STUDY

We conducted an in-laboratory pilot study to confirm the efficacy of EyeBookmark and compared the highlighting methods in terms of resumption lag.

Participants Nine volunteers (1 female) from a university participated in the pilot study, aged 20 to 37 years with

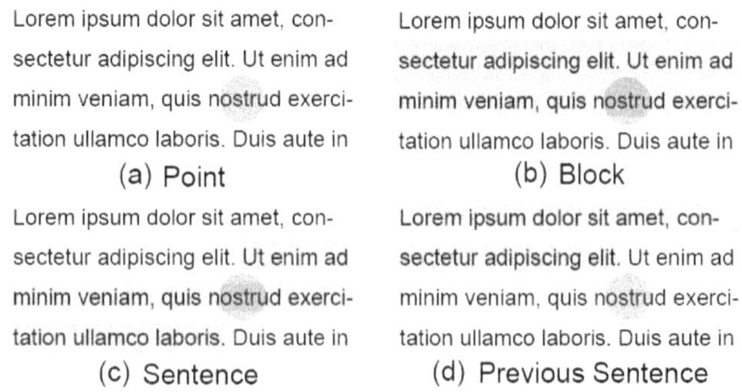

Figure 1. Four highlighting methods. For all methods, a red circle indicates the position of the last fixation before interruption. For methods (b), (c), and (d), blue markers additionally provide the context of the last reading.

normal or corrected-to-normal vision. All of them were native Korean speakers.

Apparatus A Tobii X60 binocular eye-tracker was used to collect gaze data during reading. The eye-tracker was installed in front of a 24-inch monitor with a screen resolution of 1920×1080. The eye-tracker and monitor were connected to a PC that ran a dedicated program for the pilot study. Participants were seated 65cm away from the monitor and their heads were fixed using a chin rest. Also, we implemented an I-VT fixation filter [7] to determine which sentence should be marked when getting back into reading after interruption.

Design We used a within-subjects design with five highlighting conditions: no highlighting (as a baseline condition) and four aforementioned highlighting methods. Each participant read 10 paragraphs. When reading a paragraph, one interruption occurred when a participant saw a specified target word.

During the interruption, the paragraph was hidden and a 60-sec long documentary video clip was played. After the interruption, a part of the paragraph was highlighted depending on the highlighting condition. Because we used 10 paragraphs and 5 highlighting conditions, each participant experienced each highlighting condition twice. The order of paragraphs was randomized. The order of highlighting conditions was also randomized while avoiding consecutive use of one condition.

We prepared 10 Korean paragraphs about various topics (10.4±2.2 sentences and 149.2±10.5 words). The paragraphs were shown with 24px, double-spaced, Malgun Gothic font (one of the most popular Korean fonts) contained in a rounded box with a width of 1024px.

In each trial, one word from a paragraph was chosen as a target word that triggered interruption when seen. To control the deleterious effect of interruption, the target word was randomly selected under several criteria as in [2]: all words in the first and last sentences were excluded because they brought less disruptive interruption; the first and last words of a sentence were excluded to create only mid-

	Method	Reading time (s)	# of fixations	Mean fixation duration (ms)	Mean resumption lag (s)	Answer accuracy (%)	Preference (7-point)
Pilot Study	None (baseline)	22.3 (9.3)	128.0 (37.6)	170.1 (31.4)	2.4 (0.9)	93.3	
	Point	24.3 (10.6)	136.2 (42.9)	173.9 (25.1)	1.6 (0.7)	81.3	4.6 (1.0)
	Block	26.2 (14.1)	140.3 (55.4)	179.4 (38.2)	1.2 (0.6)	88.9	5.2 (1.1)
	Sentence	23.8 (11.6)	129.0 (40.8)	178.5 (39.5)	1.3 (0.7)	88.2	5.4 (1.1)
	Prev. Sentence	28.2 (14.4)	150.1 (53.4)	180.5 (35.9)	1.2 (1.0)	88.9	3.7 (1.9)
User Study	None (easy)	26.4 (7.9)	147.0 (36.3)	177.5 (15.9)	2.0 (0.8)	90.9	
	Block (easy)	25.7 (9.1)	142.4 (42.2)	178.4 (19.6)	1.2 (0.6)	92.0	5.4 (0.7)
	Sentence (easy)	26.6 (9.0)	143.5 (43.1)	184.4 (22.5)	1.1 (0.3)	87.5	6.1 (0.9)
	None (difficult)	42.2 (14.3)	214.5 (58.9)	194.0 (28.0)	2.8 (1.5)	72.7	
	Block (difficult)	38.5 (17.9)	188.5 (55.3)	196.5 (42.0)	1.4 (0.7)	69.2	5.4 (0.7)
	Sentence (difficult)	37.1 (9.7)	189.4 (39.6)	195.2 (29.1)	1.4 (0.8)	79.2	6.1 (0.9)

Table 1. Results of pilot study and user study. Block and sentence methods significantly reduce the mean resumption lag compared to the baseline (None) condition.

sentence interruption; and the words at the extremes of each line were excluded because the fixations on those words were often missed.

Procedure At the beginning, participants were briefly introduced to tasks and highlighting methods with graphical examples as shown in Figure 1. Then, a 9-point eye tracker calibration process was conducted. Participants were familiarized to tasks using a practice paragraph and one random highlighting condition. They were not informed which highlighting condition would be used because it could introduce a bias (e.g. participants might read a paragraph more carefully if they knew no highlighting would be provided). After reading a whole paragraph with an interruption, they pressed the left mouse button to finish reading, and answered a comprehension question with three choices (one correct answer, one wrong answer, and "I don't know"). After all 10 trials, three questions about documentary video clips were given, which were not for analysis but for encouraging participants to concentrate on the clips. Lastly, we gathered feedback from the participants using a 7-point Likert scale questionnaire (1=Strongly disagree, 7=Strongly agree) and an interview.

RESULT

Among 90 trials, six trials were excluded from analysis because of excessive reading time (longer than two standard deviations from the mean) or skewed gaze pattern.

Participants' eye movements were examined using an I-VT fixation filter as shown in Table 1. The highlighting conditions were compared using ANOVA. No significant difference was found between five highlighting conditions in terms of reading time, the number of fixations, mean fixation duration, and answer accuracy ($p > .05$ for all measures). The accuracy was overall high, which implies the paragraphs were easy to comprehend.

We visually inspected the length of resumption lag for all trials without highlighting. The resumption lag was calculated by the time from the moment when the interruption ended to the moment when a reading fixation sequence within the pre-interruption text was first detected. To detect a reading fixation sequence, we used the reading detection algorithm proposed by Sharmin et al. [8]. We found a significant difference in mean resumption lag among highlighting conditions ($F_{4,\,32} = 8.001$, $p < .001$). Post hoc analysis indicated that participants could resume reading significantly faster in the block and sentence conditions than in no highlighting condition (2.4 s vs. 1.2 s, $p < .05$ for block condition, 2.4 s vs. 1.3 s, $p < .05$ for sentence condition).

Overall, participants agreed that four highlighting methods were helpful to resume reading after interruption (preference score, 6.0±0.5). Participants highly preferred the block (5.2±1.1) and sentence (5.4±1.1) methods. However, participants disagreed with the usefulness of the previous sentence method (3.7±1.9). Qualitative feedback (interviews) revealed that two far apart markers which were common in the previous sentence method might be distracting to make participants confused about where to restart reading.

Implications of the Pilot Study The block and sentence methods seemed most promising in terms of both resumption lag and preference. Therefore, we determined to use only these two methods in the user study. Also, we introduced a two-level difficulty factor to observe how the resumption lag varies according to the text difficulty.

USER STUDY

Based on implications of the pilot study, we conducted a user study to further evaluate the usefulness of the block and sentence methods with two-level difficulty of text. Apparatus and procedure were identical to those of the pilot study.

Participants 13 participants (2 females) from a university, aged 20 to 28 years with normal or corrected-to-normal vision, participated with 10,000 KRW (about $10) reward. All of them were native Korean speakers.

Design We used a within-subjects design with three highlighting conditions (no highlighting, block method, and sentence method) and two difficulty conditions (easy and difficult). Each participant read 12 paragraphs with different highlighting and difficulty conditions. Since there were six combinations of conditions, each participant experienced each combination twice. The order of combinations was determined by a balanced Latin Square.

Six easy paragraphs were chosen from the paragraphs in the pilot study (10.5±1.0 sentences and 149.8±7.9 words). Six difficult paragraphs were extracted from abstracts of M.S. theses (8.7±0.8 sentences and 149.1±6.6 words). According to the difficulty measuring formula proposed by Yun [10], the difficulty value of difficult paragraphs (grade level: 14.0±2.1) was significantly higher than that of easy paragraphs (grade level: 10.0±1.5) ($t_{10} = -3.806, p < .005$).

RESULT & DISCUSSION

For the same reason as in the pilot study, 13 trials were discarded from 156 trials. We analyzed the results of the user study using two-way ANOVA (Table 1). For all eye movement measures, no significant difference was observed between three highlighting conditions ($p > .05$ for all measures). However, as expected, all eye movement measures significantly increased in the difficult condition ($p < .05$ for mean fixation duration; otherwise, $p < .001$). No interaction effect was found.

In terms of mean resumption lag, we found a significant effect of both highlighting method ($F_{2, 24} = 15.199$, $p < .001$) and difficulty level ($F_{1, 12} = 15.416$, $p < .005$). The difficult paragraphs induced longer resumption lag. Also, post hoc analysis indicated that the block and sentence methods significantly reduced the resumption lag regardless of the text difficulty ($p < .005$ for block method, $p < .01$ for sentence method). No interaction effect was found.

When reading difficult text, participants chose wrong answers significantly more ($F_{1, 12} = 16.092$, $p < .005$). We observed a difference in answer accuracy among highlighting conditions but the difference was not significant ($F_{2, 24} = .026$, $p = .975$).

We compared the preferences of block and sentence methods using the Wilcoxon signed-rank test. Participants preferred significantly more the sentence method (6.1±0.9) to the block method (5.4±0.7) ($Z = -2.029$, $p < .05$). Also, they agreed that the highlighting was helpful to resume the reading (6.1±0.9) but it did not help to improve the comprehension (4.2±1.2), which was consistent with the result of answer accuracy. Lastly, they replied that they would use EyeBookmark for reading if possible (5.6±1.0).

In four trials (7.7%) with no highlighting condition, we found that gaze patterns of the pre-interruption and post-interruption periods did not overlap, implying that participants skipped some words. However, such cases did not happen in the block and sentence methods.

Results of the user study demonstrate that EyeBookmark successfully reduces resumption lag after interruption during reading. Although EyeBookmark did not affect reading comprehension, our results suggest that EyeBookmark helps participants not to miss any part of text.

CONCLUSION & FUTURE WORK

In this work, we present gaze-based bookmarking, EyeBookmark, which helps users to resume reading after interruption. Our user study proves the efficacy of EyeBookmark in terms of resumption lag and preference.

In our two experiments, we did not inform participants in advance whether highlighting would be provided or not. Interesting future work would be to compare the performance of different highlighting methods when participants are given the opportunity to tune their reading behavior accordingly by letting them know which highlighting method would be used in advance.

ACKNOWLEDGMENTS

This work was supported by the National Research Foundation of Korea (NRF) grant funded by the Korea government (MSIP) (No. NRF-2014R1A2A2A03006998).

REFERENCES

1. Buscher, G., Biedert, R., Heinesch, D., and Dengel, A. Eye tracking analysis of preferred reading regions on the screen. *Proc. CHI EA'10*, 2010, 3307-3312.
2. Cane, J.E., Cauchard, F., and Weger, U.W. The time-course of recovery from interruption during reading: Eye movement evidence for the role of interruption lag and spatial memory. *The Quarterly Journal of Experimental Psychology 65*, 7 (2012), 1397-1413.
3. Duggan, G.B. and Payne, S.J. Skim reading by satisficing: evidence from eye tracking. *Proc. CHI'11*, 2011, 1141-1150.
4. Inhoff, A.W. and Weger, U.W. Memory for word location during reading: Eye movements to previously read words are spatially selective but not precise. *Memory & cognition 33*, 3 (2005), 447-461.
5. Latorella, K.A. *Investigating interruptions: Implications for flightdeck performance*. National Aeronautics and Space Administration, 1999.
6. McFarlane, D.C. and Latorella, K.A. The scope and importance of human interruption in human-computer interaction design. *Human-Computer Interaction 17*, 1 (2002), 1-61.
7. Olsen, A. *The Tobii I-VT Fixation Filter*. Tobii Technology, 2012.
8. Sharmin, S., Špakov, O., and Räihä, KJ. Reading on-screen text with gaze-based auto-scrolling. *Proc. ETSA'13*, 2013, 24-31.
9. Text 2.0, http://text20.net/, Jan 2015.
10. Yun, C. A Study on the development of a readability formula in non-literary texts, 2006

The Effects of Chronic Multitasking on Analytical Writing

Danielle M. Lottridge, Christine Rosakranse, Catherine S. Oh, Sean J. Westwood, Katherine Baldoni, Abrey S. Mann, Cliff I. Nass
Department of Communication, Stanford University
450 Serra Mall, Stanford, CA 94305-2050
lottridg | being | syoh | seanjw | kbaldoni | asmann | nass @stanford.edu

ABSTRACT
Chronic multitaskers perform worse on core multitasking skills: memory management, cognitive filtering and task switching, likely due to their inability to filter irrelevant stimuli [17]. Our experiment examines effects of chronic multitasking with task-relevant and irrelevant distractors on analytical writing quality. We found a general switch cost and, when controlling for that cost, effects of chronic multitasking habits: heavy multitaskers write worse essays in the irrelevant condition and better essays in the relevant condition. Our study changes multitasking research paradigms in two fundamental ways: it studied a realistic writing scenario including access to both irrelevant and relevant distractors. We found that the effect of chronic multitasking is complex; heavy multitaskers are seduced by unrelated distractors but able to integrate multiple sources of relevant information.

Author Keywords
Multitasking; analytical writing; distractors; chronic multitasking; media multitasking index.

ACM Classification Keywords
H.1.2. User/Machine Systems: Human factors.

INTRODUCTION
Is multitasking good or bad for you? Proponents (including many employers) herald the ability to effectively juggle tasks and pressure workers to respond to messages immediately. Dissenters bemoan constant interruptions, distractions and the inability to get engrossed. Can we improve our ability to multitask? How does multitasking affect our attention span and the quality of our work?

'Practice makes perfect'—except when it comes to multitasking. Chronic multitaskers perform worse on the core executive functions of multitasking: taking in and releasing items from short-term memory stores (memory management), attending to relevant material and inhibiting irrelevant material (cognitive filtering), and inhibiting the cognitive structures required for one task and activating those required for another task (task switching) [17]. These results suggest a unique and important change in fundamental information processing. Counterintuitively, multitasking does not appear to be a problem of *attending to the right things*; rather chronic multitaskers' trouble appears to be the *inability to ignore the wrong things.*

Multitasking is studied in two main ways: field studies prioritizing external validity (e.g., [6]; what does multitasking look like in the world?) and controlled experiments prioritizing internal validity (e.g., [17]); such experiments tend to follow cognitive psychology standards, often with primary tasks related to basic cognitive function and unrelated distractors. This experiment extends that research in two fundamental ways: first, it studies multitasking experimentally in the realistic domain of essay writing; second, it exposes subjects to information streams that are either relevant or irrelevant to the task at hand.

BACKGROUND
The more people are exposed to media, the more they multitask [9]. High sensation seekers multitask more often [13]. The impact begins at a young age; in a survey of 3,461 North American girls aged 8-12, multitasking was inversely face-to-face communication, feelings of social success, and sleep [19]. When 'heavy' (chronic) media multitaskers (HMM) were compared with 'light' media multitaskers (LMM), HMM were bad at precisely the tasks at which one would expect them to be good [17]. Habitual and in-the-moment multitasking both hurt cognitive performance. Participants completing three tasks simultaneously performed worse on a subsequent memory test when compared to participants performing the same three tasks serially [26]. Multitasking contributes to cognitive overload through too much information supply and demand, interruptions, and inadequate infrastructure, thus increasing needs for planning, monitoring, reminding, and reclassifying information [14]. A study on word tasks found that people maximized productivity by switching to prioritize a continuous rate of return (an information foraging orientation) and to complete subgoals [18]. Salvucci et al. model multitasking behavior with cognitive architecture, threaded cognition and memory-for-goals theory [23]. Others suggest that people self-regulate their interruptions to maintain a flow state [1].

CHI 2015, April 18 - 23, 2015, Seoul, Republic of Korea.
Copyright 2015 ACM 978-1-4503-3145-6/15/04...$15.00.
http://dx.doi.org/10.1145/2702123.2702367

The type of task (information versus non-information) and individual differences can moderate how tasks are combined for multitasking; for example, higher versus lower order task, difficulty and information carry-over affect impact [12]. If both tasks require the same cognitive framework ('problem state'), it interferes with performance [3]. It was proposed to be more effective to multitask with tasks using different parts of the brain [24]. But fMRI studies reveal that tasks using different parts of the brain (e.g., perceptual encoding and decision-making) suffered from temporary attention limits [25]. These costs appear to increase with age, as older adults direct more attention toward irrelevant stimuli [5].

Field studies reveal that multitasking is associated with poor academic performance [22]. Multitasking students take more time to achieve the same performance as monotaskers [4], or to complete the same task [10]; texting students performed worse on exams than non-texters [7]; and students with open laptops had worse memory for lectures than those without [11]. The present research is however the first to study the causal relationship between multitasking and writing quality.

METHODS

The effects of chronic and in-the-moment multitasking on analytical writing quality were investigated with an essay task accompanied by relevant or irrelevant distractors. Undergraduates were granted course credit and categorized using top and bottom quartiles Media Multitasking Index (MMI) scores [17]. 40 HMM and 40 LMM participated; 37 were male. Participants were randomly assigned to the relevant or irrelevant condition. Gender was balanced across MMI score and condition.

Sessions consisted of groups of 5 students using laptops separated by divider boards. The task was a 30-minute GRE-style essay arguing for or against a statement on whether luxuries and conveniences of modernity strengthen character. GRE performance is a valid predictor of graduate grade point average, comprehensive examination scores, publication citation counts, and faculty ratings [15]. Text was entered through a simple editor, which included an input box for the essay and a side column with an ostensible forum including distractor links to online content. Participants were invited to post comments and told that the side column displayed comments by other participants. Predetermined comments and associated links were displayed approximately every 2 minutes. In the relevant condition, comments were related to the writing question, and included links to relevant articles. In the irrelevant condition, comments included unrelated links, such as sports news and funny videos. We recorded the number of switches between the writing and other applications (e.g. browsers) and time spent writing.

Essays were scored manually based on a standard Organization and Coherence university grading scheme. Organization was judged by presence of 1) an introduction, body, and conclusion; 2) paragraph structure; and 3) appropriate arguments. Coherence was judged by 1) connection between adjacent sentences, 2) building on ideas, and 3) contributions to over-arching argument. On a subset of 20 essays (25%), two raters (ignorant of the conditions) achieved good inter-rater reliability r = .86. Essays were also scored automatically with the Flesch-Kincaid, a widely used (e.g., US military, MS Word) indicator of writing complexity [8]. It is calculated from numbers of syllables per word and words per sentence. The lower the score, the more difficult the text to read; for example, "The cat sat on the mat" scores 116: low complexity and highly readable.

First, we investigate the correlation between number of switches between writing software and browser, time spent writing (includes editing, revising, etc), essay length and writing quality. Then, we control for number of switches to isolate effects of chronic multitasking. One MANCOVA investigates effects of between-subjects variables media multitasking (HMM/LMM) and condition (relevant and irrelevant) on time spent writing. A second MANCOVA controls for length, switches and time spent writing to examine effects on dependent variables: writing quality and Flesch-Kincaid (transformed for normality [16]). In summary, our hypotheses are:

H1. The more switches, a) the less time spent writing, b) the worse quality, and c) less complex essays.

H2. HMM will spend more time on distractors than LMM.

H3. HMM will write essays that are a) lower quality and b) less complex than those written by LMM.

RQ: Will the relevance of the distractors influence H2-3?

RESULTS

We observed a switch cost: the more participants switch, the less time participants spend writing (H1a: r =-.528, p<.001) and the worse the quality of their writing (H1b: r = -.307, p=.006). H1c was not supported. We found that time spent writing correlated with length (r=.298, p=.01) and higher complexity (r=-.306, p=.006). Length correlated with quality (r=.529, p<.001). This suggests that if given more time to write, students would likely produce longer, more complex essays and that those who write more independent of allotted time achieve higher quality essays.

Controlling for number of switches, we found an interaction effect where HMM spent a quarter of their time following irrelevant links (almost 7 min.) whereas LMM spent only 16% doing so (approx. 4.5 min.; F[1,79]=6.314, p=.01, partial η^2=0.78). In the relevant condition, both LMM and HMM spent about one fifth of their time following links.

When controlling for the number of switches and time spent writing, we observed a significant interaction between media multitasking and condition on writing quality

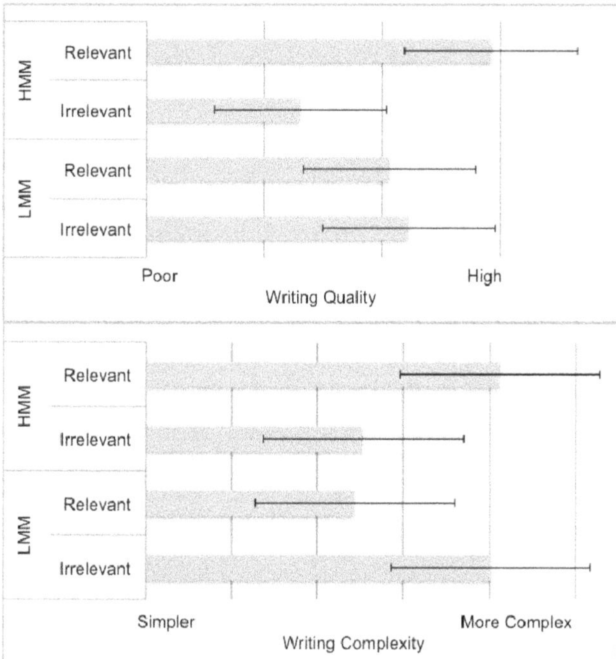

Figure 1a. Transformed writing quality
Figure 1b. Transformed Flesch-Kincaid writing complexity for HMM and LMM in the relevant and irrelevant conditions; *error bars=95% C.I.

(F[1,79]=5.859, p=.02, partial η^2=.074; Figure 1a) and Flesch-Kincaid (F[1,79]=4.348, p=.04, partial η^2=.056; Figure 1b). Complexity and quality were not correlated (r=-.121, p=.284). There were no main effects (H2, H3a, H3b).

HMM wrote the highest quality essays in the relevant condition and the poorest quality essays in the irrelevant condition, whereas LMM were unaffected ($m_{HMM\text{-}R} = 4.9$, $m_{HMM\text{-}I} = 3.9$, $m_{LMM\text{-}R} = 4.1$, $m_{HMM\text{-}I} = 4.4$). These effects are due to chronic multitasking, as in-the-moment multitasking (switches, time spent following links) is controlled for. Thus, we find differences based on chronic multitasking habits: heavy multitaskers in the irrelevant condition suffered the most in terms of essay quality and simplistic writing. However, HMM appear to use their multitasking habits in a positive way in the relevant condition, where they wrote higher quality essays with more sophisticated prose. The quality of the LMM essays was unaffected by condition, though the complexity of the writing was higher in the irrelevant condition where more time was spent writing compared to the relevant condition. The apparent danger is that HMM's behavior toward irrelevant links reflects how they tend to write in the real world: a t-test shows that HMM are much more likely than LMM to self-report multitasking during homework ($p < .001$; $m_{HMM} = 2.4$ (SD = 1.3); $m_{LMM} = .64$ (SD = .42)).

DISCUSSION AND CONCLUSIONS

In this study, we examined how heavy and light media multitaskers differ in analytical writing behavior when faced with relevant or irrelevant distractors. Our study was designed for external validity with a realistic scenario: writing essays online with access to both relevant and irrelevant information. Our study was unique in reconceptualizing switching as relevancy-dependent rather than looking only at the effects of irrelevant stimuli.

Our findings support a multi-faceted view of costs and benefits of multitasking. For both groups, writing quality suffered as a function of the number of switches between writing application and browser. Thus, in-the-moment multitasking carries a cost for writing quality. However, when controlling for switches and time spent writing, this negative effect was dependent on one's chronic multitasking habits and the type of distractors present. HMM benefited from the relevant condition and had higher writing scores. In the irrelevant condition, LMM were able to easily ignore links and spent more time writing. HMM were seduced by irrelevant content; they spent significantly less time writing and wrote poorer quality essays.

The relationship between complexity and quality is nuanced. Complexity might be sophisticated when paired with high quality but convoluted when paired with low quality. Low complexity might mean readable when paired with high quality, simplistic when paired with low quality. Our results suggest complexity is expressed differently by HMM and LMM depending on condition. HMM had high complexity and quality in the relevant condition and low complexity and quality in the irrelevant condition, suggesting that relevancy increased sophistication and irrelevancy decreased sophistication. LMM writing did not differ in quality with condition. Lower complexity in the relevant condition suggests simplicity did not affect quality. High complexity in the irrelevant condition suggests intricacy did not improve quality. The relationship between writing complexity and quality continues to be studied (e.g. [2]); our results add to this ongoing discussion.

Our study finds chronic multitaskers have advantages when using multiple streams of task-related content; they appear to have an ability to quickly integrate relevant information. This behavior fits within the theoretical framework of information foraging [20]; HMM may have developed better sampling techniques that are utilized when constrained to relevant material. Yet, as sensation seekers, chronic multitaskers fail to ignore interesting, irrelevant material; they lose time by consuming those media, and their work suffers as a result. As light multitaskers consume fewer media, the condition neither helped nor hurt.

Multitasking is good *and* bad for you. Our study found that HMM benefit when media streams are relevant and suffer when they are irrelevant. Unfortunately, HMM typically multitask with irrelevant media streams; our finding that students multitask during homework is corroborated by recent research that found students often chat online while writing essays [22]. Therefore, HMM often do not take full advantage of their integration capacity to optimize their performance. Careful construction of a context or digital environment to constrain HMM's media intake to relevant streams may thus greatly benefit their performance.

ACKNOWLEDGEMENTS
We thank Google for their support, Erina Dubois for her help, Ethan Plaut for editing, and our anonymous reviewers for their generous and constructive critiques.

REFERENCES
1. Adler, R.F., and Benbunan-Fich, R. Self-Interruptions in Discretionary Multitasking. *Computers in Human Behavior 29*, 4 (2013), 1441-1449.
2. Beers, S.F., and Nagy, W.E. Syntactic complexity as a predictor of adolescent writing quality: Which measures? Which genre? *Reading & Writing 22*, 2(2009), 185-200.
3. Borst, J.P., Taatgen, N.A., & Van Rijn, H. The problem state: A cognitive bottleneck in multitasking. *Journal of Experimental Psychology: Learning, Memory, & Cognition 36*, (2010), 363-382.
4. Bowman, L.L., Levine, L.E., Waite, B.M., and Gendron, M. Can students really multi task? An experimental study of instant messaging while reading. *Computers & Education 5,* 4 (2010), 927-931.
5. Clapp, W.C., Rubens, M.T., Sabharwal, J., and Gazzaley, A. Deficit in switching between functional brain networks underlies the impact of multitasking on working memory in older adults. *Proc. of the National Academy of Sciences 108,* 17 (2011), 7212-7217.
6. Dabbish, L., Mark, G., and Gonzalez, V. Why do I keep interrupting myself?: Self interruption, habit, and environment. *Proc. CHI* (2011), 3127- 3130.
7. Ellis, Y., Daniels, B., and Jauregui, A. The effect of multitasking on the grade performance of business students. *Research in Higher Education Journal 8,* (2010), 1-10.
8. Flesch, R. A new readability yardstick. *Journal of Applied Psychology 32,* (1948), 221–233.
9. Foehr, U.G. Media multitasking among American youth: Prevalence, pairings and predictors. *Unpublished doctoral dissertation* (2006), Stanford, CA, USA.
10. Fox, A.B., Rosen, J., and Crawford, M. Distractions, Distractions: Does Instant Messaging Affect College Students' Performance on a Concurrent Reading Comprehension Task? *Cyberpsychology & Behavior, 12*, 1 (2009), 51-53.
11. Hembrooke, H., and Gay, G. The Laptop and the Lecture: The Effects of Multitasking in Learning Environments. *Journal of Computing in Higher Education 15*, 1 (2003), 46-64.
12. Iqbal, S.T., and Bailey, B.P. Leveraging Characteristics of task structure to predict costs of interruption. *Proc. CHI* (2006), 741-750.
13. Jeong, S.H., and Fishbein, M. Predictors of Multitasking with Media: Media Factors and Audience Factors. *Media Psychology 10,* 3 (2007), 364-384.
14. Kirsch, D. A Few Thoughts on Cognitive Overload. *Intellectica 1*, 30 (2000), 19-51.
15. Kuncel, N.R., Hezlett, S.A., and Ones, D.S. A comprehensive meta-analysis of the predictive validity of the Graduate Record Examinations: Implications for graduate student selection and performance. *Psychological Bulletin 127,* 1 (2001), 162-181.
16. LaLonde, S.M. Transforming variables for normality and linearity—when, how, why and why not's. *SAS NESUG* (2005), 11-14.
17. Ophir, E., Nass, C., and Wagner, A. D. Cognitive control in media multitaskers. *Proc. of the National Academy of Sciences 106*, 37 (2009). 15583-15587.
18. Payne, S. J., Duggan, G. B., and Neth, H. Discretionary task interleaving: Heuristics for time allocation in cognitive foraging. *Journal of Experimental Psychology: General 136*, 3 (2007), 370–388.
19. Pea, R., Nass, C., Meheula, L., Rance, M., Kumar, A., Bamford, H., Nass, M., Simha, A., Stillerman, B., Yang, S., and Zhou, M. Media use, face-to-face communication, media multitasking, and social well-being among 8- to 12-year-old girls. *Developmental Psychology 48,* 2 (2012), 327-336.
20. Reader, W., and Payne, S. Allocating time across multiple texts: sampling and satisficing. *Human-Computer Interaction 22*, 3 (2007), 263-298.
21. Roberts, D.F., and Foehr, U.G. Trends in Media Use. The Future of Children. *Children and Electronic Media 18*, 1 (2008), 11-37.
22. Rosen, L.D., Carrier, L.M., and Cheever, N. A. Facebook and texting made me do it: Media-induced task-switching while studying. *Computers in Human Behavior 29*, 3 (2013), 948-958.
23. Salvucci, D. D., Taatgen, N. A., and Borst, J. P. Toward a unified theory of the multitasking continuum: from concurrent performance to task switching, interruption, and resumption. *Proc. CHI* (2009), 1819-1828.
24. Spink, A., and Park, M. Information and non-information multitasking interplay. *Journal of Documentation 61*, 4 (2005), 548–555.
25. Tombu, M.N., Asplund, C.L., Dux, P.E., Godwin, D., Martin, J.W., and Marois, R. A Unified attentional bottleneck in the human brain. *Proc. of the National Academy of Sciences 108,* 33 (2011), 13426–13431.
26. Vega, V., McCracken, K., Nass, C.I., and Labs, L. Multitasking Effects on Visual Working Memory, Working Memory and Executive Control. *ICA* (2008).

What Makes Interruptions Disruptive? A Process-Model Account of the Effects of the Problem State Bottleneck on Task Interruption and Resumption

Jelmer P. Borst[1], Niels A. Taatgen[1], & Hedderik van Rijn[2]
[1]Dept. of Artificial Intelligence and [2]Dept. of Psychology
University of Groningen
Groningen, the Netherlands
{j.p.borst, n.a.taatgen, d.h.van.rijn}@rug.nl

ABSTRACT
In this paper we present a computational cognitive model of task interruption and resumption, focusing on the effects of the problem state bottleneck. Previous studies have shown that the disruptiveness of interruptions is for an important part determined by three factors: interruption duration, interrupting-task complexity, and moment of interruption. However, an integrated theory of these effects is still missing. Based on previous research into multitasking, we propose a first step towards such a theory in the form of a process model that attributes these effects to problem state requirements of both the interrupted and the interrupting task. Subsequently, we tested two predictions of this model in two experiments. The experiments confirmed that problem state requirements are an important predictor for the disruptiveness of interruptions. This suggests that interfaces should be designed to a) interrupt users at low-problem state moments and b) maintain the problem state for the user when interrupted.

Author Keywords
Interruptions; multitasking; problem state; working memory; computational model.

ACM Classification Keywords
H.1.2 [Model and principles]: user/machine systems – human information processing.
H.5.2 [Information interfaces and presentation (e.g., HCI)]: user interfaces – theory and methods.

INTRODUCTION
The prevalence of interruptions in our society can hardly be overstated. While writing this first paragraph, I drank a cup of coffee, looked at Facebook, checked my phone for messages, had to leave the building for a fire drill, and have been asked a question by a colleague. This cartoon image – true, however – has been confirmed by a long list of observational studies [15,17,19,21,27,28,31,41]. At the same time, it is also well known that interruptions are disruptive: it takes time to resume a task and more errors are made after an interruption [3,18,20,22,23,26,32,35,45]. Given their widespread occurrence and negative effects on performance, it is crucial to gain a detailed understanding of the cognitive processes involved in task interruption and resumption: only that will enable us to develop software that can diminish the disruptive effects of interruptions.

Previous research has focused on factors that make interruptions disruptive [e.g., interrupting task complexity, duration; 13,14,18,20,22,23,34,35,46], on when users can best be interrupted [1,25,27,32], as well as on how users manage interruptions themselves [7,19,29,30,42,45,46]. To improve our understanding of interruptions, the results of these studies should be integrated into a cognitive theory. Such a theory should not only describe in detail what happens at task suspension and resumption and why some interruptions are more disruptive than others, but it should also be capable of making predictions for new tasks.

One proposal for such a theory is Altmann & Trafton's Memory for Goals theory [2]. Memory-for-goals assumes that each task has an associated task goal with a certain activation level. When a primary task is interrupted, its goal is stored in declarative memory. The activation of this goal decays during the interruption, unless it is rehearsed. When the primary task is resumed after the interruption, its goal has to be retrieved from memory, which takes time. Memory-for-goals theory made the prediction that longer interruptions lead to longer resumption processes, which was confirmed by several studies [23,34,35,45]. However, other interruption effects cannot be easily explained within memory-for-goals theory.

In the current paper we will extend memory-for-goals – and its explanatory power – by not focusing on task goals per se, but on the contents of the *problem state* associated with each task. The problem state contains information that is necessary to perform a task, and has been shown to be an important predictor of interference in multitasking [8,10,11,12,37]. By taking the contents of the problem state

CHI 2015, April 18 - 23 2015, Seoul, Republic of Korea

ACM 978-1-4503-3145-6/15/04…$15.00
http://dx.doi.org/10.1145/2702123.2702156

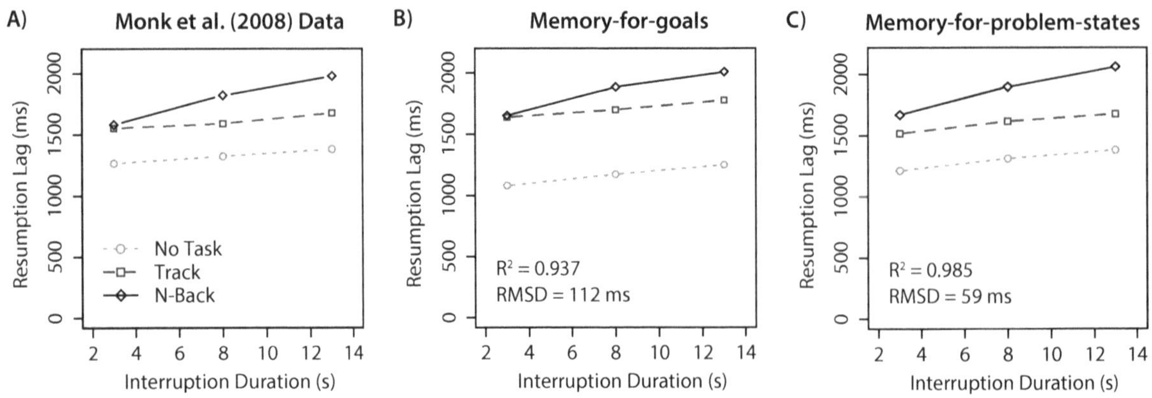

Figure 1. A) Resumption time data of [34], B) model fit of memory-for-goals [43], and C) model fit of memory-for-problem-states.

into account, this new theory, memory-for-problem-states, can explain a wide range of interruption effects. In addition, because memory-for-problem-states theory takes the form of a computational process model, it can be used to derive precise predictions about new combinations of tasks.

The remainder of this paper is organized as follows. First, we will discuss the background literature on interruptions, memory-for-goals, and on the effects of the problem state bottleneck on multitasking performance. We will then give a detailed account of memory-for-problem-states, show that it can account for an existing dataset, and derive two new predictions. Subsequently, we will test these predictions in two behavioral experiments. Finally, we will discuss the implications of our theory for interruption research and derive two recommendations for user interface design.

BACKGROUND

What Makes Interruptions Disruptive?

Researchers have identified several factors that determine the disruptiveness of interruptions. The three most consistent factors are interruption duration, the complexity of the interrupting task, and the moment of interruption.

Several studies have shown that the longer the interruption is, the longer it takes to resume the interrupted task [4,23,35], and the more errors are made after the interruption [4]. In addition, more complex interruptions (e.g., solving 17+36 as compared to 2+3; [23]) also lead to longer resumption times [13,14,20,23,35]. Both effects were nicely demonstrated by Monk et al. [35]. In their study, subjects were asked to perform a fairly complex VCR-programming task. This task was either interrupted by a blank screen, or by one of two different secondary tasks: a tracking task in which subjects had to use the mouse to track an icon on the screen, or a complex n-back task. The length of the interruptions was 3, 8, or 13 seconds. Figure 1A shows how much time it took the subjects to resume the VCR-task after an interruption. Resumption time increased with interruption duration for all three tasks and resumption costs were higher for the more complex interrupting tasks.

A third important determiner of interruption disruptiveness is the moment of the interruption in the primary task. For instance, in a related study to [35], Monk and colleagues again interrupted subjects while they were programming a VCR [34]. Depending on whether subjects were interrupted mid-subtask or between subtasks, interruptions were more or less disruptive. Likewise, Iqbal et al. interrupted subjects either at high or at low workload moments (determined by measuring pupil dilation [24] or by GOMS modeling [26]). These studies confirmed that users take less time to resume a task when interrupted at low-workload moments [25,26] (see [32] for an additional example).

To test whether users are aware that they should switch at low-workload moments, in [42] users were asked to perform a mail-and-internet task, which was interrupted by a chat task. Users were free to respond to the chat messages whenever they thought was best. The results showed that in 94% of the cases users switched at low-workload moments (low working-memory load), showing that users interrupt themselves at the 'correct' moments (see also [7,30]). Similarly, [29] showed that users self-interrupted after reducing their working memory load, and [33] that self-interruptions lead to lower interruption costs than forced interruptions (but see [29] for the opposite effect).

In summary, longer and more complex interruptions lead to higher resumption costs, especially if they interrupt the primary task at high workload moments.

Memory for Goals

Memory-for-goals theory explains these effects by assuming that each task has an associated task goal, which is stored in declarative memory when an interruption occurs [2,3]. Each task goal has an activation level, which decays when the goal is not in use. To resume the primary task after an interruption, its goal has to be retrieved from memory. Because the retrieval time of a goal is inversely related to its activation value, the longer the interruption, the more the goal's activation level will have decayed, and the longer it takes to retrieve it – explaining the interruption duration effect. To account for the effect of interrupting-task complexity, memory-for-goals assumes that users rehearse the primary task goal during an interruption to maintain its activation level. If the interrupting task is more complex, there is less time to rehearse, resulting in higher resumption costs.

In [43] and [44], Salvucci and colleagues used these mechanisms to model the VCR-data of Monk et al. [35]. Figure 1B shows the results: the model matched the data closely. For this model, Salvucci et al. had to make two important assumptions. First, the no-task condition can be resumed fastest because users do not have to reorient after the interruption. Second, users rehearse the primary task goal only for the first 2.5 seconds of the interruption, as opposed to rehearsing it during the whole interruption [44]. Otherwise, there would have been no interruption duration effect in the no-task condition: the activation of the VCR-goal would still be high at the end of the interruption due to rehearsal, independent of the length of the interruption. In the n-back condition there were fewer rehearsals than in the other conditions, because the cognitive system had to spend considerable time on the n-back task itself. As a result, the activation level of the VCR-goal was lower in the n-back condition, which therefore took more time to resume.

Although the explanation of the interruption duration effect in memory-for-goals is straightforward and accounted for several datasets [4,23,35], the explanation for the effect of interrupting-task complexity is less clear. In the example above, it had to be assumed that users rehearsed for a fixed 2.5 seconds – otherwise the model could not explain the effects in the no-task condition. A similar no-task effect was found by Hodgetts and Jones [23], who therefore concluded that it was unlikely that their subjects rehearsed at all. Furthermore, Cades et al. compared resumption times in the VCR task after a simple shadowing-task interruption, after a complex 1-back task, and after a 3-back task [13]. Although resumption was fastest after the shadowing task, there was no difference between the two n-back conditions – while it seems likely that it is harder to rehearse during 3-back than during 1-back. Finally, [29] did not find any evidence for rehearsal during interruptions in pupil dilation data, although it is well known that memory retrievals are a cause of pupil dilation [e.g., 40].

Taken together, memory-for-goals provides a simple and powerful explanation for the interruption duration effect, but its explanation for the interrupting-task complexity effect is less convincing, given that users often do not seem to rehearse during an interruption. Also, it is unclear how memory-for-goals accounts for the moment-of-interruption effect. To improve the explanatory power of memory-for-goals, we will not focus on task goals, but on the contents of the problem state associated with each task.

The Problem State Bottleneck in Multitasking

To perform a task, it is often necessary to maintain some information mentally. For instance, when solving '$4x - 8 = 20$', one needs to store the intermediate solution '$4x = 28$' before calculating the solution. This information is stored in the *problem state*, the central part of working memory that is accessible without a time cost ([5,10], comparable to the *focus of attention* in other theories, e.g., [38]). The problem state acts as a processing bottleneck in multitasking, as it can only maintain information for a single task at a time, and thus causes interference when required by multiple tasks concurrently. In a series of experiments it was shown that subjects were considerably slower and made more errors when the problem state was required for two tasks, as compared to one or none of the tasks [8,10,11,12,37]. Based on these experiments, a cognitive model was developed that gave a close account of the results. In the next section we will combine this model with the ideas behind memory-for-goals to explain task interruption and resumption.

MEMORY FOR PROBLEM STATES

The main idea of memory-for-problem-states is that both the primary and the secondary, interrupting task can have an associated problem state. If both tasks require a problem state, the problem state of the primary task is automatically stored in declarative memory during an interruption, where it starts to decay (analogously to task goals in memory-for-goals). After the interruption, the primary task's problem state has to be retrieved from memory, which takes time and can lead to errors when an incorrect (i.e. older) problem state is retrieved. As in memory-for-goals, the longer the interruption, the further the activation level of the problem state will have decayed, and the longer it takes to retrieve it from memory – explaining the interruption duration effect.

However, in contrast to memory-for-goals theory, this only occurs when both tasks require a problem state. If the primary task does not require a problem state, there is no information that can decay in memory, so there will not be an interruption duration effect – independent of whether the secondary task requires a problem state. Furthermore, if the secondary task does not require a problem state, it will not disrupt the problem state of the primary task, which will therefore again not show an interruption duration effect. This latter situation explains the effect of interrupting-task complexity: the secondary task will only disrupt the primary task's problem state if it is sufficiently complex to require its own problem state. Interestingly, memory-for-problem-states therefore predicts that it does not matter how complex the secondary task is, as long as it requires a problem state. This would for instance explain the results of Cades et al. [13], who found that although a no-task interruption was easiest, there was no difference between a complex 1-back and a 3-back interruption.

Implementation Details

Memory-for-problem-states theory was implemented in the cognitive architecture ACT-R [6], to enable quantitative predictions of reaction times and errors. This computational model is a precise implementation of our theory, and can be downloaded from http://www.jelmerborst.nl/models. The main components of memory-for-problem-states are ACT-R's problem state resource and declarative memory store. As explained above, the problem state resource is used to maintain intermediate information in a task and can store at

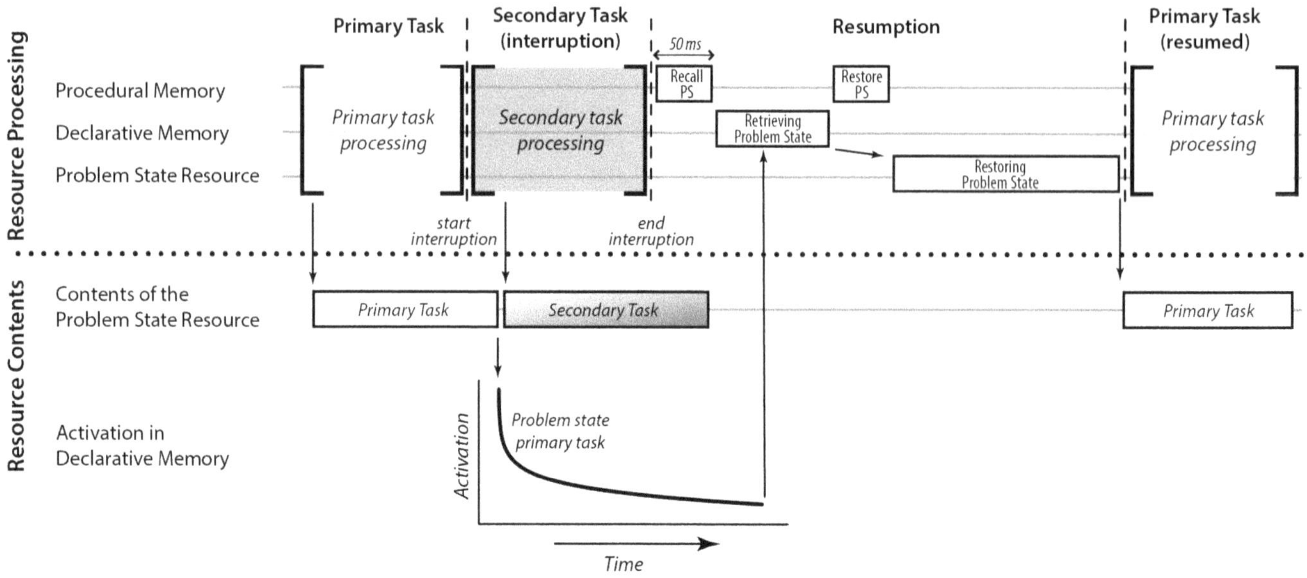

Figure 2. Interruption processing in memory-for-problem-states. Before the interruption, the primary task creates a problem state. This problem state is moved to declarative memory by the secondary, interrupting task, which requires its own problem state. After the interruption the resumption process restores the problem state of the primary task, after which the primary task can be resumed.

most a single chunk of information at a time. It is assumed that information in the problem state can be accessed instantly, without incurring a time cost. On the other hand, it was estimated that it takes 200 ms to store a new representation in the problem state resource [5,10]. When a new representation is stored, previous contents are automatically encoded in declarative memory.

Declarative memory simulates short- and long-term storage of facts. In contrast to the problem state, it contains multiple memory items. Each item has an associated activation level, representing the strength of the item in memory. Activation of an item reflects its frequency and recency of use, and decays with a power function [6]. An item that has been used more frequently in the past will have a higher activation level, as will an item that has been used more recently. The activation A_i of an item at time t is given by:

$$A_i(t) = \ln\left(\sum_{k=1}^{n}(t-t_k)^{-0.5}\right) \quad (1)$$

in which $t_1 \ldots t_n$ indicate the times when the item was used. In the case of an interruption, the problem state will be a new item in memory, and the equation can be simplified to:

$$A_i(d) = \ln(d^{-0.5}) \quad (2)$$

in which d is the time since the start of the interruption.

Retrieving an item from memory takes time. The retrieval time depends on the activation A_i of the item:

$$RT(A_i) = Fe^{-A_i} \quad (3)$$

in which F is a scale factor. The higher the activation level of an item, the faster it will be retrieved from memory. In previous work we have set F to 0.3 [8,9,10,11,12], which we will adopt in this paper, treating F as a fixed parameter. Retrieving information from declarative memory is not always successful: it can either fail altogether because the activation of an item is too low, or a similar item with a higher activation level can be retrieved. In the current paper we will not focus on these mechanisms, but they provide a possible explanation for errors after an interruption.

The final component of the models in this paper is ACT-R's procedural memory [6]. In essence, procedural memory consists of a set of *if-then* rules that govern behavior. For example, there might be a simple rule that says '*if* a fact is retrieved from declarative memory *then* store it in the problem state resource'. It takes 50 ms to 'fire' a production rule, and only a single rule can be fired at a time. For more details, including how production rules are learned, see [6].

Modeling Interruptions

Figure 2 illustrates what happens around an interruption according to memory-for-problem-states theory. It shows the situation in which both the primary and the secondary task require a problem state – for example being interrupted by a phone call while writing an article. The primary task stores a problem state before the interruption, for instance the topic of the current sentence. When the interruption occurs and the secondary task stores its own problem state (say, the date of an appointment), the problem state of the primary task is moved to declarative memory, where it starts to decay (bottom of Figure 3). After the interruption the primary task is resumed. However, first the primary task's problem state – the topic of the current sentence – has to be retrieved from declarative memory.

This resumption process is shown in detail. First, a production rule 'Recall PS' fires that notes that the primary task's problem state it not available. It therefore starts a retrieval from declarative memory. This retrieval takes a certain amount of time. When the problem state is retrieved, it is restored to the problem state resource, and the primary task can resume. Thus, the full resumption process takes 2 × 50 ms (production rules) + 200 ms (restoring the problem state) + the retrieval time of the problem state from declarative memory. The exact length depends on the duration of the interruption: the longer the interruption, the further the activation level of the problem state will have decayed, and the longer it will take to retrieve it.

Modeling Monk et al. (2008)

As a first test of memory-for-problem-states, we used it to simulate the VCR-task of Monk et al. [35]. The resulting fit is shown in Figure 1C. The model follows the memory-for-goals models of this task in that it does not attempt to make a faithful simulation of the VCR task [43,44]. Instead, it is assumed that the VCR task requires two problem states, given that it was a complex task with multiple sub-tasks.

In the no-task condition, the interruption did not require a problem state. However, because only a single problem state of the VCR-task can be maintained in the problem state resource, the second problem state of the VCR-task decays in declarative memory during an interruption. Therefore, resumption costs increase even in the no-task condition: the second problem state has to be retrieved after the interruption, resulting in increased resumption costs with longer interruptions.

Although the tracking task did not require a problem state either – there is no intermediate information to maintain in this task – it did result in higher resumption times than the no-task condition. According to the earlier models this is due to the interface of the experiment [43,44]. The tracking task was presented on the right side of the screen, while the VCR was presented on the left. In the no-task condition, participants could stay focused on the VCR during an interruption, but in the tracking condition they had to look away from the VCR. This resulted in increased resumption costs, as subjects had to refocus on the VCR task after an interruption. Note that the slopes of the resumption costs in the no-task and tracking conditions are similar, supporting the idea that the increase is due to the interface.

The n-back task incurred the greatest costs. According to the model, the n-back task required a problem state to keep track of previously presented letters. This resulted in the loss of both problem states of the VCR-task during an interruption, which decayed in declarative memory. After an interruption, both problem states had to be retrieved from declarative memory, resulting in a steeper slope of the resumption costs with interruption duration than in the other conditions, both in the data as well as in the model.

Predictions

The memory-for-problem-states model fit well to the Monk et al. dataset (R^2 and RMSD-values are reported in Figure 1). Whereas the memory-for-goals models attributed the difference between tracking and n-back to differences in rehearsal [43,44], the new model attributed it to different problem state requirements of the two tasks. Although this meant that we did not have to make somewhat ad hoc rehearsal assumptions, we did have to make the assumption that the VCR task requires two problem states.

As a stronger test of memory-for-problem-states, we will now derive two predictions, and test those predictions in two behavioral experiments. First, memory-for-problem-states claims that the interruption duration effect will only occur if both the primary and secondary task require a problem state, or if the primary task requires multiple problem states. Second, the interruption duration effect should be stronger (i.e. a steeper slope) if the primary task requires multiple problem states. Both predictions run counter to memory-for-goals, which predicts an interruption duration effect independent of the properties of the primary and secondary tasks. In addition, memory-for-goals does not predict that tasks with multiple problem states result in a stronger interruption duration effect, unless they also have multiple task goals.

To test these predictions we performed two experiments. In the first experiment we interrupted a subtraction task with an n-back task (with varying interruption durations). Both tasks could be easy (no problem state) or hard (single problem state). Memory-for-problem-states predicts that we should only find the interruption duration effect when both tasks are hard. In the second experiment a text-entry task was interrupted by an n-back task. The text-entry task required two problem states in the hard condition (but only a single task goal) leading to the prediction that resumption costs should be higher than in the first experiment, and also occur when the secondary task is easy.

EXPERIMENT 1: SUBTRACTION AND N-BACK

In Experiment 1 we used multi-column subtraction as the primary task [from 10], which was interrupted by an n-back task (Figure 3). The subtraction task had two conditions: an easy condition in which subjects did not have to carry between columns, and a hard condition in which subjects had to carry in 5 out of 10 columns. Thus, in the hard condition subjects mentally had to keep track of whether a 'carry' was in progress (solved columns were masked to ensure that subjects maintained carries mentally, Figure 3).

In the n-back task a rapid stream of letters was sequentially presented. Each letter was on the screen for 1100 ms, followed by a mask of 233 ms. The easy condition was a 1-back task: subjects had to indicate whether the current letter was the same or different as the previous letter. A response had to be made during the stimulus; no response was required to the first letter. As the mask was very brief this did not require the use of a problem state: subjects simply judged whether the shape was the same before and after the mask. The hard version was a 2-back task: subjects had to judge whether the current letter was the same as two letters

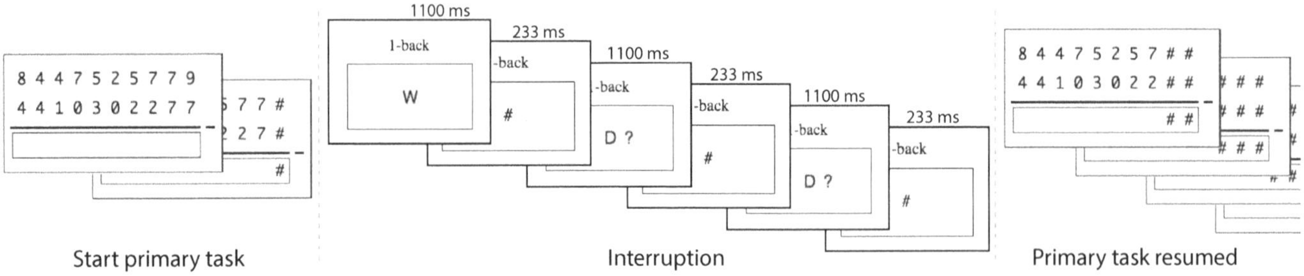

Figure 3. Easy subtraction interrupted by 1-back. The start of a trial is shown, including a 4 second interruption.

back. Thus, in the hard condition subjects needed their problem state to keep track of the letter two-back.

Stimuli for both tasks were generated anew for each subject. Half the responses on the n-back task were 'same' and half 'different'. Additionally, no more than three letters in a row could be the same. Subjects had to press 'x' or 'z' to indicate 'same' or 'different'.

Subjects

39 students of the University of Groningen participated in the experiment for course credit. Three subjects had to be excluded because they underperformed on the hard subtraction task (< 65% correct or slower than 3,500 ms per response), two subjects for underperforming on the hard n-back task (< 80% correct), and one subject because of health problems, leaving 33 complete data sets (23 female, age range 18-27, mean age 20.7). Informed consent as approved by the Ethical Committee Psychology of the University of Groningen was obtained before testing.

Procedure

Each trial started with presenting the conditions for the trial for three seconds, for example: N-Back: easy, Subtraction: hard. This was followed by the subtraction problem, which was interrupted twice by the n-back task. The points of interruption were varied between the 2nd and the 9th column, that is, subjects always started and finished with solving at least two columns. There were also at least two columns between interruptions. This yielded 15 different trial-types: the points of interruption were unpredictable to the subjects. Interruptions consisted of 3, 6, or 9 n-back stimuli, thus 4, 8, or 12 seconds. There was no relation between the length of the first and the second interruption in a trial. Finally, feedback was presented for 3 seconds, indicating the number of correct subtraction columns. Each trial ended with a 4 second fixation screen.

The experiment consisted of a practice block and two experimental blocks. The practice block started with three trials of the easy subtraction task, followed by three trials of the hard subtraction task, seven 6-step trials of the easy n-back task, and seven 7-step trials of the hard n-back task. Then the real task – including interruptions – was practiced in four trials. The two experimental blocks were identical, each consisted of 36 trials: 2 (easy/hard subtraction) x 2 (easy/hard n-back) x 3 (3/6/9 steps first interruption) x 3 (3/6/9 steps second interruption). Trial order was random. The complete experiment consisted of 72 subtraction trials: yielding 144 interruptions per subject, 12 per condition.

Statistical Procedure

A response time in the subtraction task was defined as the time between two responses, or, after an interruption, as the time between the reappearance of the subtraction task and the response. First responses of each trial were removed, as were extreme outliers (RTs <250 ms or >15,000 ms), after which data was removed exceeding three SDs from the mean per condition per subject (2.74% of the data was removed). Analyses are on correct responses only.

Results

Participant accuracy on the n-back task was above 85% in all conditions. Figure 4A shows the resumption costs in the subtraction task. Resumption cost is the extra cost after an interruption as compared to normal responses; it is plotted against n-back interruption duration. The first thing to note is that as long as subtraction was easy, resumption costs did not increase with interruption duration. However, there were fixed resumption costs of about 800 ms in all conditions. In the hard subtraction/easy n-back condition the resumption costs were slightly higher, but did not increase with interruption duration either. Resumption costs only increased with interruption duration in the hard/hard condition. A repeated-measures ANOVA (Table 1) confirmed main effects of Subtraction Difficulty and N-Back Difficulty. Furthermore, the interaction effect between Subtraction Difficulty and N-Back Difficulty was significant, but the three-way interaction between Subtraction Difficulty, N-back Difficulty, and Interruption Duration was not significant.

We subsequently performed simple effects analyses to investigate the model's prediction that we should only observe increasing costs with interruption duration in the hard-hard condition. For each n-back/subtraction condition we tested whether there was an effect of Interruption Duration. These analyses confirmed that there was no effect of Interruption Duration as long as either the subtraction task or the n-back task was easy (Fs < 1). In the hard/hard condition, we found a significant effect of Interruption Duration ($F(1,32) = 4.17$, $p = .0495$, $\eta_p^2 = .12$). Thus, resumption costs only increased with interruption duration in the hard/hard condition, and the ANOVA therefore confirmed the qualitative predictions of our theory.

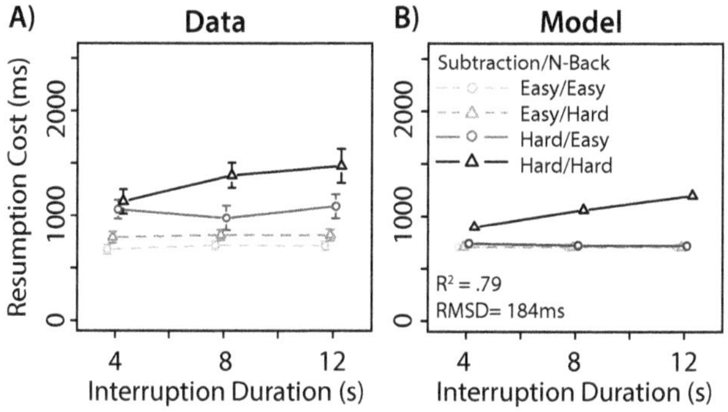

Figure 4. Resumption costs in Experiment 1 (A), and model fit (B). Error bars indicate standard error.

Source	*F*(1,32)	*p*	η_p^2
Subtraction Difficulty	33.83	< .001	.51
N-Back Difficulty	25.38	< .001	.44
Interruption Duration	3.69	.064	.10
Subtraction x N-Back	5.44	.026	.15
Subtraction x Int. Duration.	1.77	.19	.05
N-Back x Int. Duration	1.83	.19	.05
Sub. x N-Back x Int. Duration	2.51	.12	.07

Table 1. ANOVA results for Experiment 1.

Model

Figure 4B shows the quantitative fit of a memory-for-problem-states model to the data of Experiment 1 (R^2 and RMSD-values are reported in the figure). Memory-for-problem-states predicted that we should only find an effect of interruption duration when both tasks require a problem state. This is clearly shown in Figure 4B, where there is no difference between any of the conditions involving an easy task. The data shows a fixed cost of about 800 ms in all conditions. The model only predicted a fixed cost of ~355 ms. To make the effects comparable, we added 445 ms to the model results in all conditions. This is not meant to give an explanation of these costs, but only to ensure that we estimated the costs due to problem state recovery correctly.

Discussion

In Experiment 1 we tested the prediction that there should only be an effect of interruption duration on resumption costs when both the primary and the secondary task require a problem state. This prediction was confirmed by the data. Our model fit shows that memory-for-problem-states can account for the main effects in the data. However, the model underestimated the resumption costs by about 455 ms in all conditions, and did not predict the overall difference between easy and hard subtraction.

In Experiment 2 we will test the second prediction of memory-for-problem-states: when the primary task requires multiple problem states, resumption costs should be higher, and the resumption costs should increase with interruption duration even if the secondary task does not require a problem state.

EXPERIMENT 2: TEXT-ENTRY & N-BACK

In the second experiment, we used the text-entry task from [10] as the primary task, and again interrupted it with an n-back task, which used digits instead of letters. Unless noted otherwise, the design, procedure and analysis were identical to Experiment 1.

The text-entry task had two conditions: in the easy condition subjects were presented with a letter, they had to click on the corresponding button, followed by the next letter, etc. (Figure 5). In the hard version, subjects had to enter a 10-letter word. This word was shown at the start of a trial, however, as soon as subjects clicked on the first letter the word disappeared, and the rest of the word had to be entered without feedback (subjects did not see what they entered). Thus, in the hard condition subjects had to keep track of what the word was and at which position they were within the word. We assumed that they needed two problem states for this: one for the word and one for the position in the word. Each text-entry trial (entering a 10-letter string) was interrupted twice by the n-back task.

The 10 letter words for the hard version of the text-entry task were handpicked from a list of high-frequency Dutch words to ensure that similarities between words were kept at a minimum. These stimuli were also used in the easy text-entry task, except that the letters within the words were scrambled (under the constraint that a letter never appeared twice in a row). Thus, subjects were presented pseudo-random sequences of letters that they had to enter one-by-one in the easy condition. By scrambling the words, we controlled for letter-based effects, while preventing the use of strategies to predict the next letter.

Subjects

16 students of the University of Groningen participated in the experiment for course credit (12 female, age range 18–22, mean age 19.2). Informed consent as approved by the Ethical Committee Psychology of the University of Groningen was obtained before testing.

Statistical Procedure

Extreme outliers were removed from the data (RTs < 250 ms or > 10,000 ms), after which we removed data exceeding three SDs from the mean per condition per subject (in total 0.92% of the data was removed).

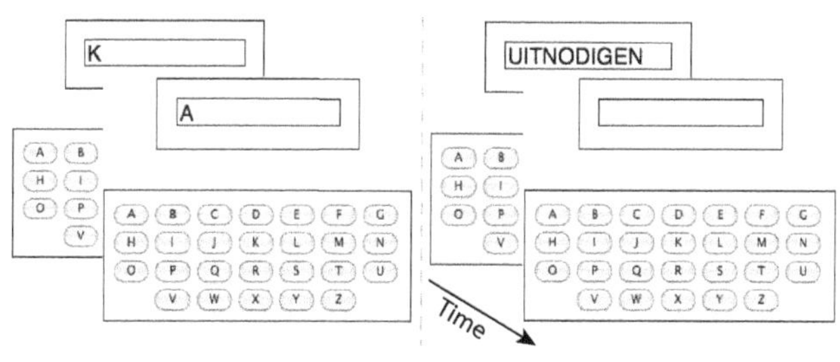

Figure 5. Interface of the easy (left) and hard (right) text-entry task.

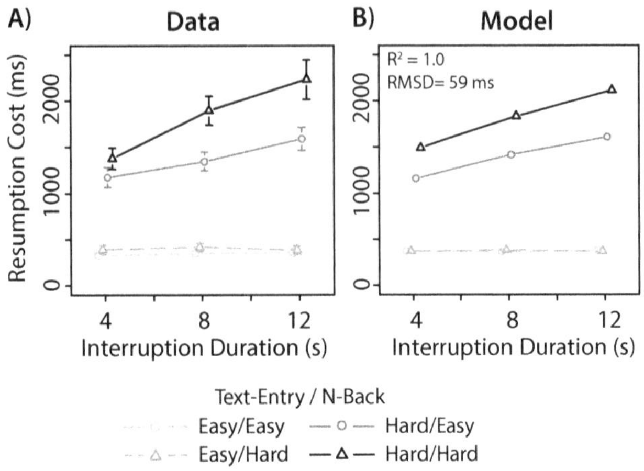

Figure 6. Resumption costs in Experiment 2 (A), and model fit (B). Error bars indicate standard error.

Source	$F(1,15)$	p	η_p^2
Text-Entry Difficulty	155.96	< .001	.91
N-Back Difficulty	18.92	< .001	.56
Interruption Duration	33.11	< .001	.69
Text-Entry x N-Back	16.24	.001	.52
Text-Entry x Int. Duration.	22.04	< .001	.60
N-Back x Int. Duration	3.75	.07	.20
Text-E. x N-Back x Int. Duration	3.18	.09	.17

Table 2. ANOVA results for Experiment 2.

Results

Participant accuracy on the n-back task was in all conditions over 90%, indicating that subjects focused on the n-back task. Figure 6A shows the resumption costs. Again, there was no effect of interruption duration as long as text-entry was easy. However, when text-entry was hard, there was clear interruption duration effect, which was stronger if the n-back task was also hard. The ANOVA (Table 2) confirmed these results: besides main effects of Text-Entry Difficulty, N-Back Difficulty, and Interruption Duration, also the two-way interaction effect between Text-Entry Difficulty and N-Back Difficulty was significant. The three-way interaction showed a trend towards significance.

Model

Figure 6B shows the fit of a memory-for-problem-states model. Because the model assumes that subjects needed two problem states to perform the hard n-back task, it predicted an effect of interruption duration also when n-back was easy, which was confirmed by the data. The effect was even stronger in the hard/hard condition – easy to see in the data (Fig. 6A) but also present in the model (Fig. 6B) – which the model explained by two problem states decaying in declarative memory instead of one, and both problem states having to be restored after an interruption.

As the data shows a fixed cost of about 400 ms in all conditions, we added this cost to the model. Again, this is not meant to give an explanation of these costs, but only to ensure that we estimated the costs due to problem state recovery correctly.

Discussion

Experiment 2 was conducted to test the second prediction of memory-for-problem-states: if a task requires multiple problem states, the resumption costs will be higher and will always increase with interruption duration, also if the secondary task does not require a problem state. This prediction was confirmed, and a memory-for-problem-states model gave a good account of the data. In addition, Experiment 2 confirmed with a new task that there is no effect of interruption duration on resumption costs as long as the primary task does not require a problem state.

GENERAL DISCUSSION

Although interruptions are ubiquitous in our society, an integrated theory of their effects is still absent. In this paper we proposed a first step towards such a theory in the form of a computational process model: memory-for-problem-states. Memory-for-problem-states is based on memory-for-goals theory [2] and on research into the problem state bottleneck [10]. It can be regarded as a more specific version of memory-for-goals: instead of focusing on general task goals, memory-for-problem-states looks in detail at the cognitive requirements of each task. For example, where memory-for-goals predicts an interruption duration effect for every task, memory-for-problem-states specified this to tasks that need a problem state. As support for memory-for-problem-states we first used it to simulate an existing dataset [35]. As a stronger test, we subsequently derived two *a priori* predictions from the model. These predictions were confirmed by two behavioral experiments, yielding strong support for our theory.

Memory-for-problem-states can account for three important factors in interruption disruptiveness: interruption duration, interrupting-task complexity, and moment of interruption. The interruption duration effect is explained by assuming that the problem state(s) associated with the primary task are stored in declarative memory during an interruption, and have to be retrieved on resumption. The longer the interruption, the further their activation in memory will have decayed, and the longer it takes to retrieve them.

The effect of interrupting-task complexity is explained by assuming that complexity can be defined as problem state requirements of the secondary task. The primary task's problem state will only be moved to declarative memory and result in higher resumption costs if the secondary task requires a problem state. Thus, a more complex secondary task that needs a problem state will result in higher costs.

Finally, memory-for-problem-states can explain moment-of-interruption effects. It was shown in multiple studies that it is better to be interrupted between tasks [25,26,34] than in the middle of a task. Memory-for-problem-states explains this by assuming that it is likely that someone has an active problem state in the middle of a task, but not between tasks. During an interruption, this problem state has to be stored in memory, and it has to be retrieved on resumption. For example, in the route-planning task in [24], information had to be maintained as a problem state during a subtask, but not between subtasks. It was shown that this was related to higher workload [24], as well as to higher resumption costs when interrupted during the subtask [25]. This problem-state explanation of the moment-of-interruption effects is also in line with the statistical model of [26], which showed that Task Level, Difficulty of Next Subtask, and Carry-Over between Subtasks, were the most important predictors of interruption disruptiveness. All three factors are clearly related to problem state requirements; especially Carry-Over is an almost identical concept.

Memory-for-problem-states does not explain all costs related to task interruption and resumption. Even in the two relatively simple experiments that we presented in this paper, we had to add a basic cost to the model results to account for the data. These costs might be due to general task reorientation costs, for instance related to task-set reconfiguration (cf. task switching, [36]). In addition, complexity is all-or-nothing in our framework: a secondary task requires a problem state or not. While this is most likely a simplification, it presents a first step to defining complexity in processing terms, which is necessary given that "the term complexity has been inconsistently defined" [35:302] in the literature. Our experiments have shown that problem state requirements are at least an important part of a full complexity definition.

To make interruption less disruptive, memory-for-problem-states makes two suggestions for user interface design. First, our theory suggests interrupting users at low-problem state moments. Where others have successfully interrupted users at low-workload moments [1,24,26,32,34], we specify that low workload should be defined as an absence of problem state usage. As Iqbal et al. have shown, these moments might be determined by using detailed task models [26] or by using physiological measures such as pupil dilation [24]. However, given that pupil dilation is sensitive to many other processes than problem state usage [29,40], task models seem preferable.

Second, our model proposes that resumption costs are due to problem state restoration. To decrease resumption costs, problem state restoration should be aided by presenting the problem state of the user in the environment. The idea of presenting cues to aid resumption is not new [16,33,39]. However, where previous approaches have sometimes recorded the entire task interface [39], we limit this to problem state information. Although this might be difficult – it is information that users maintain mentally, after all – at least in some situations it is possible [e.g., 8].

ACKNOWLEDGMENTS

This research was funded by ERC-StG grant 283597 awarded to Niels Taatgen.

REFERENCES

1. Adamczyk, P.D. and Bailey, B.P. If not now, when? In *Proc. CHI*. 2004, 271–278.
2. Altmann, E.M. and Trafton, J.G. Memory for goals: An activation-based model. *Cognitive Science 26*, (2002), 39–83.
3. Altmann, E.M. and Trafton, J.G. Timecourse of recovery from task interruption: data and a model. *Psychonomic Bulletin & Review 14*, 6 (2007), 1079–84.
4. Altmann, E.M., Trafton, J.G., and Hambrick, D.Z. Momentary interruptions can derail the train of thought. *Journal of Experimental Psychology: General 143*, 1 (2014), 215–226.
5. Anderson, J.R. Human symbol manipulation within an integrated cognitive architecture. *Cognitive Science 29*, (2005), 313–341.
6. Anderson, J.R. *How Can the Human Mind Occur in the Physical Universe?* Oxford University Press, New York, 2007.
7. Bogunovich, P. and Salvucci, D. The effects of time constraints on user behavior for deferrable interruptions. *Proc. CHI*, (2011), 3123–3126.
8. Borst, J.P., Buwalda, T.A., Van Rijn, H., and Taatgen, N.A. Avoiding the Problem State Bottleneck by Strategic use of the Environment. *Acta Psychologica 144*, 2 (2013), 373–379.
9. Borst, J.P. and Taatgen, N.A. The Costs of Multitasking in Threaded Cognition. In *Proc. ICCM*. 2007, 133–138.
10. Borst, J.P., Taatgen, N.A., and Van Rijn, H. The Problem State: A Cognitive Bottleneck in Multitasking. *Journal of Experimental Psychology: Learning, Memory, & Cognition 36*, 2 (2010), 363–382.
11. Borst, J.P., Taatgen, N.A., and Van Rijn, H. Using a Symbolic Process Model as input for Model-Based fMRI Analysis: Locating the Neural Correlates of Problem State Replacements. *NeuroImage 58*, 1 (2011), 137–147.
12. Borst, J.P., Taatgen, N.A., Stocco, A., and Van Rijn, H. The Neural Correlates of Problem States: Testing fMRI Predictions of a Computational Model of Multitasking. *PLoS ONE 5*, 9 (2010), e12966.
13. Cades, D.M., Davis, D.A.B., Trafton, J.G., and Monk, C.A. Does the Difficulty of an Interruption Affect our Ability to Resume? In *Proc. HFES*. 2007, 234–238.
14. Cades, D.M., Werner, N., Boehm-Davis, D.A., Trafton, J.G., and Monk, C.A. Dealing with Interruptions can be Complex, but does Interruption Complexity Matter: A Mental Resources Approach to Quantifying Disruptions. In *Proc. HFES*. 2008, 398–402.
15. Chisholm, C.D., Dornfeld, A.M., Nelson, D.R., and Cordell, W.H. Work interrupted: A comparison of workplace interruptions in emergency departments and primary care offices. *Annals of Emergency Medicine 38*, 2 (2001), 146–151.

16. Cutrell, E., Czerwinski, M., and Horvitz, E. Notification, disruption, and memory: Effects of messaging interruptions on memory and performance. In *Proc. INTERACT*. 2001.
17. Czerwinski, M., Horvitz, E., and Wilhite, S. A diary study of task switching and interruptions. In *Proc. CHI*. 2004, 175–182.
18. Edwards, M.B. and Gronlund, S.D. Task Interruption and its Effects on Memory. *Memory 6*, 6 (1998), 665–687.
19. Eyrolle, H. and Cellier, J.-M. The effects of interruptions in work activity: field and laboratory results. *Applied Ergonomics 31*, 5 (2000), 537–543.
20. Gillie, T. and Broadbent, D.E. What makes interruptions disruptive? A study of length, similarity, and complexity. *Psychological Research 50*, (1989), 243–250.
21. González, V. and Mark, G. Constant, constant, multi-tasking craziness: managing multiple working spheres. In *Proc. CHI*. 2004, 113–120.
22. Gould, S., Brumby, D., and Cox, A.L. What does it mean for an interruption to be relevant? An investigation of relevance as a memory effect. In *Proc. HFES*. 2013, 149–153.
23. Hodgetts, H.M. and Jones, D.M. Interruption of the Tower of London task: support for a goal-activation approach. *Journal of Experimental Psychology: General 135*, 1 (2006), 103–15.
24. Iqbal, S.T., Adamczyk, P., Zheng, X., and Bailey, B.P. Towards an index of opportunity: understanding changes in mental workload during task execution. In *Proc. SIGCHI*. 2005, 311–320.
25. Iqbal, S.T. and Bailey, B.P. Investigating the effectiveness of mental workload as a predictor of opportune moments for interruption. In *Proc. CHI*. 2005, 1489–1492.
26. Iqbal, S.T. and Bailey, B.P. Leveraging characteristics of task structure to predict the cost of interruption. In *Proc. CHI*. 2006, 741–750.
27. Iqbal, S.T. and Horvitz, E. Disruption and recovery of computing tasks. In *Proc. CHI*. 2007, 677–686.
28. Jin, J. and Dabbish, L.A. Self-interruption on the computer: A Typology of Discretionary Task Interleaving. In *Proc. CHI*. 2009, 1799–1808.
29. Katidioti, I., Borst, J.P., and Taatgen, N.A. What Happens When We Switch Tasks: Pupil dilation in multitasking. *Journal of Experimental Psychology: Applied*, (in press).
30. Katidioti, I. and Taatgen, N.A. Choice in Multitasking: How Delays in the Primary Task Turn a Rational Into an Irrational Multitasker. *Human Factors 56*, 4 (2014), 728–736.
31. Mark, G., González, V., and Harris, J. No task left behind?: examining the nature of fragmented work. In *Proc. CHI*. 2005, 321–330.
32. McFarlane, D. Comparison of Four Primary Methods for Coordinating the Interruption of People in Human-Computer Interaction. *Human-Computer Interaction 17*, 1 (2002), 63–139.
33. McFarlane, D.C. and Latorella, K.A. The scope and importance of human interruption in human-computer interaction design. *Human-Computer Interaction 17*, 1 (2002), 1–61.
34. Monk, C.A., Boehm-Davis, D.A., and Trafton, J.G. Recovering From Interruptions: Implications for Driver Distraction Research. *Human Factors 46*, 4 (2004), 650–663.
35. Monk, C.A., Trafton, J.G., and Boehm-Davis, D.A. The effect of interruption duration and demand on resuming suspended goals. *Journal of Experimental Psychology: Applied 14*, 4 (2008), 299–313.
36. Monsell, S. Task switching. *Trends in Cognitive Sciences 7*, 3 (2003), 134–140.
37. Nijboer, M., Borst, J.P., Van Rijn, H., and Taatgen, N.A. Single-task fMRI overlap predicts concurrent multitasking interference. *NeuroImage 100*, (2014), 60–74.
38. Oberauer, K. Design for a working memory. In B.H. Ross, ed., *Psychology of Learning and Motivation*. Academic Press, 2009, 45–100.
39. Renaud, K. Expediting Rapid Recovery from Interruptions by Providing a Visualisation of Application Activity. In *Proc. OZCHI*. 2000, 348–355.
40. Van Rijn, H., Dalenberg, J.R., Borst, J.P., and Sprenger, S.A. Pupil Dilation Co-Varies with Memory Strength of Individual Traces in a Delayed Response Paired-Associate Task. *PLoS ONE 7*, 12 (2012), e51134.
41. Rosen, L.D., Mark Carrier, L., and Cheever, N.A. Facebook and texting made me do it: Media-induced task-switching while studying. *Computers in Human Behavior 29*, 3 (2013), 948–958.
42. Salvucci, D.D. and Bogunovich, P. Multitasking and monotasking: the effects of mental workload on deferred task interruptions. In *Proc. CHI*. ACM Press, 2010, 85–88.
43. Salvucci, D.D., Monk, C.A., and Trafton, J.G. A Process-Model Account of Task Interruption and Resumption: When Does Encoding of the Problem State Occur? In *Proc. HFES*. Human Factors and Ergonomics Society, 2009, 799–803.
44. Salvucci, D.D. and Taatgen, N.A. *The multitasking mind*. Oxford University Press, New York, 2011.
45. Trafton, J.G., Altmann, E.M., Brock, D.P., and Mintz, F.E. Preparing to resume an interrupted task: effects of prospective goal encoding and retrospective rehearsal. *International Journal of Human-Computer Studies 58*, 5 (2003), 583–603.
46. Zijlstra, F.R.H., Roe, R.A., Leonora, A.B., and Krediet, I. Temporal factors in mental work: Effects of interrupted activities. *Journal of Occupational and Organizational Psychology 72*, (1999), 163–185.

Interruptibility of Software Developers and its Prediction Using Psycho-Physiological Sensors

Manuela Züger and Thomas Fritz
Department of Informatics
University of Zurich, Switzerland
{zueger, fritz}@ifi.uzh.ch

ABSTRACT
Interruptions of knowledge workers are common and can cause a high cost if they happen at inopportune moments. With recent advances in psycho-physiological sensors and their link to cognitive and emotional states, we are interested whether such sensors might be used to measure interruptibility of a knowledge worker. In a lab and a field study with a total of twenty software developers, we examined the use of psycho-physiological sensors in a real-world context. The results show that a Naïve Bayes classifier based on psycho-physiological features can be used to automatically assess states of a knowledge worker's interruptibility with high accuracy in the lab as well as in the field. Our results demonstrate the potential of these sensors to avoid expensive interruptions in a real-world context. Based on brief interviews, we further discuss the usage of such an interruptibility measure and interruption support for software developers.

Author Keywords
psycho-physiological, lab/field study, interruptibility

ACM Classification Keywords
H.5.m. Information Interfaces and Presentation (e.g. HCI): Miscellaneous

INTRODUCTION
In office work environments, interruptions by co-workers, emails or instant messages are common. While some of these interruptions are desired, others might incur a high cost, including long resumption lags, slower performance, negative emotions and an increase in errors due to the interruption happening at inopportune moments [6, 16]. When a co-worker is asked to assess a colleague's interruptibility into five states—from highly interruptible to highly non-interruptible—the assessment is difficult and only slightly better than chance as Fogarty et al. found in their study [17]. In addition, these assessments are generally based on cues of the colleague's social and task engagement, such as an open door, the colleague talking to someone or the use of the computer keyboard. However, especially in today's globally distributed work environments, this context information is often not available.

CHI 2015, April 18–23, 2015, Seoul, Republic of Korea.

ACM 978-1-4503-3145-6/15/04 ...$15.00.
http://dx.doi.org/10.1145/2702123.2702593

To avoid the high costs that interruptions can cause on knowledge workers, researchers have looked at automatically identifying good and bad moments for interruptions and computing a measure for a worker's interruptibility. Such an automatic interruptibility measure can then be used to better coordinate interruptions by, for instance, providing visual cues or postponing them to a more suitable moment [37]. Prior work examined the use of context-aware sensors to gather information, such as audio and video streams, keyboard and mouse interaction, or task characteristics (e.g., [17, 18, 27]).

With recent advances in psycho-physiological (aka. biometric) sensor technology, researchers have also started to investigate their use to assess a person's interruptibility in controlled environments and on small tasks. Psycho-physiological sensors have the advantage of providing more flexibility without being bound to a specific task, computer or location and are increasingly less invasive. Previous studies have shown that psycho-physiological features, such as electrodermal activity (EDA), heart rate or electroencephalographs (EEG), can be used to measure cognitive and emotional states (e.g., [9, 22]). Under the assumption that moments of high cognitive load or stress correlate with low interruptibility, studies have examined, for instance, the use of psycho-physiological sensors to calculate interruptibility from EEG data during a military exercise [36] or from a combination of heart rate variability and muscle activity on varying small tasks, such as word puzzles, mental arithmetic or racing games [12].

In our work, we aim to investigate the use of a combination of psycho-physiological sensors to automatically identify the interruptibility of a knowledge worker in a real-world working context. We build upon and extend the findings of previous research in the area by contributing two studies with software developers wearing psycho-physiological sensors: a lab study with participants working on real-world development tasks in a controlled environment, and a field study with participants working on their own tasks in their real-world office environments. In our analysis we focus on the use of psycho-physiological sensors to automatically infer the interruptibility of knowledge workers. In addition, we investigate the correlation between interruptibility, mental load and interruption lag and look at which tool support for interruptions developers desire.

The results of our studies provide evidence that psycho-physiological sensors can be used to classify the interruptibility of a software developer with high accuracy (91.5% for the lab and 78.6% for the field study). Our results also show that we can build classifiers with high accuracy for a more fine-grained set of five states of interruptibility and that psycho-physiological data is very sensitive to individuals. In addition to these results, we provide evidence for the correlations between interruptibility, mental load and interruption lag and discuss potential tool support for software developers.

RELATED WORK

Interruptibility with Context-Aware Sensors

The greater part of related work that developed an interruptibility measure used context-aware sensors, such as audio and video streams, keyboard and mouse actions, active window information, table pressure, or task characteristics. For instance, Hudson et al. were able to classify interruptibility into two states (least interruptible vs. all other states) with 78% accuracy by simulating sensors and manually coding features from audio and video recordings, such as the number of people present, who was speaking, or whether the phone was on the hook [25]. Fogarty et al. also simulated sensors by manually encoding mouse and keyboard actions, such as highlighting a line or editing code. They measured interruptibility in terms of the interruption lag—the time between the notification and the start of an interruption—during coding tasks and achieved 72% accuracy for two state interruptibility classification (interruptible and engaged) [18]. Using a pressure sensor sheet on the desk, Tani et al. were able to achieve a similar two state interruptibility classification accuracy on typing and mouse operation with easy and hard phases [43]. Different to these, Iqpbal et al. used task characteristics, such as the next subtask's difficulty, carry over of data across boundaries, and the percentage of parent task completion, to predict the cost of interruptions. They measured the cost based on resumption lag—the time needed to resume the primary task [27]. Ho et al. developed a context-aware mobile computing device to automatically detect activity transitions using accelerometers for measuring interruptibility. Their results show that messages delivered at activity transitions are better received than those delivered at random times [24].

Instead of context-aware sensors, our work uses biometric sensors to assess interruptibility. Especially with the recent advances and the development of low-cost biometric sensors with low-invasive form factors, a possible advantage is that these sensors are body-worn and not limited to laboratories, certain working environments or a specific software platform.

Biometric Sensors

An extensive amount of research investigates the link between psycho-physiological sensors and different cognitive and emotional states, such as high cognitive load or stress. The most studied sensors are electroencephalographs (EEG), eye tracking systems, sensors for electrocardiogram (ECG) or blood volume pulse (BVP), sensors measuring the electrodermal activity (EDA) and body temperature sensors.

EEG. EEG measures the aggregated electrical activity of the brain, which is caused when neurons fire. Different studies showed that certain frequency bands in the EEG data, called Alpha, Beta, Gamma, Delta and Theta can be linked to cognitive states, such as being focused, relaxed, or dreaming [9]. For instance, Gevins et al. found that an increase in theta activity and a decrease in alpha activity can be linked to an increase in memory load [19]. Kramer linked an increase in beta and decreases in alpha and theta to an increase in task engagement [30]. Several studies also used EEG devices to classify mental tasks or states of cognitive load [21, 32].

Eye Tracking. Eye trackers use the reflection of infrared light from the eyes to calculate the position of the visual focus and the pupil size. Interesting features are the pupil size, fixation duration or number of saccades. Particularly the pupil size (e.g. the peak amplitude of the pupil diameter) is an indicator for memory load or processing load, and varies with task difficulty [8]. Researchers showed that more difficult tasks demand longer processing time, induce higher subjective ratings of cognitive load and evoke greater pupillary response at salient subtasks [28]. Fixation durations and number of saccades are suitable to assess the designs of user interfaces [29].

ECG and BVP. For measuring the activity of the heart, either an ECG or BVP sensor can be used. ECG sensors measure the electrical activity of the heart using electrodes which are placed on the chest. BVP sensors, or photoplethysmographs, emit light which is absorbed by the oxyhemoglobin in the blood. The part of the light which is scattered back can be detected with a photodiode. ECG devices are more exact, but also more cumbersome to wear, therefore we chose a BVP sensor for our study. BVP can serve as a direct indicator for cognitive load [41], and can additionally be used to compute interbeat interval (IBI) and heart rate (HR).

EDA. EDA represents the skin conductivity that varies with sweating activity and can be measured by applying a small current with two electrodes. EDA has been linked to arousal, attention, emotional states, stress and anxiety [11]. In a study on text reading and arithmetic tasks imposing multiple cognitive load levels, a strong link between cognitive load and EDA was found [39].

Body temperature. Body temperature is influenced by emotions as well as stress. Vinkers et al. recently confirmed indications that stress influences body temperature in humans and found that body temperature rises with increasing stress [46]. In a study about autonomic nervous system response patterns evoked by emotions, skin temperature was demonstrated to be different in response to anger and fear [14].

Sensor combinations. Studies also applied multiple biometric sensors to measure cognitive load, task difficulty, task engagement and other cognitive states. For instance, Wilson analyzed mental workload in pilots during flight with multiple measures [47]. In prior work, we combined EDA, EEG and eye tracking to assess task difficulty in simple code comprehension tasks and found that a combination of all sensors to classify a new task achieved the highest accuracy of 84%. Haapalainen et al. combined an eye tracker, a heart rate monitor, ECG, EDA, EEG and body temperature sensors. They assessed the performance of different features to classify cognitive load on elementary cognitive tasks and found that the ECG median absolute deviation and median heat flux performed best, providing over 80% accuracy [22].

In our study, we use sensors for EEG, eye blinks, HR, BVP, EDA and body temperature due to the availability of low-cost and minimally invasive devices and their predictive power.

Interruptibility with Biometric Sensors

Fewer related work used psycho-physiological sensors to assess interruptibility. Kramer gathered EEG data during one hour of US military training and succeeded in classifying interruptibility based on labels gathered retrospectively [36]. Other researchers used measures of an eye tracker to compare mental workload during different hierarchic levels of task boundaries and were able to proof that mental workload dropped at high level task boundaries. This suggests that high level context switches are good moments for interruptions [5]. Chen et al. conducted a beeper study in which participants solved short tasks with varying difficulty. They measured heart rate variability as indicator for cognitive load and muscle activity trough EMG and calculated interruptibility using linear regression [12]. They also developed a mobile phone, which classifies interruptibility into four states combining high / low mental load with high / low movement [13]. The studies conducted by Bailey et al. [5] and Chen et al. [12] were situated in a controlled laboratory environment and used well defined and relatively simple tasks, such as document editing based on specified comments, typing a given text or solving a word puzzle. Mathan et al [36] conducted a study during military training with more complex tasks, requiring different cognitive and also physical skills.

Our work differs in that it uses real-world software development tasks requiring a multitude of cognitive skills. In our field study, participants were wearing biometric sensors while working normally in their own offices on their own software development tasks with varying difficulty and context.

Interruption Management

Some related work already used interruptibility indicators in practical applications to avoid interruptions at unsuitable moments. For instance, a decision rule based software delivered unrelated instant messages only at times of context switches that were determined based on mouse movement and window switching. In their study they achieved a five times higher answer rate to messages compared to non-mediated message delivery [4]. Chen and Vertegaal automatically set the ring tone volume of a mobile phone using an interruptibility indicator based on heart variability and muscle activity. In a six person trial they found that participants where satisfied with the chosen notification level in 83% of the cases [12]. Only recently, novel designs to handle interruptions from incoming calls on smart phones have been developed adding new actions, such as 'postpone' or 'send a message', to traditional ones, such as 'accept' and 'decline' [10]. Our work can leverage existing interruption management support by providing an automated interruptibility measure using biometric sensors.

Interruption, Resumption and Edit Lag

There are three time spans commonly used in studies concerning the effects of interruptions: interruption, resumption and edit lag. Interruption lag is the timespan between a notification and the start of the interruption [3]. Resumption lag is the timespan between the end of the interruption and the beginning of the suspended primary task, usually measured by monitoring the first mouse or keyboard action [1, 3]. Edit lag is the timespan between the end of the interruption and the first edit and represents a specialized measure of the resumption lag [40]. It is based on the assumption that interruptions in software development have a large effect and it takes minutes to regather context as opposed to resumption lag which is in the order of seconds [45].

For immediate interruptions (e.g. a phone call), the interruption lag is very short. Even short interruption lags (8s) are mitigating the disruptiveness of an interruption and can shorten the resumption lag [44]. For negotiated interruptions, the length of the interruption lag can be chosen by the interrupted person [37]. It can serve as indicator for interruptibility, following the notion of memory externalization before addressing an interruption [18]. The larger the memory load, the less interruptible a person is and the longer the interruption lag is required to find a suitable breakpoint. It has been shown that resumption lag is influenced by the availability of cues [3], the interruption length and demand [38], but not by stress, time pressure and flow [15].

In our work, we measured interruption lag, the traditional resumption lag and the specialized edit lag to report their lengths and analyze their correlation with interruptibility and mental load before the interruption.

STUDY DESIGN

To learn about the interruptibility of software developers and the use of biometric sensors to measure their interruptibility in a real-world context, we conducted two studies, a lab and a field study. The lab study was a first step to investigate whether biometric sensors can be used to measure interruptibility of software developers working on the same real-world change tasks in a controlled environment. As a second step, we conducted the field study to investigate how well results from the lab can be transferred to a real-world environment. In both studies, participants were wearing biometric sensors. Participants were interrupted at random times and asked to perform short arithmetic exercises, as well as rate their interruptibility, their mental load and the disturbance of the interruption. Figure 1 illustrates the study setup with one participant from the field study.

Psycho-Physiological Sensors

In both studies, we used two sensor devices: the Neurosky Mindband (http://neurosky.com), a headband to record electroencephalograph (EEG) and eye blink data, and the Empatica E3 wrist band (www.empatica.com) to record electrodermal activity (EDA), skin temperature, blood volume pulse, interbeat interval, and heart rate.

EEG and Eye-Related Measures

To measure the electrical brain activity and eye blinks we used the Neurosky Mindband, a low-cost and minimally invasive[1] headband with a one-channel EEG sensor. This headband works with one reference electrode at the ear and two

[1] relative to other EEG sensor devices

Figure 1. Study setup for one participant wearing the headband and wrist band in the field study. The tablet for triggering interruptions is placed next (left) to the participant's main screen.

dry electrodes placed on the forehead reading signals mainly from the pre-frontal cortex. The device records the time-varying voltage signal sampled at 512Hz as a raw wave and as a wave filtered for noise. At the same time it records the signal quality that indicates the proper placement of the device. In addition, the headband also records two proprietary measures called Attention and Meditation that are both in the range from 0 to 100, sampled at 1Hz, and meant to indicate mental focus and mental calmness or relaxation respectively.

Skin- and Heart-Related Measures

To record skin- and heart-related measures, we used the wireless Empatica E3 wrist band that integrates an EDA sensor, a photoplethysmograph and a temperature sensor. The EDA sensor is used to measure skin conductance. It consists of two electrodes that are placed at the ventral area of the wrist. By applying a small current to the skin through these electrodes, skin conductance is measured down to $0.1\mu S$ at a frequency of 4Hz. The photoplethysmograph is an optical sensor for measuring blood volume pulse (BVP), which can be used to compute interbeat interval (IBI) and heart rate (HR).

Interruptions

To trigger interruptions during the studies we used a Windows Surface 2 tablet[2] that we placed close to the participant's main monitor. For each interruption, the tablet played a sound and the display changed from a black to a white screen with a "Start" button on it. Participants were instructed to decide for themselves when to address the interruption—a technique for coordinating interruptions called "negotiated interruption" [37]. This technique usually works well and was used by others to simulate "normal" interruptions for software developers [18]. Using negotiated interruptions allows to measure interruption lag, which is the timespan between the notification and the moment a participant starts to address the interruption [2]. The interruption lag has previously been used as a measure for interruptibility, since researchers found that it corresponds to the time used to externalize the working memory before addressing the pending interruption [18].

Interruptions were composed of two parts, a mental arithmetic exercise and a set of questions on the participant's perception of the interruption on five-point Likert scales. For the arithmetic exercise participants were asked to solve a two-digit multiplication. As mental arithmetic exercises generally impose a high working memory load [33], they are considered an effective interruption for software developers [18]. After participants typed an answer into a text box on the tablet and clicked the "Ok" button, the correct solution was displayed to satisfy participants' need for closure [31]. For the question set part, the tablet application prompted participants to rate their perceived disturbance from 1 (not at all disturbing) to 5 (very disturbing), their interruptibility at the time of the notification from 1 (highly interruptible) to 5 (not at all interruptible), and their mental workload at the time of the notification from 1 (very low) to 5 (very high). After answering these questions, the tablet application displayed a black screen and participants returned to their work.

Lab Study: Participants and Method

For the lab study, all participants worked on the same three real-world code change tasks in the same controlled environment. The study took place in a quiet office room with external distractions and interruptions, except for the ones triggered as part of the study, reduced to a minimum. All participants worked at the same computer with the same integrated development environment (IDE) setup for the study.

Through personal contacts, we recruited ten graduate students, one female and nine male. All participants had their major in computer science and an average of 4.1 years ($\pm$3.8) professional and of 10.4 years ($\pm$3.2) total development experience.

The study lasted 90 minutes per participant and had three parts, a preparation phase, a 60 minutes programming session and a brief follow-up interview. In the preparation phase, we asked each participant for some demographic information. Then we helped the participant to put on the two sensor devices and had the participant watch a movie of fish swimming in a fish tank for two minutes. The movie was intended to help participants relax and to record a baseline for each participant. We used this later on to normalize the captured data, for instance, to make heart rates comparable among participants with varying resting heart rates. To familiarize participants with the interruptions, we conducted a few test runs while displaying the fish tank movie. For the main part of the study, each participant was asked to work for 60 minutes in the Eclipse IDE on three code change tasks that we explained to them beforehand. During this programming session participants were frequently interrupted after random time intervals that were between one and eleven minutes long. These time intervals model interruption frequency occurring in reality [20]. At the end of the study, we briefly interviewed each participant. In the interview, we asked participants about their perception of the primary tasks, the interruptions with the peripheral arithmetic tasks, as well as more generally about the disruptiveness of interruptions and tool support they would desire for better managing interruptions.

Project and Tasks

We chose the drawing framework JHotDraw[3] for the three code change tasks. JHotDraw is an open source project that

[2] http://www.microsoft.com/surface/en-us/products/surface-2

[3] http://www.jhotdraw.org/

has evolved over several years, is well structured and allows for easy testing due to its graphical user interface. The three study tasks were chosen to represent real code change tasks with varying difficulty levels to stress various levels of mental load and various states of interruptibility in a participant.

Adding Circles. The first task is to add a drawable figure, namely a circle, to the Draw application. The task requires to add a button with a provided icon to the toolbar and code to draw the circle. As there is already a feature for drawing an ellipse, code can be reused and the main difficulty is to identify the right places where new code needs to be inserted.

Adding Hexagons. The second task is similar to the first one, but requires to add a hexagon instead of a circle. Knowledge obtained in the first task could be reused, however, drawing a hexagon is more difficult and requires knowledge in geometry. As an optional help, a document with explanations of the geometry of a hexagon was provided.

Adding Text and URL. The third task is to add text and a clickable URL into an existing message dialog. The main task difficulty is to locate the right place in the code for implementing the functionality, and to get familiar with the Java API on message dialogs as well as user interface components.

To validate that the perceived task difficulty varied between tasks, we asked participants to rate them from 1 (very easy) to 5 (very difficult). They rated the first and third task as rather easy (2.4$\pm$0.7 and 2$\pm$1.4) and the second as rather difficult (3.9$\pm$1.0).

Field Study: Participants and Method

To learn more about interruptibility and the use of psycho-physiological sensors in the field, we conducted a study with ten professional software developers working on their own tasks and in their real-world office environments. For this study, we visited professional developers in their work places and studied them for two hours each. We did not restrict any external influences, such as interruptions by co-workers or distractions, and we did not limit the work or the participant's work setup, such as the activities they performed during work, the IDEs they used or the office layout.

We recruited ten professional software developers (1 female, 9 male) between their early twenties and late forties from four software development companies of varying size. Participants were recruited through personal contacts and recruiting emails. They had an average of 8.5 years ($\pm$7.5) professional software development experience and an average of 12.7 years ($\pm$6.0) of total development experience.

The field study lasted 2.5 hours per participant and had again three parts, a preparation phase, a main study session of 2 hours and a brief follow-up interview. As in the lab study, we first asked each participant for some demographic information. We then helped them to put on the sensors and had them watch the fish tank movie to help them relax, record a baseline and familiarize participants with the interruptions. For the main study session, participants worked on their usual tasks while being frequently interrupted after random time intervals that, again, were between one and eleven minutes long. For this session participants were told to work as usual during their work day without restriction on their activities, such as checking emails or browsing the web, and to switch tasks as they would normally do. Also, we told all participants and co-workers beforehand to interact during the session as they would usually do during their work day. At the end of the study, we again conducted a brief follow-up interview with participants on the perception of the tasks, the disruptiveness of interruptions and desired tool support.

Tasks

During the main study session, participants worked on a variety of tasks, such as the elimination of a performance bottle neck in a web application, the implementation of a user interface component, or the implementation of test cases for a business application. Most participants worked mainly on one primary task during the two hour session and only rarely switched to other small tasks. For these tasks, they used a variety of tools, such as IDEs (e.g. Visual Studio or Eclipse), revision control tools (e.g. SourceTree), web browsers (e.g. Firefox) and email or calendar clients (e.g. MS Outlook).

Data Collection and Analysis

During the course of both studies we collected data from the psycho-physiological sensor devices and data on participants' computer interaction captured through monitoring and observation. In addition, we collected participants' answers to the questions during the interruptions, their demographic information and notes from the brief follow-up interviews. We recorded a total of 30 hours of psycho-physiological data, 10 hours for the 10 lab study participants and 20 hours for the 10 field study participants. The psycho-physiological data for two lab study participants was not recorded successfully for the entire session. Therefore, we will only present the analysis and results of the 72 valid interruption samples collected from the 8 other lab study participant. The distribution of interruptions is fairly constant per study, with an average of 9 ($\pm$1.6) per person for the 1h lab study and 13.9 ($\pm$2.7) for the 2h field study.

Psycho-Physiological Data

For both studies, we captured the psycho-physiological data with the same sensors and applied the same data cleaning and analysis steps. We discuss these in the following.

EEG and Eye. The raw signal from the EEG sensor is sampled at 512 Hz. We applied a 50 Hz notch filter to remove noise and then split the signal into five commonly used brain wave frequency bands using Matlab's pwelch function: α (8-12Hz), β (12- 30Hz), γ (30-80Hz), δ (0-4Hz), and θ (4-8Hz) [23]. Additionally, we computed fractions of all combinations of frequency bands and the two ratios $\theta/(\alpha+\beta)$ and $\beta/(\alpha+\theta)$ that have previously been shown to carry information on a person's mental activity [30, 32]. Following a technique suggested by Manilov [35], we extracted eye blinks from the raw signal using a Butterworth filter and a peak finding algorithm and calculated the number of eye blinks per time unit. Finally, we used the pre-computed Attention and Meditation signals from Neurosky and extracted the minimum, maximum, mean and standard deviation.

Skin and Heart. The EDA signal generally serves as a measure for arousal and has two main components, the low frequency tonic part that changes over a period of minutes and the higher frequency phasic part that changes within seconds [42]. After filtering noise by applying an exponential smoothing filter, we used a Butterworth filter to split the EDA signal into its tonic and phasic part. From the tonic signal we extracted the skin conductance level (SCL). From the phasic signal we extracted features related to the peaks, in particular the number of peaks per time unit, the mean and the sum of peak amplitudes, and also calculated the area under the curve (AUC). Based on the skin temperature data captured from the integrated thermometer, we extracted the mean temperature and amplitude features, such as the mean and maximum. Based on the captured BVP data we calculated several features, such as the number of peaks per time unit, the mean peak amplitude as well as the heart rate, its mean and variance. Finally, from the IBI, we computed features of heart rate variability, such as the standard deviation of the signal (SDNN) and the percentage of successive IBIs with a difference greater than 20ms (PNN20) and 50ms (PNN50) [34]. All extracted features have previously been linked to various cognitive and emotional states (see Related Work).

Normalization. Since we train our machine learning classifier across participants and psycho-physiological data is very individual, we normalized the data per participant. Therefore, we collected baseline measures during the time each participant watched the relaxing fish tank movie. Normalizing a feature's value for an interruption was then done by subtracting the feature's value calculated using the baseline data from the one calculated using the interruption data.

Interruption, Edit and Resumption Lag

To calculate interruption, edit and resumption lags for participants, we needed to capture five time stamps for each interruption: when the notification for the interruption occurred ($T_{notification}$), when the participant started to address the interruption ($T_{IntStart}$), when the participant finished with the interruption (T_{IntEnd}), when the participant continued to work on her or his primary task using a mouse click or a keyboard action ($T_{FirstInteract}$) and when the participant made the first edit after the interruption ($T_{FirstEdit}$). Interruption lag can then be calculated as $T_{IntStart} - T_{notification}$, resumption lag as $T_{FirstInteract} - T_{IntEnd}$ and edit lag as $T_{FirstEdit} - T_{IntEnd}$. We captured the notification and the interruption start and end with the tablet application. For the lab study, we captured the first interaction and edit with a monitoring software that we installed on the lab study computer and which recorded screen shots and logged mouse and keyboard actions. For the field study we captured the two time stamps by observing participants interactions.

Outcome Measures

To classify interruptibility, both the interruptibility ratings and the interruption lag could serve as ground truth. Although the interruption lag might seem to be a more objective measure, we decided to use the rating in the classification for two reasons. First, the majority of prior work used the same rating and we wanted to provide a comparable measure, and second, even though interruption lags and interruptibility ratings correlate, they are distributed differently. While ratings are distributed binomially, interruption lags are distributed exponentially. This supports our observation during the studies with some participants addressing notifications quickly, regardless of their interruptibility. Therefore we believe that the ratings represent the interruptibility more accurately and independent of the participant's interruption handling behavior.

Since we are also interested in examining whether mental load and interruptibility are positively correlated as previous work suggests [7] and whether interruptions during high mental load are more disturbing, we collected participants' ratings of mental load and perceived disturbance as secondary measures. In addition, we collected the interruption, edit and resumption lags as described above to examine findings of prior work on their relation to interruptibility.

RESULTS

In this section we report on the results of automatically measuring interruptibility using psycho-physiological sensors, the links between interruptibility, mental load and the various lags as well as on the timing and support for interruptions desired by participants.

Measuring Interruptibility

To investigate the use of psycho-physiological sensors for measuring the interruptibility of knowledge workers in a real-world context, we applied machine learning to the collected data in a post-hoc analysis. In particular, we are interested in classifying interruptibility into two states (interruptible or not) as well as a more fine-grained classification using five interruptibility states from highly interruptible to not at all interruptible. For the two state classification we categorized data ratings from 1 (highly interruptible) to 5 (not at all interruptible) into two groups by labeling data with ratings of 1 to 3 as interruptible and ratings 4 and 5 as not interruptible. This categorization results in software developers being interruptible in 75% of the samples (83% for the lab and 71% for the field study). For the five state analysis we labeled data with participants' five point ratings of interruptibility. We analyzed the two data sets collected from the lab study (n=72 interruption samples) and the field study (n=139) separately.

Time Window and Classification Algorithm

To examine which time window of psycho-physiological data per interruption works best for the classification, we applied machine learning to several time windows, ranging from ten seconds to three minutes all ending with the notification (see Figure 2). Taking into consideration two and five state classification as well as lab and field study results, a time window of ten seconds works generally better than longer ones, except for the five states case of the field study in which longer time windows perform better, probably due to more frequent noise artifacts. The results also show that there are no big differences in accuracy across various time windows. In addition, we examined the use of three different machine learning algorithms: Naïve Bayes, Decision Trees and Support Vector Machine based on Weka's implementations. Overall, Naïve Bayes outperformed the other two algorithms, which is why we will focus on Naïve Bayes in the following.

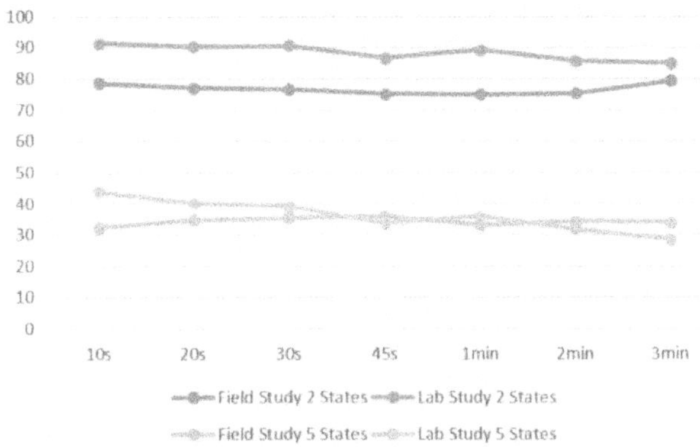

Figure 2. Classification accuracies for two and five categories using different time windows and Naïve Bayes.

Validation Methods

For the classification we used a Naïve Bayes implementation of the Weka machine learning framework [48]. We applied ten times ten-fold cross-validation, where instances of the participants were distributed randomly across the folds using stratification ('per instance' cross-validation). We chose this approach to investigate the feasibility of using psycho-physiological sensors to predict interruptibility for a development team. This method could be used in a real-world scenario by initially gathering about two hours of data per developer on the team to train a classifier and then using it to classify interruptibility based on real-time sensor data for developers on the team. To gather further insights on the generalizability and the sensitivity of the sensors across individuals, we also performed 'per participant' cross-validation. To prevent overfitting, we applied a nested correlation-based feature selection technique (Weka's CfsSubsetEval) that chooses features with high correlation with the class variable but low correlations among each other, using data from the training set of each fold.

Two and Five States Interruptibility

The results of our approach using Naïve Bayes and a ten second time window of psycho-physiological data for each interruption are presented in Table 1. For both validation methods, we calculated the accuracy, Cohen's Kappa and the standard deviation of the accuracies obtained during each fold and run. For both studies, we are able to classify the interruptibility at the sample points with high accuracy into two states (91.5% for the lab and 78.6% for the field study) as well as into five states (43.9% for the lab and 32.5%) for 'per instance' cross-validation. These classifiers perform significantly better than simple majority classifiers for both studies and number of states, except for five states classification in the field. We believe the lack of significance in the latter case is due to more frequent noise artifacts in the field that make it more difficult to distinguish between the finer grained levels. On the other hand, 'per participant' cross-validation does not result in a significant performance difference compared to a majority classifier and reveals a large variance among participants.

Tables 2 and 3 show the confusion matrices for the classification per instance, along with F-measures depicting individual class prediction performance. White cells indicate correct

	Prediction	
Truth	interruptible	not interruptible
interruptible	58.9 / 88.2	1.1 / 10.8
not interruptible	5 / 19	7 / 21
F_{lab}	0.95	0.70
F_{field}	0.86	0.58

Table 2. Confusion matrix for Naïve Bayes classification into two states using per instance cross-validation for lab and field study (lab / field) with individual class accuracies (F-measure)

	Prediction				
Truth	1	2	3	4	5
1	1.2 / 2.4	1.9 / 12.4	2.8 / 2.2	1.1 / 1	0 / 1
2	1.5 / 3.2	9.5 / 22	13.4 / 6.5	0.5 / 2.3	0.1 / 11
3	1.9 / 2.9	7.7 / 12.7	18 / 5	0.4 / 3.1	0 / 11.3
4	1 / 1.9	2 / 4.3	1.2 / 6.6	0.2 / 5.3	2.6 / 6.9
5	0.1 / 0.1	0.1 / 2.3	1 / 1.7	1.1 / 0.5	2.7 / 10.4
F_{lab}	0.19	0.41	0.56	0.04	0.52
F_{field}	0.16	0.45	0.18	0.28	0.37

Table 3. Confusion matrix for Naïve Bayes classification into five states using per instance cross-validation for lab and field study (lab / field) with individual class accuracies (F-measure)

predictions, colored cells indicate wrong predictions, where darker cells correspond to more severe errors. For the classification into five states, the confusion matrix reveals that a great part of the errors is caused by prediction of an adjacent state, and only few errors are severe, which is very promising.

Table 4 presents the features that were selected at least once by the nested feature selection and for which classifier they were used for in the per instance classification. The table shows that β, γ and the mean temperature were valuable in all scenarios. EDA related features were only chosen for the lab study data, which might be due to the more frequent occurrence of noise artifacts in the field and the short time windows chosen. Overall, these results also show that all sensors can provide value for predicting interruptibility.

Interruptibility, Mental Load and Lags

In both studies, there were significant and high positive correlations between the participants' ratings of the perceived disturbance, the mental load and the interruptibility (Pearson's $r > 0.7$, $p<0.0001$). For instance, participants' ratings on interruptibility were highly correlated with ratings on mental load in the lab (r=0.815) and in the field (r=0.702), as well as with ratings on disruptiveness in the lab (r=0.807) and in the field (r=0.741). These high correlations support the often assumed link between mental load and interruptibility, that moments of low mental load are suitable for interruptions, and that interruptions during moments of low mental load are perceived less disturbing [7].

Interruptibility was also positively correlated with the interruption lag for the lab study (Pearson's r_{lab}=0.382, $p<0.001$) and the field study (r_{field}=0.282, $p<0.001$). Participants generally took advantage of the so-called negotiated interruption, with an average interruption lag of 30.4 seconds ($\pm$7.5) in the lab study, and 44.9 seconds ($\pm$6.7) in the field study. Furthermore, 17 of 20 participants commented that they use the interruption lag to finish the current edit in most cases, which

# States	Study	Per Instance Cross-Validation			Per Participant Cross-Validation			Majority Classifier
		Accuracy	Cohen's Kappa	Stdev	Accuracy	Cohen's Kappa	Stdev	Accuracy
Two	Lab	91.5%*	0.65	0.7	74.9%	-0.11	36.0	83.3%
	Field	78.6%*	0.44	1.3	69.4%	0.22	19.7	70.7%
Five	Lab	43.9%*	0.18	2.9	37.6%	0.11	21.7	38.9%
	Field	32.5%	0.13	2.1	28.2%	0.07	14.2	32.4%

Table 1. Classification results by number of states and study (* indicates that there is a significant difference in accuracy to the majority classifier).

Sensor	Used Features
EEG	α [2L, 5L], α/γ [2F], α/δ [2F], β [2L, 2F, 5L, 5F], β/α [2L, 2F, 5L], β/γ [2F, 5F], β/δ [2F, 5F], β/θ [2L, 5L], γ [2L, 2F, 5L, 5F], γ/α [2L, 2F, 5L], γ/β [2F, 5F], γ/δ [2F, 5F], γ/θ [2F, 5L], δ [5L], δ/β [2L, 5L], δ/γ [2L, 2F, 5L], δ/θ [2L, 5F], θ [2L], θ/α [2L], θ/δ [2L], $\beta/(\alpha+\theta)$ [2F, 5F], Mean Attention [2F, 5F], Stdev Attention [2F], Min Meditation [2L]
Photoplethys-mograph	Mean Peak Amplitude BVP [2F], Sum Peak Amplitude BVP [2L, 5L], Max Peak Amplitude BVP [5F], Mean HR [2F], IBI PNN20 [2L, 2F], IBI NN50 [2F],
Temperature	Mean Temperature [2L, 2F, 5L, 5F]
EDA	Mean Phasic Peak Amplitude EDA [2L, 5L], Sum Phasic Peak Amplitude EDA [2L, 5L], Phasic Peak Frequency EDA [2L, 5L]

Table 4. Most predictive features for Naïve Bayes classification for per instance cross-validation, and their use in the classifiers (2L/2F: lab/field study two states, 5L/5F: lab/field study five states).

overlaps with Fogarty et al.'s finding that participants externalize their working memory before addressing a negotiated interruption [18]. These findings—the positive correlation between interruptibility and interruption lag and the evidence for a longer interruption lag corresponding to a higher working memory load—further support the link between interruptibility and working memory load and thus mental load.

Researchers also found a possible link between resumption/edit lag and interruption lag or interruptibility [44]. We did not find any strong support for this link across studies. There was only a significant correlation between resumption and interruption lag (r=0.275, p=0.001) in the field study and a significant correlation between edit and interruption lag (r=0.251, p=0.04) in the lab study. No other significant correlations at the level of 0.05 (two-sided) were found, including correlations with participants' ratings of interruptibility, mental load or disruptiveness.

Interruption Timing and Support

We used the follow-up interviews to learn more about the cost of interruptions at certain moments and possible tool support. In particular, we asked participants to rate certain situations that we identified in previous literature from 1 (strongly like) to 5 (strongly dislike) and found that, similar to findings of previous studies, participants like interruptions at the end of a task (1.5$\pm$0.6) but not in the middle (4$\pm$0.7), as well as they dislike them when the mental load is high (5$\pm$0) and/or the current task is difficult (4.4$\pm$0.9). In situations where participants are stuck and are not making any progress, they feel more mixed about interruptions (2.9$\pm$1.2) and several participants mentioned to dislike interruptions in these situations although they stated that interruptions would usually be beneficial for their task and for gaining a different perspective.

When we asked participants about the kind of support they desired for interruptions, they mentioned a tool that displays your interruptibility to co-workers, for instance, by using a lamp (mentioned by 7 participants), and a tool that turns interruptions on or off based on the current mental load (mentioned by 5 participants). In particular, support for in-person interruptions is more needed than for computer based ones since they are generally perceived more disruptive and cannot be ignored. However, participants also commonly mentioned that important interruptions should not be blocked even in situations of extremely high mental load, and that the company culture should be respected by the tool, e.g., a tool should not prevent interactions that foster team spirit.

DISCUSSION

The primary focus of the presented work was to investigate the use of psycho-physiological sensors to measure the interruptibility of knowledge workers in a real-world context. The results from our lab and our field study show that using these sensors, we are able to generate machine learning classifiers that can identify a software developer's state of interruptibility—for two as well as five states–with high accuracy. The fact that the results for the lab study are better than the ones for the field study is possibly an indicator for the effect that external influences can have on such sensors, but might also stem from the different sample sizes. The poor performance of 'per participant' cross-validation indicates the high sensitivity of psycho-physiological sensors to individual differences. We assume that much more data is needed to investigate whether it is possible to generalize interruptibility classification using psycho-physiological sensors across different individuals. We believe that our primary choice of 'per instance' cross-validation, for which we train a classifier with data from one team, represents a reasonable trade-off between effort, limitations and value and is applicable in a real-world scenario.

The overall high accuracy for both studies, the task variety and real-world office environment in the field study as well as the use of representative real-world tasks in the lab study, show that these sensors have great potential for measuring interruptibility in a real-world context. As main usage we imagine to display the interruptibility state in real-time via a "traffic light" lamp or IM status, which can potentially help avoiding costly personal interruptions at inopportune moments. Another possibility is to automatically adapt notification settings based on the current interruptibility, where the priority of interruptions has to be taken into account to not miss important ones. Especially the small time windows of ten seconds required to measure interruptibility with a high accuracy show that these sensors provide the possibility of a real time interruptibility index that can be used for such purposes.

Although our studies were limited to the software development domain, the mobility of these sensors allows for their use in a broad range of domains without being bound to a specific task, computer platform or location and are technically less restrictive than more context-aware sensors, such as a table top sensor or computer interaction monitors (e.g., [18, 43]). We believe that our results are therefore an encouraging step in the use of such sensors in a real-world work context and warrant further research on applying these sensors to a broader range of knowledge workers.

The results show that measures from the EEG, Photoplethysmograph, temperature and EDA sensors can all provide valuable information for classifying interruptibility. While EEG measures were selected for all classifiers, the EEG headband might be too obtrusive for long-term use. In future work, we plan to examine the use of subsets of sensors over longer periods of time to achieve a high accuracy and usability.

In addition to providing evidence for the benefits of using these sensors to measure interruptibility, the results of our study also confirm previous results on the correlation between mental load and interruptibility [7, 26], the link between interruption lag and interruptibility in setups with negotiated interruptions [18], and the findings that interruptions at task-boundaries are less disruptive [5].

CONCLUSION

In this work we investigated the use of psycho-physiological sensors to automatically classify the interruptibility of knowledge workers in a real-world context. We conducted two studies, a lab and a field study, in which we captured the psycho-physiological data of twenty participants for a total of 30 hours and interrupted them at random times. Using a Naïve Bayes classifier, we are able to predict the interruptibility of participants with high accuracy, improving significantly upon a majority classifier. Our results also confirm previous findings on the positive correlation between interruptibility and mental load, which further supports the use of psycho-physiological sensors that have already been shown to indicate states of mental load in other studies.

For future work, we aim at designing and prototyping tool support leveraging the predictive power of psycho-physiological sensors to help knowledge workers with their management of interruptions. Based on the interviews of our study, such support is highly desired for direct interruptions from co-workers, but also for computer-based interruptions, such as e-mails and instant messages.

ACKNOWLEDGMENTS

The authors would like to thank all study participants. This work was funded in part by SNF and an ABB research grant.

REFERENCES

1. Adamczyk, P. D., and Bailey, B. P. If not now, when?: the effects of interruption at different moments within task execution. In *Proc. CHI'04* (2004).
2. Altmann, E. M., and Trafton, J. G. Memory for goals: An activation-based model. *Cognitive science 26*, 1 (2002).
3. Altmann, E. M., and Trafton, J. G. Task interruption: Resumption lag and the role of cues. Tech. rep., DTIC Document, 2004.
4. Arroyo, E., and Selker, T. Attention and intention goals can mediate disruption in human-computer interaction. In *Proc. INTERACT'11*. 2011, 454–470.
5. Bailey, B. P., and Iqbal, S. T. Understanding changes in mental workload during execution of goal-directed tasks and its application for interruption management. *ACM TOCHI 14*, 4 (2008).
6. Bailey, B. P., and Konstan, J. A. On the need for attention-aware systems: Measuring effects of interruption on task performance, error rate, and affective state. *Computers in Human Behavior 22*, 4 (2006).
7. Bailey, B. P., Konstan, J. A., and Carlis, J. V. The effects of interruptions on task performance, annoyance, and anxiety in the user interface. In *Proc. INTERACT'01* (2001), 593–601.
8. Beatty, J. Task-evoked pupillary responses, processing load, and the structure of processing resources. *Psychological bulletin 91*, 2 (1982).
9. Berger, H. Uber das elektrenkephalogramm des menschen. *Archiv für Psychiatrie und Nervenkrankheiten 87*, 1 (1929), 527–570.
10. Böhmer, M., Lander, C., Gehring, S., Brumby, D. P., and Krüger, A. Interrupted by a phone call: exploring designs for lowering the impact of call notifications for smartphone users. In *Proc. CHI'14*, ACM (2014).
11. Boucsein, W. *Electrodermal activity*. Springer, 2012.
12. Chen, D., Hart, J., and Vertegaal, R. Towards a physiological model of user interruptability. In *INTERACT'07*. Springer, 2007.
13. Chen, D., and Vertegaal, R. Using mental load for managing interruptions in physiologically attentive user interfaces. In *Ext. Abstract CHI'04*, ACM (2004).
14. Collet, C., Vernet-Maury, E., Delhomme, G., and Dittmar, A. Autonomic nervous system response patterns specificity to basic emotions. *Journal of the autonomic nervous system 62*, 1-2 (1997).
15. Conard, M. A., and Marsh, R. Single and multiple interruptions increase task performance time, but don't affect stress, pressure or flow. 2010.
16. Czerwinski, M., Horvitz, E., and Wilhite, S. A diary study of task switching and interruptions. In *Proc. CHI'04* (2004).
17. Fogarty, J., Hudson, S. E., Atkeson, C. G., Avrahami, D., Forlizzi, J., Kiesler, S., Lee, J. C., and Yang, J. Predicting human interruptibility with sensors. *ACM TOCHI 12*, 1 (2005).

18. Fogarty, J., Ko, A. J., Aung, H. H., Golden, E., Tang, K. P., and Hudson, S. E. Examining task engagement in sensor-based statistical models of human interruptibility. In *Proc. CHI'05*, ACM (2005).
19. Gevins, A., Smith, M. E., Leong, H., McEvoy, L., Whitfield, S., Du, R., and Rush, G. Monitoring working memory load during computer-based tasks with eeg pattern recognition methods. *Human Factors: The Journal of the Human Factors and Ergonomics Society 40*, 1 (1998).
20. González, V. M., and Mark, G. Constant, constant, multi-tasking craziness: managing multiple working spheres. In *Proc. CHI'04*, ACM (2004).
21. Grimes, D., Tan, D. S., Hudson, S. E., Shenoy, P., and Rao, R. P. Feasibility and pragmatics of classifying working memory load with an electroencephalograph. In *Proc. CHI'08*, ACM (2008).
22. Haapalainen, E., Kim, S., Forlizzi, J. F., and Dey, A. K. Psycho-physiological measures for assessing cognitive load. In *Proc. Ubicomp*, ACM (2010).
23. Handy, T. C. *Event-related potentials: a methods handbook*. MIT Press, 2005.
24. Ho, J., and Intille, S. S. Using context-aware computing to reduce the perceived burden of interruptions from mobile devices. In *Proc. CHI'05*, ACM (2005).
25. Hudson, S., Fogarty, J., Atkeson, C., Avrahami, D., Forlizzi, J., Kiesler, S., Lee, J., and Yang, J. Predicting human interruptibility with sensors: a wizard of oz feasibility study. In *Proc. CHI'03*, ACM (2003).
26. Iqbal, S. T., and Bailey, B. P. Investigating the effectiveness of mental workload as a predictor of opportune moments for interruption. In *Ext. Abstract CHI'05*, ACM (2005).
27. Iqbal, S. T., and Bailey, B. P. Leveraging characteristics of task structure to predict the cost of interruption. In *Proc. CHI'06*, ACM (2006).
28. Iqbal, S. T., Zheng, X. S., and Bailey, B. P. Task-evoked pupillary response to mental workload in human-computer interaction. In *Ext. Abstracts CHI'04*, ACM (2004).
29. Jacob, R. J., and Karn, K. S. Eye tracking in human-computer interaction and usability research: Ready to deliver the promises. *Mind 2*, 3 (2003), 4.
30. Kramer, A. F. Physiological metrics of mental workload: A review of recent progress. *Multiple-task Performance* (1991).
31. Kruglanski, A. W. Lay epistemic theory in social-cognitive psychology. *Psychological Inquiry 1*, 3 (1990).
32. Lee, J. C., and Tan, D. S. Using a low-cost electroencephalograph for task classification in hci research. In *Proc. UIST'06*, ACM (2006).
33. Lemaire, P. The role of working memory resources in simple cognitive arithmetic. *European Journal of Cognitive Psychology 8*, 1 (1996).
34. Malik, M., Bigger, J. T., Camm, A. J., Kleiger, R. E., Malliani, A., Moss, A. J., and Schwartz, P. J. Heart rate variability standards of measurement, physiological interpretation, and clinical use. *European heart journal 17*, 3 (1996).
35. Manoilov, P. Eye-blinking artefacts analysis. In *Proc. Compsystech* (2007), 52.
36. Mathan, S., Whitlow, S., Dorneich, M., Ververs, P., and Davis, G. Neurophysiological Estimation of Interruptibility: Demonstrating Feasibility in a Field Context. In *Proc. ICACS'07* (2007).
37. McFarlane, D. Comparison of four primary methods for coordinating the interruption of people in human-computer interaction. *Human-Computer Interaction 17*, 1 (2002).
38. Monk, C. A., Trafton, J. G., and Boehm-Davis, D. A. The effect of interruption duration and demand on resuming suspended goals. *Journal of Experimental Psychology: Applied 14*, 4 (2008), 299.
39. Nourbakhsh, N., Wang, Y., Chen, F., and Calvo, R. A. Using galvanic skin response for cognitive load measurement in arithmetic and reading tasks. In *Proc. OzCHI'12*, ACM (2012).
40. Parnin, C., and Rugaber, S. Resumption strategies for interrupted programming tasks. *Software Quality Journal 19*, 1 (2011).
41. Peper, E., Harvey, R., Lin, I.-M., Tylova, H., and Moss, D. Is there more to blood volume pulse than heart rate variability, respiratory sinus arrhythmia, and cardiorespiratory synchrony? *Biofeedback 35*, 2 (2007).
42. Schmidt, S., and Walach, H. Electrodermal activity (eda): State-of-the-art measurement and techniques for parapsychological purposes. *Journal of Parapsychology 63*, 3 (1999).
43. Tani, T., and Yamada, S. Estimating user interruptibility by measuring table-top pressure. In *Ext. Abstracts CHI'13*, ACM (2013).
44. Trafton, J. G., Altmann, E. M., Brock, D. P., and Mintz, F. E. Preparing to resume an interrupted task: Effects of prospective goal encoding and retrospective rehearsal. *International Journal of Human-Computer Studies 58*, 5 (2003).
45. van Solingen, R., Berghout, E., and van Latum, F. Interrupts: just a minute never is. *IEEE software 15*, 5 (1998).
46. Vinkers, C. H., Penning, R., Hellhammer, J., Verster, J. C., Klaessens, J. H., Olivier, B., and Kalkman, C. J. The effect of stress on core and peripheral body temperature in humans. *Stress 16*, 5 (2013).
47. Wilson, G. F. An analysis of mental workload in pilots during flight using multiple psychophysiological measures. *The International Journal of Aviation Psychology 12*, 1 (2002).
48. Witten, I. H., and Frank, E. *Data Mining: Practical machine learning tools and techniques*. Morgan Kaufmann, 2005.

iSkin: Flexible, Stretchable and Visually Customizable On-Body Touch Sensors for Mobile Computing

Martin Weigel[1], Tong Lu[2], Gilles Bailly[3], Antti Oulasvirta[4], Carmel Majidi[2], Jürgen Steimle[1]
[1] Max Planck Institute for Informatics and Saarland University, Saarbrücken, Germany;
[2] Carnegie Mellon University, Pittsburgh, Pennsylvania, United States;
[3] CNRS LTCI, Telecom-ParisTech, Paris, France; [4] Aalto University, Helsinki, Finland;
{mweigel, jsteimle}@mpi-inf.mpg.de, {tlv, cmajidi}@andrew.cmu.edu,
gilles.bailly@telecom-paristech.fr, antti.oulasvirta@aalto.fi

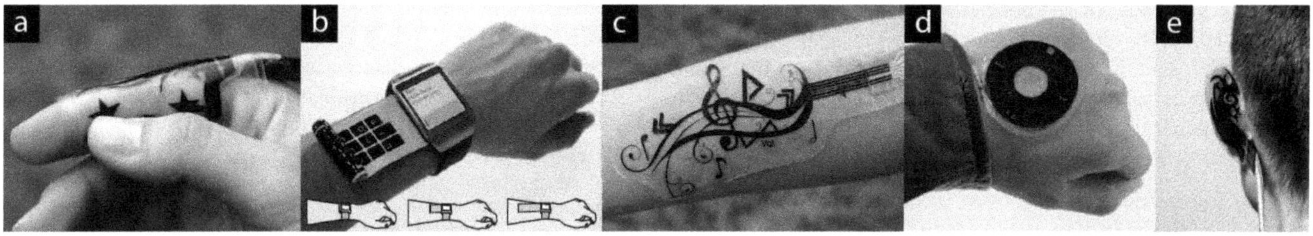

Figure 1. iSkin is a thin, flexible, stretchable and visually customizable touch sensor that can be worn directly on the skin. We present three novel classes of on-body devices based on iSkin: (a) *FingerStrap*, exemplified here with a strap on the index finger for fast, one-handed control of incoming calls; (b) *Extensions for wearable devices*, exemplified here with a rollout keyboard attached to a smart watch; and *SkinStickers*, exemplified here with (c) an input surface for a music player attached to the forearm, (d) a click wheel on the back of the hand and (e) a headset control behind the ear.

ABSTRACT
We propose *iSkin*, a novel class of skin-worn sensors for touch input on the body. iSkin is a very thin sensor overlay, made of biocompatible materials, and is flexible and stretchable. It can be produced in different shapes and sizes to suit various locations of the body such as the finger, forearm, or ear. Integrating capacitive and resistive touch sensing, the sensor is capable of detecting touch input with two levels of pressure, even when stretched by 30% or when bent with a radius of 0.5 cm. Furthermore, iSkin supports single or multiple touch areas of custom shape and arrangement, as well as more complex widgets, such as sliders and click wheels. Recognizing the social importance of skin, we show visual design patterns to customize functional touch sensors and allow for a visually aesthetic appearance. Taken together, these contributions enable new types of on-body devices. This includes finger-worn devices, extensions to conventional wearable devices, and touch input stickers, all fostering direct, quick, and discreet input for mobile computing.

Author Keywords
On-body input; Mobile computing; Wearable computing; Touch input; Stretchable, flexible sensor; Electronic skin.

CHI 2015, April 18 – 23 2015, Seoul, Republic of Korea
Copyright is held by the owner/author(s). Publication rights licensed to ACM.
ACM 978-1-4503-3145-6/15/04...$15.00
http://dx.doi.org/10.1145/2702123.2702391

ACM Classification Keywords
H.5.2. Information interfaces and presentation: User Interfaces – Input devices and strategies

INTRODUCTION
The human skin is recognized as a promising input surface for interactions with mobile and wearable devices. However, it has been difficult to design and implement touch sensors that can be placed directly on the skin. We present iSkin, an input surface for mobile human-computer interaction on the human body. iSkin is a thin, soft, flexible, stretchable and visually customizable overlay that is worn directly on the skin. It is custom-shaped and can be attached at many different locations on the body. The interactive surface is "always available" and allows for quick and discreet interactions — either standalone or as an input surface for other mobile devices. Its unique properties open up new possibilities for mobile interaction that have not been possible with existing hardware. Figure 1 shows example applications of our current implementation. One example is a very thin, yet large input area, which can be wrapped around a finger and is stretchable enough to be worn over joints. It features three touch buttons of the size of a fingertip and one linear slider with five elements. It allows for fast and direct control of mobile devices using touch input even when the hands are busy.

iSkin relates to the emerging stream of on-body interaction, e.g. [1, 6, 8, 9, 10, 16, 24, 35, 36]. It is technically based on advances in electronic skin (e-skin) and soft-matter electronics [7, 18, 30, 33], an active research field in robotics and material science. To our knowledge, our work is the first investigation into how electronic skin can be used for on-body interactions to control mobile computing devices; this includes interactive scenarios, sensing techniques, form factors and device types as well as aesthetics. We present the following main contributions:

1) The implementation of touch-sensitive iSkin, a biocompatible, stretchable soft-matter sensor. It combines capacitive and resistive sensing with a new electrode design to sense touch input with two levels of pressure. An electrode size of 8 mm led to a high signal-to-noise ratio. Study results show that the sensor remains functional under typical and extreme deformations that occur on the human body and accurately senses touch input when worn on various body locations.

2) We address visual aesthetics of the sensor, considering the important role of aesthetics for any body-worn accessory (e.g., [19, 37]). Our sensing approach is visually customizable to support aesthetic designs; the conductive traces and electrodes act as (part of) the visual artwork. This paper contributes general design patterns for sensor designers to convert graphical designs into a functional touch sensor.

3) We implement novel types of skin-worn devices, in order to explore usage and interaction scenarios of iSkin (Figure 1). These devices highlight different locations and contexts of use, different form factors, and different interactions.

The remainder of the paper starts with a review of related work, before we introduce design goals for skin-worn touch sensors. Next we present the implementation of the sensor and discuss how to realize visually aesthetic sensors. We show application examples and results from two evaluation studies. We conclude with a critical discussion on outstanding challenges for skin-worn touch sensors.

RELATED WORK

Our research is informed by prior work in the areas of electronic skin and on-skin input:

Electronic Skin

iSkin is based on recent advances in electronic skin (e-skin). E-skin makes the "effort to create an artificial skin with human-like sensory capabilities" [7]. Research in this area started with the seminal work of Lumelsky et al. [18] and Someya et al. [33]. Primary fields of study include multimodal sensor skins that allow robots to better sense their direct environment; soft prostheses that are capable of sensing contact, pressure or temperature; and health-monitoring devices [41].

Advances in e-skin [7, 32, 30] and materials science now allow for exploration of a novel application domain: on-body interaction for mobile computing. iSkin is the first investigation into this domain for the field of HCI, introducing e-skin into the recent stream of on-body interactions. Compared with temporary tattoos [14] or in the future possibly even implants [12], a skin overlay is easily attachable and detachable, which in our opinion is an important factor for its success as a consumer product.

In the materials science community, first proofs of concept have shown the technical feasibility of sensor overlays for touch sensing on the body [15, 17, 42]. Kramer et al. presented a pressure sensitive skin overlay composed of PDMS embedded with microfluidic channels of eutectic gallium-indium (EGaIn) alloy [15]. Lu et al. [17] have demonstrated the feasibility of patterning cPDMS with a laser engraver to produce an alternative to EGaIn for soft-matter sensors and circuits. This allows for tactile sensing through direct electrical contact between the circuit and human skin. However, sensing with exposed electrodes is not very reliable because skin conductance heavily varies between users and electrodes might become stained or worn through skin contact, increasing resistivity over time. Woo et al. demonstrated pressure and strain measurements using a compressible layer of EcoFlex [42]. While the measurement is continuous, the sensor is unable to differentiate between pressure and strain. Furthermore, this approach relies on microcontact printing and cleanroom microfabrication and therefore lacks possibilities for rapid customization. Our sensor adds to this body of research by capturing two levels of normal force independently of how much it is stretched, an important requirement for robust on-body input. Moreover, it is compatible with rapid prototyping in a simple lab environment and can be visually customized for an aesthetic appearance.

On-Skin Input

The HCI community has presented several sensing techniques to capture input on the skin for interaction with mobile devices. Prior work can be split into four sensing approaches. One is camera-based sensing, with RGB cameras [20, 36] or depth cameras [3, 8, 9, 21]. This allows for interacting directly on the skin, but requires direct line-of-sight to a camera and is susceptible to lighting conditions. Second, bio-acoustic sensors [10] work on many body locations and do not require a sensor overlay, at the cost of low spatial sensing resolution and single-touch-only sensing. A third approach consists of magnetic sensing [1] using magnets and Hall-effect sensor grids attached to the body. Those approaches do not require a skin overlay, but fall short in detecting precise touch-down and touch-up events. We designed iSkin to be thin and soft enough to retain much of the sensory stimulation that occurs naturally and upon touch. Finally, photo-reflective sensing [23] is based on two armbands with infrared reflective sensors. These are able to recognize deformations of skin, but do not recognize touch, which has been suggested to be the most important on-skin modality [40].

iSkin also relates to flexible sensors for smart clothing and wearables [13, 16, 27]; those support interaction in close proximity to, but not on, skin. In addition, iSkin is related to flexible touch sensors for use on objects [4, 28, 29]. These are well suited for rapid prototyping of input on non-planar surfaces. However, these approaches were not intended to be used on skin and thus are not elastic, biocompatible and robust enough for skin interaction. Finally, prior work has recognized the importance of aesthetics for body-worn interfaces [37]; we address this requirement with a visually customizable sensor.

DESIGN GOALS FOR iSKIN

This section outlines important requirements and opportunities for the design of skin-worn touch sensor overlays for mobile computing. While prior work on electronic skin has focused on addressing questions related to skin-compatibility of materials, sensing modalities and data processing, we introduce several new dimensions that are of critical importance when the sensor overlay is used as a human-computer interface. This includes locations of use, form factors of devices, visual appearance as well as input and output for control of computing devices. These goals guide our design and implementation of iSkin.

1. Skin Compatibility: The human skin is a living organ. Poorly designed sensor patches could adversely affect its physiological functions, including protection, thermal regulation, sweating, bacterial ecosystem, oxygen intake, and sensation. iSkin should be non-toxic, and easily cleanable, washable, or replaceable in order to limit the accumulation of pathogens such as bacteria. Moreover, the properties of skin vary greatly. These include thickness, stretchability (around 20%[30]), wrinkliness, oiliness, and the distribution of receptors, sweat glands, and hair follicles, which vary both across body locations and across individuals. This requires materials and adhesives that are compatible with natural skin and exhibit a high variability of form factors. iSkin should be as thin as possible to fit closely to the skin and to support localizable tactile feedback upon pressing the sensor. Moreover, iSkin needs to be lightweight, soft, flexible and stretchable to be worn comfortably during movement, stay in place and resist external stress.

2. Locations: iSkin should support placement on arbitrary locations on the body. Informed by previous work, we distinguish three primary locations:

1) Hand. If placed on the palm, sensors need to be thin and flexible to bear strong deformations. The back of the hand is less deformable. Both dorsal and palmar aspects of the hand are promising for interaction with a smartwatch [21], remote devices [3] or imaginary devices [6]. Fingers are another promising location. Prior work has started to explore wearable finger input with, for example, fingernail displays [34] and fingertip interaction [1]. However, these solutions augment only a specific part of a finger, are rigid, and are still quite thick. In contrast, iSkin can be applied over the entire finger, including the joints.

2) Arm. The forearm and upper arm provide a large surface that is often uncovered. While the forearm is easy to access, deemed socially acceptable [38] and a preferred location to touch [40], the upper arm is less preferred for touching [40].

3) Head. iSkin can be attached to the face, for instance on the cheek for capturing touch inputs with a head-mounted-display [31] or digital jewelry. It also can be worn on less visible areas, such as behind the ear (see also [16, 36]).

We demonstrate that iSkin can be worn on these locations. In addition, its flexibility allows for exploration of other on-body locations as well as use underneath or on top of clothing.

3. Device Types and Form Factors: iSkin should be easy to attach and detach, regardless of the location on the body, yet robust to movement and wear. It allows for multiple novel device types: First, it can be wrapped around a body part, similarly to a bracelet or ring (Figure 1a). Unlike rigid electronics, iSkin can be placed close to or on joints due to its stretchability. Second, iSkin can be affixed to body-worn devices (e.g. a smart-watch, Figure 1b), accessories or smart clothes (e.g. [13]). In these cases, the flexibility and stretchability of iSkin allows for rolling and folding, enlarging it on demand for larger input surfaces. Finally, iSkin can be attached directly on the skin (e.g. Figure 1c–e), similar to a patch. Skin-friendly adhesives used for cosmetics and the medical domain can be used to allow for an easy attachment. The size of devices needs to be scalable and their shape adaptable to be worn on many different locations of the body and to suit the highly varying anthropometric distributions of people with different geometries. The thin-film material of iSkin could even support ad-hoc customization through cutting, as proposed in [26].

4. Visual Customization: Visual appearance is an important requirement for social acceptability. The appearance of skin is observed by others, signaling traits related to personality, health, and social status. Many cultures have developed sophisticated traditions of decorating the skin. iSkin should thus be inconspicuous, for instance by making most parts transparent, but also customizable and aesthetically pleasing. The possibilities for aesthetic design include visual ornaments and designs inspired by the existing cultures of body art, such as tattoos and jewelry.

5. Input: iSkin should provide sufficient control to let users quickly and accurately perform input commands on the sensor surface. The sensor should also avoid accidental activation. The input possibilities include, at minimum, touch, multi-touch, pressure, and proximity sensing. Our iSkin implementation is presently able to detect two-level touch input with precise touch-down and touch-up events. Moreover, the wiring principles enable flexible layouts of input regions. This allows for multiple interaction elements, such as sliders, rotation wheels and other useful widgets.

6. Output: iSkin itself is an input interface. It allows for static visual guidance by indicating interactive areas. However, due to the flexible placement of the sensor, and especially if coupled with wireless communication, it can be combined with many additional output devices: smartphones, smartwatches, laptops, or nearby computers.

7. Interfacing and Processing: The sensor is connected with a controlling unit, which processes sensor data, supplies energy, and communicates with a nearby computer device. Advances in thin-film electronics suggest that in the future these are very likely realizable in flex and can be embedded within the flexible sensor. Presently such components need to be realized as rigid, conventional components. Scaled down, the rigid components could be attached right onto the sensor surface. While interfacing and processing is not the focus of our paper, we show that a fully functional and mobile system can be realized today.

Taking these design goals into account, realizing a touch-sensitive skin overlay is a challenging endeavor. While flexibility alone poses demands that go well beyond conventional rigid electronics, stretchability adds further significant challenges. This calls for using different base materials and new elastic conductors, novel electrode designs for soft-matter electronics and adaptation of sensing techniques. In the next section, we present the implementation of touch-sensitive iSkin that fulfills the key goals outlined in this section.

iSKIN SENSOR

This section describes manufacturing steps and our sensing implementation of touch-sensitive iSkin. We first introduce PDMS and cPDMS as promising soft matter materials for elastic user interfaces in HCI and describe how to produce and process these materials in a simple lab environment. Knowing about these materials might be helpful for the HCI community for realizing all sorts of elastic user interfaces beyond our concrete sensor implementation. Then we contribute a sensor design for capacitive and resistive sensing of on-skin touch input. Our approach is capable of distinguishing between two levels of pressure, allows for sensing of precise touch down and up events, supports flexibly shaped and freely arranged interactive areas, and last but not least, is very robust to stretching and bending.

Materials

iSkin is made of multiple layers of thin, flexible and stretchable silicone. The base material is polydimethylsiloxane (PDMS), an easy-to-process silicone-based organic polymer. PDMS is fully transparent, elastic, and a highly biocompatible material. Therefore it is widely used on or in the human body, for example in body implants. It has also been used for soft matter electronics in HCI. It is not conductive.

An elastic conductor can be realized by filling PDMS with carbon black particles, yielding cPDMS (carbon-filled PDMS). The carbon particles make the material appear black and opaque. PDMS and cPDMS are permeable to oxygen, but cPDMS does not oxidize at room temperature. Therefore the electrical resistance of the electrodes remains fairly stable over time.

Compared with other elastic conductors, such as liquid phase conductors [15], conductive meshes [11], or AgPDMS [17], cPDMS is very cheap, can be realized in a thinner form factor and neither encapsulates nor exposes harmful substances.

The cost of material for a letter-sized sheet is about $1. Therefore the sensor patch can be designed for one-time use, if desired. Alternatively, it can be used for a longer time without problems, as the material is robust, can be cleaned with water and can even be disinfected for hygienic reuse.

Fabrication

iSkin is easy to fabricate, both for prototyping purposes and in industrial production. PDMS is produced by mixing a silicone elastomer base with a silicone elastomer-curing agent (both from Sylgard 184; Dow Corning, Inc.) in a weight ratio of 10:1. For cPDMS, 13% (by weight) of acetylene carbon black powder (Alfa Aesar) is added to the uncured mixture of PDMS (weight ratio 20:1). The material can be formed to thin films using a spin-coater or thin-film applicator. We found that it helps to make the cPDMS film very thin ($\approx 100\,\mu m$), as this reduces sedimentation of the carbon black powder to the bottom of the film during curing, which would result in a lower conductivity.

The functional sensor is produced with laser-patterning using a method introduced in [17]. Figure 2 shows the composite structure of our sensor, which is composed of PDMS and cPDMS layers. Before application, the layers are laser-patterned to create conductive lines and electrodes (in cPDMS) or insulating areas (in PDMS). We use a 30W laser engraver from Universal Laser Systems (VLS 3.50) for patterning. Each layer is bonded to the composite by adding a very thin layer of uncured PDMS as connective glue. As soon as the PDMS is cured, the layers are firmly attached. To increase breathability, the final sensor could be perforated as described in [39].

On-Body Touch Sensing

Sensing touch input on the body with cPDMS faces multiple challenges. First and foremost, cPDMS is a very poor conductor. Its resistance is as high as $100\,\Omega\,m$ [22] and further decreases when it is being stretched (it even takes several hours to go back to its initial resistance). Secondly, both capacitive and resistive sensing exhibit unique challenges: permanent contact with human skin results in added capacitive coupling, while the curvature of the body disallows using the standard approach for inter-layer spacing in resistive touch sensing. In the following, we address these challenges and show how to implement robust touch sensing. We present a soft-matter electrode design that supports both projected capacitance and resistive touch sensing. Both techniques give precise real-time information about touch down and up events. Both modes combined allow for distinguishing between two levels of touch pressure. In contrast, resistive sensing alone is less prone to accidental input, as more pressure is required to trigger a touch down event.

Electrode Design

Both sensing techniques share the same physical structure, illustrated in Figure 2a: two embedded electrodes are overlaid and held apart with a spacing layer. The embedded conductive traces and electrodes are realized with cPDMS. We use solid layers of PDMS on top and on the bottom to seal off the electrodes from contact with skin and the environment. PDMS is also used for the spacing layer in between both electrodes. The spacing layer is solid at areas where no electrodes are located; it is permeable in between electrodes, to allow for pressure creating a conductive connection. At areas where no electrodes or wires are laid out, only the transparent base layer needs to be realized. The sensor is very thin: from $190\,\mu m$ at areas where no electrodes or wires are laid out to approx. $700\,\mu m$ at locations where all layers are realized. Given the high resistance of cPDMS, conductive traces need to be fairly wide. We identified the minimal width of a trace for robust conductive connection to be 1 mm.

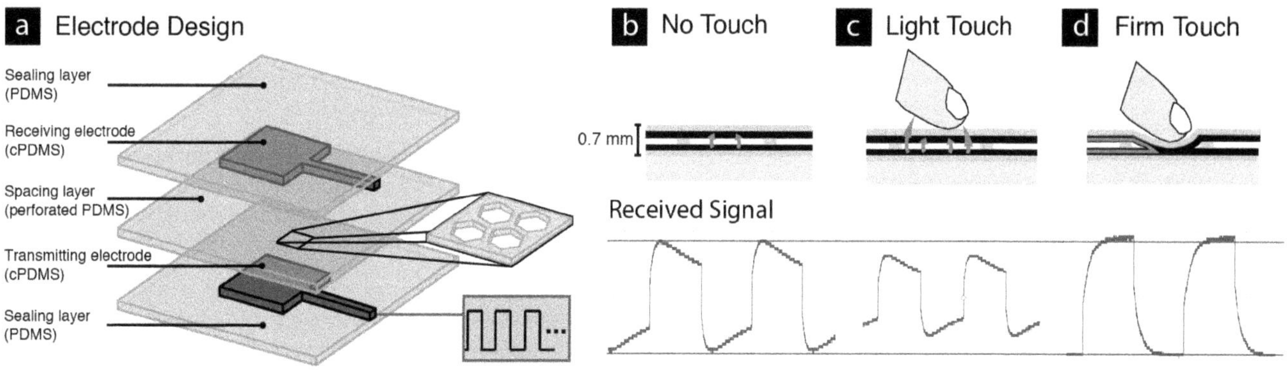

Figure 2. iSkin Touch Sensing: (a) Overview of layers in a touch-sensitive iSkin; (b) sensing without touch contact; (c) projected capacitive sensing of slight touch events; (d) resistive sensing of firm touch events.

Capacitive Sensing for Light Touch Contact

Projected capacitive sensing uses capacitive coupling between the two electrodes (Figure 2b). The bottom electrode connects to a 5 V square wave signal of 1.000 kHz generated by a wave generator (Agilent 33210A). If the sensor contains several separate touch-sensitive areas, the top electrodes are time-division multiplexed to sequentially measure the transmitted signal on each of them. The received signals are processed by a PC oscilloscope (PicoScope 6402A). Bringing a finger near the surface of the sensor changes the local electric field, which reduces the mutual capacitance. Therefore the signal amplitude decreases (Figure 2c). After calibration, the sensor can reliably detect touch events despite the high resistance of the conductor. The sensor needs to be calibrated after it is applied to the skin. It reacts on very slight touch contact, as known from commercial capacitive touch sensors.

Resistive Sensing for Firm Pressure

Resistive touch sensing relies on pressure to create a contact through the permeable spacing layer between both electrodes. A firm touch physically closes the circuit (Figure 2d). In this case, the waveform of the received signal on the upper electrode is changing, serving as a reliable indicator for firm touch.

To ensure both layers are reliably spaced apart even when they are curved or stretched, our solution uses uniform tiling with a hexagon pattern, similar to honeycombs. This improves the robustness against deformations occurring on the body while minimizing the required spacing material to decrease the required pressure for touch detection. For our prototypes we used a hexagon diameter of 1.5 mm.

Sensing of Two Levels of Touch Pressure

Combined projected capacitive and resistive sensing enables sensing of two levels of normal force: capacitive sensing detects light touches, while resistive sensing detects firm touches. The sensing techniques use the same physical electrode structure, the same sensing circuit and are performed in the same sensing cycle. Therefore, the frame rate of sensing is not reduced. Figure 2b–d shows an example of the values captured for light and firm touches.

Results from our technical evaluation below show that this approach is capable of reliably distinguishing between both pressure levels, independently of how much the sensor is stretched or bent. We consider this robust detection to be a very important requirement for successful on-body interfaces. While continuous normal force could in principle be captured using a force-sensitive resistor approach, sensor readings would be corrupted by large changes in resistance that result from stretching, which naturally occurs during use on human skin.

Interactive Widgets

The electrode design of both techniques allows for flexibly shaped interactive areas and senses precise touch down and touch up events. This allows for designing more complex widgets, such as sliders or click wheels. An example of a five-element slider is implemented in the FingerStrap (Figure 1a) and the EarSticker (Figure 1e), the click wheel as a WheelSticker (Figure 1d).

Interfacing and Data Processing

The flexible sensor patch is tethered with a ribbon cable to an Arduino-compatible microcontroller (Teensy 3.1), which is processing the data and driving the sensor. Signal measurements are time-division multiplexed with a frequency of 17 kHz. For interfacing, the sensor has a connector area, on which all pins are exposed. A custom-made rigid connector board is attached to these pins using z-axis conductive tape. Its other side is connected to wires leading to the microcontroller. An additional transparent adhesive tape on the top of the connector further stabilizes it and avoids lateral shifting of the connector board on the sensor. The connector area can be laid out anywhere on the sensor patch where no interactive area is located.

DESIGN PATTERNS FOR VISUALLY CUSTOMIZABLE SENSORS

Aesthetic visual appearance is a prime requirement for social acceptance of body-worn devices. Inspired by an example of an aesthetic sensor [5], we contribute guidelines for the development of sensors which integrate aesthetics and electronic functionality. These patterns help designers transfer an existing vector graphic into a functional sensor design. Electrodes and circuitry are laid out in a visually appealing way, following the vector graphic, while retaining their electronic functionality. Hence, the function of black cPDMS becomes two-fold: (1) providing electronic functionality, by serving as wires and electrodes for touch sensing, and (2) providing a visually appealing graphical design.

While we demonstrate these principles with cPDMS, they transfer to other conductors, such as AgPDMS, CNT-PDMS and printable inks.

Our design patterns work particularly well for connected line art, filled shapes, and silhouettes. In a first step, the designer chooses a black-and-white vector graphic to transfer into a sensor. Afterwards the graphic can be transferred into a functional sensor using a vector graphics application and the following patterns.

Fully Touch-Sensitive Graphic

To make all elements of the graphic (i.e. all black areas) touch-sensitive, the designer proceeds as follows: one pair of overlaid electrodes is created, each having the exact shape of the black part of the graphic (Figure 3a). Both electrodes are separately tethered to a connector area. To support resistive sensing, the spacing layer is perforated between the upper and lower electrodes. Hence, the entire graphic acts as one touch area. Note that the white parts of the original graphic appear transparent on the sensor and are insensitive to touch.

Correct electronic functionality puts some additional demands on the graphical design: the electrode must be one connected shape and all traces must be wide enough for a robust conductive connection. Hence, if the graphic contains disconnected components, these need to be connected with a trace. If a trace is too narrow, the designer can either scale up the entire graphic or dilate the narrow parts of the graphic. These visual changes are often subtle enough not to affect the overall appearance.

Partially Touch-Sensitive Graphic

If only some part of the graphic should be made touch-sensitive, the sensitive part can be implemented following the pattern above. Non-sensitive areas are realized with a solid spacing layer, in order to prevent resistive contact. To prevent capacitive sensing between the transmitting and the receiving electrode at non-sensitive areas, the design is slightly modified: instead of overlaying two electrodes with exactly the same shape, the visual design is realized by two non-overlapping electrodes. The top electrode realizes one half of the visual graphic, while the bottom electrode realizes the other one (Figure 3b). Due to the close proximity of the top and bottom layers, both parts appear as a uniform solid shape to the human eye.

Graphic with Multiple Sensitive Areas

Multiple touch-sensitive areas within one graphic can each be directly connected with the connector through separate traces (Figure 3c left). Some interactive areas are only addressable by having their trace go through another interactive area (Figure 3c right). In these cases the connection can be routed along the border of the area. This reduces the size of the interactive area, but leaves the visual appearance of the graphic unmodified.

Support of Fine Detail

Parts of the graphic that contain fine details, e.g. thin letters, ornaments or contours, cannot be made touch-sensitive if the visual elements are finer than the minimum width of conductive traces. While the details can still be realized and remain visible, they cannot act as a conductor for a robust connection and therefore remain insensitive.

One solution to support fine detail is to invert the graphic (Figure 3d top). The graphical elements are laid out in white while the surrounding area becomes black. Instead of the (fine) details, the (larger and wider) surrounding area is now sensitive to touch.

Another option is to add a layer of color on top of a black touch-sensitive area. This layer can add details and provide visual guidance without modifying the design of the interactive area. This allows, for example, adding labels for keys on the keyboard in Figure 3d bottom.

Non-Sensitive Visual Elements

It is possible to add insensitive visual elements, e.g., for aesthetic decoration (Figure 3e), for additional labels, or to create a coherent visual appearance. Such non-sensitive visual elements are added to the bottom electrode layer. As long as they are disconnected from other elements on the bottom layer and are not overlaid with elements on the top layer, they do not interfere with sensing.

Adjusting the Physical Shape of the Sensor

Lastly, a designer can freely choose the shape of the sensor by cutting the surrounding PDMS into the desired shape (Figure 3f). This allows for a better fit on various body parts but can also enhance the visual appearance of the sensor.

Summary

The above-mentioned patterns help designers to manually transfer a graphical design into a functional sensor. Figure 1 shows examples of sensors based on these patterns. Our presented iSkin designs use only black traces on a transparent base substrate. Future sensors could be colored by adding colored traces or areas to the (non-conductive) PDMS top layer of the sensor. A design environment for iSkin sensors can be created using the presented patterns. This environment could provide guidance to the designer, e.g., warning if traces are too narrow, or even (partially) automate the conversion of the vector graphic into a functional sensor.

APPLICATION EXAMPLES

iSkin enables several classes of interaction and supports various scenarios. We present prototypes of three novel on-body device classes. They support a wide variety of body locations demanding different sizes and shapes, different sensor designs and various degrees of flexibility and stretchability. They are organized in three groups, highlighting the flexibility in attachment of the sensor on the human skin: wrapping around body parts, attaching to on-body devices, and sticking onto the skin using biocompatible adhesives.

FingerStrap

The FingerStrap (Figure 1a) is a touch-sensitive film wrapped around the middle segment of the index finger to support microinteractions. Compared to ring-like devices, the strap

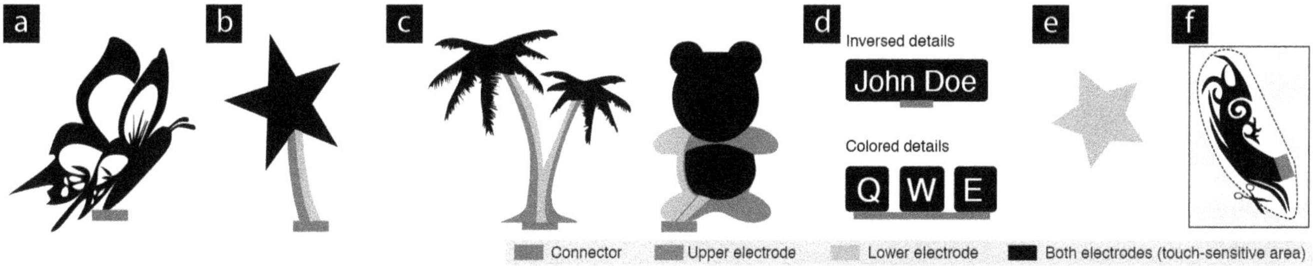

Figure 3. Design Patterns for Visual Customizations: (a) fully touch-sensitive graphic, (b) partially sensitive graphic, (c) graphic with multiple interactive areas, (d) touch-sensitive detail using inverse and color patterns, (e) non-sensitive visual elements, and (f) shape customization.

increases the input space by covering a larger area without preventing movements. It features three buttons and a touch slider with five sensitive areas, all integrated in a tattoo-like visual design. It uses resistive sensing to avoid accidental activation by requiring a certain limit of pressure. FingerStrap is especially useful when the hands are busy with a primary task (e.g. driving a car). It supports eyes-free input. Simple finger movements such as a slide of the thumb on the index finger can activate a command. It can also be used for casual interactions such as discreetly rejecting a call during a meeting or controlling a stopwatch during sports activities.

Extension for Wearable Objects

This prototype of a rollout keyboard can be attached to a smartwatch (Figure 1b). It enlarges the input space by letting the user interact on skin in the vicinity of the watch. The keyboard can be fully rolled in to be portable and can be pulled out on demand to overlay the skin of the forearm, as shown in Figure 1b. It provides a large input area for entering text using a full QWERTY keyboard with 30 keys. This highlights the possibility of sensing many interactive areas using a grid-like structure and time-division multiplexing.

SkinStickers

This class of interaction devices is useful for fast and direct selection of one or several frequent operations. While a SkinSticker can be attached virtually anywhere on the body, the forearm is suggested as a convenient location for quick and direct access [40, 38]. To attach the sensor patch onto skin, we use mastic. This is a medical-grade adhesive for use on skin. It is inexpensive (less than 0.40 USD/ml), can be easily applied, and is fully compatible with use on skin. After use, the sensor can be easily peeled off without hurting the skin and without tearing out body hair. Previous work reported successful use of ADM Tronics Pros-Aide medical grade adhesive [12]. We show three SkinStickers for different functionalities:

MusicSticker. MusicSticker supports several functionalities in a visually aesthetic design, as shown in Figure 1c. It contains five interactive areas for controlling a music player: Play, Previous, Next, Vol+ and Vol-.

ClickWheel. We have implemented a ClickWheel sticker (Figure 1d). It captures circular rotation gestures. Moreover, touching and pressing on a segment differentiates between two commands.

EarSticker. Inspired by Earput [16], EarSticker (Figure 1e) can fully exploit the flexibility, stretchability and the affordances for input on the back of the ear and the earlobe. It supports input related to audio, such as adjusting the volume.

EVALUATION

Stretchability and Bendability

We evaluated stretchability and bendability of the sensor in a controlled setup. It includes typical and extreme sensor deformations, which occur on the human body.

Methodology. We used a rectangular sensor (8.5 cm/4 cm) with an electrode diameter of 1.5 cm, conductive trace width of 1 mm and a thickness of 700 μm. This reflects the properties of the sensors in our application scenarios. The sensor was stretched by 0%, 10%, 20% and 30%. Moreover, it was bent around 3D printed cylinders of four radii: 0.5 cm, 1 cm, 2 cm, and 3 cm. These situations cover typical and extreme deformations when worn on the body. In each condition, 10 consecutive touch contacts were created using a circular shape of fingertip-sized diameter (8 mm) in resistive sensing and with a human fingertip for capacitive sensing. For each experiment we used a different sensor to avoid one experiment influencing the other. All measurements were taken with increasing stretch and curvatures.

Results. Figure 4 depicts the results for each condition. This includes changes in resistance of the circuit, the average peak-to-peak voltage readings for capacitive sensing of slight touch contact as well as the average normal pressure required for

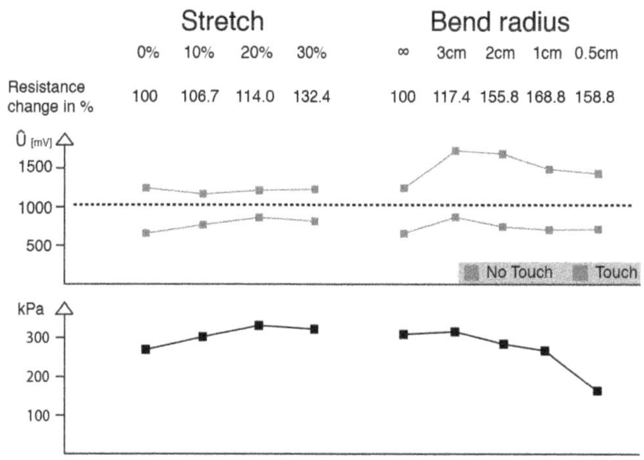

Figure 4. Results of the technical evaluation: (a) relative change in resistance, (b) measured voltage $\hat{U}$ for capacitive touch contact and no touch, (c) required pressure for resistive touch contact.

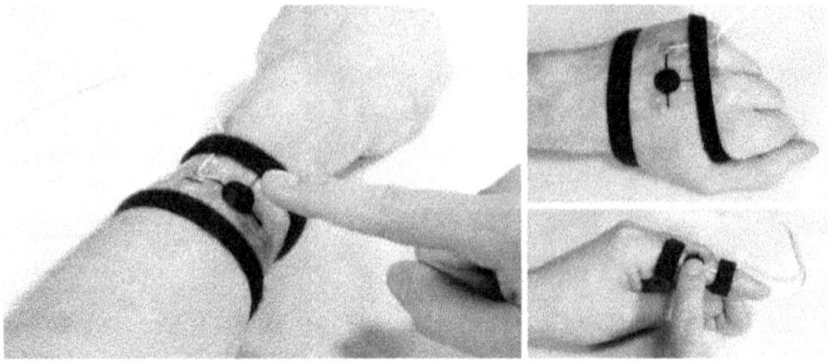

Figure 5. Study setup on the participants' forearm, back of the hand and finger. Two straps of Velcro allowed for fast and easy attachment.

creating a contact using resistive sensing. First and foremost, the data shows that in all test conditions the sensor remains functional and sensitive to touch on both pressure levels. Secondly, as indicated by the dotted line in the capacitive sensing chart, touch vs. no touch can be classified without knowledge of how much the sensor is currently stretched or bent. Thirdly, the pressure required for resistive sensing of touch remains fairly stable. A smaller bend radius decreases the required force since bending reduces the distance between the electrodes. While resistive sensing requires a firm touch, it can be a useful mode to support in addition to capacitive sensing, which reacts to very light touches. The required pressure can be tuned by changing the diameter of the hexagon pattern.

Reliability Across Body Locations

In a user study we investigate the accuracy and robustness of the touch sensor when worn on various body locations.

Methodology. Twelve voluntary participants (4f, mean age 26.8y) were recruited for the study. We used a rectangular sensor with one circular electrode having a diameter of 1.5cm, which is a recommended size for capacitive sensing elements [2]. It was attached directly on the users skin using two straps of Velcro (see Figure 5). The upper limb rested on a table to avoid fatigue effects influencing the results. Participants were seated and asked to keep arm, hand and fingers steady. We evaluated touch contact (capacitive sensing) and firm pressure touch (resistive sensing) on three body locations, reflecting the main locations identified in the design goals section: the forearm, the back of the hand, and the index finger. The order of body locations was randomized. In each condition, the task consisted of repeatedly touching the sensitive area in 1.5 s intervals, as accurately as possible. The participant was guided by an auditory metronome and received additional auditory feedback when the sensor was detecting touch contact. Participants were allowed to practice until they felt comfortable with the task. Touch events were logged on a computer with a PC oscilloscope (PicoScope 6402A). We collected a total of 4,320 touch inputs (360 per participant). Each session took approximately 15 min. The reported accuracy is the percentage of correctly recognized touch contacts (exactly one touch event recorded for one touch contact).

Results. The average accuracy was 92.5% (SD=11.2) for touch contact and 98.1% (SD=2.8) for firm pressure touch. For touch contact, it was highest on the forearm (93.0%), followed by the finger (91.2%) and the back of the hand (91.1%). For firm pressure touch, accuracy was also highest on the finger (99.2%), followed by the back of the hand (98.5%) and the forearm (97.6%). It is noteworthy that the task was more challenging than typical real-life scenarios due to the timing requirement, giving us a conservative estimate of accuracy. The lower accuracy of capacitive sensing compared to resistive sensing can be explained by the simple classification method we have used, which was merely based on measuring raw peak-to-peak voltage and did not make use of any signal conditioning. It seems quite safe to assume that a dedicated processing unit for capacitive touch sensing will lead to higher accuracies. We conclude that these results provide a lower bound, showing acceptable (91.1%) to very good (99.2%) results despite the proof-of-concept level processing of sensor data. This provides first evidence for suitability of the sensor for practical on-body input tasks.

LIMITATIONS AND FUTURE WORK

While it has been shown that the present design suffices for novel application-specific designs for touch input on the skin, four important challenges remain for future work: 1) extending input capabilities and modalities, 2) reduction of unintentional input, 3) system integration for mobile computers, and 4) investigating comfort and human factors.

First, the *size of interactive areas* of the demonstrated prototypes are comparable to a fingertip, the smallest one has a diameter of 8 mm. This size yielded a high signal-to-noise ratio (SNR) of 44.4 for capacitive (robust capacitive sensing requires ≈ 15 [2]) and 16.8 for resistive sensing. These results indicate potential for further decreasing the size of electrodes while maintaining robust sensing, but future work is necessary to provide a reliable lower bound. The prototypes also have rather low *spatial resolution* of touch sensing. This can be increased by creating denser grid-like sensing areas (e.g. used in the keyboard sensor). The smallest spacing between buttons we have tested was 1 mm. Capacitive crosstalk between electrodes turned out not to be a problem. Despite the neighboring electrode being touched, the SNR only decreased by 15.1%. This still allows for robust sensing using a naïve threshold. Future work could interpolate between the electrodes to improve resolution. Both size and resolution are limited due to the high resistance and inhomogeneity of cPDMS, which requires conductive traces to be fairly wide (we experienced 1 mm to be a good wire width). One solution would be to use AgPDMS instead of cPDMS. This would make the sensor more expensive, but the principles introduced in this paper transfer to AgPDMS. The number of available pins on the controller board could be easily increased by using multiplexers. Our sensor can simultaneously sense multiple touch contacts, making it suitable for use with multi-touch interfaces once the resolution increased.

Continuous pressure is another dimension to consider. The high and inhomogeneous resistance of cPDMS makes it very challenging, if not impossible, to use the FSR principle for reliable measurement of continuous pressure. Furthermore, stretching and deforming the material increases resistance by up to a factor of two, and it remains elevated even if the material has retracted to its original shape, regaining the original resistance only after several hours.

We envision future iSkin to sense *more modalities than touch*. iSkin could sense body movements by embedding MEMs, or access biofeedback for health-related applications [39, 41], e.g. body temperature. In addition, environmental sensing, such as air quality or UV radiation, could be included. Future iSkin could also provide visual output through an embedded thin-film display. While it has been shown that customized and deformable thin-film displays can be easily fabricated [25], it is still unclear how to produce stretchable displays.

Second, we have focused on detection performance for touch events rather than avoiding unintentional input. Future work should investigate when and how in daily use the iSkin sensor is in contact with other body parts or objects. This will allow for fine-tuning the sensor's sensitivity by tuning sensing parameters and the density of patterning of the spacer layer. Besides physical contact, also body movements can influence capacitive sensing. In our experience, typical movements do not reduce the accuracy of sensing, while a few extreme movements (e.g. a strong arm swing) require better processing, e.g. usage of a commercial capacitive touch sensors. In general, temporal and spatial input patterns can help identify and remove unintended contacts.

Third, integrating iSkin to a mobile computer is a challenge for future work. Although iSkin is a stretchable and thin touch sensor, the connector and micro-controller are still rigid. These parts could be made wireless using ad-hoc networks for communication with other body-worn devices. The electronics themselves could be either incorporated in the flexible and stretchable sensor surface or be miniaturized and attached as a small rigid pin. This would allow on-device computation and display for feedback. Instead of relying on external devices, the design of iSkin patches might also incorporate some visual display, for example by exploiting advances in thin-film displays. Moreover, audio output could be realized with integrated printed speakers. Haptic output is a further very promising channel as iSkin is directly located on the skin. For instance, temperature feedback can be quite easily realized by printing a resistor made of cPDMS.

Finally, although our results are promising in terms of comfort and safety, we see many ways to improve. In particular, future work needs to consider a more thorough exploration of the impact of skin overlays on tactile feedback. While direct-on-skin sensing can provide better sensory stimulation, skin overlays have the advantage of precisely delimiting the interaction area and providing static visual information on the interactive functionality.

SUMMARY AND CONCLUSION

This paper has contributed the design of a novel class of skin-worn touch sensors. The underlying technical solution of iSkin builds on and extends recent advances in research on electronic skin. iSkin is a proof of concept of on-skin touch sensing that bears some promise over rigid sensors and computer vision based solutions. iSkin supports touch input on the skin. While depressing the skin for input does not offer the dynamic properties of physical buttons, it does retain some of the known benefits for tactile feedback and supports eyes-free input on the body through proprioception.

The technical solution allowing this is based on embedded carbon-doped electrodes and combined capacitive and resistive sensing. A technical evaluation showed that this solution supports bending around radii of 5 mm and stretching by 30% and is therefore well suited for on-body interaction.

The design of iSkin supports the customization of touch sensors to specific applications and body locations, desired visual appearance and button layouts. This has allowed us to create applications to very challenging body parts, like the index finger or the back of the ear. Moreover, while we are far from a generic controller for mobile devices, we can already cover some essential aspects like unidimensional selection tasks and text entry.

We hope that this paper will stimulate future research on electronic skin for mobile human-computer interaction, leading to multimodal input-and-output skins that improve interaction with mobile devices in a wide variety of tasks and activities.

ACKNOWLEDGMENTS

This work has partially been funded by the Cluster of Excellence on Multimodal Computing and Interaction within the German Federal Excellence Initiative.

REFERENCES

1. Chan, L., Liang, R.-H., Tsai, M.-C., Cheng, K.-Y., Su, C.-H., Chen, M., Cheng, W.-H., and Chen, B.-Y. FingerPad: Private and Subtle Interaction Using Fingertips. In *ACM UIST '13* (2013).
2. Davison, B. Techniques for Robust Touch Sensing Design. `http://ww1.microchip.com/downloads/en/AppNotes/00001334B.pdf`. Accessed: 2015-01-01.
3. Dezfuli, N., Khalilbeigi, M., Huber, J., Müller, F., and Mühlhäuser, M. PalmRC: Imaginary Palm-based Remote Control for Eyes-free Television Interaction. In *EuroiTV '12* (2012), 27.
4. Gong, N.-W., Steimle, J., Olberding, S., Hodges, S., Gillian, N. E., Kawahara, Y., and Paradiso, J. A. PrintSense: A Versatile Sensing Technique to Support Multimodal Flexible Surface Interaction. In *ACM CHI '14* (2014), 1407–1410.
5. Gong, N.-W., Zhao, N., and Paradiso, J. A. A Customizable Sensate Surface for Music Control. 417–420.
6. Gustafson, S. G., Rabe, B., and Baudisch, P. M. Understanding palm-based imaginary interfaces. In *ACM CHI '13* (2013), 889.
7. Hammock, M. L., Chortos, A., Tee, B. C.-K., Tok, J. B.-H., and Bao, Z. 25th Anniversary Article: The Evolution of Electronic Skin (E-Skin): A Brief History, Design Considerations, and Recent Progress. *Advanced Materials 25*, 42 (2013), 5997–6038.
8. Harrison, C., Benko, H., and Wilson, A. D. OmniTouch: Wearable Multitouch Interaction Everywhere. In *ACM UIST '11* (2011), 441.
9. Harrison, C., Ramamurthy, S., and Hudson, S. E. On-body Interaction: Armed and Dangerous. In *ACM TEI '12* (2012), 69.

10. Harrison, C., Tan, D., and Morris, D. Skinput: Appropriating the Body As an Input Surface. *Communications of the ACM 54*, 8 (2011), 111.

11. Hawkes, E., An, B., Benbernou, N. M., Tanaka, H., Kim, S., Demaine, E. D., Rus, D., and Wood, R. J. Programmable matter by folding. *In PNAS 107*, 28 (2010), 12441–12445.

12. Holz, C., Grossman, T., Fitzmaurice, G., and Agur, A. Implanted user interfaces. In *ACM CHI '12* (2012), 503.

13. Karrer, T., Wittenhagen, M., Lichtschlag, L., Heller, F., and Borchers, J. Pinstripe: Eyes-free Continuous Input Anywhere on Interactive Clothing. In *ACM CHI '11* (2011), 1313.

14. Kim, D.-H., et al. Epidermal Electronics. *Science 333*, 6044 (2011), 838–843.

15. Kramer, R., Majidi, C., and Wood, R. Wearable tactile keypad with stretchable artificial skin. In *IEEE ICRA '11* (2011), 1103–1107.

16. Lissermann, R., Huber, J., Hadjakos, A., and Mühlhäuser, M. EarPut: Augmenting Behind-the-ear Devices for Ear-based Interaction. In *ACM CHI EA '13* (2013), 1323–1328.

17. Lu, T., Finkenauer, L., Wissman, J., and Majidi, C. Rapid Prototyping for Soft-Matter Electronics. *Advanced Functional Materials* (2014).

18. Lumelsky, V. J., Shur, M., and Wagner, S. Sensitive skin. *IEEE Sensors Journal* (2001), 41–51.

19. McCann, J., Hurford, R., and Martin, A. A Design Process for the Development of Innovative Smart Clothing That Addresses End-User Needs from Technical, Functional, Aesthetic and Cultural View Points. In *IEEE ISWC '05* (2005), 70–77.

20. Mistry, P., Maes, P., and Chang, L. WUW - wear Ur world. In *ACM CHI EA '09* (2009), 4111.

21. Nakatsuma, K., Shinoda, H., Makino, Y., Sato, K., and Maeno, T. Touch Interface on Back of the Hand. In *ACM SIGGRAPH '11* (2011).

22. Niu, X., Peng, S., Liu, L., Wen, W., and Sheng, P. Characterizing and Patterning of PDMS-Based Conducting Composites. *Advanced Materials 19*, 18 (2007), 2682–2686.

23. Ogata, M., Sugiura, Y., Makino, Y., Inami, M., and Imai, M. SenSkin: Adapting Skin as a Soft Interface. In *ACM UIST '13* (2013).

24. Ogata, M., Sugiura, Y., Osawa, H., and Imai, M. iRing: Intelligent Ring Using Infrared Reflection. In *ACM UIST '12* (2012), 131.

25. Olberding, S., Wessely, M., and Steimle, J. PrintScreen: Fabricating Highly Customizable Thin-film Touch-displays. In *ACM UIST '14* (2014), 281–290.

26. Olberding, S., Yeo, K. P., Nanayakkara, S., and Steimle, J. AugmentedForearm: Exploring the Design Space of a Display-enhanced Forearm. In *AH '13* (2013), 9–12.

27. Perrault, S. T., Lecolinet, E., Eagan, J., and Guiard, Y. Watchit: Simple gestures and eyes-free interaction for wristwatches and bracelets. In *ACM CHI '13* (2013), 1451–1460.

28. Rendl, C., Greindl, P., Haller, M., Zirkl, M., Stadlober, B., and Hartmann, P. PyzoFlex: Printed Piezoelectric Pressure Sensing Foil. In *ACM UIST '12* (2012), 509–518.

29. Rosenberg, I. D., Grau, A., Hendee, C., Awad, N., and Perlin, K. IMPAD: An Inexpensive Multi-touch pressure Acquisition Device. In *ACM CHI EA '09* (2009), 3217–3222.

30. Sekitani, T., Kaltenbrunner, M., Yokota, T., and Someya, T. Imperceptible Electronic Skin. *SID Information Display 30*, 1 (2014), 20–25.

31. Serrano, M., Ens, B. M., and Irani, P. P. Exploring the Use of Hand-To-Face Input for Interacting with Head-Worn Displays. In *ACM CHI'14* (2014).

32. Someya, T. *Stretchable Electronics*. Wiley-VCH, 2013.

33. Someya, T., Sekitani, T., Iba, S., Kato, Y., Kawaguchi, H., and Sakurai, T. A large-area, flexible pressure sensor matrix with organic field-effect transistors for artificial skin applications. *In PNAS 101*, 27 (2004), 9966–9970.

34. Su, C.-H., Chan, L., Weng, C.-T., Liang, R.-H., Cheng, K.-Y., and Chen, B.-Y. NailDisplay: Bringing an Always Available Visual Display to Fingertips. In *ACM CHI '13* (2013), 1461–1464.

35. Sugiura, Y., Inami, M., and Igarashi, T. A Thin Stretchable Interface for Tangential Force Measurement. In *ACM UIST '12* (2012), 529–536.

36. Tamaki, E., Miyak, T., and Rekimoto, J. BrainyHand:: A Wearable Computing Device Without HMD and It's Interaction Techniques. In *AVI '10* (2010), 387–388.

37. Vega, K., and Fuks, H. Beauty Technology: Muscle Based Computing Interaction. In *ACM ITS '13* (2013), 469–474.

38. Wagner, J., Nancel, M., Gustafson, S. G., Huot, S., and Mackay, W. E. Body-centric design space for multi-surface interaction. In *ACM CHI '13* (2013), 1299.

39. Webb, R. C., Bonifas, A. P., Behnaz, A., Zhang, Y., Yu, K. J., Shi, H. C. M., Bian, Z., Liu, Z., Kim, Y.-S., Yeo, W.-H., Park, J. S., Song, J., Li, Y., Huang, Y., Gorbach, A. M., and Rogers, J. A. Ultrathin conformal devices for precise and continuous thermal characterization of human skin. *Nature Materials 12* (2013), 938944.

40. Weigel, M., Mehta, V., and Steimle, J. More Than Touch: Understanding How People Use Skin As an Input Surface for Mobile Computing. In *ACM CHI '14* (2014), 179–188.

41. Windmiller, J. R., and Wang, J. Wearable Electrochemical Sensors and Biosensors: A Review. In *Electroanalysis* (2013).

42. Woo, S.-J., Kong, J.-H., Kim, D.-G., and Kim, J.-M. A thin all-elastomeric capacitive pressure sensor array based on micro-contact printed elastic conductors. *J. Mater. Chem. C 2* (2014), 4415–4422.

Cyclops: Wearable and Single-Piece Full-Body Gesture Input Devices

Liwei Chan* Chi-Hao Hsieh† Yi-Ling Chen* Shuo Yang†
Da-Yuan Huang* Rong-Hao Liang* Bing-Yu Chen*
National Taiwan University
*{liweichan, yilingchenntu, d99944006, rhliang, robin}@ntu.edu.tw
†{p121225, yangs}@cmlab.csie.ntu.edu.tw

ABSTRACT
This paper presents Cyclops, a single-piece wearable device that sees its user's whole body postures through an ego-centric view of the user that is obtained through a fisheye lens at the center of the user's body, allowing it to see only the user's limbs and interpret body postures effectively. Unlike currently available body gesture input systems that depend on external cameras or distributed motion sensors across the user's body, Cyclops is a single-piece wearable device that is worn as a pendant or a badge. The main idea proposed in this paper is the observation of limbs from a central location of the body. Owing to the ego-centric view, Cyclops turns posture recognition into a highly controllable computer vision problem. This paper demonstrates a proof-of-concept device and an algorithm for recognizing static and moving bodily gestures based on motion history images (MHI) and a random decision forest (RDF). Four example applications of interactive bodily workout, a mobile racing game that involves hands and feet, a full-body virtual reality system, and interaction with a tangible toy are presented. The experiment on the bodily workout demonstrates that, from a database of 20 body workout gestures that were collected from 20 participants, Cyclops achieved a recognition rate of 79% using MHI and simple template matching, which increased to 92% with the more advanced machine learning approach of RDF.

Author Keywords
Full-body gesture input; posture recognition; single-point wearable devices; ego-centric view

ACM Classification Keywords
H.5.m. Information Interfaces and Presentation (e.g. HCI): Miscellaneous

INTRODUCTION
Body gestural input has emerged as a popular natural user interface and become widely accessible since the release of Microsoft Kinect. Recently, more depth-sensing cameras have enabled reliable body tracking, but they have a limited working distance owing to the cameras' imaging fields-of-view.

CHI 2015, April 18–23, 2015, Seoul, Republic of Korea.

ACM 978-1-4503-3145-6/15/04 ...$15.00.
http://dx.doi.org/10.1145/2702123.2702464

Figure 1. Cyclops is a wearable single-piece bodily gesture input device that captures an ego-centric view of the user. With Cyclops worn at the center of the body, the user plays a racing game on the mobile phone with hand and foot interactions. The user pushes forward an imaginary gear stick on his right to trigger a nitro turbo.

To free users from the location constraints, novel wearable devices that are dedicated to partial body-centric inputs, such as arm [20], foot, palm [6], and finger-based [5] touch or gestural interactions, have been developed and demonstrated. Other research works have developed full-body motion capture by distributing motion sensors [19][15][32] around body parts of the user. However, wearing these sensors is commonly inconvenient, even though they are incorporated into motion-capture suits.

Recent research has developed full-body gestural input using single devices. Smart phones, for example, have been utilized for recognizing coarse-grain activities [18] such as walking, running and sleeping. Allowing for more interactivity, single wireless units that are carried by users [7] or arm-worn accelerometers [25] have been demonstrated for the recognition of motion gestures.

Cyclops
We present Cyclops, a single-piece wearable device that sees a user's bodily postures through an ego-centric view of the user. Figure 1 demonstrates the Cyclops device, and an example of the device's view of the user performing hand and foot interactions in a racing game. This ego-centric view offers two benefits. First, because Cyclops is fixed on a user's body, the ego-centric view presents a registration-free image, allowing body gestural recognition using simple template matching

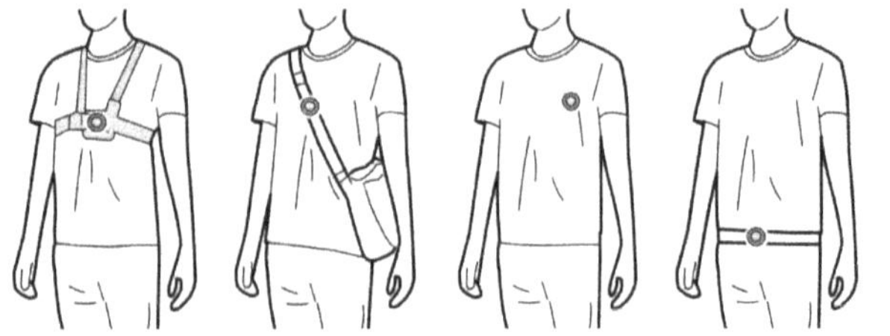

Figure 2. Cyclops can be worn around the middle of the body. Different placements favor head or foot interactions.

and motion history images. Second, a user's limbs enter the ego-centric field of view from outside of it, allowing foreground limb extraction to be more independent of cluttered backgrounds since the limbs are identified as foreground objects that penetrate the outermost rim of the image.

Figure 2 shows different ways to put on Cyclops as a wearable device. Displacement of the device toward the upper or lower body further facilitates head or foot interactions. Users can move the device according to the task at hand.

Contributions

The main contribution of this paper is the concept of full body gestural recognition using a fisheye ego-centric view of the user. To demonstrate the idea, this work (1) presented a proof-of-concept prototype and (2) evaluated the potential of the ego-centric view for full-body gestural recognition using motion history images with template matching and random decision forest methods.

RELATED WORK

This work concerns body-centric interactions that are identified using wearable devices, concentrating on full-body gestural recognition with single-point sensing techniques.

Body Inputs Using Wearable Cameras

Body-mounted cameras for monitoring gestural interactions have been extensively studied. Previous research [22] has demonstrated that locating cameras at various positions on the body enables unique interactions. Head-mounted cameras [24][36][8], for example, yield a mobile interaction space that is under the user's perspectives, but they do not support eye-free interactions. Attaching cameras to the body rather than to the head or close to the eyes, provides more dedicated interaction spaces. For example, attaching cameras to the shoulders [13] or chest [23][12], can turn users' palms into interactive surfaces, and facilitate hand gestural input. A camera on a wrist can be used track hand gestures [38][17]. A camera on a foot, pointing upward [2], provides an interaction space that incorporates the user's upper body. However, none of these developments can be used to sense the motions of feet so none supports the identification of full-body gestures. The goal of this work is to identify full-body motion gestures using single-piece wearable device.

Body Inputs Using Wearable Low-Level Sensing

Light-weight wearable devices, rather than cameras, can be used in low-level sensing. To make the body a touchable interface, capacitive sensing is integrated with users' clothing [28]. Scott et al. [31] proposed the recognition of foot gestures using a phone in a pocket. EarPut [21] instrumented the ear as an interactive surface for touch-based interactions using capacitive sensors.

Much research on body input is dedicated to hand-based interactions. Data gloves have been widely studied [35][4] in the field of HCI, and other techniques have been developed. Analyzing the sound that bounces through bones [14][26] allows tapping on the skin to be detected by acoustic sensors that are worn on the arm. SenSkin [27] made the skin into a touch interface by sensing skin deformation that is caused by the application of a force tangentially to the skin. PUB [20] facilitated touch interactions on the forearm by using a distance sensor on the wrist. Touche [30] enabled discrete hand gestures using swept frequency capacitive sensing. Saponas et al. [29] enabled hand gestural interaction by analyzing forearm electromyography. uTrack [6] enabled touch interaction on the palm by magnetic localization. FingerPad [5] used magnetic tracking to turn the index fingertip into a touch interface.

Depending on purpose and application, low-level sensing techniques be implemented on certain parts of the body. However, full-body motion input requires a body sensor network of sensors that are distributed on body parts [15][16], which may be inconvenient for users to put on.

Full-Body Gestures Using Single-point Devices

Activity recognition using single-point devices, such as smart phones, has been widely explored [18][10]. Relevant research has focused on the coarse-grain classification of daily activities such as walking, running, sitting, standing, and sleeping, using inertial sensors in smart phones. Real-time recognition is not their main concern. More recent research, RecoFit [25] has allowed repetitive exercises to be recognized in an interactive manner using a single arm-worn inertial sensor. Humantenna [7] enabled the identification of whole-body motion gestures by treating the human body as an antenna.

A single-point device involves minimal instrumentation. Previous research in this area, however, suffer from focusing on only limited motion gesture sets and an inability to detect static bodily gestures. Owing to its fisheye lens, Cyclops can recognize a rich set of static and moving full-body gestures.

HARDWARE PROTOTYPE

235-Degree Super Fisheye Lens

The main component of Cyclops is an ultra wide-angle camera that sees the user's limbs. Figure 3 displays the three tested types of wide-angle lens. Two are wide-angle lenses from GoPro[1] and Super Fisheye[2], and the other is an omnidirectional lens from Omni-Vision[3]. Each lens is positioned at the center of the user's chest, observing him adopting five body postures.

[1]http://www.gopro.com/

[2]http://www.superfisheye.com/

[3]http://www.omnivision.com/

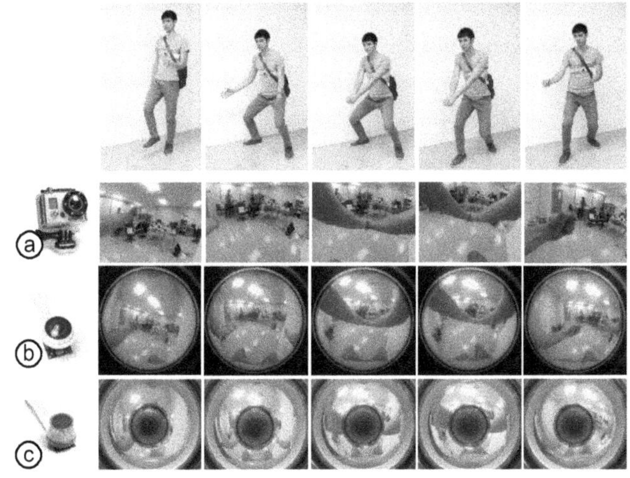

Figure 3. Comparison of three wide-angle camera lenses for observing five bodily gestures. (a) Go-Pro (180 degrees) wearable camera, (b) SuperFisheye (235 degrees), which was used in the Cyclops prototype herein, and (c) Omni-Vision, an omni-directional lens.

GoPro is a wearable imaging device that is equipped with an 180 degrees wide-angle lens, designed to capture the first-person experience of the wearer. The device can see the user's hand gestures but barely observes the user's head and legs. The 180-degree images thus obtained are presented as a reference, to suggest the need for a device with a wider viewing angle to capture full body interactions. Super Fisheye is the fisheye lens with the widest field-of-view that we could obtain commercially: it has a 235 degree field-of-view, and so easily captures the user's head and legs. Lastly, Omni-Vision, a omni-directional lens, has the widest field of vision at the expense of central vision. This omni-directional view clearly observes all limbs, but not those parts of the limbs that enter the central region. Accordingly, the Super Fisheye lens was chosen in the presented implementation owing to its ultra-fisheye field-of-view.

Enabling 235-Degree Field-of-view

The Raspberry Pi NOIR camera module's original field-of-view is about 90 degrees and not wide enough to cover the full 235-degree field-of-vision of the Super Fisheye Lens. Our previous prototype that used an unmodified NOIR camera module with the super fisheye lens achieved a field-of-vision of only 190 degrees. To fully realize the potential of the 235-degree lens, the original lens of the NOIR camera module was replaced with an 110-degree lens, as shown in Figure 4. Specifically, the lens in the NOIR camera module on the left the figure was removed. A 3D-printed ring-shaped connector formed a bridge between the 110-degree lens and the 235-degree lens.

Cyclops Wearable Device

To simplify foreground extraction, Cyclops was implemented with infrared imaging and active infrared illumination. Although color images could also be used to extract bare body limbs, they are more affected by various colors of clothing.

Figure 5 presents the components of our hardware prototype. The super fisheye lens with its 235-degree field of view

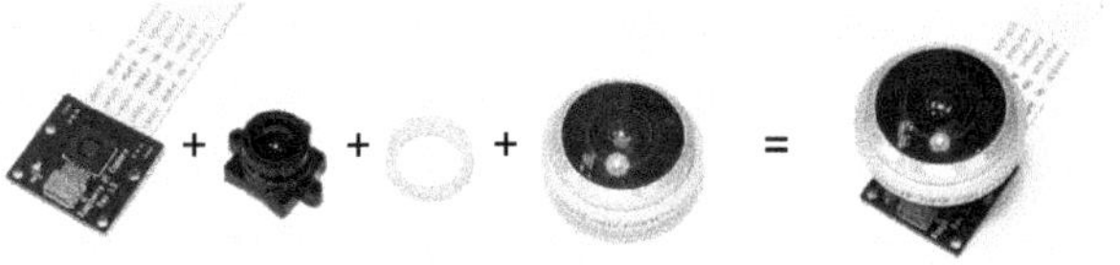

Figure 4. Cyclops' ultra-fisheye field-of-view is realized by firstly replacing the lens in the NOIR camera module with a 110-degree lens, and then bridging it with a 235-degree super fisheye lens.

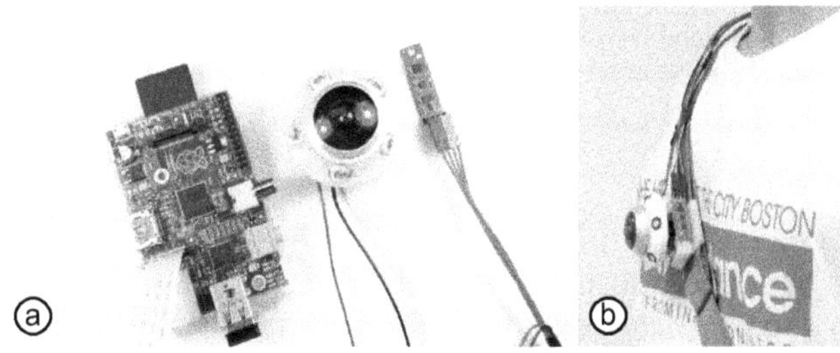

Figure 5. The Cyclops hardware comprises a super fisheye lens, an infrared illuminator around the lens, a Raspberry Pi NOIR camera module, and a 9-DOF inertial motion sensor. The Raspberry Pi module can stream the camera frames wirelessly at interactive speed.

provides an ego-centric view. Five infrared LEDs were attached around that lens to provide uniform illumination. The Raspberry Pi NOIR camera module captures infrared images which are then streamed wirelessly to a remote PC for further image processing. Notably, the Raspberry Pi NOIR camera module can see both visible and infrared light. To facilitate the extraction of limbs from images, an 850nm filter is added to block visible light and only infrared reflection from foreground objects such as limbs is accepted. A nine-DOF inertial motion sensor (IMU) is utilized to re-orient the fisheye images such that users need not worry about incorrectly putting on the wearable device, such as by putting it on upside down. The orientation data such as pan, pitch and yaw that are obtained by the IMU sensor are also applied in body gestural recognition in the experiments and applications.

The resulting prototype is packed with a 3D printed case, measuring about two inches in every dimension (width, height and length), excluding the Raspberry Pi and mobile power supply. The flexible data wire that connects the camera module to the Raspberry Pi is 90 cm long, which is long enough to allow the Raspberry Pi module and a mobile power supply to be stored in a fanny pack that is worn by the user.

Raspberry Pi streams images from the camera wirelessly over WiFi using the GStreamer Multimedia Framework. GStreamer[4] provides real-time streaming with an average delay of less than 300ms. In the implementation, a remote laptop receives approximately 20 frames per second from Cyclops, and the streaming delay is acceptable for our applications that run at an interactive speed.

RECOGNIZING BODILY GESTURES

Despite extensive research in this area, gesture recognition remains a challenging problem to solve in computer vision.

[4]GStreamer: http://gstreamer.freedesktop.org/

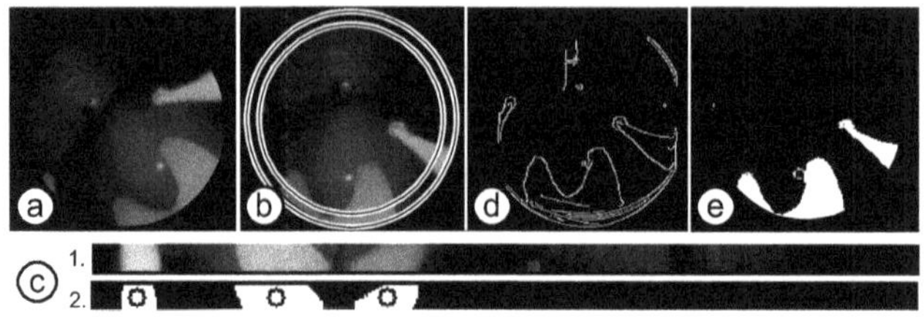

Figure 6. Image processing of the proposed algorithm for labeling components in the image as limbs. Accordingly, the limbs are extracted as a foreground image where they enter the fish-eye image. Notice that the source image in (a) is re-oriented using the information that is provided by the IMU.

Owing to its ego-centric image acquisition pipeline, Cyclops benefits from a sequence of *registration-free* input images from which the essential foreground objects (i.e. limbs) can be reliably identified using basic image processing techniques. Information about the motion of the user can then be further encoded into temporal templates in the form of a low-resolution, grayscale image. This work demonstrates that such compact representation of human actions is very effective for gestural recognition and the corresponding image classification problem can be effectively solved by standard pattern recognition and machine learning methods.

Based on the similar approach proposed in [37], we also take advantage of motion history image (MHI) and random decision forest (RDF) to identify stationary and moving bodily gestures. In the following, the process of foreground extraction will firstly be described. Based on this identification of the foreground limbs, two types of MHI [3] will be generated to represent the temporal motion in a single image. Bodily gestures will be shown to be recognized reasonably well using MHIs with straightforward template matching, and that the recognition rate can be increased by exploiting the RDF-based method [33].

Foreground Extraction

Figure 6 illustrates our image pre-processing pipeline. The basic idea is to extract foreground images from where the limbs enter the ego-centric view at the edge of the fisheye image. This strategy avoids dealing with non-limb foregrounds in the central part of the image. Firstly, the source images (Figure 6a) are re-oriented using the information that is provided by the IMU. Then, as highlighted in Figure 6b, the process is begun from a circular strip at the edge of the fisheye image. Figure 6c displays a straightened version of the circular strip. Then, Otsu thresholding is applied to the strip image to extract the foreground regions that potentially contain limbs. To separately identify limbs that overlap in the image, a vertical erosion along the length of the strip is performed to remove weak connections. The resulting connected components are further processed as follows.

From the geometric center of each component in the strip image, its corresponding position in the source image (Figure 6b) is identified, and used as a seed from which a foreground region is grown by performing image flooding. The Canny edge map of the source image, as shown in Figure 6d, is utilized to block the flooding operation. Figure 6e presents the overall foreground image that is obtained by aggregating all foreground regions. In simple cases, favorable results are obtained even in a cluttered environment. In complex cases, however, incorporating depth information from the infra-red image [11] or using a time-of-flight depth camera may be helpful. The foreground masks are used to compute the MHIs discussed in the next subsection.

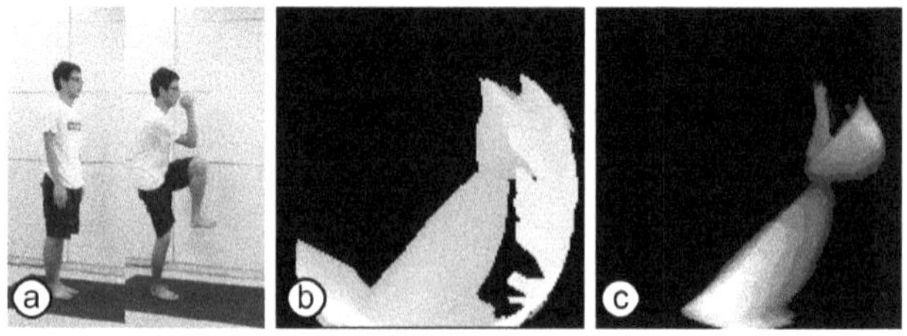

Figure 7. Examples of dMHI and iMHI that are generated from a sequence of images of a user performing a workout.

Motion History Image

Briefly, MHI is an image template in which non-zero pixels simultaneously record the spatial and temporal aspects of motion. A larger intensity value indicates more recent motion and intensity decays over time. MHI and many of its variations [1] have been extensively investigated in the field of action recognition. One key factor that affects the performance in MHI is image registration, which constitutes a difficult problem in the field of computer vision.

Like [37], we adopt two types of MHI in our implementation - the difference-MHI (dMHI) and the integral-MHI (iMHI). Specifically, for each incoming frame I_t at time t in an image sequence, we first resize I_t into a lower resolution of 75×75 and then compute the foreground mask I_t^m with the aforementioned foreground extraction algorithm. The dMHI is obtained by setting the pixels within I_t^m to 255 and decaying the rest pixels with a constant. To form the iMHI, foreground masks are summed up by $\sum_{i=0}^{k-1} w_{k-1-i} I_{t-i}^m$, where $w_i = \frac{2i}{k(k-1)}$ are the weighting coefficients, k is the number of past frames kept in the history, and i is the frame index. Figure 7 shows an example of dMHI and iMHI generated from a sequence of the user performing a workout gesture (right hand and left leg crunching while standing).

Random Decision Forest for Gesture Classification

RDF is a generic and powerful learning algorithm that has been used with much success in computer vision and medical image analysis applications [9]. One of the most notable examples is the Kinect body tracker [33]. Briefly, a forest is an ensemble of T decision trees, each comprising internal and leaf nodes. Each internal node is associated with a *split function* f_θ and a threshold τ. At test time, for a data point $\mathbf{x}$ arriving at an internal node, its corresponding *feature* is evaluated using f_θ and compared to τ. Based on the comparison result, $\mathbf{x}$ is assigned to either the left child or the right child of the current node. The above operation is repeated until $\mathbf{x}$ reaches a leaf node, where a predictor function is pre-learned and stored. The final classification of $\mathbf{x}$ is made by aggregating the results of all trees in the forest. In the following, we describe two different approaches of applying RDF classifiers to accomplish gesture recognition with Cyclops.

Standard RDF Classifier

The motion representation of MHI discussed above contains crucial information for gesture recognition and the framework of RDF-based classifiers [33, 37] can be readily applied to accomplish this task. Following [37], to classify a pixel $\mathbf{x}$ in a motion template image, we leverage the intensity differences of MHIs as features, as formulated below,

$$f_{\mathbf{u},\mathbf{v}}(I, \mathbf{x}) = I(\mathbf{x} + \mathbf{u}) - I(\mathbf{x} + \mathbf{v}), \quad (1)$$

where $\theta = (\mathbf{u}, \mathbf{v})$ are offset vectors relative to $\mathbf{x}$ and $I(\cdot)$ denotes the intensity value at a specific pixel location of a given MHI. The intuition behind this feature selection function is that it enables f_θ to learn the spatial extent and configuration of body parts in the motion signature image. At training time, randomly generated offset vectors are evaluated to obtain the feature values by Equation (1). For each internal node, the pair of $\mathbf{u}, \mathbf{v}$ and a corresponding threshold that best separates the labeled training data are kept. More details on applying RDF classifier to gesture recognition are referred to [33, 37].

Multi-layered RDF Classifier

In [34, 11], multi-layered decision forests are proposed to accomplish gesture recognition or depth estimation on mobile devices.The basic idea behind these approaches is to exploit expert forests trained for a particular task (e.g., roughly classify an image into several levels of quantized depth) and only those images corresponding to a particular class are forwarded to a second forest, trained only on examples from this class. Each of the forests then needs to model less variation and hence can be comparatively well performed.

Since Cyclops aims to handle full-body gestures, it is thus possible for the gesture recognizer to deal with rich and diverse gesture types. However, building a training database that covers all gestural variations to train a single classifier is a non-trivial but essential task for any machine learning algorithms. Inspired by [34, 11], we also propose a multi-layered architecture of RDFs with Cyclops. Differing from previous methods, which focus on a single source of input data (e.g., images), our observation is that additional orientation data captured while actions are being performed are potentially useful to facilitate the task of gesture classification.

Continuous orientation signatures are particularly useful when dealing with a specially purposed gesture set, such as a body workout. These gestures are carefully designed and very likely to yield distinct patterns of body orientation across different classes. For example, the orientation signatures of the standing gestures beginning with horizontal tilting differ from those of the face-down gestures beginning with a series of downward tilting. With the built-in IMU module, it is thus very simple to establish *two*-layered RDFs for Cyclops.

1. First layer: before training, the gesture set needs to be roughly divided into N categories according to their orientation patterns. For each motion category, we collect a set of orientation signatures for training. Specifically, *pitch* and *yaw* angles from n consecutive timestamps are concatenated into a vector $\mathbf{o} \in \mathbb{R}^{2n}$. During training, one dimension of $\mathbf{o}$ is randomly selected as a feature. In other words, f_θ is equivalent to an axis-aligned hyperplane in the feature space that separates the incoming data into two disjoint sets.

2. Second layer: we train N standard RDF classifiers for each motion category with the training data limited to the MHIs belonging to a certain category.

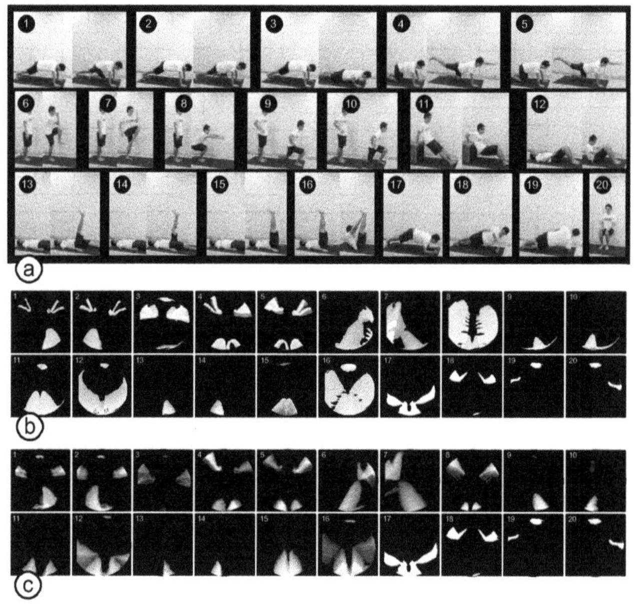

Figure 8. Four types of workout exercises. (a) A total of 20 captured moving and stationary bodily gestures. (b) and (c) shows examples of dMHIs and iMHIs, respectively, of bodily gestures in workout, as observed by Cyclops.

At test time, an orientation signature $\mathbf{o}'$ is firstly classified by the *single* first-layer forest. Once the motion category of $\mathbf{o}'$ is determined, the corresponding MHI I' is forwarded to the corresponding second-layer forest, by which the final gesture type is solely determined.

SYSTEM EVALUATION

To evaluate the performance of Cyclops, we chose to conduct a study on a body workout data set consisting of a wide variety of full-body gestures. In the following, we describe the experimental settings, data preparation procedures, and evaluation results.

Experimental Settings

The study included 20 exercises, which comprised both moving exercises and stationary postures, and were categorized into four types. As presented in Figure 8a, three of the four types of exercises involved motion; these comprised face-down (1-5), six standing (6-11), and five lying-down (12-16) exercises. The last group of exercises involved four stationary postures (17-20).

In a pilot study, we observed that loose clothing may occasionally block the Cyclops' view. Additionally, the images

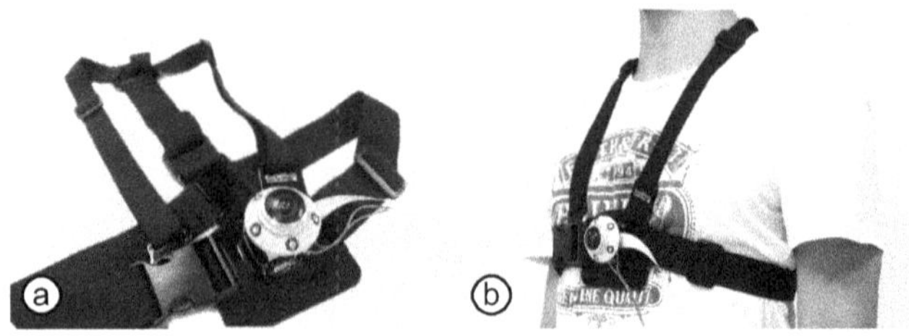

Figure 9. The Cyclops device is set firmly on the chest mount harness to fit a wide range of users.

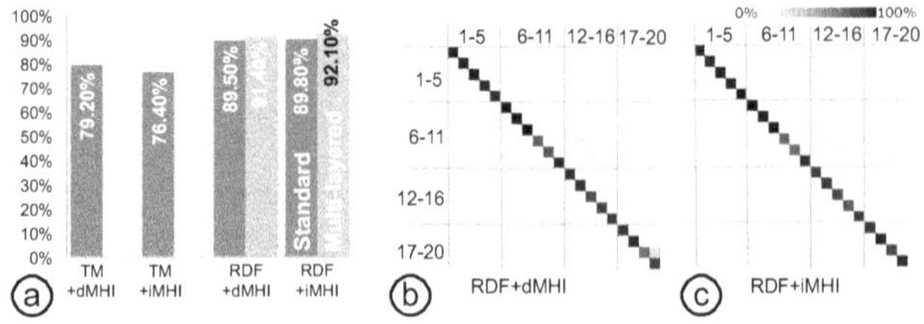

Figure 10. (a) Recognition rates of workout gestures achieved by Leave-one-person-out cross-validation with various algorithms. (b)(c) Confusion matrices of gesture recognition obtained using RDF + dMHI and RDF + iMHI, respectively.

observed by Cyclops from female and male participants differed greatly, mainly because the camera was easily occluded by the chests of female participants, below or above which Cyclops must be worn. Hence, to exclude these unfavorable factors from evaluation, only male participants were recruited and asked to be dressed properly.

Participants

Twenty participants were recruited from our department to perform the workout gesture set. They were aged between 21 and 25 (mean = 24.2, std = 2.95). Their heights (mean = 175.5 cm, std = 5.48 cm), weights (mean = 68.4 kg, std = 10.21 kg), and BMI values (mean = 22.1, std = 2.92) were recorded. All participants were able to perform the entire workout set without any problems.

Training Data Acquisition

At the beginning of this study, every participant received a 10-minute training. The experimenter firstly helped the participants put on the Cyclops device, and then explained the exercises to be performed. To ensure that all participants wore Cyclops properly, a 3D-printed hinge was made to fix the device firmly to a chest-mounted harness as shown in Figure 9. Following the experimenter, the participants had to physically perform dry runs of all of the workout exercises to ensure that they fully understood the details.

During the study, a monitor prompted example videos of each trial exercise to the participants. As soon as the participant was ready to perform the action, he notified the experimenter. A beep sound was then played to indicate that the participant should perform the action; meanwhile both the image and the accompanying orientation (yaw, pitch, and roll) data, provided by the IMU sensor, were recorded. Upon completing an action, the participant had to stay stationary until a second beep was heard, indicating the end of the recording. This procedure simplified the segmentation of the captured data. The above process was repeated for each exercise until the entire workout set was completed. The participant then took a rest before performing a second round of the workout.

Each participant performed two rounds of the entire workout set, and each exercise in the workout set was performed twice. Hence, each participant generated 20 (exercises) $\times$ 4 (repetitions) $=$ 80 labeled images (either dMHI or iMHI) and orientation data sequences.

Performance Evaluation

A technical evaluation was carried out to determine the recognition rates achieved by applying 1) basic template matching, 2) standard RDF classifier and 3) multi-layered RDF classifier with both dMHI and iMHI motion signatures. *Leave-one-person-out* cross-validation was performed on the workout dataset to evaluate the performance of each method. For each subject, 1520 training images and 80 test images were utilized to measure the accuracy of the evaluated method to predict the unknown gestures. The obtained recognition rates are then averaged to indicate the overall performance.

Notably, a non-gesture class must be included for a deterministic classifier like RDF. However, the non-gesture class is more difficult to define in this study than in the work of [37], because Cyclops captures full-body gestures. In a body workout exercise, some random bodily motions may even partially coincide with the workout gestures. To limit the uncertainty that could be introduced by an invalid non-gesture class, the non-gesture class was not included in this evaluation.

Performance of Template Matching

Served as a baseline approach for comparison, template matching (TM) is implemented straightforwardly by measuring the distance between two MHI images as the summation of pixel-wise absolute differences of intensity values. For each test image, the label of the MHI image in the training set with the smallest distance is returned as the gesture type. As shown in Figure 10a, the average recognition rates of applying template matching to iMHI and dMHI achieved 76.4% and 79.2%, respectively. This reasonably good performance is accounted for by the registration-free images captured by Cyclops, which considerably simplified the recognition tasks.

Performance of Standard RDF Classification

To obtain the standard RDF classifiers, the following parameters were used to train a three-tree forest for each of the 20 subjects. For each training image, 2000 sample pixels were randomly selected as data points. All the data points were passed to the root node to start the recursive training process. For each intermediate node, 2000 candidate features generated by Equation (1) and 50 candidate thresholds per feature were adopted to determine the best split function. Tree node splitting stops at the maximal level of 19 or the information gain is less than a prescribed threshold in terms of Shannon entropy (we empirically set it to 0.01). In our current C++ implementation, the tree trainer was run on a single core of i-7 3.4 GHz CPU and training a forest took around six hours. We have also tried to accelerate RDF training by concurrently training individual trees with OpenMP. The training time can

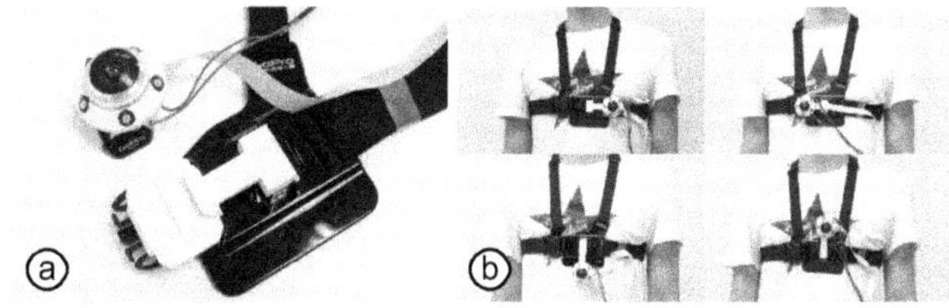

Figure 11. A detachable hinge was designed to offset the placement of the Cyclops device unfavorably.

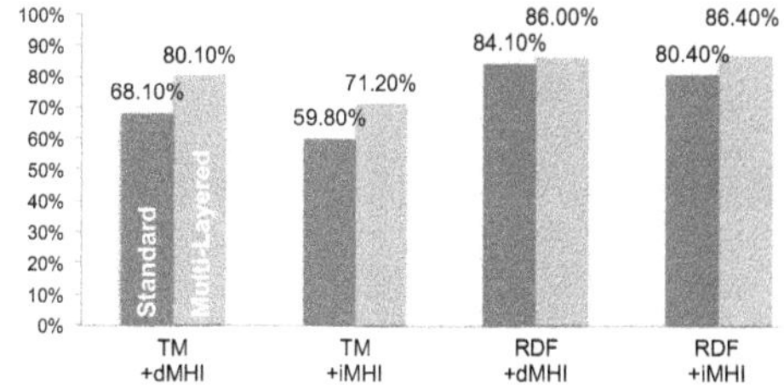

Figure 12. Recognition rates of various gesture recognition algorithms after offsets are applied to Cyclops. Blue/green bars indicate the performance obtained with/without IMU orientation information, respectively.

be further reduced to between 2 and 3 hours. Since the computation of RDF classifiers mainly involves pixel operations, we believe that the computation efficiency can be further significantly enhanced by GPU acceleration.

As shown in Figure 10a, standard RDF classifier increases the recognition rates to nearly 90% for both motion signature representations. Figure 10bc shows the confusion matrices of recognizing workout gestures using dMHI and iMHI, respectively. The gesture classifier worked generally well for most classes. The cases of false recognition mainly involved some face-down and lying-down exercises, which are visually similar to their MHI representations and therefore difficult to be distinguished from each other. In the next evaluation, IMU orientation data will be utilized to deal with such gestures more effectively.

Performance of Multi-layered RDF Classification

Before training, the 20 workout exercises were first divided into three motion categories[5]. The IMU data associated with each category are then used to train the first-layer RDF. Specifically, the following parameters are adopted: number of trees $T = 3$, depth = 10, temporal length of orientation signatures $n = 150$, 100 candidate features, and 20 candidate thresholds per feature. Owing to its simplicity, the first-layer training can typically be completed in just a few seconds. The second-layer RDFs can be obtained just as the standard RDF except that the training data set is reduced for each category.

Unlike [11], which obtains depth estimates by aggregating results from both depth classification and regression forests, the gesture type is solely determined by the second-layer RDF in our system. Therefore, a highly accurate first-layer classifier is essential. Under the same leave-one-person-out cross validation setting, the first-layer RDF achieved a relatively high average recognition rate of 98%, indicating fairly successful coarse-grained classification. Moreover, we observed a slightly increased average recognition rate for the second-layer MHI-based classification, indicating that gesture classification by categories is simplified when compared with the full workout set. When combined, the two-layer classifiers achieved an overall recognition rate of 92.1% and 91.4%, corresponding to dMHI and iMHI respectively (shown in the green bars in Figure 10a).

[5]The orientation signatures of stationary gestures are similar to the other three types of motion gestures, respectively.

Applying Offset to Cyclops

In this experiment, the effect of applying an offset to the Cyclops device on recognition performance is investigated.

Test Data Acquisition

To acquire data under offset conditions, four detachable hinges (Figure 11) were fabricated; each introduced a 30-mm offset from the original location in the up, down, left or right direction. Ten participants were recruited from the original participant poolto perform the entire workout set once under all four offset conditions. The offset data sets were used as the test sequences, and the non-offset data sets of the same participants were used to train the RDF classifiers.

Evaluation Results

Figure 12 presents the effects of offsetting the placement of Cyclops on the human body. Since offsetting the Cyclops' camera compromises the characteristics of registration-free images, the fact that the performance of template matching was considerably degraded is unsurprising. RDF classifiers still achieved acceptable performance of above 80%. Notably, the IMU orientation signature is unaffected regardless of how the device is displaced. As a result, two-layered classification consistently improved the overall performance in all test cases.

EXAMPLE APPLICATIONS

The proposed proof-of-concept device is demonstrated with four applications - interactive body workout, mobile racing game, wearable VR gaming and tangible toy interaction.

Interactive Body Workout

Figure 13 shows the interactive body workout application. The user performs workout routines at home while Cyclops monitors progress and provides vocal instructions concerning subsequent actions. For example, Cyclops counts the sit-ups performed by the user; encourages the user to speed up or slow down, and, when the exercise is complete, (Figure 13 a-b), instructs the user to prepare for leg crunches (Figure 13c-f). Static and motion gesture recognitions are based on the iMHI+RDF method, as described in the Evaluation section.

Hand and Foot Interactions in Mobile Gaming

Cyclops enriches gaming on mobile devices by incorporating hand and foot interactions. Figure 14 presents an example of a racing game on mobile phones. The user holds the

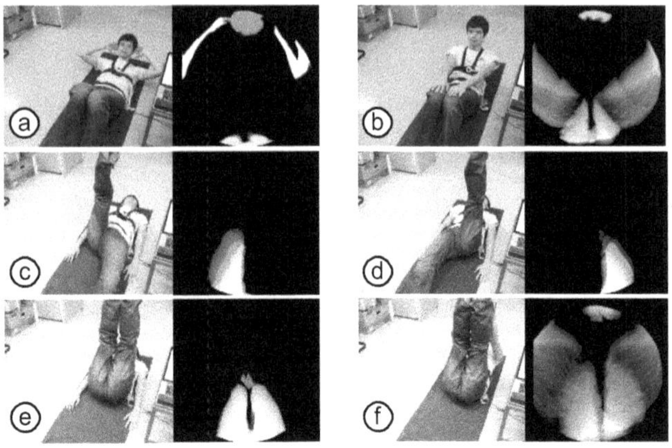

Figure 13. Interactive body workout applications track the user's performing workout exercises, and provide interactive instructions. (a-b) The workout tracker counts the sit-ups and provides suggestions to help the user maintain a good pace. (c-f) The tracker provides hints to the user concerning the next step in a four-step leg crunch exercise.

mobile phone as if holding an steering wheel, and the steering is monitored by the motion sensors of the phone. Moving the phone closer to the body results in an engaged view (Figure 14a), and pushing it away results in a second-person view (Figure 14b). Pushing the right-hand forward as if pushing forward a gear stick triggers nitro turbo (Figure 14c), and pushing the left leg out brakes the car.

The application is implemented with a VNC client on the mobile phone, which displays the racing game that is being run on a remote PC. The same remote PC processes Cyclops' video stream, performs gesture recognition using iMHI+RDF, and feeds back to the racing game with a keyboard simulator.

Wearable VR Snowball Fight Game

Recent developments in virtual reality (VR) have led to immersive gaming with wearable VR headsets such as Oculus Rift. However, most current interaction methods use gamepads, or allow limited body input using external image sensors but they still suffer from the line-of-sight problem.

This application of Cyclops enables the use of omnidirectional body motion gestures in immersive virtual reality gaming. Figure 15 presents a snowball fight game. The user, wearing Cyclops and an Oculus Rift VR headset, plays the game in the first-person view. In the game, enemies appear in all possible directions and throw snowballs toward the player. User interactions include throwing back snowballs by swinging one's arms (Figure 15a), throwing a giant snowball by swinging both arms (Figure 15b), and avoiding a ball by squatting or leaning to the left or the right (Figure 15cd).

The application is implemented with Unity3D and Oculus Rift VR headsets. Cyclops recognizes the player's motion gestures using dMHI+RDF and uses the actions to drive corresponding action scripts in the Unity3D game. The 9-DOF IMU of the Cyclops device tracks the player's orientation and leaning directions.

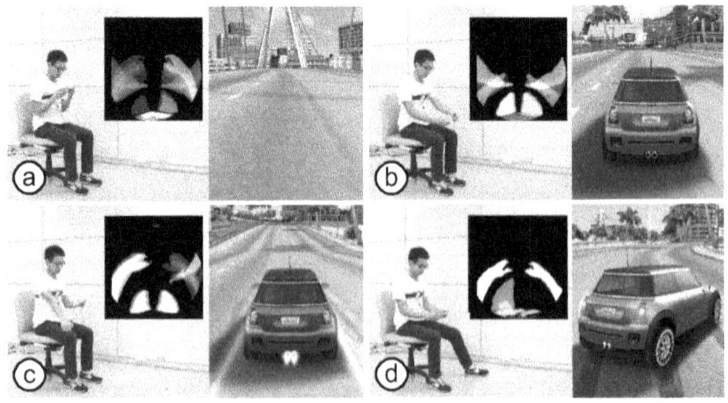

Figure 14. Hand and foot interaction in a mobile racing game. (a) Moving the phone closer to the body provides an engaged view. (b) Pushing the phone away enables a second-person view. Users can (c) push an imaginary gear stick on his right to trigger nitro turbo, and (d) step to the left to brake.

Tangible Toy Interaction

Attaching Cyclops to a stuffed toy turns the toy's body posture into an interactive controller. Figure 16 demonstrates the interaction with a display stuffed toy. A mobile display is embedded in the face of the toy. The Cyclops device tracks the motion gestures of the toy's limbs using iMHI+RDF and triggers facial expressions using the mobile display on the toy's face. Waving its hand causes the toy say 'Hi' with a smiling face (Figure 16a). Moving both of the toy's legs back and forward displays a running face (Figure 16b).

DISCUSSION AND LIMITATIONS

Cyclops is a single-piece wearable device that allows full-body posture inputs. We believe that the ultra-wide-angle view of users' body gestures will pave the way to a new generation of wearable motion capture devices. Therefore, this work seeks to establish the feasibility of this idea by demonstrating a proof-of-concept prototype. In the following, we discuss the main challenges and limitations faced by the current prototype system in two aspects.

Computer vision challenges

Like all existing vision-based projects, Cyclops faces the challenges that are typically faced by computer vision techniques, such as cluttered backgrounds and varying lighting conditions. To mitigate these challenges while validating the benefits of wearable devices that capture full-body gestures, Cyclops was implemented using an infra-red camera with active illumination, and the experiments were conducted in a controlled environment. In the future, Cyclops can be realized with advanced depth sensing techniques, such as time-of-flight distance estimation, to overcome the challenges.

Social acceptance by gender

Previous research [22] has demonstrated that social acceptance of wearable devices differs between genders. Female users were less accepting of Cyclops. In the pilot test, Cyclops inevitably yielded more occluded images owing to its ego-centric view. Female users tended to report feeling uncomfortable with putting the device on the chest. Currently, the prototype is relatively bulky. In the future, Cyclops will

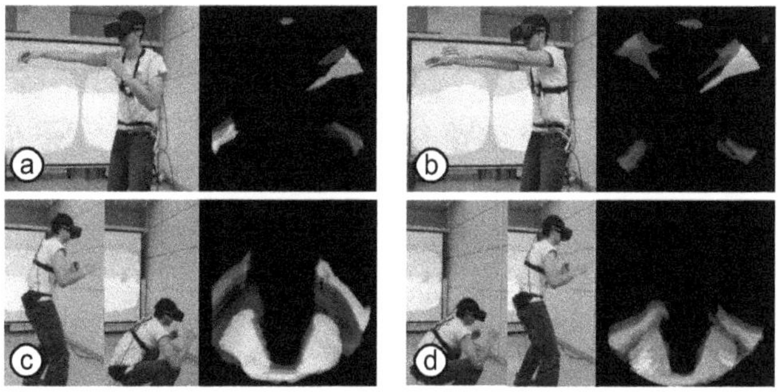

Figure 15. Cyclops supports omni-directional body motion gestures for immersive virtual reality. (a) The user flings a snowball by swinging his right arm; (b) throws a giant ball by swinging both arms, and (c)(d) avoids a ball by squatting or leaning to the left or to the right.

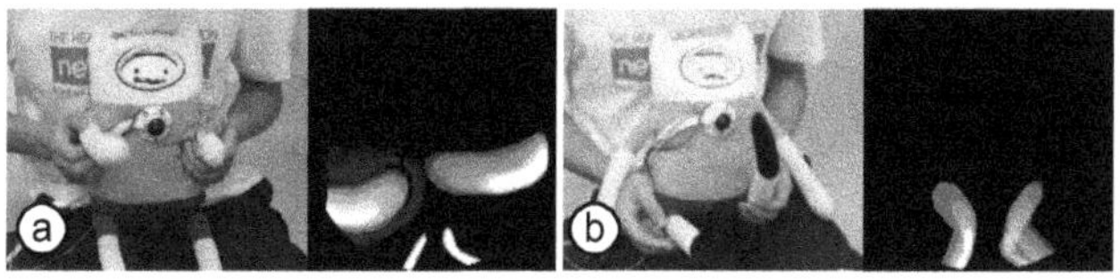

Figure 16. Attaching Cyclops to a stuffed toy enables a user to interact with the whole body of the toy. (a) The toy says 'Hi' with a smiling face when its hands are waved, and (b) displays a running face when its legs are made to run.

be made small enough to fit the wearable forms that are presented in Figure 2.

CONCLUSION

This paper presented a single-piece wearable motion-capture device. The use of Cyclops, as a proof-of-concept device, in full-body posture recognition, is demonstrated. The main contribution is the idea of determining body posture using an ego-centric perspective of the user, using only a single-piece motion-capture device.

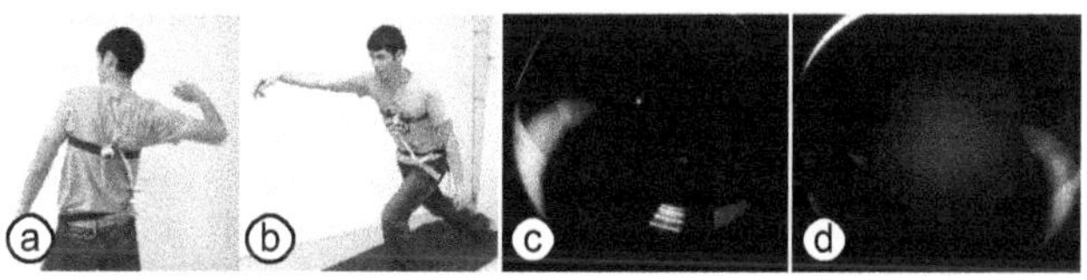

Figure 17. The strengths and limitations of Cyclops arise from its fisheye field-of-view. (a-b) Cyclops fails when it cannot see the motion of the body, such as in ball pitching. (c-d) This problem, however, can be solved by using another Cyclops that is worn on the back of the user.

Cyclops allows many body postures to be observed, owing to its fisheye field-of-view. Like other devices that use cameras, however, Cyclops yields uncertain results concerning postures in which limbs are out-of-sight. Figure 17 shows a user's ball-pitching posture. The pulling back of the pitching hand is invisible to Cyclops. This problem can be solved by adding another Cyclops to the user's back, as displayed in Figure 17. Future works will incorporate into Cyclops a pair of fisheye lenses in a wearable chest mount, yielding a blind spot-free wearable motion capture device.

ACKNOWLEDGMENTS

We gratefully acknowledge the helpful comments of the Associate Chairs and the anonymous reviewers. This paper was partially supported by National Science Council of Taiwan under NSC103-2218-E-002-014 and MOST103-2218-E-002-024-MY3, and also supported by Ministry of Science and Technology, National Taiwan University and Intel Corporation under Grants MOST102-2911-I-002-001, NTU103R7501, and NTU103R104130.

REFERENCES

1. Ahad, M. A. R., Tan, J. K., Kim, H., and Ishikawa, S. Motion history image: Its variants and applications. *Mach. Vision Appl. 23*, 2 (Mar. 2012), 255–281.
2. Bailly, G., Müller, J., Rohs, M., Wigdor, D., and Kratz, S. Shoesense: A new perspective on gestural interaction and wearable applications. In *Proc. ACM CHI '12* (2012), 1239–1248.
3. Bobick, A. F., and Davis, J. W. The recognition of human movement using temporal templates. *IEEE Trans. Pattern Anal. Mach. Intell. 23*, 3 (Mar. 2001), 257–267.
4. Bowman, D. A., Wingrave, C. A., Campbell, J. M., and Ly, V. Q. Using pinch gloves for both natural and abstract interaction. In *Proc. HCI International '01* (2001), 629–633.
5. Chan, L., Liang, R.-H., Tsai, M.-C., Cheng, K.-Y., Su, C.-H., Chen, M. Y., Cheng, W.-H., and Chen, B.-Y. Fingerpad: Private and subtle interaction using fingertips. In *Proc. ACM UIST '13* (2013), 255–260.
6. Chen, K.-Y., Lyons, K., White, S., and Patel, S. utrack: 3d input using two magnetic sensors. In *Proc. ACM UIST '13* (2013), 237–244.
7. Cohn, G., Morris, D., Patel, S., and Tan, D. Humantenna: Using the body as an antenna for real-time whole-body interaction. In *Proc. ACM CHI '12* (2012), 1901–1910.
8. Colaço, A., Kirmani, A., Yang, H. S., Gong, N.-W., Schmandt, C., and Goyal, V. K. Mime: Compact, low power 3d gesture sensing for interaction with head mounted displays. In *Proc. ACM UIST '13* (2013), 227–236.
9. Criminisi, A., and Shotton, J. *Decision Forests for Computer Vision and Medical Image Analysis*. Springer, 2013.
10. Dernbach, S., Das, B., Krishnan, N. C., Thomas, B., and Cook, D. Simple and complex activity recognition through smart phones. In *IEEE IE '02* (June 2012), 214–221.
11. Fanello, S. R., Keskin, C., Izadi, S., Kohli, P., Kim, D., Sweeney, D., Criminisi, A., Shotton, J., Kang, S. B., and Paek, T. Learning to be a depth camera for close-range human capture and interaction. *ACM Trans. Graph. 33*, 4 (July 2014), 86:1–86:11.

12. Gustafson, S., Bierwirth, D., and Baudisch, P. Imaginary interfaces: Spatial interaction with empty hands and without visual feedback. In *Proc. ACM UIST '10* (2010), 3–12.

13. Harrison, C., Benko, H., and Wilson, A. D. Omnitouch: Wearable multitouch interaction everywhere. In *Proc. ACM UIST '11* (2011), 441–450.

14. Harrison, C., Tan, D., and Morris, D. Skinput: Appropriating the body as an input surface. In *Proc. ACM CHI '10* (2010), 453–462.

15. Junker, H., Amft, O., Lukowicz, P., and Tröster, G. Gesture spotting with body-worn inertial sensors to detect user activities. *Pattern Recogn. 41*, 6 (June 2008), 2010–2024.

16. Keally, M., Zhou, G., Xing, G., Wu, J., and Pyles, A. Pbn: Towards practical activity recognition using smartphone-based body sensor networks. In *Proc. ACM SenSys '11* (2011), 246–259.

17. Kim, D., Hilliges, O., Izadi, S., Butler, A. D., Chen, J., Oikonomidis, I., and Olivier, P. Digits: Freehand 3d interactions anywhere using a wrist-worn gloveless sensor. In *Proc. ACM UIST '12* (2012), 167–176.

18. Kwapisz, J. R., Weiss, G. M., and Moore, S. A. Activity recognition using cell phone accelerometers. *SIGKDD Explor. Newsl. 12*, 2 (Mar. 2011), 74–82.

19. Lee, J., and Ha, I. Real-time motion capture for a human body using accelerometers. *Robotica 19*, 6 (Sept. 2001), 601–610.

20. Lin, S.-Y., Su, C.-H., Cheng, K.-Y., Liang, R.-H., Kuo, T.-H., and Chen, B.-Y. Pub - point upon body: Exploring eyes-free interaction and methods on an arm. In *Proc. ACM UIST '11* (2011), 481–488.

21. Lissermann, R., Huber, J., Hadjakos, A., and Mühlhäuser, M. Earput: Augmenting behind-the-ear devices for ear-based interaction. In *Proc. ACM CHI EA '13* (2013), 1323–1328.

22. Mayol-Cuevas, W. W., Tordoff, B. J., and Murray, D. W. On the choice and placement of wearable vision sensors. *Trans. Sys. Man Cyber. Part A 39*, 2 (Mar. 2009), 414–425.

23. Mistry, P., and Maes, P. Sixthsense: A wearable gestural interface. In *Proc. ACM SIGGRAPH ASIA '09 Sketches* (2009), 11:1–11:1.

24. Mistry, P., Maes, P., and Chang, L. Wuw - wear ur world: A wearable gestural interface. In *Proc. ACM CHI EA '09* (2009), 4111–4116.

25. Morris, D., Saponas, T. S., Guillory, A., and Kelner, I. Recofit: Using a wearable sensor to find, recognize, and count repetitive exercises. In *Proc. ACM CHI '14* (2014), 3225–3234.

26. Mujibiya, A., Cao, X., Tan, D. S., Morris, D., Patel, S. N., and Rekimoto, J. The sound of touch: On-body touch and gesture sensing based on transdermal ultrasound propagation. In *Proc. ACM ITS '13* (2013), 189–198.

27. Ogata, M., Sugiura, Y., Makino, Y., Inami, M., and Imai, M. Senskin: Adapting skin as a soft interface. In *Proc. ACM UIST '13* (2013), 539–544.

28. Rekimoto, J. Gesturewrist and gesturepad: Unobtrusive wearable interaction devices. In *Proc. IEEE ISWC '01* (2001), 21–.

29. Saponas, T. S., Tan, D. S., Morris, D., Balakrishnan, R., Turner, J., and Landay, J. A. Enabling always-available input with muscle-computer interfaces. In *Proc. ACM UIST '09* (2009), 167–176.

30. Sato, M., Poupyrev, I., and Harrison, C. Touché: Enhancing touch interaction on humans, screens, liquids, and everyday objects. In *Proc. ACM CHI '12* (2012), 483–492.

31. Scott, J., Dearman, D., Yatani, K., and Truong, K. N. Sensing foot gestures from the pocket. In *Proc. ACM UIST '10* (2010), 199–208.

32. Shiratori, T., Park, H. S., Sigal, L., Sheikh, Y., and Hodgins, J. K. Motion capture from body-mounted cameras. In *Proc. ACM SIGGRAPH '11* (2011), 31:1–31:10.

33. Shotton, J., Fitzgibbon, A., Cook, M., Sharp, T., Finocchio, M., Moore, R., Kipman, A., and Blake, A. Real-time human pose recognition in parts from single depth images. In *Proc. IEEE CVPR '11* (2011), 1297–1304.

34. Song, J., Sörös, G., Pece, F., Fanello, S. R., Izadi, S., Keskin, C., and Hilliges, O. In-air gestures around unmodified mobile devices. In *Proc. ACM UIST '14* (2014), 319–329.

35. Sturman, D. J., and Zeltzer, D. A survey of glove-based input. *IEEE Comput. Graph. Appl. 14*, 1 (Jan. 1994), 30–39.

36. Tamaki, E., Miyaki, T., and Rekimoto, J. Brainy hand: An ear-worn hand gesture interaction device. In *Proc. ACM CHI EA '09* (2009), 4255–4260.

37. Taylor, S., Keskin, C., Hilliges, O., Izadi, S., and Helmes, J. Type-hover-swipe in 96 bytes: A motion sensing mechanical keyboard. In *Proc. ACM CHI '14* (2014), 1695–1704.

38. Vardy, A., Robinson, J., and Cheng, L.-T. The wristcam as input device. In *Proc. IEEE ISWC '99* (1999), 199–202.

Bodyprint: Biometric User Identification on Mobile Devices Using the Capacitive Touchscreen to Scan Body Parts

Christian Holz, Senaka Buthpitiya, Marius Knaust
Yahoo Labs, Sunnyvale, CA
{christianh, senaka, mariusk} @ yahoo-inc.com

ABSTRACT

Recent mobile phones integrate fingerprint scanners to authenticate users biometrically and replace passwords, making authentication more convenient for users. However, due to their cost, capacitive fingerprint scanners have been limited to top-of-the-line phones, a result of the required resolution and quality of the sensor. We present *Bodyprint*, a biometric authentication system that detects users' biometric features using the same type of capacitive sensing, but uses the touchscreen as the image sensor instead. While the input resolution of a touchscreen is ~6 dpi, the surface area is larger, allowing the touch sensor to scan users' body parts, such as ears, fingers, fists, and palms by pressing them against the display. Bodyprint compensates for the low input resolution with an increased false rejection rate, but does not compromise on authentication precision: In our evaluation with 12 participants, Bodyprint classified body parts with 99.98% accuracy and identifies users with 99.52% accuracy with a false rejection rate of 26.82% to prevent false positives, thereby bringing reliable biometric user authentication to a vast number of commodity devices.

INTRODUCTION

Mobile phones now store a manifold of sensitive user data, such as photos, emails as well as login credentials to access personal data on the web, including finances and shopping portals. To protect such data from theft and unauthorized access, mobile devices implement lock screens to verify the user's identity and authenticate their use of the device.

Lock screens commonly ask the user to enter a PIN to unlock [4,8]. Unfortunately, only a small percentage of mobile phone users actually protect their device using a PIN [13]. A commonly cited reason is that PIN codes impede convenience and ease of access [3]. Graphical passwords ease the memorization and entry of PIN codes, but are subject to eavesdropping and find only limited acceptance [8].

Researchers have thus sought to replace PIN codes to protect mobile devices, such as to identify users from behavioral biometrics [5] or analyzing the characteristics of gestures users perform with the device [12]. Alternative approaches leverage the front-facing cameras in mobile devices to implement face [1] or iris recognition [7].

CHI 2015, April 18 – 23 2015, Seoul, Republic of Korea
Copyright 2015 ACM 978-1-4503-3145-6/15/04...$15.00
http://dx.doi.org/10.1145/2702123.2702518

To balance reliable and strong authentication with the convenience of use, some recent phones have started to integrate capacitive fingerprint scanners as part of the enclosure (e.g., iPhone 5S and up, Samsung Galaxy S5). However, capturing fingerprints requires high-quality sensors, which incurs considerable cost in the manufacturing process. Fingerprint scanners have thus been reserved for top-of-the line mobile devices only. Several research prototypes have further explored touch-based authentication by identifying users during contact with the touchscreen itself [9,10,11].

In this note, we present *Bodyprint*, a biometric authentication system that uses the capacitive sensor of commodity touch*screens* to detect users' biometric features—the same type of sensing that fingerprint scanners use. Whereas fingerprint scanners exist only in a small number of devices, all current smartphones feature capacitive touchscreens, ready to run Bodyprint for authenticating user access.

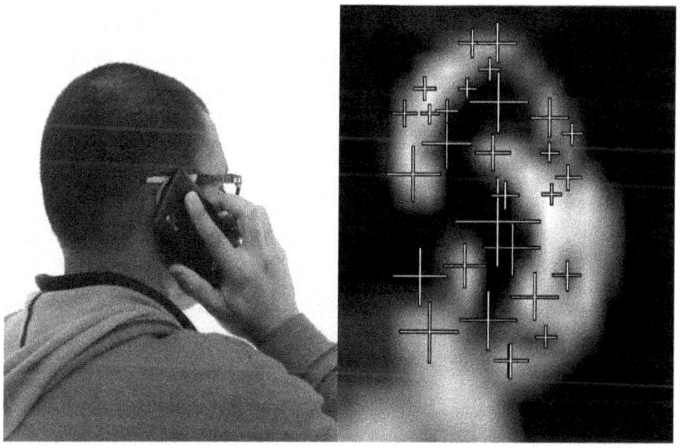

Figure 1: *Bodyprint* brings biometric authentication to commodity mobile devices using the capacitive touchscreen as a low-resolution, but large-area image sensor to reliably identify users based on their ears, fists, or grips when pressed against the touchscreen. (left) To accept an incoming call, the user places the touchscreen onto his ear. (right) Bodyprint extracts features from the raw capacitive image to identify the user.

BODYPRINT: SENSING BIOMETRICS WITH THE SCREEN

Figure 1 shows the use of Bodyprint to accept an incoming call. (a) The user touches the phone to his ear and (b) Bodyprint captures the raw capacitive image from the touch sensor, extracts features and matches them against a user database, and identifies the user to authenticate access.

Bodyprint replaces password entry on mobile devices with biometric authentication. Since the input resolution of commodity touchscreens at ~6 dpi is two orders of magnitude lower than that of fingerprint scanners, Bodyprint scans body parts with proportionally bigger structural features as shown in Figure 2: ears, fists, phalanges, fingers and palms. Bodyprint appropriates the capacitive touchscreen as an image sensor and thus has the potential to run on most if not all currently available touch-based phones.

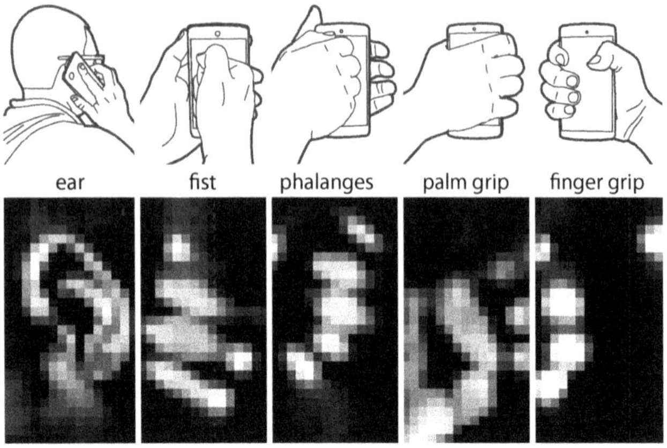

Figure 2: Bodyprint identifies users through these body parts and characteristic poses when touching the screen.

A key benefit of Bodyprint is the usage of the flat touchscreen *surface* to capture an image of the body part, which conveniently solves the challenge of projection for matching images. When pressed against the screen, a body part has a 1–1 mapping to the screen's sensor cells. This mapping remains *constant* over time, such that scanned parts will always exhibit the same dimensions on the device. Using the contact surface for scanning also frees Bodyprint from accommodating image captures from various angles, as is a requirement when using camera-based scanning [1].

CONTRIBUTION

Our main contribution is technical: We demonstrate the feasibility and reliability of the touchscreen as an image sensor with sufficient resolution to capture users' biometric features that are adequate for robust user identification. We require no additional hardware or dedicated sensors, just the capacitive touchscreen, which is the largest component in smartphones today. Our identification algorithm is designed to identify users with high precision and robustness using low-resolution images as input, running in real-time on commodity phones to authenticate access, which brings biometric user identification as a replacement for passwords from high-end devices to *all* current smartphones.

BODYPRINT'S ALGORITHM AND IMPLEMENTATION

We implemented Bodyprint on an LG Nexus 5 phone, which features a Synaptics ClearPad 3350 touch sensor. Through rooting the Android phone and modifying the touchscreen module in the kernel source, we activated Synaptics debug mode and now obtain the capacitive values from the sensor: a 27×15px 8-bit image across a 4.95″ surface (6.24 dpi) at 30fps. Figure 2 visualizes the raw data from the sensor as a "depth" image that captures the proximity of skin to the surface with limited depth resolution.

Bodyprint robustly identifies users despite the low resolution of the input sensor. We accomplish this by processing the sequence of consecutive raw images that result from a *trial*, gathering images between activating the debug mode and detecting touches. Our algorithm has three steps: preprocessing, body part classification, and user identification. Figure 3 shows an overview over our implementation.

Step 1: Preprocessing (raw values to 3×4 key frames)

For each raw image in a trial, Bodyprint first generates three representations using logarithmic, linear and exponential tone mapping. Each mapping accentuates contours and gradients at different intensity levels, enhancing the information in the low-resolution images from the touch sensor.

Depending on the average pixel intensity of an image, the image is sorted into one of five brightness buckets. The purpose of the five buckets is to collect sensor images depending on the body part's proximity to the touchscreen during a trial (i.e., low-intensity images correspond to hovering body parts, high intensities to body parts in contact). We then merge all frames within each bucket into a single image, stretch intensities to the full range, discard the lowest-intensity bucket and scale the remaining four images 16 times using cubic interpolation. This results in 3 tone mappings × 4 buckets = 12 images. Finally, we derive the SURF descriptors [2] of the features resulting from Hessian corner detection, arriving at a set of 12 *key frames* per trial.

During training, Bodyprint inserts each of the 12 key frames into two databases. The user database stores each key frame along with the user's name, body part, and trial ID. The body part database contains 12 groups of features for each body part, corresponding to each of the 12 key frames, thereby combining all features across all trials.

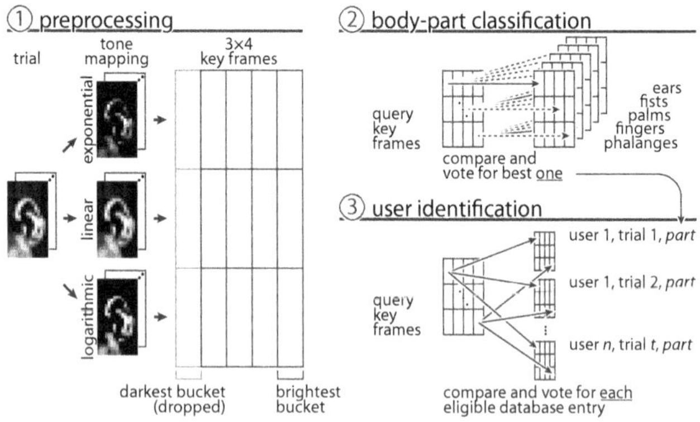

Figure 3: Overview over Bodyprint's algorithm.

Step 2: Body-part classification

The purpose of body part classification is to reduce the search space of the ensuing identification. Although trials may be misclassified as wrong body parts at this stage, we discard false positive matches during user identification.

To classify the body part of a query trial, Bodyprint assigns a body part from the database to each query key frame by comparing it to the respective key frame group in the database. For each body part, we search the database for a best-matching feature f_j of a SURF feature f_i in the query key frame, then search the query key frame for a best match of f_j using L2 distance, and obtain $f_{i'}$. If the two searches produce the same result, i.e., if $f_i = f_{i'}$, we add (f_i, f_j) to the set of matched features for that key frame. If more than half of the features in a query key frame match, we derive the average L2 distance of the matches of that body part. Otherwise, we reject the key frame from voting for that body part. After repeating this procedure for all body parts and key frames, we assign the body part with the lowest L2 distance to each key frame, resulting in a 3×4 set of voted-on body parts.

Each of the 12 key frames now votes for one body part in the database. Bodyprint classifies the query trial as the body part with the highest number of votes if the ratio of votes and number to all voting key frames is above the threshold "body part vote percentage." Otherwise, Bodyprint discards the entire trial and stops the subsequent user identification.

Step 3: User identification using classified body parts

To identify a user, Bodyprint implements a multi-step voting procedure. Each key frame in the query trial can vote for multiple users in the database (similar to Bootstrapper [14]). We additionally check the transformation between the query trial and database trials to reject false positive matches. We repeat this process for each key frame k_l in the database where tuple l = (user, body part, trial ID), but limit body part to the body part determined in Step 2.

First, we compare each query key frame to each key frame k_l. For each feature f_j in a query key frame, we determine the two features f_{j1} and f_{j2} in k_l with the lowest and the second-lowest L2 distance. If the distance between (f_i, f_{j1}) is smaller than 70% of the distance between (f_i, f_{j2}), we add f_i to the set of good matches [2]. If this results in less than 10 good matches, we prevent this query key frame from voting for the currently-tested combination of (user, trial ID).

Next, we calculate the best rigid 2D transformation to rotate the good matches in the query key frame onto the respective features in the database key frame, but exclude other transformations, such as scaling and shearing. If the average error of the transformation is less than the "rotational error threshold," we count a vote for that user.

By iterating across all (user, trial ID) combinations in the database, each key frame can vote as many times for a user as there are trials for that user's body part. We thus normalize each user's votes by the number of those trials. Finally, we sum the votes per user across all key frames. If the vote winner receives less than a fraction of all votes ("user vote percentage threshold"), we reject the query trial. This is how Bodyprint robustly rejects false positive matches.

The use of the previous three thresholds allows us to balance between two extremes: high security of the system, resulting in a higher false rejection rate, and low false rejection rate, which always produces a match after each trial, but risks lower authentication precision. If a trial is rejected, Bodyprint prompts the user to retry. Upon repeated rejection, Bodyprint resorts to regular password entry.

APPLICATIONS

We implemented two applications that use Bodyprint, which we demonstrate in our video figure. Figure 1 shows our first application, which authenticates the user by their ear for an incoming call. Once the user touches their ear onto the screen, Bodyprint identifies the user, confirms or rejects them for the call, and plays auditory confirmation.

Our second application extends Bodyprint to two people and implements the four-eye principle for locking sensitive documents; accessing them then requires the presence of both people. To lock a document, a user pushes the 'lock' button for an open document. Bodyprint requests that all parties shake the phone, which provides the touchscreen with their palm prints. Bodyprint identifies each user and locks the document using their identities. To unlock a document later, a user needs to provide their palm print to the touchscreen again and Bodyprint will prompt for the other user to also be authenticated to reveal the document.

TECHNICAL EVALUATION

We evaluated Bodyprint's performance for each of the 5 body parts shown in Figure 2. We recruited 12 participants (ages 24–53, 4 female) and demonstrated each of the 5 poses to them once. During the evaluation, participants held the Nexus 5 phone as demonstrated and performed 12 trial repetitions. Between trials, participants put the phone down on a table. We did not verify the correctness of performed poses or ask for retries. Overall, we collected 864 trials.

Evaluation methodology

We tested the performance of our algorithm with 12-fold cross validation, which evaluated two aspects: identifying a known user and rejecting an unknown user who is trying to authenticate. In each fold, all of one participant's trials were withheld from the training data set, such that Bodyprint's body part and user database contained 11 trials for each of the remaining 11 participants. We then tested the trained system with the 11 withheld trials from participants in the databases as well as all 12 trials of the withheld participant. Bodyprint then attempted to correctly identify the user of the system or reject the user when it determined the trial to represent an unknown user. We repeated the full 12-fold cross validation varying the three tunable thresholds explained above in unison linearly through each one's range.

Results

Figure 4 plots Bodyprint's false rejection rate against authentication precision. The false rejection rate represents the likelihood of a user to be prompted to retry. Precision is the probability of a known user being correctly identified and unknown users being rejected. The ROC-like curves illustrate the tradeoff for all threshold settings: A precision of 99.5% leads to a false rejection rate of 26.8% using any of the five body parts. Or, for a false rejection rate of 0.2%, Bodyprint achieves 86.1% precision. Limiting the body parts to the ear only boosts the precision of our algorithm to 99.8% with a false rejection rate of only 7.8%.

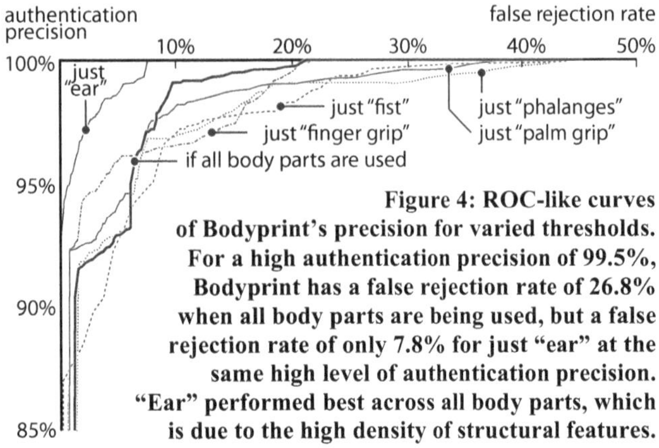

Figure 4: ROC-like curves of Bodyprint's precision for varied thresholds. For a high authentication precision of 99.5%, Bodyprint has a false rejection rate of 26.8% when all body parts are being used, but a false rejection rate of only 7.8% for just "ear" at the same high level of authentication precision. "Ear" performed best across all body parts, which is due to the high density of structural features.

Battery consumption of the touchscreen debug mode

We repeatedly measured the time to fully discharge the Nexus 5 running Bodyprint fulltime with and without Synaptics' debug mode enabled. In both cases, the phone was in airplane mode and a wake lock kept the screen on. In debug mode, the phone turned off after ~15 hours on average compared to ~18 hours on average in regular mode.

Discussion and limitations

The results from our evaluation demonstrate that Bodyprint can be tuned for very high identification precision (99.6%) for applications that require secure authentication, such as accessing sensitive data. In this case, Bodyprint achieves this high precision by strictly rejecting potential false positives, which naturally leads to increased false rejection rate for known users. Alternatively, Bodyprint's thresholds can be set to facilitate quick unlocking, such that each trial will be matched (low false rejection rate), albeit at reduced precision (86.1%). To achieve the results shown in Figure 4, applications that have ~10 known users require a minimum of 11 training samples per user and body part.

When run fulltime, Bodyprint accounts for a 17% overhead on the battery of the device. In reality, however, Bodyprint activates the touch sensor's debug mode only when a user is authenticating, which takes only a few seconds.

CONCLUSIONS

We presented Bodyprint, a password replacement for commodity mobile devices to identify users biometrically from the features of their body, thus possibly increasing the convenience of logging in and authenticating. Users thereby press a body part against the large touchscreen of the device, from which Bodyprint obtains the raw capacitive image, extracts features, and identifies body parts and users.

Bodyprint appropriates the capacitive touchscreen of mobile devices as an image sensor and accommodates their low input resolutions through an increased false rejection rate, but not reduced precision or increased false positives. Bodyprint identified users with 99.5% precision in an evaluation with 12 participants with a false rejection rate of 26.8% across all body parts, but as low as 7.8% for ear-only matching, which is explained through the increased presence of structural features in the human ear [6].

Since all current touchscreens use capacitive sensing, Bodyprint brings reliable biometric authentication to a vast number of commodity devices. In the case that future touchscreens support higher input resolutions, up to a point where they may detect the fine structure of fingerprints, Bodyprint will readily incorporate the higher level of detail of sensor data, which will not only extend our approach to further body parts, but likely reduce false rejection rates at the same high levels of authentication precision.

ACKNOWLEDGEMENTS

We thank Dan Odell, Scott Lin and Mitesh Patel for feedback.

REFERENCES

1. Abate, A.F., Nappi, M., Riccio, D., Sabatino, G. 2D and 3D face recognition. *Pattern Recognition Letters (28):14*, 2007.
2. Bay, H., Ess, A., Tuytelaars, T., Van Gool, L. Speeded-up Robust Features. *Proc. CVIU '07,* 346–359.
3. Ben-Asher, N., Kirschnick, N., Sieger, H., Meyer, J., Ben-Oved, A., Möller, S. On the need for different security methods on mobile phones. *Proc. MobileHCI '11.*
4. Biddle, R., Chiasson, S., Van Oorschot, P. Graphical passwords: Learning from the first twelve years. *ACM Computing Surveys*, (44)4, 2012.
5. Bo, C., Zhang, L., Li, X., Huang, Q., Wang, Y. SilentSense: silent user identification via touch and movement behavioral biometrics. *Proc. MobiCom '13.*
6. Burge, M. and Burger, W. Ear biometrics. *Biometrics* 273–285, Springer US, 1996.
7. Cho, D., Park, K.R., Rhee, D.W., Kim, Y., Yang, J. Pupil and Iris Localization for Iris Recognition in Mobile Phones. *Proc. SNPD '06*, 197–201.
8. Everitt, K., Bragin, T., Fogarty, J., Kohno, T. A comprehensive study of frequency, interference, and training of multiple graphical passwords. *Proc. CHI '09.*
9. Harrison, C., Sato, M., Poupyrev, I. Capacitive Fingerprinting: Exploring User Differentiation by Sensing Electrical Properties of the Human Body. *Proc. UIST '12.*
10. Holz, C. and Baudisch, P. Fiberio: A Touchscreen that Senses Fingerprints. *Proc. UIST '13*, 41–50.
11. Holz, C. and Baudisch, P. The Generalized Perceived Input Point Model and How to Double Touch Accuracy by Extracting Fingerprints. *Proc. CHI '10*, 581–590.
12. Kirschnick, N., Kratz, S. and Moller, S. An improved approach to gesture-based authentication for mobile devices. *Proc. SOUPS '10.*
13. Kurkovsky, S. and Syta, E. Digital natives and mobile phones: A survey of practices and attitudes about privacy and security. *Proc. ISTAS '10,* 441–449.
14. Richter, S., Holz, C., Baudisch, P. Bootstrapper: Recognizing Tabletop Users by their Shoes. *Proc CHI '12.*

NailO: Fingernails as an Input Surface

Hsin-Liu (Cindy) Kao, Artem Dementyev, Joseph A. Paradiso, and Chris Schmandt
MIT Media Lab
Cambridge, MA, USA
{cindykao, artemd, joep, geek}@media.mit.edu

ABSTRACT

We present NailO, a nail-mounted gestural input surface. Using capacitive sensing on printed electrodes, the interface can distinguish on-nail finger swipe gestures with high accuracy (>92%). NailO works in real-time: we miniaturized the system to fit on the fingernail, while wirelessly transmitting the sensor data to a mobile phone or PC. NailO allows one-handed and always-available input, while being unobtrusive and discrete. Inspired by commercial nail stickers, the device blends into the user's body, is customizable, fashionable and even removable. We show example applications of using the device as a remote controller when hands are busy and using the system to increase the input space of mobile phones.

Author Keywords

Capacitive touch; printed electronics; beauty technology; gesture recognition; wearable electronics

ACM Classification Keywords

H.5.m. Information Interfaces and Presentation (e.g. HCI): Miscellaneous

INTRODUCTION

In this Ubiquitous Computing era, we have witnessed increasing levels of technology embedded in our surroundings, blurring the boundary between physical and digital worlds. Moving beyond environments, the near-ubiquity and miniaturization of sensor devices enables technology close to our bodies, redrawing the line between technology and ourselves. In ways, people have started to view on-body devices as extensions of self [8]. Pushing this notion, Holtz et al. [7] implanted interfaces under the human skin, exploring interfaces that are *with the user at all times* and truly *always-available*. However, as medical purpose implants already raise social, ethical, and privacy concerns [4], the acceptability of implanting for pure interaction purposes are still left in question. Drawing inspiration from the multi-billion dollar cosmetic industry, we present a solution towards acceptable implant-like interfaces in the form of cosmetic extensions.

CHI 2015, April 18 - 23 2015, Seoul, Republic of Korea
Copyright is held by the owner/author(s). Publication rights licensed to ACM.
ACM 978-1-4503-3145-6/15/04$15.00
http://dx.doi.org/10.1145/2702123.2702572

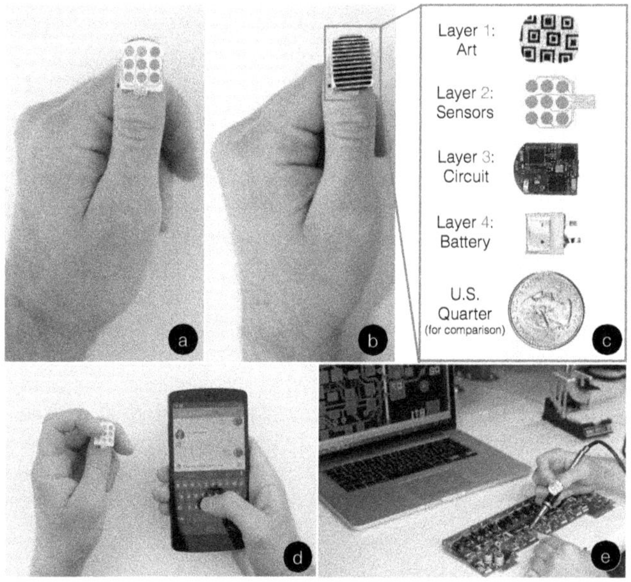

Figure 1. NailO prototype and applications: (a) Miniature and wireless prototype worn on the fingernail. (b) Sensor customization with additional nail art layer. (c) NailO is made of 4 layers. Each layer is shown individually, stacked on top of each other. (d) NailO used to increase input space of a mobile phone. (e) NailO used as remote controller for one-handed input, when the hands are busy.

Products such as nail art stickers and fake eyelashes are widely accepted as extensions to the body for decoration and self-expression. They seamlessly blend into our physical bodies when attached, and are easily removable. As people already wear these products for fashion purposes, we propose embedding technology into these products to extend their functionality and utility to interaction.

To afford usability in the form of cosmetic extensions, three main design themes must be realized: First, the interface should be small and unobtrusive. It should be designed with technology that can be miniaturized to the size of cosmetic products. When worn, it should be comfortable to an extent its existence could be forgotten. Second, the interface should afford natural interactions. The interactions should be simple, intuitive and require minimal cognitive mapping, building on natural body gestures. Third, the interface should be appealing and easy to wear. Like clothing and accessories, the interface can be easily customized. The mounting and removal process should also be simple and similar to existing cosmetic processes. As no device exists that satisfies the above criteria, our work is motivated to do so.

To the best of our knowledge, there is no device that leverages the fingernail as input interface. As a first step towards the vision of cosmetic-inspired wearables, we present NailO (Figure 1), a nail-like capacitive sensing interface to augment the fingernail into a robust yet fashionable input device.

The contributions of the paper are as following:

1. We present a novel input interface that leverages fingernails as input surface and develop a nail-mounted wireless and real-time capable prototype.
2. We perform user studies to assess performance and appeal.
3. We implemented scenarios to explore interactions.

RELATED WORK

Nail and finger mounted devices: Researchers have explored nail mounted outputs such as small displays [9]. For inputs, nail mounted cameras [5] were demonstrated. Furthermore, FingerPad project [3] presented Hall effect sensors to turn the fingertip into a touchpad. However, the project does not leverage the nail as an input surface, and requires bulky finger-mounted hardware. We are not aware of any project that leverages fingernails for input. All of the above-mentioned projects were wired for power and communications. In this project, we demonstrate a wireless and easy-mounting hardware solution. In contrast, rings as input were explored by a number of projects, such as magnetically tracking the rotation of the ring [2] and ring-mounted accelerometers [11].

Beauty Technology: Vega et. al. presented the vision of merging technology into beauty products as a new form of wearable computing [10]. Our work continues this vision and goes beyond the capabilities of decorative on-body electronics; NailO affords functional gesture input.

Capacitive Sensing with Printed Circuits: Conductive Inkjet Printing has created a low-cost and versatile solution for capacitive sensing [6]. Inspired by the paper-like form factor of printed circuits, we apply this technology to a sticker-like nail interface.

THEORY OF OPERATION

Capacitive touch sensing

NailO uses projected capacitance to sense finger touch gestures. In this method, the capacitance is measured on each electrode independently. During a touch event, a capacitor is formed between the finger and the sensing electrode. This capacitance is sensed indirectly by charging and discharging a resistor-capacitor (RC) circuit. With a known resistor, the charge time of an RC circuit is proportional to the capacitance. We choose capacitive sensing over resistive because a custom sensor can be fabricated with accessible technology.

Electrode Layer Design

We designed several conductive electrode patterns to fit the size of a fingernail and manufactured it using low-cost, roll-to-roll Conductive Inkjet Technology [1]. Drawing inspiration from the electrode designs for capacitive touch screens, we prototyped spatially separated electrodes in both single layer and two layers. For the single layer, each electrode represents a different touch coordinate pair and is connects individually to a controller (Figure 2, layer 2). When the electrodes are in two layers, they are arranged in a layer of rows and a layer of columns; the intersections of each row and column represent unique touch coordinate pairs. Because of difficulties of making two-layer in conductive inkjet technology we chose the single layer design. The two layer design is more appropriate for flex PCB technology.

PROTOTYPE

Hardware

Figure 2 presents the NailO system design. We constructed the hardware such that it fits on a fingernail. The hardware consists of four layers (top to bottom): (1) A decorative nail sticker layer for users to customize sensor appearance, (2) the matrix of sensing electrodes, (3) a printed circuit board (PCB), as shown in Figure 3 consisting of an ATmega328 (Atmel) microcontroller and MTCH6102 (Microchip) capacitive touch controller. The samples are transmitted to a laptop or a phone using Bluetooth Low Energy chip nRF8001 (Nordic). (4) a 10 mAh lithium-polymer battery powered the circuit.

With the mean power consumption of 4.86 mA, the device can wirelessly transmit data for at least 2 hours. This represents the worst case scenario, as no power optimization was performed. The battery life can be greatly increased by implementing a sleep scenario, e.g., waking up and transmitting when a touch event is detected.

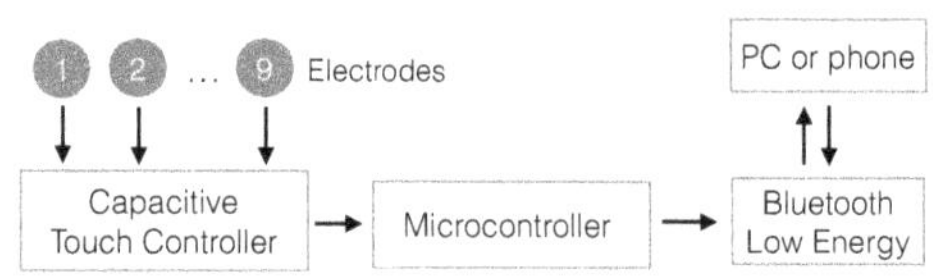

Figure 2. The system design.

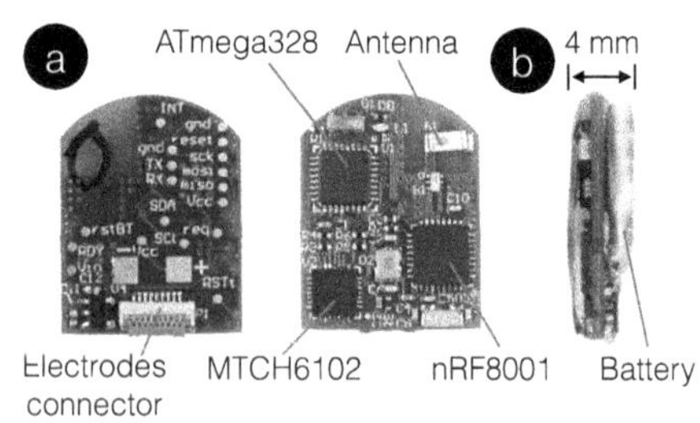

Figure 3. (a) PCB top, bottom. (b) side view of NailO's 4 layers.

Software

To embed the software on-chip for future iterations, we choose a thresholding algorithm over machine learning for a lightweight solution. However, from our pilot studies we found the baseline capacitive sensor values to differ between people, and therefore included an initial calibration phase to find the optimal parameters for each user. After calibration, the system feeds the optimal parameters to the gesture detection algorithm. The electrode matrix is presented as a Cartesian coordinate. For the 3 x 3 sensor grid, the sensor at the lower left corner is set as the coordinate origin. The software

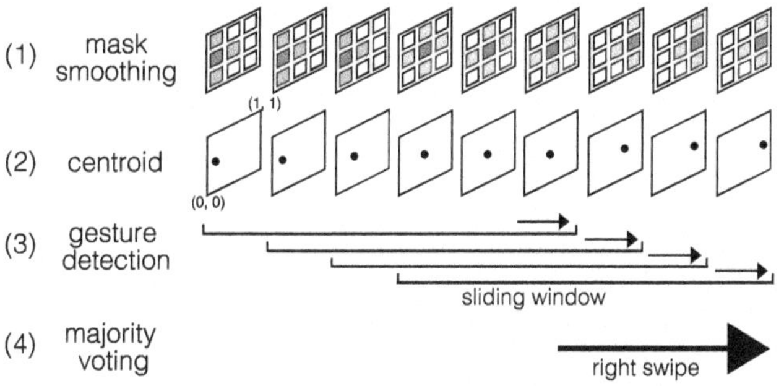

Figure 4. Software: Gesture detection algorithm.

reads in sensor data at around 30 frame/sec, feeding it into the algorithm. As shown in Figure 4, the gesture detection algorithm consists of four main steps, (1) spatial mask smoothing on the raw sensor values for each frame, (2) centroid calculation for each frame, (3) applying a sliding window to calculate centroid position change for gesture detection, (4) majority voting to output detected direction.

USER STUDY

Protocol

We recruited 10 participants (5 male, 5 female) from ages 21 and 28 (mean 25.5). 5 gestures were tested (Figure 5). Each study took about 40 minutes, and had two phases:

(1) *User study*: We mounted the electrode layer on the index finger of the user's dominant hand with cosmetic nail tape. Users were asked to perform swipe gestures with their middle finger using the 3x3 single layer electrodes. The participants had the option to choose a decorative nail sticker layer to apply on top of the electrodes. The 5 tested gestures include left/right swipe, top/down swipe, and long press (Figure 5). We choose this gesture set as they are commonly used input interactions which require low cognitive load.

For calibration, we collected 5 data sets for each gesture, sampling 40 data samples in a 2 sec interval for each data set. The data collection time took around 1 min. The calibration data was used to compute the optimal parameters.

For evaluation, on-screen instructions prompted participants to perform specific gestures. Each gesture was tested 12 times with a total of 60 gestures.

(2) *Post-study interview*: We elicited qualitative feedback towards the system: which gestures were favorable/unfavorable; preference for sensor appearance customization, and how the participant would use a nail-mounted sensor in everyday life. This feedback assisted us in the design of applications for NailO.

Results and Discussion

Accuracy: Accuracy is defined as the number of correctly detected gestures divided by the total number of gestures. The accuracy due to chance was 20%. The system achieved mean accuracy of 92.3% (SD: ±6.8%). Misdetection mostly occurred in the swipe down gesture. The nail curvature caused several right-hand participants to shift left towards the end of the swipe down gesture, resulting in lower accuracy.

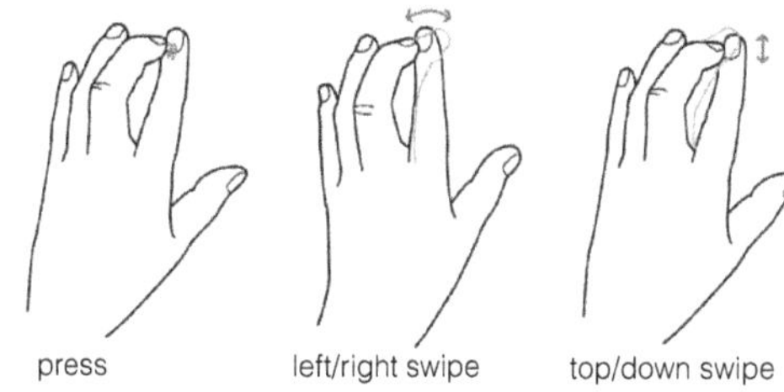

Figure 5. Gestures used in the user study

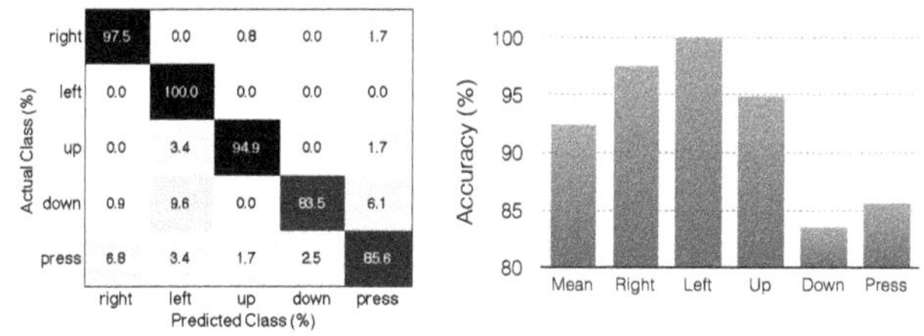

Figure 6. User study results. Left: confusion matrix for all participants. Right: overall mean accuracy and accuracies for individual gestures.

Alternative gestures: From the pre- and post-study interviews, the participants suggested alternative gestures, as depicted in Figure 7. We observed that participants with different hand structures preferred different fingers to perform gestures. Swiping with the middle finger was difficult for participants with middle and index fingers of similar length. Users found elongating the middle finger straining; these participants suggested thumb-based interactions. However, participants with longer middle fingers found the tested gesture natural and comfortable. For future iterations, we plan to manufacture the sensors for all ten fingers, allowing participants to select the nail sensor placement based on individual preference. Is it also necessary to print the electrode substrate in different sizes to fit different users.

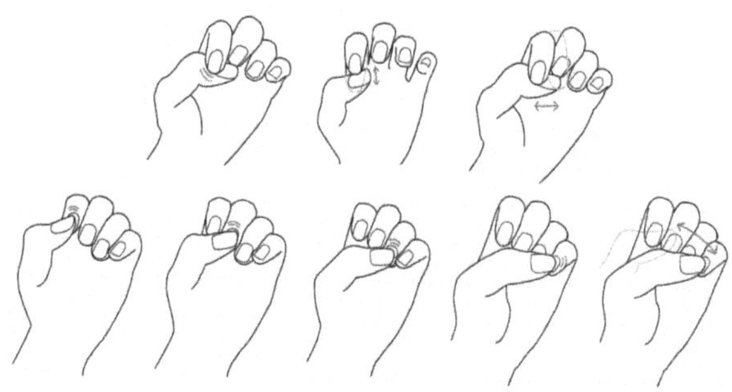

Figure 7. Alternative gestures (1) Thumb gestures (2) NailO on multiple fingers for continuous cross-finger gestures, and also discrete input.

Customizing the sensor: 8 out of 10 participants found it appealing to attach a nail sticker on top of the electrodes. Female participants were especially enthusiastic; they expressed they were more likely to use NailO on a regular basis if they could customize the designs. During the study, they carefully selected nail art designs which reflected their fashion style. Two of the male participants were also receptive to the nail decorations, but preferred simple, single-colored designs.

Other male participants either found the idea of decorating their nails unattractive, or preferred the cyborg look of the electrodes and chose to leave them exposed. One user also suggested a realistic nail design.

False Positives: For NailO to be worn in everyday life, it is important to avoid accidental recognition of gestures, i.e., false positives. We propose the use of an activation gesture, a 2-second press, before any other gestures can be performed. For activation to happen the mean of all electrodes has to remain above a predefined threshold for 2 seconds. With 5 participants (male: 3, female: 2) activation gesture was detected with 100% accuracy. Also, participants found the gesture intuitive and easy to perform. Futhermore, we found that the activation gesture was never detected accidentally when participants performed the swipe and press gestures.

APPLICATIONS

Building on participant feedback from the study, we show two use cases for NailO in Figure 1 and the accompanying video.

1. Remote control: *(1) Hands-full scenario*: As our fingers are dexterous, they have capability for simple interactions even when both hands are occupied. We developed an application for electrical engineers to navigate PCB designs on devices while both hands are occupied with soldering. Without having to break from the soldering process, they can zoom into the on-screen board layout with long press, and navigate by swiping in four directions.

(2) Private and subtle interaction: For scenarios where gesture or speech input are socially awkward or privacy intrusive; NailO affords gestures that are implicit and attract minimal attention. An example scenario is simple interactions with devices while in meetings. As it is considered impolite to openly interact with technology in these situations, NailO affords basic input to subtly control unexpected prompts from devices, such as rejecting a phone call.

2. Expanding the input space: Fingernails are an easily accessible location, so they have great potential to serve as an additional input surface for mobile and wearable devices. Such devices are typically small and thus are difficult to use for complex input. We present a mobile typing application where the user does not have to switch between different keyboards. When typing with the English keyboard, the user can employ nail swipe gestures to input punctuation or emoticons without having to alternate keyboards.

LIMITATIONS AND FUTURE WORK

Hardware: The envisioned form factor of NailO should be comparable to that of a commercialized nail art sticker. To achieve this, we are prototyping a flex PCB version of the circuit with an integrated electrode layer. The flex PCB will conform to the curved surface of the nail. The battery life is the limiting factor for the size and lifetime of the device; we plan to explore wireless powering options, to remove the battery and allow perpetual operation.

Input and Output: Beyond including the gestures in Figure 7, with flex PCB we can prototype robust 2 layer electrodes, turning the NailO into a X-Y coordinate touchpad. Along with the addition of an accelerometer, we can expand the input space to contact-less gestures. The system can also become an output device with the addition of LEDs or vibrators.

CONCLUSION

In this paper we present NailO, a novel nail-mounted input surface. The miniaturized hardware fits on a fingernail and wirelessly transmits data. We show that the system can detect gesture inputs in real-time with high accuracy (>92%). Also, we explored interaction scenarios using NailO as a remote control in "hands-full" or privacy-sensitive use cases. NailO also broadens input space when coupled with mobile devices. Further, NailO's customizable features fuses functional wearable electronics and cosmetics, which appealed to study participants. NailO is our first exploration; we plan to augment other cosmetic extensions to continue our study of cosmetic-inspired wearable technologies.

REFERENCES

1. `http://www.conductiveinkjet.com/`.
2. Ashbrook, D., Baudisch, P., and White, S. Nenya: subtle and eyes-free mobile input with a magnetically-tracked finger ring. In *Proc. of CHI '11*, 2043–2046.
3. Chan, L., Liang, R.-H., Tsai, M.-C., Cheng, K.-Y., Su, C.-H., Chen, M. Y., Cheng, W.-H., and Chen, B.-Y. Fingerpad: private and subtle interaction using fingertips. In *Proc. of UIST '13*, 255–260.
4. Denning, T., Borning, A., Friedman, B., Gill, B. T., Kohno, T., and Maisel, W. H. Patients, pacemakers, and implantable defibrillators: Human values and security for wireless implantable medical devices. In *Proc. of CHI '10*, 917–926.
5. Galeotti, J., Horvath, S., Klatzky, R., Nichol, B., Siegel, M., and Stetten, G. Fingersight: fingertip control and haptic sensing of the visual environment. In *Proc. of SIGGRAPH '08*, 16.
6. Gong, N.-W., Steimle, J., Olberding, S., Hodges, S., Gillian, N. E., Kawahara, Y., and Paradiso, J. A. Printsense: a versatile sensing technique to support multimodal flexible surface interaction. In *Proc. of CHI '14*, 1407–1410.
7. Holz, C., Grossman, T., Fitzmaurice, G., and Agur, A. Implanted user interfaces. In *Proc. of CHI '12*, 503–512.
8. Luhrmann, T. What students can teach us about iphones. `http://salon.com/a/sT_weAA`. Salon May 30, (2010).
9. Su, C.-H., Chan, L., Weng, C.-T., Liang, R.-H., Cheng, K.-Y., and Chen, B.-Y. Naildisplay: bringing an always available visual display to fingertips. In *Proc. of CHI '13*, 1461–1464.
10. Vega, K., and Fuks, H. Beauty technology: body surface computing. In *IEEE Computer Apr'14*, 71–75.
11. Wu, J., Pan, G., Zhang, D., Qi, G., and Li, S. Gesture recognition with a 3-d accelerometer. In *UIC '09*. Springer, 25–38.

Exploring Subtle Foot Plantar-based Gestures with Sock-placed Pressure Sensors

Koumei Fukahori
The University of Tokyo
Tokyo, Japan
furaga@is.s.u-tokyo.ac.jp

Daisuke Sakamoto
The University of Tokyo
Tokyo, Japan
d.sakamoto@acm.org

Takeo Igarashi
The University of Tokyo
Tokyo, Japan
takeo@acm.org

ABSTRACT
We propose subtle foot-based gestures named *foot plantar-based (FPB) gestures* that are used with sock-placed pressure sensors. In this system, the user can control a computing device by changing his or her foot plantar distributions, e.g., pressing the floor with his/her toe. Because such foot movement is subtle, it is suitable for use especially in a public space such as a crowded train. In this study, we first conduct a guessability study to design a user-defined gesture set for interaction with a computing device. Then, we implement a gesture recognizer with a machine learning technique. To avoid unexpected gesture activations, we also collect foot plantar pressure patterns made during daily activities such as walking, as negative training data. Additionally, we evaluate the unobservability of FPB gestures by using crowdsourcing. Finally, we conclude with several applications to further illustrate the utility of FPB gestures.

Author Keywords
User-defined gesture; foot plantar sensing device; sock-placed interface; hands-free interaction.

ACM Classification Keywords
H.5.2. Information interfaces and presentation, e.g., HCI: User Interfaces - Input devices and strategies

INTRODUCTION
We use our hands to control computing devices (e.g. personal computers and mobile devices). However, in life, our hands often get busy, so we are not always able to use them. Some examples are: 1) when the user's hands are busy such as during cooking or carrying bags with both hands, 2) when upper-body space is limited for use such as in a crowded train, or 3) when the user's fingers are stiff with cold.

To address this, a number of interaction techniques using foot-based gestures have been proposed such as kicking

CHI 2015, April 18-23, 2015, Seoul, Republic of Korea.
Copyright 2015 ACM 978-1-4503-3145-6/15/04...$15.00.
http://dx.doi.org/10.1145/2702123.2702308

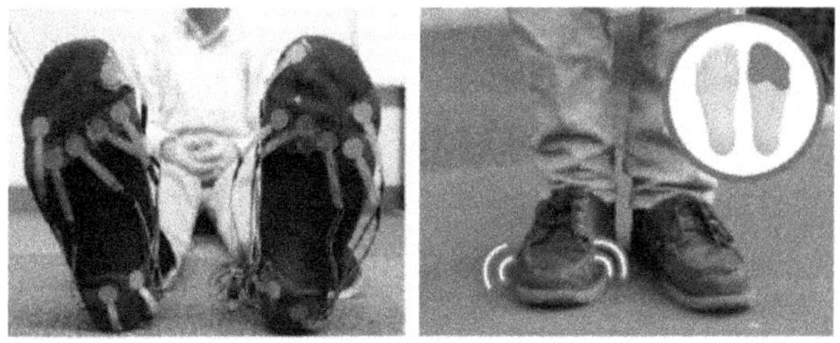

Figure 1. Left: user wearing sock-placed pressure sensors named *Sockswitch*. Right: performing gesture of pressing floor with toes in shoes.

gestures [1], toe/heel rotations [24], and tapping the floor [3]. However, due to the fact that these foot-based gestures require users to move their feet largely, they are not private and sometimes serve as an annoyance to people around the user. Therefore, it is difficult to use these gestures in a public space, e.g. in a train or on the street. In this work, we propose subtle foot-based gestures named *foot plantar-based (FPB) gestures* used with sock-placed pressure sensors (Figure 1). The user can control a computing device by changing the pressure distributions under his/her feet, e.g., by pressing the floor with his/her toe. FPB gestures are subtle; they are suitable for use especially in a public space and are able to be used both in and out of shoes.

There are three goals in this study: designing a suitable FPB gesture set for interaction with a computing device, implementing a gesture recognizer for FPB gestures (we use a machine learning technique for the gesture recognition), and evaluating how unobservable FPB gestures are. To achieve these goals, we conducted four studies. In the first study, we asked 20 participants to design an appropriate FPB gesture set for 29 operations. On the basis of the collected gesture ideas, we designed a user-defined gesture set [29] that consists of 15 FPB gestures. The second and third studies were for collecting training data for our gesture recognizer. In the second study, we collected foot plantar pressure patterns appearing when performing FPB gestures. We measured the pressure patterns of participants with simple sock-placed pressure sensors called *Sockswitch* (Figure 1, Left). In the third study, we collected foot plantar pressure patterns appearing during daily activities such as walking. We use the pressure patterns to avoid unexpected gesture activations made during daily activities. As a result, the accuracy of the gesture classification was 91.3%, and the accuracy of the binary classification of a FPB gesture and daily motion was

99.4%. In the last study, we asked crowd workers to watch videos where an actor is performing foot-based gestures and to guess which gesture was performed. The result of this study confirmed that FPB gestures are significantly more difficult to observe than other foot-based gestures.

Finally, we conclude with showing several applications to further illustrate the utility of our system. In summary, the main contributions of this research are:

- Designing a user-defined FPB gesture set.
- Implementing a FPB gesture recognizer that can prevent unexpected gesture activations during daily activities.
- Evaluating how unobservable FPB gestures are.

RELATED WORK

Foot Plantar Pressure Measurement System

A number of devices for sensing pressure distributions between the feet and the floor have been proposed. These devices can be categorized into two classes: sensing floors and footwear (shoe-placed or sock-placed) sensors. A sensing floor is a floor that contains pressure sensors underneath. For example, Paradiso et al. proposed Magic Carpet [15], which detects the pressure and position of the feet by using a grid of piezoelectric wires and a pair of Doppler radars. Richardson et al. proposed Z-tiles [20], interlocked tiles that contain a number of force-sensitive resistor sensors. Augsten et al. [3] used frustrated total internal reflection (FTIR) and front diffused illumination (front DI) to allow a camera beneath a floor to capture foot pressure images. These sensing floors can precisely detect a user's foot plantar pressure distribution and the position where the user stands. However, because these techniques are limited to a fixed position, it is difficult to use them outdoors such as in a train.

A number of footwear (shoe-placed or sock-placed) pressure sensors have been proposed ([25, 28] and a survey paper is [19]). These footwear devices have several pressure sensors on their foot plantar. However, these sensors have mainly been used in specific application domains such as physiotherapy [9, 12] and sport science [11, 22] for passive monitoring. In contrast, we use sock-placed pressure sensors to actively control computing devices.

Foot-based Gesture Interaction

Many researchers have been exploring interaction techniques with the foot. Pearson et al. [17] proposed a foot operated cursor-positioning device called the "planar slide mole" and assessed its performance against a mouse for target selection. Takeuchi [26] proposed foot tap gestures to operate a map navigating system. Several researches have proposed foot-based interaction techniques to move around virtual reality (VR) environment [6, 10, 13]. Scott et al. [24] evaluated the use of four foot gestures: lifting a toe/heel and foot rotations pivoting the heel/toe. Alexander et al. [1] conducted user studies and propose suitable foot gesture patterns for controlling mobile devices. As an example of systems using footwear pressure sensors, Paradiso et al. [16] proposed a dance system where a user can control background music by using foot-based gestures. As another example, Papetti [14] proposed a sandal-placed foot tapping interface with audio-tactile feedback. Although these foot-based gestures allow the user to control devices comfortably, these gestures are too large; they are not private and sometimes serve as an annoyance (eyesore) to people around the user. In contrast, the FPB gestures we propose are subtle; they are private and not annoying to others.

A supplemental feature of Multitoe [3] is most similar to our system. The system uses a sensing floor, and the user can control a PC game by changing his or her foot plantar pressure distributions. We extend this idea to design a user-defined gesture set for various interactions with computing devices, and to implement a gesture recognizer that works even in real-world applications.

Subtle and Private Input Device

Several subtle interaction techniques have previously been proposed. Costanza et al. [7] used electromyography (EMG) to detect subtle motionless gestures for mobile computing. Saponas et al. [23] extended this idea and proposed a gesture set for use in real-world applications. Wolf et al. [30] explored how microinteractions such as hand gestures allow executing a secondary task without interrupting the primary tasks such as controlling mobile applications while driving. Amento et al. [2] proposed a wrist-mounted bio-acoustic device for sensing fingertip gestures. The freedom of fingertip gestures has been expanded to allow users to point to a 3D position (uTrack [5]) and to use a fingertip as a touchpad (FingerPad [4]). These subtle interaction techniques usually use the hands for interaction. Therefore, these techniques are limited for use in situations where the user's hands are busy. On the other hand, brain-computing devices have been proposed [18, 27]. Using these devices, a user can control a computer only by thinking of a command in his or her mind. However, it is currently difficult to recognize a command precisely. In contrast, our FPB gestures can be used even when the user's hands are busy and can be recognized relatively precisely.

User-defined Gesture Set

User-defined gestures are designed by asking users to design a gesture that they believe is suitable for each computing operation. This approach works effectively when an input device is not common and it is not clear how users want to handle it. This approach has been used to design gestures for tabletop [29] and mobile devices [21] and to design (large) foot-based gestures such as moving a foot leftward and tracing a circle with it [1]. We also adapt this approach to design a suitable FPB gesture set.

DESIGNING A USER DEFINED GESTURE SET

We first design a FPB gesture set for 29 operations in 6 categories (Table 1). The 29 operations are based on

Alexander et al.'s work [1]. They investigated an appropriate "large" foot-based gesture set, e.g., kicking and tracing a circle with a foot, for controlling mobile devices. We refer mainly to their operation list because our motivation is similar to their research.

Study 1: Collecting Gesture Ideas for the 29 Operations

To design a gesture set, we first conduct a guessability study. We ask 20 participants to think and generate an appropriate gesture idea for each of the 29 operations.

Procedure

We show participants the 29 operations one by one and ask them to consider a FPB gesture that they believe is most appropriate for each operation. The categories of gestures are always presented in the same order; the gestures in those categories are presented randomly. During this study, participants wear a head mounted display (HMD) and a pair of earphones (Figure 2, Right). We use HMD and earphones for the study because they are private output methods, which are suitable for a subtle and private input technique. The HMD shows a video and the earphones plays a sound that explains each operation. For example, when we show a participant the operation "*answer phone call,*" the HMD shows the call screen of an iPhone 5 (Figure 2, Left), and the earphones play a ringtone.

To minimize the bias on generating FPB gesture ideas, we showed as general as possible interfaces to participants (e.g., rectangles in a grid pattern for *"item selection"* category). However, only *"answer/ignore phone call"* may be strongly biased because the two operations shows horizontally aligned buttons (Figure 2, Left). Therefore, we also tested vibration interface without screen (Left-bottom in Table 1).

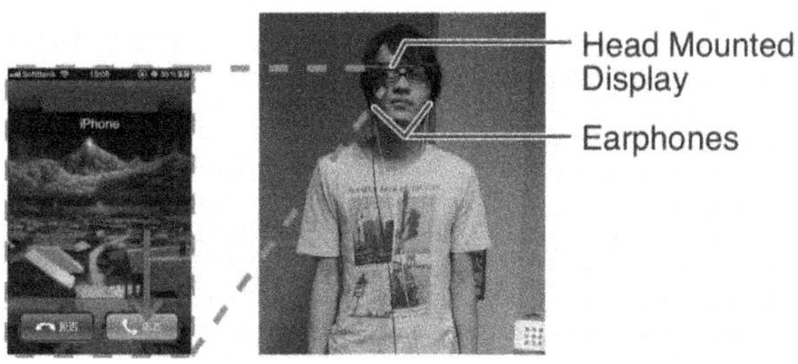

Figure 2. A participant wears HMD and earphones. The HMD is showing a video for *"answer phone call"*.

The participants propose a FPB gesture by performing the gesture while orally explaining it. Also, we give five instructions: 1) participants need to execute each operation without shifting or lifting their foot plantar, 2) they can use both feet if necessary, 3) they need not worry about conflicts of gestures among the operations, 4) they need not worry about technical issues in gesture recognition, and 5) they can say "no idea" if they cannot come up with any FPB gesture. We manually sketch the proposed gestures like illustrations in Table 1.

Participants

Twenty volunteers between 23 - 59 years old (average was 26.8 years old) participated in the study. All of them were Japanese. Only one participant was left-footed. Only two participants regularly use a foot-based input device (a dance game in a game center). No participants had any injury that would inhibit foot movement.

Result

We obtained 17 - 20 gesture ideas for each operation and observed 563 gesture ideas in total. The participants said "no idea" 17 times. The supplemental material A shows the gesture ideas we obtained for each operation.

Gesture Selection Process and Algorithm

Next, we choose a user-defined gesture set based on the 563 gesture ideas collected in Study 1. To remove the subjective selection process, we design an algorithm for selecting gestures automatically. We can see the gesture selection process as an energy minimizing problem. Intuitively, we follow three rules (Figure 3): 1) choose a gesture that many participants proposed for each operation, 2) choose symmetric gestures for a symmetric operation pair, and 3) avoid choosing the same gesture (or similar gestures) for multiple operations. However, we do not care about conflicts among operations that are seldom executed in the same situation, e.g., *"Next track"* in media control and *"Next page"* in browser navigation.

Formally, we minimize the following energy function for

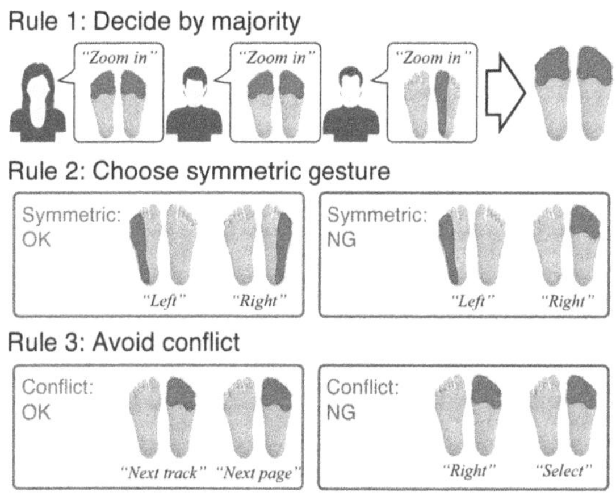

Figure 3. Three rules for designing our user-defined gesture set

mapping L from a set of operations O to a set of FPB gestures G.

$$\min_{L:O\to G} E_{Agree} = \min_{L:O\to G} -\sum_{i\in O} |P_{iL(i)}|$$

$$\text{s.t} \quad \{i,j\} \in S_O \Rightarrow \{L(i), L(j)\} \in S_G,$$

$$\exists C_O \in \{C_O\},\ \ i,j \in C_O \Rightarrow L(i) \neq L(j), \{L(i), L(j)\} \notin I_G$$

1. Item selection					2. Map navigation				
Left	Right	Up	Down	Select	Move viewpoint leftward	Move viewpoint rightward	Move viewpoint upward	Move viewpoint downward	Rotate map clockwise
2. Map navigation			**3. Media control**					**4. Phone control**	
Rotate map counter-clockwise	Zoom in	Zoom out	Play/pause	Previous track	Next track	Volume up	Volume down	Answer phone call	Ignore phone call
4. Phone call		**5. Browser navigation**					**6. Gesture recognition**		
Answer phone call (call with vibration)	Ignore phone call (call with vibration)	End phone call	Home screen	Previous page	Next page	Focus address bar	Activate	Deactivate	
							x 2	x 2	

Table 1. Our user-defined gesture set designed through Study 1

$|P_{ig}|$ is the number of participants that proposed a gesture g for an operation i, S_O is a set of symmetric operation pairs, S_G is a set of symmetric gesture pairs, and C_O is a set of operations that should not be in conflict with each other. I_G is a set of similar gesture pairs, e.g., the upper-left and upper-right gestures in Table 2. We enumerate the elements of each set in the supplemental material B.

Implementation

We implement a solver of the energy minimizing problem in C#. The basic strategy is: 1) enumerate possible gesture pairs for each symmetric operation pair (or gestures for an operation without any symmetric counterpart) and 2) accept the gesture pairs one by one in the order of the total number of participants that proposed the two gestures. If a gesture pair conflicts with already accepted operation-gesture mappings, it is rejected.

Result

The gesture set consisted of 15 different FPB gestures (Table 2). Each illustration means a FPB gesture of pressing the floor with the part (parts) highlighted in red. For example, the upper-left in Table 2 means the FPB gesture of pressing the floor with the left toe (i.e., each illustration shows foot plantar in a mirror.). There was one gesture assigned into multiple operations, i.e., $|C_O| < 29$. However, in practice, any conflict will not happen because the operations arc seldom used in the same situation. Thus, we suppose that our system understands which operation should be executed depending on the situation.

In this study, participants preferred FPB gestures made using the right foot because most of them were right-footed. In fact, the left-footed participant tended to propose gestures by using the left foot. In practice, it is better to allow users to freely switch which foot to use for performing each FPB gesture.

FOOT PLANTAR-BASED GESTURE RECOGNITION

We implement a gesture recognizer for the 15 FPB gestures designed in Study 1. We use a machine learning technique (support vector machine, or SVM) for the gesture recognition. To collect training data (foot plantar pressure patterns), we conduct two data collection studies. In the first study (Study 2), we measure foot plantar pressure patterns while participants perform FPB gestures. We use the pressure patterns in Study 2 as positive training data. In the second study (Study 3), we measure plantar pressure patterns while participants perform daily activities, such as walking or standing up. We use the pressure patterns in Study 3 as negative training data to avoid unexpected gesture activations during daily activities. Our gesture recognizer is implemented in C# and running on a 2.5GHz CPU (Quad Core) and 8GB RAM computer.

Sockswitch: Sock-placed Pressure Sensors

For sensing foot plantar pressure distributions, we develop a simple foot plantar pressure measurement system named *Sockswitch* (Figure 4, Left). Sockswitch is a pair of socks, each of which has a microcontroller (ATmega328P on Arduino Fio) connected to eight force-sensing resistor (Interlink Electronics, FSR 402) pressure sensors. As a pre-resistor of each FSR, we set 330 Ω resistor in a circuit. We follow Wertsch et al.'s work [28] to decide the arrangement of the sensors (Figure 4, Right). We place sensors 1 - 7 according to their work and append sensor 8 to sense the movements around the user's little toes. Pressure data is sampled every 50 milliseconds. The data is transmitted to the host computer by wireless (ZigBee serial) connection.

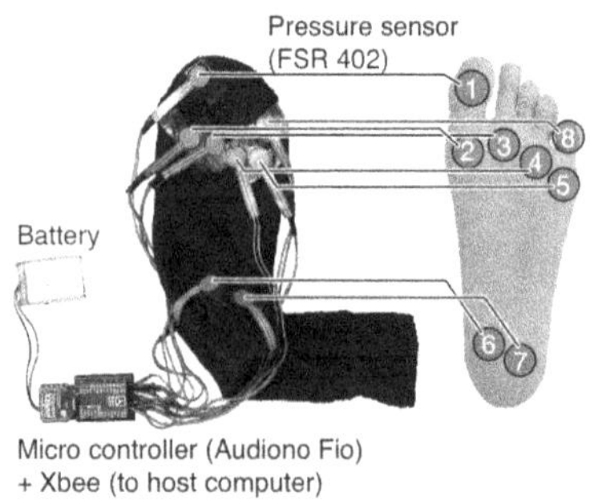

Figure 4. Left: Sockswitch system configuration. Right: locations of pressure sensors for one foot.

Gesture Recognition Algorithm

Our gesture recognizer analyzes the pressure data received from Sockswitch and recognizes FPB gestures. In our approach, our recognizer directly recognizes 14 FPB gestures except *"double pressing with right toe"* (lower-right of Table 2). The system notices that the double pressing gesture is performed when the single pressing gesture (middle-left of Table 2) is performed twice in 0.5 seconds. This is a process similar to a click and double clicks on computing devices.

We show the process of our gesture recognition in Figure 5. First, when our system receives time series data of pressure distribution from Sockswitch, it calculates $I(t)$ as the intensity of movement of each foot. Our system segments a time span, where $I(t)$ is more than a threshold (0.1) (plus a 200ms buffer on either end).

$$I(t) = (f_i(t) - E_i(t) - f_j(t) + E_j(t))\ \max(0, \frac{df_i}{dt}(t))$$

$$\text{s.t.} \quad \{i,j\} = \max_{i,j \in sensors} f_i(t) - E_i(t) - f_j(t) + E_j(t)$$

$f_i(t)$ is the pressure value of sensor i at the time t. $f_i(t)$ has been normalized from raw data from FSR 402; range of [0, 1023] as integer into [0, 1] as float. $E_i(t)$ is an exponential moving average (EMA, $\alpha = 0.3$) of $f_i(t)$. $E_i(t)$ is used as a baseline of $f_i(t)$. The baseline $E_i(t)$ adaptively changes according to the user's body weight and barycentric position of the user. Therefore we do not conduct any pre-calibration for our gesture recognition.

Next, our system classifies each segment (a movement of the foot plantar) into "a daily motion" or "a FPB gesture" with SVM. We use 146 features for the classification. The features include the maximum and minimum value of each pressure sensor (32 features), the inner product of $I(t)$ and the time derivative for each pressure ($\int I(t)\frac{df_i}{dt}(t)dt$, 16 features), and the minimum of the summation of the pressure values on each foot plantar (2 features). We also calculate a 64-point discrete Fourier transform (DFT) of the waveform of each pressure sensor and use the amplitude and the phase of the three lowest frequency components ($16\times3\times2 = 96$ features). We use an open source library, LIBSVM[1], for the implementation of SVM. We use the pressure data obtained in Study 2 as training data of a FPB gesture and one obtained in Study 3 as a daily motion.

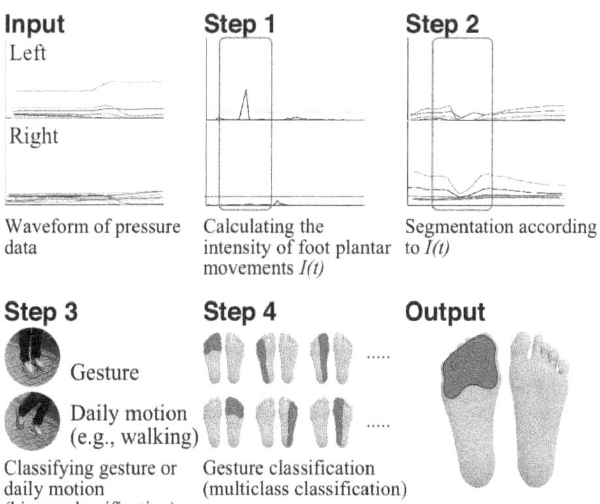

Figure 5. Workflow of our gesture recognition

Finally, if the segment is classified as a FPB gesture, the system classifies it into one of the 14 FPB gestures with another SVM. We use the same 146 features described in the previous paragraph. We use the pressure data obtained in Study 2 as training data for each gesture.

Study 2: Collecting Pressure Patterns during FPB Gestures

Procedure

We asked each participant to wear Sockswitch and to perform the 14 FPB gestures (*"double pressing with right toe"* excluded from the 15). We show each gesture one by one in random order, and the participants perform the gesture. Each gesture is shown 10 times during the study; each participant performs FPB gestures 140 times in total. Our system measures foot plantar pressure patterns while each participant is performing the gestures. During the study, we also videotape them for later verification.

Participants

Five volunteers between 22 - 24 years old (average was 23.4 years old) participated in the study. Only one participant was left-footed. No participant regularly uses a foot-based input device. No participant had any injury inhibiting foot movement. Their foot sizes were between 25.5 and 27.5 cm (average was 26.4 cm). Their body weights were between 51 and 85 kg (average was 62 kg)

Result

We obtained $10 \times 5 = 50$ pressure patterns for each gesture and 700 patterns in total. To evaluate the classification accuracy, we used the two cross validation protocols proposed in [24]: within-participant stratified cross

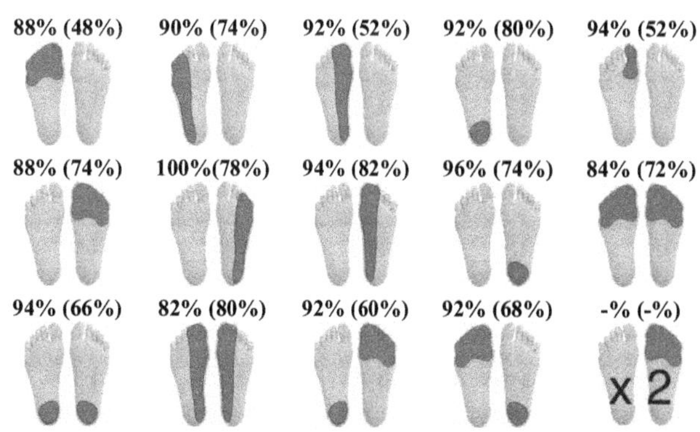

Table 2. Gesture classification accuracy on WP (outside parentheses) and LOPO (in parentheses).

[1] http://www.csie.ntu.edu.tw/~cjlin/libsvm/

validation (WP) and leave-one-participant-out cross validation (LOPO). WP assumes user-dependency and LOPO assumes user-independency respectively. Table 2 shows the classification accuracies on the two protocols.

Overall, the average accuracy of the 14 FPB gestures was 91.3% on WP and 56.2% on LOPO. This means that our gesture classifier is strongly user-dependent. In other words, FPB gestures can be classified accurately if using the training data from the same user.

Study 3: Collecting Pressure Patterns during Daily Activities

Procedure

We asked each participant to wear Sockswitch and go to a university co-op to buy something to drink as a reward. We follow them with holding a PC to record the sensor data from Sockswitch. First, each participant sits down on a chair in our lab. After we start the measurement, he stands up, go to the store, buys a drink, goes back to our lab, and sits down on the chair again. Then, we finish the measurement. Through this study, we could collect pressure patterns made while sitting, standing up, walking, stopping, and so on. During the study, we also videotape participants for later verification.

Participants

Five volunteers, who had participated in Study 2, participated in this study. Each study was performed soon after Study 2.

Result

We obtained 1824 seconds of pressure data in total. We segmented all of the pressure data by executing the segmentation process (the upper row of Figure 5), yielding 299 pressure patterns. Table 3 shows the accuracies of binary classification of FPB gesture and daily motion on WP and LOPO.

Overall, the accuracy on WP was 99.4% and that on LOPO was 58.0%. This means the binary classification is also strongly user-dependent. On the other hand, the precision of FPB gesture and the recall of daily motion were surprisingly good on both of the two protocols. This is because sensor values for walking were completely different from those for standing. For example, 1) each data segment was long, 2) the max value of $I(t)$ in the segment was large, and 3) all sensor values change synchronously.

	Precision	Recall	F-measure
FPB gesture	0.99 (0.97)	1 (0.41)	0.99 (0.58)
Daily motion	1 (0.41)	0.98 (0.97)	0.99 (0.58)

Table 3. Accuracy of binary classification of FPB gesture and daily motion on WP (outside parentheses) and LOPO (in parentheses).

EVALUATING UNOBSERVABILITY OF FOOT PLANTAR-BASED GESTURES

The key idea of FPB gestures is making foot-based gestures difficult to observe. FPB gestures should not be observed by people around the user. In this section, we conduct a user experiment to measure how unobservable FPB gestures are by testing the following three hypotheses:

H.1. It is more difficult to identify which FPB gesture was performed than other foot-based gestures.

H.2. It is more difficult to notice the user's foot movement while he or she is performing a FPB gesture than other foot-based gestures.

H.3. It is as difficult to notice the user's foot movement while he or she is performing a FPB gesture as while the user is doing nothing.

In this study, we compare the unobservability of FPB gestures with one of Alexander et al.'s gestures [1] and Scott et al.'s gestures [24].

Study 4: Evaluating Unobservability of FPB Gestures by Using Crowdsourcing

We conduct a user experiment on a crowdsourcing service named *CrowdFlower*[2]. We evaluate the unobservability of 35 gestures in 4 categories: 15 FPB gestures, Alexander et al.'s 13 gestures [1], Scott et al.'s 6 gestures [24] and performing no gesture (Table 4).

Category 1. FPB gestures (15 gestures)
See Table 2
Category 2. Alexander et al.'s gestures (13 gestures)
Single tap
Double tap
Double tap forward/leftward/rightward (3)
Trace a clockwise/counter-clockwise circle (2)
Trace a clockwise/counter-clockwise arc (2)
Kick forward/backward/leftward/rightward (4)
Category 3. Scott et al.'s gestures (6 gestures)
Up toe
Up heel
Rotate foot leftward/rightward pivoting toe (2)
Rotate foot leftward/rightward pivoting heel (2)
Category 4. No gesture (1 gestures)
Do nothing

Table 4. 35 gestures in 4 category evaluated in Study 4

Procedure

Crowd workers are asked to watch a video of a trained user performing a foot-based gesture and to try and guess which gesture was performed (Figure 6). We show each video by using <video> tag of HTML 5. The workers can watch a video repeatedly. For this study, we prepare 35 videos; each video shows an actor performing one of the 35 gestures. The length of each video was less than 10 seconds. The workers answer which gesture was performed in a five-choice question. The five choices consist of the correct

[2] http://crowdflower.com

answer, three dummy answers, and "no gesture was performed". The dummy answers are randomly selected from the same category of the correct answer. For example, if the correct answer is any of the FPB gestures, the dummy answers are also any of the FPB gestures. Also, the workers answered how confidently they answered the question on a 5-level Likert scale ("Definitely," "Very probably," "Probably," "Possibly," and "Not sure").

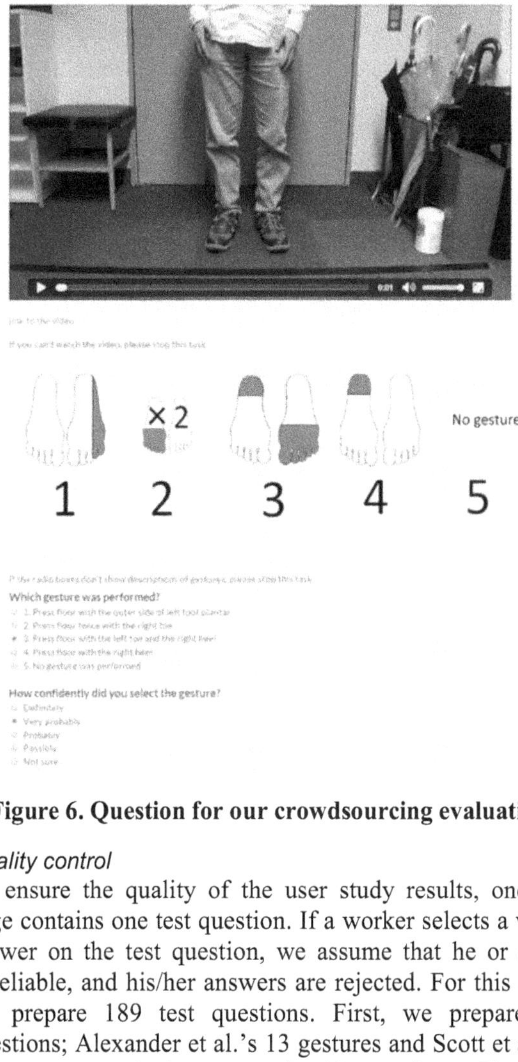

Figure 6. Question for our crowdsourcing evaluation

Quality control

To ensure the quality of the user study results, one task page contains one test question. If a worker selects a wrong answer on the test question, we assume that he or she is unreliable, and his/her answers are rejected. For this study, we prepare 189 test questions. First, we prepare 190 questions; Alexander et al.'s 13 gestures and Scott et al.'s 6 gestures respectively appear in 10 questions. Then, we asked two lab members to answer the 190 questions. We used the 189 questions that both of the lab members answered correctly as our test questions.

Questions and crowd workers

We prepared 3700 questions (+189 test questions). The 34 foot-based gesture videos respectively appear in 100 questions, and the no-gesture video appears in 300 questions. The 300 questions for the no-gesture video consist of 3 sets × 100 questions. Each question has four dummy answers and the dummy answers in each set are selected from the same category (FPB gestures, Alexander et al.'s gestures or Scott et al.'s gestures). A task consists of five questions including one test question. A crowd worker can take 25 tasks (100 answers and 25 answers for test questions) at maximum. The workers can stop their tasks in the middle. Overall, 909 workers participated in this study, and the average number of answers was 4.1. We paid the workers 5 cents for a task, and the total cost of this crowdsourcing was $162.

Result

We evaluated the unobservability of gestures with three metrics: accuracy, number of questions wrongly answered as "no gesture was performed," and confidence for each answer on a 5-level Likert scale. Accuracy means how difficult it was to identify each gesture, the number for "No gesture" means how difficult it was to notice the actor's foot movement while he was performing each gesture, and confidence means the subjective difficulty of each question.

Figure 7 shows the averages of each category for the three metrics. For example, the averaged accuracy of FPB gestures was 68.9%, and the other categories' accuracies were above 94%. To compare the averages among categories, we performed a non-parametric multiple comparison test (Steel-Dwass test [8]). As a result, there were statistical significances ($p < 0.05$) between FPB gestures and the other foot-based gestures in all metrics (black annotations in Figure 7). This means that FPB gestures were significantly more difficult to identify and notice (H.1 and H.2). On the other hand, for number of "No gesture," the average of FPB gestures was significantly smaller than that for no gesture (red annotations in Figure 7). This means that a lot of workers could notice the actor's foot movement when performing FPB gestures (against H.3).

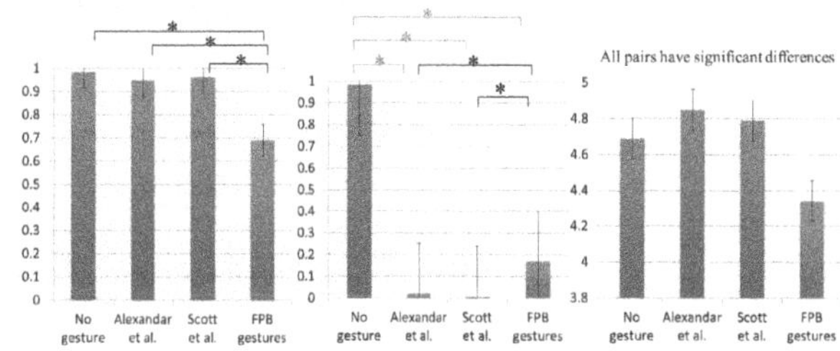

(a) Accuracy (b) # of "No gesture" (c) Confidence

Figure 7. Result of Study 4 for each category

To compare each gesture, we also performed a Steel-Dwass test among the 37 question sets (34 × 100 questions for the foot-based gestures and 3 × 100 questions for no gesture). We show the p-value of each pair in the supplemental material C. Then, for each FPB gesture, we counted the number of other foot-based gestures, Alexander et al.'s and Scott et al.'s, that were significantly different from the FPB gestures in accuracy ($p < 0.05$, the last row of Table 5). Nine FPB gestures were significantly different (more difficult to observe) from most of the 19 other foot-based gestures in accuracy (≥ 18). On the other hand, three FPB gestures had almost no differences with other gestures ($\leq$

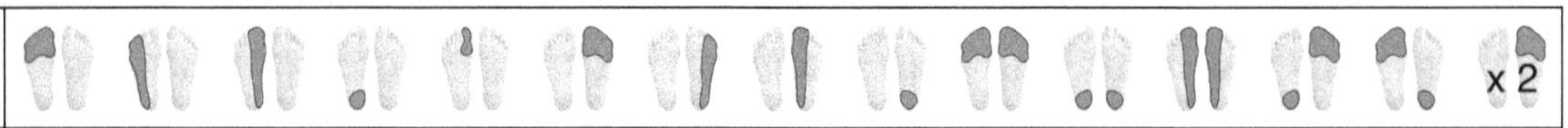

Accuracy	74%	55%	59%	59%	57%	74%	60%	59%	67%	84%	78%	83%	66%	60%	88%
# of "No gesture"	17%	23%	24%	15%	20%	16%	16%	21%	22%	11%	13%	13%	17%	20%	7%
Confidence	4.5	4.1	4.4	4.1	4.2	4.4	4.3	4.3	4.4	4.6	4.5	4.6	4.0	4.2	4.7
Differences with large gestures	12/19	19/19	19/19	19/19	18/19	12/19	19/19	19/19	18/19	1/19	7/19	1/19	19/19	19/19	0/19

Table 5. Result of Study 4 for each FPB gesture

1). This is likely because the three gestures are difficult to perform subtly, and the actor unconsciously moved his feet largely. The small number of differences for *"pressing the floor with both heels"* (= 7) is due to the same reason. The two gestures of pressing with the left or right toe also had relatively few differences (= 12). We consider this is because we recorded each video from the front of the actor; the movements of the toes were more visible than those of the other parts of the foot plantar.

APPLICATION

The design of the FPB gestures is aimed at hands-free interaction with subtle foot movements. They are suitable for controlling mobile devices in a public space such as answering/ignoring a phone call on a crowded train. Likewise, they are suitable for use in situations where we cannot or should not use our hands, e.g., scrolling the web page of a recipe while cooking or browsing a slide during a presentation with hand gestures like in a TED presentation. Here, we briefly present some possible applications with FPB gestures.

Secure Interface

Because FPB gestures are subtle, they may be used for security systems such as ATMs. As a proof of concept, we implemented a GUI application for inputting a secret number (Figure 8-a, left). In this application, users wear a head mounted display (HMD), and the HMD shows a number pad. Users control a cursor on the number pad by using the five FPB gestures in the item selection category (Table 1). We designed this interface by asking the 20 participants of Study 1 to design an interface for inputting numbers (we asked after Study 1) and choosing one that the most participants proposed.

As a simpler application, we also implement a password input system for unlocking a smartphone (Figure 8-a, right). The user can unlock a smartphone by performing several FPB gestures in pre-defined order.

Supporting PC control

FPB gestures can be used to support our PC work. For example, a participant in Study 1 commented *"I want to use FPB gestures to switch desktop windows while working on PC"*. We agree with his idea because it is tiring to move the user's hand from keyboard to mouse and then click an icon on task bar. Also, pressing Alt + Tab repeatedly until the target window appears is time-consuming. As a solution of this problem, we implemented a Windows service application where the user can switch desktop windows by performing FPB gestures (Figure 8-b). For example, in the accompanied video, a user is writing a thesis with TeX. He switches to bash by pressing a floor with the right-heel, to a pdf viewer with the right-toe and to a text editor with the left-heel.

Gaming interface

Our participants often said that they wanted to play a game with FPB gestures. To achieve this, we implemented a simple rhythm game (Figure 8-b). The main objective of this game is to press the floor with the foot plantar, following notes of music scrolling from the front. Each note is represented as an illustration of the left foot plantar or one of the right foot plantar. Users are required to press the floor with the left or right foot plantar.

Interface for Wearable Devices

It is possible to use FPB gestures to control a head-mounted display (HMD) such as Google Glass. Currently, voice recognition and hand-based gestures are proposed as the main input methods. However, these methods can be heard or seen by people around the user, which is not private and sometimes serves as an annoyance. In contrast, because FPB gestures are difficult to observe, they are suitable for use as an input method for HMDs, particularly in a public space.

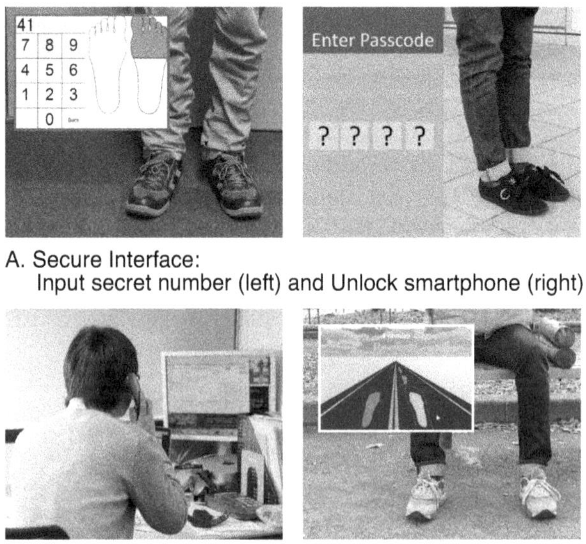

A. Secure Interface:
Input secret number (left) and Unlock smartphone (right)

B. Supporting PC control C. Gaming interface

Figure 8. Applications for FPB gestures

DISCUSSION

In this research, we conducted three studies to design and implement a FPB gesture system with sock-placed pressure sensors. From the result, our system successfully recognized FPB gestures with avoiding unexpected gesture activations during daily activities. The accuracy of the gesture classification was 91.3%, and the accuracy of the binary classification between a gesture and a daily motion was 99.4%. Though the number of participants of Study 2 and 3 is small, we consider that our concept, FPB gesture recognition with sock-placed sensors, was proven.

Then, we conducted a user study to evaluate how unobservable FPB gestures are (Study 4). The result confirmed that FPB gestures are significantly more difficult to observe than other foot-based gestures. On the other hand, the accuracy of FPB gestures was 68.9%. This percentage seems too large. However, in this study, we supposed one of the most severe situations; each video showed only the actor's lower-body and workers could watch the same video as many times as they wanted. In daily life, when we look at a person, we usually look at his/her upper body and can look at his/her movement only once. Considering this, we believe that the accuracy of 68.9% is small enough to confirm that FPB gestures are absolutely difficult to observe.

The result of Study 4 also shows that it is easy to notice that the user somewhat moves his foot while performing a FPB gesture. This seems to be against our motivation that a user can perform FPB gestures without being noticed. However, in daily life, our foot plantar frequently moves subtly during standing and sitting (see people around you). Thus, even if others notice the user's foot movement, they could not know whether the movement is a FPB gesture or a daily motion.

We used sock-placed pressure sensors for sensing foot plantar pressure distributions. However, it was possible to use shoe-placed pressure like *FootLogger*[3]. We used sock-placed sensors because they can cover wider situations rather than shoe-placed sensors. For example, in most Asian countries, people take off their shoes indoors but do not take off their socks. Further, a participant of Study 3 pointed out that sock-placed sensors are better because they can be stretched and worn by users even if their foot sizes are different. In fact, the five participants of Studies 2 and 3 (their foot sizes were 25.5 - 27.5 cm) could wear the same sock-placed sensors.

FPB gestures can be performed with subtle foot movements. However, in some cases, large foot gestures such as kicking forward and tracing a circle with the foot, might be more intuitive and easier to perform than FPB gestures. In practice, it would be better to allow users to use both FPB gestures and large foot gestures and to choose which gesture to use depending on the situation.

Limitation and Future Work

In Studies 1, 2, and 3, all of the participants performed tasks while wearing low-heel shoes such as sneakers. However, if they were wearing high heels, gesture ideas and foot plantar pressure patterns would differ from the ones we obtained. Further, all of the participants in Study 1 were Japanese, which might bias FPB gesture ideas. It is future work to explore how shoes and cultural differences affect the design of the FPB gesture set and FPB gesture recognition.

In Study 3, we mainly collected pressure patterns during walking. Therefore, it might not be enough to prevent unexpected gesture activations during various activities, such as exercising or driving a car. Our gesture recognizer would be more robust if we collect pressure patterns during such activities as negative training data.

To perform a FPB gesture, a user needs to add force to the pressure sensors on his or her foot plantar. Therefore, it is difficult to perform a FPB gesture such as when sitting with folded legs. However, this problem would be addressed by attaching strain gage sensors along the foot fingers and detecting how each finger is hooked. It is future work to implement a FPB gesture recognizer with those additional sensors.

In this paper, we focused on subtle foot-based gestures used when a user is stopping (standing or sitting). However, we can consider ones used during walking or running, e.g., swinging the feet with adding force around the thumbs or the little toes. It is future work to explore subtle foot-based gestures when a user is moving.

Seven participants of Study 1 pointed out that FPB gestures are not suitable for executing complex operations such as map navigation. They said that it is difficult to perform FPB gestures quickly, and it is tiring to perform them many times. We consider that it is most suitable to use FPB gestures to execute a simple operation such as answering a phone call or playing/pausing a music player.

CONCLUSION

We proposed foot plantar-based (FPB) gestures, an interaction technique that uses sock-placed pressure sensors. We designed a user-defined gesture set and implemented a SVM gesture recognizer for FPB gestures. Our gesture recognizer can avoid unexpected gesture activation during daily activities such as walking. The accuracy of the gesture classification was 91.3%, and that of the binary classification of a FPB gesture and a daily motion was 99.4%. We also evaluated how unobservable each FPB gesture is and confirmed that FPB gestures are significantly more difficult to observe than existing foot-based gestures. Finally, we showed several applications of FPB gestures to illustrate their utility.

ACKNOWLEDGMENTS

This work was supported by JSPS KAKENHI Grant Number 26240027.

[3] http://vandrico.com/device/3l-labs-footlogger

REFERENCES

1. Alexander, J., Han, T., Judd, W., Irani, P., and Subramanian, S., Putting Your Best Foot Forward: investigating real-world mappings for foot-based gestures. In *Proc. CHI'12*, 1229-1238.
2. Amento, B., Hill, W., and Terveen, L. The Sound of One Hand : a wrist-mounted bio-acoustic fingertip gesture interface. In *Proc CHI EA'02*, 724–725.
3. Augsten, T., Kaefer, K., Meusel, R., Fetzer, C., Kanitz, D., Stoff, T., Becker, T., Holz, C., and Baudisch, P. Multitoe: high-precision interaction with back-projected floors based on high-resolution multi-touch input. In *Proc. UIST '10*, 209-218.
4. Chan, L., Liang, R.H, Tsai, M.C., Chang, K.Y., Su, C.H., Chen, M.Y., Cheng, W.H., Chen, B.Y. FingerPad: private and subtle interaction using fingertips. In *Proc. UIST'13*, 255-260.
5. Chen, K.Y., Lyons, K., White, S., Patel, S. uTrack: 3D input using two magnetic sensors. In *Proc. UIST'13*, 237-244.
6. Choi, I., and Ricci, C. Foot-mounted gesture detection and its application in virtual environments. In *Proc. IEEE Internationa Conference on System, Man and Cybernetics '97*, 4248-4253.
7. Costanza, E., Inverso, S.A., Allen, R., and Maes, P. Intimate Interfaces in Action: assessing the usability and subtlety of EMG-based motionless gestures. In *Proc. CHI '07*, 819-828.
8. Dwass, M. Some k-sample rank-order tests. In *Essays in Honor of Harold Hotelling*. 198–202.
9. Edgar, S., Swyka, T., Fulk, G., and Sazonov, E.S. Wearable shoe-based device for rehabilitation of stroke patients. In *Proc. IEEE Engineering in Medicine and Biology Society'10*. 3772-3775.
10. Haan, G.D., Griffith, E.J., and Post, F.H. Using the WiiBalance Board TM as a low-cost VR interaction device. In *Proc. VRST '08*, 289-290.
11. Holleczek, T., Ruegg, A., Harms, H., and Troster, G. Textile pressure sensors for sports applications, In *Journal of Sensors '10*, 732-737.
12. Luo, Z.P., Berglund, L.J., and An, K.N. Validation of F-Scan pressure sensor system: a technical note. In *Journal of rehabilitation research and development 98*, 186–191.
13. Matthies, D.J.C., Muller, F., Anthes, C., and Kranzlmuller, D. ShoeSoleSense: proof of concept for a wearable foot interface for virtual and real environments. In *Proc. VRST'13*, 93-96.
14. Papetti, S., Fontana, F., Civolani, M., Berrezag, A., and Hayward V. Audio-tactile display of ground properties using interactive shoe. In *Proc. HAID'10*, 117-128.
15. Paradiso, J., Abler, C., Hsiao, K.Y., and Reynolds M. The Magic Carpet: physical sensing for immersive environmentse. In *Proc. CHI EA '97*, 1997.
16. Paradiso, J., Hu, E., and Hsiao, K.Y. Instrumented footwear for interactive dance. In *Proc. the XII Colloquium on Musical Informatics '98*, 89-92.
17. Pearson, G., and Weiser, M. Exploratory evaluation of a planar foot-operated cursor-positioning device. In Proc. *CHI '88*, 13-18.
18. Pike, M.F., Major, H.A., Porcheron, M., Sharples, S.C., and Wilson, M. L. Measuring the effect of think aloud protocols on workload using fNIRS. In *Proc. CHI '14*, pp. 3807–3816, 2013.
19. Razak, A.H.A., Zayegh, A., Begg, R.K., and Wahab, Y. Foot plantar pressure measurement system: a review. In *Journal of Sensors 2012*, 9884–912.
20. Richardson, B., Leydon, K., Fernstrom, M., and Paradiso, J.A. Z-Tiles: building blocks for modular , pressure-sensing floorspaces, In *Proc. CHI '04 EA*, 1529-1532.
21. Ruiz J., Li, Y., and Lank E., User-defined motion gestures for mobile interaction. In *Proc. CHI'11*, 197-206.
22. Salpavaara, T., Verho, J., Lekkala, J., and Halttunen, J. Wireless insole sensor system for plantar force measurements during sport events. In *Proc. IMEKO XIX World Congress on Fundamental and Applied Metrology'09*, 2118-2123
23. Saponas, T.S., Tan, D.S., Morris, D., Balakrishnan, R., Turner, J., and Landay, J.A. Enabling always-available input with muscle-computer interfaces. In *Proc. UIST '09*, 167-176.
24. Scott, J., Dearman, D., Yatani, K., and Truong, K.N. Sensing foot gestures from the pocket. In *Proc. UIST '10*, 199-208.
25. Sensoria. http://www.sensoriafitness.com/
26. Takeuchi, Y. Gilded Gait: reshaping the urban experience with augmented footsteps. In *Proc. UIST '10*, 185-188.
27. Tan, D. S., and Nijholt, A. *Brain-Computer Interfaces: applying our minds to human-computer interaction*. Springer, 2010.
28. Wertsch, J.J., Webster, J.G., and Tompkins, W.J. A portable insole plantar pressure measurement system. In *Journal of Rehabilitation Research and Development '92*, 13-18.
29. Wobbrock , J. O., Morris, M. R., and Wilson , A. D. User-defined gestures for surface computing. In *Proc. CHI '09*, 1083–1092, 2009.
30. Wolf, K., Rohs, M., Naumann, A., Müller, J., Laboratories, D.T., and Berlin, T.U. A taxonomy of microinteractions: defining microgestures based on ergonomic and scenario-dependent requirements. In *Proc. INTERACT '11*, 559-575.

Classification Accuracy from the Perspective of the User: Real-Time Interaction with Physiological Computing

Stephen H. Fairclough
Liverpool John Moores University
Byrom Street, Liverpool, UK
s.fairclough@ljmu.ac.uk

Alexander J. Karran
Liverpool John Moores University
Byrom Street, Liverpool, UK
alexander.j.karran@gmail.com

Kiel Gilleade
Liverpool John Moores University
Byrom Street, Liverpool, UK
gilleade@gmail.com

ABSTRACT
The accurate classification of psychophysiological data is an important determinant of the quality when interacting with a physiological computing system. Previous research has focused on classification accuracy of psychophysiological data in purely mathematical terms but little is known about how accuracy metrics relate to users' perceptions of accuracy during real-time interaction. A group of 14 participants watched a series of movie trailers and were asked to subjectively indicate their level of interest in a binary high/low fashion. Psychophysiological data (EEG, ECG and SCL) were used to create a binary classification of interest via a Support Vector Machine (SVM) algorithm. After a period of training, participants received real-time feedback from the classification algorithm and perceptions of accuracy were assessed. The purpose of the study was to compare mathematical classification accuracy with the perceived accuracy of the system as experienced by the users. Results indicated that perceived accuracy was subject to a number of psychological biases resulting from expectations, entrainment and development of trust. The F1 score was generally a significant predictor of perceived accuracy.

Author Keywords
Physiological Computing; EEG; Psychophysiology; tagging media

ACM Classification Keywords
H.1.2. User/Machine Systems; H.5.1 Multimedia Information Systems; H.5.2. User Interfaces; I.2.6 Learning; I.5.1 Models

CHI 2015, April 18–23, 2015, Seoul, Republic of Korea.

http://dx.doi.org/10.1145/2702123.2702454

INTRODUCTION
Psychophysiological data can be collected implicitly during human-computer interaction and used to represent the affective or cognitive state of the person. This dynamic and quantified representation of the user represents a basis for adaptive software mechanics. The same logic can be applied to the derivation of media tags during the passive consumption of movies, music or still images. In this case, psychophysiological data is collected and classified as the person experiences the media, which are subsequently classified to yield tags related to emotional experience [1]. This form of implicit human-centred tagging [2] provides a method for understanding human behavior and the effects of media on the user – as well as enabling a number of interactive media applications, such as interactive narratives tailored to induce a specific psychological state in the viewer [3]. This type of implicit interaction represents a form of physiological computing [4] constructed upon a generic control loop [5].

Physiological computing as implicit interaction
Research on human-centred tagging of media has focused on the measurement of emotional states [6], which may be categorized as discrete states (happy, angry, calm etc.) or within the two-dimensional space of the circumplex model [7]. The generation of affective tags provides a useful means to: (1) assess whether media produced the intended emotional state, and (2) to assemble a repertoire of media over a period of time known to induce specific emotional states in that particular individual. The former represents a 'test audience' usage case where automated psychophysiological quantification effectively replaces subjective self-report. The second instance emphasizes the construction of personalised database (of media clips) via human-centred tagging that may be utilized to elicit desirable emotional states and mitigate undesirable ones, e.g. affective music player [8]. Recent work in the domain of cultural heritage [9] departed from this tradition by measuring a psychological state of interest as a cognitive-affective state. In this example, measures from EEG and autonomic psychophysiology were combined to operationalize the degree of interest elicited by exposure to media. Interest is defined as a combination of: (1) attention, (2) stimulation and (3) high levels of either

positive or negative emotion. Tagging media with respect to items that elicit high interest can be used to create personalised and engaging trajectory through any information space [10]. This approach is concerned with the classification of magnitude along a single psychological dimension (high vs. low levels of interest) as opposed to the categorization of discrete emotional states.

Classification accuracy

Current research on the classification of psychophysiological data places enormous emphasis on the application of machine learning algorithms in this context [11]. The general methodology for the construction of a classifier is to generate a training set, which is subsequently used to train a classifier and represents a template for all subsequent acts of categorisation. The first obstacle for classification is the derivation of an optimal set of training data. It is hoped that training data provides a good mapping in terms of a quantitative discrimination (between the states to be classified) and lead to a reduction of classification errors. Those factors most likely to actively contribute to classification errors are:

1. The influence of noise from non-psychological sources, noise is a 'fact of life' for ambulatory psychophysiology
2. The degree of divergence between the estimated mapping provided by the training set and the best mapping possible. This factor is determined by the representativeness of the training set. The degree of divergence between what is measured by the system now and what was measured during training is called Bias.
3. The sensitivity of the classifier to the training set. It is important to note that different approaches to signal classification differ with respect to their susceptibility to specific and idiosyncratic qualities of the training dataset. The degree of sensitivity to the training set exhibited by the classifier is called Variance.

Therefore, a good dataset for training may be defined as one that encompasses the full range of physiological responses for classification and has been acquired under realistic conditions. The acquisition of such a dataset often requires a sustained period of monitoring and a cumulative approach to data collection, i.e. training dataset becomes more inclusive as data is acquired over time/episodes of usage. The accumulation of training data over a period of time should reduce bias and variance as the resulting data that informs the process of classification is both representative and generalizable [12].

Perceived accuracy & user experience

The quality of the classification emerging from the training dataset is generally assessed using 'hard' markers of mathematical accuracy, e.g. cross-validation. It is assumed that accurate classification as represented by a mathematical index will translate into good performance with respect to the categorization of psychological states within the context of human-computer interaction. This assumption disregards the obvious fact that users of physiological computing systems will possess varying degrees of subjective self-awareness. The co-existence of 'hard' markers of classification accuracy (from the system) and 'soft' markers of subjective self-awareness is characteristic of interactions with physiological computing systems. The combination of 'hard' and 'soft' markers of classification accuracy yields a third category of accuracy – which equates to the perceived accuracy of the system from the perspective of the user (see [4] for a more detailed discussion).

The perceived accuracy of the classification engine is an important determinant of the user experience. A system that is perceived to be accurate in the short-term will create a positive impression that encourages further use. In the long-term, an acceptable level of perceived accuracy will engender trust in the technology [13]. The question of what is an acceptable level of accuracy for a physiological computing system has been addressed by previous research [14,15]. These authors simulated various levels of accuracy with respect to control of an input device and task difficulty respectively in order to explore levels of user acceptance and tolerance for system error.

Current study

The current paper will focus on the relationship between perceived classification accuracy and mathematical accuracy of a physiological computing prototype working in real-time. A system was designed to make a binary (high/low) classification of the interest level experienced by the user during the viewing of 40 movie trailers. Data from EEG, ECG and skin conductance level were collected, quantified and classified in real-time. Classification of psychophysiological data was achieved using a Support Vector Machine (SVM) working on a subject-dependent basis, i.e. a SVM was generated that was specific to each individual participant.

The training dataset used to generate the SVM classifier was obtained at four different points in time as each participant viewed the series of movie trailers. The initial system build for classification was achieved on the basis of a small dataset whereas the final system build utilized a significantly larger training dataset for classification. Four system builds are included in the experimental design in order to explore how the acquisition of training data influences both 'hard' and 'soft' markers of classification accuracy.

At the end of each movie trailer, the participant was required to provide a subjective binary estimate of interest and subsequently received feedback on the classification of interest produced by the system.

The purpose of this paper is to assess users' perceptions of psychophysiological classification based upon real-time feedback within the context of an interaction with a working system. We also wished to explore the feasibility of subject-dependent classification where the classification algorithm for psychophysiological data is trained to each user following a brief period of initial exposure. The focus of current research in this field is on 'hard' mathematical markers of classification accuracy that are often derived on a retrospective basis [11]. Our contribution is to study the association between these 'hard' markers and the perception of accuracy from users who have received explicit feedback from the system during a real-time interaction.

The study was designed to explore four research questions:

1. How does the accumulation of training data influence both mathematical classification accuracy and perceived classification accuracy? It is assumed that both estimates of classification will improve over each successive build of the system (due to the cumulative acquisition of training data and an associated reduction of variance and bias in the training set)
2. How do user perceptions of accuracy change with sustained exposure to the system? Is there evidence for any systematic bias?
3. For subject-dependent classification of psychophysiology in real-time, how long is required for a system to generate a sufficient corpus of data to train a classifier?
4. What is the relationship between mathematical accuracy and perceived accuracy? Do users tend to over- or under-estimate classification accuracy?

SYSTEM DESCRIPTION

Conceptual Model

The conceptual model for the system used in the study is illustrated in Figure 1. Four types of measure are collected from the participant, each one maps onto three process sub-components, which are forwarded to the classification engine in order to categorise the level of interest as high or low. The concept of interest is divided into three types of process: (1) activation, i.e. does the content stimulate the autonomic nervous system? (2) cognition, i.e. does the content engage novel problem-solving and consolidate memory formation in the rostral prefrontal cortex of the brain, and (3) valence, i.e. does the content provoke a strong positive or negative emotional response (see [10] for a detailed description of how the concept of interest and associated measures were derived). If psychophysiological data indicates that content is stimulating, cognitively engaging and emotionally provocative, it is deemed to be of interest to the user. The activation processor is indexed by autonomic indicators, such as heart rate (HR) and skin conductance level (SCL). The level of electrocortical activation from the EEG signal over the rostral prefrontal cortex [16] was used as a measure of cognition. Valence was represented by frontal EEG asymmetry [17].

Measures from the physiological sensors were forwarded to the component processors. These features were used as inputs to the classification engine in the composite model that expressed interest as a binary (high/low) state. The output from the classification represents a control input for a hypothetical process of software adaptation.

Real-time interest classification

A data processing pipeline was designed to: (1) extract the relevant psychophysiological features, (2) quantify each category of psychophysiological response, (3) classify the response as a binary state of interest and label this response. Because the system works in real-time on a subject-dependent basis, an initial exposure of the participant to video clips was used to train the first build of the SVM classifier. The classifier was re-trained on a new data set three times after this initial build, e.g. every 7-9 movie trailers, in order to deliver a steady accumulation of the training dataset.

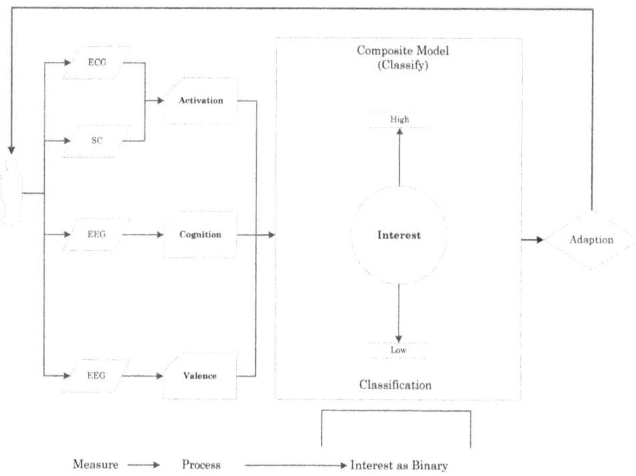

Figure 1. System Model

Due to the complexity of the application framework two elements have been extracting from the overall structure to highlight how they functioned within the application. The first element took the form of a video player sub-window, which also acted as the means for gathering and processing the subjective responses to each 60sec video after viewing. Execution of the video player function drew a clip from the pool of video material. After the video had been displayed a new window appeared to prompt the user to deliver a subjective response (high/low interest). These responses were processed and forwarded to the export module for association with psychophysiological responses for that particular video.

The second element received feature vector output from the data export process and checked whether it was necessary to construct a new version of the classifier. If true, a check was performed to determine if the current request corresponded with the first build of the classifier. If this condition was satisfied, a further check was performed to determine whether two instances of both classes (i.e. two examples of high and low class data) existed within the training dataset. If true, a classifier was constructed. However, if a classifier already existed and a new classifier build was required, then data collected for the current stimulus period (i.e. corresponding to approx. 10 movie trailers) was added to the existing training set and a new classifier was constructed based upon this aggregated dataset. If no new classifier build was required, the train classifier process was bypassed and new vectors were classified and output.

Data acquisition

Psychophysiological data was imported in real-time from two ambulatory physiological sensor technologies: the Nexus X MkII © (used to capture autonomic ECG and SCL responses) and the Enobio © (used to capture EEG responses). These data were buffered internally and the process pipeline split into two top-level protocols to process autonomic data and EEG data respectively.

Physiological responses from the autonomic system were measured using the Electrocardiogram (ECG, sampled from the torso) and SCL (distal phalanges, second and forth finger, non-dominant hand). Both channels were sampled at 512Hz. Three channels of electroencephalographic (EEG) data were recorded, measuring alpha (8-12Hz) and beta (13-30Hz) activity, using the Enobio wireless 3-channel sensor (sampled at 250Hz) with ground contacts on left ear lobe and inner ear (Starlabs Inc). A mobile sensor forehead band was fitted and nasion aligned to ensure sensor placement at Fp1, Fp2, Fpz and electrodes attached.

The autonomic data processor included filtering for both electrocardiogram (ECG) and skin conductance level (SCL) of a 0.5 to 35Hz bandpass and 35Hz lowpass respectively. The ECG data was subsequently forwarded to a beat detection process in order to determine the mean and standard deviation of the inter-beat-interval (IBI). The filtered SCL data was forwarded to the epoch analysis module to produce the mean and standard deviation of SCL. The resulting derivatives from ECG and SCL were forwarded to a feature store for eventual output.

Data analysis

The EEG data processor performed filtering (Bandpass 0.05-35Hz) and epoch analysis on three channels of EEG activity derived from Fp1, Fp2 and Fpz. These data were subjected to a Fast Fourier Transform (FFT) analysis to determine the total amplitude spectra of the signal in the alpha and beta bandwidths. Data from the FFT were forwarded to calculate cognition and valence. The former was expressed as a ratio of electrocortical activation (β/α) at sites Fp1, Fp2, and FPz. Valence was represented by frontal EEG asymmetry, which is expressed as the difference between the natural logs (ln) of the total power in the alpha band of the right and left hemispheres. The resulting eight derivatives (see Table 1) are forwarded to the feature store and exported to the train classifier process

Measure	Signal Derivatives for Classification
Heart Rate	IBI (mean) IBI (s.d.)
Skin Conductance	SCL (mean)
EEG	Ratio β/α (Fp1) Ratio β/α (Fp2) Ratio β/α (Fpz) $\ln(\alpha FP2)-\ln(\alpha FP1)$

Table 1. A list of measures and those signal derivatives used as input to the classification algorithm.

All derivatives were extracted from a 60 second epoch (i.e. duration of each movie trailer) to deliver a total of 40 stimulus events. For autonomic measures features were captured using a 12sec data window with a moving window of 6sec. For EEG, features are captured using a 12sec of data with moving 6sec window. This approach was used to construct a feature vector every 6sec resulting in 10 -1 (due to the overlapping data 12 second data windows) per sixty seconds stimulus epoch. This approach delivered a potential of $360 - (n * 9)$ classification vectors, where n equals the total number of vectors used to train the classifier initially.

Classification

The training of the classifier occurred within MatLab using the deployment command line processor for real-time data interaction

To train and ascertain estimated performance of the classifier in real-time, the sequential minimal optimisation [18] and hold-out cross-validation methods are used on the aggregated training data. The hold-out cross-validation method partitions the data into two parts, by randomly assigning data to either training or testing sets, ensuring that the classifier is trained and tested with novel data and is analogous to a real world task. This method of cross-validation has been shown to provide a more accurate assessment of potential classifier performance in comparison to k-fold cross-validation when applied to small datasets, such as those gained from real-time applications [19]. When coupled with a loose grid search algorithm, these methods form the basis for the training and parameterisation of the SVM in real-time, providing the optimal settings for the box constraint and sigma values of the SVM radial basis function (RBF) kernel for each new instance of training data as the system is used. That is, for each new build of the system, training data is aggregated and cross-validated to create a new classifier in real-time, in this instance to prevent over fitting of the classifier to the training data and reduce computation time the box constraint and sigma values are set to a maximum of 2.

Using this approach a feature vector was constructed every 6 seconds resulting in 10 -1 (due to the overlapping data 12 second data windows) classification vectors per sixty second stimulus epoch. This gave a potential of 360 – (n * 9) classification vectors, where n equals the total number of vectors used to train the classifier initially. Thus, nine classifications were performed in real-time per stimulus epoch and a majority vote was performed between class outputs at the end of each epoch to determine the resulting class for that epoch.

METHODOLOGY

Participants

16 participants (9 female) aged 19-25yrs. took part in the experiment. However, only 14 participants data were used for analysis. Data from two participants were excluded because their responses did not meet a criterion that was required to train a classifier on four occasions. Specifically, these two participants did not produce the required instances of high and low classes over the maximum 10 videos needed to train the system (i.e. the number of videos remaining in the database was insufficient to permit three further iterations of the classifier). All procedures and measures were approved by the University Research Ethics Committee prior to data collection.

Experimental design

The experiment was designed as a repeated measures study (i.e. the same participants took part in all build sessions). A "Wizard of Oz" [20] prototyping approach was derived in order to convey feedback to the user in real-time. The application included four build phases over the course of the experiment designed to investigate how the accumulation of data into the training set influenced classification accuracy:

- build 1 was the initial classifier training phase and required responses from at least two of each of the target classes (high and low)
- build 2 aggregated the database of responses from build 1 into a new training data set and the SVM was re-built
- build 3 aggregated the responses from builds 1 and 2 into a new training data set and the SVM was re-built
- build 4 aggregated the responses from the previous 3 builds and into a new training data set and the SVM was re-built

Materials

The stimulus material took the form of movie video trailers from four genres of film: science fiction, comedy, action and horror. The presentation of each movie trailer lasted 60 seconds; each genre contained 10 trailers. Videos were displayed on a 42" LCD TV screen at 720p resolution and audio was reproduced through television stereo speakers at an easy listening volume of 70 dB. Participants sat at an approximate distance of 1m directly in front of the television and within easy reach of a computer connected mouse. Video display and user interactions were captured using a computer with two display outputs; one screen output the video and subjective response collection application interface and the other displayed the classifier interface. The presentation order of the movie trailers was randomised for each participant, with each video presentation drawing from the pool of 40 until all material was exhausted.

Procedure

After receiving instruction about the experimental procedure, participants were required to provide written consent. Electrodes were placed on the torso for ECG and on the distal phalanges of second and forth finger of the non-dominant hand for SC. Participants were asked to sit comfortably but remain as still as possible.

The experimental procedure was completed in two parts, initial training (build 1) and subsequent instances of classification/feedback. During the build 1 mode a video trailer of 60 seconds duration randomly chosen from a pool of 40 was displayed to the participant. After each video, participants were shown a simple interface on screen that asked "was this content interesting? Yes/No." Once feedback was received, another screen appeared to allow the next video in the sequence to be played ("Play next video? Yes/No"). This procedure was repeated until the experimenter received a message indicating that a classifier was being constructed.

Once a classifier had been constructed, the sequence of events was as follows:

(1) participant views movie trailer

(2) participant provides a subjective rating of whether the movie trailer was rated as high or low interest. This rating was added to the training dataset for subsequent builds of the classifier

(3) The system provides feedback (high/low interest) to the experimenter for that item based on the current build of the classification algorithm

(4) Feedback from the system is conveyed verbally to the participant by the experimenter.

This mode of interaction continued during builds 2-4.

The experimenter was the same person throughout the trial and it was made clear to the participants that he was simply a conduit to system feedback.

RESULTS

The classification accuracy of the system was measured in mathematical terms using holdout cross-validation (as described above) and the F_1 score. The holdout method of cross-validation uses the entire dataset as both training and testing data by splitting the data arbitrarily according to criteria; that is, data is randomly assigned to either training or testing according to the "set size" determined before classification (in this case 60% training, 40% testing). The dataset contains both the classification vectors (observations) and its associated label (subjective judgments), testing the SVM model involves classifying the remaining (40%) novel instances of test data, to determine accuracy. The labels (subjective judgments) associated with the test vectors (observations) are known to the experimenter but unknown to the SVM model.

The perceived accuracy of the system was expressed as the degree of agreement between the binary classification produced by the system in real-time and subjective self-assessment from the user. Perceived accuracy was expressed as a percentage figure (i.e. % of agreement) and in terms of four categories of outcome:

- True Positive (both system and participant rated the movie as high interest)
- False Positive (system rated the movie as high interest but participant produced a rating of low interest)
- True Negative (both system and participant rated the movie as low interest)
- False Negative (system rated the movie as low interest but participant produced a rating of high interest).

Research Question 1: How does the accumulation of training data influence classification accuracy over successive builds of the system?

The first question posed by the study addressed the relationship between the accumulation of training data and mathematical accuracy (and the perception by the user of mathematical accuracy). The classification engine was build through four phases. The first build was based upon a relatively small number of stimuli (movie clips) and is assumed to produce the lowest level of classification accuracy. By the same logic, it is assumed that the fourth and final build would deliver the highest level of accuracy because it is based upon the largest corpus of training data.

A univariate ANOVA was conducted to assess the influence of build on mathematical accuracy. This analysis revealed no significant influence of build on either index of mathematical accuracy [$F(3,11)=1.40$, $p=.30$]. A second ANOVA was performed to explore the influence of build on perceived accuracy. This analysis revealed a marginal main effect [$F(3,11)=3.15$, $p=.06$]; post-hoc analyses indicated that perceived accuracy was significantly higher for build 1 and 4 compared to build 2 ($p=.04$), in addition, perceived accuracy increased during build 4 compared to build 3 ($p=.05$). These finding suggest that perceived accuracy followed a quadratic pattern over the number of builds, being high at build 1, falling by 10% at build 2 and rising to original level by build 5. All descriptive statistics are illustrated in Figure 2.

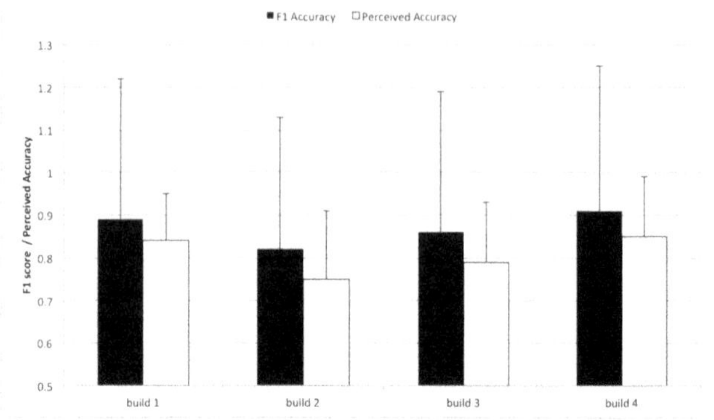

Figure 2. Means and standard deviation for mathematical accuracy (F1) and perceived accuracy over four successive system builds (N=14).

Research Question 2: How does perceived classification accuracy change over successive builds and sustained exposure to the system?

The second question concerned the effect of each build on user perceptions of accuracy with respect to pattern of responses, i.e. True Positive, False Positive, True Negative, False Negative. A 4 (build) x 2 (positive/negative) x 2 (true/false) ANOVA was conducted on these data. This analysis indicated a greater frequency of positive responses ($M=3.04$) compared to negative responses ($M=0.95$) [$F(3,11) = 105.7$, $p<.01$], i.e. participants tended to indicate high rather than low interest. In addition, there were a greater number of true (i.e. correct) responses ($M=3.23$) compared to false responses ($M=0.75$) [$F(3,11) = 106.3$, $p<.01$].

A significant interaction between positive/negative response category and true/false [$F(3,11) = 11.06$, $p<.01$] revealed a higher number of correct ($M=5.12$) compared to false responses ($M=0.96$) in positive/high interest category. A significant interaction between build and true/false [$F(3,11) = 8.56$, $p<.01$] indicated that the number of correct responses was higher during build 4 ($M=4.04$) compared to build 2 ($M=2.75$) or build 3 ($M=2.93$). These findings suggest a general bias towards positive (i.e. high interest) cases and true (i.e. correct) responses from the participants. It was also apparent that participants perceived the frequency of correct responses (in both positive and negative categories) to peak following the fourth and final build of the classification algorithm. The effect of build on positive responses is illustrated in Figure 3.

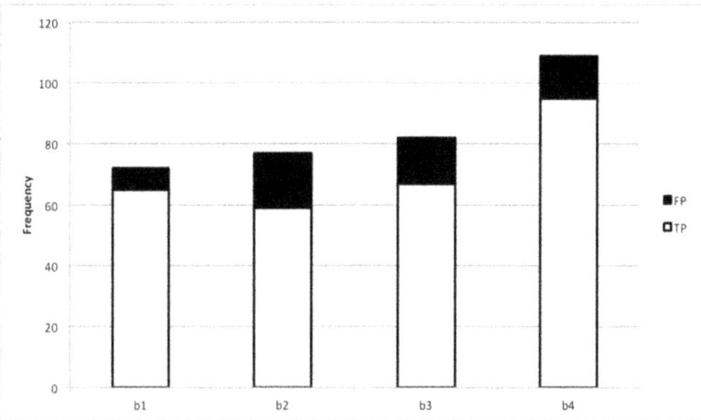

Figure 3. Frequency of True Positives (TP) and False Positives (FP) over four successive builds of the classification algorithm (N=14).

Research Question 3: How long is required to train a subject-dependent classifier?

The study was designed to train a classification algorithm to the individual on a subject-dependent basis using data from initial exposure to the system. There is a question regarding the feasibility of this approach with respect to user acceptance, i.e. can a classifier be created for all participants within a short period of time. We found that the system took an average of 7 videos (i.e. 7 minutes) to construct the SVM. The maximum number of videos was 12 but this was an upper limit imposed by the experimental protocol (see *Participants* section for further explanation). The minimum number of videos used to create the SVM was 4.

Research Question 4: What is the relationship between mathematical classification accuracy and perceived accuracy?

The final question to be explored concerns the relationship between mathematical measures of classification accuracy and users' perceptions of accuracy during interaction. There are two aspects to be investigated, the first concerns the differential between perceived accuracy and mathematical accuracy, i.e. do users tend to over- or under-estimate with respect to mathematical classification accuracy. A difference score was calculated to express the differential between perceived accuracy and mathematical accuracy [Perceived Accuracy – Mathematical Accuracy], i.e. positive score indicates that perceived accuracy was greater than mathematical accuracy. The mean difference score illustrates that estimates of perceived accuracy were generally between 4-9% lower than the F1 score but variability was substantial. A 4 (build) x 2 (index of mathematical accuracy) ANOVA was performed to explore the impact of build number on this differential. No significant differences were found with respect to influence of build number (see Table 2 for descriptive statistics).

The second aspect of this analysis relates to the degree of association between perceived classification accuracy and its mathematical analogue. There is also a secondary issue related to whether the degree of association between perceived and mathematical accuracy changes over time with each successive build, i.e. does the association between 'hard' and 'soft' markers of accuracy change with each successive build. A series of Pearson's r correlations were calculated to express the degree of association between mathematical and perceived accuracy over all four builds of the classification algorithm. The resulting r scores (Table 4) demonstrate a positive correlation for F1 that is statistically significant in the case of all but the second build phase.

Build	F1 *r*	Mean Diff.
1	0.58*	.09 [.29]
2	0.37	.04 [.30]
3	0.82**	.05 [.24]
4	0.73**	.07 [.27]

Table 2. Pearson's r correlation coefficients between mathematical classification accuracy and perceived accuracy. Mean Diff. refers to the differential score produced when mathematical accuracy was subtracted from perceived accuracy, standard deviation in parentheses. * p<.05, **p<.01 (N=14).

DISCUSSION

The purpose of this study was to explore the relationship between mathematical classification accuracy and the perception of accuracy from users during a real-time interaction with explicit feedback. In addition, the experiment was designed to explore how the size of the training dataset influenced both 'hard' and 'soft' markers of classification accuracy.

The system was designed to classify psychophysiological data in real-time on a subject-dependent basis. The classification algorithm (SVM) was initially created for each individual based upon exposure to an average of seven movie trailers of 1min duration. After the initial build of the classifier (build 1), the SVM was rebuild every 7-9 movie trailers to yield three subsequent versions of classifier, each one based upon on cumulative increase of training data.

The effect of system builds on classification accuracy

Due to high levels of bias and variance in the initial training set, it was assumed that both mathematical accuracy and perceived accuracy would be poor during build one and exhibit a linear increase as the training dataset used to train the classifier increased over successive builds. The analysis of both markers of mathematical accuracy (Figure 2) revealed no significant support for this prediction. It was notable that a high (e.g. 89%) level of mathematical accuracy was achieved during the first build based upon approximately seven minutes of data collection. This finding is encouraging with respect to designing a system upon a process of subject-dependent classification where each algorithm is created dynamically for each user.

The absence of any subsequent increase in mathematical accuracy could be a 'ceiling effect' i.e. the high level of accuracy accomplished during build one left little room for further improvement. Alternatively the 40min duration of the experiment may have been insufficient to observe the effect of exposure/data collection on classification accuracy. Extending the period of exposure and size of the training dataset beyond the current experiment represents one avenue for further research.

The perceived accuracy of the classification engine tended to fluctuate over the four builds (Figure 2). The statistical analysis support a view that perceived accuracy increased during the final build compared to builds 2 and 3. High level of perceived accuracy observed during build one could reflect a 'halo effect' due to the novelty of the system and the incorporation of technical apparatus, such as sensors. When participants progressed to the second build phase, perceived accuracy dropped by 9%, a trend that was mirrored by the F1 score (Figure 2). The decline of perceived accuracy during the second build may reflect how increased exposure to the system classification led to a less optimistic (and more accurate) appraisal of the capabilities of the technology. This type of analytic understanding of a technical system informs the development of trust between user and technology [13].

Factors influencing perception of system accuracy

It is important to note that positive responses (high interest) were more frequent than those in the negative (low interest) category. This is unsurprising given that our participants watched movie trailers, which are designed to pique the interest of the viewer. However, this imbalance did bias the participant to perceive classification accuracy in terms of the more frequent (high interest) category. If we consider the ratio of true (correct) to false (incorrect) responses in the positive category (Figure 3), participants experienced one incorrect response for every 9.3 classifications during the first build. This was the highest accuracy recorded by participants and represented an initial positive bias. This index fell to one error for every 3.3 classifications during the second build phase (Figure 3). The proportion of incorrect responses in the positive/high interest category subsequently decreased during builds 3 (one error per 4.5 classification) and 4 (one error per 6.8 classifications). Given that negative responses (low interest) were relatively infrequent, it is argued that the proportion of correct responses in the high interest category were largely responsible for driving the perceived classification accuracy.

The number of classifications judged to be correct (in both high and low interest categories) significantly increased during the fourth and final build compared to builds 2 and 3. In addition, the correlation between mathematical scores of classification accuracy and perceived accuracy were positive and significant during final two builds of the system (Table 2). It can be argued that build four represented instances of classification based upon the largest training dataset, where bias and variance are both reduced, and convergence between mathematical and perceived measures of accuracy was a natural consequence of this factor.

Alternatively, the presence of class imbalance within our classification system may have functioned as a form of implicit bias. Participants learned that output from classification tended to favour the 'high interest' category, which represented a subtle mechanism of entrainment whereby participants tended to choose the positive category without conscious realization. It is also possible that participants treated the experiment as a game where the goal was to correctly match their response with one produced by the system. Hence, participants were predisposed towards the high interest category, which in turn leads to the creation of classification engine with an implicit bias towards this category - and repeated feedback from the system both reinforces and amplifies this bias towards the high interest category. A final possibility is that participants tended towards agreement with the system classification during the fourth build due to fatigue accumulated during the test session.

Methodological issues

This issue of class bias with respect to binary classification presented a dilemma for assessment of the current system. The obvious solution is to create a balanced training set where both outcomes are equally likely but that can be problematic where bias is an inherent property within a database. Even if the classification system were initially trained using perfectly balanced data, bias would eventually creep into the classification engine when it was re-trained according to the preferences of the individual. A systematic exploration of class bias using this type of subject-dependent classification based upon an incremental training dataset is one topic for further work. The issue of bias due to feedback could be explored systematically by varying the protocol used in the current study. For example, the results of each classification could be withheld from the participant and shared at the end of the experiment.

The current study used a protocol where system feedback was conveyed to participants via the experimenter. This form of feedback was selected due to the technical limitations of the system and was far from ideal. The presentation of feedback at the interface is likely to exert a strong influence on the perception of accuracy. The use of a human agent introduces an unwelcome level of 'experimenter bias' into the experience of the participants.

It was surprising that perceived accuracy and mathematical scores of accuracy were generally within 10% of one another (Table 2). There was a general tendency for perceived accuracy to be higher than mathematical accuracy. The study does indicate that F1 score was generally a good predictor of perceived accuracy; it was significantly positively correlated with perceived accuracy in all but one of the four builds (Table 4). The results of the correlation suggest that F1 score from a classification engine may provide a reasonable estimate of perceived accuracy from users but more research is required to support this claim.

CONCLUSION

The purpose of this study was to explore the relationship between mathematical and perceived classification accuracy using psychophysiological data in a real-time application. It was found that mathematical accuracy remained stable throughout the experiment whilst perceived accuracy showed some fluctuation related to bias and developing expectations from the user. The study indicated that perceived accuracy tended to be an over-estimation of mathematical accuracy (F1 score) but there was a high degree of positive correlation between F1 and perceived accuracy.

ACKNOWLEDGEMENTS

This work was partly funded by the European Commission as part of ICT-2009.4.1 (Digital Libraries and Digital Preservation) under the ARtSENSE project (270318).

REFERENCES

1. Soleymani, M, Pantic, M & Pun, T. 2012. Multimodal emotion recognition in response to videos. IEEE Transactions on Affective Computing, 3(2), 211-223.
2. Soleymani, M. & Pantic, M. 2012. Human-centred implicit tagging: overview and perspectives. In Proceedings of the 2012 IEEE International Conference on Systems, Man and Cybernetics, 3304-3309.
3. Gilroy, S. W., Porteous, J., Charles, F., Cavazza, M., Soreq, E., Raz, G., Ikar, L., Or-Borichov, A., Ben-Arie, U., Klovatch, I. & Hendler, T. (2013). A Brain-Computer Interface to a Plan-Based Narrative. In F. Rossi (ed.), *IJCAI*, 633-2
4. Fairclough, S.H. 2009. Fundamentals of physiological computing. Interacting With Computers, 21, 133-145.
5. Fairclough, S.H. & Gilleade, K.E. 2012. Construction of the biocybernetic loop: a case study. In *Proceedings of the 14th ACM international conference on Multimodal interaction* (ICMI '12). ACM, New York, NY, USA, 571-578.
6. Koelstra, S., Mühl, C., Soleymani, M., Lee, J., Yazdani, A., Ebrahimi, T, Pun, T., Nijholt, A., and Patras, I. 2012. DEAP: A Database for Emotion Analysis ;Using Physiological Signals. IEEE Transactions on Affective Computing, 3(1), 18-31.
7. Russell, J.A. 1980. A circumplex model of affect. Journal of Personality and Social Psychology, 39(6), 1161-1178.
8. van der Zwaag, M.D., Janssen, J.H & Westerink, J.H.D.M. 2013. Directing physiology and mood through music: validation of an affective music Player, IEEE Transactions on Affective Computing, 4(1), 57-68.
9. Karran, A.J., Fairclough, S.H. and Gilleade, K.E. 2013. Towards an adaptive cultural heritage experience using physiological computing. In CHI '13 Extended Abstracts on Human Factors in Computing Systems (CHI EA '13). ACM, New York, NY, USA, 1683-1688.
10. Karran, A.J. & Kreplin, U. 2014. The drive to explore: physiological computing in a cultural heritage context. In Fairclough, S.H. & Gilleade, K. (Eds.) Advances in Physiological Computing. Springer. 169-195.
11. Novak, D., Mihelj, M. & Munih, M. 2012. A survey of methods for data fusion and system adaptation using autonomic nervous system responses in physiological computing. Interacting With Computers, 24, 154-172.
12. Lotte, F., Congedo, M., Lécuyer, A., Lamarche, F. & Arnaldi, B. 2007. A review of classification algorithms for EEG-based Brain-Computer Interfaces. Journal of Neural Engineering, 4, R1-R13.
13. Miller, C. A. 2005. Trust in adaptive automation: The role of etiquette in tuning trust via analogic and affective methods. Paper presented at the First International Conference on Augmented Cognition, Las Vegas, NV.
14. Van de Laar, B, Bos Plass-Oude, D., Reuderink, B., Poels, M. & Nijholt, A. 2013. How much control is enough? Influence of unreliable input on user experience. IEEE Transactions on Cybernetics, 43(6), 1584-1592.
15. Novak, D., Nagle, A. & Riener, R. 2014. Linking recognition accuracy and user experience in an affective feedback loop. IEEE Transactions on Affective Computing, 5(2), 168-172.
16. Ramnani, N. & Owen, A.M. 2004. Anterior prefrontal cortex: insights into function from anatomy and neuroimaging. Nature Reviews Neuroscience, 5, 184-194.
17. Coan J.A., Allen J.J. 2004. Frontal EEG asymmetry as a moderator and mediator of emotion. Biological Psychology. 67(1) 7-49.
18. Platt J.C. 1999. Fast training of support vector machines using sequential minimal optimization. In Advances in kernel methods, Bernhard Schlkopf, Christopher J. C. Burges, and Alexander J. Smola (Eds.). MIT Press, Cambridge, MA, USA 185-208
19. Isaksson, A., Wallman, M., Göransson, H. & Gustafsson, M.G. 2008. "Cross-validation and bootstrapping are unreliable in small sample classification". Pattern Recognition Letters, 29(14), 1960-1965
20. Kelley, J. F., "An iterative design methodology for user-friendly natural language office information applications". ACM Transactions on Office Information Systems, March 1984, 2:1, pp. 26–41.

Examining the Reliability of Using fNIRS in Realistic HCI Settings for Spatial and Verbal Tasks

Horia A. Maior*†, Matthew Pike*, Sarah Sharples‡ and Max L. Wilson*

*Mixed Reality Lab
University of Nottingham
Nottingham, UK

†Horizon Centre for Doctoral Training
University of Nottingham
Nottingham, UK

‡Human Factors Research Group
University of Nottingham
Nottingham, UK

{horia.maior, pike, sarah.sharples, max.wilson}@nottingham.ac.uk

ABSTRACT

Recent efforts have shown that functional near-infrared spectroscopy (fNIRS) has potential value for brain sensing in HCI user studies. Research has shown that, although large head movement significantly affects fNIRS data, typical keyboard use, mouse movement, and non-task-related verbalisations do not affect measurements during *Verbal* tasks. This work aims to examine the *Reliability* of fNIRS, by 1) confirming these prior findings, and 2) significantly extending our understanding of how artefacts affect recordings during *Spatial* tasks, since much of user interfaces and interaction is inherently spatial. Our results show that artefacts have a significantly different impact during Verbal and Spatial tasks. We contribute clearer insights into using fNIRS as a tool within HCI user studies.

ACM Classification Keywords

H.5.2 [Information interfaces and presentation]: User Interfaces. - Graphical user interfaces

Author Keywords

functional near-infrared spectroscopy; fNIRS; brain-computer interface; human cognition; BCI

INTRODUCTION

Recent research has shown functional near-infrared spectrsocopy (fNIRS) to be a highly suitable brain sensing technology for typical HCI user studies, providing an objective, non-intrusive measure correlating to what is known as human Mental Workload. Solovey et al. [10] showed that some typical interactions, like typing on a keyboard and using a mouse, did not create significant artefacts in fNIRS measurements during Verbal memory tasks, as long as forehead and major head movements were avoided. Further, Pike et al. [7] showed that only non-task-related verbalisation created additional workload measured with fNIRS during Verbal memory tasks. This work aims to explore the reliability of fNIRS data as a measure of mental workload, by 1) replicating the prior findings of Solovey et al. [10] and Pike et al. [7], and 2) extending our understanding of how these artefacts affect *Spatial* tasks, since much about user interfaces and interaction involves Spatial working memory [8]. We hypothesised that each artefact would have different measurable affects on spatial tasks than with verbal tasks.

CHI 2015, April 18 - 23 2015, Seoul, Republic of Korea

ACM 978-1-4503-3145-6/15/04...$15.00.
http://dx.doi.org/10.1145/2702123.2702315

Mental Workload

Mental Workload (MWL) is a concept used to describe how much mental effort is being experienced by an individual when completing a task. Baddeley and Hitch first proposed that Working Memory (WM) was composed of multiple components [2]. The model distinguishes between two types of encodings: Spatial (Visuospatial Sketchpad) and Verbal (Phonological Loop). Using this model as a foundation, we can develop tasks to target each of these encoding types, allowing us to investigate whether measurement techniques can detect them.

The Multiple Resource Model (MRM) proposed by Wickens [12] illustrates how resource limitations and coordination affects the interrelation of MWL in tasks. Wickens describes that necessary resources are limited, and aims to illustrate how elements of the human information processing system such as attention, perception, memory, decision making and response selection interconnect.

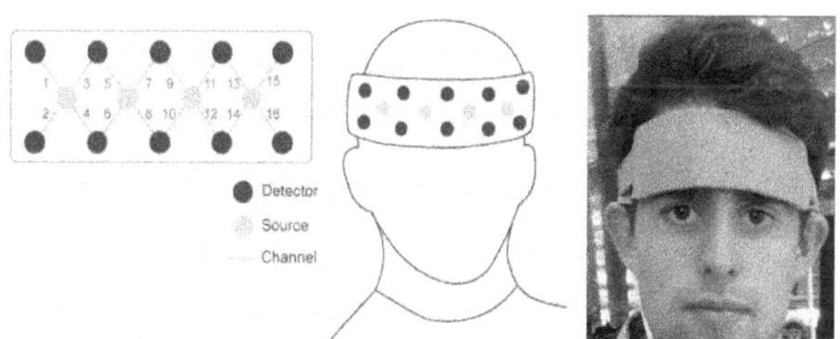

Figure 1. Source detector diagram and placement.

Measuring Mental Workload

A wide variety of measures are used to capture MWL. Subjective measures (e.g. questionnaires, think aloud protocols, interviews, and NASA-TLX scale [3]) are useful for capturing a user's perception of a system and are minimally intrusive if applied infrequently. Objective measures (e.g. task performance, secondary measures, physiological changes) are

		Control	Artefacts				
			Head Movement	Typing	Mouse Movement	Facial Movement	Verbalising
Task	Verbal	✓HbO	℧	✓HbO			✓HbO
	Spatial	✓HbO	✓Hb	℧			✓HbO
	Non-Replicated Conditions, Replicated Conditions, Novel Conditions						

Table 1. Results and Contributions of the current and Solovey et al. study. ✓HbO means fNIRS is fine to use in the presence of the investigated artefact, best measure to use HbO. ℧ means that the artefact needs to be avoided or filtered.

complex methods, but do have the potential to provide a real-time continuous measure of the user's state. To be valuable for HCI research however, the equipment should be non-intrusive, ideally allowing "normal" interaction with the system.

fNIRS offers the potential to provide continuous, detailed insight into human mental workload, enabling an objective means of detecting overload conditions during complex tasks in a minimally intrusive manner. Our fNIRS device (Figure 1) allows for the easy and direct application to an individual's forehead, targeting the prefrontal cortex; an area of the brain typically associated with Working Memory [2, 4]. fNIRS measures the change in Oxygenated (HbO) and Deoxygenated (Hb) haemoglobin as the body responds to the individuals' cognition (when measured on the head).

Reliability of fNIRS

Sharples and Megaw [9] state the appropriate criteria for MWL measures as being: Validity, Reliability, Generalisability, Sensitivity, Interference, Diagnosticity, Selectivity, Granularity/Bandwidth, Feasibility of use, Acceptability/Ethics and Resources. Pike et al., Maior et al. and Peck et al. [7, 5, 6] provide evidence of fNIRS correlating with NASA-TLX, a widely used measure of MWL (**Validity**). fNIRS is inherently generalisable as it simply measures oxygenation and is not specific to a particular domain (**Generalisability**).

Afergan et al. [1] demonstrated the ability to distinguish between different workload states (**Sensitivity**) during a UAV simulation task. Additionally, the study identified workload changes over time (**Bandwidth**). Pike et al [7] identified non-related verbalisations as being a contributing factor to increased mental workload (**Diagnosticity**). Solovey et al [10] demonstrated that fNIRS was able to distinguish between common human behaviours (typing, mouse movement, head and facial movement) and a Verbal Memory task (**Selectivity**).

fNIRS has been deployed in a number of studies and has caused minimal **Interference**, with many reporting ecological validity whilst using fNIRS (also demonstrating **Feasibility of use, Acceptability/Ethics** and **Resources**)[7, 10, 1]. In this context however we are particularly interested in exploring the **reliability** of fNIRS within HCI.

As fNIRS is an emerging technology in this field, replicating the findings of existing work is one step towards establishing the reliability of the technology.

EXPERIMENT DESIGN

The aim of this study is to identify the reliability of fNIRS as a measure of MWL in the context of HCI. We have chosen to replicate the work of Solovey et al. [10] and Pike et al. [7] on *verbal* memory, but significantly extend our understanding of the impact of artefacts on fNIRS measurements, by also examining *Spatial* tasks. Reliability of the measure is one of the criteria identified by Sharples and Megaw [9] as being appropriate for measuring MWL. In this study we followed much of the original procedure as described by Solovey et al., we did however remove some of the behaviours under study deciding instead to focus on the behaviours that had the greatest impact on the fNIRS signal (Typing and Head Movement). We included another human behaviour in our study - Verbalisation, a common part of HCI studies that was absent in the original study, but studied by Pike et al. [7].

In this study we also addressed the issue of memory encoding types and how the artefacts under study can affect these different encodings. In the original study, the task of memorising a 7 digit number was Verbal since the encoding of the digits would reside within the Phonological Loop of Baddeley and Hitch's model of WM [2]. To understand the impact of a different encoding, we introduced a Spatial task of memorising a 6x6 grid. This task will be encoded in the Visuospatial Sketchpad (according to the same model [2]), allowing us to investigate whether there are differences in results according to the encoding type of the task.

The study had 4 conditions, which were tested under both task types: 1)Task Only (No Artefact), 2)Task + Head Movement, 3)Task + Typing, 4)Task + Verbalising. We followed the same repeated measures, within-participants approach as the original study to compare conditions.

Participants

Fifteen participants (11 male, 4 female) with an average age of 22.06 (SD = 2.31) were recruited to take part in the study. All participants had normal or corrected vision and reported no history of head trauma or brain damage. The study was approved by the school's ethics committee. Participants provided informed consent and were compensated with gift vouchers.

Tasks and Study Procedure

The study procedure closely followed that of the original study by Solovey et al. Participants were asked to memorise a 7 digit number for the Verbal Task and then submit the number using an on-screen form. For the Spatial Task, participants were required to memorise a 6x6 black and white grid (Figure 2), and recreate the grid using an on-screen form. Participants completed 8 experiments (3 Artefact conditions and 1 Control (No Artefact) condition, under 2 tasks), with each experiment composed by 8 trials. Each trial started with 15s rest, followed

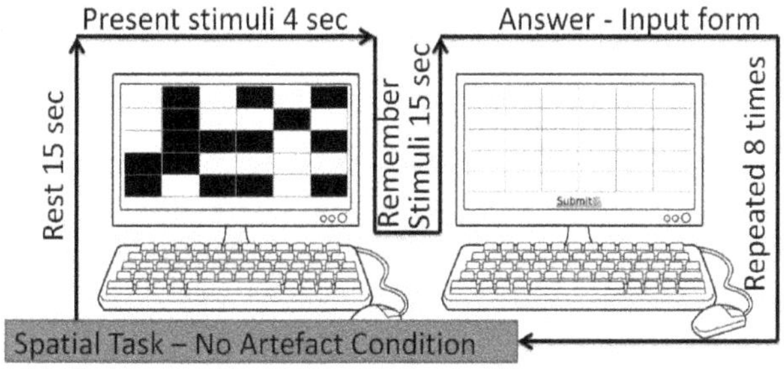

Figure 2. Experiment Procedure with Spatial Task

by 4s presented stimuli (Verbal number or Spatial grid), 15s remembering the stimuli, and ended with an input form for answering the remembered stimuli. For the artefact conditions the 15s remembering period also included performing the specific artefact, and an additional 15s period of performing the artefact alone was performed after the task.

Measurements and Equipment

In this study we have collected two types of measures, namely brain activity using fNIRS and task performance.

fNIRS data was recorded using an fNIRS300 device and the associated COBI Studio recording software provided by Biopac Systems Inc. Using the Matlab Toolbox NIRS-SPM [13] we applied filtering algorithms to remove high-frequency noise, physiological artefacts such as heartbeats and motion derived artefacts. Finally we separated each trial according to the condition under test (rest/ task/ artefact) considering the slow hemodynamic response [11], and averaged the data accordingly.

Task performance for both task types was calculated using 2 measures: Absolute performance - where an answer is simply correct or not, and Relative Performance - where answers were scored according to distance from the target answer (calculated with Levenshtein distance).

RESULTS

Performance data

No significant difference between conditions was reported by Solovey et al. in task performance, where the number of correct (in-place) digits was used as the dependent variable. We hypothesised that non-related verbalisation will negatively impact performance during the Verbal task, as demonstrated by Pike et al. [7]. Based on Wickens MRM [12], we expect no performance differences under Spatial conditions as the resources are complementary. However, a within participants, one-way repeated measure ANOVA with LSD correction, revealed that participants performed significantly worse under the typing artefact compared to all other conditions during the Verbal task ($N = 15, p < 0.05$). Participants also performed significantly worse in the Verbalisation artefact condition compared to the no artefact one during the Spatial task ($N = 15, p < 0.025$). The findings disprove our hypothesis, but do lead to an interesting discussion; For the Verbal task, the greatest interference was typing, which could be interpreted as being a Spatial input modality since the keys have a physical mapping. Whereas for the Spatial task, the verbalising artefact had the greatest interference providing a **crossing** of resource modalities, which is the opposite of our original hypothesis.

Experiments: No artefacts

The main observation we wanted to reproduce in this experiment was distinguishing between states of rest and cognition, a distinction described as "fundamental" in the original study. We hypothesised that in addition to reproducing the distinction in the Verbal task (as identified by Solovey et al.), we would also identify the difference in the 2 states for our Spatial task. For both Verbal and Spatial tasks, a paired-sample t-test, within participants, revealed significant differences over multiple channels between rest periods and task periods. In both task conditions HbO was significantly higher in 13 out of the 16 channels of data, with $N = 15, p < 0.05$. Our results are in line with those identified by Solovey et al. and with our hypothesis regarding the Spatial task. We note that our results favoured HbO over Hb in the detection of these states. To provide an interesting visual representation of fNIRS ability to distinguish between rest and cognitive states, Figure 3 visualises a participant's fNIRS data (ch.1) for the no artefact experiment (consisting of 8 trials hence the 8 peaks in HbO data).

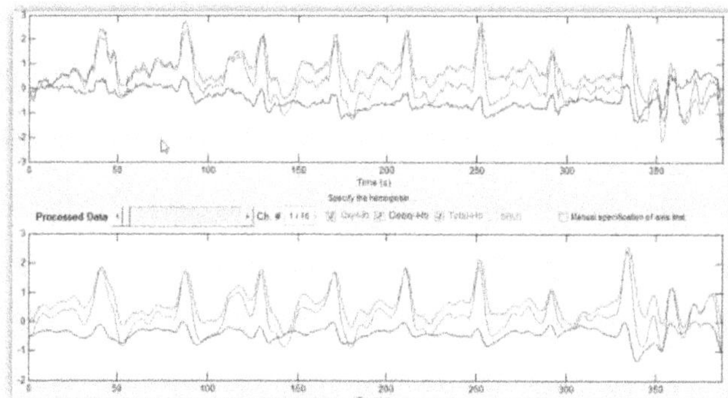

Figure 3. Oxygenation level peaks for 8 Verbal trials.

Experiments: With artefacts

Our interest here lies in distinguishing cognition in the presence of artefacts (Table 1 provides the summary of our findings). To achieve this, we combine the following three stages: rest periods, artefact (alone) periods, and cognitive task under artefact into paired comparisons. We have applied a series of one-way repeated measure ANOVAs within participant design with LSD correction for each of the artefact conditions.

Head Movement Artefact - For the Verbal task we were not able to significantly distinguish between participants at rest and participants performing the cognitive task in the presence of major head movement, as reported by Solovey et al. We were however able to distinguish between participant at rest and participants performing just the artefact ($Hb, p < 0.025$), indicating that head movement is detrimental to the fNIRS signal. We were also able to distinguish between cognition in the presence of head movement and performing the artefact alone ($Hb, p < 0.01$), indicating the potential for filtering of this artefact in the future. Accordingly, we advise the sampling of major head movements as a part of studies involving a Verbal task. For the same artefact (head movement) under the Spatial task our results suggest that we could relax the restrictions. For the Spatial Task we report significance in Hb for all comparisons ($p < 0.05$) indicating that Spatial based tasks are less prone to head movement artefacts.

Keyboard Input Artefact - For the typing condition we were able to distinguish between rest and task periods ($HbO, p < 0.05$) during the Verbal Task. During the Spatial Task, the difference was not significant. Potential for filtering exists again due to the significance difference between the remaining two comparisons (rest vs artefact and artefact vs cognitive task = $HbO, p < 0.05$). The findings suggest that keyboard input does not affect the fNIRS signal during verbal tasks, however, it should only be controlled for the spatial ones.

Verbalisation Artefact - There were significant differences between rest and cognition periods for both Verbal and Spatial tasks ($HbO, p < 0.01$ Verbal Task and $HbO, p < 0.025$ Spatial Task) in the presence of verbalisation artefact. This finding implies that fNIRS could be reliably used in the presence of Verbalisation artefacts, confirming the findings of Pike et al. [7]. The results also show that Verbalization artefact is the most compatible with fNIRS for a typical HCI Settings.

CONCLUSIONS

In this study we sought to replicate and extend the work performed by Solovey et al., investigating the effect of common human behaviours on fNIRS ability to distinguish states of cognition from other states. Our aim in doing so was to prove the reliability of fNIRS as a measure and extend our understanding of artefacts effects on different task types (Verbal *and* Spatial). The fundamental finding confirmed by this study is that we are able to distinguish between cognitive and rest states in both Verbal (as confirmed by Solovey et al.) and Spatial tasks. The two types of tasks, however, were differently affected, according to the two key fNIRS measures, for each artefact. Our addition of a Spatial task, therefore, provided a greater understanding of fNIRS' ability to distinguish cognition under tasks using such encodings. Further, our inclusion of the verbalisation artefact also provided this greater understanding for an additional, but very common user study behaviour. These findings contribute towards a body of evidence to suggest that, in a HCI context, fNIRS is a indeed valuable measure. To provide further practical advice to other researchers about fNIRS reliability and portability, future work might examine other untested artefacts, such as: age of participants, interface familiarity, task expertise etc.

ACKNOWLEDGMENTS

This work was partially supported by the EPSRC ORCHID project (EP/I011587/1) and the Horizon Centre for Doctoral Training at the University of Nottingham (EP/G037574/1).

REFERENCES

1. Afergan, D., Peck, E. M., Solovey, E. T., Jenkins, A., Hincks, S. W., Brown, E. T., Chang, R., and Jacob, R. J. Dynamic difficulty using brain metrics of workload. In *Proc. SIGCHI*, ACM (2014), 3797–3806.
2. Baddeley, A. D., and Hitch, G. Working memory. *The psychology of learning and motivation 8* (1974), 47–89.
3. Hart, S. G., and Staveland, L. E. Development of nasa-tlx (task load index): Results of empirical and theoretical research. *Human mental workload* (1988).
4. Kane, M. J., and Engle, R. W. The role of prefrontal cortex in working-memory capacity, executive attention, and general fluid intelligence: An individual-differences perspective. *Psychonomic bulletin & review 9*, 4 (2002), 637–671.
5. Maior, H. A., Pike, M., Wilson, M. L., and Sharples, S. Continuous detection of workload overload: An fnirs approach. In *Contemporary Ergonomics and Human Factors 2014: Proceedings of the international conference on Ergonomics & Human Factors 2014, Southampton, UK, 7-10 April 2014*, CRC Press (2014), 450.
6. Peck, E. M., Yuksel, B. F., Ottley, A., Jacob, R. J., and Chang, R. Using fNIRS Brain Sensing to Evaluate Information Visualization Interfaces. In *Proc. SIGCHI*, ACM (2013).
7. Pike, M. F., Maior, H. A., Porcheron, M., Sharples, S. C., and Wilson, M. L. Measuring the effect of think aloud protocols on workload using fnirs. In *Proc. SIGCHI*, ACM (2014), 3807–3816.
8. Robertson, G., Czerwinski, M., Larson, K., Robbins, D. C., Thiel, D., and Van Dantzich, M. Data mountain: using spatial memory for document management. In *Proc. UIST*, ACM (1998), 153–162.
9. Sharples, S., and Megaw, T. *The definition and measurement of human workload.* In Wilson, J.R. & Sharples, S. (Eds) Evaluation of Human Work. Boca, 2015.
10. Solovey, E. T., Girouard, A., Chauncey, K., Hirshfield, L. M., Sassaroli, A., Zheng, F., Fantini, S., and Jacob, R. J. Using fNIRS brain sensing in realistic HCI settings: experiments and guidelines. In *Proc. UIST*, ACM (2009), 157–166.
11. Villringer, A., and Chance, B. Non-invasive optical spectroscopy and imaging of human brain function. *Trends in neurosciences 20*, 10 (1997), 435–442.
12. Wickens, C. D. Multiple resources and mental workload. *The Journal of the Human Factors and Ergonomics Society 50*, 3 (2008), 449–455.
13. Ye, J. C., Tak, S., Jang, K. E., Jung, J., and Jang, J. NIRS-SPM: statistical parametric mapping for near-infrared spectroscopy. *Neuroimage 44*, 2 (2009), 428–447.

StructJumper: A Tool to Help Blind Programmers Navigate and Understand the Structure of Code

Catherine M. Baker, Lauren R. Milne, Richard E. Ladner
Computer Science & Engineering
University of Washington
{cmbaker, milnel2, ladner}@cs.washington.edu

ABSTRACT

It can be difficult for a blind developer to understand and navigate through a large amount of code quickly, as they are unable to skim as easily as their sighted counterparts. To help blind developers overcome this problem, we present StructJumper, an Eclipse plugin that creates a hierarchical tree based on the nesting structure of a Java class. The programmer can use the TreeView to get an overview of the code structure of the class (including all the methods and control flow statements) and can quickly switch between the TreeView and the Text Editor to get an idea of where they are within the nested structure. To evaluate StructJumper, we had seven blind programmers complete three tasks with and without our tool. We found that the users thought they would use StructJumper and there was a trend that they were faster completing the tasks with StructJumper.

Author Keywords

Blind Programmers; Screen Reader; Navigation; Accessibility; Code Structure

ACM Classification Keywords

H.5.2 [**Information Interface and Presentation**]: User Interfaces

INTRODUCTION

Computer programmers rely on the use of visual aids when programming [11], especially in an integrated development environment (IDE) such as Eclipse. These visual aids range from using different colors for syntax highlighting to using indentation within the code to indicate scope. The use of visual aids present difficulties for blind programmers, as they are unable to quickly access the same information available to sighted developers. In fact, blind developers have more difficulties navigating and understanding the structure of code than their sighted counterparts [6, 9, 11].

CHI 2015, April 18 - 23 2015, Seoul, Republic of Korea
Copyright 2015 ACM 978-1-4503-3145-6/15/04…$15.00
http://dx.doi.org/10.1145/2702123.2702589

Figure 1. Screenshot of StructJumper with source code file on top and tree of nesting structure on bottom.

Screen readers only allow blind programmers to have access to a single line of code at a time. Therefore, to move around in the code, the programmers are limited to a few options: using the arrow keys to go through each line of code, using the outline or package explorer to navigate to a specific method and then navigating within the method line by line, or using a search mechanism. Despite these difficulties, the space of accessible developer tools and studying the practices of blind programmers is still a young field.

Smith et al. created a tool to allow blind programmers to navigate the hierarchical structure of a program, specifically the tree structure of files in the Eclipse IDE [9]. Our tool, StructJumper, expands on this work by creating a hierarchical tree of the nesting structure of a program (see Figures 1, 2 and 3) to allow users to both navigate within the program and gain an understanding of the structure of code within the program. We create one tree per Java file, and the root of each tree is an invisible node corresponding to the file. A node is a child to another node if the code of the child node is nested within the code of the parent node. Inner nodes represent classes, methods or statements, and leaf nodes are code sections without any changes in nesting. We include these code sections in the tree, because we want to allow users to easily switch between coding and finding where they are in the tree structure, so every line of code must be contained within a node on the tree.

StructJumper allows the user to quickly discover in which nested structure a particular line of code she is working on. She can do so by pressing a key in TreeView to jump to the node corresponding to the current location. Moreover, it allows the user to switch between being able to make edits within the code and gaining contextual information without losing her place. We present a prototype of our plugin for Eclipse for a single programming language (Java) and evaluate our tool in a user study with seven blind developers. We had participants perform a variety of code exploration tasks both with and without our tool.

With our evaluation, we aim to answer the following research questions:

(1) Does StructJumper make it easier for a blind programmer to navigate the code?

(2) Does StructJumper make it easier for a blind programmer to understand where they are within the code?

To evaluate StructJumper, we had seven blind programmers complete three tasks related to navigation and answer questions about the context of a line of code. We found that the users in the study thought our tool was useful for navigation and for understanding the structure of code.

Our contributions are:

(1) The StructJumper tool itself, available as a plugin to Eclipse.

(2) The results from our evaluation of our tool, which show that StructJumper is useful in helping blind developers navigate code and gain an understanding of which statements a line of code is nested within.

(3) Insights into how designers should create similar navigational tools for blind programmers.

BACKGROUND AND RELATED WORK

Practices and Challenges for Blind Programmers

The space of blind developer tools and the investigation of the blind developer programming practices is still a young field. Mealin et al. [6] interviewed eight blind developers and highlighted several practices employed by and challenges faced by blind developers. They found that despite issues with integrating screen readers with the complexities of integrated development environments (IDEs), five of the eight blind developers had used an IDE such as Eclipse or Visual Studio. However, the researchers found that blind developers rarely used and were not aware of the tools available to them within these complex IDEs [6]. This could be because it is more difficult for blind developers to explore the user interface of IDEs or the extra tools are not accessible. However, it could also be that the added complexity of the environment detracts more than the extra functionality adds in total usefulness. In our evaluation, the programmer is aware of the navigation tool and it is accessible, allowing us to explore the benefit provided: the ability to better understand the structure of the code.

Blind developers also indicated that they often had a difficult time getting an overview of the code. For example, skimming the code is not possible due to the linear nature of the screen reader. They tend to rely more heavily on API documentation and header files to get an idea of how the code is structured, although this is not useful if the code is not well-documented. Blind developers also use the find function to gain structural information by searching through common keywords (e.g. public, private, if etc.), which is often more time-consuming than skimming the code [6]. The researchers noted that none of the blind developers mentioned using other code navigation tools, such as moving the cursor back to the last edited text position. It was unclear whether this was because the developers did not know about these tools or because they did not find them useful. Blind developers found it difficult to search through the code to find variables or methods, especially since it requires moving the cursor to a specific line in order to have the screen reader read it aloud. Therefore, they could not easily alternate between editing the code and finding the piece of information that they need [6]. Based on the challenges presented in this paper, we decided to develop a better way to navigate through code and made the design choice to allow the user to switch between her location in the code and the nested tree structure without moving her cursor and losing her place.

Audio Based Programming Tools

There has been some prior work on creating accessible tools for blind developers. Stefik et al. created Sodbeans, a new programming IDE, which relies on audio cues to convey information such as complier errors or changing the values of variables while debugging. Sodbeans' auditory cues are built on three principles that we will also apply to the screen reader cues given by StructJumper: 1) they are short, 2) they are "browsable" (i.e. you can browse through the cues by only listening to the beginning of each cue), and 3) the important information comes first [12]. Another group created Audio Programming Language (APL), a new programming language specifically designed to help teach people who are blind how to program [8]. Stefik et al. used Sodbeans at a programming camp for blind high schoolers, but their evaluation focused on the efficacy of the curriculum and not Sodbeans itself [12]. Similarly, the focus of the evaluation of APL was on the ability of the student to learn programming concepts [8]. In contrast, as we evaluate StructJumper, we are trying to determine the effect of the nesting level navigation on experienced programmers who are already well-versed in programming concepts.

Another challenge mentioned by blind developers is using debugging tools, as most debugging tools do not work well with screen readers. Stefik et al. integrated an audio debugging tool in the Sodbeans IDE [12]. The same research group [10] also created a debugging tool for Microsoft's

Visual Studio IDE, which used sonification (non-speech audio) to aid developers. In a feasibility study, they found that blind developers were able to understand the sonification cues the majority of the time. Although not designed specifically for blind developers, Vickers et al. [13] added auditory cues to debugging tools by mapping the entry, exit and evaluation of program constructs (if, while, for, etc...) in Pascal to different musical cues. They found that sighted people learning programming found this useful to find bugs. Although the authors found that the audio cues were useful, they only used a small number of cues to map onto a small number of constructs. Other work suggests that auditory cues are difficult to understand and learn [7], so it seems likely that using audio cues would only be useful to convey short information, but not be useful to convey more complex information, so we chose not to rely on non-verbal audio cues for our navigation tool.

There has also been work on navigating through large projects in a non-visual manner. Smith et al. [9] wrote an Eclipse plugin to navigate the hierarchal structure of files in the Eclipse IDE and found that both blind programmers and sighted programmers who could not see the screen found it to be useful. We would like to expand on this idea by extending it to work on structures within the code, specifically to move between nesting levels.

Stefik et al. explored the use of audio cues to indicate the lexical scoping relationship between program statements [11]. These relationships were determined dynamically and the cues played when a change in scope was detected as the program executed. We created a similar static tool, which generates a tree that can be used to navigate through source code without running the program.

Navigation Aids for Screen Readers

Although there has been minimal research into tools for blind developers and ensuring that screen readers work well with IDEs, there have been useful research efforts on navigating web pages and textual documents with screen readers [1, 15]. In early work by Asakawa et al. [1] on developing an add-on to a screen reader that could read web pages, the researchers found that navigation was important to the design of the screen reader. Unlike navigation in IDEs, many controls allowed users to skip between links or lines on a page or skip directly to the first or last link.

With current standard screen readers, users can use controls to switch between header types (e.g. h2 and h3) and then skip from header to header on web pages. In a 2012 survey by WebAIM [14], 61% of 1782 respondents reported using headers as the main form of navigation when trying to find information on a lengthy web page, as opposed to using the find feature, navigate using links, landmarks or simply reading the page. Additionally, 82% of respondents found having different heading levels either useful or very useful when navigating a web page. However, in order to allow users to navigate using this structural information, webpage creators must provide it. The Web Content Accessibility Guidelines 2.0 [15] provides guidelines to help developers create accessible pages. The guidelines require that "Information, structure, and relationships conveyed through presentation can be programmatically determined or are available in text," and that "Headings and labels describe topic or purpose" [15]. Headers are particularly important for navigation and understanding content on a webpage.

Our plugin works similarly by designating certain parts of the code as key structural parts of the code (e.g. method and class declarations, control flow lines, etc.), which serve similar purposes as the headers on a website. Although there are tools available that can move between nesting levels in IDEs today, to the best of our knowledge no one has studied whether they are useful for navigation by blind developers, and they do not provide the ability to switch between navigation while still maintaining the current position of the cursor, which is useful for blind developers.

Code Navigation

While there have been many researchers who have looked into code navigation, many of the techniques would not be helpful for blind programmers. One of the most common techniques to help programmers is to make more information visible to provide the programmer better context such as providing a fisheye view of the code [5].

Other researchers have focused on allowing users to rearrange code in order to help them be able to navigate quicker [3,4]. While it may be beneficial for blind programmers to be able to rearrange their code, it does not help with the problem of navigating within those code sections.

STRUCTJUMPER DESIGN AND IMPLEMENTATION

We created StructJumper, a plugin for Eclipse. We chose to use Eclipse for a couple of reasons. Eclipse is a mainstream IDE that is used commonly by both blind and sighted programmers. As it is common for programmers to work in groups, having a common IDE is beneficial. Additionally, Eclipse is open source and has good support for creating and adding plugins.

For the plugin, we are combining two concepts that have already been used in software development. This first concept is turning code into a tree structure. This has been done with Abstract Syntax Trees (AST). We are using a simplified version of an AST, as we do not want to overwhelm the programmer with too much information. Grouping code together at a certain nesting level is not a new concept and is frequently done by visual cues (e.g. indentation or highlighting). We are just adjusting this method to be in a format accessible to blind programmers.

The plugin creates a hierarchical tree of the code based on nested structure (Figures 2 and 3). Nodes are broken into two categories: code sections and statements that precipitate a change in nesting. Code sections are sequential lines of code that are all within the same level of nesting. They can

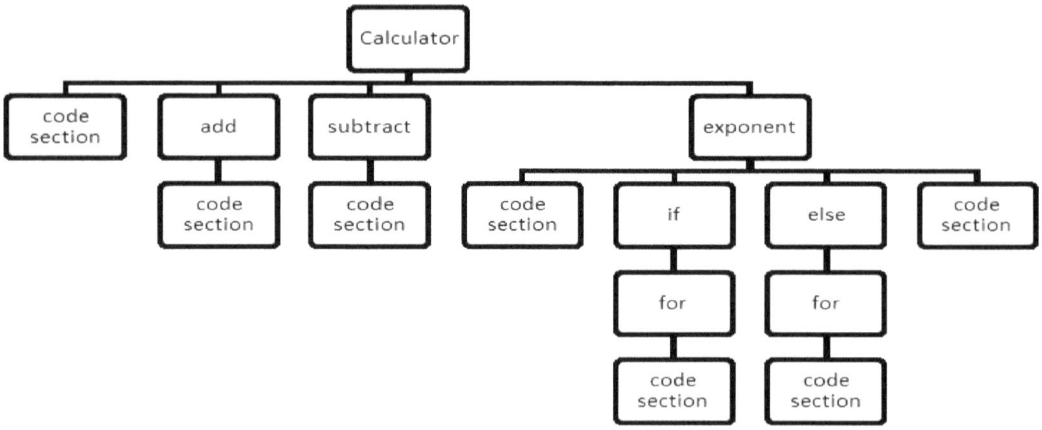

Figure 2. The tree created from the code in Figure 3. Code sections have no further nesting. Note in this image, the first code section corresponds to the code containing the member variable declared at the beginning of the Calculator class.

```
public class Calculator {
        private String display;
        public int add(int a, int b) {
                return a+b;
        }
        /**This method subtracts b from a*/
        public int subtract(int a, int b) {
                return a-b;
        }
        public double exponent(int a, int b) {
                double answer = 1.0;
                if(b>=0) {
                        for(int i = 0; i<b; i++) {
                                answer = answer*a;
                        }
                }
                else{
                        for(int i = 0; i<b; i++) {
                                answer = answer/a;
                        }
                }
                return answer;
        }
}
```

Figure 3. This is the code of a simple calculator class, which is turned into the tree in Figure 2.

only be a leaf on a tree, not a parent to other nodes. A procedure call is not included as a separate node in the tree, but within the containing code section.

The tree is created in a separate window so that a programmer can use StructJumper both to navigate as well as to gain contextual information. This is further enabled by the key commands (Table 1). One of the major decisions we made was what should happen when you enter and exit StructJumper.

On entering, there were two options, (1) update the selected node to the one that represents the cursor location or (2) to leave it on the previously selected node. There are good arguments for either, but based on limitations of the screen reader, we decided to leave the cursor on the previously selected node (option 2).

On exiting there were also two options. (1) update the cursor location to that of the selected node or (2) leave it at its previous location. Work by Mealin [6] shows that being able to get information (such as a method name) while leaving the cursor in the current location is valuable to programmers and that many blind programmers create workarounds to gain this functionality by using an text buffer. Therefore, we allowed for both options to be possible with 'E' updating the cursor location and 'Ctrl+F7' leaving the cursor in the previous location.

In Eclipse, the Package Explorer window has a similar layout, but only includes class, fields and methods. As we wanted to make sure that our tool used the same mental model as all the other parts of Eclipse, we used that model for our tool as opposed to one similar to Figure 2. While this was inspiration for the layout and key selection choice, we made one change in how the arrow keys work. In the Package Explorer, if a user presses the down arrow key when the selection was on "TreeParent" (Figure 4) then the selection moves to "children." To avoid moving the selection onto a further nested statement without the programmer being aware, the programmer has to use the right arrow to move to a child. If the user presses the down arrow, the selection would move from "TreeParent" to the next item at the same nesting level, "ViewContentProvider."

When the user is in navigation mode, the screen reader reads relevant and unique cues (such as method names) first and then provides the rest of the information, so that users can quickly navigate and skim through code as suggested by Stefik et al [12]. In order to present the most important information first, we reordered the presentation of several lines of code that are in the tree.

For a method, we first present the name, followed by the input, return type, and then any modifiers or annotations. For a class declaration, we first present the name, then what it extends and implements, followed by the modifiers.

Figure 4. This is an example of a portion of what the Package Explorer in Eclipse would show.

When necessary, keywords are inserted to distinguish the end of one type of item and the start of the other. For instance the keyword "return type" would be added in between the input and return type to more easily distinguish the difference. Other lines of code are read as is, as they already have the important keywords first. For example, the subtract method in Figure 3 would be read "*subtract, Input: int a, int b, Return type: int Modifiers: public Comments: /**This method subtracts b from a*/.*" The plugin is written in Java, and currently only parses Java code.

EXPERIMENT DESIGN

To evaluate StructJumper, seven blind programmers completed three tasks, while using StructJumper and without the tool. After they had completed the tasks, we asked them questions about their experience.

Participants

We conducted the study with seven blind programmers, one of whom was female. Participants were recruited using emails lists and our contacts. The average age of the participants was 24.1 (SD = 4.9). The programmers had an average of 7.8 years of programming experience (SD = 3.9), with a minimum experience of 3.5 years. Additionally, the participants had an average of 2.8 years of experience with Eclipse (SD = 2.6) and 3.8 years of experience with Java (SD = 2.8). The minimum experience for Java and Eclipse was 0.5 years.

Table 1. A table of the keyboard shortcuts that can be used to navigate in the tree and the code editor.

Key	Action
Ctrl+F7	Switches between tree and editor and leaves the cursor/selected node at previous location (Eclipse Built-In Command)
Left Arrow	Go to parent
Right Arrow	Go to first child
Up Arrow	Go to previous sibling
Down Arrow	Go to next sibling
C	Go to node representing cursor location
T	Go to top of the tree
U	Update the tree
E	Switches to the editor and updates the cursor location to that of the current node

Set-Up

The study was conducted remotely, allowing each participant to use their own computer set-up. The participants used a variety of screen readers including JAWS, NVDA, and Window Eyes. By conducting the study remotely, the participants were able to use the settings in which they are comfortable, such as talking speed or amount of punctuation to speak. Using the screen sharing abilities of Skype and Google Hangouts, the researchers were able to watch and record as the participants completed the tasks and track their progress.

Procedure

Before the study, the participants were asked to fill out demographic information and install StructJumper. Participants were not given access to the code until minutes before we started the study.

The study was divided into three parts, completing a series of tasks with our tool, completing a series of tasks without our tool and the post-session interview. There were two different code bases and each code base had three tasks that were similar to each other. The participants completed the tasks on one code base using our tool and one code base without our tool. The order of the code bases and whether they used our tool first or second was counterbalanced.

As common advice to improve programming skills is to read other people's code, we selected two trending repositories from GitHub. The code bases were selected as they each had a long file (600-800 lines of code), which was well commented, on which navigation would not be a trivial task. The two repositories chosen were the ZXing[1] repository which scans QR codes and the other was MPAndroidChart[2] which creates charts and graphs for Android applications. The ZXing file selected is code that searchs the image for FinderPatterns which are markers in the corners of QR codes. The MPAndroidChart file is the code that creates Pie Charts in Android applications.

As the users were unfamiliar with the StructJumper, the users were first given a short tutorial on how to use the tool. They were given a description of the tree created and an overview of the key commands that could be used with the tool. Then, they could practice using the tool on a toy code base that did a variety of matrix calculations. Once they felt

[1] https://github.com/zxing/zxing

[2] https://github.com/PhilJay/MPAndroidChart

familiar with the tool, they were asked to follow a series of directions to check if they knew each of the key commands.

Before completing the tasks, users were given a chance to familiarize themselves with the code. The participants could spend up to 15 minutes becoming familiar with the code. Users were given the option to use StructJumper in order to familiarize themselves as well as their own methods.

Once they were familiar with the code, the participants completed three tasks. The tasks were selected to get at the two goals of the tool: improving understanding of nesting information and improving navigation within code. There were two navigation tasks, which had non-obvious so that the users would need to navigate more to determine the correct answer. There was one context task, which was nested deeply so that it was possible to either miss a condition or to add a condition to their answer. The tasks were similar for each code base. For the StructJumper tasks, participants were asked to use the tool, but did not have to use it exclusively.

Mealin [6] mentioned that search was a technique that some blind programmers use to navigate in the code. To simulate exploring code in which you may or may not know keywords to look for, we phrased the two feature location tasks different. One of the feature location task's answer could be found by using search on the keywords included in the question (referred to as the *With Keywords* task). The other feature location task purposefully did not use keywords that would allow the answer to be found using search (referred to as the *Without Keywords* task). In this way, we can investigate the differences in the use of StructJumper when search is effective or is not effective for navigation.

The third task, regarding which conditions were necessary for a line to execute, involved a deeply nested line of code (referred to as the *Conditions* task). In both code bases, the line was within three if statements or for loops and there was at least one other if statement on the same level as an if statement necessary for the line to execute.

The three tasks for the ZXing code were:

1. *With Keywords:* Find the location in the code where we skip more than the normal number of rows of the image in our search for finders patterns
2. *Without Keywords:* Find the location in the code where after we have found all the potential finder patterns, we determine which are most likely the actual finder patterns
3. *Conditions:* What are the conditions necessary for line 463 to execute?

The three tasks for the MPAndroidChart code were:

1. *With Keywords:* Find the location in the code where the text for each slice of the pie chart is added
2. *Without Keywords:* Find the location in the code where the size of all the chart slices are determined
3. *Conditions:* What are the conditions necessary for line 300 to execute?

The tasks were timed and the answers were recorded for later analysis. The task time started when the investigator had finished reading the questions and ended when the participant had stated their answer and stopped looking through the code.

The answers were evaluated on a 3 point scale. Participants received 3 points on the feature location tasks if they found the correct location in the code, 2 points if they found a similar or related section of code, 1 point if it was loosely related or similar, and 0 points if it was not at all related or similar to the correct answer.

For the *conditions* tasks, the participants were awarded full points if they correctly identified all the conditions and did not add any conditions. If any conditions were missing or erroneously added, a point was subtracted per condition. If a participant had more than 3 errors, they were just given a 0. It was not possible to get negative points.

Once they had completed the three tasks, the participants were asked to rate their experience completing the tasks on a seven point semantically anchored scale. They were asked:

1. How easy the tasks were to complete: 1 – Very Hard to 7 – Very Easy
2. How frustrating the tasks were to complete: 1 – Very Frustrating to 7 – Not at all Frustrating
3. How well they knew where they were in the code while completing the tasks: 1 – No idea where they were in the code to 7 – Always knew where they were in the code

After both sets of tasks had been completed, the participants were asked to reflect on the differences in their experience completing the tasks both with and without StructJumper.

Design and Analysis

We used a 2x2 within-subjects factorial design with factors of the code base and whether or not StructJumper was used. Each participant completed three tasks for each code base. We presented the tasks in the same order for each code base, but the order was counterbalanced for each participant using a Latin square. Participants completed a total of 6 tasks for a total of 42 tasks completed altogether.

While analyzing completion task completion time, we used a mixed-effects model analysis of variance with a fixed effect of *Tool*, with *Participant* modeled as a random effect. For the semantically anchored scale data, we looked at the descriptive statistics.

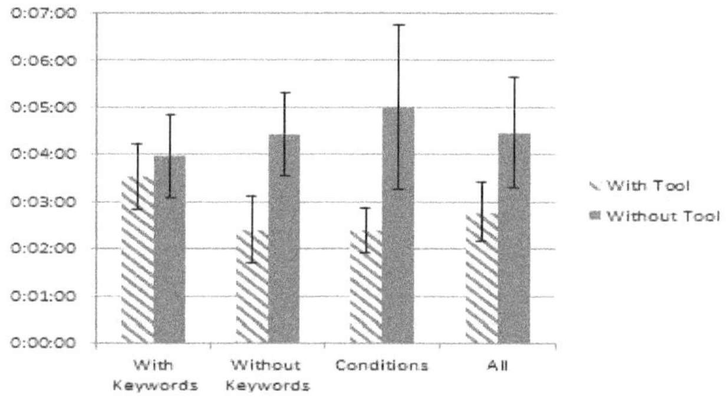

Figure 5. This chart shows the average completion time that it took participants to complete the three tasks broken down by type. The bars represent the standard error.

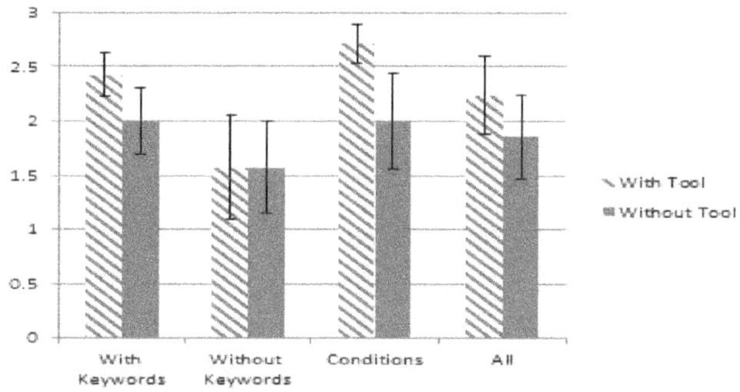

Figure 6. This chart shows the average score for all participants on the three tasks broken down by task. The bars represent the standard error.

RESULTS

To analyze the results, we used task completion times, task scores, and reported semantically anchored scale values. We found that participants were faster using StructJumper and had a better experience while using our tool as they were less frustrated and were more aware of where they were in the code.

Task Completion Time

Participants completed all of the tasks in an average time of 3 minutes and 38 seconds. Participants were faster with StructJumper (mean = 2m 47s, SD = 1m 41s) than without (mean = 4m 28s, SD = 3m 7s). While *Tool* did not have a statistically significant effect on *Time*, there was a trend in this direction ($F(1,6) = 5.783$, $p = .053$). The largest difference in time for the tasks came on the *conditions* task (see Figure 5) where participants performed faster with StructJumper (mean = 2m 24s, SD = 1m 16s) than without (mean = 5m 1s, SD = 4m 34s).

Task Score

The average score for participants was 2.0 (SD = .99). There was no significant effect of tool on score ($F(1,6) = 1.038$, n.s.). The average score with StructJumper was 2.2 (SD = .94), and 1.9 (SD = 1.01) without. The largest difference in task score was on the third task, (Figure 6), where participants received higher scores using StructJumper (mean = 2.7, SD = .49) than without (mean = 2.0, SD = 1.15). It is not surprising that participants performed better on this task, as providing the nesting context was one of the main goals for StructJumper. When participants did the completion task without the tool, two participants missed at least one condition and one participant added an extra condition, and one participant made both of these mistakes. With StructJumper, only two participants made errors, where one missed a condition and one added a condition.

On the feature identification tasks of *With Keywords* and *Without Keywords,* many of the participants found related or similar sections of code. Full credit was achieved on 10 out of the 28 feature identification tasks.

For example, one of the tasks asked the participants to find the section of code where the code skipped more than the normal number of rows in the search through the image. For this task, many participants found sections of code that determined how many rows of the image to skip instead of where the actual skip happened.

Another task asked participants to find where the most likely finder patterns were identified from all the potential finder patterns that were found. One participant found a section of code that identified if a single section of the image is likely a finder pattern.

Participants may have found related sections of code as opposed to the correct answer because our tasks purposefully contained as little information about the correct code section as possible. We made this decision in attempt to mimic a real life situation where the programmer is searching for a certain feature or action in a newer or unfamiliar code base. This choice may have added difficulty for users to locate the correct section of code, and thus caused users to find a section that is similar or related.

Participant Experience

We gathered insights on participant experience by asking three semantically anchored scale questions after each set of three tasks. We asked about how easy they found the tasks to complete, how frustrated they felt completing the tasks and how well they knew where they were in the code.

For how easy they found the tasks to complete, there was no difference in the average. The average score was 4.1 for both. However, the standard deviation was larger with the tool, than without the tool (SD = .83 vs. SD = 1.64).

When asked about their frustration when completing the tasks, the average was higher with the tool. For this semantically anchored scale, a higher number was less frustrating. The average was 4.3 without the tool (SD = 1.67) and 5.0 with the tool (SD = 1.4).

The largest difference however, was when the participants were asked about how well they knew where they were in the code (see Figure 7). The average was higher with the tool on this question as well. Once again, a higher number

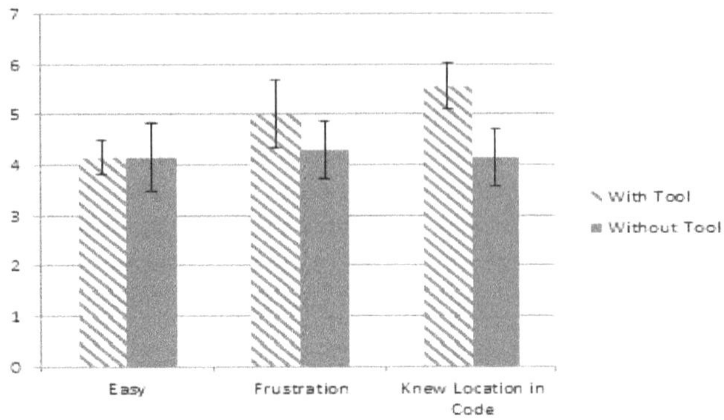

Figure 7. This chart show the average score for the participants for the semantically anchored questions. A higher value is better for all three questions. The bars represent the standard error.

is better as it meant they knew more often where they were in the code (1 was they never knew where they were and 7 was they always knew where they were). The average without the tool was 4.1 (SD = 1.12) and the average with the tool was 5.6 (SD = 1.40).

One thing that stood out about the responses for the question about how well they knew where they were in the code was the number of people who felt like they always knew where they were (response of 7) or almost always knew where they were (response of 6). Without the tool, nobody indicated they always knew where they were and only one person indicated that almost always knew where they were. Conversely, with the tool, two people always knew where they were and another three people almost always knew where they were.

QUALITATIVE RESULTS

After they had completed the sets of tasks with and without StructJumper, the participants were asked to reflect on completing the tasks themselves, their ability to complete the tasks, their knowledge of where they were in the code, and their understanding the code. Participants were asked if they would use StructJumper, and if so, for what types of tasks. Five of the participants indicated that they would use the tool.

To analyze the qualitative results, we looked at the interviews for concrete examples provided by the participants on how StructJumper changed the experience of completing the tasks and for examples on how the participants indicated that they would use the tool. Themes that were brought up by multiple participants were included in the results.

Quicker and Easier

As found in our results, there was a trend that StructJumper may have reduced the task completion time. In fact, six participants said that felt that they were able to navigate through the code faster and easier:

It's much easier than reading code. It's far more efficient because I'm reading relevant information. I don't have to read the complete code.

They mentioned that they were able to find the relevant information from the tool and skip between methods. When they were deep within a method, they were able to get information about where they were more quickly than without StructJumper.

Better Understanding of the Layout

Six participants indicated that the tool helped them with their understanding of how the code was laid out and how the statements were related to each other. Participants also felt that it helped them get a broad overview of the code.

This was particularly seen in the *conditions* task. As one participant was asked to complete the *conditions* task without StructJumper, they said:

I don't know how to see that in Eclipse. For that matter, in fact, I don't know how to see it in any of the IDEs I've worked in. Short of reading the code using brute force.

Another participant mentioned as they started the *conditions* task that this was one case where they would definitely want to use the tool as it made it a lot easier. This was also a common type of task that participants mentioned in the interviews that that the tool would be helpful for.

Participants also indicated that StructJumper was useful for gaining a broad understanding of the code. One participant indicated that they would be likely to use this to skim the code a few times before reading the code line by line when first introduced to a large, new code base.

Lack of Cues

Two participants mentioned that StructJumper was helpful when there is a lack of cues to indicate how far a statement is nested in the code. There were two cases of this mentioned by participants.

For instance, one participant mentioned Python. The participant mentioned that in languages like Java, there are cues, such as curly braces, to indicate the start and end of a nesting level. These cues make knowing how far nesting a statement is possible. Without these cues, the participant indicated that it is much harder to know where the statement was. Therefore, expanding this concept to a language like Python could potentially have a large impact on a blind programmer.

Another participant indicated a similar sentiment about the lack of cues. In order to have the screen reader speak cues such as the braces, the settings of the screen reader need to be set to speak all the punctuation. However, the participant said:

I really hate changing the punctuation verbosity of my JAWS, on my screen reader, to most or all. So it's always set at none. So I don't even know braces and stuff like that.

And it's just that since I read through the code so many times and I understand it so well that I can figure out, ok well here has to be a brace or here is where the indentation changes. So I never use a feature ever to actually notify me. It's really annoying. So that one thing that this tool really helps with. I know, ok, well this condition, it's within the other condition, within that loop. So it kind of helps that way.

As participants were completing the tasks, we saw some change the verbosity of the punctuation level as they were completing the tasks as they may only use that level of punctuation verbosity for programming and it may be the case that others would prefer not to have to have the screen reader read all the punctuation all the time.

Change in Focus

One of the prompts we asked the participants to reflect on was whether or not the tool affected their ability to understand the code. A few brought up that it removed the number of things that they would have to focus on as they were going through the code, which may make it easier to understand. For example, some participants mentioned that it allowed them to focus less on the little details of how to navigate or keep track of where they are in the code. One participant said:

You know, the navigation part, you know, without it, I was more focusing on that probably. How do I navigate, how do I get to the next thing, what keywords can I use to easily jump to where it needs to go? So, you know, without having to do that, you know, maybe I was focusing more on understanding what the code actually does.

Another participant indicated that they would use the tool when they were trying to understand the code. They said that it was useful when:

Trying to keep track of what level you're on basically... If I'm reading through code and trying to remember how many right braces you have remaining, how the different conditionals are related to each other.

It allowed them to see the relationship between blocks of code more easily. For instance, one participant indicated that is made it easier for them to know which conditionals a statement in the code it was nested under.

Unfamiliar Code

Multiple participants indicated that this tool would be more helpful for unfamiliar code than for code they know well. Many indicated that this was because, for code in which they are familiar, they already know the keywords they can use to jump to a section of code or what statements are under which conditionals. StructJumper aims to help provide this information, so it helps them learn when they first see a code base.

In familiar code, the biggest benefit this tool may add is the ability to navigate more quickly to that line, as mentioned by one participant. The tool can be used to skip lines and the user can quickly skip through code as they know each where the section is nested. This could be better than a keyword search as frequently the keywords may not be unique to that section of code only, and far better than moving through code line by line.

Programming Use

There were some participants who mentioned use cases for the tool that were more related to coding and finding errors in code. Some participants mentioned that this might be good at finding errors such as improperly matched braces. Another area that a participant suggested it might be useful to use it to skim over the logic for errors, such as looking at what the switch cases are to determine why the correct case is not getting called.

One participant mentioned that in his work, he might receive feedback from customers about the functionality of the application. He could then use the tool to navigate to a section of code where the functionality in question is and then fix the problem or make the requested change.

The researchers are interested in investigating the use of this tool for programming by conducting follow-up studies.

DISCUSSION

We believe the lack of significant effect of the tool on time comes from some variation in the participants. For 8 of the 21 tasks, participants were slower with our tool than without. Of the 8 slower tasks, 2 were on C*onditions* tasks, 3 were on the *With Keywords* task and 3 were on the *Without Keywords* tasks.

We attribute this variation to a variety of reasons. In one case, the participants only found one of the conditions without the tool and with the tool found all three and spent more time double-checking them. Two of the participants that were slower on some tasks with the tool did not use anything like the package explorer or outline. They were efficient with a line-by-line navigation approach. All but one other of the participants used either the package explorer or the outline and may be more accustomed to using a similar tool.

For some participants, it was not clear what made them slower with the tool than without the tool. It may be that they were more efficient with their current method. It could also be that they just found the navigation task that they received while using the tool more difficult.

One of the limitations of this work is that it only looks at navigation within unfamiliar code. As programmers will spend much of their time navigating through code that they have been working on and is familiar to them, this study does not look at one of the main use cases. We cannot know if the benefits we saw in this study will carry over to navigation in familiar code.

FUTURE WORK

The evaluation of StructJumper focused only on navigational tasks as that is its main purpose, but it would be interesting to learn how participants use this tool to perform different coding tasks as well. Some participants mentioned its use in debugging to try and find logical errors as well as navigation to find problem sections of code. In addition, the researchers could learn by having StructJumper used in the wild. This would allow us to look at how its use might change with familiar programs versus unfamiliar programs.

Additionally, it would be interesting to research whether this tool is beneficial to sighted programmers and investigate how their use of the tool varies from blind programmers. Much of the benefit of the tool is overcoming the difficulties that screen readers have in jumping many lines of code, which can be done more easily with sight and visual clues like indentation. However, there may be benefits for sighted programmers to only look at the included lines of code and ignore other code sections as they are collapsed on the tree.

CONCLUSION

We created StructJumper, an Eclipse plugin that allows blind programmers to quickly navigate through the code and see the how specific statements are nested within the code. We ran a user study with seven blind programmers and found that there is a trend that the tool has an effect on the time it took users to complete the tasks.

We also found that participants were positive about the tool and that they would be interested in continuing to use the tool. The participants found it quicker to navigate through the code and, thought that StructJumper provided valuable information about the conditionals that apply to a line of code.

ACKNOWLEDGMENTS

This material is based upon work supported by the NSF Graduate Research Fellowship under Grant Nos. DGE-0718124 and DGE-1256082 and NSF grant IIS-1116051.

REFERENCES

[1] Asakawa, C. and Itoh, T. 1998. User interface of a Home Page Reader. In *Proc. of ACM conference on Assistive technologies* Assets '98. ACM, New York, NY, USA, 149-156.

[2] Austin, J. 2013. Want a Great Scientific Career? Choose Computer Science. From http://sciencecareers.sciencemag.org/career_magazine/previous_issues/articles/2013_03_25/caredit.a1300053.

[3] Bragdon, A., Zeleznik, R., Reiss, S.P., Karumuri, S., Cheung, W., Kaplan, J., Coleman, C., Adeputra, F. and LaViola, J.J. Jr.. 2010. Code bubbles: a working set-based interface for code understanding and maintenance. In *Proceedings of CHI '10*. ACM, New York, NY, USA, (April 2010), 2503-2512.

[4] Henley, A.Z. and Fleming, S.D. 2014. The patchworks code editor: toward faster navigation with less code arranging and fewer navigation mistakes. In *Proc. of CHI '14*. ACM, (April 2014), 2511-2520.

[5] Jakobsen, M.R. and Hornbaek, K. 2006. Evaluating a Fisheye View of Source Code. In *Proc. CHI '06*, ACM Press, (April 2006), 377-386.

[6] Mealin, S., Murphy-Hill, E. 2012. An exploratory study of blind software developers. *Visual Languages and Human-Centric Computing (VL/HCC), 2012 IEEE Symposium on*. IEEE, (September 2012), 71-74.

[7] Palladino, D. and Walker, B. 2007. Learning rates for auditory menus enhanced with spearcons versus earcons. In *Proc. of International Conference on Auditory Display* (Montreal, Canada June 26-29, 2007) ICAD '07.

[8] Sánchez, J., Aguayo, F. 2005. Blind learners programming through audio. In *CHI'05 extended abstracts on Human factors in computing systems*, ACM, (April 2005), 1769-1772.

[9] Smith, A., Cook, J., Francioni, J., Hossain, A., Anwar, M., and Rahman, M. 2003. Nonvisual tool for navigating hierarchical structures. In *SIGACCESS Access. Comput.*77-78 (September 2003), 133-139.

[10] Stefik, A., Alexander, R., Patterson, and Brown, J. 2007. WAD: A Feasibility study using the Wicked Audio Debugger. In *Proceedings of the 15th IEEE International Conference on Program Comprehension* (ICPC '07). IEEE Computer Society, Washington, DC, USA, 69-80.

[11] Stefik, A., Hundhausen, C., and Patterson, R. 2011. An empirical investigation into the design of auditory cues to enhance computer program comprehension. In *International Journal of Human-Computer Studies*, 69 12, (December 2011), 820-838.

[12] Stefik, A., Hundhausen, C., and Smith, D. 2011. On the design of an educational infrastructure for the blind and visually impaired in computer science. In *Proceedings of the 42nd ACM technical symposium on Computer science education*, ACM, (March 2011), 571-576.

[13] Vickers, P. and Alty, J. 2002 When Bugs Sing. In *Interacting with Computers*, 14 (6). 793-819. ISSN 0953-5438

[14] WebAIM, 2012. Screen Reader User Survey #4 Results. From http://webaim.org/projects/screenreadersurvey4/.

[15] W3C, 2008. Web Content Accessibility Guidelines (WCAG) 2.0, From http://www.w3.org/TR/WCAG20/

An Interactive System for Data Structure Development

Jibin Ou
ETH Zürich
jou@student.ethz.ch

Martin Vechev
ETH Zürich
martin.vechev@inf.ethz.ch

Otmar Hilliges
ETH Zürich
otmar.hilliges@inf.ethz.ch

Figure 1: We contribute a novel way of debugging, allowing the user to directly interact with a program's live heap. The heap graph is abstracted using a method for online parametric heap abstraction which allows us to only visualize the algorithm's essential operation. The user can change and refine these automatic abstractions interactively. Our system can be used during regular development (left) and in a classroom setting using a pen+touch user interface (right).

ABSTRACT

Data structure algorithms are of fundamental importance in teaching and software development, yet are difficult to understand. We propose a new approach for understanding, debugging and developing heap manipulating data structures.

The key technical idea of our work is to combine deep parametric abstraction techniques emerging from the area of static analysis with interactive abstraction manipulation. Our approach bridges program analysis with HCI and enables new capabilities not possible before: i) online automatic visualization of the data structure in a way which captures its *essential operation*, thus enabling powerful local reasoning, and ii) fine grained pen and touch gestures allowing for interactive control of the abstraction – at any point the developer can pause the program, graphically interact with the data, and continue program execution. These features address some of the most pressing challenges in developing data structures.

We implemented our approach in a Java-based system called *FluidEdt* and evaluated it with 27 developers. The results indicate that *FluidEdt* is more effective in helping developers find data structure errors than existing state of the art IDEs (e.g. Eclipse) or pure visualization based approaches.

CHI 2015, April 18 - 23 2015, Seoul, Republic of Korea
Copyright ©2015 ACM 978-1-4503-3145-6/15/04... $15.00
http://dx.doi.org/10.1145/2702123.270231

Author Keywords

debugging; program analysis; software development

ACM Classification Keywords

D.2.6 Programming Environments; H.5.2 User Interfaces

INTRODUCTION

Data structures and algorithms are at the core of modern software systems and are a staple of computer science curricula worldwide. It is via data structures and algorithms that students are first exposed to many of the core concepts in computer science. However, despite decades of research and teaching, understanding the underlying operation of even small data structure algorithms remains as difficult and as cognitively demanding as ever. Even shorter programs can perform complex and difficult to understand manipulations on the program's heap. Thus data structure manipulating algorithms are an interesting case for HCI research as they are well understood *in principle* yet are very hard to master *in practice*. To crystalize some of the issues associated with their development, we conducted a series of interviews with colleagues involved with the data structures class at our University as well as a thorough analysis of hundreds of online posts related to this topic (found on Stack Overflow*). The results of our study clearly illustrate a diverse set of errors and misunderstandings involving linked lists, arrays, trees and other structures – the complete catalog can be accessed via supplementary materials.

*http://stackoverflow.com

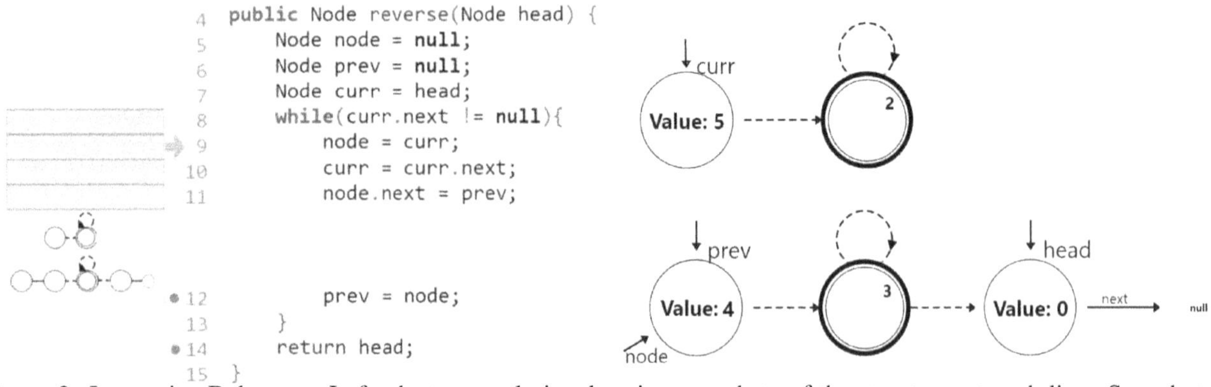

Figure 2: Interactive Debugger. Left: the temporal view keeping snapshots of the structures at each line. Snapshots can be collapsed and expanded on demand and are aligned with lines of code. Middle: the code (in this case, an attempt at reversing a linked list). Right: the abstracted heap view. Red dots indicate break points, yellow arrow indicates the current line.

Our study firmly reinforces that complex pointer manipulations are a key source of confusion in understanding existing algorithms, in discovering and repairing errors, and even in explaining how algorithms work. Unfortunately, despite the universal importance of these algorithms, there is still little tool support for effectively understanding their operation.

In this paper we introduce a new approach and a complementary tool for interactive debugging and development of data structure manipulating algorithms. Our approach bridges the areas of HCI and program analysis. The key technical idea of our work is based on a novel combination of parametric predicate abstraction techniques emerging from the area of static analysis with *interactive* abstraction manipulation. Our tool has two benefits. First, it automatically visualizes the data structure in a way which *captures its essential operation* while abstracting the rest. This is an important feature which enables *local reasoning*, meaning that even though the data structure may contain a large number of nodes, at any given time only the (small number of) nodes relevant to the current program context are kept concrete. Second, our tool provides the developer with fine grained controls over *which data is visualized* – the developer can pause the program, interact with the data structure (e.g. abstract, concretize, modify), and continue program execution with the new structure. This enables one to try various hypotheses for the algorithm operation.

We envision our approach being useful in a wide range of settings including the classroom but also in the increasingly common search-and-modify code development setting. For instance, in this setting, a developer will usually i) search online for the particular functionality (e.g., an AVL tree), ii) try to understand what the suggested program does [16], and iii) modify the program according to their needs. Proliferation of online source code repositories such as GitHub and sites such as Stack Overflow, along with other web resources have made step i) almost instant. Further, the HCI research community has come up with a number of tools to better integrate the usage of web resources and the development process [5, 9, 22, 28]. Step ii) is most time consuming and challenging as the developer is not familiar with the code and even short algorithms can admit many different implementations. Worse, step iii) cannot be accomplished until step ii) is thoroughly completed. We believe that our tool can be very effective in reducing the cost of the search-and-modify loop by drastically reducing the time for step ii).

In our experimental user study, we show that our system makes it easier and faster to detect data structure errors than modern debuggers found in IDEs such as Eclipse or Visual Studio.

Main contributions:

- A method for online and automatic parametric heap abstraction, enabling *local reasoning* by focusing developer attention on the essential parts of the data structure.
- A fine grained interface for *interactive heap abstraction manipulation* involving visual representation of (abstract) objects and gestures for navigation and modification.
- An implementation of our approach in a system called *FluidEdt* and an experimental results indicating increased efficiency in finding errors over existing IDEs.

SYSTEM OVERVIEW

The user interface consists of i) a temporal view containing (easily accessible) structures recorded at each program point (left), ii) the code view in the middle (here showing a program attempting a list reversal), and iii) the main drawing canvas where the (abstract) heap is rendered on the right.

Temporal View

The temporal view captures a visual history of (abstract) shapes. At every point this history keeps a snapshot of the current heap. To prevent visual clutter, the snapshots are initially collapsed (similar to [18]) and the user can expand a thumbnail for any snapshot, or drag it onto the *heap view* to restore it. This feature enables relational reasoning by comparing heap structures at different execution points. We currently keep the most recent snapshot at a program point, usually effective for common programming scenarios (if needed, the system can record more snapshots). We note that static analyzers have also successfully used forms of recency abstractions [2].

Code View

The code view shows the part of the program currently being inspected. As with traditional IDEs, red dots indicate break points while a yellow arrow indicates the current line (in this case line 9). Beyond giving the user a simultaneous view onto code and data, this view also links together temporal and heap views. Here, snapshots are aligned with the line of code they belong to. The code shows a short but challenging example: (a faulty) algorithm which attempts to perform linked list reversal. A typical Java implementation of this algorithm only takes about 10 lines of code, yet despite its simplicity, developers struggle with this problem – there are hundreds of threads on this topic on StackOverflow. Many of these are lengthy discussions with many answers (which themselves often need to be corrected). Almost all threads include some form of graphical depiction illustrating the algorithm operation.

Abstracted Heap View

This view renders an abstraction of the data structure and allows for interactive manipulation. It aims to distill the *essential* parts of the structure while abstracting the rest, enabling *local reasoning*. Here the view shows an abstraction of the concrete structure arising at line 9 – abstract nodes are shown with thick bold edges, while abstract edges are denoted by dashed lines. An abstract node can contain a number of concrete nodes (indicated by its label). Similarly, an abstract edge may contain a number of concrete edges. In this example we have two abstract nodes, one with 2 concrete nodes and another with 3. Note how the abstract shape already conveys much useful information: we immediately see that the list is disconnected into two parts and that `head` points to the last element of one of the structures. Importantly, regardless of the size of the concrete list, it will still be collapsed into this shape *automatically*, greatly reducing irrelevant details (e.g. the size of the list).

Suppose the programmer inspects the structure and finds that the structure captures her intuition of how the algorithm should work. Naturally, she may then set a breakpoint, say at line 12, run the program, and inspect the new structure arising at that line. To allow programmers to better understand the changes between program lines (e.g. lines 9 to 12), we smoothly animate these transitions in the displayed graph. In particular, nodes that were concrete in one frame and will be abstracted next, are moved smoothly into the new abstract node and vice versa. This feature is crucial for users to understand the temporal effects on the heap during program execution. Further, as the developer steps through the code (or reaches breakpoints), our system will automatically update the abstraction. The abstract structure at line 12 then is:

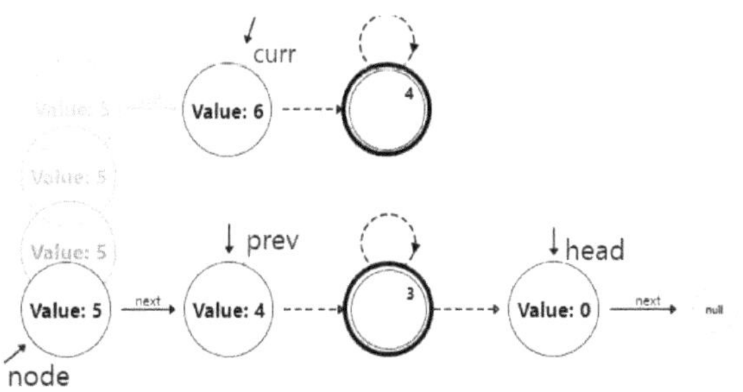

The animation indicates the movement of a node to the front of the second structure while `curr` advanced towards the abstract node, necessitating concretization. The rest of the structure remains the same. The programmer now inspects the structure and assuming it conforms to their intuition, sets a breakpoint at line 14 resulting in the following structure:

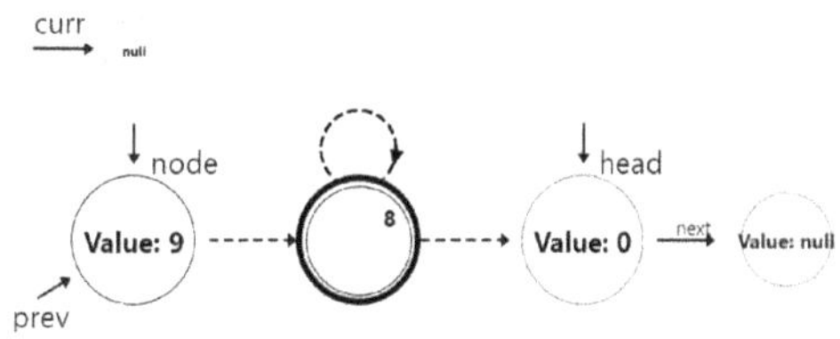

We now clearly see the algorithmic error: `head` points to the end rather than the beginning of the list and hence the algorithm returns an incorrect result! Note how it is unnecessary to know what is in the middle of the list (the abstracted part) to know that an error has occurred.

Interactions and Usage Scenarios

We envision our tool being useful in at least two separate but related scenarios. The first scenario is regular development of new code. This scenario usually happens on a regular desktop PC with a large monitor, mouse and keyboard. The main form of interaction with *FluidEdt* in this scenario is likely to be focused on stepping through code, comparing (abstract) snapshots and specifying the visual abstraction levels.

The second scenario focuses on code understanding rather than writing new code from scratch. In particular, it applies to the classroom where code snippets are provided by the instructor for students to experiment with the program on their own devices. Today almost all students own personal touch screen devices and bring them to class. Towards this, we designed a set of touch and pen gestures that allow one to directly interact with the data of a program. Similar approaches have been used successfully to foster understanding of complex issues such as mathematical equations [30] and multivariate datasets [23], suggesting that direct, physical manipulation of complex and abstract data aids understanding.

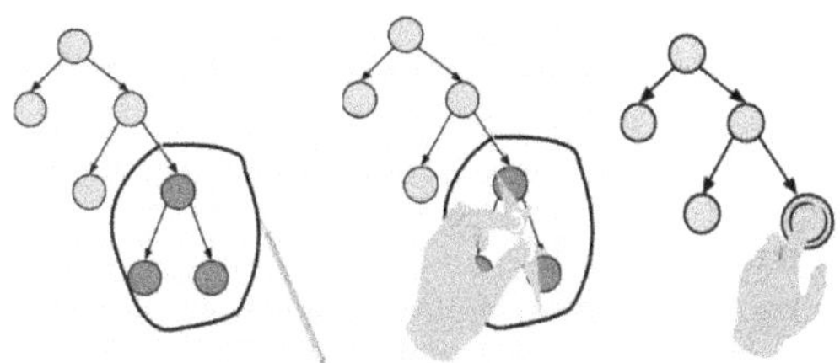

Figure 3: Pen+Touch gestures for heap manipulation

We provide a succinct set of gestures allowing users to interact with the heap. Fig. 3 illustrates how different tasks are allocated to pen and touch respectively. Touch is mainly used to pan and zoom the canvas and to arrange the nodes spatially, in case the automatic layout does not suit the user. The user can also select abstract nodes in order to inspect the values encapsulated by the node. The stylus is primarily used to select multiple nodes simultaneously by circling them (Fig. 3, left). Selected nodes can either be moved together, or be abstracted by a pinch gesture performed directly on the selection (Fig. 3, middle). Abstracted nodes can be concretized by double tapping the node (Fig. 3, middle).

Concrete Heap	Abstracted Heap	Abstracted Heap after: `y := y.n`

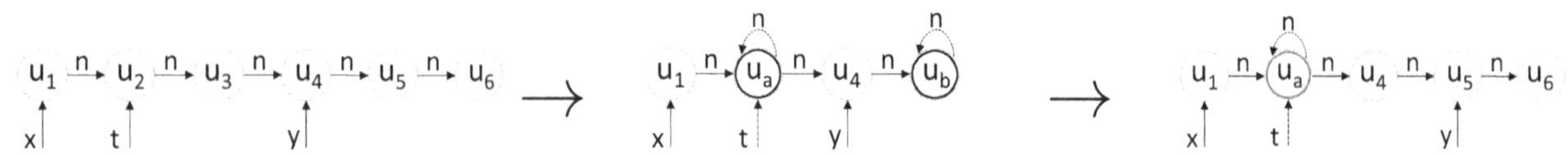

(a) (c) (e)

	u_1	u_2	u_3	u_4	u_5	u_6
$x(u)$	1	0	0	0	0	0
$y(u)$	0	0	0	1	0	0
$r_{n,x}(u)$	1	1	1	1	1	1
$r_{n,y}(u)$	0	0	0	1	1	1
$t(u)$	0	1	0	0	0	0

(b)

	u_1	u_a	u_4	u_b
$x(u)$	1	0	0	0
$y(u)$	0	0	1	0
$r_{n,x}(u)$	1	1	1	1
$r_{n,y}(u)$	0	0	1	1
$t(u)$	0	1/2	0	0

(d)

	u_1	u_a	u_4	u_5	u_6
$x(u)$	1	0	0	0	0
$y(u)$	0	0	0	1	0
$r_{n,x}(u)$	1	1	1	1	1
$r_{n,y}(u)$	0	0	0	1	1
$t(u)$	0	1/2	0	0	0

(f)

Table 4: The figure shows how the concrete linked list in (a) is abstracted into the shape in (c) via the abstraction predicates x, y, $r_{n,x}$, $r_{n,y}$ and how the abstraction in (c) is updated when performing the statement `y := y.n` resulting in (e).

ABSTRACTION BY EXAMPLE

We now present an intuitive understanding of the core techniques underlying our approach (formal explanations are provided later). The three core features of our approach are: i) how to perform abstraction of a concrete graph (used to perform the abstraction of the heap upon starting the program), ii) how the abstraction is updated when stepping through the program, and iii) how we support interactive user driven abstraction manipulation. Our machinery is inspired by techniques developed in the static analysis community [24], but departs from these in a number of important ways.

A key ingredient of a parametric abstraction are predicates – logical formulas which given a (concrete) heap evaluate to 1 (i.e. $true$) or 0 (i.e. $false$). These predicates capture information which we would like to preserve in the abstracted graph. Predicates are the knobs for controlling what information should be abstracted away. Roughly speaking, we abstract the heap in a way that relevant predicates (abstraction predicates) are kept concrete. We now illustrate how to abstract the concrete list in Table 4(a) into the abstract list sin Table 4(c).

Step 1: select predicates

We first select the relevant predicates for our problem. By default, we use local pointer variables as *points-to* predicates – these have proven useful in enabling local reasoning [24], a key to understanding intricate data structure behavior. We usually instantiate new *points-to* predicates corresponding to the local pointer variables in the stack frame as well as few other predicates we found generally applicable (based on our experimental study). Of course, the user can switch-off predicates at any point if they do not find them useful. For our example, we used five unary predicates: $x(u)$, $y(u)$, $t(u)$, $r_{n,x}(u)$ and $r_{n,y}(u)$. That is, we use points-to predicates x, y, t and reachability predicates (as we may be interested in keeping precise information of what is reachable from pointers x and y). Out of these five, all are abstraction predicates except $t(u)$ meaning that t's value need not be kept concrete. We selected $t(u)$ on purpose to illustrate how one can obtain $1/2$ values (edges carrying $1/2$ information are dashed in the pictures). For our list reversal in Fig. 2, the automatically selected abstraction predicates will be `curr`, `prev`, `node` and `head`.

Step 2: predicate evaluation

Next, we evaluate each of the selected predicates on each concrete node. The result of this evaluation is shown in Table 4(b). In the general case where the predicates can be arbitrary logical formulas, the evaluation process involves evaluating logical formulas (as done in [24]). However, in our case, the predicates have a pre-defined meaning (that is, they have a fixed logical formula) and hence we can evaluate them with graph algorithms specific to their particular meaning.

Step 3: direct abstraction

After predicate evaluation, the next step is to perform abstraction. Using our abstraction approach, we obtain the predicate values shown in Table 4(d). The basic idea of abstraction is conceptually simple: all nodes which share the same set of predicate evaluations for the *abstraction predicates* are collapsed into an abstract node. For example, nodes u_2 and u_3 are collapsed into the same abstract node u_a because they both share the exact same valuations for all four of the abstraction predicates. Similarly, nodes u_5 and u_6 are collapsed into the same abstract node u_b. However, node u_4 is *not* abstracted into u_a or u_b because $y(u_3) \neq y(u_4)$. It is important to note that all of the abstraction predicates remain with *concrete* values, that is, they still evaluate to 0 or 1 for the abstracted node u_a and u_b. However, the values of the non-abstraction predicates such as $t(u)$ need not be kept concrete, and as we can see, indeed, it now evaluates to $1/2$ for u_a (because there were two concrete nodes u_2 and u_3 for which t evaluates to 1 and 0 respectively).

Step 4: visualize

Once the new matrix is obtained, we can now visualize that matrix – the result is shown in Table 4(c). Here, if for a given abstract node, the predicate evaluates to 1, we show the node, otherwise (if its $1/2$ or 0) it is omitted from the picture. To reduce clutter, in our figure we do not show $r_{n,x}$ or $r_{n,y}$.

On-demand abstraction updates

Now suppose that starting from the shape shown in Table 4(c), the programmer performs one step by executing `y := y.n`. If we proceed naively, y would end up pointing to the abstract node u_b and it may be confusing to the programmer what exactly is inside u_b. To avoid this, we automatically concretize node u_b on-demand – the system will observe that the abstraction predicate y now evaluates to $1/2$ and will concretize the node, splitting it into two abstract nodes where y will evaluate to 0 on one of the abstract nodes and to 1 on the other node (in our example, there are only two concrete nodes hence we fully concretize u_b but this need not be the case with all other unary predicates and shapes). Note that node u_a still stays abstracted as it is not relevant to the current "local view". The result of this step is shown in Table 4(f) and the visualization in Table 4(e). We argue that this gradual update of the abstraction *on demand* helps developers in understanding the algorithm as it focuses on the local changes to the data while abstracting the uninformative complexity of the heap.

Stepping into functions

When we step into a function, the previous predicates are still used to maintain the abstract shape, but we identify the new stack pointers and add the corresponding points-to predicates corresponding to these pointers as abstraction predicates.

Manual abstraction interactions

We allow the user to control the abstraction by selecting nodes which are to be abstracted and to concretize existing nodes. This enables users to customize the heap view to the particular intuition they have about the algorithm at a given point. The machinery for these manual interactions is similar to what is discussed above and is elaborated in the next section.

A note on predicates

In general, predicates can be arbitrary logical formulas. However, in our work, we decided against supporting arbitrarily defined predicates for two reasons: i) we do not expect developers to write complex logical formulas, and ii) perhaps more importantly, automatically abstracting arbitrary logical formulas is computationally expensive [24] and not suitable for an interactive environment. Therefore, in our approach we still use the abstraction semantics as described above (same as in [24]), but we work with a set of predefined predicates that can be instantiated. We provide the full set of built-in predicates in the Appendix. Our set of built-in predicates was derived from our detailed experimental evaluation and inspecting various programming forums, in which we found it to naturally captures programmer's intentions. We do note however that there is nothing inherent in our parametric approach that precludes us from adding more predicates. We note that the user can extend this list with other predicates without requiring any change to our (parametric) system.

ABSTRACTION FORMALLY

In this section, we present a more formal discussion of how our abstractions work: the abstraction representation, the initial abstraction of the program, the update of the abstraction when a piece of code is executed and how we combine predicate abstraction with user level manipulations of the shape.

Abstraction representation

To capture the abstraction and the concrete nodes that are connected with it, our system maintains the four maps described below. These four maps are continually updated during program navigation:

- $\alpha_N(v) : CN \to AN$: the map maintains a mapping from a concrete to an abstract node.
- $\alpha_E(e) : CE \to AE$: the map maintains a mapping from a concrete to an abstract edge.
- $\gamma_N(v) : AN \to \mathcal{P}(CN)$: reverse map from an abstract node to a *set* of concrete nodes.
- $\gamma_E(e) : AE \to \mathcal{P}(CE)$: reverse map from an abstract edge to a *set* of concrete edges.

Here, we use CN to denote the set of concrete heap nodes, AN to denote the set of abstract nodes, CE to denote the set of concrete edges and AE to denote the set of abstract edges. We note that such maps are *not* naturally maintained by static tools such as TVLA (Three-Valued Logic Analyzer, a tool implementing the approach in [24]) because the concrete nodes are not available (the entire purpose of static analysis is to soundly approximate these concrete nodes with abstract nodes). Maintaining such maps is unique to our setting.

In a static analysis setting (e.g. TVLA), abstraction is done entirely based on predicates without the option of interactively modifying the abstract shapes. In our case however, modification of the abstract shape is a first class operation and therefore we need to address the challenge of combining such modifications with the standard predicate abstraction – a challenge which simply does not arise in the pure static analysis setting.

Computing the initial abstraction

Initially, when the program starts, we have a concrete heap G and a current set of pointer variables. A natural problem then is how to abstract this initial shape (as the shape may be too large due to the input test case, etc). Algorithm 1 shows how to perform the initial abstraction. Here, we use $Preds$ to denote the set of predicates that we use for abstraction. First, at step 1, the algorithm starts by evaluating each predicate on each node (object) in the concrete graph (we already illustrated this step on an example). Because the graph is concrete, the resulting value of the evaluation can only be 0 ($false$) or 1 ($true$). Then, in step 2, it groups all nodes which have the same value for *all* of the predicates. Finally, at step 3, we update the node and the edge abstraction and concretization maps accordingly – this is done via the auxiliary functions described in Algorithm 2. For readability purposes, we slightly abuse notation and write $f(a) = b$ for $f' = f[a \to b]$ followed by $f = f'$.

Updated abstract shapes

Once an abstract shape is computed, it is important to define what happens to it as the user steps through the program. In particular, we need to define how such shapes are transformed during program execution. For instance, if the user steps over a large function (which results in some concrete heap), we need to define how the new abstract shape is computed. Note that in practice, the function over which the user has stepped over may not even be subject to instrumentation (e.g a native method in Java). Therefore, we cannot adopt the approach of TVLA

// create temporary maps
$NodePredVals = \textbf{new}\ (CN \rightarrow Preds \rightarrow \{0,1\})$
$PredValNodes = \textbf{new}\ (Preds \rightarrow \{0,1\} \rightarrow \mathcal{P}(CN))$
// step 1: compute predicate values for each node
foreach $node \in G.nodes$ **do**
  foreach $pred \in Preds$ **do**
    $NodePredVals(node)(pred) = pred(node)$
  end
end
// step 2: build equivalence classes
foreach $node \in G.nodes$ **do**
  $PredVals = NodePredVals(node)$
  $PredValNodes(PredVals) \cup = \{node\}$
end
// step 3: create the abstract maps: nodes and edges
foreach $(\_, nodes) \in PredValNodes$ **do**
  $abstractNodes(nodes)$
end
$abstractEdges(G.edges)$

Algorithm 1: Creating an abstraction.

abstractNodes$(nodes)$ {
$absNode = createUniqueAbstractNode()$
foreach $n \in nodes$ **do**
  $\alpha_V(n) = absNode$
  $\gamma_V(absNode) \cup = \{n\}$
end
}
abstractEdges$(edges)$ {
foreach $e \in edges$ **do**
  $absEdge = \langle \alpha_V(e.source), \alpha_V(e.target)\rangle$
  $\alpha_E(e) = absEdge$
  $\gamma_E(absEdge) \cup = \{e\}$
end
}

Algorithm 2: Auxiliary functions.

foreach $an \in range(\alpha_V)$ **do**
  foreach $pred \in Preds$ **do**
    if $pred(an) = 1/2$ **then**
      $N_1 = \{cn \mid cn \in \gamma_V(an) \wedge pred(cn) = 1\}$
      $N_0 = \{cn \mid cn \in \gamma_V(an) \wedge pred(cn) = 0\}$
      $abstractNodes(N_0)$
      $abstractNodes(N_1)$
      $abstractEdges(dom(\alpha_E))$
    end
  end
end

Algorithm 3: Focusing / Refining the abstraction.

Statement	Updated Map
$new\ edge\langle e\rangle$	$\alpha'_E = \alpha_E \cup (e,e)$, $\gamma'_E = \gamma_E \cup (e,\{e\})$
$del\ edge\langle e\rangle$	$dom(\alpha'_E) = dom(\alpha_E) \setminus \{e\}$ $\gamma'_E = \gamma_E[(\alpha_E(e)) \rightarrow \gamma_E(\alpha_E(e)) \setminus \{e\}]$
$new\ node\langle v\rangle$	$\alpha'_V = \alpha_V \cup (v,v)$, $\gamma'_V = \gamma_V \cup (v,\{v\})$
$del\ node\langle v\rangle$	$dom(\alpha'_V) = dom(\alpha_V) \setminus \{v\}$ $\gamma'_V = \gamma_V[(\alpha_V(v)) \rightarrow \gamma_V(\alpha_V(v)) \setminus \{v\}]$

Table 5: Updating the abstraction and concretization maps.

which defines the effects of a statement on the abstract shape (as we may not have the statement available). We next describe a 3-step process for computing this new abstract shape.

Step 1: compute shape differences

Given the initial graph C and the new graph C' resulting from stepping over statements, we compute their heap difference. That is, we compute the quadruple $\langle newEdges, delEdges, newNodes, delNodes\rangle$ denoting the set of new edges in C' not in C, the set of deleted edges from C not in C' (and similarly for nodes).

Step 2: update maps

We next update the abstraction and concretization maps defined earlier: we iterate over the sets and update the map accordingly. The rules for updating the maps for each of the four cases (added edge, deleted edge, new node, deleted node) are described in Table 5. For instance, if a new edge is created, we add that edge to the abstraction and concretization maps.

Step 3: focus maps

Simply updating the maps in step 2 is not enough. The reason is that a useful unary predicate may suddenly evaluate to $1/2$ in the new abstract graph and we would like these predicates to be concrete (an example of that was shown in the overview section). A predicate evaluates to $1/2$ if the abstract node contains two concrete nodes where the predicate evaluates to 0 for one node and to 1 for the other. In Algorithm 3, we show how to focus the values of these predicates. Here, if a node is evaluated to $1/2$, we concretize the node into two sets of nodes and then re-abstract these sets of concrete nodes as before using the auxiliary functions (and update the maps). As a result, we end up with a more intuitive abstract graph.

Interactive Abstraction Manipulation

Manual abstraction manipulations (e.g. via pen+touch) involve selection of nodes to be abstracted or concretized. Both of these operations update the maps as discussed so far – for instance, the interactive abstraction works via the two functions shown in Algorithm 2. Note that these operations may change the values of the selected abstraction predicates as they will now be evaluated on the new (possibly abstract) structure.

IMPLEMENTATION

We implemented our approach described so far in a prototype system called *FluidEdt* targeting Java (we built an Eclipse plug-in to query the heap information). The plug-in sends the heap information to the front-end which processes and renders the graph. The front-end is built as a stand alone Windows app.

For the graph rendering component, we used a customized version of the GraphX framework†. AvalonEdit‡ is used to format the code view. We implemented a communication protocol to initially transfer the graph data from back-end to front-end and to incrementally transfer heap modifications (i.e. the delta between two shapes) at each program step.

In general, when we step in or out of a function, we simply copy the abstract maps – nothing else needs to be changed. By default, all predicates in the new function are disabled, but the user is free to enable them as she wishes. Because stepping in or out of a function does not change the maps, this entails that the only time we compute differences between heap graphs is when the graphs belong to the same function.

In addition to the abstraction and concretization, we support data *allocation* and *modification*. For *data modification*, one can change a node's primitive value or connect two nodes together. For *data allocation*, we allow the user to create new nodes on-demand without changing the code. This is useful in a debugging scenario where the programmer wishes to check if certain data configurations behave well (i.e. do not exhibit bugs) when starting from particular program points. Our implementation automatically updates the current program state in order to reflect these graphical changes allowing the program to continue running with the new heap state. Currently we do not persist these changes but leave this for future work.

EXPERIMENTAL EVALUATION

Our literature review and analysis of online forums has revealed that the two main sources of confusion – and hence errors – are complexity of data structures and complex pointer manipulations. In this section we report findings from a controlled experiment assessing the benefits of our design in respect to these difficulties. Our hypotheses are:

H1: Visualizing the heap of a running program improves code understanding and makes it *faster for developers to find errors* in the program code, compared to a *standard debugger*.

H2: Automatic and user driven abstraction of the heap graph will further improve code understanding. Hence, developers will be *faster to find errors* with these features than when using either a *standard debugger* or a *pure visualization*.

Experiment

To evaluate the hypothesis, we conducted a controlled experiment comparing our interface (***FluidEdt***) with i) the standard debugger of Eclipse IDE§ (**Eclipse**), and ii) a reduced version of *FluidEdt* that does visualize the heap but has no abstraction & concretization functionality (**Viz**). This variant also forbids the user to interact with the heap graph.

To test our hypothesis we asked experienced developers to try and find errors in programs. To avoid learning effects we chose an across-groups design i.e., each participant worked with each of the three **interfaces** but performed a different task in each condition. The experiment was conducted on a desktop PC (Core i7 CPU 3.4GHz) running Windows 8.1, equipped with a 19" monitor and an additional Wacom Cyntiq HD 24 tablet providing touch and pen input to drive the touch enabled UI. The resolution was set to 1920×1200.

Participants

We recruited 27 participants (3 female, 24 male) from our institution, mostly students (2 undergrad, 20 grad) and 5 postdocs from the computer science (CS) department. By selecting CS students only we aim to control the variance in programming skills (inline with prior experiments [3, 14]). Participants' ages ranged from 22 to 35 years ($M = 24$) and their self reported programming experience ranged from 2 to 7+ years ($M = 4.3$) with weekly programming activities ranging from 3 to 40 hours ($M = 17.3$). All participants reported 2 or more years of experience using some IDE.

Tasks

Each participant had to complete three tasks in total. Each of the tasks was performed with a different *interface* and to avoid learning effects each participant worked with different programs for each task. Participants were given a description of the expected program behavior and were told that the program contained at least one error. We designed the tasks such that they fall into three levels of difficulty from easy to hard.

T1: 10 lines of Java code reversing a singly-linked list. The code contained two bugs. First, it returns the tail of the reversed list (not the head). Second, after reversal the last node is missing from the list due to early-loop termination.

T2: 30 lines of Java code which reverse a linked-list from index m to n (not the whole list). The sole program error introduces a cycle into the list.

T3: 200 lines of Java code implementing an AVL-tree including insertion of new values and tree re-balancing. This code contained four errors but all of them were very similar so that once one is found all can be fixed. The errors cause entire subtrees to be detached from the tree during re-balancing. However, the error is not in the re-balance method but caused by wrong assignment of the method's return value (the sub-tree).

A description of the data-structures was read to the participants and we provided them with a set of sensible inputs to test the code. All participants managed to complete the tasks within the allotted 20 minutes.

Procedure

We used a $3 \times 3 \times 1$ between-subjects design with **tct** the dependent variable and with **interface** and **task** as the independent variables. Presentation order of conditions was counterbalanced using a Latin Squares design. Participants were split into three groups so that each task was only performed once per participant (and per interface). Resulting in a total of nine participants per *interface* × *task* combination and a total of 81 debug sessions (lasting 20 minutes each). Before each trial the participants were given written instructions on how to use the interface, were allowed to ask questions and to practice. During this warm-up phase they used different code, unrelated

† `https://github.com/panthernet/GraphX`
‡ `http://avalonedit.net/`
§ `https://www.eclipse.org/`

to the programs used in the actual experiments. As metric for **tct** we measured the time before the participants localized the error in the code and provided an appropriate fix for the error. We also encouraged participants to think out loud and performed an exit interview to gather qualitative feedback.

Results

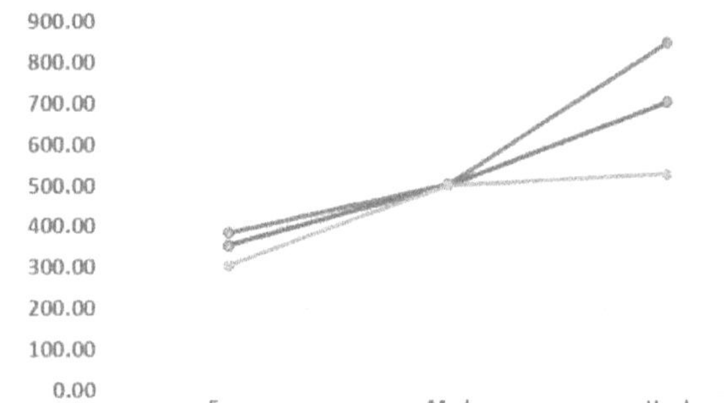

	Easy	Med	Hard
Eclipse	385.55	504.89	848.44
Viz	354.55	501.89	705.11
Ours	305.33	502.00	529.89

Figure 7: Task completion time in seconds as function of the task difficulty. The two interfaces with heap visualization perform significantly better than the standard debugger. Our system *FluidEdt* (referred to as Ours in the figure) is significantly faster than the other two in the hardest task.

We performed a two-way ANOVA which yielded stat. significant main effects for *interface* ($F_2 = 9.2, p = .0002$) *task* ($F_2 = 51.79, p = .0001$) and for the interaction *interface* $\times$ *task* ($F_4 = 5.8, p = .0004$). This suggests that the task difficulties are indeed different, that the interface has a significant effect on **tct** and that the difference between the means depends on the interaction between interface and task difficulty. Fig. 7 summarizes the mean **tct** across all tasks and interfaces. Indicating that both interfaces with heap graph visualization are faster than the standard debugger and that our tool performs better with increasing task difficulty. Note that the definition of 'difficulty' used here is not rigorous and the three tasks can not be placed equidistant along this dimension. Informally, the 3rd task (tree) seems more challenging than the others for several reasons: i) the program contains more code (>200 LOC), ii) the data structure is richer and inherently recursive, and iii) the program makes frequent use of nested operations.

Interestingly, there is evidence from the static analysis literature that trees are more difficult to reason about than lists, for two reasons: i) the invariants for trees (i.e. the predicates needed for verification) are more complicated to state and update, and ii) the number of states of a tree is much larger than a list. We believe our approach is particularly helpful for these more complex tasks due to its ability to abstract away the complexity of the data structure to allow for temporal comparison.

To further analyze these effects we performed post-hoc pairwise comparisons. These reveal that ***FluidEdt*** and **Viz** are statistically significantly faster than **Eclipse** ($p = .0036$ and $p = .0001$ respectively), allowing us to accept **H1**. While ***FluidEdt*** ($M = 452$ sec) was faster than **Viz** ($M = 487$ sec), these differences are not stat. significant ($p = .15$), and does not allow us to accept **H2**. However, the graph in Fig. 7 suggests a clear benefit in using our tool with increasing difficulty. This is also supported by the main effect on the *interface* $\times$ *task* interaction. To crystalize where these differences came from we performed two 2×2 ANOVAs, comparing *T1*vs.*T2* and *T2* vs.*T3* respectively. This time only the second ANOVA (T2$\times$T3) revealed a main effect for *interface* ($F_2 = 6.583$), showing that ***FluidEdt*** ($M = 529$ sec) is stat. significantly faster than **Viz** ($M = 705$ sec $p = .003$) for the hard task.

In summary the experimental data suggests that visualizing the heap graph of a running program does benefit debugging efficiency (**H1**) and that our mechanisms for automatic abstraction and concretization alongside the possibility to directly interact with the heap graph are indeed useful. In particular, our tool outperforms the baseline interfaces in the hard task suggesting that the utility of our mechanism increases with task difficulty.

Qualitative Results

Here we briefly summarize insights that we gathered from think aloud commentary during the debugging sessions and from the exit-interviews. Overall users reacted positively to our interface. All participants uniformly found that the visualization is helpful in understanding the data structure saying e.g., *"It helps me to form an [mental] image of the data structure"* or simply *"It helped me to find the problem in the data structure, without even looking at the code"*. Furthermore, participants commented (without a direct experimenter question) that they think this would be helpful to learn/teach basic algorithms in introductory CS classes. A total of 16 participants also commented that the tool is particularly *"useful for complex data structures"*. One participant commented that he has to deal a lot with data structures when working on OS kernel code and often finds himself drawing depictions of data structure state on paper during this work, further validating our approach beyond introductory CS education.

In terms of automatic and user driven abstraction all participants but one preferred the interface with these capabilities over the "pure" visualization. The single outlier commented that he simply wants to see all the data and found it too work intensive to concretize abstract nodes by hand. 28 out of 30 participants ended up refining the initial abstraction using the pen & touch interface with the remaining two using the mouse and keyboard only. Participants found the possibility to interact "directly" with the data compelling and thought that it allows them to more quickly reconcile their mental model of the structure with the rendering on-screen. In particular, participants often simple changed the visual layout of the graph in order to better understand the program state. While participants found the automatic abstraction useful, almost all of them would manually concretize at least one of the abstract nodes fully at the beginning of each session. When asked why they had done this they said they simply wanted to verify that the initial data structure was populated correctly with the input data. This visual check is currently laborious and points to the need for a fast way to preview the content of an abstract node without having to concretize the whole structure one-by-one.

Finally, the participants would have liked to see a tighter integration between visualization and code views. For example, most users found that selecting an edge in the graph view should also highlight the variable in the code view. A further area for improvement that got commented on frequently was the limited code editing and navigation capabilities of our tool. In fact many participants preferred our tool to find the bug but would switch back to Eclipse to fix the bug. This suggests that there are opportunities in either integrating our approach into a regular IDE or to combine it with recent more visual approaches for code navigation (e.g., [3, 7, 14]).

Implications for information vizualisation

To the best of our knowledge, there is currently no graph layout algorithm that meets the many requirements that arise from visualizing the dynamics of an evolving data structure. Most layout algorithms have no means to enforce temporal consistency as the graph changes over time. In our case these changes can be dramatic, e.g., if a large part of the heap gets abstracted or concretized from one timestep to another. Occasionally this is not reconcilable with the automated layout algorithm and temporal consistency is broken with the algorithm rendering an entirely new graph view. This is clearly not ideal and users commented on this frequently. It is paramount to keep the parts of the structure that the user was (or is) inspecting in the same location and to preserve the relative spatial arrangement over time. This requirement necessitates entirely new graph layout algorithms that incorporate temporal consistency into their formulation. User modifications are another difficult topic. Currently we cannot guarantee that manually positioned nodes will stay in the same place when stepping through the program – an interesting item for future work.

RELATED WORK

Our work spans the two areas of HCI (developer support tools) and programming languages (e.g. program analysis). Here we briefly survey some of the most related work.

Development Tools

Both the software development process [8, 21] as well as development tools have been of long standing interest to HCI. In particular, debugging and bug isolation strategies have seen significant attention [15, 27]. In particular, Gilmore highlights the importance of understanding debugging as an essential part of program development [10].

There is now a lot of evidence in the literature that code development does not happen in isolation and programmers often encounter problems that they can only overcome with external resources [17]. Hence, recent work has focused on supporting developers in code understanding related activities where several challenges arise: i) developers need to find appropriate code examples (e.g., [13, 19]), and ii) then they need to reconcile program output and their understanding of its operation [16], and finally iii) adapt the examples to their own needs [29]. Tools have been developed that allow users to work backwards from program output in order to understand code behavior and to isolate bugs in the code [16].

Furthermore, many approaches attempt to more tightly integrate resources found on the web with programming related activities [13, 19, 28]. In particular, example driven development [4, 12] has received much attention recently. Others have tried to auto-generate useful code-snippets [9]. While in spirit these works are similar to ours, they tend to focus solely on the program code while we treat both code and data as first class citizens. This is especially critical in the context of data structure development, a fundamental area which has not received much research attention in the HCI community.

Heap Analysis and Visualization

Over the years, there has been substantial amount of work on static and dynamic program analysis with the goal of better program understanding, bug finding or verification. Representative works here are deep static analysis abstractions popularized by the TVLA approach [24] and runtime techniques for visualizing and/or abstracting the heap [1, 20].

In general, static verification is a very challenging problem often requiring significant manual annotations. And while our setting is quite different (i.e. we allow user manipulation of the abstract shape not possible in TVLA), we draw inspiration from the predicate based parameterized approach used in their work. However, existing works are typically not interactive, that is, the user cannot control the abstraction or interact with it in meaningful ways. Further, these approaches do not provide practical evidence that the particular visualization and/or hardcoded abstraction is actually useful.

We note that there are many variants on the above works found in the research literature, however from our perspective, all of these variants share the same limitations described above.

Program visualization for educational purpose

There exist a number of approaches to generate or compose fixed, mostly pre-computed animations of algorithms. These are aimed at teaching (e.g., [6, 11, 26]) and supporting code understanding purposes. Sorva et al. [25] provide an excellent overview which we refer the interested reader to.

Many of these tools have been evaluated quantitatively and qualitatively and results indicate that visualizing program behavior is beneficial for code understanding and learning. Furthermore, there seems to be evidence that interactivity and being able to use and edit own code is beneficial [25]. In our work we build on these findings.

However, our system differs from prior work in that we allow not only interact with the code but also enable complex interactions with the data (e.g. mechanisms for automatic abstraction of large data structures). This makes our approach scale to complex real-world settings.

DISCUSSION AND FUTURE WORK

Our approach bridges program analysis techniques with HCI and leverages online automatic abstraction and visualization of the data structure in a way which captures its *essential operation*, thus enabling powerful local reasoning. Local reasoning is key to understanding the core data structure algorithm operation as it strips away irrelevant details. In addition, we provide a fine grained mechanism for manually modifying the abstracted view using pen and touch gestures – this enables the developer to pause the program, carefully interact with its data, and then resume program execution, thus allowing them to try out various hypotheses.

Our experimental evaluation has shown this to be a very effective mechanism particularly for more complex structures and in combination with our user interface that gives developers interactive control over the abstraction.

Based on the quantitative and qualitative feedback we elicited we believe this is an exciting first step in the right direction. However, there are also many limitations and plentiful areas left for future research. Perhaps the most interesting and promising idea would be to extend our approach to generic and more complex programs. We believe this would require a combination of our user interface with an approach that is better suited for the debugging of control flow and program logic. Furthermore, we discovered that current graph layout algorithms are not well suited for our purposes as they do not allow for incremental and user edit preserving layouts. We believe this to be another interesting area for future research.

CONCLUSION

In this work we proposed a new approach for understanding, debugging and developing heap manipulating data structures. We implemented our approach in a tool called *FluidEdt* and evaluated it against modern debuggers. Our tool begins to address some of the most pressing challenges in developing data structures – we obtained a categorization of these after performing a thorough experimental study spanning online forums and interviews with students and staff involved with teaching data structures at our university.

Our work bridges the areas of program analysis and HCI by combining deep parametric abstraction techniques arising from the area of static analysis with interactive fine grained abstraction manipulation via pen and touch gestures. Based on our experimental user study, we believe this to be a fruitful direction towards reducing the difficulties that developers – beginners and experts alike – encounter when dealing with heap manipulating algorithms.

REFERENCES

1. Aftandilian, E. E. et al. Heapviz: interactive heap visualization for program understanding and debugging. In *Proc. SOFTVIS '10*, 2010, p.53–62.
2. Balakrishnan, G., and T. Reps. Recency-abstraction for heap-allocated storage. In *Proc. SAS'06*.
3. Bragdon, A. et al. Code bubbles: A working set-based interface for code understanding and maintenance. In *Proc. CHI '10*.
4. Brandt, J. et al. Example-centric programming: integrating web search into the development environment. In *Proc. CHI '10*.
5. Brandt, J. et al. Two studies of opportunistic programming: Interleaving web foraging, learning, and writing code. In *Proc. CHI '09*.
6. Brown, M. H., and M. A. Najork. Algorithm animation using 3d interactive graphics. In *Proc. UIST '93*.
7. DeLine, R., and K. Rowan. Code canvas: Zooming towards better development environments. In *Proc. ICSE '10*.
8. Détienne, F. *Software Design–Cognitive Aspect*. Springer, 2002.
9. Galenson, J. et al. Codehint: Dynamic and interactive synthesis of code snippets. In *Proc. ICSE '14*.
10. Gilmore, D. J. Models of debugging. *Acta Psychologica 78*, 13 (1991), 151 – 172.
11. Guo, P. J. Online python tutor: Embeddable web-based program visualization for cs education. In *Proc. SIGCSE '13*.
12. Hartmann, B., M. Dhillon, and M. K. Chan. Hypersource: Bridging the gap between source and code-related web sites. In *Proc. CHI '11*.
13. Hoffmann, R., J. Fogarty, and D. S. Weld. Assieme: finding and leveraging implicit references in a web search interface for programmers. In *Proc. UIST' 07*.
14. Karrer, T. et al. Stacksplorer: Call graph navigation helps increasing code maintenance efficiency. In *Proc. UIST '11*.
15. Katz, I. R., and J. R. Anderson. Debugging: An analysis of bug-location strategies. *SIGCHI Bull. 21*, 1 (Aug. 1989).
16. Ko, A. J., and B. A. Myers. Extracting and answering why and why not questions about java program output. *ACM Trans. Softw. Eng. Methodol. 20*, 2 (Sept. 2010), 4:1–4:36.
17. Ko, A. J., B. A. Myers, and H. H. Aung. Six learning barriers in end-user programming systems. In *Proc. VL/HCC '04*.
18. Lieber, T., J. R. Brandt, and R. C. Miller. Addressing misconceptions about code with always-on programming visualizations. In *Proc. CHI' 14*.
19. Mamykina, L. et al. Design Lessons from the Fastest Q&A site in the west. In *Proc. CHI '11*.
20. Marron, M. et al. Abstracting runtime heaps for program understanding. *Trans. Softw. Eng.*.
21. Mayer, R. E. The psychology of how novices learn computer programming. *ACM Computing Surveys (CSUR) 13*, 1 (1981), 121–141.
22. Oney, S., and J. Brandt. Codelets: Linking interactive documentation and example code in the editor. In *Proc. CHI '12*.
23. Rzeszotarski, J. M., and A. Kittur. Kinetica: Naturalistic multi-touch data visualization. In *Proc. CHI' 14*.
24. Sagiv, M., T. Reps, and R. Wilhelm. Parametric shape analysis via 3-valued logic. *ACM Trans. Program. Lang. Syst.*.
25. Sorva, J., V. Karavirta, and L. Malmi. A review of generic program visualization systems for introductory programming education. *Trans. Comput. Educ.*.
26. Stasko, J. Tango: a framework and system for algorithm animation. *Computer 23*, 9 (Sept 1990), 27–39.
27. Weiser, M. Programmers use slices when debugging. *Commun. ACM 25*, 7 (July 1982), 446–452.
28. Wightman, D. et al. Snipmatch: Using source code context to enhance snippet retrieval and parameterization. In *Proc. UIST '12*.
29. Yeh, R. B., A. Paepcke, and S. R. Klemmer. Iterative design and evaluation of an event architecture for pen-and-paper interfaces. In *Proc. UIST '08*.
30. Zeleznik, R. et al. Hands-on Math: A Page-based Multi-touch and Pen Desktop for Technical Work and Problem Solving. In *Proc. UIST '10*.

Polymorphic Blocks: Formalism-Inspired UI for Structured Connectors

Sorin Lerner **Stephen R. Foster** **William G. Griswold**
University of California, San Diego
{lerner, srfoster, wgg}@cs.ucsd.edu

ABSTRACT
We present a novel block-based UI called *Polymorphic Blocks*, in which a connector's shape visually represents the structure of the data being passed through the connector. We use Polymorphic Blocks to add visual type information to block-based programming environments like Blockly or Scratch. We also use Polymorphic Blocks to represent logical proofs. In this context, if we erase all symbols, our UI becomes a puzzle game, where solving the puzzle amounts to building a proof. We show through a user study that our Logical Puzzle Game is faster, more fun, and more engaging than an equivalent pen-and-paper interface.

Author Keywords
Proofs; Games; Block-based Programming Environments.

ACM Classification Keywords
H.5.2. Information Interfaces and Presentation (e.g. HCI).

INTRODUCTION
Blocks that snap into place are commonly used in UIs for novice visual programming environments such as Scratch [5], Blockly [2], App Inventor [1], and TinkerBlocks [6]. A key component of these block interfaces is the UI mechanism for connectors, and the most common such mechanism consists of shaped ports, making blocks akin to jigsaw puzzle pieces. For example, Blockly uses a groove reminiscent of jigsaw puzzles for ports where values can be transmitted, and a semi-circular groove for ports where statements can be connected. Scratch uses circular ports for integers, angled ports for booleans, and a small flat trapezoid for statements.

Although these shaped ports provide some form of visual feedback about the kind of information being passed through the port, typically environments only use a handful of shapes, and as a result, these shaped ports do not visually expose the full structure of the data being passed through them. For example, in most block-based visual programming environments, the shape for an integer, a boolean, a list of integers, and a list of booleans would look exactly the same (in particular, it will be the "value" shaped port).

CHI 2015, April 18–23, 2015, Seoul, Republic of Korea.

ACM 978-1-4503-3145-6/15/04 ...$15.00.
http://dx.doi.org/10.1145/2702123.2702302

In this paper, we present a new block-based UI called *Polymorphic Blocks* that is better suited for visualizing the structure of information passed through connectors. There are two key insights behind Polymorphic Blocks that lead to its flexibility and expressive power.

First, the shape of connectors in Polymorphic Blocks are produced through a compositional translation process that can map complex recursive structures into unique shapes. This allows Polymorphic Blocks to visually represent complex structures such as types of the form *List*[*int*] and *Pair*[*int, bool*], as well as complex logical formulas.

Second, we allow the shape of connectors in Polymorphic Blocks to include *Colored Polymorphic Ports*, which work as follows: when a shape is connected to a Polymorphic Port of a certain color, the port in question takes on the shape it is connected to, and furthermore, all Polymorphic Ports of the same color also change to that shape. As a simple example, suppose we want a Polymorphic Block that takes two parameters which must be of the same type, for example (int, int) or (bool, bool) but not (int, bool). The Polymorphic Block to encode this operation would have two input Polymorphic Ports of the same color, and when one is connected to a shape, say the shape of bool, the other will also change to that shape, indicating that henceforth only the shape of bool can be passed to the other parameter.

In the context of block-based visual programming interfaces, Polymorphic Blocks can visually represent complex types such as *List*[*int*], *List*[*bool*], *Pair*[*int, bool*], as well as parametric types such as *List*[T], *Pair*(T_1, T_2), and higher-order types, such as function types. In this setting, Polymorphic Blocks have a theoretical grounding, in that they correspond precisely to the notion of *parametric polymorphism* (alternatively called *generics*) from the programming languages community, a kind of type polymorphism found in languages like Java, C#, Standard ML, OCaml, F#, Haskell and Scala.

Even more interestingly, it turns out that Polymorphic Blocks are applicable beyond block-based visual interfaces. In particular, we will show how Polymorphic Blocks can be used as a novel visual interface for building logical proofs, where each block represents an inference rule, and connectors represent formulas. If the logical formulas are hidden, and only the visual connectors are left, the resulting interface turns into a visual Puzzle Game where solving the puzzle amounts to completing the logical proof. This application, which we find intriguing and exciting, has possible implications for the future crowdsourcing of interactive proofs in theorem provers like Coq.

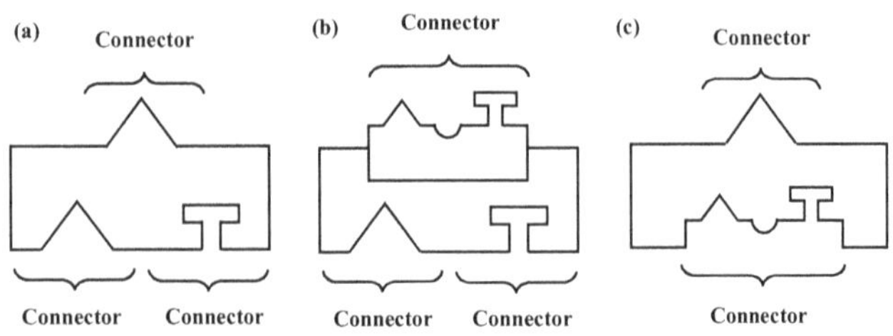

Figure 1. Examples of Polymorphic Blocks: (a) shows a block with some simple connectors; (b) shows a block with more complex connectors.

Finally, the design of Polymorphic Blocks was heavily guided by the formalism of type theory and logical proofs. We discuss this notion of *formalism-inspired UI design* further throughout the paper, showing both its benefits and pitfalls.

In summary, our contributions are as follows:

- We present the idea of Polymorphic Blocks, a novel UI mechanism for visualizing the structure of data passed through connectors.
- We implement Polymorphic Blocks in two settings: (1) a typed version of Blockly and (2) a visual interface for building logical proofs.
- By means of a user study, we evaluate Polymorphic Blocks as a visual interface for building logical proofs in a Puzzle Game. Our results show that participants are able to understand the mechanics of Polymorphic Blocks through self-guided experimentation, and are able to quickly build logical proofs. Furthermore, our results also show that, while Polymorphic Blocks do not teach all aspects of logical proofs in a class-room setting, they lead to faster completion times, and are more fun and engaging than a traditional pen-and-paper interface.
- Finally, we discuss our results and techniques within the context of several possible applications and in relation to existing HCI theories, pointing out lessons learned from our formalism-inspired design.

OVERVIEW

We start with an overview of how Polymorphic Blocks work through a set of increasingly more complex examples.

Basics of Blocks and Connectors. Figure 1(a) shows a very simple example of a Polymorphic Block. Each polymorphic block has a set of *connectors*, with each connector representing one of the block's inputs or outputs. For example, the block in Figure 1(a) has three such connectors, two on the bottom, and one at the top. Each connector has a shape, which intuitively represents the structure of the data being passed through that connector. For example, the block in Figure 1(a) could be used to represent a computation that takes two inputs from below, and produces one output above. In this case, the shape of the connectors would represent the types of the values being passed through the connectors, for example the triangle could be *int* and the "T" could be *bool*. The block in Figure 1(a) would then represent a computation that takes an *int* and a *bool*, and produces an *int*. To start, let us assume that two blocks can be connected through a connector only if the shape of the connector matches exactly. For example, a block producing a triangle on top could be connected to the bottom-left connector of the block in Figure 1(a). In this way, shaped-connectors provide a jigsaw-puzzle metaphor which enforces that correctly typed values are passed along each connector.

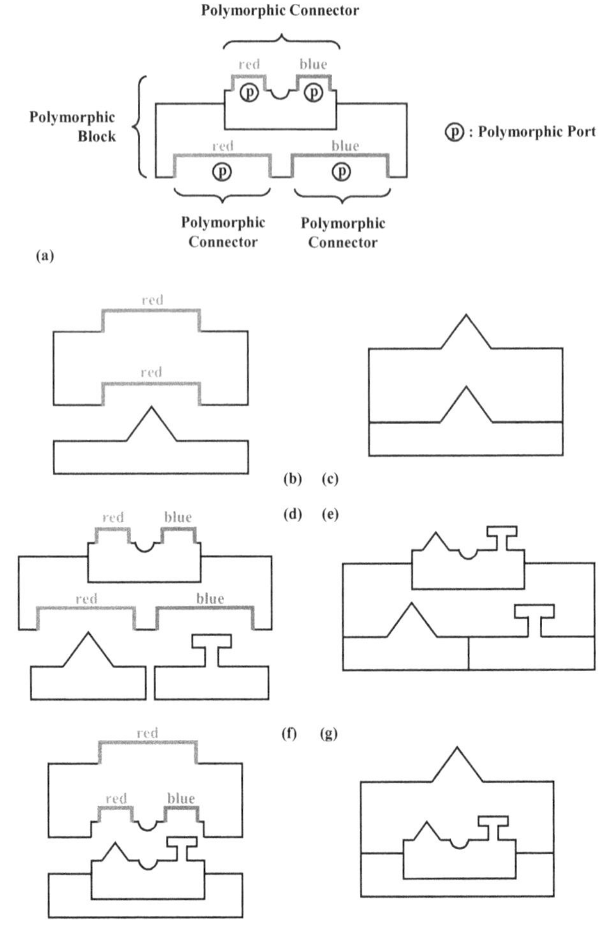

Figure 2. Examples of Polymorphic Ports: (a) shows an example containing Polymorphic Ports with each constituent part labeled; (b) shows two blocks before they are connected and (c) shows what happens after these blocks are connected; similarly for (d)-(e) and (f)-(g).

More Complex Shapes for Connectors. One of the key insights in Polymorphic Blocks is that the shape of connectors are produced through a compositional translation process which can map complex recursive structures into unique shapes. Figure 1(b) shows a block with a connector on top that is produced by this translation process. The shape of the top connector is produced by the combination of two simpler shapes (the triangle and the "T") together with a semi-circle. If we continue with the domain where blocks are computations and shapes are types, the semi-circle could represent the notion of a "pair". In this case, the block in Figure 1(b) represents a computation which takes an *int*, represented as a triangle, and a *bool*, represented as a "T", and produces a value of type *Pair[int, bool]*, i.e. a pair of an *int* and a *bool* (an example: the computation which takes an *int* and a *bool* and creates a pair out of them). Figure 1(c) shows another example, which could represent a computation that takes a

Basic exprs with types	In Polymorphic Blockly
int 0	
bool true	
T cond$(bool, T, T)$	
$List[T]$ list(T, T, T)	
$Pair[T_1, T_2]$ pair(T_1, T_2)	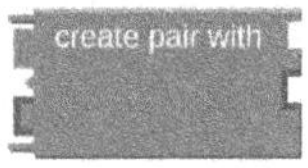
T_1 first$(Pair[T_1, T_2])$	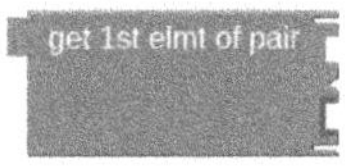
T_2 second$(Pair[T_1, T_2])$	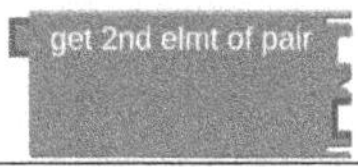

Figure 3. Basic expressions and their corresponding Polymorphic Blocks

Expression	In Polymorphic Blockly
cond$(\ldots, 0, \ldots)$	
list$(0, \ldots)$	
list(true, ...)	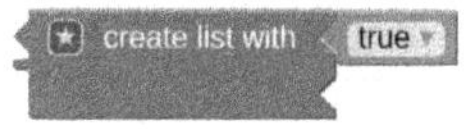
pair$(0, \ldots)$	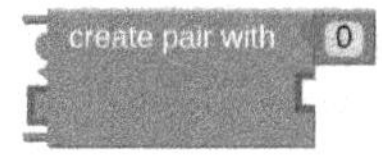
pair$(0, true)$	
first(pair(0, true))	
list(cond(...), ...)	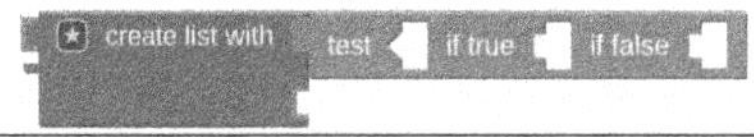

Figure 4. Complex expressions and corresponding Polymorphic Blocks

Pair[int, bool] and produces an *int* (e.g.: the computation which returns the first element of an *int, bool* pair).

Note that the semi-circle here acts as what we call a *shape constructor*: it takes two shapes on either side and glues two together into a larger shape. We support arbitrarily many shape constructors, and later in the paper we will see another example, namely a "V" shaped dent. We can also easily support shape constructors with arities other than 2.

It's important to note that when a shape constructor like the semi-circle combines two shapes into a larger one, the two constituent shapes themselves can be complex shapes built out of shape constructors. As a result, the shapes of connectors are produced from a recursive visual language capable of expressing arbitrarily complex shapes. Through this lens, the shapes of connectors represent an underlying structure corresponding to a language of recursive mathematical terms. These mathematical terms are made up of: function symbols (which correspond to shape constructors) and constants (which correspond to basic shapes). In our instantiations of Polymorphic Blocks, this language of terms will be: (1) the language of type expressions for typed Blockly, and (2) the language of formulas for our visual proof environment.

Polymorphic Ports. Another key insight of Polymorphic Blocks is that the shape of connectors are allowed to include *Colored Polymorphic Ports*. Figure 2(a) shows an example containing Polymorphic Ports, with each constituent part labeled, and where the color of the port is also labeled (for readability on black-and-white printouts). Polymorphic Ports work as follows: when a shape is connected to a Polymorphic Port of a certain color, the port in question takes on the shape it is connected to, and furthermore, all Polymorphic Ports of the same color also change to that shape. For example, Figure 2(b) shows two blocks before they are connected, and Figure 2(c) shows what happens after these blocks are connected – similarly for (d)-(e) and (f)-(g).

INSTANTIATION TO THE BLOCKLY DOMAIN

Now that we have presented an overview of the ideas behind Polymorphic Blocks, we show how these ideas can be used in practice. We start by showing how Polymorphic Blocks can be used to enhance block-based programming environments with a visualization of program types.

We use the Blockly visual programming editor [2] as the vehicle for our demonstration, but the ideas can be applied to any block-based editor. Blockly is a block-based editor similar in many ways to Scratch, where blocks representing computations can be snapped together to create programs. Below are sample blocks from the traditional Blockly UI:

The shape of all connectors is a groove reminiscent of jigsaw puzzles. Note that values flow right-to-left.

We extend Blockly with Polymorphic Blocks to produce *Polymorphic Blockly*, where the shape of connectors represent the types of values flowing through those connectors. Figure 3 shows several basic expressions with their types, along with the Polymorphic Block for the expression – "basic expression" here means that the representation in Polymorphic Blockly is a single block. We use the Java and C style of writing types for functions, where the return type is written first, followed by the name of the function, followed by the types of parameters. We use the naming convention T (with possible subscripts) for type variables, akin to the generics found in Java. Because values in Blockly flow right-to-left, the connectors of Polymorphic Blocks are on vertical edges, as opposed to horizontal edges. Note that all the Polymorphic Blocks in Figure 3 use red and blue for port colors, and this is because Figure 3 shows how each block appears when it is created in isolation (i.e.: without other blocks on the screen). More generally, our implementation keeps tracks of what port colors are in use, and generates unique colors for ports when a new Polymorphic Block is created, with red and blue just being the first two colors. As a result, if one were to create multiple blocks on the same screen, we would in fact see many more port colors than in Figure 3. The importance of generating port colors in this way will be explained shortly.

Integer values are represented using a semi-circle, boolean values using a triangle. Note that semi-circle here is not used as a shape-constructor, as is done elsewhere in the paper – here semi-circle is just a basic shape. The `cond` function is a conditional similar to the "?" operator in C, and its Polymorphic Block encodes the fact that the types of the two parts of the conditional should be the same. The $List[T]$ type is represented by adding a single small side-ways "l" next to the shape of the T type. The $Pair[T_1, T_2]$ is represented by putting a small triangular wedge between the shapes of T_1 and T_2, and then surrounding the entire shape using two slim barriers. Note that the "create pair" block has a single output connector which is visually large because it represents a pair, and similarly, the "first" and "second" blocks have a single large input connector each.

Figure 4 shows some more complex examples involving multiple Polymorphic Blocks. The occurrence of "..." in an expression indicates that the given part of the expression has not been filled in yet (or in the Blockly perspective, has not yet been connected to another block). In the first two examples, once an integer is connected to the red Polymorphic Port, all red ports take on the semi-circular shape representing integers. The same happens when a triangular boolean value is connected to the red port, as shown in the third example. The next few examples in Figure 4 show pairs.

The last example shows what happens when two colored Polymorphic Ports are connected. In this example, we created a `cond` block, which Polymorphic Blockly built with a red port, and then a `list` block, which Polymorphic Blockly built with blue port (since the red color was already in use in the `cond` block). When the red output of `cond` is connected to the blue input of `list`, the red shape connected to the blue input of `list` is propagated to all blue ports of `list`, producing the final result shown in Figure 4. Note how the red Polymorphic Port is now *global*, in that it spans multiple blocks. This underscores the importance of generating unused colors when creating blocks: the interpretation of colors is not block-local, and we must therefore avoid coloring conflicts.

Parametric Polymorphism. From a programming language perspective, Polymorphic Blockly implements a typing discipline called *parametric polymorphism* (alternatively called *generics*). Parametric polymorphism manifests itself in the type system as unconstrained type variables, for example in the declaration $List[T]$ `reverse`$(List[T])$, where T is an unconstrained type variable that can be instantiated to any type. Generics in Java and C# were initially introduced to enable parametric polymorphism, although generics have since increased in expressiveness to encode more complex kinds of polymorphism. Parametric polymorphism is also at the core of programming languages like Standard ML, OCaml, F#, Haskell and Scala. Polymorphic Blocks encode exactly the notion of parametric polymorphism, with Colored Polymorphic Ports acting as unconstrained type variables. Furthermore, the *Hindley-Milner* type inference algorithm [18], which is at the core of type systems for Standard ML and OCaml, falls out "for free" from the way that Polymorphic Ports get matched against shapes when blocks are connected.

INSTANTIATION TO THE PROOF DOMAIN

It turns out that Polymorphic Blocks are applicable well beyond block-based programming environments. In this section, we show how Polymorphic Blocks can be used to build a novel visual environment for manipulating logical proofs. The shape of connectors will represent formulas, and Polymorphic Blocks will represent inference rules, the proof steps that manipulate formulas. This user interface to logical proofs is entirely visual, completing eschewing symbols. As a result, it lends itself very well to becoming a *Puzzle Game*, which we call the Proof Puzzle Game

We focus on a particular kind of proof system called *natural deduction*, which was introduced by Gentzen in 1934 to closely mimic the "natural way" in which humans think. For simplicity, we consider here the subset of natural deduction involving implication and conjunction. Nonetheless, since what we show here is how to encode the syntactic manipulations of inference rules using Polymorphic Blocks, the ides can easily be extended to more complex forms of natural deduction, and more broadly to other inference systems.

Short Tutorial on Natural Deduction

We start with a quick overview of natural deduction. In the subset we are considering, a formula ϕ is a boolean predicate defined according to the following grammar:

$$\begin{array}{lll} \phi & ::= v & \text{boolean variables, e.g.: } x, y, z \\ & ::= \phi \Rightarrow \phi & \text{implication} \\ & ::= \phi \wedge \phi & \text{conjuction} \end{array}$$

Note that the variables above are *boolean* variables, meaning that their interpretation is either *true* or *false*.

Examples: (1) x (2) $x \wedge y$ (3) $x \Rightarrow y$ (4) $x \Rightarrow (y \wedge z)$

A *judgment* J has the form $\Gamma \vdash \phi$, where Γ is a comma-separated list of formulas. It essentially states: "using logical reasoning, it is provable that if all assumptions in Γ are true, then ϕ is also true".

Examples: (1) $x, y \vdash x \wedge y$ (2) $x \wedge y \vdash y \wedge x$

To establish that a judgment holds, proof systems like natural deduction make use of *inference rules*. Inference rules correspond to logical steps in a proof, allowing certain judgments to be concluded from other judgments. An inference rule has the form:

$$\frac{J_1 \quad \cdots \quad J_n}{J}\ \textit{Name}$$

The interpretation is that if judgments J_1 through J_n (called premises) hold then judgment J holds. The simplest example of a judgment is the *Assume* rule, which has no premises:

$$\frac{}{\ldots,\ A,\ \ldots \vdash A}\ \textit{Assume}$$

The A above is a so called *meta-variable*, which can stand in for any formula (A is a *meta-variable* to distinguish it from boolean *variables* like x, y, z). The "..." is just an informal way of saying that there can be other formulas in the list. For example, the *Assume* rule can be used to establish the judgment $x, y, z \vdash y$, where A is instantiated to y.

Inference Rule	In Proof Game
$\dfrac{A \vdash B}{\vdash A \Rightarrow B}\ \textit{ImpI}$	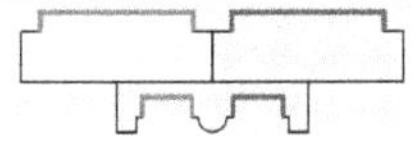
$\dfrac{\vdash A \quad \vdash B}{\vdash A \wedge B}\ \textit{AndI}$	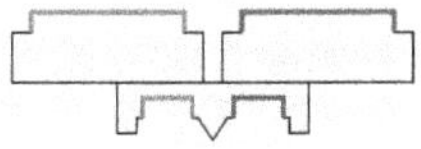
$\dfrac{\vdash A \wedge B}{\vdash A}\ \textit{AndE}_1$	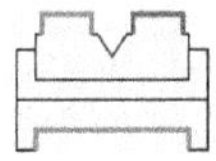
$\dfrac{\vdash A \wedge B}{\vdash B}\ \textit{AndE}_2$	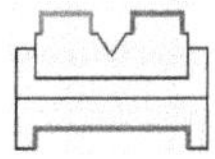
$\dfrac{\vdash A \quad \vdash A \Rightarrow B}{\vdash B}\ \textit{ImpE}$	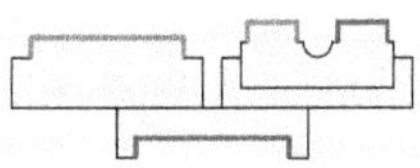

Figure 5. Inference rules with corresponding Polymorphic Blocks

The left column of Figure 5 shows some additional natural deduction inference rules – the right column shows the corresponding Polymorphic Block, and can be ignored for now. Because we will apply inference rules bottom-up, it's easiest to read rules starting at the bottom. For example, the first rule says: "to prove $A \Rightarrow B$, assume A and prove B". This rule is traditionally called *ImpI*, or "Implication Introduction", because when reading the rule top to bottom, we are "introducing" an implication. The second rule says: "to prove $A \wedge B$, we need to prove A and we need to prove B". The "E" in the names of the other rules stands for "elimination".

The inference rules shown here are not the most general versions – instead we show the simplest form of each rule, which corresponds directly to the Polymorphic Blocks shown in the right column of Figure 5. The most general version of each rule has an additional Γ "context" at the left of the $\vdash$, to allow the rule to be applicable in settings where the set of assumptions is non-empty.

A formal proof is a tree of connected inference rules, which is rooted at the bottom with the judgment to prove, and grows upward as inference rules are connected. The proof is complete when all branches are topped with an *Assume* rule. For example, here are two complete proofs in natural deduction:

$$\dfrac{\dfrac{}{x \vdash x}\ \textit{Assume}}{\vdash x \Rightarrow x}\ \textit{ImpI} \qquad \dfrac{\dfrac{\dfrac{}{y \vdash y}\ \textit{Assume} \quad \dfrac{}{y \vdash y}\ \textit{Assume}}{y \vdash y \wedge y}\ \textit{AndI}}{\vdash y \Rightarrow (y \wedge y)}\ \textit{ImpI}$$

Natural Deduction in Polymorphic Blocks

We now describe how to encode natural deduction using Polymorphic Blocks. Each inference rule is represented as a block; each formula is represented as a connector, where the shape of the connector encodes the formula; each meta-variable is represented as a Polymorphic Port.

Let's first start with a single judgment. Figure 6 shows several examples of judgments that we may want to prove, and the corresponding encoding using Polymorphic Blocks. From the first row of Figure 6, we can see how the different variables are encoded: x as a triangle, y as a "T" and z as a hook-like shape. The list of formulas on the left of the $\vdash$ is shown in yellow, whereas the formula on the right of the $\vdash$ is shown in pink. Although this difference in color is not strictly necessary, it helps to visualize how the blocks line-up. The remaining rows show how $\Rightarrow$ and $\wedge$ are encoded. In particular, $\phi_1 \Rightarrow \phi_2$ is represented by adding a semi-circle between the shapes of ϕ_1 and ϕ_2, and $\phi_1 \wedge \phi_2$ is represented by adding a "V" between the shapes of ϕ_1 and ϕ_2.

Judgment	In Proof Game
$x, y, z \vdash x$	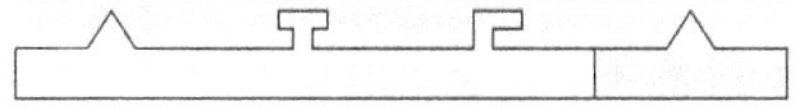
$\vdash y \Rightarrow y$	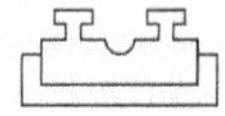
$\vdash x \Rightarrow (y \Rightarrow x)$	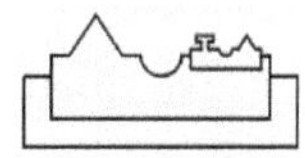
$x \wedge y \vdash y \wedge x$	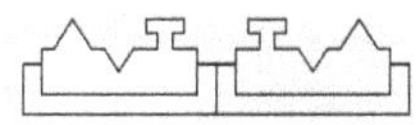

Figure 6. Judgments with corresponding Polymorphic Blocks

Finally, we can return to Figure 5, and look at the blocks in right column. In these blocks, formulas are encoded as connectors, and meta-variables are encoded as Polymorphic Ports of different colors. The structure of each block mimics faithfully the structure of the corresponding inference rule. As was mentioned previously, Figure 5 shows the most basic version of the inference rules, without any Γ "context" to the left of the $\vdash$. We encode additional context to the left of the $\vdash$ by extending the block with additional connectors, each one being a Polymorphic Port. For example, here is a version of the *ImpI* rule which has been extended *once*:

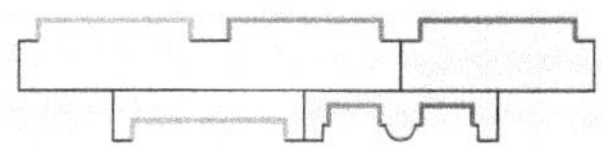

This rule now applies when there is a single formula to the left of the $\vdash$ on the bottom. We provide the player of the game with explicit buttons to add and remove these kind of additional "context" connectors.

Recall the complete proofs we showed previously in natural deduction for $\vdash x \Rightarrow x$ and $\vdash y \Rightarrow (y \wedge y)$. Using Polymorphic Blocks, these two proofs would look as follows:

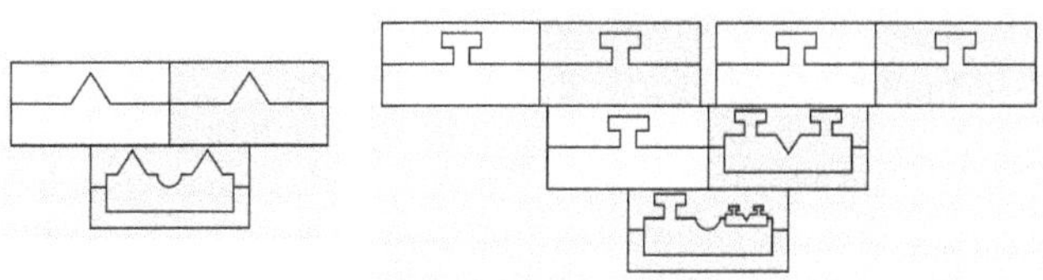

Additional UI for Game

The Proof Puzzle Game contains a few additional UI mechanism to make Polymorphic Blocks easier to work with, and the game more playable, which we describe here.

Assume rule. Although the *Assume* rule can be encoded purely using Polymorphic Blocks, this encoding requires the user to create a block with the right number of connectors and in the right order, using a variety of block manipulation primitives for adding/removing "context" connectors. Preliminary testing showed that while players were able to create the right *Assume* blocks, it was more tedious than the intuition behind the *Assume* rule. Intuitively, the *Assume* rule is applied by finding the formula on the right of the $\vdash$ somewhere in the list on the left of the $\vdash$. We designed a UI for *Assume* that mimics this intuition: users simply double click on the two connectors that the *Assume* rule is meant to discharge, and the system automatically creates the *Assume* block in one step.

Port Animation. Having users understand the semantics of Polymorphic Ports is crucial: when a port of a given color is connected to a shape, all ports of that color take on that shape. We found through preliminary trials that players had trouble keeping track of the changes if they happened all at once. Inspired by the animated transitions of Heer and Robertson [14], we created an animation where the new shape of a colored port "flies" from the place where the connection was made to all the other occurrences of that colored port. For example, below on the left we show two blocks before they are connected, and on the right we show the animation that occurs when the blocks are connected as a "trail":

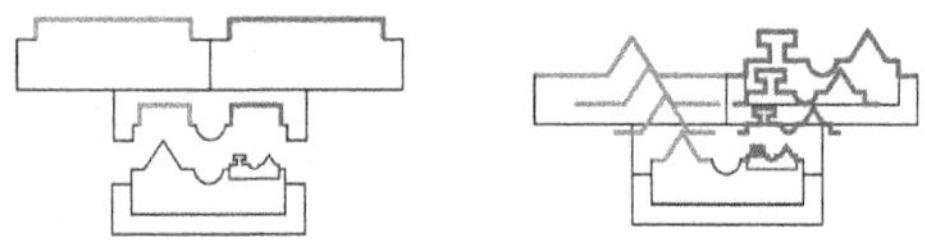

This animation makes it much easier to understand the semantics of Polymorphic Ports through visual observation.

Curry Howard Isomorphism

Although our two applications of Polymorphic Blocks seem disparate, they are in fact connected through a concept called the *Curry-Howard Isomorphism* [18]. The Curry-Howard isomorphism establishes a correspondence between types and programs on the one hand and formulas and proofs on the other. For example, the type $Pair[T_1, T_2]$ corresponds to the conjunction $T_1 \wedge T_2$, and the pair function in Figure 3 corresponds to the *AndI* rule from Figure 5. In our setting, the Curry-Howard isomorphism is reified as follows: types and blocks in Polymorphic Blockly have corresponding formulas and blocks in the Proof Game, and vice-versa. For example, the Polymorphic Block for the pair function in Figure 3 is isomorphic to the Polymorphic Block for *AndI* in Figure 5 (where the left-side of a block in Figure 3 is the bottom-side in Figure 5). Similarly, the block for first is isomorphic to the block for $AndE_1$, and the block for second is isomorphic to the block for $AndE_2$. This correspondence through the Curry-Howard isomorphism provides a better understanding of how our two seemingly disparate applications of Polymorphic Blocks are in fact related.

EVALUATION

Our goal in evaluating Polymorphic Blocks is two fold. First, we want to understand how easy Polymorphic Blocks are to use. Second, we want to understand how Polymorphic Blocks compare to a more traditional encoding. To evaluate these research questions, we must pick a domain in which to study Polymorphic Blocks. We pick the Proof Domain, embodied in the Proof Puzzle Game, for the following reasons.

Focus. The Proof Puzzle Game allows us to more narrowly focus on Polymorphic Connectors: since formulas are erased in the game, the only mechanics still in play are those of Polymorphic Connectors. For example, there is no notion of code or code understanding that interferes with our study of how subjects understand and interact with Polymorphic Connectors. Furthermore, Polymorphic Connectors in the Puzzle Game are *essential* – there is no way to remove them, since they have become the primary mode of interaction.

Complexity. The Proof Puzzle Game is a more complex domain as far as the Polymorphic Connectors are concerned, so it will push the limits of the UI further.

Novelty. The Proof Puzzle Game is a more novel domain. As the section on Related Work will explain in further details, while there has been previous work attempting to encode type polymorphism in block-based UIs (although none has achieved the expressiveness that we achieve), there has far less work on designing and evaluating our kind of encoding of logical formulas and logical proofs.

Now that we have focused on a domain, our evaluation goals can be reified as two hypotheses:

1. **Hypothesis 1: Ease of understanding.** The mechanics of Polymorphic Blocks in our Puzzle Game can quickly be understood through self-guided experimentation.
2. **Hypothesis 2: Comparison to traditional encoding.** Our encoding of natural deduction as a Puzzle Game using Polymorphic Blocks leads to (a) smaller completion times and (b) better engagement than a traditional encoding of natural deduction using symbolic inference rules.

Experimental Methodology

More specifically, we gathered 30 high-school students who agreed to be part of our study, and randomly split them into two groups of 15 each. We invited the first group to a session where participants solved a set of proof exercises encoded in the Puzzle Game using Polymorphic Blocks. We call this the Game group. We invited the second group to a session where participants solved the *exact same set* of proof exercises using symbols and inference rules on paper. We call this the Symbols group. Groups were not told a priori what was going to be covered in the session. Participants of each group also completed a common survey at the end of their session. Because of last minute cancellations from study participants, 14 participants attended the session for the Symbols group, and 10 participants attended the session for Game group.

We use the Game group to evaluate Hypothesis 1, and a comparison of the Game vs Symbols group for Hypothesis 2.

Teaching Style. Study participants had no previous knowledge of natural deduction proofs or the Puzzle Game. As a result, we made use of *tutorials exercises* to teach participants how to build proofs, both in the Game group and the Symbols group. A tutorial exercise is an exercise in which participants are guided to the solution step by step. Such exercises are used to teach new concepts, for example a new puzzle piece or inference rule. In the Game group, tutorial exercises are implemented using an in-game tutorial that guides participants through the solution. In the Symbols group, tutorial exercises are implemented using a lecture-style approach where an instructor shows the solution step by step on a tablet computer connected to a projector. We intersperse tutorial exercises and non-tutorial exercises to create a pedagogical progression of proof exercises.

Furthermore, the Symbols group also received a 30 minute lecture at the beginning of the session to introduce the concepts of formulas, inference rules, and proofs. This lecture presentation, along with the lecture-style tutorials for the Symbols group, were designed with the level of polish comparable to a well prepared lecture for an undergraduate class.

Interface Differences. Participants in the two groups used very different interfaces, offering different tradeoffs. Game participants, through the computer interface, get more *immediate* feedback, whereas the Symbols participants get more *customized* feedback (since it's help from a human instructor). To help reduce these differences, we provided the Symbols group with as much immediate feedback as we could, both through peer instruction (participants worked in pairs) and through checking the correctness of each exercise on the spot (which is not the way traditional exercises are done, and in some sense brings a gamification feel of "level completion" to the pen-and-paper interface). As a result, the Symbols group ended up receiving a learning experience using the best pedagogical practices, including interactive example-based material, peer learning, and quick feedback.

Session Structure and Recorded Data. Each session, which ran 3 hours, started with a main part consisting of required exercises, followed by an open-ended part, in which participants were given a set of "optional" exercises (to test engagement). We recorded completion times, number of exercises solved, amount of help required, and an exit-survey at the end with questions about their experience.

Hypothesis 1: Ease of Understanding

Based on both informal observations, and various measurements that we describe in more detail below, we found that Game participants were able to easily understand the dynamics of the Game through the help of tutorials and experimentation. In fact, all participants finished all puzzles, including the ones in the open-ended session.

The in-game tutorial appropriately guided users through the solution of puzzles involving new pieces. The average time spent on a tutorial level was 22 seconds, far less than the 48 seconds spent on average on non-tutorial puzzles.

Connecting Puzzle pieces. To evaluate the extent to which study participants understood the mechanics of connecting puzzle pieces, we collected the total number of times users tried to connect pieces and out of this total, the number of times they tried to connect pieces that did not match. We only consider the counts for non-tutorial levels, since tutorial levels explicitly ask players to connect pieces that don't match for pedagogical purposes. We recorded a total of 541 connection attempts, out of which 4 failed, for a success rate of 99%. Each of the 4 failed attempts occurred in a puzzle that immediately followed a tutorial level, hinting at the fact that the introduction of new pieces causes cognitive load which in turn leads to failed connection attempts. At the same time, we can also see that participants learn quickly from the failed connection attempts, since beyond the one puzzle immediately following a tutorial, they stop making connection mistakes. This leads us to conclude that participants can quickly understand the connection semantics of Polymorphic Blocks from tutorial levels and from their own mistakes.

UI for Assume. Recall that double clicking on matching connectors is a technique that we use for applying the puzzle equivalent of the *Assume* rule. To evaluate the effectiveness of the double-clicking interface, we collected the total number of double-clicking attempts, and of these, the number of failed attempts (a failed attempt occurs because the two connectors did not match). There were a total of 260 double-clicking attempts in non-tutorial levels, of which 53 failed, leading to 80% success rate. Here again, many of the failed attempts occurred right after a tutorial, and the main source of errors stems from confusion as to whether a sub-part of the connector can match. Still, despite these confusions, participants were able to play the game effectively, in essence because the confusion was limited in scope (to puzzles right after tutorial levels and to a handful of additional ones).

Help provided. Participants needed relatively little help to solve the puzzles, and the help was at a higher level than understanding the mechanics of Polymorphic Blocks. Instead it had to do with strategic decisions about what piece to use (keep in mind that the search space is unbounded). We provided two kinds of feedback when participants asked for help. First, if the proof became so big that it was obviously wrong, we told participants to restart the puzzle from scratch. We did this 5 times. Second, if only a small portion of the proof was wrong, we either narrowed down the pieces that participants should look at, or told them to undo the last step, and think carefully about the next step. We did this a total of 7 times. One key observation is that these two kinds of feedback are *extremely uniform*, and can easily be automated.

Hypothesis 2: Comparison of Symbols vs Game Group

Solve time. When pairs in the Symbols group did exercises on paper, they were placed in front of a laptop computer, which not only displayed the exercises to perform but also measured the amount of time taken on each exercise. To make sure exercises were solved correctly, each pair would raise their hand when they were done with an exercise, and we would check their solution. If the solution was correct, we would advance them to the next exercise using a secret key combination on the keyboard; if the solution was not correct, we would give them feedback (the nature of the feedback will be described shortly). Figure 7 shows the average completion time in seconds for each of 29 non-tutorial puzzles, for the Game group and the Symbols group. The Game group has significantly faster completion times overall.

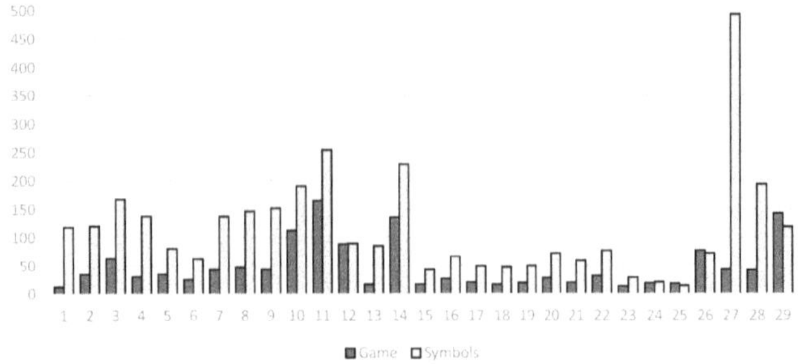

Figure 7. Exercise completion times in seconds for the Game and Symbols group; x-axis: the sequential # of the exercise; y-axis: average time in seconds. The Game group was faster than the Symbols group.

Help provided. We helped participants when they thought they finished an exercise, in which case we helped them understand what they did wrong. We also helped participants when they raised their hand, and stated that they were stuck. The kind of feedback we provided varied, but mostly included: clarifications about which inference rules to apply; clarifications about how to apply a given inference rule; clarification about how substitution works.

Recall that we helped Game participants a total of 12 times (for 5 pairs). In the Logic group, we helped participants a total of 16 times (for 7 pairs). Although the number of times we provided help per pair is similar, the help for the Game group was much easier to administer and would be far easier to automate. This is because the Game group received stylized uniform help, whereas the Symbols group received more customized help. Furthermore, Symbols participants were given a 30 minute lecture at the beginning, including what amounts to instructions on "strategies" for doing proofs. As there is no equivalent in the Game group, this lecture can be considered as additional help that the Symbols group received.

Engagement. To measure engagement, we want to understand the extent to which participants are willing to continue doing exercises if left to their own devices. To this end, following the regular session we presented participants with a new set of 15 exercises, and told them to work for at least 5 minutes, after which they could choose to continue working, or do something else. Figure 8 plots the percentage of pairs who completed each of the 15 exercises in this open-ended session, for the Game group and for the Symbols group. In the Symbols group, there is steady drop-off in the number of solved exercises. In addition to this quantitative data, we also noticed qualitatively that many groups started to browse the web, look at their phones, and play games online. On the other hand, in the Game group, all pairs went past the five minutes, and all groups solved all the exercises. In fact, we noticed that one pair started re-playing some puzzles *after* the were done with the study, without any prompting from us.

Both the quantitative and qualitative data suggest that the Puzzle Game is indeed more engaging. To better understand why this is the case, we can turn to the survey results. In particular, one of the questions on the survey asked participants to rate how fun the experience was on a 5-point Likert scale. The average Symbols response was 3.6, whereas the Game group was 4.3. This difference in the "fun-ness" rating

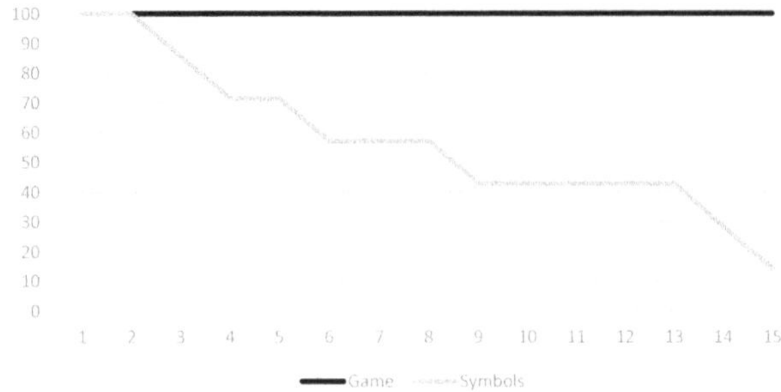

Figure 8. Percentage of pairs who completed each one of the 15 exercises in the open-ended session, for the Game and Symbols group; x-axis: sequential # of the exercise; y-axis: percentage of pairs who completed the exercise. The Game group was more engaged than the Symbols group.

is likely the root explanation for the better engagement. Furthermore, the survey results can also help us understand what led the Game group to have fun. In particular, the survey included a question "What does this experience remind you of?" In response to this question, Game participants consistently used gaming metaphors like "jigsaw puzzle", "Tetris", "oneline puzzle game", whereas Symbols participants consistently used school metaphors like "Math", "Class", "Proofs", and "lecture". This shows that our gamification strategy was successful, in that the Proof Puzzle Game puts participants in a gaming frame of mind. In turn, this is likely an important contributor to the Game participants having more fun.

In summary, our results point to the following conclusion: the Game group had a more Game-like experience, which in turn was more fun, and as a result led to more engagement.

DISCUSSION OF APPLICATIONS

We now discuss our techniques and results in the context of several possible applications.

Learning Logic. Our visualization and gamification of proofs has potential applications for math education. However, it is important to understand some subtle nuances in our results. Although the Puzzle Game is more fun and engaging, it does *not* teach all aspects of symbolic proofs. For one, it does not teach the symbols; but more importantly, it does not teach the full extent of *unification* and *substitution application* because the Game does these automatically (*unification* matches two expressions to determine which meta-variables map to which formulas; *substitution application* replaces a meta-variable with a given formula). Instead, the Puzzle Game focuses on teaching high-level strategies, for example how to pick the right puzzle piece (proof rule), a non-trivial aspect of proof building given the infinite search space.

As a result, we would not expect learning in the Puzzle Game to transfer to the symbolic domain without some additional teaching. The same also holds in the other direction: we don't know if learning in the symbolic domain with pen-and-paper would help learn the Puzzle Game. These questions of knowledge transfer, although interesting and worth investigating, are not the focus of this paper. Instead, our goal in the study was to use a common set of metrics to compare and understand two different encodings, a novel encoding, and a traditional one. In this respect, our experiments support the following characterization of the trade-offs: while Polymorphic Blocks do not teach all aspects of logical proofs, they lead to faster completion times, and are more fun and engaging than a traditional pen-and-paper interface.

Our results then point to a hybrid approach for further investigation: the Puzzle game can provide a fun and engaging first look, whereas a pen-and-paper example-driven lecture can complete the knowledge about *unification* and *substitution application*. Future work can further explore the viability of this hybrid approach through educational studies.

Types in Visual Programming Environments. Our visualization of types in Blockly can bring the traditional benefits of static types to block-based languages: 1) it would steer programmers away from mal-formed programs 2) it would help programmers quickly see which operations can (or cannot) be connected together. More specifically, once students are faced with many types, they really need to understand the input/output types for each block. Our techniques would provide a constant visual reminder of these types, as opposed to a textual description only visible on the side or in a pop-up.

Although our participants were only exposed to the proof domain, our study also focused narrowly on the mechanics of Polymorphic Blocks, since that's the only mechanics visible to the player (who is not exposed to formulas or proofs). As such, we have reason to believe that our results would generalize to the typing domain, in that the mechanics of Polymorphic Blocks can also be understood in that domain. Future work can investigate this further with additional user studies.

Crowdsourcing Proofs. Our gamification of proofs could lay the foundation for crowdsourcing proofs via gamification, a direction inspired by the Verification Games project [10] on crowdsourcing software verification. Crowdsourcing formal proofs is particularly interesting in light of *Foundational Verification*, a technique that has shown increasing promise in the past decade. In this technique, the programmer writes programs in a proof assistant like Coq, and then interactively proves these programs correct, in full formal detail. Experimental studies have shown that software built this way is far more reliable than software written in a traditional way. The main challenge is that building the proofs is still a painstakingly manual and difficult-to-automate process. The hope is that our work on gamification of proofs can pave the way for crowdsourcing of Foundational Verification proofs.

DESIGN PRINCIPLES AND RECOMMENDATIONS

The Polymorphic Blocks Puzzle Game instantiates five visual design principles: (a) colors and shapes, which are common in the design of virtual manipulatives for math; (b) the Animated Transitions of Heer and Robertson [14]; (c) Direct Manipulation Interfaces [15], most notably giving the impression of manipulating actual puzzle pieces; (d) exploiting cultural conventions, in that we leverage the popular visual cues of jigsaw puzzles and Tetris; (e) Interface Metaphor [8], in which the UI is made similar to a domain already familiar to the user, thus providing intuition on how to interact with the UI.

In our experience, colors and shapes (a) were central in helping users see what shapes match. However, as the complexity of formulas/proofs grow, colors and shapes suffer from scalability issues, which could be addressed in a variety of ways. To avoid overly long connectors, we could add a mechanism to selectively collapse/expand nested shapes. To reduce color conflicts, we note that colors need only be unique within a set of connected blocks, allowing some color re-use. Furthermore, we could continually re-color based on the current viewport so that visible ports use highly contrasting colors.

As stated earlier, we also found that the Animated Transitions of Heer and Robertson (b) were critical in helping users understand the semantics of Polymorphic Ports. Without these animations, too many visual changes would occur at once, and the user would not be able to follow what happened.

Finally, we found that our Interface Metaphor (puzzles for logic) was effective in part because it caused a change in cognitive mindset. In particular, Interface Metaphors vary in how accurately they map elements of the UI to the target domain, with our interface being very close to a precise one-to-one mapping. Larkin and Simon [16] suggest that such a precise mapping may lead to an ineffective diagram representation, as effectiveness is attributed precisely to *differences* in the structure and efficiency of operations. Nonetheless, we found that our puzzle metaphor was effective in part because it leads to a different cognitive state, in two different ways: (1) through the use of cultural conventions, our puzzle pieces put users in a "gaming" (rather than "classroom") state of mind, leading to a predisposed state of enjoyment; (2) the game focuses the user's attention on higher-level strategic thinking.

In addition to leveraging existing principles, our work points to the following more unique principles/recommendations.

Formalism-inspired Design. Our work illustrates how a mathematical formalism (proof theory) can guide an HCI design, yielding several benefits. A well-chosen formalism can be simple, concise, uniform and general, which has the potential to confer similar properties to the UI. The UI's semantics is clean and unambiguous as it is grounded in a mathematical formalism. Finally, one can potentially exploit the connection between the formalism and the cognitive mindset of the user: familiarity with the formalism could help understand the UI, or understanding the UI could help learn the formalism. At the same time, our work also hints at the dangers of following the formalism blindly. Recall that a direct encoding of the Assume rule led to a tedious UI, which we addressed by adapting the UI to match the logical intuition. Our strategy can then be summarized as *formalism-inspired* design: we focus on bringing the structure/intuition of the formalism into the UI, without exposing the symbolic formalism to the user.

Formulas as Shapes. Our work shows that shapes with colored ports can represent formulas with variables. Shape shifting of ports becomes variable substitution. This new visual metaphor can be used for any kind of mathematical expression, and could be applicable beyond polymorphic blocks.

RELATED WORK

Block-based Visual Programming Environments. There are a variety of block-based visual programming environments [5, 2, 1, 6], and our encoding of types using Polymorphic Blocks could be applied to any of them. We note here two projects that attempt to add types to block-based visual programming environments, although we could not find peer-reviewed papers. First, there is undergraduate honors thesis on *TypeBlocks* [19]. Although *TypeBlocks* uses shapes to represent types, it does not use colors to represent type variables: all type variables look the same and thus *TypeBlocks* doest not implement full parametric polymorphism. Second, there is a Blockly-based editor for the Bootstrap educational program [3]. Instead of using shapes to represent types, their system uses colors to represent types, while keeping connector shapes as in Blockly. Unfortunately, colors are not compositional through the use of constructors the way shapes are, in the sense that it's not clear what color could be used to represent the "list" of another color, or the "pair" of two other colors. For this reason, it's not clear how type constructors are handled in a general way. With respect to these two lines of work, Polymorphic Blocks distinguish themselves by using *both* shapes and colors: shapes to distinguish types, and colors to distinguish type variables. Furthermore, we show how Polymorphic Blocks are applicable *beyond* block-based programming environments, namely for encoding proofs.

Interfaces for proofs. There have been a variety of tools built for interactively building proofs, for example Pandora [7], Panda [13], Theorema [21] and DeduceIt [12]. However, all these tools expose symbolic formulas, something which our gamification approach does not. There has been *one* attempt at gamifying logic *without* exposing formulas: Benkmann built a visualization of natural deduction as a dominos-style game [4] (we could not find a peer reviewed paper). Each formula is mapped to a colorful pattern on a domino tile, and placing domino tiles next to each other is equivalent to applying inference rules. This approach, which is very different from ours, is not evaluated through a user study, and does not generalize to block-based programming environments.

Games with a purpose, for example ESP [20], FoldIt [9], and Verification Games [10], use gamification to leverage human-based computation through crowdsourcing. *Educational Games*, for example Refraction [17] and Codespells [11], use gamification to teach material like fractions or coding. The techniques and domain of our Proof Game are different from these previous games, and our interface is also applicable beyond the gaming interface (i.e.: Polymorphic Blockly).

Acknowledgments. We would like to thank Nadir Weibel and Scott Klemmer for their feedback. This work was supported in part by NSF grant CCF 1423517.

REFERENCES

1. App inventor. `http://appinventor.mit.edu/`.
2. Blockly. `https://code.google.com/p/blockly/`.
3. Bootstrap block editor. `http://bootstrap-block-editor.appspot.com/`.
4. Natural deduction visualized as a game of dominoes. `http://www.winterdrache.de/freeware/domino/`.
5. Scratch. `http://scratch.mit.edu/`.
6. Tinkerblocks. `http://www.tinkerblocks.org/`.
7. Broda, K., Ma, J., Sinnadurai, G., and Summers, A. Pandora: A reasoning toolbox using natural deduction style. *Logic Journal of the IGLP 15*, 4 (2007), 293–304.
8. Carroll, J. M., Mack, R. L., and Kellogg, W. A. Interface metaphors and user interface design. In *Handbook of Human-Computer Interaction*, M. Helander, Ed. Elsevier Science, 1988, 67–85.
9. Cooper, S., Khatib, F., Treuille, A., Barbero, J., Lee, J., Beenen, M., Leaver-Fay, A., Baker, D., and Popović, Z. Predicting protein structures with a multiplayer online game. *Nature 466*, 7307 (Aug. 2010), 756–760.
10. Dietl, W., Dietzel, S., Ernst, M. D., Mote, N., Walker, B., Cooper, S., Pavlik, T., and Popović, Z. Verification games: Making verification fun. In *FTfJP 2012: 14th Workshop on Formal Techniques for Java-like Programs* (Beijing, China, June 12, 2012), 42–49.
11. Esper, S., Foster, S. R., and Griswold, W. G. Codespells: Embodying the metaphor of wizardry for programming. In *Proceedings of the 18th ACM Conference on Innovation and Technology in Computer Science Education*, ITiCSE '13 (2013).
12. Fast, E., Lee, C., Aiken, A., Bernstein, M. S., Koller, D., and Smith, E. Crowd-scale interactive formal reasoning and analytics. In *Proceedings of the 26th Annual ACM Symposium on User Interface Software and Technology*, UIST '13 (2013).
13. Gasquet, O., Schwarzentruber, F., and Strecker, M. Panda: A proof assistant in natural deduction for all. A gentzen style proof assistant for undergraduate students. In *Tools for Teaching Logic - Third International Congress, TICTTL* (2011).
14. Heer, J., and Robertson, G. Animated transitions in statistical data graphics. In *IEEE Information Visualization (InfoVis)* (2007).
15. Hutchins, E. L., Hollan, J. D., and Norman, D. A. Direct manipulation interfaces. *Hum.-Comput. Interact. 1*, 4 (Dec. 1985), 311–338.
16. Larkin, J. H., and Simon, H. A. Why a diagram is (sometimes) worth ten thousand words. *Cognitive science 11*, 1 (1987), 65–100.
17. Martin, T., Smith, C. P., Andersen, E., Liu, Y.-E., and Popović, Z. Refraction time: Making split decisions in an online fraction game. In *American Educational Research Association Annual Meeting (AERA)* (2012).
18. Pierce, B. C. *Types and Programming Languages*. MIT Press, Cambridge, MA, USA, 2002.
19. Vasek, M. *Representing Expressive Types in Blocks Programming Languages*. Undergraduate honors thesis, Wellesley College, 2012.
20. von Ahn, L., and Dabbish, L. Labeling images with a computer game. In *Proceedings of the SIGCHI Conference on Human Factors in Computing Systems*, CHI '04, ACM (New York, NY, USA, 2004), 319–326.
21. Windsteiger, W. Theorema 2.0: A graphical user interface for a mathematical assistant system. In *CEUR Workshop Proceedings* (2012), 73–81.

Investigating Genres and Perspectives in HCI Research on the Home

Audrey Desjardins[1], Ron Wakkary[1,2], William Odom[1]
[1] Simon Fraser University, Surrey, British Columbia, Canada
[2] Eindhoven University of Technology, Eindhoven, Netherlands
{adesjard, rwakkary, wodom}@sfu.ca

ABSTRACT
The home and domestic experiences have been studied from multiple points of view and disciplines, with an array of methodologies in the past twenty-five years in HCI. Given the attention to the home and the volume of research, what further areas of research might there be? Based on a critical analysis of 121 works on the topic, we present seven genres of domestic technology research in HCI: social routines in the home, ongoing domestic practices, the home as a testing ground, smart homes, contested values of a home, the home as a site for interpretation, and speculative visions of the home. We articulate dominant research perspectives in HCI, and we offer two complementary perspectives about how to investigate the domestic experience in future research: the material perspective and the first person perspective.

Author Keywords
Home; domestic; critical analysis; reflective HCI.

INTRODUCTION
Since the 1990s, the HCI community has increasingly focused on understanding the complex and evolving ways interactive technologies are situated within the home and their implications for domestic experience. As focus expanded beyond the workplace to the messy contexts of everyday life, it became necessary to critically revisit the assumptions, methods, and underlying values guiding the design of interactive systems [31,44,61,84]. This has led to the adoption of many new methods and approaches to better understand and remain sensitive to the intimate, private nature of the home. Since then, a wide range of research has emerged that has focused on, for example, how social routines bring a sense of social order to everyday life [18,19,82], how family members negotiate communication and coordination practices [12,26,58,72], how resources are consumed and managed [15,67,91], and the social nature of work that unfolds in various domestic sites (e.g., in the kitchen [7,37,83]). There has also been a movement to investigate the experience of mundane everyday practices, such as watching TV [76] or knitting and gardening [36]. Several design and research initiatives have focused on provoking experiences of reflection and interpretation in the home [34,43,55]. In some cases prior works have questioned what constitutes 'the home' and the diverse experiences that unfold within it [5,6,65,66,94]. After nearly twenty-five years of research, now is a timely opportunity to critically reflect on the genres of approaches that have been adopted to understand the complex intersection of the home, domestic experience, and interactive technology.

CHI 2015, April 18 - 23, 2015, Seoul, Republic of Korea

ACM 978-1-4503-3145-6/15/04 $15.00
http://dx.doi.org/10.1145/2702123.2702540

This paper is a critical literature review of HCI and interaction design research on the home and domestic experiences. Specifically, this paper offers 3 contributions. First, it presents a cohesive analytical summary of the current state of research on the home. We present genres of research that have emerged and become concrete. We unpack the genres by highlighting the questions researchers ask and how they proceeded to answer these questions. Second, it articulates different underlying epistemological commitments adopted in each genre and critically reflects on 2 dominant perspectives: the anthropocentric view and the 3rd person view. Third, it proposes two complementary perspectives to help expand the HCI community's attention to new areas of domestic technology research: the material perspective and the first person perspective.

THE HOME
Researchers have investigated the concept of 'the home' for over a century. This work spans many different fields and disciplines; among these, social sciences, humanities, and architecture have given special attention to exploring this concept. While their aims vary, one thing they hold in common is the belief that the home is a rich, complex, nuanced, and multifaceted setting for everyday life [2,73]. Central to this conceptualization of the home is the notion that there are multiple coexisting meanings the home carries at the psychological, social, cultural and political levels [56,57,73]. More recently, the HCI community has turned to the home along with all the complexities and subtleties that are bound to it. Using a variety of approaches, HCI researchers have focused on the social life and practices that shape domestic experience, as well as the complex and evolving role of technologies in the domestic sphere.

The ways in which HCI has investigated the home

Methodologies for investigating the home and domestic experiences have also dramatically increased in the past decade. Commonly used to understand the social life and practices in the home are ethnographic methods (e.g. [14,77,87,90]) and ethnomethodology inspired studies [17,18,62,81,82]. Both describe in nuanced detail the observed practices in the home as a way to inform the design of future domestic technologies [20]. Field studies and prototype deployments (e.g. [10,27,34,45,48,58,63]) involve testing a new technological artifact or prototype in a real setting with participants in their home [11]. In addition, we found less prominent but still very present additional methodologies in HCI domestic technology research: cultural probes [8,28,34] and technology probes [45,53,63,68], smart home experiments [50,69,71,83], and participatory design [54,59,68]. The complex topic of everyday domestic experiences has inspired researchers to refine and reinvent investigative approaches for the home as is evident in the diversity of methodologies we encountered.

OUR METHODOLOGY

Our work is inspired by and draws on these diverse and, at times, divergent aspects of people's experiences at home. We aimed to keep a broad description and definition of the home to reflect this diversity of views and methods. Our analytic approach involved creating genres that were constructively defining yet neither rigid nor hermetic. In this way, it is possible for an individual work to span multiple genres. In the following sections, we describe 7 genres of research on the home in HCI that surfaced from our critical review of 121 peer-reviewed conference papers, journal articles, book chapters and books (all of which focused on the broad topic of technology in the home).

Selection of works

Works were selected firstly by searching in the ACM Digital Library for the keywords 'home', 'domestic', 'house', and 'everyday'. We added research found by searching specific activities performed in the home using the keywords 'cooking', 'cleaning', 'watching TV', 'video conferencing with family members', 'gardening', 'repair', 'home network', 'kitchen', 'health at home', and 'religion'. In addition, we surveyed general visions of domestic technology with the keywords 'sustainable living'[1], 'ubiquitous computing', and 'smart homes'. Motivated by our own and the HCI community's growing interest in design oriented research, we completed our selection by exploring alternative methods for designing domestic technologies, such as speculative design and critical design.

From this first selection, we branched out to include the relevant references cited in the original articles. Finally, we culled our list to include the most cited papers (according to Google Scholar), and eliminated papers that presented ideas that we felt were redundant within the corpus of research. Our goal was to create a broad landscape of the types of technologies designed for the domestic settings and to represent the range of views on what constitutes the home in order to build strong genres of domestic technology research. We do not claim to present an exhaustive list of related research done in the field, but rather we aim at representing the past and current research genres for conducting research in the home setting. A full list of the 121 references can be found on this paper's ACM Digital Library webpage (Appendix A). Finally, it is important to note that our sample is drawn primarily from North American and European research, which creates a western view of the home, a clear limitation of our analysis.

Analysis

For each work, we read the resource and summarized the goal of the research, the methodology used, the focus of the analysis, and the results presented. As we were going through this process, we created categories for research approaches. These categories are what we came to call *genres* of research on domestic experience (similar to and inspired by DiSalvo et al. [23]). To create our genres, we looked at what the goal of each work was, what questions researchers asked, and the types of things focused on in their research. The process of creating the genres followed a constant back and forth between defining the genres and seeing how they applied to the entire corpus of literature.

In addition to analyzing the works' research questions and orientations, we also wanted to know what researchers were concerning themselves with in the home. As we read the works, we took note of the type of data that was collected and what the object of this data was. This formed the basis for our description of the *objects* of the study. Moreover, we were interested not only in the textual descriptions of the results, but also in the visual reports of study findings. We conducted a preliminary visual analysis of the graphical elements that were added in each work. We took note of the format of those elements (photograph, line drawing, photomontage, floor plan, etc.) as well as the topic or focus of the visual element (people in the home, artifacts in the home, visual interface of a technological artifact, etc.). In this paper, we present some results of this visual analysis as complementary data to our original analysis, in the cases where results elevate our understanding of a genre.

We delved deeper into our analysis by identifying the inquirer's *commitments* vis-à-vis the domestic experience, for each question asked in each genre. Each genre resulted in multiple epistemological commitments; after a thorough thematic analysis, we crystalized these into 5. We then further categorized our 7 genres based on related commitments (this is summarized in Table 1).

[1] Sustainability is a major concern in the design of domestic technologies (e.g. [15,34,67,74,91]) and we found that it cut across almost all genres of research. In this paper, we do not report specifically on this topic, however we acknowledge its high importance in our corpus of literature.

GENRES OF RESEARCH ON THE HOME

We present seven genres of research on the topic of the home that are present in the CHI community. We focus specifically on the types of questions each genre asks and what is analyzed.

Social routines in the home

An influential and prominent theme in HCI research centers on the social routines and work of everyday home life. In this genre, authors tend to agree that the home is a complex collection of interrelated social routines that the HCI community needs to understand before designing interactive technologies. Researchers have articulated the crucial need to gather rich and detailed descriptions of social routines in the everyday life of the home, often using ethnomethodology inspired ethnography [18,19,61,62,75,82]. Authors of this genre have asked questions such as:

- How is the home socially organized?
- What are the elements of the social machinery that support everyday life in the home?

With an underlying goal of informing the design of domestic technology, specific attention was given to particular routines that touch on the organization and the communication within the home; two identified areas that could benefit from interactive technologies. Researchers have looked at current, often analog, systems in the home such as the positioning and migration of letters, calendars, and how documents are positioned in the home [18,75]. In the corpus of work within this genre, researchers have given an essential place to artifacts and systems as a way to reveal to social aspects of domestic life. This is evidenced by the use of photographs featuring artifacts in participants' homes. In addition, annotated maps and diagrams were also presented to represent results on where activity centers and coordinate displays [19] are and where it would be beneficial to install interactive technologies.

Ongoing domestic practices

Ongoing domestic practices refer to the wide variety of activities that people perform at home. In our corpus of works, practices are generally described in the form of observational contextual studies, often ethnographic studies, that focus on richly describing and interpreting activities, artifacts and interactions. The goal of these descriptions is to provide enough information to highlight opportunities and challenges in designing interactive technologies for those practices. Authors of works that characterize this genre have asked questions such as:

- How do practices configure the home experience?
- How do people describe and reflect on the various domestic practices they perform?
- What is the role of artifacts and technologies in the practices of the domestic experience?

Authors have described activities, materials and interactions with artifacts involved in the practices of, amongst others, gardening [36], pottering [78,93], religious practice [90,92], health monitoring [1,39], interpersonal communication [3,4,26], domestic networks management [38], and resource consumption [74]. Works in this genre often rely on an ongoing relationship between participants and researchers as a way to gain an insider's understanding of the more intimate aspects of domestic practices. This is illustrated in how researchers present results in the participants' voices, using a significant amount of verbatim quotes to support the description they provide of everyday practices. Furthermore, the commonly used method of home tours and personal artifact inventories resulted in an understanding of ongoing practices in terms of supporting artifacts. Figures included photographs where study participants were seen to be active and present in a situation within the home, as well as where they were interacting with artifacts, as illustrated, for example, by Ames et al.'s photographs of their study of family videochat [3] (fig. 1).

Figure 1. Pictures of people performing domestic practices [3,36].

The home as testing grounds

The home as testing grounds for new domestic technologies is a central part of how the HCI community investigates how to design for the home. This is an important shift departing from observational studies of *what is,* to move towards exploring *what could be* in the home. Field studies and prototype deployments are common in HCI and in the context of the home [11,80]. Questions in this genre typically include:

- How is this new designed technology used, appreciated, and adopted in domestic setting?
- What are the new activities, routines, and behaviors surrounding this new technology?

In this genre, focus is placed on the newly designed artifact and its introduction in the home. Researchers give attention to how social routines and ongoing practices might be affected by this new addition to the home, with an eye toward how changes occur. For example, Forlizzi and DiSalvo [27] explored how the introduction of a Roomba, an autonomous cleaning robot, might transform the practices and values surrounding cleanliness in the home. Other field studies have looked at new technologies for family calendars [59,68], interpersonal communication and messaging [12,44,48,58,72], and the use of surface computing in the home [52]. This genre has also seen some exploratory testing about different ways of engaging with technology in the home, such as through ludic engagement

[10,34], slowness [63], and discovery [55], relating closely to the genre of *home as a site for interpretation*, described in a following section.

In order to investigate the ways newly designed technologies might shape everyday life, authors have looked at the instances in which they were used, the position of the prototypes in the home, as well as reflections by participants in interviews. Demonstrating the prominence of the design artifact oriented view of this genre, figures showing how and where a prototype was placed in homes (fig. 2) were meant to reveal the importance of the relationship between the new artifact and the unique and intimate home of the participants. This can also be seen as a move to situate bespoke design artifacts outside of the studio or gallery, and situate them more directly in the contexts of people's everyday lives. Moreover, log data from the study usage allowed researchers to test the usability and functionality goals that are also part of this genre.

Figure 2. Pictures are taken of the deployed prototypes in the home environment [12,33,55,63].

Smart homes and home automation

The genre of smart homes and home automation is concerned with the design of the smart home itself as well as the applications and systems that are part of the home. Harper defines the smart home as "*a residence equipped with computing and information technology which anticipates and responds to the needs of the occupants, working to promote their comfort, convenience, security and entertainment through the management of technology within the home and connections to the world beyond*" [41:17]. To conduct research on smart homes, teams of researchers have built living labs (e.g. [47,51,69,71]), houses where participants can stay for a short period of time and live within this technological environment. This genre asks questions along the lines:

- What is a smart home?
- How do people live in, maintain, and install a smart home?

Studies of people in living labs have focused on their simulation of everyday routines, with an emphasis on the ways in which people utilize the various capacities of the smart home both holistically and in details (for example the usability of a specific user interface [51]). Interestingly, even though researchers looked at people's behavior in the living labs, they have rarely described the home in a similar fashion as the genres of *social routines* or *ongoing practices*. The figures included in research further support this claim and we would argue that this genre foregrounds developing technological aspects of smart homes over eliciting people's long-term lived experiences in such settings. Figures, when used, usually consisted of floor plans of the houses, sensor positioning diagrams, visual interfaces, and pictures of the exterior of the living lab house (fig. 3). Finally, in order to understand how people maintain and install home automation systems 'in the wild', researchers have also observed and interviewed people who are in the process of transforming their home or who have lived with home automation systems for some time [13,14,90]. Here, researchers paid attention to the roles played by family members, the inherent social dynamics and the material implications of home automation systems.

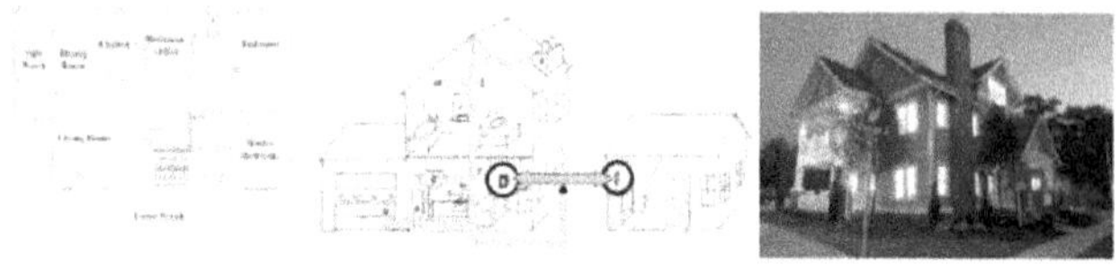

Figure 3. Smart home floor plan [50], sensing diagram [58], and the Aware Home by Georgia Tech [58].

Contested values of a home

The genre of contested values of a home is constituted of works that have touched on the assumptions the HCI community has about what is considered the home and what isn't. For example, Bell and Dourish [6] have articulated and reflected on the qualities of 'the shed'. In this, they have argued that by defining what is at the edges of the home (with qualities like masculine, dangerous, secret, chaotic), we might further our understanding of the home itself. Authors in this genre ask questions including:

- What have we overlooked when we talked about the home?
- How can we go beyond common assumptions about what the home is in a way that can tell us more about how to design interactive domestic technologies?

Authors have aimed at going beyond the traditional meaning of the home by investigating alternative family structures [64], ways of living beyond the Western European world [5,7], mobile ways of living [66,89,94], temporal qualities of the home [24], and gendered visions of the home [6,16]. This genre also provides alternative views on how, when, and why we should (and should not) introduce technologies in the home. For instance, Grimes and Harper [37] propose celebratory technologies for the kitchen instead of technologies concerned with the problematic aspects of eating, such as diets or the lack of cooking skills. Likewise, Taylor, Wyche and colleagues [78,93] have looked at the activity of pottering and conclude that sometimes, technology might not be a solution in itself for some domestic practices. This genre often relies on critique and argumentation, typically drawing from literature in fields outside of HCI, to present those new ideas and how they relate to HCI.

The home as a site for interpretation

Within the genre of the home as a site for interpretation, authors have embraced the unique, nuanced, private, messy, and creative environment of the home and aimed at designing domestic technologies that support interactions that go beyond achieving tasks and efficiency. Researchers have created and studied technologies that encourage playfulness [30,31] exploration [34], discovery [55], reflection [63], interpretation [33], speculation [43] and provocation [25] when installed in householders homes. Here, researchers have aimed to answer questions like:

- How can we encourage reflection and interpretation about technology in the home?
- How can we create technology that reflects the intimate, complex, and nuanced character of the domestic experience?
- How do people react to, use, and explore with new technologies designed for interpretation in the home?

The approach often taken by researchers is to develop finished technological artifacts with a high design quality that can be lived with for a period of time. When deployed, researchers investigated the behaviors, the attitudes (interpretation, creativity, reflection, etc.), and the adoption (or rejection) of the design artifact. Deployments were often reported in terms of researchers' observations and what participants have said about their life with the prototype. The type of interaction and the cycles of engagement with prototypes was also of interest, particularly for the long term studies of the History Tablecloth [32], the Indoor Weather Stations [34] and the Photobox [63] for which authors articulated the different phases the homeowners went through in a cycle of initial excitement, disappointment, and persisting attachment.

The attention to detail and craft that went into the creation of these artifacts show a different kind of sensibility to the way the HCI community designs domestic technologies. This is highlighted by how these artifacts were presented in our corpus (fig. 4): the use of a white background draws attention to design details in terms of the form, materials, and composition that collectively communicate the quality and craft of these kinds of design artifacts.

Figure 4. The white background in these photographs gives emphasis to the design artifacts themselves prior to becoming integrated into a domestic setting [34,35,55].

Speculative visions of the home

The final genre we present is speculative visions of the home, which is concerned with *potential domestic futures* rather than a present (or near present) conceptualization of the home. Speculative concepts and sketches offer glimpses into alternative visions of what the home could be in the future. Examples are Weiser's vision of ubicomp [88], Tolmie et al.'s [82] concept of unremarkable computing, and various descriptions of the smart home of the future [47,50]. This genre often asks questions such as:

- What is the home of the future?
- How should we configure technology for the domestic experience of the future?

Similarly to the genre *contested values of a home*, with speculative visions, authors explore ideas and critiques of current research with the aim of broadening the field. For example, Aipperspach et al. [2] present radical new design concepts that challenge the continuing trend towards homogeneous and undifferentiated domestic environments. Moreover, Gaver and Martin [29] present nine speculative sketches which represent provocative ideas for domestic information appliances as a starting point for a discussion with their project partner. Finally, Taylor et al. [77] combine ethnographic studies with sketched explorations of the findings as a way to pursue the dialogue between the research materials and future designs.

This genre is particularly defined by works that use visual methods to present and share their new concepts, such as workbooks, sketches [29], and sketchbooks [2]. The treatment of these images, particularly the inclusion of line drawings, photo montages, and the mélange of black and white with a few carefully chosen colors, demonstrates a strong design sensibility, but more importantly proposes concepts that are just at the right level of fidelity to suggest something that does not exist yet (fig. 5).

Figure 5. Illustrations are used for communicating ideas about potential future domestic technologies [2,8,29,78].

ANALYSIS OF THE GENRES

Describing HCI research on the home, domestic experience and interactive technology in terms of 7 genres provided us with two main anchors for understanding the field more comprehensively. First, it enabled us to identify *questions* the HCI community has been implicitly and explicitly asking about domestic experiences. In this, we have uncovered questions about the different configurations and definitions of the home, how social machinery and everyday practices constitute the home, what the experience of the home is, and how technology is used and lived with in the home. Second, the genres supported a description of the *objects* of the studies conducted. We reported on a focus on the visible acts that constitute routines and practices, often portrayed through images of people in action or verbatim quotes. We have also seen an important emphasis on artifacts and technologies in the home, strongly supported by a vast amount of photos of objects in situ.

Epistemological Commitments and Perspectives

Now, we expand our analysis of the genres by articulating the *epistemological commitments* adopted when asking the questions, as seen in table 1. Each commitment shapes the way research is conducted and how results are uncovered.

Table 1. Epistemological commitments and respective genres

Commitments	Genres
Objective observer	Social routines, testing grounds, smart homes, interpretation
Third person observer	Ongoing practices, testing grounds, smart homes, interpretation
Relayed informant	Ongoing practices, testing grounds, interpretation
Author interpreter	Contested values, speculative visions
Experimenter	Testing grounds, interpretation

The *objective observer* commitment is similar to a bird's eye view: it is removed from the study situation and relies on factual visible accounts to report on domestic life. In the *third person observer* commitment, the researcher observes, asks questions, and sometimes participates in home life, allowing a deep look into the routines and practices of everyday life. The *relayed informant* commitment is characterized by a participant's verbatim quotes (from interviews or photo/text/video diaries) as relayed and selected by the researcher. In the *author interpreter* commitment, questions are asked by an attributable author who builds a reasoned argument about the domestic experience. Finally, the *experimenter* commitment refers to the questions a designer of research artifacts might ask while developing prototypes that are deployed to observe the effects of new technologies in the home.

We have also observed how two dominant perspectives emerged, as high-level patterns of epistemological commitments and genres. Since they continually surfaced as meta-level categories, it became clear they were best viewed as *dominant* perspectives that could further refine our understanding of research conducted in the home.

Dominant perspective: The anthropocentric perspective

Our analysis revealed the first dominant perspective to be an *anthropocentric perspective* that is the view that the home is uniquely human. Researchers in all 5 epistemological commitments either looked at people and their activities in the home, or investigated artifacts and technologies from the point of view of their users (householders and family members in this case). Arguably HCI research is concerned with understanding both humans and computers, and eventually interaction. However, in almost all the works of our corpus, data and analysis were centered on human experience such as people's lives, experiences, routines, activities, challenges, and motivations. Even the study of artifacts was shifted to, influenced by, or looked at through the lens of people (e.g. the focus on human usability in visual interfaces or on the impacts on human social routines in technology deployments). Although we agree that the human perspective on the home is fundamental and only natural, we see the potential if not validity of asking about alternative perspectives that do not prioritize such a human point of view. We explore this in our notion of a *material perspective* that we outline in the following section.

Dominant perspective: The observer/interpreter perspective

The second dominant perspective that was revealed through our analysis is the predominant role of the *observer/interpreter*. The commitments of the *objective observer*, the *third person observer* and the *relayed informant* all take a view from a third person outside the domestic situation or technology studied. In the *observer/interpreter* perspective, the author is accountable for the ideas she articulates in her research no matter if she is relaying information in the voice of participants or through observations. In this case, the researcher plays the role of choosing what to include (and exclude) and how to frame quotes or images in order to better support claims based on their analysis. A concern with this perspective might be the mediating role played by the intermediary position the researcher takes between the lived experience of the home and the construction of knowledge about the home. We note that the views of the *author interpreter* and the *experimenter* commitments already offer a step towards choosing a more personal voice for presenting research work, either through argumentation or through the voice of the designer. In the complementary perspective of *first person view of the home*, we push this idea of a personal voice even further.

COMPLEMENTARY PERSPECTIVES

The two complementary perspectives we present below are a result of our analysis. They are our attempt to answer the question of what more we can understand in HCI research of the home and more specifically, what set of underexplored commitments and emergent genres might be productive in HCI. Discussing complementary perspectives in relation to the dominant perspectives was not meant as oppositional but rather was a helpful way to sharpen our exploration of new perspectives. In addition, we do not aim to be exhaustive nor do we mean to suggest these are the two 'missing' perspectives from the existing literature on domestic technologies. Rather, we propose them as possible perspectives and critical mechanisms for framing and expanding future initiatives targeted at the home in HCI.

A material perspective of the home

This perspective centers on a non-human object perspective within the home or, in other words, the *material views of the home*. Recent and growing scholarship on object oriented ontology [40] and speculative realism—a branch of philosophy that critiques and proposes an alternative to the anthropocentric view of the world [9,22]—serves as a rationale to support this new perspective. In general, this post-phenomenological work champions an egalitarian view of all 'things' in the world, both human and non-human. Relatedly, philosophers of technology [46,85] have acknowledged the non-neutral ways artifacts meditate between human beings and reality. Viewing the home through the perspective of non-human objects could strongly support HCI in more critically considering the complexity bound to the objects we, as a community, produce, what they do, and their collective effects. Although this perspective could be adopted for several research domains in HCI, we believe it would especially benefit research on the home by moving away from traditional emphasis on humans, to acknowledge and critically engage the substantive role that objects play in shaping the domestic reality, a reality humans experience.

Investigating what non-human objects experience, see, live, and understand about the home is an endeavor that will require new ways of inquiring about the home. For example, a question like 'how does a fridge experience domestic life?' will likely call for alternative data collection and analytical and speculative approaches. Hidden cameras (e.g. the BinCam project [79]) and pet cams [49] (fig. 6) offer means of a material perspective to data collection. Inherent challenges of a material perspective will influence the ways in which research strategies and methods can be appropriately developed for this emerging area and will be a key issue framing future work.

Another intriguing dimension of the material perspective on the home is the way in which it offers a radically different scale of time for thinking about the home. For example, a house's life can span many human lifetimes and family heirlooms can be passed down for many generations [24,70]. A reflection on this alternative scale might lead HCI to investigate questions such as 'How will a domestic technology exist in 200 years?' and 'How ought we design material objects today with the idea in mind that they would be discovered or used in 200 years?' This deeper critical capacity for situating the home within a bigger temporal spectrum offers the potential to profoundly shift our thinking about the role of technologies in domestic life.

Figure 6. Views from a parcel in the mail [21], a pet cam [49] and a fridge cam (our own photograph).

A first person view of the home

A first person view of the home is the most direct way to study the domestic experience. A primary question that can be asked from a subjective perspective could be: 'Are our personal experiences of the same home different?'. Investigating the same home, space, and events with two (or more) people's experiences can lead to potentially radically different understandings of what the home is. In that case, how can the HCI community design for variations on the same theme in a home? In addition to building on HCI's understanding of the multiple meanings of the home, this perspective can be beneficial by revealing how a single setting can lead to diverse experiences.

First person views of the home can also be gained through the eyes of the researcher/author herself. Autobiographical design—"*design research drawing on extensive, genuine usage by those creating or building the system*" [60:514]—and auto-ethnography—a branch of cultural anthropology defined by the researcher studying 'his own people' [42]—are strong starting points to construct first person research as an HCI researcher. Although this method could also be used in a variety of contexts, we believe that for sensitive settings like the home, seriously considering the researcher's (and designer's) personal experience, needs, and desires can profoundly elevate the richness and value of research. For instance, Gaver's [30] Video Window is an example of how designing for oneself can produce a uniquely rich and deeply textured understanding of the effect a technology can have in the home, and the kinds of experiences this object might (or might not) lead to.

A first person view will require new modes of collecting, interpreting, analyzing, and representing data. The quantified self and life logging movements are already popular trends where people can constantly record facts about their everyday lives, such as step counts, calories spent, hours of sleep, etc. First person photography and video, and personal experience photo essays might also be visual ways to investigate the subjective experience of domestic life. Like in the material perspective of the home, first-person research methods will also carry complexities, such as the need to appropriately communicate the kinds of epistemological commitments that come with personal accounts, which vary considerably compared with more traditional or dominant approaches in HCI.

One determining characteristic of first person research is the fact that research can happen over long periods of time. By being constantly with oneself, one can reflect and investigate her relations to artifacts and domestic experience in ways that are impossible with other perspectives. This is a major opportunity to investigate further the lived-with qualities of artifacts in the home. Lived-with qualities [86] need time to emerge as they arise more through the day-to-day living together with the artifact than from specific punctual interactions, similarly to how one dwells with furniture in the home. Lived-with qualities construct a focus that can lead to a significantly new way of understanding technologies in the home and we argue that first person research might be one of the most appropriate perspectives to take for those investigations.

FUTURE RESEARCH AND CONCLUSIONS

In this paper, we have presented 7 genres of research for domestic technologies, highlighting the questions the HCI community has been asking about the domestic experience and the ways in which to design interactive technologies for the home. By looking at the epistemological commitments from which those questions are asked, we identified two dominant and two complementary perspectives that can lead us to fruitful reflections about technology in the home. The complementary perspectives offer exciting and potentially fruitful starting points for future research about the home. By shifting perspective to a material perspective, future research can bring a strong counterpart to HCI's vast and detailed research in how *people* experience domestic technology. In addition, by removing the observer's interpretation, 1st person research may lead to more personal, genuine, and nuanced first-hand experience of what it is like to live with technology at home.

ACKNOWLEDGMENTS

All images appearing in this paper were used with the permission of the authors themselves. We thank the Social Sciences and Humanities Research Council (SSHRC) of Canada for their support.

REFERENCES

1. Aarhus, R. and Ballegaard, S.A. Negotiating Boundaries: Managing Disease at Home. In *Proc. CHI'10*, ACM (2010), 1223–1232.
2. Aipperspach, R., Hooker, B., and Woodruff, A. The Heterogeneous Home. In *Proc. UbiComp'08*, ACM (2008), 222–231.
3. Ames, M.G., Go, J., Kaye, J. "Jofish," and Spasojevic, M. Making Love in the Network Closet: The Benefits and Work of Family Videochat. In *Proc. CSCW'10*, ACM (2010), 145–154.
4. Anderson, B., McWilliam, A., Lacohee, H., Clucas, E., and Gershuny, J. Family Life in the Digital Home — Domestic Telecommunications at the End of the 20th Century. *BT Technology Journal 17*, 1 (1999), 85–97.
5. Bell, G., Blythe, M., and Sengers, P. Making by making strange: Defamiliarization and the design of domestic technologies. *ACM TOCHI. 12*, 2 (2005), 149–173.
6. Bell, G. and Dourish, P. Back to the shed: gendered visions of technology and domesticity. *Pers. Ubi. Comput. 11*, 5 (2007), 373–381.
7. Bell, G. and Kaye, J. Designing Technology for Domestic Spaces: A Kitchen Manifesto. *Gastronomica: The Journal of Food and Culture 2*, 2 (2002), 46–62.
8. Blythe, M. and Monk, A. Notes Towards an Ethnography of Domestic Technology. In *Proc. DIS'02*, ACM Press (2002), 277–281.
9. Bogost, I. *Alien phenomenology, or, What it's like to be a thing.* University of Minnesota Press, Minneapolis, 2012.
10. Boucher, A. and Gaver, W. Developing the drift table. *interactions 13*, 1 (2006), 24–27.
11. Brown, B., Reeves, S., and Sherwood, S. Into the Wild: Challenges and Opportunities for Field Trial Methods. In *Proc. CHI'11*, ACM Press (2011), 1657–1666.
12. Brown, B., Taylor, A.S., Izadi, S., Sellen, A., Kaye, J.J., and Eardley, R. Locating Family Values: A Field Trial of the Whereabouts Clock. In J. Krumm, G.D. Abowd, A. Seneviratne and T. Strang, eds., *UbiComp 2007*. Springer Berlin Heidelberg, 2007, 354–371.
13. Brush, A.J.B., Lee, B., Mahajan, R., Agarwal, S., Saroiu, S., and Dixon, C. Home Automation in the Wild: Challenges and Opportunities. In *Proc. CHI'11*, ACM Press (2011), 2115–2124.
14. Chetty, M., Sung, J.-Y., and Grinter, R.E. How Smart Homes Learn: The Evolution of the Networked Home and Household. In J. Krumm, G.D. Abowd, A. Seneviratne and T. Strang, eds., *UbiComp 2007.* Springer Berlin Heidelberg, 2007, 127–144.
15. Chetty, M., Tran, D., and Grinter, R.E. Getting to Green: Understanding Resource Consumption in the Home. In *Proc. UbiComp 2008*, ACM Press (2008), 242–251.
16. Cowan, R.S. The "Industrial Revolution" in the Home: Household Technology and Social Change in the 20th Century. *Technology and Culture 17*, 1 (1976), 1–23.
17. Crabtree, A., Mortier, R., Rodden, T., and Tolmie, P. Unremarkable Networking: The Home Network As a Part of Everyday Life. In *Proc. DIS'12,* ACM Press (2012), 554–563.
18. Crabtree, A. and Rodden, T. Domestic Routines and Design for the Home. In *Proc. CSCW 13*, 2 (2004), 191–220.
19. Crabtree, A., Rodden, T., Hemmings, T., and Benford, S. Finding a Place for UbiComp in the Home. In A.K. Dey, A. Schmidt and J.F. McCarthy, eds., *UbiComp 2003*. Springer Berlin Heidelberg, 2003, 208–226.
20. Crabtree, A., Rodden, T., Tolmie, P., and Button, G. Ethnography Considered Harmful. In *Proc. CHI'09*, ACM Press (2009), 879–888.
21. Davoli, L. and Redström, J. Materializing Infrastructures for Participatory Hacking. In *Proc. DIS'14,* ACM Press (2014), 121–130.
22. DiSalvo, C. and Lukens. Nonanthropocentrism and the Nonhuman in Design: Possibilities for Designing New Forms of Engagement with and through Technology. In M. Foth, ed., *From Social Butterfly to Engaged Citizen: Urban Informatics, Social Media, Ubiquitous Computing, and Mobile Technology to Support Citizen Engagement*. MIT Press, 2011, 421–435.
23. DiSalvo, C., Sengers, P., and Brynjarsdóttir, H. Mapping the Landscape of Sustainable HCI. In *Proc. CHI'10*, ACM Press (2010), 1975–1984.
24. Dong, T., Ackerman, M.S., and Newman, M.W. "If These Walls Could Talk": Designing with Memories of Places. In *Proc. DIS'14,* ACM Press (2014), 63–72.
25. Dunne, A. and Raby, F. *Design Noir: The Secret Life of Electronic Objects.* Springer, 2001.
26. Elliot, K., Neustaedter, C., and Greenberg, S. Time, Ownership and Awareness: The Value of Contextual

Locations in the Home. In M. Beigl, S. Intille, J. Rekimoto and H. Tokuda, eds., *UbiComp 2005*. Springer Berlin Heidelberg, 2005, 251–268.

27. Forlizzi, J. and DiSalvo, C. Service Robots in the Domestic Environment: A Study of the Roomba Vacuum in the Home. In *Proc. HRI'06,* ACM Press (2006), 258–265.
28. Gaver, B., Dunne, T., and Pacenti, E. Design: Cultural probes. *interactions 6*, 1 (1999), 21–29.
29. Gaver, B. and Martin, H. Alternatives: exploring information appliances through conceptual design proposals. In *Proc. CHI'00*, ACM (2000), 209–216.
30. Gaver, W. The Video Window: My Life with a Ludic System. *Pers. Ubi. Comput. 10*, 2-3 (2006), 60–65.
31. Gaver, W. Designing for Homo Ludens, Still. In T. Binder, J. Löwgren and L. Malmborg, eds., *(Re)Searching The Digital Bauhaus*. Springer London, 2009, 163–178.
32. Gaver, W., Bowers, J., Boucher, A., Law, A., Pennington, S., and Villar, N. The History Tablecloth: Illuminating Domestic Activity. In *Proc. DIS'06*, ACM (2006), 199–208.
33. Gaver, W., Sengers, P., Kerridge, T., Kaye, J., and Bowers, J. Enhancing Ubiquitous Computing with User Interpretation: Field Testing the Home Health Horoscope. In *Proc. CHI'07*, ACM (2007), 537–546.
34. Gaver, W.W., Bowers, J., Boehner, K., et al. Indoor weather stations: investigating a ludic approach to environmental HCI through batch prototyping. In *Proc. CHI'13*, ACM Press (2013), 3451–3460.
35. Gaver, W.W., Bowers, J., Boucher, A., et al. The Drift Table: Designing for Ludic Engagement. *Ext. Abstracts CHI'04*, ACM Press (2004), 885–900.
36. Goodman, E. and Rosner, D. From garments to gardens: negotiating material relationships online and 'by hand.' In *Proc. CHI'11*, ACM Press (2011), 2257–2266.
37. Grimes, A. and Harper, R. Celebratory Technology: New Directions for Food Research in HCI. In *Proc. CHI'08*, ACM Press (2008), 467–476.
38. Grinter, R.E., Edwards, W.K., Chetty, M., et al. The Ins and Outs of Home Networking: The Case for Useful and Usable Domestic Networking. *ACM TOCHI, 16*, 2 (2009), 8:1–8:28.
39. Grönvall, E. and Verdezoto, N. Beyond Self-monitoring: Understanding Non-functional Aspects of Home-based Healthcare Technology. In *Proc. Pervasive and Ubiquitous Computing*, ACM (2013), 587–596.
40. Harman, G. *Tool-Being: Heidegger and the Metaphysics of Objects.* Open Court Publishing, 2002.
41. Harper, R., ed. *Inside the smart home.* Springer, London ; New York, 2003.
42. Hayano, D. Auto-Ethnography: Paradigms, Problems, and Prospects. *Human Organization 38*, 1 (1979), 99-104.
43. Helmes, J., Taylor, A.S., Cao, X., Höök, K., Schmitt, P., and Villar, N. Rudiments 1, 2 & 3: Design Speculations on Autonomy. In *Proc. TEI'11*, ACM Press (2011), 145–152.
44. Hindus, D., Mainwaring, S.D., Leduc, N., Hagström, A.E., and Bayley, O. Casablanca: Designing Social Communication Devices for the Home. In *Proc. CHI'01*, ACM Press (2001), 325–332.
45. Hutchinson, H., Mackay, W., Westerlund, B., et al. Technology probes: inspiring design for and with families. In *Proc. CHI'03*, ACM Press (2003), 17–24.
46. Ihde, D. *Technics and Praxis: A Philosophy of Technology.* Springer, 1979.
47. Intille, S.S. Designing a home of the future. *IEEE Pervasive Computing 1*, 2 (2002), 76–82.
48. Judge, T.K., Neustaedter, C., and Kurtz, A.F. The Family Window: The Design and Evaluation of a Domestic Media Space. In *Proc. CHI'10*, ACM Press (2010), 2361–2370.
49. Keeney, C. *Petcam: The World Through the Lens of Our Four-Legged Friends.* Princeton Architectural Press, New York, 2014.
50. Kidd, C.D., Orr, R., Abowd, G.D., et al. The Aware Home: A Living Laboratory for Ubiquitous Computing Research. In N.A. Streitz, J. Siegel, V. Hartkopf and S. Konomi, eds., *Cooperative Buildings. Integrating Information, Organizations, and Architecture.* Springer Berlin Heidelberg, 1999, 191–198.
51. Kientz, J.A., Patel, S.N., Jones, B., Price, E., Mynatt, E.D., and Abowd, G.D. The Georgia Tech Aware Home. *Ext. Abstracts CHI'08*, ACM Press (2008), 3675–3680.
52. Kirk, D., Izadi, S., Hilliges, O., Banks, R., Taylor, S., and Sellen, A. At Home with Surface Computing? In *Proc. CHI'12*, ACM (2012), 159–168.
53. Kirk, D.S., Izadi, S., Sellen, A., Taylor, S., Banks, R., and Hilliges, O. Opening Up the Family Archive. In *Proc. CSCW'10*, ACM Press (2010), 261–270.
54. Lee, H.R. and Šabanović, S. Weiser's Dream in the Korean Home: Collaborative Study of Domestic Roles, Relationships, and Ideal Technologies. In *Proc. Pervasive and UbiComp*, ACM (2013), 637–646.
55. Lim, Y., Kim, D., Jo, J., and Woo, J. Discovery-Driven Prototyping for User-Driven Creativity. *IEEE Pervasive Computing 12*, 3 (2013), 74–80.
56. Marcus, C.C. *House As a Mirror of Self: Exploring the Deeper Meaning of Home.* Nicolas-Hays, Inc., 2006.
57. Moore, J. Placing Home in Context. *Journal of Environmental Psychology 20*, 3 (2000), 207–217.
58. Mynatt, E.D., Rowan, J., Craighill, S., and Jacobs, A. Digital Family Portraits: Supporting Peace of Mind for Extended Family Members. In *Proc. CHI'01*, ACM Press (2001), 333–340.
59. Neustaedter, C. and Bernheim Brush, A.J. "LINC-ing" the Family: The Participatory Design of an Inkable Family Calendar. In *Proc. CHI'06* ACM Press (2006), 141–150.
60. Neustaedter, C. and Sengers, P. Autobiographical Design in HCI Research: Designing and Learning Through Use-it-yourself. In *Proc. DIS'12,* ACM Press (2012), 514–523.

61. O'Brien, J. and Rodden, T. Interactive Systems in Domestic Environments. In *Proc. DIS'97,* ACM Press (1997) 247–259.
62. O'Brien, J., Rodden, T., Rouncefield, M., and Hughes, J. At Home with the Technology: An Ethnographic Study of a Set-top-box Trial. *ACM TOCHI 6*, 3 (1999), 282-308.
63. Odom, W.T., Sellen, A.J., Banks, R., et al. Designing for Slowness, Anticipation and Re-visitation: A Long Term Field Study of the Photobox. In *Proc. CHI'14*, ACM Press (2014), 1961–1970.
64. Odom, W., Zimmerman, J., and Forlizzi, J. Designing for Dynamic Family Structures: Divorced Families and Interactive Systems. In *Proc. DIS'10,* ACM Press (2010), 151–160.
65. Palen, L. and Hughes, A. When Home Base is Not a Place: Parents' Use of Mobile Telephones. *Personal Ubiquitous Comput. 11*, 5 (2007), 339–348.
66. Petersen, M.G., Lynggaard, A.B., Krogh, P.G., and Winther, I.W. Tactics for Homing in Mobile Life: A Fieldwalk Study of Extremely Mobile People. In *Proc. MobileHCI'10*, ACM (2010), 265–274.
67. Pierce, J., Schiano, D.J., and Paulos, E. Home, Habits, and Energy: Examining Domestic Interactions and Energy Consumption. In *Proc. CHI'10,* ACM Press (2010), 1985–1994.
68. Plaisant, C., Clamage, A., Hutchinson, H.B., Bederson, B.B., and Druin, A. Shared Family Calendars: Promoting Symmetry and Accessibility. *ACM TOCHI 13*, 3 (2006), 313–346.
69. Randall, D. Living Inside a Smart Home: A Case Study. In R. Harper, ed., *Inside the Smart Home*. Springer London, 2003, 227–246.
70. Rodden, T. and Benford, S. The Evolution of Buildings and Implications for the Design of Ubiquitous Domestic Environments. In *Proc. CHI'03*, ACM (2003), 9–16.
71. De Ruyter, B. *365 days' Ambient Intelligence research in HomeLab.* 2003.
72. Sellen, A., Harper, R., Eardley, R., et al. HomeNote: Supporting Situated Messaging in the Home. In *Proc. CSCW'06*, ACM Press (2006), 383–392.
73. Sixsmith, J. The meaning of home: An exploratory study of environmental experience. *Journal of Environmental Psychology 6*, 4 (1986), 281–298.
74. Strengers, Y. Negotiating everyday life: The role of energy and water consumption feedback. *Journal of Consumer Culture 11*, 3 (2011), 319–338.
75. Swan, L., Taylor, A.S., and Harper, R. Making Place for Clutter and Other Ideas of Home. *ACM TOCHI. 15*, 2 (2008), 9:1–9:24.
76. Taylor, A. and Harper, R. Switching On to Switch Off. In R. Harper, ed., *Inside the Smart Home.* Springer London, 2003, 115–126.
77. Taylor, A.S. and Swan, L. Artful systems in the home. In *Proc. CHI'05*, ACM Press (2005), 641–650.
78. Taylor, A.S., Wyche, S.P., and Kaye, J. "Jofish." Pottering by Design. In *Proc. NordiCHI'08*, ACM (2008), 363–372.
79. Thieme, A., Comber, R., Miebach, J., et al. "We'Ve Bin Watching You": Designing for Reflection and Social Persuasion to Promote Sustainable Lifestyles. In *Proc. CHI'12*, ACM (2012), 2337–2346.
80. Tolmie, P. and Crabtree, A. Deploying Research Technology in the Home. In *Proc. CSCW'08*, ACM Press (2008), 639–648.
81. Tolmie, P., Crabtree, A., Rodden, T., Greenhalgh, C., and Benford, S. Making the home network at home: Digital housekeeping. In L.J. Bannon, I. Wagner, C. Gutwin, R.H.R. Harper and K. Schmidt, eds., *ECSCW 2007.* Springer London, 2007, 331–350.
82. Tolmie, P., Pycock, J., Diggins, T., MacLean, A., and Karsenty, A. Unremarkable computing. In *Proc. CHI'02*, ACM Press (2002), 399–406.
83. Tran, Q.T., Calcaterra, G., and Mynatt, E.D. Cook's Collage. In A. Sloane, ed., *Home-Oriented Informatics and Telematics*. Springer US, 2005, 15–32.
84. Venkatesh, A. Computers and Other Interactive Technologies for the Home. *Commun. ACM 39*, 12 (1996), 47–54.
85. Verbeek, P.-P. *What Things Do: Philosophical Reflections on Technology, Agency, and Design.* Penn State Press, 2005.
86. Wakkary, R., Desjardins, A., and Hauser, S. Unselfconscious Interaction in the Home: A Construct. *Interacting With Computers*, (Submitted for publication).
87. Wakkary, R. and Maestri, L. The resourcefulness of everyday design. In *Proc. C&C'07*, ACM (2007), 163–172.
88. Weiser, M. *The Computer for the 21st Century.* 1991.
89. Winther, I.W. Homing oneself: home as a practice. *Haecceity Papers 4*, 2 (2009).
90. Woodruff, A., Augustin, S., and Foucault, B. Sabbath Day Home Automation: "It's Like Mixing Technology and Religion." In *Proc. CHI'07*, ACM Press (2007), 527–536.
91. Woodruff, A., Hasbrouck, J., and Augustin, S. A Bright Green Perspective on Sustainable Choices. In *Proc. CHI'08,* ACM Press (2008), 313–322.
92. Wyche, S.P. and Grinter, R.E. Extraordinary Computing: Religion As a Lens for Reconsidering the Home. In *Proc. CHI'09*, ACM Press (2009), 749–758.
93. Wyche, S.P., Taylor, A., and Kaye, J. Pottering: A Design-oriented Investigation. *Ext. Abstracts CHI'07*, ACM Press (2007), 1893–1898.
94. Zafiroglu, A. and Chang, M. Digital Homes on Wheels: Designing for the Unimagined Home. *Personal Ubiquitous Comput. 11*, 5 (2007), 395–402.

Building Change: Constructive Design of Smart Domestic Environments for Goal Achievement

Ryan Brotman[1], Winslow Burleson[2], Jodi Forlizzi[3], William Heywood[1], Jisoo Lee[4]
[1]The Design School, Arizona State University, Tempe, AZ, USA, ryan.brotman@gmail.com
[2]College of Nursing, New York University, New York, NY, USA, wb50@nyu.edu
[3]HCI Institute, Carnegie Mellon University, Pittsburgh, PA, USA, forlizzi@cs.cmu.edu
[4]School of AME, Arizona State University, Tempe, AZ USA, Jisoo.Lee@asu.edu

ABSTRACT
This paper presents the *constructive design research (CDR)* of smart domestic environments comprised of smart home infrastructure, smart domestic artifacts and digital services. CDR is an approach that focuses on imagining futures and learning through the making and testing of prototypes to construct new knowledge about how people engage with the world. While the body of research on smart domestic environments includes a wealth of human-centered research, the use of CDR is marginal. Our work demonstrates how such a process engages residents in activities to imagine why people might value smart domestic environments and how they might want to interact with them. Through goal setting activities, paper prototyping, and field-testing of resident designed technology probes, we present use cases, design principles and experiential insights. After sharing these findings, we introduce the emergence of smart domestic environments as possessing persuasive, personified and artful qualities.

Author Keywords
Constructive design; participatory design; Internet of Things; smart homes; domestic technologies; prototyping; persuasive technologies

ACM Classification Keywords
H.5.m. Information interfaces and presentation

INTRODUCTION
Research on smart domestic environments incorporates a number of methodologies, including living labs [11, 13, 25], ethnography [4, 16, 27, 28, 29] and field-testing of new technologies in the homes of residents [10, 17, 21, 23, 25, 26]. Living labs often explore the implementation of embedded systems, distributed I/O and machine learning to make the home itself intelligent. Ethnographic research on home life centers on human-derived systems of domestic activity and, in many cases, situates such environments as mostly passive platforms for supporting human intelligence. Field-testing of new technologies sits somewhere in-between the two other methodologies depending on the rationale of the research. Through these methodologies wages a debate on what smartness is within the home, as well as whom and/or what should possess agency.

This paper introduces a new perspective to this conversation by engaging residents in a constructive design research (CDR) [14] process to address three questions: 1) Why would residents want a smart domestic environment? 2) What do they want such environments to do? 3) How do such environments potentially impact resident behavior? CDR emphasizes making and evaluating prototypes to envision futures and create new knowledge about how people desire to engage with the world [14]. Our approach uses constructive design research in three iterative prototyping cycles. The first two phases focus on conceptual modeling and low-fidelity participatory prototyping [5, 19, 31], while the final phase field-tested technology probes [10].

As a research approach steeped in interaction design, CDR fundamentally examines desired systems of mediation [14]. Our primary contribution is a reconceptualization of *smartness* through this lens of mediation between residents and their built environment to articulate a rationale for smart domestic environments. This new focus on mediation assumes that both residents and the built environment (by virtue of being thoughtfully designed by people) contain a latent intelligence. To explore mediation, we constrained our research to goal-directed behavior in the home. Designing with this boundary allowed participants to explore *why* and *how* they engage in intellectual processes, such as reasoning, reflection, coordination, creativity and learning within the home and how a future of smart domestic technologies could contribute to those processes. This study resulted in use cases, design principles and insights suggesting smart domestic environments can be persuasive [6], personified, and artful [28].

RELATED WORK
The past several decades of research on smart domestic environments have yielded a body of work far too large to

CHI 2015, April 18 - 23, 2015, Seoul, Republic of Korea
Copyright 2015 ACM 978-1-4503-3145-6/15/04...$15.00
http://dx.doi.org/10.1145/2702123.2702602

summarize within the limits of this paper. Instead, we focus on the current state of research methodologies to situate CDR. Prior to such comparison; it is paramount to note that CDR is defined as a research perspective capable of employing many methodologies. Living labs, ethnography and field-testing are viewed as methodologies that may be all be utilized as part of CDR.

Traditionally, a living lab of a domestic environment consists of a simulated home space where researchers can run controlled research and development efforts. The Georgia Tech's Aware Home [13] and MIT's PlaceLab [11] exemplify this tradition. According to [9], living labs can inform the overall user testing strategy by examining bounded social interaction and assessing usability issues. However, a living lab diminishes in value in its ability to account for social complexity of the real world [9]. More recently, efforts such as Schwartz et al.'s study of consumptive feedback and home energy management systems (HEMS) challenge both the definition and limitation of living labs by implementing new technologies in resident domiciles while maintaining experimental controls [25]. This evolving definition employs similar practices to a number of less experimentally rigorous studies involving technology probes [10], including the Digital Family Portraits [23] HomeNote [26], Tableau Machine [21] and EmotoCouch [17] projects.

Living labs may serve as an actionable methodology for CDR because both constrain the real world. CDR does so to enable a design space for the production of prototypes. Yet, several differences present themselves. For most living labs, knowledge generation takes place through the deployment and evaluation of prototypes. For CDR, knowledge generation begins with the act of prototyping as well as the deployment and evaluation of prototypes. Additionally, when CDR is deployed through use of a co-design methodology, it can also enable a bottom-up process for end users to deconstruct systems of domestic practice through participatory prototyping. Such work is exemplified by Westerlund et al.'s use of modeling clay to engage residents in prototyping [31], as well as the paper prototyping work of Neustaedter & Brush [19] and Elliot et al. [5] of domestic coordination systems. When applied so, CDR, much like the ethnographic work of [16, 29] can generate models for domestic systems. For living labs to apply to CDR, issues of knowledge generation through making and the targeted use of co-design must be accounted for.

However, ethnography is challenging to align with CDR. As stated previously, CDR constrains sociocultural systems to create a design space. Such constraints contrast ethnography, which seeks to observe and report sociocultural systems in their entirety. CDR attempts to account for such constraints, through iterative design cycles, during which boundary conditions adapt in response to new information. Additionally, ethnography's observational nature positions the approach as one concerned with understanding present circumstances. CDR, which takes an interventionist stance, challenges design researchers, be they professionals or lay people, to create hypothetical designs that represent potential futures. In short, ethnographic studies focus on human activity, while constructive design studies focus on human intent, making the former methodology a potential compliment to CDR studies, but rarely a direct component of them.

STUDY OVERVIEW

CDR revolves around the act of prototyping. Beaudouin-Lafon and Mackay define prototypes as a, "concrete representation of part of or all of an interactive system," [1]. Koskinen et al. maintains a loose definition of what constitutes a prototype, referencing a range of low and high fidelity instantiations, including affinity diagrams, scenarios, concept sketches, Wizard of Oz systems and fully interactive systems [14]. What separates CDR prototypes from the general notion of prototypes is the rationale behind them. Within engineering and computer science, prototypes prove and refine new technologies. Within the context of CDR, prototypes imaginatively embody human values, reasoning, sensuality and interaction that inform why and how people may desire to engage with the world [13]. Additionally, as a research perspective emerging from interaction design, CDR typically explores relationships of sociotechnical mediation [14]. These qualities serve as the foundation for our research design.

Participants

Our interest in personal goals as a focus for design led to a solicitation of young adults as research participants. Nurmi demonstrated that young adults possess a greater heterogeneity of goals than middle-aged adults and elders, with a focus on sociality, personal and career development, finding mates and creating families [20]. A longitudinal study on goal dynamics supported these findings by demonstrating that as people transition from young adults to middle-aged adults both a reduction in goal counts and heterogeneity occur [24]. Young adults are also plagued by ambiguity that decreases the likelihood of goal attainment [15]. Because of the voraciousness of young adults to attain goals and their lack of clarity on how to do so, this life phase is a fertile area of exploration for our research. Participant selection occurred through online solicitation. Twenty participants, ranging in age from 22 to 31, with 8 male and 12 female, completed the first two prototyping iterations. Three of the original sample completed the third iteration.

Study Design

The research unfolded over two months, with the following phases: 1) conceptual modeling 2) paper prototyping 3) technology probe field-testing. Our initial discussions with participants revealed two key issues. First, people often have difficulty explaining their personal goals and what achieving them entails. Second, current smart domestic technologies are often small boxes that plug into power outlets, get affixed to walls and, in many cases, require specialized PC peripherals, or are hidden within forms of historically dumb technologies such as televisions. These product forms do little to communicate their functionality, methods of interaction or intent to their users.

We addressed these challenges by infusing our approach with action research and co-design methods. Action research facilitates learning opportunities for participants, allowing them to act as lay researchers [8]. Co-design emphasizes the role of participants as lay designers who collaborate to create prototypes [5, 19, 31]. Participant activities were designed to inspire self-discovery about personal goals and to generate insights about smart domestic environments through prototyping.

During phase one, participants completed Little et al.'s Personal Project Analysis (PPA) workbook to explore personal goals [15]. After participants completed the workbook, we exposed them to the notion of smart domestic environments through examples of academic projects such as the *Aware Home* as well as consumer products such as the *Nest* thermostat. Participants then chose a personal goal they believed smart domestic technologies could assist with. Content analysis of the chosen personal goals provided a set of use cases.

During phase two, participants completed PhotoVoice [30], PICTIVE mapping [18] and psychocartographic [7] exercises to produce a collage of their solution. Affinity diagramming and content analysis of collages yielded design principles.

During phase three, participants field-tested technology probes [10] based on their paper prototypes for one week. Use logs and interview transcripts were collected. Content analysis stimulated insights into how residents experience smart domestic environments for goal achievement.

CONCEPTUAL MODELING OF PERSONAL GOALS

Participants first completed a Personal Project Analysis (PPA) workbook that elicited and ranked personal goals. This activity addressed our first research question by stimulating personal reflection on participants' goals and to understand why residents may desire smart domestic environments. Workbook activities began with a divergent thinking exercise, asking participants to "Take 10 minutes to list out as many personal goals as possible." Participants were asked to choose a maximum of 10 top goals. Each selected goal was then ranked on a 0-10 scale across 27 statements. Statements ranged from "How happy are you when you work towards this goal?" to, "A lot of people know about this goal." to "Achieving this goal is the most important thing in my life right now." After rating their goals, participants chose one goal for which to prototype a smart domestic environment application.

Participants selected a wide variety of personal goals, ranging from "learn to play 'Blackbird' on my guitar" and "grow tomatoes" to "build a new bike" and "eat healthier". Nineteen of the 20 personal goals selected for co-design sessions could be clearly categorized, with three focusing on exercise (participants 5, 11 and 18), three focusing on diet (participants 3, 12 and 14), 11 focusing on learning and/or new skills development (Participants 1, 2, 4, 6, 7, 8, 9, 10, 15, 16, 19), one focusing on intrapersonal development (participant 20) and one focusing on interpersonal communication (participant 13). Participant 17's project, "Spend less time online", intersected all of these categories. As learning new skills was the most frequent and varied type of goal, we further divide them into subcategories shown in figure 2.

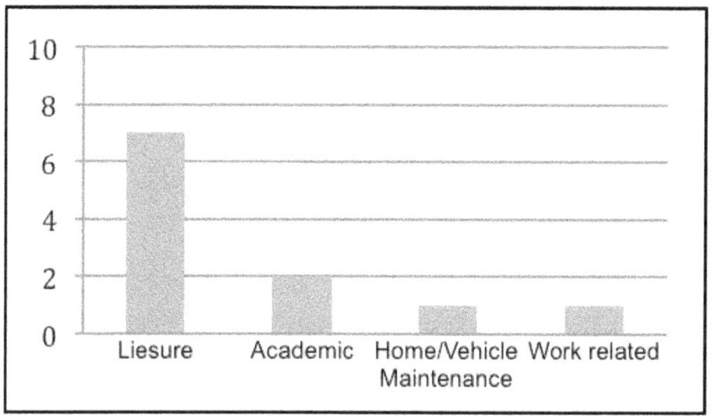

Figure 1. Frequency of *learn new skills* goals by category.

The 20 personal goals collectively suggest three use cases: (1) Promote Making: Support of creative practice resulting in a tangible artifact; 2) Self-Improvement: Foster personal growth through assimilating new knowledge and/or skills; and (3) Keep Me On Task: Recognize what I need to be doing and provide real-time support. These use cases serve as a basis for understanding why young adults would want to live within a smart domestic environment, namely to assist with the structuring of activity fostering creativity, growth and productivity.

PAPER PROTOTYPING

The paper prototyping phase addressed participant perceptions about functionality and interaction. It began with a photoVoice exercise, where participants captured and commented on photographs of their homes in relation to their chosen goal. We then mounted prints of the photos onto poster boards to create initial collages of their homes.

During the co-design sessions, participants completed a semi-structured interview and PICTIVE interaction mapping and psychocartography activities to further create their smart domestic environment collage (figure 2). The interview expounded on participants' chosen personal goals, focusing on translation into domestic practice and the role of the home environment in supporting that domestic practice. We viewed this interview as a grounding exercise that allowed participants as lay designers to begin to weave a design scenario by translating their chosen goals into tangible practices within their home lives.

The PICTIVE interaction mapping activity consisted of choosing and sequencing paper tokens onto the home interior montage. Each token represented a specific input or output modality or device use. Participants placed the tokens on their home interior collages by either choosing from a pre-defined set of interactions based on the Game-as-Life--Life-as-Game (GaLLaG) [2] distributed computing prototyping platform, or sketching new interactions on a blank token. Predefined interaction tokens included the use of mobile phones, tablets, smart televisions, desktop and laptop computers, automation of lights and appliances, detection of furniture use and entry/exit from a room and interaction with web content. Participants were also encouraged to further describe interactions through hand sketching and writing directly on the collages.

The psychocartography activity focused on hypothesizing how interactions could mediate behavior. Participants mapped representations of cognitive and emotional behaviors onto physical spaces. Participants were again given paper tokens containing either cognitive or emotive icons and attribution labels taken from PPA goal assessment. Participants were also provided blank tokens to define additional behaviors. For each token placed on the collage, participants ascribed a positive or negative modifier to it to indicate whether they felt their design would increase or decrease the specified behavior.

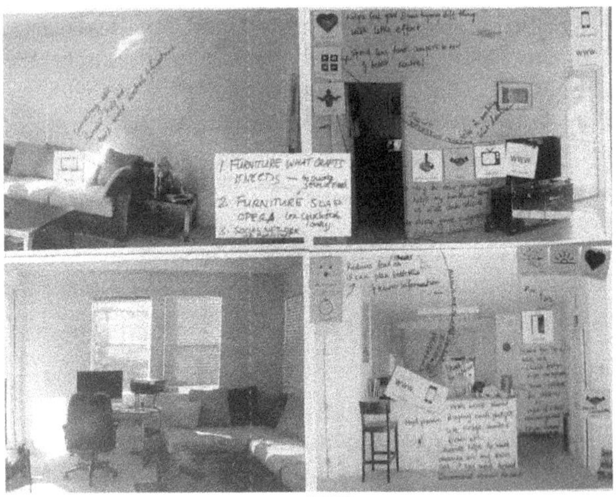

Emotion token Cognition token

Interaction token

Figure 2. Collage example with token categories.

During the 20 co-design sessions, 396 interview notes were transcribed, and 152 annotated PICTIVE interaction tokens and 147 psychocartographic tokens were catalogued. Interview notes and tokens underwent two rounds of unconstrained affinity diagram clustering with triangulation occurring across the research team, third party experts and participant collaboration.

DESIGN PRINCIPLES FOR SMART DOMESTIC ENVIRONMENT PROTOTYPING

Through our analysis, we created three design principles for smart domestic environments to mediate goal-oriented behavior. They address our second research question of describing what participants want these systems to do:

Mediate ambiguity – Reveal resources to accomplish the goal at hand. Psychocartographic tokens that consistently appeared across participant collages were *control* (the perception that a desired outcome is within one's control), *difficulty* (the perceived degree of difficulty to attain a goal given skills and resources), *progress* (The perception of making gains towards goal completion), *success* (a person's perception of whether or not they will succeed at attaining their goal) and *uncertainty* (The degree to which a person feels uncertain about what to do next with regards to attaining a personal goal). These tokens indicate that participants require assistance in defining what success entails, feedback on where they stand in achieving that success, as well as potential next steps in continuing their pursuit. In terms of intellectual processes, this principle relates to reflection and planning. Examples of notes informing this principle are, "Can I do it, and if so, what does success look like," stated P14 on eating healthier, while P15 admitted uncertainty on playing keyboard at a public venue, "I want to perform publicly, but I'm not sure how that is going to happen." P20 conveyed, "I felt like I'm out of control because when I sit down to fulfill my vision, I don't know what the steps to complete it are," with regards to completing her autobiography.

GaLLaG interactions designed to mediate ambiguity consistently focused on curating and provisioning of digital content to show examples of people completing similar tasks as well as promoting participant reflection on the desired outcomes of their designed service provisions. In most cases, such content constituted videos sent directly to their existing devices in response to environmental triggers such as time of day, location in the home and use of specific domestic artifacts.

Guidance and accountability – Provision digital, physical and social resources that support the actions of residents in real-time. Psychocartographic tokens that consistently appeared across participant collages were *absorption* (the degree to which a person feels completely immersed when engaged in a goal related activity), *autonomy* (The degree to which a person perceives goal attainment as solely the function of their individual actions), *control, difficulty*, *stage* (A person's perception of where they fall on a scale ranging from concept, planning, action or completion relating back to a goal), *success*, *support* (A person's perception of if, and how other social agents support the attainment of the goal) and *visibility* (How visible goal related activities are to people close to the person pursuing the goal) [15]. These tokens indicate that participants require either in-situ, just-in-time interaction to scaffold activity and inspire a sense of continued personal responsibility concerning achievement of their goals. In terms of intellectual processes, this principle relates to learning. Examples of notes contributing to this principle include, "With the fitness thing, I need someone to do it with me," as stated by P11 concerning his goal of working out five times per week; "I just want someone to guide me through it," as stated by P18 with regards to creating a fitness routine; and, "It makes me feel like when I get help, my time matters more because someone else is invested," as stated by P13 with regards to keeping in touch with old friends. A number of previous systems have been developed to address issues of scaffolding resident activity, yet these projects primarily focus on support of activities of daily living for frail populations [13]. Such system behavior also seems relevant for young adults within the context of learning support. These back and forth interactions between actors that occur during scaffolding relates to Cialdini's model of reciprocity and influence [3].

For guidance interactions, participants chose environmental cues such as lights turning off and on to signal activity locations; text messages, video and audio providing just-in-time content; automation of appliances and augmentation of non-computational objects to cue resources needed to attain a goal. Accountability occurred in two ways. First, through automated communications to friends, family and peer groups updating them on participant efforts. Second, through participants creating positive and negative incentive structures that often involved accessing or restricting digital content in response to participant efforts.

Time and timing – Structure the start points, durations and end points of activities. Psychocartographic tokens that consistently appeared across participant collages were *control*, *stress* (the degree of stress a person feels when engaging in activities related to a goal), *difficulty* and *time adequacy* (the degree to which a person perceives they have enough time to make meaningful gains towards attaining a goal). These tokens serve as indicators regarding how participants perceive time to mediate their behavior. In terms of intellectual processes, this principle relates to coordination. P1 stated that learning to play "Blackbird" on her guitar, "depends entirely on time allocation," while P13 referenced the challenge with keeping in touch with her old friends was in "finding continuous time" necessary to stay connected to people who live far away and are not a part of her daily life. P19 recognized her proclivity towards delaying activity related to her goal, stating, "[Procrastination] It's like a personal epitaph of mine."

Interactions involving time involved call-to-action and completion-of-action prompts. Call to action prompts, in most cases, came from audio speakers embedded in the environment. Participants either chose to record messages in their own voice, play audio clips from movies, or play songs. Completion of action prompts either happened through pop up windows on their devices, text messages or remote audio. In addition to these prompts, this principle includes scheduling time and setting durations of activity.

FIELD TESTING SMART DOMESTIC ENVIRONMENTS SUPPORTING GOAL ATTAINMENT

We explored our third research question by understanding to what extent resident-designed interventions had the desired impact on participants' goal-oriented behavior. We chose which applications to field test based on a participant's willingness to allow system installation in their homes and the ability of the development team to build the applications within a time frame in which the participant's goal would not lose relevance. Three applications were built for P1 (referred to as "Rachel"), who wanted to learn how to play "Blackbird" on her guitar; P17 (referred to as "Jamie"), who sought to spend less time online; and P20 (referred to as "Sarah"), who struggled to complete her autobiography.

We used the GaLLaG rapid prototyping platform (figure 3) to build our applications [2]. The platform consists of Indigo home automation software, which serves as the communication hub for GaLLaG objects, allowing for scripting of interaction between devices and logging user data via an SQLite database. Through the "Digital GaLLaG Space", developers can produce programs using a variety of languages including Applescript, Objective C, JavaScript, Python and Ruby. Program commands can travel through web services to the GaLLaG server and out to "physical GaLLaG space" devices to trigger interactions.

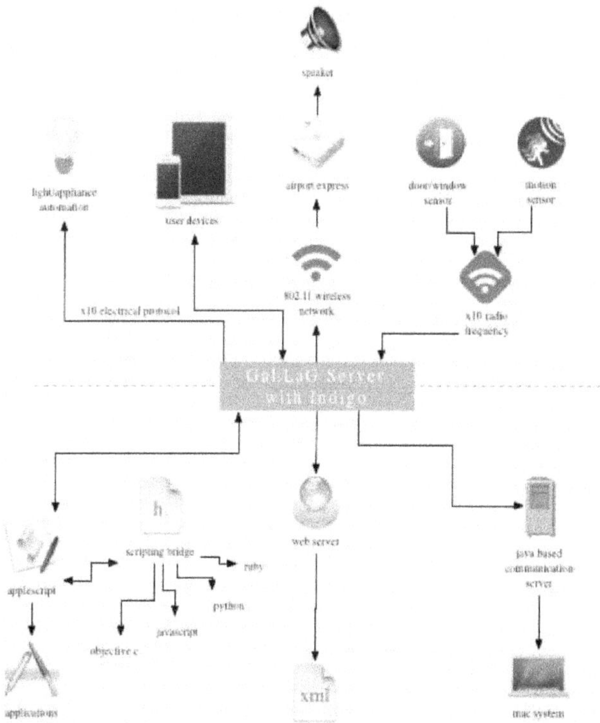

Figure 3. Game-as-Life, Life-as-Game System Architecture

Field test one: Learn to play "Blackbird" on my guitar
Rachel chose to design a prototype to assist her in learning to play The Beatles song "Blackbird" on her acoustic guitar. She reported this project as one that she started during the summer of 2011, but as new priorities such as her degree and an internship consumed her time, she let the project fall to the wayside. Despite the lapse of commitment to the project, she reported it as important to her because playing guitar provided an escape from her more serious activities and allowed her to do something physically immersive, inducing a semi-meditative state.

During the course of the co-design session, Rachel divulged a number of motivational needs. First, she expressed a need to feel like she was making progress on mastering the song. When asked how she defined "mastery", she responded with being able to play the song from start to finish without making a mistake while keeping tempo. This frustration manifested on the collage with placement of psycho-cartographic tokens representing *anger, stress, difficulty* and *challenge*. She reported feeling like she had lost control over the project because she no longer practiced. She also reported that she used to practice with her boyfriend and that he would encourage her to practice. However, since moving across country for an internship, she had lost that form of physically present social support, which decreased her willingness to engage in the project.

Her scenario begins with waking up in the morning to a custom alarm clock playing "Blackbird". The song plays through a pair of remote speakers placed in her bedroom. Rachel can press a button on her nightstand to pause the audio. Rachel conveyed that her morning routine consists of going downstairs to the kitchen to make an espresso immediately after getting out of bed. The song follows her through her house during this routine. This start to her day provides an ambient reminder to practice.

Mid-day, Rachel receives an email at work containing a link to an online video of another amateur musician playing "Blackbird". During prototyping, Rachel stated that, "Seeing someone else playing the song, and listening to their version of it, will make me feel like I can do it too."

In the evenings, Rachel's home recognizes her arrival and turns on a light in her living room to illuminate her acoustic guitar, which sits on a stand next to a desk with a laptop on it. To turn the light off, Rachel must pick her guitar up.

When Rachel picks up the guitar, the light shuts off and guitar tablature for "Blackbird" appears on a laptop next to the guitar. Recording software and a practice timer also launch. During the co-design session, Rachel defined the ability to record her sessions so that if she made significant improvements on playing the song, she could send the video to her boyfriend. Placing the guitar back on the stand resets the system for the next day. Figure 4 presents multiple images of Rachel's application.

"While the system was installed in my place, I practiced three times that week. It's more than I've practiced in the last year," Rachel stated. Rachel also reported that she felt more immersed in the project because of the ongoing dialogue her application engaged her in throughout the day by waking up to "Blackbird" and sending her videos of other musicians playing the song.

Rachel also reported that she felt the system reduced feelings of *anger*, *difficulty* and *challenge*, but increased feelings of *stress*. Rachel associated this stress to a perceived increase in pressure to practice the song because of the tangible presence of her prototype. "You have this thing in your living room, exerting a sort of physical presence as you go about your day... Although, once I sat down and got into it, I was in it and felt good." This pressure created a tension for Rachel as she explained that, " – Felt like there were more important things I could have been spending my time on, but that light was always on. Sometimes, it was a pain in the ass, but again, once I sat down to play, it felt good." Little et al.'s work on personal project ecosystems positions personal goals a set of objects that require people to make decisions on resource allocation in relation to one another [15]. One resource is time. This tension of Rachel's echoes this viewpoint.

With regards to our design framework, Rachel's project falls under the *Self Improvement* use case, which involves learning new knowledge and skills. Her application contains a number of tasks that fall under the three design principles. Audio playback of "Blackbird" in the morning and midday email link to other musicians covering the song are instances of the *Mediate Ambiguity* principle because they represent what she is trying to accomplish. The automation of her practice space demonstrates a series of interactions meant to guide her through a practice session exemplify *Guidance and Accountability*. Automation of the light next to her guitar and the practice session completion notification are prompts that fall under *Time and Timing* while sending the video of her practice session to her boyfriend is meant to increase her accountability by creating social visibility of her actions.

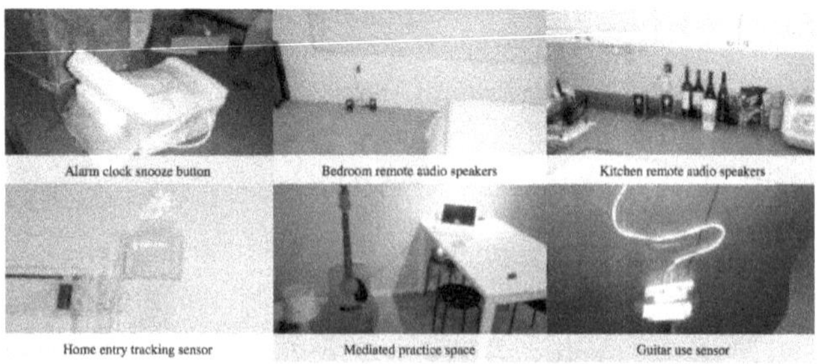

Figure 4. Probe for Rachel's goal to learn how to play "Blackbird" on her guitar.

Field test two: Spend less time online

Jamie chose to design a prototype to assist her in spending less time online during her evenings at home in order to pursue other activities. These activities included experimenting with recipes for cooking vegetables; practicing latte art; completing a collage of Arizona, meeting friends outside of her home and working out. She stated that she spent much of her time online simply meandering from website-to-website, losing her entire evening to the web. Psychocartographic tokens representing *hope, happiness, love, time adequacy, anger* and *support.*

The prototype Jamie designed begins with the system recognizing it is a weekday evening, she is at home, and that she has been on her laptop for almost an hour. At the end of the hour, the prototype restricts her access to her blogs, social media sites and online shopping sites.

For the purpose of maintaining a rapid implementation timeline, the capability to restrict Jamie's access to Internet service accounts was role played remotely (WoZ) by a researcher. A remote researcher received a notice of Jamie's laptop usage, prompting the researcher to change the passwords to Jamie's web services.

Upon restricting web access, Jamie receives a text message randomly prompting her to engage in one her desired activities. A variety of sensors affixed to white box goods, appliances and infrastructure track Jamie's adherence to the prompt. In the cases where collaging, cooking vegetables and latte art were chosen digital media in the form of tutorial videos and music to enhance the atmospheric aesthetics were used to support the experiential aesthetics of the activity.

For meeting friends outside of the home, the prototype sent a text message to a predefined list of friends eliciting a meet up. This interaction was also done via WoZ, with a researcher sending the messages in response to a system prompt. Both environmental and mobile device sensors infer if Jamie leaves the house and determines if she meets her friends. If prompted to work out, the same sensors were used to determine adherence to the prompt

During her exit interview, Jamie reported a perceived increase in hope, *joy, time adequacy* and *support* and a decrease in *anger*. Feelings of *love* remained the same. She stated the prototype felt, "— like a roommate constantly telling me to get out from behind my computer and be active. I think having someone else, or some*thing* else - other than my own free will was really powerful in helping me spend less time online."

Additionally, Jamie reported that the system made her more conscious of how much time she spends on her computer throughout the course of her entire day. "I was much more aware of when I got on my computer, and the time I was wasting, essentially, not doing other things I have been wanting to do that I didn't think I had time for."

Jamie's application intersects all three use cases. First, the application keeps her on task by keeping her off line. Second, both the creative practice and self-improvement use cases are reflected by which activity she is prompted to take on. Completing her collage of Arizona falls under creative practice, while learning to cook vegetables, making latte art and exercising all instances of self-improvement. The one anomaly is the prompt for Jamie to socialize with her friends. The restriction of her online content, various instruction sets regarding her activities and tracking of real world artifact use (her exercise shoes) relate to guidance and accountability, while the various prompts on her laptop and phone represent timing interactions. Providing example images of vegetables and latte art exemplifies mediation of ambiguity by illustrating the end results of her efforts.

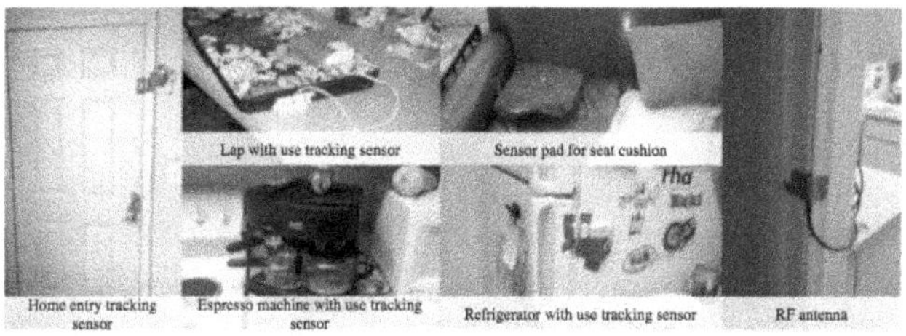

Figure 5. Probe for Jamie's goal to spend less time online.

Field test three: Finish writing my autobiography

Sarah chose to design a prototype that supports her writing her autobiography. This goal began as a school assignment. However, as she began to pen her personal history, the assignment took on a life of it's own, becoming deeply meaningful to her. This increase in meaning led to a need to make her story perfect, which led to writer's block and incompletion of the assignment. Her instructor gave her an extension on the assignment and she continues to struggle with completing her story. As with both Rachel and Jamie, Sarah stated that she had a problem with structuring her time in a manner that allowed her to make consistent gains on writing her autobiography. Additionally, she often preferred to write in public venues, such as coffee shops, because her home was a distraction. The one exception to feeling sidetracked at home was in the morning because her roommates were either still asleep or away from home. Sarah also reported a number of general interests, including extreme sports, electronic music and comedic movies that were used to ground design of incentives. During her psychocartography exercise, Sarah thought her application would increase feeling of *hope*, *happiness* and *love* towards writing, while reducing feelings *sadness* and *stress*.

Sarah's application supports two scenarios. One scenario takes place on Friday through Monday Mornings when she writes at home, while the other takes place on Tuesday through Thursday nights, when she writes away from home.

The Friday through Monday morning scenario begins when motion and audio sensors determine Sarah is awake. An hour afterwards the system plays a song chosen by Sarah prior to the field test from the server laptop to prompt a writing session. Her desk lamp turns on and an additional prompt to sit at her desk and write for 60 minutes displays on her computer screen. The system recognizes Sarah sitting at her writing desk through a pressure sensitive seat cushion installed on her chair. Once Sarah completes 60 minutes of writing, the desk lamp turns off to notify her that she has completed her writing for the day. As a reward, the prototype sends Sarah an email with a link to an extreme sports video. Additionally, the system allots times for impromptu breaks of up to 15 minutes total time. If Sarah does not sit down to write, or once sitting, leaves for longer than the break time, the application bans Sarah's Facebook access for 24 hours.

On Tuesday through Thursday evenings, a similar scenario occurs, the system recognizes when Sarah returns home in the evening (as opposed to waking up in the morning) and the location of writing changes to one of several pre-defined potential public venues within biking distance of Sarah's house. Once the application recognizes Sarah is at home in the evening, it sends her a text message with a writing location. Sarah has an hour to arrive at the location and write. The GPS of her phone recognizes her arrival.

Sarah's application failed to both incentivize writing and bolster her desired behavior change. Instead, Sarah refused to adhere to her prototype, ignoring the system's calls to action and incentives. With the exception of the first day of installation, Sarah failed to write her autobiography, initially resulting in six days of restricted Facebook access. During what was supposed to be Sarah's exit interview, she requested to keep the system for an additional week to, "get back on track." During the second week of testing, she did not write at all, resulting in an additional seven days of restricted Facebook access.

When asked about her lack of adherence to her prototype, Sarah stated, "I just didn't have the time. I felt so overwhelmed with my current courses, work, and just life, that I didn't use the system." Despite abandoning the prototype, Sarah did state that simply having it physically in her home made her feel more aware of both the goal, as well as her failure to make gains towards completing it. "It's really weird but I actually feel more depressed about the whole thing [writing her autobiography] because I have this cool stuff in my room and that people built this thing for me and here I am not doing what I'm supposed to do…I feel really bad about the whole thing."

Banning Sarah's Facebook access also failed to motivate adherence. Sarah stated that she found the tactic frustrating because she would forget that her access was blocked and attempt to access the social network only to have her entry denied. "At first, I saw it as a reminder to get going…you know, an oh shoot kind of moment. But after a couple days, I just gave up and resigned myself to it. It's like, at some point, oh well…"

The positive incentive of sending an extreme sports video to Sarah in response to her successful completion of a writing session was also an ineffective motivator. When asked why, Sarah responded, " I really don't know. When I received the video of the UFC knockout on the first day, I thought it was cool. Again, once I just kept not writing, I just completely shut down. Facebook didn't matter. The videos didn't matter."

In contrast to Sarah's negative emotional experience, she reported that the prototype increased her clarity around what she needed to do to complete the project on her own, "I know the hours that were scheduled for me to write everyday would have resulted in completing my autobiography. I just need to do it already"

Sarah's application illustrates a *keep me on task* use case. Sarah reported that she already knew both how to write and what she wanted to write, she just did not actually engage in the act of writing. She used remote audio cues in the form of movie clips and music as well as automation of her desk lamp and text messages to create timing prompts. Tracking of her writing sessions as well as incentives through restriction and access to digital media demonstrate attempts at creating accountability. While no single interaction represented mediating ambiguity, Sarah perceived the application in its entirety as a means of such mediation with regards to her time management. This perception is reflected in her previous comments regarding a perceived renewed understanding of how to complete her autobiography in the future.

DISCUSSION

By engaging in a CDR, participants set goals, made paper prototypes, and field-tested applications of smart domestic environments. In addition to the discussed use cases and design principles, field-testing resulted in a number of insights regarding these applications. These findings include smart domestic environments as persuasive agents; personifying the home; and that act as artful systems.

Smart domestic environments as persuasive agents

Many of the interactions between young adults and smart domestic environments involved acts of persuasion. The design principle *Time and Timing* aligns with Fogg's spark, facilitator and signal triggers for prompting behavior [6] while *Mediating ambiguity* and *Guidance and accountability* often dealt with in situ nudging [12] and implementing incentive structures. Nudging through the use of calls-to-action was prevalent across the entire paper prototyping population, speaking to the *Keep Me on Task* use case. The use of media, such as remote audio, to manipulate environmental aesthetics for a more conducive creative atmosphere pervaded instances of the *Promote Making* use case. Such manipulation can be viewed as a persuasive method for sustaining activity. Instances of persuasive interaction for the *Self-Improvement* use case also included nudging, and in some cases, manipulation of environmental conditions. In addition, the use of digital media tutorials deployed *in situ* permeated many of the personal goals falling under this use case.

The work of [22] aptly demonstrates the potential dangers of prompts and incentives. Like them, we mistrust a future in which residents mindlessly move from one prompt to the next, incentivized by rewards like media access. We do find the question of how a smart domestic environment should engage with temporality, ambiguity (either fostering it or removing it) and incentives a necessity for future research. These issues suggest a need for more nuanced relationships between domestic and persuasive technologies.

Smart domestic environments that personify the home

A finding that emerged from the deployment of our technology probes was the personification of the home. Rachel unknowingly acknowledged the transformation of her home into a social agent when she states that her house sent her the link to the "Blackbird" cover instead of referencing the agent as a computer application.

This personification of the home continued through both Rachel's and Jamie's description of their applications exerting a presence. For Rachel, this presence induced an influence akin to peer pressure, creating additional stress that spurred her to practice playing guitar. Jamie, however, perceived the system as a roommate, encouraging her to engage in her real world activities. Unlike the other two participants, Sarah did not think of her application as an agent, but as a system someone installed in her home. One area of future work is an exploration of the relationships between adherence, interaction and system personification as Sarah's experience with her application was largely negative, while Rachel and Jamie's were positive.

Smart domestic environments that act as artful systems

Finally, each of the technology probes was designed in accordance with the participant's paper prototype. While many designers argue that end users do not know what they want when asked to design a solution, we chose to build to end user specifications as a means of understanding if, how and in what ways the reality of living with their applications aligned with the designs they put to paper. We viewed the prototyping process as not only about end user creation of personalized distributed computing systems for their homes, but also as prototyping "artful systems" [28] for home life. By treating distributed computing no differently than any other resource in the home, we allowed participants to determine their own computationally augmented artful system. Through the process of co-design, participants demonstrated an ability to weave digital I/O into their built environment to create new types of organizing systems [28] populated with spatially situated augmented artifacts, responsive infrastructure and media.

However, as demonstrated, there are a number of shortcomings with these systems. First, systems could not adapt in response to participant behavior. Second, while co-design centered on creating artful systems, once installed in the homes' of participants, the systems were far from "artful" in that end users could not reconfigure them as needed to account for changes in desires and domestic routine. Third, in cases where participants developed incentives, they gravitated towards brusque interactions similar to Sarah's (rewards and punishments associated with resource accessibility, a la revoking Sarah's Facebook) that oversimplify strategies and tactics associated with motivating behavior change. Further exploration into the role of incentives relating to these systems is another trajectory for future work. Collectively, these challenges introduce new opportunities for machine learning and context awareness, end user tools for both long term planning and improvisation, and reflective tools that allow residents to better wield computational systems as part of their artful systems. As such future work proceeds, we expect the boundary conditions for prototyping to adapt, with residents perceiving different use cases.

CONCLUSIONS

We have presented a CDR approach for exploring the role of smart domestic environments in support of goal-oriented domestic practices of young adults. Through this process, residents made prototypes they perceived as not only supporting their daily home life, but also fostering behavior change. From these studies we derived use cases and design principles that foster setting and achieving personal goals. Many emergent interactions aligned with previous work in persuasive technologies. A number of insights also emerged on how residents perceived the presence of their prototypes.

Through these contributions, we demonstrate the use of CDR as an approach for examining home life and domestic technologies. Our work is another step towards articulating the rationale and interactional qualities that mediate relationships between residents and smart domestic environments. Sociocultural, economic and life stage factors may introduce new, interesting stratifying criteria for replicating this study's methodology. Additional, longitudinal field tests of technology probes could prove useful in understanding topics such as novelty bias, use life cycles and the potential for fostering healthy, happier and more productive lives.

REFERENCES

1. Beaudouin-Lafon, M. and Mackay, W. Prototyping tools and techniques. *The human-computer interaction handbook: fundamentals, evolving technologies and emerging applications*, Lawrence Erlbaum Associates, NY, USA, 2007.
2. Burleson, W., Ruffenach, C., Jensen, C., Bandaru, U and Muldner, K. Game as life - life as game. In *Proc IDC 2009*, ACM Press, 272-273.
3. Cialdini, R. *Influence: The psychology of persuasion (Revised ed.)*, Harper Press, New York, NY, USA, 2006.

4. Crabtree, A., and Rodden, T. Domestic routines and design for the home. *Computer Supported Cooperative Work (CSCW)*, *13*(2), (2004) 191-220.

5. Elliot, K., Neustaedter, C., and Greenberg, S. Using location to embed technology into the social practices of home In *Proc TIE 2007,* ACM Press, (2007), 79-86.

6. Fogg, B. Persuasive Technologies: *Using Computers to Change What We Think and Do*. Morgan Kaufman, CA, USA, 2002.

7. Foland, A., and Lewicka, M. Psi-Map: Psychological method for psycho-cartographic research. In *Poster 10th EU Congress of Psychology,* SPA Press (2007).

8. Hayes, G. The relationship of action research to human-computer interaction. *ACM Transactions on Computer-Human Interaction 18,* 3 (2011) 15.

9. Hornecker, E. and Nicol, E. What do lab-based user studies tell us about in-the-wild behavior?: Insights from a study of museum interactives. In *Proc DIS 2012, ACM Press* (2012), 358-367.

10. Hutchinson, H., Mackay, W., Westerlund, B., Bederson, B., Druin, A., Plaisant, C. and Eiderbäck, B. Technology probes: inspiring design for and with families. In *Proc CHI 2005*, ACM Press (2005), 17-24.

11. Intille, S., Larson, K., Beaudin, J., Nawyn, J., Tapia, E. and Kaushik, P. A living laboratory for the design and evaluation of ubiquitous computing technologies. In *Proc CHI 2005*, (2005), 1941-1944.

12. Kalnikaite, V., Rogers, Y., Bird, J., Villar, N., Bachour, K., Payne, S. and Kreitmayer, S. How to nudge in Situ: designing lambent devices to deliver salient information in supermarkets. In *Proc UbiComp 2013,* ACM Press (2013), 11-20.

13. Kidd C., Orr, R., Abowd, G., Atkeson, C., Essa, I., MacIntyre, B., Mynatt, E., Starner, T. and Newstetter, W. The aware home: A living laboratory for ubiquitous computing research. In *Cooperative buildings. Integrating information, organizations, and architecture*. Springer (1999) 191-198.

14. Koskinen, I., Zimmerman, J., Binder, T., Redstrom, J., and Wensveen, S. *Design research through practice: From the lab, field, and showroom*. Morgan Kaufman, MA, USA 2011.

15. Little, B., Salmela-Aro, K. and Phillips, S. (2007). *Personal project pursuit: Goals, actions and human flourishing (1st ed.)*. Lawrence Erlbaum Associates, NY, USA 2007.

16. Mateas, M., Salvador, T., Scholtz, J. and Sorensen, D. Engineering ethnography in the home. In *Proc CHI 1996,* ACM Press (1996), 283-284.

17. Mennicken, S., Scott, J., Brush, A. and Roseway, A. Finding roles for interactive furniture in homes with EmotoCouch. In *Proc Ubicomp 2014,* ACM Press (2014), 923-930.

18. Muller, M. PICTIVE—an exploration in participatory design. In *Proc CHI 1991*, ACM Press (1991), 225-231.

19. Neustaedter, C. and Brush, A. LINC-ing the family: The participatory design of a family calendar. In *Proc CHI 2006,* ACM Press (2006), 141-150.

20. Nurmi, J. Age differences in adult life goals, concerns, and their temporal extension: A life course approach to future-oriented motivation. *International Journal of Behavioral Development*, *15*(4), (1992) 487-508.

21. Pousman, Z., Romero, M., Smith, A. and Mateas, M. Living with tableau machine: A longitudinal investigation of a curious domestic intelligence. In *Proc Ubicomp.* ACM Press (2008), 370-379.

22. Purpura, S., Schwanda, V., Williams, K., Stubler, W. and Sengers, P. Fit4life: The design of a persuasive technology promoting healthy behavior and ideal weight. In *Proc CHI 2011.* ACM Press, (2011), 423-432.

23. Rowan, J. and Mynatt, E. Digital family portrait field trial: Support for aging in place. In *Proc CHI 2005,* ACM Press (2005), 521-530.

24. Salmela-Aro, K., Aunola, K. and Nurmi, J. E. Personal Goals During Emerging Adulthood: A 10-Year Follow Up. *Journal of Adolescent Research*, *22*(6), (2007) 690-715.

25. Schwartz, T., Stevens, G., Jakobi, T., Denef, S., Ramirez, L., Wulf, V., & Randall, D. (2014). What People Do with Consumption Feedback: A Long-Term Living Lab Study of a Home Energy Management System. *Interacting with Computers,* (2014) 1-26.

26. Sellen, A., Harper, R., Eardley, R., Izadi, S., Regan, T., Taylor, A. and Wood, K. HomeNote: Supporting situated messaging in the home. In *Proc CSCW 2006* ACM Press (2006), 383-392.

27. Taylor, A., Harper, R., Swan, L., Izadi, S., Sellen, A. and Perry, M. Homes that make us smart. *Personal and Ubiquitous Computing 11*, 5, (2007) 383-393.

28. Taylor, A. and Swan, L. Artful systems in the home. In *Proc CHI 2005*. ACM Press, (2005), 641-650.

29. Venkatesh, A. (1996). Computers and other interactive technologies for the home. *Communications of the ACM*, *39*(12), 47-54.

30. Wang, C. and Burris, M. Photovoice: Concept, methodology, and use for participatory needs assessment. *Health education & behavior 24,* 3 (1997), 369-387.

31. Westerlund, B., Lindqvist, S., and Sundblad, Y. (2003, September). Co-designing with and for Families. In *Proc COST269*, (2003), 290-294.

uCap: An Internet Data Management Tool For The Home

Marshini Chetty[1], Hyojoon Kim[2], Srikanth Sundaresan[3], Sam Burnett[2], Nick Feamster[4], and W. Keith Edwards[2]
[1]University of Maryland, College Park, marshini@umd.edu
[2]Georgia Institute of Technology, {joonk; keith}@gatech.edu, sburnett@google.com
[3] International Computer Science Institute, srikanth@icsi.berkeley.edu
[4]Princeton University, feamster@cs.princeton.edu

ABSTRACT
Internet Service Providers (ISPs) have introduced "data caps", or quotas on the amount of data that a customer can download during a billing cycle. Under this model, Internet users who reach a data cap can be subject to degraded performance, extra fees, or even temporary interruption of Internet service. For this reason, users need better visibility into and control over their Internet usage to help them understand what uses up data and control how these quotas are reached. In this paper, we present the design and implementation of a tool, called *uCap*, to help home users manage Internet data. We conducted a field trial of *uCap* in 21 home networks in three countries and performed an in-depth qualitative study of ten of these homes. We present the results of the evaluation and implications for the design of future Internet data management tools.

Author Keywords
Data caps; bandwidth caps; home networking tools

ACM Classification Keywords
H.5.m. Information interfaces and presentation (e.g., HCI): Miscellaneous.

INTRODUCTION
Internet service providers (ISPs) are instituting a variety of policies to discourage heavy use to cope with network congestion [10]. One of the more prevalent—and controversial—policies is to impose a data cap on a subscriber; such a cap limits on the amount of data that a customer can consume during a billing cycle. A user who exceeds the cap can face higher usage fees, degraded performance, and even disruption of service [3,12]. Many ISPs around the world already impose data caps on their subscribers [25]. There is even some speculation that the Internet may now be subject to pricing tiers [19], a practice already present in larger "backbone" ISPs in the Internet core [33]. Data caps and other forms of usage-based pricing have angered consumers [27]. For example, Comcast, a major United States (US) ISP, announced in May 2014 that it would institute "data caps" on all of its customers, and later withdrew the announcement after public backlash. More importantly, data caps have highlighted the fact that users have no idea about how much data they are using, let alone how to manage their Internet data usage.

CHI 2015, April 18-23, 2015, Seoul, Republic of South Korea.
Copyright 2015 ACM 978-1-4503-3145-6/15/04...$15.00.
http://dx.doi.org/10.1145/2702123.2702218

Specifically, users need more visibility into and control over how the applications they use consume their available data budgets. Without better tools, users cannot manage how (and when) data-hungry applications such as video, automated backup, and other cloud-based services use the network [15] and can sometimes make decisions that have more serious ramifications, such as forgoing critical software updates simply because they might consume a large (or unknown) amount of data [20].

In this paper, we report on the user-centered design, implementation, and evaluation of *uCap*, a data cap management system that we deployed in 21 home networks in three countries (South Africa, India, and the United States). In addition to the empirical measurements that we gathered from these homes reported in Grover *et al.* [14], we performed a qualitative study in ten of the homes to evaluate which aspects of the tool users found most effective. *uCap* runs directly on a user's home router. It provides real-time visibility into and control over network traffic usage in the home. *Visibility* exposes the websites, devices (and by proxy users) that are sending and receiving large amounts of data, and when they are doing so. *Control* allows a user to actually do something about data usage such as by limiting the amount of data a particular device might be able to send. We present three contributions: (1) we introduce a tool for Internet data management in home networks, (2) we present the results of the *uCap* field trial, and (3) we discuss implications for the design of future tools of this nature.

Designing and implementing *uCap* presented many challenges, the most significant of which involved developing a *usable* system on an extremely resource-constrained device. Most home routers have a fraction of the memory and processing power of a "normal" computer and thus cannot support arbitrarily sophisticated monitoring capabilities or elaborate user interfaces. To cope with these constraints, we designed a system that placed only critical functions on the home router and offloaded more complex functions to a separate software system. This system interfaced with the router and permitted the necessary visibility into data usage and control over Internet traffic, yet offloaded the more expensive operations such as analysis of traffic data and presentation of data in a graphical user interface. This design decision introduced more latency, making it more challenging to offer users real-time feedback and introducing a design tradeoff.

Our field trial of *uCap* suggests users desire more information about how ISPs implement usage-based policies and that the additional visibility that *uCap* provides often gives users a much richer understanding about the applications and devices that consume data on the network. We also found that users generally did not use *uCap* to control the usage of different devices; instead, they relied on social mechanisms to do so. Additionally, in contrast to our expectations about users' desire for privacy of Internet data, we discovered that many wanted more fine-grained information about usage (*e.g.*, the specific application that was consuming traffic, as opposed to just the Internet destination). Overall, our study results imply that users are receptive to Internet data management tools, but the designs can be improved to better fit into the home environment. With Internet pricing mechanisms in flux, our results suggest that developing usable tools that provide consumers visibility and control over their Internet usage is an important area with a rich set of HCI research problems.

BACKGROUND AND RELATED WORK

Various forms of *data caps*, also known as bandwidth or usage caps, exist around the world [25,26]. Many ISPs in US are implementing usage-based pricing [32]; in South Africa, *all* service plans had data caps through the end of 2010 [2]. Caps range from as little as 1–2 GB per billing cycle to several hundred GB. ISPs may enforce caps by degrading (or terminating) a user's connection when they have exceeded the usage cap or by imposing additional fees [18]. Caps that cut users off from the Internet are typically called "hard caps"; other caps are often called "soft caps".

Researchers have demonstrated that users adapt depending on how bandwidth is priced [30,31]. Sen *et al.* performed a study of time-dependent pricing and allowed users to schedule activities depending on the price of bandwidth (*e.g.*, deferring data-intensive activities to off-peak hours). They found that users were often willing to reschedule activities when data prices were cheaper. Instead of experimenting with alternative pricing schemes, *uCap* provides users with better visibility and control over how applications and devices can make efficient use of their *existing* service plans. Rather than requiring users to interact via a single client device, *uCap* runs on the home router and thus can help users monitor and control usage from *all* devices in the home network. Sambasivan *et al.* displayed the cost of accessing a link in search results to mobile Internet users in Ghana, allowing users to choose whether to click a link based on its cost and their current data balance. This work provided information about pricing for a single mobile device; *uCap* provides information about usage across an entire home network.

uCap applies insights from our previous study of users' experiences with managing data caps in the home [3]. This study highlighted the need for a tool that helps users manage an ISP data cap by tracking usage and identifying the devices, online activities, and users that consume the most data and controlling their usage. Yet, merely demonstrating the need for such a tool does not solve the problem of *creating* a useful one. A usable data cap management tool must grapple with issues of privacy in the home [22]; the flexibility and fine-grained control that the system could provide vs. the risk of distracting users with minutia like bits and bytes [8]; coping with continually changing requirements and usage patterns; and accounting for users of varying technical abilities to both understand the information presented and implement effective usage controls [29]. Such a system must also help users visualize and control "invisible" data consumers, such as automated applications and services that consume data in the background, without the user's knowledge [14].

uCap takes advantage of several trends: (1) the shift towards providing users more control over their home networks, (2) the open-sourcing of software for home routers, and (3) the ability to implement complex network functions in separate network control programs. First, to address various problems users have managing their networks [7,13,15], different systems have addressed problems related to device configuration [34], congestion [4], performance, and access control [5,17,24]. Yet, none of these systems address network management problems related to managing data usage in the face of data caps. Second, the rise of open-source software—specifically OpenWrt [35]—for home routers has made it possible to write software that dramatically improves the monitoring and control capabilities of these (resource constrained) devices. Third, the rise of Software Defined Networking (SDN) [9] and associated software—including OpenFlow-controlled software switches such as Open vSwitch [28] that can run on home routers—makes it possible to implement complex monitoring and control functions and integrate them with elaborate interfaces.

UCAP DESIGN AND IMPLEMENTATION

The conclusions from our prior work [3] provided the initial requirements for a data cap management system. Using those guidelines as a starting point, we performed a user-centered design of *uCap* from June 2011 to June 2012.

System Design

Although home routers provide an ideal location for performing both monitoring and control, they are also underpowered and thus introduce significant constraints. For example, a typical NetGear router might have 16 MB of flash storage, 512 KB of RAM, and a 500 MHz processor, making it considerably more resource constrained than even a smartphone. There are some trends that suggest movements towards more powerful home routers (e.g., Comcast's recent acquisition of SkyDog [21]) but these vendors compete on price and have little incentive to create more powerful devices in the short term. Such constraints presented us with some serious choices concerning design tradeoffs: we wanted a responsive, usable, intuitive interface that could operate on a commodity home router.

SDN helped us navigate this tradeoff. Briefly, SDN allows a network device (in this case, the home router) to be controlled by a high-level software program that *runs as a separate control system, typically on a separate device.* Separating the router's forwarding behavior from its control logic and interfaces allowed us to separate the more complex logic and interface code from the router itself. This design choice did result in more delays between the control systems and the router (and slightly slower responsiveness), but it enabled us to design an interface and control system that would not have been possible on the router itself.

Rather than run a controller in each home, we ran a single controller at a central location that managed the logic and front-end interfaces for all deployed routers. This decision made it easier for us to deploy the system in homes, since deployment only required installing a home router, as opposed to an additional server. We ensured that if a user's router loses connectivity to the controller, the router would forward traffic normally, to ensure that connectivity problems or controller malfunction do not interfere with the user's Internet connectivity. More details on the technical implementation are described in Kim *et al.* [16], and all of our code is available on GitHub.

Interface Design

We iterated on the system architecture based on feedback on an initial prototype from network experts at a major conference and an HCI event held at our institution [11,16]. For example, we changed the front-end technologies and back-end communication to improve implementation efficiency. We found that users liked the real-time data usage information and seeing a bar chart of their devices' data usage against the device's data cap as well as numeric values of data usage. Potential users also told us that they enjoyed setting and seeing the immediate effects of caps on devices. Once we had a working data tracking and control system, we iterated on interface design ideas from our previous work [3] and this prototype.

We created a series of sketches and higher-fidelity mockups for uCap. Networking and HCI experts performed a heuristic evaluation of these designs in several design-critique sessions. We found that tracking data usage for and setting limits on individual users would require too many changes to the way users currently get online in the home (e.g., requiring all users to use a login mechanism prior to using the Internet). Thus, we shifted our focus to tracking and controlling devices, domain names, and overall household usage, rather than individual users. We also received feedback on how to improve the overall interaction design, such as placing all the control information in one tab and placing real-time and historical data usage information in separate tabs. We used this feedback to create our final system, *uCap* (a play on "you set the caps"), which allows users to monitor data usage and set mini-caps on home networked devices.

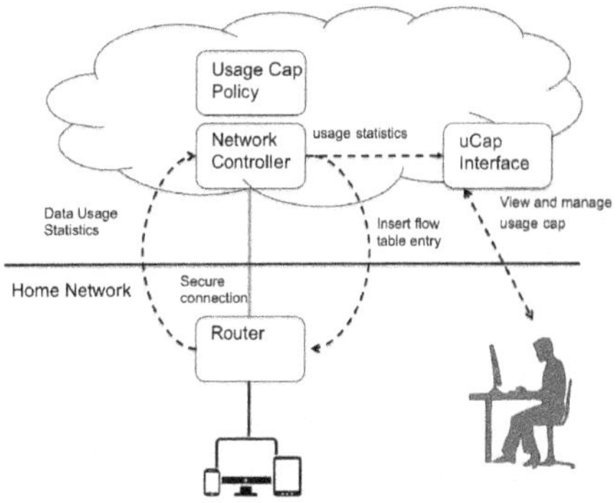

Figure 1. Implementation: Separating control logic and interface from the resource constrained router.

Implementation

We implemented the uCap interface in HTML5 and JavaScript; the router runs custom firmware based on OpenWrt [35]; this firmware runs an OpenFlow-enabled software switch that exchanges both traffic statistics and control messages with an SDN controller that is based on Pyretic [23]. As shown in Figure 1, the router collects the data, aggregates traffic data at a one-minute granularity, and sends reports to a controller that maintains usage statistics and implements controls according to policies that the user sets. A user interacts with the front-end webpage to monitor usage patterns and set usage policies through a webpage that communicates the resulting policies with the controller. If a user sets a usage cap for a specific home device, uCap tracks the cap and prevents a device from accessing the network if it exceeds its cap.

Although the statistics we collect anonymize most destinations for user traffic, uCap helps users track their usage to popular sites by "whitelisting" destinations that are in the Alexa top 100 sites in the United States (excluding pornographic and spam sites) [1]. Users can add or remove sites from this list. uCap only tracks the second-level domain for each site. For example, uCap monitors usage to *.google.com, but not finer-grained information about traffic to "subdomains" (*e.g.*, mail.google.com). We logged all user-initiated actions in the uCap system to help us study how users interact with the system.

To protect user privacy, uCap hashes the second half of each device's Media Access Control (MAC) address with a cryptographic hash that is based on a unique key on the router. The router maintains a mapping between the original and hashed MAC addresses, but it only communicates with the controller using the hashed (*i.e.*, anonymized) MAC addresses of the devices; the router never stores the actual device MAC addresses.

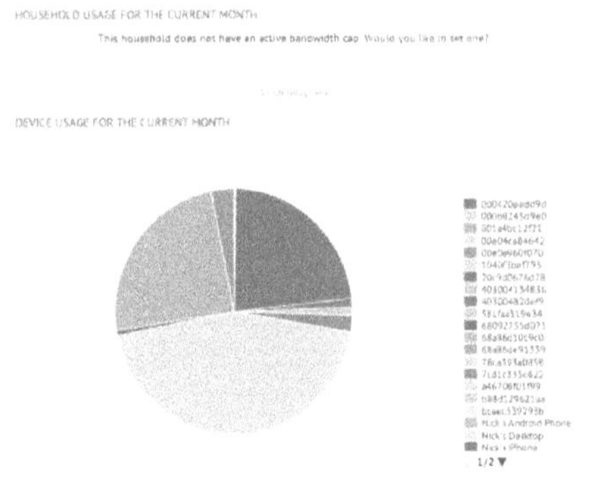

Figure 2. Household and device usage for current month.

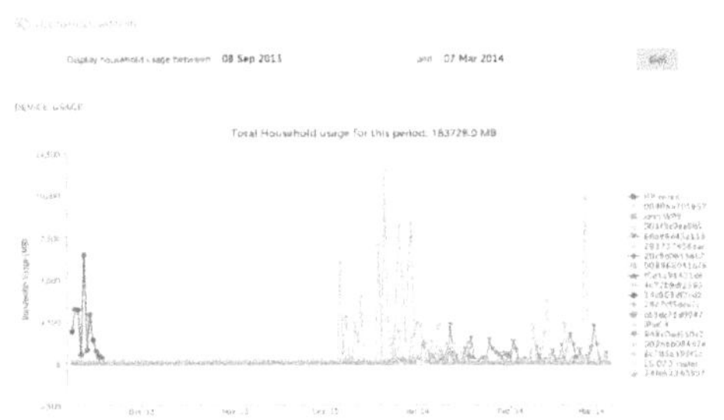

Figure 3. Monthly usage history timeline per-device.

Figure 4. Per-device usage and cap settings.

uCap Features

Overall Household Usage: Users first need to understand how the household is consuming data, in near real time. Once users log into *uCap*, they land on a *Network Tab* by default. As seen in Figure 2, in the *Overview* part of this tab, we provide users with a bar graph of the percentage of the total household data cap used to date. The bar reflects cumulative usage from the start of the billing cycle (or the start of the month, if the billing cycle is unspecified) and updated in real time. The data usage resets at the beginning of the billing cycle. This tab also shows a pie chart illustrating each device's contribution to overall data usage.

A user can set billing cycle information, household cap, and time zone in the *Network Manager* tab. When the household usage reaches the cap, the bar is colored red. We do not enforce the household cap because *uCap* may not be exactly aligned with the ISP's tracking system, and we did not want to prevent users from using the Internet.

Data Usage of Devices and Online Activities: Once users know the overall trends of data usage, they need to see specific information about data usage of devices and online activities in real time and over time so that they can adjust their usage patterns. Thus, in *uCap*, in the *Network Tab,* a list of devices currently online on the home network is always visible. When a user clicks on a device, he or she is taken to a page for that particular device. This screen shows the amount of data used by the device in real time in megabytes (MB). If a user sets a usage cap for a specific device, the percentage of usage towards the cap is shown as a bar graph. When the device reaches or exceeds the specified cap, this bar is colored red. Users can also choose to set a notification threshold (*e.g.*, 50%, 80%). If device usage reaches this percentage of the cap, *uCap* sends the user a warning. Finally, users can rename their devices (*e.g.*, "Jack's laptop") and personalize each device's avatar.

uCap also provides a historical view of usage in a *History & Status Tab,* as shown in Figure 3, which allows a user to view data usage by devices on the home network over time. The usage is shown as a line graph over the default period of the last week. Users can also select any date range over which to view their data and choose which devices to visualize. The page also shows top ten domains responsible for the most data usage in the selected date range.

Controls to Set Device Specific Data Caps: To effect change over data usage, *uCap* allows users to set mini-caps on devices on their home network and our system enforces these caps. In the *Network Tab->Manager,* shown in Figure 4, the user sees a list of devices on the home network and each device's current data usage in real time. Users can set caps on the devices and remove the caps for one or multiple devices at a time. Existing caps can also be enabled or disabled. If a device reaches a cap set by the user, it is blocked from accessing the Internet. The users can still access the *uCap* website even if they are capped to allocate more data to devices or disable the cap. On the *History & Status* Tab, users can see a log of all device caps that were set or removed over the selected date range.

Users can personalize their profiles in a *Settings* Tab. In a *Support* tab, *uCap* provides a help manual and allows users to both adjust system settings and send bug reports.

UCAP STUDY

Recruiting Process: We created a promotional website and Facebook page for *uCap* and a Google Forms signup page. We then publicized these sites and actively recruited participants via Facebook, Twitter, mailing lists, broadband forums, and our contact networks. We attempted to recruit

#	Household Composition	Annual Household Income (USD)	# Internet Enabled Devices	Cost	Cap (GB)	Location	Approx. Length of Participation in Study
H1	Male [UX research] (25-34)	$35K-$50K	>10	~$62	250	US	15 months
H2	Male [CTO of ISP] (35-44) & partner	Undisclosed	>10	~$48	300	US	19 months
H3	Female [Research Scientist] (35-44) & two children	$50K-$75K	9	~$40	40	US	16 months
H4	Male [Grad student] (25-34) & partner	$50K-$75K	>10	~$47	U	US	19 months
H5	Male [Grad student] (25-34) & 3 roommates	$100K-125K	9	~$90	300	US	19 months
H6	Male [Research manager] (35-44) & wife	$100K-125K	>10	~$32	75	IN	3 months
H7	Male [IT engineer] (25-34) & wife	Undisclosed	7	~$110	U	ZA	11 months
H8	Male [Technician] (18-24), mother & brother	<$8K	7	~$49	U	ZA	4 months
H9	Male [IT support] (18-24), mother, aunt, & sister	<$8K	6	~$66	U	ZA	11 months
H10	Male [IT manager] (25-34) and wife	>$25K	7	~$50	130	ZA	4 months

Table 1. Participant Demographics (occupation, age range and household members, Cost is self-reported and may include Internet and phone costs, line rental, and bundles per month, U is uncapped, US is USA, IN is India, ZA is South Africa).

more technical users who could easily install the *uCap*-enabled router and who were already interested in their home networks, regardless of whether they had a data cap. By focusing first on this demographic, we could work on the design of the system itself, with our ultimate goal being to extend this work to the general population. We also looked for participants in multiple geographic locations to determine whether different Internet environments affect *uCap* use. Although this approach yielded fewer users in any single country, it provided more diversity in the types of environments we could study.

We recruited 21 households: 13 in United States, 6 in South Africa, and one in India. Ten of these households also participated in an in-depth qualitative study. These participants used *uCap* between June 2012 and February 2014, some over the entire period and some for parts of the period. After we gained informed consent from participants' entire households, we mailed them a router with instructions on how to swap it for their existing router (or, in South Africa, to plug it in behind their existing ADSL router).[1] When participants received and installed their routers, we created *uCap* accounts for them and showed them how to use the system. All participants were compensated with the router.

Privacy Challenges: uCap's collection of personal information introduces challenges related to privacy. To mitigate risk, all of our data collection and consent processes were reviewed by our institution's review board. The lengthy consent process and user anxiety about data collection made it difficult to recruit a large sample of users. We expect future studies involving collection of user data in home networks to face similar challenges.

Method: All ten households that participated in the qualitative study completed a demographic survey and a pre-study survey about their Internet usage habits, their service plan, and their experience with data caps. We interviewed participants both before and after they used *uCap* and had them complete a post-study survey about their experiences. The final interviews focused on how participants used *uCap* and their experiences with monitoring data usage. All interviews were conducted over Skype and audio-recorded. We also logged all user-initiated actions on the *uCap* website and collected per-device usage information, as well as data usage of whitelisted websites.

We transcribed all pre- and post- study interviews and used a thematic inductive analysis to find the themes across the data [6]. The primary author performed the initial analysis, and the themes were discussed with the research team to arrive at a consensus. We also performed a triangulated analysis, comparing measured network usage and interaction with *uCap* to the users' reports of their behavior.

Participants: Table 1 summarizes the participant demographics. We had a mix of household types (couples, one single person, and families), but the primary person we interacted with and interviewed was typically a (male) head of the household who had a technical background. Four households had an unlimited service plan, and six households had a bandwidth cap.

FINDINGS

We discuss users' desires for a data cap management tool prior to using *uCap*, the results of the field trial, and users' privacy concerns about Internet data management tools. We did not observe any significant differences between countries; capped and uncapped users had different concerns, as we explain below.

[1] Because the South African users did not necessarily use the router as their main router, not all of their home devices may have connected to the network via this router. As such, uCap's measurements of their data usage may not have been as accurate as for the US users.

Before uCap: Desires for a Data Cap Management Tool

Our participants all reported using the Internet regularly in the interviews and surveys for email, work activities, and entertainment including either gaming, file sharing, and downloading or streaming movies and music. Echoing some findings from our earlier study [6], they all struggled to understand their data usage over the course of the month, what activities and which devices were using up data on their networks and desired more *control* over data usage.

Generally, participants signed up to use *uCap* to gain more insight into their data usage, beyond what was available to them already via their ISP or existing tools. Some used *uCap* to learn more about data usage of various devices and applications. Users sometimes wanted to ensure that devices or websites were not consuming excessive data. In other cases, users wanted to know more about the relative costs of comparable services. For instance, one household (H4) mentioned they wished to compare usage of two streaming services, HBO versus NetFlix, to determine which was worth the subscription fee.

Users with "hard caps" wanted to use *uCap* to see why they were exceeding their quota. Households that had used previous tracking tools (7 of the 10 in the study) wanted to see how *uCap* compared to these tools, particularly since setting up tracking often involved significant effort or time investment. For instance, H8 developed his own monitoring tool to show him graphs of data usage in his home. Others experimented with existing tools such as NetWorx (H9) but found that these tools were only able to track one PC not other devices such as an Xbox [36] or experienced issues installing the tools on machines used for work (H6). Only one household (H5) had previously used a router-based tool to monitor data usage. Users noted that existing tools were difficult to set up, did not provide adequate visualization, or did not present per-device usage.

To sum up, all participants expressed a desire to track their data usage and most had tried to use existing tools but found these tools were lacking in terms of either setup or the information and control that the tool offered.

Lack of Transparency into ISP Policies and Accounting

Our participants also complained about the lack of transparency that ISPs provide into data usage. For instance, H8 told us that his ISP profiles "heavy" users to determine how to shape users connections including those on unlimited plans. However, this profiling was not transparent, making it difficult for the user to trust the ISP: "*They also implemented a threshold for a week period: They used to have a threshold, every seven days which was for my account 20 Gigs in seven days. If you pass that you get warning. Now they work on a 5 star system. Depending on network load and your usage, it figures out your star [rating] as well as what shaping moves to apply to your account.*"

Five households (H2, H5, H6, H8, and H9) discussed using their ISPs' websites to check aggregate use but also commented on how these tools did not satisfy their needs. For example, H2 lamented: "*I don't feel like I have a lot of control in that situation. Because all they just say is a net number and I don't know where it's coming from and if I go over the number and I am charged, I don't really have a lot of control on that.*" Participants often did not trust the accuracy of ISP tools because they did not give details at a fine level of granularity; for example, they lacked a daily usage breakdown. In one case, H5 reached the usage quota and checked the router's logs to better understand the usage patterns: "*There was one day a few months ago where we ended up blowing through the bandwidth cap and when we checked on the router, the router said that we had consumed something like 80 gigs in a part 24 hour period, which, given our speeds, I don't think was actually possible.*"

Others questioned whether ISPs have an incentive to notify them about whether they are going over the cap because many ISPs collect "overage charges" when the usage cap is exceeded. Some simply did not understand how or when ISPs would enforce the caps. An example of this concern is expressed by H1 who talked specifically about running way over the cap and not feeling any consequences: "*They haven't actually been enforcing it. So I have been definitely passing over a terabyte a month sometimes and yet I've not received a few notifications.*"

Some participants worried about whether they had subscribed to the right data plan and whether a data cap would affect them. For instance, H4 wanted to make sure that the household would be within the cap: "*I really had no way of knowing how much I should be signing up for and what plan I should be signing up.*" In some cases, participants wanted to know if they could switch to a cheaper plan or decrease costs by sharing the connection with others: "*I live in a fairly small apartment building and I have a neighbor upstairs and one of the things I've been wondering was whether or not we could share Internet.*" (H3)

Thus, before using *uCap*, participants expressed a strong desire for transparency into how ISPs track and enforce the cap, a distinct distrust in ISPs in general, and doubt about how to pick the service plan that best suits their needs.

uCap Usage in the Field Trial

Table 2 shows the number of times each participant accessed *uCap* during the study, according to our logs. This usage is slightly lower than the usage reported on the surveys but from both data sources, it appears that users accessed the web interface infrequently. Yet, all but one of the households (H3) told us that they found the information on *uCap* to be helpful and that they actively used the system when they wanted more information on data usage (much like one checks a bank statement).

In particular, self-identified "heavy" users who faced the possibility of exceeding their usage caps used *uCap* regularly. For instance, when their ISP notified them that they would enforce the cap in December 2013, H5 turned to *uCap*: "*Since then we've been monitoring our usage on uCap pretty closely and obviously uCap had months of data prior to December of last year and so we were sort of comparing the numbers over the summer 2013 of Comcast versus uCap*". The exception, H3, felt that the system was not helpful because her household was not hitting its cap. In another case, an OpenWrt bug causing instability in Wi-Fi connections led to one participant (H6) to stop using *uCap* altogether, even though this household found *uCap* helpful.

	# Logs	Estimated Use	Actual Use (uCap)
H1	112	1 TB	916 GB
H2	21	40-50 GB	72 GB
H3	9	-	-
H4	39	80-100 GB	105 GB
H5	19	400-450 GB	529 GB
H6	7	50-60 GB	66 GB
H7	4	-	-
H8	9	-	-
H9	11	-	-
H10	5	-	-

Table 2. *uCap* Usage Logs and Estimated vs. Actual Monthly Data Usage Per Household.

All participants said that they found the system was easy to install, since enabling *uCap* merely entailed replacing the home router and did not require other configuration changes to the network or devices. H1's quote summarizes the collective positive feedback on why our participants found it helpful: "*I don't think that anything else has provided that level of transparency to home networks*."

Another quote suggests the type of use envisioned for *uCap* beyond the study period by H4: "*I anticipate that I'm going to keep using it. Kind of more infrequently that I used to. Just checking in maybe once every few weeks.*" He emphasized: "*So it's the kind of tool I really liked having. I can see it becoming an invaluable resource for me.*"

Many participants asked for a version of *uCap* for mobile devices that provided more options for push notifications about data usage. Overall, *uCap* was well received.

Tracking Overall Household Usage and Learning Patterns

Most participants told us that they found tracking the overall household data usage useful for learning patterns of use. For example, in a quote typical of those we heard, H1 explains: "*So I was actually kind of surprised with how much data I was using. I posted it on some of my social media accounts. I was like check it out guys I'm using over a terabyte a month.*"

For the half of our households that used *uCap* as their primary router—for which we also had a self-reported estimate of monthly data usage—we calculated the actual monthly data usage (Table 2). Interestingly, all of these five households gave fairly accurate estimates of monthly data usage. For households H2, H5, and H6, we suspect that this is because they had used previous tools to track their usage. Others may simply be well-informed, or it may be that *uCap* gave them more awareness about their usage.

Participants were sometimes confused because the real-time data and the historical data were not always consistent. Two participants (H2 and H5) were worried that the usage reflected did not match up with the reported usage from their ISP. This inconsistency resulted because our real-time and historical data are tracked by two separate components, creating slightly different data counts. Furthermore, *uCap* itself consumes data, but we opted not to show this data usage because it represented a minimal 0.4% of total usage on average. For these reasons, the data usage reported by *uCap* differed slightly from the user's actual usage.

Participants also felt that the real-time usage units (GB for the household and MB for individual devices) were too coarse-grained. For example, H1 talked about how incremental changes were hard to notice and correlate with the real-time usage, since many actions such as checking email do not consume much data and were thus difficult to see on the progress bar. "*Most applications don't use the multiple gigabytes or megabytes when you're watching it. So it's hard to notice the incremental changes that smaller actions on the network do, checking emails and things like that.*"

Participants liked the pie chart showing the device breakdown in the *Network Overview Tab* but found that it became cluttered after awhile, as it continued to accumulate many unidentified devices. We did not provide a way to delete or remove transient devices (*e.g.*, those belonging to guests), but doing so would improve the user experience. For example, Grover *et al.* [14] revealed that one dominant device typically consumes the bulk of traffic in a home (60% on average), thus showing the top 5 devices may provide sufficient information to identify data "hogs".

Most participants did not mention frequently using the *Network Tab->Devices* page for individual devices. A few had tried to set notification emails but had trouble with receiving emails. Others did not realize that it was possible to set notifications. In summary, participants found household-wide tracking helpful but noticed discrepancies between the real-time and historical information. They also suggested ways to de-clutter the interface.

Tracking Device Data Usage and Starting Conversations

Participants consistently told us that they found the history view most useful for tracking individual devices' data usage. For example, H6 talked about comparing different devices' usage over time. H5 talked about how he liked *uCap*'s breakdown by MAC address and how he would use this information as a conversation starter with other household members: "*Because uCap breaks down the usage by MAC address if there was a huge spike in bandwidth, I would ask the roommate associated with that MAC address if they had done anything. And the reason for that was not to restrict them from using the Internet right. Because it becomes pointless if basically you prohibit yourself from using the Internet in the normal way.*

But the question was more to make sure that they were the ones responsible for it as opposed [to processes they are unaware of]".

Similarly, H2 described how he discovered that their overall data usage was not very high and that the data "hogs" he suspected were not using as much as they thought: "*I actually discovered my Apple TV used less data than it actually used. I was expecting it to be more chatty than it actually was. And watching movies didn't kill me as bad as I thought.*" In fact, after using *uCap*, this participant said his usage pattern changed because he was *less* worried about exceeding his usage cap. Now, he said, "*When a provider tells me that you know [you have] 300 gigs or whatever I guess. And then I do a simple calculation, then I get worried about using it. Having information saying that it really wasn't as impactful as I thought it was, it actually made me use the service more.*"

In many cases, *uCap* confirmed what users perceived about usage of specific devices before they used the tool. Many of our participants also mentioned that they discovered new and interesting things about their home network data usage patterns. A participant in H4 explains: "*Every once in a while there would be weird spikes where a particular device would use twice as much data as it had ever used before. And so there was always a little mystery with that. Usually it was just things like the device downloading updates, things like that.*".

Others said that *uCap*'s list of online devices and their usage history gave them a sense of security about whether the data cap was being abused by unauthorized users. In H7, *uCap* alerted the household to a virus: "*I was actually able to find out that my wife's laptop was infected. Actually, yes because the amount of data it was using was far more than her looking at YouTube*".

This same participant and others expressed surprise at how much data an iPad and an Android phone use. "*When you actually see how much data that device uses just when you're at home sleeping and the phone is charging. It's quite scary*". Participants also commented on how they enjoyed seeing what devices such as the Wii or Xbox used and how easy *uCap* made it to see the usage: "*It makes it a bit easier for normal home users to actually monitor all their various devices that are actually using bandwidth. So you know things like smart phones and stuff like that where you can't specifically monitor that kind of traffic without having some kind of a proxy* ". (H9)

In summary, participants found *uCap* useful for illuminating per-device usage (particularly background traffic) and the tool reassured them that trusted devices were on the network using data. Participants also suggested that showing usage by time-of-day would be helpful.

Tracking Data Usage for Online Activities

Participants had mixed feelings about the panel showing the top-ten domains using data in a month. Some users liked the information that it provided but also noticed that the "other" category reflected a lot of usage. (*uCap* categorized traffic to any destination not explicitly whitelisted as "other", since any destinations outside of the Alexa top 100 were anonymized and, hence, could not be categorized.) Others felt the top-ten domains did not tell the users much about their data usage. For example, H4 noticed NetFlix did not show up as the biggest data hog.: "*It didn't really give me as much information as I was hoping for. Like whenever I would use NetFlix, it didn't show up as coming from NetFlix, cause the data is sort of by Amazon usually, but so was a lot of other stuff on the Internet. So basically we would just end up with Amazon, 2 Gigabytes*". In fact, since NetFlix is actually hosted on a content distribution network (CDN), such as Amazon Web Services, the domain reflecting NetFlix usage would show up as amazonaws.com or akamai.com, not as netflix.com. (In fact, amazonaws.com consistently shows up in the top five most popular domains according to Grover *et al.* [14].)

Most of all, participants wanted more detail on top website and application usage, contrary to what we would have expected given privacy concerns. For example, H2 wanted a per-protocol breakdown of traffic. Others wanted usage in terms of activities such as "watching a YouTube video".

Participants liked having the ability to modify the whitelist, but some were suspicious that what was displayed was not the same as what was tracked. To sum up, participants wanted more detailed information on data usage, even at the expense of privacy. Additionally, they wanted data usage to reflect the everyday online activities they engage in to make the information easier to interpret.

Controlling Data Usage By Mediating Behavior

Interestingly, none of our participants regularly used the features to set caps on their devices. Only four of the ten (H1, H6, H7, H8) tried the capping functions at all; those four felt that imposing a "hard cap" on a device was not useful or necessary for controlling use within the home. Some suggested that capped devices be throttled instead or redirected to a page explaining what happened. Participants also told us they often used the per-device data to decide whether to start a dialogue about data usage with other household members.

In a typical example given by participants, when Apple TV was discovered not to be a data hog as suspected in H2, the participant consciously did not mention this to his partner, the primary Apple TV user: "*He watched a ton of movies on Apple TV and I thought that that would put us in jeopardy and when the number showed that it didn't, I never said anything to him about it.*" In summary, rather than relying on the system for control, users relied on conversations to manage data usage, with uCap providing a starting point to chat.

Privacy Concerns With Tracking Home Data Usage

In designing uCap to protect privacy, we inadvertently compromised usability. For example, obscuring device MAC addresses made it more difficult to identify and rename devices, and withholding certain data about per-application usage also obscured useful information.

Most participants said they did not want ISPs tracking the same data uCap collects; a few stated they only trusted the research team with the data. Some felt that the ISP should not have access to the type and number of devices a user has. Others felt the ISPs could monetize the information or charge them for using certain types of traffic. A few worried that ISPs would track illegal downloads or sell the data. Most mentioned that cloud storage presented a security threat from outsiders. For example, thieves might target households with many devices.

In particular, storing uCap data outside the home at a central location created anxiety: "*Having all your data logged on a sever, your whole usage patterns, and everything it's a bit nerve-wracking.*" (H8). H6 reflects these concerns: "*Who has access to it? And what is the control, my control over that data? And what are they using the data for?*" Users also worried about how an ISP could use the data to control usage, such as blocking traffic. Our participants had conflicting ideas about what they wanted uCap to show, notions of what data should be private, and who should have access to this data. These attitudes are striking because ISPs can *already* gather much of the data that was cause for concern. This naïveté highlights a gap between users' perceptions and discomfort about what data might be collected about them and ISPs' *current* capabilities for gathering this very data.

DISCUSSION

Our field trial showed that uCap helps users understand more about their households' data use, as well as what devices (and often by proxy, people) and activities consume network data. This visibility helped participants react to in-the-moment situations (*e.g.*, "Do I need to curb usage now?") and see trends over time. Our participants also suggested minor improvements, such as allowing users to remove devices no longer present on the network or providing more visibility into how ISPs charge for data to enable better auditing. To our surprise, participants also wanted more information about the data usage of online activities that was in direct conflict with their anxieties about keeping this data private from others and ISPs.

As the Internet of Things and a greater reliance on the cloud introduces more background traffic, and as ISPs continue to implement data caps and other pricing mechanisms [19], developing tools that help users manage their Internet data will only become more important. Given that the home network is a complex socio-technical system, these solutions must not just provide technical capabilities; they must also mesh with how people operate in home environments. For instance, our users did use *uCap* for controlling data usage, but not with the mini-caps as we expected; instead, users either self-mediated (*i.e.*, reduced usage) or mediated others' behavior with social means.

Implications for Design of Data Cap Management Tools

Placing the *uCap* controller in a central location made *uCap* easier to deploy, but users remained concerned about privacy and the granularity of the data that the tool collects. Future Internet data cap management tools should store the tracked data in the home to minimize privacy and security risks. Future tools can improve tracking online activities by providing more detail on time-of-day usage and intuitive summaries about usage of specific applications (*e.g.*, NetFlix). Doing so requires better activity characterization of web traffic in real time, which should be easier if the controller is situated in the home. It also requires better application identification mechanisms, to allow flows to be associated with "watching YouTube".

Finally, since our study focused on technically savvy users, the interface and visualizations may need to be adjusted for a more general audience in future studies. For instance, *uCap* could include cost information, as in SmartBrowse [26], or compare usage to activities that use the same amount of data (*e.g.*, "you used 1 GB of data, which is roughly one episode of a TV show"). The tool could also depict usage averages and reference points such as past consumption patterns. These mechanisms can help make the tool more accessible to a more general audience. Ultimately, the lessons from the uCap study may apply to other settings beyond the home where there are also no dedicated system administrators such as libraries and small businesses.

CONCLUSION

We presented the creation and evaluation of *uCap*, a home Internet data cap management tool. In our field trial, we found users want better ways to manage data and our participants were positive about using *uCap* to help them do so. Our findings suggest that creating tools that fit into users' everyday Internet usage patterns is difficult without extensive field trials of this nature. Future research could improve the existing interfaces we designed, address the challenges of providing detailed data usage information without compromising user privacy, and extend our work to a more general user population. Our study also emphasizes the increasing value of creating tools to provide consumers with visibility and control over Internet data usage.

ACKNOWLEDGMENTS

This work was supported by NSF Awards CNS-1059350, CNS-1346723, CNS-1405781, CNS-1422680, and a Google Focused Research Award. We thank our participants and other contributors: Victoria Ayo, Michael Dandy, Zuiena Kabir, Rebecca Rouse, Boris de Sousa, Hyewon Suh, Bethany Sumner, and Steve Woodrow.

REFERENCES

1. Alexa. Top websites in USA. http://www.alexa.com/topsites/countries/US.
2. Chetty, M., Banks, R., Bernheim Brush, A.J., Donner, J., and Grinter, R.E. Under Development: While the meter is running: computing in a capped world. *Interactions 18*, 2 (2011), 72–75.
3. Chetty, M., Banks, R., Brush, A.J., Donner, J., and Grinter, R. You're capped: understanding the effects of bandwidth caps on broadband use in the home. CHI 2012, ACM (2012), 3021–3030.

4. Chetty, M., Banks, R., Harper, R., Regan, T., Sellen, A., Gkantsidis, C., Karagiannis, T., and Key, P. Who's hogging the bandwidth: the consequences of revealing the invisible in the home. CHI 2010, ACM (2010), 659-668.
5. Chetty, M., Haslem, D., Baird, A., Ofoha, U., Sumner, B., and Grinter, R. Why is my internet slow?: making network speeds visible. CHI 2011, ACM (2011), 1889–1898.
6. Corbin, J. and Strauss, A. *Basics of Qualitative Research*. SAGE, 2008.
7. Crabtree, A., Mortier, R., Rodden, T., and Tolmie, P. Unremarkable networking: the home network as a part of everyday life. DIS 2012, ACM (2012), 554-563 .
8. Davidoff, S., Lee, M.K., Yiu, C., and Zimmerman, J. Principles of smart home control. UbiComp 2006, Springer-Verlag (2006), 19-34 .
9. Feamster, N., Rexford, J., and Zegura, E. The Road to SDN. *Queue 11*, 12 (2013), 20–40.
10. Federal Communications Commision. Policy Issues in Data Caps and Usage-Based Pricing. (2013), 1–26.
11. Georgia Institute of Technology. GVU Fall Research Showcase. 2011.
12. Government Accountability Office. Eshoo Shares Preliminary Findings of Study on Broadband Data Caps with FCC 2014. http://eshoo.house.gov/press-releases/eshoo-shares-preliminary-findings-of-study-on-broadband-data-caps-with-fcc/.
13. Grinter, R.E., Edwards, W.K., Chetty, M., et al. The ins and outs of home networking: The case for useful and usable domestic networking. *ACM TOCHI* 16, 2 (2009), 8–28.
14. Grover, S., Park, M.S., and Sundaresan, S. Peeking behind the NAT: an empirical study of home networks. IMC 2013, ACM, 377-390.
15. Kawsar, F. and Brush, A.J.B. Home computing unplugged: why, where and when people use different connected devices at home. Ubicomp 2013, ACM (2013), 627-636.
16. Kim, H., Sundaresan, S., Chetty, M., Feamster, N., and Edwards, W.K. Communicating with caps: managing usage caps in home networks. SIGCOMM 2011 Demo,ACM (2011), 470–471.
17. Yiakoumis, Y., Katti, S., Huang, T., McKeown, N., Yap, K., and Johari, R. Putting Home Users in Charge of their Network. Ubicomp 2012, ACM (2012), 1114-1119.
18. Lasar, M. *It could be worse: data caps around the world.* Ars Technica, 2011.
19. Lohr, S. *F.C.C. Is Deluged With Comments on Net Neutrality Rules*. *New York Times*, 2014. http://www.nytimes.com/2014/07/16/technology/a-deluge-of-comment-on-net-rules.html.
20. Lucey, P. How Data Caps Are Bad for Cybersecurity. http://oti.newamerica.net/blogposts/2014/how_data_caps_are_bad_for_cybersecurity-117644.
21. Lunden, I. Comcast Acquired PowerCloud Systems, Gears Up For Smart Home Play. *TechCrunch*, 2014. http://techcrunch.com/2014/07/14/comcast-skydog/.
22. Mazurek, M.L., Arsenault, J.P., Bresee, J., et al. Access Control for Home Data Sharing: Attitudes, Needs and Practices. CHI 2010, ACM (2010), 645–654.
23. Monsanto, C., Foster, N., Rexford, J., and Walker, D. Composing Software Defined Networks. NDSI 2013, ACM (2013), 1–13.
24. Mortier, R., Rodden, T., Tolmie, P., and Lodge, T. Homework: Putting interaction into the infrastructure. UIST 2012, ACM (2012), 197-206.
25. OECD. *Average data caps by country (GB) logarithmic scale, September 2012*. 2012.
26. OECD. *Prevalence of explicit bit/data caps amongst surveyed offers by country, September 2012*. 2012.
27. OToole, J. Comcast plans data caps for all customers. *CNN*, 2014. http://money.cnn.com/2014/05/15/technology/comcast-data-limits/.
28. Pfaff, B., Pettit, J., Amidon, K., Casado, M., Koponen, T., and Shenker, S. Extending Networking into the Virtualization Layer. Hotnets 2009, (2009).
29. Poole, E.S., Chetty, M., Grinter, R.E., and Edwards, W.K. More than meets the eye: transforming the user experience of home network management. DIS 2008, ACM (2008), 455–464.
30. Sambasivan, N., Lee, P., Hecht, G., and Aoki, P.M. Chale, how much it cost to browse?: results from a mobile data price transparency trial in Ghana. ICTD 2013, ACM (2013), 13-23.
31. Sen, S., Joe-Wong, C., Ha, S., and Bawa, J. When the price is right: enabling time-dependent pricing of broadband data. CHI 2013, ACM (2013), 2477-2486 .
32. Sen, S., Joe-Wong, C., Ha, S., and Chiang, M. A survey of smart data pricing: Past proposals, current plans, and future trends. *ACM Computing Surveys (CSUR)*, (2013).
33. Valancius, V., Lumezanu, C., Feamster, N., Johari, R., and Vazirani, V.V. How many tiers?: pricing in the internet transit market. SIGCOMM 2011, 194–205.
34. Yang, J., Edwards, W.K., and Haslem, D. Eden: supporting home network management through interactive visual tools. UIST 2010, ACM, 109-118.
35. OpenWRT. https://openwrt.org/.
36. NetWorx. http://www.softperfect.com/products/

Mediating Attention for Second Screen Companion Content

Timothy Neate
FIT Lab, Swansea University
Swansea, SA2 8PP UK
tdjneate@gmail.com

Matt Jones
FIT Lab, Swansea University
Swansea, SA2 8PP UK
mattjonez@gmail.com

Michael Evans
BBC R&D
Salford, M50 2LH UK
michael.evans@rd.bbc.co.uk

ABSTRACT
There is increasing interest in providing content to users on secondary devices while they watch TV. This material, termed companion content, can be anything from textual information, to interactive quiz games. It can be delivered throughout a broadcast and often directly relates to specific scenes in a show. This new scenario has exposed a challenging design space for creators of both the content and the enabling technology. A key question when introducing content on a secondary device is how much it detracts from, or enhances, the show the user is currently engaged with. To examine this, we investigated methods for mediating attention from the TV and onto a secondary device. By examining a typical use case we have been able to gain new insights into how best to design additional stimuli to alert users to companion content from both a broadcasting, and an HCI perspective.

Author Keywords
Companion content; second screens; attention; TV; Alerts

ACM Classification Keywords
H.5.m. Information Interfaces and Presentation (e.g. HCI): Miscellaneous

INTRODUCTION
Multi-screen TV experiences are becoming increasingly prevalent, whether instigated by the broadcaster or as an independent behaviour by the viewer. We might browse the web for related content on our phone or computer whilst watching TV; perhaps Googling an actor we recognise in a show when we cannot place him. However, the material we browse is not necessarily related to the content we are viewing. As described in the work of Rooksby et al. [6], this relationship between the two devices often becomes a complex web of related, semi-related, and non-related content.

A desire to leverage this dual screen interaction and enhance the user experience (UX) of TV, has led to broadcast content providers developing companion content. Regardless of the application, we believe that the design of attention across devices should be a part of the craft of TV making – primary and companion content should enhance, and not disrupt, each other. A potential innate tension in using second screens to enhance the UX of TV is the fact that content on the secondary device can clearly have a distracting effect on the attention available for the primary content. Therefore, it is crucial to understand methods by which TV producers and engineers can design and deploy companion content without detracting from the experience as a whole. Though much research has considered visual attention for TV-based scenarios, for example the recent work of Valuch et al. [9] and Vatavu et al. [10], no work has explored the notion of how we may mediate attention from the motion-rich television to the companion content. Therefore, in this paper we explore methods for attracting a user's attention between screens from an objective and subjective standpoint so that we may begin to consider how we may orchestrate companion content.

CHI 2015, April 18–23, 2015, Seoul, Republic of Korea.

ACM 978-1-4503-3145-6/15/04 ...$15.00.
http://dx.doi.org/10.1145/2702123.2702278

BROADCASTING IN AN IP WORLD
From both the production and the audience perspective, the notion of what TV broadcasting *is* is undergoing significant change. The main technical driver for this is the end-to-end use of IP networks. The UX trend is heading away from scheduled programmes that are identical for everyone. Traditional linear production of TV involves the capture of signal-based assets, from cameras, microphones and other sources, together with a live, concurrent or post-production editing and compositing phase, where those media assets are used to construct a bundled programme. This piece of content is then delivered, in an essentially identical form, for equivalent consumption by each member of the audience: the programme is an immutable block.

Conversely, IP-based broadcasting – featuring data-format agnostic bi-directional communication between audience and broadcaster is not constrained in this way. Creating and broadcasting content as a related set of media and data objects, together with curatorial decisions describing its recombination, means that TV content can be made responsive to a number of human factors and use cases. This lends itself to significant new possibilities for media experiences such as those discussed in depth by Armstrong et al. [1], but more pertinently, such methods of broadcast yield considerable possibilities for second screen experiences.

The terminology of second screens and companion content refers to a spectrum of dual screen TV use cases. Essentially, companion content is second screen material that embellishes the primary TV experience, such as factual text or interactive games. Broadcasters and the HCI community have developed numerous examples of this type of experience in recent years. Two notable examples have formed some preliminary UX considerations for this design space: a companion application for tablets to support experimental studies alongside

(a) (b) (c)

Figure 1: Examples of content and stimuli used: (a) shows an icon indicating companion content in the bottom right of the TV, (b) shows a user watching the companion content along with the show, and (c) shows this second screen content close up.

No.	Type	Description
1	Content appears	Content simply appears on tablet
2	Content shakes	Content shakes on tablet
3	Earcon	User notified with musical sound
4	Auditory icon	User notified with related sound
5	On TV	Icon appears on bottom right of TV
6	On TV & shaking	Icon shakes in bottom right of TV

Table 1: Methods used to attract the attention from the TV.

the nature programme Autumnwatch [1], and a quiz game to accompany the programme Antiques Roadshow [2].

For Autumnwatch, companion content appeared on a second screen during the TV broadcast. To explore this use case more systematically, Brown et al. [3] observed gaze across both screens while users watched this content. The findings indicate that, unlike task-based scenarios, where division of attention is divided more equally between the screens [5], users focus primarily on the TV and only intermittently pay attention to companion content. This study implied that with such a focus on the primary (TV) screen, it is critical to design for a positive second screen experience without disrupting the UX of the programme.

ATTENTION MEDIATION METHODS

The aim of this experiment was to find the best methods for getting a user's attention to transfer to the companion content in the most efficient and preferable way. To this end we developed methods and tested them in a typical scenario.

Design of Stimuli

As described in Table 1, there were 6 methods tested – one (baseline) where the content just appears on the tablet (no. 1), one animated visual method on the tablet (no. 2), two auditory methods on the tablet – an earcon (no. 3) and an auditory icon (no. 4) (both defined in [2]). Also, there were two methods that notified the participants on the TV itself by providing an icon (Figure 1a) – one stationary (no. 5), and one animated (no. 6).

We designed the shaking visual alerts on the device (no. 2) and on the TV (no. 6) to best gain attention and negate change blindness [8]. As peripheral vision is poor, in terms of acuity, but tuned to detect motion (specifically horizontal) [4] we designed them to shake diagonally to attract a user's gaze. To avoid the content going unnoticed and combat the auditory equivalent of change blindness we designed two types of auditory notifications – one totally disjunct from the sounds in the show (no 3); and a more related type (no. 4). The earcon (no. 3) featured a musical sound, which was designed to be totally different from the sounds associated with the show (natural sounds, incidental music, and presenters speaking); and, the auditory icon (no. 4) featured related sounds – for example, the sound of a river running when a fish is in shot on the TV.

METHOD

We recruited 18 participants from general staff mailing lists at the BBC. Their ages ranged from 25 to 48, with a mean of 36 (σ = 7.24), with 11 identifying as male and 7 female. Users reported an average of 2.53 hours of TV viewing per day (σ = 1.43), 16 (89%) of the participants stated that they engaged with mobile devices while watching TV, and 10 (56%) stated that they are easily distracted by other electronic devices while watching TV.

We conducted the study in a usability lab, rigged as a generic living room. The participants were in a typical scenario for such a viewing experience – sitting on a sofa in front of a 42 inch modern TV with a tablet computer (iPad 2) on their lap. As depicted in Figure 2, participants were filmed from directly in front by a camera on top of the TV, and also from above the iPad, allowing for us to make recordings of the participants and use them for analysis. The participants were first talked through the study and then asked to fill in the consent and demographics forms. They then watched the television show, which was an excerpt from Autumnwatch – similar to content used by Brown et al. [3]. During this, second screen content was introduced at 2 to 4 minute intervals to complement the programme. This content was simple images and textual information (as in Figure 1c). Each time a piece of content appeared it was accompanied by an attention mediating method (for example the content appeared on the tablet and shook). Upon completion, the user was asked to fill in a post-study questionnaire that allowed us to gauge their impressions.

[1] Autumnwatch app – http://goo.gl/hI3UJs (accessed 18/6/14)
[2] Antiques roadshow app – http://goo.gl/I1IfOj (accessed 18/6/14)

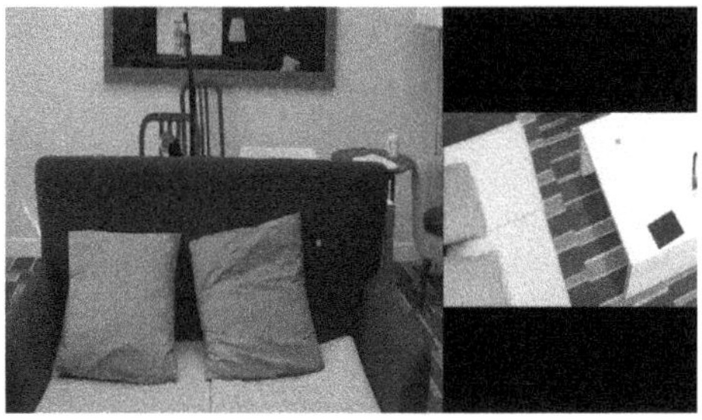

Figure 2: Camera angles used for analysis: the left side (TV mounted camera) allowed for a good view of the participant's gaze, and the right side allowed for us to determine when new content had appeared.

In terms of experimental design, we used a Latin square arrangement to ensure that the participants were exposed to the methods in a different order each time so that we could observe their effect irrespective of the content on the TV or the tablet. Reaction times were our primary objective metric. To observe these, we inspected the time between the content appearing on the tablet and each participant's attendance to it. By analysing the video (Figure 2) we could track the participants' eyes and easily infer where they were looking and at exactly what time. To ensure consistency we adhered to a strict set of criteria to classify the participants' gaze, and verified our results with a second sampled analysis, and with an external party. We then framed our objective findings by using a post-study questionnaire to gauge how much the methods got their attention and to assess what they preferred.

RESULTS

In this section we describe the objective findings (reaction times). We then discuss the participants' subjective impressions of the stimuli by analysing their ratings, and briefly discuss their comments.

Objective Analysis

Figure 3 shows that peripheral methods (on-device auditory and visual stimuli) resulted in the fastest overall reaction times from the participants, and that notifying the participants on the television resulted in the slowest. We conducted ANOVA to examine the data and found significant overall variance ($F(6,17) = 2.826$, $p = .037$). Moreover, upon conducting post-hoc tests on the stimuli conditions, we find significant differences between the Earcon and the stimuli appearing on the television, both static ($p = .001$), and shaking ($p = .020$), and also compared to the content appearing on the device ($p = .041$). Notably, a shaking alert on the iPad appears to attract attention to the tablet quicker than the non-animated cue, but the opposite occurs on the TV.

Participants' Impressions

Participants were asked to describe how well they believed different cues had performed in attracting their attention to the tablet. As shown in Table 2, 11 participants (62%) strongly agreed that the earcon was most effective at attracting their attention, followed by the auditory icon. Both were preferred to the content simply appearing without additional stimuli – significantly so for the earcon ($Z = 2.59$, $p = .005$).

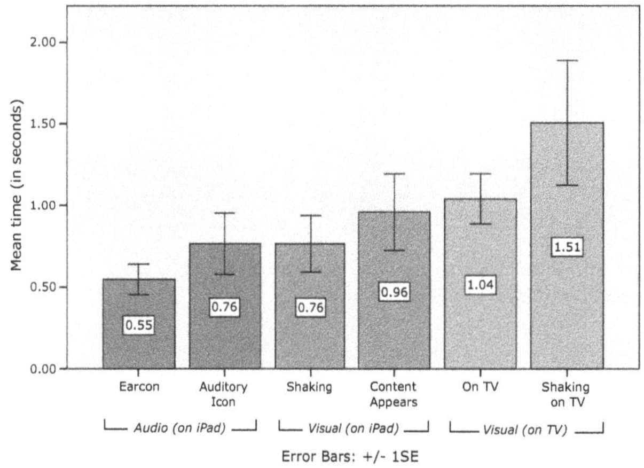

Figure 3: Participants' reaction times in ascending order.

In terms of subjective preferences, auditory icons (the sounds that related directly to the show) were most favoured, significantly more so than the content simply appearing ($Z = 2.03$, $p = .021$). Also, approval of both TV-based alerts was significantly higher than the no alert case ($Z = 2.16$, $p = .016$ and $Z = 1.86$, $p = .032$ for non-shaking and shaking respectively). Several participants noted that they used the notification on the TV to delay when they viewed second screen content, for example – "*I think the TV icon was best, I can look at the 2nd device in my own time then*".

	Missed	Strongly disagree	Disagree	Neutral	Agree	Strongly agree
Content appears	2	0	2	1	7	6
Content shakes	6	1	0	0	4	7
Earcon	4	0	0	0	3	11
Auditory Icon	3	1	0	0	5	9
On TV	3	0	3	2	3	7
Shaking on TV	4	0	1	2	3	8

Table 2: Participants' reported attention gained for each method. Darker colours indicate higher frequencies.

The uncued (content appears) case scored very poorly, and comments from the participants imply that they believed that they would miss the content if not alerted to it – "*[I] was constantly checking to see if I'd missed it.*" – "*It felt a little surprising just to discover content*". On the other hand, the highest scoring method, the auditory icon, was mostly praised because of its ability to link the show to the second screen content, for example – "*It felt [a] more sympathetic and complimentary way of identifying that more content was available.*" and "*it felt less intrusive*". Conversely, it was apparent that some participants found audio distracting in general and would have preferred more discreet methods such as vibration. Notably, we found a correlation between how much a user believed something got their attention, and how much they liked it (Spearman's $\rho = .384$, $p < .001$).

Table 3 shows that a notable proportion (39%) did not notice the notification shake on the TV. Some comments indicated that they did not notice such subtleties because their attention

	Missed	Strongly Disagree	Disagree	Neutral	Agree	Strongly agree
Content appears	2	1	6	3	4	2
Content shakes	3	0	0	9	5	1
Earcon	1	0	4	4	7	2
Auditory Icon	2	0	1	5	6	4
On TV	4	0	1	4	7	2
Shaking on TV	7	0	1	4	2	4

Table 3: Participants' reported preference for each method. Darker colours indicate higher frequencies.

had already been diverted to the tablet – "*because it happened at the same time [as the alert on the tablet] I felt unprepared. The [secondary] device caught my attention*".

DISCUSSION

Reaction time data and the subjective feedback indicate that auditory methods performed best at quickly attracting users' attention to companion content. Likely causes of this observation are: a) we process auditory information significantly faster than visual [7], b) that peripheral stimuli (in general) cause a strong disjunct from the TV show, and c) that, in the case of the earcon, its lack of ecological coherence with the TV content forms a more explicit highlighting of change in the content on the tablet. Note, however, that reaction time may not be the most important measure: the subjective data shows that not only do participants' opinions vary greatly, but also that the fastest method (the earcon) for getting attention onto the tablet is not generally as favoured as the auditory icon.

We believe there are two reasonable explanations for the notifications on the TV being the slowest: Firstly, several participants reported that they used it as a method of delaying a voluntary switch of attention. Secondly, main screen alerts attracted (and split) participants' attention first delaying a shift of attention to the second screen. Moreover, we believe that the shaking effect on the TV did not aid the participants in noticing the content on the iPad quicker was because its motion focused their gaze onto the TV and away from the tablet in their periphery.

CONCLUSIONS AND DESIGN IMPLICATIONS

This paper investigates methods for attracting attention to companion content when a user is engaged with the related TV programme. We found that users react quicker to the availability of refreshed second screen content when alerted by means of peripheral stimuli – especially through the modality of sound. In addition, users much prefer their attention to be mediated, to insure against missing parts of primary content (constantly glancing at the tablet to check for new content), or second screen content (missing it because they are too focused on the TV).

Interestingly, our findings indicated that many participants liked alerts on the TV itself, as it supported consciously delaying shifting their attention to the companion content until a moment of their choosing. Designers of dual screen user experiences should consider how closely in time the companion content needs be synchronised to the main screen content and cue the user appropriately. If, for example, the content is relevant to only a few seconds of the show, a designer may wish to use attention mediating techniques which have been found to cause more involuntary, faster attendance to the second screen, such as peripheral/auditory methods. However, if the relevance of the content to the notification cues spans minutes rather than seconds, then perhaps methods that use notifications on the main TV screen may be more beneficial, as these will allow users time to choose when to look at them.

ACKNOWLEDGEMENTS

We would like the participants who took part in our experiment and the reviewers for helping us improve this paper. Timothy Neate is funded by an EPSRC DTA scholarship (EP/L504865/1) and the BBC UX partnership.

REFERENCES

1. Armstrong, M., Brooks, M., Churnside, A., Evans, M., Melchior, F., and Shotton, M. Object-based broadcasting: Curation, responsiveness and user experience. In *Proc. Int. Broadcasting Convention* (2014), 12.2.
2. Blattner, M., Sumikawa, D., and Greenberg, R. Earcons and icons: Their structure and common design principals. *Human-Computer Interaction 4* (1989), 11–44.
3. Brown, A., Glancy, M., Evans, M., Jones, R., Jay, C., and Harper, S. Hci over multiple screens. In *CHI EA '14* (2014), 665–674.
4. Fahle, M., and Wehrhahn, C. Motion perception in the peripheral visual field. *Graefe's Archive Ophthalmology*, 229 (1991), 430–436.
5. Grudin, J. Partitioning digital worlds: Focal and peripheral awareness in multiple monitor use. In *Proc. CHI*, ACM (2001), 458–465.
6. Rooksby, J., Rost, M., Morrison, A., Bell, M., Chalmers, M., and Smith, T. Practices of parallel media: Using mobile devices when watching television. In *Workshop at CSCW – Designing with Users for Domestic Environments: Methods, Challenges and Lessons Learned* (Feb. 2014).
7. Shelton, J., and Kumar, G. P. Comparison between auditory and visual simple reaction times. *Neuroscience and Medicine 1* (Sept. 2010), 30–32.
8. Simons, D., and Levin, D. Change blindness. *Trends in Cognitive Sciences 7*, 1 (1997), 261–267.
9. Valuch, C., Ansorge, U., Buchinger, S., Patrone, A. R., and Scherzer, O. The effect of cinematic cuts on human attention. In *Proc. TVX*, ACM (2014).
10. Vatavu, R.-D., and Mancaş, M. Visual attention measures for multi-screen tv. In *Proc. TVX*, ACM (2014).

Social Media Effectiveness for Public Engagement: Examples of Small Nonprofits

Youyang Hou and Cliff Lampe
School of Information
University of Michigan
{youyangh, cacl}@umich.edu

ABSTRACT
Social media sites are increasingly adopted by small nonprofit organizations (NPOs) to help them meet their public engagement goals. However, several characteristics of small organizations make it hard for them to effectively use social media sites. We present findings from interviews with 26 small NPOs' social media professionals on how they use multiple social media sites to support public engagement. Small NPOs use multiple social media sites to engage with different stakeholders toward various ends. However, these NPOs are not using social media to its full potential with regard to community-building and action mobilization. Several challenges in small NPOs, such as ineffective measurement of social media performance, deficient organizational resources, and lack of control over work, lead to strong tensions between social media engagement strategies and outcomes. Drawing on these findings, we present several practical implications for the design of successful public engagement social media tools.

Author Keywords
Nonprofit organization; social media; organization

ACM Classification Keywords
H.5.3. Information Interfaces and Presentation: Group and Organization Interfaces

INTRODUCTION
Organizations are increasingly using social media to interact with their internal and external stakeholders. Big corporate organizations have used enterprise social media like Yammer and SocialText to support a vast amount of knowledge-sharing and work coordination [9]. Externally, organizations have also used social media sites such as Facebook and Twitter as public engagement tools. For instance, advertisers exploit the power of online social networking to raise awareness about their products, and government agencies also leverage social media to support government services [3].

CHI 2015, April 18 - 23, 2015, Seoul, Republic of Korea
Copyright 2015 ACM 978-1-4503-3145-6/15/04$15.00
http://dx.doi.org/10.1145/2702123.2702557

Recently, social media have also been increasingly adopted in small organizations such as charities, small businesses, and community groups. Social media are especially beneficial for these small organizations in providing cheap and easy ways to allow their campaigns to go viral online and reach a global audience—something previously only available in large organizations with more resources to devote to such efforts.

When using social media for public engagement, all organizations face certain shared barriers, such as dealing with different stakeholders and needing social media training and expertise. As new social media sites appear and evolve, another challenge is to efficiently manage multiple social media sites. For small organizations, this becomes even more challenging because they are unable to confront the overhead involved in learning and managing multiple social media systems.

During our research with a group of small NPOs that focus on advocacy work related to local water and environmental issues, we found that they well represent small organizations in social media use. They face a unique set of needs and constraints distinct from those of large organizations. First, small NPOs are constrained by limited financial resources that affect long-term technology planning and access to technical expertise. Second, small NPOs are tight in human resources and depend heavily on volunteers to fulfill their day-to-day operations, creating a cooperative dynamic that is different from that of corporate organizations where all work is done by paid employees. Third, small NPOs face competition with large NPOs and organizations, both in terms of getting public funding and capturing attention on social media sites [28]. Finally, small NPOs often involve various stakeholders who are more loosely connected to the organization overall [21]. All of these factors lead to a complex assortment of coordination and communication challenges.

By studying how a group of small environmental NPOs use multiple social media sites, we aim to answer four central questions in regard to social media use for public engagement in small organizations. What are the factors that influence small NPOs' decision-making regarding social media adoption? How do small NPOs use various social media sites to achieve different public engagement goals? How do small NPOs assess the effectiveness of different social media for public engagement? And what are the organizational challenges that influence how social media support their public engagement goals? Close examination of these challenges can enable small organizations to use different social media tools more effectively for public engagement, and provide design implications for complex social media management in an organizational context. Although we are specifically focused on small NPOs, the need to develop social media strategies with organizational constraints is an issue that all small organizations face.

Related Work

Social Media Use in Organizations

Social media sites have been used widely within organizations as tools for building social capital by providing access to new people and knowledge [26], sharing knowledge [29], and building relationships [7]. Diverse affordances of social media sites such as visibility, editability, persistence, and association have provided rich opportunities to support organization communication [29]. Recently, others have also found that organizations use multiple social media sites to complement each other for communication and knowledge sharing across different work role boundaries [14, 35]. Social media use in organizations has also evolved over time, with the trend being that more social media sites are used to support different aspects of organizational work [36].

Not all social media channels used in the organizational context exist entirely within the organizations. Previous researchers have also explored the value of social media sites in terms of communicating and engaging with stakeholders outside of organizations. Many public sectors such as government agencies actively use social media to engage with citizens to enhance government openness and transparency [3]. Business sectors are also interested in making use of social media to promote sales [11].

Compared with traditional organizations, small organizations face more challenges in leveraging social media sites to fulfill their organizational goals, such as building networks and mobilizing actions. For instance, Robson et al. [23] used Facebook and Twitter to promote a citizen science project, but the contribution of these sites to the effort was less than that of face-to-face communication. Self-organized small organizations were also constrained by limited experience and informal networks when they used social media for action mobilization [1].

NPOs and ICTs Use

NPOs are a critical component of civil society because they serve the public good and social welfare, organized around such issues as healthcare, shelter, and environmental protection. There are 1.5 million NPOs in the United States, about three quarters of which are small NPOs whose annual budgets are under 1 million dollars a year. These small NPOs share and cultivate knowledge and caring for localized areas and they impact and engage local communities. Like other organizations, NPOs have adopted information and communication technologies (ICTs) such as email, databases, websites, etc., to facilitate and improve activities such as volunteer management, internal information management, public relations and fund-raising activities [15, 18]. On the other hand, small NPOs have relatively limited budgets to purchase technology and training [12, 15], while their dynamic and fluid information needs, stakeholders, and work contexts pose various challenges for how ICTs can support their coordination and information management [27, 32].

Social Media Use for NPOs Public Engagement

Recently, many NPOs have started to use social media sites to reach out directly to their audiences around the topics and activities associated with their missions. Social media sites provide many useful affordances for public engagement, such as low-cost platforms, rapid information dissemination channels, and rich interactive features [20]. As a result, social media sites, especially Facebook and Twitter, have been broadly used by NPOs and may have great potential to support NPOs in relationship building and collective action mobilization [17].

Public relations researchers have analyzed the content of large NPO social media sites and derived several categories of engagement-related content strategies. For instance, one study [33] examined 275 large NPOs' Facebook pages and categorized their social media practice into disclosure, information dissemination and involvement. Other research [10, 13] analyzed the content of several large NPOs' Twitter pages and categorized them into three main public engagement functions: information, community, and action. The information messages mainly aimed to increase awareness of the organizations' causes among both current and potential supporters. Community messages aimed to maintain a sense of community through social media interaction. Finally, many messages attempted to convert social media interactions into some other form of advocacy actions, such as fund-raising or attending a face-to-face meeting.

Nevertheless, NPOs lack proper strategies to make use of the technology affordances in their social media platforms to enact these public engagement goals. For instance, Sommerfeldt et al. [25] found that NPOs websites were commonly tailored to highly involved audiences, thus missing the opportunity to extend their reach to new audiences. Other research has suggested that NPOs often do not fully employ the interactive affordances of social media, instead treating social media as a one-way broadcasting platform rather than a two-way interactive tool [13, 31, 34]. However, it is less clear which contextual factors influence NPOs' effective use of social media sites.

One contextual factor is how NPOs perceive and assess the effectiveness of social media sites in achieving their initial communication and engagement goals. In fact, evaluating social media outcomes and utilities is not as straightforward for NPOs as it is in enterprise sectors, where outcomes can be assessed directly using the standard return of investment (ROI) metrics. In NPOs, on the other hand, assessment is conducted within a context of uncertain and there are various outcomes that are hard to measured or quantify, such as awareness, volunteers, and funding. A survey conducted by Idealware [30] showed that about only half of US NPOs measured their social media performance; but that for all of those who did, they found a correlation with positive social media outcomes. However, it was still unclear what exact metric NPOs relied on, and whether these measurements accurately reflected their public engagement performance.

Another group of contextual factors tie to several organizational factors that influence NPOs' social media adoption and use. Previous literature has revealed that the adoption and performance of social media sites in large NPOs is related to organizational strategy, capacity and governance [18]. In addition, resource limitations, mis-coordination, blurring between personal and organizational accounts, as well as low media literacy may prevent NPOs from actively using social media [4, 20, 22]. However, it is unknown which factors influence small NPOs' social media adoption, and how these organizational factors directly influence their efforts at public engagement via social media platforms.

METHODOLOGY

Participants

We recruited 27 social media "point persons" (9 males) from 26 small environmental NPOs in the United States (2 participants were from the same NPO). The average age of participants was 41 (SD=14.7). 15 participants were communication and marketing specialists, 6 participants were project or executive directors, and 6 participants were technical specialists. All of the NPOs had an average of 15 staff numbers (SD=12.3). To protect the anonymity of participants, we refer to all participants using number IDs.

We used a purposive sampling strategy based on a sampling frame generated by a group of environmental conservation researchers. Most of the NPOs we interviewed focus on issues surrounding waterways and watersheds, though some take a broader environmental approach, in which water issues are only one facet of their work. The nonprofits fall into three general categories: affiliate and university (6), network and policy (11), and community NPOs (12). Affiliate and university organizations are programs associated with larger governmental agencies or universities. Network and policy organizations primarily advocate for policy change surrounding environmental issues on a statewide or regional level. Community organizations are often dedicated to their local waterway(s) and organize at a community level.

We invited people who worked directly with their NPO social media sites to participate in our interview. We identified the individual participants from the NPOs' website or through referral by their coworkers who were listed as the NPO contact. Participants were recruited through emails, organizational website contact pages, phone calls, and private messages sent through Facebook. We continued recruiting participants until we achieved saturation regarding their use of social media sites. By looking at one group of NPOs with similar missions, we were able to identify and analyze common patterns of social media practice without introducing uncertainty related to the effects of highly different missions, scale, or geographic regions.

Data Collection and Analysis

Semi-structured Interview

We conducted semi-structured phone interviews [2] with each NPO social media point person. The average interview lasted 45 minutes. We conducted all interviews singly or in a team of two, and all researchers used the same interview protocol, which was designed around the following areas of interest: (1) The background and goal of the NPO and the participant's role in the organization; (2) The nature of the work undertaken by the participant, with emphasis on how they managed their social media sites; (3) The strategies that the participant and the organization utilized for different social media sites; (4) How participants perceived and assessed the effectiveness of social media sites for their organization; (4) Who constituted their audience on social media sites and how they reached out to that audiences; and (5) The challenges that they had in their organization when using social media.

The interview data were collected from Nov 2013 to March 2014. The interviews were recorded and transcribed verbatim and coded using NVivo 10 [19]. Using a constant comparative coding strategy, we iteratively and inductively developed a coding scheme related to NPOs' use of social media sites. We used coding strategies such as initial coding, process coding, and in-Vivo coding. We initially developed a set of codes inductively merged from data related to different social media sites (e.g., Facebook, Twitter, YouTube, LinkedIn), social media strategies (e.g., scheduling posts, multimedia, initiating conversation) and organizational factors (e.g., resource allocation, teamwork, multiple roles). During the initial coding, we used analytical memos to examine themes and patterns (e.g., control over social media, fluid workforce). After the coding, we used data analysis tools such as the case-ordered descriptive meta-matrix and the variable-by-variable matrix to further describe and explain the data [16], and deductively categorized NPOs' social media strategies into three key functions of public engagement: *information*, *community* and *action* [13].

Content Analysis

To further understand the strategies that small NPOs articulated in the interview, we conducted a content analysis of their Facebook public page and Twitter account during Sept 2014. We sampled the 30 most recent posts for each NPO's Facebook and Twitter page. Two coders coded 26 Facebook accounts and 23 Twitter accounts. Deductively drawing on previous literature about the three key functions of NPOs public engagement: information, community and action [13], we developed a coding schema that contained 9 social media post categories in 3 overarching categories (Table 1).

OVERVIEW OF SMALL NPOS SOCIAL MEDIA USE

In our research, we found that small NPOs used a wide range of social media sites. Many NPOs (13/26) had their own blogs built from WordPress or Drupal, which were an important place to update organizational news, policy issues, and educational resources. Almost every NPO used social networking sites such as Facebook (25/26, followers: 2747±952), Twitter (23/26, followers: 1871±498), LinkedIn (7/26, followers: 180±87) and Google+ (4/26, followers: 41±26). Finally, many NPOs also explored media sharing sites such as Pinterest (4/26, followers: 83±29), Flickr (4/26), Instagram (2/26, followers: 269±75), YouTube (12/26, followers: 130±92), Podcast (2/26) and Vimeo (1/26) to post multimedia content to engage with their audience.

Adoption of Social Media Sites

Small NPOs' decisions regarding the adoption of social media sites were driven mainly by the needs of different stakeholders. First, they considered if their existing members or potential audience were already on the sites. Facebook, for example, was perceived as the platform that most of their targeted group used: "When we launched our Facebook page, tons of our members liked our Facebook page. And I did our Twitter account within the exact same week, and people were making Twitter accounts to follow me" (P8). Second, NPOs were compelled by the social comparison with peer organizations to adopt these platforms; as one participant put it, "otherwise you're just gonna get left behind" (P3). Third, they were motivated to demonstrate to funders that they were making efforts to reach out to people in order to satisfy their funders' expectation. Finally, NPOs selected social media in the hope of expanding their reach to include audiences gathered in different social media channels. For instance, P13 told us the reason that their organization wanted to use Pinterest was to "attract people who are just kind of interested in healthy living or just interested in nontoxic products… at least get people to use it not for advocacy purposes, using it for kind of lifting the general knowledge about what green living would be like".

Engage with a Diversity of Stakeholders

NPOs worked with a variety group of stakeholders through social media sites, and the interaction with different stakeholders segmented based on the affordances of social media and the popularity of social media among the stakeholders.

NPO Members: NPO members are local citizens who show an interest in the NPO's cause and sign up for membership, which usually includes sharing their contact information with the NPO. Membership size among the NPOs we examined ranged from 450–17000, and members were the most reliable sources for financial support and event participation. As a consequence, one of the most vital motivations for using social media was to expand membership. For daily communication, however, NPOs mainly used email and newsletters to communicate directly with the members.

Volunteers: Volunteers are important workforces for NPOs, supporting their organizational activities. Social media sites enabled NPOs to post about volunteers recruitment information and give recognition and thanks to volunteers who helped with previous events or activities. In addition, they also frequently posted photos of volunteer activities in Flickr, Instagram, and Facebook albums, and shared these images through social networking sites like Facebook and Twitter.

Funders: NPOs used social networking sites to engage with funders by posting donation information and giving recognition and thanks to donors. Nevertheless, as financial donors are usually older adults who are relatively less active on social media sites, NPOs felt the most effective way to contact and engage with funders was still traditional via communication channels such as email lists and face-to-face meetings.

Other organizations: NPOs (9/26) frequently use social media to strengthen existing partnerships with other organizations by cross promoting one another on social media—for example, liking each other's content, reposting each other's posts, promoting each other's events, sharing news and tools from other's sites, and recognizing and congratulating each other's work. NPOs saw this as a way to "scratch each other's back" (P11), to support and build relationship with other organizations, get updated about each other's working progress, and especially "double the poll of viewers" (P11) and expand the follower influence on social media sites. At the same time, some NPOs did feel as though they were primarily connected to other organizations, and still didn't reach out to the general public enough.

Reporters: Building a positive relationship with reporters and media has long been an important outreach and communication goal for NPOs (6/26), as reporters can help to attract press attention and disseminate information. Twitter was perceived as the primary platform for media reporters to reach out to NPOs. Reporters frequently use Twitter features such as retweet, favorite and @ to interact with NPOs, pick up their tweets as news sources, or ask questions on Twitter, which greatly increased NPOs' online influence. Additionally, NPOs' social media point persons proactively interacted with reporters in order to strengthen the relationship. As one interviewee explained, one might use the NPO's social media to "post [reporters'] work, credit their work, try to generate discussions with the individual reporters, and say to them by name" (P20).

DIVERSE STAKEHOLDERS AND ENGAGEMENT GOALS: INFORMATION, COMMUNITY, AND ACTION

Small NPOs leveraged multiple social media sites to engage with a variety of stakeholders and their social media practice and activities fell into three engagement goals discussed in previous literature [10, 13]: disseminating information about their causes and the organization; building community and engaging with different stakeholders; and mobilizing action like donation and volunteering work. NPOs actively leveraged different social media sites to fulfill these engagement goals and connected with diverse stakeholders, yet the actual effectiveness of social media for public engagement remained unclear and insufficient.

Increasing Awareness of Information

NPOs shared a huge amount of information regarding environmental issues and organizational updates via a variety of social media sites in order to increase awareness of their organization and its mission. A content analysis (Table 1) of NPOs' Facebook and Twitter pages illustrated that about half of their social media posts were related to an information goal: news and updates of their website and organization, educational resources and environmental tools, as well as multimedia content such as photo or videos.

NPOs commonly used multiple social media sites together to support the information engagement goal. NPOs frequently shared updates from their websites and blogs, tutorials or educational videos from YouTube, and photos from Flickr or Instagram. NPOs also used blogs to aggregate information from the social networking sites and provide longer form content on interesting topics:

> The features that primarily go into the blog site actually originate on the day to day news items that I tweet out. And then I compile those in the weekly blog summary under various headings, such as agriculture or water quality or biodiversity. So it's an aggregate. If there are more, what I see as more significant issues, then I'll do a separate article about those significant breaking issues and then sometimes summarize those in a paragraph or two within the weekly issue. (P2)

Multimedia content was also a popular strategy among NPOs. Most participants (13/26) told us that the most effective strategy to solicit shares and comments was to post appealing photographs, usually containing cute animals or beautiful nature scenes. NPOs frequently posted such media content on Flickr, Pinterest, and/or Instagram and shared through social networking sites. Participants felt that the practice helped to provide "a better entry point" (P20) for the public to learn more about NPOs.

Building Community

While the purpose of the first engagement goal is to disseminate information, another set of social media practices involve building stronger ties with existing stakeholders and local communities. Content analysis (Table 1) illustrates the types of community posts tied to this goal: interaction with other organizations, conversation with public, giving recognition and thanks, and live posting about volunteer events. NPOs proactively posted questions and discussion topics to prompt interaction and conversation with their audience. For instance, P26 described their experience of posting questions online:

Engagement goals	Code type	Facebook (N=25)	Twitter (N=23)
Information	News and updates	218 (29.0%)	171 (24.8%)
	Education, tools	113 (15.1%)	84 (12.2%)
	Media	47 (6.2%)	29 (4.2%)
Community	Other organization	29 (3.8%)	73 (10.6%)
	Conversation	24 (3.2%)	54 (7.8%)
	Giving recognition and thanks	44 (5.8%)	59 (8.6%)
	Live posting	37 (4.9%)	46 (6.7%)
Action	Event	162 (21.6%)	74 (10.7%)
	Call for action	78 (10.4%)	100 (14.5%)

Table 1. Content analysis on NPOs Facebook and Twitter

> We ask a question, and when they respond, we can become close to them through being actively engaged with what they're saying. You have to build up to a point where people feel almost safe, and that it's going to be alright if they're wrong.

Many NPOs found that *hashtags* on Twitter—created using the "#" symbol, with users collaboratively contributing content to the hashtag—were particularly helpful to initiate such discussion, as the hashtag format "speaks in ways a sentence can't" (P20). Nevertheless, many NPOs also said that despite using these strategies in their social media, their followers were still not active in participating in the conversations.

Lastly, NPOs frequently posted photos taken during about their work and events, such as conferences or volunteer events, which demonstrated their endeavors and accomplishments to their audience. In some cases, they made use of the "real time," live properties of Twitter and Facebook by providing live postings of events, with positive results:

> That issue went to court and there were very few people who could take time off during the day to sit and listen to this court hearing even though everybody was extremely interested in the outcome of this debate, and what the judge was gonna say. So I was able to live tweet that court hearing. The Twitter stream that I was posting got a gigantic spike of followers and people were really tuning in to hear that play. (P18)

Mobilizing Actions

For most NPOs, the ultimate goal of social media use was to mobilize an audience by providing enough *information* and building a sufficient sense of *community* to spur people into potential *actions*, such as becoming a volunteer member, donating money, or signing a petition. For instance:

> The bigger question becomes, are they going to sign the letter to congress, or are they going to sign the letter to the Wisconsin legislature when there's an issue going on that they can take action on? Or are they more of just a casual supporter? And that's something we're trying to get a handle on but we don't quite know. (P20)

In our content analysis, we also found that NPOs frequently posted about actionable items: event information, fund-raising, advocacy, social media campaigns, or direct calls for action (Table 1). But while NPOs have tried to mobilize actions through social media sites, they typically remain disappointed with the ability of such sites to transform online engagement into "real" *action*, whether in the form of attending an event or providing financial support, particularly when the NPO has directly asked for such actions. They noted that "liking a Facebook page is not an engagement" (P9), and felt it did not lead to actual action outside the site. They thought the problem was that the social media audience was not "tuned to hear the message" (P7), and seemed to lack the motivation to take real actions:

> We invited people to participate on social media. They loved the pictures and the quotes that people were sending in about the river. But we didn't get a single person to print out the form and put a check with it and send it to us from any of the platforms we used electronically. (P7)

Instead of social media sites, many NPOs (21/26) mentioned that traditional communication tools like email lists or even face-to-face interactions are still more effective in mobilizing people, especially previous volunteers and donors, into *action* like fund-raising and signing a petition. They reported usually getting pretty good results with such "traditional" calls for action. P3 described one example when they asked people for an advocacy action:

> More recently we did ask people to call their local congressmen about the Water Resources Development Act. I was sort of surprised the emails I got. People were forwarding to me the responses they got from the congressman, when they did call.

Evaluating Social Media Effectiveness: Mismatch with Real Engagement

One challenge for small NPOs is to define and measure the "success" of social media sites in terms of public engagement. NPOs paid close attention to basic metrics like number of followers, shares and likes, and growth trends of their social media sites. These metrics reflected the size of audiences and how much interaction occurred on their social media sites, and thus spoke to the *information* and *community* goals of public engagement.

> I think people like some of the news stories that we post and if we post something fun like, "We just got a million dollar grant from the EPA," a lot of people tend to like those things. Sort of a "Yay. Congratulations." The like button's like a virtual high five. (P19)

Many participants (13/26) also noted that they had been using social media analytics tools like Facebook Insights, Klout, and Urchin to further track the demographics and behaviors of visitors to social media sites. However, they generally did not have formalized routines or strategies for using these analytic tools, and only looked at anecdotal information rather than tracking numbers systematically. Participants repeatedly tell us that although such analytic tools provide numerous metrics, they are too complicated to interpret:

> Facebook is crazy. They measure every little click that anybody does. But it's hard for me to capture that information and present it to our board members to explain whether the performance of our social media are improving or needs boosting. (P18)

Furthermore, participants noted that the analytical tools gave them little information about their performance in terms of achieving the *action* goal. They had no idea whether social media visitors were being effectively transformed into highly engaged members or donors. Even if they were succeeding in this goal, there was no way for them to compare the list of social media visits with the lists of volunteers, members, or donors. Without having clear methods in place to match these sets of information, they felt it was extremely hard to further engage these audiences. For instance, P9 noted that it was hard for their NPOs to compare their Facebook audience with their existing membership list, and that the data from Facebook itself was not quite useful:

> For this post the people that like the thing 20 people out of the 329 likers we have here, I don't know who they are. They don't show up on email lists. I know that they're mostly local, which is good, because that means that they saw us somewhere, or picked up one of our bookmarks somewhere, and liked the page. But we need to figure out how to connect these people with our organization. They're disconnected from other parts of communication that you have. …

THE ORGANIZATIONAL CONTEXT OF SMALL NPOS' SOCIAL MEDIA USE

We have observed that small NPOs seek to achieve a complex assemblage of public engagement goals with different stakeholders. However, distributed coordination with multiple sites, a diverse and fluid workforce, time, funding, expertise constraints, and organizational policy all factored into decisions about which social media to use and how social media sites were used by small NPOs for public engagement.

"All hands on deck" for Social Media Management

In small environmental NPOs, there was usually a shortage of labor for social media management. Participants noted that they commonly "wear a lot of hats" (P14) and were responsible for a variety of communication and public relation tasks. Social media management work, though important, was only one small component on the long list of such tasks. As a result, most NPOs did not have one person wholly dedicated to social media management, but rather distributed the responsibility across a group of staff members.

This "all hands on deck" approach to social media management took several different patterns. The first mode was that each staff member would manage one official social media page that he or she was familiar with. The challenge, as a result, was to coordinate between different social media pages. In the second mode, multiple staff members had administrative access to the official social media page(s) and anyone could edit and maintain the sites' content. When there were multiple people working collaboratively on these social media sites, the challenge became how to coordinate among people and conduct quality control. Nevertheless, most organizations did not have a rigorous policy about coordination and quality control; instead, staff members just had to trust that each person would be responsible when posting something:

> We don't have a process of running something by the whole team because that's too slow. We just have to trust each other's judgment, and each of us do it. If there's something that I do have a question about, it's easy for me to run it by somebody if I want, but it's not required. (P14)

In the third mode, small NPOs encouraged certain staff members such as outreach specialists to create a personal account separate from the official account, usually on Twitter, to post about their work, expertise, and experiences related to the NPO's causes. The official account and the specialist accounts frequently reposted each other's content and attracted their own audience, which expanded the overall NPO's influence "like a big web" (P16). This strategy was also perceived as effective way to make the organization feel more real and accessible:

> So it does allow you to peek behind the curtain of our organization, kind of humanize people. But again, not in a frivolous way, and then I think that builds the interest that we naturally have. We're just naturally curious about other people. (P16)

In addition to the full-time staff, NPOs often relied on their temporary workforce, such as interns or volunteers, to manage their social media sites. These short-term workers were temporary, their schedule frequently changed, and their work discontinued after they left the job. For instance, P9 told us that her organization's use of Twitter was based entirely on one worker's expertise: "We used Twitter for nine months that we had the social networking intern last year. And then when she left we didn't use Twitter. "

Constraints in Time, Funding, and Expertise

The work of social media management is characterized by pragmatic constraints in terms of time and human and financial resources. Time constraint was the primary concern of most NPOs. Even though social media were initially perceived as an easy, low-cost way to communicate, most NPOs (15/26) still felt that social media sites were very time consuming and that they lacked the time to make use of them fully. Consequently, NPO point persons normally only focused on only one or two social media channels, even when they saw other new or alternate social media sites as potentially useful:

> As a smaller organization, a Twitter and a Facebook Page is pretty much all we can handle at this moment. I think as far as social media go, that we have to devote our time to quality over quantity when it comes to that. (P26)

Social media management was also limited by financial resources in small NPOs. NPOs cannot afford to hire dedicated staffs to manage social media channels, nor can they hire social media or marketing firms to help with social media management techniques. Many participants (6/26) also complained about Facebook with regard to its new Newsfeed algorithm, which charges NPOs to promote their posts in users' newsfeeds. Because NPOs did not have the budget for social media advertising, this dramatically limited the organic reach of their Facebook page:

> Facebook also has its sharing algorithm which is very different than it used to be a few years ago. And I think that its limits to how many of your supporters see your post. Their promote scheme where they're trying to charge for increased visibility of your post, I think is absolutely killing the platform for non-profits. I just really think that Facebook should have an exemption for 501 [c] [3] recognized non-profits, that our pages shouldn't have to be subjected to promote functions. We should be able to have all of our supporters be able to see all of our posts at all times for free. (P18)

Finally, NPOs' social media channels were constrained by their internal lack of expertise in differentiating their use of different social media sites. Several participants (9/26) noted that they posted the exact same content in both Facebook and Twitter pages and used automatic synchronizing tools to link different sites, despite the significant differences between the two sites in terms of audiences and features. Other participants, however, pointed out problems in using such auto-link strategies across different sites:

> But the one thing that we never ever do for any reason, ever upon penalty of me being very angry is, you never, ever, ever, post on Facebook what's on Twitter. Facebook and Twitter are not synonymous. The platforms don't work together, so stop trying to make them work together. (P10)

The Politics of Social Media Management

Small NPOs had their own organizational policy or guidelines that regulated their social media use regarding the approval of content, ownership of social media sites and interaction with social media followers. However, these organizational norms and routines did not always work collaboratively with their social media practice and public engagement goals.

For many small NPOs, the decision to adopt social media sites required approval or was decided by higher-level organizations or managers. P22 worked for a local branch of a national NPO, and explained that the former was strictly constrained by the latter's rules regarding which sites could be used by each level:

> Twitter goes to our Ohio account. Facebook, we're not able to do that. We have a blog, but we don't have any control over that, we just submit things to it once in a while. Flickr, we can't

> have one of those. So those are national, I don't think we're allowed to. We don't have very much available to us. Instagram is another one. (P22)

In addition, many participants noted that they had a complex approval process regarding the content strategies and actions in social media sites, to make sure that posts were considered "appropriate" and without any typos, errors, or mistakes. Furthermore, this approval process regarding which features or content strategy to use has greatly influenced their interaction and engagement with social media audiences. For instance, P26 talked about how their director's preference and approval processes limited the organizations' ability to use social media for public engagement:

> Our main director doesn't like hashtags for some reason. I think they're a great tool to use when you're using Twitter. Now, on my personal account, I use them a lot. When it comes to responding to different posts from other organizations, it's kind of hard to go through that approval process. We'll like on Facebook or favorite something that somebody says on Twitter, but we won't necessarily respond in words. (P26)

DISCUSSION AND DESIGN IMPLICATIONS

Our findings provide a background for understanding the challenges for small organizations in using social media to engage with diverse stakeholders and enact different public engagement goals. Small organizations need to better understand and evaluate the success of their social media performance, especially given the lack of awareness and information regarding their social media audiences and whether social media can foster long-term, productive relationships with those audiences. Small organizations also face several within-organization challenges that sometimes hinder their engagement goals. These all call for significant design and research trajectories to support complex social media use for public engagement in small organizations.

Managing Social Media Multiplexity for Engagement

The challenges of engaging diverse stakeholders for small organizations involve not just one single social media platform, but a complex social media ecosystem. In this research, we provided evidence of how small NPOs perceived the effectiveness of different social media sites: Facebook was seen as effective at engaging general public audiences, Twitter was seen as particularly useful for engaging other organizations and reporters, and blogs were seen as effective at aggregating diffused information scattered across other social media platforms. These insights extend prior work examining NPOs' use of social media in understanding their practices in a single social media platform [10, 13, 34] and discussion about the effectiveness of different social media sites in advocacy [20].

However, using multiple social media sites requires time, a relatively stable workforce, proper collaborations between organizational staff, and expertise to be usable to small organizations. Most small organizations are constrained in their capacities to be able to manage and fully maximize the power of multiple social media platforms. These findings indicate that social media platforms such as Hootsuite, Sprout, and Storify should better support heterogeneous content strategies, audiences, and stakeholders of organizational social media sites. Social media management systems should be designed not only to provide tools to manage multiple sites, but also to provide guidance on how to make use of the unique affordances of each site to engage with different stakeholders. Visualization tools should provide straightforward and integrated summaries of individual and overall performance of different social media platforms. In addition, there is also a need for tools to track interactions with different stakeholders, such as the number of RTs, @s, and conversations with other organizations, reporters, and donors.

Connecting Information, Community, and Action

We found that, like large NPOs, small NPOs seek to fulfill different engagement goals through social media sites. Social media are seen as promising for increasing *information* and awareness, but less effective at engaging with *community*, or mobilizing people into the types of *action* that the organizations want to engender. These results echo previous literature, which found that NPOs failed to utilize social media for dialogic communication [25] and faced the challenge of "slacktivism" [5], in which participants only take minimum support efforts online without devoting real actions.

In addition, another challenge for small organizations is the lack of accurate feedback regarding their social media performance. Though social media analytic tools exist that aim to measure social media success, these tools primarily target business sectors that measure the return on investment (ROI) of technology use such as sales and brand value. Most of these tools are also not free, which limits small organizations' ability to use them.

These findings have many implications for the design of social media analytic assessment tools for public engagement. There is, in particular, an absence of metrics that assess social media's connection to important outcomes such as fund-raising and volunteer recruitment. In addition to measuring the ROI of social media sites, it is also critical to support connections between social media performance and public participation performance. There is a need to connect social media analytics tools with more situated traces and records of which social media followers are really engaged and motivated to *actions*, possibly through organizational information system and metadata of volunteers and donors' information, such as linking to online volunteer recruitment management tools (e.g., VolunteerMatch.com) and fund-raising sites (e.g., giveforward.com), as well as existing volunteer or donor email lists. These tools should also help aggregate detailed demographic and background information of participants to help small organizations better target and filter highly motivated audiences and mobilize them from "likers" to engaged actors.

Supporting Organizational Social Media Management

In this paper, we also highlighted several organizational factors that influenced social media use in small organizations' public engagement practice. It is crucial for HCI researchers to acknowledge these constraints when aiming to design social media tools for small organizations. It is also important pragmatic information for small organizations who want to facilitate their social media sites' engagement with diverse communities.

We found that there were typically multiple people involved in NPOs' social media management, either through dividing work between staff members, or sharing responsibilities with multiple staff, specialists, and volunteers. This strategy poses potential problems related to coordination and quality control; it can also blur the boundaries between personal and organizational accounts [24]. In addition, existing social media sites are usually designed for one account per organization or person who manages the public account. As a result, there is a need for social media management tools that support multiple users and multiple accounts, and provide the necessary links or distance between official and unofficial organizational social media accounts. In order to support efficient social media management within small NPOs, the design of organizational social media platforms should also effectively incorporate the organizational internal workflow with different social media sites, such as drafting, editing, approval, and scheduling posts.

Additionally, organizational norms and routines, such as unwieldy, slow, and/or hierarchical approval processes also prevented small organizations from being creative in content strategies, being interactive in communication strategies, and, in some cases, even adopting useful social media channels. In general, participants expressed a desire for greater flexibility and autonomy regarding social media sites decision and strategies. The influence of organizational norms and culture reflected the influence of power-oriented structures on the use of technology in the adaptive structuration theory [6] and was found in social media use in other organizational contexts [8, 12]. This suggests that small organizations should identify and resolve tensions between different constituents and coordinate to find the best strategies to use social media for public engagement goals. Our findings also indicate that the design of organizational social media management tools should provide proper editing or management rights to certain aspects of work and organizational staff, e.g., which type of work should be approved by which group of people, in order to mitigate conflicts between the organizational power and efficiency of social media management.

Limitations

There are several limitations of the current study. First, the study was based on 26 small environmental advocacy NPOs. We did not compare their social media performance (i.e., number of followers) with the general population of US NPOs. This means that the results may not be directly applicable to other small NPOs. Another limitation is that we only interviewed the social media point person in small NPOs, and thus it is mainly the viewpoints of social media point persons that are represented. We did not look, for example, at the viewpoints of managers, activists, or outreach specialists, which could vary based on their power status in the organization [8]; nor did we talk to the recipients of messages, such as volunteers, other organizations, or the general public. Future work should investigate the perceptions of these other stakeholders in order to identify shared and divergent experiences and perceptions.

CONCLUSION

Our study provides a comprehensive analysis of how social media sites are adopted, used, and constrained in small NPOs for their public engagement goals. The small NPOs we examined sought to leverage the availability of multiple social media sites to disseminate information to new audiences, build community with different stakeholders, and mobilize people into action related to advocacy missions. We found that the NPOs' efforts to use social media sites were not fully successful in initiating conversations and mobilizing actions. Our paper has argued that the design of social media platforms intended to support public engagement must address organizational issues such as the diversity and fluidity of workforce, constraints in time, funding, workforce, and expertise, as well as the need to mitigate organizational politics inconsistent with small organizations' public engagement goals. The design of social media tools must be carried out with particular sensitivity to the specific needs of small organizations needs to achieve their public engagement goals in the complex and constrained organizational context.

REFERENCES

1. Anduiza, E., Cristancho, C. and Sabucedo, J. M. Mobilization through online social networks: The political protest of the indignados in Spain. *Information, Communication & Society 17*, 6 (2014), 750-764.
2. Bernard, H. R. and Bernard, H. R. *Social research methods: Qualitative and quantitative approaches*. Sage, 2012.
3. Bertot, J. C., Jaeger, P. T. and Hansen, D. The impact of polices on government social media usage: Issues, challenges, and recommendations. *Government Information Quarterly 29*, 1 (2012), 30-40.
4. Briones, R. L., Kuch, B., Liu, B. F. and Jin, Y. Keeping up with the digital age: How the American Red Cross uses social media to build relationships. *Public Relations Review 37*, 1 (2011), 37-43.
5. Christensen, H. S. Political activities on the Internet: Slacktivism or political participation by other means. *First Monday 16*, 2 (2011).
6. DeSanctis, G. and Poole, M. S. Capturing the complexity in advanced technology use: Adaptive structuration theory. *Organization science 5*, 2 (1994), 121-147.

7. DiMicco, J., Millen, D. R., Geyer, W., Dugan, C., Brownholtz, B. and Muller, M. Motivations for social networking at work. In *Proc. CSCW 2008*, ACM Press (2008), 711-720.
8. Foster, D., Lawson, S., Wardman, J., Blythe, M. and Linehan, C. Watts in it for me?: Design implications for implementing effective energy interventions in organisations. In *Proc. CHI 2012*, ACM Press (2012), 2357-2366.
9. Gibbs, J. L., Rozaidi, N. A. and Eisenberg, J. Overcoming the "ideology of openness": Probing the affordances of social media for organizational knowledge sharing. *Journal of Computer-Mediated Communication 19*, 1 (2013), 102-120.
10. Guo, C. and Saxton, G. D. Tweeting Social Change: How Social Media Are Changing Nonprofit Advocacy. *Nonprofit and Voluntary Sector Quarterly 43*, 1 (2014), 57-79.
11. Hoffman, D. L. and Fodor, M. Can you measure the ROI of your social media marketing? *Sloan Management Review 52*, 1 (2010).
12. Le Dantec, C. A. and Edwards, W. K. The view from the trenches : Organization , power , and technology at two nonprofit homeless outreach centers. In *Proc. CSCW 2008*, ACM Press (2008), 589-598.
13. Lovejoy, K. and Saxton, G. D. Information, community, and action: How nonprofit organizations use social media. *Journal of Computer-Mediated Communication 17*, 3 (2012), 337-353.
14. Matthews, T., Whittaker, S., Badenes, H. and Smith, B. A. Beyond end user content to collaborative knowledge mapping: Interrelations among community social tools. In *Proc. CSCW 2014*, ACM Press (2014), 900-910.
15. Merkel, C., Farooq, U., Xiao, L., Ganoe, C., Rosson, M. B. and Carroll, J. M. Managing technology use and learning in nonprofit community organizations: Methodological challenges and opportunities. In *Proc. CHIMIT 2007*, ACM Press (2007), 8.
16. Miles, M. B. and Huberman, A. M. *Qualitative data analysis: An expanded sourcebook*. Sage, 2013.
17. Miller, D. and Miller, D. M. Nonprofit Organizations and the Emerging Potential of Social Media and Internet Resources. *SPNHA Review 6*, 1 (2011), 4.
18. Nah, S. and Saxton, G. D. Modeling the adoption and use of social media by nonprofit organizations. *New Media & Society 15*, 2 (2012), 294-313.
19. NVivo *NVivo qualitative data analysis software*. QSR International Pty Ltd, City, 2012.
20. Obar, J. A., Zube, P. and Lampe, C. Advocacy 2.0: An analysis of how advocacy groups in the United States perceive and use social media as tools for facilitating civic engagement and collective action. *Journal of Information Policy 2* (2012), 1-15.
21. Powell, W. W. and Steinberg, R. *The nonprofit sector: A research handbook*. Yale University Press, 2006.
22. Quinton, S. and Fennemore, P. Missing a strategic marketing trick? The use of online social networks by UK charities. *International Journal of Nonprofit and Voluntary Sector Marketing 18*, 1 (2013), 36-51.
23. Robson, C., Hearst, M., Kau, C. and Pierce, J. Comparing the use of social networking and traditional media channels for promoting citizen science. In *Proc. CSCW 2013*, ACM Press (2013), 1463-1468.
24. Skeels, M. M. and Grudin, J. When social networks cross boundaries: A case study of workplace use of Facebook and Linkedin. In *Proc. CSCW 2009*, ACM Press (2009), 95-104.
25. Sommerfeldt, E. J., Kent, M. L. and Taylor, M. Activist practitioner perspectives of website public relations: Why aren't activist websites fulfilling the dialogic promise? *Public Relations Review 38*, 2 (2012), 303-312.
26. Steinfield, C., DiMicco, J. M., Ellison, N. B. and Lampe, C. Bowling online: Social networking and social capital within the organization. In *Proc. C&T 2009*, ACM Press (2009), 245-254.
27. Stoll, J., Edwards, W. K. and Mynatt, E. D. Interorganizational coordination and awareness in a nonprofit ecosystem. In *Proc. CSCW 2010*, ACM Press (2010), 51-60.
28. Thrall, A. T., Stecula, D. and Sweet, D. May we have your attention please? Human-rights NGOs and the problem of global communication. *The International Journal of Press/Politics 19*, 2 (2014), 135-159.
29. Treem, J. W. and Leonardi, P. M. 7 social media use in organizations. *Communication Yearbook 36* (2012), 143.
30. Using Facebook to Meet Your Mission : Results of a Survey. http://www.idealware.org/facebook_survey.
31. Uzunoğlu, E. and Misci Kip, S. Building relationships through websites: A content analysis of Turkish environmental non-profit organizations' (NPO) websites. *Public Relations Review* (2013), 1-3.
32. Voida, A. Shapeshifters in the voluntary sector exploring the human-centered-computing challenges of nonprofit organizations. *Interactions* (2011), 27-31.
33. Waters, R. D., Burnett, E., Lamm, A. and Lucas, J. Engaging stakeholders through social networking: How nonprofit organizations are using Facebook. *Public Relations Review 35*, 2 (2009), 102-106.
34. Waters, R. D. and Jamal, J. Y. Tweet, tweet, tweet: A content analysis of nonprofit organizations' Twitter updates. *Public Relations Review 37*, 3 (2011), 321-324.
35. Yuan, Y. C., Zhao, X., Liao, Q. and Chi, C. The use of different information and communication technologies to support knowledge sharing in organizations: From email to microblogging. *Journal of the American Society for Information Science and Technology 64*, 8 (2013), 1659-1670.
36. Zhang, H., De Choudhury, M. and Grudin, J. Creepy but inevitable? The evolution of social networking. In *Proc. CSCW 2014*, ACM Press (2014), 368-379.

Exploring Barriers to the Adoption of Mobile Technologies for Volunteer Data Collection Campaigns

Sunyoung Kim
School of Engineering and Applied Science
Harvard University
Cambridge, MA
sunyoungkim@seas.harvard.edu

Jennifer Mankoff
Human-Computer Interaction Institute
Carnegie Mellon University
Pittsburgh, PA
jmankoff@cs.cmu.edu

Eric Paulos
Electrical Engineering and Computer Sciences
University of California, Berkeley
Berkeley, CA
paulos@berkeley.edu

ABSTRACT
Volunteer campaigns for data collection make it possible for non-profit organizations to extend their ability to monitor and respond to critical environmental and societal issues. Yet mobile data collection technologies that have the potential to lower the costs and increase the accuracy of volunteer-collected data are not commonly used in these campaigns. In this paper we conduct a series of studies that reveal the complex issues affecting technology adoption in this domain. First, we surveyed and interviewed existing volunteering campaigns to map out current technology usage within volunteer campaigns. Next, we provided two organizations with a customizable tool for data collection (Sensr) and studied its use and non-use across six real volunteer-driven campaigns over six months. Our study explored success and failure across the first few phases of the campaign lifecycle (campaign creation, initial deployment, and adoption). Our results highlight the impact of resource constraints, cognitive factors, the depth of volunteer engagement, and stakeholders' perspective on technology as important factors contributing to the adoption and usage of mobile data collection technologies. We use these findings to argue for specific design features to accelerate the adoption and use of such tools in volunteer data collection campaigns.

Author Keywords
Public participation; data collection; mobile technology; nonprofit organizations; citizen science

ACM Classification Keywords
H.5.m. Information interfaces and presentation (e.g., HCI): Miscellaneous.

CHI 2015, April 18 - 23, 2015, Seoul, Republic of Korea
Copyright 2015 ACM 978-1-4503-3145-6/15/04...$15.00
http://dx.doi.org/10.1145/2702123.2702378

INTRODUCTION
Volunteer data collection has the potential to extend the scale and reach of non-profit organizations engaged in monitoring and tracking data in our everyday lives. Yet traditional tools used for volunteer data collection introduces the risks of error and data loss and limits the ability of remote volunteers to participate in data collection [28]. Mobile technology offers an opportunity to improve volunteer data collection campaigns, as it can save effort, reduce risk associated with traditional modalities (e.g., loss of paper forms), and minimize errors during data entry and analysis. Nevertheless, volunteer organizations, many of which are small nonprofits, often do not make use of mobile data entry applications. For example, a 2012 survey of general mobile technology use in nonprofit fieldwork showed an adoption rate of only 14% [16]. An understanding of the reasons behind this could help to support the integration of mobile technology into volunteer data collection campaigns.

The primary contributions of this paper are a survey of existing volunteer campaigns, a 6-month mobile study covering development, deployment, and use of a mobile application within six campaigns *in situ*, and the resulting design implications for mobile data collection tools.

First, we surveyed existing volunteer campaigns and their technology use practices using an online questionnaire and interviews to map out the current technology landscape. Most participating organizations did not use mobile solutions and viewed resources as a primary obstacle to using technology. While this is clearly a barrier that should be addressed, the goal of our second study was to explore what *other* barriers exist, assuming the resources to create or identify appropriate technology are available. Thus, our second study involved a 6-month deployment of Sensr, a system to support creating custom mobile data collection applications without requiring in-house technical expertise, hardware, or additional licensing costs [11]. We worked with two local nonprofit organizations that were beginning or continuing six separate campaigns over the course of the study. Unlike most previous work that observes existing technology-use practices, we investigated the cycle from assessment to creation to appropriation of, or failure to adopt mobile solutions *in situ*. Our second study revealed two factors that significantly influence mobile technology adoption: the depth of volunteer engagement in a campaign and stakeholders' perspective on technology. Based on these two studies, we make recommendations for the design of future volunteer data collection campaigns and the mobile software that may support them.

In the rest of the paper, we first revisit literature that has explored advanced technology adoption practices in nonprofits. Next, we briefly describe Sensr, the mobile-tool authoring platform. After explaining our study methods, we describe our findings, and conclude by outlining and discussing implications for leveraging mobile technology in volunteer campaigns.

RELATED WORK

Information Technology (IT) use in nonprofit organizations can enhance mission-related outcomes and organizational performance [9]. However, nonprofits lag behind for-profits in investment and adoption of technology [24]. The average technology budget in nonprofits is less than 5% of the total budget, and over 50% of small nonprofits did not plan to adopt any new technology [18]. Potential reasons for the minimal use of technology in nonprofits identified in the literature include financial and technical constraints [23], lack of understanding the social context into which technologies are deployed [29], the organizational cost of creating and preserving the knowledge necessary to make effective use of deployed IT [13], and diversity in organizational structure, scope, and application area [23].

In the case of volunteer data collection activities (we include *citizen science* [26] in this category), resource constraints are particularly salient for non-profit organizations that may survive on fundraising alone, because these activities typically benefit from the development of custom mobile applications that are specific to the data being collected. An ideal solution to this is a tool for rapid creation of custom data collection applications without programming. Recently, several variations on this theme have been created (e.g., [1,10,15,22]), including Sensr, which we used in our second study [11].

Some examples of projects that have successfully adopted custom mobile applications include eBird [28], and Creek Watch [12]. These projects demonstrate the advantages of technological support for data collection, including scalability, centralization, and a wider variety of sensing capabilities, since people can report on indirect measures such as neighborhood health and community living conditions [5], and urban planning issues [4]. Other examples include COASST[1], MLMP[2], CoCoRaHS[3], etc.

[1] COASST, http://depts.washington.edu/coasst/

[2] MLMP, http://www.mlmp.org/

[3] CoCoRaHS, http://www.cocorahs.org/

However, very little is known about the success of these tools in campaigns, and even less is known about the reasons why they may have *not* been used. While we know that multi-stakeholder collaborative systems often fail due to complex socio-technical reasons [8,19], the specific socio-technical factors that may affect volunteer data collection campaigns are not well known.

Theoretical framework in IT adoption

A theoretical approach to understanding IT adoption has been an important research agenda in Information Systems research [30]. While resource constraints (i.e. the ability to build technology) may seem like an obvious barrier to IT adoption on the surface, there are several decades of research, starting with Grudin [8], showing that failures in the adoption of technology by organizations cannot be solely explained by technical problems. Among a significant body of research in Information Systems and Human-Computer Interaction to acceptance and usage of new systems, a widely employed model is Structuration Theory, which characterizes technology adoption through a combination of individual acts and social forces [6]. It regards an individual's perceptions of a technology, rather than its capabilities, as a key influencer in technology adoption. For instance, Orlikowski explains that the "appropriation of technology is strongly influenced by users' understandings of the functionalities of a technology, rather than the properties itself" [19]. Further, she said that individual perceptions are shaped through personal experience and social interactions, which shape the way people use technology [20]. In this regard, Leonardi revealed the gap between what a technology is capable of doing and what people interpret a technology as capable of doing [14].

SURVEY TO EXPLORE EXISTING CAMPAIGNS

We first surveyed existing campaigns through an online questionnaire and interviews to map out the current technology landscape in volunteer data collection activities.

Methods

Our recruitment target was nonprofit organizations that collected data from volunteers (described in the invitation as "your organization coordinates a volunteer activity and collects data from volunteers"). We sent out emails to 900 nonprofits listed in a local nonprofit directory[4] asking them to participate in our online questionnaire. The questionnaire had four parts: Organization's structure and its members; Data collected from volunteers; Volunteer activities and work process; and Technology used in volunteer activities. We also asked if a representative of the organization would be willing to participate in an interview.

Next, we conducted interviews with representatives from organizations that answered the questionnaire and had active volunteer activities at the time of recruitment. One

[4] http://www.pittsburghcares.org/

staff member (e.g., executive director, leader or manager) participated in an interview of one to two and a half hours in length. All interviews were audio recorded and transcribed. We analyzed the data using a thematic analysis to reveal patterns across data sets important informed by Grounded Theory [27]. We used open coding to identify concepts that were significant in the data. As a group, we categorized related concepts, created during open coding, into themes that emerged as patterns within the data.

Participants

Forty-six organizations of the 900 we contacted filled out the online questionnaire. Some possible explanations for the low response rate include out-of-date websites, busyness, and the limited scope of this study to organizations with volunteer data collection efforts. A variety of organizations participated in the survey, including animal protection, conservation, education, healthcare, and science. Among the organizations that responded, 77% had 10 or fewer staff members.

Among those forty-six, eleven organizations participated in the interviews. Those organizations fell under one of two topical areas based on their goal: environmental activism organization (EA) and community mobilization organization (CM). We did not recruit organizations based on these two types, but rather the types emerged through the analysis process. While these types might not cover the entire domain of volunteer organizations, these types represent important purposes for which they seek public engagement for data collection.

Table 1 summarizes the participating organizations. To protect anonymity, we refer to each organization with the type acronym and a randomized number (e.g., EA1-birds for environmental activism group 1 for bird counting).

Type	Site ID	Description of site's programs	# of staff	# of volunteers
Environmental Activism	EA1-birds	Bird counting	7	1,000
	EA2-birds	Bird counting	5	1,500
	EA3-dumping	Cleaning illegal dumping	3	2,000
	EA4-water	Water quality monitoring	6	300
	EA5-water	Water quality monitoring	7	500
Community mobilization	CM1-reuse	Waste reclaiming	5	200
	CM2-dev	Community development	9	500
	CM3-bike	Bike-safe community	7	3,000
	CM4-dev	Community development	11	300
	CM5-shale	Protest against Fracking	4f	2,000
	CM6-food	Eliminating hunger	12	14,000

Table 1. A list of interview-participating organizations

Results

To better understand the technology landscape, we began by probing the types of technologies in use in participating organizations for interacting with volunteers (staying in touch, collecting data, etc.). Our focus was on exploring perceived challenges in the adoption of technology for data collection, especially mobile technology.

Staying In Touch

Eight interviewed organizations said that they used social media to post news about upcoming activities, and to communicate with volunteers. However, while social media are powerful for communication, organizations cannot easily manipulate the communication data because it is stored in a third-party's database (e.g., Facebook's server).

Collecting Data and Measuring Its Quality

While the campaigns varied greatly in their goals with respect to what volunteers would gain and how the organization would benefit, the types of data to collect were fairly evenly distributed between qualitative and quantitative data (See Chart 1). However, the interview data revealed a difference in expectations about data collection across different types of organizations. Our interview data also showed that the meaning of *quality* varied across organizations, and was not always synonymous with accuracy. We will return to the complex topic of quality in the discussion section.

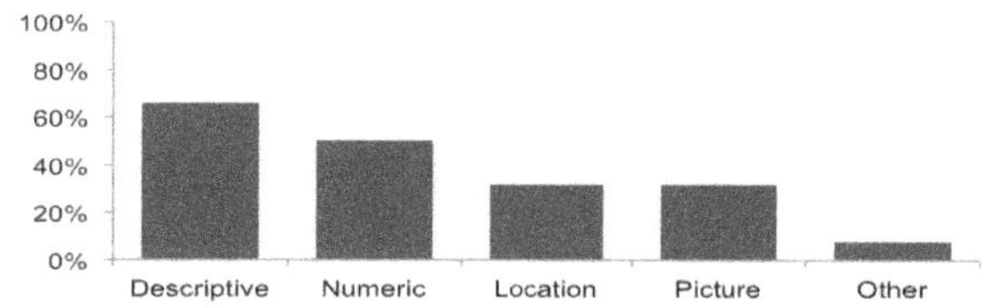

Chart 1. Questionnaire: Data format in campaigns (multiple-choice questions)

Interview participants from *Community Monitoring* organizations collected subjective information about community conditions and neighborhood issues (e.g., feedback on new community facilities). This information helps to shape the focus of campaigns, such as highlighting problems that the organization should address. Therefore, contextual details such as location and demographics were valuable additions to such data because they helped to organize the data. Many organizations used free-form media, such as email and online bulletin boards, although such tools are not well suited to collecting structured data. For these organizations, data is most meaningful and representative when the quantity becomes large enough to identify a trend. Therefore, the *volume* of data submission is regarded as a barometer of data quality.

Conversely, participants from *Environmental Activism* organizations primarily reported seeking factual, standardized, and numeric data (e.g., numeric water quality data). Volunteers were required to follow carefully defined protocols when collecting data. This typically involved a combination of pen-and-paper for manual data capture and IT for digital sharing: people write down their observations out in the field, and then email their findings to a program coordinator. For these organizations, the *accuracy* of data is the barometer of data quality. However, with such protocols in place, volunteer-collected data was sometimes not entirely trusted among our participants, even though prior work has shown that the quality of novice-collected data is as valid and credible as professional-collected data [3].

"I wouldn't even bother looking at that data if I know that volunteers collected the information." (EA5-water)

This tendency was particularly conspicuous among EM organizations. Perhaps for this reason, participants from EM organizations described volunteer data collection campaigns as educational outreach that would increase volunteers' sense of achievement and engagement and train novice volunteers for "real" data collection.

Technologies Used for Data Collection

Conventional communication media were a dominant tool for data submission (e.g., email and web-based submission). Pen and paper were also used, but in that case data retrieval was hard and data needed to be digitized manually. Both processes are time-consuming and prone to human error. In addition, 58% of organizations reported data being submitted in person and 40% by phone (See Chart 2).

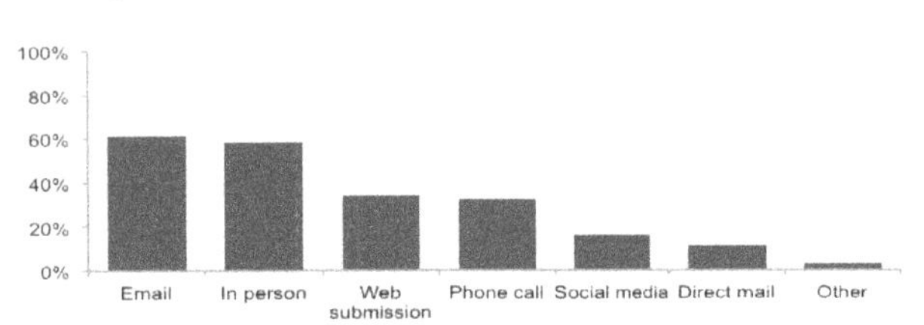

Chart 2. Questionnaire: Technology used for data submission (multiple-choice questions)

Interviews revealed that technologies with a large temporal distance between capturing and sharing data were more likely to cause data to go missing. One solution that came up is for the coordinator to remind volunteers, something that may not scale well.

"For now, it's manageable to call, because it is small, around twenty [volunteers]. But it's going to grow pretty quickly. If it gets larger, that will become really cumbersome to call everyone and to email everyone" (EA3-dumping)

In contrast, mobile technologies were seen as bridging this gap by allowing data to be reported as they happened.

The thing about being out on a bike is that when you come into some issues, if you have a mobile device, you can think about it right there and report it right there." (CM3-bike).

At the same time, some participants concerned that they might diminish authentic field experience, and introduce errors and/or distract.

"Birds are not going to stay dormant. You watch it and take notes on it, and that bird is already leaving. Also, I find it distracting to use my cellphone in the field because then I read emails, and I send text messages. So, I prefer not to actually do any logging in the field on my phone." (EA1-birds)

Lastly, interview participants could not easily imagine the applications of mobile technology when initially asked. But often once one idea came up, other ideas easily followed.

"If you hover over a section on a map, the device would tell you more about the section." (CM3-bike)

"[If] you can tell yourself like 'I recycled 20 pounds this month'. That would help us with quantifying activities both creativity-wise and recycling-wise." (CM1-reuse)

Summary

Overall, this study highlights both some value and some difficulties that might affect the adoption of mobile technology for data collection. For some organizations, the *quality control process* is crucial, while for others the *quantity of data collected* is more important. Mobile technology can potentially contribute both a process and a just-in-time ability to report information. However, participants also had concerns about its impact on the field experience. Thus, our first study did not give clear answers about the likelihood that mobile data collection technology would be adopted.

DEPLOYMENT TO EXPLORE A CAMAPIGN LIFECYCLE

To more deeply understand the adoption of mobile technology in volunteer data collection campaigns, we investigated the first few phases of the campaign lifecycle through a six-month deployment of Sensr [11], a mobile tool for rapidly creating and deploying custom data collection applications. In this section, we first briefly describe Sensr, and then explain the study methods and participating organizations with their campaigns.

Sensr: a mobile-tool authoring platform

While the entire description of Sensr can be found in [11], here we briefly describe the key features. Sensr consists of

Figure 1. Left two: Screenshots of Sensr web & mobile. Data entered in the fields on the left appears on a replica iPhone screen (left). Drag and drop widgets from a predefined set onto replica iPhone screen to design a mobile tool (right). Right: From left to right, a list of projects a user added, a page to find a project, a project main page, and a data-reporting form

two parts: a website where an author creates and manages a mobile tool for a campaign, and a mobile application where volunteers explore and participate in the campaign.

To create a mobile campaign, an author (typically a staff member in an organization) lays out a data collection interface by dragging and dropping widgets from a predefined palette onto a replica iPhone screen (See Figure 1 left). We provide widgets for a photo, radio buttons (two or three options), and a freeform text entry field. The author can rearrange the order of widgets, delete a widget, and edit labels. Additionally, the system automatically captures sensor data such as a timestamp and location. The final interface is automatically converted into a mobile application.

To participate in a campaign, volunteers download the Sensr app to a smartphone (See Figure 1 right). Volunteers search for campaigns that are interesting, and subscribe to the campaigns that they want to contribute data to.

Method

We recruited two organizations that expressed needs for mobile technology use but were struggling with its adoption. For anonymity, we refer to them as CleanUp and AirQuality. We worked with each organization to investigate the use of mobile technology in six campaigns, summarized in Table 2.

We visited each organization every two weeks for six months to conduct semi-structured interviews. The first two visits were to understand existing campaigns and describing Sensr. The remaining visits focused on understanding how organizations determine, evaluate, and use (or decline to use) mobile technology. Protocols for interview questions were centered on the following areas:

- Staff's knowledge and experience in technology use
- Participatory environmental campaigns and volunteers
- The use practices of new mobile tools created via Sensr

We interviewed one staff member at a time, and interviewed one or two staff members per visit. In both organizations, one staff member managed the entire process of one campaign or more independently. Each interview lasted 1.5 hours on average. In total, 13 interviews were conducted with CleanUp and 10 interviews with AirQuality (See Table 2). All interviews were audio-recorded and transcribed.

Participating Organizations

Among those who participated in the interviews and the organizations that we had previously worked with, two local organizations were selected to participate in the deployment study.

CleanUp Organization: Eliminating Illegal Dumping

The CleanUp organization works with community members to eliminate illegal dumping. Its primary campaigns were where volunteers clean up dumping from the sites (*Dumpsite cleanup campaign*), and from the riverbanks (*Riverbank cleanup campaign*). Before cleanup, sites were assessed to plan an event, and after cleanup, sites were monitored to prevent them from becoming trashed again. While staff assessed most sites, the organization recently launched a campaign to engage the public in a visual assessment of a local watershed (*Watershed assessment campaign*). For monitoring the cleaned sites, they ran a *Stewardship program*. Lastly, they created a new campaign to receive public dumpsite reports, *Dumpsite reporting campaign*. They have three full-time staff (an executive director, a program coordinator, and an outreach coordinator) and two part-time. All had experience with using basic IT tools for tasks such as web browsing, word processing, and email.

AirQuality Organization: Advocating for Clean Air

The AirQuality organization educates the public, raises awareness, and advocates for laws and regulations regarding environmental issues to improve air quality in the region. They operate a few campaigns, including *Bicycle air-monitoring campaign* that asks cyclists to collect urban air quality. In addition, they created a new campaign to allow citizens to report neighborhood air-quality issues, *Air-pollution reporting campaign*. They have four full-time staff (an executive director, two lawyers, and a policy & outreach coordinator) and three part-time staff. The policy & outreach coordinator was experienced in advanced IT tools.

Org	Campaign	Coordinator (Interviewee)	# of Inter view s
Clean-Up	Watershed assessment	Outreach coordinator (OC)	3
	Stewardship campaign*	Program coordinator (PC)	12
	Dumpsite reporting*	Program coordinator (PC)	6
	River cleanup	Outreach coordinator (OC)	4
Air-Quality	Bicycle air quality monitoring	Policy & outreach coordinator (POC)	4
	Air pollution reporting*	Policy & outreach coordinator (POC)	11

Table 2. Campaigns and coordinators that we interviewed
(The campaigns marked with * created mobile tools using Sensr.)

Campaign Case Studies

We analyzed the data using a case-based method [17]. Because each campaign (and the staff member running it) is unique, this method helps to contextualize the data being presented. Our discussion section draws themes across the cases together for further insight. Note that each campaign had a single primary coordinator, listed in Table 2, who was also the sole interviewee in quotes for that campaign.

CleanUp Campaign: Watershed Assessment

Two months into our study, the CleanUp org launched a campaign to produce assessment maps of a local creek. A group of one expert and several volunteers was formed to walk through a creek to conduct visual assessment. The outreach coordinator (OC) was the coordinator of this campaign and interviewee for this case.

The coordinator planned to use a camera to record pictures, an inventory sheet to write down a description about the spot, and a photo sheet to mark the ID number of the spot where the photo was taken. Locations were marked on a paper map (See Figure 3). Thus, she planned to form a group of four or more volunteers so that each volunteer would conduct one task. After one month, in which over 250 items were recorded over 2 miles of creek, the coordinator determined that the assessment procedure was too slow: their initial plan was to complete assessing the entire 18 miles within three months. Thus, she revised the process to reduce the number of volunteers to two.

"We are mostly expediting the recording process. Because we were filling it out for each thing we saw on the sheet. It's a lot of paper and a lot of actions for information." (OC)

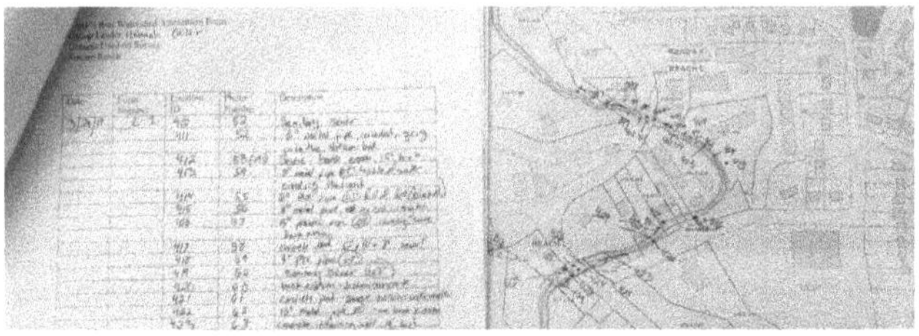

Figure 3. An assessment sheet and a printout map with spots marked used for the watershed assessment project

She explored Sensr for two weeks, and decided not to use it because of the distrust on smartphone's GPS accuracy.

"We will just take pictures and record it on a map for the location, because GPS will not be accurate enough. We are looking at a very fine level accuracy.... We have maps that were made for us in a very small scale." (OC)

In the end, this project did not use any computing technologies except a camera.

CleanUp Campaign: River Cleanup

The outreach coordinator runs a campaign, aiming to clean up the city's rivers and shores twice a month from April to October. The schedule for the entire year is planned out early in the year. Planning includes selecting locations, preparing a boat, and recruiting volunteers.

Selecting locations is a particularly important part of the planning, as it determines where trash is, estimates the amount of trash in the river, and finds the closest riverbank to embark to load/unload the collected trash and volunteers. The existing process was that the boat pilot drove on the river and wrote down a description of spots.

This campaign was originally run by the program coordinator (PC), who was very positive about the potential of GPS to simplify the process.

"[we] try to guess and try to write down the closest from the landmark to estimate." (PC)

However, as with the previous campaign, the outreach coordinator who currently runs the river cleanup campaign did not want to use a mobile tool. She believed that the boat pilot was skilled enough to determine the location without any technical supports. She trusted human capabilities and believed that pen-and-paper would be more convenient.

CleanUp Campaign: Stewardship Campaign

In the CleanUp stewardship campaign, volunteer stewards monitor cleaned-up sites regularly to prevent them from being trashed again. A steward visits each site once or twice a month walking around and checking whether there is new dumping, and then reports the condition to the program coordinator (PC), who runs this campaign.

Most reports were made through emails by the 25 stewards. But the program coordinator sometimes had to call stewards to gather data, because stewards sometimes forget to report back about their fieldwork after returning home. Thus, she was looking for a systematic channel through which stewards report data. She created a mobile tool to allow stewards to report findings on the go using Sensr with the goal of addressing the time lag in reporting.

"That will be helpful for [stewards] as they go through the busy day, stopping by the place to report things to us. People will not have to wait until they get back and email me." (PC)

The created tool consisted of a photo, three text fields (site name, reporter's name, general comments) and two multiple-choices (litter: minimal or extensive, dumping: yes or no) (See Figure 4).

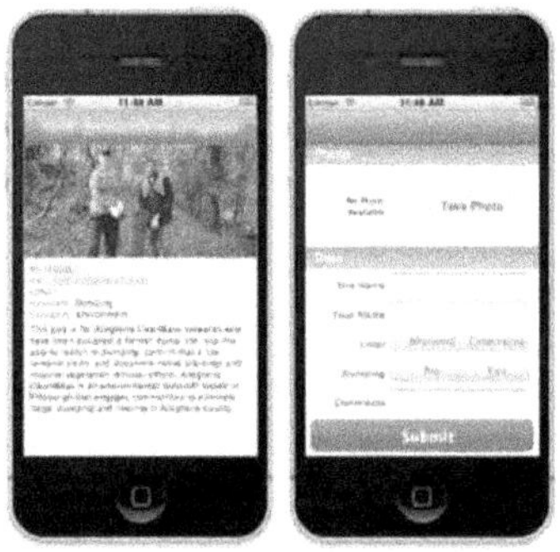

Figure 4. Mobile stewardship project

The program coordinator was extremely positive at the start of the deployment because she felt the mobile tool would help her to manage this campaign more easily. She expected that a mobile tool would provide volunteers with a clear idea of how they are expected to do without much verbal explanation.

"With the app, people clearly know more of what to do. 'I have this app. I am putting my data here.' Otherwise, it's like what am I doing, how am I reporting it to you?"

She also felt that the mobile app made the campaign more official and more in line with social norms.

"With the proliferation of apps for everything, not having an app is a deficit. Someone might say 'you don't have an app for that'? ... It seems more official because we have some technology. I like to be able to say like 'do you want to be a

steward? Now, we do have an app. We do have a way to make it easy if you have a smart phone!'" (PC)

This mobile tool was deployed for four months in this study. During the 4-month deployment, 10 reports were made through this tool. One reason for the small number of reports is that reporting is only done monthly or bimonthly. Another reason is that Sensr only supported iOS. Seven stewards who were using Android devices and eleven who were not using smartphones could not participate.

We attempted to support volunteers without iOS devices by creating a web form for data submission, but this interface created additional confusion for users. Most volunteers did not understand how to use it on a mobile platform. In other words, the "mobile app" metaphor did not adequately map across onto web-based interface. After trying to adopt the web data-submission page for two weeks, the program coordinator decided to stop using it.

"People are saying like 'I don't know what's going on'. So it ... discourages people, and they give up." (PC)

Consequently, she had to keep the conventional ways of emailing and calling for non-iOS device users. Despite this, the program coordinator felt that it still reduced her work in the ways she had predicted.

"It has decreased the number of emails and reminders that I have to send out. It's more convenient for me because I am not being bombarded with separate requests and updates in my email. Also, it is nice not to have to worry as much about the data coming in, because it's all right there at one place. Especially for pictures it's really helpful, because I have a whole record right there, picture, picture, picture. It is great to have all of them in one place, rather than in an email and downloading them." (PC)

CleanUp Campaign: Dumpsite Reporting

Satisfied with a mobile tool for the Stewardship campaign, the same coordinator decided to launch another mobile tool, one to enable the public to report newly discovered dumpsites. The CleanUp org was already receiving occasional reports from the public about new dumpsites through emails or phone calls. The program coordinator wanted a mobile tool that could function as an alternative channel for people to report new dumpsites on the go. So, she created a mobile tool using Sensr. It consisted of a photo, four fields (city, neighborhood, nearest road, comments, email) and one multiple-choice question (tire: yes or no) (See Figure 5).

The program coordinator announced this mobile campaign via email, social media, and its homepage to volunteers. The tool was deployed for two months. During the deployment, 21 volunteers registered to the campaign, and 6 reports were made through this tool. These reports primarily came from stewards who were already using a mobile tool for the stewardship campaign. We learned that the majority of dumpsite reporters are one-time reporters, for whom installing and learning a mobile tool was too much overhead.

"For the person that comes to me and says one dumpsite behind his house, it doesn't make much sense for that person to download it and go through the whole process. So, it looks like not as convenient for the regular people." (PC)

Figure 5. Mobile stewardship project

Hence, the program coordinator did not expect this tool to be widely used by the public. Interestingly, she intended to keep operating it, not only because it was useful to ongoing volunteers, but also for the perceived value of a campaign having its own custom technology.

"Whenever someone does the dumpsite reporting to us, I will say like 'hey in the future you can use this app that helps you doing it easily.'" (PC)

AirQuality Campaign: Bike Air Quality Monitoring

The bicycle air-quality monitoring program collects air quality data in the region from cyclists. This campaign already made use of custom technology, an air quality sensor to attach on the recruited cyclists' bikes. With the data, the AirQuality org aimed to present a sampling of the region's air quality to illustrate where the problem areas are. A part-time staff member operated this campaign, and the policy & outreach coordinator (POC) managed the data and was the primary interviewee.

The POC was a technology expert. He managed technical tasks in the organization, including updating a webpage, posting news on social media, and maintaining computing facilities. The policy & outreach coordinator and the part-time staff used a third party system (not Sensr) to allow cyclists to report air pollution while riding a bike.

Data provided by this sensor was seen as supplementary evidence for effective communication with other stakeholders, rather than to be used in-house for assessing air quality. He trusted the accuracy of the sensed data but did not expect that the data would provide new information.

"I personally don't need monitors to see the data. I know it without a monitor. But other people like political leaders and businessmen won't believe me unless I show them a nice fancy map." (POC)

Whereas Sensr was not needed for this campaign, the POC decided to create a campaign, described next, through which the public could report issues related to air pollution.

AirQuality Org Campaign: Reporting Air Pollution

The AirQuality org created a mobile campaign through which the public can report air pollution. While the campaign itself was new, the idea was not new, as they were already receiving reports about air pollution from the public through an email or phone call occasionally. The mobile tool was designed as an alternative way to collect reports. Because they were receiving reports via emails and phone calls, they sought a systematic channel through which they could manage reports.

The policy & outreach coordinator created the mobile tool using Sensr and announced it via mailing list, social media, and the organization homepage to their volunteers. The tool consisted of a photo, two multiple-choice questions (Pollution type: mobile or stationary, email from us: yes or no) and one field (email) (See Figure 6).

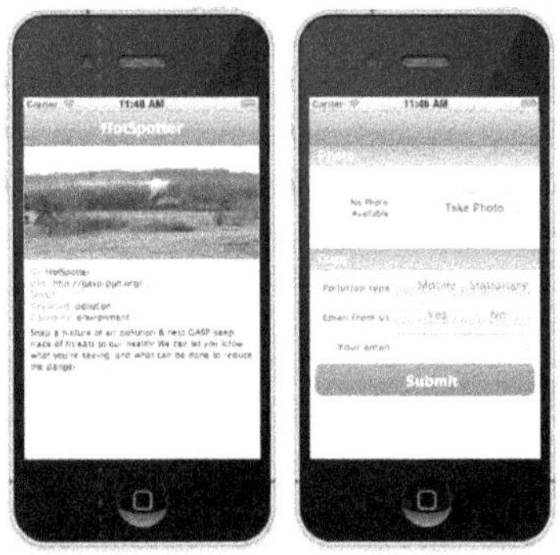

Figure 6. Air pollution source reporting campaign

During the three-month deployment, 27 volunteers registered to this campaign, but only 7 reports were made through this tool. We had several discussions with the coordinator to explore possible reasons why it was not used much. Similar to the Dumpsite Reporting campaign, it seemed this campaign consisted mostly of one-time reports, for which volunteers preferred email or phone:

"They are usually people we never heard of. People don't think about air pollution until it affects them. Then, they freak out, research, find us, and email or call us... we give them some answer, and usually we never hear again from them." (POC)

Additionally, POC said that volunteers were dissatisfied with short yes-no questions. He also said that the descriptive information is less useful for the organization, but powerful and persuasive to share within community members to promote collective action.

"People don't want to share a small piece of data, but want to share a whole experience about what happened and their thoughts. In this way, people feel that their actions are more meaningful than submitting a line of short sentences." (POC)

The AirQuality org had volunteers who were regular participants in monitoring air pollution. However, unlike the volunteers for the CleanUp org, the active volunteers in the AirQuality or did not make use of Sensr but kept their own way of reporting data.

"They have their own ways to make a report, because they have been doing this for years. So, I think the people that would have been very excited to use this are already set [in their ways]." (POC)

Similar to the OC for CleanUp, volunteers' beliefs and attitudes about technology as well as their relationship to the campaign itself strongly affected their use of Sensr.

DISCUSSION AND DESIGN IMPLICATIONS

Our two studies, taken together, reveal a landscape of participation that matches our expectations about the impact of individual perception and attitude on technology use. In total, our studies included over fifty interviews, deep explorations of the potential value of Sensr across six separate campaigns, and the construction and deployment of four separate data collection applications. Our results help to tease apart a range of specific issues and ground our understanding of how technology adoption plays out in resource-constrained, small non-profit campaigns.

Our findings touch on some of the key issues that may need to be considered in designing mobile data collection tools for small non-profit organizations. At a high level, it is critical to bring the viewpoints of multiple stakeholders into the design process (e.g., using participatory design [2,25] or Value-sensitive design – an approach to account for human value throughout the design process [7]).

Specifically, our data revealed four factors that could directly influence design.

1. Quality Control, Trust, and Authenticity are an issue for any data collection task. However, our data highlight how notions of *data quality* can vary widely based on the perceptions of individuals involved, the goals of the organization, and the structure of a campaign. For example, quality was expressed across our studies in terms of specificity, quantity, novelty, ability to appeal to funders, accuracy, and trust (in technology and/or volunteer participants). In addition, even when quality was raised as the primary issue, underlying issues were often visible, such as lack of familiarity with the capabilities of technology or a concern about losing control of tasks when using technology. *Thus, it is critical to figure out what "quality" means before designing for it.*

2. Individual Beliefs and Attitudes towards Technology are sure to have an impact on the use of various technologies. For example, one participant was concerned about a social expectation of there being "an app for that" as a sign of the realness of a campaign. *What was unexpected in our data is the degree to which personal opinions dominated decision-making within the organizations we studied.* Personal propensity and organizational context are known to be strongly associated with the adoption of technological innovations [28]. Perhaps because of their small size, the attitudes of individuals reigned supreme in our data. One explanation is the lack of social interaction (among staff) around the technology – over time in other settings. It has been shown that workers may improve their interpretations about technology through social interaction [14]. It might be because organizations are operated under a traditional hierarchical structure that made it hard for new technical interventions to merge into the existing structure. Another reason might be because elements of Sensr may have biased towards a more flat organizational structure rather than a hierarchical one. This opens up the opportunity to discuss how such community data collection tools need to support existing organizational structures. *In all, systems need to allow alternative flows of information and improved transparency.*

3. The presence of volunteers requires special consideration. Multiple stakeholders are a given in organizational contexts, and volunteers have a unique relationship to the organizations we studied. They are not accountable in the same way that a staff member may be. In addition, volunteers are often unpaid and in some cases completely transitory. Our data suggests that it is critical to pay attention to whether participation is *recurrent* (as with structured, periodic field events) or *sporadic* (as with one-time reports of air quality or dumping issues).

Data collection tools may serve communities best by designing multiple entry points to participate through dedicated apps like Sensr as well as lightweight social media such as Twitter. Customized tools like Sensr will serve a critical role in providing a richer experience of the data, campaign, and community in recurrent activities, whereas lightweight tools (e.g., Twitter) will serve to lower the barrier to participation and provide a scaffolding mechanism for individuals into data collection systems. *As such, our findings suggest that an application installation and its associated overhead is better suited to recurrent participants, while a lighter-weight interaction may be necessary for sporadic participants.*

4. Need for Narrative was another interesting finding. The recording and reporting of data varied from logging raw values to descriptive stories and contextual narratives. This related to how satisfied participants felt about their recorded data. For example, repeated volunteers facilitated formally structured tools for data submission, whereas transitory volunteers sought a narrative input mechanism to share the entire story of what they experienced. While most existing data collection systems are suited to formal, structured data collection efforts, a richer narrative-based input mechanism should be another design consideration for future digital volunteering systems. For example, perhaps a collection of stories could become the basis of a brochure or feed into an annual report for potential funders. In addition, a flexible mechanism that supports data flow between volunteers and organizers in both directions should be considered. For example, an organization can notify volunteers with a follow-up on data. This mechanism will increase volunteers' feeling of engagement and allow organizations to grasp richer contexts about the issue of concern. *Thus, a tool could help organizations to scaffold participation over time by leveraging volunteers' existing proclivities for data entry into new and beneficial types of data.*

LIMITATIONS

A limitation of our data is its focus on only two organizations in the second study, and the fact that our studies did not continue to track technology use beyond the initial diffusion of that technology into the volunteer community. Because of the small number of organizations in the study, our discussion and results should be interpreted as a starting point for exploring mobile data collection adoption. In addition, because Sensr did not support every feature/platform organizations may have wanted, it is possible that Sensr itself might have influenced adoption in ways that are difficult to tease out. Lastly, while previous work has studied volunteers (e.g., [21,31]), one of the unique features of our work was to study an underrepresented stakeholder in mobile data collection: the campaign organizing staff. Ideally, this study would be complemented by a volunteer perspective, something not present in our paper.

CONCLUSION

Despite the increased usage of mobile technology across many wide economic and cultural demographics, application specific mobile data collection applications have yet to be widely adopted. There is a clear opportunity here, since mobile technology has the potential to provide information that could be of great value in community based data collection tasks. Photos, GPS location, and other sensors could be easily leveraged to enhance existing data collection tools. However, the technical skills required to effectively develop these custom mobile data collection applications still remain well outside the ability of most non-profit organizations.

Building on prior work which points to the importance of a range of social factors in technology acceptance (e.g., [8,13,14]), our contribution is an analysis of the factors that should be considered in the design of custom mobile technology for data collection in small non-profits. Through a series of survey studies, we first mapped out current technology use in volunteer campaigns. Then, in the six-month deployment study, we removed the issue of technical difficulty to allow other more subtle problems to rise to the surface. Our findings reveal important issues such as personal interpretation about, comprehension of, and propensity to accept technological interventions as barriers. Extending existing theoretical approaches to the design of technology, this work suggests identifying different perspectives, needs, benefits, and skills of multiple stakeholders that constitute volunteer campaigns, incorporating these into the process of designing novel mobile volunteering systems. We are hopeful that our work can motivate future research on mobile technology and digital volunteerism.

ACKNOWLEDGMENTS

We appreciate the valuable input of our anonymous reviewers. We also would like to thank all the study participating organizations. This work was supported by NSF IIS-1211047 and NSF IIS-1217929.

REFERENCES

1. Aanensen, D. M., Huntley, D. M., Feil, E. J., & Spratt, B. G. (2009). EpiCollect: linking smartphones to web applications for epidemiology, ecology and community data collection. *PloS one*, 4(9), e6968.
2. Carroll, J. (2004). Completing design in use: Closing the appropriation cycle. *ECIS 2004*, pp.44
3. Cohn, J. P. (2008), Citizen Science: Can Volunteers Do Real Research? *Bioscience* 58:192–197.
4. Corburn, J. (2003). Bringing local knowledge into environmental decision making improving urban planning for communities at risk. *J. of Planning Educ. and Research*, 22(4), 420-433.
5. Corburn, J., Osleeb, J., & Porter, M. (2006). Urban asthma and the neighbourhood environment in New York City. *Health & Place*, 12(2), 167-179.
6. DeSanctis, G., & Poole, M. S. (1994). Capturing the complexity in advanced technology use: Adaptive structuration theory. *Org. Science*, 121-147.
7. Friedman, B. et al. (2013). Value sensitive design and information systems. In *Early engagement and new technologies: Opening up the laboratory* (pp. 55-95). Springer Netherlands.
8. Grudin, J. (1988). Why CSCW applications fail: problems in the design and evaluation of organizational interfaces. In *CSCW'88* (pp. 85-93).
9. Hackler, D., & Saxton, G. D. (2007). The strategic use of information technology by nonprofit organizations: Increasing capacity and untapped potential. *Public Administration Review*, 67(3), 474-487.
10. Hartung, C., Lerer, A., Anokwa, Y., Tseng, C., Brunette, W., & Borriello, G. (2010). Open data kit: Tools to build information services for developing regions. *Fourth Inter. Conf. on Info. and Comm. Tech. and Dev.* (p. 18)
11. Kim, S., Mankoff, J., & Paulos, E. (2013). Sensr: evaluating a flexible framework for authoring mobile data-collection tools for citizen science. *CSCW'13* (pp. 1453-1462).
12. Kim, S., Robson, C., Zimmerman, T., Pierce, J., & Haber, M. (2011). Creek watch: pairing usefulness and usability for successful citizen science. *CHI'11* (pp. 2125-2134).
13. Le Dantec, C. A., & Edwards, W. K. (2008). The view from the trenches: Organization, power, and technology at two nonprofit homeless outreach centers. *CSCW'08* (pp. 589-598).
14. Leonardi, P. M. (2009). Why do people reject new technologies and stymie organizational changes of which they are in favor? Exploring misalignments between social interactions and materiality. *Human Communication Research,* 35(3), 407-441.
15. Liu, S. Iacucci, A.A., & Meier, P. Ushahidi Haiti & Chile: Next Generation Crisis Mapping. *American Congress on Surveying and Mapping,* August 2010.
16. MAP & Idealware. (2012). *Unleashing innovation: Using everyday technology to improve nonprofit services.* St. Paul, MN
17. Miles, M.B. and Huberman, A.M. *Qualitative data analysis: An expanded sourcebook.* SAGE publications, Inc, 1994
18. NTEN (2011), Technology: the Smart Investigation, http://blog.techimpact.org/10-nonprofit-tech-stats-on-digital-planning/
19. Orlikowski, W. J. (2000). Using Technology and Constituting Structures: A Practice Lens for Studying Technology in Organizations. *Org. Science,* 11(4), 404–428.
20. Orlikowski, W. J. (2005). Material works: Exploring the situated entanglement of technological performativity and human agency. *Scand. J. of Info. Systems,* 17(1), 6.
21. Raddick, M. J., Bracey, G., Gay, P. L., Lintott, C. J., Murray, P., Schawinski, K., ... & Vandenberg, J. (2010). Galaxy zoo: Exploring the motivations of citizen science volunteers. *Astronomy Educ. Review*, 9(1), 010103.
22. Ramanathan, N., Alquaddoomi, F., et al. (2012). ohmage: An open mobile system for activity and experience sampling. *Pervasive Health,* IEEE, 2012.
23. Saeed, S., Rohde, M., & Wulf, V. (2011) Conducting ICT research in voluntary organizations: Reflections from a long term study of the european social forum, *The J. of Community Informatics, 7(3).*
24. Schneider, J. A. (2003). Small, minority-based nonprofits in the information age. *Nonprofit Management and Leadership*, 13(4), 383–399.
25. Schuler, D. & Namioka, A. (1993). Participatory design: Principles and practices. *Erlbaum Associates Inc.*
26. Silvertown, J. (2009). A new dawn for citizen science. *Trends in ecology & evolution*, 24(9), 467-471.
27. Strauss, A. L. and Corbin, J. *Basics of Qualitative Research.* Sage Publications, 1990.
28. Sullivan, B. L., Wood, C. L., Iliff, M. J., Bonney, R. E., Fink, D., & Kelling, S. (2009). eBird: A citizen-based bird observation network in the biological sciences. *Biological Conservation*, 142(10), 2282-2292.
29. Voida, A., Harmon, E., & Al-Ani, B. (2011). Homebrew databases: Complexities of everyday information management in nonprofit organizations. *CHI'11* (pp. 915-924).
30. Wastell, D. G., & McMaster, T. (2008). Organizational dynamics of technology-based innovation: diversifying the research agenda. *J. of Info. Tech.*, 23(2), 63-70.
31. Wiggins, A., & Crowston, K. (2011). From conservation to crowdsourcing: A typology of citizen science. *HICSS'11* (pp. 1-10).

"Everyone Is Talking about It!": A Distributed Approach to Urban Voting Technology and Visualisations

Lisa Koeman
ICRI Cities
University College London
London, UK
lisa.koeman.12@ucl.ac.uk

Vaiva Kalnikaitė
Dovetailed
23 King Street
Cambridge, UK
vaiva@dovetailed.io

Yvonne Rogers
UCL Interaction Centre
University College London
London, UK
y.rogers@ucl.ac.uk

ABSTRACT
The deployment of technology interventions, such as public displays and mobile apps, in community settings has been found to engage people in sharing and comparing their opinions. Our research is concerned with how to extend this to community-wide participation by devising and deploying multiple voting devices and visualisations. We present an in-the-wild study where a number of shopkeepers along a street participated by placing a novel voting device in their shops to collect locals' opinions. Results were displayed outside the shops, on the pavement. This distributed set-up was found to promote public debate on local issues, particularly around the perceived divide between people on either end of the street. We outline our design process and describe the impact of distributing voting devices and situated visualisations in a local community.

Author Keywords
Opinion gathering technology; public visualisations; in-the-wild study; design

ACM Classification Keywords
H.5.m. Information Interfaces and Presentation (e.g. HCI): Miscellaneous

INTRODUCTION
How can public technology facilitate civic engagement and community building? Active participation and communication are key to the functioning of geographical communities, and ultimately democracy, as they ensure that local views are heard and discussed — and potentially taken into account during decision making processes. Motivated by growing concerns about social connectedness in cities [17], interventions have often focused on engaging community members in becoming more familiar with one another, with the aim of stimulating participation and communication. A number of projects have attempted to spark civic discourse in communities by deploying input technology (for example voting devices) and publicly broadcasting the output (for example via public digital screens). Though many studies have successfully managed to attract people to the technology, they have been limited in how far they reach out to facilitate 'electronic democracy'. In particular, most have only made use of a single location for input and output. As a result, the ability of the technology to engage with people in the community is limited to people happening to pass by, or those who are aware of, that specific location. Similarly, projects with specific technical requirements have limited participation to, for example, people in the possession of RFID-enabled transport passes (e.g. [2]) or mobile phones (e.g. [18]).

While it is generally easy to involve a small number of active community members, reaching out to a wider number of the population is far more challenging. How can we engage people living on the 'poorer' part of the street, elderly residents, those working nightshift and those only working in the area to take part? In other words, how can we design urban technology interventions for more community-wide engagement? Our research describes how using a more distributed approach can help bridge the gap, by deploying a number of urban voting technologies and visualisations throughout a community setting. While using a single input and output location has several advantages, including the ability to encourage people to congregate at one place, the relatively low maintenance and costs, and the ease of data collection (especially capturing conversation), it also has limitations. In particular, people may not be aware of its existence. We argue that a decentralised approach can be more pervasive, providing multiple entry-points for more people to notice and take part. Furthermore, by facilitating multiple congregations at different locations, more localised conversation can take place.

We present a case study in which low tech input devices were positioned inside shops and cafes, and visualisations were displayed all the way along a high street, enabling customers and passers-by to vote on locally-relevant questions generated by the community and view the results. The aim of the deployment was to encourage people to reflect on local issues and generate conversations about their perceptions about the area and the community. The results from an in-the-wild study of the technology intervention showed our dis-

CHI 2015, April 18 - 23 2015, Seoul, Republic of Korea

ACM 978-1-4503-3145-6/15/04... $15.00
http://dx.doi.org/10.1145/2702123.2702263

tributed approach not only facilitated much conversation and reflection, but also evoked several other behaviours, including curiosity, comparison, and competition with neighbouring shops and cafes along the street.

We outline the design process and then discuss how the situated voting technology and visualisations affected the community in different ways. We discuss how engagement was encouraged and which aspects of our design proved key in this process. Finally, we highlight the importance of spreading technology throughout a physical locale, such as a high street or town centre, for encouraging community-wide public debate.

RELATED WORK

New technologies, such as public displays, interactive installations and sensors are providing new opportunities for civic engagement, also known as urban informatics[9]. While a range of different projects have been conducted in recent years, a popular area of study is the use of technology to encourage social connectedness in cities. This direction is primarily inspired by claims that cities are becoming less and less connected (e.g. [17]). Discourse and reflection on personal opinions and the viewpoints of other people have been deemed important in the process of connecting people and fostering communities. For this reason, researchers have started exploring the role opinion gathering (and sharing) technology can have in the urban environment. A number of studies have used technology to gather and share personal opinions publicly [1, 6]. While these initial deployments made use of conventional input technology, like a keyboard, more recent interventions have explored bespoke technology — allowing people to express themselves in more creative ways. For example, Fortin et al. [8] allowed people to talk into a digital megaphone. Speech recognition was used to parse what people said, and a word cloud-like visualisation was presented on a nearby building. Fischer et al. [7] developed a similar installation, allowing people to 'shoot' messages onto a wall using a digital slingshot. The use of body movement to cast a vote has also been investigated, including the use of arm gestures [24] and feet presses [20].

Fewer developments have taken place in the presentation of the gathered data, with virtually all studies making use of either digital screens (e.g. [4, 6, 10, 11, 12, 13, 18, 20, 21, 23, 27]) or projections (e.g. [8, 19, 24]). While these two display techniques allow for the presentation of live data, display blindness [16] and glare have been known to limit what people see and hence subsequent engagement. The vast majority of these opinion gathering and sharing studies are aimed at generating civic discourse (e.g. [13, 20, 24]) and facilitating e-democracy (e.g. [4, 23, 25]).

To enable technology interventions to be used more community-wide, however, and by people from different ages, backgrounds and living in different areas, consideration needs to be given to how best to design and deploy the technologies that are intended to gather opinions and facilitate conversation. Design considerations include, for example, accessible design of the input technology and accessible, understandable feedback as output. A practical example of this is the consideration of whether to use digital screens and projections. As many digital screens and projections are known to be best visible in a dark setting, deploying these output technologies can limit participation to people able to view them at nighttime.

Study	Year	Input location(s)	Output location(s)
Ananny et al. [1]	2004	Web	1
Behrens et al. [2]	2014	1	1
Braun et al. [4]	2013	1	1
Brignull et al. [6]	2003	1	1
Fischer et al. [7]	2013	1	1
Fortin et al. [8]	2014	1	1
Gianluca et al. [10]	2013	1	1
Hosio et al. [11]	2012	1	1
Kriplean et al. [12]	2012	1	1
Leong et al. [13]	2009	1	*"Various"*
Schroeter [18]	2012	SMS	1
Simm et al. [19]	2012	SMS/Web	1
Steinberger et al. [20]	2014	1	1
Steins et al. [21]	2011	1	1
Tang et al. [22]	2008	SMS	1
Taylor et al. [23]	2012	3	3
Valkanova et al. [24]	2014	1	1
Vlachokyriakos et al. [25]	2014	2	Web
Whittle et al. [27]	2010	1	1

Table 1. Overview of studies in which opinion gathering technology is situated in public spaces, together with their number of input (e.g. voting technology) and output (e.g. visualisation of votes) locations.

When deployed in the urban environment, the spatial dimension of inclusiveness also needs to be taken into consideration: how can people easily access the technology? And perhaps even more importantly, how will they find out about its existence in the first place? Most studies have provided one input location and one output location, as shown in Table 1. While the deployment of technology at one key location can prove sufficient, it does require the existence of such a key location — for example a popular public square or train station. As a result, this approach is by default less applicable to residential neighbourhoods or other areas where there is not an obvious 'common place' that is frequented by a large proportion of the local community. In those settings, it is important to find out which locations people do visit regularly. A nearby high street is often frequented by many people within a local community, and as such local shops can be used as a location for input and output — as demonstrated by Taylor et al. [23]. In addition to providing communities with goods and services, high streets have fulfilled an important social role throughout history. Mehta et al. [14] describe this role as follows: *"The biggest competitive advantage of the neighbourhood commercial street is its ability to support social interaction as a part of the daily routine"*.

RESEARCH AIMS

The aim of our research was to explore how a distributed approach to urban voting technology and visualisation can engage a geographic community. By a distributed approach we

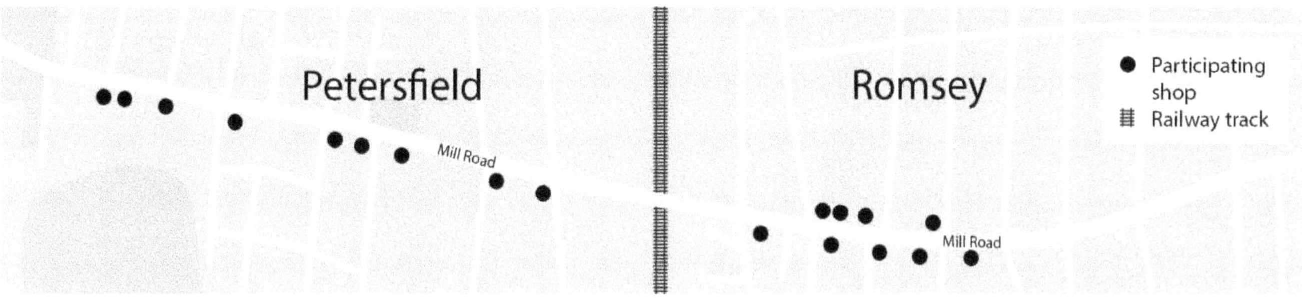

Figure 1. Overview of participating shops in both the Petersfield and Romsey areas of Mill Road (Cambridge, UK).

mean a deployment using multiple input and output locations — as opposed to the use of a single input and output location. Specifically, we were interested in whether a distributed approach can trigger a community to talk about unspoken local perceptions more openly? And can having distributed locations for the technology intervention encourage people to venture into different parts of the community, including areas they do not usually visit?

CASE STUDY: VISUALISING MILL ROAD

We chose a high street, in the heart of a UK city, called Mill Road as the focus of our study (coined 'Visualising Mill Road'). The street is a bustling community locale with many shops and cafes. But in addition, a railway bridge divides Mill Road into two areas: Petersfield (the part of the street closest to the city centre) and Romsey (see Figure 1). While Petersfield was primarily built by the University of Cambridge, Romsey historically had a more 'working class' demographic, resulting in socio-economic and political differences between residents of the two areas. Though a quiet street in the past, the arrival of the railway line in the 19th century drastically changed the character of Mill Road. Nowadays, it is a nationally renowned street, popular for not only its range of independent shops, but also the many local festivities. Despite having a large number of community groups, the divide between Petersfield and Romsey appears to persist. We were interested in how residents and visitors would share their opinions on different aspects of the street, and what they would think of the opinions of others. Our approach was to provide distributed voting technology and situated public visualisations, in order for people to discover more about the perceptions of others — and how those compare with their own. Key to this approach was the goal of engaging a broad range of people into thinking about the local perceptions. Did they think the same or different? Did they know what the others thought about them, especially those living, shopping and working on the two sides of the railway tracks? How ingrained were their views about each other? How could the technology intervention provide them with a better awareness of their community?

Initial community meetings

At the start of the study, we arranged several meetings with Mill Road community groups, to gather more information on the history, characteristics and challenges of the street. Members from several community groups participated, including a group dedicated to Mill Road's history, a group dedicated to 'bridging the divide' and a group involved in organising local festivities. Several people were actively involved in more than one group. During this pre-study, it became apparent how strong the divide between the Petersfield and Romsey areas is in everyday life. Despite efforts from a community group to bridge the divide, both shopkeepers as well as local residents stated they *"rarely go to the other side of the bridge"* and that they believed people on both sides of Mill Road had the same attitude towards *"not wanting to go over the bridge"*. The shop owner of one of the street's oldest shops explained: *"The bridge divides. I suppose it is really a lack of familiarity, actually. Because lots of people don't go over there. I do go more now, but years ago I never used to go – it was like the two sides of the Thames, you know. The North and the South. It still has a slightly different feel over there. Which is interesting, same as London, curiously enough. What exactly it boils down to, I don't know"*. Another shopkeeper added: *"People talk like going over the bridge like it is going to another world"*. From the conversations with these shopkeepers and local residents it emerged that the divide between the two halves of Mill Road plays an important role in everyday life. We also found that the views about 'the other side' are not often explicitly discussed, despite the fact that everyone seemed to feel strongly about this topic. This lack of discourse was also brought up by members of local community groups.

To explore whether the perceived differences between the two areas of Mill Road could be made more open, we discussed with active community members, who wanted people to move between the two areas more, the possibility of gathering and visualising people's perceptions publicly, along Mill Road. To do so, we suggested creating voting devices, allowing people to express their views. The aggregated views would then be presented back to the community via public visualisations, located near the voting devices. It was collectively decided that the voting devices would be situated along the street, in the different shops, as there was a strong belief held by members of the community groups that the shops along Mill Road act as a social hub. One local community organiser expressed it as follows: *"I believe the shops are the social glue of the Mill Road community"*. Based on suggestions from the community groups, council representative and local trade organisation, a list was made of 'shops to approach'. To ensure a variety of demographics would be able to encounter the voting devices, a range of different types of shops was selected. In addition, an attempt was made at selecting comparable shops

Petersfield	Romsey
Charity shop	Charity shop
Charity shop	Flower shop
Local supermarket	Local supermarket
Liquor shop	Greengrocers
Café	Café
Takeaway	Café
Electronics shop	Café
Computer shop	Homeware
Oriental supermarket	Delicatessen shop

Table 2. Overview of participating shops

on both sides of the railway bridge (see Table 2). Where possible, the same type of shop was approached: a charity shop, local supermarket and cafe on both sides. Whenever this was not an option, shops with a similar number of customers were selected. In total, we approached 23 shops along Mill Road. Of these, 18 agreed to participate. Shopkeepers of the participating shops were given an explanatory leaflet about the project and told the voting devices would be placed on their countertop with the aim of collecting opinions from the community. In addition, they were asked to provide suggestions for questions they would like to pose via the devices.

Questions and statements

Based on our conversations with the community groups, shopkeepers and local residents, we identified a set of topics that they considered to be relevant to explore the divide and their community as a whole. These topics were then discussed and iterated with the community groups. After several iterations, a set of 7 questions and statements was finalised:

Q1: How do you feel today? (i.e. *happiness*)
Q2: How well do you know your neighbours? (i.e. *neighbourliness*)
Q3: Mill Road is safe (i.e. *safety*)
Q4: Mill Road feels like home (i.e. *community*)
Q5: I like to shop locally (i.e. *local shopping*)
Q6: Mill Road is buzzing today (i.e. *street buzz*)
Q7: I know lots of people around here (i.e. *social ties*)

A number of shopkeepers and residents indicated they wanted to think about relevant questions for a longer period of time. We therefore decided to gather further suggestions during the deployment. The following two questions were later included, based on their additional suggestions:

Q8: I am happier on this side of the bridge (i.e. *localism*)
Q9: The future of Mill Road is bright (i.e. *future*)

For the purpose of community-wide participation, all suggestions had to comply with one condition: the topic had to be of relevance to people along the whole street. As such, suggestions that were only relevant to the (commercial) interests of one shop or person were omitted. It was also decided that the questions and statements had be kept short, to allow people to read them at a glance. Slightly ambiguous topics like safety were not clarified (e.g. road safety, risk of pickpocketing) with the hope this would encourage further discussion.

Voting technology

To gather opinions of people in the Mill Road area, we designed, built and deployed a set of novel voting devices. We

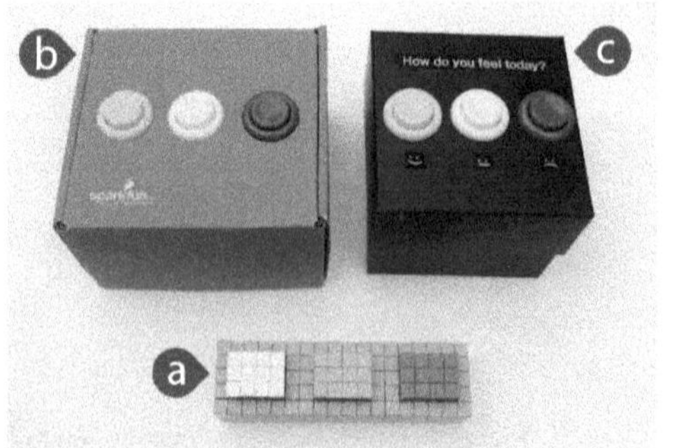

Figure 2. Voting devices: a) lo-fi Lego prototype, b) hi-fi prototype, c) final version.

aimed to make them attractive, appealing and easy to use by everyone – simply, at the press of a button. To this end we thought a device that was tangible and evocative would be effective. We chose not to design a data collection device to run on an existing technology, such as a touch screen, mobile phone app or web-based interface as this would mean having to ask people to download an app or the shopkeepers to set up and maintain a touch screen in their shop or café. Instead, we chose to design a device that was salient and obvious how to use — by basing it on the familiar input interaction of pressing a button to communicate a choice. Due to its simplicity and familiarity, this type of interaction requires no learning for the vast majority of people. To enable the voting device to be clear to people of different ages and backgrounds requires the questions being asked to be concise and the options to answer them straightforward. The device also has to be low maintenance and robust for it to be able to be used in a range of shops. To fit into the setting of a shop it also has to be able to stand on the counter, without taking up a lot of space or looking out of place, while still being noticed by customers.

After a few iterations, we designed a compact device that contained a set of large colourful buttons designed to attract attention. Each question was placed above the buttons. Below them were smiley faces, intended to provide a canonical set of answers: agree, neutral or disagree. The device only allows one of three choices to be selected. This constraint was intended to provoke public discussion around the voting devices between shoppers and shopkeepers. A low fidelity Lego prototype of the voting device (see Figure 2a) was presented during meetings with local community members, together with sketches of the final version. The feedback elicited during these sessions suggested that the concept of three large smiley face buttons, in order from happy to sad, was entirely clear. However, it also emerged that the device as a whole would have to be larger in size, both to attract attention as well as to display the question in a more readable manner. Based on these findings, a larger high fidelity prototype was built, using a cardboard box (see Figure 2b). Though the initial idea was to use 3D-printed or wooden boxes, the high fidelity prototype revealed that strong cardboard was a suitable, cheaper and more practical material. The final voting devices (see Figure 2c) were built from black cardboard boxes, with Microsoft Gadgeteer hardware modules and an SD card to store a log of all button presses. Devices were connected to the mains. Shops that were unable to provide a plug point were given a battery-powered device. Neutral but bright colours were selected for the arcade game buttons, to avoid negative colour-emotion associations. The questions and smiley faces were created using a label printer.

Public visualisations

To make the visualisations accessible to a broad range of community members, we chose to make use of simple representations. We wanted to make it obvious the visualisations conveyed something about the community, and the collected votes, rather than being an art installation. In addition, the visualisations were designed to provoke members of the community to reflect on what they meant and for them to provoke further discussion about the perceived social divide on Mill Road. The public visualisations were designed to be placed in front of the participating shops along the street, on both sides of the railway track, in a way that would catch people's attention as they walked up and down the street. This way, the placement of the visualisation reveals from which shop or café the data is collected. In addition, to ensure we did not compromise people or shops, we decided to only visualise relative data, which allows for comparison between visualisations without revealing sensitive and distracting data about the popularity of shops.

During the sketching process it emerged that making use of the road would cause significant delays, as not only the city council but also the national Highways Agency would have to approve it. When it emerged such approval would involve closing off the road and taking out insurance for all people involved, it was decided that using the pavement would be a more realistic option. An Isotype-inspired visualisation consisting of rows of ten human-like figures was created and informally discussed with members of the community groups to ascertain readability and clarity. For each question posed via the voting device, a row was added, with each figure representing 10% of the votes. Percentages were rounded to 'whole figures'. These figures were coloured in, matching the colours used for the buttons on the voting device (the neutral colours yellow, white and blue, representing happy, neutral and sad). In addition, a keyword summarising the question was added at the front of the row (see Figure 3). This more ambiguous description was chosen to minimise clutter and encourage interaction between residents and shopkeepers to discuss what was meant by it. The visualisation was meant to convey enough information about the question and accompanying votes but also to encourage people to visit the corresponding shop to find out more about what it meant and how it was derived.

The visualisation was stencilled on the pavement through the use of non-permanent brightly coloured chalk spray. This method of presentation was previously demonstrated to successfully communicate data in the Tidy Street project [3, 26]. More obvious presentation choices would have included the use of digital displays or digital projections, however, keeping in mind display blindness, electricity requirements and the need for visualisations to appear clearly in bright sunlight, we opted for this novel, eye-catching and low tech approach. The aim was to attract people's attention while walking into

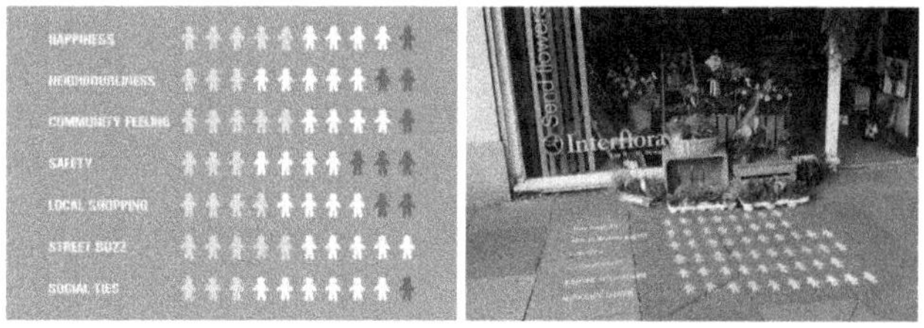

Figure 3. Left: sketch of the visualisation of votes cast within a participating shop, with each figure representing 10% of the votes. Right: visualisation outside a shop.

shops or cafés while not being offensive or appearing as art or vandalism. A benefit of using chalk in this way is that it stays there for a while. Natural elements such as wind and rain cause the chalk to slowly fade, thereby creating an organic way of ending the project. Besides providing a gradual ending, the use of chalk also pacified shop owners and members of the city council, as they trusted all visualisations would automatically disappear again. The visualisations were created using laser cut polyester stencils and were placed at the doorstep of the participating shops. They were updated when the question on the voting device was changed. A final comparative visualisation was created on the bridge to allow for comparison between the Petersfield and Romsey area as a whole. For this visualisation, the data from the different sides of the railway track was aggregated, and shown as a bubble chart. This visualisation was also discussed with members of local community groups, to ensure it was easy to interpret. To avoid compromising people or shops, only relative data was shown. Furthermore, the decision was made to only show data relating to the positive (happy smiley) votes, thus focusing on the positivity from both sides of Mill Road.

In-the-wild study

The voting devices, together with a small explanatory poster, were deployed in 18 different shops along Mill Road. All devices were placed on the shop counters with the idea that the period of waiting that often takes place before customers pay and leave the shop would be an ideal time to quickly voice their opinion. Shopkeepers were asked to decide upon the exact location of the device on the counter, informed by their knowledge of customer behaviour.

The devices were deployed for 24 days in order to enable sufficient time for each question to be posed, discussed and new questions to be suggested by the community. It also allowed for a gradual build up of the visualisations, for the project to be publicised and for a range of people to come in and participate, take a look, and discuss. During the first two weeks, the questions on the devices were changed every other day and the data from the previous question was collected from the SD memory cards in the boxes. This process was done at the end of the afternoon, to coincide with the closing time of the majority of the shops. Shopkeepers were asked to only vote once a day themselves. They were also told that they did not have to encourage customers to vote, but that were free to do so if they would like to, and that they were not in any way responsible for the safekeeping of the voting device. The visualisations outside the shops were sprayed onto the pavement on alternating days, by a team of four local artists accompanied by the researchers. This was done at dawn, when all businesses were still closed and there was little traffic. The comparison visualisation on the railway bridge was created after the data from the seventh question was collected (see Figure 6). Permission was sought from the local council beforehand, to ensure the chalk graffiti visualisations would not be removed by street cleaners.

To see how the distributed voting technology and public visualisations engaged this urban community, an in-the-wild study was conducted. A mixed method approach was adopted, and the following data was collected: (i) logged votes from the devices; (ii) observations in situ, both inside the shops as well as outside, near the shop and bridge visualisations throughout the deployment; (iii) brief semi-structured interviews were conducted with shopkeepers and customers when the shops were visited to replace the question and collect the data from the voting device (iv) additional more extensive semi-structured interviews were conducted with shopkeepers, at the end of the study. A total of 43 semi-structured interviews were carried out with shopkeepers (23 from Romsey, 20 from Petersfield) and 22 with customers and passers-by (12 from Romsey, 10 from Petersfield).

FINDINGS

Throughout the deployment, the 18 voting devices and public visualisations attracted a lot of attention in the Mill Road area. The visualisations lured people into the shops, who then asked the shopkeepers what was going on. Once aware of the project, people returned regularly to answer the different questions and to view and compare results, as observed by the shopkeepers and the researchers present. Some even ventured across the bridge to find out more about the results 'on the other side'. The project sparked conversations on the various topics addressed via the posed questions both inside the shops, and outside near the visualised results — including topics not usually spoken about. From the observations and interviews, it emerged that the study triggered discussions on previously 'hidden' topics. In the following sections these findings will be described in more detail, starting with an analysis of the factors that encouraged participation, followed by descriptions of the votes and the types of engagement the project elicited.

Factors encouraging engagement

The eye-catching visualisations and voting buttons successfully enticed people to ask questions and participate. However, two additional factors were found to greatly encourage community-wide engagement: the participating shopkeepers and the media.

By leveraging on the existing social role of the shops along Mill Road, described as 'social glue' by a community organiser, the shopkeepers acted as community champions. As all shops had an existing customer base, using them as input locations embedded the project in the existing community practices. Furthermore, many shopkeepers voluntarily took up an active role in encouraging customers to vote. The variety of the shops involved proved crucial for engaging a broad range of people. For example, while students and families with young kids frequented Shop P3, Shop R9 had a significantly older group of regular customers. The shopkeeper explained many come from a nearby retirement housing complex: *"They came in the other day to say* "What is it? What have we missed?". *So we told them about the question, they came in, did the box [i.e. voting device] and they will be back at the end of the week."*. Apart from age, demographic differences like cultural background, location of residence and the amount of time people have lived in the area also varied greatly between the customers of the different shops. For instance, while Shop R8 sells very common products, and as a result is primarily frequented by local residents, Shops P5 and P9 sell highly specialised products — attracting customers from all over the city and beyond. Similarly, while some of the older shops have many customers the shopkeepers have known for years (many of them having been born in the area), some of the cafes and newer shops attract people that have only started living near or on Mill Road in recent years.

The local media and social media also played an important role in raising awareness of the project. During the deployment, the project was featured in local radio shows and newspapers. Via Facebook and Twitter, people discussed the results and shared photos of the visualisations. This media activity directly impacted participation. For example, after a front page publication in the city's newspaper, shopkeepers noticed an increase in people coming into their shops, asking if they could cast their vote. One shopkeeper explained: *"It is getting to be known that this thing is going on. People realise that something is happening, and they are curious about it"*.

Votes

In total, 11610 votes were cast during the deployment, of which 4879 (42%) were identified as genuine (i.e. not obvious repeat votes; a vote cast within 5 seconds of the previous vote was classified as a repeat vote and discarded). The number of presses peaked during the second day of the deployment, with 388 genuine presses. As to be expected, the least votes were cast on Sundays and Mondays. The majority of button presses occurred during the daytime, particularly between 11:00 and 18:00. The number of votes differed greatly between shops, as shown in Table 3, with local supermarkets and shops with long opening hours receiving far more votes than any other shops. The type of votes also differed slightly per area, with relatively more 'happy' votes being cast in the Romsey area for each question (as shown in Figure 4).

Types of engagement

To identify the types of engagement, a thematic analysis [5] was conducted on the collected data. Five different types of engagement with the distributed voting devices and visualisations were identified, which we have labeled as curiosity, contemplation, conversation, comparison and competition.

Curiosity

From the moment the voting devices were deployed and the visualisations started appearing on the pavement, people became curious about what was going on. From our observations it became apparent that the majority of people walking

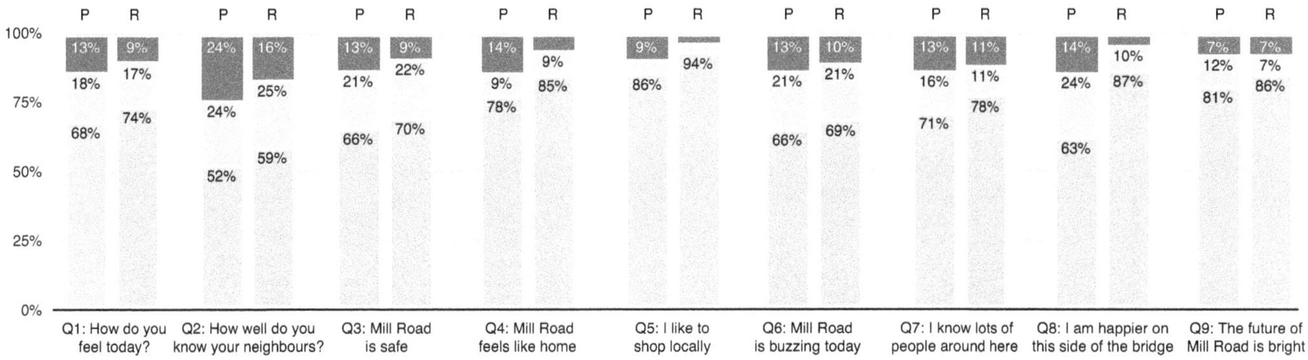

Figure 4. Comparison of votes per question per area (P = Petersfield, R = Romsey). Happy votes shown in yellow, neutral in grey and sad in blue.

Ques.	Q1	Q2	Q3	Q4	Q5	Q6	Q7	Q8	Q9
Days	3	2	2	2	2	2	2	3	6
P1	30	15	16	0	24	13	16	17	27
P2	11	5	1	6	19	2	8	12	18
P3	42	31	25	21	16	25	19	25	58
P4	90	14	23	31	37	0	35	40	43
P5	162	76	49	62	73	66	12	0	0
P6	90	23	35	27	38	10	20	2	0
P7	29	8	7	12	52	8	3	34	41
P8	23	2	2	10	12	2	14	13	35
P9	65	40	30	43	35	19	27	18	66
R1	177	85	78	110	133	52	99	88	102
R2	81	72	24	79	35	55	32	31	0
R3	13	13	9	7	15	3	7	0	0
R4	57	11	17	22	37	14	26	39	55
R5	23	14	13	27	25	19	25	20	32
R6	20	14	2	6	12	17	6	11	20
R7	57	27	30	42	31	25	28	42	102
R8	16	38	33	21	40	24	24	0	0
R9	14	8	14	8	14	17	7	0	24
Total	999	496	408	534	648	371	408	392	623

Table 3. Overview of votes (excluding obvious repeat votes) per shop (P = Petersfield, R = Romsey) and the deployment length of each question. Question number legend can be found in Figure 4.

down the street noticed the visualisations, and many stopped to have a look. Shopkeepers started noticing passers-by coming into their shop to ask questions about the project. Several shopkeepers commented on the benefits they believed this had for them, including a shopkeeper at Shop R6: *"I think it is probably actually beneficial to us, because people are curious, they see the little stick people and because we are one of the shops that has a box [i.e. voting device] they come in. And then they may buy something."*. Passers-by and local residents also started explaining the visualisations to one another. This behaviour was observed by the researchers at several occasions. The owner of Shop R3 noted: *"There is always someone out there explaining it to someone else"*.

Curiosity remained high throughout the deployment, with even those already familiar with the project returning to vote and view the updates regularly (*"They've literally run in, said* "what's the question?", *answered it and gone again"*). During conversations with passers-by, it emerged that many people had been casting their vote on a daily basis, even if they were not buying anything from one of the shops. A number of shopkeepers took an active role in encouraging curiosity, by ensuring their customers would see the voting device. In one shop, this meant the owner placed the voting device at an angle to increase visibility, in another shop the owner used her battery operated voting device to regularly approach all customers at the different tables in her cafe.

Towards the end of the study, when the summary visualisation was sprayed onto the pavement of the railway bridge that connects the two parts of Mill Road, the initial response was far less noticeable. During the informal conversations we had with customers, shopkeepers and passers-by, it emerged many people had heard of the visualisation and the final results through word of mouth — but had not yet seen it themselves. All indicated they would visit it later that day or week, an action that often seemed to require conscious planning. The stark difference in the level of response towards the shop visualisation and summary visualisation suggested people were still resistant to walk to or across the bridge from both sides. While the bridge is one of the few places that is visited by both sides of the street, few people cross it regularly, and our results also showed that likewise, few people made the effort to go out of their way to visit the summary visualisation.

Contemplation

From the informal conversations with passers-by, customers and shopkeepers, it emerged the questions and results from the Visualising Mill Road project had made them reflect upon a) their views and what these views are based on, and b) the changes on Mill Road over the years. The latter was mainly the case for people who have been living in the area for a long period of time, with many reflecting on their youth (e.g. *"Mill Road has changed a lot in terms of the kind of feel of the place. When I was kind of around 16, 17, 18, it was always seen as a really dodgy area and over time it has become much more sort of multi-cultural and therefore a more accepting area."*; *"They used to warn you, you must not go down to Romsey, it is a very rough area. I don't think that's true now."*). Reflections on the questions and results also made some people doubt their own views (e.g. *"Maybe it is just a feeling [that she finds the other side of the road unsafer], I don't know."*; *"I don't know if [my view on the divide between the two areas] is perception or reality"*; *"One or two people,*

Figure 5. Passers-by looking at and discussing the visualisations sprayed on the doorstep of the participating shops

in pressing the button, were suddenly questioning themselves, as to how they should answer - and therefore, you posed a question to them, which up to that moment, they did not seem to have considered").

Conversation

During the observations it became clear that the questions displayed on the devices led to many discussions between customers and shopkeepers, which in turn drew other people into these conversations (cf. [6]). For example, in Shop P2, P7, R1, R7 and R9, it was observed that customers started sharing anecdotes of unsafe situations that they had experienced or heard of on Mill Road. The ambiguity of the questions also resulted in additional discussions. In Shop R7, a customer asked the shopkeeper *"What kind of safety would they mean? Traffic or something else?"*, which was followed by a conversation on the different types of unsafe situations on Mill Road. In the informal conversations and semi-structured interviews the occurrence of these discussions was further confirmed by shopkeepers: *"You have got everyone talking about it!"*; *"It has encouraged people to talk about their environment"*; *"It has definitely made people talk about issues, like community, safety, general trendiness of Mill Road itself. Most people wouldn't bat an eyelid, normally"*; *"It has been a really good talking point"*. The majority of the shopkeepers indicated that the question on safety led to most discussion, followed by the question on neighbourliness.

The voting devices and visualisations appeared to generate different types of discussion. Whereas the conversations held inside the shops largely focused on personal perceptions and the sharing of anecdotes, the conversations around the visualisations tended to be towards comparisons with others. For example, comparison of one's own perceptions versus those of the other customers of that shop, as well as comparisons between shops and areas. In many ways, the visualisations provided people with evidence to vindicate or refute their individual prejudices, and as a result reactions to the discussions were often focused on either agreement (e.g. *"[nods while looking at results] we are the safer side"*) or surprise (e.g. *"I am surprised neighbourliness did not score more positive, this is a very friendly area"*). The results from the voting results sparked most debate, as the findings were contrary and surprising to what most people had assumed: the side that is historically seen as poorer and more unsafe (Romsey) voted more positively for all questions.

Figure 6. Passers-by looking at the visualisation on the railway bridge, representing the differences in votes between Petersfield and Romsey

Comparison

The situated visualisations successfully supported three types of comparisons: between questions, between shops, and between areas. The use of relative data, rounded to tens, allowed people to easily compare and remember results between different locations (e.g. *"I was really interested to see that at [shop] there's a 100% neighbourliness. You know, 10 little men, in yellow. Whereas some of the other places, quite nearby, are not saying that. Like the [shop] just here, I think there is only one or two for neighbourliness"*). This encouraged a number of people to visit 'the other side of the street', to see how the results there compared to those on 'their' side. News about the differences between the two areas spread rapidly, with people on both sides sharing their findings, and the latest hearsay, in gossip-like conversations in the different shops and cafes (e.g. *"I have heard some rumours that it is more positive on the other side of the bridge [Romsey] than it is from over here"*). The unexpected outcome, with Romsey scoring more positively on all questions, fuelled speculation (*"Maybe everyone gets positive here and then moves to that side of the bridge [and votes there]?"*), as well as pride (*"We are the best side"*; *"Good. That disproved the local theory then, doesn't it?"*).

Competition

The ability to vote in different locations and compare results also promoted a sense of competition. This feeling was present at a shop-level (e.g. a shopkeeper was observed asking a customer to please vote positively, as they had *"so many blue people outside already"*. The customer did not comply, as he did not agree with Q4 because in his view there are many drunk and homeless people frequenting Mill Road) as well as at an area-level (e.g. *"A lot of my customers have been quite possessive about insisting "this is the happy side, this is the strong community side""*). By voting multiple times, some customers as well as shopkeepers attempted to influence the results. While most shopkeepers explicitly said they did not vote themselves and instead focused on getting customers to vote, two admitted to casting repeat votes (*"The first time I saw it I had a bit of a symphony [on the buttons]. But yeah, I've been a good boy [since]"*, *"Sometimes I might press it twice, between you and me"*).

DISCUSSION

Based on these findings, we argue that if there is not one central place that unites a geographical community, distribution to a number of places that have existing social functions (e.g. pubs, libraries, stations, etc.) can provide a solution. Key to community-wide participation is the integration of technology into the rhythms and routines of the community. Below, we discuss five core lessons learnt for the design of opinion gathering and sharing technology interventions facilitating more community-wide engagement:

Simple input technology

The use of physical voting devices offers an *accessible, simple, and familiar design*, which can be readily understood by people who may or may not be familiar with modern technology. This proved crucial for the participation of young kids and elderly people (cf. [23]). In addition, such simple voting devices can easily be placed in many different locations. A limitation of using such simple devices is the possibility of enabling people to vote more than once [23, 25]. However, it is possible to reduce such noise by further developing criteria for removing false positives (e.g. people voting in quick succession) and false negatives (e.g. 'slow' repeat votes from one individual).

Community-generated questions and statements

Involving different community groups, shops, and local residents, in generating questions and statements makes them more accessible and *relatable to the community*, including local residents and visitors. While this may require considerable investment of time, it ensures that the questions and statements will be more relevant and topical, and thereby more likely to spark public debate.

Controversial topics

Including controversial subjects is a good way of triggering debate in a community. They can often relate to prejudices around socio-demographics, such as socio-economic status and race. As these themes are universal, yet highly personal, they can engender rich discussions. It can help to *identify topics that are not spoken about, yet many people feel strongly about*, such as, a perceived differences and divides in a community.

Multiple community champions

Involving shopkeepers by placing the voting devices in their shops can ensure that the technology is *embedded in the existing community practices*. Furthermore, it can enable *multiple community champions* to be involved and to encourage different community members to participate, thereby eliciting different perspectives.

Simple public visualisations

Relative data is a powerful representation method to use when designing public visualisations intended to be understood by everyone. This kind of representation can capture the essence of the data collected and show at a glance difference in opinion, enabling both those familiar and unfamiliar with information visualisations to compare results between questions, shops, and areas. Furthermore, situating them close to the input devices shows where the opinions were derived [15] which allows passers-by to *link the output to the input* at the various locations.

The system presented in this paper, and systems like this, have the potential to facilitate community consultation and to evoke community-wide public debate. In the context of local politics, such technology can play an important role in decision making processes — both top-down (e.g. council asking for community's input) and bottom-up (e.g. local activists polling the community). Whereas often a subset of active people are involved in these processes, systems like these allow for low effort, community-wide involvement. Several local residents and shopkeepers of Mill Road expressed seeing value in the use of situated voting technology as a tool, to be used when issues arise in the community. However, a range of challenges need to be overcome in order for such a distributed system to become a widely accepted method of encouraging and facilitating civic participation, such as the need for more reliable and actionable data and coordination between sites.

CONCLUSION

Accessible community technology, such as the one we have described and studied in this paper, can play a valuable role in engaging a range of people in a community to participate in, for example, local discourse and decision making. We have presented an in-the-wild study using multiple voting devices and public visualisations distributed along a street. Our novel approach has shown how affordable, low tech solutions, that can be easily set up and placed throughout a locale can lead to more community-wide involvement, especially when the technology is embedded in existing community practices. Our study has also shown how this approach can help address sensitive issues that can arise in a community. In sum, our distributed approach offers an engaging way of encouraging and facilitating civic participation, offering much potential for opening up public debate and challenging local perceptions.

ACKNOWLEDGMENTS

This work is funded by ICRI Cities. We would like to thank the Cambridge City Council, Mill Road community groups, shops, artists and residents for participating. Thanks to Nicolas Villar for technical support, and to the reviewers for their valuable feedback.

REFERENCES

1. Ananny, M., and Strohecker, C. Textales: Creating interactive forums with urban publics. *Handbook of Research on Urban Informatics: The Practice and Promise of the Real-Time City, IGI Global, Hershey, PA* (2009).
2. Behrens, M., Valkanova, N., Fatah gen. Schieck, A., and Brumby, D. P. Smart citizen sentiment dashboard: A case study into media architectural interfaces. In *Proceedings of the 3rd ACM International Symposium on Pervasive Displays*, ACM (2014).
3. Bird, J., and Rogers, Y. The pulse of tidy street: Measuring and publicly displaying domestic electricity

consumption. In *Workshop on Energy Awareness and Conservation through Pervasive Applications (Pervasive 2010)* (2010).

4. Braun, L., Rivera, J., Mello, J., Hindi, K., Lin, L., Patel, K., and Mathew, A. Skywords: an engagement machine at chicago city hall. In *CHI Extended Abstracts* (2013), 2839–2840.
5. Braun, V., and Clarke, V. Using thematic analysis in psychology. *Qualitative research in psychology 3*, 2 (2006), 77–101.
6. Brignull, H., and Rogers, Y. Enticing people to interact with large public displays in public spaces. In *Proceedings of INTERACT*, vol. 3 (2003), 17–24.
7. Fischer, P. T., Hornecker, E., and Zoellner, C. Smslingshot: an expert amateur diy case study. In *Proceedings of the 7th International Conference on Tangible, Embedded and Embodied Interaction*, ACM (2013), 9–16.
8. Fortin, C., Neustaedter, C., and Hennessy, K. The appropriation of a digital speakers corner: Lessons learned from the in-the-wild deployment of mégaphone. *Proceedings of 2014 ACM Conference on Designing Interactive Systems* (2014).
9. Foth, M., Choi, J. H.-j., and Satchell, C. Urban informatics. In *Proceedings of the ACM 2011 conference on Computer supported cooperative work*, ACM (2011), 1–8.
10. Gianluca, S., Milano, M., Saldivar, J., Nasir, T., Zancanaro, M., and Convertino, G. Agora2. 0: enhancing civic participation through a public display. In *Proceedings of the 6th International Conference on Communities and Technologies*, ACM (2013), 46–54.
11. Hosio, S., Kostakos, V., Kukka, H., Jurmu, M., Riekki, J., and Ojala, T. From school food to skate parks in a few clicks: using public displays to bootstrap civic engagement of the young. In *Pervasive Computing*. Springer, 2012, 425–442.
12. Kriplean, T., Morgan, J., Freelon, D., Borning, A., and Bennett, L. Supporting reflective public thought with considerit. In *Proceedings of the ACM 2012 conference on Computer Supported Cooperative Work*, ACM (2012), 265–274.
13. Leong, T. W., and Brynskov, M. Co2nfession: engaging with values through urban conversations. In *Proceedings of the 21st Annual Conference of the Australian Computer-Human Interaction Special Interest Group: Design: Open 24/7*, ACM (2009), 209–216.
14. Mehta, V. Look closely and you will see, listen carefully and you will hear: Urban design and social interaction on streets. *Journal of Urban Design 14*, 1 (2009), 29–64.
15. Moere, A. V., and Hill, D. Designing for the situated and public visualization of urban data. *Journal of Urban Technology 19*, 2 (2012), 25–46.
16. Müller, J., Wilmsmann, D., Exeler, J., Buzeck, M., Schmidt, A., Jay, T., and Krüger, A. Display blindness: The effect of expectations on attention towards digital signage. In *Pervasive Computing*. Springer, 2009, 1–8.
17. Putnam, R. D. *Bowling alone*. Simon & Schuster, 2001.
18. Schroeter, R. Engaging new digital locals with interactive urban screens to collaboratively improve the city. In *Proceedings of the ACM 2012 conference on Computer Supported Cooperative Work*, ACM (2012), 227–236.
19. Simm, W., Whittle, J., Nieman, A., Portman, A., and Sibbald, J. Ourcity: Understanding how visualization and aggregation of user-generated content can engage citizens in community participation. In *Sixth International AAAI Conference on Weblogs and Social Media* (2012).
20. Steinberger, F., Foth, M., and Alt, F. Vote with your feet: Local community polling on urban screens. In *Proceedings of the 3rd ACM International Symposium on Pervasive Displays*, ACM (2014).
21. Steins, C., Peschel, C., Warnke, D., and Borning, A. Playful civic engagement using large public displays.
22. Tang, A., Finke, M., Blackstock, M., Leung, R., Deutscher, M., and Lea, R. Designing for bystanders: reflections on building a public digital forum. In *Proceedings of the SIGCHI Conference on Human Factors in Computing Systems*, ACM (2008), 879–882.
23. Taylor, N., Marshall, J., Blum-Ross, A., Mills, J., Rogers, J., Egglestone, P., Frohlich, D. M., Wright, P., and Olivier, P. Viewpoint: empowering communities with situated voting devices. In *Proceedings of the 2012 ACM annual conference on Human Factors in Computing Systems*, ACM (2012), 1361–1370.
24. Valkanova, N., Walter, R., Vande Moere, A., and Müller, J. Myposition: Sparking civic discourse by a public interactive poll visualization. In *Proceedings of the 17th ACM conference on Computer supported cooperative work & social computing*, ACM (2014), 1323–1332.
25. Vlachokyriakos, V., Comber, R., Ladha, K., Taylor, N., Dunphy, P., McCorry, P., and Olivier, P. Postervote: Expanding the action repertoire for local political activism. *Proceedings of 2014 ACM Conference on Designing Interactive Systems* (2014).
26. Webb, F. Tidy St: Shining a light on community energy efficiency. [On-line]. Accessed August 2014. Available: `http://www.theguardian.com/environment/blog/2011/apr/12/energy-use-households-monitor-electricity`, 2011.
27. Whittle, J., Simm, W., Ferrario, M.-A., Frankova, K., Garton, L., Woodcock, A., Binner, J., Ariyatum, A., et al. Voiceyourview: collecting real-time feedback on the design of public spaces. In *Proceedings of the 12th ACM international conference on Ubiquitous computing*, ACM (2010), 41–50.

Design Challenges in Supporting Distributed Knowledge: An Examination of Organizing Elections

Nina Boulus-Rødje
IT University of Copenhagen
Denmark
nbou@itu.dk

Pernille Bjørn
IT University of Copenhagen
Denmark
pbra@itu.dk

ABSTRACT
This paper identifies the design challenges for creating collaborative technologies supporting the practices of *organizing elections*. We ethnographically investigate the distributed nature of knowledge as enacted between heterogeneous groups over the course of three elections in Denmark. We 1) identify fundamental characteristics of elections, 2) provide a comprehensive account of the distributed nature of knowledge in organizing and executing elections, and 3) point to new challenging areas for human-computer interaction (HCI) design supporting distributed collaborative knowledge practices. We found that organizational pattern of elections complicates the embodiment of nomadic knowledge, which is crucial for managing the effective organization of an election. Thus, one of the relevant design challenges is finding out how to support the timely distribution of large amounts of information, while still ensuring it is appropriately divided and delivered to various groups participating in planning and executing elections.

Author Keywords
Organizing election; Nomadic knowledge; Voting; Denmark; Knowledge practice; Embodiment

ACM Classification Keywords
H.5.3. Group and Organization Interfaces [Computer-supported cooperative work]

INTRODUCTION
The majority of CHI research investigating election focuses on comparing paper-based voting to different types of electronic voting machines, such as direct-recording electronic voting machines, or Internet voting systems [4, 8, 9, 12]. Results include new technologies for casting and counting ballots, and concerns of usability [5], mostly within the USA with only few exceptions [8]. Research includes the role of social media in elections, campaigning, and voters decisions [6, 15]. However, there are, yet, no studies in CHI of the collaborative work involved in *planning and executing* elections; behind the scenes work of election officials. The few studies of election officials [4] examine the influence of officials on voters. We provide an ethnographic account of the knowledge practices of election officials when planning and executing elections, with the aim of informing design of collaborative systems supporting temporary electoral management bodies.

CHI 2015, April 18–23, 2015, Seoul, Republic of Korea.

http://dx.doi.org/10.1145/2702123.2702458

It is crucial to investigate the distributed nature of the knowledge sharing practices involved in organizing an election, as well as the practices by which knowledge is created, produced, and transformed. An election is a transient event and up to two years may pass between each one. A key challenge is the creation of relationships that support knowledge practices across diverse communities from various organizations over long and interrupted periods of time. Knowledge practices have been fundamental for the CHI community [3, 20], and previous research has investigated *routine work* and the practice of *experts* in different domains, such as healthcare and aircraft repair [18, 20, 24]. Organizing elections involves practices that require a high degree of knowledge. Nonetheless, temporary electoral management bodies depend heavily on novices with only few experts, whose expertise may not remain consistent over time. This makes the knowledge sharing practices in elections uniquely interesting.

In this paper, we focus on knowledge practices involved in organizing elections. We examine the enactment of knowledge in planning and executing elections, and the means by which knowledge is shared and distributed during elections. Thus, our interest lies in how the distributed nature of knowledge matters for the collaborations involved in election work – spanning organizational, geographic, and cultural boundaries, and temporal patterns. Our research question is: What are the ways in which the distributed knowledge used in organizing elections is enacted, and which channels are used for sharing knowledge?

Investigating this research question, we present empirical data from a longitudinal ethnographic study of the organization and execution of elections in Denmark. The first author conducted extensive fieldwork during three elections: a 2011 parliamentary election, a 2013 municipal and regional election, and 2014 European Union election and referendum. Our focus has been on understanding the users: the election officials (i.e., municipal workers and volunteers) collaborating to make elections happen. We unpack the user practices by analyzing each election, focusing on various knowledge sharing practices involved, and artefacts used for organizing and executing elections. We conduct a cross-case analysis [7] by comparing and contrasting knowledge practices involved in all three elections, and unpacking how the use of technologies changed over time.

A fundamental characteristic of elections is their transient nature. Organizing elections never truly become routine work since more than two years can pass between each election. This makes it challenging to recollect knowledge and experiences from past elections. Also various types of elections exist, each based upon different legal frameworks providing different complexities. Our data show that a key challenge in organizing elections is managing the efficient and timely distribution of a large amount of information, ensuring the appropriate knowledge is delegated to a large number of people in a relatively short time. The intermittent pattern of elections requires intensive periods of collaboration followed by long breaks. We argue that this organizational pattern complicates the practice of embodiment of nomadic knowledge, which is crucial for managing an effective organization of an election.

The paper is structured as follows: First, we present relevant literature on knowledge practices in collaborative settings. Second, we present our empirical case, followed by an analysis of our results and an identification of the different knowledge sharing practices in each election. Finally, we discuss the knowledge practices in elections and the relevant design challenges.

THE DISTRIBUTED NATURE OF KNOWLEDGE

Within CHI, election research focus on political campaigning and predicting election outcomes through social media [11], informing voters decisions [22], and following political agendas [13]. Our study shift the focus from what is happening *front-stage* when there are elections, to the collaborative work that takes place behind the scenes before, during and after elections. Thus, we are not focusing on activities related to *participating* in elections (e.g., following political debates, casting a ballot, etc.), but on *planning and executing* elections (e.g., ordering ballots, placing polling booth). We, therefore, shift the user-focus from *voters and politicians*, to *municipal workers* who hold legal responsibility and accountability for elections and have to collect and communicate information to volunteers and political representatives participating in executing elections. Our aim is to provide an ethnographic account of knowledge practices informing the design of collaborative technologies supporting the work of temporary electoral management body.

The distributed nature of knowledge is fundamental for CHI and CSCW research; both of which aim to design systems that can support collaborative practices. When mutually interdependent participants are engaged in collaborative work, the knowledge and expertise required becomes part of a shared activity [3]. The distributed nature of cooperative work has been unpacked in various domains, such as navigation [16]. Research on knowledge in CHI typically follows a technological orientation and has a micro-empirical focus on knowledge practices. The focus is to unpack the complex nature of knowledge practices, while keeping in mind that knowledge and work are closely intertwined [3]. We emphasize that "knowledge is situated in people and in locations, and that the social is an essential part of using any knowledge" [3, p. 532]. While computational repositories play an important role, the use of technologies for knowledge sharing is *not* merely about externalization of knowledge in the form of information technology artefacts. Instead, the capability to get the work done and solve problems is primarily based on discussions among knowledgeable actors [1, 20].

To investigate the enactment of knowledge practices, we use the notion of *nomadic knowledge* as an analytical lens to better understand the dispersed interdisciplinary activities of the heterogeneous groups organizing elections. *Nomadic knowledge* refers to "knowledge that mainly travels as it is used frequently on different occasions, but rarely used by the same set of actors again" [23, p. 537]. This notion drives our investigation of knowledge as community-bound, without being dependent upon specific individuals. Consequently, investigating knowledge includes examining how knowledge practices are integral part of organizing elections. The notion of nomadic knowledge directs our research towards investigating the complexity in "mastering" the organization of elections, since this requires the full attention of many actors, who are involved in time-critical decisions. The nature of "mastering" such a task can result in later complication in how the knowledge is collected for later use, in new situations, and by a different set of actors [23].

The notion 'nomadic knowledge' was originally introduced in the context of studying knowledge practices related to organizing a social forum of political activist organizations [16]. One of the main differences between our work and previous work is the legal framework in which the election officials operate within. These special conditions provide a high level of responsibility to which all election officials must adhere. The legal framework includes formal documents, protocols, artefacts, procedures, and subjective material, all of which are necessary for organizing, executing and documenting the process. Thus, the accountability of the election work introduces new challenges (e.g. documenting decisions), but also new opportunities (e.g., access to additional materials from past events for sensemaking processes).

When identifying and analyzing the specific characteristics of knowledge practices in organizing elections, a key challenge concerns the *reliability and authoritativeness* of the information. Since it is rarely exactly the same group of people who organize and execute each election, re-contextualization of information becomes immensely critical [14]. It is, therefore, important to investigate the critical activities involved in transferring responsibility and information from previous elections. This includes studying how participants assess the information, and how they situate it within its original institutional context. It requires paying attention to how traces are de-contextualized and re-contextualized across elections. Thus, understanding the reuse of information becomes critical [2]. Furthermore, in order to find the appropriate context for reuse of information, the *embeddedness* of previously held knowledge must be considered. It is critical to consider how connections across the distributed nomadic knowledge network are re-configured to become relevant and actionable within the context of the current election.

Empirical Case

Despite the high level of expertise necessary for organizing an election, Denmark does not have a permanent, central, and independent electoral management body. Instead, there is a decentralized electoral structure operating under the supervision of the Ministry of Economic Affairs. For each election, the local authorities have an electoral secretariat responsible for delegating and coordinating electoral activities, such as determining who is eligible to vote, coordinating advance voting, counting votes, procuring electoral material, aggregating voting results, and recruiting participants. These tasks are delegated to several administrative units who regularly report to the electoral secretariat. This delegation of electoral responsibilities to local authorities causes various organizational challenges, making it difficult to maintain electoral consistency.

Data Sources

The first author did a four-year ethnography on elections in Denmark. Data sources comprise extensive fieldwork of three elections in Copenhagen Municipality (the largest municipality in Denmark), focusing on the tasks of municipal workers, volunteers, and representatives from political parties. The elections were a 2011 parliamentary election; a 2013 municipal and regional election; and a combined 2014 referendum and European Union election.

A variety of data collection methods were used, including observations, shadowing, interviews, participation in formal and informal meetings with various groups, attendance in two election courses (14 hours total), and gathering documents from the ministry, municipality, and the media. In total, the first author spent 220 hours of observation sessions before, during, and after Election Day throughout three different elections. In addition, seven formal interviews (one to two hours each) were conducted with key municipal employees, and 15 informal conversations (lasting 15–35 minutes each) were conducted with municipal employees, volunteers, and representatives from political parties. All interviews and informal conversations were either fully or partially transcribed.

Data Analysis

The data analysis focused on how the distributed knowledge required in executing elections was organized by the diverse set of participants. Particularly, we identified situations where complexities in collecting and using information were encountered. We first synthesized the data through thick descriptions [21] for each election, focusing on the various knowledge sharing practices of those involved in organizing and executing elections. Then, we conducted a cross-case analysis [7], comparing and contrasting knowledge practices across the three elections. We found gradual changes in the knowledge practices across the elections. These changes resulted in distributing the knowledge from one person to several people, enabling information to be accessible from different locations. Finally, we applied the notion of nomadic knowledge [23] in order to identify the unique characteristics of the knowledge practices enacted in elections.

RESULTS

The process of organizing elections is complex caused by external pressure to reduce cost, adopt new technologies, and produce election results rapidly. Finding effective ways to better plan, monitor, and control elections is very topical. Copenhagen Municipality has experimented over the years with different strategies for gathering information about election management and execution. Below we analyze the different strategies, and identify the practices, technologies, and artefacts deployed. But first, we provide a description of the fundamental characteristics of organizing elections.

The Key Characteristics of Organizing Elections

Elections are fundamental to democracy and have specific characteristics. These characteristics are related to an election as an *event*, an election as an *organizational entity*, and an election as a *knowledge practices*.

An Event of Uniqueness, Urgency & Celebration

While similarities exist between elections, each election is a novel event with unique challenges. These challenges can take different forms. In the 2013 municipal and regional election, one of the challenges was related to the size of the ballots, which were very long as there were many different parties and candidates running. Due to the long list of parties and candidates on the ballots, voters tended to spend more time searching for their candidate on the list, and election officials spent relatively longer time sorting and counting these long and heavy ballots. Thus, the size and weight of the ballots increased the time and effort involved in casting, sorting, and counting the ballots. The material properties of the ballots also increased the effort required for packing and transporting them. In the 2013 election it was not the ballot size, which was a challenge, instead several computers crashed in one of the polling stations, and in the 2011 parliamentary election, many ballot boxes stored in a school were damaged in a flood. Therefore, election officials spend a considerable amount of time trying to manage these unexpected hurdles.

Despite unexpected challenges, there is always a high level of urgency and pressure to organize and execute quickly. A key person in organizing elections described it as "*having one shot left in the gun, so you better get it right. [...] There is no time...for mistakes and the deadlines are very tight. You know how important [the election event] is, and we must make it work. You cannot miss or fail in an election.*" There is no space for error during the ramp up to an election. This is why backup procedures and control mechanisms are crucial for the election apparatus, in an attempt to avoid and minimize the likelihood for mistakes. Furthermore, ideally, nothing should be postponed or cancelled. Over the course of organizing elections, the urgency in solving problems quickly gradually increases. The pressure reaches its peak a day after Election Day, when final results are announced.

Election officials often describe Election Day as a solemn day when democracy is celebrated. Municipal employees display high dedication to the task of organizing elections, in spite of the many extra hours they spend working during these periods. Some municipal workers perceive working on elections as a prestigious obligation. There are even small competitions between some of the polling stations, such as competing for the fastest results of the rough count. The high level of time pressure in election and the demanding extra hours of intensive work create immense personal challenges. Two municipal workers said that they miss having a proper dinner at home, and seeing their families and kids. One of the municipal employees explained that some people decline repeated participation because of the demanding nature of the work. A key person in organizing elections described the election atmosphere in the following way: "[*An election resembles situations with] outside pressure, such as the downsizing of an organization, creating enormous internal pressure, which then causes [employees] to stand closely together and support one another.*" Organizing an election is compared to a crisis type event at work, during which co-workers must put other duties aside to support each other during tense and critical periods.

Organizational entity: Sub-groups of distributed people

Elections in Denmark depend increasingly on volunteers who collaborate with representatives from political parties to complete the various tasks for Election Day. The municipality is responsible for providing information to these heterogeneous groups from different organizational backgrounds, consisting mostly of non-experts. The collaboration is coordinated through the division of tasks into various sub-processes for particular sub-groups. This strategy and structure requires a careful orchestration of all individual processes and their relations. The coordination strategy of task division and standardization allows for the management of a large number of sub-processes by a large number of sub-groups. To accommodate this strategy, a hierarchical organizational structure is created, where lines of command are explicitly articulated in order to be able to trace back to all the small details involved in each process. The ability to trace all sub-processes is crucial in elections since this visibility ensures the trustworthiness of the results. Knowledge and responsibilities are distributed across the organizational structure, making it difficult to "hack" elections. Few individuals have a completed overview of the entire chain of processes. Most people involved only know few small and highly specified sub-processes. A key election official described organizing and executing elections as: "*a complicated coordinative process with a large number of small gears and cogwheels, which need to fall in place and where everyone is responsible for solving their own small task*".

Coordinating all the cogwheels involves managing inter-organizational coordination across several institutions and organizations: schools, police departments, taxi companies, postal services, Statistics Denmark, and others. All of these organizations play important roles in making an election a reality. Each of the organizations mentioned are not part of one single entity and the impact of their work is not confined to one location. For example, the postal service in Denmark is responsible for ensuring that all advanced votes sent via letters are distributed to the appropriate municipality. Similarly, a complex chain of coordination mechanisms is required to ensure that all polling stations (e.g., libraries and schools) are set up for Election Day.

This organizational structure means that all participants involved cannot gather in one room to learn their assigned tasks. Also, many election officials – particularly volunteers – do not participate in recurrent elections. Due to the temporal pattern of elections and the large time lapse between elections, it is impossible for the new volunteer to "observe" and gain skills from experienced volunteers. Therefore organizing elections is characterized by discontinuous collaboration between distributed yet interdependent actors engaged in articulation work directed at connecting the temporal, geographical and organizational discontinuities. This setup complicates the development of routine practices. Once an activity develops into a routine, the task is completed and put aside until next election.

During the election period municipal employees normally continue to attend to their other responsibilities. Thus, tasks related to organizing an election are added to the list of their daily tasks. Such structure causes "ordinary tasks" to pile up. Therefore, as soon as an election is completed, most employees discontinue with tasks related to the election in order to catch up with their routine duties. This structure leaves no space for reflecting on the election experience, nor for offering suggestions for improvements in the future. Furthermore, the period of time between elections makes it difficult for participants to remember in detail their past experiences. Many municipal workers say they feel the need to start from scratch each time. The temporal staffing complicates the execution of election.

Still, previous experience is extremely valuable in organizing elections, thus they try to recruit municipal workers with previous election experience. Recruiting experienced people allows for the use of personal networks, which is critical because certain tasks depend on other people from other organizations. Networking also eases communication across organizations. For instance, the coordination of various election tasks is much easier if an election secretary (responsible for administrating an election in a polling station) is already familiar with the local school and election officials.

Distributed Knowledge in Elections

Capturing all the information required in one place in impossible. It is also difficult to map all the sub-groups and sub-processes taking place during elections. The knowledge required to conduct elections is complex, scattered, and distributed. We learned that there are only two people in the municipality who know the entire organizational apparatus that elections require. Thus, identifying best practices for knowledge sharing is an immense challenge.

The challenge is that a large amount of information needs to be communicated within a short time frame to different groups of people, in a range of organizations, and with diverse backgrounds. Knowledge sharing for elections requires distributing manageable and digestible information to volunteers, since many are also working their regular day jobs and do not have the time or resources to process large volumes of information. Furthermore, information must be organized in a comprehensive way so that first-time participants can understand their instructions. Finally, participants are under time pressure and must quickly learn their tasks. Therefore, information regarding sub-tasks is typically divided into smaller, dedicated entities, ensuring that each group is not required to know all details about elections but only what is relevant to their tasks. Expertise becomes distributed according to specific delegated tasks. The process of organizing elections depends on diverse sets of experts (e.g., legal experts, elections experts, and technology experts), who are working from within various government institutions and locations. Knowledge of organizing elections is dispersed and distributed. Therefore, translating and tracing information, while making it useful across expertise and practices, is an important yet complex task when organizing elections. Texts describing election processes tend to be encumbered by legal language, due to the various laws and regulations that apply. This jargon needs to be translated into everyday terminology.

In the process of transcending across divides in the election hierarchy, information also acquires different states of urgency. Critical information at one point in time can be considered completely irrelevant later. For example, on the morning of Election Day, an election committee's focus is on providing information to election officials on how to instruct and assist voters on processes such as receiving a ballot, scanning election cards, managing or responding to journalists, and using the digital voter machines. Such information, provided by the election secretary on the morning of Election Day, is completely irrelevant by the end of the day. Then, the focus shifts to methods of sorting and counting in-person votes and advance votes, as well as handling invalid votes.

Organizing elections can be generally divided into three main phases: pre-election, Election Day, and post-election. Each phase has particular aims and processes. Key tasks in the pre-election phase include ordering election material (e.g., ballots and election books), organizing advance voting (e.g., organizing home visits for those unable to attend elections, providing technical training, organizing the process of checking whether advance votes are valid, and updating election books to signal who voted in advance and prevent from double voting). Key tasks relevant to Election Day include identifying polling stations, recruiting volunteers and representatives from political parties, assigning election officials to polling stations (ensuring a mixture of representatives from various political parties and volunteers), setting up polling stations (e.g., the technical infrastructure and the ballot booths), arranging meals for all polling stations, and more. Finally, tasks relevant to the post-election phase include processes related to orchestrating the fine count, which takes place a day after Election Day. In Denmark, ballots are first counted the evening of Election Day by volunteers and representatives from political parties. This is called a "rough count," meaning counting votes by parties. The fine count is conducted the following day by municipal workers, who recount the ballots for parties and for candidates. Therefore, all election material need to be packed and transported into one central place where it is unpacked to be ready for the fine count. Municipal employees have to be assigned to the fine count, and meal, equipment, and supply arrangements must be made.

2011 Parliamentary Election

As a new initiative in 2011, the Center for Public Expertise Development (COK) organized a course led by two experienced employees from another municipality to prepare Danish municipal employees for the parliamentary election. The intention was to ensure that all employees were familiar with recent laws and regulations. The course also encouraged employees at the different municipalities to exchange knowledge and discuss their own experiences. This initiative was deemed highly useful by the employees, because the course exposed them to various local inspiring practices and traditions across the different municipalities.

Parliamentary elections are the most complicated elections in terms of organizational logistics. While many Western countries are suffering from declining participation in parliamentary elections, Denmark continues to maintain stable and relatively high election participation rates.

Furthermore, while in other countries, parliamentary elections take place within a pre-defined time frame (e.g., every four years), this is not the case in Denmark. Here the prime minister can announce a parliamentary election at any point in time, up to a maximum of four years from the previous election. This practice makes it difficult to plan ahead. In 2011, the prime minister's announcement of a parliamentarian election allowed the municipalities only *three* weeks to prepare. Thus, the election allotted an exceptionally short amount of time for planning and preparation. This presented additional challenges in coordinating the large number of voters, election officials, volunteers, polling stations, and election material.

Technologies for Knowledge Sharing in 2011

During the parliamentary election, various collaborative artefacts were used for sharing information. This included local guidelines and instructions created by the municipality and given to different groups. Some guidelines were printed and handed out during various meetings; others were distributed via email. The sheer *volume of emails sent to election workers was enormous: 11 emails with 28 attachments* in total were sent during the pre-election phase. Other important communication tools used were dedicated cell phones provided to key election officials, e.g. election secretaries and technical support staff.

An intensive series of meetings was held over the course of the three weeks leading up to Election Day. Meetings among election team members and meetings with representatives from different teams were conducted to ensure information was communicated both within and across the teams. For example, there were several meetings with the election secretaries, who hold administrative responsibility for their assigned polling station. There were also several meetings to rehearse for the fine count day that follows Election Day (including separate meetings with specific teams assigned to conduct the fine count). As well, there was a special meeting with election secretaries and city hall employees responsible for packing and unpacking election material. Finally, one last meeting was held two days before Election Day to discuss the election in general.

The election in 2011 also presented an unusual situation because the head of elections – responsible for organization elections in Copenhagen – was retiring. There was a concern that all her knowledge and expertise would be lost. This inspired the municipality to – using their words – "collect and capture" her knowledge about organizing elections in a more systematic and comprehensive manner. At the time, there were incomplete bits and pieces of information scattered across various repositories in a range of formats and communicated via different channels. The information was not written in any comprehensive or extensive way that could help in specifying the tasks and practices of various groups. Thus, the newly appointed head of elections began gradually collecting the information while, striving to familiarize herself with the new tasks. Collecting information while simultaneously developing an understanding of how to orchestrate election was an enormous challenge.

2013 Municipal and Regional Election

The 2013 Municipal and Regional election brought about several unexpected challenges. This includes, a surprisingly high level of voters attendance, which was a result of various national and local campaigns organized by different organizations to encourage more people, particularly youth, to vote for the municipal and regional election. In addition, the high number of candidates resulted in very large and heavy ballots. Moreover, the design of the ballots was newly revised, thus a new small box was added next to every candidate's name and the voters were expected to mark their cross in the little box. These changes led long queues at the voting booths and increased complications for sorting and counting the ballots. This meant that some large polling stations in Copenhagen were unable to complete their rough count during the evening of Election Day.

During this election, the municipality strived to have different teams working more independently of each other. The centralization of the advanced-votes process was a major change. The day before the election, the election officials at the various polling stations opened the envelopes containing advanced votes. Advance votes arrive with cover envelopes, and the letters are examined. The advance vote identifiers are checked against the electoral register. If a voter does not appear on the register (e.g., if they had passed away after casting a vote), the vote would not be included. Other reasons for the rejection of advance votes include incorrect completion of the cover letter. Centralizing this process required all election officials to gather in one location and execute the process of examining advance votes together. Previously, various sub-teams conducted the task independently and without coordination. Since the municipality knew well in advance the date of the election, preparation began early. Reducing time pressure and ensure better planning, meetings were held a few months in advance of Election Day.

Technologies for Knowledge Sharing in 2013

Due to the challenges encountered with the information and communications strategies of the 2011 election, Copenhagen Municipality acknowledged that new initiatives were required to organize information in a more systematic way. Therefore, the municipality created a new position solely dedicated to the task of collecting information from the various experts with the aim of creating more detailed guidelines organized in knowledge repository. The person hired for this position did not have previous experience with running elections, and took this opportunity to familiarize herself with required election tasks during the 2013 municipal and regional election. To avoid the previous situation of drowning in emails, the municipality had purposefully strived to send fewer emails with attachments to election officials, attempting instead to gather the information in one place.

The newly hired election consultant, together with key officials from the municipality, began gathering information and updating the various guidelines well ahead of Election Day. Since new information continued to pour in from various channels (e.g., updates from the ministry), the team creating these guidelines waited until the last possible days to compile all the information into a 60-page binder. The binder was given to the election secretaries responsible for the polling stations. The election secretaries were left with only a short time to familiarize themselves with the tasks and regulations outlined in the binders.

During separate interviews, two highly experienced municipal election secretaries said they normally read through the guidelines and summarize important items in handwritten notes. This process of summarizing and synthesizing the most important information was viewed as an immensely crucial analytical process in facilitating navigation through the huge amount of information received, which officials were required to remember in a short time. The summaries were critical for election officials and were useful in how personally tailored they were. Such summaries cannot be easily formalized and standardized as their content depends on the election secretary's particular experience and knowledge.

Currently, the standardized guidelines embed a hierarchal structure, reflecting the chronological order in which the tasks occur. An experienced election secretary proposed redesigning these guidelines to process-oriented structure, reflecting upon how often a process is used. The secretary explained that there were a large number of details that had to be memorized; thus, it would be easier to navigate through the information by way of the most pertinent and recurrent activities. In other words, certain information is more important and/or used more often, thereby it needs to be more easily and quickly retrievable. For example, it is important for an election secretary to know what to do in situations where a voter behaves inappropriately (e.g., displaying violent behavior). However, this information can be included towards the end of the guideline, since the likelihood of occurrence is very low. The municipal employee also pointed out that including the rationales behind the various tedious and mundane tasks could help clarify election officials of their importance, and encourage them to avoid workarounds.

Typically, during elections, officials become so immersed in their election work, gathering a wealth of knowledge and experience, that they tend to come up with various ways to improve current practices. These suggestions often "disappear" after elections because these are quickly forgotten as election officials are busy going back to their daily jobs. These suggestions and this knowledge is contextual and temporal. Therefore, to "capture" these unique embodied experiences, Copenhagen Municipality began organizing evaluation meetings right after Election Day to ask for feedback from officials.

2014 Referendum and EU Elections

The 2014 referendum and European Union (EU) elections presented the challenge of organizing two elections in one polling location. These elections were two separate events, since not all voters are eligible to vote in both elections. Unlike other types of elections, referendums and EU elections do not usually have high voter turnout, nor do they involve lengthy ballots. However, organizing double elections brought organizational and logistical challenges.

During the evaluation meeting, a new strategy was proposed, to help support knowledge sharing in elections. Accordingly, it was suggested to allow volunteers to observe an election as this could provide them with a better understanding of their upcoming roles and duties. In a previous election, some volunteers had left before the final completion of the fine count, not fully carrying out their duties. Volunteers are required even after the polling stations close, as this is when the rough count begins.

Technologies for Knowledge Sharing in 2014

The municipality began developing a common digital repository in the form of an intranet application, which was meant to contain all the guidelines well in advance of Election Day. This should provide more time for election officials to familiarize themselves with the regulations, tasks, and responsibilities.

The digital repository marks a clear change in knowledge sharing practices, *away* from a centralized approach (in which information is located only in the hands of a few municipal workers) and *towards* a distributed approach (in which knowledge is accessible directly through the common repository). Thus, the responsibility of accessing information is shared among election officials and volunteers. Paper-based guidelines are still printed and binders are still assembled before an election, to ensure crucial information reaches the correct individuals.

DISCUSSION

Our cross-case analysis (Table 1) demonstrate the different attempts to manage nomadic knowledge in the three cases, each providing different fundamental structures (centralized, semi-centralized, or distributed), imposing different design challenges for IT systems supporting election officials work practices, in terms of information sources, authorships, and interpretations. Also, we identified predictable (long ballots are common in municipal elections) and emergent (damaged ballot box) challenges across the elections. IT systems supporting the election officials must take both into account by minimizing the predictable challenges while leaving space for the emergent challenges.

Election	2011 Parliamentary	2013 Municipal and Regional	2014 Referendum and EU
Voter turnout	87.7%	69.1%	55.85% (Ref) 56.32% (EU)
Time	3 weeks	3-6 months	3-6 months
Knowledge practices	Centralized approach Many meetings, emails, guidelines	Semi-centralized approach Centralized binder Fewer meetings held over a longer period of time Evaluation meeting	Distributed approach Centralized binder Fewer meetings held over a longer period of time Gradual use of Intranet
Challenges	Damaged ballot boxes Head of election retiring	High voter turnout Long ballots Long waiting lines New head of election Ballot redesigned	Orchestrating two elections in one polling station

Table 1. Cross case analysis across the three elections.

Close examination of our data reveals that no-single person has all the required expertise. Rather, know-how is distributed across participants with different backgrounds and areas of responsibility. Expertise is delegated and distributed, causing knowledge to become nomadic [23]. The process of organizing elections depends upon various governing authorities. Thus, information communicated to the various actors needs to be readable and digestible to a wide range of users, without mutual understanding of the entire election apparatus. Few have a complete insight into the practices of elections, making it difficult to design technologies that support the reuse of information across elections. Instead of completeness, election practices emerge in transient situations, where various participants gather and connect their practices. The complexity increases when examining elections as recurrent events and investigating how knowledge travels across these disparate events. Thus, the practices of assessing the reliability and authoritative of information is critical. When reusing decontextualized material from previous election, it is important to determine the original institutional context and whether the material was officially sanctioned [14]. Likewise, in recurrent elections, the practices of de-contextualizing and re-contextualizing [2] information from previous elections becomes critically important to the organization of updated election practices. The creation of new knowledge in election practices is not a matter of "processing" objective information [19]. Rather, knowledge practices depend on connecting the tacit and often highly subjective insights gained from the embodied experiences and practices of election work participants. Thus, creating new knowledge repositories is about mobilizing commitment and embodied knowledge in actual technology. The question is: how can this embodied and nomadic knowledge be assembled and put into practice when most participants are volunteers and do not participate in recurrent events? Designing technology for organizing elections is also complicated by the lack of routine work and standardization.

Clearly, the nature of knowledge in organizing elections is nomadic [23], as it transcends locations, time, and people. Furthermore, the same groups of people rarely use the same information, which creates a challenge in localizing the exchange of information to meet different needs at different times. Also the nature of nomadic knowledge means that most participants have little interest in retaining it once the election is over. Participants tend to forget their specific practices and embodied experiences, which also implies that this knowledge often "disappears." Disparity exists between the need for specified knowledge and practices, and the general interest in documenting these for later use. This imbalance is important if we are to design for collaborative technologies supporting this work.

Finally, to make the information about organizing elections useful, it is critical to address the reuse of information. Extraneous information details are removed to support different and specific local needs, thus re-contextualization concerns creating new relevant links; thus, embedding the knowledge within their local contexts. We heard several key election officials explain how they synthesized and de-contextualized information gathered from the weighty guidelines they received. They summarized the most relevant segments into short handwritten notes, re-embedded into the guidebooks. This analytical process of first synthesizing and then re-embedding the information was viewed as important for these highly experienced election secretaries, as it allowed them to become familiar with this information in a short period of time and to navigate through the vast amount of information. This process is not only about embedding information, but also a process of re-embodying the knowledge and practices relevant to organizing and executing elections. In a discussion with one of the key municipal employees, he used the metaphor of giving birth to illustrate the immense embodied challenge that participating in election work entails. He explains that elections is like giving birth: One can read a lot about it to try to gain familiarity with the processes and procedures, but one does not really know what it is actually like until experiencing it in practice. This statement reflects upon how the aspect of embodiment of knowledge and practice are seen as highly important.

Previous election research investigate the role of blogs, fundraising tools, the use of social media in political campaigning, and whether new tools make elections more transparent to voters [11]. Others, examine what kind of information systems could facilitate voters in collective information gathering, sharing, and filtering, supporting decision making [22]. Furthermore, social media use has been explored in relation to interactions between voters with political disagreements [13] and in crowd-sourced fact-finding support for public dialogue in democratic societies [17]. Thus, previous studies focus on the collaborative practices and use of technologies among candidates, voters, and *elected* officials. Our work addresses a different set of participants (users); namely *election* officials and how they organize elections. Thus, while previous research focus on the collaboration between voters, our research focus on election officials. Secondly, while previous research on knowledge management [22] in elections also point to the challenges of collecting and re-using information across elections, they focus on a different group of *users*, different *type of information* used for a different *purpose*. These knowledge management studies [22] focus on voters sharing information about the different political parties and supporting voters in making an informed decision when casting their ballot [17]. Our study focuses on election officials sharing information across elections about how to organize, plan and execute an election while ensuring legal framework and correct conduct are adhered to. It is exactly the legal framework and the level of responsibility in organizing the nomadic knowledge which distinguish our work from previous work on nomadic knowledge in political activist organizations [23]. The special conditions identified in our cases demonstrate the high level of responsibility to which election officials must adhere. The legal framework includes formal documents, protocols, artefacts, procedures, and subjective material, all of which are necessary for organizing, executing and documenting the process. Accountability introduces certain constraints for design of systems supporting due processes, but also opportunities for sharing and reusing information through access to materials from past events supporting sensemaking.

Designing for Distributed Knowledge in Elections

Similarly to Robertson et al [22], we adopt a user-centered perspective on the larger context of planning and executing elections, which includes the activities of the non-political participants when coordinating administrative practices ensuring that elections follow due processes demanded by the legal framework. Our users are the municipal workers in Copenhagen who currently explore new opportunities for a digital repository supporting knowledge exchange in elections. It supports sharing information to a diverse group of people quickly and has potential to standardize information and practices allowing for easier navigation. However, common repository does not support knowledge sharing practices by default; it is not simply about "capturing" and "displaying" information. The repository must address the challenges of informal knowledge, embodied knowledge, emergent and contextual knowledge, improvisations, and other crucial skills that are used when organizing elections. Strategies of standardization risk stripping away the embodied knowledge of experienced election officials. This acquired knowledge is crucial for dealing with the unexpected contingencies that inevitably occur in every election. When designing collaborative technologies to support nomadic knowledge in elections, it must support the collective and dynamic process of active remembering, interpretations, re-contextualization, and internalization of knowledge as it emerges across professions, geography, and temporal disruptive patterns. Through the first author's engagement with the field site, these concerns were included in the discussions about design strategies for the repository. It was concluded that instead of written textual descriptions of efficient method to sort and count ballots, a short video could possibly more easily convey this information enabling information sharing across organizational actors during elections, and across temporal discontinuities between election periods.

Previous research on political campaigning discusses whether new technologies can level the field between amateurs and the professionals [10]. In our case, introducing a new technology is not about leveling the field, because the hierarchy in knowledge sharing is critical for the coordination and interpretation of information, which must persistent in new design. The challenge persists that the type of information material required to organize and execute elections remains somewhat absent, or rather, not so easily available. Municipal employees carry out different tasks before, during, and after Election Day, thus they are often bound to particular locations where these tasks take place. This means that municipal employees rarely have the possibility to observe the various tasks taking place across different geographical locations.

The first author produced large amount of video and audio material documenting the various activities scattered across different locations. This material is currently being incorporated into the design of the digital repository, aiming to ease the communication of the large amount of information to election officials. This is the first step towards the creation of a common knowledge repository. While building such a repository is promising, it does not solve all the organizational challenges that elections present. It is important to also acknowledge elements of embodiedness of knowledge and practice required for the election process to function.

FINAL REMARKS

We investigated the distributed knowledge practices and artefacts used in organizing elections. We found that the orchestration of elections is of a distributed nature spanning organizational and geographical boundaries. Retaining the consistency and continuity of knowledge practices is difficult. Elections are a standardized part of democracy; still organizing elections vary causing the exchange and reuse of information across elections in Denmark to be challenging. Each election is characterized by new groups of volunteers, municipal employees etc. These findings unpack the design implications for collaborative technologies that support the elections management.

ACKNOWLEDGMENTS

Funded by DemTech grant 10-092309: Danish Council for Strategic Research, Programme Commission on Strategic Growth Technologies. We thank Copenhagen Municipality.

REFERENCES

1. Ackerman, M., Pipek, V. and Wulf, V. *Sharing Expertise: Beyond-Knowledge Management*. MIT Press, Cambridge, MA, 2002.
2. Ackerman, M. and Halverson, C. Organizational Memory: Processes, Boundary Objects, and Trajectories. *Comput Support Coop Work 13*, 2 (2004), 155–189.
3. Ackerman, M., Dachtera, J., Pipek, V. and Wulf, V. Sharing Knowledge and Expertise: The CSCW View of Knowledge Management. *Comput Support Coop Work*, *22* (2013), 531–573.
4. Alvarez, R., Hall, T. and Llewellyn, M. Are Americans confident their ballots are counted? *Journal of Politics* 70 (2008), 754–766.
5. Bederson, B., Lee, B., Sherman, R., Herrnson, P. and Niemi, R. Electronic voting system usability issues. In *Proc. CHI 2003*, ACM Press (2003).
6. Bouillot, F., Poncelet, P. and Roche, M. Frence presidential elections: What are the most efficient measures for tweets? In *Proc. PLEAD 2012*, ACM Press (2012)
7. Boulus, N. and Bjørn, P. A cross-case analysis of technology-in-use practices: EPR-adaptation in Canada and Norway. *Int J Med Inform*, 79, 6 (2008), 97-108.
8. Boulus-Rødje, N. Mapping the Literature: socio-cultural, organizational and technological dimensions of e-voting technologies. *Lecture Notes in Informatics* (2012), 205ff.
9. Byrne, M., Greene, K. and Everett, S. Usability of voting systems: Baseline data for paper, punch cards, and lever machines. In *Proc. CHI 2007,* ACM Press (2007).
10. Carpenter, K., Nardi, B., Moore, J., Roberson, S., Foot, K., Drezner, D., Benson, I. and Jett, Q. Online political organizing: Lessons from the field: Panel. In *Proc. CSCW 2004*, ACM Press (2004).
11. Carpenter, K., Roberson, S., Foot, K., Nardi, B., Drezner, D., Jett, Q., Moore, J. and Benson, I. Online political organizing: Lessons from the field: Panel. In *Proc. CSCW 2004*, ACM Press (2004).
12. Everett, S., Greene, K., Byrne, M., Wallach, D., Derr, K., Sandler, D. and Torous, T. Electronic voting machines versus traditional methods: Improved preference, similar performance. In *Proc. CHI 2008*, ACM Press (2008).
13. Grevet, C., Terveen, L. and Gilbert, E. Managing political differences in social media. In *Proc. CSCW* 2014, ACM Press (2014).
14. Heath, C. and Luff, P. Documents and Professional Practice: "Bad" Organizational Reasons for "Good" Clinical Records. In *Proc. CSCW 1996*, ACM Press (1996)
15. Hellström, J. and Karefelt, A. Participation through mobile phones: A study of SMS use during the Ugandan general elections 2011. In *Proc. ICTD 2012*, ACM Press.
16. Hutchins, E. *Cognition in the wild*. MIT Press, Cambridge, Massachusetts, 1995.
17. Kriplean, T., Bonnar, C., Borning, A., Kinney, B. and Gill, B. Integrating On-demand Fact-checking with Public Dialogue. In *Proc. CSCW 2014*, ACM Press (2014).
18. Lutters, W. and Ackerman, M. Beyond Boundary Objects: Collaborative Reuse in Aircraft Technical Support. *Comput Support Coop Work*, 16, 3 (2007), 341-372.
19. Nonaka, I. The knowledge-creating company *Harvard Business Review*, 85, 7/8 (2007), 162.
20. Pipek, V., Wulf, V. and Johri, A. Bridging Artifacts and Actors: Expertise Sharing in Organizational Ecosystems. *Comput Support Coop Work 21* (2011), 261–282.
21. Randall, D., Harper, R. and Rouncefield, M. *Fieldwork for design: Theory and practice*. Springer, London, 2007.
22. Robertson, S. Voter-Centered Design: Towards a voter decision support system. *ACM Transactions on Computer-Human Interaction 12*, 2 (2005), 263-291.
23. Saeed, S., Pipek, V., Rohde, M. and Wulf, V. Managing nomadic knowledge: a case study of the European social forum. In *Proc. CHI 2010,* ACM Press (2010).
24. Spence, P. and Reddy, M. Beyond Expertise Seeking: A Field Study of the Informal Knowledge Practices of Healthcare IT Teams. *Comput Support Coop Work*, *21* (2011), 283–315.

The Politics of Measurement and Action

Kathleen H. Pine
University of California, Irvine
Irvine, CA
khpine@uci.edu

Max Liboiron
Memorial University of Newfoundland
St. John's, NL, Canada
mliboiron@mun.ca

ABSTRACT
Contemporary decisions about the management of populations, public services, security, and the environment are increasingly made through knowledge gleaned from 'big data' and its attendant infrastructures and algorithms. Though often described as 'raw,' this data is produced by techniques of measurement that are imbued with judgments and values that dictate what is counted and what is not, what is considered the best unit of measurement, and how different things are grouped together and "made" into a measureable entity. In this paper, we analyze these politics of measurement and how they relate to action through two case studies involving high stake public health measurements where experts intentionally leverage measurement to change definitions of harm and health. That is, they use measurement for activism. The case studies offer a framework for thinking about of how the *politics* of measurement are present in user interfaces. It is usually assumed that the human element has been scrubbed from the database and that significant political and subjective interventions come from the analysis or use of data *after* the fact. Instead, we argue that human-computer interactions start *before* the data reaches the computer because various *measurement interfaces* are the invisible premise of data and databases, and these measurements are political.

Author Keywords
Measurement; science and technology studies; quantification; data; evaluation; politics

ACM Classification Keywords
H.5.m. Information Interfaces and Presentation (e.g. HCI): Miscellaneous

INTRODUCTION
In the 21st century, the capacity of big data to capture massive volumes of increasingly fine-grained information, and the ability for algorithms to pull patterns from that data, is being deployed to make large-scale decisions about the management of populations, economies, the environment, security, and public services. "Big Data" and its algorithms are popularly thought to change knowledge practices and make connections in all domains, providing an informational "planetary nervous system" [53]. Databases have come to shape the very contours of our knowledge and decision-making, and thus hold the potential to shift how we know the world and act in it. Given this link between data and action, recent years have seen an intensification of interest in data, data infrastructures, and algorithms as well as other information infrastructures both within the CHI community and without, particularly in terms of how the organization of information exerts an oft-invisible hand in shaping human action, power, and culture [2, 3, 4, 7, 8, 24, 46, 60, 61].

This rich body of work, which often draws deeply from Science & Technology Studies (STS) dating back to Suchman's quintessential work [61], critically interrogates what David Ribes and Steven Edwards refer to as the "commodity fictions" of data [53: 147]. Based on Foucault's commodity fiction of power [19], the commodity fiction of data is the belief that data and context are separate-able, making data a free-floating, harvestable entity. This belief assumes data are given-in-advance of discovery, are "natural" objects—even natural resources—that can circulate and aggregate irrespective of their origins. However Ribes and Edwards point out that research consistently shows that data is never actually "raw" but is instead always socially and culturally situated [24]. Data – and its attendant processes of measurement, database production, stabilization, curation, maintenance and use – reproduce power dynamics, knowledge systems, and culturally-based assumptions [6, 16, 17, 24, 25, 41, 51, 54]. Thus, scholarship on the politics of data has expanded to include studies of data infrastructures as complex sociotechnical entities with a recent interest in algorithms as the artifacts that "make [datasets] intelligible [13: 10]" [see also 3, 33, 46, 51].

Yet data are not the deepest layer of analysis in this debate. Beneath this are the practices and premises of data creation that populate datasets themselves, shaping human-computer interactions even before data reaches the computer. Our research focuses on measurements, the artifacts and practices that form some of the smallest units of quantification underlying data, algorithms, and other vectors of representation. To this end, we present an analytical framework for thinking about measurement as a

CHI 2015, April 18 - 23 2015, Seoul, Republic of Korea

ACM 978-1-4503-3145-6/15/04...$15.00
http://dx.doi.org/10.1145/2702123.2702298

vector for political action through two cases of high stakes measurements drawn from medicine and environmental health. The first case follows the measurement of severe maternal morbidity via units of blood transfused in maternity wards, a measurement that is under development today; and the second case looks at the measurement of water quality during cholera epidemics in the nineteenth century. These cases allow an analysis of the politics of information by highlighting how the characteristics of measurement are used *intentionally* by experts to redefine indicators of health and harm. In each case, we assert that advocates use measurement to make a previously invisible form of harm visible, then focus on metrics that promote affective visions of crisis—what we call *charismatic data*— to spur specific managerial actions can address the newly visible problem. The intentional leveraging of measurements by activists for specific action-oriented goals is a unique contribution to the existing literature.

RELATED WORK

We will review the complete range of how different literatures have recognized the politics of measurement, then narrow things down to the specific genre of politics our study engages in. At its core, measurement entails categorization and the judgment of characteristics through abstracted descriptions of entities. While measurement does not necessarily have to be quantitative, we are focused in this paper on quantitative descriptions. Measurement is "the delimitation and fixation of our ideas of things, so that the determination of what it is to be a man or a circle is a case of measurement" [44: 313]. Morgan Robertson, a scholar who works for the US Environmental Protection Agency and thus is deeply invested in adjudicating measurements, calls measurements "coherent abstracts" resulting from "a process of creating socially-necessary abstractions that are adequate to bear value...The construction of abstract spaces, the definition of boundaries between types of things that allow nature to be segregated out in a typology, are matters of measure" [56: 2-3]. These judgments, delimitations, abstractions, and constructions are political.

Human computer interaction literature on the politics of artifacts has pointed out that all technology is inherently political; that is, technologies are built in particular politically-infused social systems for particular political ends whether intentional or not [31, 64, 65]. For example, by embedding certain types of tasks but not others in the design of collaborative workflow technologies for nurses, such technologies enable certain practices and constrain others, thus becoming a device for social control [4, 61]. Our work illuminates the politics of measurements as key artifacts shaping the design and management of information technology. Since computing technologies such as databases, algorithms, and information entry interfaces, are designed around measurements; the development of measurements and the politics they embody can shape HCI design before it has even begun.

Thus, measurements are political artifacts that cannot only launch action, but are actions in and of themselves. Margaret Morrison's study of mathematical and engineering models highlights the interventionist aspects of measurement in her definition of measurement, which "involves some type of causal interaction with the material world via instruments" [41: 35]. Measurement is causal because when the quantitative descriptions of a thing such as size, number, or temperature are recorded, these measurements simultaneously determine and affirm the boundaries and characteristics of the thing being measured, judging it to be one thing and not another, measurable in some terms and not others. Measurement always involves the enactment and re-enactment of ontologies through what appears to be merely description (see more in the section *Measurements Make Things* below).

To investigate the ramifications of measurement, we are going to start by reviewing some of the literature mentioned above in more detail. This review occurs in three related sections: politics and power; how measurements make, rather than merely describe, the world; and how value and moral judgments are part of measurement. We will then use two case studies to see how these concepts play out in situations of health and harm. Finally, in the discussion, we create a framework for thinking through the links between measurement and action, particularly in terms of *charismatic* measurements consciously designed to resonate with certain values and morals, and thus launch specific actions. Since major decisions in the 21st century are based on big data and the proliferation of measurement, investigating the qualitative work of quantitative measurements is crucial for understanding how decisions at the "end" of data analysis have already begun before data collection, during measurement, even when they are not intentional.

Politics and Power

Studies of the politics of measurement have a long legacy. In *Seeing Like a State*, historian James Scott states that "legibility has [long been] a central problem in statecraft," and modern bureaucracies are characterized by the development of "a measure, a metric, that would allow it to 'translate' what [the state] knew into a common standard necessary for a synoptic view," the top-down view required to govern populations [57: 3-4]. Likewise, in *The Politics of Large Numbers*, statistician and sociologist Alain Desrosières writes that modern statistics is the "recombining of scientific and administrative practices" [17: 9]. As such, citizens, trees, hospitals, and other entities of interest have long been measured, counted, aggregated, organized, judged, and archived in a calculus of governance. Measurement and its manipulation as central techniques in governance and control has been a strong theme in research that lays bare the political work of quantification [5, 7, 17, 18, 25, 51, 56, 57]. In line with this work, our case studies are about politics proper: the use of measurement by a governing body or its agents to affect change within its jurisdiction.

Measurements are not just political in the sense that they are used in governance; they are also political in that they exercise covert political power by bringing certain things into spreadsheets and data infrastructures, and thus into management and policy, while leaving other things out. Sociologist Stephen Lukes [in Scott, 58] refers to this latent power to shape political agendas as a mobilization of bias, or the ability to shape agendas before overt political conflict even emerges. This view is summed up in the truism, "You can't manage what you can't measure" an its inverse, "you can only manage what you do measure."

One of the main themes in research on power, politics and data is how certain things, particularly things that are not of interest to the state or other institutions designing and collecting data, are systematically left out of data infrastructures, and thus left out of the political sphere. Case studies in the literature include the early European state not counting any qualities of trees that were not amenable to units of lumber, a choice that made for a sickly forest over the long term [57]; un-charismatic flora and fauna such as seaweed being left out of ecological evaluations and thus out of environmental policies and protection [6]; and through a seemingly rational use of normal statistical methods, the City of New York removing people of color and women from post-Hurricane Sandy survivor surveys [39]. In each case, certain entities are *unintentionally* excluded from measurement, and thus from circulation in science, policy, and management in the pursuit of other interests and values.

Measurements Make Things

The power and politics of measurement via leaving things out is further complicated by how the interplay of inclusion and exclusion *makes* things. Measurements create certain possibilities for action and exclude other possibilities; this is why it is crucial to examine not only the politics underpinning the design of measurements, but how measurements are linked to action, carrying the interests of their designers into the world.

Science and technology studies theorist Geoffrey Bowker writes, "the database itself will ultimately shape the world in its image: it will be performative. If we are only saving what we are counting, and if our counts are skewed in many different ways [such as what gets counted and what does not], then we are creating a new world in which those counts become more and more normalized" [5: 675]. It becomes normal, natural even, that some entities and qualities are measured and some are not. Soon it becomes normal to think of trees as lumber, and soon instead of "nature" they are called "natural resources" [57: 13]. Certain measurements become the norm, are taken for granted, and eventually we do not recall how those measurements were chosen over others in the first place. Our daily lives are full of seemingly natural measurements, from the caloric content of food [43] to the miles per gallon performance of our vehicles [36], despite their constructed and even contested nature, demonstrating how measurements enter into vernacular usage and are accepted as legitimate, unquestioned descriptions of the things being represented.

Not only do measurements make certain things normal, they also make new things entirely. For example, in "The Making and Molding of Child Abuse," Ian Hacking describes how the concept of "child abuse" was invented in Denver in 1961 by pediatricians after their publication of "The Battered-Child Syndrome" [26]. Once "child abuse" was on the books as something to be counted—it became a medical category by 1965—the counting began in earnest until it seemed there was an epidemic in America: 7000 in 1967, 1.1 million in 1982, doubling to 2.4 million in 1989. Child abuse became a concrete social problem via measurement. Like our case studies, "child abuse" is a category that made a previously "invisible" form of harm manifest. Once "recognized," it became a national crisis.

Moral Measurements, Judgment, and Qualculation

When measurements make things, the practice of measurement also encapsulates moral judgments about these things. To understand how measurement is linked with action, it is necessary to understand measurement as a moral act, one that embodies a particular set of values and principles of conduct.

STS scholars [10, 11, 42] link calculation and judgment in their term 'qualculation.' Qualculation is the act through which judgment and calculation, and their vested values, are stabilized into standardized things. The term qualculation denotes that quantitative calculation always already involves qualitative judgment. The results of a popular algorithm ranking hotels, for example, is inseparable from the practices of qualitative assessment that users engage in concert with the particular design of a tripadvisor interface which provides a certain scale structure and specific categories for reviewers to exercise judgment on (location, sleep quality, rooms, cleanliness, etc.) [11, 45]. Ingunn Moser and John Law explain:

"Judgment and calculation [...] have much in common. This is because each makes relations between elements that are materially heterogeneous and different in kind. Each needs to simplify those heterogeneities and order – perhaps homogenise – them. Each, therefore, works by setting limits to what will count as "information". Each does this by setting boundaries to what is taken to be important and what is not. In short, we are arguing that judgment and calculation both work by arraying and manipulating entities within a single spatio-temporal frame. In this way they achieve what we will call qualculability [42: 59]."

For Moser & Law, measurement is one of a number of highly impactful descriptive practices along with classification, counting, and naming that make groups of diverse things into one kind of thing. Messy realities are framed and stabilized so that they may circulate in the world as homogenous units. These choices are value-based judgments. To return to the case of child abuse, a number of different behaviors were grouped together into one kind. It was judged that battery, willful neglect, sexual abuse, and incest against children were all one kind of thing. Through measuring these behaviors and grouping them under the term 'child abuse,' they were deemed morally wrong, thus identification of these actions was linked to a moral imperative for society to address and mitigate these behaviors.

The following case studies highlight how measurement makes something in the world that was not there before, even as they may aim to "merely" describe the thing under measurement. We have multiple aims. The first is to demonstrate how measurement makes certain things visible, and others invisible, thus creates and delimits certain spaces for action and closes off other possibilities. As noted above, other scholars have also looked at qualculation through this framework; we are extending this analysis by focusing on how this process occurs in high stake situations of health and harm. Second, in each case study we show how the qualitative, value-based aspects of measurement have be used intentionally for positive ends, rather than following most research on the topic that highlights how unreflective use of measurement and other forms of qualculation can lead to negative politics. In our cases, measurement is employed to make visible what was invisible in an attempt to intervene in a system with the aim of promoting health and well-being. If all measurements are political, we argue for both critical reflexivity in their construction and deployment, and an ethical stance that foregrounds their use for good.

CASES

We present two case studies: one on measures of maternal health for healthcare provision for hospitals, and one on measures of environmental health through sewage contamination of drinking water. These are chosen because in both cases, scientists and health professionals used their profession to intentionally advocate for change through measurement. The cases are overt in how change makers link quantitative measurement to qualitative action, thereby making the mechanics of the practice explicit to analysis and research for cases where the politics are less explicit: they are extreme but quintessential examples.

Case study 1: Measuring Severe Maternal Morbidity

Introduction

Our first case is drawn from Pine's ongoing ethnographic work on information practices in maternal and child healthcare [47, 48, 49], and specifically current development of a measurement of severe maternal morbidity. The severe maternal morbidity measure is directly linked to efforts from medicine, public health, and social justice groups to impact the high incidence of maternal mortality in the U.S., the number of women dying directly of pregnancy or childbirth related causes. In recent years maternal health has been adopted as an indicator of a country's health, development, and economic progress more broadly; improving maternal health through reducing maternal mortality was adopted as one of the United Nation's eight Millennium Development Goals in 2000. Maternal mortality received significant media attention in the United States in 2010, when the World Health Organization published a report revealing that the incidence of maternal mortality had decreased globally in the past 20 years but had doubled in the United States, ranking the U.S. number one among developed countries for maternal mortality, and even worse than some developing countries [66]. The data also revealed deep ethnic disparities in outcomes as African American women had a rate of death four times higher than other ethnic groups.

Invisible Harm

However, obtaining the precise U.S. maternal mortality rate has proven quite difficult in practice. A number of difficulties have been encountered. Bowker and Starr [7] have described the difficulty of accurately recording cause of death in general, and maternal death data is of notoriously low quality [15]. Even where pregnancy or childbirth are directly responsible for mortality, cause of death is often listed differently, such as "cardiac arrest" [23]. Further, the gross number of deaths is quite low, even if the rate is high compared to other countries. Maternal mortality is measured as a ratio of the number of deaths per 100,000 pregnancies. There is a perceptual issue in that while the ratio has risen dramatically over the past two decades, the fact that the gross number is low has lead to a tendency to discount maternal mortality as a true social problem by both medical professionals and the general public. In particular, infant mortality has received much more attention in quality improvement efforts than maternal mortality. Human rights and feminist activists point out that this may be exacerbated by pervasive underlying discrimination that places fetal rights above those of women exemplified by the ongoing abortion debate and legal cases that pit fetal rights to healthcare against those of their mothers.

Additionally, hospital culture has proven challenging for highlighting the severity of material mortality as a medical problem. There is a common belief in hospitals that obstetrical emergencies are lightweight and less pressing than other kinds of emergencies. For example, a blood bank manager interviewed during fieldwork explained that she feels efforts to improve operational and system responses to obstetrical hemorrhage are a waste of effort because "gunshot wounds to the chest are the real emergencies" for blood banks, while obstetrical hemorrhage is not, though both require blood. As a result of this culture and the interpretation of the ratio, activists from a number of realms have found it difficult to both impact the maternal mortality rate and impress the importance of the issue on both professionals and the general public.

In trying to affect maternal health more broadly, a recent strategy has been to develop a measure of maternal morbidity rather than mortality – that is, on maternal health and wellbeing rather than death rates. Maternal health activists and quality improvement advocates argue that maternal mortality represents only "the tip of the iceberg" in terms of severe maternal health events, and the number of women who experience severe morbidity (resulting in both short and long term impairment) is estimated to occur at a rate 50 times higher than mortality. Focusing on severe maternal morbidity additionally creates a much larger pool of data and thus a larger dataset with greater statistical power from which to measure structures, processes, and outcomes related to maternal health and harm. The thought is that if morbidity can be impacted, the more elusive mortality rate will be affected as well. Thus, making maternal morbidity visible via measurement is an explicit effort to draw attention to substandard material conditions of healthcare in both medical and public spheres.

In 2008, the American Center for Disease Control (CDC) [14] proposed a potential algorithm for identification and classification of severe maternal morbidity cases based on algorithms developed by Callaghan, Creanga, & Kuklina [9] and Kuklina et al [35]. Each of these potential algorithms encapsulates a number of measurements, including a number of pieces of administrative information such as length of stay in hospital, unit of admission, along with 25 diagnosis and procedure codes that may be related to maternal health events (i.e. acute myocardial infarction, aneurism) drawn from International Classification of Disease (ICD) data applied by medical coders after a stay in the hospital. At present, some states are working to implement this measure although it is not yet required by law or by the hospital accreditation body.

The Activist Measurement

A state-funded quality improvement collaborative has recently decided to focus on data related to blood transfusions as a primary indicator of maternal morbidity in Pine's hospital and data center field sites. Obstetric hemorrhage is the leading cause of preventable maternal mortality. This is not simply a medical move, but an attempt to make obstetric emergency visible in very visceral terms: blood. The severe maternal morbidity measurement is based on the number people who receive four or more blood products, and total number of blood products each person in this sample received. Describing morbidity in terms of blood evokes an image of crisis. Moreover, in the hospital, blood is a precious resource that is expensive in both fiscal terms and in human resources required to acquire (from direct donors and larger regional blood banks), store, manage, and coordinate fragile and limited blood supplies. Further, accurate blood transfusion data can only be collected with the explicit buy-in of hospital blood banks. The current construction of the blood unit-based severe morbidity measure shapes a need for collaboration between obstetrical units, quality improvement units, and blood banks, which the statewide quality improvement agency hopes will naturally create increased dialogue between these units thus increasing the salience of obstetric hemorrhage as an urgent priority for blood banks, one of the most important departments within the hospital.

Measuring blood loss and replacement is now being materialized in the design of hospital information systems. Blood loss constitutes a substantial design challenge for both clinicians and designers of computer interfaces for obstetrical work. This is because accurately quantifying blood loss is difficult to do in practice. In some hospitals, a new pop-up calculating scale has been introduced in the Electronic Health Records (EHR) that helps clinicians accurately quantify blood loss. When a hemorrhage is documented, clinicians access a calculator that automatically subtracts the weight in grams of blood- soiled items from the pre-programmed tare weight of sheets, towels, and gauze, and produces a running tally of quantified blood loss. As the SMM measure is further developed around number of blood products transfused, designers are grappling with a way to develop calculators in the EHR interface which will depict both quantified blood loss and also the total number of products transfused, further shaping information entry into the computer system in ways that shift organizational behavior and shape it around a blood-based notion of health and harm. In short, these user interfaces will naturalize the measure of blood designed to address high material mortality and morbidity rates.

Conclusion

The blood measurement involves counting the number of blood units given to patients who receive 4 or more units of blood from an obstetrical hemorrhage. This measurement is an active local effort to label and count blood in order to stabilize "severe maternal morbidity" as a problem. When multiple sites use this measurement, they will make maternal morbidity visible and comparable, thus creating a new artifact—a coherent abstraction of 'maternal morbidity'— where there was previously none. The design of the calculator in the EHR system materializes the loss of blood of hemorrhaging patients in a way that requires weighing blood soaked items—gone are the days of estimating blood loss visually. Thus the development of the Severe Maternal Morbidity measure centered around blood loss and transfusion, and subsequent design of the calculator, requires a change in observation practices and new attention to blood loss. Our case study also shows how this calculator and its subsequent iterations, which might appear to be a benign design element, is the result of advocacy.

This measurement is an explicit attempt at intervention on many fronts. Blood loss is not only scary in the wider social imaginary, but units of blood given are understood in the social order of the hospital as denoting "dire emergencies." Making blood loss visible via measurement thus explicitly makes "harm" by denoting that there is an acceptable amount of blood loss and an atypical, pathological amount of blood loss. Maternal health is materialized as an emergency involving the potential for massive pathological bleeding, thus presents a moral imperative for action on the part of the medical establishment to stop blood loss and on the public to pay attention to a deadly crisis in the United States.

Case study 2: Previous Sewage Contamination (PSC)

Introduction

In the mid-nineteenth century, increased industrial activity and urbanization in Britain and the United States lead to the contamination of waterways used for public water supplies by industrial chemicals and sewage. In addition to sewage, effluents of inner-city tanneries, slaughterhouses, reduction plants, breweries, paper milling and textile manufacturing compounded the "filth problem" by dumping their waste into the public water sources from which drinking water came. Cholera epidemics increased in number rather than decreasing after the industrial revolution in Britain and the United States. Governments in both countries agreed something had to be done. In Britain, the 1887 *Rivers Pollution Prevention Act* decreed

There is no such thing as absolutely pure water in nature, and the waters met with in our springs, lakes, rivers, and sewers, form a series gradually increasing in dirtiness; there is actually no definite line of demarcation separating the purest spring water from the filthiest sewage.... It is, therefore, obvious that, for the purposes of efficient legislation, an arbitrary line must be drawn between waters which are to be deemed polluting and [those deemed non-polluting]. [Rivers Pollution Commission]

Scientists were asked to determine this "arbitrary line" to say whether a waterway was fit for consumption. In London, this line was often whether or not the water had been filtered in new state-of-the-art filtration systems.

Invisible Harm

While the norm for safe drinking water metrics became whether water had been filtered and if a specific number bacteria were found in a sample (the number varied by jurisdiction), in the professional opinion of Edward Frankland, a British water chemist for the British Royal Institution, science was not up to the task [20, 21, 22]. Frankland believed that water analysis could not define the safety of water, chiefly because the presence and habits of germs, a new concept in the field, were still largely unknown. Frankland believed germs could potentially withstand filtration, chemical reagents, dilution, condensation, and other popular purification methods. Thus, even if a bacteriological test found no living germs in a sample, Frankland reasoned that a few germs may have survived purification and were just not present in the sample taken. These resilient germs could start an epidemic. Between 1831 and the time of Frankland's first writing on the topic, over 43,000 people in London had died of cholera [63].

The Activist Measurement

Thus, in 1867, Frankland introduced the concept of "previous sewage contamination," or PSC, in London's water quality metrics. PSC was meant to represent the amount of sewage a river had received upstream [22]. It was a number obtained by measuring the total amount of nitrogen compounds in a water sample, which in turn indicated the amount of organic material that had been in the water. This organic material could come from sewage or peat or other sources; science could not differentiate between them, and Frankland maintained the differentiation was "hygienically irrelevant" [22: 113-17]. PSC was meant to indicate whether there had ever potentially been sewage in the water, and thus indicated a health danger regardless of whether the water had been purified.

In effect, PSC was a measurement used to advocate for a definition of safety that differed substantially from the status quo. At the time, post-purification was the preferred standard for measurement of safety. Thus, In contrast to post-purification, PSC was an activist measurement, one that sought to link measurement to a particular mode of action [28, 29]. As a member of several Royal commissions on water quality, Frankland had the ability to instate PSC in water analysis reports received by Londoners, materializing the measurement as a commonplace information artifact used by citizens to understand water quality. His idea was that citizens and other stakeholders would understand the measurement to mean they were drinking feces—not urine, because disease-causing germs such as cholera and yellow fever had been explicitly linked to solid sewage—and become disgusted, fearful, or enraged to the point of demanding better water quality from their government. PSC would be present in any purified water since all local waterways were used as extensions of sewers (and had other organic materials in them besides), meaning the PSC metric effectively made sewage contamination an intractable problem of urban planning. Affecting change toward "better water" via this measurement would entail either changing the source of London's water supply, or the legislated cessation of all sewage disposal into waterways. The latter was Frankland's goal.

Conclusion

PSC was an explicitly, intentionally political measurement that sought the complete revolution of sewage disposal practices. It aimed to make danger visible where people had previously seen safe drinking water, an intervention premised on the notion that science was not yet capable of making judgments of safe drinking water, and that any amount of organic matter (nitrates) indicated a possible germ, and therefore the single seed of an epidemic. It grouped together all indicators of organic contaminants, effectively homogenizing them as "previous sewage contaminant" even if they had been from peat or textile manufacturers, and these homogenized units circulated through bureaucracies and into the public sphere. In effect, PSC was a lever for banning raw sewage disposal into local waterways; it was action-by-measurement.

If you work monitoring water quality at a water treatment plant today, you would measure and log nitrates among other common contaminants. But there is no category for PSC. As a consumer of water, your yearly water quality report does not contain an entry for PSC. Again, you might see a numerical value beside "nitrates," but this number does not indicate harm or even potential harm. Despite Frankland's best efforts, PSC did not change practices of dumping sewage into waterways, nor did the measurement itself endure in water quality monitoring infrastructures. This is partly because science became able to detect safe or unsafe water and epidemics of cholera and yellow fever become less common. Yet, even today, the presence of water-borne endocrine disruptors in the form of pesticide runoff, plastic leachates, and flushed synthetic hormones are thought to cause forms of harm that science is unable to track definitively [37], but there is no indicator for these contaminants in day-to-day data collection practices. The absence of an interface that can receive these measurements makes their invisibility all the more concrete and likely to continue. It is a sort of ignorance by design [34, 52] where it becomes impossible to see certain harms because the tools and interfaces that would detect and receive them look for other things, and so they remain out of scientific, political, and public consciousness. What the interface doesn't include shapes action. Thus, Frankland's fight remains relevant to contemporary issues of measurement and how it endures in information systems with ramifications for interventions around health and contamination.

DISCUSSION

Other researchers have shown how qualculations create "things," or ontologies, which are then programmed into databases, ICTs, and management structures (i.e. see [1, 2]). Our research adds nuance to this discussion by looking at how activist and advocate groups have recognized this and leveraged it for social change in the realm of health. In particular, we show how measurements are linked to actions in the broader world by redefining harm and health and their attendant crises. Our two main assertions are:

1) Some data is more "charismatic" than others, meaning it inspires action more than other forms of evidence, because of both pre-existing social and cultural values and affective modes of representing crisis.

2) All data is already interested and value-laden, and some groups of people are using this explicitly for social change, but the value-laden nature of measurement and thus of data is true in all cases.

Charismatic Measurements

It is no coincidence that the agents in our examples chose blood and feces as their objects of measurement, for both are *charismatic*. We use charisma to mean the characteristic of inspiring devotion so strong that it moves an audience to action [50]. Measurements get their power to move people to action from qualculation—the values, judgments, and fears that are already salient in a culture, which are then "baked into" the measurement. Blood already signals fear and crisis, both in the popular imagination and in the hospital emergency hierarchy. Feces are already disgusting and dangerous, particularly in the nineteenth century, and must be segregated from human consumption at all costs. Returning to Hacking's example, child abuse is already morally abhorrent at the moment of its inception as a category of violence. All these measurements have a terrifying charisma.

Elsewhere, the second author has discussed "charismatic data" [37], information that is simultaneously scientific evidence and proof of a moral imperative, and thus has the potential to launch action the way other data may not. Blood-based maternal morbidity rates and Previous Sewage Contamination (PSC) are charismatic measurements in this way. By purposefully choosing blood as the measure of maternal morbidity and presence of feces as the measure of dangerous water, the agents in our case studies were attempting to make a problem manifest that had heretofore been invisible, and thus introduce solutions that may not have been viable before. Their efforts to make a type of harm apparent through measurement made a new entity. That entity was crafted in such a way that it was actionable.

For example, crafting the measure of maternal morbidity through blood transfusions made the problem of maternal morbidity a certain sort of crisis, which then has specific attendant solutions. Harm is constructed and made visceral in the measurement. Further, harm is tied to a specific material resource: blood. 'Making' morbidity through a measurement of transfused blood units casts maternal morbidity as an organizational problem. The measurement itself affords certain solutions to the problem; adequate treatment of morbidity involves first staunching blood loss, and second transferring blood supplies from the blood bank to the site of care, rapidly and effectively replacing blood that is lost to prevent grave harm and perhaps even impending death. At a macro level, the crisis involves prioritization at the administrative level as a consumer of valuable resources. The measurement itself, which is being built into algorithms and schemes for healthcare systems management and quality improvement [49], lends itself to evaluations of medical practice and organizational performance, particularly inter-unit coordination. Now maternal morbidity, and by extension, maternal mortality, can be managed. Likewise, calling all organic matter Previous Sewage Contamination made any suspicious material a dangerous entity that had to be completely absent, rather than present in small numbers, to achieve safe drinking water. Now the urban water supply had to be managed differently.

Measurement and Action

In both cases, the measurements leveraged action by mapping into preexisting values. Measurements are a "technique of definition" that distills something amorphous into something essential [37], and by doing so, "having exposed its true nature, [one can] skillfully excise its root causes" [55: 159]. In the making and remaking of things and establishment of what is usual and average, normal and pathological, countable and measurable, entities and their attendant problems are presented in certain ways. Hacking [26] describes the link between measurement and action via labeling theory: "people act and decide under descriptions, and as new possibilities for description emerge, so do new kinds of action [p. 255]." When child abuse became something to be measured, it allowed policy to work in places it could not before. When blood is the measure of harm, the problem of maternal health rises in importance within the hospital and public sphere, allowing more resources and attention, and ideally fewer maternal deaths in the United States. When there is sewage rather than "organic matter" in the water, a municipality may shift from filtration to the regulation of dumping in waterways. Thus, qualculation delimits the kinds of actions towards that entity that make sense, and those which do not, determining the types of action that are likely to take place in both expert communities and policy circles. As such, measurement is always linked to action.

However, we do not want to let the charisma of blood and feces obfuscate the point that while our examples might be extreme, they are also quintessential. nAll qualculations are inherently political; they make the things they are describing, are infused with values and judgment, and are intimately tied to action. Using charismatic examples based in activism and advocacy makes the implicit explicit and, most importantly, available for action.

CONCLUSION

Returning to Bowker's [5] point that "the database will shape the world in its image," we are at a key moment in which to excavate the sociocultural and sociopolitical underpinnings of measurement. If successful, measurements and their modes of action are interred in data structures [1], which are increasingly woven into almost all aspects of our daily activities. Nigel Thrift [62] calls for attention to how the increasingly qualculated world is shaping the "background hum of thinking," our invisible cognitive processes, and how they will be changed by current developments in database capacity and attendant information and communication structures. This background hum includes, often invisibly, the judgments, assumptions, and values of various decisions that have been interred in information infrastructures through measurement. This is political. This is as true of overt and intentional qualculations like blood-based maternal morbidity measures or Previous Sewage Contamination as it is for every other form of data and measurement. As we seek more things to measure to meet the capacities of Big Data, and as we come to use this data to make decisions on grander and grander scales, we need to be aware of these underlying structures and our own role in shaping them as interventions in the world. Our case studies of maternal mortality metrics and Previous Sewage Contamination add to the wider conversation about the politics of information by highlighting cases where these characteristics of measurement are used intentionally by advocates and activists to redefine, via measurement, the indicators of health and harm.

ACKNOWLEDGMENTS

We are indebted to Ellie Harmon and Melissa Gregg for their helpful comments in developing drafts of this paper. We also thank Morgan Ames in her capacity as editor of the Ethnography Matters blog for her help in editing a blog post that captured some of the early ideas presented in this work. We thank Christine Wolf who helped with data collection for the severe maternal morbidity case. We are indebted to sources who were further helpful in constructing the cases presented, including Christine Morton as well as the Chemical Heritage Foundation. We thank the Intel Science and Technology Center for Social Computing. Portions of this work were supported by the Agency for Healthcare Research and Quality grant R36 HS20753, National Science Foundation Grant 1319897, and the Center for Organizational Research.

REFERENCES

1. Agre, P.E. (1994) Surveillance and capture: two models of privacy." *The Information Society,* 10, 101–127.
2. Agre, Philip E. (1994). Accountability and Discipline: A Comment on Suchman and Winograd. *Computer Supported Cooperative Work,* 3(1), 31–35.
3. Barocas, S., Hood, S., & Ziewitz, M. (2013). Governing algorithms: a provocation piece. *SSRN Electronic Journal.*
4. Bjørn, P., & Balka, E. (2007). *Health Care Categories Have Politics Too: Unpacking the Managerial Agendas of Electronic Triage Systems.* ECSCW '07.
5. Bowker, G.C. (2000). "Biodiversity Datadiversity." *Social Studies of Science,* 30, 643–683.

6. Bowker, G.C. (2008). *Memory Practices in the Sciences*. Cambridge: The MIT Press.
7. Bowker, G. C., & Star, S. L. (1999). *Sorting Things Out: Classification and Its Consequences*. Cambridge: MIT press.
8. Boyd, D., & Crawford, C. (2012). Critical questions for big data. *Information, Communication & Society* 15 (5), 662–79.
9. Callaghan, W.M., Creanga, A.A., & Kuklina, E.V. (2012). Severe maternal morbidity among delivery and postpartum hospitalizations in the United States. *Obstetrics and Gynecology,* 120(5), 1029–36.
10. Callon, M. (2007). What does it mean to say economics is performative? In MacKenzie, D. A., Muniesa, F., & Siu, L. (Eds.). Do economists make markets?: on the performativity of economics. Princeton: Princeton University Press.
11. Callon, M., & Law, J. (2005). "On Qualculation, Agency, and Otherness." *Environment and Planning D: Society and Space* 23(5), 717–33.
12. Canguilhem, Georges. (1991). *The Normal and the Pathological*. Cambridge: MIT Press.
13. Cardon, D. (2013). Présentation. *Dossier Politique Des Algorithmes, Réseaux* 177(1), 9–21.
14. Centers for Disease Control. Severe Maternal Morbidity in the United States - Maternal and Infant Health - Reproductive Health. Accessed September 19, 2014. http://www.cdc.gov/reproductivehealth/MaternalInfantHealth/SevereMaternalMorbidity.html.
15. Deneux-Tharaux, C., Carmona, E., Bouvier-Colle, M.E., & Bréart, G. (2006). Postpartum Maternal Mortality and Cesarean Delivery. *Obstetrics and Gynecology* 108(3), 541–48.
16. Dourish, P. (In Press). "NoSQL: the shifting materialities of database technology." *Computational Culture*.
17. Desrosières, A. (2002). *The Politics of Large Numbers: A History of Statistical Reasoning*. Cambridge: Harvard University Press.
18. Douglas, M. (1986). *How Institutions Think*. Syracuse: Syracuse University Press, 1986.
19. Foucault, M. *Power/Knowledge: Selected Interviews and Other Writings, 1972-1977*. 1st American Ed edition. New York: Vintage, 1980.
20. Frankland, E. (1880). *Water Analysis for Sanitary Purposes*. N.p.
21. Frankland, E. (1877). *Experimental Researches in Pure, Applied and Physical Chemistry*. J. Van Voorst.
22. Frankland, E., and Royal Institution of Great Britain. (1867). *On the Water Supply of the Metropolis*. N.p.
23. Gaskin, I.M. (2008). Maternal death in the United States: a problem solved or a problem ignored? *The Journal of Perinatal Education* 17(2), 9–13.
24. Gitelman, L. (2013). *Raw Data Is an Oxymoron*. Boston: MIT Press.
25. Hacking, I. (1990). *The Taming of Chance*. 1st edition. Cambridge England ; New York: Cambridge University Press.
26. Hacking, I. (1991). The making and molding of child abuse. *Critical Inquiry*, 253–288.
27. Hacking, I. (1999). *The Social Construction of What?* Cambridge: Harvard University Press.
28. Hamlin, C. (1990) *Edward Frankland: The Analyst as Activist*. Berkeley: University of California Press.
29. Hamlin, C. (1990). *A Science of Impurity: Water Analysis in Nineteenth Century Britain*. Berkeley: University of California Press.
30. Haraway, D.J. (1989). *Primate Visions: Gender, Race, and Nature in the World of Modern Science*. Psychology Press.
31. Irani, L., Vertesi, J., Dourish, P., Philip, K., & Grinter, R. E. (2010). Postcolonial computing: a lens on design and development. In *Proc. SIGCHI 2010*, 1311-1320.
32. Irwin, S., & Jordan, B. (1987). Knowledge, practice, and power: court-ordered cesarean sections. *Medical Anthropology Quarterly* 1(3), 319–34.
33. Karasti, H., Baker, K.S., & Halkola, E. (2006). Enriching the notion of data curation in E-Science: data managing and information infrastructuring in the Long Term Ecological Research (LTER) Network." *Computer Supported Cooperative Work,* 15(4), 321–58.
34. Kleinman, D.L. & Suryanarayanan, S. (2013). Dying bees and the social production of ignorance. *Science, Technology & Human Values* 38(4), 492–517.
35. Kuklina, E.V., Whiteman, M.K., Hillis, S.D., Jamieson, D.J., Meikle, S.F., Posner, S.F., & Marchbanks, P.A. (2008). An enhanced method for identifying obstetric deliveries: implications for estimating maternal morbidity. *Maternal and Child Health Journal* 12(4), 469–77.
36. Larrick, R.P., & Soll, J.B. (2008). The MPG illusion. *Science,* 320, 1593–1594.
37. Liboiron, M. (2012). Terrible and charismatic waste. *Peabody Museum of Archaeology & Ethnology*.
38. Liboiron, M. (2013). Plasticizers: a twenty-first-century miasma. In *Accumulation: The Material Politics of Plastic*, 2013.
39. Liboiron, M. (2015). Disaster data, data activism: grassroots Responses to Representing Hurricane Sandy," in *Extreme Weather and Global Media*, Eds. Julia Leyda and Diane Negra, Routledge.

40. MacKenzie, D. (2006). Is economics performative? Option theory and the construction of derivatives markets. *Journal of the History of Economic Thought*, 28(1), 29-55.
41. Morrison, M. (2009). Models, measurement and computer simulation: the changing face of experimentation. *Philosophical Studies* 143, 33–57.
42. Moser, I., & Law, J. (2006). Fluids or flows? Information and qualculation in medical practice. *Information Technology & People*, 19(1), 55-73.
43. Mudry, J.J. (2009). *Measured Meals: Nutrition in America*. SUNY Press.
44. Nagel, E. (1931). On the Logic of Measurement. *Thesis (PH.D.)—Columbia University, Source: American Doctoral Dissertations,*.
45. Orlikowski, W. J., & Scott, S. V. (2013). Knowledge eclipse: producing sociomaterial reconfigurations in the hospitality sector. In: Tsoukas, H., Nicolini, D. and Carlisle, P., (eds.) How Matter Matters: Objects, Artifacts, and Materiality in Organization Studies. Oxford: Oxford University Press.
46. Pasquale, F. (2013). The emperor's new codes: reputation and search algorithms in the finance sector. Governing Algorithms Conference, May 16, 2013.
47. Pine, K. (2012). Fragmentation and choreography: caring for a patient and a chart during childbirth. *Proc. CSCW 2012,* 887-896.
48. Pine, K.H., & Mazmanian, M. Institutional logics of the EMR and the problem of 'perfect' but inaccurate accounts." *Proc CSCW,* 283–294.
49. Pine, K.H., Wolf, C.T., & Mazmanian, M.. The Work of Re-use: Quality Measurement in Healthcare Organizations. CSCW '14 Workshop: Sharing, Re-Use and Circulation of Resources in Cooperative Scientific Work.
50. Potts, J. (2009). *A history of charisma*. Basingstoke, UK: Palgrave Macmillan.
51. Porter, T.M. (1996). *Trust in Numbers: The Pursuit of Objectivity in Science and Public Life*. Princeton: Princeton University Press.
52. Proctor, R., & Schiebinger, L.L. (2008). *Agnotology: The Making and Unmaking of Ignorance*. Palo Alto: Stanford University Press.
53. Ribes, D., & Jackson, S.J. (2013). Data bite man: the work of sustaining a long-term study." In *"Raw Data" Is an Oxymoron*, 147–66. Cambridge: MIT Press.
54. Richards, T. (1993). *The Imperial Archive: Knowledge and the Fantasy of Empire*. Verso.
55. Rittel, H.W.J., & Webber, M.M. (1973). Dilemmas in a general theory of planning." *Policy Sciences,* 4, 155–69.
56. Robertson, M. (2012). Measurement and alienation: making a world of ecosystem services. *Transactions of the Institute of British Geographers* 37, 386–401.
57. Scott, J.C. (1998). *Seeing Like a State: How Certain Schemes to Improve the Human Condition Have Failed.* Yale University Press.
58. Scott, J. (1994). *Power: Critical Concepts*. Taylor & Francis.
59. Smolan, R. (2012). *The Human Face of Big Data.* Sausalito: Against All Odds Productions.
60. Steiner, C., & Dixon, W. (2012). *Automate This: How Algorithms Came to Rule Our World.* New York: Portfolio/Penguin.
61. Suchman, Lucy. (1993). "Do Categories Have Politics?" *Computer Supported Cooperative Work,* 2(3), 177–190.
62. Thrift, N. (2004). Movement-Space: the changing domain of thinking resulting from the development. *Economy and Society* 33(4), 582–604.
63. "A Healthy Nation? Timeline." UK National Archives, n.d. http://www.nationalarchives.gov.uk/education/victorianbritain/healthy/timeline2.htm.
64. Vertesi, J. (2011). Transnational, never neutral: regulatory politics and the deployment of technological systems, workshop paper for Transnational HCI workshop at CHI 2011, Vancouver, BC, Canada.
65. Winner, L. (1986): 'Do Artifacts have Politics?' In L. Winner (ed.): The Whale and The Reactor: A Search for Limites in an age of High Technology, University of Chicaga Press, Chicago, 1986, pp. 28-40.
66. World Health Organization. *Maternal Mortality* Accessed September 19, 2014. http://www.who.int/mediacentre/factsheets/fs348/en/..

Beyond Participatory Production: Digitally Supporting Grassroots Documentary

David Philip Green[1], Simon J. Bowen[1], Chris Newell[2], Guy Schofield[1], Tom Bartindale[1], Clara Crivellaro[1], Alia Sheikh[3], Peter Wright[1], Patrick Olivier[1]

[1] Culture Lab, Newcastle University, Newcastle Upon Tyne, UK
{d.p.green, simon.bowen}@ncl.ac.uk

[2] School of Arts and New Media, Hull University, Scarborough, North Yorkshire, UK
c.newell@hull.ac.uk

[3] BBC Research & Development, London, UK
alia.sheikh@rd.bbc.co.uk

ABSTRACT

We conducted a study to explore the values and qualities of 'grassroots documentaries', framed around the production of two parallel documentary films with a London-based opera company. A team of professional filmmakers produced one film and the other was an exploratory form of grassroots documentary. We studied the different production activities through observations, interviews and a reflective workshop at the end of the study and evaluated the resulting films. Our analysis reveals critical insights that could inform the next generation of technological systems to support user-generated video content (UGVC) production, particularly in collaborative contexts such as grassroots communities.

Author Keywords

Video; Film; Documentary; Grassroots; Collaboration; Participation; UGC; UGVC; Production; Creativity

ACM Classification Keywords

H.5.m. Information interfaces and presentation (e.g., HCI): Miscellaneous.

INTRODUCTION

The medium of documentary film provides a rich platform for communicating ideas and an effective tool for scaffolding debate around social, political and environmental issues [34]. Its evolution over the last century has resulted in well-defined genres and narrative conventions that help audiences structure their interpretations of documentary films. John Grierson's definition of documentary as the "creative treatment of actuality" [17] is amongst the most widely accepted and broadest definitions but, in the aftermath of media convergence and the democratization of publishing [22], the term *treatment* presents the question *by whom?*

CHI 2015, April 18 - 23 2015, Seoul, Republic of Korea

ACM 978-1-4503-3145-6/15/04...$15.00
http://dx.doi.org/10.1145/2702123.2702203

At the grassroots level, recent technological developments in areas such as consumer tools for video production (in smartphones, for example) have broadened opportunities for participation in documentary video production activities. This is evidenced in the quantity and variety of *user-generated video content* (UGVC) seen on YouTube [35], social networks and video blogs. In addition to this abundance of publicly available UGVC, some is also produced that does not find an audience far beyond those who produce it [26]. This expanding dataset has prompted questions within Media Studies concerning audiences' abilities to find meaning within this "sea of data" [13]. Its variable quality has provoked some to question whether user-generated content is "trash or treasure" [2] and inspired new tools to support visual literacy [36]. Pioneering work within HCI in relation to documentary has largely focused on single user-producers [4] or tools that reduce the barriers-to-entry for professional tools, often by reimagining them for consumer devices [15]. A recent backlash against mobile phone recordings at live performances [18] has raised important questions about the social context of UGVC production, particularly at-scale and in sensitive situations, when the video production activities are unorganized and potentially disruptive. As new ways of structuring and searching media content emerge, what can we learn from documentary production practices? Do certain key values help professional documentary producers produce meaningful content? Can we leverage our understanding of documentary production processes to help overcome the organisational and social challenges facing UGVC producers and support motivated communities to organize their collaborative UGVC-production activities around a kind of 'grassroots' production model? What are the fundamental differences between professional and non-professional video production processes, the different *values* brought to these processes and the essential *qualities* that distinguish UGVC from professional content in this context, and vice-versa? To explore these questions, we conducted a study with a community-of-practice, framed around two documentary productions, one by a team of professional documentary producers and a second by members of the same community-of-practice. We supported the second documentary using a series of subtle interventions, designed to facilitate a 'grassroots production'. The study culminated in a workshop, at which we explored the relative *values* of the two production processes and the different *qualities* of the content produced for each. In this paper, we report findings from this study and discuss design implications for future tools and infrastructure to support grassroots documentary and collaborative UGVC production.

BACKGROUND

Professional Documentary Productions.

Professional documentaries are usually made by teams of skilled specialists in various roles. The necessary skills and knowledge of the different roles can be learned formally (e.g. at film school) or, more commonly, on-the-job, often over many years, in various different roles before specializing in a role such as director, sound-engineer, editor or producer. These films often have a production budget that has been sourced and allocated by a 'producer' in advance of filming. Professional filmmaking typically follows a well-known, industrial production workflow, within which hierarchical roles structure the filmmaking processes and support the collaborative aspects of the production. Professional documentaries usually possess *narrative coherence* and some degree of *aesthetic consistency*. From a variety of literature on the subject [30], we can break the professional production workflow into five sequential activities, representing a kind of filmmaking "blueprint", which we will use to explore alternative models:

Commissioning: subject matter, intended outcomes/ deliverables, timescales and budgets defined, usually by a 'producer'.

Pre-Production: detailed planning / decisions made about *what* and *who* to film, *when*, *where* and *how*. Narrative structured in documents produced by a 'director'. Equipment reserved and personnel recruited.

Production: video and audio materials obtained, interviews conducted, archive and other materials gathered and a 'director' oversees the creation of narratives.

Post-Production: materials are collated and arranged into a sequence along with graphical elements and music by an 'editor', generally using digital video editing systems such as AVID or Adobe Production Suite.

Distribution: the film is released, either online or licensed to festivals, broadcasters and screening venues.

Participatory Documentaries

Participatory documentaries are a form of professional documentary that include their human subjects in the production process by providing the skills and/or tools necessary for them to shoot and edit video, often through workshops or longitudinal engagements with subjects. Many participatory documentaries explicitly claim to help produce a more authentic representation of the subject [28]. Several innovative and successful collaborations between professional documentary producers and groups of UGVC producers, such as *Life in a Day (2009), 18 Days in Egypt (2011)* and *My Afghanistan (2012)*[1] illustrate the potential to frame UGVC within participatory documentaries. In these examples, professionals maintained overall control of the workflow, but delegated roles to non-professionals using techniques such as crowdsourcing. Typically, professional editors build linear narratives from the variety of crowdsourced UGVC, often around common themes, using storytelling conventions such as a three-act structure and story-arcs. Post-production techniques such as color-correction and audio mastering help create stylistic consistency, often in ways that are aligned to a particular genre. In *Life in a Day*, the narrative is based around the chronological sequence of the day when all of the submissions were filmed. Participatory documentaries are often praised for their insightfulness and poignancy and their "empowering" nature compared with traditional, ethnographic or fly-on-the-wall documentary production methods [28] but they have also catalyzed an ongoing discourse about the effect of documentary filmmaking upon their subjects; one that began almost a century ago with revelations that sequences from Flaherty's *Nanook of the North* (1922), had been staged for ease-of-filming (a one-sided igloo is said to have been constructed to allow the filmmakers to shoot interior shots of Inuits "at home" [29]). Evoking the lower rungs of Arnstein's 'Ladder of Participation' [3], Milne et al. describe these impositions by filmmakers upon their subjects as the result of a "filmmaker-victim-paradigm" [31]. Even within the participatory production model, this fundamentally imbalanced power relationship prevails. Where user-participation is enlisted in the *production* stage, the paradigm remains in the *pre-* and *post-production* stages. As yet, no practicable workflow has presented a solution that does not require substantial investment in training or ongoing support. Critics such as Nash [32], exploring aspects of documentary ethics and audience participation note various participatory production roles, but questions remain about the extent to which participatory productions are more, or less, "empowering" than traditional ethnographic documentaries [31].

Grassroots Documentaries

'Grassroots' films rarely resemble professional films since they are generated in response to various relatively independent video production activities, which are themselves responsive to wider goals of a community; for example an activist group wishing to highlight a campaign or a particular issue, or a community-of-practice wishing to share their practice with others. As such, they often lack coherency and consistency. Historically, grassroots documentaries have been distinguished from professional documentaries by virtue of their intention; "conveying arguments or information to a targeted audience, rather than evoke aesthetic or narrative pleasure." [20] A rare example of a professional-quality 'grassroots' documentary, *Kony 2012*[2], began as a 'grassroots' production (by the charity Invisible Children), but ultimately became an 'independent' film. Independent films are professional-quality films made

[1] Life in a Day - 18 Days in Egypt - My Afghanistan

[2] Kony 2012

without external resources, often by devoted amateur filmmakers who invest significant personal resources into a project. In the example of *Kony 2012*, one individual took ownership and committed significant personal resources to the project, as well as securing financial investment to enlist professional support. In this research, we consider grassroots documentaries to be those that must be realized without significant investment of this kind since we are aiming to maximize accessibility and minimize barriers-to-participation.

Much of the existing research in this area draws inspiration from professional processes. Life Mirror [27] presents a prototype crowdsourced commissioning tool and Wreck-a-Movie [23] succeeded in pioneering crowdfunding. Some innovative systems, such as [7], have explored using video metadata to algorithmically generate films, in doing so signposting new challenges around generating meaningful metadata. However, as [19] notes, technocentric systems can often fail to appeal beyond the tech-curious. Kelliher suggests, "Storytelling requires appropriate tools and technologies for promoting competency and fluency of expression, along with the development of carefully designed supporting structures for engaging audiences and building communities of active participants." [25] Many existing tools and technologies, by automating skilled processes, could be said to undermine - rather than promote - competency. Automatic exposure settings on most consumer cameras, for example, leave many oblivious to the roles of shutter speed, aperture and ISO and whilst tools are manifold, Kelliher's call for "supporting structures" tends to be overlooked. To connect with audiences, some structure is needed, but the challenge presented by the filmmaker-victim paradigm is the need for a more user-centric structure. As with any user-centered design challenge, we must strive to understand the user, or in this case *the users,* since grassroots implies an inherently collaborative approach. The notion of *produsage*, or "the collaborative, iterative, and user-led production of content by participants in a hybrid user-producer role" [8] presents a conceptual starting point for our study, but we also draw upon broader citizen-led, DIY and 'grassroots' media approaches [11].

CASE STUDY

We designed an 'in-the-wild' study, in collaboration with *Popera*, an independent, London-based opera company with approximately forty-two members, several of whom were active producers of UGVC. However, despite coming from a wide variety of creative backgrounds, none had formal training in filmmaking or video production. As a company of professional creative practitioners, the levels of visual literacy within the company were high, so they presented an opportunity to study the complex social challenges of collaborative UGVC (rather than basic visual creativity, which has been studied in detail elsewhere within HCI). At the beginning of the study, thirty members, including three members of the directorate, were embarking upon a production of the Rogers and Hammerstein operetta 'The Mikado' at a prestigious London theatre. *Popera* therefore presented a clearly defined community-of-practice with whom a study could be developed and a clear subject around which it could be structured. We worked closely with *Popera's* co-directors to design a study that would address our research questions, but also provide useful documentary materials for the company. During our first meetings, *Popera's* directors expressed an interest in capturing rehearsals for 'The Mikado'. Our aim for the study was to explore the differences between two different documentary production models: a traditional (non-participatory) 'professional' model and an exploratory 'grassroots' model. Thus, we commissioned *two parallel documentaries* about the three-month rehearsal period leading up to the first performance of 'The Mikado'. The 'professional' film ('*Pro-Film'*) was produced by '*RHMedia*', a small London-based film production company. The 'grassroots' film ('*Pop-Film*') was produced by the *Popera* community, supported by a *production assistant* (PA), who was recruited by the researchers from the half of the *Popera* community not directly involved in 'The Mikado' to assist with the research. This semi-experimental setup was designed pragmatically to synchronize the production activities and the timescale of the research. However, we aimed to retain the complexities of both productions in the study design, to reflect the complexities of real-world collaboration and co-creation within communities as much as possible.

Study Design

We designed the study to consist of two phases, based on the ***values*** and ***qualities*** of the two films. Firstly, we would examine the production activities of each of the two films, framed around the broader question of "what *values* are brought to these activities by those involved?" Thereafter, we would examine the documentary materials themselves, framed around the question of "what *qualities* can these artifacts be said to possess?" The film productions would provide a scaffold for discussions with participants (in both productions) about their values and experiences. This would culminate in a reflective workshop with all participants at the end of the process, at which we hoped to compare the two processes and their end-products and, through doing so, identify the values and qualities within each model – and any *limitations* within each - that might reveal opportunities for new ways to support grassroots documentary production.

Commissioning the films

Both films were produced over the same three-month period and began with an identical brief:

> *"The world of the opera is famed for its stirring music, melodramatic plots and grand sense of spectacle, but it remains overlooked by many, dismissed as exclusive or ostentatious. It is considered by many to be one of the finest art forms and some operatic performances by performers such as Maria Callas and Luciano Pavarotti have attained the status of legendary moments in performance history.*
>
> *To what extent do these opera stereotypes reflect what is actually happening in a modern opera company? How much do we really know about modern opera?*
>
> *With behind-the-scenes access to Popera's forthcoming production of The Mikado, we would like you to produce a 10-*

15 minute documentary film that documents the activities leading up to the performance, showing the different facets of contemporary opera."

Both teams were invited to submit their finished films to the researchers at the end of the study and encouraged to consider 'the general public' as the film's target audience.

'Designing' Popera Film

To help initiate and maintain the study, and to support the grassroots production, three minimally supportive interventions by the research team were implemented. The *first intervention* was the provision of the brief (above), which was designed to be suitably instructive yet open to interpretation. The *second intervention* was the provision of several commonly available production tools. Smartphones were offered to all participants and a basic upload portal set up (*Jotform*, synchronized to *Dropbox*), which allowed videos to be uploaded with optional metadata. Researchers manually transferred this footage daily to *WeVideo*, a free, online collaborative video editor. This provided a central online resource where everyone could review the videos emerging from the process and/or produce a basic edit from the footage. A two-page help sheet was distributed to all participants at the beginning of the study to explain how to access and use the upload portal and the *WeVideo* platform. The *third intervention* was the appointment of PA, who was known personally to many within the company and also had no formal filmmaking training or experience. The role was designed to facilitate liaison between the three main project parties; the research team, *RHMedia* and the *Popera* community, including relaying questions and/or concerns to the research team, where necessary. PA was briefed on the research objectives and asked to keep a diary of activities relating to the project over the course of 10 x three-hour sessions during the study. PA was paid for their involvement, but no other incentives were offered since we wanted to reflect a grassroots scenario as closely as possible and minimize 'artificial' motivations for participation.

Interviews

Over the three months, during the production, we attended eight 3-4 hour rehearsal sessions and conducted informal, unstructured interviews with four participants (all female singers from the cast) and two members of the board. The unstructured approach to the interviews was designed to contrast the interventions in the grassroots production and covered topics such as documentary ethics, the value of reflexive-documentation and professional-documentation and participants' previous experiences of UGVC. These interviews lasted between 20 and 40 minutes and were conducted at the rehearsal and performance venues in London. In addition, three semi-structured interviews with PA allowed us to monitor the project's progress throughout. We also conducted a semi-structured telephone interview with *RHMedia*, to understand their proposed production methods for *Pro-Film*.

User Workshop

At the end of the three-month production period, after the opera performance run, a four-hour workshop featured three activities, designed to explore questions of ***values***, ***qualities*** and ***limitations*** respectively. 11 participants attended the workshop: four members of *RHMedia* and seven members of *Popera* (two artistic co-directors, four female singers and PA). Two representatives from the national broadcasting corporation also attended. The design of the workshop was inspired by work by Hook et al. [21], in which video materials were presented back to their producers as a means of stimulating discussion about production methods that may otherwise have been difficult to articulate due to their tacit or routine nature.

Activity 1 focused on the processes involved in the production of each film. In separate, parallel groups, we began by presenting the groups' own films back to them. They were then asked to represent their production processes as flow diagrams on flipcharts, using Post-it notes and marker pens to identify *activities* and *roles*. Facilitators encouraged the group to consider how the other team's workflow may have differed.

Activity 2 focused on the films themselves. The groups were each shown the other group's film and asked to complete a questionnaire designed to elicit evaluation and comparison of the two films. Afterwards, the groups were asked to consider how they might re-edit their film if they had access to the other team's material and this was prototyped using printed screenshots representing clips from each film.

Activity 3 brought the two groups together to critically reflect upon the two previous activities. With the groups together, we first reflected upon the different production processes and, secondly, upon the films themselves. The activity took the form of a round-table discussion, with questions and visual materials generated in the previous activities used to stimulate the conversation.

Data Analysis

In total, 6 hours of interviews and 5 hours of workshop activities were transcribed. From the workshop, we also generated two 'workflow diagrams' and 'paper prototype' re-edits of two 'hybrid' films incorporating the other film's rushes. Eleven questionnaires, PA's diary and notes taken during the process provided additional data. Throughout the process, we conducted member-checking exercises by reflecting upon the findings with members of *Popera*, including members of the directorate, and an academic specializing in digital media. This ongoing reflective process culminated in an inductive thematic analysis [3] of the data, which we discuss in the 'findings' section. In the following section we describe the two films, focusing on the production activities and the resulting documentary materials.

THE TWO FILMS

1 - Pro-Film

Production Activities (Pro-Film)

RHMedia, led by '*Zen*', a 'self-shooting' producer/director, were recruited in liaison with a national broadcasting corporation to ensure the production followed - as closely as possible - professional production protocols and ensure the finished product was of broadcast standard. To achieve this, they were given a budget of £4,500 by the researchers; a figure suggested by the broadcasting corporation as appropriate for an undertaking of this scale. *Zen*, in the role of 'director', took responsibility for the film's day-to-day management and creative direction. During initial contact with the researchers, *Zen* requested specific stylistic advice and eventually agreed to produce a "*BBC The One Show-style insert*" (a self-contained, interview-led piece with 'cutaway' shots and a clear, linear, beginning/middle/end structure). *Zen* carried out some preliminary research into the subjects of opera, The Mikado and *Popera* and produced a 'treatment document' (an interpretation of the brief). *Zen* described this *pre-production* stage as "*designing the film*", using a basic set of tools, "*Word, Excel, email and a telephone.*" For the *production* stage, *Zen* recruited a crew of individuals to the roles of *sound-engineer, lighting technician/2nd camera* and *editor*, who were paid on a day-rate basis determined by *Zen*, who also took responsibility for delegating tasks throughout the production. A team of three worked together during filming days (*Zen + sound-engineer + lighting technician/2nd cameraman*). Production took place over three days towards the end of the three months (fig 3), primarily based on the crew's availability, but also reflecting *Zen*'s opinion that "*there would be more going on to film.*" The final day of filming was the night of the first performance. During *post-production*, a team of two were involved (*Zen + editor*), although the editor carried out the majority of the post-production work, during the week between the first performance and the submission deadline, over four non-consecutive days. *RHMedia* used a variety of professional equipment, the majority of which was owned, although some was hired-in. The final 24-minute film was submitted in a broadcast-quality HD format (video figure – part 1). The representatives from the national broadcaster commented that although it was longer than the requested length, the criteria outlined in the brief had otherwise been met.

Documentary Materials (Pro-Film)

Pro-Film used a combination of interviews and behind-the-scenes footage to present an overview of the opera production, focusing on the first night performance, via 'portraits' of people in key roles within the opera. RHMedia's 'house style' (shallow depth-of-field, subtle cinematography, dynamic editing) and a consistent compositional and lighting style provided visual consistency (Fig 1). The audio from the filmed interviews provided a linear narrative structure for the film, focusing on the personalities of seven interviewees (four performers, the set designer, the director and one of the artistic co-directors). The interviews were punctuated by sequences of 'cutaway' shots that showed various aspects of the behind-the-scenes activities taking place during their three days of filming. Overlapping responses of interviewees provided a variety of perspectives on short 'themes' throughout such as 'working with the director', 'working with Popera' and 'the dress rehearsals'.

Fig 1 - Stills from *Pro-Film*

2 - Pop-Film

Production Activities (Pop-Film)

The production of '*Pop-Film'* did not follow a recognizable structure. The artistic co-directors of *Popera* took responsibility for distributing the brief to the company at the beginning of the project but during the workshop, existing communication issues within *Popera* – particularly relating to emails – were blamed for "*confusion about what was expected*". The brief had been sent to the company as part of "*a very long email*", which the majority of participants confessed to "*not reading*" - "*The first thing was an email from the artistic director but it wasn't very clear.*" Despite this, some participants began filming activities almost immediately; inside rehearsal venues (during rehearsals), during breaks and at home. Participation was limited exclusively to video production, throughout (i.e. nobody edited). Over the three months of the study, four (of thirty) members of the community took part multiple times, filming on various occasions and uploading clips via the portal (multiple times each). Six other members filmed on several occasions and uploaded clips (once each). In total, 112 clips were uploaded to the project ranging in length from 2 seconds to 6 minutes and 50 seconds. A total of approximately 77 minutes of footage was submitted, primarily consisting of interviews, on-stage footage at rehearsal venues and early rehearsals, which took place in open-plan venues without props or lighting. An unexpected outcome (since it was not explicitly requested in the brief) was that PA produced the most material for the film. In total, PA shot 29 minutes (37%) of the footage produced. Many of the remaining members of the community featured in videos but otherwise did not take part.

Documentary Materials (Pop-Film)

Pop-Film was unfinished at the time of the workshop. PA had assembled an ad-hoc sequence of clips in WeVideo totalling five minutes (video figure part 2) during a one-off session described as "*trial-and-error*"; although others had logged-in, none had proceeded to edit anything. PA's assembly of clips functioned as '*Pop-Film*' for the purposes of the workshop, but other rushes (unedited clips) were shown within *WeVideo* and from *Dropbox* (in some cases, clips had not been transcoded). At the workshop, *RHMedia* spent approximately 15 minutes reviewing and discussing the rushes, alongside the unfinished film. The rushes (Fig 2) were almost exclusively anthropocentric, handheld, static wide shots. All had used the on-board microphones in their devices for audio-capture, so there was some background and handling noise. The shots were varied, but included wide-shots of action on-stage, primarily in 'interview style' setups.

Fig 2 - Stills from *Pop-Film* (taken from unedited rushes)

FINDINGS

Responses from the Community

In general, the majority of members of the *Popera* community felt that video documentary was a desirable way of capturing and sharing their experiences. Some, however, voiced concerns about capturing 'private' aspects of the rehearsal process. Two members of the community objected to any film about opera rehearsals, "*because performers need a safe environment in which they feel comfortable enough to take risks.*" But these concerns were ultimately 'overruled' as consent was included in their contracts. Another interviewee described "*fears*" resulting from "*injudicious*" uploading of media to Facebook; "*they have a habit of just posting things at random and they'll post every hideous photograph they've taken.. because of this everybody gets scared.*" PA explained that some members of the community "*were concerned that by making a documentary, our main goal might have been to demystify theatre and take away the magic of it.*" A solution was proposed reflectively by PA; "*I don't understand why it has to be about 'demystifying theatre' – why can't it be you talking about who you studied singing with, your experience on your journey with your vocal technique, or about how you prepared, how you learned music, or how you learned to pronounce Italian?*" Before the conclusion of the study, additional consent was obtained from all participants who were filmed for either film.

We present the remaining findings in chronological order to reflect chains of cause-and-effect in each of the two films. We begin with the different motivations of those involved and subsequently address the production activities observed and, ultimately, the two different outcomes. Our thematic analysis revealed a set ten themes, which related to various manifestations of values, qualities and limitations within each film. Further analysis revealed five approximate pairings within these themes, corresponding with the chronological sequence of events. We have used these themes to structure the findings, alluding to the pairings using ellipses. Reflecting upon our interventions in *Pop-Film*, we determined that the differences we observed were clearly related to the fundamental differences in approach and did not introduce any identifiable bias within the data. We discuss the implications of these findings in the final discussion section.

Directorial Vision in Pro-Film...

As director of *Pro-Film*, *Zen* provided leadership and a common sense of purpose to the crew and, through this, maintained a high level of control over the production and the resulting film. *Zen*'s pre-production 'designs', included writing the interview questions, which "*were the same for each subject*". Responses to these questions directly informed the choices of cutaways and ultimately structured the narrative of the final film. *Zen*'s influence was also perceivable in the film's aesthetic, via *RHMedia*'s 'house style', as well as specific personal stylistic influences such as, "*I wanted to try and use the style of interview they used in 'Carrier'...*" (a US television documentary).

...Diverse Motivations in Pop-Film

Within *Popera*, the absence of clear leadership and structure, coupled with a diverse range of motivations resulted in independent activities in *Pop-Film* that did not correspond with any of the organized roles in *Pro-Film*. The "*rigidly hierarchical*" (PA) structure of *Popera* was initially reflected in the production of *Pop-Film*, as leadership was automatically assumed by the creative co-directors, who took responsibility for distributing the brief to the community via email. This hierarchy did not translate to the film production however and the *Popera* community's motivations for participating were revealed to be diverse. The artistic co-directors were motivated by the end product(s), "*publicizing the company and reaching a broader audience*", but this was not shared by other participants, who had independent reasons for wanting to take part, as illustrated by the following responses,

"*I thought it was a great idea, but I did it more for myself... I saved all the videos for myself in the future so I can think 'who was I when I was doing that role?'*"

"*My inner researcher came out and, almost like an experiment, I would be interested in looking at things like 'how does your attitude vary throughout the process?'*"

These participants brought elements of *reflexivity/personal development* and *ethnography*, respectively, to the process. Other participants were motivated by a sense of duty; PA said, "*outside of my own personality, I filmed because I was hired*". Others were indirectly influenced this way, "*I did it because I had* PA *breathing down my neck...*" but for many it became more personal over time, "*...but I thought it was interesting and I would have liked to have done more.*" One participant reported that the filmmaking process had an unexpected social value in aiding the establishment of personal relationships. "*I felt as though, when I had a camera, I could approach people with more of a sense of purpose and, by interviewing them, I got to know them.*" Another participant suggested a process that might draw upon these personal relationships, "*It would've been really* *nice to have videos from everyone and, from that, figure out what questions to ask and you would catch that person in their own time."*

Concentrated Efforts in Pro-Film…

From the outset, *RHMedia* were business-like, process-driven and pragmatic in their approach. Their commitment to the project was quantified from the outset, financially (by the budget) and chronologically (by the timescale provided). *Zen* explained, *"when we spoke on the phone and worked out how much money there was available to make this, then I went away and did the maths and worked out what we could actually achieve with that." RHMedia*'s activities were concentrated around clear roles and processes (e.g. the *editor* and *director* collaborated on the *editing process*). Filming days were organized around availability and costs and, over three intense, long days, more than 14 hours of rushes were obtained.

…Ad-Hoc Responsiveness in Pop-Film

Whilst *RHMedia*'s production was organized around scheduled activities, *Popera*'s production activities were more *ad-hoc* and *responsive*. Although their primary commitments were to the opera production, simply 'being there' throughout the rehearsals gave members of *Popera* the flexibility to begin filming almost immediately. They were also able to film responsively, whenever they were not participating in the opera activities – which was often. The rushes submitted to *Pop-Film* covered the majority of the different activities that took place during the rehearsal period, including two months of early sessions that *RHMedia* missed (Fig 3), which were described as a crucial element missing from *Pro-Film* and one of *Pop-Film*'s key qualities.

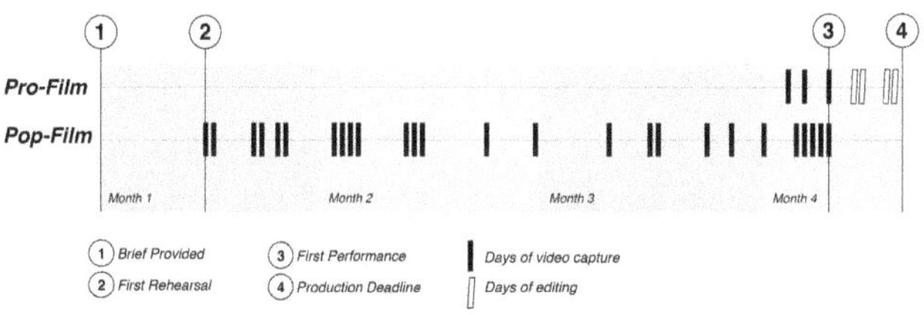

Fig 3 – Comparison of production timelines

Participants in *Pop-Film* tended to operate independently from one another, but two kinds of collaborative activities were observed, each characteristically different to those within *RHMedia*. Firstly, collaborations aligned more closely with personal relationships within the community. A 'turn-taking' approach was observed between four members of the cast, who took turns to informally interview each other during their lunch break. Secondly, PA collaborated with participants in a kind of *support* role, or in some cases, acting as 'interviewer' for individuals who wanted to appear in the film, but did not want to engage in the production activities.

Objectivity in Pro-Film…

At certain points during filming, *RHMedia* failed to observe informal expectations, such as where was acceptable to stand and which backstage areas were out-of-bounds at certain times. One member of *Popera* described this as a "*breach of rehearsal etiquette*". These contextual sensitivities were well known by the community, but not by the production team. The result was that restrictions were imposed upon *RHMedia*'s access to certain areas at certain times, which *Pop-Film* producers were not subject to. On reflection, *Zen* suggested a more traditional ethnographic approach, "*One way to change that would be more planning… if we'd been there throughout the rehearsal process, then you would be so much more comfortable with our presence.*" However, with their limited resources, *RHMedia* had insufficient time to build up trust with Popera. This did, however, enable them to maintain an *objective* (i.e. 'outsider') perspective, which was seen by many as a positive quality, "*nice to have an outside view (questions from non-singers/opera people)*".

…Contextual Sensitivity in Pop-Film

Within the community, particularly over the intensive rehearsal period, the *Popera* community built up relationships of "*trust, bonding and building an interest*". However, these took time to develop. "*When you're with people for the first four weeks, you're just getting to know them … the more you work with people, the more you understand them … If it had gone on longer, I think we'd have got more videos … now we're really interested in each other, but you have to build that first*". This trust was reflected in the experience of being interviewed for *Pop-Film*, which was described as "*more natural, not always feeling like you had to say the 'right' thing.*" Greater *contextual sensitivity* also meant that in addition to knowing when was (and when wasn't) appropriate to film, *Popera* participants also instinctively knew what would be interesting to capture. *Popera*'s rushes included a variety of elements missed by *RHMedia*, including songbooks, sheet music, instruments, orchestra members, props, breaktime activities and moments such as the "sitzprobe", when the orchestra and the performers rehearse together for the first time. The idea of contextual sensitivity also extended to collaborative activities; in both examples of collaboration (above) consent was socially negotiated, rather than prescribed upon the "victim" in advance.

Technical Quality in Pro-Film…

Many professional productions use hired equipment since cameras have quickly started to become obsolete. In this case, *RHMedia* used their own equipment. *Zen's* reasons came down to "*balancing the value of working with people that you trust and paying them the rates you want and getting the best technical quality possible….*" The value *RHMedia* placed on technical quality was also reflected in their criticism of *Pop-Film*, which primarily focused on its technical shortcomings, "*poor quality images and sound*" "*I found it hard to concentrate on the user doc because of quality issues*".

…Familiar Apparatus in Pop-Film

Despite being offered high quality smartphones, participants from *Popera* all preferred to use their own devices, citing "*familiarity*" as the main reason. The preference for using personal apparatus over technically superior tools further emphasizes that *Popera* were not motivated by technical quality in the same way as *RHMedia*. Instead, they preferred to use what they already had, in ways that they were used to. When the participants who had filmed in 'portrait' were questioned as to why they had done so, one explained "*because that's the way the phone's shaped*". Most contributing participants used only the basic video camera functionality (as opposed to third party apps such as *Instagram* or *YouTube Capture*) and although some (but not all) uploaded it to the portal, even fewer logged into *WeVideo* and nobody except PA attempted to edit it. This replicates findings within other studies of non-professional media producers, where users have disengaged at the editing stage [26]. The reasons given here for not editing included usability, "*the portal was difficult to use*" and "*I couldn't find all the videos on there... I knew there were tons of my videos that I couldn't find*". Others cited the project's overall lack of clarity as their main reason for not continuing, "*I understood what to do, but the 'why' was missing – the incentive.*"

Coherency and Consistency in Pro-Film...

Overall, *Pro-Film* was considered by the majority of participants to be "*better quality*" than *Pop-Film* and reviews were unanimously positive, "*made me want to go and see the performance*". *Pro-Film* was commended for "*the variety of aspects covered*", "*overall quality*", "*really good interviews... very slick and well-edited*" and "*the technical quality of the sound*". However, it was considered by some to be repetitive, "*too many interviews covering similar material*", particularly in its praise of the director "*too much gushing positivity!*" and for lacking footage "*of earlier rehearsals and it overlooked other aspects like orchestration, audience reactions and other cast members*". Despite minor criticisms, *Pro-Film* possessed a number of recognizable qualities such as a *coherent* linear narrative in an aesthetically *consistent* style.

...Intimacy and Realism in Pop-Film

Although *Pop-Film* lacked the coherence and consistency of *Pro-Film*, it provided a more *realistic*, *intimate* portrayal of the rehearsals. *Pop-Film* was commended by the *RHMedia* team for "*the endearing qualities of the amateur effort*"; "*it was, by its nature, genuine*", "*natural... genuine*", "*a personal touch*", "*the smartphone footage was low-key and therefore more natural*", "*more varied – more candid*", "*everything was real...*" These qualities are reminiscent of popular documentary movements such as *cinema verité* and Direct Cinema, which valued "realism" above all [12]. *Pop-Film* was also praised for its intimacy in capturing "*little details*" such as "*kneepads during rehearsals*" and for giving "*access to the cast and behind the scenes that was not possible for the professional crew to obtain*". *RHMedia* criticised *Pop-Film*'s "*lack of structure*", but despite being given access to the rushes of the film – PA's "trial-and-error" within *WeVideo* was chosen as the primary basis for judgment. During workshop activity 2, *RHMedia* dismissed all of the shots that had been filmed in portrait but *Zen* claimed the editorial value of some of the other (landscape) rushes from earlier rehearsals would overcome their technical shortcomings and he would have used them in *Pro-Film*.

DISCUSSION

Our study revealed distinctive *qualities* in the two films produced and a variety of *values* and motivations amongst the producers and participants. Whereas *Pro-Film* was more *coherent* and *objective*, *Pop-Film* was more *realistic* and *intimate*. From an identical brief, the two productions were characterized by clear differences in approach, which reflected the values of their producers. *RHMedia*'s production followed a typical professional workflow model, with planned activities, skilled individuals in co-ordinated roles and sophisticated tools employed towards a shared objective: the production of a coherent, broadcast standard narrative documentary. Where *RHMedia* valued leadership and a common sense of purpose, resulting in a finished documentary product, the *Popera* community's values were shown to be relatively heterogeneous, reflecting a diversity of motivations, some of which reveal new potential uses for UGVC within documentary contexts. The outcome of this was less coherent. Within *Popera*, diverse motivating factors resulted in independent production activities that were relatively ad-hoc and made use of less sophisticated - yet more familiar - personal devices. By virtue of their physical proximity to, and familiarity with, the subject, *Popera* were more attuned to contextual sensitivities during filming and were afforded a greater degree of trust by their peers within the subject community. They were thus able to cover a significantly broader scope of activities and mobilise quickly in response to relevant activities. Whilst their proximity introduced a degree of subjectivity to the footage, it also captured more natural behavior. In contrast, *RHMedia* produced a more objective film , but had limited resources, and faced barriers of access and trust, resulting in less comprehensive coverage.

Within this study, 'coherence' and 'realism' were mutually exclusive qualities, attributed to *Pro-Film* and *Pop-Film* respectively. Participatory documentaries (and some forms of ethnographic documentary) can be said to possess "the best of both worlds" as coherence is provided by professionals (during *pre-* and *post-production*) and intimacy comes from the subjects/participants (during *production*). In the 'grassroots' model we simulated, neither *pre-* nor *post-production* stages were realized. We saw in *Pro-Film* that these stages provided structure to the production activities and the film respectively, so an implication of overcoming the "filmmaker-victim paradigm" appears to be 'realism' at the expense of 'coherence'.

One solution to this problem would be to design new ways of supporting equivalent *pre-* and *post-production* activities within grassroots communities. However, we have shown that *pre-production* does not require specialist tools and instead relies on specialist skills that cannot be learned quickly. *Post-production* is already supported by a variety of tools, but most (like *WeVideo*) are built upon professional editing paradigms. We suggest that tools such as these are of limited use outside the context of the supporting workflow, but persist via a "task-artefact cycle" [9], which by emulating professional tools, channels UGVC producers into processes originating within professional workflows. As we have seen, this is unsustainable without a level of skill and resources beyond the reach of most grassroots producers. We propose that in order to design tools to support collaborative UGVC production (as in grassroots documentaries) we need to reconsider not just the artefacts required, but also the tasks involved, which may not be equivalent to professional production processes and workflows. To do this and preserve the qualities of intimacy and realism, we need to overcome the paradox of structuring ad-hoc production activities. One potential avenue, suggested by [7] is to consider new forms of metadata capture that provides ad-hoc media with an inherent structure. From our findings, we suggest the challenge will also be to remain sensitive to the heterogeneity of multiple participants, who may have different motivations and varying degrees of consent and trust. A potentially more difficult challenge will be to design systems that draw upon "familiar" practices of potential participants (bearing in mind that such familiarities might be contextually specific, as *Popera*'s "rehearsal ettiquette"). Also, when considering social aspects, we should not necessarily presume that the formal structure of the community will be reflected in the collaborations around video production.

As an alternative solution, we might ask, *what does an incoherent documentary look like?* Joutsen suggests, "interesting results often arise from the process of making a film, rather than the product" [23]. In *Pop-Film*, one participant saw video production activities as a chance to develop social relationships. Another identified a value in UGVC, not as a 'product' but rather as a 'process' that might support, for example, more insightful interview questions, or personal reflection. An insider/outsider role such as PA, might be leveraged to enable these kinds of processes. We have seen that wide audiences are not always a motivation for UGVC production, so we might consider alternative distribution strategies or metrics of success. 'Impact' (measurable achievements), 'virality' (rapid acceleration of popularity) and 'filmanthropy' (shining light on a tough subject) challenge the dominant financial and reach-based metrics of success. *Pop-Film* was considered a failure in the workshop and a paradigm shift was necessary to consider the value of their unedited rushes for the purposes of the study. *RHMedia* did not consider the 'montage aesthetic' of *Pop-Film's* rushes within *WeVideo*, or the corresponding conversations amongst the group about what to view next, to be a desirable end result. The term 'documentary' implies an edited product, but a growing body of evidence suggests UGVC is rarely edited. The paradigm shift towards non-linear or modular distribution facilitated in the workshop does, however, resonate with certain cultural shifts in documentary studies. Alluding to early pioneers of film editing techniques, Dovey and Rose suggest "our technological moment produces the need for a new generation of Eisensteins and Kuleshovs to bring montage aesthetics to the database." [13]. Gaudenzi, in her thesis on the "Living Documentary" [16] describes, "an artifact made of heterogenous components". Interactive documentaries thus provide a design space to enable diverse motives, heterogeneous activities and varying degrees of consent to co-exist in a 'living' system with the potential to be both 'coherent' and 'intimate'.

Reflecting critically upon our methods reveals two potential limitations. Firstly, although the measures described in the Study Design section were designed to minimize the artificiality of the setup, the 'grassroots' model we sought to explore was partially pre-determined by the researchers. Secondly, our "in-the-wild" approach necessitated a high level of responsiveness during the study, even compared with other user-centered design studies. As we have already discussed, this was acknowledged within the study design and provided a rich source of data but ultimately, it presented significant logistical challenges to the research team. Similar studies in future may wish to focus the study on smaller participant groups or focus on a particular theme (such as those identified in our thematic analysis).

CONCLUSION

By exploring the relative *values* and *qualities* of two parallel documentaries, we observed varying approaches and two very different outcomes. These differences suggest that support for meaningful UGVC production and/or grassroots documentary might require fundamentally different production structures. There is evidence to suggest that elements of the traditional professional documentary production workflow are well-supported by equivalent tools for non-professionals. However, the "supporting structures" suggested by Kelliher [25], are relatively under-developed and UGVC currently tends to be absorbed into professional productions, or lost in the "sea of data" [13]. Hence, we propose a new paradigm that is more sensitive to *various production contexts*, *heterogeneous motives*, *levels of consent* and *social dynamics within the community,* to better reflect the inherent qualities and values of grassroots communities and UGVC producers. We have identified unique qualities that set UGVC apart from professional video content: 'realism', a tendency to capture more intimate, natural behavior, its potential role as a research tool and its constructive role within the social dynamics of a community. However, we have found that these qualities are not valued as highly within professional production systems and have therefore not been valued highly in the design of existing production tools. The aim of this study was to understand and develop design recommendations for the next generation of systems to support grassroots documentaries. Much could be gained from observing emerging models of production such as interactive, non-linear productions and considering that narrative and aesthetic coherence are just two of any number of qualities that documentaries might possess.

ACKNOWLEDGMENTS

This research was funded by the AHRC Creative Exchange Knowledge Exchange Hub. Thanks also to Mariya Krywaniuk, Nezih Savaşkan, Kate Flowers and Paul Need.

REFERENCES

1. Allan, S., Citizen Journalism (Global Crises and the Media), First printing Edition. New York: Peter Lang Publishing, 2009.
2. Alluvatti, G. M. et al., "User Generated (Web) Content: Trash or Treasure?", Proc' IWPSE-EVOL '11, Szeged, Hungary. pp 81-90. 2011.
3. Arnstein, Sherry R. "A Ladder of Citizen Participation," JAIP, Vol. 35, No. 4, July 1969. pp. 216-224. 1969.
4. Barry, B. 2003. The Mindful Camera: Common Sense for Documentary Videography. In Proc' MM'03. ACM, New York, NY, USA, 648-649. 2003.
5. Bhimani, J. et al., Vox Populi: Enabling Community-Based Narratives through Collaboration and Content Creation. In *Proc' EuroITV '13*. ACM, New York, NY, USA, 2013. 31-40.
6. Braun, V., & Clarke, V. Using Thematic Analysis in Psychology. *Qualitative Research in Psychology*, *3*(2), 77–101. 2006.
7. Bocconi, S. et al., Vox Populi: A Tool for Automatically Generating Video Documentaries. In Proc' HYPERTEXT '05. ACM, New York, NY, USA, 292-294. 2005.
8. Bruns, A. "Towards Produsage: Futures for User-Led Content Production" in F. Sudweeks, et al. (eds) Proc' Cultural Attitudes towards Communication and Technology, pp. 275-284. 2006.
9. Carroll, John M. et al., The Task-Artifact Cycle. In *Designing Interaction*, John M. Carroll (Ed.). Cambridge University Press, New York, NY, USA 74-102. 1991.
10. Chamberlain, A., Research in the Wild: Understanding 'In The Wild' Approaches to Design and Development. In *Proc'* DIS 12. ACM, New York, NY, USA, 795-796.
11. Cinehack, Available from http://www.cinehack.com/, Accessed: 10th September 2013
12. Cousins, M. and MacDonald, K. (eds.), Imagining Reality (revised edition), Chatham, Faber, 2006.
13. Dovey, J. et al. "We're happy and we know it: Documentary: Data: Montage". Studies in Documentary Film. vol 6. no 2. pp. 159-166, June 2012.
14. Durrant, A. et al., Design to Support interpersonal communication in the special educational needs classroom. In Proc IDC '13. ACM, New York, NY, USA, 46-55. 2013.
15. Engström, A. et al. "Producing Collaborative Video: Developing an Interactive User Experience for Mobile TV", Proc' uxTV'08, Oct 2008.
16. Gaudenzi, S., "The Living Documentary: from representing reality to co-creating reality in digital interactive documentary". PhD Dissertation. Goldsmiths, University of London, UK, 2013.
17. Grierson, J. "The Documentary Producer", Cinema Quarterly vol.2 no. 1. pp. 8-24.
18. Hann M. (10th April 2003), "Yeah Yeah Yeahs launch pre-emptive strike at phone-wielding gig-goers", Available http://www.guardian.co.uk/music/shortcuts/2013/apr/10/yeah-yeah-yeahs-phones-gigs, Accessed: 10th September 2013
19. Heim, J. and Brandtzæg P. B. "Patterns of Media Use and the Non- professional Users". Supporting non-professional users in the new media landscape. Workshop at CHI '07, ACM, 2007.
20. Hing-Yuk Wong, C., in Gerstner, David A. and Staiger, Janet, *Authorship and Film*, London, Routledge. 2003.
21. Hook, J. et al, A VJ Centered Exploration of Expressive Interaction. In Proc. of CHI'11, ACM, pp.1265-1274.
22. Jenkins, H., *Convergence Culture: Where Old and New Media Collide*, New York, USA: NYU Press. 2008.
23. Joutsen, A. et al., "Wreck A Movie: empowering the masses for film productions"| Proc' MindTrek '08, ACM, New York, NY, USA, 141-144. 2008.
24. Juhlin O. et al., "Mobile Broadcasting – The Whats and Hows of Live Video as a Social Medium", Proc MobileHCI'10, September 2010, pp.35-43.
25. Kelliher. A., Everyday cinema. In Proc' SRMC '04. ACM, New York, NY, USA, 59-62. 2004.
26. Kirk, D. et al. "Understanding Videowork", Proc'CHI2007. ACM, pp.61-70, 2007.
27. LifeMirror, Available http://www.catalystproject.org.uk/content/lifemirror, Accessed: 10th September 2013
28. Lunch, N., Lunch C., Insights into Participatory Video: A Handbook for the Field, Oxford: Insightshare, 2006. Available http://insightshare.org/resources/pv-handbook, Accessed: 10th September 2014
29. Macdonald, K, and Cousins, M., Imagining Reality, London: Faber and Faber, 2006.
30. Millerson, G. Television Production, 13th Ed. Woburn, MA, Focal Press, 2009.
31. Milne E-J. et al. (eds.), Handbook of Participatory Video. Altamira Press: Plymouth, 2012.
32. Nash, K., et al., *New Documentary Ecologies: Emerging Platforms, Practices and Discourses,* Palgrave. 2014.
33. Puikkonenetal. A. "Practices in Creating Videos with Mobile Phones". MobileHCI'09, ACM, 2009.
34. Waugh, T. "Challenge for Change: Activist Documentary at the National Film Board of Canada"
35. You Tube https://www.youtube.com/yt/press/en-GB/statistics.html, Accessed: 10th September 2014
36. Weilenmann, A., et al. Mobile video literacy: negotiating the use of a new visual technology. *Personal Ubiquitous Comput.* 18, 3 (March 2014), 737-752. 2014.
37. Where the Water Meets the Sky (Review), Available from https://camfed.org/latest-news/films/where-water-meets-sky/, Accessed: 10th September 2014
38. Life Mirror (Review), Available from http://www.infolab21.lancs.ac.uk/news_and_events/news/002026/a-radical-new-way-to-create-film, Accessed: 10th Sept 2014.

Designing Political Deliberation Environments to Support Interactions in the Public Sphere

Bryan Semaan[1], Heather Faucett[2], Scott P. Robertson[3], Misa Maruyama[4], Sara Douglas[4]

[1]School of Information Studies
Syracuse University
Syracuse, NY, 13244
bsemaan@syr.edu

[2]Department of Informatics
University of California, Irvine
Irvine, CA, 92697
hfaucett@uci.edu

[3]Information and Computer Sciences Department
[4]Communication and Information Sciences Program
University of Hawaiʻi at Mānoa
{scott.robertson, misattm, sarad}@hawaii.edu

ABSTRACT

Little is known about the challenges and successes people face when piecing together multiple social media to interact in the online public sphere when: seeking information, disseminating information, and engaging in political discussions. We interviewed 29 US citizens and conducted 17 talk-out-loud sessions with people who were using one or more social media technologies, such as Facebook and Twitter, to interact in the online public sphere. We identified a number of challenges and workarounds related to public sphere interactions, and used our findings to formulate requirements for new political environments that support the interactions in the public sphere. Through evolving requirements generation, we developed a new political deliberation technology, dubbed *Poli*, which is an integrated social media environment with the potential to enable more effective interactions in the public sphere. We discuss several remaining questions and limitations to our tool that will drive future work.

Author Keywords
Political deliberation; public sphere; design; social media

ACM Classification Keywords
H.5.m. Information interfaces and presentation (e.g., HCI): Miscellaneous.

INTRODUCTION

Social media tools hold promise as valuable online environments for citizens who wish to engage in the political deliberation process. A variety of platforms exist, such as Facebook and Twitter, where people can construct information feeds or discuss political issues and topics in a distributed online public environment [e.g. 32].

Researchers have studied the use of social media from a variety of perspectives, e.g. "social searching" [22] and social capital [7]. Social media tools allow people to interact with others in various ways in the social sphere, as human capabilities are often enhanced via the ability to explore, connect, exchange and coordinate to a much greater degree than is available offline [11]. As social media continues to be widely adopted, we believe that they could be valuable tools for supporting people who wish to actively engage in the political deliberation process.

Little is known about the challenges citizens face when piecing together multiple social media for the purpose of seeking, disseminating and discussing political information. Here, "politics" refers to the broad range of information and activities around civic engagement, where civic engagement includes all the ways in which individuals deal with concerns of the public that are beyond being purely private or personal [11]. For example, for some citizens, political interactions can be scoped around political elections, whereas for others, political interactions may be related to their duties as citizens or to their subjective positions about political issues—motivations and interactions may vary from person to person. Social media technologies have varying affordances, and as such, depending on a user's civic goals, one technology may be better suited to achieving their goals than another.

To our knowledge, researchers have not yet explored the real world experiences, challenges and successes of citizens who are using multiple social media technologies for political deliberation. Yet, it is clear that there is great need for social media environments that integrate a variety of online spaces and enable more effective civic engagement. In this paper, we are interested in investigating how and under what circumstances citizens use multiple social media technologies to engage in the political deliberation process. Moreover, through our analysis of empirical data of real world social media use for civic engagement, we describe how we developed an integrated social media

CHI 2015, April 18 - 23, 2015, Seoul, Republic of Korea Copyright 2015 ACM 978-1-4503-3145-6/15/04...$15.00
http://dx.doi.org/10.1145/2702123.2702403

environment, dubbed Poli, which aids people in their ability to seek and disseminate information, and engage in discussions in the online public sphere.

INTERACTIONS IN THE ONLINE PUBLIC SPHERE

According to Habermas [15, 16], deliberative democracy can only exist in the public sphere, which he described as "a domain of our social life in which such a thing as public opinion can be formed". In this view, the public sphere is a democratic space that facilitates open, reasoned and reflexive interaction and communication among different kinds of publics.

Dahlgren [6] describes how a public sphere can only be successful if it enables and supports three types of citizen interactions: (1) people's ability to access diverse information from media and other citizens, (2) people's ability to freely disseminate diverse information and opinions to media and other citizens, and (3) people's ability to engage in rational discussions with media and other citizens. Others have added that in addition to the three interactions defined by Dahlgren, another type of citizen interaction centers around (4) people's ability to take action in union with or against social institutions [11].

The social networking components of many online sites are often described as a new type of socio-technical public sphere for civic discourse [5, 6, 27]. The Pew Internet and American Life project has shown increasing use of the Internet and social media for political activity [30]. Raine and Smith [30] found that 25% of their interview respondents used social media to discuss or debate political issues with others. Thirty percent of respondents said that their friends post occasionally about politics and 25% said that they have become more involved politically as the result of information in their social networking feeds.

Online Political Deliberation: Limits to Interaction

Political deliberation platforms are often criticized for not engaging a representative sample of participants [e.g., 13, 14] nor encouraging interaction between individuals who hold dissimilar political perspectives [2, 36, 40]. This leads to the question of whether or not current Internet tools are satisfying the participatory needs of citizens.

Research in this area, which has generally focused on singular social media platforms and spaces devoted to politics, e.g. Obama's Facebook timeline, has been divided as some have found the emerging interactions to be diverse [e.g. 35], whereas others have found that such online spaces are leading to polarization, as users are only exchanging information and ideas with people who share the same political perspectives [e.g. 10]. However, the online public sphere does not exist in any one given online space; rather, it is distributed across online technologies.

Dahlgren [6] points out that the multiple spaces available on the Internet for social interaction and political deliberation form a "sprawling public sphere," by which he means spread out across various online spaces. People may be using different media for varying purposes. For example, citizens can discuss politics with others using one medium, and disseminate information and opinions in another tool. Even within a given medium people have access to different audiences. For example, Facebook users can interact with friends and family via their personal newsfeed, but they may also be members of public and private political groups where they share information and opinions and engage in lively discussions.

Research on political deliberation across multiple social media technologies has found that citizen interactions across online spaces (both political and non-political) are depolarized in nature [e.g. 32]. Semaan and colleagues [32], for example, reported how although some people may be limited in their ability to interact in one technology, they often use a combination of tools to enact deliberation that stays true to Habermas' vision. This implies that several challenges exist with respect to people's ability to appropriate social media technologies as public spheres.

Current social media technologies were not designed to serve as spaces devoted to political information sharing and discourse. In fact, there may be negative social consequences associated with the political activities in the online public sphere afforded by social media. Whereas a healthy public sphere is predicated upon people's ability to share information and opinions, and engage in rational discussions, the other members of the "online public" may negatively impact people's ability to interact. People may refrain from participating freely for fear of being unfriended, unfollowed, or hidden by other members of their networks [30]. In fact, polarizing political posts are one of the main reasons why people remove friends or hide friends' activities [30].

A critical challenge is developing new tools and approaches that help participants engage in diverse interaction and take opposing views into account, assess their own contributions and the contributions of their peers, and deliberate on issues through positive discourse. Earlier research has explored and evaluated various online political deliberation platforms [e.g., 5, 13, 14, 17, 23] and has explored novel approaches and interfaces [20, 21].

Designing Political Deliberation Environments

Recent scholarship has investigated how political deliberation can be facilitated or enhanced through online platforms [e.g. 1, 3] or through hybrid environments combining online and offline interactions [e.g. 12]. Researchers hypothesize that online political environments can be improved if they promote deliberation and accountability [e.g. 8, 33]. More specifically, by incorporating these approaches into online political deliberation environments, people may share knowledge and engage in discussions, provide constructive feedback on ideas and perspectives even when they do not agree, and help foster a sense of civic identity through idea generation and collective action [e.g. 1, 3, 4, 19, 33, 38].

Researchers who have developed online political information browsers, or described features that should be integrated into online deliberation platforms [25, 31, 37, 38, 39], have highlighted the importance of online tools in facilitating public sphere interactions. Robertson and colleagues [31] developed an information browser that organized information topically using a drop-down menu, and the simple design intervention showed dramatic differences when contrasted head-to-head with a "free query" interface akin to Google search. Wright and Street [39] considered how user interface design, such as the use of moderation or deliberative polls, support higher-level engagement in discussion forums. Karlsson [18] observed that higher-level participant engagement positively contributes to whether an individual will consider another participant's views.

Other researchers have argued for hybrid deliberation models that integrate offline and online interactions. For example, Gordon and Manosevitch [12] observed that by using online environments to augment in-person deliberation, the qualities of face-to-face interaction that are difficult to reproduce online, such as trust and rationality, could be maintained while integrating the positive aspects of online deliberation, e.g. access and scale.

Previous work, however, has not considered the challenges citizens face when piecing together multiple social media technologies for political deliberation. Many insights and design considerations could be gleaned from understanding how and under what circumstances people use multiple social media to interact in the online public sphere. In this paper, we describe an empirical study where we sought to understand how and under what circumstances people were using multiple social media technologies to engage in the online public sphere. Using our data, we designed a new political deliberation environment—Poli—which integrates a variety of social media and takes into account the various challenges people experienced when interacting in the sprawling online public sphere.

METHODOLOGY

The data presented in this paper is from an on-going larger study in which we are following social media users across several political elections to understand how they use social media to participate in the political deliberation process. This element of the larger study is longitudinal, including interviews and in-lab talk-aloud observation sessions as data points.

Participants and Recruitment

The 29 interviewees were U.S. citizens ranging in age from 18 to 67, with 14 participants being male and 15 female. The subjects were of diverse educational backgrounds ranging from having no college to having completed a doctorate, as well as diverse job characteristics including professors, journalists and students. Interviews were conducted in two phases. In Phase I from May 2012 until December 2012, 21 subjects were interviewed. Phase II is ongoing with 8 subjects having been interviewed since the beginning of February 2013. Participants of the talk-aloud protocol were recruited from the sample of interviewees. Seventeen subjects took part in these in-lab sessions including 9 males and 8 females. All participants used one or more social media technologies. The tools used, included: Facebook, Twitter, Google+, blogs, online forums such as Reddit, online news sites and YouTube.

Multiple avenues for recruitment were used, including fliers posted on a major university campus, weekly advertisements published by a local news agency and social media outlets such as Facebook, Twitter and Craig's List. In addition, snowball sampling was conducted after each interview. Participant eligibility was determined by an interest in politics as well as use of at least one social media outlet. All subjects were given a $20 dollar Amazon gift card as compensation for their participation in the study.

Data Collection

Interviews for this study were semi-structured and lasted between 45 minutes to 2.5 hours. Each interview was conducted in-person (in the lab or at the participant's home, at the discretion of the participant) or over the phone. After each interview, the first author asked the interviewee if he could follow or "friend" him or her using his personal social media accounts to conduct observations of the participant's social media activity.

In Phase I, participants were asked to identify which social media they used for political interaction, how and for what reason they used said social media for political interaction, the activities they used each media for, who (if anyone) they deliberated with, how often each media was used, which features they used and why, and their motivation(s), if any, for using one or multiple social media outlets.

Phase II interviews were built on the findings of Phase I. During this set of interviews, however, more directed questions about the tools used, how each was used, and motivations for use (such as information dissemination, information seeking, and discussion) were asked.

In hour-long talk-aloud observation sessions, participants were recorded using Morae as they engaged in their typical online political deliberation behavior. Observations took place during the month leading to the U.S. general election in November 2012. This allowed us to better understand the interactions people engaged in that were not visible when observing an individual's online activity vicariously. Following these sessions we asked our informants additional questions about their browsing and posting behavior, which we used to further triangulate with our interview data.

Data Analysis and Evolving Requirements Generation

Each interview and talk-aloud session was recorded and transcribed. The coding process was continuous, with the research team meeting on a weekly basis to discuss reoccurring themes found in each data set. Coding was conducted by the lead author using an approach from grounded theory [34]. A grounded theory-based iterative and inductive analysis of our observations and interview transcripts using coding and memoing was also performed.

During this time, phenomena were identified, named, and categorized and themes were generated. From this, several codes emerged, many of which were related to the challenges participants reported experiencing when using multiple social media, as well as the methods participants used to work around the reported complications. The codes were merged into several overarching categories, which are described in the following section. With each subsequent interview, these codes were fed into evolving requirements generation, ultimately culminating in a set of requirements for a tool, which we used to develop Poli.

DESIGNING FOR POLITICAL DELIBERATION

Through interviews, in-lab observations and talk-out-loud sessions with politically-minded social media users, we identified several problems inhibiting people's ability to successfully access information, disseminate information and engage in political discussions in the online public sphere. We also observed various ways in which our informants worked around these issues.

Information Access: Challenges and Workarounds

One of the primary interactions in the public sphere, and a major component of the political learning process, deals with people's ability to seek political information across the political spectrum. Our informants used a variety of social media technologies, including Facebook, Twitter, Google+, YouTube, blogs, and online forums, through which they were both inactively "encountering" and actively searching for relevant political information concerning political candidates and a variety of issues. The tools at their disposal, however, posed several challenges with respect to their ability to search for and access information.

Challenge to information seeking: Unstructured access to information. We found that people often encountered political information by accident—through serendipitous encounters when scanning their social media feeds. Importantly, they were made aware of diverse issues and topics that they may not have otherwise encountered through more deliberate searches, as the information they were exposed to was being disseminated by people within their networks, or through the blogs and online forums they frequented.

Challenge to information seeking: Information overload. One major challenge with Facebook concerned information overload. The mixture of non-political and political posts that comprised people's Facebook newsfeeds limited their ability to access political information. In order to search for political information, significant cognitive overhead was required as people had to manually peruse their newsfeeds with the intention of seeking out political information. Our informants expressed a desire to be able to filter their feeds by type, which would have allowed them to more effectively seek out political information.

Challenge to information seeking: Inadequate search and filtering tools. Another issue experienced by our informants dealt with how well social media supported their ability to search for political information and create structured information feeds. Unlike social media tools like Twitter and Google+ that allow users to more effectively search for political information, the search functionality available within Facebook was inadequate. Our informants who attempted to use the search functionality often found that Facebook search attempts were mostly connected to Internet search tools like Google, as opposed to connecting to information being posted by people in their networks. Moreover, our studies were conducted before Facebook adopted Twitter-like hash tags as searchable metadata, meaning Facebook content about a certain topic was even less findable than it is today.

Moreover, whereas Twitter users can create structured information feeds by searching keywords anonymously, the way in which Facebook is tied to users' real life identities restricted its use as an information tool. In order for users to actively "follow" the information being disseminated by politicians and news agencies with varying perspectives, they were required to "Like" a respective candidate or agency's profile. The act of "Liking" implied that their personal political perspectives aligned with the account, even when the user did not agree with its political stance. When users "Liked" a candidate or media agency that did not align with their personal perspectives, they often met backlash from members of their social networks

Challenge to information seeking: Network effects. Another issue people experienced dealt with their dependency on the people with whom they were connected for political information and news. When people perused their Facebook feeds, or accessed information in online forums and blogs, they were relying on people within their networks for diverse information. In some cases this was not problematic, as people had developed social networks consisting of people with diverse political views, or were actively participating in online forums and reading blogs that spanned the political spectrum. In other cases, however, in alignment with recent work investigating people's desire to seek alternative perspectives [10], our informants had purposefully developed homogenous social networks so as to avoid being exposed to viewpoints and perspectives with which they did not agree.

Information access workaround: Constructing information feeds using external aggregation tools. Whereas some of our informants relied solely on Facebook as a tool for political information, in other cases people adopted multiple social media technologies. By using alternative social media platforms, they were able to develop structured information feeds that spanned the political spectrum.

Some of our informants were tailoring the information environment to more effectively consume information across the political spectrum. They aggregated information by creating structured information and opinion newsfeeds from media agencies, politicians and lay citizens, even when the information they were receiving did not align with their personal political beliefs. They wanted to receive timely information spanning the political spectrum in an effort to understand varied political perspectives on both a local and national level.

Some of our informants, however, felt that using multiple tools posed challenges. When they "followed" several political candidates and news agencies, their feeds were difficult to navigate due to an excessive amount of information. In order to further structure their feeds and more effectively consume political information, some informants used external aggregation tools like Tweetdeck. These users organized their feeds in a variety of ways. For example, our most expert users structured their feeds by local, national and global politics, as well as by "political slant", e.g. right- or left-leaning, thus allowing themselves to more easily consume political information.

Information Dissemination: Issues and Workarounds

One of the primary interactions in the public sphere, as described by Dahlgren [6], deals with people's ability to disseminate political information across the political spectrum. Our informants used a variety of social media technologies, including Facebook, Twitter, Google+, YouTube, blogs, and online forums, through which they could disseminate information. The tools at their disposal, however, posed several challenges with respect to their ability to actively disseminate information.

Challenge to information dissemination: Negative interactions associated with audience and identity. Our informants were using multiple social media tools to disseminate diverse political information and personal perspectives about candidates, issues or events that were emerging locally, nationally and globally. However, two major challenges limited their ability to freely distribute cross-ideological information.

First, the presence of family and friends in their networks (this was dependent on how they constructed their networks in any given tool and was most prevalent on Facebook) limited their ability to freely share information and opinions. Consistent with what has been reported in other studies [30], posting content that was counter to the perspectives of people in their networks often led to negative interactions, arguments and unfriending.

Moreover, the way in which some tools, especially Facebook, were tied to their real world identity further limited their ability to post. Goffman [9] discusses how people tend to create and manage impressions of themselves that they want to make publicly visible. When interacting with others our actions influence people's impression of us, and thus we conduct ourselves in a certain way in order to manage how we are perceived. Similarly, our data suggests that when people were posting information that conflicted with their personal perspectives even if they simply wanted to make people aware of alternative perspectives, the act of posting said perspectives led to negative interactions because what they were posting did not align with the expectations of what people in their network thought they *should* be posting.

Information dissemination workaround: Network-switching as a form of identity management. In order to freely share political information, our informants began using alternative social media technologies where they could disseminate information in a more impersonal manner. For example, whereas tools like Facebook are highly associated to personal identity, people adopted and/or switched to tools such as Twitter where they could target more impersonal networks.

Political Discussion: Issues and Workarounds

One of the primary interactions in the public sphere, as described by Dahlgren [6], deals with people's ability to engage in rational and reasoned political discourse. Our informants used a variety of social media technologies through which they could interact with others. The tools at their disposal, however, posed several challenges with respect to their ability to engage in positive interactions.

Challenge to political discourse: Audience management. Although some of our informants were engaging in fruitful political discussions with people in their personal networks, may of our informants described how social media technologies like Facebook did not support their ability to engage in rational discourse as their friends and family often argued with them as opposed to trying to understand their views [c.f. 30]. Furthermore, social media tools like YouTube mostly consisted of messages of flaming and support, so people did not feel that interacting in those spaces could yield constructive interactions.

Challenge to political discourse: Political self-efficacy. Whereas the majority of our informants were "political junkies", some described how they did not feel comfortable engaging in political discussions in the online public sphere because they did not feel as if they were knowledgeable enough to contribute. This was especially an issue when people wished to engage in discourse with known discussants, such as family, friends and friends-of-friends.

Challenge to political discourse: Interaction context. Another issue experienced by our informants dealt with the lack of interaction context afforded by some social media technologies. Interaction context refers to the ability to view and understand an entire discussion over time, as well as understand the current event or set of events surrounding and leading to any given discussion. This was especially prevalent in Twitter, where "tweets" were oftentimes seen as "coming out of the blue," thus lacking contextual cues.

Political discourse workaround: Seeking, creating and managing online spaces. In order to engage in rational discussions, our informants often sought networks where they perceived the audiences to be more receptive to alternative perspectives. Whereas many people experienced issues interacting with family and friends on Facebook, they sought alternative networks through other tools, such as Twitter, blogs and Google+, where they could interact with others via more impersonal networks. Although some of the discussions they were having in these alternative spaces were not conducive to positive discourse, they did not feel the negative implications as they, first, did not know many of the people with whom they were interacting and, second, could move on and continue to seek others who were willing to interact in a positive manner.

Other informants constructed their own online spaces through social media to engage in reasoned political discourse. People created Facebook groups, blogs and other spaces where they could invite people from diverse backgrounds, as well as control who was allowed to engage in discussions, and establish and enforced a set of rules to promote positive discursive behavior.

Political discourse workaround: Audience, anonymity and self-efficacy. Our informants also chose tools where they could interact anonymously. This served two major functions. First, the ability to move in and out of their real world identity enabled interaction without the negative consequences associated with engaging people in their personal networks. Second, the ability to interact anonymously served as a low-barrier to entry, where people could engage even when they did not feel as if they had mastery of any given topic. This enabled them to more actively learn, as well as develop the necessary skills to more effectively engage in positive political discourse—thus improving their political self-efficacy.

Poli: An Integrated Political Deliberation Environment Supporting Diverse Public Sphere Interactions

Our informants were able to assemble suitable deliberation environments to accomplish their own personal goals by combining multiple tools with varying affordances. However, this may be beyond the average users' capabilities. Based on our findings, we identified several requirements for an environment conducive to diverse interactions in the public sphere, which include:

- An integrated information environment that automatically aggregates information across social media technologies.
- An environment that exposes users to diverse political information and discussants with alternative viewpoints.
- Serendipitous exposure to diverse political information.
- Information browsing and filtering capabilities by: topic, sentiment, geographic location and political orientation.
- The ability to judge the impact of personal posts and the posts of others.
- The ability to understand and view interaction context.
- The ability to manage identity (i.e. by switching in and out of anonymity when posting and engaging in discussions).

We will now elaborate on the design of Poli, which was designed to feel like a single experience, and describe how it functions as a political deliberation environment conducive to the three main interactions—information access, information dissemination and rational discourse—in the public sphere as defined by Dahlgren [6].

Diverse information exposure through automated aggregation: Serendipity as an interaction paradigm. Rather than rely on the diversity of a user's network, or their willingness or ability to utilize available tools and construct varied information feeds, we developed Poli first and foremost as a diverse information platform. In order to do so, we first created an in-lab tool that collects political information across social media technologies, and stores them in a database. We used this tool as a back-end to our constantly evolving political deliberation environment.

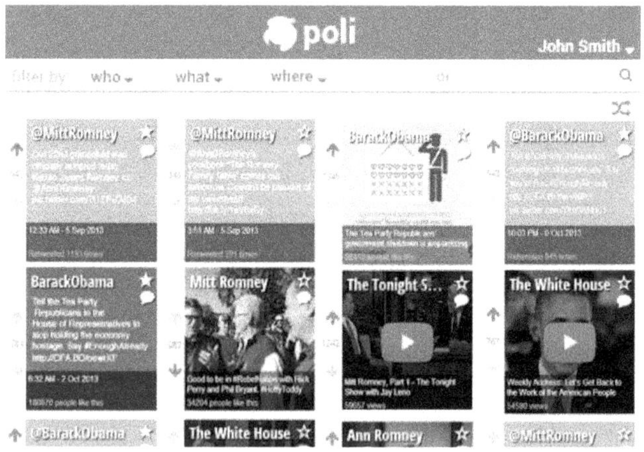

Figure 1: The main view of Poli.

The tool aggregates information from multiple sources from a variety of perspectives, and pulls this information and presents it to users in a serendipitous fashion (Figure 1) both randomly or according to our internal rating system. The main view of Poli automatically aggregates and exposes users to political information from multiple social media technologies (i.e. Facebook, Twitter and YouTube). The information is presented in a tiled format and spans political ideologies, and exposes users to diverse perspectives from candidates, media networks, and lay citizens (i.e. highly rated comments). Each tile includes the source of the content, a headline, the date the content was posted and the number of times it was retweeted, "Liked" or viewed. If a user sees a "headline" and is interested in exploring it further, they can click the tile and either view the discussion around any given post as is being discussed by the Poli community (Figure 3), or link out to the post in the native social media environment and investigate how the community in any tool is discussing the topic.

As we found in our sample, and has been corroborated by other studies [c.f. 25], exposure to diverse information can lead people to become more actively interested in understanding alternative perspectives. We designed Poli to promote positive behavior change. For example, our informants described how they became more interested in understanding differing views after first being exposed to them—especially when they learned of perspectives on issues that they were otherwise unaware of.

Structured information search and filtering. We designed Poli with the capability to search for and filter information by: topic, sentiment, geographic location and political orientation.

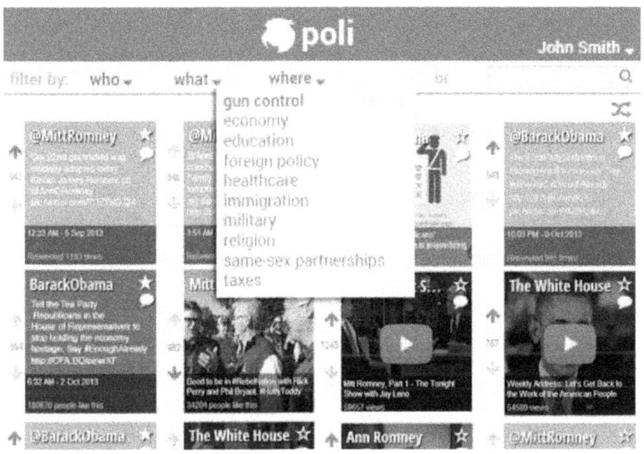

Figure 2: Structured information search capabilities.

Poli integrates previous work on a "drop-down browser" for political information searching [31] which showed that providing users with options for exploring candidates and issues greatly increased the number of searches that users performed, the complexity of their queries, and the quantity and breadth of information to which they were exposed. The drop-down browser allowed users to take advantage of recognition memory to access information about candidates for office and to think of important election issues. The browser automatically constructed queries that filtered information based on the union of a candidate and an issue. This allowed users to adopt a strategy whereby they could perform either issue-based searches or candidate-based searches through menu selection. By enabling strategic and structured searches, the complexity of the task was reduced.

The drop-down browser filtered only on candidate names and election issues. In contrast, Poli has the capability to search for and filter information by topic, sentiment, location, and political orientation. This potentially allows even more sophisticated searches. As with the drop-down browser, these filters are applied by drop down menus, depicted in Figure 2, as follows:

- The *Who* menu includes parties and names of individuals.
- The *What* menu includes topics, such as gun control, economy, etc.
- The *Where* menu includes the ability to filter by geographic location.
- The *Or* menu allows people to filter by sentiment. People can view how people felt about any given topic or candidate. This menu is available in every search view, and gives people the ability to filter by sentiment utilizing a variety of combinations, e.g. by candidate and feelings towards a candidate, and how people in a specific geographic location feel about a topic.
- The *Search Box* allows people to construct their own search queries and connects to social media data aggregated within Poli that spans various sources.

Identity management: Supporting reasoned and diverse information dissemination and discussions. Poli provides users with the ability to post anonymously or by using their real world identity associated with any given social media technology. Thus, we not only designed the environment to aggregate across social media tools, but we also integrated the posting functionality across tools, so that people could choose to post to Facebook or Twitter from within our tool.

Figure 3: Political discourse: Supporting identity management and positive discursive interactions.

Importantly, we also developed a rating system, where users can "up vote" a comment, similar to the way in which the rating system in Reddit works. Users can rate one another's posts and, over time, as user posts are rated more highly their reputation score also increases accordingly. Users, in turn, can earn a reputation over time (Figure 3).

Although reputation systems have their faults, they also have a variety of benefits in the context of political communication [26]. As elaborated by Towne and Herbsleb [37], first, reputation systems provide an important feedback loop, providing users with a way to improve their skills, knowledge, and how they construct their posts and interact with others. Moreover, whereas some communities like YouTube are considered highly polarized and posts are considered to typically fall into the categories of "cheerleading" or "rants", a rating system allows for an easy way to filter posts or decide whether or not to pay attention to a post—especially if a post has a severely negative rating.

The ability to judge impact. Another design consideration was to allow people to judge the impact of their posts. The peer recognition provided by the rating system we developed could act, first, as a motivation for people to participate, and second, as a motivation for people to construct thoughtful posts and replies. Rather than speaking to a tight-knit audience of friends, family and acquaintances, users would be able to speak to a loose aggregate of politically minded and ideologically-diverse individuals. We believed this can help foster a sense of positive community building and increased self-efficacy, as users can learn to develop more constructive and rational posts over time. People can also use humor and political memes to generate discussion and judge the impact of such posts. This can also as act as a motivation to learn more and integrate more facts (i.e. links to outside sources via websites) or humor into their posts depending on their experiences and ratings.

Interaction context and political discourse. Poli also effectively solves the various issues our informants described with respect to the lack of interaction context. When people discuss a Facebook or Twitter post, they can see a timeline of the entire threaded conversation from first to last post (similar to the way in which Discussions emerge through Facebook). They can also view an entire conversation sorted by rating. Importantly, they can construct a post using any tool with which they have an account, post anonymously or using their true identity, and write short posts (using Twitter) or longer posts (when connected to Facebook, their blog or Google+).

DISCUSSION AND FUTURE WORK

In this study we focused on a group of highly motivated, civically engaged social media users. These users appropriated multiple technologies for political deliberation, experienced several challenges in interacting in the public sphere, and found suitable workarounds. We utilized our findings to formulate requirements for, and develop a new, social media environment devoted to political deliberation—Poli—taking into account the real world experiences of those who were able to string together multiple tools to suit their deliberation goals across the "sprawling" public sphere.

Poli at this point is in the initial design and prototyping phase. While the design has been guided by input from users, an iteration through which users assess the new tool has not yet occurred. In the iteration step we will be concerned with several questions related to both user experience and task success.

User Experience and Task Success

With regard to user experience, in future evaluation studies we will be concerned with whether Poli engenders interest and engagement. These are two critical impasses to political participation. We anticipate that the dynamic features will contribute to interest in politics. Another experience measure that we will be concerned with is enjoyment. We seek to change users' sense of the political participation process from one of a duty or chore to one that is more enjoyable.

With regard to task success, we will assess whether Poli increases the diversity of information to which users are exposed. Filtering on multiple dimensions has the potential to expand the range of information sources, but it also has the potential to narrow searches to only the topics of interest of each user. Similarly, the addition of a social commenting component has the potential to either broaden or narrow information exposure depending on the commenters' political predilections.

Another task factor that we will assess is success in finding information relevant to the voting decision. Again, the diversity of information available can be overwhelming, and we hope that users can stay on task, create useful query filters, and sample appropriate information.

In addition to looking for experience- and task-related performance measures, we will be interested in what strategies Poli enables for users. With the drop-down browser, researchers observed both candidate-centered search and issue-centered search [31]. With Poli, we might find "sentiment-centered search" in which a user looks for all of the good things about a candidate or for all the bad things about a candidate. Maruyama et al. [24] noted that people using Twitter while watching a political debate "took the temperature" of the crowd in terms of their overall sentiment. We might find the same behavior with Poli, in which users search in order to essentially crowdsource sentiment about candidates and/or issues.

Environment Evolution and Current Limitations

Poli's functionality is centered on its ability to integrate the information feeds from multiple social media channels. At this point our tool only aggregates what is specified by the research team. This will work for the purpose of experiments and testing, but this also raises several challenges and questions that need to be further explored through careful research and experimentation. For example, how can we leverage the Poli community to assist with data aggregation? How can we develop a tool that automatically aggregates the broad spectrum of political information being disseminated across social media technologies?

Moreover, our tool also filters by sentiment. However, our sentiment analysis is mostly hard coded. Existing sentiment analysis tools, such as Linguistic Inquiry and Word Count (LIWC), provide basic word counts and percentages of words in affective, part-of-speech and semantic categories [28, 29]. Word categories have been psychometrically tested [29] and the analyses have been documented to work well given large bodies of text but the tool does not support the accurate analysis of single sentence structures. Moreover, social media data is unique in that people often use affectively charged jargon, such as humor and sarcasm, which is difficult to detect using sentiment tools. This leads to questions about how we can best determine the sentiment of social media data, and how we can adapt sentiment machine languages to better support the analysis of social media data.

CONCLUSION

The public sphere is not confined to any single tool and thus it exists, as Dahlgren [6] asserts, as a "sprawling" public sphere. Civically engaged users are aware of the sprawling nature of the online public sphere and have developed strategies to deal with it. As designers, we have developed a new political environment that can help people more effectively engage in political interaction in the online public sphere, building on previous work on designing for deliberation [e.g. 33, 37, 39] while also taking into account the experiential data derived from our politically minded informants.

Whereas we have designed and implemented a new online environment to aid citizens throughout the political deliberation process, our work also raises important questions that we hope to address in the future.

1) To what extent can technology address a lack of political engagement? What model of political interaction is most conducive to positive interaction—hybrid, online-only or face-to-face?

Given that people are using multiple social media to interact in the public sphere, Poli could serve as a channel that can help people with the daunting task of traversing multiple platforms. Real world testing is required to compare Poli to existing practices, as well as hybrid models.

2) What is considered political in nature?

We designed Poli to be general and allow people to use the environment based on their needs. Our belief is that although in some cases people have well-established perspectives or positions, such as is often the case with Presidential elections, the benefits of exposure to diverse information moves beyond elections. In our work we have found that people have altered their perspectives when given the opportunity to truly engage positively with people holding differing views, especially when they put themselves in the other person's shoes. Of course this may not hold true for elections, as people will typically vote by party, but other topics exist that are considered political where people may feel they have an opinion, but could change as a result of exposure to alternative ideas, facts, and opinions, when presented in a rational manner.

This research evokes many questions that remain unanswered, and it will become increasingly important for us, as a research community, to continue to study users of social media as closely as possible.

ACKNOWLEDGMENTS

This research was funded by NSF award No. IIS-1064852. Any opinions, findings and conclusions or recommendations expressed in this material are those of the authors and do not necessarily reflect the views of the National Science Foundation.

REFERENCES

1. AbouAssi, K., Nabatchi, T., and Antoun, R. 2013. Citizen participation in public administration: Views from Lebanon. *Inter. J. of Pub. Admin.*, 36(14), 1029-1043.

2. Adamic, L., and Glance, N. (2005). The political blogosphere and the 2004 U.S. election: Divided they blog. *In Proc. of IWLD*, 36-43.

3. Brabham, D. C. (2008). Crowdsourcing as a model for problem solving an introduction and cases. *Convergence: the international journal of research into new media technologies*, 14(1), 75-90.

4. Coleman, S., and Moss, G. (2012). Under construction: the field of online deliberation research. *Journal of Information Technology & Politics*, 9(1), 1-15.

5. Dahlberg, L. (2001). The Internet and democratic discourse: Exploring the prospects of online deliberative forums extending the public sphere. *Information, Communication & Society*, 4(4), 615-633.

6. Dahlgren, P. (2009). *Media and political engagement: Citizens, communication, and democracy*. University Press, Cambridge, MA.

7. Ellison, N., Steinfield, C., and Lampe, C. (2007). The benefits of Facebook "friends:" Social capital and college students' use of online social network sites. *Journal of Computer-Mediated Communication*, 12 (4), 1143-1168.

8. Fung, A., and Wright, E. (2001). Deepening democracy: Institutional innovations in empowered participatory governance. *Politics & Society*, 29(1), 5–41.

9. Goffman, E. (1959). *The Presentation of Self in Everyday Life*. Doubleday, Carden City, NY

10. Gilbert, E., Bergstrom, T., and Karahalios, K. (2009). Blogs are echo chambers: Blogs are echo chambers. *In Proc. of HICSS-42*.

11. Gordon, E., Baldwin-Philippi, J., and Balestra, M. (2013). Why we engage: How theories of human behavior contribute to our understanding of civic engagement in a digital era. *Berkman Center Research Publication*, 21.

12. Gordon, E., Manosevitch, E. (2010). Augmented deliberation: merging physical and virtual interaction to engage communities in urban planning. *New Media and Society*, 12, 763-778.

13. Graham, T., and Wright. S. (2014). Discursive equality and everyday talk online: The Impact of 'superparticipants.' *JCMC*, 19(3), 625–642.

14. Graham, T. (2008). Needles in a haystack: A new approach for identifying and assessing political talk in non-political discussion forums." *Javnost*, 15(2), 17–36.

15. Habermas, J. (1984). *The theory of communicative action: Reason and the rationalization of society*. Heneimann, London.

16. Habermas, J. (1991). *The structural transformation of the public sphere: An inquiry into a category of bourgeois society*. MIT Press, Cambridge, MA.

17. Jensen, J. (2003). Virtual democratic dialogue? Bringing together citizens and politicians. *Info. Pol.*, 8(1-2), 29–47.

18. Karlsson, M. (2011). What does it take to make online deliberation happen?: A comparative analysis of 28 online discussion forums. In *E-Participation to Online Deliberation: Proceedings of the Fourth International Conference on Online Deliberation*, 142–156.

19. Kies, R. (2010). *Promises and Limits of Web-Deliberation*. New York, NY: Palgrave Macmillan.

20. Klein, M. (2012). Enabling large-scale deliberation using attention-mediation metrics. *Computer Supported Cooperative Work*, 21(4-5), 449-473.

21. Kriplean, T., Morgan, J., Freelon, D., Borning, A., and Bennett, L. (2012a). Supporting reflective public thought with Considerit." *In Proc. of CSCW '12*.

22. Lampe, C., Ellison, N., and Steinfield, C. (2006). A face (book) in the crowd: Social searching vs. social browsing. *In Proc. of CSCW'06*.

23. Macintosh, A., Robson, E., Smith, E., and Whyte, A. (2003). Electronic democracy and young people. *Social Science Computer Review*, 21(1), 43–54.

24. Maruyama, M., Robertson, S., Douglas, S., Semaan, B., Faucett, H. (2014). Hybrid Media Consumption: How Tweeting During a Televised Political Debate Influences the Vote Decision. *In Proc. of CSCW'14*.

25. Munson, S., and Resnick, P. (2010). Presenting diverse political opinions: how and how much, *In Proc. of CHI'10*.

26. Noveck, B. S. (2009). *Wiki government: How technology can make government better, democracy stronger, and citizens more powerful*. Harrisonburg, VA: Brookings Institution Press.

27. Papacharissi, Z. (2010). *A private sphere: Democracy in a digital age*. Polity Press, Malden, MA.

28. Pennebaker, J.W., Francis, M.E. and Booth, R.J. (2001). *Linguistic Inquiry and Word Count: LIWC (2nd Edition)*. Mahwah, NJ: Lawrence Erlbaum Associates.

29. Pennebaker, J.W., Mehl, M.R., and Niederhoffer, K.G. (2003). Psychological aspects of natural language use: Our words, our selves. *Ann. Rev. of Psych.*, 54, 547-577.

30. Raine, L., and Smith, A. (2012). *Politics on social networking sites*. Pew Internet and American Life Project.

31. Robertson, S., Wania, C., Abraham, G., and Park, S.J. (2008). Drop-down democracy: Internet portal design influences voters' search strategies. *In Proc. of HICSS'08*.

32. Semaan, B., Robertson, S., Douglas, S., Maruyama, M. (2014). Social Media Supporting Political Deliberation Across Multiple Public Spheres: Towards Depolarization. *In Proc. of CSCW'14*.

33. Smith, G. (2009). *Democratic Innovations: Designing Institutions for Citizen Participation*. Cambridge, United Kingdom: Cambridge University Press.

34. Strauss, A. L. and Corbin, J. M. (1998). *Basics of Qualitative Research: Techniques and Procedures for Developing Grounded Theory*. Sage, CA.

35. Stromer-Galley, J. (2004). Diversity of political conversation on the Internet: Users' perspectives. *Journal of Computer-Mediated Communication*, 8(3).

36. Sunstein, C. (2002). The law of group polarization. *Journal of Political Philosophy*, 10(2), 175-195.

37. Towne, B., and Herbsleb, J. (2012). Design considerations for online deliberation systems. *Journal of Information Technology & Politics*, 9(1), 97–115.

38. Wright, S. (2012). Politics as Usual? Revolution, Normalization and a New Agenda for Online Deliberation. *New Media & Society*, 14(2), 244–261.

39. Wright, S., and Street, J. (2007). Democracy, deliberation and design: The case of online discussion forums. *New Media & Society*, 9(5). 849-869.

40. Zuckerman, E. (2014). New media, new civics? *Policy and Internet*, 6(2), 151-168

Debating Poverty Porn on Twitter: Social Media as a Place for Everyday Socio-Political Talk

Phil Brooker[1], John Vines[2], Selina Sutton[3], Julie Barnett[1], Tom Feltwell[4], and Shaun Lawson[4]

[1] University of Bath, UK, {p.d.brooker, j.c.barnett} @bath.ac.uk

[2] Culture Lab, School of Computing Science / [3] Faculty of Medical Sciences, Newcastle University, UK,{john.vines, selina.sutton} @ncl.ac.uk

[4] University of Lincoln, UK, {tfeltwell, slawson} @lincoln.ac.uk

ABSTRACT

This paper presents an empirical investigation of how people appropriated Twitter for socio-political talk in response to a television (TV) portrayal of people supported by state welfare and benefits. Our findings reveal how online discussion during, and in-between, TV broadcasts was characterised by distinctly different qualities, topics and user behaviours. These findings offer design opportunities for social media services to (i) support more balanced real-time commentaries of politically-charged media, (ii) actively promote discussion to continue after, and between, programming; and (iii) incorporate different motivations and attitudes towards socio-political concerns, as well as different practices of communicating those concerns. We contribute to the developing HCI literature on how social media intersects with political and civic engagement and specifically highlight the ways in which Twitter interacts with other forms of media as a site of everyday socio-political talk and debate.

Author Keywords

Social media, politics; television; welfare; live-tweeting.

ACM Classification Keywords

H.5.m. Information interfaces and presentation (e.g., HCI): Miscellaneous.

INTRODUCTION

The use of social media as a place for civic engagement has received significant recent attention from the HCI research community (e.g. [7, 10, 17, 32, 26, 47]). Much of this work has focussed on how social media can be used by groups to support debate and action around social and political concerns. Such research has often concentrated on understanding and supporting patterns of online behaviours that are aligned with *activism* and with fostering and promoting political *participation*. The study of online platforms, including social media, as places that support more casual *everyday* socio-political talk is an area that has received less attention by HCI researchers until recently (e.g. [40]). This is in contrast to scholars from other disciplines, e.g. from media, communications, and politics, who have, for considerable time, explored the theoretical implications of everyday political discourse on the Internet and social media (e.g. [8, 24, 28]). Researchers from these disciplines have recently argued that a *talkative electorate* is a cornerstone of civic society (e.g. [21]) and of deliberative democracy [16]. However argument continues as to whether social media facilitate this [18].

In this paper, we study the ways in which old and new media converge to galvanize everyday socio-political talk, discussion and debate. We are motivated by characterisations of a talkative electorate [21] and of observations regarding the 'mediatization of everything' [25], including political debate, in everyday life. Our aim is to understand the actions of users who simultaneously engage with 'traditional' broadcast media (i.e. television (TV)) and 'new' interactive media (i.e. social media and micro-blogging) through everyday casual 'social TV' [11] practices of live-tweeting and second screening. In doing so, we expose design opportunities for digital systems to support everyday political talk, with the longer term aim of equipping a talkative electorate with useful interactive, social digital tools and platforms.

We situate our work within an analysis of 124,008 Tweets related to the UK TV show *Benefits Street*: a documentary series about the residents of a particular street in the UK city of Birmingham, many of whom were reportedly in receipt of state unemployment and other welfare benefits. The series was extremely controversial and received widespread media attention in the UK, with the programme makers being accused of generating a 'poverty porn' [29] depiction of welfare claimants for the gratification of prime-time TV audiences [20]. During its original run, the broadcaster actively encouraged Twitter discussion via an 'official' hashtag *#benefitsstreet* shown in the opening credits. Our dataset, comprised of tweets using this hashtag over a portion of the original run, shows that commentary and discussion on the issues raised in the programme persisted beyond the periods of broadcast themselves. As such, our analyses of the data are intended to explore how

CHI 2015, April 18 - 23 2015, Seoul, Republic of Korea
Copyright 2015 ACM 978-1-4503-3145-6/15/04...$15.00
http://dx.doi.org/10.1145/2702123.2702291

everyday talk about politics and casual socio-political commentary operates through social media. In a quantitative analysis of the data, we were able to identify two different periods of Twitter activity related to whether the show was being broadcast and 'live tweeted' [39] or discussed between broadcasts in a more reflective manner. Our qualitative analysis demonstrates the differences between those periods in how Twitter acts as a platform for both abuse of the people represented and to support discussion related to the wider political narratives surrounding welfare in the UK.

We contribute to existing HCI in two ways. Firstly, we provide an understanding of the ways in which Twitter might be supportive of a 'talkative electorate'. We show that the observed social TV practices of live tweeting enables socio-political discussion and everyday talk as a response to broadcast media that contains provocative political material. Secondly, we contribute towards an understanding of the design space for the development of social media and social TV services which could more seamlessly support vigorous, balanced, reflective and dialogical socio-political talk.

RELATED WORK

The Digital Public Sphere and Everyday Talk

Research that is interested in the ways that citizens engage with political issues is theoretically dominated by recourse to Habermas's notions of the public sphere [23] and its place in deliberative democracy [16]. In simple terms the public sphere can be thought of as 'society engaged in critical public debate' [23]. Habermas's deliberations are also conceptually grounded in Marx's political theory and emphasize that all citizens should have inclusive and equal access to such debate. A range of researchers drawn from fields including politics, communications, media and computer science, have argued for and against the importance of social media as platforms that are supportive of the public sphere in a democratic society. Perhaps despite Habermas's own warnings, many have put forward very positive claims in this regard (e.g. [37, 43] and [31] who argue that Twitter was directly instrumental in political upheaval in the Middle East). Underlying criticisms of such claims pivot on evidence that platforms such as Twitter are capable mainly of supporting information *delivery* rather than *debate* (e.g. as evidenced through limited replies, and retweets) but most especially that digital platforms have inherent asymmetric power distributions [18] and can be easily dominated, or manipulated, by privileged individuals, communities and corporations. Fuchs [18, p.200] reminds us of Habermas's principle that 'individuals (should) have the same formal education (and) material resources for participating in the public sphere'. Though the former argument can be contested empirically (e.g. [46]) it is difficult to argue that platforms such as Twitter can be used equally effectively by each and every citizen.

Recently a number of communications scholars (e.g. [21, 27]) have eschewed grand claims that digital tools may implement a Habermassian public sphere, but instead have suggested that online platforms such as social media might usefully facilitate a *talkative electorate*. This is to say they provide a means for citizens to engage in everyday political talk. Jackson et al [27] suggest that 'civic culture requires a talkative electorate where discussion is a way of making evident a sense of connection between citizens and the democratic process'. Graham and Wright [21] further assert that it is through 'participation in informal political talk whereby citizens become aware of other opinions, discover important issues...test new ideas, and develop and clarify their preferences'; Graham most recently [22] suggests that 'it is through such talk whereby citizens achieve mutual understanding about each other and the political and societal problems ... they face'. A number of researchers (e.g. [24]) have identified the high levels of conflict and disharmony that emerge when discussing politics in online settings. Whereas this can be problematic it is also frequently argued that conflict is a cornerstone of deliberative democracy, and therefore digital systems should not be explicitly designed to remove this [4, 18].

HCI, politics and mediatization

Over the last decade, social action and political discourse has also emerged as an important area of study within HCI. Commonly, this work has focused on how digital technology is appropriated to support social movements (e.g. [7, 47]) or deliberately designed to facilitate engagement in social action or political (e.g. [10, 17, 32]). In a similar vein, there has been strong interest in the ways in which critical [14], participatory [3] and more recently adversarial [9] design practices can raise questions about social norms, politics and democracy. Therefore, work in and around HCI has frequently focused on the ways technology may support activism or social change, with a view to empowering specific groups or communities to engage in activities, i.e. how technology supports practices that can be labelled as active political participation or civil engagement [15]. In contrast, relatively little HCI work has discussed the role of 'armchair' or 'everyday' online socio-political discussion. An exception is Semaan et al's [40] recent analysis of interactions across multiple online platforms (the "sprawling public sphere"), revealing how users seek out diverse information and discussants online in an everyday political context. In this paper we focus on similar themes, and are also motivated by the *mediatization* of political engagement i.e. the increasing prevalence of how media (e.g. TV) and mediated communications (e.g. social media) interact with one-another thus shaping and transforming everyday life – including politics [25].

Social Computing, Political Talk and TV

CSCW and social computing researchers have taken the opportunity to analyse large datasets containing political talk from social media platforms. This includes studies of social media use during societal upheaval [26], and of online sentiment mining during political elections [46]. Of particular relevance here however is a subset of such work which has focused on the analysis of data in the context of simultaneous social media use and TV viewing: a practice variously termed 'live tweeting' [39], 'second screening' [12] or 'co-viewing' [11]. Anstead et al have studied how interaction between social media and broadcast TV has formed an emergent 'viewertariat' [2] where Twitter provides a space for discussion in response to televised live political debates [2] and controversies [1]. Doughty et al [11] show how tweet length and frequency may signify differing engagement with TV content, suggesting responses to political material are lengthier and more considered. Doughty et al [13] have also discussed how live tweets related to a controversial TV show demonstrated a high degree of socio-political discussion related to the minority community portrayed in the broadcast. In particular, they suggest that this mix of media acted as a catalyst for online abuse and 'Othering' which might be explained through computer-mediated communication theories such as online disinhibition [44]. Their work highlights the ways in which broadcast media such as TV encourages a high degree of discussion and debate online even when the broadcast content does not contain an explicit political message. However, the authors [13] suggest that this, in the context of their study, was essentially problematic due to the abusive nature of much of the discussion. Our stance is somewhat contrary to this in that we argue *all* everyday political talk as something to be supported, encouraged, yet also openly contested.

CASE STUDY: BENEFITS STREET

The focus of our study is the British broadcast TV show *Benefits Street*: a documentary series first aired in early 2014, which documented the lives of the residents living on James Turner Street in Birmingham, England. Across five 60-minute episodes, the series follows the lives of residents as they look for work, deal with problems within families and between neighbours, and engage in petty crime. The dominant narrative from the show is that many of the street's residents are dependent on welfare payments; this is set against a backdrop of 'austerity' imposed on UK society following the global financial crisis, as well as an ongoing program of controversial reforms designed to reduce the UK's overall welfare and unemployment benefit spending.

Poverty Porn

It has commonly been argued that Benefits Street is an instance of 'poverty porn' [20]—a portrayal of the poor in order to cause sympathy or outrage to other segments of the public [34]. It has been noted how these portrayals, although undeniably complex, tend to make those in poverty feel victimized, stigmatized and objectified [41]. Jensen [29] further argues that such media leaves little room for constructing critical perspectives, resulting in a state of 'making the social world appear self-evident and requiring no interpretation' [5].

Our Research Focus

Our aim was to understand the ways in which Twitter is supportive of a talkative electorate. In particular, we wanted to observe social TV practices of live tweeting and second screening as enablers of socio-political discussion and 'everyday talk'. We selected Benefits Street as an example of broadcast media that contains stimulating, provocative political material centred upon a number of current concerns for the UK electorate – namely those of austerity, welfare reform and the negative perception of communities that are supposedly supported by benefits. Moreover, Benefits Street received a significant amount of media interest prior to, and during, its broadcast. This precipitated considerable public interest and thus high viewership figures for the programme (in fact the highest ratings for the broadcaster Channel 4 in two years). This resulted in significant public discourse and awareness of the show, its socio-political content and wider political framing. Following [13] we expected that Benefits Street would provoke a good deal of abusive and divisive talk, given commonly highlighted views regarding poorer communities in the UK [30]. We were particularly interested in understanding how these views were countered by more reasoned and critical debate and discussion.

Overall Approach to the Research

Quantitative and qualitative methods were used to analyse 124,008 Tweets related to Benefits Street. We began our data collection and analysis using the Chorus visual analytic suite*. Chorus provides a means of collecting and generating visualisations of Twitter data based on text mining principles and techniques. Our visual analysis of the data was in two stages: (i) we conducted a time-oriented analysis that provided details of tweet frequency and identified periods of greater and lesser activity; (ii) we used Chorus' text mining and visualization features to perform a topic-based analysis to generate clusters of tweets based on their semantic content. From here, using insights drawn from the topical clustering, we performed an inductive thematic qualitative analysis [6] on data sub-sets to develop a rich understanding of the talk surrounding Benefits Street.

DATA COLLECTION AND INITIAL VISUAL ANALYSIS

We used Chorus to collect tweets containing the hashtag #benefitsstreet. Chorus uses the Twitter Search API [45] to acquire tweets; though our own experience is that the API will return most tweets containing a #hashtag (except those from restricted accounts), it should be noted that Twitter themselves state "Not all Tweets will be indexed or made available via the search interface". Our dataset consisted of 124,008 tweets posted between 21:52 on the 13th of January 2014 (towards the end of the broadcasting of the second episode) to two days past the broadcast of the penultimate fourth episode at 23:45 on the 29th January 2014. Within this dataset, there were 6,788 unique users and 2,911 @mentions directed to other users or as part of a retweet.

* www.chorusanalytics.co.uk

Timeline Analysis

To begin our explorations we adopted a 'time-dependent' view of the data. This, as might be expected, highlighted two distinct periods of activity as shown in Figure 1—'peaks' during broadcast (signified by prominent spikes in tweet volume) and 'off-peak' periods between broadcasts. While previous research (e.g. [39]) has often discarded tweets that lie significantly outside of broadcast periods, we were interested in this data, as we assumed it would contribute to an understanding of everyday talk.

Figure 1 – Timeline View of quantity of #benefitsstreet tweets. Red bars denote periods defined as 'peak'.

We noted that rises in tweet volume during 'peak' periods occurred between 20:00 and 01:30 across the day of the programme's broadcast (i.e. an hour before broadcast to 01:30 the following morning), with 'off-peak' periods occurring outside of those times. By defining these peak and off-peak periods, we were able to split the dataset into two sub-sets such that we could look at each period in isolation in our topic analysis. The 'peak' period dataset consists of 76996 tweets, propagated by 5,155 users and featuring 1846 different @mentions. The 'off-peak' period dataset consists of 47012 tweets, propagated by 3,501 users and featuring 1,764 different @mentions.

Clustering of #benefitsstreet talk

From our analysis of tweet frequencies, we inductively derived a research question: in addition to being produced at different times and in different volumes, do tweets in different periods (i.e. in 'peak' or 'off-peak' conversation) reflect different thematic concerns? To explore this we used Chorus' 'cluster explorer' functions to ascertain the key topics within these 'peak' and 'off-peak' periods. The topical maps (see Figure 2) compute an index of co-occurrence values—the frequency with which a given word appears with all other key words in the dataset. Note that Chorus uses a 'stop list' of common words such as "is" and "to" and so on. A given co-occurrence value can be thought of as a probability that, within a particular data set, one word will be found with another in a tweet. Chorus then uses these values as a way of locating individual terms on a 2D map in relation to each other. Words that commonly feature in tweets together are located close to each other on the map, forming clusters that may be thought of as representing distinct semantic aggregations, or topics. Hence, we used Chorus' clustering of commonly co-occurring words as an entry point into the data corpus.

We then used the topical 'peak' and 'off-peak' maps (shown in Figure 2) to further filter the data by extracting terms featured in the single largest topical cluster from each. This reflects a visual analytic approach to Chorus' cluster maps wherein we visually identified a selection of keywords (appearing in =>1% of tweets) associated with clusters and compiled datasets containing those terms. Through extracting the single largest point of clustering in each dataset, we are left with a refined dataset for each period, consisting of only the key topics that tweeters most frequently commented on. This resulted in 24,759 'peak' and 24,746 'off-peak' tweets in total.

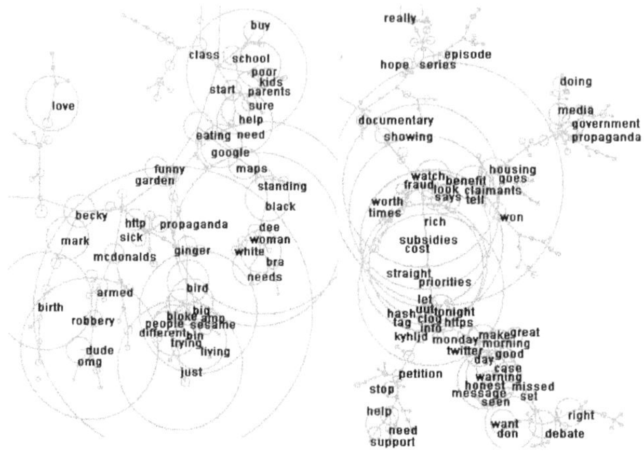

Figure 2. Clustering of discussion using Chorus. Left: 'Peak' Clusters. Right: 'Off-Peak' Clusters.

THEMATIC ANALYSIS

Our two refined peak and off-peak data sub-sets were then used as the basis for an inductive thematic analysis. Two researchers initially took a randomised assignment of 20% of each sub-set and coded these independently. Individual tweets were summarised using one or two-word codes through a process of open coding [6]. Once completed, the researchers met to share codes and identify commonalities and differences. From here, 29 codes were agreed upon and used to code the remaining data. Once completed the two researchers met once more to cluster codes around themes that characterise the data. The analysis generated 5 themes: *abusing, critiquing and judging*; *appreciating, defending and contesting*; *politics of public spending*; *politics of fear and propaganda*; and *fiction and reality*. These are now discussed in the following sections, with the quantity of tweets coded in a theme provided in parenthesis.

Abusing, critiquing and judging

The most frequently occurring codes in our analysis (15,832 peak, 8,924 off-peak) related directly to people featuring regularly in the programme: primarily *"White Dee"*, *"Fungi"*, *"Black Dee"*, *"Mark"*, *"Becky"* and *"the Romanians"*. The most retweeted comments during the peak period were directly critical of those portrayed; for example, 776 tweets related to White Dee's lack of wearing a bra. Other comments would be predominantly negative in their sentiment and comprise of observations related to the appearance of the residents and the ways in which their homes and James Turner Street itself were presented: e.g.

"White d looks like she hasn't brushed her teeth since 1984"; *"Why does that Becky always look like that she is wearing the same clothes"*; *"How people live in shit conditions is absolutely beyond me. Clean your house you dirty scutters"*. While in many respects the comments in this cluster of data might be considered abusive, there were more subtle commentaries associated with stereotypes related to British distinctions in social class. The comments on how *"dark and dingy"* and *"empty"* the resident's homes appeared in the show seemed to reflect class distinctions and expectations. This was noted further by comments on the brand of clothes some residents wore (*"someone tell that dude helly hensen went out in the 90's!!"*), the ways in which some residents left their doors open or unlocked for neighbours to walk in and out (*"Why are the people in #benefitsstreet unable to close their front doors?"*) and how children were seen to *"roam the street"* or sit around on garden walls (*"Women encouraging her kids to sit on ye wall and go on benefits when they finish school"*).

A smaller subset of peak data (8,526) related to critiques and judgements made on the characters in relation to their motivations to find employment. Comments questioned how much the residents desired to find work or their inability to keep jobs when they are offered to them (*"Mark from #benefitsstreet is an absolute loser. Find a job for the kids"*). Another recurring issue was the ways in which some characters were seen to live beyond their means. Tweets referred how some characters owned premium consumer goods while struggling to pay for food, energy and clothing: "*She got no money for food and stuff but sits there with an iPhone 5s?; Here is a mad idea stop smoking and buying cheap cider and buy some fucking food*". A further implication here is that these individuals are unable to make informed decisions or prioritize aspects of their life. In one scene, Fungi was seen contacting his estranged daughter for the first time in several years; as he made a phone call to her, he was seen to drop both his phone and a beer can held in his other hand. Comments reacting to this scene chastised his prioritization of not spilling his beer over saving his phone from hitting the ground (*"I'm trying to call my daughter, this is such a big moment for me, I'm so emotional.... FUCK I'VE DROPPED MY BEER, DAMMIT!!")*. In a similar vein, White Dee was frequently chastised for not supporting her daughter in her sporting achievements (*"Wants the best for her kids but can't be arsed to go see her daughter run in a school sports event"*) or in her desire to find employment: *"White Dee disparaging her children for wanting to work, not claim benefits. Nice parenting."*.

Appreciating, defending and contesting

While the peak data was characterised by overwhelmingly abusive and critical comments of the people in the show, there were also examples of Twitter users being more complimentary to the residents. For example, some tweets conveyed sympathy (*"Find it genuinely sad that people have to use food banks in England in 2014 or go hungry!"*) and concerns for their welfare (*"Funghi is breaking my heart. I hope he really does turn his life around"*). There were also positive attributes in the ways in which the residents engaged with each other (*"Say what you like about these people but the community they have is wonderful. They don't have much but they have each other"*) and their ability to respond to personal challenges (*"White Dee's daughter is a fantastic, smart young lady. I wish her well in her future"*).

It was notable how the frequency of positive comments increased off-peak in comparison to the immediate reactions alongside the live broadcast (2,587 peak, 10,243 off-peak). During the off-peak period there were clusters of data around the terms "live", "work", "job" and "welfare", "poverty", "giving a voice" and "hostility". Moreover, the word "welfare" was connected to much more sympathetic representations of benefits claimants as a general group (i.e. not specifically linked to the people in the programme). Other comments during the off-peak period responded to the ways in which other Twitter users had vilified residents' spending. For example, it was suggested that people should be free to spend their money as they wish (*"It's stupid and selfish to say people receiving money from the welfare state cannot smoke cigarettes or drink alcohol"*) and that they should not be criticised for having treats (*"what's so wrong with somebody eating a Mcdonalds all of a sudden? God forbid the poor can have a treat"*). Furthermore some tweets actively defended the residents in reference to a feeling that the programme was misrepresenting them. Comments referred to how the production process had edited footage to meet popular stereotypes: *"Regardless of what people think of those 'scroungers' the truth is their vulnerable and channel 4 have set them up"*, and that the documentary's portrayal of living on benefits was one-sided and simplistic: *"There is a basic level of living that all need. #benefitsstreet ignores that, instead going for blame & shame"*.

As well as more balanced commentaries on the issue of welfare and the lives of the people in the programme, over the course of the off-peak period, tweets started to link to points made in wider debates related to welfare and benefits. The off-peak data in general was characterised by a greater use of URLs (51% of tweets compared to 25% in peak data) as many Twitter users started to refer to blog posts and pro-welfare organizations detailing the social challenges associated with job loss and living on benefits: *"Don't be taken in by badly researched programmes like #benefitsstreet Get clued up on the real facts on welfare! (URL)"*; *"Benefits claimants are shortchanged by £35bn a year, says thinktank Demos #benefitsstreet #austerity #welfare (URL)"*. Others started to use the #benefitsstreet hashtag to express agreement with views portrayed on other shows discussing Benefits Street: *"Paul O'Grady just nailed it on The One Show, talking about the exploitation of #benefitsstreet"*. One of the results of this contestation was a series of campaigns to create *"more accurate portrayals"* of living on welfare, and petitions to promote changes to welfare legislation. Such tweets typically included URLs to blogposts and campaigns, or to websites where people could sign petitions: *"Read @MairAB alternative to #benefitsstreet on our blog: #reallondonlives"*; *"Think the debate on benefits needs to change? Join #weallbenefit campaign"*.

Politics of public spending

While many of the tweets associated with the spending habits of the residents were direct commentaries on their behaviour, there was also discussion and comment around wider welfare issues. In the peak data, a cluster of tweets related directly to the ways in which residents were *"a drain on society"*; *"It is truly shocking to see so much money is spent on paying people to .. sit on their arses all day."* Somewhat surprisingly, one section of broadcast content that precipitated this discussion was when a family was shown accessing a food bank—a charitable service that provides food to people in extreme poverty. It was here where we started to see wider narratives emerge that were related to the welfare state as well as feelings of anger in relation to judgements people make when using resources given, or allocated, to them. Some comments would refer to how the residents were spending *"my money"* inappropriately: *"At least the people on #benefitsstreet are putting my money to good use, wide screen tv's, phone contracts and endless booze and fags"; "It's a good feeling paying for people to sit on their arses and get drunk all day. Enjoy spending my money".*

During the peak period, a smaller number of tweets (1,280) referred to state spending beyond welfare and benefits. This included bank subsidies (*"Make everyone think unemployed people are scroungers, and let the bankers and tax-dodgers get away with it"*), politician's expenses (*"On next week's #benefitsstreet how MP @nadhimzahawi claimed £35000 to heat his stables"*) and low-tax rates for the rich (*Let's get our facts right – subsidies to the rich cost us 54x as much as benefit fraud*). However, it was notable how these discussions emerged more prominently in the off-peak period (9,380). During this period, the terms 'benefits' featured in 5,016 tweets, 'fraud' in 3,379, 'rich' in 3,194 and 'subsidies' in 2,803. While 'benefits' still occasionally referred to the content of the show, we saw more frequent occurrence of its use as a strongly anti-rich (though not necessarily pro-benefits) sentiment. This is due partly to those tweets reminding people to compare benefits fraud against subsidies for the rich, and partly due to several using the same terminology to equate the two: *"#benefitsstreet on C4, exploiting the poor when they could make a show about bankers and MPs the REAL benefits cheats"*. Also, the discussions surrounding who was benefitting from taxation often involved referring to external sources or attempts to incite reactions across Twitter users and other programming. For example, tweets within this topic commonly featured a link to a website[†] intended to redress the focus on benefits fraud with factual information about the state burden of tax subsidies for the rich. Others made attempts to incite discussion by using @mentions to politicians, banks and organisations or individuals that had received subsidies, bailouts and tax-breaks from the UK Government.

Politics of Fear and Propaganda

It was also notable how the peak and off-peak data differed in the ways in which users reflected on the motivations of the broadcasters and production team (265 peak, 3,267 off-peak). As above, some comments appreciated that the portrayal of the residents was purposely edited so as to incite discussion and reactions. Thus, some tweets raised critical questions about the accuracy of the ways the residents were being portrayed, and whether this was done purely to increase viewership of the show: *"C4 are using naive and vulnerable people to get higher ratings, exploiting their lack of education, media misrepresentation"*. During the off-peak data, this was prominently discussed on Twitter following an interview with the show's producer on another TV channel discussing its popularity: *"Productions 1st response to whether proud of #BenefitsStreet was to talk ratings. Says it all really"*. Indeed the overall feeling here was that the producers had attempted to vilify and propagate fear of an already marginalized social group without due consideration of the impact this may have on both the individuals and on the wider population: *"Time to portray a small minority as being like all Benefit Claimants #benefitsstreet"; "Hate crime against disabled people doubled since 2008. Linked to media distortion"*.

As well as considering the broadcaster's motivations, questions were raised about who had funded and commissioned the series. Channel 4 sits in the unusual position of being publically owned but funded via advertising; this led to speculation on how much involvement the government had in commissioning the show—leading to calls that it was an act of state propaganda[‡]: *"The govt who owns the broadcaster that showed #BenefitsStreet have a vested interest – cuts or abolition to welfare."; "AGENDA: demonise those on welfare; introduce reforms; desensitise injustice; fabricate consensus ... ACTION: propaganda"*. As such, the *"shaming"* of people on the show was seen to be a purposeful way of deflecting blame away from government policy: *"Shame on a Government which pushes programmes like #benefitsstreet & then does this little to help them in to work!"*.

Fiction and reality

Our final theme related to the framing of the documentary as fiction or a form of *reality TV*. While Benefits Street was framed as a documentary, many people saw it as staged, or scripted, "entertainment" (6,792 peak, 2,565 off-peak). This was manifest in tweets where users would explain how they were *"settling down"* to watch it, how they *"couldn't wait for next weeks episode"* or speculation about *"what trouble Fungi will get into next"*. A large number of tweets that were clustered around this theme compared Benefits Street to a number of UK 'scripted reality' shows that have come to prominence over the last five years: *"#benefitsstreet is a much better show than #towie and #MadeInChelsea; I suspect that #benefitsstreet needs to be seen not as a Documentary but as scripted reality tv show like #theonlywayisessex #towie was"*. These comments in some respects exposed debate over how

[†] www.parasite-street.co.uk

[‡] This feeling was exacerbated when the government minister responsible for welfare reform suggested that the reaction to Benefits Street justified the changes to welfare in the UK. E.g. see http://bit.ly/1dWWH47

much of the show was real, or carefully edited and orchestrated, by the production company. The blurred distinction between documentary, fiction and reality was explicitly referred to by some users: *"is this even real?"; "It's just telly entertainment, use your brain"*. The fact that the show was seen as entertainment meant that serious events were met with amusement: *"how can fungi firstly do armed robery on McDonald's and secondly get caught robbing the place bahahhahaha #WorstCriminalEver"; "funny as fuck, robbing a mcD's with a sawn off shotty an getting caught hahaha"* While reactions like these are not surprising given the resident's on-screen portrayal, it also highlights the ways in which Twitter reactions sometimes trivialized serious issues.

DISCUSSION

In the following sub-sections, we reflect on our findings. In particular, we discuss the ways in which Twitter acted as a site that supports different forms of talk regarding Benefits Street, poverty porn and welfare, and the ways in which evidence was used to counter the provocative content of the broadcast material and other users' tweets; finally we offer a series of design sensitivities derived from our findings.

Second Screening and Everyday Talk About Benefits

Our findings highlight the diverse qualities of socio-political talk on Twitter in relation to Benefits Street. It is common for the findings of studies of second-screening and live-tweeting to highlight ways in which users primarily act in response to merely what they see before them. This is in part why analyses of live tweets can be used as a way of predicting broadcast content [42], or as ways of generating 'ratings' [36]. We saw similar spikes in relation to on-screen events in Benefits Street. However, we also observed Twitter being appropriated as a site of discussion around the socio-political issues in the show, or those surrounding it. Users embodied a range of opinions and perspectives on the political content of Benefits Street, evoking many of the qualities of an online talkative electorate. In some respects, users' talk was still based on immediate readings of the political dimensions of the show. Yet others went beyond just accepting the way in which benefits claimants were being portrayed and invoked alternative narratives and readings of the content. For some, the show was seen very much as propaganda, which they were able to interpret and question, thus contesting Jensen's [29] assertion mentioned earlier. But more subtly, this type of questioning was illustrated by the ways in which the terms 'welfare' and 'benefits' came to be defined in multiple ways through online discussion. While live tweeting reflected a definition of 'benefits' associated with those in receipt of state welfare payments, in the off-peak data we started to see how this was replaced with greater explicit discussion of the term 'welfare'. In this way, the terms 'benefits' and 'welfare' became loaded with different emotive contents (one negative, one positive) despite semantically referring to the same thing. This highlighted a significant shift in the ways in which issues to do with the politics of state welfare was being discussed—from seeing the people of James Turner Street as *receivers of benefits* to the state *looking after their welfare*. This was juxtaposed with a shift in the association of the word "benefits" with tax-breaks for the rich, politicians' expenses and bank bailouts. Unlike [31], we saw that the discussion alongside Benefits Street was an attempt at more than using Twitter to propagate views and information—more akin to [40], it was used by some to actively seek those with diverging views and attempt to promote and provoke reasoned discussion. However, contrasting with [40] rarely did discussion manifest in ways that were not polarised, likely due to the limited overlap between peak and off-peak Twitter users.

Countering with Mediatized Evidence

Our findings also highlighted how the emergence of more explicitly socio-political talk was often associated with increased referencing to external sources— e.g. tweets from beyond the #benefitsstreet hashtag, the introduction of other prominent Twitter user handles into the discussion, and of course weaving in discussion from commentaries from TV and radio, news sites and blog posts. It was also notable how the references to external sources increased outside of the peak periods. As noted, during the peak period, 25% of tweets included a URL to another data source. However, in the off-peak period, this doubled, along with dramatic increases in the cross-fertilisation of different hashtags related to other programming (e.g. #bbcqt appearing 1,195 times). We consider these noteworthy for two reasons.

Firstly, references to external sources were used to counteract the portrayal of people in the programme. This included links to alterative narratives of experiences of living on welfare payments, to campaigns about the biases inherent in the show and petitions for more representative portrayals. On other occasions, links to third-party sources highlighted the problematic impacts such portrayals can have on the disenfranchised, or the economic impact of other forms of government spending. Throughout both peak and off peak datasets, it was clear that the use of external links was a primary form of countering the portrayal of benefit seekers with evidence. While studies of socio-political talk on Facebook groups have highlighted how the features of that site draw people towards focusing, closing and excluding discussion [7], here we saw Twitter being appropriated to distribute alternative perspectives on benefits. This is more pronounced during off-peak periods, where users indulge in a 'mediatizing move' where they decentralise the topic of Benefits Street and connect it to wider issues across a range of media. In many respects, this evidence was being produced to counter what was considered as a lack of evidence on other users' behalf, or even a lack of evidential basis in the documentary itself. This also reflects prior work noting that more considered comments on Twitter tend to be produced more slowly and are thus less likely to be immediately responsive to the media under discussion [11].

Secondly, the peak dataset was characterised by tweets demonstrating practices consistent with 'live tweeting' an event. Users during 'peak' periods tended not to rely on outside resources to reinforce their statements and claims—rather, they were voicing opinions and comments for purposes that did not require this level of referential support. As noted, these tweets were typically remarks on the specifics of events in the programme rather than connecting to wider debates or contexts. This gives us a depiction of the 'peak' period of tweeting as being one typified by kneejerk reactions grounded in the experience of watching the programme unfold in real-time—resulting in discussion which is tightly and centrally organised around issues arising in the programme. These users also rarely tweeted outside of these periods—suggesting that once they were done watching the show, then so was their interest and commentary. This highlights how much—but not all—of our data is heavily mediatized political talk [27], in that much of it was temporally related to media representations. As such, we might assume that kneejerk tweeters rarely engaged, or came into contact, with the evidenced based commentaries that increased in number during the off-peak periods. Therefore, while some users offer evidence of alternative accounts and understandings of the issues being discussed, these likely do not reach those whose opinions they may be challenging and contesting.

Designing for an Online Talkative Electorate

Our findings present opportunities for designing technologies that might further support political talk and debate. Here we present a series of sensitivities that could drive forward the (re)design of social media platforms with a view to enhancing the potential to support more balanced, nuanced and reflective everyday socio-political talk. In constructing our sensitivities (listed below), we draw on DiSalvo's notion that 'the political is a *condition* of life' which is 'expressed and experienced in the dealings between people and organizations in a multiplicity of ways including debate, dissensus and protest' [9, p.8]. We build on this in the specific context of everyday talk emphasised by our study. It was clear during our analysis that while there is much socio-political 'talk', this does not always translate into 'talkative'. As such, we present a number of design principles with which to promote talkative qualities through encouraging contestation and dissensus, which are fundamental parts of the democratic process [16].

Encountering talk: One immediate way of addressing the disconnection between the different qualities of talk arising from commentaries on #benefitsstreet would be to simply raise awareness that different types of talk are occurring. This could be implemented through the notion of 'encountering'—to be suddenly confronted with a comment or tweet that has been determined as distinctly divergent from views previously expressed. This evokes work such as ConsiderIt [18], which confronts users with diverging opinions in order to support greater deliberation around state elections. However, here we wish to illustrate the potential of this occurring more prominently in everyday online discussion, rather at the point of explicit witting engagement with political debate.

Contrasting talk: Developing the above, we also might imagine ways of providing simple tools that allow different forms and modes of talk be visually contrasted with one-another. In simple terms, one way of incorporating this into an existing micro-blogging service like Twitter would be to present subsets of 'trending' hashtags associated with a particular program (e.g. #benefitssteet #scroungers or #benefitsstreet #bbcqt) which are likely to confront users with different aspects of the discussion that are occurring. This might act as a means to demonstrate that trending topics may in fact be representative of a much larger range of different views which might be worth consideration. This suggestion, of course, also draws on well-known aspects of the 'filter-bubble' problem [38] commonly generated by collaborative social platforms and recommender systems, as well as other suggestions (e.g. [33]) on how to solve it.

Contesting talk: A related quality that may be beneficial to support is the contestation of talk. We saw how while there was clearly contestation from some Twitter users of other peoples' posts, in many respects this was lost in the mass of peak tweets, or because of a lack of awareness. We might imagine that a social media service could have a 'contestation' feature. This might have similar functionality to a 'report' button—however, this would not be done for the purposes of complaining to administrators but instead to raise awareness of a post e.g. due to its controversy or because it represents a poorly articulated view. A contested tweet may be 'pinned' alongside a live tweeted discussion for more users to see and be prompted to responded to.

Interpretative talk: One finding was that while some users posted reflective commentaries on Benefits Street, a large number of peak time tweets simply responded directly to what the show presented to them. As such, it would be interesting to explore ways of prompting deeper and more interpretative interrogations of media. For example, we could envisage a social media service that asks specific questions. In the case of Benefits Street this might be questions such as "Who do you believe funded this programme?"; "Have the issues of state welfare affected anyone you know personally?" This could be used to drive the design of *companion apps* for specific events and programming that might use existing social media services but overlay discussion with other media and content.

Evidencing talk: We saw how those tweets that drew on third-party evidence when making comments were often more critical of the content of the show; in particular using their evidence to present a case for alternative perspectives on the issue under discussion. We argue that encouraging users to evidence certain tweets would be a provocative way of engaging them in both reflection upon their comments and also promoting greater engagement from others. We could imagine a scenario where for certain hashtags those adding comments would be prompted to submit evidence as URLs. However, as [7] highlights in the appropriation of media and 'like' functions on Facebook, we might consider accompanying apps designed specifically for evidence-based talk, which provide a rich range of media objects to be attached and made immediately accessible as part of an ongoing conversation—such as the incorporation of images, videos, and data visualisations. This might support contestation in the form of uploading evidence that contradicts certain statements (e.g. graphs of public spending; videos of welfare claimants volunteering for work) or provoke reflection i.e. highlighting the ways that a much wider sphere of individuals rely on welfare. As well as evidencing, however, it is important to scaffold others engagement — therefore, richly emphasising the evidence in discussion and prompting others to read, view and actively respond to this would be critical.

Maintaining talk: Finally, an issue that is particularly problematic in the context of promoting debate and discussion alongside TV programming is keeping discussion alive once a broadcast is over. In the context of Benefits Street, we did see discussion continue—however, it was separate from that found when the programme was broadcast—and indeed, in many cases this appeared to be discarded when the next episode started. One possible way to maintain talk could be to link those commenting in different time periods more explicitly. This would support more asynchronous interaction and discussion—and would potentially bridge the gap in audiences between responsive 'kneejerk' reactions and more reflective commentaries. For example, we might imagine certain tweets or comments that visibly 'last', 'hang' or 'persist' in relation to a specific hashtag. Alternatively, we could see carefully constructed 'evidencing talk' that is timed to be repeatedly deployed during a 'live tweeting' event. Related to this, work in [35] shows how companion apps can assist in maintaining attention and recognition across instances of broadcasts.

CONCLUSION

We investigated how Twitter discussion and TV interact with one-another in ways that support socio-political talk. Our findings highlight how online discussion during, and between, TV broadcasts was characterised by distinctly different qualities, topics of discussion and user behaviours. A large amount of what we saw could be characterised as being abuse; or, perhaps, jokingly pejorative. This behaviour was mostly targeted towards people depicted in the programme, as well as towards the broader social class that those individuals supposedly represent. This reflects the findings of prior work on the 'Othering' of minorities on Twitter [13]; but it also reflects a substantive body of research showing that current attitudes towards the poor in the UK are unsympathetic at best and hostile at worst [30]. While at one level such talk is abuse, or at best an illustration of problematic stereotypes that permeate society, as everyday talk it is also inherently socio-political.

While social media sites like Twitter provide an way of propagating such socio-political talk, and indeed talk that counters these points of view, much could be done to facilitate more balanced, nuanced and reflective—but also deliberative—debate. Through opening up a space for exploring how talk might be contrasted, contested, interpreted, evidenced and maintained, we have suggested practical directions to inform future design work. Looking further forward, generating a deeper understanding of how digital platforms and interaction design can contribute to political engagement, debate and activism is an increasingly urgent line of research for the HCI community. Our own work for instance, raises broad questions about how class, welfare, and poverty are debated in a mediatized society; we call for further research, in particular, which investigates cross-platform, as well as cross-media, engagement with these issues, as well as recognition that the constant shifting picture of social media use (e.g. uptake of media sharing services such as Instagram) will demand new approaches to users studies, data collection and interpretation.

REFERENCES

1. Ampofo, L., Anstead, N., O'Loughlin, B. Trust, confidence & confidentiality: Citizen responses on twitter to opinion polls during the 2010 UK general election. *Information, comm & soc*, 14 (2011), 850-871.
2. Anstead, N., and O'Loughlin, B. The emerging viewertariat and BBC Question Time: *The International Journal of Press/Politics*, 16 (2011), 1-23.
3. Björgvinsson, E., Ehn, P., and Hillgren, P. A. Agonistic participatory design: working with marginalised social movements. *CoDesign*, 8 (2012), 127-144.
4. Blumler, J. G., & Coleman, S. (2001). Realising democracy online: A civic commons in cyberspace (Vol. 2). London: IPPR.
5. Bourdieu, P. (1999) *On Television.* London: New Press.
6. Braun, V. & Clarke, V. Using thematic analysis in psychology. *Qualitative Research in Psychology*. 3 (2006), 77 – 101.
7. Crivellaro, C., Comber, R., Bowers, J., et al. A pool of dreams: Facebook, politics and the emergence of a social movement. *Proc. CHI '14*, ACM, 3573-3582.
8. Dahlberg, L. The Internet and democratic discourse: Exploring the prospects of online deliberative forums extending the public sphere. *Information, Communication & Society*, 4(2001), 615-633.
9. DiSalvo, C. *Adversarial design*. MIT Press, 2013.
10. Disalvo, C., Nourbakhsh, I., Holstius, D., et al. The neighborhood networks project: a case study of critical engagement and creative expression through participatory design. *Proc. PDC '08*, ACM, 41-50.
11. Doughty, M., Rowland, D., and Lawson, S. Co-viewing live TV with digital backchannel streams. In *Proc. EuroITV '11*, ACM, 141-144.

12. Doughty, M., Rowland, D., Lawson, S. Who is on your sofa? TV audience communities and second screening social networks. *Proc. EuroITV '12*, ACM, 79-86.
13. Doughty, M., Lawson, S., Linehan, C., et al. Disinhibited abuse of othered communities by second-screening audiences. *Proc. TVX '14*, ACM, 164-171.
14. Dunne, A., and Raby, F. *Hertzian Tales.* RCA Press, London, UK, 2005.
15. Ekman, J., and Amnå, E. Political participation and civic engagement: Towards a new typology. *Human affairs*, 22 (2012), 283-300.
16. Elster, J. (Ed.). (1998). *Deliberative democracy* Cambridge University Press.
17. Foth, M., Parra Agudelo, L., Palleis, R. Digital soapboxes: towards an interaction design agenda for situated civic innovation. *Proc. UbiComp '13*, 725-728.
18. Freelon, D., Travis, K., Morgan, J., Bennett, W., and Borning, A. Facilitating Encounters with Political Difference: Engaging Voters with the Living Voters Guide. *Proc. JITP '11*, paper 5.
19. Fuchs, C. *Social media: A critical introduction.* 2013.
20. Gold, T. After Benefits Street, it's another round of poverty porn – with added celebrity. *The Guardian*, London, 2014: http://tinyurl.com/neoza7q
21. Graham, T and Wright S. Analysing 'Super-Participation' in Online Third Spaces in: Cantijoch, M., Gibson, R. & S. Ward (eds.) Palgrave Macmillan, 2014.
22. Graham, T. Everyday Political Talk in the Internet-Based Public Sphere. To be published in: Stephen Coleman and Deen Freelon (Eds). *Handbook of Digital Politics*. Cheltenham, UK: Edward Elgar (forthcoming).
23. Habermas, J. *The structural transformation of the public sphere.* MIT Press, 1991.
24. Halpern, D., and Gibbs J. Social media as a catalyst for online deliberation? Exploring the affordances of Facebook and YouTube for political expression. *Computers in Human Behavior,* 29 (2013), 1159-1168.
25. Hjarvard, S. (2013). *The mediatization of culture and society*. Routledge.
26. Howard, P.N., Duffy, A., Freelon, D., Hussain, M., Mari, W. & Mazaid, M. Opening Closed Regimes: What Was the Role of Social Media During the Arab Spring?. 2011. Seattle: PIPTI.
27. Jackson, D., Scullion, R., & Molesworth, M. (2013). 15 'Ooh, politics. You're brave'. Politics in everyday talk. *The Media, Political Participation and Empowerment*.
28. Janssen, D., and Kies, R. Online forums and deliberative democracy. *Acta política*, 40. 2005. 317-335.
29. Jensen, T. Welfare Commonsense, Poverty Porn and Doxosophy. *Sociological Research Online*, 19(2014), 3.
30. Jones, O. *Chavs: The demonization of the working class.* Verso Books, London, 2012.
31. Lotan, G., Graeff, E., Ananny, M., et al. The Arab Spring| the revolutions were tweeted: Information flows during the 2011 Tunisian and Egyptian revolutions. *International Journal of Communication*, 5, 2011 31.
32. Massung, E., Coyle, D., Cater, K., et al. Using crowdsourcing to support pro-environmental community activism. *Proc. CHI '13*, ACM, 371-380.
33. Munson, S.A., Lee, S.Y. and, Resnick. P. Encouraging Reading of Diverse Political Viewpoints with a Browser Widget. *Proc ICWSM '13*. AAAI.
34. Mooney, G. *Stigmatising poverty? The 'Broken Society' and reflections on anti-welfarism in the UK today*. Oxfam, London, 2011.
35. Nandakumar, A., and Murray, J. Companion apps for long arc TV series: supporting new viewers in complex storyworlds with tightly synchronized context-sensitive annotations. *Proc of TVX 2014*, ACM, 3-10.
36. Nielsen. The follow back: understanding the two way causal influence between Twitter activity and TV viewship. http://tinyurl.com/ps59dmk
37. Papacharissi, Z. (2002). The virtual sphere The internet as a public sphere. *New media & society*, 4(1), 9-27.
38. Pariser, E. *The filter bubble: What the Internet is hiding from you*. Penguin, London, 2011.
39. Schirra, S., Sun, H., and Bentley, F. Together alone: Motivations for live-tweeting a television series. In *Proc. CHI '14*, ACM Press, 2441-2450.
40. Semaan, B. C., Robertson, S. P., Douglas, S., & Maruyama, M. Social media supporting political deliberation across multiple public spheres: towards depolarization. *Proc CSCW 14*. 1409-1421. ACM Press.
41. Seymour, D. *Reporting poverty in the UK*. Joseph Rowntree Foundation, London, 2009.
42. Shamma, D., Kennedy, L., & Churchill, E. Tweetgeist: Can the twitter timeline reveal the structure of broadcast events. *CSCW Horizons*. 2010.
43. Shirky, C. Political Power of Social Media-Technology, the Public Sphere, and Political Change, *The. Foreign Aff.,* 90, 28. 2011.
44. Suler, J. The Online Disinhibition Effect. *CyberPsychology & Behavior*, 7 (2004), 321-326.
45. Twitter. The Search API. Available at https://dev.twitter.com/rest/public/search
46. Tumasjan, A., Sprenger, T. O., et al. Predicting Elections with Twitter: What 140 Characters Reveal about Political Sentiment. *Proc of ICWSM '10*, 178-185.
47. Wulf, V., Aal, K., Ktesh, I.A., et al. Fighting against the wall: social media use by political activists in a Palestinian village. *Proc. CHI '13*, ACM, 1979–1988.

Recognizing Depression from Twitter Activity

Sho Tsugawa
University of Tsukuba
Ibaraki 305-8573, Japan
s-tugawa@cs.tsukuba.ac.jp

Yusuke Kikuchi
Kwansei Gakuin University
Hyogo 669-1337, Japan
bfc72150@kwansei.ac.jp

Fumio Kishino
Kwansei Gakuin University
Hyogo 669-1337, Japan
kishino@kwansei.ac.jp

Kosuke Nakajima*
Osaka University
Osaka 565-0871, Japan
nakajima.kosuke@ist.osaka-u.ac.jp

Yuichi Itoh
Osaka University
Osaka 565-0871, Japan
itoh@ist.osaka-u.ac.jp

Hiroyuki Ohsaki
Kwansei Gakuin University
Hyogo 669-1337, Japan
ohsaki@kwansei.ac.jp

ABSTRACT
In this paper, we extensively evaluate the effectiveness of using a user's social media activities for estimating degree of depression. As ground truth data, we use the results of a web-based questionnaire for measuring degree of depression of Twitter users. We extract several features from the activity histories of Twitter users. By leveraging these features, we construct models for estimating the presence of active depression. Through experiments, we show that (1) features obtained from user activities can be used to predict depression of users with an accuracy of 69%, (2) topics of tweets estimated with a topic model are useful features, (3) approximately two months of observation data are necessary for recognizing depression, and longer observation periods do not contribute to improving the accuracy of estimation for current depression; sometimes, longer periods worsen the accuracy.

Author Keywords
Social media; Depression; Twitter; Machine learning

ACM Classification Keywords
H.5.m. Information Interfaces and Presentation (e.g. HCI): Miscellaneous

INTRODUCTION
Depression has become recognized as a major public health problem around the world [21]. A 2012 survey conducted by the World Health Organization (WHO) suggests that depression affects 350 million globally [21]. Among other associated problems, depression can lead to suicide [32], and so the high number of people with depression is considered to be a serious problem. Also in Japan, depression and suicide are recognized as serious problems. An OECD (Organisation for Economic Co-operation and Development) report shows that the standardized suicide rate per hundred thousand people in Japan is 20.9 in 2011, which is much higher than OECD average of 12.4 [24]. Suicide of young people is particularly serious since for 15–39 year old people in Japan, the top cause of death is suicide [15]. To cope with such a serious problem, the government of Japan is making strong efforts on the care of depression [15] since depression is considered to be a major cause of suicide [32].

Before depression can be effectively treated, it must be recognized in individuals [18, 34, 36]. The WHO reports that the majority of people who need treatment for depression do not receive it [21]. Even during visits with primary care physicians, depression is often unrecognized and undiagnosed; as a result, many people with depression do not receive adequate treatment [36]. Hence, for the effective treatment of depression in the population, it is important that people know how to recognize symptoms of depression in themselves and those around them.

Several measures for estimating signs of depression in individuals have been proposed in the form of questionnaires [2, 17, 30, 40]. Among such questionnaires, there are many scales for estimating severity of depression: the Center for Epidemiologic Studies Depression Scale (CES-D) [30], Beck's Depression Scale (BDI) [2], Zung's Self-rating Depression Scale (SDS) [40], and Hamilton's Depression Rating Scale (HDRS) [17] are the more popular. Results on these scales are obtained from answers to the questionnaires, either through self-reporting or third-party observation.

These subjective measures are widely used and are expected to achieve high estimation accuracy. Nevertheless, developing techniques for recognizing depression in individuals by using objective, rather than subjective, information is important. One reason for this is that questionnaires are often costly, and sometimes significantly so. In contrast, a method for recognizing depression in individuals by examining objective information, such as records of daily activities, could be applied for a very low cost in many cases. A technique to identify symptoms of depression in individuals from objec-

*Currently with Mitsubishi Electric Corporation

CHI 2015, April 18–23, 2015, Seoul, Republic of Korea.

http://dx.doi.org/10.1145/2702123.2702280

tive information would hasten recognition of depression by individuals and thereby allow earlier access to effective treatment.

As objective information for identifying depression in individuals, we focus on large-scale records of users' activities in social media. In recent years, social media has become increasingly popular, and therefore both large-scale and fine-grained records of users' activities are available [26]. Many researchers are interested in analyzing such large-scale data, and prior analyses have used those for purposes such as estimating the future movement of stock market indices and predicting the results of elections [6, 23, 38, 39, 33]. Since social media are often used for expressing emotions, the records of users' activities are a promising source for information that could be used to recognize symptoms of depression in the users.

The use of data from social media to estimate severity of depression in social media users has been studied before. For example, Tsugawa *et al.* [37] found that frequency of word usage in messages (hereinafter, tweets) on the popular microblogging service Twitter could be used for recognizing depression among users. Pioneering work by De Choudhury *et al.* [14] describes how to construct support vector machine (SVM) classifiers that can be used to identify users with depression using features obtained from the records of individual users' activities on Twitter. That research shows the potential for recognizing symptoms of depression in a user by examining the user's social media activities.

The results of prior research suggest that the use of social media for recognizing depression is a promising approach. However, research into these techniques is just beginning, and so extensive evaluation is necessary. As an example, the sensitivity of results to the period over which a user's social media activities are analyzed is not yet known. Additionally, the generality of the results of [14] should be verified by analyzing other datasets. It should be important to share and accumulate the results from several datasets among researchers particularly in such an emerging research field.

In this paper, we extensively evaluate the effectiveness of using a user's social media activities for estimating degree of depression. As ground truth data, we use the results of a web-based questionnaire for measuring degree of depression; this questionnaire was completed by the Twitter users who agreed to participate. From these data and user activity histories, we investigate the relation between features of each user's activity and that user's score on the depression questionnaire. We construct several models to predict users with depression from the features of the user's activity. For this purpose, we use SVM and investigate the estimation accuracy of the models. Our main contributions are summarized as follows.

- We show that features obtained from user activities can be used to predict depression of users with an accuracy of 69%, which is similar to the rate in [14]. While De Choudhury *et al.* [14] use data about English-speaking users, we use data about Japanese-speaking users. Together, these results suggest that the use of data from social media is an effective approach for users with different backgrounds (here, English-speaking and Japanese-speaking users).

- We show the effectiveness of using topics, as identified in tweets by a topic model [5], as features for the SVM. Our results show that applying a simple bag-of-words model (i.e., word frequencies) to tweets results in overfitting, but using topics inferred from word frequencies prevents overfitting and improves estimation accuracy.

- We investigate the relation between the number of tweets used for estimation and the estimation accuracy. We suggest an appropriate amount of tweets for recognizing depression. Additionally, we find that about two months of observation data are necessary for recognizing depression, and longer observation periods do not contribute to improving the accuracy of estimation for current depression; sometimes, longer periods worsen the accuracy.

RELATED WORK

In the areas of medicine and psychology, several questionnaire-based measures for rating depression in individuals have been proposed [2, 17, 30, 40]. CES-D [30], BDI [2], and SDS [40] estimate the severity of depression in individuals from the self-reported answers to 20 questions. HDRS uses the answers given by a third party to 17 questions for the same purpose [17].

Approaches that use objective information, such as log data about an individual's activities to estimate depression severity have been studied recently. Resnik *et al.* [31] propose a method for identifying depression in individuals by analyzing textual data from essays written by the individuals. Resnik *et al.* obtain topics for the essays by applying a popular topic-extraction model, latent Dirichlet allocation (LDA) [5]. By using the discovered topics as features in machine learning, depression severity is estimated. That research is an important work that shows the potential for using texts written by an individual to estimate severity of depression in that person. However, the essays are typically difficult to obtain.

Due to the widespread adoption of social media and the availability of large-scale data from social media, approaches that use such data for depression screening are receiving increased attention from researchers. Moreno *et al.* [22] shows that college students display symptoms consistent with depression on Facebook, a popular social networking service. Park *et al.* [27] analyze differences between Twitter users with and without depression by analyzing their activities. In Park *et al.* [28], a similar analysis is performed by analyzing data from Facebook. Using multiple regression analysis, Tsugawa *et al.* [37] show that frequencies of word usage on Twitter are useful features for recognizing depression among users. The main objective of such research is to clarify which features that can obtained from user activity are useful for estimating the severity of depression.

De Choudhury *et al.* [14] are pioneering in demonstrating the estimation accuracy that could be achieved by using activities on Twitter to predict depression among users. In their study,

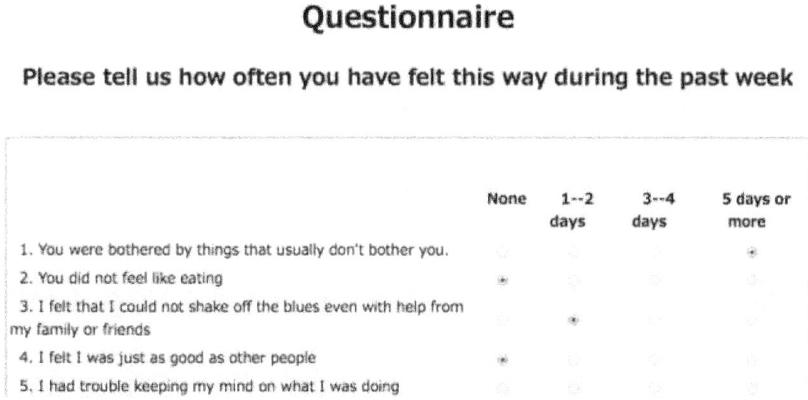

Figure 1. A screenshot of our website. The questionnaires to determine degree of depression (CES-D questionnaires) were completed by participants through their web browsers. (Originally all messages shown in this figure were written in Japanese.)

De Choudhury *et al.* obtained training data for machine learning by appealing to large numbers of people for help (popularly known as crowdsourcing). Then, models that could be used to predict risk of depression were identified from several features obtained from the records of user activity on Twitter by using SVM. Experimental results show that depression can be recognized among users with an accuracy of approximately 70%. Such approaches are applied to prediction of postpartum depression from Facebook and Twitter data [11, 13]. De Choudhury *et al.* have also proposed a method for estimating the depressive tendencies of populations by a similar approach [12]. Twitter data are also suggested to be effective for estimating health-related statistics [10, 29].

Our study builds on the mentioned prior work and contributes to enhancing methods for predicting depression risk from objective information, particularly large-scale data from social media. Research into using social media data for recognizing depression in individuals is just beginning, and so whenever possible the effectiveness of such approaches should be validated for several datasets. In this study, we adopt an approach similar to that in De Choudhury *et al.* [14] and apply it to Japanese-speaking Twitter users. Note that this is not the first study on depression of non-English social media users since differences between Korean social media users with and without depression have been analyzed in [27, 28]. This study extends the prediction framework of [14] to Japanese-speaking users. We also examine the effectiveness of using topics of tweet messages as a feature for estimating depression risk. Additionally, we investigate the effects on accuracy of observation period and number of data items used for estimation; this has not yet been fully investigated.

METHODOLOGY

Data Gathering

In this study, we gathered information on depression levels of Twitter users and their activity histories. To do this, we published a website to administer a questionnaire and disseminated information about the website over Twitter[1]. In contrast to De Choudhury *et al.* [14], who collected data from English-speaking users through crowdsourcing, this study collected data from Japanese-speaking volunteers. This approach was used to investigate the extent to which depression risk can be estimated for a population different from the population considered by the prior research [14]. Figure 1 shows a screenshot of our website.

The website collected the responses to a questionnaire to evaluate the degree of depression of the Twitter users who participated (hereinafter, the participants) and to collect the histories of participants activities on Twitter. The activity histories of participants were collected through the Twitter application programming interface (API)[2], and the questionnaires to determine degree of depression were completed by participants through their web browsers.

Before data collection, visitors to the website were presented with a written explanation of the aims of the experiment, the information that would be collected, and how that information would be handled. Those who consented to become participants after receiving the explanation logged into their individual Twitter accounts through the OAuth authorization process. Next, participants were surveyed on gender, age, occupation, and history of depression, following which they answered a questionnaire designed to evaluate degree of depression. A message called the "kokoro score," ("kokoro" is a Japanese word meaning "heart") determined on the basis of answers to the questionnaire and information in the collected tweets, was displayed to participants after completion of the questionnaire (Fig. 2). Experiment participants were able to tweet the message displayed, which made it possible to promote the website over Twitter by word-of-mouth in a type of snowball sampling.

The CES-D questionnaire was used to evaluate the degree of depression [30]. In the CES-D test, participants answered 20 questions on a Likert-type 4-point scale. Each answer was assigned a score of 0-3 points, with the sum of the points from all answers used as the score to estimate likelihood of depression. Several standards exist by which to determine the appro-

[1]Administration of the website and processing of the obtained data were performed under the approval by the ethical committee in the organization to which authors belong.

[2]`https://dev.twitter.com/docs/api/1.1`

Figure 2. A screenshot of our website showing *kokoro score* to user Mr. ABC. Several candidate messages for display were prepared in advance, and a message was selected from among these and displayed to the participant according to the questionnaire answers and textual information contained in the tweets. The aim of this message was to provide participants an incentive to answer the questionnaire. (Originally all messages shown in this figure were written in Japanese.)

priate cutoff score for identifying depression. In this research, we regarded a score of 22 points or higher as indicating active depression and a score of 21 points or lower as indicating no active depression; these are the same values as used in [14] and give a cutoff score of 22. In addition, answers to BDI [2], a depression scale used with characteristics similar to CES-D, were collected to ensure the reliability of data. For each participant, scores were calculated on both scales, with poor correlation regarded as indicating unreliable answers. The time taken to answer the questionnaires was also recorded, and those completed in too brief a time were excluded. After each participant answered the questionnaire, the activity history of that participant on Twitter was collected from Twitter by using the API. At most 3,200 tweets were collected for each participant, and the number of users following the participant and being followed by the participant were recorded. Tweets published after the questionnaire was taken were discarded.

The website was opened to the public on 4 December 2013, at which time the authors publicized it on their Twitter accounts. Between 4 December 2013 and 8 February 2014, 219 people participated in the experiment. After eliminating participants who did not tweet and participants who answered the questionnaire in fewer than 30 seconds (as previously mentioned, to ensure the reliability of the questionnaire answers), 214 sets of answers remained. Only the first set of answers was used for participants who completed the questionnaire more than once. As a result, data about 209 experiment participants (male: 121; female: 88) aged 16 to 55 (mean: 28.8 years; standard deviation: 8.2 years) were analyzed. The correlations between CES-D score and BDI score for these participants were high, 0.87, and there were no participants with uncorrelated scores, so the data for all 209 participants were used; excluded datasets are not discussed any further. Figure 3 shows the histogram of CES-D scores of 209 participants. Among the participants, 81 (resp. 128) were estimated to have (resp. not have) active depression, for an incidence of approximately 39%. This incidence is similar to that found by De Choudhury *et al.* [14], who identified depression in approximately 36% of participants. Table 1 gives statistics on the activity histories of participants.

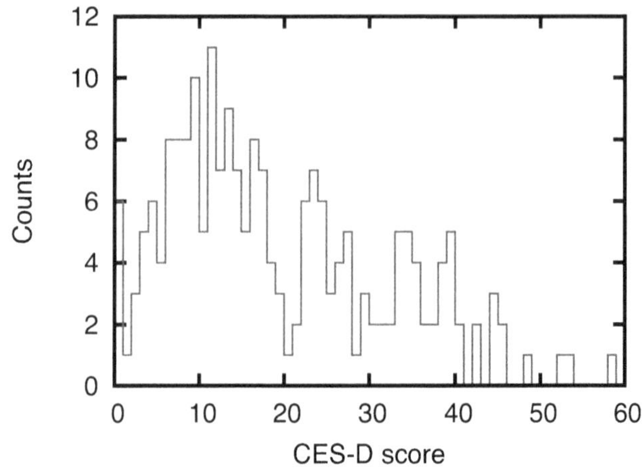

Figure 3. Histogram of CES-D scores of 209 participants

Table 1. Basic statistics about activities of participants

	Mean	Median	Std. dev.
Num. of tweets	2749.1	3191	850.2
Num. of tweets per day	18.0	7.8	27.5
Days spanned by tweets	569.2	348.2	502.0

Features for Recognizing Depression

It is possible to extract various features from the activity histories of Twitter users. This section explains what kinds of features are used to estimate degree of depression and the way in which these quantities are extracted. Table 2 shows the features used in this study. A detailed explanation of each feature follows.

The frequencies of words in a tweet (i.e., its bag of words) are used as a basic feature relating to the content of the tweet. Tsugawa *et al.* showed that the word frequencies are useful for identifying depression [37]. MeCab [20] was used to for morphological stemming and categorization of the Japanese tweet text to obtain accurate word frequencies. Particles, auxiliary verbs, adnominal adjectives, and visual symbols were excluded for extracting content words. Words used by only

Table 2. Features used for predicting depression

Name	Description
bag of words	Frequencies of words used in the tweet
topic	Ratio of tweet topics found by LDA [5]
positive	Ratio of positive-affect words contained in the tweet
negative	Ratio of negative-affect words contained in the tweet
hour	Hourly posting frequency
tweet frequency	Tweets per day
num. of words	Average number of words per tweet
RT	Overall retweet rate
mention	Overall mention rate
URL	Ratio of tweets containing a URL
followee	Number of users following
follower	Number of users followed

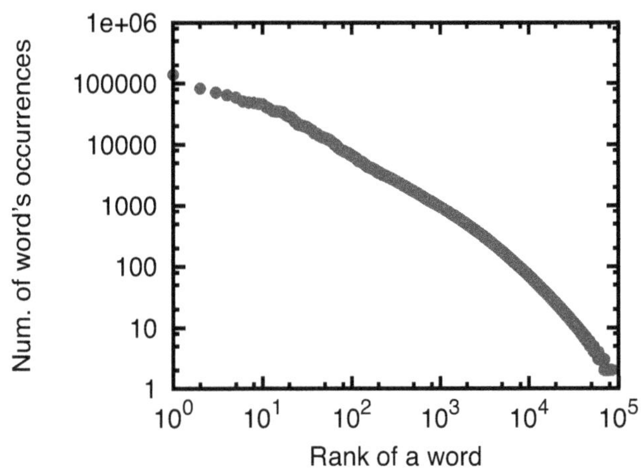

Figure 4. Distribution of word frequencies: Rank of a word based on its frequency vs. the total number of the word's occurrences in all tweets

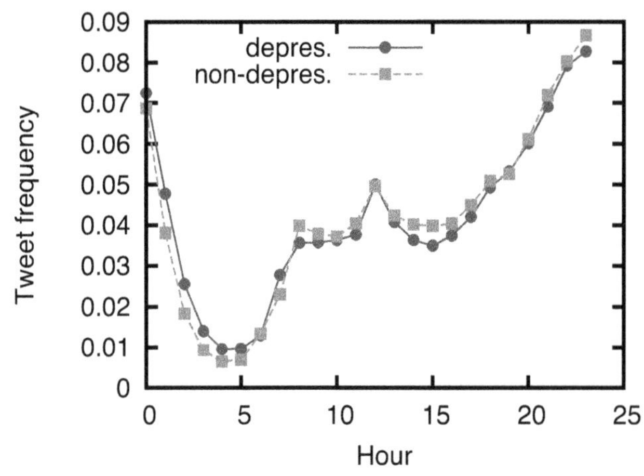

Figure 5. Hourly posting frequency: Comparison between participants with and without depression

one participant were also excluded, resulting in a total of 84,255 distinct words. However, most of these words were rarely used, and the distribution of word frequencies is extremely biased (see Fig. 4). Because words with a low rate of use were regarded as unlikely to be associated with depression for most users, the frequencies of only the 20,000 words with the highest rate of use (corresponding to 25 or more uses across all participants) were used as a feature in this study. Furthermore, because the number and length of tweets differed by participant, the word frequencies were normalized by the total number of words in the tweets.

The topics of the tweets of each user, as estimated by using a representative topic model LDA [5], were used as a second feature relating to the content of the tweets. With LDA, the distribution of topics in each document is estimated from the word frequencies in each text through unsupervised learning on the assumption that the text and the words in it are generated according to a particular topic [5]. In LDA, the number of topics to identify and a set of documents (as bags of words) are used as input, and a topic distribution is output for each document. As mentioned in Related Work Section, the topics of essays written by university students were estimated by using LDA and found to be useful in evaluating degree of depression [31]. From that study, topics are expected to be a useful feature. A set of all tweets of each user was used as the user document for input in LDA, and the 20,000 words selected as described above were used as the words. We used LDA with collapsed Gibbs sampling [16]. As the parameters of LDA, we used $\alpha = 50/K$ and $\beta = 0.1$, where K is the number of topics [16]. All extracted topics were used as the features.

The ratio of positive words and the ratio of negative words used in the tweet text are used as the final features relating to tweet content. Users with depression are intuitively expected to use negative words more frequently than users without depression do. To categorize words, a dictionary of affective words [19], which is compiled by manual evaluation of a dictionary of positive and negative words extracted according to a technique proposed in the literature [35], is used. The dictionary contains 760 positive words and 862 negative words.

The user's timing of tweets, frequency of tweets, average number of words, retweet rate (rate of republishing other users' tweets), mention rate (rate of directly referencing at least one other user), ratio of tweets containing a uniform resource locator (URL), number of users being followed, and number of users following are used as features independent of the content of the tweet. The relative ratios of tweets posted during each hour of the day were used to characterize the timing of tweets; the number of posts per day was used as the posting frequency; and the ratio of qualifying tweets to all tweets were used for the retweet ratio, mention ratio, and ratio of tweets containing a URL. These features are used in prior research [14].

RESULTS

Comparison of Features between Users with and without Depression

Differences in the features described in the previous section according to the presence or absence of depression were investigated. A complete discussion of individual-level differences in word frequencies and topics according to the presence of depression would be lengthy and could obfuscate the underlying results. Accordingly, in this section we focus on features other than the bags of words and topics. In the next section, we use the bags of words and topics to predict depression among participants and check those results.

First, a comparison was made of the posting frequency by time for all participants (Fig. 5). Figure 5 shows that the posting frequency was the highest at 11 p.m. and the lowest at 4 a.m. through 5 a.m. (all times are Japan Standard Time) among all participants, independent of the presence of depression. Almost no difference was found in posting frequency of the two groups. This differs from the results of [14], in which

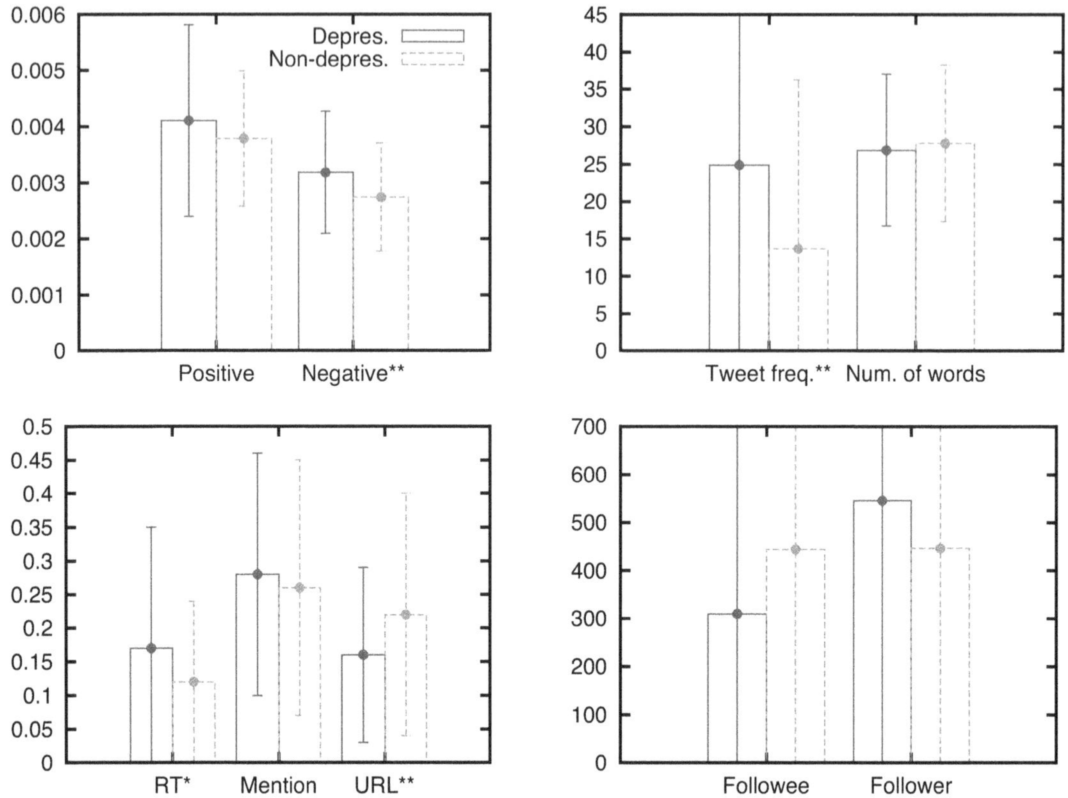

Figure 6. Feature means: Comparison between participants with and without depression (: $p < 0.01$, * : $p < 0.05$)**

a large difference between participants with and without depression was observed in relative frequencies by time. The difference in observed trends suggests that the feature relating to posting time is not robust.

Next, the averages of each feature, partitioned by depression status, are examined (see Fig. 6). A significant difference between the two groups was found for the relative ratio of negative words, posting frequency, retweet rate, and ratio of tweets containing a URL. Individual t-tests confirmed significant differences in these features according to the presence of depression, with a significance level of 5%. Furthermore, although not statistically significant in our study, a numerical difference can be seen between groups in the number of followees and followers. These features were found to be significant in [14], and these are expected to be useful features in the general case. Similarly, although a significant difference was observed in mention frequency in [14], no such difference was observed in this study. This suggests that mention frequency is not a robust feature, in the same way as posting time. The differences between this study and [14] might be caused by the cultural differences between Japanese-speaking and English-speaking users. However, further investigations are necessary to clarify the reason of the differences; i.e., whether these are really due to the cultural differences, or just due to the differences of the participants.

The above analysis identifies several features that may be helpful in recognizing depression in Twitter users. In the next section, we investigate the accuracy of estimating the presence of active depression from these features.

Prediction Accuracy

In this section, we investigate the degree of accuracy with which the presence of active depression can be ascertained from the features extracted from a user's activity history. Classifiers were constructed by machine learning with SVM for estimating the presence of active depression, and their classification accuracy was evaluated by 10-fold cross-validation. Several classifiers were constructed from the extracted features, and the classification accuracy of each was investigated. The precision, recall, F-measure, and accuracy of the estimations (where the CES-D scores are taken as ground truth with a cutoff score of 22) are used as indices to evaluate classification accuracy. The precision is the proportion of participants with depression among those classified as having depression; the recall is the proportion of participants with depression who were classified as having depression; the F-measure is the harmonic mean of the precision and the recall; and the accuracy is the rate of correct classification across all participants. We note here that classifying all participants as not having depression yields precision, recall, F-measure and accuracy of 0, 0, 0, and 0.61, respectively. In the complementary case, in which all participants are classified as having depression, the corresponding values are 0.39, 1, 0.56, and 0.39, in the same order.

Table 3 shows the classification accuracy of the constructed model. The classification accuracies are the average values given by 10-fold cross-validation carried out 100 times. There are a large number of combinations of all features, so only the results of the most accurate models and those models useful for discussion are shown. A radial basis function kernel was used for the SVM kernel.

Table 3 shows that the presence of active depression can be estimated by the most accurate model with 0.61 precision, 0.37 recall, 0.46 F-measure and 66% accuracy. Because the research of De Choudhury *et al.* and that of this study use different data, a simple comparison cannot be carried out, but these accuracies can be considered to be comparable level to those reported by De Choudhury *et al.* [14]. Since similar results were obtained from different datasets, estimating the presence of depression by examining users' activity histories on Twitter can be considered to be a useful technique.

Looking at the features used, it is found that the estimation accuracy of models using the bag of words as a feature is low. The cause of this may be that this approach results in overfitting. When using the bag of words feature, the feature dimensions are too high, which is known to degrade performance. In Tab. 3, limiting the number of words to 2,000 (rather than 20,000) improves accuracy with the bag of words feature, which confirms that overfitting is occurring. However, even after this adjustment, accuracy with that feature is low in comparison to the accuracy of models without it. In contrast, models using topics as a feature achieved a high accuracy. This means it may be possible to improve estimation accuracy by reducing the dimensions to the broad feature of topics, rather than using the narrow feature of word frequencies. Not only topics but also other features (positive, negative, tweet frequency, RT, URL, followee, and follower from Tab. 2) were found to result in more accurate models than using the bag of words, and these additional features may be useful when predicting the presence of depression. Together with topics, models using the number of followees and the posting frequency achieved the highest accuracy of the models investigated here.

Looking at the number of topics in the topic model, it was found that accuracy was the highest in this experiment when the number of topics was set at 10. This is probably because using a very small number of topics lowered the expressiveness of the model using a large number of topics made it difficult to capture the predominant topics.

Effects of the Amount of Data on Prediction Accuracy

Next, we varied the quantity of tweets used for learning and estimation, and investigated the resulting estimation accuracy in order to find the quantity of data needed to make accurate predictions. Features were extracted using the N most-recent tweets (prior to study participation) and applied these features to model learning and prediction. For users with fewer than N tweets, all available tweets were used. Here, we discuss the results for the following models: the 10-topic model (Model 1); a model using the features positive, negative, tweet frequency, RT, URL, followee, and follower (Model 2); and a 10-topic model including the features positive, negative, tweet frequency, RT, URL, followee, and follower with the highest estimation accuracy from the previous section (Model 3). Figure 7 shows the relation between N (the number of tweets used) and the F-measure (used to representing estimation accuracy).

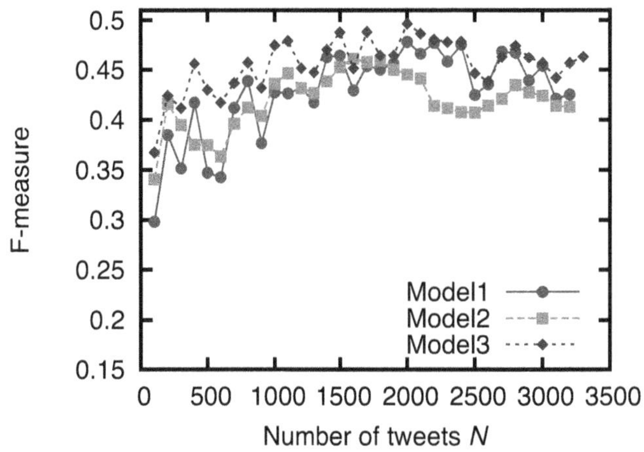

Figure 7. Number of tweets used for training and prediction vs. F-measure

From these results, it is found that the F-measure reaches approximately 0.45 when the number of tweets used is approximately 500–1000, and it remains almost unchanged even when the number of tweets used is further increased. This implies that observing around 500–1000 tweets is sufficient for recognizing depression, and observation of a higher number of tweets contributes negligibly to estimation accuracy.

The time span over which tweets were observed was also controlled, and the F-measure was calculated to assess the resulting estimation accuracy. The tweets used in learning and prediction were limited to those made in the W weeks prior to the day on which the participant answered the questionnaire, and the previously mentioned models were used for prediction. Figure 8 shows the relation between the time span W and the F-measure.

From this result, it is found that the F-measure reaches 0.4–0.5 when the tweets of the prior 6–16 weeks (1.5–4 months) are used, and lengthening the time span does not improve this; in some cases, longer time spans result in worse results. This indicates that using tweets from the most recent 6–16 weeks is sufficient for recognizing depression, and observations spanning a longer period may be less accurate. This could be because out-of-date information may not reflect the current state of depression; in such cases, the additional data do not contain information useful for prediction. The highest accuracy is achieved when using tweets from the recent 8 weeks, and the presence of active depression can be estimated by Model 3 with 0.64 precision, 0.43 recall, 0.52 F-measure and 69% accuracy.

Table 3. Classification accuracy of constructed models

Features	Precision	Recall	F-measure	Accuracy
bag of words (20,000 words)	0.04	0.0005	0.024	61%
bag of words (2,000 words)	0.58	0.13	0.21	62%
5 topics	0.50	0.13	0.21	61%
10 topics	0.55	0.35	0.43	64%
20 topics	0.54	0.33	0.41	63%
positive + negative + tweet frequency + RT + URL + followee + follower	0.57	0.33	0.41	64%
10 topics + positive + negative + tweet frequency + RT + URL + followee + follower	0.61	0.37	0.46	66%

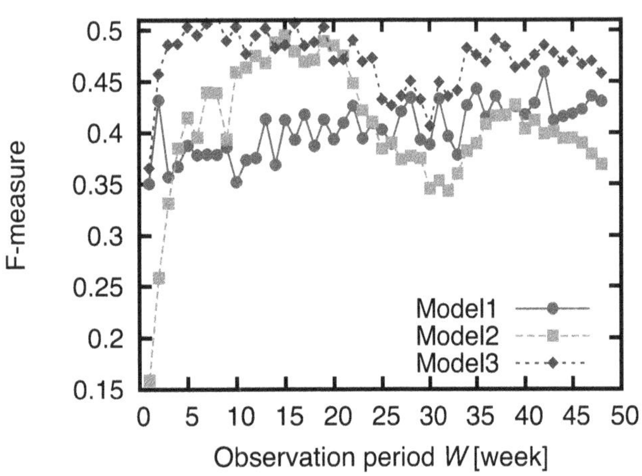

Figure 8. Observation period W [week] vs. F-measure

DISCUSSION

This study investigated the degree to which the activity history of Twitter users is useful in recognizing depression. The results showed that the activity history of users can be used to recognize the presence of depression with an accuracy of approximately 69%. The fact that similar results were obtained between user groups with different languages and backgrounds, as here and in [14], strongly suggests that using social media activity is a valid approach to recognizing depression. Sociological studies show that the rate of self-disclosure of Japanese is lower than that of American (e.g., [1]); i.e., Japanese people talk less about themselves than American people. In contrast, Japanese people post tweets very frequently. The ratio of Japanese tweets around the world is 14% in 2011[3] although the population of Japanese is only 130 million. It should be noted that using social media data is an effective approach for people with such different cultural backgrounds. Note that we do not claim that our models achieved higher performance than those in [14], but just claim that our models achieved comparable performance with [14]. While it is difficult to directly compare the results in [14] and ours since the data are different from each other, the values of precision and recall reported in [14] are higher than ours.

[3] `http://semiocast.com/en/publications/2011_11_24_Arabic_highest_growth_on_Twitter`

There were several challenges to apply the framework of [14] to Japanese-speaking twitter users, and these challenges might affect the performance of our models. Our models didn't include several features used in [14]. Choudhury *et al.* [14] show that usage of 1st person pronoun and usage of 3rd person pronoun are useful features. However, as linguistic researches discuss (e.g., [25]), Japanese personal pronouns are significantly different at least from those in the Western languages. Japanese have a large number of forms for each person pronoun. For instance, in [25], 21 types of Japanese 1st person pronoun are listed, and we can observe more variety of forms of pronoun in social media texts. Moreover, the subject words are often missing in Japanese texts, and using pronouns for subject words is sometimes unnatural particularly in twitter-like short and casual texts. We therefore decided not to include such features in our models. Moreover, to the best of our knowledge, there are no available standard Japanese dictionaries like ANEW lexicon [7], and we therefore used a simple list of positive and negative words. These limitations might affect our model performance.

While linguistic-based features and some dictionary-based features were not used in our study, we adopted a topic modeling approach and demonstrated the usefulness of it. Our experimental results showed that the model including topics as the features of SVM achieves 2% higher accuracy and 0.05 point higher F-measure than the model without topics (see Tab. 3). Resnik *et al.* [31] show the usefulness of a topic model when recognizing depression by analyzing essays written by university students. This study extends that result to Twitter. A single tweet is short, but because a large number of tweets (around 1,000 here) can be used, it is possible to extract topics successfully, which should make Twitter data useful for recognizing depression. Using topic model is expected to be a promising approach also for recognizing depression of non-Japanese twitter users since Resnik *et al.* [31] have already shown the usefulness of a topic model to English documents, and topic modeling approaches are successful in other tasks such as predicting stock market prices [33] and public health statistics [29] from social media text data. We therefore expect that the accuracy of the model found in [14] could be increased by including topics as a feature.

The experimental results of this paper suggest that the length of the selected activity history is important. De Choudhury *et al.* [14] set the observation period at one year, but our experimental results indicate that accuracy is likely to be improved by adjusting this period appropriately. However, the period of tweets that is informative may differ by user. A more detailed analysis is necessary to isolate per-user differences.

This study has some limitations. First, there is still room for further improvement of the features used. De Choudhury *et al.* [14] reduced the dimensions of high-dimensional features by using principal component analysis and treated the results as SVM features. They also applied data abstraction techniques such as using the average, variance, and entropy of the features for each day. It is important to verify how effective these techniques would be on the data of this study.

It may also be important to demonstrate what kind of machine learning method is most effective for the purpose of recognizing depression. Rather than using only SVM, the use of the newest machine learning frameworks, such as deep learning [3, 4] and ensemble learning [8, 9], is expected to have the potential to further increase estimation accuracy. In particular, deep learning is known to be able to extract useful features from within a large quantity of features. The bag of words and other features that could not be applied effectively in this study may be more effective if deep learning is used in place of SVM.

Finally, this experiment was carried out using information from only 209 users; it is important to determine the degree to which the accuracy increases (if at all) by increasing the number of users to a larger number, such as 1,000 or 10,000 people. Collecting a large quantity of learning data is difficult to do because of the data characteristics, but the collection of larger-scale learning data may be important to obtain the best possible results from the approach described here.

CONCLUSION

This study investigated how useful the various features extracted from Twitter user history are for recognizing depression, and the degree of accuracy with which the presence of active depression could be detected by using these features. Our aim was to establish a method by which to recognize depression by analyzing the large-scale records of users' activities in social media. The following specific results were obtained: depression can be recognized in users with an accuracy of approximately 69%; topics extracted by a topic model are useful features; around two-months observation is sufficient for the tweets used in learning and prediction; and long observation periods may decrease accuracy.

The estimation of user depression over time is suggested for future research. The ability to estimate daily variations in depression may be a useful tool for self-diagnosis as well as for diagnosis by a medical professional. Determining techniques that could be used in a medical context to identify depression from social media users' activities is an important future task.

ACKNOWLEDGMENTS

The authors would like to thank participants of the experiments and ethical committee members. This work was partly supported by JSPS KAKENHI Grant Number 26870076 and Leave a Nest research grant Fuji Xerox award.

REFERENCES

1. Barry, D. T. Cultural and demographic correlates of self-reported guardedness among East Asian immigrants in the US. *International Journal of Psychology 38*, 3 (2003), 150–159.
2. Beck, A. T., Ward, C. H., Mendelson, M., Mock, J., and Erbaugh, J. An inventory for measuring depression. *Archives of General Psychiatry 4*, 6 (June 1961), 561–571.
3. Bengio, Y. Learning deep architectures for AI. *Foundations and Trends in Machine Learning 2*, 1 (Jan. 2009), 1–127.
4. Bengio, Y., Courville, A., and Vincent, P. Representation learning: A review and new perspectives. *IEEE Transactions on Pattern Analysis and Machine Intelligence 35*, 8 (Aug. 2013), 1798–1828.
5. Blei, D. M., Ng, A. Y., and Jordan, M. I. Latent dirichlet allocation. *The Journal of Machine Learning Research 3* (Jan. 2003), 993–1022.
6. Bollen, J., Mao, H., and Zeng, X. Twitter mood predicts the stock market. *Journal of Computational Science 2*, 1 (Mar. 2011), 1–8.
7. Bradley, M., Lang, P., and Cuthbert, B. Affective norms for english words (ANEW). *Gainsville, Fla, NIMH Centre for the Study of Emotion and Attention, University of Florida* (1999).
8. Breiman, L. Bagging predictors. *Machine Learning 24*, 2 (Aug. 1996), 123–140.
9. Breiman, L. Random forests. *Machine Learning 45*, 1 (Oct. 2001), 5–32.
10. Culotta, A. Estimating county health statistics with twitter. In *Proceedings of the SIGCHI Conference on Human Factors in Computing Systems (CHI'14)* (Apr. 2014), 1335–1344.
11. De Choudhury, M., Counts, S., and Horvitz, E. Predicting postpartum changes in emotion and behavior via social media. In *Proceedings of the SIGCHI Conference on Human Factors in Computing Systems (CHI'13)* (Apr. 2013), 3267–3276.
12. De Choudhury, M., Counts, S., and Horvitz, E. Social media as a measurement tool of depression in populations. In *Proceedings of the 5th Annual ACM Web Science Conference (WebSci'13)* (May 2013), 47–56.
13. De Choudhury, M., Counts, S., Horvitz, E. J., and Hoff, A. Characterizing and predicting postpartum depression from shared facebook data. In *Proceedings of the 17th ACM Conference on Computer Supported Cooperative Work & Social Computing (CSCW'14)* (Feb. 2014), 626–638.
14. De Choudhury, M., Gamon, M., Counts, S., and Horvitz, E. Predicting depression via social media. In *Proceedings of the 7th International AAAI Conference on Weblogs and Social Media (ICWSM'13)* (July 2013), 128–137.

15. Government of Japan. White paper on goverment measures for suicide, June 2014. Also available as http://www8.cao.go.jp/jisatsutaisaku/whitepaper/index-w.html (in Japanese).

16. Griffiths, T. L., and Steyvers, M. Finding scientific topics. *Proceedings of the National Academy of Sciences of the United States of America 101*, Suppl 1 (Apr. 2004), 5228–5235.

17. Hamilton, M. Development of a rating scale for primary depressive illness. *British Journal of Social & Clinical Psychology 6*, 4 (Dec. 1967), 278–296.

18. Houston, T. K., Cooper, L. A., Vu, H. T., Kahn, J., Toser, J., and Ford, D. E. Screening the public for depression through the Internet. *Psychiatric Services 52*, 3 (Mar. 2001), 362–367.

19. Inui, T., Umezawa, Y., and Yamamoto, M. Complaint sentence detection via automatic training data generation using sentiment lexicons and context coherence. *Journal of Natural Language Processing 20*, 5 (Dec. 2013), 683–705. (in Japanese).

20. Kudo, T. Mecab: Yet another part-of-speech and morphological analyzer. http://mecab.sourceforge.net/.

21. Marcus, M., Yasamy, M. T., van Ommeren, M., Chisholm, D., and Saxena, S. Depression: A global public health concern. Tech. rep., WHO Department of Mental Health and Substance Abuse, Oct. 2012. Also available as http://www.who.int/mental_health/management/depression/who_paper_depression_wfmh_2012.pdf.

22. Moreno, M. A., Jelenchick, L. A., Egan, K. G., Cox, E., Young, H., Gannon, K. E., and Becker, T. Feeling bad on Facebook: Depression disclosures by college students on a social networking site. *Depression and Anxiety 28*, 6 (June 2011), 447–455.

23. O'Connor, B., Balasubramanyan, R., Routledge, B. R., and Smith, N. A. From tweets to polls: Linking text sentiment to public opinion time series. In *Proceedings of the 4th International AAAI Conference on Weblogs and Social Media (ICWSM'10)* (May 2010), 122–129.

24. OECD. Health at a glance 2013, Nov. 2013.

25. Ono, T., and Thompson, S. A. Japanese (w)atashi/ore/boku 'I': They're not just pronouns. *Cognitive Linguistics 14*, 4 (2003), 321–348.

26. Pak, A., and Paroubek, P. Twitter as a corpus for sentiment analysis and opinion mining. In *Proceedings of the 7th International Conference on Language Resources and Evaluation (LREC'10)* (May 2010), 1320–1326.

27. Park, M., Cha, C., and Cha, M. Depressive moods of users portrayed in twitter. In *Proceedings of the ACM SIGKDD Workshop on Healthcare Informatics (HI-KDD'12)* (Aug. 2012), 1–8.

28. Park, S., Lee, S. W., Kwak, J., Cha, M., and Jeong, B. Activities on Facebook reveal the depressive state of users. *Journal of Medical Internet Research 15*, 10 (Oct. 2013), e217.

29. Paul, M. J., and Dredze, M. You are what you tweet: Analyzing twitter for public health. In *Proceedings of the 5th International AAAI Conference on Weblogs and Social Media (ICWSM'11)* (July 2011), 265–272.

30. Radloff, L. S. The CES-D scale a self-report depression scale for research in the general population. *Applied Psychological Measurement 1*, 3 (1977), 385–401.

31. Resnik, P., Garron, A., and Resnik, R. Using topic modeling to improve prediction of neuroticism and depression. In *Proceedings of the 2013 Conference on Empirical Methods in Natural Language Processing (EMNLP '13)* (Oct. 2013), 1348–1353.

32. Rihmer, Z. Can better recognition and treatment of depression reduce suicide rates? A brief review. *European Psychiatry 16*, 7 (Nov. 2001), 406–409.

33. Si, J., Mukherjee, A., Liu, B., Li, Q., Li, H., and Deng, X. Exploiting topic based twitter sentiment for stock prediction. In *Proceedings of the 51st Annual Meeting of the Association for Computational Linguistics (ACL'13)* (Aug. 2013), 24–29.

34. Simon, G., Goldberg, S., Tiemens, B., and Ustun, T. Outcomes of recognized and unrecognized depression in an international primary care study. *General Hospital Psychiatry 21*, 2 (Mar. 1999), 97–105.

35. Takamura, D., Inui, T., and Okumura, M. Extracting semantic orientations using spin model. *IPSJ Journal 47*, 2 (Feb. 2006), 627–637. (in Japanese).

36. Tiemens, B., Ormel, J., Jenner, J., Van der Meer, K., Van Os, T., Van Den Brink, R., Smit, A., and Van den Brink, W. Training primary-care physicians to recognize, diagnose and manage depression: does it improve patient outcomes? *Psychological Medicine 29*, 04 (July 1999), 833–845.

37. Tsugawa, S., Mogi, Y., Kikuchi, Y., Kishino, F., Fujita, K., Itoh, Y., and Ohsaki, H. On estimating depressive tendency of twitter users from their tweet data. In *Proceedings of the 2nd International Workshop on Ambient Information Technologies (AMBIT'12)* (Mar. 2013), 29–32.

38. Tumasjan, A., Sprenger, T., Sandner, P., and Welpe, I. Predicting elections with twitter: What 140 characters reveal about political sentiment. In *Proceedings of the 4th International AAAI Conference on Weblogs and Social Media (ICWSM'10)* (May 2010), 178–185.

39. Zhang, X., Fuehres, H., and Gloor, P. Predicting stock market indicators through twitter "I hope it is not as bad as I fear". *Procedia-Social and Behavioral Sciences 26* (2011), 55–62.

40. Zhung, W. W. K. A self-rating depression scale. *Archives of General Psychiatry 12*, 1 (1965), 63–70.

You Tweet What You Eat: Studying Food Consumption Through Twitter

Sofiane Abbar, Yelena Mejova, Ingmar Weber
Qatar Computing Research Institute, PO 5825, Doha, Qatar
{sabbar,ymejova,iweber}@qf.org.qa

ABSTRACT
Food is an integral part of our lives, cultures, and well-being, and is of major interest to public health. The collection of daily nutritional data involves keeping detailed diaries or periodic surveys and is limited in scope and reach. Alternatively, social media is infamous for allowing its users to update the world on the minutiae of their daily lives, including their eating habits. In this work we examine the potential of Twitter to provide insight into US-wide dietary choices by linking the tweeted dining experiences of 210K users to their interests, demographics, and social networks. We validate our approach by relating the caloric values of the foods mentioned in the tweets to the state-wide obesity rates, achieving a Pearson correlation of 0.77 across the 50 US states and the District of Columbia. We then build a model to predict county-wide obesity and diabetes statistics based on a combination of demographic variables and food names mentioned on Twitter. Our results show significant improvement over previous CHI research [10]. We further link this data to societal and economic factors, such as education and income, illustrating that areas with higher education levels tweet about food that is significantly less caloric. Finally, we address the somewhat controversial issue of the social nature of obesity (Christakis & Fowler [6]) by inducing two social networks using mentions and reciprocal following relationships.

Author Keywords
Dietary Health; Obesity; Food; Twitter; Social Networks

ACM Classification Keywords
H.3.1 Content Analysis and Indexing; H.3.5 Online Information Services; J.3 Life and Medical Sciences: Health

INTRODUCTION
Food is a part of our daily lives that determines our well-being, health, and longevity. It is an important social activity and an expression of our culture and beliefs. The study of dietary habits is important for both cultural understanding and for monitoring public health. Heart disease, diabetes, osteoarthritis, and even cancer have all been linked to weight gain[1] and the US Center for Disease Control and Prevention (CDC) estimates some 35.7% of adults in US are obese[2], with medical care and other expenses associated with obesity costing up to $190 billion a year [5]. To best address this issue, public health awareness campaigns use data on dietary behavior across various segments of US population to tailor their messages to particular focus groups [13]. Having detailed and accurate data on the cultural and individual behaviors that lead to unhealthy dietary habits is necessary for effective intervention programs.

Until now, large-scale dietary studies of food consumption used questionnaires and food diaries to keep track of the daily activities of their participants, which can be intrusive and expensive to conduct [12]. Alternatively, social media is notorious for providing its users with a means of documenting the minutiae of their daily lives, including their dietary choices.

Can we use social media – and Twitter in particular – to get insights into dietary habits of an entire country? After all, tweeting "I'm having a sandwich" has become a classic example of the "pointless babble" commonly found on Twitter.[3] Recent research into recipe search logs in US [27] and China [30] were able to show temporal and spatial peculiarities of regional cuisines, suggesting that dietary habits may be closely linked to culture, as it is propagated geographically. However, such studies lack demographic and other personal information of their users, and are limited to coarse-grain geo-spacial analysis. In this work we make a case for using social media to monitor dietary habits at both national and personal scale. We perform a large scale analysis of 210K Twitter users in the United States, tracking their 502M tweets. We augment this data using a variety of sources which allows us to consider the nutritional value of the foods mentioned in these tweets, demographic characteristics of the users who tweet them, their interests, and the social network induced by

CHI 2015, April 18–23, 2015, Seoul, Republic of Korea.
Copyright © 2015 ACM 978-1-4503-3145-6/15/04 ...$15.00.
http://dx.doi.org/10.1145/2702123.2702153

[1] `http://www.nhlbi.nih.gov/health/health-topics/topics/obe/risks.html`

[2] `http://www.cdc.gov/obesity/data/facts.html`

[3] A 2009 study found that 40% of all tweets fell under the label of "pointless babble", see `http://www.pearanalytics.com/blog/2009/twitter-study-reveals-interesting-results-40-\percent-pointless-babble/`. This study is feeding, pun intended, on a lot of such tweets.

their interactions. We show that these food mentions reflect the state of national health by correlating them with the state-wide obesity and diabetes rates, finding a substantial correlation at 0.77 and 0.66, respectively. We also compare our food-based lexicon with previous CHI research [10], and show that our lexicon outperforms the generic LIWC one. Additionally, the single caloric value estimator (which does not require training) achieves the same performance as the model trained using 64 categories of LIWC.

But is the data sensitive enough to pick out more personal dietary variations? To answer this question, we use demographic information from the 2010 US Census, extrapolate users' gender using their screen names, and characterize users' zip codes as being either urban or rural. We find gender differences among the Twitter users, with women generally tweeting about less caloric foods than men. Estimated education level also proves to be a significant factor, with fewer calories being mentioned in areas with higher education levels. Not only do we see a difference in the density of the foods mentioned by users, but we also find qualitative differences in their dietary selections. Alcoholic beverages tend to be mentioned in urban environments, whereas pizza and chocolate are popular in the rural ones. Users' self-disclosed interests are also related to their diets, with those who mention an interest in cooking decreasing the chance of being obese by 1.5%, which is in line with research showing that lack of cooking at home gives rise to obesity [11].

Does social network influence personal dietary habits of users? Unlike traditional surveys that focus on isolated, randomly chosen individuals, social networks come with a *network* structure. The links of this network allow to analyze individuals not just in isolation, but in the context of their social circle. It has been suggested in [15] that social trends can spread in society much like diseases, resulting in a *social infection*. By inducing two kinds of social networks – one using reciprocal communication and another using following relationships – we show the assortativity in the dietary habits of users far beyond that which would be expected by chance.

Barring several limitations, which we outline in the Discussion section, we hope this study provides a case for the use of social media in public health monitoring in the dietary domain. We show that it is possible not only to detect indications of country-wide health trends, but zoom in on demographic and interest groups, potentially informing public health awareness campaigns.

RELATED WORK

Unlike in the animal kingdom, as omnivores, humans make nutritional selection not only based on their physiological needs, but also based on their culture and identity. As Fischler [14] puts it, by selecting and cooking food, one "transfers nutritional raw materials from the state of Nature to the state of Culture". The rules which are applied to food differ according to one's nationality, gender, and age, and social circumstances of the meal dictate its content, timing, and atmosphere. Below we outline the latest attempts to track public health using social media, and most notably nutritional research, which has been mostly thus far focused on recipe websites.

Recently, Twitter has been used as a source of data for public health monitoring, such as for tracking flu-like symptoms [3, 9, 21], adverse side-effects of drugs [4], tobacco use [19], and county-level health statistics [10] . Using a text classifier, Sadilek & Kautz [21] detect tweets which mention the user being sick. They find that the higher social status of the users, the better their health, with poverty, education, and race (originating from the census data) explaining 8.7% of the variation in observed health. The most predictive variables were proximity to polluted sites and encounters with sick individuals. Culotta [10] uses well-defined lexicons such as LIWC and some demographic variables about users to predict county-wide health statistics (e.g., *Obesity* and *Diabetes*) of the top 100 most populous counties in the US. Prier et al. [19] use LDA to find topics related to tobacco, such as addiction recovery, other drug use, and anti-smoking campaigns. Paul & Dredze [18] apply an Ailment Topic Aspect Model to tweets to discover mentions of various ailments, including allergies, obesity, and insomnia. More generally, life satisfaction has been mined from Twitter by Schwartz & Eichstaedt et al. [22], who evaluated their approach using phone survey data. Using LDA, they find word topics which correlate with demographics and socio-economic status, and provide insights into the sources of well-being, such as donating money and having rewarding jobs. These efforts, including those utilizing other social media websites like Craigslist [16], have aimed to augment the current data collection practices, making them faster, cheaper, and potentially more accurate.

In this paper we focus on the dietary choices of a large population of social media users. Culture-specific ingredient connections have been discovered by Ahn et al. [2] who mine recipes to create a "flavor network". Temporal nature of food consumption has been explored by West et al. [27], who mine logs of recipe-related queries. Using Fourier transforms, they illustrate the yearly and weekly periodicity in food density of the accessed recipes, with different trends in Southern and Northern hemispheres, suggesting a link between food selection and climate. Focusing on users who decided to go on a diet (as signified by them adding a book on dieting to their shopping cart), authors show the dip in caloric value per serving of the recipes users search for, and a gradual return to the pre-diet levels. Geographical distribution of food has been explored by Zhu et al. [30], who, unlike [27], find climate (operationalized using temperature) to have little correlation with ingredient use, while finding geographical proximity to be a key factor in shaping regional cuisines. A recent work by Wagner et al. [26] on german-language recipe site shows similar negative relation between recipes and geographic distance of their seekers. We also find caloric content of foods mentioned in text a useful quantification of dietary selections, but unlike these studies, we relate it to public health statistics in order to validate its use. Furthermore, the nature of social media, unlike the recipe search logs, allows us to enrich our data with information on user demographics, interests and social network. In particular, our work on user interests echoes that in [7], where interests of Facebook users were found to be related to their BMI. However, we take a more general approach to detecting user interests, using the network of the Twitter users.

Social nature of obesity has been hypothesized by Christakis & Fowler [6], who tracked a densely interconnected social network of 12,067 people across 32 years. They found a person's chances of becoming obese increased by 57% if he or she had a friend who became obese in a given interval. These effects were not seen among neighbors in the immediate geographic location, emphasizing the importance of social ties. They provide three explanations for the collective dynamics of obesity: *homophily* which is a tendency of people to associate with people who are similar to them, *confounding* which occurs when people share attributes or jointly experience events, and *induction* which refers to a person-to-person spread of behaviors and traits. These findings have been contested, however, by Cohen-Cole & Fletcher [8], who claim "social network effect" becomes negligible once "standard econometric techniques are implemented". Recently, Silva et al. [23], who use Foursquare checkins to gauge food culture similarity between geographical locales, also found that countries closer in geographic proximity are not necessarily similar in their check-in behavior. In this work we examine both demographic and social aspects of food tweeting behavior, and provide some support to the social affinity that is not local in geographic sense.

DATA

We begin by collecting 50M tweets through the Twitter Streaming API[4] using a keyword filter over a span of 2013/10/29 – 2013/11/29. Keywords were selected to match as many food-related tweets as possible (covering eating, food, cooking and cuisine). The list of keywords contains also the names of the top 10 fast-food brands in the US (e.g., McDonald's and Starbucks). Then we selected all geo-tagged tweets and filtered out those that are not posted from the US. The result was a collection of 892K tweets posted by 400K users from the US. A uniform sample of 210K users who contributed from the US was randomly generated. We requested for each user in the sample (through different Twitter APIs) the profile (i.e., name, description, location, # tweets, # followers, etc.), their latest 3.2K tweets, and up to 5K followers as well as 5K friends. This process resulted in a collection of 503M historical tweets, 44.5M followers (173M links), and 32.1M friends (180M links).

We take several bootstrapping steps in order to improve our detection of food-related tweets and to extend our list of keywords. First, we examine the 1,000 most frequent terms used in the tweets detected by the initial list, and hand-select other 118 terms unambiguously related to food. This new "food" filter was now applied to the users' historical tweets. We then label a subset of tweets detected using these two filters, as well as a sample of those which were not thus far identified as food-related, in order to train a classifier. Using CrowdFlower[5] crowdsourcing platform, we published a total of 2,157 tweet examples, collecting 3 annotations for each tweet. The task was fairly easy, with 95.9% agreement. The training set, consisting of 583 positive and 1,574 negative examples, was used to train a unigram Naive Bayes classifier.

[4] `https://dev.twitter.com/docs/streaming-apis`

[5] `https://crowdflower.com`

Finally, we select 500 most popular terms in the tweets the classifier deems to be on food-related topic and further enrich them with nutritional information – mainly calories per serving. To estimate this value, we search a nutritional information website[6] using the identified food keyword, such as *pizza*. We then average the per-serving caloric values for the top 25 returned entries (which in this case would be pizzas of different brands and with different toppings). We then manually check the validity of the resulting entries, excluding ambiguous ones such as *plain* and *cured*. The final list contains 460 entries and is available online[7].

In terms of food twitting activity, we detect weekly periodicity, as well as some major holidays: Thanksgiving, Fourth of July, and Valentine's Day. Weekly periods spike on Saturday and are at lowest on Mondays.

Now, we can use this list to perform longest n-gram matching to detect the foods in the tweet text, and aggregate their caloric content. Upon manual examination of 800 tweets containing these foods, we found 70% of tweets to mention some food, and out of these 63% either explicitly or implicitly being about food consumption and another 12.5% wishing for a food. Most false matches happened when the foods were used in figurative sense ("they scattered like fish") or referring to others ("chocolate man"), though many of these references may still reveal cultural relationships with food, such as reference to Thanksgiving as "turkey day". The most frequently mentioned foods in our dataset are *pizza*, *chocolate*, *chicken*, *ice cream*, and *apple*. Among the top drinks are *coffee*, *beer*, *wine*, and *tea*. We then get the food that most distinguishes a given state, by first considering the top 200 most popular foods in each state, and computing the difference in probability of each word from that of appearing in the overall food-related corpus – a technique similar to feature selection for a binary classification – to find the term most likely to be found in tweets of one state, and not the others. We find local peculiarities like California *wine*, Florida *orange*, Maryland *crab*, and Alaskan *salmon*. We also find possible erroneous matchings, as in the case of New York *apple* (from "Big Apple") and Missouri *arrowhead*. These special cases, having particular prevalence in specific localities, attest the difficulty of identifying the proper context in a limited-length text of tweets. We leave further tuning of our food lexicon for future work.

STATE-LEVEL CORRELATIONS

Although the cyclical nature of food consumption and major holidays can be detected in this data, there is still a concern whether the data sampling is representative of US population or, at least, useful to detect *differences* in food consumption. Thus, we correlate the caloric values of foods mentioned in tweets per each state to the obesity rates[8] (from 2012) and the incidence of diabetes[9] (2005 – 2007), as measured by Centers for Disease Control and Prevention (CDC). Obesity is defined

[6] `http://caloriecount.about.com/`

[7] `http://bit.ly/1whhowz`

[8] `http://www.cdc.gov/obesity/data/adult.html`

[9] `http://www.cdc.gov/mmwr/preview/mmwrhtml/mm5743a2.htm`

Table 1: Pearson and Spearman correlations of tweet caloric value to state obesity and diabetes rates.

	Obesity		**Diabetes**	
	Pearson	Spearman	Pearson	Spearman
All	0.772***	0.784***	0.658***	0.657***
Food	0.629***	0.643***	0.538***	0.517**
Beverage	0.762***	0.786***	0.646***	0.622***
Alcoholic bev.	0.445*	0.430*	0.073	−0.007

Significance: $p < 0.0001$ ***, $p < 0.001$ **, $p < 0.01$ *

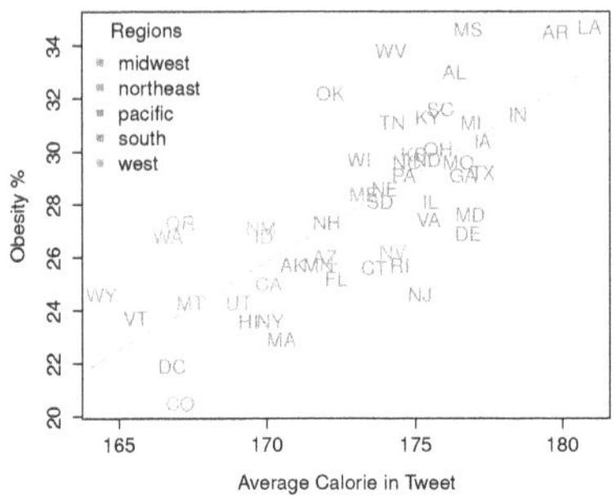

Figure 1: Caloric value of foods mentioned in tweets versus obesity rates.

by Body Mass Index (BMI) – a person's mass divided by the square of their height – with BMI > 30 considered obese.

Table 1 shows Pearson product-moment correlation r and Spearman rank correlation coefficient ρ between the average caloric density of tweets and these health statistics across the $50+1$ US states (including Washington DC). For each tweet, we use exact string matching to identify the foods (many of which would result in erroneous matches otherwise) and, if more than one is found, average their caloric value. In *all* we consider all entries, we also differentiate between solid foods and non-alcoholic and alcoholic beverages. The correlation is the highest when we consider all foods, with the Pearson correlation of 0.772 with obesity and 0.658 with diabetes. For both ailments, beverage caloric value alone has higher correlations than solid food alone. However, the importance of alcoholic beverages differs drastically, with being somewhat correlated with obesity at 0.445 and having no statistically significant relationship with diabetes. The reasons for this differentiation may be physiological, but also cultural. In the next section we also illustrate the association of alcohol with urban locales.

We further explore the relationship between obesity and caloric value of the mentioned foods in Figure 1, where we color the states according to their geographic region. The grey dashed line shows the linear regression line. We find the Southern states to be in the upper right corner, with Louisiana (LA) and Arkansas (AR) in the extreme right.[10] The clustering of the Southern, Midwest, and Northeast states suggests a common food culture between spatially proximal populations. These findings are supported by earlier work on recipe search in Germany [26] and ingredient use across China [30], who find that geographically closer cuisines shared more ingredients (with a few exceptions such as Hong Kong, which has a historical diversion from Chinese culture). Likewise, we notice Washington DC to be somewhat removed from its geographic neighbors, potentially due to the influence of the peculiar urban culture. We explore the effects of culture, personal interests, and demographics on the dietary habits of Twitter users in the next section.

COUNTY-WIDE MODEL FITTING

Despite the inherent sparsity problem observed at county-level as compared to the state level, we found a Pearson correlation of the caloric value of all foods with obesity at 0.501 and diabetes 0.447 for counties with at least 100 users. For counties with at least 200 users ($N = 191$), the correlations were even better with 0.605 for obesity and 0.498 for diabetes. Encouraged by this results, we wanted to investigate further the extent to which food mentions could capture county-wide health signals such as obesity and diabetes. To this end, we designed an experiment that compares our "food mention" model to the one presented in [10]. Similarly to the paper we train a regression model using different kinds of variables to predict obesity and diabetes rates at county level.

Culotta's model [10] uses lexicon categories along with a selection of demographic variables to predict county-level health statistics of the top 100 most populous counties in the US. Their experimental study revealed a strong predictive accuracy of demographic variables which can be improved if combined with linguistic variables derived from LIWC[11] (Linguistic Inquiry and Word Count) lexicon.

To enable the comparison with Culotta's model, we first build a user model with the following variables:

- LIWC categories: For each user, we compute a binary vector of LIWC categories extracted from her Twitter profile. A LIWC category (e.g., *Social*, *Family*) takes the value of 1 if the user mentions at least one word in her profile that belongs to the category, 0 otherwise.
- Food names: For each user, we compute a binary vector of Food names mentioned in her tweets. We use our hand-crafted dictionary of food names and apply an exact matching to the tweets.
- avgCal: this variable reflects the average caloric value computed across all food names mentioned by the user in her tweets.
- Demographic variables: Each user is assigned a list of five demographic variables derived from census data related to the county to which she belongs. These variables are: *Under_18* (proportion of people under the age of 18), *Over_65* (proportion of people above the age of 65) , *Female* (proportion of females), *Afro-Hispanic* (proportion of Afro-American and Hispani), and *Income* (log of median household annual income).

[10]See **http://content.time.com/time/health/article/0,8599,1909406,00.html** on why that may be the case.

[11]**http://www.liwc.net/index.php**

Next, we aggregate user models at the level of counties. We generate for each county, a vector of LIWC categories (64), food names (461), and demographic variables (5). The weight of a given food name (resp. LIWC category) reflects the proportion of users in that county who mentioned that food name (resp. LIWC category). Note that unlike Culotta's work where only the top 100 most populous counties (based on census data) are considered, we have retained all counties with at least 100 users (346 counties).

We run a series of regressions using various models (features) to predict obesity and diabetes scores of the 346 counties. We consider six models: **Demog** (demographic variables), **Liwc** (LIWC categories), **Calories** ($avgCal$ variable), **Food** (food name variables), **Liwc-Demog** (LIWC categories and demographic variables), and **Food-Demog** (food names and demographic variables). For each model, we use a five fold cross-validation to assess the generalization of its accuracy. Folds are selected in a way that prevents counties from the same state to appead simultaneousely in both training and test sets. Finally, we use Ridge regression in order to reduce over-fitting, espacially in models with large number of variables (e.g., Food (461)).

Figure 2 shows the Pearson's correlations (which are all statistically significant) achieved by different models along with their corresponding SEM (standard error of the mean) scores. Recall that the SEM score is equal to the corrected standard deviation of the sample divided by the root square of the size of that sample. **Food-Demog** model, which combines food names and demographic variables, is found to outperform Culotta's model **Liwc-Demog** which combines LIWC linguistic variables with Census demographics. If fact, **Food-Demog** achieves held-out correlations of 0.775 for obesity and 0.804 for diabetes while **Liwc-Demog** achieves respectively 0.679 and 0.708 for the two health statistics. Surprisingly, the simple **Food** model based on our handcrafted dictionary of food names significantly outperforms the **Liwc** model. Also, we notice that **Calories** model which has only one variable achieves reasonably good correlation scores (0.450 for obesity and 0.398 for diabetes) compared to **Liwc** (0.470 for obesity, 0.380 for diabetes) which has 64 variables. Note that we also tried a baseline using top 1,000 most frequent hashtags in our dataset and find very low correlations with the county-wide obesity and diabetes rates of around 0.06. Finally, we built another baseline that uses generic tweet statistics, including number of tweets, retweets, number of replies, and number of hashtags. This baseline achieved comparable correlations (0.38 for obesity and 0.44 for diabetes) to those of the "Calories" model.

Finally, we observe that **Food** model significantly outperforms – the aggregated – **Calories** model for the prediction of both obesity and diabetes. Yet, **Calories** model has several advantages. First, **Calories** model is much simpler than all the other models as it relies on a single variable ($avgCal$) and does not require any model fitting. Second, the model is easily interpretable and arguably closer to the "root cause" of obesity and diabetes. Third, the caloric value of food has shown very strong correlations at the state level. Next, we use

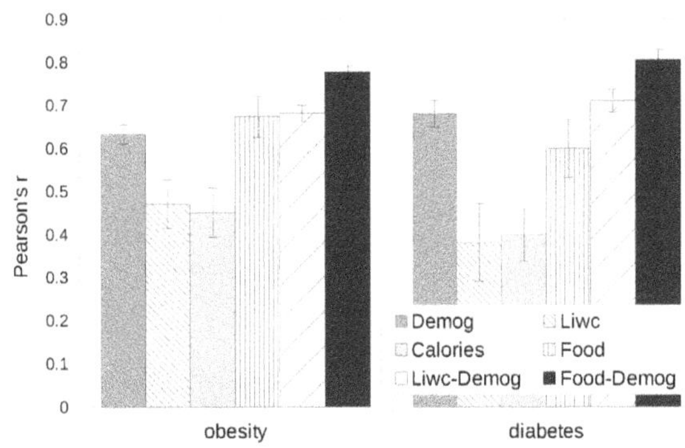

Figure 2: Held-out Pearson's correlation with standard error of the mean (SEM) for the different models. Demog: uses the five demographic variables. Liwc: consists of 64 LIWC categories, Calories: consider only one variable avgCal. Food: consists of 461 food names. Liwc-Demog: combines LIWC categories and demographic variables. Food-Demog: combines food names and demographic variables.

Calories model and the best-performing model **Food-Demog** to zoom in to the personal, user level of analysis.

CHARACTERIZING USERS

Income, Education and Gender

The effect of obesity in US has been shown to vary according to income, education, and gender. According to CDC, whereas among men, obesity prevalence is generally similar at all income levels, higher income women are less likely to be obese than their low income counterparts[12]. Motivated by these statistics, we map the income and education figures from 2010 US Census[13] to zip codes from which Twitter users sent their messages. As the statistics are broken down into bins (such as "\$10, 000-\$14, 999" for income and "Some College" for education), we computed a weighted average of these values using the mean of each bin. Finally, we associated each user with the zipcode most frequently associated with their tweets.

We supplement this with a per-user gender classification using Genderize API[14] on users' screen names. The API uses a database of names from major social networks, and produces the most likely gender associated with a first name, which can be *male*, *female*, or *none* when the gender cannot be detected. Among our users we detect 37.2% as female, 32.1% as male, and the remaining 30.7% were labeled as none. Concerned about the latter group, we run a crowdsourced experiment on CrowdFlower to tag a random subset of 1,331 accounts as belonging to a real person or not. Whereas the female and male users had low numbers of non-personal accounts (2.57% and 3.49% respectively), over a quarter of "none" gender – 26.69% – were such accounts. For this reason, we exclude these users from further analysis, with 128,487 data points remaining. Notice that we did not remove users with "none" gender from the previous computation of correlations because

[12] `http://www.cdc.gov/nchs/data/databriefs/db50.pdf`
[13] `www.census.gov/2010census/data/`
[14] `http://genderize.io/`

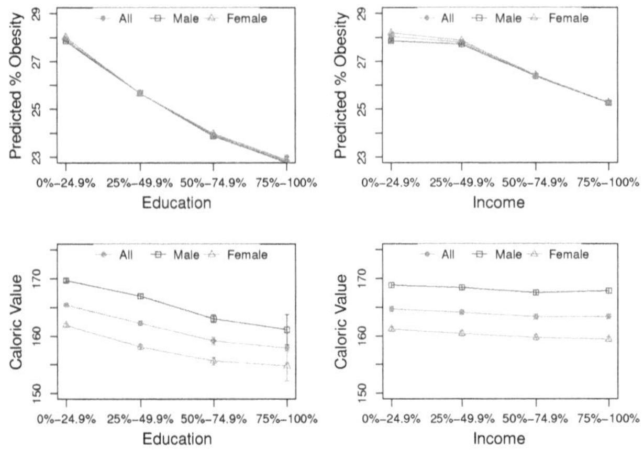

Figure 3: Average predicted obesity and caloric value of tweets of four quartiles divided by education (Bachelor degree attainment, and income level), with 95% CI.

of their limited impact on the results. For instance, removing these users brings Pearson correlation between caloric values of all food and obesity from 0.772 (all users) to 0.741.

Figures 3 shows an exploration of the dimensions of gender, educational attainment (likelihood of a Bachelor's degree) and median household income. Two variables are plotted: the likelihood of obesity (estimated using the model built in the previous section) the average caloric values of the tweets produced by each user. We find that although the trends differ in for the genders in the kind of heaviness of food they tweet, the distinction is not present in the obesity rates. It is understandable, given gender-mixed populations on which the model was trained. We witness a stronger negative correlation for educational level with both the caloric values and the estimated obesity rates. These trends echo those found by USDA, which finds obesity prevalence increase as education decreases (though more so for women).

Next, we mapped the zip codes to major metropolitan areas (top 100 US cities by population) and labeled all of these as "urban". We find 36,196 (26.9% of all) users to be in these urban areas. Although one may suppose eating at restaurants (in urban areas) may result in tweets mentioning more caloric food, we find quite the opposite. There is a significant (at $p < 0.001$) distinction between the two populations, with users in rural areas having an average of 164.8 calories in their tweets, and urban 161.6.

The above distinctions are identifiable not only in the caloric value of the foods mentioned in the tweets, but in the foods themselves. Figure 4 shows the distinguishing foods between users in rural and urban areas, computed using probability differences such that the foods which are popular in one area but not in another get a higher score. Urban food vocabulary distinguishes itself with alcoholic drinks (*wine* and *beer*), and more uncommon foods like *avocado* and *crab*, whereas the rural cuisine emphasizes *pizza* and common deserts like *chocolate* and *ice cream*.

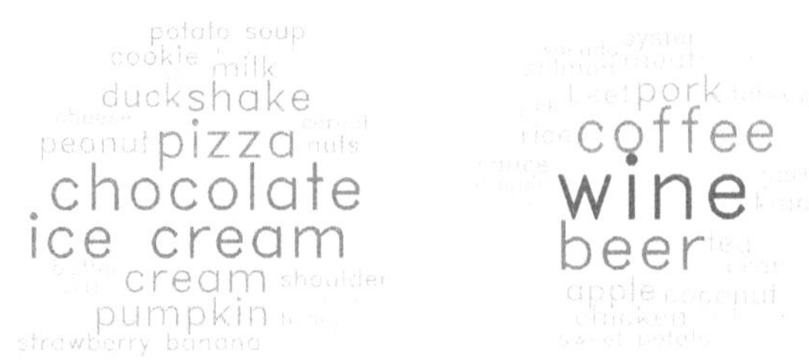

(a) Rural (b) Urban

Figure 4: Distinguishing foods between rural and urban users.

Interests

There are, of course, other factors which contribute to one's diet. For instance, people who are interested in healthy eating and organic food, or those with families would consciously alter their diets. To detect individuals with such interests, we compiled a high-precision keyword lists to detect users interested in, or at least mentioning cooking, dieting, organic food, and health. We also detected users who mentioned being a family member (being a father, mother, having kids, etc.). These filters were then applied to user profiles.

The above method can be used to detect interests users feel comfortable declaring in their profile, however not all user characteristics can be extracted. We take a different approach to detect users who declare themselves to be overweight by the use of hash tags such as `#fatgirlproblems` or `#fatguyproblems`. These are typically used by users in self-reference, for example "*I have more pictures of food than I do selfies .. #fatgirlproblems*" Doing this, we detected 10,797 users using at least one such tag.

Table 2 shows the difference in estimated obesity of population for which a variable has been detected (say, mentioning sports) from that where the variable was not detected, as well as the number of instances found for the class. Thus, if the difference is positive, the class has a higher chance of obesity by that many percentage points. Note that for this experiment only users whose names resulted in an identified gender were used (totaling in 128,487 data points). We find that people who are interested in cooking and organic food decrease their likelihood of obesity by 1.3 and 2.1 percentage points, respectively. Although our *on diet* keyword filter produced a low recall – of only 107 users – the chance of decrease is near 1%. The detection of `#fatproblems` hashtags resulted in 10,797 matches, but we see only a moderate (although statistically significant) positive change in the obesity rate.

We go further and identify fine-grained interests as in [1]. Using WeFollow[15], we collect a list of users who are judged to be prominent in some area. For each of the 61 areas such as *TV*, *Science*, or *Football*, we collected top 200 users, having the highest prominence score (ranging from 0 to 100) in their area. We compute a user's aggregate interest score for an area of interest by summing over the scores of the prominent users they follow. However, following behavior differs among the

[15] `http://wefollow.com/`

Table 2: Difference between the estimated obesity rate while considering profile factors (mean rate at factor = 1 minus mean rate at factor = 0), and # of non-zero instances.

factor	f_1 - f_0	p-value	non-zero n
`#fatproblems`	+0.3	0.0000	10797
Student	0.0	0.3695	2709
Family	+0.3	0.0000	8014
Cooking	-1.3	0.0000	637
Organic	-2.1	0.0005	49
On Diet	-0.9	0.0174	107
Health/Sport	-0.2	0.0138	3181

Table 3: Top 15 factors by the magnitude of the coefficient in a linear regression modeling the predicted obesity rate using interests as determined by following WeFollow users. For binary variables, the number of non-zero instances is given.

Factor	Coefficient	Sign.	non-zero n
(Intercept)	26.98593	***	
tvshows	0.80296	***	4267
education	0.63017	***	1904
business	0.62499	***	1962
sports	0.49467	***	11423
nfl	0.35523	***	6111
entrepreneur	-0.23009	**	5530
music	-0.28651	***	20364
baseball	-0.29567	**	1990
animals	-0.29867	**	1510
travel	-0.36032	***	3220
news	-0.47807	***	9266
blogger	-0.68136	***	7209
football	-0.92379	***	4691
media	-1.08349	***	6782
tech	-1.15935	***	3804

$p < 0.0001$ ***, $p < 0.001$ **, $p < 0.01$ *

various areas. For example, an average aggregate score for *Social Media* is 311, whereas that for *Cats* is only 64. Thus, we consider a user to have an interest in an area if the aggregate prominence score of her friends in that area is at or above the mean score of all users potentially interested in that area. Using these variables we construct a linear regression model. Table 3 shows the top significant factors by the magnitude of the coefficient. Among these we see interest in TV shows and general sports categories to have positive relationship with obesity, whereas interest in football (soccer) and technology has the opposite effect. Recall that these interest scores do not stem from the text of the tweets, but from the user's following network. In that way, they provide a glimpse of a users' interests which may be not be available in their tweets, but which still may provide some indication of the user's dietary health.

Our findings partially confirm a previous study on Facebook interests of users in US and New York metropolitan area [7] in which it was found that a greater proportion of the population with interest in television was associated with higher prevalence of obesity. However, our observations of interests in sports is less straightforward, with *sports* and *NFL* categories positively relating to obesity, whereas the Facebook study finds activity-related interests to be associated associated with a lower predicted prevalence of obese and/or overweight people. The separation between watching and participating in sports would shed more light on this discrepancy.

SOCIAL NATURE OF FOOD

Social circumstances play an important role in how we consume our food, and which food we consume. We attempt to discern the relationship between social interactions, expressed in the text of the tweet and in the follower network of the user, and users' eating behavior (operationalized by predicted probabilities of obesity and diabetes, frequency of food mentioning, and caloric value of tweets). We first study the impact of two types of relationship networks on the obesity and diabetes scores of users. Then, we use a threshold model to quantify the circumstances under which a user would get exposed to higher obesity and diabetes risks. Finally, we look at the influence of friends at varying degrees of closeness.

User-level obesity, diabetes and food frequency

In this section, we focus on the impact of social relationships on obesity, diabetes and the amount of food related tweets. For each user, we compute the fraction of tweets citing at least one food name. To estimate the obesity and diabetes scores at individual levels, we use the **Food** model that relies on food names only. For training a model, each user is assigned the obesity and diabetes rates of their county. A Ridge regression is used to learn the models and predict individual user scores. Predicted scores could be seen as a user's risk level of obesity and diabetes, based on the food mentioned in their tweets.

Note that for the following analysis we deliberately discarded demographic variables. Friends on Twitter are also likely to live in close proximity [24] and hence are likely to share similar estimates of demographic variables, based on geographic census data. So friends are likely to be similar along this dimension. However, we are more interested in observing the connection between social network closeness and propensity to share "unhealthy tweeting behavior", such as the use of food names associated with higher obesity levels.

User Networks

We explore the social nature of eating habits by constructing two social networks, namely *Friendship network* (FN) and *Mention network* (MN). The Friendship network relates to the structural aspect of Twitter. In FN, two users are considered to be "friends" only if they follow each other. This definition follows the principal of mutual reachability introduced by Xie et al. [28] to identify real-life friends from Twitter. Alternatively, Mention network relates to the behavioral aspect of users. Here, a user a (mentioner) has a link to user b (mentionee) only if a has mentioned b in at least one tweet.

Note that users without gender have been removed from both MN and FN, and only links between users with a known gender (i.e. *male* or *female*) in the initial set of US users are considered. Table 4 provides some statistics on the two networks.

Obesity and Diabetes Activation (Spread)

Focusing on obesity, we ask to which extend does being connected to users with a high likelihood of obesity and diabetes

Table 4: Description of Friendship and Mention networks

Network	# Links	# Users
Friend	295, 285	84, 599
Mention	378, 801	85, 144

(based on the food names they tweet) increases the likelihood of a user for these two health issues? A threshold model postulates that a success or failure of a social diffusion process depends on the reaching of a certain critical number of adopters [25]. This model has been used, for example, to model the adoption of a particular notation for source attribution on Twitter [17]. Following the idea of "social activation", we label users beyond the 90th percentile (i.e. the top 10%) in terms of obesity and/or diabetes scores as "*active*" users. Then, for every user we calculate the number of active users to whom they are connected in both friendship and mention networks. Finally, we compute the activation probability (i.e., the probability of being an *active* user) given that a user is connected to x *active* users.

Figure 5 shows the activation probability scores of users as a function of the number of their *active* friends. As expected, the probability of showing a strongly increased probability of obesity, estimated by the food names mentioned, increases as the number of friends with high obesity scores increases. This increasing trend is particularly pronounced for up to four active friends. Though the standard errors of the computed probabilities increase dramatically beyond this point, with only few users having more than five active friends, there seems to be a plateau effect. The same behaviour is observed in the activation graph of diabetes.

To alleviate the influence of *content spread phenomena* in which people may tweet about a food name just because their friends tweeted about it, we removed all tweets that are "replies to" or "retweets of" other tweets. We trained a new **Food** model and run our activation algorithm which resulted in the same activation curve as Figure 5. Thus, although we cannot exclude offline motivational effects, excluding them from data does not affect our results. We also investigate the effect of *geography* to make sure that the activation process is not the result of people living in the same region as their friends. We removed from the social graph all friendship links between users living in the same US state. We observed a small drop in activation probability scores, yet the increasing trend function of the number of active friends was still there.

Clique-ness Analysis

Another way to assess the influence of social connections on users' dietary habits is to take into consideration the strength of user connections. Here, we define the link strength between any pair of users (a, b) having an edge in the mention network or the friendship network as the fraction of their common friends in the same network. As mentioned in the dataset description (section Data), we have collected up to $5,000$ friends for each of the 210K US users, leading to a user-friend bipartite graph with $\approx$180M links. Then, we use Jaccard index to compute the similarity of the friend sets between all pairs of users in both networks. Based on the computed scores, users and their links are assigned to different bins corresponding to different Jaccard index intervals. As expected, the distribution of Jaccard scores is heavily skewed. For instance, more than 71.6% of the total number of links have a strength score lower that 0.1 in the mention network.

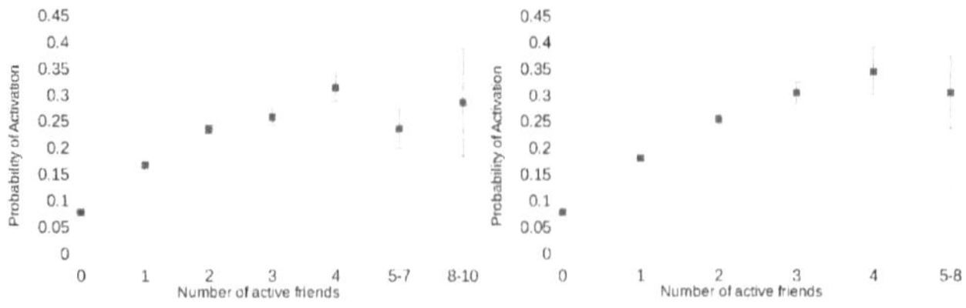

(a) Obesity spread in FN (b) Obesity spread in MN

Figure 5: Obesity activation probabilities function of the number of "*active*" friends in Friendship Network (FN) and Mention Network (MN).

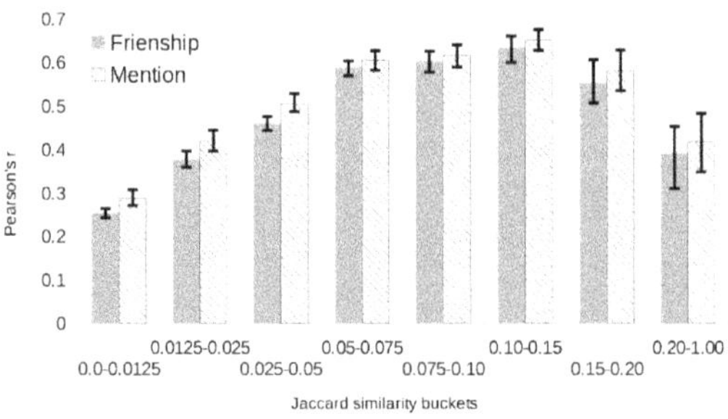

Figure 6: Pearson correlation of the fraction of food related tweets between users and their friends, bucketed by Jaccard similarity in mentions and friendship networks. The 95% confidence intervals (CIs) are computed using a bootstrap test, iterated 1,000 times. CIs correspond to the 2.5^{th} and 97.5^{th} percentiles obtained over the bootstrapping process.

In order to check whether tightly connected friends share a higher degree of content similarity, we correlate the fraction of food tweets of each user to that of their friends within each bin. Figure 6 shows the bins from most dissimilar users ($[0.0, 0.0125]$) to those most similar in terms of ego-network overlap. Note that the intervals are not normalized due to the highly skewed distribution of the data, with the last bin of $[0.2, 1.0]$ having only $5,428$ users in Mentions and $5,076$ in Friendship networks. We witness an increase in the correlation of the food-related tweet fraction of users and their friends as network overlap increases until the last two buckets – those with users sharing the most friends.

Upon manual examination, we find highly related users to be in the same social locales, such as students in the same university or school. The phenomena may also be related to the shape of the *exposure curve*, as proposed by Romero et al. [20], which models the rise of initial interest as the number of exposures increases, and the decrease after over-exposure to a phenomenon.

DISCUSSION & FUTURE WORK

Using data from social media to study sociological phenomena and to "nowcast" variables such as obesity rates has both advantages and disadvantages compared to traditional survey-based methods. Two of the most commonly given advantages include cost and timeliness. Data for hundreds of thousands of users can be obtained at relatively low cost, and this data can be collected, aggregated and analyzed in a matter of days or even hours, rather than weeks or months for comparable surveys. However, in addition to these two quantitative differences, there is also an important qualititative advantage: the availability of network information. Having access to even a subset of people that a given person interacts with makes it possible to look for evidence of social mechanisms such as homophily. In the health domain, having data on the strength of such effects makes it possible to consider *social* interventions. Rather than trying to change unhealthy behavior of individuals by providing information and incentives derived solely from their own behavior, information about their friends' physical activity or healthy dietary choices could be provided. Similarly, altruistic incentives of the type "Run a total of 30km this week and your friend @JohnDoe has a chance to win an iPhone" could be based on automatically derived, intricate knowledge of a user's social circle. Or if a set of friends are planning a physical activity, they may be encouraged to invite others from their social circle.

The availability of rich data related to hobbies and interests is also a potential advantage for studies using social media. Public health initiatives targeting various segments of population already exist, such as UK's Change 4 Life (`http://www.nhs.uk/change4life`) targeting parents and USDA's MyPlate on Campus for university students (`http://www.choosemyplate.gov/MyPlateOnCampus`). In our study, we link users' obesity likelihood, inferred by a model combining demographic estimates with food names mentioned on Twitter, to their interests, such as TV shows, sports, and movies. The relationship between each of these activities and food would help target population segments which are especially at risk, and maximize the return on media advertising expenditures. But it is our vision that automated tools will help provide personalized messages to social media users, providing context-aware, real-time information, suggestions, and motivation. For instance, if a user tweets about an intention to exercise, links to tutorials and videos can be suggested. The development of these approaches first requires automated assessment of a user's dietary behavior, and this paper takes first steps in that direction.

Of course, sociological studies which use social media also have significant drawbacks. Typically, such studies suffer from a user sampling bias with an over-representation of affluent and tech-savvy demographic groups. This bias can be more pronounced when only users with GPS-enabled devices are considered. Indeed, the users in our subset come from neighborhoods with average household income at $85,117$, well above the US average of $51,017$ in 2012[16]. Similarly, our users come from locations where the average percentage of people with a Bachelor degree or above is at 23.71%, slightly higher than the nationwide percentage of 22.23% observed in Census database. This, however, may be an artifact of the aggregation of census statistics (which are binned for each district in a range with no other distributional information), and a more fine-grained analysis may improve these numbers. Still, our sample did closely resemble the nationwide gender proportions, with female slightly outnumbering male (53%, compared to 51% nationwide). Despite this shortcoming, we find a substantial correlation between several types of models using both the actual food names or the the caloric density of the foods mentioned in tweets and state-wide obesity and diabetes rates. This suggests that, in aggregate, social media does provide useful insights into national dietary health, even though the underlying data might not be representative.

It is an advantage of big data analysis that high-precision methods, such as hand-crafted keyword filters, can be effectively applied to glimpse a phenomena of interest. Yet, such approaches are not robust under temporal changes in the vocabulary, and may suffer from low recall. For example, the `#fatproblems` hash tags are a convention for people to admit (often humorously) to feeling overweight. However, there may be many more subtle (and more serious) ways one can detect self-image expressions. Being able to identify with high accuracy users that are overweight would allow a more fine-grained validation of our techniques, in addition to the state-level validation that we currently focus on.

Despite the significant relationship between food mentions and their caloric value in the tweets and health problems, one needs to be careful not to assume that the user consumed every food about which they tweeted. In fact, it is difficult to extrapolate whether the tweet is about an actual dining experience, even if we detect a mention of food. A crowd-sourced effort to label a training set of tweets for detecting dining experiences has shown the task to be difficult, with user agreement at 78%, and the resulting trained classifier producing noisy output. We leave determining the exact nature of the food mention in a tweet to future work.

Another concern is whether the tweets are about foods not normally eaten by their writers, that is, written on special occasions or on special topics. Thus, we checked the intervals at which the users in our dataset tweet, finding the top 1% tweeting at a median of 18.8 food tweets per week, and the median overall to be at 1.2 food tweets per week. This suggests that our users at least do not tweet just about their birthday cake, but are actively engaged on a weekly basis. Although in our analysis we normalize our data per user, we still may have unusual very-active users who tweet differently than the rest. Thus, we check the overlap between the top mentioned food between the top 1% and the bottom 50%, and find 43 out of 50 foods overlap. Finally, even the top foods we find are every-day ones, like *pizza*, *coffee*, and *chicken*. These findings encourage us that we capture at least in part the day-to-day dietary habits of Twitter users.

Our analysis describes correlations, not causations. However, we believe that insights gained from this type of analysis are required before deciding where to drill deeper through, ide-

[16] `http://www.census.gov/prod/2013pubs/p60-245.pdf`

ally, controlled experiments. Targeting Twitter users with a particular behavior could also be a promising step for interventions such as public health awareness campaigns.

Finally, active promotion of dietary habits were studied by Yom-Tov et al. [29], who track the dissemination of pro- and anti-anorexia photos on Flickr and the emerging social networks. They find the two groups to interact mostly within each respective community, but for pro-recovery group to tag their content with terms which would ensure their content is visible to pro-anorexia users. Such fine-grained analysis is beyond the scope of our current study, but the direct social influence in terms of verbal and non-verbal interactions is an enticing future direction of this research.

CONCLUSIONS

In this paper we describe a large-scale study of the Twittersphere, as it allows us to monitor US-wide nutritional behavior. We show that the foods mentioned in the daily tweets of users are predictive of the national obesity and diabetes statistics, with values of $r = .77$ and $r = .66$ across the 50 US states and the District of Columbia. We show how the calories tweeted are linked to user interest and demographic indicators, and that users sharing more friends are more likely to display a similar interest toward food. More needs to be done to develop sensitive and accurate tools for user characterization, with both textual and social network information available. As a documentation of users' interests, opinions, and behaviors, this study is another example of the potential Twitter has for public health research.

REFERENCES

1. Abisheva, A., Garimella, V. R. K., Garcia, D., and Weber, I. Who watches (and shares) what on youtube? and when?: using twitter to understand youtube viewership. In *WSDM* (2014).
2. Ahn, Y.-Y., Ahnert, S. E., Bagrow, J. P., and Barabási, A.-L. Flavor network and the principles of food pairing. *Nature Scientific reports* (2011).
3. Aramaki, E., Maskawa, S., and Morita, M. Twitter catches the flu: Detecting influenza epidemics using twitter. In *EMNLP* (2011).
4. Bian, J., Topaloglu, U., and Yu, F. Towards large-scale twitter mining for drug-related adverse events. In *SHB* (2012).
5. Cawley, J., and Meyerhoefer, C. The medical care costs of obesity: an instrumental variables approach. *Journal of health economics 31*, 1 (2012), 219–230.
6. Christakis, N. A., and Fowler, J. H. The spread of obesity in a large social network over 32 years. *New England journal of medicine 357*, 4 (2007), 370–379.
7. Chunara, R., Bouton, L., Ayers, J. W., and Brownstein, J. S. Assessing the online social environment for surveillance of obesity prevalence. *PloS one 8*, 4 (2013), e61373.
8. Cohen-Cole, E., and Fletcher, J. M. Is obesity contagious? social networks vs. environmental factors in the obesity epidemic. *Journal of Health Economics 27*, 5 (2008), 1382 – 1387.
9. Culotta, A. Lightweight methods to estimate influenza rates and alcohol sales volume from twitter messages. *Language Resources and Evaluation* (2013), 1–22.
10. Culotta, A. Estimating county health statistics with twitter. In *CHI* (2014).
11. Cutler, D. M., Glaeser, E. L., and Shapiro, J. M. Why have americans become more obese? *Journal of Economic Perspectives 17* (2003), 93–118.
12. de Castro, J. M. Seasonal rhythms of human nutrient intake and meal pattern. *Physiology & behavior 50*, 1 (1991), 243–248.
13. Donohew, L., Ray, E., and Donohew, L. Public health campaigns: Individual message strategies and a model. *Communication and health: Systems and applications* (1990), 136–152.
14. Fischler, C. Food, self and identity. *Social science information 27*, 2 (1988), 275–292.
15. Gershenson, C., Gasca-González, O. O., Delgado-Reyes, L., Pérez-Cruz, J. C., Orozco-Gómez, L. P., Hernández-Salazar, L., Moguel-Ancheita, S., Ramírez-Moreno, M. A., Morales-Cruz, M. V., Cortés-Gastélum, M. A., et al. Epidemiology and social networks. *Cir Cir 79* (2011), 199–200.
16. Haimson, O. L., Brubaker, J. R., and Hayes, G. R. Ddfseeks same: Sexual health-related language in online personal ads for men who have sex with men. In *CHI* (2014).
17. Kooti, F., Mason, W. A., Gummadi, K. P., and Cha, M. Predicting emerging social conventions in online social networks. In *CIKM* (2012).
18. Paul, M. J., and Dredze, M. You are what you tweet: Analyzing twitter for public health. In *ICWSM* (2011).
19. Prier, K. W., Smith, M. S., Giraud-Carrier, C., and Hanson, C. L. Identifying health-related topics on twitter. In *Social computing, behavioral-cultural modeling and prediction.* Springer, 2011, 18–25.
20. Romero, D. M., Meeder, B., and Kleinberg, J. Differences in the mechanics of information diffusion across topics: idioms, political hashtags, and complex contagion on twitter. In *WWW* (2011).
21. Sadilek, A., and Kautz, H. Modeling the impact of lifestyle on health at scale. In *WSDM* (2013).
22. Schwartz, H. A., Eichstaedt, J. C., Kern, M. L., Dziurzynski, L., Agrawal, M., Park, G. J., Lakshmikanth, S. K., Jha, S., Seligman, M. E., Ungar, L., et al. Characterizing geographic variation in well-being using tweets. In *ICWSM* (2013).
23. Silva, T. H., Vaz de Melo, P. O. S., Almeida, J., Musolesi, M., and Loureiro, A. You Are What You Eat (and Drink): Identifying Cultural Boundaries by Analyzing Food and Drink Habits in Foursquare. In *ICWSM* (2014).
24. Takhteyev, Y., Gruzd, A., and Wellman, B. Geography of twitter networks. *Social networks 34*, 1 (2012), 73–81.
25. Valente, T. W. Social network thresholds in the diffusion of innovations. *Social networks 18*, 1 (1996), 69–89.
26. Wagner, C., Singer, P., and Strohmaier, M. Spatial and Temporal Patterns of Online Food Preferences. In *WWW* (Republic and Canton of Geneva, Switzerland, 2014).
27. West, R., White, R. W., and Horvitz, E. From cookies to cooks: insights on dietary patterns via analysis of web usage logs. In *WWW* (2013).
28. Xie, W., Li, C., Zhu, F., Lim, E.-P., and Gong, X. When a friend in twitter is a friend in life. In *WebSci* (2012).
29. Yom-Tov, E., Fernandez-Luque, L., Weber, I., and Crain, S. P. Pro-anorexia and pro-recovery photo sharing: a tale of two warring tribes. *Journal of medical Internet research 14*, 6 (2012).
30. Zhu, Y.-X., Huang, J., Zhang, Z.-K., Zhang, Q.-M., Zhou, T., and Ahn, Y.-Y. Geography and similarity of regional cuisines in china. *PloS one 8*, 11 (2013), e79161.

Rethinking the Mobile Food Journal: Exploring Opportunities for Lightweight Photo-Based Capture

Felicia Cordeiro[1], Elizabeth Bales[1,2], Erin Cherry[3], James Fogarty[1]
[1] Computer Science & Engineering
[2] Human Centered Design & Engineering
DUB Group, University of Washington
{felicia0, lizbales, jfogarty}@cs.washington.edu
[3] Computer Science
University of Rochester
erinc@cs.rochester.edu

ABSTRACT
Food choices are among the most frequent and important health decisions in everyday life, but remain notoriously difficult to capture. This work examines opportunities for lightweight photo-based capture in mobile food journals. We first report on a survey of 257 people, examining how they define healthy eating, their experiences and challenges with existing food journaling methods, and their ability to interpret nutritional information that can be captured in a food journal. We then report on interviews and a field study with 27 participants using a lightweight, photo-based food journal for between 4 to 8 weeks. We discuss mismatches between motivations and current designs, challenges of current approaches to food journaling, and opportunities for photos as an alternative to the pervasive but often inappropriate emphasis on quantitative tracking in mobile food journals.

Author Keywords
Personal Informatics; Self-Tracking; Food Journals; Photos.

ACM Classification Keywords
H.5.m. Information interfaces and presentation (e.g., HCI).

INTRODUCTION
Food choices are among the most frequent and important health decisions in everyday life, yet it remains notoriously difficult to understand our food choices. People eat in many different contexts and have widely varying motivations and constraints on food. Being mindful of the quality and quantity of food choices is a crucial component of a healthy life [35,36], and food journals can be effective for monitoring food intake [8,15]. The implications of food also go beyond health, as food is central to our daily experiences and our relationship with food varies according to personal contexts and goals [14]. But food journals impose high burdens that detract from their potential benefit [11,12]. Effective food journaling is thus a grand challenge for personal informatics.

CHI 2015, April 18 - 23 2015, Seoul, Republic of Korea

http://dx.doi.org/10.1145/2702123.2702154

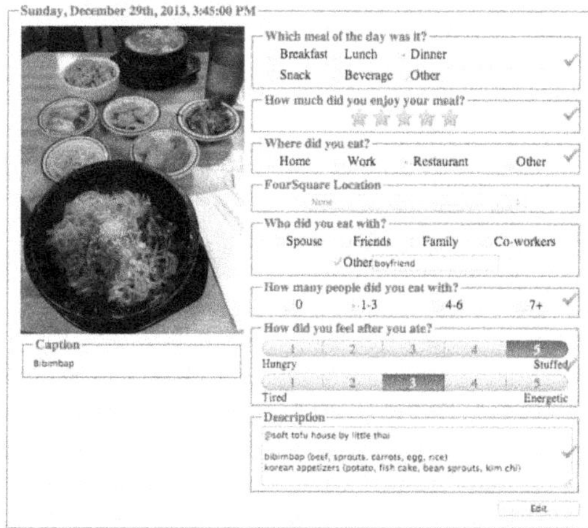

Figure 1. An entry in our lightweight photo-based food journal. No calorie or nutrition information is shown, as the journal instead logs meal enjoyment, location context, and social context.

Automated sensing has proven powerful in some domains of human activity, but remains out of reach for food despite recent advances [1,3,18,27,29,32,38]. It is also unclear whether automation is desirable, as it may undermine in-the-moment awareness created by food journaling [36]. Some existing methods involve taking photos of food as an intermediate step toward collecting underlying nutritional information [18,27,38]. We step further back, asking what people want to capture about food and what value photos themselves might provide in a lightweight food journal.

Our work examines lightweight photo-based capture and reflection, reconsidering the common assumption that a quantitative approach is required. We first present a survey examining how people define healthy eating, experiences and challenges with existing food journals, and how people interpret the healthiness of food presented as either photos or nutrition labels. We then present interviews and field deployments of a lightweight, photo-based mobile food journal. A total of 27 people with varying food goals from two distinct trials use our application to journal for between 4 to 8 weeks. We explore reactions to a design focused on food photos in lieu of nutritional information and examine the value of food photos with regard to their goals. Finally, we discuss our results in the context of rethinking challenges and opportunities in the design of mobile food journals.

The specific contributions of our work include:

- Examination of how people define healthy eating, their experiences and challenges with food journaling, and their interpretation of nutritional information that can be captured in a journal. This includes surveying 257 people to define healthy eating and to rate the healthiness of foods presented as either photos or nutrition labels.
- A field study examining a lightweight photo-based food journal. Specifically, we build and deploy DECAF with 27 people with varying food goals from two distinct trials, each for between 4 to 8 weeks. We examine the challenges participants encounter in journaling relative to their prior methods, the value they find in photos, and differences according to their food goals.
- Discussion of opportunities for lightweight photo-based capture and reflection in mobile food journals. In contrast to quantitative designs, our results suggest an opportunity for qualitative capture and reflection to help support the diversity of goals that people bring to food journaling.

RELATED WORK

We review six areas of related work: benefits, traditional methods, challenges, automation, photos and alternative representations, and alternative views on food journals.

Benefits of Food Journaling

Food journaling can provide benefit across many areas of health. Hollis et al. found weight-loss patients who kept regular food journals lost twice as much weight as patients who kept no records [16]. Reflective analysis of daily food intake and symptom progression is critical in diabetes management, thus motivating food journals and more comprehensive health monitoring systems that help scaffold understanding and interpreting collected data [21,22]. Similarly, food journals and elimination diets are critical tools in identifying and managing food allergies [15,30]. In addition to creating a record, journaling can encourage healthier choices by increasing in-the-moment awareness. Prior studies have found increased mindfulness encouraged journalers to avoid consuming unhealthy foods [17,36].

Traditional Food Journaling Methods

Early methods used lengthy interviews and questionnaires to understand patient eating habits [24]. Recall and paper diaries remain popular in the medical community [7], but mobile devices have become powerful journaling tools. Early research proposed using mobile devices to provide real-time feedback on daily calorie budgets [33]. Outside the medical community, many common commercial phone applications now support using food databases to journal calories and other nutritional information relative to a daily budget (e.g., MyFitnessPal, Lose It!). A person journals food by searching for each component of a meal in the database and then entering portion information. Many applications also allow storing custom recipes, shortcuts for commonly eaten foods, or using barcode scanners to quickly enter packaged foods. Others strive to simplify journaling using a point system (e.g., Weight Watchers).

Challenges of Food Journaling

The high level of engagement required for food journaling can quickly lead to fatigue and reduced compliance [4,12]. Choe et al. found self-trackers across a variety of domains encounter key difficulties in tracking too much information or information that is irrelevant to their goals, contributing to fatigue and abandonment [10]. In research reviewed later in this paper, Cordeiro et al. examine barriers and negative nudges in current food journals [11]. Another important problem is data hoarding, the practice of completing many delayed entries at once [31]. Our interest in photo-based journals is partially motivated by a desire to examine how photo-based capture might reduce fatigue, but also that temptation to hoard might be reduced because a person can only take a photo of food before or during its consumption.

An additional food journaling challenge is the accuracy of journaled nutrition information. Journaled calories can be inaccurate by 20% to 50% [19,20], due to difficulty finding appropriate entries in food databases, unreliable entries in those databases, and difficulty estimating portions [11,35]. Inaccurate estimates are problematic for people relying on them to make decisions relative to a daily budget, especially when combined with errors in estimating calorie expenditure. This plays a role in a popular backlash against gaining weight while following the guidance of popular fitness devices [34].

Automating Food Journals

Researchers have investigated automating food journaling by detecting chewing sounds [1,29] or scanning grocery receipts [23]. Others have proposed automatically capturing meal photos using wearable devices, such as SenseCams [3,32]. In addition to automatic image capture, there have been several attempts to automate nutrition entry, including crowdsourcing nutrient estimates [27] and using computer vision to recognize foods [18,38]. But visually similar foods can have vastly different nutritional profiles (e.g., due to the presence of condiments not visible in a photo, according to whether the food is homemade or processed). As previously noted, full automation may also undermine the mindfulness benefits of food journaling [36]. We designed our photo-based journal to lower the burden of journaling while still requiring active involvement in data capture.

Photos and Alternative Representations in Food Journals

Prior work has proposed food photos to simplify journaling. Photos can be used for estimating nutrient content and portion sizes [6,26] or directly for reflection [5,13]. Zepeda and Deal compare food journaling with paper versus a camera, finding in-the-moment photos increase awareness of unhealthy eating [37]. Frost and Smith develop a system to support diabetes patients in taking and viewing photos in conjunction with visualizations of blood glucose levels, including but not limited to food photos [13]. They report some participants observed trends between foods consumed and blood glucose. Research has also explored other representations for food journals, often intended to simplify capture. Andrew et al.'s POND journaled according to food components (e.g., grains, vegetables, sodium, solid fats, added sugar) and allowed circumventing database search by directly journaling components [2]. Mattila et al. present a multi-dimensional wellness diary that emphasized minimal entry designed for long-term self-tracking, finding sustained usage they argue contrasts with what could be expected of more burdensome journals [25]. We build upon these prior results to examine direct use of photos for lightweight capture and reflection in support of a variety of food-related goals, focusing on contrasts to challenges reported by participants with prior journaling methods.

Alternative Views on Journaling

Many food journals are designed with a focus on persuasion and behavior change, but research has critiqued this as a limiting view. Purpura et al. present Fit4Life, a fictional persuasive system promoting healthy behavior and ideal weight, then use it to discuss issues of control and coercion in self-tracking [28]. Baumer et al. similarly argue a focus on prescriptive persuasion is limiting, then create VERA to explore open-ended social awareness as an alternative approach [5]. More focused on food, Grimes and Harper critique what they term "corrective technology" and suggest "celebratory technology" as an alternative, noting that food journaling can be used as a reflective task to capture positive aspects related to food, such as time spent with family and friends, moments of creativity, and meaningful exchanges [14]. We build on these perspectives of personal empowerment, in that our focus on qualitative capture and reflection in a photo-based journal allows people to interpret their journal according to their personal goals.

FOOD JOURNALING SURVEY

We conducted a survey of 257 people (162 female) of which 141 had current or past food journaling experience. Respondents were recruited from university and local mailing lists, Facebook groups, and Fitbit and MyFitnessPal forums. The median age was 30 years (range: 19 to 70). The majority of respondents (64%) had Body Mass Index (BMI) scores within the normal range, with 10 people opting out of providing height and weight information. Table 1 shows additional survey participant demographics.

All survey respondents were first asked "*What does healthy eating look like to you?*" They were then asked to rate the healthiness of 9 foods on a scale of 1 (Very Unhealthy) to 7 (Very Healthy), using food images or the corresponding nutrition labels. The images and nutrition labels represented the same foods but were presented in a random order. The foods correspond to a range of nutritional profiles, selected to fall into four groups: (1) foods that look healthy in a photo, but unhealthy on a nutritional label (avocado, salmon, mixed nuts), (2) foods that look unhealthy in a photo, but look healthy on a nutritional label (waffles, mac and cheese), (3) foods that look healthy on both (apple, cucumber), and (4) foods that look unhealthy on both (burger, cake). The nutrition labels presented the nutritional information for a single serving. Figure 3 shows a sample food photo and corresponding nutritional label. We note that food is complex, and the medical community has no

	Past Journalers	**Current Journalers**
Gender	69 Female, 25 Male	36 Female, 11 Male
Age	M: 34, SD: 9.5, Min/Max: 21/70	M: 34, SD: 11.7, Min/Max: 19/64
BMI	M: 25, SD: 4.6, Min/Max: 17/43	M: 28, SD: 7, Min/Max: 19/53
Length Journaling	Median: 2-3 months, Min/Max: 1 week / 2+ years	Median: 7-12 months, Min/Max: 1 week / 2+ years
Benefits of Journaling	I feel better about myself (17), it helps me lose weight (35), it makes me think about my eating decisions (75), it helps me find patterns (42), it helps me have a record (44)	I feel better about myself (14), it helps me lose weight (34), it makes me think about my eating decisions (40), it helps me find patterns (23), it helps me have a record (22)
Methods of Journaling	Paper (45), MyFitnessPal (18), Weight Watchers (13), Other Mobile (22), Desktop / Website (19), Fitbit (2), Other(18)	Paper (2), MyFitnessPal (25), Weight Watchers (3), Other Mobile (7), Desktop / Website (4), Fitbit (7), Other (2)
Accuracy of Journal (Remember to log...)	all of their food (30), most of their food (45), 75% of their food (14), 50% of their food (3), mostly forgot (1)	all of their food (20), most of their food (16), 75% of their food (8), 50% of their food (1), 25% of their food (1), mostly forgot (1)
When Meals are Logged	after eating (48), end of the day (19), when remember (8), before eating (4), other (6)	after eating (21), when remember (6), before eating (12), other (4)
Method of Calorie Journaling	64 used calorie journaling: 37 used databases, 31 used the internet, 25 used nutrition labels, 18 estimated on their own, 8 used a book or other resource	40 used calorie journaling: 28 use databases, 19 use the internet, 23 use nutrition labels, 2 estimate on their own, 3 use a book or other resource

Table 1. We surveyed current and past journalers to examine their perspectives on healthy eating and their experiences with current food journaling methods.

single objective measure for rating food healthiness [9]. This survey targets respondent *perceptions* of healthiness.

Past and current journalers were further asked to respond to questions about their goals for food journaling, their journaling methods, the benefits received from journaling, as well as experiences and difficulties in journaling. Respondents who no longer journaled were additionally asked questions targeting their reasons for stopping. We used open coding techniques on open-ended questions to extract themes and gain an understanding of trends.

SURVEY RESULTS

We present survey results in four sections: healthy eating as defined by respondents, food journaling barriers, when and why past journalers stop journaling, and comparing healthiness ratings between photos and nutrition labels. Additional analysis of responses regarding current and past food journaling practices is available in [11], with this paper focusing on their relevance to photo-based food journaling.

What Does Healthy Eating Look Like

Responses to "*What does healthy eating look like to you?*" identified a variety of perspectives, summarized in Figure 2. Responses include consensus around several themes: eating more vegetables (77%), more fruit (53%), or more protein (33%), maintaining a balanced diet (29%), and avoiding processed foods (29%).

In contrast, we note only 24 (9%) respondents mentioned calories. Calories are probably the most pervasive metric for weight-loss and nutrition journaling, but reducing food to such a single numeric value often loses the dimensions respondents said were important (e.g., eating more vegetables, eating more fruit, having a balanced diet,

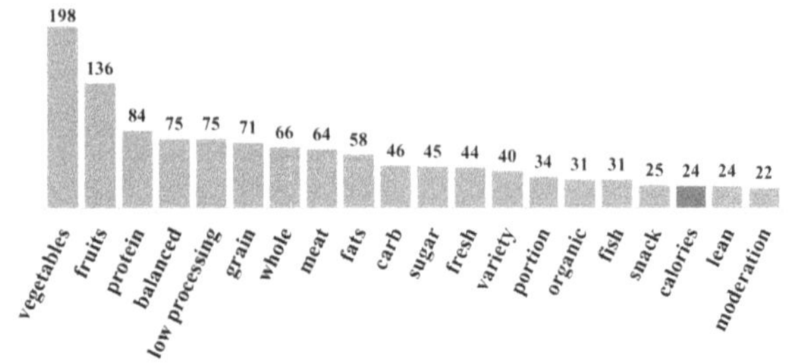

Figure 2. The 20 most frequent survey responses to "*What does healthy eating look like to you?*" Respondents identify a variety of themes, in contrast to a focus on calories in many current food journaling applications.

having a low processed diet). This suggests a mismatch between how people define healthy eating versus the information highlighted in many current food journals.

Food Journaling Challenges

The most cited reason for not journaling was forgetting, with 54% of respondents having missed an entry for this reason. However, forgetting was far from the only reason respondents did not journal. Even when they remembered they should journal, 40% reported choosing not to journal a food that was too difficult to enter. Additional reasons for not journaling included not knowing what was in a meal (40%) or social contexts (20%), such as not wanting to journal in front of friends. This shows that forgetting is not the only challenge in current approaches to capture, thus suggesting opportunities for new designs. But 13% of respondents further reported they intentionally avoided journaling when they ate something unhealthy or did not want to record exceeding a calorie budget: "*Sometimes I feel like not logging things because I know it's really unhealthy.* =(" (P117). This is problematic in that deciding against capture undermines later reflection or analysis.

Although respondents reported packaged food and fast food were the easiest to journal with their prior tools, that conflicted with how they defined healthy eating (e.g., to eat less processed foods). Most journaling applications allow adding entries for foods not found in a database, but many respondents found this tedious. Some even reported avoiding food that was hard to track, instead turning to packaged food: *"They weren't on the list. I just avoided eating things that were hard to log."* (SP132). This exposes a concern that journaling can artificially limit food choices by incentivizing foods that are easier to track, even though those foods may not support journaler goals. Cordeiro et al. discuss this as a negative nudge in current journals [11].

When and Why Did Past Journalers Stop

Of 141 respondents with prior food journaling experience, 94 no longer kept a food journal. Their most common method was paper (48%), and they reported keeping a journal for a median of between 2 to 3 months. In contrast, current journalers primarily used technology (98%) and reported journaling for a median of 7 to 12 months. This suggests technology-simplified journaling is supporting longer-term journaling. The most commonly stated reason for stopping was reduced value over time (37%), either because a new habit was established or a goal was reached. Other reasons included journaling requiring too much effort (25%), being too time consuming (16%), and a loss of motivation (10%). Reasons for stopping were often complex with many factors contributing to the decision.

SP27 was representative of encountering multiple barriers and ultimately deciding to abandon journaling: *"It was too time consuming and tedious. I also did not know what to enter if I ate out, so I often did not enter data and that compounded. I also felt embarrassed to do it in front of friends so I stopped. It seemed like more work than it was worth."* We further discuss these general challenges to food journaling in Cordeiro et al. [11], with the remainder of this paper focusing on our lightweight photo-based food journal.

Comparing Food Representations

We hypothesized food representation impacts perception of healthiness. We tested this by asking respondents to rate 9 food photos and their corresponding nutrition labels on a scale of 1 (Very Unhealthy) to 7 (Very Healthy). We also asked which representation made it easier to determine.

When asked which representation made it easier to determine healthiness, 46% of respondents selected photos, 22% selected nutrition labels, and the remainder had no preference. For participants that preferred photos, many expressed having an image in their mind of what healthy and unhealthy looked like, but knowing less about nutritional contents: "*I think I have roughly accurate pictures in my mind of what a healthy vs. not healthy food looks like, but I'm realizing I don't really know the nutritional makeup of any of these things with any sort of decent accuracy*" (SP190). Many respondents that preferred photos also reported advantages of photos over nutrition labels, such as being able to determine portion sizes, the method of cooking, or whether food was processed: "*I have a hard time understanding size, and whether or not the food is heavily processed, which pictures convey*" (SP170) and "*photographs reveal quality*" (SP179). The respondents that preferred nutritional labels generally worried about pictures hiding condiments and wanted precision in calorie counts, two points we revisit in examining field study responses.

To further examine respondent interpretation of food representations, we calculated the skewness of healthiness rankings for each food in each representation, using the adjusted Fisher-Pearson standardized moment coefficient with a 0.9 cutoff. The skew allowed us to determine the general trend in how respondents perceived the healthiness of each food and compare that trend across representation. The results of these comparisons fell into three groups, shown in Figure 3. We found foods that (1) had the same skew in both representations (e.g., hamburgers rated unhealthy in both, cucumbers rated healthy in both), (2) foods with skew in the photo but no skew in the label (e.g., salmon rated healthy in the photo, but had no skew in labels), and (3) opposing skew (e.g., mixed nuts rated healthy

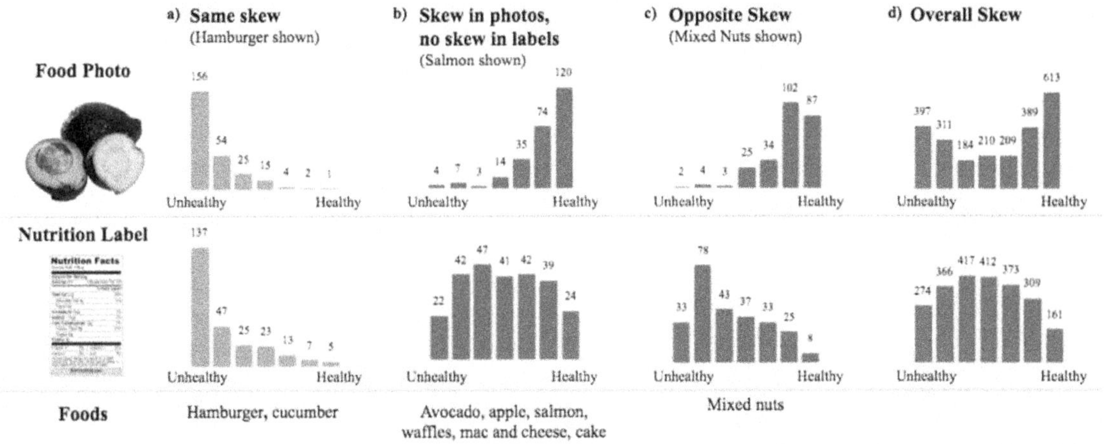

Figure 3. Respondents rated the healthiness of the same foods represented using Food Photos or Nutrition Labels. We found a) foods with agreement in skew in both representations, b) foods with skew in only the photo representation, c) foods with opposing skews in the representations, and d) more extreme ratings for Food Photos.

in the photo, but unhealthy in labels). Consistent with our finding that calories are not primary in how many define healthy eating, these differences in skew show that low-level nutritional information often does not correspond with how people consider food healthiness.

In the photo representation, all foods had either a positive or negative skew. In contrast, only three foods had skew in the nutrition labels representation. Figure 3d illustrates the combined respondent ratings across all foods. Respondents overall ranked photos toward extremes (i.e., "very healthy" or "very unhealthy"). Nutrition labels for the same foods received a broader range of scores. We tested whether photos yield more extreme ratings using a chi-squared test, bucketing ratings in (1, 2, 6, 7) as *extreme* and ratings in (3, 4, 5) as *neutral.* Respondents were significantly more likely to give food an *extreme* rating with a photo representation than with a nutritional label representation $X^2(1, 4626) \approx 624$, $p < .001$. Food photos thus allowed respondents to develop a stronger opinion of the healthiness of foods, while nutrition labels left them unsure. This supports our prior discussion of respondent statements they prefer photos because they understand healthiness but are often unsure how to interpret nutritional information.

FIELD STUDY OF A LIGHTWEIGHT FOOD JOURNAL

Our survey reveals challenges in food journal design, mismatches between journals versus how people define healthy eating, and opportunities for photo-based capture. Because of the survey method, responses were based in recollections and hypothetical foods. We complement this with a field study examining photo-based journaling with the food that journalers encounter in their everyday lives.

We conducted our field study by developing a food journal organized around photos and does not include calories or nutrition information. We deployed it with 27 people to examine: (1) the impact of photo-based capture on food journaling challenges, (2) what value photos provide absent nutritional details, and (3) how journaling challenges and the value of photos vary according to journaler goals.

Figure 4. The DECAF mobile interface, showing a blank journal entry (left) and a scrolling journal view (right).

The DECAF Food Journal

We conduct our field study using a lightweight, photo-based journal, DECAF (*Diary of Emotion, Context, And Food*). It consists of two components: (1) a mobile application for easy food capture, and (2) a website for providing details and reflection. At the time of eating, a journaler simply opens the application and adds an entry with an "I Am Eating" button. Mobile journal entries can include a picture of the food, a description, and a rating of current mood (as seen in Figure 4). The myDECAF.org website allows providing additional detailed information about an entry, such as which meal of the day, the meal enjoyment rating, meal location, how many and with whom it was eaten, feelings after eating, and a description of the meal components (as seen in Figure 1). DECAF explicitly and intentionally does not log calories or other nutritional details, as our focus is on participant response to photo-based capture and reflection in comparison to prior journaling techniques.

Procedure

Participants installed DECAF on their own phone. We encouraged them to use the application for in-the-moment journaling and to then visit the website nightly to provide additional details. Participants were compensated $20 for every week they journaled their food and provided details on the website. The study consisted of a one-hour pre-study session, use of the journal for four weeks, and a one-hour post-study session. Some participants who kept thorough journals were given the option to continue for up to 4 more weeks, with an additional one-hour interview.

In the initial session, we interviewed participants about their health goals, past journaling experiences, and eating routines. In the post-study session, we asked multiple choice and Likert scale questions and then a semi-structured interview. The interview began by asking participants to reflect on their four weeks of DECAF usage. We finished with a series of questions about advantages, disadvantages, difficulties, and valuable aspects of any prior journaling methods as well as those for photo-based journaling with DECAF. We transcribed the semi-structured interviews and used open coding techniques to extract themes.

Participants

We recruited 27 participants to use DECAF for between 4 and 8 weeks (not including 3 drop outs). Participants ranged in age from 21 to 64 years (M: 39, SD: 13) and had a range of health goals and journaling experience. Although all field participants indicated a general goal of wanting to make healthier food choices, their specific goals ranged from substantial weight loss to transitioning their diet to be vegan or vegetarian. Participants were in two trials:

Trial 1 consisted of 14 participants (after 2 drop outs) from the Seattle area. Participants were recruited from university and local mailing lists based on interest in food journaling. This trial included several people on vegetarian, vegan, and low-processed food diets. 10 people had previous food journaling experience. This trial ran November to January.

Trial 2 consisted of 13 participants (after 1 drop out) recruited from the University of Rochester Medical Center using ResearchMatch. All had a BMI >= 25, indicating they were overweight or obese. As in Trial 1, we recruited based on interest in food journaling, and 10 had previous experience. This trial ran January to February.

FIELD STUDY RESULTS

We present our field deployment results in terms of usage, the impact of lightweight journaling on challenges, the value of photos, and differences by journaler food goal.

Usage

Common challenges with long-term food journaling include compliance and data hoarding. Estimating compliance is difficult as there is no ground truth as to what food was consumed. To approximate compliance, we examine the journaling rate. Participants journaled for an average of 5.2 weeks, a total of 3569 entries, an average of 3.5 entries per participant per day. This suggests overall high usage.

We expected in-the-moment photo-based journaling to minimize hoarding, as a photo can only be taken before or during food consumption. To detect hoarding, we logged the eating time and the journaling time, then compared the timestamps. We defaulted the eating time to "Now" and asked participants to change it to match when they ate. Participants generally journaled within 10 minutes of eating (86% of all entries). Because 94% of entries created within 10 minutes of eating contained photos of the food, they were not susceptible to hoarding. In contrast, a journal entry created more than 30 minutes after eating normally did not contain a photo (12% of all entries were created more than 30 minutes after eating, only 20% of which include a photo). When delayed entries did contain a photo, it was often of dirty plates or empty wrappers. Although such photos would be difficult or impossible for transcription by an automated system or by other people, participants reported they supported their ability to remember what they ate.

Impact of Lightweight Journaling on Challenges

Similar to our survey findings, all field participants with prior food journaling experience reported their prior techniques made packaged food and fast food easiest to log, with home-cooked meals being more challenging. In contrast, photo journals lowered this barrier and leveled the playing field among meal types. Taking a picture is equally difficult regardless of preparation, and participants rated all food types at the same difficulty. 60% of field participants with prior journaling experience reported they sometimes did not journal a meal with their prior technique because it was too difficult. With photo-based journaling in DECAF, only 22% reported not journaling because it was too difficult. Participants still reported difficulty when food is eaten over time (e.g., appetizer, main dish, dessert) or in a sampling manner (e.g., a buffet, at a party). These types of meals require several entries throughout dining, increasing burden and the likelihood of forgetting or choosing to not journal [11].

With many journaling methods, it is difficult to log a meal if a journaler does not know the exact ingredients. 65% of field participants with prior experience reported not journaling with their prior technique because they did not know the ingredients. Knowing meal composition does not impact the ability to journal a meal with photos, and none of our participants reported not journaling for this reason.

There are also often social challenges surrounding food journaling. 55% of field study participants with prior journaling experience reported this was a challenge with their prior technique. Although publicly taking photos of food with phones has become more accepted, participants reported similar challenges with photo journals. 52% reported feeling awkward photographing food in front of others. The types of meals reported as most socially awkward to photograph were restaurant meals, dinner at a friend's house, and food at a party. We note these are also contexts in which food often comes over time, and so this challenge may interact with the above challenge.

Finally, although participants reported photo-based capture reduced barriers to journaling, simply forgetting to journal remains a challenge. 95% of participants with prior experience reported forgetting to journal with their prior technique, and 93% of participants reported sometimes forgetting with DECAF. Because there is no ground truth in either case, we cannot determine if reducing barriers with photo-based capture impacts the frequency of forgetting. But this clearly remains a challenge for food journal design.

Value of Photos

Photos provide rapid capture, but people also need to obtain value from the data they capture. DECAF explicitly and intentionally does not log calories or other nutritional details, as we explore the value people obtain directly from the photos themselves. Of the 3569 entries journaled in the deployment, 3136 (88%) included photos. Many said photos were the most salient feature: "*the strength was obviously the photos*" (FP34), "*I think the pictures were great. With pictures you, even if there are no words there, you understand a lot*" (FP11). During the final interview, we asked participants to talk aloud as they reflected on the most recent weeks of their journal. Many described looking only at photos, ignoring other information they collected: "*I'm totally just looking at the picture*" (FP4), "*I'm just looking at the picture, that's the interesting thing*" (FP11).

Who, What, Where, How

Photos were not merely "*the interesting thing*", as interview participants reported that photo context supported much richer recall (e.g., where a meal was eaten, what other tasks had been accomplished that day, who was eaten with, and the preparation and makeup of the food). FP9 stated "*I can know what I ate, what I typically eat, I can remember the events, I can understand myself better*". Photo background often contained enough detail that participants knew where they had eaten (as in Figure 5c): "*[mom] actually has nice tablecloths and really nice plates, so I know it's her house*" (FP11), "*you can see my counter*" (FP3). Participants also reported purposely including context so they could later know where they had eaten (e.g., FP4 included her laptop when eating at work).

Some participants expressed an emotional connection to photos that captured happy times they had with friends and family: "*Having the picture reminded me of how I was feeling that day, and the context around it*" (FP10). Some also reported purposely including people in photos so that they could better remember those times (as in Figure 5a). FP11 said "*I purposely got my boyfriend's hand [in the photo], because I wanted to remember that he was there*".

Survey respondents had expressed concern that nutritional labels often do not provide the preparation of food, such as what oils were used or the level of processing. Conversely, some had expressed concerns that photos might hide condiments or other high-calorie portions of a meal. In our field study, we found participants could use their photos in seeing or remembering these details of food they had eaten. FP13 was on a low-processed diet, and described being able to tell if her food met her goal by quickly scanning photos for wrappers: "*From my pictures it's pretty obvious to me if it was prepackaged or not.*" Similarly, some participants

Figure 5. Participant photos supported rich recall, including a) with whom food was eaten, b) details of food that was eaten, c) context of where food was eaten.

reported scanning photos for color as an indication of the presence of more vegetables. Several said photos helped with determining portion sizes: "*It gave you an idea of what your portions are [...] 'Wow, I ate way too much pasta in that bowl.'*" (FP24). Finally, participants reported using cues in the photos to remember food that was not actually in the photo: "*an empty muesli bowl looks different than an empty salad bowl, because my salad dressing always has balsamic vinegar in it, so it's kinda brown, whereas muesli is kinda white*" (FP5). Overall, participants reported they could flexibly interpret photos during reflection, including remembering context that would be difficult or impossible to recover with an automated system or by another person.

Triggers and Trends

Participants were able to use photos in making deeper connections that attributed cause to context. They often identified the places they were at and the people they were with as influences in why they made certain food choices: "*[the photos] reminded me of what I ate and what was the situation*" (FP6), "*I know I ate all of these cookies because my friend came to visit*" (FP11). Participants were also able to use photos in picking out higher-level trends confirming beliefs they had about themselves: "*I eat too much pizza*" (FP10), "*I have salad for lunch every single day*" (FP5), "*For breakfast, I eat lots of the same things*" (FP4). They also identified previously unrecognized patterns: "*I don't branch out as much as I thought I did, even when I go somewhere new, I kind of get what I always get somewhere else*" (FP10), "*I eat a lot of the same thing, and I eat kind of boring*" (FP19), "*I'm surprised at how many times I'm seeing things that I consider an exception to my diet!*" (FP4), "*I didn't eat as many fruits and vegetables as I thought*" (FP16). Identifying triggers and trends can be an important use of a food journal in improving eating habits and identifying new goals. Participants used photos for this, but more explicit support could add lightweight tagging in support of more active sorting and filtering mechanisms, without imposing calories or nutritional details.

Awareness and Mindfulness

Wilde and Garvin define increased awareness of behavior as one of two complementary components in self-tracking [36]. Photo-based captured encouraged participants to journal at the moment of eating, which they found helped them think about their food choices: *"The simple action of logging makes me think about what I eat and how much of it"* (FP6). Participants reported taking photos created additional mindfulness because they did not want unhealthy food to appear in their journal: "*The fact that there would be a picture made me have healthier snacks*" (FP19), "*Do I really want to eat this? I'm capturing this image*" (FP17), *"I didn't want to take a picture of chips, or a bunch of really bad food, so I guess that kinda helped me make more healthy food choices, just the act of taking a picture"* (FP2), "*when I had to take a picture of it, I was more worried about what was in the picture, that there should be some fruits and vegetables*" (FP16). Such reactions suggest calorie budgets or detailed nutritional information are not necessarily required for healthier in-the-moment decisions. If people already know what is healthy, the mindfulness of journaling can itself encourage healthier choices.

Differences by Goal

Our field study included two separate trials with participants with varying goals. Trial 1 contained participants with a general interest in food journaling, while Trial 2 contained only participants that were overweight or obese and trying to lose weight. Because our system did not contain calories or other nutrition details, we expected different reactions from participants according to their health goals. Although most participants across both trials saw value in photos as part of a food journal, we found differences in how the photos were used and the benefits they provided. Trial 1 participants generally found the lack of calories to be a strength, while most Trial 2 participants felt they needed calorie information to reach their weight goal: "*I need to know calories*" (FP24), "*calories and nutrients, the things in the food really matter to me the most*" (FP19), "*I think someone starting out really needs [calories]*" (FP20).

After using photo-based journaling, some Trial 2 participants changed their view, seeing additional value: "*I think you can tell a lot from the pictures. You might not have your calorie count. But, am I eating something too fattening? Is my portion too large?*" (FP28). When reflecting on their diary at the end of the study, several had strong reactions to actually seeing the photos of what they were eating: "*When I would get on the computer, I would look at the diary and realize that I was on a really bad road. I realized what I was eating for the last month. It was awful!*" (FP24) and "*The history was kind of a wake up call for me*" (FP25).

Several Trial 2 participants liked photos in conjunction with calorie information: "*I would LOVE if I could see the picture on MyFitnessPal*" (FP26). Many also decided to additionally track calories using other methods, using photos as a quick way to capture the foods consumed for later lookup: "*easier to figure out what the calories are from the pictures*" (FP22) and *"For some meals, it's just really easy to take a picture.... Rather than sit there and type in every ingredient*" (FP20). We have noted prior work uses photos as an intermediate capture to support later calorie entry, and our results support such a usage. But our broader results also show this should not be required nor assumed as the primary usage, and journals should instead support a variety of goals enabled by photo-based capture.

DISCUSSION

We found that photo-based capture and reflection can directly support a variety of food journaling practices in support of diverse goals. We now discuss our results relative to challenges participants reported with their prior techniques.

Journaling Without Judgment

13% of survey participants and 45% of field participants reported that in their prior journaling they sometimes chose not to journal because food exceeded their calorie budget or because the food was unhealthy. In contrast, none of our field participants reported avoiding journaling an entry for this reason. Photo-based journaling supported capture while avoiding creating feelings of failure and judgment: *"[DECAF was] easier because there were no calorie counts, no judgments, but still makes you aware"* (FP14). Such reactions suggest a potential for some separation between in-the-moment capture and more goal-oriented reflection. We have noted the act of journaling itself creates mindfulness, but that "bad" moments can create a sense of judgment that undermines capture and therefore later reflection. This is especially damaging if failing to capture those "bad" moments prevents a journaler from correctly diagnosing a trigger, identifying a trend, or achieving a goal. A design opportunity exists for considering how to support capture of "bad" moments while promoting outside-of-the-moment reflection in the context of goals.

Role of Personalization

Field participants wanted to track aspects of their diet that were not supported by DECAF or other existing journals. These include whether a food was organic or grass-fed, the level of processing of a food, and the oils used when cooking. 37% of our survey participants with prior journaling experience reported they stopped journaling due to reduced value over time, so providing mechanisms to set and track varied personal goals could help journalers stay motivated. People change their goals over time, and there is an opportunity for systems that allow people to change the goals of their journaling. For example, many participants mentioned trying to lose weight and then keep it off while eating more nutritiously. These are two distinct goals, and the support a system should provide when a person is trying to lose weight may be different than when trying to maintain weight and eat nutritiously. Journals should be configurable to support evolving personal goals.

Active Reminders

The top reported reason for not journaling food in our survey was simply forgetting. Although using photos as a capture mechanism lowered the journaling barrier, our field participants also struggled with remembering to log. Future systems could combine lightweight capture methods with automatic reminders to log. For example, research is examining detection of visual or audio characteristics that correspond to eating [1,3,29,32]. Another possibility would be using journal history to identify routines that can prompt reminders at likely eating times. In contrast to proposals for automated journaling, a combination of lightweight capture and active reminders could keep journalers involved in capture, thus providing the benefits of mindfulness while reducing the burden of remembering to journal.

Journaling During Transitions

Long-term compliance is often a goal in self-tracking, but our results suggest targeted journaling at critical times may provide benefits without requiring long-term adoption. We administered the study over a time containing food-related holidays (American Thanksgiving, Hanukkah, Christmas) as well as New Years Day (when many set health goals). For our student participants, the study also spanned the university transitions of finals week, winter break, and a new quarter. A trend in our interviews was a persistent optimism that, although their eating was not currently ideal, in the future it would be easier: "*I want to go back to the normal. The past month is a lot different and a lot of times I couldn't really have the food I wanted to eat.*" (FP9). Although optimism can be good, it can also encourage people to postpone changing behaviors because they hope it will be easier if they just wait a bit longer. Targeting journaling during times of transition may help people navigate these times with a higher level of awareness and help them implement habits in their new environment that can persist after journaling has ended.

Robustness to Missing Data

Survey respondents and field study participants reported many reasons for not logging a meal with prior techniques (e.g., forgetting, it being too difficult, not knowing the ingredients). Missed entries are particularly problematic for calorie-based food journals, as the primary feedback is quantitative (e.g., a sum relative to a budget, an average over the past week). Missed entries make this inaccurate, so one missed entry can derail an entire day or more of journaling: "*it showed the amount of calories you took in that week but if you didn't fill out most of the week it was sort of useless. So then I started with a lot of effort but as it started to go down, it sort of snow balled from there*" (FP2). As reported by Cordeiro et al. [11], participants reported that with prior techniques they often would not bother journaling after missing a single meal in a day, sometimes leading them to abandon journaling: "*Too hard to remember to do it after every meal. Then I got discouraged once I got behind and was never able to catch up again.*" (SP81).

In contrast, participants reported that forgetting to photograph a meal did not devalue journaling other meals, as each represented a self-contained data point. By focusing on a data presentation that does not require long periods of perfect compliance, missing a meal did not initiate longer periods of non-journaling. This suggests robustness toward missing data should be considered in the design of food journals. Even if photos are not a primary format, alternative presentations could better preserve value and motivation for journaling in the face of missing data.

Interpretability of Data Representation

Prior work finds calorie journals are inaccurate by as much as 20% to 50% [19,20], and 46% of our survey respondents preferred food represented as photos over nutrition labels. Even respondents with prior food journaling experience expressed difficulty interpreting nutrition labels without the context of the foods. Although that context is available during capture of the food a person eats, many journals remove the context in daily or weekly summaries that focus on a summary of calories or other nutritional details. The result is often a journal that is both inaccurate and difficult to interpret in the context of a person's goals.

In contrast to measurement, photos emphasizes capture. Field study participants reported diverse value in photos as their primary data representation. Although some with specific weight-related goals also wanted calories, most felt photos provided information about what was eaten, how the food was cooked, with whom food was eaten, and the context surrounding the meal. Participants were able to interpret their journals to quickly determine whether they thought it was a healthy or unhealthy week, a personal judgment that can be difficult with nutritional summaries. Participants were also able to identify trends and triggers that would have been masked in a nutritional summary. Photo-based representation is thus familiar and interpretable, allowing journalers to leverage existing food knowledge. Although there are important questions about how to help people improve food knowledge, our results show an opportunity for designs to exploit existing knowledge in support of diverse food-related goals.

CONCLUSION

People bring a variety of goals to food journaling, and they report prior techniques fail to support or even undermine their self-tracking. Our work has examined direct use of photos in a food journal to support capture and reflection. We deployed a lightweight photo-based food journal with 27 participants for between 4 to 8 weeks. Participants report photos ease capture, present information that is important to them (e.g. food variety, level of processing, vegetables), and support reflection to identify triggers and trends. Our work thus provides support for photo-based journaling to augment or sometimes replace methods focused on calories or other nutritional details. Photos can support journaling relevant to a variety of food-related goals, while also removing or reducing barriers associated with common methods.

ACKNOWLEDGEMENTS

We thank Daniel Epstein, Julie Kientz, and Sean Munson for their feedback. This work was funded in part by the Intel Science and Technology Center for Pervasive Computing and by the National Science Foundation under awards OAI-1028195 and SCH-1344613.

REFERENCES

1. Amft, O., Stäger, M., Lukowicz, P., and Tröster, G. Analysis of Chewing Sounds for Dietary Monitoring. *UbiComp 2005*, 56-72.
2. Andrew, A.H., Borriello, G., and Fogarty, J. Simplifying Mobile Phone Food Diaries: Design and Evaluation of a Food Index-Based Nutrition Diary. *PervasiveHealth 2013*, 260-263.
3. Arab, L., Estrin, D., Kim, D.H., Burke, J., and Goldman, J. (2011). Feasibility Testing of an Automated Image-Capture Method to Aid Dietary Recall. *Eur J Clin Nutr, 65*(10), 1156-1162.
4. Barrett-Connor, E. (1991). Nutrition Epidemiology: How Do We Know What They Ate? *Am J Clin Nutr, 54*(1 Suppl), 182S-187S.
5. Baumer, E.P.S., Katz, S.J., Freeman, J.E., Adams, P., Gonzales, A.L., Pollak, J., Retelny, D., Niederdeppe, J., Olson, C.M., and Gay, G.K. Prescriptive Persuasion and Open-Ended Social Awareness. *CSCW 2012*, 475-484.
6. Bird, G. and Elwood, P.C. (1983). The Dietary Intakes of Subjects Estimated from Photographs Compared with a Weighed Record. *Hum Nutr Appl Nutr, 37*(6), 470-473.
7. Burke, B.S. (1947). The Dietary History as a Tool in Research. *J Am Diet Assoc, 23*(12), 1041-1046.
8. Burke, L.E., Wang, J., and Sevick, M.A. (2011). Self-Monitoring in Weight Loss: A Systematic Review of the Literature. *J Am Diet Assoc, 111*(1), 92-102.
9. Chahoud, G., Aude, Y.W., and Mehta, J.L. (2004). Dietary Recommendations in the Prevention and Treatment of Coronary Heart Disease: Do We Have the Ideal Diet Yet? *Am J Cardiol, 94*(10), 1260-1267.
10. Choe, E.K., Lee, N.B., Lee, B., Pratt, W., and Kientz, J.A. Understanding Quantified-Selfers' Practices in Collecting and Exploring Personal Data. *CHI 2014*, 1143-1152.
11. Cordeiro, F., Epstein, D.,Thomaz, E., Bales, E., Jagannathan, A.K., Abowd, G., and Fogarty, J. Barriers and Negative Nudges: Exploring Challenges in Food Journaling. *CHI 2015*, To Appear.
12. Craig, M.R., Kristal, A.R., Cheney, C.L., and Shattuck, A.L. (2000). The Prevalence and Impact of 'Atypical' Days in 4-Day Food Records. *J Am Diet Assoc, 100*(4), 421-427.
13. Frost, J. and Smith, B.K. Visualizing Health: Imagery in Diabetes Education. *DUX 2003*, 1-14.
14. Grimes, A. and Harper, R. Celebratory Technology: New Directions for Food Research in HCI. *CHI 2008*, 467-476.
15. Heizer, W.D., Southern, S., and McGovern, S. (2009). The Role of Diet in Symptoms of Irritable Bowel Syndrome in Adults: A Narrative Review. *J Am Diet Assoc, 109*(7), 1204-1214.
16. Hollis, J.F., Gullion, C.M., Stevens, V.J., Brantley, P.J., Appel, L.J., Ard, J.D., Champagne, C.M., Dalcin, A., Erlinger, T.P., Funk, K., Laferriere, D., Lin, P.-H., Loria, C.M., Samuel-Hodge, C., Vollmer, W.M., and Svetkey, L.P. (2008). Weight Loss During the Intensive Intervention Phase of the Weight-Loss Maintenance Trial. *Am J Prev Med, 35*(2), 118-126.
17. Kanfer, F.H. (1970). Self-Monitoring: Methodological Limitations and Clinical Applications. *J Consult Clin Psych, 35*(2), 148-152.
18. Kong, F. and Tan, J. DietCam: Regular Shape Food Recognition with a Camera Phone. *BSN 2011*, 127-132.
19. Lansky, D. and Brownell, K.D. (1982). Estimates of Food Quantity and Calories: Errors in Self-Report among Obese Patients. *Am J Clin Nutr, 35*(4), 727-732.
20. Livingstone, M.B., Prentice, A.M., Strain, J.J., Coward, W.A., Black, A.E., Barker, M.E., McKenna, P.G., and Whitehead, R.G. (1990). Accuracy of Weighed Dietary Records in Studies of Diet and Health. *BMJ, 300(*6726), 708-712.
21. Mamykina, L., Mynatt, E., Davidson, P., and Greenblatt, D. MAHI: Investigation of Social Scaffolding for Reflective Thinking in Diabetes Management. *CHI 2008*, 477-486.
22. Mamykina, L., Mynatt, E.D., and Kaufman, D.R. Investigating Health Management Practices of Individuals with Diabetes. *CHI 2006*, 927-936.
23. Mankoff, J., Hsieh, G., Hung, H.C., Lee, S., and Nitao, E. Using Low-Cost Sensing to Support Nutritional Awareness. *UbiComp 2002*, 371-376.
24. Marr, J.W. (1971). Individual Dietary Surveys: Purposes and Methods. *World Rev Nutr Diet, 13*, 105-164.
25. Mattila, E., Pärkkä, J., Hermersdorf, M., Kaasinen, J., Vainio, J., Samposalo, K., Merilahti, J., Kolari, J., Kulju, M., Lappalainen, R., and Korhonen, I. (2008). Mobile Diary for Wellness Management - Results on Usage and Usability in Two User Studies. *IEEE Trans Inf Technol Biomed, 12*(4), 501-512.
26. Nelson, M., Atkinson, M., and Darbyshire, S. (1996). Food Photography II: Use of Food Photographs for Estimating Portion Size and the Nutrient Content of Meals. *Br J Nutr, 76*(1), 31-49.
27. Noronha, J., Hysen, E., Zhang, H., and Gajos, K.Z. Platemate: Crowdsourcing Nutritional Analysis from Food Photographs. *UIST 2011*, 1-12.
28. Purpura, S., Schwanda, V., Williams, K., Stubler, W., and Sengers, P. Fit4Life: The Design of a Persuasive Technology Promoting Healthy Behavior and Ideal. *CHI 2011*, 423-432.
29. Rahman, T., Adams, A.T., Zhang, M., Cherry, E., Zhou, B., Peng, H., and Choudhury, T. BodyBeat: A Mobile System for Sensing Non-Speech Body Sounds. *MobiSys 2014*, 2-13.
30. Sicherer, S.H. and Sampson, H.A. (2010). Food Allergy. *J Allergy Clin Immunol, 125*(2 Suppl 2), S116-S125.
31. Stone, A.A., Shiffman, S., Schwartz, J.E., Broderick, J.E., and Hufford, M.R. (2003). Patient Compliance with Paper and Electronic Diaries. *Control Clin Trials, 24*(2), 182-199.
32. Thomaz, E., Parnami, A., Essa, I., and Abowd, G.D. Feasibility of Identifying Eating Moments from First-Person Images Leveraging Human Computation. *SenseCam 2013*, 26-33.
33. Tsai, C.C., Lee, G., Raab, F., Norman, G.J., Sohn, T., Griswold, W.G., and Patrick, K. (2007). Usability and Feasibility of PmEB: A Mobile Phone Application for Monitoring Real Time Caloric Balance. *Mobile Netw Appl, 12*(2-3), 173-184.
34. Urist, J. My Fitness Band Is Making Me Fat: Users Complain of Weight Gain with Trackers. *Today.com*, July 16, 2014.
35. Wansink, B. and van Ittersum, K. (2007). Portion Size Me: Downsizing Our Consumption Norms. *J Am Diet Assoc, 107*(7), 1103-1106.
36. Wilde, M.H. and Garvin, S. (2007). A Concept Analysis of Self-Monitoring. *J Adv Nurs, 57*(3), 339-350.
37. Zepeda, L. and Deal, D. (2008). Think Before You Eat: Photographic Food Diaries as Intervention Tools to Change Dietary Decision Making and Attitudes. *Int J Consum Stud, 32*(6), 692-698.
38. Zhu, F., Bosch, M., Boushey, C.J., and Delp, E.J. (2010). An Image Analysis System for Dietary Assessment and Evaluation. *ICIP* 2010, 1853-1856.

Collective Sensemaking in Online Health Forums

Lena Mamykina, Drashko Nakikj, Noemie Elhadad
Columbia University, Department of Biomedical Informatics
622 W. 168th Street, New York, NY 10032
{om2196, dn2311, ne60}@cumc.columbia.edu

ABSTRACT
Online health communities collect vast amounts of information and opinions in regards to health and wellness management. However, these opinions are usually stored within lengthy and loosely structured discussion threads; synthesizing information in these threads can be challenging. In this mixed-methods study, grounded in the theoretical perspective of collective sensemaking, we examined patterns of communication within an online diabetes community TuDiabetes. The results of the study suggest that members of TuDiabetes often construct shared meaning through deep discussions, back and forth negotiation of perspectives, and resolution of conflicts in opinions. However, unlike participants of other sensemaking communities, members of TuDiabetes often value multiplicity of opinions rather than consensus. We use study results to draw implications for the design of computing platforms for facilitating collective sensemaking that promote construction of shared knowledge yet embrace diversity of opinions.

Author Keywords: Online health communities, collective sensemaking, diabetes

ACM Classification Keywords: H5.3. Group and Organization Interfaces: Web-based Interaction

INTRODUCTION
With the growing prevalence of chronic diseases and disorders such as cancer, diabetes and autism, more individuals are turning to peers and often seek support and advice online [4]. According to the 2009 Pew Report, close to one third of all Americans had accessed social media for questions related to health [9]. Yet despite the high popularity of online health forums, the progress in platforms that support them has been slow. The vast majority of these forums continue to rely on traditional discussion boards, in which users propose new topics for discussion and invite others to respond. The resulting discussion threads can include hundreds of individual contributions, many of them stating diverse opinions, with different degrees of relevance to the original post. Synthesizing and comprehending this information can be challenging, particularly for newcomers, and lead to information overload and disengagement [20].

CHI 2015, April 18 - 23 2015, Seoul, Republic of Korea

ACM 978-1-4503-3145-6/15/04…$15.00
http://dx.doi.org/10.1145/2702123.2702566

Over the years, there emerged several novel types of platforms that facilitate knowledge construction and sharing within communities of peers. For example, in Wikipedia, individuals engage in collaborative writing of articles on topics of mutual interest [21]. This often involves coordination, negotiation, and resolution of differences in opinions [22]. In Question and Answer sites (Q&A) such as Stack Overflow, individuals ask questions on topics of interest, receive answers from others, and identify the best answers through voting [23]. Both of these approaches have been shown successful in inspiring collective construction of knowledge and shared understanding. However, there remains a question as to whether these novel platforms can help to facilitate information sharing and learning within online health communities.

In order to examine how individuals in online health communities share information and learn from each other, we conducted a study of TuDiabetes, an online forum for individuals with diabetes (both Type 1 and Type 2). It was created in 2008 and has over 30,000 members. TuDiabetes' computing platform includes such features as public profiles, public and private forums that preserve discussion threads, live chat, and blogs, among others.

We approached our study from the theoretical perspective of sensemaking and, in particular, collective sensemaking [43]. Sensemaking is chiefly concerned with how individuals make sense of dynamic social environments and situations [40],[41]. Collective sensemaking shifts focus from an individual to communities of peers and examines how members of these communities create shared knowledge structures and build meaning together [43]. Previously, Swartz used a similar collective intelligence perspective to examine transformation of facts on Wikipedia [38]. Building upon this work, we set out to examine whether and how individuals in TuDiabetes construct shared knowledge structures, and how their style of engagement compares to the one found within Wikipedia and Stack Overflow. Our mixed-methods approach included qualitative interviews with members of the community, quantitative analysis of patterns of interactions within TuDiabetes forums, qualitative analysis of 30 of the most popular discussion threads, and deep discourse analysis of 2 of these threads.

The study revealed that similarly to authors in Wikipedia, and participants of Stack Overflow, members of TuDiabetes often engage in deep discussions on topics of mutual interest, examine different opinions, and seek to resolve conflicting perspectives, thus exhibiting all defining properties of collective sensemaking. The study also suggested that the three attributes of collective sensemaking in online forums include: 1) lateral engagement between participants, 2) reflection on previously stated perspectives, and 3) transformation of ideas throughout the posts in the thread. Further, the study suggested that certain properties of individuals' posts, for example reference to a contentious topic or generalized presentation of a personal problem, are likely to lead to inspired discussions and can serve as triggers for collective sensemaking. However, and somewhat in contrast with Wikipedia authors and participants of Stack Overflow who usually seek consensus, members of TuDiabetes often value multiplicity and diversity of perspectives, rather than agreement among contributors.

The study also showed that the organization of posts in threads often obscures traces of collective sensemaking from members not actively participating in these discussions. A common reading strategy reported by study participants—random sampling of posts throughout a thread—breaks rich structures of shared meaning and can leave individuals with a fragmented perspective on a topic. To address these limitations, we propose that new platforms for collective sensemaking can help individuals to engage in more explicit construction of shared artifacts, help individuals to express how their contributions relate to previous perspectives, and generate visual summaries of collective sensemaking using a combination of computational text analysis and information visualization.

BACKGROUND

Sensemaking and Collective Sensemaking

Sensemaking is an approach to conceptualizing and investigating how individuals make sense of complex, dynamic, often social environments and situations [40],[41]. Over the years, researchers explored sensemaking in many different contexts [28] from education [37], [6], to organizational science [40]. In HCI, sensemaking is often viewed as individuals' interaction with vast amounts of information in the context of professional analytics and Web 2.0 technologies [34], [10].

Collective and collaborative sensemaking shift focus onto groups of individuals making meaning together. In *collaborative sensemaking* groups actively work on pursuing common goals (e.g. [31]). In *collective sensemaking*, individuals use each other to collectively make sense of new information, rather than work towards a common goal (e.g., [5]). A related body of work on *collective intelligence* often focuses on its products and associated extrinsic benefits [25].

There exist several theoretical accounts of collective sensemaking. Wenger argues that collective sensemaking involves two interrelated processes: participation and reification [43]. *Participation* refers to the social experience of membership in social communities and active involvement in social enterprise. *Reification* refers to the "process of giving form to our experience by producing objects that congeal our experience into "thingness" (p.58). This perspective is consistent with the views espoused by the proponents of Distributed Cognition (DC) that is concerned with propagation of representational states across a series of representational media [14], [19].

Computing Platforms for Collective Sensemaking and Collective Intelligence

To date researchers in HCI and related fields developed a host of approaches to promoting individual as well as collective sensemaking. Tools for individual sensemaking focus on ways to represent information [32], [11] and organize search results [1]. Entity Workspace supports sensemaking by allowing users to explore a large collection of documents, highlight important terms, annotate content, and organize information [3].

In recent years Wikipedia presented a fertile ground for investigation of collective sensemaking and intelligence [25], [7], with different studies focusing on coordination of work [21], styles of leadership [45], and issues related to content ownership [12]. A recent analysis by Swarts suggested that collective intelligence in Wikipedia is accomplished through the "back and forth writing, editing, and revising, through periods of negotiation and article stability." [38] Consistently with this account, in our study we specifically focused on the evidence of "back and forth" engagement between members of TuDiabetes.

A somewhat alternative approach to supporting collective sensemaking is offered by social Question and Answer sites (Q&A). In Q&A sites large distributed groups of individuals ask questions and provide answers on topics of mutual interest and negotiate shared meaning through voting, comments and discussions [13], [16], [27], [24], [17], [23].

Tools that explicitly target collaborative sensemaking often focus on collaborative information seeking on the Web. For example CoSense system [30] specifically targets individuals engaged in active teamwork, rather than members of loosely organized communities. Finally, tools for distributed sensemkaing [8] help individuals to benefit from the sensemaking activities of others; however in distributed sensemaking these individuals neither collaborate nor coordinate their sensemaking activities.

Information sharing within online health forums

Previous studies of online health forums mostly focused on information seeking [26], [35], emotional support [42] and seeking and coordinating help [36], rather than on transformation of ideas, negotiation of meaning, and resolution of conflicts. A recent study by Huh and Ackerman of another diabetes forum, dLife.com, specifically examined individuals' interactions around seeking and receiving help [18]. These researchers suggested that individuals operationalize their experiences using their personal illness trajectories. In addition, they argued that individuals develop common understanding in regards to diabetes self-management through alignment of personal histories and opinions. Zhou et al provided a detailed account of unique issues faced by the members of a Chinese online diabetes community, Sweet Home, for example the need to negotiate two different approaches to medicine, Western and traditional Chinese, and the struggle to meet social expectations [44]. The study presented here builds upon these works and suggests a number of contentious issues negotiated by the international membership of TuDiabetes. Moreover, it carefully examines the process through which this negotiation is accomplished: what factors serve as triggers, the steps involved in the process, and the different contributions members make to advance the overall discussion.

METHODS

This study used a mixed-methods approach. First, we conducted qualitative open-ended interviews with administrators and active user of TuDiabetes (n=9). The interviews focused on individuals' experiences with the community, their ways to characterize discussions that resulted in new knowledge and insights, issues of trust, and the impact of the platform on users' engagement, among others. Second, we used quantitative methods to examine a set of 20,000 discussion threads (out of 22,180 available). In addition, we conducted thematic analysis of 30 of the most popular threads with the specific focus on patterns of participants' engagement. We used our working definition of collective sensemaking as back and forth negotiation of meaning to rate the most popular threads on their degree of collective sensemaking (high, medium, low). We then specifically examined what attributes differed between threads exhibiting different degrees of collective sensemaking. Finally, we conducted detailed discourse analysis of two threads from the most popular list ("How Soon on Insulin?" and "At the End of the Rope") and inductively coded each post based on its contribution to the discussion. To preserve participants' identity, in the rest of the paper, we use P1-P9 to refer to participants of the interviews, and M1-M9 to refer to members who contributed to the discussion threads we analyzed.

GENERAL PATTERNS OF ENGAGEMENT

The analysis of the discussions showed patterns consistent with much of the previous research on online communities. Most of the variables we examined followed a similarly skewed distribution, with the bulk of the data gathering within a small range of dominant values and a long tail. For example, most of the discussions included only a few members (between 1 and 10, including the initiator of the thread); only a small percentage of the discussions had more then 30 participants. Similarly, most of the discussions had between 0 and 30 replies, however, several reached over 1K replies. Most users posted only once, fewer contributed between 2 and 6 posts, and only a few posted on a regular basis; their contributions could amount to tens of thousands of posts during their membership with the community.

Similarly, when examining posts per user within discussions, most users contributed to a given discussion only once. However, a fair number contributed between 2 and 8 posts, and a few individuals contributed more than 8 posts to a given discussion. Most of the discussions

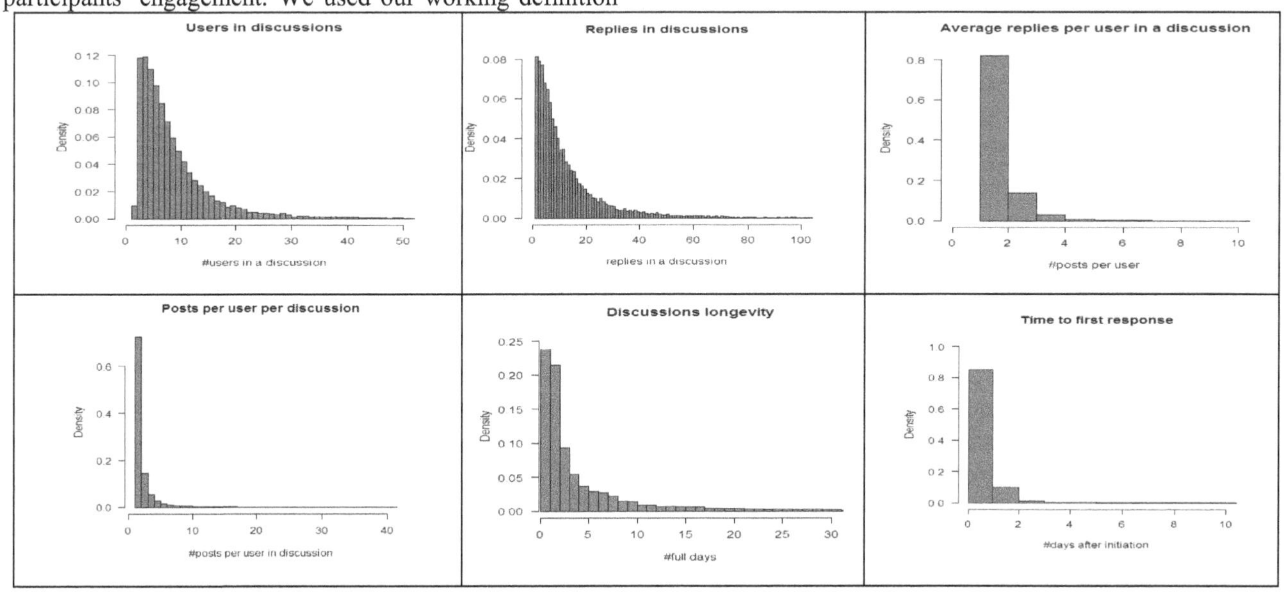

Figure 1: a) number of users in a discussion; b) number of replies in a discussion; c) average number of replies per user; d) posts per user per discussion; e) discussion longevity; f) time to first response

did not stay active beyond the first day; a fair number stayed active for about a week, and the oldest still active discussion was initiated almost 6 years ago. TuDiabetes is a very active forum – almost 90% of the initial posts received their first reply within the first day.

ANALYZING POPULAR DISCUSSIONS

Qualitative analysis of 30 of the most popular discussion threads on TuDiabetes revealed several distinct categories:

Opinion/experience polls (n=13) started with posts that sought opinions or experiences of others on a topic of interest. *Statement of strong opinion* threads (n=2) were initiated with posts that stated a strong opinion in regards to a certain issue. *Ice-breakers* included simple games usually not related to diabetes (n=7). *Bonding threads* (n=3), asked individuals to share their experiences related to diabetes in general, rather than to any aspect of it in particular. A*nnouncements* of new events from TuDiabetes leadership (n=2) usually led to a roll call with members responding and committing to participating. *Personal issue* threads (n=3) were initiated by individuals seeking advice in regards to a specific personal issue.

These popular threads varied greatly in their longevity (from 3 days to over 6 years), the number of posts (from 64 to 24,193), and in the reply rate, from 1 post every 5 days to 91 posts per day (on average). We found an interesting metric to be a ratio of views to replies, which indicated both the level of interest in the topic among members of the community, and the effort required for participation in the discussion. For example, many ice-breakers had low view/reply ratio, suggesting that most members who viewed this thread posted their own reply. In contrast, opinion polls, particularly on controversial topics had a very high view/reply ratio with many people viewing the thread, but only few replying to it. In regards to collective sensemaking, we classified 8 of the threads as "High CS", 7 threads as "Medium CS" and 13 threads as "Low CS". Most of the community building threads (ice-breakers and bonding) were classified as having a low degree of collective sensemaking; opinion/experience poll threads were almost evenly split between "High CS" and "Medium CS", as were personal issue threads.

COLLECTIVE SENSEMAKING ON TUDIABETES

The makings of a great discussion

The first question we sought to address in this study was what members of TuDiabetes considered to be a great discussion. Previous research in online health communities suggested that individuals come to these forums seeking either information or emotional support and companionship [26]. Similarly to that classification, our interviewees differed in what they valued in a discussion. Some stressed the emotional support members received from others.

P1: To me [the great discussions] are the ones where people really come out to support one another, you know. If somebody posts that they're having a really hard time and they get an outpouring of love and support from lots of different community members.

Others valued diversity and multiplicity of perspectives, which exposed them to different experiences and opinions.

M7: I know an awful lot about my insulin but I don't know anything about your insulin or your insulin and so that is interesting to me.

Yet others valued conversations where individuals engaged in deep discussion with each other, examined different perspectives, and sought consensus on an issue of common interest. Consistently with the literature on collective sensemaking discussed above, we used this last perspective as a working definition of collective sensemaking in online health communities. Of note, the interviews suggested that both diversity and consensus (or at least attempts to arrive at one) were important, but in different contexts. For example, in discussions regarding values and personal experiences, unlikely to find a resolution, multiplicity of opinions was highly desirable. In contrast, in discussions about more objective topics, such as new scientific discoveries related to diabetes, deeper engagement between participants was perceived as more valuable than many superficially expressed perspectives.

P2: If it's the type wars [discussion about differences between type 1 and type 2 diabetes] then the fact that 10 people have posted 70 times means nothing to me. If it's a type wars and there have been 70 people who have posted 70 times that's very important to me. On the other hand, if it has been a scientific news that might be out there and 10 people have posted 70 times that might be very interesting to me, but if it's a scientific issue and 70 people have posted 70 times that probably means nothing to me, because they are not really drilling on that particular subject; but in the former case, 10 people posted 70 times on a scientific issue, means that they are probably drilling on the subject and I am probably going to learn something.

Attributes of collective sensemaking

Given our working definition of collective sensemaking, our first question was what attributes of a discussion thread indicate presence of collective sensemaking. Our analysis suggested that the discussion threads classified as exhibiting high collective sensemaking had the following properties: *1) lateral engagement between participants, 2) reflection on previously stated perspectives, and 3) transformation of ideas throughout the posts in the thread.*

Lateral engagement between participants. One of the most obvious indicators of collective sensemaking was the *depth of the replies in the thread.* Multiple levels of replies usually indicated that participants not only expressed their own individual perspectives but also engaged in the back and forth negotiation of meaning. For example, in many of the opinion/experience polls, individuals often interrogated each other's perspectives, weighting evidence or sharing relevant experiences. In contrast, many ice-breakers included only first-level replies, and showed no engagement between participants. Importantly, however, level of depth was not always a sufficient indicator of collective sensemaking. When most of the back and forth discussions occurred between the person who initiated the discussion and those who responded, individuals' ideas and recommendations rarely developed beyond their original form. In contrast, when different respondents engaged with each other, their exchanges often focused on clarifying, enriching, and otherwise developing their initial ideas.

Reaction to previous perspectives. Many posts in threads with a high degree of collective sensemaking began with *reflection on previously stated perspectives*. For example, below are two replies in the "How Soon to Insulin?" thread, one that reinforces a previously proposed solution, and another that contradicts it:

M1: I agree with what everyone else has said; you need to be antibody tested to see if you are T1.

M2: I second everything that has been said here ... except the criticism of Humulin.

These simple references placed new posts in the context of other contributions and helped to move the discussion forward. In contrast, in "At the End of the Rope…" most of the new posts lacked such reference and seemed independent from each other, often leading to high redundancy in the thread. Any similarity in opinions and recommendations could only be recognized through critical reading and comparison.

Transformation of ideas. Perhaps most importantly, many posts within high collective senesmaking threads not only reflected on the previously proposed perspectives, but also *developed those ideas beyond their original form*. Consider the following sub-discussion from the thread "How Soon to Insulin!" that focused on comparative advantages and disadvantages of a particular type of insulin, Humulin. This sub-thread began when the initiator of the original post mentioned that she was prescribed Humulin taken at bedtime. This choice, however, was quickly called into question:

M3: I wonder at her decision to put you on Humulin rather than using one of the newer insulins.

Many subsequent posts took a similarly skeptical view of Humulin; however, instead of simply restating their disagreement with the endocrinologist's choice, each of them contributed a new perspective on Humulin's specific limitations, for example its unpredictability and its ability to lead to hypoglycemia (low blood glucose levels).

Yet, another replies highlighted its positive aspects, for example its ability to "handle" high-protein meals:

M2: It may not be the flashiest and newest thing around, but it definitely has its valid uses. I haven't found anything else that handles high-protein meals anywhere near as well.

In our analysis we found that all three of these characteristics are necessary to recognize collective sensemaking; *absence of either one of them puts collective sensemaking into question*. For example, lack of lateral exchange between participants in a thread de-emphasizes the possibility of any shared understanding among participants. Absence of reflection on the previously stated perspectives obscures connection between posts, turning a thread into a list of unconnected opinions and recommendations. And finally, if there is no transformation of ideas, and each new posts simply agrees or disagrees with previously expressed perspectives, the thread becomes an elaborate way of community voting more typical for Q&A sites, or a debate between individuals holding opposing positions, rather than richer forms of collective sensemaking.

Types of contributions to collective sensemaking

The next question in this study was regarding different types of contributions to collective senesmaking. A detailed discourse analysis of two discussion threads suggested a number of *conversational moves*—different types of contributions each individual post made to the overall discussion (Table 1). Importantly, individual posts were rarely limited to a single move and often included multiple moves simultaneously.

Many discussion threads began with a post that *asked a question*. These types of posts, however, could appear anywhere in the conversation, when members sought new information or clarification of previous positions. Often, questions were replied to with posts that *stated different perspectives* on the topic of interest. Notably, these could take a form of an opinion (for example, "it's never too early to start on insulin") or a recommendation (for example, "I think you should ask your endo for insulin right away"). At times, however, instead of directly answering the question, answers attempted to *reframe the problem* in somewhat different terms. For example, instead of answering whether early introduction of insulin is appropriate, this type of post could suggest correctness of diagnosis as a more important question. Other posts suggested a *new topic for discussion* that was related to the original question, yet took the discussion in a different direction. For example, in a thread about early introduction of insulin, one of the replies mentioned low carb diet as a way to stabilize BG levels in addition to medication. Other posts *suggested resources*, such as useful websites or books, often without stating their authors' opinion on the topic of interest.

While the five categories above focus on the nature of the individual posts, the next five categories focus more on the relationships between posts. The first category includes moves that express direct *agreement or disagreement* with previously stated perspectives. These moves can often be complemented by presenting an *argument or evidence* for a previously stated perspective; however, often we found that individuals continued presenting new arguments long after the perspective was stated. When differences in opinions created conflicts, individuals often attempted to

Conversational move	Example
1. Asking a question	Anyone else in a similar situation or have any advice?
2. Statement of a perspective	I think it is perfectly fine to move to insulin.
3. Reframing the problem	I strongly encourage you to ask for a full panel of antibody testing and a c-peptide test to determine if you are Type 1
4. Introducing new topic	Btw, even with insulin I still have to eat a low carb diet to keep my bg as stable as possible, you may end up having to do that anyway.
5. Suggesting resources	Gary Scheiner's "Think Like a Pancreas" and John Walsh's "Using Insulin" are good resources.
6. Agreement/disagreement with previously stated position	I agree with what everyone else has said, you need to be antibody tested to see if you are T1
7. Presenting argument for/against previously stated position	There was a study I saw a note about in a Diabetes Forecast "sidebar" that showed that T2 put straight onto insulin had better control or something to that effect
8. Further developing previously stated position	Humulin R may have a role as a supporting player or even as a primary insulin if cost is the issue but it is being prescribed for use before bed rather than before meals
9. Personal reconciliation	Dear, im sorry if i offended you
10. Synthesis of previously stated perspectives	You have gotten some excellent advice here at TuD, and I am glad you have an appointment with your endo. It is important to get testing to see if you have Type 1 diabetes, but the most important thing is getting excellent treatment and care.

Table 1: Types of contributions to a discussion; 6-10 specifically indicate contributions to collective senesemaking

reconcile differences, make amends, or to phrase their opinions in milder terms. In some cases, individuals, often community moderators, attempted to *synthesize and summarize* previously stated perspectives.

What triggers collective sensemaking

Our next question focused on the conditions under which collective sensemaking occurred, and on different factors that appeared to contribute to it. The study suggested four main factors that appeared to be associated with collective sensemaking: *1) reference to a contentious topic; 2) contentious or strongly expressed opinion; 2) statement of a personal question in generic terms; and 3) involvement of core members of the community.*

Contentious topic. There are a number of contentious topics that almost inevitably provoke engaged discussion within the community. The appropriateness of low carbohydrate diet for diabetes self-management, the nature and significance of differences between T1 and T2 and which of these conditions is "worse", and advantages and shortcomings of early introduction of insulin therapy – these questions are continuously debated within TuDiabetes and healthcare community at large. Some participants became wary of these ongoing debates that often involve emotional reaction from members, but rarely get resolved or lead to any consensus.

M2: There are certain topics that apparently must be debated and redebated endlessly. Every few months this discussion starts up again. Everyone restates their positions, nobody changes their mind, and everyone jockeys to have the last word. Broken records. Makes me tired.

However, new members of the community often felt that these debates were enormously educational, exposed them to many diverse opinions, and often inspired them to try new approaches in their own self-management.

M6: I know it's been discussed and debated in the past, but just reading through these 8 pages over lunch, I've gleaned a lot of new information that is great!

Contentious posts. In addition to contentious topics, posts that expressed strong opinions even on mundane topics tended to generate a lot of discussion:

P1: I think for a lot of people, you know, you see a thread and you chime in with what you want to say about it and then you're kind of done with it unless you're mad, and then you say what you want to say and then you wait 15 minutes and go see if anybody replied so that you can reply again.

However, in both of these cases, intensive back-and-forth engagement between participants did not always lead to collective sensemaking, for example if their posts did not include transformation of ideas.

Generalizing personal problems. Third, we found that the framing of the question in the post initiating the discussion had a significant impact on the patterns of engagement between participants. This became particularly apparent in threads in which the initiating post presented a personal challenge and asked for advice. For example, initial posts in both "At the End of the Rope…" and "How Soon to Insulin" asked for advice on a specific personal challenge. However, in "At the End of the Rope…", the initial post presented the problem in a rather idiosyncratic way, which made it difficult to construct a more general question of interest to others. In contrast, the initial post in the "How Soon to Insulin" thread formulated a more general question: whether it is appropriate to introduce insulin as the first treatment option. This generalization inspired others to not only respond to the original question, but also engage in negotiation of a more generalizable answer.

Involvement of core members. Finally, we found that while the topic and the framing of a question had a significant impact on the patterns of engagement among participants, ultimately it often came down to who posted the question, and who was involved in the discussion. As many other online communities, TuDiabetes has a core group of members who actively contribute to blogs and forums and who often recognize each other's names. These individuals are usually highly opinionated and outspoken; their voices were persistent in all of the threads included in our analysis. Moreover, they have a level of comfort and familiarity with each other that often leads to a deeper engagement.

P2: If a person is plugged into a site, that is they are common posters in that area, they are far more likely to get more and more comments back. The more plugged in you are, the more regulars will comment back to you.

Dimensions of Collective Sensemaking

Together with persistent patterns, there were also considerable differences between threads with a high degree of collective sensemaking. We discuss these differences along two different but related dimensions: whether these threads included exchange of information or personal experiences, and whether they sought consensus or diversity in opinions.

Information-driven threads often evolved around general concepts of high interest to the community, for example, the appropriateness of severe reduction of carbohydrates for individuals with diabetes. In these threads, most of the back and forth negotiation of perspectives focused on presenting and critiquing new arguments and evidence supporting either of the contrasting positions:

M7: Here are some studies to look at: 1) Link between obesity and inflammation. 2) Link between chemicals secreted by fat tissue and insulin resistance. 3) Another study along the same lines as the one above, but regarding different inflammatory chemicals.

M8: The first link has a lot of "could" in it...

In contrast to this, most of the posts in ***experience-driven threads*** included descriptions of individuals' personal experiences related to the topic of interest. For example, in a different thread with the focus on low carbohydrate diet, the participants mostly shared their personal stories, and what worked and did not work for them. In these situations, the participants use similar back and forth mechanisms to relate to each other's experiences and point similarities and possible explanations.

M9: I like to be in the upper 80s because after 8:30, I start to climb to 120ish until 11:00 when it magically goes down and stays down if I eat right. If I start out in the 80s it doesn't climb as high. So I have dawn phenomenon but it doesn't kick in until after 8:30?

M10: M8, same thing happens to me. If I don't eat & inject right away, up, up & away. Not a morning person either.

Perhaps as a result, these two threads exhibited different attitudes towards consensus. In the first one, individuals holding different perspectives presented new information and evidence, trying to convince other members to agree with their point of view. In contrast, in the second thread, a consensus, even temporary, was neither sought, nor deemed necessary. Instead of trying to convince each other, participants of this thread shared different perspectives and experiences, together creating a rich and multifaceted picture of this complex issue.

Impact of the platform

TuDiabetes is built using a commercially available platform for discussion forums that has a number of distinct features that appeared to have an impact on collective senesmaking within the community. Most importantly, it supports sub-threading of discussions: individuals can reply to the initial post, thus appending their contribution to the bottom of the main thread, and also to different posts within the thread, thus creating sub-discussions. This allows individuals to explore issues of mutual interest in greater depth, and enables that back and forth that we perceived as indicative of collective senesmaking. However, the platform also has a few limitations that often lead to confusion.

First, as is common for most discussion threads, because all of the posts in a thread are made in a textual form with no meta-data (users can tag discussion threads but not individual posts), users must read the entire thread to understand how each individual post contributes to the discussion. For any thread with a large number of posts this may present a challenge.

Because the initial post in a discussion thread is immediately followed by a "Reply" button with an open text field, users often felt compelled to compose their own reply before reading the existing discussion. However, after perusing the discussion later on, many users restated their perspective as a response to a particular post. This often resulted in redundant posts that made the thread longer, but contributed little to collective sensemaking. Those who read other posts and wished to reply to the main thread, had to return back to the initial post; adding reply to the last post in a thread created a sub-discussion. As a result, many users did both: added their reply to the bottom of the thread (thus creating or extending a sub-discussion), and then repeated it again in the main thread. In addition, the platform imposes a limit of 9 replies within a sub-discussion and removes the option to continue the sub-thread beyond that. As a result, additional replies were sometimes added not to the last post in the sub-thread, but to the previous posts, essentially putting replies out of order.

In regards to thread presentation, all the posts in a thread are displayed in chronological order, but within their original sub-discussion structure. As a result, when reading through the thread, individuals could read posts added to sub-discussions several years later before seeing posts added to the main thread much earlier.

These limitations, combined with a rather ineffective search function, made it difficult to peruse discussion threads with over 20 or 30 posts, which was noted in many of our interviews. Those who actively participated in a discussion could follow its structure by seeing it unfold in real time. However, synthesizing the main topics and opinions in a discussion they were not a part of was both labor-intensive and time-consuming.

M8: Well, the challenge is the amount of words you have to read in order to find the consensus. ... so if I go on and I want to know if there is a discussion that is going on, it's easy for me to follow it, hour by hour, minute by minute but if I want to look at it even one month later, it's very very difficult to figure it out because you have to read it all.

The participants mentioned several different strategies to exploring threads they did not participate in. Some started reading from the beginning of the thread (in chronological order) and read until they "got bored" or reached a point of saturation. Others read in the reverse chronological order, starting with the most recent posts and going backwards. Yet the most common strategy appeared to be random sampling. In this strategy, the participants skimmed through the thread, reading a few messages from the beginning of the thread, a few from the middle, and a few more from the end. Many participants who reported relying on this strategy felt that it gives them an idea of how the thread evolved over time. However, this common strategy made it difficult to benefit from the rich back and forth of collective sensemaking, and could result in a fragmented or skewed perspective on the opinions in the community.

DISCUSSION

Collective sensemaking with different platforms

The underlying question for this work was what technological platforms are best suited for facilitating individuals' interactions in online health forums. First, the study suggested that traditional discussion boards are ill-suited to supporting collective sensemaking. The rich back and forth negotiation among members is often buried in the volume of posts in the threads, and is usually only apparent to those who participated in the discussion. The random sampling method for reviewing long discussion threads, common among members of the community, breaks internal structures of meaning and can lead to a distorted or incomplete perspective on the topic of the discussion.

Given the limitation of the discussion boards, one might wonder whether such platforms as Wikipedia, or Stack Overflow present a more suitable alternative to the traditional discussion boards. The results presented here suggest that there are indeed many similarities between the types of engagement we observed on TuDiabetes, and others observed within Wikipedia [38] and Stack Overflow [23]. Similarly to members of these communities, members of TuDiabetes often engaged in deep discussions, back and forth negotiation of meaning, and resolution of conflicts in opinions. In addition, individuals together created shared artifacts, as their negotiated opinions left permanent traces in the discussion threads. In a way, these traces fulfill Wenger's requirement for reification through construction of shared artifacts [43].

However, together with these similarities, there are also deep epistemological differences between Wikipedia, Stack Overflow, and TuDiabetes. Wikipedia's style of engagement implies that knowledge is socially constructed through active collaboration between individuals. Somewhat in contrast to this, the design of Stack Overflow implies that knowledge is a property of an individual, and the role of the community is to recognize the "best answer", rather than collectively construct it. Further, both Wikipedia and Stack Overflow value consensus and lead their users towards agreement through collaborative writing and editing or through voting. At the end, there is only one Wikipedia article on any given topic, and one most popular answer on Stack Overflow, however unstable it might be. Similarly to Wikipedia, the style of engagement in TuDiabetes implies that knowledge is distributed among many individuals, and is often brought into existence through active back and forth negotiation of different perspectives. However, members of TuDiabetes value both diversity of opinions and agreement among members. Often the main benefit of the forum is in exposing individuals to the richness and multiplicity of different perspectives, which help them to construct their own personal views.

Implications for computing systems

As a result of our analysis, we propose that tools for facilitating collective sensemaking in online health communities could take several different forms.

First, they can help individuals to engage in a more explicit collective production of shared artifacts in a way that encourages negotiation, yet does not require consensus. In recent years, shared content collections, such as Pinterest [46] gained substantial popularity. In a similar way, members of TuDiabetes could create collages of content related to topics of mutual interest that reflect their perspectives and views. Such collectively constructed collages could serve as shared artifacts and further reinforce reification.

Second, computing tools can help individuals to be more explicit about how their posts contribute to the overall discussion thread. For example, using the taxonomy of contribution types presented in this paper, members can be more explicit on whether they present a new perspective, agree or disagree with others, provide evidence or recommend new resources by assigning it an appropriate tag. Moreover, these tools could also facilitate polling opinions of others through voting, making distribution of opinions more apparent.

Finally, there is a significant and growing body of work on using computational approaches, such as natural language processing (NLP), data mining, and machine learning, to computationally analyze text within discussion threads. In computational linguistics, new methods focus on the design of novel statistical models for tasks such as event detection [2], sentiment analysis [29], and modeling of the topics of discussions [33] as well as predicting the structure of discourse [39]. Taking these trends further, Hoque et al used a combination of NLP and data visualization techniques to visualize salient properties of discussion threads, such as topics discussed and sentiment towards these topics [15]. The framework suggested in this paper can provide foundation for new approaches to facilitating collective sensemaking using computational text analysis and interactive visualizations. Specifically, the three main attributes of collective sensemaking proposed here—lateral engagement between participants, reflection on previous perspectives, and transformation of ideas—can suggest new directions for computational analysis of text. Some of these methods already exist (e.g. detection of agreement and of topic transformation); others still need to be developed. These methods can then be used to inform visualizations of discussion threads that draw individuals' attention to areas of debate, or to areas where discussion pivots and may warrant further examination.

CONCLUSION

In this study we used a mixed-methods approach to investigating how members of an online diabetes community, TuDiabetes, share information and learn from each other. The study showed that members of TuDiabetes often engage in deep discussions, back and forth negotiation of meaning, and resolution of conflicts in opinions. In addition, individuals together create shared artifacts, as their expressed perspectives leave permanent traces in the discussion threads. However, unlike participants of other popular sensemaking communities, members of TuDiabetes often value multiplicity and diversity of opinions rather than consensus. We identified a number of design directions for computing platforms that facilitate collective sensemaking and construction of meaning, yet embrace diversity of perspectives.

ACKNOWLEDGEMENTS

This work was funded in part by the National Science Foundation grant #1422381. We are grateful to Emily Coles and all members of TuDiabetes community who took part in this study.

REFERENCES

1. Baldonado, M.Q.W. and Winograd, T. SenseMaker: an information-exploration interface supporting the contextual evolution of a user's interests. *Proceedings of the SIGCHI conference on Human factors in computing systems*, ACM (1997), 11–18.
2. Benson, E., Haghighi, A., and Barzilay, R. Event discovery in social media feeds. *Proceedings of the 49th Annual Meeting of the Association for Computational Linguistics: Human Language Technologies - Volume 1*, Association for Computational Linguistics (2011), 389–398.
3. Billman, D. and Bier, E.A. Medical sensemaking with entity workspace. ACM (2007), 229–232.
4. Chen, A.T. Exploring online support spaces: using cluster analysis to examine breast cancer, diabetes and fibromyalgia support groups. *Patient education and counseling 87*, 2 (2012), 250–257.
5. Coburn, C.E. Collective Sensemaking about Reading: How Teachers Mediate Reading Policy in Their Professional Communities. *Educational Evaluation and Policy Analysis 23*, 2 (2001), 145–170.
6. Duffy, M. Sensemaking: A Collaborative Inquiry Approach to 'Doing' Learning. *The Qualitative Report*, (1995).
7. Ferron, M. and Massa, P. Collective memory building in Wikipedia: the case of North African uprisings. *Proceedings of the 7th International Symposium on Wikis and Open Collaboration*, ACM (2011), 114–123.
8. Fisher, K., Counts, S., and Kittur, A. Distributed sensemaking: improving sensemaking by leveraging the efforts of previous users. *Proceedings of the SIGCHI Conference on Human Factors in Computing Systems*, ACM (2012), 247–256.
9. Fox, S. *The Social Life of Health Information.* Pew Research Center, 2011.
10. Furnas, G.W. and Russell, D.M. Making sense of sensemaking. *CHI '05 extended abstracts on Human factors in computing systems*, ACM (2005), 2115–2116.
11. Gotz, D. The ScratchPad: sensemaking support for the web. *Proceedings of the 16th international conference on World Wide Web*, ACM (2007), 1329–1330.
12. Halfaker, A., Kittur, A., Kraut, R., and Riedl, J. A jury of your peers: quality, experience and ownership in Wikipedia. *Proceedings of the 5th International Symposium on Wikis and Open Collaboration*, ACM (2009), 15:1–15:10.
13. Harper, F.M., Moy, D., and Konstan, J.A. Facts or friends?: distinguishing informational and conversational questions in social Q&A sites. ACM (2009), 759–768.
14. Hollan, J., Hutchins, E., and Kirsh, D. Distributed cognition: toward a new foundation for human-computer interaction research. *ACM Trans. Comput.-Hum. Interact. 7*, 2 (2000), 174–196.
15. Hoque, E. and Carenini, G. ConVis: A Visual Text Analytic System for Exploring Blog Conversations. *Computer Graphics Forum 33*, 3 (2014), 221–230.
16. Hsieh, G. and Counts, S. mimir: a market-based real-time question and answer service. ACM (2009), 769–778.
17. Hsieh, G., Kraut, R.E., and Hudson, S.E. Why pay?: exploring how financial incentives are used for question & answer. ACM (2010), 305–314.
18. Huh, J. and Ackerman, M.S. Collaborative help in chronic disease management: supporting individualized problems. *Proceedings of the ACM 2012 conference on Computer Supported Cooperative Work*, ACM (2012), 853–862.
19. Hutchins, E. *Cognition in the Wild.* A Bradford Book, 1996.
20. Jones, Q., Ravid, G., and Rafaeli, S. Information Overload and the Message Dynamics of Online Interaction Spaces: A Theoretical Model and Empirical Exploration. *Information Systems Research 15*, 2 (2004), 194–210.

21. Kittur, A. and Kraut, R.E. Harnessing the wisdom of crowds in wikipedia: quality through coordination. *Proceedings of the 2008 ACM conference on Computer supported cooperative work*, ACM (2008), 37–46.
22. Kittur, A., Suh, B., Pendleton, B.A., and Chi, E.H. He says, she says: conflict and coordination in Wikipedia. *Proceedings of the SIGCHI Conference on Human Factors in Computing Systems*, ACM (2007), 453–462.
23. Mamykina, L., Hartman, B., and Hripcsak, G. Drawing design lessons from the fastest Q&A site in the West. (2011).
24. Mendes Rodrigues, E. and Milic-Frayling, N. Socializing or knowledge sharing?: characterizing social intent in community question answering. ACM (2009), 1127–1136.
25. Nagar, Y. What do you think?: the structuring of an online community as a collective-sensemaking process. *Proceedings of the ACM 2012 conference on Computer Supported Cooperative Work*, ACM (2012), 393–402.
26. Nambisan, P. Information seeking and social support in online health communities: impact on patients' perceived empathy. *Journal of the American Medical Informatics Association 18*, 3 (2011), 298–304.
27. Nam, K.K., Ackerman, M.S., and Adamic, L.A. Questions in, knowledge in?: a study of naver's question answering community. ACM (2009), 779–788.
28. Naumer, C.M., Fisher, K.E., and Dervin, B. Sense-Making: A Methodological Perspective, a position paper for CHI 2008 workshop on Sensemaking. (2008).
29. Pang, B. and Lee, L. Opinion Mining and Sentiment Analysis. *Found. Trends Inf. Retr. 2*, 1-2 (2008), 1–135.
30. Paul, S.A. and Morris, M.R. CoSense: enhancing sensemaking for collaborative web search. *Proceedings of the 27th international conference on Human factors in computing systems*, ACM (2009), 1771–1780.
31. Paul, S.A. and Reddy, M.C. Understanding together: sensemaking in collaborative information seeking. *Proceedings of the 2010 ACM conference on Computer supported cooperative work*, ACM (2010), 321–330.
32. Qu, Y. A sensemaking-supporting information gathering system. *CHI '03 extended abstracts on Human factors in computing systems*, ACM (2003), 906–907.
33. Ritter, A., Cherry, C., and Dolan, B. Unsupervised modeling of Twitter conversations. *Human Language Technologies: The 2010 Annual Conference of the North American Chapter of the Association for Computational Linguistics*, Association for Computational Linguistics (2010), 172–180.
34. Russell, D.M., Furnas, G., Stefik, M., Card, S.K., and Pirolli, P. Sensemaking. *CHI '08 extended abstracts on Human factors in computing systems*, ACM (2008), 3981–3984.
35. schraefel, m. c., White, R.W., André, P., and Tan, D. Investigating web search strategies and forum use to support diet and weight loss. *Proceedings of the 27th international conference extended abstracts on Human factors in computing systems*, ACM (2009), 3829–3834.
36. Skeels, M.M., Unruh, K.T., Powell, C., and Pratt, W. Catalyzing social support for breast cancer patients. *Proceedings of the 28th international conference on Human factors in computing systems*, ACM (2010), 173–182.
37. Stahl, G. *Group Cognition: Computer Support for Building Collaborative Knowledge.* MIT Press, 2006.
38. Swarts, J. The collaborative construction of "fact" on Wikipedia. *Proceedings of the 27th ACM international conference on Design of communication*, ACM (2009), 281–288.
39. Wang, L., Lui, M., Kim, S.N., Nivre, J., and Baldwin, T. Predicting thread discourse structure over technical web forums. *Proceedings of the Conference on Empirical Methods in Natural Language Processing*, Association for Computational Linguistics (2011), 13–25.
40. Weick, K.E. *Sensemaking in Organizations.* Sage Publications, Inc, 1995.
41. Weick, K.E., Sutcliffe, K.M., and Obstfeld, D. Organizing and the Process of Sensemaking. *Organization Science 16*, 4 (2005), 409–421.
42. Welbourne, J.L., Blanchard, A.L., and Boughton, M.D. Supportive communication, sense of virtual community and health outcomes in online infertility groups. *Proceedings of the fourth international conference on Communities and technologies*, ACM (2009), 31–40.
43. Wenger, E. *Communities of Practice: Learning, Meaning and Identity.* Cambridge University Press, Cambridge, 1998.
44. Zhou, X., Sun, S., and Yang, J. Sweet Home: Understanding Diabetes Management via a Chinese Online Community. *Proceedings of the 32Nd Annual ACM Conference on Human Factors in Computing Systems*, ACM (2014), 3997–4006.
45. Zhu, H., Kraut, R.E., Wang, Y.-C., and Kittur, A. Identifying shared leadership in Wikipedia. *Proceedings of the 2011 conference on Human factors in computing systems*, ACM (2011), 3431–3434.
46. Pinterest. *Pinterest.* http://www.pinterest.com.

Opportunities and Challenges for Data Physicalization

Yvonne Jansen[1], Pierre Dragicevic[2], Petra Isenberg[2], Jason Alexander[3],
Abhijit Karnik[3], Johan Kildal[4], Sriram Subramanian[5], Kasper Hornbæk[1]
[1]University of Copenhagen, [2]Inria, [3]Lancaster University, [4]Nokia, [5]University of Bristol
jansen.yv@gmail.com, {pierre.dragicevic, petra.isenberg}@inria.fr, {j.alexander, a.karnik}@lancaster.ac.uk, johan.kildal@nokia.com, sriram@cs.bris.ac.uk, kash@di.ku.dk

Figure 1: Examples of data physicalizations: (left) population density map of Mexico City co-created by Richard Burdett and exhibited at the Tate Modern (photo by Stefan Geens), (center) similar data shown on an actuated display from the MIT Media Lab [70], and (right) spherical particles suspended by acoustic levitation [61]. All images are copyright to their respective owners.

ABSTRACT
Physical representations of data have existed for thousands of years. Yet it is now that advances in digital fabrication, actuated tangible interfaces, and shape-changing displays are spurring an emerging area of research that we call *Data Physicalization*. It aims to help people explore, understand, and communicate data using computer-supported physical data representations. We call these representations *physicalizations*, analogously to visualizations – their purely visual counterpart. In this article, we go beyond the focused research questions addressed so far by delineating the research area, synthesizing its open challenges, and laying out a research agenda.

Author Keywords
Data physicalization; visualization; tangible user interfaces; shape-changing interfaces; physical visualization

ACM Classification Keywords
H.5.m. Information Interfaces and Presentation (e.g., HCI): Miscellaneous

INTRODUCTION
More than 7000 years ago, the Sumerians used clay tokens to represent quantitative data well before inventing written language [59]. The Incas never even developed a writing system but relied on Quipus – complex assemblies of knotted ropes – for data storage and retrieval [3]. Scientists in the 19th century used physical representations as essential teaching and research aids [15] for organic chemistry and thermodynamics. Today, designers are crafting data sculptures to convey meaning and emotion in data [79]. All such physical representations help people think about, explore, and share data.

CHI 2015, April 18–23, 2015, Seoul, Republic of Korea.

ACM 978-1-4503-3145-6/15/04 ...$15.00.
http://dx.doi.org/10.1145/2702123.2702180

Similarly, for centuries people have been developing visualizations for flat surfaces, such as maps or genealogies printed on papyrus, paper, tapestries, and now computer screens. Yet, recent and anticipated technological advances in digital fabrication, tangible user interfaces [63], shape displays [54], and programmable matter [30] are radically changing the fidelity and flexibility with which data can be made physical (see Figure 1) while decreasing the cost of doing so. We see an unprecedented opportunity to create new forms of physical representations – they will be self-reconfigurable, freely manipulable, and will eventually support data analysis tasks as complex as performed on today's desktop computers.

This article identifies *Data Physicalization* as an emerging research area that uses physical data representations to help people explore and communicate data. So far work in this area has been scattered and has focused on specific questions, thus an overview is needed to establish this area and to advance its research. We illustrate the current and future potential of physicalizations through usage scenarios and discuss their possible benefits. We clarify how this area relates to other domains such as Visualization [10] and Tangible User Interfaces [31] by illustrating its focus on data analysis (versus other forms of interface usage) in a physical form (versus visual presentation only). We then synthesize a research agenda for Data Physicalization detailing challenges such as how to encode data physically, how to support interaction, what enabling technologies are needed, and how to evaluate physicalizations.

WHAT ARE DATA PHYSICALIZATIONS?

We propose that:

> A *data physicalization* (or simply *physicalization*) is a physical artifact whose geometry or material properties encode data.

For instance, the physicalization in Figure 1–left is a wooden three-dimensional model of Mexico City where height encodes population density. The photo in the middle shows a physicalization of similar data, but dynamic. Here, the physicalization is used as a detail view to explore a larger information space displayed on an adjacent large screen [70]. While the photo on the right is a technology demonstration, it shows the potential to use free-floating particles to encode data [61].

The above definition should be taken as a working definition. A similar definition has been given for *physical visualizations* [34], and the terms can be used interchangeably. We prefer *physicalization* as it aligns with neologisms such as *sonification* and *haptification* [56] without favoring one specific sense. By extension, we also refer to physicalization as the process of producing physicalizations (to *physicalize* is to give data physical shape), and as a research area. These three meanings are consistent with the way *visualization* is currently informally employed by the Visualization community. However, the lack of an explicit distinction can easily generate confusions that we wish to avoid here. To reinforce this we use capitalization when referring to research areas.

Other Examples of Physicalizations

The idea of turning data into physical artifacts is not new, with many physicalizations already in everyday use [15]. Today's physicalizations are mostly static, but can offer potential perceptual, cognitive, and communicative value that neither paper nor computer displays may be able to offer.

An example of current use of physicalizations is shown in Figure 2–left, where Kevin Quinn, a chief engineer at General Motors, uses a custom Lego-based board to oversee and update problems and progress in production lines (tinyurl.com/mwilson2012). To him, two important benefits of this physicalization are the constant availability of information and the motivational factor for his engineers who like to see the progress of their work publicly reflected on the board.

Medical doctor and public speaker Hans Rosling (Figure 2–right) uses physical representations to emphasize his messages during his presentations (tinyurl.com/roslingBox). He uses physicalizations for their communicative and perhaps persuasive power. In the shown example, he discusses the divide between the world's rich (blue box) and poor (green boxes) and illustrates possible effects of policy changes by moving these boxes between piles. His physicalizations are useful and effective in communicating information which individuals may find difficult to comprehend due to unfamiliar magnitudes and scales. It can also carry a shock value.

Future Usage Scenarios For Physicalizations

To further illustrate the potential of data physicalizations, we provide three usage scenarios which are fictional and to a large extent ignore current technological limitations.

Figure 2: Manually-updated physicalizations used by an automotive engineer (left, image © General Motors) and by Hans Rosling during a public talk (right, image © TED).

Science Museum

A visitor to a museum walks into a room which describes the earth's changes in climate. She picks up stones that physicalize the change of temperatures on Earth backwards in time. She can get a good sense of the differences between ice ages and hotter periods – but when she gets to the volcanic beginnings and the stones quickly heat up, she drops them. At the hurricane diorama, miniature hurricanes of the past 50 years move over a map of North America covered in dense fog, with only the eyes of the storms allowing a peak inside. The visitor places her hands over two of the eyes, and the differences in pressure give her the sensation of the intensity of the hurricanes at their peak. She reaches into the eye of the stronger hurricane and feels a strong drag on her hand when it crosses the eyewall. She can easily judge how devastating it was.

Explaining Complex Systems

A government analyst developed an improved multi-variate model that predicts the economic position of her country. During a meeting, she physicalizes past and predicted time-series data for indicators such as GDP, income tax rates, and unemployment, into line charts (physicalized as wires). Uncertainties in the system are illustrated by wires expanding into cones that cover the ranges of plausible values. To illustrate the requirements for ensuring a 2% growth in GDP, the analyst deforms and compresses the GDP cone and shows the effect on tax revenue. Once she has reached a realistic growth objective, the dynamic physicalization is frozen and static 3D printed models are created for the policy makers in the audience.

Neurosurgical Planning

A neurosurgeon scans the brain of a patient who suffers from an asymptomatic tumor. He physicalizes the data into a visually and haptically realistic brain model made of programmable matter (i.e., microscopic particles that can dynamically re-arrange themselves and change their properties [30]). With a caress, he makes the brain semi-translucent to reveal the tumor's localization. He then takes a scalpel and cuts the brain into slices. He lays the slices side-by-side to identify and mark the tumor's tendrils. He then stacks the slices again and they re-assemble back into a monolithic object. With a poking gesture, he then turns the brain into a 3D connectivity graph to reveal functional correlations between brain regions. He pulls dense clusters of links apart to see them more clearly. After this sequence of explorations he gains the insight that the tumor may soon affect important perceptual and cognitive brain functions and recommends immediate scheduling of surgery.

THE BENEFITS OF DATA PHYSICALIZATION

We see many possible benefits of physicalization on the perceptual, cognitive, and societal levels. We discuss some of them here. Currently, however, the empirical literature offers scant evidence about the merits and possible limitations of data physicalizations. Consequently, this discussion draws upon the insights from other fields. We later identify the lack of empirical studies as a major element of the research agenda for Data Physicalization. For now, we note that these potential benefits need to be traded off against the costs of data physicalizations, in particular the cost of creating them.

Leveraging our Perceptual Exploration Skills

Humans have evolved a highly complex sensorimotor system that allows them to efficiently extract information from the physical world [9]. We explain why physicalizations can tap into these skills more deeply than classical computer setups.

Active Perception: A major benefit of physicalizations is that they better exploit our *active perception* skills. Perception has evolved as an active process, that is, it strongly relies on motor control [20]. For example, a physical object like a hand-sized physicalization can be visually inspected by turning it around, by moving it closer, or by taking it apart. A large-scale physicalization can be explored by walking around. In contrast, on-screen visualizations need to explicitly support active perception by coupling input with output devices, that is, by being "interactive", possibly introducing usability issues. For example, visual exploration of large information spaces typically requires navigation tools such as pan-and-zoom. Although powerful, these tools are often inconsistent across applications and constantly need to be rediscovered and learned.

Depth Perception: Another benefit of physicalizations is their better leverage of our *spatial perception skills*. Since physical objects give rich cues of shape and volume, 3D data can be perceived with less effort and more accuracy on physicalizations than on computer displays – even stereoscopic ones [34].

Non-visual Senses: While vision is a dominant sense, it is not the only way by which we explore the world. As our earlier scenarios illustrated, touching a physical object can reveal a whole set of additional information such as texture, stiffness, temperature, and weight [27] – it becomes a haptic display of information [38]. Hearing also provides information on object properties [11]. Even smell or taste can can signal warning or invitation. All senses can participate in information gathering and they each have unique characteristics that can be leveraged by physicalizations. Touch, for example, requires close contact with the object, meaning that materials can be manipulated to influence our emotional states [27]. Physicalizations can take advantage of these additional sensory channels to convey a larger range of meanings than a simple visual display.

Intermodal Perception: The idea of conveying data to several senses has been around (e.g., [26,42,56]) but has typically followed a *multimodal* approach, where multiple output devices address the senses separately. In contrast, data physicalization follows an *intermodal* approach [64] that guarantees cohesive and realistic multisensory experiences. When inspecting physical objects, perceptual senses are tightly coupled and work hand-in-hand. For example, stroking a surface produces sounds that nuance tactile information on texture [9, Chap 7]. A rich repertoire of gestures is available for gathering both visual and non-visual information. Lateral hand motions can reveal an object's texture, holding it unsupported can reveal its weight, while following contours can reveal the details of its shape [38]. Informative sounds can also be produced by knocking an object or by scratching its surface [4, 11]. These are all "built-in interaction techniques" and none of them need to be explicitly implemented and documented. Such interactions are hard to emulate with output devices (e.g., [35]).

Making Data Accessible

Since physicalizations can address non-visual senses, they can make data analysis more accessible to visually-impaired people. Traditional approaches use raised paper to convey maps and charts [12, 16], or cork boards with pins and rubber bands to teach mathematical functions [41]. Novel interactive systems are trying to improve these techniques [41, 42] but often follow a multimodal approach and thus do not fully leverage our perceptual exploration skills. With physicalizations, visually-impaired data analysts may be able to explore data through the geometry and material properties of data artifacts in more ways than possible with currently established techniques. For instance, they could explore physicalizations with both hands to gain an overview, possibly using tactile pre-attentive cues [10] to identify interesting features that they could then explore in detail. At the same time, such physicalizations could be designed to remain compatible with visual exploration and thereby foster collaboration between sighted and unsighted analysts.

Cognitive Benefits

We expect physicalizations to benefit cognition and learning. Physical representations have been widely used in classrooms, for example, to teach basic mathematics [19] and chemistry [77]. A large body of evidence from educational psychology suggests that manipulable physical representations facilitate understanding and learning [48]. Part of this research is motivated by the embodied cognition thesis, according to which cognition is supported by the body and the physical world [7]. Similar arguments have been made for the benefits of tangible user interfaces [48,63]. Although the artifacts used in classrooms and educational psychology studies are typically not physicalizations (i.e., they do not convey *data*), we assume that some of their cognitive and educational benefits will transfer to physicalizations. Given the key role of physical manipulation in learning, we believe this to be especially true for rearrangeable and interactive physicalizations [33].

Bringing Data into the Real World

Apart from their perceptual and cognitive benefits, physicalizations allow individuals and groups to relate to data in new ways. The Tangible User Interface community has already pointed out that embedding physical artifacts in the space around us offers possibilities beyond those of virtual objects [28]. In comparison to screen-based visualizations, physicalization can similarly offer to bring data to many more places and aspects of our social lives. In particular, since physicalizations can be anywhere and are always "on", they can be used as ambient data displays and support casual visualization [53]. Furthermore, data is increasingly present in museums and art galleries in the form of *data sculptures* [15], that is, physicalizations created by designers and artists whose purpose is to communicate meaning and elicit reflection on data [43]. Meanwhile, more and more makers and fabrication enthusiasts physicalize data for sharing or for personal purposes [68]. Even fashion is being impacted, as people are already wearing personal data in the form of jewelery (e.g., www.meshu.io).

Engaging People

An emerging challenge in information visualization – particularly in the area of data journalism – is to engage large audiences with data [14]. There is anecdotal evidence that physicalizations may aid individuals in engaging with and communicating information to others more effectively than with digital representations. Our earlier example showed Hans Rosling using physicalizations to communicate world statistics (see Figure 2–right). The growing popularity of data physicalizations in many societal domains indicates a strong potential for fostering public engagement. This popularity suggests that data physicalizations pique interest, and this interest could in turn be leveraged to have people spend more time and effort exploring and understanding important and complex data.

Summary

We have put forward several arguments suggesting that physicalizations can be beneficial. We do not expect them to be beneficial in all situations, but the number of favorable situations will undoubtedly increase as technology advances. The increasing popularity of physicalizations provides another argument for studying them, irrespective of their practical merits and drawbacks. Flat surfaces – such as paper and later computer screens – have long been the primary media for visualization, but this is rapidly changing. While data physicalization is becoming part of our society, scientific research is lagging behind. The TUI community is only starting to consider data exploration scenarios [18], while the Visualization community only recently started to explore physical designs [75] and carry out studies on physicalizations [34, 66].

DATA PHYSICALIZATION AS A RESEARCH AREA

So far we covered data physicalizations as artifacts. We discussed why such artifacts can be beneficial, and hinted at how current and future technology will allow us to create more powerful interactive data physicalizations.

We now discuss Data Physicalization as a research area. We show that it is not simply a subset of existing fields, but a new research area that opens up new research questions and challenges beyond what existing fields are concerned with.

We propose to think of *Data Physicalization* as:

> a research area that examines how computer-supported, physical representations of data (i.e., physicalizations), can support cognition, communication, learning, problem solving, and decision making.

Data Physicalization relates to two broad topics: *(i)* the support of data analysis through visualization and *(ii)* the support of human-computer interaction through physical objects.

Data Physicalization and Visualization

Data Physicalization is related to the fields of Information Visualization (InfoVis) and Scientific Visualization (SciVis). Since the two fields are most often separated by the type of data they address [44], we use *Visualization* as an umbrella term for *"the use of computer-supported, interactive, visual representations of data to amplify cognition"* [10]. This definition includes four aspects closely related to Data Physicalization: a focus on external representations, computing, interaction, and the ultimate goal of enhancing humans' cognitive abilities to deal with data. One key difference is that Data Physicalization does not explicitly focus on the visual channel but instead attempts to tap into perceptual exploration skills more broadly.

Another important difference is that Data Physicalization excludes systems that convey data *solely* through flat visual displays, although it does include hybrid setups such as deformable visual displays [1, 17, 58, 65], provided the *geometry or material properties of the display surface encode data*. Consistent with our definition of data physicalizations, the focus is on the physicality of data representation, not on the physicality of interaction. Thus most setups involving multi-touch and large display surfaces are not the focus of Data Physicalization, despite the "physicality" of direct touch interaction and locomotion in space. However, the field is clearly concerned with how touch – both as input and sensory modality – and locomotion can support data analysis with physicalizations.

While Data Physicalization is concerned with physicalizations whose construction or actuation is *computer-supported*, interaction with physicalizations can also take place in the physical world without computer assistance [34]. Furthermore, handmade physicalizations of which many historical examples exist [3, 15, 59] may not involve computers at all, but are relevant to Data Physicalization when they can inform and inspire the design of modern, computer-supported physicalizations.

Data Physicalization and TUI

The area of Tangible User Interfaces (TUI) studies interactive systems that *"give physical form to digital information, employing physical artifacts both as representations and controls for computational media"* [71]. While this view clearly emphasizes the physical representation of information, the physical representations themselves are generally not meant for data exploration and analysis tasks. Several TUI systems have been developed for such tasks, but they typically use physical objects as *controls*, while the data itself is visualized on a screen [72] or top-projected [49, 73]. Although controls can encode information through their physical arrangement, this information entirely originates from the user and is not meant to be explored to gain insights as in Figure 2–left. Thus it does not constitute data in the Visualization sense [10].

Overall, there is large overlap between TUI and Data Physicalization, though they differ in focus. While both necessarily involve input and output and share many concerns, the former mostly focuses on information *input* and *manipulation* tasks (with output being used to assist in the task) while the latter mostly focuses on information *output* and *exploration* tasks (with input being used to assist in the task). The area of TUI has been remarkably productive in addressing technological and theoretical challenges, and its work will be important both to implement data physicalizations and inform their design. Conversely, simple data exploration scenarios have started to be used to illustrate actuated TUIs [70], suggesting that the idea of data physicalization is making its way into the community and may well become a major drive for TUI research.

Examples of Data Physicalization Research

Several research papers have already started to address questions raised by Data Physicalization. Early on, Vande Moere and colleagues pointed out the potential of data sculptures as a medium and the need to study them more deeply [43,75,79]. Later, several papers were published in Visualization and HCI venues that investigate empirical [34], design [67,69], and conceptual [32,33,75,79] questions regarding physicalizations, as well as specific application domains [68]. However, the physicalizations investigated are static and none of this work involves novel input and output technologies. Conversely, as far as we know, none of the work on new user interface technologies explicitly addresses Data Physicalization questions.

ENABLING TECHNOLOGIES

The area of Data Physicalization both depends heavily on available technologies, and can contribute to shaping the emergence of future technologies. Research has already demonstrated the process for composing and creating one-off static physicalizations using fabrication technologies [68,69]. Dynamic physicalizations, on the other hand, require computer-driven control of physical geometry or of material properties.

A range of technologies for controlling physical geometry have been explored in the area of shape-changing interfaces [54,58], many of which could be used to implement dynamic data physicalizations. Several systems offer discretized shape control through arrays of motorized bars [18,52], winch-actuated wires [15], or tiltable tiles [1]. Complex dynamic geometries can be also created by assembling actuated modules [30,60]. Alternatively, continuous shape deformation can be achieved through, e.g., pneumatic or hydraulic actuation [17,78], or shape-memory alloys [58]. Microrobotics can also be used to position multiple physical objects on a 2D plane [21,45,57], while free 3D positioning through levitation is currently being researched [39,61]. Physical geometry encoding can be complemented with color encoding through the use of deformable visual displays [47,65], sets of actuated visual displays [1], or projection mapping [5]. Finally, technologies also exist for dynamically controlling material properties such as stiffness [17,35,54], weight [46], or transparency [17], all of which can be used as additional dimensions to encode data.

While many of the above systems are bulky and only allow limited control over geometry and material properties, they lay the foundation for the promise of programmable matter [30].

RESEARCH AGENDA

Data Physicalization brings with it many research questions and challenges regarding the design, implementation, and evaluation of physicalizations. We split up open research questions into four main themes: *(i)* how to convey data effectively, *(ii)* how to employ animation and support interaction, *(iii)* covering specific applications, and *(iv)* evaluation methodologies.

Designing Physical Data Representations

Three main challenges are involved in creating perceptually effective physical designs to convey digital data: *(a)* understanding the design space of physical data representations, *(b)* understanding the perceptual effectiveness of different approaches, and *(c)* finding out how to implement these designs.

Charting the Design Space – Physical Variables

Data Physicalization and Visualization share the problem of finding suitable transformations from digital data to human-readable representations. The standard *visual encoding* process in Visualization maps each data point to a *visual mark* (i.e., a graphical primitive) and each data attribute to a *visual variable* (e.g., position, area, length, or hue) [13]. If we want to create physicalizations that are meant to be readable – as opposed to purely artistic data sculptures [36] – we need a similarly principled way of encoding data.

Researchers have begun to address this challenge by applying 2D and 3D visual encodings to physicalizations [69]. However, classical visual encodings largely ignore the multisensory nature of physical exploration that we previously highlighted as a benefit. Visual variables can be complemented with haptic variables such as resistance, friction, and temperature [22]. Roberts and Walker suggested the identification and use of such variables for each of our five senses [56]. However, considering senses separately does not fully capture the way information is encoded and accessed in the physical world [64]. For example, a smooth surface like glass or metal tends to be highly reflective, feels cold when touched, and silent when caressed. All these cues together participate in the perception of a single integrated physical property, "smoothness".

We argue that instead of studying individual sensory (e.g., visual or haptic) variables, it is necessary to study how they can be combined in physicalizations. We propose to call physical properties such as smoothness, hardness, or sponginess, *physical variables*. Physical variables are *not* inherently haptic, nor visual. They are also typically perceived *actively*, through exploratory actions involving hand, head, and body movements [20,33]. Identifying, exploring, and classifying physical variables is a research challenge that will be key to understanding the design space of data physicalizations.

Understanding what is Effective

When engaging in the design of physicalizations, one needs to know the design space of physical variables but also how effective they are at encoding and communicating data.

Perceptual studies in Visualization [13] have resulted in guidelines on how visual variables are best employed. For example, *length* as a visual variable is known to be perceptually effective at conveying quantitative values, while *color hue* is not [13]. Although initially developed for flat media, we can use many of these guidelines as a starting point for designing physicalizations. Yet, work on visualizations for wall-sized displays [6] cautions against a direct transfer. It showed that certain viewing angles change the effectiveness of visual variables and suggests that different effects may be found as well for data physicalizations. Work has also suggested that 3D spatial encodings are perceived more effectively when made physical than when shown on a screen [34].

In addition to studying how the use of visual variables transfers to non-flat spatial encodings, guidance is needed for conveying data to non-visual senses. Besides informal guidelines for haptic variables [22], we are unaware of any guideline for using physical variables. Data Physicalization needs to develop empirical guidelines similarly to those in Visualization, and consider similar questions such as: what are the just-noticeable differences that a physical variable can convey? Can it convey quantitative, ordinal, or nominal data best? Are there physical variables that can be perceived pre-attentively? Importantly, studies need to assume an active – rather than a fixed and passive – observer [20]. Also, the many interactions between the senses that physical variables address, as well as the interactions between the variables themselves, likely make their study very challenging compared to the study of visual variables.

Besides perceptual efficiency, discoverability and recognizability also need to be considered. While the presence of visual cues is easy to detect, the presence of physical cues like weight may not be. Physicalizations should be designed so that users can quickly identify which physical variables convey information, and how. This requires understanding to what extent people's experience in perceiving the physical world can be transferred to physicalizations, and how much requires explicit learning. Data physicalization researchers may need to be involved in developing new data encoding conventions, as well as helping promote *physicalization literacy*.

There are other aspects of data physicalization design besides the choice of appropriate physical encodings. For example physical size: a large physicalization such as in Figure 1–left can convey large amounts of data and be explored collaboratively. However, it cannot be manipulated and examined like a hand-sized physicalization [34]. Thus the effects of form factor and size will also need to be better understood.

Finally, the potential support for engagement previously discussed will also need to be studied. It is unclear which physical representations would contribute most to an engaging experience. Processing fluency – the ease with which an observer can decode an object – has also been shown to affect people's preferences [55]. Thus other qualities of physical variables need to be studied besides their perceptual effectiveness.

Implementation Challenges

Digital fabrication technologies greatly facilitated the process of prototyping and creating static physicalizations [68, 69] but even the most elaborate digital fabrication machines available today have not been built with data physicalization in mind. Multi-material 3D printers can interleave different source materials to gain some form of control over properties such as color, opacity, or deformability, but the range of materials available is still very limited [25, 47]. Much more research is needed before machines can accurately render physical variables such as thermal conductivity, weight, smell, or taste.

A further challenge is to ensure reproduction fidelity of physical variables across different machines. Materials also need to be chosen such that the variable they encode does not "run out" or depletes due to repeated user interactions. This requires careful consideration, as certain properties like temperature or deformation can change the value of the encoded variable after successive use. One way of addressing physical variable depletion is through *active physicalizations*, where an external energy source can be used to maintain a physical variable such as temperature at a desired value.

Active physicalizations can address other hard problems of physicalization implementation, such as free positioning in 3D space. While an on-screen visualization can have free-floating objects, physicalizations are subject to gravity. Technologies have been explored to address this, such as the use of magnetic fields [39], bubbles [62], or acoustic levitation [61] (see Figure 1–right). However, fine control over 3D geometry is hard and no technology exists yet that can successfully physicalize data encodings as simple as 3D scatterplots.

Finally, prototyping and building physicalizations involve complex workflows, ranging from laborious and low-fidelity manual crafting to custom programming (less laborious but requires expertise) to fully automatic (lower entry requirements but little control over the design) [69]. Thus, one challenge is to characterize possible fabrication workflows and classify them as to their benefits and drawbacks, including how fast physicalizations can be created or replicated, how accurate they are, how expensive the required material is, their environmental impact, and which skills are required to create them.

Supporting Animation and Interactivity

While physical encodings are important to convey a dataset effectively, building dynamic data physicalizations can help support not only reusability across datasets, but also a wider range of analytical and communication tasks. Here, we discuss two main challenges: *(a)* how to design effective dynamic physicalizations, and *(b)* how to implement them.

Designing Dynamic Physicalizations

So far we considered a fixed dataset with a fixed physical representation. Most on-screen visualization systems are however *dynamic*, and are therefore able to visually reflect (1) changes in datasets, (2) changes in data operations such as filtering and aggregation, (3) change from one data representation to another, (4) changes in visualization settings such as color scales and sorting order, and (5) view transformations such as pan, zoom, or rotate [33]. These operations can be either triggered by the system (they are *animated*) or by the user (they are *interactive*). Much research is needed on how to support similar features on data physicalizations.

Previous work on animated visualizations examined how to turn abrupt visual changes into animated transitions [24]. Although we expect most dynamic physicalizations to support animated transitions by design, it remains a challenge to design them such that they appropriately convey the changes to the observer. In particular, it remains unknown whether optimal settings for timing apply to animations in 3D space and animations of other physical variables, and what the perceptual limits of concurrent changes in these variables are.

Designing interaction with physicalizations is likely even more challenging. As discussed before, a key characteristic of physicalizations is their *built-in* support for interaction techniques that generally need to be explicitly implemented on regular displays. A hand-held 3D physicalization can be manually turned around. Modular physicalizations can be disassembled, reassembled, rearranged, aligned, thus already covering a range of analytical tasks [33, 67]. We call such interactions *physical interactions* to contrast them with what we call *synthetic interactions* requiring sensing, actuation, and computation.

The primary research challenge in designing effective interactive physicalizations is to find *how to best combine physical with synthetic interactions*. For example, with modular or malleable physicalization designs based on LEGOs or clay, a range of tasks can be manually accomplished through physical interaction, including updating datasets (see Figure 2–left), filtering data, or even changing their representation. At the same time, computer assistance is clearly desirable in many cases to accomplish repetitive or computational tasks.

Designing synthetic interaction techniques for physicalizations may require readapting – or more likely reinventing – interactive visualization. For example, should we support dynamic filtering through physical range sliders [72], or through more physical, direct manipulation gestures [18]? Some functionalities may not map to any manipulative gesture. Filtering on non-encoded dimensions, for example, will likely require alternative interaction mechanisms, such as symbolic gestures or instruments. Regardless, Data Physicalization will need to study ways of smoothly integrating synthetic with physical interaction, while avoiding "Midas Touch" issues common in gesture-based interfaces [40]. A key question is how much automation is necessary, and whether automation can be used in a way that preserves the cognitive benefits offered by physical object manipulation.

As with physical encodings, recognizability and discoverability of interactions are important. While synthetic interactions that rely on direct manipulation or familiar controls can convey their function through physical affordances (e.g., a handle or a switch), not all interaction styles can be easily expressed with affordances. Examples include symbolic and/or mid-air gestures [18]. The most effective interaction designs for data exploration also likely depend on factors such as the type of data, the size of the physicalization, and the number of users.

Implementation Challenges

While we often speak of computer displays as being *dynamic* displays, we want physicalizations to be more generally *reconfigurable*. Reconfigurability is required to switch datasets, to physicalize dynamic data (e.g., from a streaming source), or to get different perspectives on the same dataset. Recall that these operations can be either automatically triggered by the system (*animation*), or invoked by the user, either via sensing and actuation (*synthetic interaction*) or through purely physical manipulation (*physical interaction*).

Reconfigurability is required to implement rich *physical interactions*. For example, a modular 3D bar chart supports reordering [32], and a LEGO-based physicalization could support even more tasks. However, limited reconfigurability can be desirable. Information as to which states and operations are meaningful can be conveyed as physical constraints, by adding mechanical features such as attachments [69] or bindings [67]. Physical constraints have been already used in TUIs [72] but largely remain to be explored for physicalizations.

Actuated physicalizations can switch physical states without human intervention. Actuation provides support for *animation*, and once combined with sensing, for *synthetic interaction*. A key element to consider from the implementation perspective is the degree of *self-reconfigurability* of hardware technologies, as well as the *speed* with which the devices can reconfigure themselves. Self-reconfiguration taxonomies [54, 58] are key to better understanding to what extent different technologies can support data physicalization. For example, 2.5D shape displays [18] can support 3D bar charts of a certain size as well as solid terrain visualizations, but not 3D scatterplots. Although such devices are ultra-fast and can support slick interactions once combined with sensing, support for other physical representations requires a higher degree of self-reconfigurability. The technological complexity required is high, and much more research is needed to achieve full spatial flexibility [30].

Novel technologies are also needed to dynamically convey variables other than geometry. Prototypes exist that can dynamically control softness [17, 54] or weight [46], but more work is needed before we can "actuate" a range of physical variables such as reflectivity, porosity, rugosity or taste. The ultimate physical display that can dynamically control not only its shape and colors, but also its material properties still belongs to science-fiction, but is an exciting goal to pursue.

More work is also needed to better understand the practical trade-offs between different technologies, especially between digital fabrication and actuated devices. Despite its many benefits, actuation only supports temporal multiplexing, that is, showing a single dataset or view of a dataset over time. In contrast, many passive physicalizations (analogously to paper print-outs) can be easily duplicated, produced in different versions, arranged side-by-side, and explored. As passive physical objects they are both permanent and disposable, two properties that are lost when switching to actuated technology.

Finally, over-arching the above technological challenges is the importance of making the value of physicalizations greater than their construction cost (e.g., time, money) [74]. Only when this benefit is achieved can physicalizations become mainstream. The cost of producing data physicalizations can be reduced with appropriate tools that aid in their construction, both for static [69] and for dynamic physicalizations.

Application-Specific Challenges

Even though physicalizations promise many possible benefits, we expect them to apply differently depending on application scenarios. Thus, we need to identify the application areas that can draw immediate benefit in relation to the required cost and effort of creating them, and to understand the trade-offs involved [74]. Gaining such an understanding may also help develop physicalizations that target large audiences [14].

Consider education as an example. As mentioned earlier, physical artifacts have been shown to facilitate learning [19, 48]. Physicalizations could further help students understand data from topics such as meteorology, history, physics, or chemistry [15, 77], or help them learn about data representations [75]. They could support a way of learning that is not purely auditory or visual. Students could share and compare data objects, and even author their own [29, 75]. Yet we need to understand how such physicalizations should be designed to best support collaborative learning activities. It is also an open question to which extent *physicalization literacy* has to be taught to students before they can begin to understand physical encodings less familiar than 3D bar charts.

Using a physicalization will likely not remain a solitary activity [23]. Physical objects can easily be shared as long as collaborators are co-located [68], but in many cases people work over a distance. With current visualization tools, we can create snapshots to share by email or on paper, or to show during talks. Static physicalizations could be similarly shared through fabrication instructions, or dynamic physicalizations could be remotely synchronized. Many challenges are involved in identifying and implementing appropriate solutions.

Evaluation-Specific Challenges

Evaluating physicalizations is both important and difficult. On a methodological level, Data Physicalization shares challenges with HCI and Visualization on how to conduct evaluations.

Given the focus on data representation, many of the evaluation issues are shared by the Visualization community [37,50,74]. A pending challenge is to find appropriate ways of studying how people engage in data exploration when no clear task is defined [10]. Another concerns the choice of criteria for assessing the merits of data representations that go beyond pure time and error metrics. For example, the benefits of the physicalizations used by Rosling (Figure 2–right) likely lie in their pedagogical and persuasive power. Other criteria relevant to physicalizations include the insights gained from interacting with them [51], the extent to which they promote engagement and behavior change, their memorability [8], and the affective responses they elicit [26]. Taking inspiration from work on visualization evaluation scenarios [37], it also seems important to explore methodologies for understanding how people reason, collaborate and communicate with physicalizations.

In terms of research methods, comparative evaluation is of importance – in particular to empirically establish the benefits of physicalizations. A difficulty lies in the proper phrasing of research questions and choice of experimental manipulations. It is important to identify a fair alternative presentation method (or *modality*) as a baseline of comparison. Regular computer displays are an important baseline, but others include paper and ink, whiteboards, or advanced computer displays such as stereoscopic or volumetric displays. All these baselines need to be tested before we can claim to have strong formal evidence for the merits of physicalization.

It is also crucial, yet difficult, to only manipulate the presentation modality in order to avoid experimental bias. Data encodings should be kept the same or similar across modality conditions for comparisons to be informative [34]. Support for interaction should also be kept as similar as possible. For instance, it would be unfair to compare a static physical visualization with an on-screen visualization system augmented with rich and powerful interaction techniques. Technological advances in actuated physicalizations will make it possible to support similar interaction functionality, but keeping interaction styles comparable across presentation modalities while balancing ecological validity will remain a challenge.

Another example of a potential confound is physical size. It is already known that display size can have an effect on data exploration efficiency [2]. Therefore, when evaluating the effects of *physicality*, physical size has to be kept the same for the comparison to be fair, e.g., wall-sized on-screen visualizations need to be compared to room-sized physicalizations.

Finally, the issues of exploring, evaluating, and implementing physicalizations all are linked and we need new methods to address them concurrently. For example, how can we investigate a range of synthetic interactions without being subject to current technical limitations? One possibility is to use *proxy technologies* [32], for instance, building static physicalizations for gesture elicitation studies [76] to inform the design of synthetic interactions with future actuated physicalizations.

CONCLUSION

Data Physicalization is an emerging area of research that examines how computer-supported, physical renditions of data can support cognition, communication, learning, problem solving, and decision making. It is related to and bridges traditional fields such as Visualization and Tangible User Interfaces through its combined focus on data exploration and analysis with physical data representations, we call *physicalizations*.

We outlined many possible benefits of physicalizations in use and multiple research challenges and opportunities that remain to be addressed. The goal of this paper is to open the discussion about Data Physicalization as a research area, by providing a first working definition of physicalization artifacts and an initial proposition of the area's research focus.

Data Physicalization is a particularly exciting research area as many questions remain unanswered and much can be learned from related disciplines. Visualization researchers, for example, can find novel contexts to apply their knowledge on the design of data representations, psychologists can contribute methodologies and studies for understanding how physical interactions influence cognition, hardware enthusiasts can work on novel ways to implement powerful shape-changing dynamic physicalizations, and Tangible and Human-Computer Interaction researchers can contribute knowledge on how to best design and implement interactions for physical data representations. There also remain many fruitful application domains to be explored for both serious data exploration with physicalizations as well as more casual use. Data Physicalization research is truly at its beginning and researchers now have the great opportunity to shape and influence it.

With this paper, we hope to inspire the creation of a community around research on Data Physicalization that will begin to address the outlined as well as new and emerging challenges and opportunities. We hope the outcome will be exciting examples of how our thinking, learning, problem solving, or communication can be enriched with data physicalizations. See the dataphys.org website for further developments.

ACKNOWLEDGMENTS

We thank Benjamin Bach for his help on the neurosurgical planning scenario. This work has been supported by the EC within the 7th framework programme through the FET Open scheme's GHOST project (grant #309191) and by the Danish Council for Strategic Research (grant #10-092316).

REFERENCES

1. Alexander, J., Lucero, A., and Subramanian, S. Tilt Displays: Designing display surfaces with multi-axis tilting and actuation. In *Mobile HCI* (2012), 161–170.
2. Andrews, C., Endert, A., Yost, B., and North, C. Information visualization on large, high-resolution displays: Issues, challenges, and opportunities. *Information Visualization 10*, 4 (2011), 341–355.
3. Ascher, M., and Ascher, R. *Mathematics of the Incas: Code of the Quipu*. Dover Publications, 2013.
4. Barrass, S. Digital fabrication of acoustic sonifications. *J. Audio Eng. Soc. 60*, 9 (2012), 709–715.
5. Benko, H., Wilson, A. D., Zannier, F., and Benko, H. Dyadic projected spatial augmented reality. In *Proc. UIST* (2014), 645–655.
6. Bezerianos, A., and Isenberg, P. Perception of visual variables on tiled wall-sized displays for information visualization applications. *TVCG 18*, 12 (2012), 2516–2525.
7. Borghi, A. M., and Cimatti, F. Embodied cognition and beyond: acting and sensing the body. *Neuropsychologia 48*, 3 (2009), 763–773.
8. Borkin, M., Vo, A., Bylinskii, Z., Isola, P., Sunkavalli, S., Oliva, A., and Pfister, H. What makes a visualization memorable? *TVCG 19*, 12 (2013), 2306–2315.
9. Calvert, G., Spence, C., and Stein, B. E. *The Handbook of Multisensory Processes*. MIT Press, 2004.
10. Card, S., Mackinlay, J. D., and Shneiderman, B., Eds. *Readings In Information Visualization: Using Vision To Think*. Morgan Kaufmann Publishers, 1999.
11. Carello, C., Wagman, J. B., and Turvey, M. T. Acoustic specification of object properties. In *Moving Image Theory: Ecological Considerations*. Southern Illinois University, 2005, 79–104.
12. Challis, B. P., and Edwards, A. D. N. Design principles for tactile interaction. In *Haptic Human-Computer Interaction*. Springer, 2001, 17–24.
13. Cleveland, W. S., and McGill, R. Graphical perception: Theory, experimentation, and application to the development of graphical methods. *J. Am. Stat. Assoc. 79*, 387 (1984), 531–554.
14. Danziger, M. Information visualization for the people. Master's thesis, MIT, 2008.
15. Dragicevic, P., and Jansen, Y. List of physical visualizations. dataphys.org/list, 2012.
16. Edman, P. *Tactile Graphics*. AFB, 1992.
17. Follmer, S., Leithinger, D., Olwal, A., Cheng, N., and Ishii, H. Jamming user interfaces: Programmable particle stiffness and sensing for malleable and shape-changing devices. In *Proc. UIST* (2012), 519–528.
18. Follmer, S., Leithinger, D., Olwal, A., Hogge, A., and Ishii, H. inFORM: Dynamic physical affordances and constraints through shape and object actuation. In *Proc. UIST* (2013), 417–426.
19. Froebel, F. *The Education of Man*. A. Lovell & Co, 1885.
20. Gibson, J. J. *The Ecological Approach to Visual Perception*. Psychology Press, 1986.
21. Gilpin, K., Koyanagi, K., and Rus, D. Making self-disassembling objects with multiple components in the Robot Pebbles system. In *ICRA* (2011), 3614–3621.
22. Griffin, A. L. Feeling it out: the use of haptic visualization for exploratory geographic analysis. *Cartographic Perspectives*, 39 (2001), 12–29.
23. Heer, J., Ham, F., Carpendale, S., Weaver, C., and Isenberg, P. Creation and collaboration: Engaging new audiences for information visualization. In *Information Visualization*, LNCS. Springer, 2008, 92–133.
24. Heer, J., and Robertson, G. G. Animated transitions in statistical data graphics. *TVCG 13*, 6 (2007), 1240–1247.
25. Hiller, J., and Lipson, H. Design and analysis of digital materials for physical 3d voxel printing. *Rapid Prototyping Journal 15*, 2 (2009), 137–149.
26. Hogan, T., and Hornecker, E. How does representation modality affect user-experience of data artifacts? In *Haptic & Audio Inter. Design*. Springer, 2012, 141–151.
27. Hornecker, E. The role of physicality in tangible and embodied interactions. *Interactions 18*, 2 (2011), 19–23.
28. Hornecker, E., and Buur, J. Getting a grip on tangible interaction: a framework on physical space and social interaction. In *Proc. CHI* (2006), 437–446.
29. Huron, S., Jansen, Y., and Carpendale, S. Constructing visual representations: investigating the use of tangible tokens. *TVCG 20*, 12 (2014), 2102–2111.
30. Ishii, H., Lakatos, D., Bonanni, L., and Labrune, J.-B. Radical Atoms: Beyond Tangible Bits, toward transformable materials. *Interactions 19*, 1 (2012), 38–51.
31. Ishii, H., and Ullmer, B. Tangible Bits: towards seamless interfaces between people, bits and atoms. In *Proc. CHI*, ACM (1997), 234–241.
32. Jansen, Y. *Physical and Tangible Information Visualization*. PhD thesis, Université Paris-Sud XI, 2014.
33. Jansen, Y., and Dragicevic, P. An interaction model for visualizations beyond the desktop. *TVCG 19*, 12 (2013), 2396–2405.
34. Jansen, Y., Dragicevic, P., and Fekete, J.-D. Evaluating the efficiency of physical visualizations. In *Proc. CHI* (2013), 2593–2602.
35. Kildal, J. Kooboh: Variable tangible properties in a handheld Haptic-Illusion box. In *Proc. EuroHaptics'12*. Springer, 2012, 191–194.
36. Kosara, R. Visualization criticism—the missing link between information visualization and art. In *Proc. IV* (2007), 631–636.
37. Lam, H., Bertini, E., Isenberg, P., Plaisant, C., and Carpendale, S. Empirical studies in information visualization: Seven scenarios. *TVCG 18*, 9 (2012), 1520–1536.
38. Lederman, S. J., and Klatzky, R. L. Hand movements: a window into haptic object recognition. *Cogn. Psychol. 19*, 3 (July 1987), 342–368.
39. Lee, J., Post, R., and Ishii, H. ZeroN: Mid-air tangible interaction enabled by computer controlled magnetic levitation. In *Proc. UIST* (2011), 327–336.
40. Lee, J. C. In search of a natural gesture. *ACM Crossroads 16*, 4 (2010), 9–12.
41. McGookin, D., Robertson, E., and Brewster, S. Clutching at straws: using tangible interaction to provide non-visual access to graphs. In *Proc. CHI* (2010), 1715–1724.

42. McGookin, D. K., and Brewster, S. A. SoundBar: Exploiting multiple views in multimodal graph browsing. In *Proc. NordiCHI* (2006), 145–154.
43. Moere, A. V. Beyond the tyranny of the pixel: Exploring the physicality of information visualization. In *Proc. IV* (2008), 469–474.
44. Munzner, T. Process and pitfalls in writing information visualization research papers. In *Information Visualization*. Springer, 2008, 134–153.
45. Murata, S., Yoshida, E., Kamimura, A., Kurokawa, H., Tomita, K., and Kokaji, S. M-TRAN: Self-reconfigurable modular robotic system. *TMECH 7*, 4 (2002), 431–441.
46. Niiyama, R., Yao, L., and Ishii, H. Weight and volume changing device with liquid metal transfer. In *Proc. TEI* (2014), 49–52.
47. Olberding, S., Wessely, M., and Steimle, J. Printscreen: fabricating highly customizable thin-film touch-displays. In *Proc. UIST* (2014), 281–290.
48. O'Malley, C., and Fraser, S. Literature review in learning with tangible technologies. Tech. rep., Futurelab, 2004.
49. Piper, B., Ratti, C., and Ishii, H. Illuminating clay: A 3-D tangible interface for landscape analysis. In *Proc. CHI* (2002), 355–362.
50. Plaisant, C. The challenge of information visualization evaluation. In *Proc. AVI* (2004), 109–116.
51. Plaisant, C., Fekete, J., and Grinstein, G. Promoting insight-based evaluation of visualizations: From contest to benchmark repository. *TVCG 14*, 1 (2008), 120–134.
52. Poupyrev, I., Nashida, T., Maruyama, S., Rekimoto, J., and Yamaji, Y. Lumen: interactive visual and shape display for calm computing. In *SIGGRAPH Emerging Technologies* (2004), 17.
53. Pousman, Z., Stasko, J. T., and Mateas, M. Casual information visualization: Depictions of data in everyday life. *TVCG 13*, 6 (2007).
54. Rasmussen, M. K., Pedersen, E. W., Petersen, M. G., and Hornbæk, K. Shape-changing interfaces: a review of the design space and open research questions. In *Proc. CHI* (2012), 735–744.
55. Reber, R., Schwarz, N., and Winkielman, P. Processing fluency and aesthetic pleasure: Is beauty in the perceiver's processing experience? *Personality and Social Psychology Review 8*, 4 (2004), 364–382.
56. Roberts, J. C., and Walker, R. Using all our senses: the need for a unified theoretical approach to multi-sensory information visualization. In *VisWeek Workshop* (2010).
57. Romanishin, J., Gilpin, K., and Rus, D. M-blocks: Momentum-driven, magnetic modular robots. In *Proc. IROS*, IEEE/RSJ (2013), 4288–4295.
58. Roudaut, A., Karnik, A., Löchtefeld, M., and Subramanian, S. Morphees: Toward high "shape resolution" in self-actuated flexible mobile devices. In *Proc. CHI* (2013), 593–602.
59. Schmandt-Besserat, D. *How Writing Came About*. University of Texas Press, 1996.
60. Schweikardt, E., and Gross, M. D. roBlocks: A robotic construction kit for mathematics and science education. In *Proc. ICMI* (2006), 72–75.
61. Seah, S., Drinkwater, B., Carter, T., Malkin, R., and Subramanian, S. Dexterous ultrasonic levitation of millimeter-sized objects in air. *UFFC 61*, 7 (2014), 1233–1236.
62. Seah, S. A., Martinez Plasencia, D., Bennett, P. D., Karnik, A., Otrocol, V. S., Knibbe, J., Cockburn, A., and Subramanian, S. SensaBubble: A chrono-sensory mid-air display of sight and smell. In *Proc. CHI* (2014), 2863–2872.
63. Shaer, O., and Hornecker, E. Tangible user interfaces: Past, present, and future directions. *Found. Trends Hum.-Comput. Interact. 3* (2010), 1–137.
64. Spelke, E. S. The development of intermodal perception. In *Handbook of Infant Perception*. Academic Press, 1987, 233–273.
65. Steimle, J., Jordt, A., and Maes, P. Flexpad: highly flexible bending interactions for projected handheld displays. In *Proc. CHI* (2013), 237–246.
66. Stusak, S., and Aslan, A. Beyond physical bar charts: An exploration of designing physical visualizations. In *Proc. CHI-EA* (2014), 1381–1386.
67. Stusak, S., Tabard, A., and Butz, A. Can physical visualizations support analytical tasks? In *Posters of IEEE InfoVis* (2013).
68. Stusak, S., Tabard, A., Sauka, F., Khot, R., and Butz, A. Activity sculptures: Exploring the impact of physical visualizations on running activity. *TVCG 20*, 12 (2014), 2201–2210.
69. Swaminathan, S., Shi, C., Jansen, Y., Dragicevic, P., Oehlberg, L., and Fekete, J.-D. Supporting the design and fabrication of physical visualizations. In *Proc. CHI* (2014), 3845–3854.
70. Tang, S. K., Sekikawa, Y., Leithinger, D., Follmer, S., and Ishii, H. Tangible cityscape, 2013. tinyurl.com/tcityscape.
71. Ullmer, B., and Ishii, H. Emerging frameworks for tangible user interfaces. *IBM Syst. J. 39* (July 2000).
72. Ullmer, B., Ishii, H., and Jacob, R. J. K. Tangible query interfaces: Physically constrained tokens for manipulating database queries. In *Proc. INTERACT* (2003), 279–286.
73. Underkoffler, J., and Ishii, H. Urp: A luminous-tangible workbench for urban planning and design. In *Proc. CHI* (1999), 386–393.
74. Van Wijk, J. J. The value of visualization. In *Proc. VIS* (2005), 79–86.
75. Vande Moere, A., and Patel, S. The Physical Visualization of Information: Designing Data Sculptures in an Educational Context. In *Visual Information Communication*. Springer, 2010, pp. 1–23.
76. Wobbrock, J. O., Morris, M. R., and Wilson, A. D. User-defined gestures for surface computing. In *Proc. CHI* (2009), 1083–1092.
77. Wu, H.-K., and Shah, P. Exploring visuospatial thinking in chemistry learning. *Science Education 88*, 3 (2004), 465–492.
78. Yao, L., Niiyama, R., Ou, J., Follmer, S., Della Silva, C., and Ishii, H. PneUI: Pneumatically actuated soft composite materials for shape changing interfaces. In *Proc. UIST* (2013), 13–22.
79. Zhao, J., and Vande Moere, A. Embodiment in data sculpture: A model of the physical visualization of information. In *Proc. DIMEA* (2008), 343–350.

Exploring Interactions with Physically Dynamic Bar Charts

Faisal Taher[1], John Hardy[1], Abhijit Karnik[1], Christian Weichel[1], Yvonne Jansen[2], Kasper Hornbæk[2], Jason Alexander[1]
School of Computing and Communications, Lancaster University, United Kingdom
{f.taher, j.hardy, a.karnik, c.weichel, j.alexander}@lancaster.ac.uk
Department of Computer Science, University of Copenhagen, Denmark
{yvja, kash}@di.ku.dk

ABSTRACT
Visualizations such as bar charts help users reason about data, but are mostly screen-based, rarely physical, and almost never physical and dynamic. This paper investigates the role of physically dynamic bar charts and evaluates new interactions for exploring and working with datasets rendered in dynamic physical form. To facilitate our exploration we constructed a 10×10 interactive bar chart and designed interactions that supported fundamental visualisation tasks, specifically: annotation, navigation, filtering, comparison, organization, and sorting. The interactions were evaluated in a user study with 17 participants. We identify the preferred methods of working with the data for each task (e.g. directly tapping rows to hide bars), highlight the strengths and limitations of working with physical data, and discuss the challenges of integrating the proposed interactions together into a larger data exploration system. In general, physical interactions were intuitive, informative, and enjoyable, paving the way for new explorations in physical data visualizations.

Author Keywords
Shape-changing interfaces; physical visualizations; tangible user interfaces; information visualization; shape displays.

ACM Classification Keywords
H.5.m. Information interfaces and presentation (e.g., HCI): Miscellaneous.

INTRODUCTION
Effective visualizations help users "*use vision to think*" [3] and aim to improve reasoning about data. They increase the effectiveness of our ability to process information by transforming it into visual structures that leverage our biological ability to detect patterns and trends. While todays visualizations are optimised for 2D screens and computers, the information visualization community has begun to discuss how to design 3D visualizations for physical devices and non-traditional inputs [15, 17, 18, 23].

As part of this effort, researchers have investigated the benefits of 3D physical charts in comparison with 3D on-screen visualizations [16] and found that the rich qualities of physical objects can play an important role in the data inspection process. Huron et al. [13] showed how people construct, manipulate, and update visualizations based on tangible tokens. Other examples include data sculptures [1] and tactile cartographic maps [27]. The main drawback of current physical visualizations is that they are inert, being either fabricated (i.e. laser cut [15], 3D printed [3], constructed from passive building blocks [13]) and thus disconnected from the data-source once constructed. Shape-changing interfaces (i.e. Relief [22], inFORM [6]) have the potential to alleviate these drawbacks. However, the community lacks an understanding of how data can be interacted with to achieve effective and intuitive data exploration with physically dynamic displays.

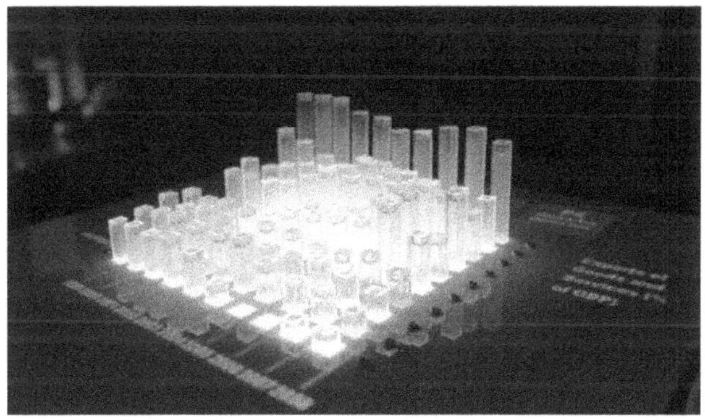

Figure 1 – EMERGE using actuating physical rods and RGB LEDs to display international export data.

This paper presents a first exploration of user interactions with data using our custom built dynamic bar chart: EMERGE (Figure 1). EMERGE contains self-actuating rods capable of RGB colour output and touch detection for pushing and pulling of the data itself, in addition to traditional touch detection on the surrounding surface. As a first step towards guidelines for designing physically dynamic data we carried out a user study with 17 participants and investigated fundamental interaction tasks that are common in data exploration scenarios: annotation, filtering, organisation, and navigation. Within these we

CHI 2015, April 18 - 23, 2015, Seoul, Republic of Korea
Copyright 2015 ACM 978-1-4503-3145-6/15/04…$15.00
http://dx.doi.org/10.1145/2702123.2702604

explore directly manipulating data points (e.g. by pulling to select data points), as well as using gestures on projected axis labels (e.g. moving rows of data by dragging labels). These explorations form the baseline for more complex and diverse interaction techniques.

The key contributions of the paper are (a) the identification and design of 14 baseline interaction techniques designed to be used with physically dynamic bar charts, (b) a user study that evaluates these interactions, determining ones that are most preferred and effective, and (c) a discussion of important design considerations and challenges for physically dynamic visualizations.

RELATED WORK

Physical data visualizations, or 'Physicalizations' [17], are informed by two strands of research: visualization [15, 25] and tangible and shape-changing interfaces [22]. Below we review these strands to argue that few papers have used dynamic, physical interfaces to visualize data, and that no study we are aware of has investigated the possibilities and usefulness of interactions for such interfaces. We also outline the research questions for this paper.

Static Physical Visualizations

Physical visualizations aim to extend the benefits of visualizations by tapping into active perception skills and integrating sensory information in addition to the visual sense. Jansen and Dragicevic [16] curate a *list of physical visualizations*[1] that includes examples more than six millennia old. These are mostly used to show quantity in physical form, for instance by mapping a number to physical height. Paneels and Roberts [26] reviewed approaches that focus on haptic data visualization, such as using audio, texture/friction, and enclosures to show quantity.

Previous research has examined the efficiency of physical visualisation [15] and approaches for designing physical visualizations [35]. Jansen et al. [15] found that hand-held 3D printed physical visualizations improved users' efficiency at information retrieval tasks, with physical touch and visual realism key being advantages. Stusak and Aslan examined various physical visualization prototypes and found that these representations can support analytical tasks through mature design, emphasising the importance of stability and affordances [35].

Physical visualizations can also increase the accessibility of data to blind or low-vision users [3, 7, 19, 24]. Examples include tactile pin arrays to show graphics [39], VizTouch [3] that allows blind users to 3D print visualizations of line graphs, and tactile maps [27] that show cartographic data using physical properties (physical height corresponds to elevation of the terrain).

Other physical visualizations have more artistic aims. The term 'data sculptures' [1] describes visual pleasing artefacts that communicate information, such as jewellery that shows internet connection rates. Khot et al. [30] describe Sweatatoms, a 3D modeling and printing system that can turn activity patterns in sports into 3D objects that support reflection and aesthetic pleasure. Stusak et al's 'activity sculptures' artistically visualised running activity for discussion and reflection [36].

Physical visualizations, such as those described above, have a range of potential benefits over their purely visual counterparts [16, 25, 38]. First, as physical objects they can be manipulated more directly than through a mouse or even through touch screens [16]. Second, the interplay of vision and touch can facilitate cognition [15]. Finally, the physical modality opens a range of new interaction possibilities compared to on-screen visualizations.

Dynamic Physical Visualizations

While static, physical visualizations are useful and attractive, they must be fabricated before use. Modifications of their physical form are often limited once created and many of the computational and interactive benefits of screen-based visualizations are lost. Work into tangible user interfaces (TUIs) and shape-changing interfaces has attempted to address these disadvantages by showing non-static data.

Shape displays typically have a physical equivalent of pixels, either binary (on/off) or continuous (being able to show a range of values). Typical examples include Sublimate [21], Relief [22, 23], Lumen [28], Feelex [14], Taxel [18], inFORM [6], Tilt Displays [1], and Physical Charts[2]. These physical pixels are often implemented via motorized pins that can extrude from a surface; pneumatics [10] and shape-memory alloys [5] can serve a similar purpose. These extrusions can be mapped to data values. Resolution varies from a few (<10) pixels to inFORM's 900 motorized pins. Although these papers mainly demonstrate systems, they do show tasks relating to visualization, including showing bar chart data (Physical Charts), mathematical functions [6] and wind tunnel flow [21].

The interactions for shape displays often use well-known input, such as direct touch, and pulling and pushing [6, 23]. Relief [23] supports free-hand gestures to interact with 3D models: the user performs hand gestures to translate, scale, and rotate models. In addition to direct touch, inFORM [6] supports remote gestural interaction and the use of on-surface objects to control interactions such as menu selections. While free-hand gestures are useful in many scenarios, they do not capitalise on the rich haptic dimension touted as a key benefit of physical visualizations,

[1] http://dataphys.org/list (last accessed 07/01/2015)

[2] http://research.microsoft.com/en-us/um/cambridge/projects/physicalcharts/ (accessed 23/12/2014)

nor do they support the delicate manipulation of data observed in by Jansen et al. [16].

Open Questions for Physically Dynamic Bar Charts

The above literature instigates several research questions regarding physically dynamic bar charts. In particular, the following two questions are crucial for interaction design. First, it is an open question how physically dynamic bar charts should support tasks in visualization, such as comparing specific values [2] or gaining an overview of a dataset [33]. Previous work has suggested multiple task models for use in visual data analysis [2, 11], yet these are directed towards 2D data visualizations.

Second, it is unclear which interactions with physically dynamic bar charts are useful and usable. In contrast to previous work on static physical visualizations and data sculptures, support for user interaction is as crucial as the ability of the interface to actuate itself. Further, the key aim of these artefacts is to help users think about data and the focus is *on* the visualizations, rather than on the control. This poses questions such as: are the useful interactions with static physical visualizations (e.g., [16]) transferrable to dynamic physical visualizations? Thus, identifying useful interactions with physical dynamic graphs is still very much an open question, beyond the straightforward uses of touch, pushing/pulling, and mid-air gestures.

IMPLEMENTATION

To investigate data analysis tasks and interactions, we developed a dynamic physical bar chart: EMERGE. Our design follows that of the inFORM system [6], differing through details such as the inclusion of LEDs, hardware control architecture, and software model.

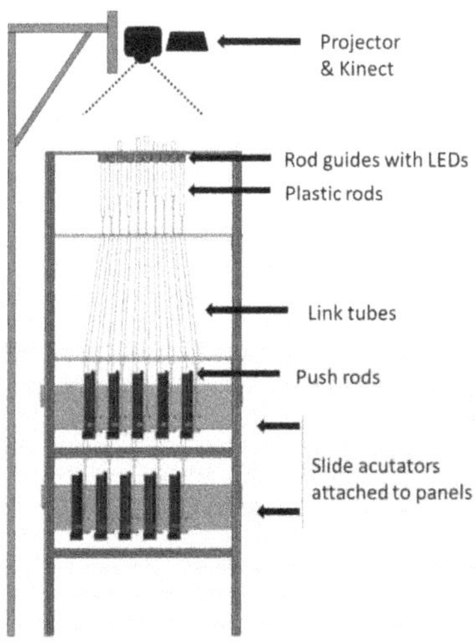

Figure 2 – The setup of the EMERGE system.

Hardware

The hardware consists of a 10 × 10 array of actuated plastic rods that are individually linked to 100 motorized potentiometer sliders. The sliders provide 100mm travel length. The linkage consists of push-rods supported by hollow tubes such that the sliders at the bottom are able to control the plastic rods at the top.

The sliders are stacked in two layers to minimize the size footprint (0.55×0.44×1.20m). Each rod is illuminated by a dedicated RGB LED (WS2812B) attached to rod guides, which are designed to keep them vertically stable. Additionally, a Microsoft Kinect® and projector were mounted above the system to project information (i.e. axes, labels, and controls) and detect touch interaction on the surface surrounding the rods.

Software

The EMERGE software stack is shown in Figure 3. The overall software architecture separates three logic layers: application, model, and firmware. The separation between application and model uses the model-view-controller pattern to allow multiple applications to connect simultaneously. This was useful in the debugging and development of applications.

The application layer consists of multiple user study applications and a 3D viewer/simulator. The study applications are written in HTML5 and hosted by the Ubi Displays toolkit [9] to map the projection and detect touch on the surrounding surfaces. The EMERGE API (model) is written in C# and used to manage the state of the actuators and LEDs. It also handles calibration, animation, and touch detection, which was based on the changes in potentiometer readings (thereby enabling push and pull interactions). The model communicates with the EMERGE Driver—an ABI (Application Binary Interface) that interfaces with the control firmware for sliders and LEDs.

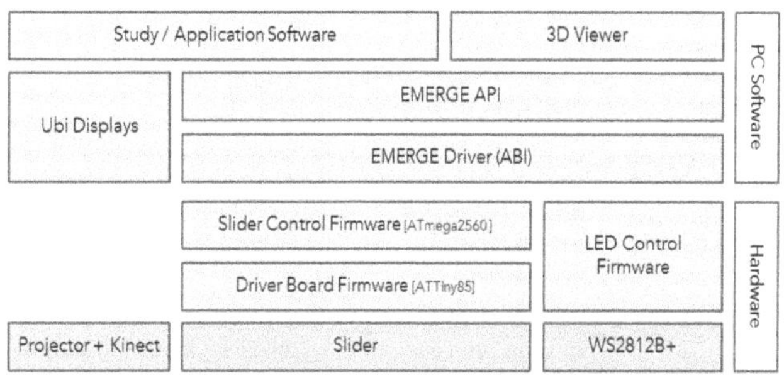

Figure 3 - The EMERGE software stack. Application layer: orange; Model layer: blue; Firmware: green; hardware: red.

The control firmware consists of 2 Arduino Mega2560 (sliders) and a single Arduino Uno (LEDs). These send and receive data frames from the ABI via USB. Connected to the Mega2650s, are 17 bespoke motor driver boards. Each driver board carries 3 ATTiny84 microcontrollers that control the position of 6 sliders at ≈8Mhz using a PID controller. When selected on an SPI bus, these update the PID set point and report byte position values back to the ATmega2560s.

APPROACH

To reason about effective methods for exploring data with dynamic physical visualizations, we first needed to evaluate interactions that are specific to this type of display. We present a series of novel methods for interacting with physical data and test whether they are useful and usable. Our investigations are based on Heer and Shneiderman's taxonomy [11], and explore different types of commonly used visualization tasks such as annotation, organization, filtering, and navigation. A user study was structured to elicit formative feedback about the usefulness and usability of specific features, capturing initial reactions and experiences. We specifically avoided early experimentation as others have warned against this approach [8, 12], especially given the immaturity of this area.

Task Structure

We focus on 'physicalizing' data using bar charts as they map naturally to our hardware setup and have been used for previous studies on physical visualizations due to their low requirements for visualization literacy [15]. We base our exploration on Heer and Shneiderman's taxonomy for visual data analysis [11]. This taxonomy structures the required interactive dynamics for visual analysis tasks into three high-level categories: *Data and View Specification*, *View Manipulation*, and *Process and Provenance*. These break down into sub-categories, which we utilize to derive tasks that are relevant and applicable in a physical space.

Table 1 provides an overview of the task-sets that we adopted from Heer and Shneiderman's taxonomy (expressed in parentheses) of visual data analysis tasks [11]. Each task-set consists of multiple tasks/interactions.

Table 1 – Task-sets and interaction techniques explored during the user study.

Task	Overview	Interaction Techniques
Annotation *(Process & provenance)*	Selecting and marking individual data points.	Point, pull, press.
Filtering *(Data view & specification)*	Hiding and refining data for enhanced perception and comparison.	Swipe away, manual press, assisted press, press shortcut, and press to compare.
Organization *(View manipulation)*	Data arrangement by moving rows and columns.	Drag and drop with immediate transition and hide-all with transition, press with instant transition and hide-all with transition.
Navigation *(View manipulation)*	Controlling the view of large data sets.	Scroll, directional arrows, directional press, and paging.

Tasks such as *Coordinate* from *View Manipulation*, and *Share* and *Guide* from *Process and Provenance* are not applicable to our setup, and are therefore excluded. *Coordinate* typically concerns multiple views of data, whereas we experiment with one view. *Sharing* involves actions such as exporting data, which is software-based, and *Guiding* leans towards helping users through workflows. Complex task explorations such as *Sort* and *Derive* from *View Manipulation* are, for now, excluded as we first need to understand basic interactions rather than, for instance, exposing patterns and forming data models. Further, *Record* typically involves showing historical data (e.g. through undo or redo features) and forms part of a larger 'data explorer' system, rather than a fundamental interaction.

Participants

The user study was carried out with 17 participants (6 female) with a mean age of 27 years. None of the participants had previous experience interacting with shape-changing displays. Two participants had previously seen demonstrations of shape-changing technology. Each session lasted approximately 40 minutes and participants were compensated £8 for their time.

Materials

We utilized the EMERGE system (as described in the previous section), which enables users to interact with an actuating interface of LED-lit rods (representing the bars of bar charts). Information such as labels were projected around the bars of the shape-display (e.g. see Figure 4).

Procedure

Participants were welcomed individually and introduced to the EMERGE system. A short demographic questionnaire was initially provided. Participants were then asked to carry out a number of task-sets pertaining to annotation, organisation, filtering, and navigation. We explored a variety of interactions for each task-set, some of which were adapted from Jansen et al. [15] (e.g. physically selecting data points of interest). The data sets were downloaded from Jansen et al's [15] materials page[3], and included country indicator data. The data sets consisted of HIV prevalence, GDP percentage in exports, annual electricity consumption, and a UK rainfall dataset downloaded from the MET office website[4] (as we required a larger data set for the Navigation task). The data shown to users was encoded as follows: each row is discerned by a unique colour, and the height of a rod represents a numerical value (i.e. the y-axis value). The study procedure included the following steps:

- To elicit initial thoughts and perceptions, and before showing any interactions for a task-set, participants were asked how they could achieve the task. This followed an informal guessability approach [40] to gather insights without being influenced by demonstrations. Participants were shown a sample data set with interactivity disabled.
- Interaction techniques were then demonstrated to participants. They were also asked to carry them out to build familiarity. A task was then verbally given to participants by the experimenter. We were interested in participant behaviours and feedback whilst carrying out

[3] http://www.aviz.fr/phys (last accessed 7/01/2015)
[4] http://www.metoffice.gov.uk/climate/uk/datasets/ (last accessed 22/09/2014)

the interactions rather than in how accurately they were able to carry out the task.

- The ordering of task-sets and interaction techniques were counterbalanced in order to reduce the influence on subsequent tasks.
- Immediately after participants carried out a task, they filled out a 5-point Likert scale questionnaire, and asked to comment on what they found useful and problematic.
- At the end of a session, a short discussion was carried out in order to receive any additional insights.

Each session was recorded using audio and video to document participant feedback and interaction behaviours with the EMERGE system.

EXPLORING PHYSICAL BAR CHART INTERACTIONS

We used EMERGE as a test-bed for exploring user interactions with physically dynamic bar charts. Below, each of the task-sets (see Table 1) is described along with the results from the user study.

Annotation

Annotation (see Figure 4) allows users to select and mark data-points for later reference [11]. This is useful when users wish to document and return to subsets of data, or to communicate interesting observations. During the study, we asked participants to mark single data points using three techniques: point, pull, and press. The data set used for this task was the electricity consumption in 10 different countries (rows) between 1971 and 1998 (columns).

- *Point:* Users position one finger on the row label and a second finger on the column label projected beside the physical columns. All data points are dimmed except the intersection point, which is marked by a unique colour (e.g. white). Participants were asked to select the year and country with the highest electricity consumption in the complete data set.
- *Pull:* Users pull the data point that they wish to select. The selected data point becomes emphasized by dimming the unselected data points. Participants were asked to select the year in which Qatar had the highest electricity consumption.
- *Press:* Similar to *Pull*, however, users press the data point (similar to a tap) to select it. Participants were asked to select the year in which Iceland had the lowest electricity consumption.

Results and Feedback

Participants preferred the *press* technique for annotating data points (5-point *Likert M*: 4.29, *SD*: 0.99, see Figure 5). This also matched all 16/17 participants' initial perceptions of how they would select an individual data point. One participant stated they would prefer to pull a column in order to "pick out" the value.

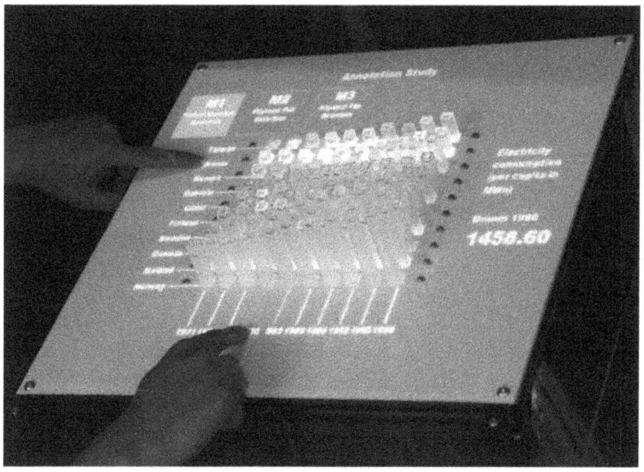

Figure 4 - The annotation task. Here the user is using the *Point* technique to select a data point.

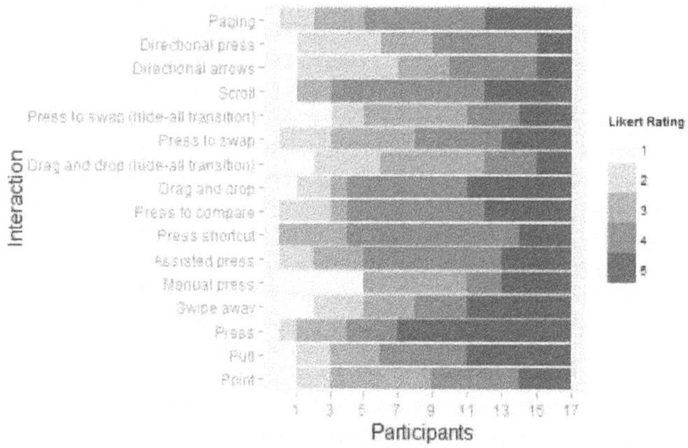

Figure 5 - Likert scale ratings for helpfulness of interaction techniques. Range = 1: Strongly Disagree, 5: Strongly Agree.

"This was my favourite technique as it was very simple to use. I like how only that particular point is highlighted with colour to make it easier to see. It feels more like I am actively selecting the data point I want to see, more than when I just touched the screen."

The visual feedback (i.e. dimming the unselected data points) also allowed participants to distinguish the selected data point from the others (as commented by 5 participants). Although users will be physically aware of selecting a data point, the visual confirmation (as feedback) is necessary to confirm the selection.

Filtering

Data filtering allows users to control the items displayed and enables focus by eliminating irrelevant data [33]. Filtering is particularly useful in a setup of physical bars. Zacks et al. [41] found that for height estimates of bar charts printed on paper, distortions introduced by neighbouring elements were most problematic. Therefore, clearing the display of unneeded bars can aid users to correctly read and compare values. Although Zacks et al.'s [41] observations were based on printed bar charts, we expect similar issues with physical bars. The data set used for this task was the export percentage of goods and services in 10 different countries (rows) between 1999 and 2008 (columns). During the study we explored filtering irrelevant rows using the techniques below (see Figure 6):

- *Swipe away:* Swipe the projected row label off the edge of the surface to hide the row. Participants were asked to hide eight selected rows that were deemed irrelevant and to state a general comparison overview between the remaining two countries.
- *Manual press:* Directly and manually push down all irrelevant data points. Similar to *swipe away*, participants were asked to press down the data points of eight different rows and compare the GDP of the remaining two.
- *Assisted press:* Similar to manual push, except the system detects downward pressure and hides the pressed data point. Participants were asked to hide the row with the highest exports percentage.
- *Press to compare:* This technique explores pressing down on any data point on two rows, which then hides all other rows. Participants were asked to press and compare the GDP of two selected countries.
- *Press shortcut:* The data point at the beginning of each row acts as a control point. Once this data point is pressed, the remainder of the data in the row becomes hidden. Participants were asked to hide eight different rows and compare the GDP of the remaining two.

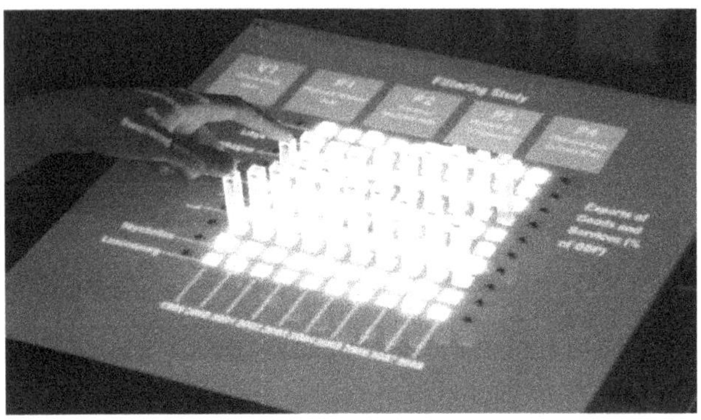

Figure 6 - Filtering task showing the *press to compare* technique.

Results and Feedback

All 17 participants initially stated that they would prefer to only tap the row labels that they are interested in observing and comparing, which would subsequently hide the other irrelevant rows. The study showed that the *press shortcut* technique was preferred by most participants (*Likert M*: 4, *SD*: 0.63). This was regarded to be especially useful when smaller numbers of rows are required to be hidden.

"I found this one the best way, as it was easy, you weren't relying on touch screen and you had to click the column closest to the name so it was good for accuracy."

We also found that using the *press to compare* technique was preferred for comparing smaller data sets such as two rows (*Likert M*: 3.94, *SD*: 1.06). This builds on the premise that it is more efficient to select a small set of rows that are of interest, rather than hiding multiple irrelevant rows.

"I wanted this for the previous comparison task and it did not disappoint. It also helped cut down on the sheer amount of repetitive selection, since it makes more sense to select the 20% of objects I want rather than the 80% I don't."

A noteworthy outcome of studying the filtering techniques is that, unlike participants' initial perceptions of how to filter data (i.e. tapping the projected labels), both highly rated interaction techniques involved physical interaction with the data points. Furthermore, it is clear that a tradeoff is required between hiding small amounts of data versus a larger amount of data.

Organization

This task-set explores user preferences for organizing data sets and points in the physical space (see Figure 7). Although Heer and Shneiderman's [11] taxonomy describe *Organize* in terms of multiple views, we adapt this concept and look at organization within a single view. For instance, users might want to bring some data closer to them (e.g. from the last row to the first row). The data set used for the organization task was prevalence of HIV in 10 countries (rows) between 1920 and 2012 (columns). The following interaction techniques were explored:

- *Drag and Drop:* Analogous to drag-and-drop on touch devices, users touch-down on a row label and drag it to a new position. Participants were asked to compare HIV prevalence between two countries by organizing the rows and placing them next to each other.
- *Press to swap:* Users simultaneously select a target row by tapping on a column, and select the destination by tapping on a column in a different row. Similar to d*rag and drop*, participants were asked to compare two countries side-by-side.

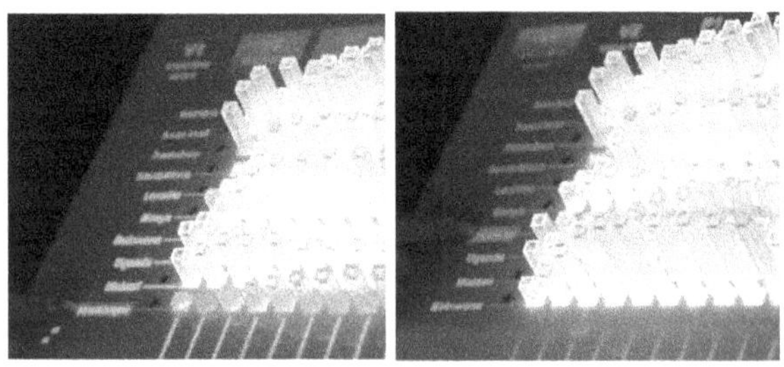

Figure 7 – The organize task, showing the *drag and drop* technique.

In addition, we use the organisation task techniques to explore how users would like to see physical data transitions (i.e. visual feedback of the data points 'moving' to another location). Participants were asked to compare different rows (to the ones above) for techniques involving the transitions. Both interaction techniques had the following transition options:

- *Instant transition:* New data simply replaces old data (bars immediately adjust to correct new heights).
- *Hide-all and transition:* All irrelevant rows hide at the beginning of a swap action; the selected and target rows swap values, then the other rows re-emerge.

Using the nominal dataset, participants were asked to compare various combinations of data by moving the comparison rows/points beside each other.

Results and Feedback

All 17 participants initially stated that they would prefer to drag a row by touch the projected labels to reorder them. The study confirmed their initial perceptions and it was clear that dragging the label was the preferred method (*Likert M* 3.88, *SD*: 1.22).

"This interaction has a sequential logic and this seems to facilitate this task ... It is also easier to look at the labels as opposed to interacting with the columns directly in rearranging data."

The *hide-all and transition* technique scored low in both organize techniques (*drag and drop,* and *press to swap*). Participants preferred to have faster feedback rather than wait for a more drawn-out transition.

"I don't think the added animation was very helpful - prefer instant reaction. Also the travel of the row isn't the important bit."

One participant also stated that in a professional setting, accidentally selecting the incorrect rows, and having to wait for the transition to finish, would be embarrassing.

Navigation

Navigation typically involves exploring data sets in more detail (e.g. geographic maps that present an overview, but also further details on data subsets). One of the limitations of developing shape-changing display is the high cost to achieve higher resolution due to the one-actuator-per-column architecture (e.g. as faced by inFORM [6]). Therefore, these displays require mechanisms to allow users to navigate large data sets. The rainfall data set was used for this particular reason during our study, showing 10 different regions within the UK (rows) between 1920 and 2012 (columns). This allowed participants to look at trends over time (i.e. 92 years) by navigating through the data. The following techniques were investigated (see Figure 8):

- *Scrollbars:* scrollbars, identical to those found on the desktop were projected on the x-axis. Tapping within the scrollbar trough moved the dataset to that location. All of the data points were also shown (to show continuity) until the selected position was reached. Participants were asked to identify any patterns and relationships that can be observed between the entire dataset (i.e. 1920 to 2012) between regions in the North and South of the UK.
- *Directional Arrows:* Projected left and right arrows were shown on the EMERGE surface. Analogous to the desktop environment, tapping on the arrows moved the all data set rows by a single column. Participants were asked to compare rainfall between two regions during a specific year.
- *Directional Press:* All the data points on the right-half and left-half act as navigation mechanisms; when pressed, the data set shifts on column to the left or right. Participants were asked to compare rainfall between two regions during a specific year.
- *Paging:* Similar to *Direction Press,* all the data points on the right-half and left-half act as navigation mechanisms for shifting the data set by one page, that is, 10 columns to the left or right. The term paging is used because of the 10×10 grid of the EMERGE display. Participants were asked to compare rainfall between two regions during a specific year.

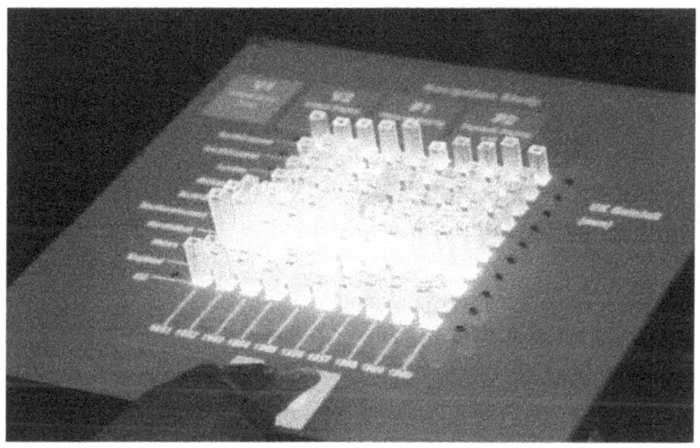

Figure 8 - The navigation task, showing the *scroll* technique.

Results and Feedback

The initial user perceptions stage showed that 15/17 participants prefer to navigate a large data set by using a scrollbar display combined with a swipe gesture. Intriguingly, two participants stated that they would prefer to physical shift the columns to the left or right to view the next or previous data points. The study showed that the *scrollbar* technique was preferred (Likert *M*: 4, *SD*: 1).

"It was very simple and you could scroll a lot quicker if you had to jump say, 40 years. It took a little while for the [scrollbar] to catch up with where you wanted it to be, but I found this interesting as you got to see the bar chart changing over time."

Furthermore, by showing the actual values whilst the data is scrolling was useful for allowing participants to look at trends over time.

"The [transition] that followed the projected scrollbar was most useful as it also showed progress towards the intended date. The tangible interface indicated certain patterns

between the years which were interesting to observe (such as seasonality)."

Although the ratings were lower for the single-column navigation tasks, participants stated that this would be more useful for more fine-grained control of the data. It is therefore necessary to support continuous data navigation, as well as to allow more fine-grained control.

"Simpler for fine tuned detail. A combination of this and scroll bar would simulate the standard web scroll bar, this would cut down the learning curve."

DISCUSSION

The user study demonstrated a number of insights from user feedback and observed behaviours that indicate how bar charts can be effectively combined with shape-changing technology. We discuss the following themes: gestural vs. physical interaction, combining interaction modalities, effect of preconceptions, user reactions, technological challenges, limitations, and future directions.

Gestural vs. Physical Interaction

The interaction techniques explored during the user study comprised of directly touching the data points (or the plastic rods) as well as using gestures such as swiping to manipulate data. There was no clear difference in user preferences (i.e., the Likert scale ratings) for directly touching the rods and using gestures; each provides strengths and weaknesses based on the context of use. For instance, it was far more effective for participants to directly press and annotate a data point rather than to use gestures. In contrast, larger gestures such as row organization benefits from dragging their corresponding projected labels. The positive feedback received from physical interactions removes uncertainty about whether users might feel that they are interfering with the data points. This provides designers with more freedom to integrate different types of interactions.

Combining Interaction Modalities

We developed a number of insights on combining interactions for physically dynamic bar charts. For instance, we found that switching between overview and more fine-grained interaction modalities is highly useful. The *scrolling* technique in the navigation task revealed that all participants noticed a clear distinction over time between the northern and southern regions of the UK (i.e. more rainfall in the north). However, it is important to be able to switch to a mode that allows scrolling through one data point at a time (e.g. if users want to compare specific years). One participant commented that they would like to expand a data point showing rainfall by year and region into the months that make up the yearly value. Similarly, the filtering task necessitated the ability to combine the *press to compare* technique with *press shortcut* to hide a row. One participant's comment particularly highlights this:

"I did like this and felt it was easier to be sure I had selected the right rows for what I wanted to see. I would like this method alongside being able to keep only the rows I wanted, depending on how many I wanted to keep/hide."

Effect of Preconceptions

Each participant was initially asked, before being shown any techniques for the tasks, how they would achieve, for instance, selecting an individual data point or organizing rows by moving the furthest one closer to them. All responses consisted of using swipe, drag or tap on a projected label, similar to the interactions on touch-screen devices. The prevalence of touch-screen devices have provided users with preconceptions of how to carry out interactions such as scrolling, selecting, etc. As a result, these interactions have become familiar and intuitive. An interesting outcome from the study concerns the filtering task, where participants initially suggested that actions such as using swipe or tapping on a row label would be preferred. However, after exploring direct touch interactions with the data points, the opinions shifted to the more physical side. Whilst designers should capitalize on the familiarity of touch-screen gestures and incorporate them into shape-changing displays, it is also important to realize that physical interactions can expand the interaction space in innovative ways.

User Reactions

As shape-changing displays are uncommon, we were interested in how users physically approach and react to this type of technology. During the study, we observed that nearly all participants were surprised or startled by the actuation (e.g. by moving back, moving their hands out the way), as well as from the noise generated by the motors. Three out of seventeen participants also moved around the system to carry out their interactions. For instance, one participant moved to the side of the display to select press down on two rows to compare them (filtering task). Another participant bent down to align themselves and select the highest value in a row (annotation task). We believe that movement around the system was likely reduced by the fixed text alignment of the labels, and therefore, to encourage users to move around the display, text orientation could be adjusted based on user position.

Limitations and Technological Challenges

For this first study, we chose to focus on fundamental low-level tasks and a limited number of interaction techniques. Further studies will be necessary to explore the possible interaction space for physically dynamic graphs (including different variations of actions and gestures, and combinations of tasks and techniques). The EMERGE system uses a grid of 10×10 data points and therefore only a limited amount of data could be presented to participants. Thus, the scalability of the interactions studied requires further investigation. A higher resolution might, for instance, afford different types of interactions (pagination might suffice rather than scrolling during navigation). Finally, we excluded vertical axis data (essentially the y-axis) and it is therefore difficult to anticipate how this might change user interactions and behaviours.

There were numerous technological challenges during the development of the EMERGE system, such as choosing an appropriate actuation speed, selecting an appropriate spacing for the plastic rods, as well as determining the size of the entire setup. The user study showed, for instance, that almost all participants were sometimes hesitant to interact with the system either due to the speed of actuation (e.g., when hiding data points, the rods actuated downwards quite rapidly) or due to the noise generated by the actuators. The spacing between rows and columns was also fixed and predetermined by technological constraints. The large actuator size also forced us to increase the height of the system to reduce angles and enable smooth actuation.

Generalizability and Future Directions

The findings from the user study have identified baseline interactions that users prefer, and for which data manipulation tasks they prefer them. For instance, smaller interactions such as annotation afforded physical interaction, whereas larger motions such as row organization afforded touch-screen style swipe interactions. We believe that understanding such interactions with fundamental data manipulation tasks can aid researchers to incorporate them in the development of similar systems.

There are numerous avenues for further work with physical interactions, data analysis tasks, and system functionality. We intend to carry out deeper explorations into the physical aspect, such as data manipulation with external objects, multi-finger input, and pressing over time. More complex task explorations are required (e.g. from Heer and Shneiderman's taxonomy [11]) such as undo/redo, different types of filtering (e.g. thresholding), and combining interactions (annotation with filtering). Furthermore, we require controlled studies with performance metrics (e.g. task completion times, accuracy) to measure how well users can analyze data by using physical visualizations.

CONCLUSION

The key objective of this paper was to uncover means through which physically dynamic bar charts can support data analysis-based interaction techniques. The user study provides initial insight into physical data exploration by testing 14 interaction techniques that formed part of four task-sets: annotation, filtering, organization, and navigation. We report on several ways of combining interaction modalities, utilizing the physicality of the system, incorporating familiar interactions (i.e. from touch-screens), and discussing the challenges that arise from this type of technology. By exploring these fundamental interactions we hope to lay the groundwork for future investigation into physically dynamic data visualizations.

ACKNOWLEDGEMENTS

This work forms part of GHOST, a project funded by the European Commission's 7th Framework Programme, FET-Open scheme (grant #309191). Thank-you to Matthias Schittenhelm, Leanne Bates, Pauline Anthonysamy, and John Vidler for their help at various stages in this project.

REFERENCES

1. Alexander, J., Lucero, A., & Subramanian, S. (2012). Tilt displays: designing display surfaces with multi-axis tilting and actuation. In *Proc. MobileHCI,* pp. 161-170.
2. Brehmer, M. and Munzner, T. (2013). A multi-level typology of abstract visualization tasks. *Visualization and Computer Graphics, IEEE Transactions on 19*, 12, pp. 2376–2385.
3. Brown, C. and Hurst, A. (2012). VizTouch: automatically generated tactile visualizations of coordinate spaces. In *Proc. TEI*, pp. 131–138.
4. Card, S.K., Mackinlay, J.D., and Shneiderman, B. (1999). *Readings in Information Visualization: Using Vision to Think.* Morgan Kaufmann Pub.
5. Coelho, M., Ishii, H., & Maes, P. (2008). Surflex: a programmable surface for the design of tangible interfaces. In *CHI'08 EA,* pp. 3429-3434.
6. Follmer, S., Leithinger, D., and Ishii, A.O.A.H.H. (2013). inFORM: dynamic physical affordances and constraints through shape and object actuation. In *Proc. UIST*, pp. 417–426.
7. Fritz, J. P., & Barner, K. E. (1999). Design of a haptic data visualization system for people with visual impairments. *IEEE Transactions on Rehabilitation Engineering*, 7(3), pp. 372–384.
8. Greenberg, S. and Buxton, B. Usability evaluation considered harmful (some of the time). (2008). In *Proc. CHI*, pp. 111–120.
9. Hardy, J., Ellis, C., Alexander, J., & Davies, N. (2013). Ubi Displays: A Toolkit for the Rapid Creation of Interactive Projected Displays. In *The International Symposium on Pervasive Displays.*
10. Harrison, C., & Hudson, S. E. (2009). Providing dynamically changeable physical buttons on a visual display. In *Proc. CHI,* pp. 299-308.
11. Heer, J. and Shneiderman, B. (2012). Interactive Dynamics for Visual Analysis. *Commun. ACM 55*, 4, pp. 45–54.
12. Hornbæk, K. Some Whys and Hows of Experiments in Human–Computer Interaction. (2013). *Foundations and Trends in HCI 5*, 4, pp. 299–373.
13. Huron, S., Jansen, Y., and Carpendale, S. Constructing Visual Representations: Investigating the Use of Tangible Tokens. (2014). *IEEE Transactions on Visualization and Computer Graphics 20*, 12, 1.
14. Iwata, H., Yano, H., Nakaizumi, F., and Kawamura, R. (2001). Project FEELEX: adding haptic surface to graphics. In *Proc. SIGGRAPH*, pp. 469–476.
15. Jansen, Y., Dragicevic, P., and Fekete, J.-D. (2013). Evaluating the Efficiency of Physical Visualizations. In *Proc. CHI*. pp. 2593-2602.

16. Jansen, Y. and Dragicevic, P. (2013). An Interaction Model for Visualizations Beyond The Desktop. *Visualization and Computer Graphics, IEEE Transactions on 19*, 12, pp. 2396–2405.

17. Jansen, Y., Dragicevic, P., Isenberg, P., Alexander, J., Karnik, A., Kildal, J., Subramanian, S., Hornbæk, K. (2015). Opportunities and Challenges for Data Physicalization. In *Proc. CHI.*

18. Kyung, K.-U., Lim, J.M., Lim, Y.-A., et al. (2011). TAXEL: Initial progress toward self-morphing visio-haptic interface. *IEEE World Haptics*, pp. 37–42.

19. Lederman, S.J. and Campbell, J.I. (1982). Tangible graphs for the blind. *Human Factors: The Journal of the Human Factors and Ergonomics Society 24*, 1, pp. 85–100.

20. Lee, B., Isenberg, P., Riche, N.H., and Carpendale, S. (2012). Beyond Mouse and Keyboard: Expanding Design Considerations for Information Visualization Interactions. *Visualization and Computer Graphics, IEEE Transactions on 18*, 12, pp. 2689–2698.

21. Leithinger, D., Follmer, S., Olwal, A., et al. (2013). Sublimate: state-changing virtual and physical rendering to augment interaction with shape displays. In *Proc. CHI*, pp. 1441–1450.

22. Leithinger, D. and Ishii, H. (2010). Relief: a scalable actuated shape display. In *Proc. TEI* pp. 221–222.

23. Leithinger, D., Lakatos, D., DeVincenzi, A., Blackshaw, M., and Ishii, H. (2011). Direct and gestural interaction with relief: a 2.5 D shape display. *Proceedings of the 24th annual ACM symposium on User interface software and technology*, pp. 541–548.

24. Manshad, M.S., Pontelli, E., and Manshad, S.J. (2012). Trackable interactive multimodal manipulatives: towards a tangible user environment for the blind. In *Proceedings of the 13th international conference on Computers Helping People with Special Needs - Volume Part II*, Springer-Verlag, pp. 664–671.

25. Moere, A.V. (2008). Beyond the tyranny of the pixel: Exploring the physicality of information visualization. *Information Visualisation,* pp. 469–474.

26. Paneels, S., & Roberts, J. C. (2010). Review of Designs for Haptic Data Visualization. *IEEE Transactions on Haptics*, 3(2), pp. 119–137.

27. Perkins, C. (2002). Cartography: progress in tactile mapping. *Progress in Human Geography 26*, 4, pp. 521–530.

28. Poupyrev, I., Nashida, T., Maruyama, S., Rekimoto, J., and Yamaji, Y. (2004). Lumen: interactive visual and shape display for calm computing. *ACM SIGGRAPH Emerging technologies*, 17.

29. Rasmussen, M.K., Pedersen, E.W., Petersen, M.G., and Hornbæk, K. Shape-changing interfaces: a review of the design space and open research questions. In *Proc. CHI,* pp. 735–744.

30. Khot, R. A., Hjorth, L., and Mueller, F. (2014). Understanding Physical Activity through 3D Printed Material Artifacts. In *Proc. CHI.*

31. Roudaut, A., Karnik, A., Löchtefeld, M., and Subramanian, S. (2013). Morphees: Toward High "Shape Resolution" in Self-Actuated Flexible Mobile Devices. In *Proc. CHI.*

32. Shah, P. and Hoeffner, J. (2002). Review of graph comprehension research: Implications for instruction. *Educational Psychology Review 14*, 1, 47–69.

33. Shneiderman, B. (1996). The eyes have it: A task by data type taxonomy for information visualizations. In *Proc. IEEE Symposium on Visual Languages,* pp. 336–343.

34. Spence, I. (1990). Visual psychophysics of simple graphical elements. *Journal of Experimental Psychology: Human Perception and Performance 16*, 4, pp. 683–692.

35. Stusak, S., & Aslan, A. (2014). Beyond physical bar charts: an exploration of designing physical visualizations. In *CHI'14 EA,* pp. 1381-1386.

36. Stusak, S., Tabard, A., Sauka, F., Khot, R., & Butz, A. (2014). Activity Sculptures: Exploring the Impact of Physical Visualizations on Running Activity. *IEEE Transactions on Visualization and Computer Graphics*, 99, 1.

37. Tversky, B., Morrison, J.B., and Betrancourt, M. (2002). Animation: can it facilitate? *International Journal of Human-Computer Studies 57*, 4, pp. 247–262.

38. Tversky, B. (2001). Spatial schemas in depictions. *Spatial schemas and abstract thought*, pp. 79–111.

39. Wall, S.A. and Brewster, S. (2006). Sensory substitution using tactile pin arrays: Human factors, technology and applications. *Signal Processing 86*, 12, pp. 3674–3695.

40. Wobbrock, J. O., Morris, M. R., & Wilson, A. D. (2009). User-defined gestures for surface computing. In *Proc. CHI,* pp. 1083-1092).

41. Zacks, J., Levy, E., Tversky, B., and Schiano, D.J. (1998). Reading bar graphs: Effects of extraneous depth cues and graphical context. *Journal of Experimental Psychology Applied 4*, pp. 119–138.

42. Zhao, J. and Moere, A.V. (2008). Embodiment in data sculpture: a model of the physical visualization of information. *Proc. DIMEA*, pp. 343–350.

Evaluating the Memorability of Physical Visualizations

Simon Stusak, Jeannette Schwarz, Andreas Butz
Human-Computer Interaction Group, University of Munich (LMU)
Amalienstr. 17, 80333 Munich, Germany
simon.stusak@ifi.lmu.de, jeannette.schwarz@gmail.com, butz@ifi.lmu.de

ABSTRACT
Physical Visualizations are currently mostly used in casual contexts, e.g., as artistic data sculptures. However, their measurable benefits for traditional information visualization are largely unexplored. As a step in this direction, we compared the memorability of physical visualizations to that of digital visualizations. We conducted a user study with 40 participants in which we measured the recall of three types of information immediately after exploration and with a delay of two weeks. The results show that the physical visualization led to significantly less information decay within this time span. Our results build on known effects from cognitive psychology and provide a first indicator for measurable benefits of physical visualizations regarding memorability.

Author Keywords
physical visualization; evaluation; memorability.

ACM Classification Keywords
H.5.2 User Interfaces: Evaluation/Methodology

PHYSICAL VISUALIZATIONS
Information Visualization (InfoVis) helps users to explore and understand large amounts of abstract data. While digital visualizations are well-explored, *physical visualizations* which map data to physical form instead of pixels recently started to attract attention [6, 7, 11]. Reasons for this are the progress in digital fabrication technologies, such as laser cutters and 3D printers [12], as well as recent developments in the field of shape changing displays (e.g., [4]). The fact that such technologies are becoming increasingly commonplace, prompts further research on how digital and physical visualizations can complement one another and to explore areas in which physical visualizations can have benefits.

Jansen et al. [7] compared physical 3D bar charts to their on-screen counterparts and found that physical outperformed on-screen 3D bar charts, but 2D visualizations performed best for all of the tested low-level information retrieval tasks. In their outlook they suggest, that future studies should investigate other factors than pure performance.

CHI 2015, April 18 - 23 2015, Seoul, Republic of Korea
Copyright is held by the owner/author(s). Publication rights licensed to ACM.
ACM 978-1-4503-3145-6/15/04 $15.00
http://dx.doi.org/10.1145/2702123.2702248

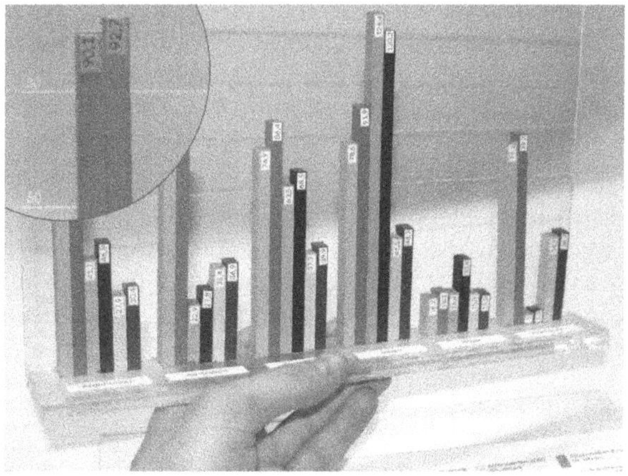

Figure 1. Static physical bar chart which was used in our study and a close-up on the bars' labeling and the background panel.

Visualizations can actually extend human memory [13], and memorability therefore is a frequently discussed topic in InfoVis (e.g., [1, 5]). There are indications that visual and haptic perception are processed dependently [9] and that vision and haptics share common abstract representations of the shape and structure of objects [3]. Furthermore it has been shown that spatial layouts, which were learned through haptic and visual exploration, are stored within a common reference frame: Haptic experiences were able to influence memories that were acquired visually [8]. Previous studies also revealed that physical objects were recalled more frequently than pictures, and pictures more often than words [2].

All of this suggests that a physical representation, for example of a bar chart, could generate a more detailed representation in the subjects' memory and hence be more memorable than its digital on-screen representation.

In a study with 40 participants we compared a physical bar chart (see figure 1) to the same chart displayed on a tablet screen. Memory performance was measured by a questionnaire about the visualizations' content, once immediately after exploration, and again after two weeks. The results show that the modality of the visualization significantly influenced the loss of information during two weeks (see figure 3): Subjects using the physical visualization forgot less information in the category of *extreme values* than those who used the digital visualization.

PRE-STUDY
To discover first tendencies and test the study procedure, we conducted a pre-study with a between-groups design and 3 independent variables: modality (physical, digital), memorization (implicit, explicit) and time (immediately, delayed).

Data Sets

As an abstract data set we chose country indicator data from the Human Development Report (HDR)[1] on the topics of *social integration* and *population trends*. Two data sets were extracted, both consisting of the values for six countries and six different subtopics per country (2x36 values in total). We expected these topics to be interesting to a wide audience, but at the same time not too well known publicly, in order to minimize the effect of previous knowledge. The complexity of the data set was kept on the one hand at a level where the recall of the entire content was rather difficult, but on the other hand not too complicated to avoid a situation in which reading difficulties would distract from the actual content.

Visualization Type

As a visualization, we chose a static vertical bar chart, which is well-known and easily understood by people without experience in InfoVis. It should therefore not influence the experiment's results by either a novelty effect or difficulty in interpretation. A static visualization was chosen in order to investigate just the effects of the modality of the visualization, rather than specific interactions with it.

Visualization Modalities

The final design of the digital bar chart can be seen in figure 2. It was shown on an Apple iPad (2048*1536 px., 264 ppi) in full screen display. We chose a tablet instead of a classic desktop setting in order to create conditions similar to the physical visualization. Both had a similar size and weight and could be held conveniently in one or both hands.

The physical visualization prototype (see figure 1) was built from 8mm acrylic glass using a laser cutter and colored with acrylic paint. The layout and colors of the physical visualization matched those of the digital visualization. Numeric values on the bars, labels for countries as well as the legend were printed on self-adhesive foil. The bars had engraved lines as a reading aid. In addition, a 28*17 cm acrylic panel with engraved numeric values and lines served as a background.

Procedure and Participants

The study took place in an isolated and quiet room. After a questionnaire about demographic data and previous experience with visualizations, subjects started with the *reading phase*: In a counterbalanced order one of the visualizations was presented to each participant. The experimenter encouraged them to read the visualization and think aloud about all content-related issues. Subjects in the *explicit memorization* group were told to memorize the facts because they would be asked about them again later. For the *implicit memorization* group, this ahead warning was not given.

The experimenter checked a list of facts (e.g., all country names and categories) every participant was supposed to speak out loud during the *reading phase*. If items were missing the experimenter asked predefined questions in order to complete the participant's knowledge (e.g., which countries

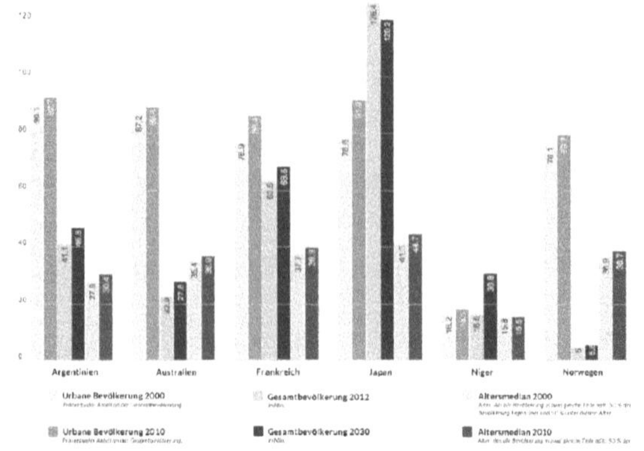

Figure 2. The static digital bar chart which was used in our study.

are shown in the visualization?). After the reading phase, subjects filled out a questionnaire collecting qualitative data and another one for subjective memory assessment.

The *recall phase* started directly after the questionnaires. Subjects were asked to freely recall everything they remembered about the visualizations. When they did not know any more facts, the experimenter asked predefined questions to support the recall process. The *recall phase* was videotaped, transcribed and a recall score was calculated for each participant: One point was given for each correct fact, 0.5 points if facts were only little explicit or too vague.

Out of the 24 participants, eight were female. The average age was 25 (range: 23-27). Participants received a 10 Euro voucher for an online shop.

Results

The pre-study revealed first tendencies and gave us confidence in the general study design. In total, scores for subjects that used the physical visualizations were higher (M=29.58, SE=8.54) than for the digital visualizations (M=22.25, SE=6.42). The results between physical (M=22.58, SE=9.22) and digital (M=19.5, SE=7.96) converged if only the scores of the delayed *recall phase* were taken into account. *Explicit memorization* (M=25.95, SE=3.22) and *implicit memorization* (M=25.875, SE=2.49) led to similar scores overall, independent of the visualization modality. This was contrary to our assumption that subjects would recall more facts when explicitly told to memorize them. We also observed that users did not frequently interact haptically with the physical visualization. While the visualization was often held in both hands, almost nobody traced the bars with their fingers. Users often tilted the visualization in order to have a better perspective and use the guiding lines on the background panel.

MAIN STUDY

The main study was based on the procedure of the pre-study, but parts were modified according to the findings from the pre-study. We kept the between-groups design, but reduced the number of independent variables to one: visualization modality (physical, digital). We only tested *implicit memorization* and measured recall both immediately and after two weeks for all participants. A *memorability score* was defined

[1] http://hdr.undp.org/

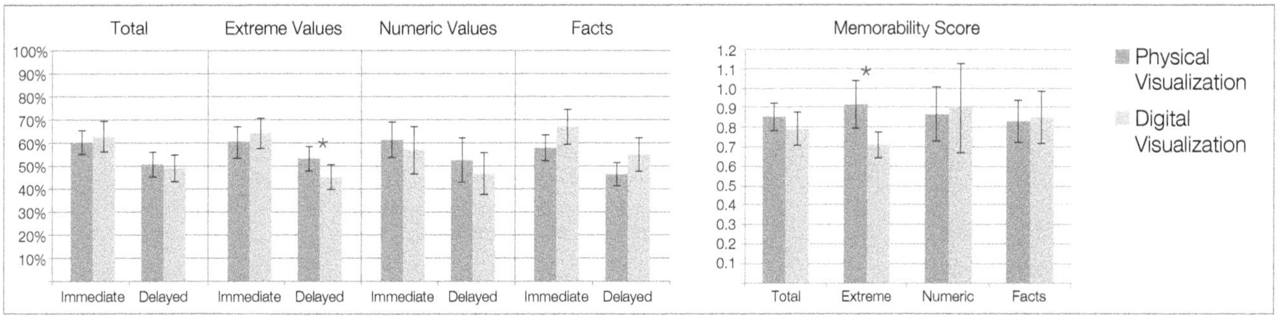

Figure 3. Results of main study: percentage of correct answers for *immediate* and *delayed* recall as well as the calculated *memorability score (delayed recall/immediate recall)*, with 95% CIs.

as the ratio between the scores for delayed and immediate recall: If, for example, a subject recalled 60% immediately and 45% after 2 weeks, this resulted in a memorability score of 0.75. Using the absolute difference instead of the ratio actually leads to the same overall results.

Data Sets and Visualizations

We used the same data set as in the pre-study. The layout of both the physical and digital visualizations were modified for better readability according to participants' suggestions in the pre-study. We also made changes to the design of the physical visualization to encourage haptic exploration by splitting it into two parts: legend and bars (see figure 1). The latter consisted of a small base which contained all the bars as well as the labels and background panel with the scales. The panel, however, could easily be removed and held in one hand while the other hand could explore the bars.

Procedure and Participants

The questionnaires at the beginning and the end of the study were shortened to reduce study duration. Unclear questions were rephrased. The most important changes were made in the *recall phase*: Instead of asking subjects to recall all remembered facts verbally and transcribing the results, an online quiz assessed each subject's performance in order to gain a more comparable memory score and to exclude possible influences by the experimenter (e.g., differently phrased questions). The quiz consisted of three question categories:

- *extreme values*: Questions which country had the maximum/minimum value were asked for each category, in total 24 questions (e.g., "Which country has the most trust in its government?"). Answers were chosen from a list of the six used countries, as well as "I don't know".
- *numeric values*: Questions about specific numeric values, in total 12 questions (e.g., "In Brazil, only 15% have trust in their government."). Answers were chosen from a drop-down list including "true", "false" and "I don't know".
- *facts*: General questions about the underlying data, in total 14 questions (e.g., "Germany has more trust in its government than Brazil."). Answers were chosen from a drop-down list including "true", "false" and "I don't know".

Participants did not receive any feedback on their performance, nor were they told the correct answers to the quiz. They were informed that they would have to fill out another questionnaire in two weeks, but not that it would be the same. However, some participants suspected there would be another memory test. For the delayed *recall phase* participants received a link to the same quiz via e-mail two weeks later and completed it at home.

For the recall score, we counted all correct answers. We decided against subtracting one point for each wrong answer as only few subjects chose the "neutral" option "I don't know".

Out of the 40 participants, 17 were female. The average age was 23.5 years (range: 18-32). All participants were students of a technical subject. Participants received a 15 Euro voucher for an online shop.

Results

The results of the *immediate* and *delayed* recall score and their ratio, the *memorability* score are depicted in figure 3. The *immediate recall* score for the *digital* modality (M=62.80, SE=3.19) was higher than for the *physical* (M=59.91, SE=2.54) modality. The reverse was true for the *delayed recall*, where the physical visualizations (M=50.68, SE=2.68) performed better than the digital ones (M=48.96, SE=2.85). A breakdown into the three question categories revealed, that the *delayed recall* score for the *physical* modality (M=53.13, SE=2.51) in the category of *extreme values* was higher than for the *digital* (M=45.21, SE=2.55). An independent t-test identified a significant difference, $t(38)=2.21$, $p=0.033$, $r=0.34$. None of the other categories showed any significant differences.

As indicated by the *memorability* score, subjects who used the physical visualizations remembered more information (M=0.85, SE=0.03) than those using the digital visualizations (M=0.79, SE=0.04). Again we found a significant difference for the question category of *extreme values* between *physical* (M=0.91, SE=0.06) and *digital* (M=0.71, SE=0.03), $t(38)=3.092$, $p=0.004$, $r=0.45$.

Participants spent slightly more time in the *reading phase* with the physical visualization (M=19.27m, SE=1.50) than with the digital one (M=17.62m, SE=1.00). The mean score for the subjective memory was higher in the *physical* group (*digital*: M=64.15, SE=2.52 / *physical*: M=66.85, SE=1.92).

After the reading phase, subjects were asked to rate aspects such as memorability or readability on 5-point Likert scales (from 1=*very bad* to 5=*very good*). Those who used the physical visualization found the information significantly more *memorable* (*MODE*=4, M=3.85, SE=0.17) than those who used the digital visualization (*MODE*=3, M=3.10, SE=0.14), $t(37.165)=-3.41$, $p=0.002$, $r=0.489$. Participants furthermore had significantly more *fun* reading the physical visualization (*MODE*=4, M=3.95, SE=0.17) than the users in the digital group (*MODE*=3, M=3.25, SE=0.16), $t(37.873)=-2.99$, $p=0.005$, $r=0.438$.

CONCLUSION AND FUTURE WORK

We compared the memorability of a physical and a digital 2D bar chart. In a user study with 40 participants and a between-groups design, we tested recall immediately after exploration and again after two weeks. While the number of correct answers did not differ significantly between groups in each single comparison, participants who used the physical visualization forgot significantly less information within the two weeks. Particularly facts about maximum and minimum values could be remembered better, when they were perceived from a physical visualization.

The extreme values in the physical visualizations might have been derived from their visually recalled and imagined shape [8]. The fact that spatial layouts can be memorized better in a physical setting is another plausible explanation: Participants might have remembered where high and low bars were situated, and which country and category was at that position. This would explain why better scores for the physical visualization were achieved in the category of extreme values. Scott [10] argues that pictures are better remembered than object names because they are more distinctive. For physical visualizations this aspect could particularly apply for the extreme values because of the vivid physical height of the bars. As we used a rather simple static bar graph built from acrylic glass, which is for example commonly used in museum installations, we believe that a novelty effect hardly could impact the results.

The slightly longer reading times for the physical visualization cannot be excluded as an explanation for the reduced decay. However, in our opinion it seems unlikely that this causes such a large effect only for the memorability of extreme values and only for delayed recall. As another limiting factor, the study procedure involved optional predefined questions and the verbal expression of all facts the subject saw, in order to ensure that each participant had the same knowledge before the interrogation. This process of verbal expression might have helped some users more to remember the facts than the actual visualization itself. However, this potentially confounding factor should be independent of the modality. A clearer approach for future studies could be to give the subjects certain tasks that induce the same knowledge implicitly.

Furthermore most participants only held the physical visualization in their hands, but did hardly explore it haptically. The use of a more handy physical visualization or tasks that more clearly require haptic interaction could change this in further studies, and we expect that this will even increase the observed effect.

Our results suggest that physicality alone was able to increase the memorability of visualizations for a particular kind of information. Although there are many criteria other than memorability according to which the value of physical visualizations need to be judged (e.g. fabrication costs, interactive exploration, etc.), this is a promising preliminary result for both casual and traditional InfoVis. Physical visualizations could in addition enter areas such as advertisement, journalism or education in general, where it is desirable to present memorable information.

REFERENCES

1. Bateman, S., Mandryk, R. L., Gutwin, C., Genest, A., McDine, D., and Brooks, C. Useful junk?: the effects of visual embellishment on comprehension and memorability of charts. In *Proc. CHI '10*, ACM (2010), 2573–2582.
2. Bevan, W., and Steger, J. A. Free recall and abstractness of stimuli. *Science 172*, 3983 (1971), 597–599.
3. Easton, R. D., Greene, A. J., and Srinivas, K. Transfer between vision and haptics: Memory for 2-d patterns and 3-d objects. *Psychonomic Bulletin & Review 4*, 3 (1997), 403–410.
4. Follmer, S., Leithinger, D., Olwal, A., Hogge, A., and Ishii, H. inFORM: dynamic physical affordances and constraints through shape and object actuation. In *UIST '13*, ACM (2013), 417–426.
5. Healey, C. G., and Enns, J. T. Attention and visual memory in visualization and computer graphics. In *Proc. VIS '12*, vol. 18, IEEE (2012), 1170–1188.
6. Jansen, Y., and Dragicevic, P. An interaction model for visualizations beyond the desktop. In *Proc. VIS '13*, vol. 19, IEEE (2013), 2396–2405.
7. Jansen, Y., Dragicevic, P., and Fekete, J.-D. Evaluating the efficiency of physical visualizations. In *Proc. CHI '13*, ACM (2013), 2593–2602.
8. Kelly, J. W., Avraamides, M. N., and Giudice, N. A. Haptic experiences influence visually acquired memories: Reference frames during multimodal spatial learning. *Psychonomic bulletin & review 18*, 6 (2011), 1119–1125.
9. Kerzel, D. Visual short-term memory is influenced by haptic perception. *Journal of Exp. Psychol.: Learning, Memory, and Cognition 27*, 4 (2001), 1101–1109.
10. Scott, K. G. Clustering with perceptual and symbolic stimuli in free recall. *Journal of Verbal Learning and Verbal Behavior 6*, 6 (1967), 864–866.
11. Stusak, S., Tabard, A., Sauka, F., Ashok Khot, R., and Butz, A. Activity Sculptures: Exploring the Impact of Physical Visualizations on Running Activity. In *Proc. VIS '14*, vol. 20, IEEE (2014), 2201–2210.
12. Swaminathan, S., Shi, C., Jansen, Y., Dragicevic, P., Oehlberg, L., and Fekete, J.-D. Supporting the design and fabrication of physical visualizations. In *Proc. CHI '14*, ACM (2014), 3845–3854.
13. Ware, C. *Information visualization: perception for design*. Elsevier, 2013.

Personality as a Predictor of User Strategy: How Locus of Control Affects Search Strategies on Tree Visualizations

Alvitta Ottley
Tufts University
alvittao@cs.tufts.edu

Huahai Yang
IBM Research - Almaden
huahai.yang@gmail.com

Remco Chang
Tufts University
remco@cs.tufts.edu

ABSTRACT
Individual differences matter. While this has been the theme for many recent works in the Visualization and HCI communities, the mystery of how to develop personalized visualizations remains. This is largely because very little is known about *how* users actually use visualizations to solve problems and even less is known about how individual differences affect these problem-solving strategies. In this paper, we provide evidence that strategies are indeed influenced by individual differences. We demonstrate how the personality trait locus of control impacts strategies on hierarchical visualizations, and we introduce design recommendations for personalized visualizations.

Author Keywords
visualization; individual differences; strategy; personality; locus of control

ACM Classi cation Keywords
H.5.2 Information Interfaces and Presentation (e.g. HCI): User Interfaces

INTRODUCTION
There is no optimal visualization design. However, research advocating this notion is still in its infancy and has primarily focused on correlating individual differences to users' speed and accuracy [7, 10, 14]. While these results do highlight differences between groups of users, they give us little to no insight into *how* or *why* groups of users differ. Many open questions remain. For instance, *Do user groups adapt different problem-solving strategies? How can we choose between existing tools?* and *How can we design new tools to better facilitate users needs?*

We hypothesize that the observed differences in users' speed and accuracy are due to differences in their strategies. Furthermore, we believe that users' strategies can be uncovered by analyzing their interaction patterns and that these strategies are mediated by cognitive traits. By better understanding how individuals use visualizations, the community can begin to design tools that target users' specific cognitive needs.

CHI 2015, April 18–23, 2015, Seoul, Republic of Korea.

http://dx.doi.org/10.1145/2702123.2702590

In this paper, we focus on the personality trait locus of control (LOC) and how it impacts users' search strategies - their data exploration path as they perform searches using a given visualization. LOC describes the extent to which an individual believes that he is in control of external events. Individuals with internal LOC (*Internals*) tend to believe that events are influenced by their own actions, while individuals with external LOC (*Externals*) are more likely to blame outside factors such as luck. LOC has been shown to consistently correlate with performance when using visualizations [2, 7, 10, 14].

We present results from a user study where we captured participants' mouse interactions as they completed simple search tasks using two popular hierarchical visualizations (Figure 1). Overall, we found a strong correlation between LOC and strategies. An initial analysis found that Externals were almost twice as fast as Internals when using the indented tree visualization and conversely, Internals were almost twice as fast as Externals when using the dendrogram.

Further analysis demonstrated that the search patterns for the two groups of users (Internals and Externals) differed significantly, and even within groups, we found that search patterns differed across visualizations. Altogether, our results provide evidence that Externals are less efficient when a visualization affords open exploration than when a visualization provides a guided/restricted exploration.

We make the following contributions:

- We demonstrate how personality (LOC) affects users' speed and search strategies.
- We introduce recommendations for designing personalized visualizations based on the observed user strategies.

RELATED WORK
The impact of LOC has been explored for many decades beyond the Visualization and HCI communities, and research suggests that the differences between Internals and Externals are quite vast. Internals tend to have a strong sense of self-efficacy allowing them to take control even when faced with difficult problems. Conversely, Externals believe that they have no control over external events, making them far more likely to adapt to situations. However, because of this perceived lack of control, Externals are also more likely to give up when faced with difficulty.

Past research corroborates this. Internality has been shown to correlate with increased effectiveness at work [8], better academic performance [4] and greater ability to cope with stress [1]. LOC also affects learning style. Cassidy and Eachus [3] showed that Internals are more likely to practice deep learning, while Externals are more likely to practice surface learning. In the medical community, LOC has been shown to affect patients' recovery outcomes. Fisher and Johnstion [5] found that users with external LOC were more likely to become discouraged and give in to their disability.

LOC and Visualization

In the visualization community, Green and Fisher [7] and Ziemkiewicz et al. [14] showed a significant correlation between LOC and users' speed and accuracy when using visualizations. More recent work by Ottley et al. [10] demonstrated the solidity of the relationship between LOC and performance on visualization tasks. By using psychological priming to temporarily alter a user's LOC, they showed how changes in LOC can predictably influence a users' performance on visualization tasks.

More recent work by Brown et al. [2] captured click stream data as users performed a visual search task with an interactive visualization system, and successfully used machine learning techniques to classify users based on their LOC. By using mouse interactions as features, this work by Brown et al. [2] suggests that LOC also impacts users' strategies.

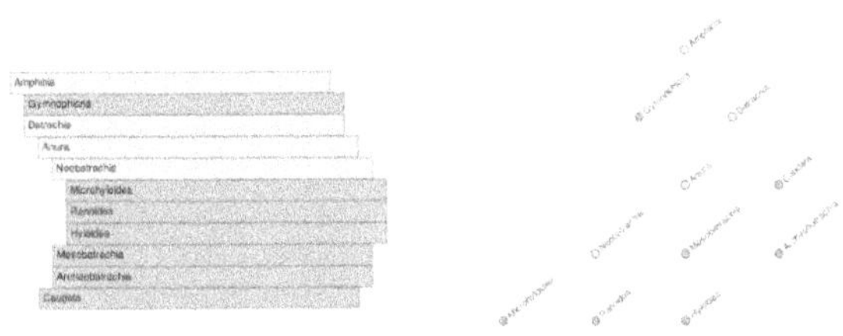

(a) Indented Tree (b) Dendrogram

Figure 1: The two visualizations used for our experiment.

EXPERIMENT DESIGN

Grounded by existing work, our experiment examines exactly how LOC impacts strategies. To test participants' LOC, we used the LOC inventory from the International Personality Inventory Pool [6]. We recruited 54 participants over Amazon's Mechanical Turk service (28 males). Participants' age ranged from 20 to 60 with an average age of 33 years. Only 16% of our participants self reported to be familiar with interactive visualizations and 66.7% self reported to have at least a college education.

Each participant was only able to complete the task once and was paid a base pay of $1 plus a bonus for every section successfully completed. A successful participant received a total of $5. This method of renumeration was chosen to dissuade participants from simply clicking through the task to be paid, thus increasing the reliability of our data.

Visualizations

Participants completed search tasks using two hierarchical visualizations: an indented tree (Figure 1a) and a dendrogram (Figure 1b). These particular visualizations were chosen because they are typical representations of hierarchical data [12], are commonly used in real world scenarios and have been extensively studied in the visualization community [7, 10, 14]. The indented tree uses indentation to depict hierarchy while the dendrogram uses a classic node-link structure.

With the exception of the layout, all other the design features were consistent across the two visualizations. Participants were able to explore the datasets by clicking parent nodes to expand their children. Clicking an already expanded node "hides" that subtree. If a user clicks a parent node to expand a "hidden" subtree, the subtree would be restored to its former state.

Datasets

We used two different datasets; both were subsets of a full taxonomic tree retrieved from National Center of Biotechnology Information's Genome database [9]. Each dataset was a phylogeny tree where the leaf nodes were actual species. By hovering over a leaf node, participants were able to access attributes of the species.

Tasks

For the main task, participants performed two simple search tasks (one with each visualization) where they were instructed to find a species under a specified classification with a specified attribute. For example:

> Under the classification "Pelophylax", find the species with the lowest length value.

Procedure

Prior to beginning the experiment, participants completed the LOC survey. The main task was divided into two sessions, one for each visualization. For each session, the participants were first given an opportunity to interact and familiarize themselves with the visualization (a third dataset was used for the trials). They were then instructed to take as long as they needed to interact with the visualization to find the target species.

Once they found the species, they clicked "Ready to Answer" and were then able to enter the species name in the text field provided. At this point, they were no longer able to interact with the visualization and we recorded their search times, mouse clicks, hovering and scroll events. After the main tasks, each participant completed usability and demographic surveys.

RESULTS

Each participant performed 2 search tasks (one with each visualization), resulting in a total of 108 trials. To filter the inherent "noise" in our Mechanical Turk data, our analysis only includes trials where the participant successfully found the target (91 trials).

The average time spent completing the task was 259 seconds (σ = 207.7) with an average of 75 clicks (σ = 11), and the overall accuracy rate was 68% (75.6% with the indented tree and 62% with the dendrogram). While participants were slightly more accurate with the indented tree, the observed difference was not statistically significant ($\chi^2(1, N= 91)= 1.92, p = .166$).

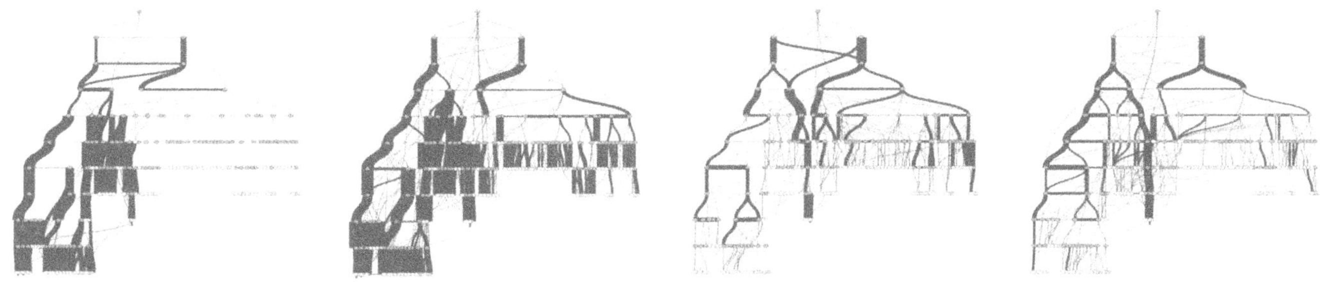

(a) Externals with indented tree (b) Internals with indented tree (c) Externals with dendrogram (d) Internals with dendrogram

Figure 2: The figures above show the aggregated exploration paths for users who were successful in locating the target. We grouped users based on a median split of their LOC scores and the visualization design used. For ease of comparison, we used a dendrogram to visualize the exploration paths of both visual designs used in our experiment. The weight of the links represent the percentage of users from that group who traversed that link during their search.

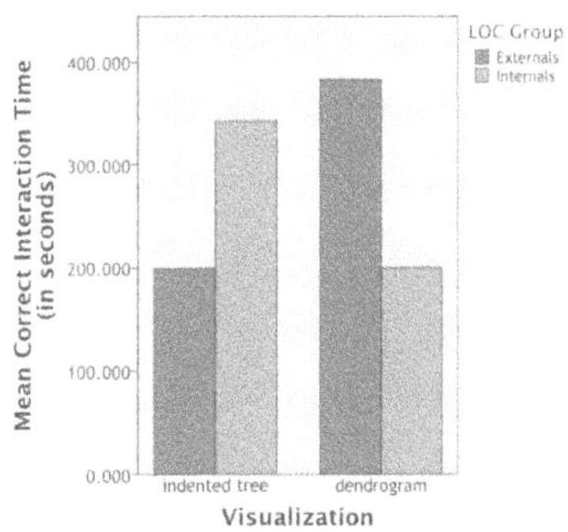

Figure 3: Mean correct response time for the two LOC groups across the two visualization designs.

Interaction Time

We divided participants into two groups based on the median split of their LOC scores. We then ran a 2x2 Univariate Analysis of Variance on the log interaction times to test for differences between the two LOC groups (Externals vs. Internals) across the two visualization designs (indented tree vs. dendrogram). Our overall model was significant ($F(3, N{=}91) = 3.189$ $p = .03$) and the interaction between LOC group and visualization was also statistically significant ($F(1, N{=}91) = 9.297$ $p = .003$).

Figure 3 summarizes our interaction time findings. Taking a closer look at interaction times, we found that Externals were almost two times faster with the indented tree visualization (Figure 1a) than the Internals. The Externals were also almost two times faster with the indented tree than they were using the dendrogram (Figure 1b). Interestingly, we observed the exact opposite effect with the Internals.

Strategies

During the experiment, a user explored a non-leaf node by clicking to expand or collapse its children and explored a leaf node by hovering to view its attributes. For our analysis we recorded each participant's mouse click and mouse hover events.

With this data, we were then able to reconstruct each user's exploration path as they searched for the target species. This analysis was performed manually using a visualization tool that we developed specifically for this study, and utilizes animation and juxtaposition to compare different exploration paths. Figure 2 summarizes our findings.

In general, we found that visualization design influences a user's strategies. When using the indented tree visualization, most participants explored the tree in a top-down fashion, resulting in a search strategy that resembles a depth-first search. Search patterns with the dendrogram were usually less structured and were often a combination of depth-first and breadth-first search.

Again, we separated participants into LOC groups. When using the indented tree visualization, Externals tended to be very strategic and explored the tree in top-down fashion, following the search strategy afforded by the visualization design (Figure 2a). While this strategy logically follows the indented tree's top-down design, we found that Internals were far less likely to adopt this strategy (Figure 2b). This resulted in a more exploratory but less effective search strategy.

Conversely, when using the dendrogram visualization, we found that Externals adopted more sporadic search techniques, resulting in much slower interaction times (Figure 2c). On the other hand, Internals performed a combined depth- and breadth- first search that proved quite effective with the dendrogram (Figure 2d).

DISCUSSION

While we seldom think about a user's personality traits when designing interfaces, the current work demonstrates why they must be considered. Between the tested designs, no design was suitable for all users. We found that Externals performed better with the indented tree but the Internals were more effective with the dendrogram. When asked which visualization they preferred using, 78% of Externals reported to prefer the indented tree over the dendrogram and 63% of Internals said they preferred the dendrogram.

These results are consistent with the LOC construct. Internals prefer control and tend to struggle when a visualization does not fit the their mental model of a problem [14]. While both visualizations were fully exploratory, the design of the indented tree best facilitates a top-down exploration and users who adapted this strategy were fastest (see figure 2a). This design property is subtle, still it proved to be a hindrance for the Internals. Conversely, since Externals in general do not believe that they can influence external events, they are more adaptable and were able to adopt the top-down search strategy afforded by the indented tree.

The scenario was reversed for the dendrogram visualization. The dendrogram proved to be more versatile and as a result, the Internals excelled with this visualization. They were able to freely search in a manner that best fit their mental model of the data. Unfortunately, this versatility was incompatible with the Externals. Their perceived lack of control coupled with the lack of guidance may have been too overwhelming.

Our design implication follows directly from this finding. When designing for Internals, designers should ensure that designs are flexible to users' mental models. Internals perform better when a visualization allows them to explore the data freely and doesn't impose a strategy. However, the needs of Externals are quite different. While they are in general more flexible and are likely to adapt to novel designs, our findings suggest that adapting to a flexible system may be overwhelming. Unlike Internals who take control of difficult situations, Externals are more likely to feel hopeless and may give up. Thus, it is essential to provide guidance (implicit or explicit) to Externals.

That said, LOC is a multidimensional construct and there are also many other cognitive traits and states that may impact performance on visualization systems [11]. Thus, it is important for us to better understand how these factors, individually and collectively, impact the usability of our designs. There is also evidence that certain traits can be detected from users' interactions [2, 13]. Future work can expand this existing research by exploring how systems can automatically detect and adapt to an individual's specific needs.

CONCLUSION

Altogether, we have demonstrated that individual differences, specifically the personality trait locus of control, do impact both interaction times and search strategies. We believe that our work is a significant step toward fully understanding *how* individual differences affect visualization use and how we can begin to design visualizations that better facilitate users' cognitive needs.

ACKNOWLEDGMENTS

This material is based upon work supported by the National Science Foundation under Grant No. IIS-1218170.

REFERENCES

1. Anderson, C. R. Locus of control, coping behaviors, and performance in a stress setting: A longitudinal study. *Journal of Applied Psychology 62* (1977), 446–451.
2. Brown, E. T., Ottley, A., Zhao, H., Lin, Q., Souvenir, R., Endert, A., and Chang, R. Finding waldo: Learning about users from their interactions. *IEEE Symposium on Visual Analytics Science and Technology (VAST)* (2014).
3. Cassidy, S., and Eachus, P. Learning style, academic belief systems, self-report student proficiency and academic achievement in higher education. *Educational Psychology 20* (2000), 307–320.
4. Findley, M. J., and Cooper, H. M. Locus of control and academic achievement: A literature review. *Journal of Personality and Social Psychology 44* (1983), 419–427.
5. Fisher, K., and Johnstion, M. Experimental manipulation of perceived control and its effect on disability. *Psychology and Health 11*, 5 (1996), 657–669.
6. Goldberg, L. R., Johnson, J. A., Eber, H. W., Hogan, R., Ashton, M. C., Cloninger, C. R., and Gough, H. G. The international personality item pool and the future of public-domain personality measures. *Journal of Research in Personality 40*, 1 (2006), 84–96.
7. Green, T. M., and Fisher, B. Towards the personal equation of interaction: The impact of personality factors on visual analytics interface interaction. In *IEEE Symposium on Visual Analytics Science and Technology (VAST)*, IEEE (2010), 203–210.
8. Judge, T. A., and Bono, J. E. Relationship of core self-evaluations traits–self-esteem, generalized self-efficacy, locus of control, and emotional stability–with job satisfaction and job performance: A meta-analysis. *Journal of Applied Psychology 86* (2001), 80–92.
9. National Center for Biotechnology Information. NCBI genome database. http://www.ncbi.nlm.nih.gov/genome/. Accessed 11/18/2010.
10. Ottley, A., Crouser, R. J., Ziemkiewicz, C., and Chang, R. Manipulating and controlling for personality effects on visualization tasks. *Information Visualization* (2013).
11. Peck, E. M., Ottley, A., Yuksel, B. F., Chang, R., and Harrison, L. ICD 3: Towards a 3-dimensional model of individual cognitive differences. *ACM BELIV 12: Beyond Time and Errors: Novel Evaluation Methods for Information Visualization* (2012).
12. Shneiderman, B. The eyes have it: A task by data type taxonomy for information visualizations. In *Visual Languages, 1996. Proceedings., IEEE Symposium on*, IEEE (1996), 336–343.
13. Steichen, B., Carenini, G., and Conati, C. User-adaptive information visualization: using eye gaze data to infer visualization tasks and user cognitive abilities. In *Proceedings of the 2013 international conference on Intelligent user interfaces*, ACM (2013), 317–328.
14. Ziemkiewicz, C., Ottley, A., Crouser, R. J., Yauilla, A. R., Su, S. L., Ribarsky, W., and Chang, R. How visualization layout relates to locus of control and other personality factors. *Visualization and Computer Graphics, IEEE Transactions on 19*, 7 (2013), 1109–1121.

*Sketch*Sliders: Sketching Widgets for Visual Exploration on Wall Displays

Theophanis Tsandilas[1,2]
fanis@lri.fr
[1]INRIA
F-91405 Orsay, France

Anastasia Bezerianos[2,1]
anab@lri.fr
[2]Univ Paris-Sud & CNRS (LRI)
F-91405 Orsay, France

Thibaut Jacob[1,2,3]
thibaut.jacob@telecom-paristech.fr
[3]Telecom ParisTech & CNRS (LTCI)
F-75013 Paris, France

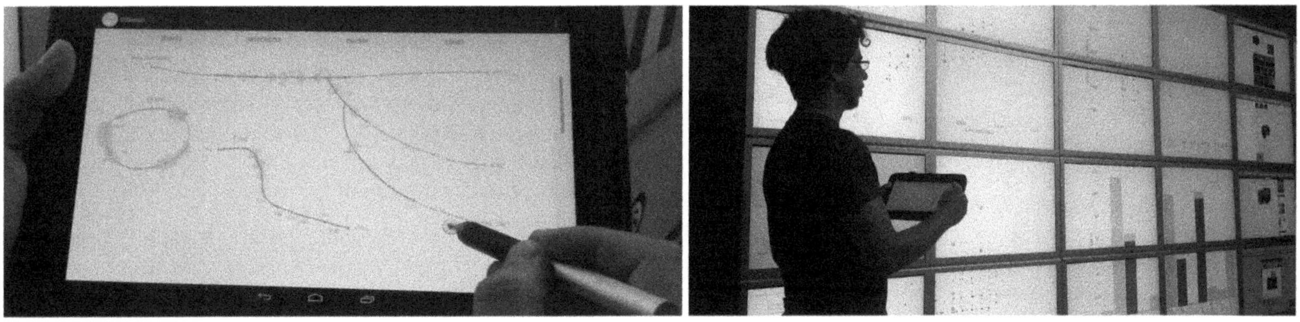

Figure 1. ***Sketch*Sliders (left) allow users to directly sketch visualization controllers to explore multi-dimensional datasets. We explore a range of slider shapes, including branched and circular, as well as shapes that express transformations. *Sketch*Sliders control visualizations on a wall display (right).**

ABSTRACT

We introduce a mobile sketching interface for exploring multi-dimensional datasets on wall displays. We demonstrate the idea of *Sketch*Sliders, range sliders that users can freely sketch on a mobile surface to customize their exploration. A small combination of sketches and gestures allows the creation of complex interactive sliders, such as circular sliders for periodic data, slider branches for detailed interaction, and fisheye transformation sliders. We augment sliders with a suite of tools, such as markers, slider cursors, and approximate views of data distributions. Our designs are inspired by a design study with three visualization experts and validated through a user study with six experts using our system. Our findings indicate that our sketching interface accommodates a wide range of exploration strategies, helping users customize as well as focus their visual explorations.

Author Keywords

Data visualization; sketching interfaces; wall displays

ACM Classi cation Keywords

H.5.m. Information Interfaces and Presentation (e.g. HCI): Miscellaneous

INTRODUCTION

High-resolution wall-sized displays [3, 6, 24] allow users to view a large amount of visual information, and thus have applications in a wide range of domains related to visual data analysis and exploration. Nevertheless, choosing appropriate techniques to explore data in such environments is not a simple matter. Viewers are often mobile, moving away to get an overview of complex visuals, and coming up-close to see details [3]. Exploring complex datasets also requires access to a large number of interactive controls in order to manipulate multiple dimensions and adjust their visual parameters.

We introduce a mobile sketching interface (Figure 1) that decouples control and visualization in a wall environment. Instead of having users interact with a large set of predefined exploration widgets, we let them customize their exploration by *sketching the controllers* that best suit their needs. To demonstrate the approach, we focus on range slider controllers, *Sketch*Sliders. We show how with a small gesture vocabulary users can: creatively use sketching to adjust exploration properties, such as precision, by drawing controllers of various sizes and shapes; focus on parts of the data by changing the control resolution in dense areas of data; explore variations of controllers by grafting alternative paths; and bookmark important results and points. Due to the nature of sketching, users can naturally customize the controller's appearance and its effect on the exploration. For example, they can draw larger sliders and branches for a finer control, circular sliders for periodic data, or shapes that describe transformation functions to focus on a smaller range of the data.

Our designs were inspired by design sessions with three visualization experts, whose feedback reinforced our choice of sketch-based range sliders as a versatile controller. Our sketching interface was then evaluated by six visualization experts. Our findings verify the flexibility of sketching controllers. They also demonstrate how the approach can accommodate different visual exploration strategies, and effectively support data exploration in interaction with wall displays.

CHI 2015, April 18 - 23, 2015, Seoul, Republic of Korea

http://dx.doi.org/10.1145/2702123.2702129.

Our main contributions are:

- We allow users to sketch directly the interactive controllers they require to conduct data exploration. We illustrate the potential of the approach with range sliders.
- We design mechanisms for sketching interactive sliders of arbitrary forms, including circular, branched and transformation sliders, that support complex queries over multiple data dimensions and multiple levels of control granularity.
- We introduce an environment that combines visualization plots on a wall display with mobile devices for sketching controllers. We study how experts use such a setup.

RELATED WORK

The search for appropriate interactions for wall displays has been largely investigated in HCI, focusing on questions mostly related to specific tasks, such as pointing [24] and maintaining awareness [6]. Recent work has looked at the use of mobile devices as an interaction medium that supports mobility. For example Smarties [10] customizes programmatically mobile interfaces to control a wall, while Jansen et al. [18] combine mobile devices with tangible controllers to explore visualizations. Our approach differs, as we allow users to customize their exploration interface using sketching.

Sketch-based input has been used among others for 3D modeling [17], note taking [14], and for domain specific applications such as MathPad2 [21] and Mus*ink* [28]. We focus here on two relevant research directions: using sketching to create interfaces, and sketching specifically for visual exploration.

Sketching to Create Interfaces

Wong [33] explains that sketching by hand to prototype interfaces allows users to ignore graphic details, focusing instead on the main goal and nature of the interaction. This is of special interest in data exploration, as often there is no clear goal (and thus an ideal interface), and hypotheses are formed progressively as users generate insight into their data [26].

SILK [20] was the first to allow users to sketch several interface controllers (buttons, sliders), and make them active by automatically detecting them and generating code. It relates to our work, as interface components are sketched, but are then "beautified" by the system, losing their informal and custom look. Given Wong's suggestions [33] and comments from our participants, this custom drawing and appearance is important in visual exploration.

Monet [23], allows users to sketch items and their states to create continuous widgets, keeping their informal look. They explore how to define new widgets and their states by example, while we examine how to customize existing widgets through sketching to aid visual exploration.

Sketching in Information Visualization

Sketching has been used in visualization as a visual rendering style (e.g. [34]), but less work has been done on using sketching as input for data exploration.

QuerySketch [30] and QueryLines [25] allow users to search and query data by sketching the desired result of their queries in the form of a graph. Relaxed selection techniques [16] go further by providing ways to implicitly define the level of similarity between sketches and real data. These approaches target mainly time-series data, focusing on searching for predefined patterns, rather than open exploration as we do.

In Transmogrification [7] selected regions from a 2D visualization can be transformed into a destination shape defined by sketching. This technique does not focus on interactive controllers. It rather acts directly on the visualization. Nevertheless, it relates to our work, as we also explore how an arbitrary slider shape can deform a visualization.

SketchStory [22] uses a small set of sketched gestures and touch interactions to construct a story for presentation and communication purposes. This tool does not support data exploration per se, it is rather a tool for helping play back the results of data exploration to others.

NapkinVis [9] uses sketching gestures to rapidly generate different types of charts, focusing mainly on data visualization authoring, not exploration. More relevant to our approach is SketchVis [8] that allows users both to load and to create visualizations using sketching, but it also provides simple ways of conducting data exploration. Users can switch between different data views, select specific data categories, or apply simple functions such as averages or maximum. SketchVis was later used in a Wizard of Oz study [29] to better understand the interplay between touch and pen interactions. Our work delves into using sketching for more complex query types during exploration, focusing in detail on one type of interactive controller, range sliders.

GOALS, CONCEPT AND DESIGN SESSIONS

Visual exploration and analysis tasks [2], such as filtering and range-selection, consist of selections and dynamic queries [1]. These are predominantly performed using slider widgets, each representing one data dimension. Our goal was to combine the simplicity of such widgets with the expressive power of sketch-based data exploration. We were particularly interested in identifying meaningful roles that shaped controllers can take, and explore how users could make use of sketching to augment controllers with new functions.

To explore this direction, we recruited three information visualization experts outside the research team, and ran an hour-long semi-structured design session with each of them. Their experience in visualization design and exploration ranged from 5 to 10 years. We first explained the main goal of the session, and then gave them three examples of sketch interaction, namely how to draw a straight slider and define new ranges to filter a data set, and how to sketch a data transformation function to acquire overview or details. These are fundamental tasks in visual exploration [27].

The experts then explored a multi-dimensional dataset. Their task was left intentionally open to encourage exploration, and was run in a *Wizard of Oz* setting. Participants had to think aloud, explaining what they were sketching on paper and what the expected behavior on the visualization was. One experimenter simulated this behavior on a real visualization

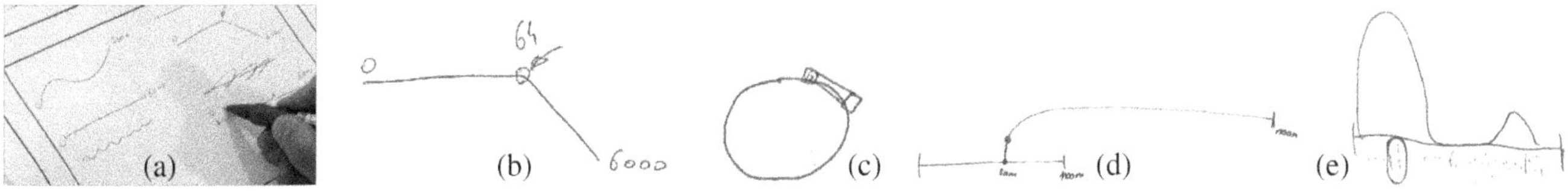

Figure 2. Designs from our three experts: (a) customized sliders, (b) bended slider with a mark, (c) circular slider, (d) grafting a slider, and (e) a slider combining different granularity ranges.

using controllers on her machine. A small brainstorming session followed, to discuss sketch interactions that could benefit data exploration in the context of our experts' own work.

Participants gravitated naturally to variations of sliders as their main interaction tool to narrow down their exploration, further validating our choice to focus on this controller. They all felt that sketching sliders for filtering data provided several benefits for visual exploration:

Customization (B1). Each stroke is unique. This aspect of sketching can be used to visually differentiate one slider from another (Figure 2a). Moreover, as the shape of a stroke can be arbitrary, one can encode information inside it, for example bending the slider in a given point of interest (Figure 2b).

Granularity (B2). The length of sketched slider affects the level of its control on the data. Long sliders allow fine-grained control and more precise filtering of data, while smaller ones are only appropriate for coarse-grained control. Two experts commented on how they often need both fine and coarse-grained control, e.g., for timelines that contain periods with both heavy and low activity. Each expert sketched a different solution to this problem. One created a coarse-grained slider and then *grafted* on top of it a second fine-grained slider (Figure 2d). The other expert drew a bulge at the location he required finer control (Figure 2e).

Parametrization (B3). Sketched sliders can support multiple ranges, giving users the possibility to filter the visualization in a discontinuous manner. This is occasionally a constraint in existing predefined range sliders. Another way of parametrizing a slider is to write by hand possible slider extremums or link specific data values to specific locations of the slider, which controls completely the mapping between the slider and the data. All our experts suggested a variation of this.

Special Shapes (B4). Our experts took advantage of the fact that they can sketch sliders in any shape they wanted. One expert sketched a circular slider to be used in the exploration of periodic dimensions such as hours of the day or angle values (Figure 2c). In this way, the slider represents a complete period with no start or end.

Reusability (B5). All participants requested the ability to deactivate controllers while still have them accessible for later use, either "faded-out" on the canvas or in a separate side panel. These solutions ensure that users keep copies of their sketched components, allowing them to explore alternative aspects of their data without losing their past work.

Annotation (B6). All our experts appreciated how a sketching environment naturally supports annotating and bookmarking of important information that is crucial for long term visual analysis tasks. Such an environment can combine notes on the analysis process taken by users, as well as traces of the interaction exploration, e.g., sketched controllers and values, that led to specific insights and findings.

One motivation behind our work is the need for an interface that is mobile, to accommodate users working in front of high-resolution wall displays. Nevertheless, all experts commented that a tool for sketching controllers would be valuable even in desktop environments, where visualization systems are often overloaded with numerous controllers.

SYSTEM OVERVIEW

We designed a sketch-based interface for data exploration that implements many ideas from our design sessions. The interface runs on mobile devices and communicates with a visualization dashboard on a high-resolution wall display (see Figure 1). The dashboard displays plots such as scatterplots and bar charts that present different views of a dataset. Plots are completely synchronized (coordinated views). If data points are selected or filtered, these effects are applied to all plots.

Users can sketch sliders on the mobile interface to explore different data dimensions, and create queries to filter data. Queries are communicated through the network to a server, which propagates the appropriate data filters to a wall cluster for rendering. Figure 3 shows the effect of filters on the two dimensions of a scatterplot. Blue points are data points inside all active filter ranges, while pale orange ones are outside.

Our setup supports personal exploration (tablet) over a shared viewing space (wall). This decoupling serves two main goals. First, users can move freely around the wall display and interact with sliders at the desired viewing distance and level of data overview. Second, large datasets can be comfortably visualized on a visualization cluster without overloading the limited capacities of personal devices. To a lesser extent, the setup accommodates wall displays that lack touch support.

Interacting with Gestures

Our sketch-based interface runs on Android devices, tablets and smartphones. Its design combines free writing, sketching of interactive controllers, and interaction with gestures. Since our interaction model only requires the use of a passive stylus or a finger, we combine stroke delimiters [13], crossing-based selection [4], and simple gesture recognition [32] to correctly infer the type and function of pen strokes.

Delimiters. We use dwells as delimiters to identify special command-strokes. As seen in Figure 4, a dwell invokes a contextual menu with a list of possible actions, e.g., create a

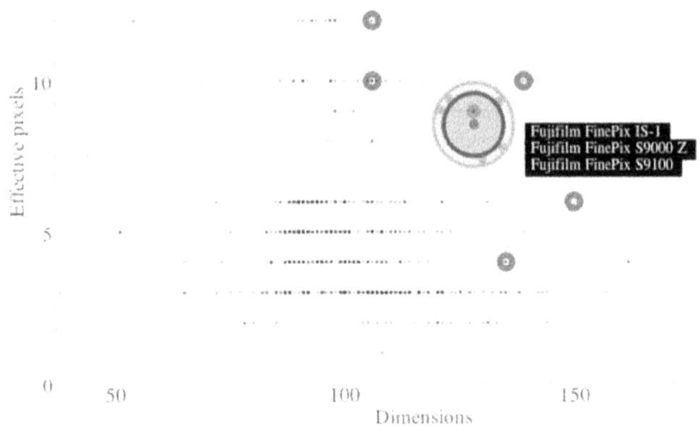

Figure 3. A scatterplot displays filtered points that represent camera models. Blue points are inside the active filter ranges, pale orange points are outside. A red area cursor can point to, and select, blue data points. Circled points correspond to previous selections. The dots in the ring around the cursor communicate the relative position of selected points.

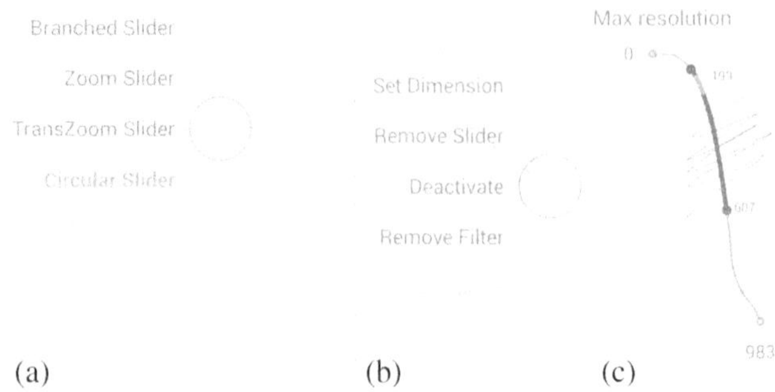

Figure 4. Combining crossing, dwelling, and gesture recognition. (a) Dwelling after drawing a curve activates a contextual menu that lets the user create a new slider. In this example, the system has recognized a circular form and therefore suggests a "Circular Slider" in addition to other types. (b) Dwelling after crossing a *Sketch*Slider shows a contextual menu with a set of possible actions. (c) Scribbling out a filter.

new slider. We found that short dwells of 250 to 350 ms do not disrupt the flow of regular writing. Hinckley et al. [13] report that dwells result in fewer errors but are slower than pigtails. But since pigtails interfere with symbols of regular handwriting, we only use them in conjunction with crossing.

Crossing-Based Selection. Users can cross existing interactive components and then dwell to choose a function from a context menu, e.g., deactivate or activate a slider, remove a filter or a marker, and change a filtering dimension.

Gesture Recognition. We facilitate interaction by recognizing three special forms of gestures: zig-zag scribbles, circular strokes, and pigtails. Zig-zag gestures serve as erasers of individual or groups of strokes as well as erasers of interactive slider components, e.g., whole sliders and filters. Circular strokes are generally considered as candidates for periodic sliders unless their trace crosses a slider, in which case they create slider cursors. Finally, pigtails create filters. We give more details about these features in the next section.

Pointing on the Wall Display and Data Selection

Users can activate additional functionality through bezel and contextual menus to reconfigure the plots on the wall display. They can also interact directly with their filtered content by turning the mobile device into a touch pad. As shown in Figure 3, we support pointing and selection through a circular area cursor with *excentric labeling* [12], for previewing and selecting data points directly on the plots. Users can pinch with two fingers to resize the area cursor and reduce or increase the active area of selection. We use the GlideCursor [5] and the acceleration function of Nancel et al. [24] to control the cursor position on the wall display.

Implementation

Our application has been built on Java for Android 4.3. The visualization software on the wall runs on Processing 1.5 - 2.0 and uses the Most Pixels Ever library[1] for spanning the charts on multiple machines and screens on the wall display, and a modified giCenter Utilites library for the charts[2]. Our wall consists of 32 30-inch LCDs arranged in a 8   4 matrix (size 5.5 x 1.8m and effective resolution 20480 x 6400 pixels) and is driven by a cluster of 16 computers. A Java server takes care of the communication between the Android and the wall application through the Open Sound Control protocol[3].

SKETCHSLIDERS

As regular sliders, *Sketch*Sliders control specific dimensions of a dataset, but can take arbitrary shapes. We have explored a number of designs that take advantage of their free form, including periodic sliders, grafted sliders, and transformation sliders whose path describes a fisheye function. *Sketch*Sliders can serve as classic controllers, but also as alternative mechanisms for direct data exploration. As we support embedded data distributions, slider cursors, and markers, users can focus on the tablet to complete part of their tasks without having to frequently move their attention to the wall display.

Basic SketchSliders and Filters

After drawing the path of a *Sketch*Slider, a popup dialog asks the user to assign a data dimension. We support both ratio and ordinal dimension variables (numerical, or textual sorted in alphabetical order). For ratio variables, we differentiate between decimals and integers. We also differentiate between periodic, e.g., months, and non-periodic variables (Figure 5).

When first created, a slider extends between the two extrema values of the dimension's active range. Users can interactively change the active range (*B3*) by long-pressing the label of the starting or ending extremum value, and then dragging it leftwards or rightwards. This decreases or increases the associated value, but also updates the range of the data dimension on the plots of the wall display. This way, users can control the charts by zooming in within a subrange of a dimension.

Figure 5 shows examples of *Sketch*Sliders and explains how users interact with their widgets. Sliders can host one or more interactive filters (*B3*), that define the union of ranges or individual values. Filter ranges are shown in blue. We support *delta filters* and *range filters*, created with pigtailed strokes that cross either once or twice the path of a slider. A delta

[1] http://github.com/shiffman/Most-Pixels-Ever-Processing
[2] http://www.gicentre.net/software/#/utils/
[3] http://opensoundcontrol.org

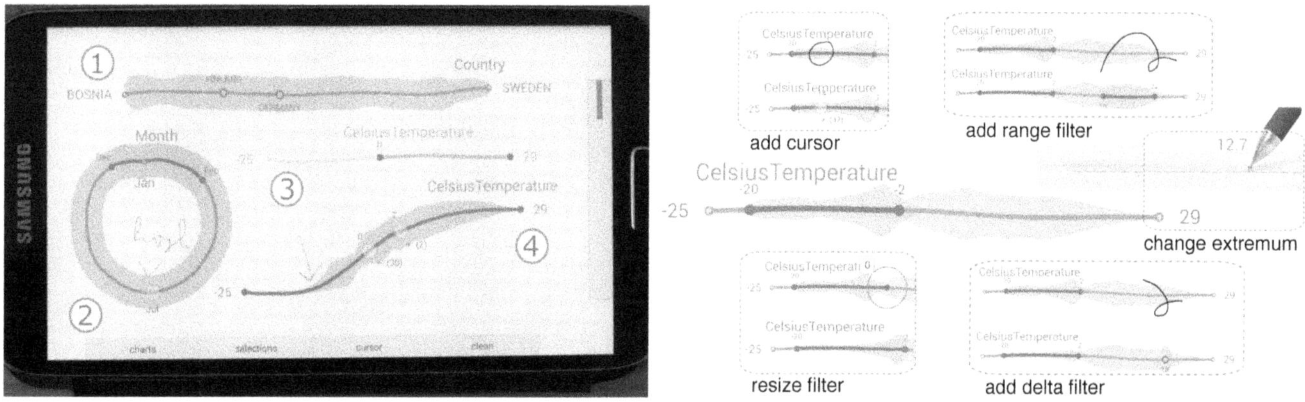

Figure 5. Left: Four *Sketch*Sliders on the screen of a 5-inch Samsung Galaxy S4: (1) a slider over an ordinal variable (Country), (2) a circular slider over a periodic variable (Month), (3) a slider that is currently inactive, and (4) a slider over a ratio variable (Temperature). The query of the three active sliders selects winter mean temperatures for Finland and Germany. Slider 4 shows how the distribution of active temperatures (blue) leans towards lower values. Right: Gestures and interactions to create and manipulate basic slider widgets: add a cursor (crossing circle), add a range or a delta filter (crossing pigtail), change a slider extremum, and resize a filter. Observe how active (blue) density distributions change in response to these actions.

filter has a single control point and represents either a unique value (ordinal variables), or a small delta range around a value (ratio variables), whose precision depends on the slider size and range of values. Range filters have two control points, and determine an active range between two values. Users can manipulate the control points to change the start and end values, or pick and move the entire range along the slider.

For complex queries involving multiple data dimensions, users can create multiple *Sketch*Sliders. Their result is the intersection of the results of the individual sliders' queries. During data exploration, users may draw several sliders and switch between them by deactivating ones or activating others (*B5*). Our implementation allows for a single active slider for each dimension. Sliders become automatically inactive when a new slider for the same dimension is drawn.

Guided by the results of our design study (*B4*), we support circular sliders dedicated to periodic variables (Figure 5: Left). Circular sliders have no ends, and thus do not constrain the translation of their filters. For example, a single range filter can specify the winter months, from December to February.

Embedded Density Distributions

We augment *Sketch*Sliders with density distributions that appear as shadows along the path of each slider, and communicate data overviews. We get inspiration from *scented widgets* [31], but opt for a different visualization approach that derives from *violin plots* [15]. Violin plots show a density trace that extends symmetrically along the length of a box plot. The density trace provides rich information about the underlying distribution, and when compared to histogram-based visualizations [31] it results in less visual clutter. It can also better generalize to curved paths of arbitrary shapes.

As with histograms, this approach requires the selection of an interval (bin) width h. We try to optimize h by considering the type of the slider's variable (ordinal, integer, decimal) and its range. For a given range, longer *Sketch*Sliders contain a larger number of intervals, and thus show more detailed density distributions. Density distributions are normalized between zero and the highest available density. We visualize two distributions: (1) a static distribution of the entire dataset within the slider's range (in light orange), and (2) a dynamic one of the active data subset, defined by the filters of the currently active sliders (in blue). A dynamic distribution is updated every time the user adds, removes or changes a filter on an active *Sketch*Slider. This allows users to directly observe the effects of their filters on multiple dimensions.

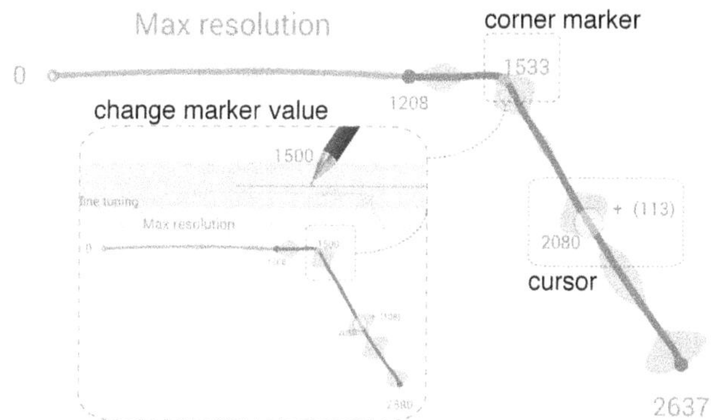

Figure 6. Corners can serve as markers of values of interest. As with extrema, the user can adjust the value of a corner by long-pressing and dragging its label along the horizontal axis. A slider cursor reveals both the value of its center and the number of active data points it covers.

Density distributions are approximate but can support data exploration directly on the mobile surface. For instance, users can draw multiple sliders to get quick information about how data points are distributed along different dimensions, and identify areas of interest within the sliders' ranges, common tasks in data analysis [2]. Thus, users can focus on their actual filters without having to continuously shift their attention to the wall display. Or, the distributions can help users identify functional dependencies between dimensions as they manipulate filters of different sliders. For example, the Temperature slider in Figure 5 (Left) shows that registered winter temperatures for Finland and Germany lean towards the low range of values and include a high proportion of negative values.

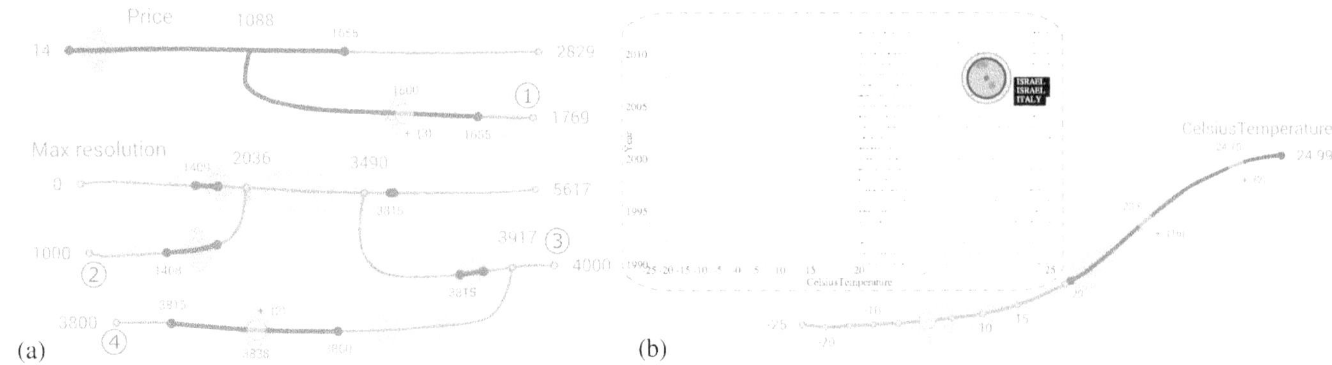

Figure 7. (a) Branched *Sketch*Sliders. Branches (1, 2, 3, 4) serve as proxies, providing a more detailed view of a range. A branch can start from (1, 3) or end at (2, 4) the main slider or another branch. (b) A Transformation *Sketch*Slider applies a fisheye deformation to a scatterplot. The slider contains grid lines that correspond to the transformed grid of the scatterplot. In this example, the transformation allows for zooming into the range of temperatures between 20 and 25° C. For this range, the user can make more precise selections on the scatterplot and the slider itself.

Slider Cursors and Markers

A *Sketch*Slider can host one or more *slider cursors* that serve as one-dimensional navigation widgets. Slider cursors can move along the length of a slider and display the data value that corresponds to its centre, aiding value retrieval tasks [2]. Similarly to the 2D area cursor on the wall charts, they also serve as data-point selectors. As seen in Figure 6, a slider cursor covers a delta area over the slider's range, and counts the active data points queried by the filters. Users can tap on the + symbol to display the list of the covered data points, and optionally, add a subset of these points to their selections. The granularity of the cursor depends on the length of the *Sketch*Slider and its range of values.

Since *Sketch*Sliders can take any shape, distinctive features can act as *markers* of values of interest, as suggested in our design study (*B1*). We enhance this property by running a corner detection algorithm that automatically identifies corners on the slider's path and displays their value. As with extrema values, users can long press on a marker label to further adjust its value. Figure 6 shows that changing the value of a marker shifts the extreme values (one or both) of the slider and adjusts its scale, ensuring that the slider remains linear.

Grafting: Branched Sliders

We apply the concept of grafting from our study (*B2*), in a new slider type, *branched* sliders. Branched sliders support infinite nesting of branches to allow multiple levels of granularity within a slider's range. Grafting a branch is similar to creating a new *Sketch*Slider, but the stroke for the new branch has to cross an existing slider or branch. The joint point can be either the starting or the ending extreme of the branch, depending on the direction of the stroke that creates it. Thus, branches can form arbitrary tree and polytree structures. We also allow for closed branches between any two points of the root slider or a branch. Note that the extrema values of a branch cannot exceed the extrema values of its parent.

As seen in Figure 7a, branches act as slider proxies, and filters have copies in all the branches of a slider. The user can manipulate any of these copies according to the level of intended precision. By grafting branches and adjusting their extrema, users can zoom in partial ranges of the slider. The density distribution of a branch reflects its individual range rather than the range of the root slider, offering a different view of the data. As users zoom in a subrange, distributions get more fine grained, while filters and cursors become more precise. This can reveal distribution anomalies or clusters, that are important components of data analysis [2]. For example, branches 1, 3, and 4 in Figure 7a reveal small clusters of data points not visible on the root slider. Notice how the filter on branch 4 has increased in length and granularity compared to its original copy on the root slider. Branched sliders let users dig incrementally into ranges of a dimension, without removing the trace of previous explorations.

Transformation Sliders

Sketching is commonly used for drawing curves to communicate trends or mathematical functions. Inspired by our study (*B2*), the path of *transformation* sliders similarly describes an 1D transformation function. To define transformations over slider paths, we use a curvilinear l-y coordinate system, where l is the arc length of the partial curve at point $p(x, y)$. This approach overcomes the problem of curves that do not describe valid functions in Cartesian coordinates.

We examine *focus+context* transformation functions that affect the dimensions of plots on the wall display. More specifically, peaks of a slider curve represent areas of focus while valleys represent areas of context. To model this behavior, we define a fisheye function $F(y, g) = (1 - g)f(1) + gf(y)$, where $y \in [0, 1]$ is the vertical curve position normalized between the higher and lower extreme of the curve, while $g \in [0, 1]$ is a gain function. In our implementation, the gain is $g = h/h_{max}$, where h is the height of the curve and h_{max} is a maximum height value. Finally, f is a monotonically increasing function. We produce a more aggressive fisheye deformation by taking an exponential function $f(y) = a^y$.

Figure 7b shows a *Sketch*Slider that applies a fisheye transformation to the x−axis of a scatterplot. We can see that the transformation applies to the scatterplot but also to the slider itself. This means that values are not uniformly distributed along the path of the slider, i.e., they are sparser around peaks and denser around valleys. Similarly, the granularity of slider

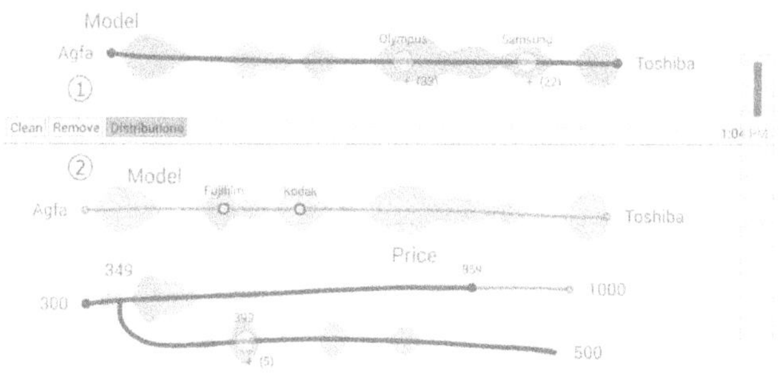

Figure 8. A document can consist of multiple sections, where each section (1, 2) forms a unique query. A movable bar (separator) denotes the bottom of a section and includes functionality for managing the section.

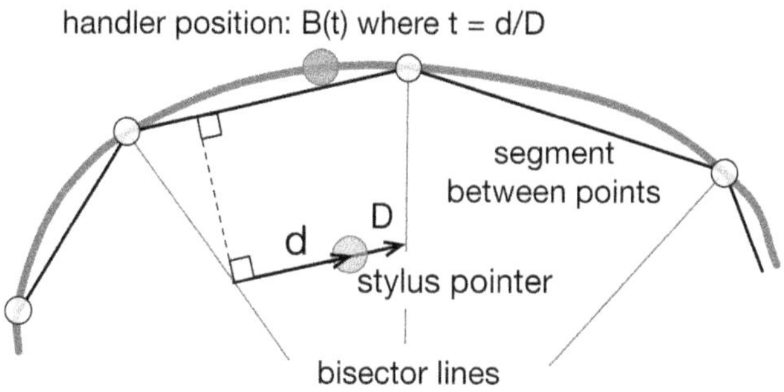

Figure 9. Deriving the position of a handle (blue circle) on the cubic Bézier curve of a slider from the position of the pen (red circle).

widgets varies along the slider. As a result, delta filters and cursors become more precise closer to higher peaks.

To apply a fisheye transformation over the slider's path, we divide it into small arcs and estimate the transformed value $v(l) \in [0, 1]$ at position l as the sum of its partial delta values:

$$v(l) = \sum_{k=1}^{i-1} \Delta v(l_k, l_{k+1}) + \Delta v(l_i, l) \tag{1}$$

We then approximate the fisheye transformation value for a position s within each arc i as a linear function $F(s) = F_i + \lambda_i s$, where F_i is its value at the start point of the arc and $\lambda_i = (F_{i+1} - F_i)/(l_{i+1} - l_i)$. Based on this approximation, we can calculate the delta values in Equation 1 as follows:

$$\Delta v(l_k, l) = \beta \int_{l_k}^{l} F(s)ds = \beta(F_k \delta l + \frac{\lambda_k \delta l^2}{2}) \tag{2}$$

where $\delta l = l - l_k$. The parameter β is a normalization factor derived from Equations 1 and 2 by setting $v(L) = 1$, where L is the total slider length.

Exploration Sections

A user can divide an exploration session into sections, where each section can contain any number of sliders that form a query. Sections let users start a new exploration without losing the history of their previous queries (*B5*). New sections are created by drawing a long horizontal line with a pigtail. This creates a *separator* (Figure 8) that serves as the lower boundary of a section. The widget can be dragged up or down to adjust the size of two adjacent sections.

CURVE MODELING AND DRAGGING

We model the path of *Sketch*Sliders and range filters as cubic Bézier curves. We uniformly decrease the number of path points, which results in smoother curves and better performance. We also use cubic Bézier curves to model the trace of distributions, by connecting density points between bins at the normals of the *Sketch*Sliders. If the lines of two neighboring density points intersect, we consider a single density point at their intersection, avoiding the creation of path loops.

Figure 9 explains how we derive the position of a handler, e.g., a slider cursor, on the Bézier curve from the position of the finger or stylus pointer when dragging the handler. We find the line that crosses the pointer and is parallel to the closest segment between two consecutive path points. We then take the vector $\vec{D}$ defined by its intersection with the previous and the next bisector of the between-segment angles. We also take the position $\vec{d}$ of the pointer on this vector. From this, we derive the t parameter of the corresponding Bézier curve $B(t)$ as the normalized pointer position $t = d/D$. To deal with slider curves that contain closed loops, we can set a threshold distance that avoids accidental jumps between non-neighboring segments.

In contrast to our approach, DimpVis [19] simply takes the minimum-distance point to project the position of the finger to a path. Dragicevic et al. [11] have proposed a more generic solution by modeling curvilinear dragging as an optimization problem that minimizes a 3D instead of a 2D distance. Our solution is less generic, yet fast and simpler, while it still results in very smooth behavior for meaningful slider shapes.

USER STUDY

To validate our prototype we conducted a user study with six visualization researchers (2 female), who used regularly visual analytics tools, recruited through chain-sampling. Their experience in visualization research and analysis ranged from 2 to 15 years (median 10), and their age from 24 to 41 (median 34.5). All reported being highly familiar with the visualization plots used in our study and the notion of range sliders. Three had taken part in our early design study.

Goals: The goal of the study was threefold: (*G1*) verify the findings from the design study regarding the value of sketching controllers for visual exploration; (*G2*) observe how experts can appropriate *Sketch*Sliders; and (*G3*) examine the benefits and shortcomings of divided attention. We wanted to observe how the sketching interface supports visual exploration in combination, but also in separation, from the wall.

Setup: Participants were seated in front of the wall display, which displayed three scatterplots and one bar chart. Participants interacted with the plots using a Nexus 10-inch tablet running our prototype (Figure 10). We also provided a capacitive pen. We chose a seated setup, as opposed to free walking, to ensure user comfort for the duration of the study, and to avoid any confounds due to uncomfortable hold positions of the tablet without proper hand support.

Figure 10. Study setup with wall display and *Sketch*Sliders on a tablet.

T1	Tell us your observations about the distribution of Prices (e.g. extremes, clusters, similarities or gaps inside clusters at low detail).
T2	Which camera Models are in the Price range 3000-6000? Approximate as much as you can the most frequent Max resolution values for them.

Table 1. The two open tasks. T1 was conducted by using both the wall and the tablet. For T2, participants were asked to not look at the wall.

Procedure and Tasks: Each session lasted approximately one hour and was videotaped. Participants were given a detailed training session of 20-30 minutes, using a dataset on the history of temperatures in different countries. They then performed alone, using a think-aloud protocol, two open exploration tasks on another dataset. The two open tasks (Table 1) were related to a multidimensional camera dataset with a total of 1038 digital cameras and 13 dimensions. For the second task, participants were asked to not look at the wall. We expected that this would encourage them to explore the capabilities of *Sketch*Sliders in more depth, and assess their strengths and limitations both with and without the wall. The session was followed by a semi-structured interview.

Results

We report here on observations gathered during the study and participants' responses during the interview.

G1: Value of Sketching in Visual Exploration

All participants were very enthusiastic about sketching their own controllers as needed. They each commented on different aspects, which we briefly summarize here:

Customization. Participants reinforced findings from our design study, stating that sketched sliders can be *"customized to what I need"*, *"easy to tell apart"*, and *"feel personal"*. As one participant mentioned *"there is something very compelling about sketching your own tools"*.

Personal space. All participants could envision sharing the wall plot result but would be reluctant to share the sliders themselves. As one participant mentioned, *"it is similar to sharing my notes, I would be reluctant, it is too personal"*.

Flexibility. All participants appreciated the flexibility of sketching different shapes and sizes to: (i) better fit their view of the data, *"this is vertical [indicating a dimension on a plot] so I drew a vertical slider"*; (ii) focus on parts of the data as needed, *"I can focus either with branches or transformation, you don't have that in other interfaces"*; and (iii) generally allow users to feel that the interface can accommodate their needs. As one participant stated *"existing interfaces are not exible enough, they only show you predefined controllers"*.

Annotation. All participants mentioned they liked the ability to be able to sketch controllers and also take personal notes related to their analysis and findings (see Figure 11a,b). However, three participants stated that they would have preferred a different mode for analysis and a different one for annotation, as in some cases they wanted to use gestural marks, such as circling a slider, as a free-form note to indicate emphasis.

G2: Use of Sketch*Sliders functionality by Experts*

Participants were able to effectively use the interface without aid, adopting different strategies to perform their tasks and using different combinations of *Sketch*Sliders' functionalities.

Branches. Five participants used extension branches to increase the granularity of their exploration. As P1 mentioned *"I draw a branch when I couldn't interact precisely [with the slider], and adjusted its end to be more precise"*. Branches were also used to compare different parts of the data. P2 explained that *"I made a second branch to see if I have the same detailed pattern as in the other [branch]"*. P4 combined branches with other strategies to explore different aspects of the data. She drew multiple sliders for the same dimension and adjusted their ranges. She then compared their effect on the wall plots by switching between them. As the activation and deactivation of sliders happens through a contextual menu, she asked for a faster way to do so.

Transformation sliders. Four participants used transformation sliders to focus on part of their data. As P6 mentioned, this gave *"a better view of the densely packed data points in this range"*. Figure 11a shows how P6 used a transformation slider to focus on the lowest range of camera prices, while he filtered release dates with a regular slider. This participant did not use any branches, as he could complete the tasks with transformation sliders by adjusting their extremes. Others used transformation sliders early on to get a quick view of clusters in their data, or to focus on some interesting areas of certain dimensions, while using branched sliders for others.

Slider cursors. Participants made a frequent use of the slider cursor and found it very useful. Some created a large number of these cursors (Figure 11) to locate items within an area of the slider and then display them as selected on the wall. Two participants commented that they would have liked to change the cursor's size, as they could do with the wall cursor.

Density distributions. All participants mentioned that slider distributions were helpful to *"identify possible high level patters"*, *"get a quick overview of data"*, or to *"quickly see how much data are filtered"*. P1 stated that the distribution was enough on its own for a high level and approximate data exploration. On the other hand, P4 and P5 suggested showing individual points rather than distributions at fine granularity, as they *"expected clusters not points, and was not sure if I should focus more"*. P4 observed that the rendering can be misleading, expecting that data are normally distributed within the range covered by bins. A possible solution to this problem is to use beeswarm-like visualizations[4] when the number of data points around a bin becomes very low.

[4] http://www.cbs.dtu.dk/~eklund/beeswarm/

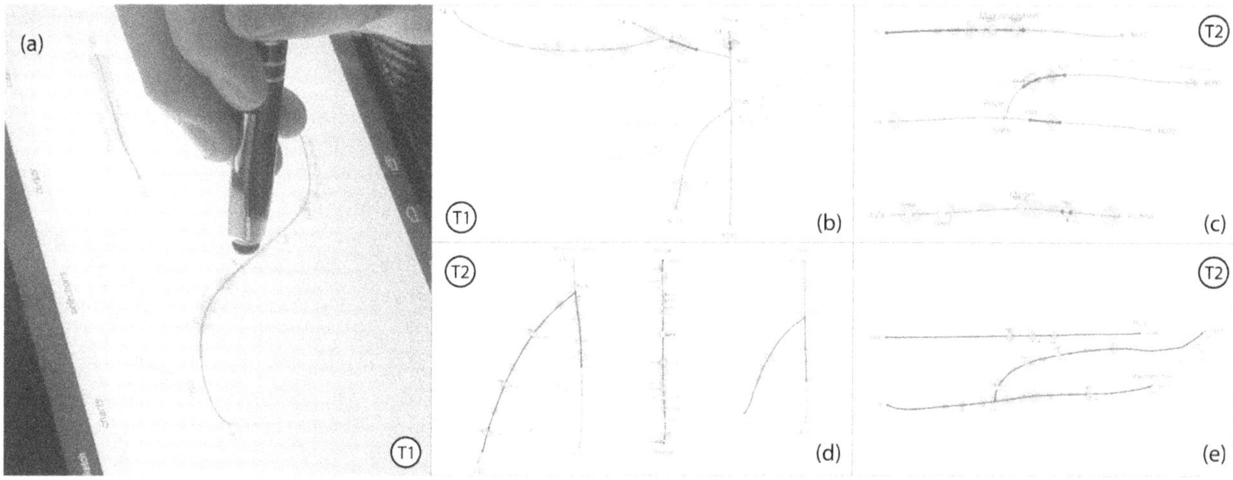

Figure 11. Complex queries sketched by different participants of our study. P6 applies a filter to lower prices by using a transformation slider (a). Use of a mix of simple and branched *Sketch*Sliders by P2 (b, d), P3 (c), and P4 (e). We indicate the task (T1, T2) for which the query was created.

G3: Exploration using Sketch*Sliders and Wall Display*

All participants mentioned that the combination of sketching controllers and decoupled wall plots worked really well for visual exploration and were *"very well integrated"*. According to P5, *"the setup really works well for me, they are complementary, as you cannot show all the information on the tablet, and I don't really want to directly interact with the wall all the time"*. Observing how participants worked on task T1, we were able to identify the following strategies.

Participants found that sketching one controller at a time helped their analysis process. P1 used almost exclusively the tablet, as plots on the wall *"are at first overwhelming, too much data"*. She explained that sketching sliders as needed let her *"focus on one dimension, and see the result on other dimensions [using the slider distributions], which reduced my cognitive load"*. She explained that the interface *"helped me filter not just my data, but also my controllers"*.

A similar sentiment was expressed by P3, who explained that *"existing interfaces are too cluttered and it is hard to decide where to focus on, here I can focus on one thing, and drawing a slider is a way for myself to decide what will be most likely of interest next"*. It is interesting to note that P3 and P6 completed the task by focusing mainly on the wall, manipulating their sliders eyes-free. According to P6, this helped him *"avoid splitting attention"* between the two displays.

P2, P4, and P5 divided their analysis between tablet and wall. They used slider distributions for approximate answers, and the wall for detailed ones. P4 mentioned she always *"checked to see the result [of a slider] on the plots"*, while P2 explained that *"when I wanted detail I would go here [plots]"*.

Overall, participants were very enthusiastic, and were able to retain and use the interface successfully. Their choices on what controllers to create, and how to explore data using the tablet and wall varied greatly. Clearly experts have their own analysis approaches, and one interface does not fit all. Given the varied ways our setup was used, we feel *Sketch*Sliders are flexible enough to support different working styles.

CONCLUSION AND PERSPECTIVES

We presented *Sketch*Sliders, range sliders that users can freely sketch directly on a mobile, in order to parametrize and customize their exploration of data on a wall display. With a small combination of sketches and gestures users can create complex interactive components, such as slider branches and data transformation sliders, to investigate detailed aspects and subsets of their datasets. Apart from their natural custom shape, our sketched sliders are enhanced by interaction aids such as slider cursors, markers and distribution visualizations.

Results from a user study with visualization experts indicate that *Sketch*Sliders are flexible, support different exploration strategies, while the fact that they are sketched as needed can focus and aid the visual analysis. Our system currently does not support collaboration. Nevertheless, participants indicated that the sketched sliders are very personal, and although they would be willing to share their results on the wall visualization, they are less open to sharing the controllers themselves. This opens interesting questions regarding sharing mechanisms and privacy that need further study.

We were motivated by a scenario where users view large datasets on wall displays, and require mobile interaction support. Nevertheless, our experts commented that sketching customized controllers can be useful even in desktop settings, where visualizations are usually laden with numerous inflexible controls. We plan to investigate further how users can sketch and use sliders directly on their visualizations.

One benefit of *Sketch*Sliders is the combination of regular note taking that is crucial in data exploration, and the trace of the interactive controllers and their values that were used to reach insights. This coupling of analysis process and recording could be further enhanced. We could envision users taking snapshots of their data to add to their sketched environment, and detailed history mechanisms for reverting to previous steps in their exploration. These "traces" of the interaction exploration could then be used as a logging mechanism for analysts, or shared with others without sharing the data themselves that could be too large or sensitive.

REFERENCES

1. Ahlberg, C., Williamson, C., and Shneiderman, B. Dynamic queries for information exploration: an implementation and evaluation. *CHI '92*, ACM (1992), 619–626.
2. Amar, R., and Stasko, J. A knowledge task-based framework for design and evaluation of information visualizations. *Symposium on Information Visualization*, INFOVIS '04, IEEE (2004), 143–150.
3. Andrews, C., Endert, A., Yost, B., and North, C. Information Visualization on Large, High-resolution Displays: Issues, Challenges, and Opportunities. *Information Visualization 10*, 4 (2011), 341–355.
4. Apitz, G., and Guimbretiere, F. Crossy: A crossing-based drawing application. *UIST '04*, ACM (2004), 3–12.
5. Beaudouin-Lafon, M., Huot, S., Olafsdottir, H., and Dragicevic, P. Glidecursor: Pointing with an inertial cursor. *AVI '14*, ACM (2014), 49–56.
6. Bezerianos, A., Dragicevic, P., and Balakrishnan, R. Mnemonic rendering: an image-based approach for exposing hidden changes in dynamic displays. *UIST '06*, ACM (2006), 159–168.
7. Brosz, J., Nacenta, M. A., Pusch, R., Carpendale, S., and Hurter, C. Transmogrification: Causal manipulation of visualizations. *UIST '13*, ACM (2013), 97–106.
8. Browne, J., Lee, B., Carpendale, S., Riche, N., and Sherwood, T. Data analysis on interactive whiteboards through sketch-based interaction. *ITS '11*, ACM (2011), 154–157.
9. Chao, W. O. NapkinVis: Rapid Pen-Centric Authoring of Improvisational Visualizations. *IEEE InfoVis Poster* (2009), 1–9.
10. Chapuis, O., Bezerianos, A., and Frantzeskakis, S. Smarties: An input system for wall display development. *CHI '14*, ACM (2014), 2763–2772.
11. Dragicevic, P., Ramos, G., Bibliowitcz, J., Nowrouzezahrai, D., Balakrishnan, R., and Singh, K. Video browsing by direct manipulation. *CHI '08*, ACM (2008), 237–246.
12. Fekete, J.-D., and Plaisant, C. Excentric labeling: Dynamic neighborhood labeling for data visualization. *CHI '99*, ACM (1999), 512–519.
13. Hinckley, K., Baudisch, P., Ramos, G., and Guimbretiere, F. Design and analysis of delimiters for selection-action pen gesture phrases in scriboli. *CHI '05*, ACM (2005), 451–460.
14. Hinckley, K., Zhao, S., Sarin, R., Baudisch, P., Cutrell, E., Shilman, M., and Tan, D. Inkseine: In situ search for active note taking. *CHI '07*, ACM (2007), 251–260.
15. Hintze, J. L., and Nelson, R. D. Violin plots: A box plot-density trace synergism. *The American Statistician 52*, 2 (May 1998), 181–184.
16. Holz, C., and Feiner, S. Relaxed selection techniques for querying time-series graphs. *UIST '09*, ACM (2009), 213–222.
17. Igarashi, T., Matsuoka, S., and Tanaka, H. Teddy: A sketching interface for 3d freeform design. *SIGGRAPH 2007 Courses*, SIGGRAPH '07, ACM (2007).
18. Jansen, Y., Dragicevic, P., and Fekete, J.-D. Tangible remote controllers for wall-size displays. *CHI '12*, ACM (2012), 2865–2874.
19. Kondo, B., and Collins, C. Dimpvis: Exploring time-varying information visualizations by direct manipulation. *Trans. Vis. Comput. Graph. PrePrints*, IEEE (2014), 2003–2012.
20. Landay, J. A. Silk: Sketching interfaces like krazy. *CHI '96*, ACM (1996), 398–399.
21. LaViola, Jr., J. J., and Zeleznik, R. C. Mathpad2: A system for the creation and exploration of mathematical sketches. *SIGGRAPH '04*, ACM (2004), 432–440.
22. Lee, B., Kazi, R. H., and Smith, G. Sketchstory: Telling more engaging stories with data through freeform sketching. *Trans. Vis. Comput. Graph. 19*, 12 IEEE (2013), 2416–2425.
23. Li, Y., and Landay, J. A. Informal prototyping of continuous graphical interactions by demonstration. *UIST '05*, ACM (2005), 221–230.
24. Nancel, M., Chapuis, O., Pietriga, E., Yang, X.-D., Irani, P., and Beaudouin-Lafon, M. High-precision pointing on large wall displays using small handheld devices. *CHI '13*, ACM (2013), 831–840.
25. Ryall, K., Lesh, N., Lanning, T., Leigh, D., Miyashita, H., and Makino, S. Querylines: Approximate query for visual browsing. *CHI EA '05*, ACM (2005), 1765–1768.
26. Saraiya, P., North, C., and Duca, K. An insight-based methodology for evaluating bioinformatics visualizations. *Trans. Vis. Comp. Graph. 11*, 4 IEEE (2005), 443–456.
27. Shneiderman, B. The eyes have it: A task by data type taxonomy for information visualizations. *Symposium on Visual Languages*, IEEE (1996), 336–.
28. Tsandilas, T., Letondal, C., and Mackay, W. E. Musink: Composing music through augmented drawing. *CHI '09*, ACM (2009), 819–828.
29. Walny, J., Lee, B., Johns, P., Riche, N. H., and Carpendale, S. Understanding pen and touch interaction for data exploration on interactive whiteboards. *Trans. Vis. Comput. Graph. 18*, 12 IEEE (2012), 2779–2788.
30. Wattenberg, M. Sketching a graph to query a time-series database. *CHI EA '01*, ACM (2001), 381–382.
31. Willett, W., Heer, J., and Agrawala, M. Scented widgets: Improving navigation cues with embedded visualizations. *Trans. Vis. Comp. Graph. 13*, 6 IEEE (2007), 1129–1136.
32. Wobbrock, J. O., Wilson, A. D., and Li, Y. Gestures without libraries, toolkits or training: A $1 recognizer for user interface prototypes. *UIST '07*, ACM (2007), 159–168.
33. Wong, Y. Y. Rough and ready prototypes: Lessons from graphic design. *CHI '92*, ACM (1992), 83–84.
34. Wood, J., Isenberg, P., Isenberg, T., Dykes, J., Boukhelifa, N., and Slingsby, A. Sketchy rendering for information visualization. *Trans. Vis. Comput. Graph. 18*, 12 IEEE (2012), 2749–2758.

Two-Level Personas for Nested Design Spaces

Anke Dittmar
Department of Computer Science
University of Rostock, Germany
anke.dittmar@uni-rostock.de

Maximilian Hensch
Department of Computer Science
University of Rostock, Germany
maximilian.hensch@uni-rostock.de

ABSTRACT
The persona approach is often treated as a single user-centered design method, but there are variations and adaptations for different design contexts which go beyond local customization. This paper discusses a set of dimensions and success criteria for describing the different persona uses, presenting a new framework. It then specifically investigates personas in the context of end-user development. Professional designers need to consider the design space for potential end-user tools. In addition they need to understand that their users are often designers themselves (they are designer-users), requiring that they also consider the design spaces of their users. Two-level personas are introduced to make professional designers more aware of such nested design spaces. A two-level persona consists of one first-level persona and a set of second-level personas to additionally represent complex designer-user relationships. The effectiveness of the approach is investigated in an exploratory empirical study. The results suggest that two-level personas add value when designing end-user design tools.

Author Keywords
Personas; two-level personas; user-centered design; design spaces; end-user development; empirical studies.

ACM Classi cation Keywords
H.5.m. Information Interfaces and Presentation (e.g. HCI): Miscellaneous

INTRODUCTION
Mary[1] *has been working for 32 years at John Brinckman elementary school. She especially likes to teach general studies because of the practical exercises she can include in the course. She often thinks she should just take the kids to her garden to show them that there are other things in life than Gameboys* ™ *and smartphones. The eight and nine-year-olds she teaches seem to completely depend on them. She used to complain about this technology fixation to her son Christian who is also a teacher, but he didn't seem to share her fears. Some weeks ago, he stopped her complaints by switching on his laptop to show her some data his class had collected from a recent biology field trip. On this trip he was fortunate that all students had a mobile phone so that they could use the app he had created to document different plants in the field. Christian said that he would install the design tool he used to create his plant classification app on her laptop so that she could create apps too. He explained it is easy to use and that she will finally have a use for the birthday present he gave her years ago! Mary felt somewhat ashamed after this conversation. Her son was right, the laptop had seldomly been used; although, she did use it to look through the family pictures and she also sometimes played solitaire on it after coming home from school feeling tired...*

Mary is 54 years old, she is divorced and has a 29-year-old son named Christian who works as a secondary school teacher in another town. Mary is not a person, she is a persona - a hypothetical archetype of users, a concept introduced by Cooper into the domain of interactive systems design in the late 1990s [8]. Because of its focus on the users' behaviors, goals and needs, the persona method has been extensively investigated in the context of the user-centered design approach. Still, the method is "new enough not to be fully fixed and [is] open to change" [41]. The discussion of the benefits and the limitations of personas is often guided by either faith or skepticism, claim or counter-claim [28]. However, personas have been applied in specific projects in many different ways that are beyond local customizations [16], and Floyd et al. recommend not to treat the approach as a single design method but as "different methods which are appropriate for different contexts" [16]. We will consider this further in the background section along with suggestions on a more differentiated view of personas to support a refined debate about the applicability of the approach and about appropriate adaptations for different design contexts.

This paper investigates personas in the context of end-user development [27, 24], and more specifically, in the context of end-user design tools which allow users to design their own applications for their own work situations. We call these users *designer-users* to emphasize their dual role. An example would be a design tool that enables designer-users to create mobile applications for in-situ data collections. Researchers applying the experience sampling method [26] could use such a tool to develop applications for study; alternately, teachers may wish to design a tool for their students to collect data during a field trip. The professional designers (referred to simply as *designers* henceforth) of such end-user design tools need

[1]Readers who prefer a more straightforward introduction can skip this paragraph at first, and come back later.

CHI 2015, April 18 - 23 2015, Seoul, Republic of Korea
Copyright 2015 ACM 978-1-4503-3145-6/15/04...$15.00
http://dx.doi.org/10.1145/2702123.2702168

to be aware that their users (the designer-users) act as designers themselves. They have to understand not only the goals and needs of their designer-users, but also the designer-users' potential end users (referred to as *end-users* henceforth) and the relationship between the designer-users and the end-users. The design tool would therefore ideally be created with the end-user applications under consideration. In the example, the designers must consider the needs of the researchers and teachers as both users and designers, the participants and students as end-users, and, most importantly, they must understand the relationship between researchers and study participants, or between teachers and students. (This relationship is referred to as the *designer-user relationship* henceforth.) For example, a researcher may wish to establish a respectful relationship with the study participants. An appropriate design tool could support this by offering him or her the opportunity to design an app which allows participants to cancel the in-situ data collection at any time.

In the paper, the term *nested design spaces* is introduced to refer to design spaces as they occur in the above described situations. Design spaces in general are conceptual spaces designers navigate to understand design problems and to find good solutions [2, 29, 48]. Nested design spaces emphasize that designers have to be aware of their own design space of potential end-user design tools and of the impact that has on the design space possibilities for designer-users. *Two-level personas* are suggested for a better understanding of nested design spaces. A two-level persona consists of an individual persona representing a group of designer-users (a first-level persona) and other personas representing groups of end-users of their products (second-level personas). The two-level persona description also contains information that is important to understanding the relationship between the first-level and second-level personas. With respect to the example design tool for in-situ data collections referred to above, the introductory description of Mary (a designer-user) could be the basis for a first-level persona representing a group of teachers. It would need to be supplemented by second-level personas representing various groups of students (end-users), and give a sense of the design challenges Mary faces. This explicit representation of the designer-users, their end-users, and the designer-user relationship, puts extra emphasis on the complex nature of the situations to which an end-user design tool is applied and encourages the consideration of assumptions and mutual expectations that exist there.

The effectiveness of two-level personas in comparison to 'classical' individual personas is investigated in an exploratory empirical study presented in the second part of the paper. Two teams of graduate students were given the same design task in an early-design project. While the first group used three individual personas representing designer-users, the second group worked with two two-level personas. Although both groups actively used their personas, the results suggest more consensus between the members of the second group. They developed a clearer picture of the relationship between the designer-users and their end-users in the design task than the first group. This helped them, in particular, to develop more ideas on how their design tool could support designer-users in designing the navigation of their applications. While the effectiveness of two-level personas has to be investigated in further studies, this paper finishes with general implications of using two-level personas in the user-centered design approach.

BACKGROUND

Personas are user representations intended to establish empathy and understanding of the potential or actual users of interactive systems in designers. Personas work because they draw on the human ability to make predictions about a person's behavior based on a precise description of their background and goals [19]. The ubiquitous generative nature of personas makes them an effective tool for communication in (multidisciplinary) design teams [19]. The empathetic focus enabled by personas helps designers create clean and coherent systems [35] instead of systems "that supposedly fit everyone but in the end fit no one" [12]. This 'elastic user' problem became better understood through the persona concept.

Persona as Umbrella Term

Floyd et al. point out that there is an ongoing debate on the usefulness of the persona approach, which is hampered by the fact that it is considered as a single method that is either accepted or rejected [16]. The authors provide one of the few attempts to view the benefits and drawbacks of existing variants of the method in a more differentiated way. Seven persona types are identified, among them Cooperian initial and final personas [8], Pruitt-Grudin personas [38, 37, 19], and Norman's ad-hoc personas [35]. The persona types are characterized by a set of seven attributes concerning their empirical basis, the quality of the persona description, their permanence, and the intentions of their use. A similar approach is taken here, but instead of persona types, a set of dimensions and success criteria has been extracted from a broader range of literature, which includes conceptual work (e.g. [8, 9, 19, 38, 37]), critical reviews of the method (e.g. [7, 30, 45]), case studies (e.g. [41, 11, 20, 39]), and empirical studies on the effectiveness of personas (e.g. [3, 28, 31]). While persona variants can be described along the dimensions suggested above, the additional success criteria help to observe or assess effects of the use of the different persona approaches (see Table 1 for our framework). Our approach emphasizes that the persona method is not a panacea [30]. Rather, its application is influenced by the specific constraints of a design project, and that typically the project's goals and objectives can be supported to only a certain extent by persona use.

THE CONTEXTUALIZED PERSONA FRAMEWORK (CPF)

In this section, each of the dimensions we identified is discussed in more detail together with the success criteria. We start with the dimensions concerning the user representation.

Presentation Style

Persona descriptions are typically structured narratives, often accompanied with a picture, and sometimes with other visual material (e.g. [11]). The presentation style has a profound impact on the empathy with end users as experienced by the designers who use them (C1). According to Cooper [8] and Grudin and Pruitt [18], designers engage better with specific and precise descriptions that include personal details

Dimensions	Success Criteria
User Representation	- Empathy with users (C1)
Presentation style Empirical basis Structure and content	- Effectiveness for describing user groups (C2)
Practical Implementation	- Effectiveness for capturing design problems (C3)
Integration in the design process Involvement in creation and use Skills of persona users	- Effect on other design representations (C4) - Shared tool (C5) - Maintenance costs (C6)

Table 1. Dimensions and success criteria of persona usage.

than with aggregated user data. Studies suggest that even subtleties, such as the type of a portrait picture of a persona, have an impact (according to Long [28], photographs work better than illustrations). Nielsen criticizes that when personas are used, designers are often faced with flat character descriptions, but that these need to be 'rounded' [33]. Information about physiology (e.g. sex, age, appearance), sociology (e.g. occupation, education, home life), and psychology (e.g. ambitions, frustrations, attitudes to life) have to convey multidimensional characters that belong to and interact with a culture [33]. This rounded depiction is believable and evokes the designers' empathy and reasoning about plausible user behavior. In contrast, 'elastic personas' (describing almost anyone) fail to constrain the design space [22].

Narrative personas have their costs though (C6) and an ad-hoc persona is an example of a less detailed user description using bulleted key points, which, despite its sparseness, can still can be a useful temporary tool for some design activities (e.g., role-playing exercises [35]). Some authors further criticize that too much background information in personas may decrease the number of represented users (curse of dimensionality [7]) or that it may distract designers from actual design problems.

Empirical Basis

A persona models "a small portion of the potential user space" [7]. Existing approaches differ in how representative user groups are identified and how the link between empirical data and personas is documented. Originally, Cooper et al. used material from interviews and ethnographic studies to identify behavioral patterns from which an initial set of personas was constructed and then, in a next step, condensed to a manageable set of prioritized personas [9]. In [38], a large amount of qualitative and quantitative data is made accessible to all project members and used to generate personas. Persona segmentation can be based on different forms of purely quantitative analysis (e.g. [44, 25]) or on explicit assumptions about user groups [37, 13], or they can be constructed in an ad hoc manner [35]. The need for a better integration of quantitative and qualitative data in persona construction is demonstrated in [43].

The empirical basis of persona construction greatly influences the effectiveness of personas for describing user groups (C2). Generally, personas have a potential for stereotyping, which is more evident in descriptions based on designers' intuition rather than on user data [45]. Chapman and Milham point out that the accuracy of a persona is generally difficult to verify [7]. To mitigate this problem, Faily and Fléchais apply grounded theory and argumentation tools to document how empirical data and personas are related, and to make the construction process more traceable [14]. Checks with stakeholder representatives are suggested in [46].

Structure and Content

In order to address specific classes of users and design problems more adequately (C2, C3), several adaptations of the personas' structure and content are reported in the literature. Often, relevant domain-specific information have to be added to a single persona (e.g., clinical information in [47]). Typically, projects are supported by sets of typed personas (e.g., primary, secondary, and negative personas [9]) with each type having a different function in the design process. Personas in such sets are mostly not related and focus on descriptions of typical individual users [9]. There are a few exceptions. For example, Putnam et al. suggest creating *family personas* for a better understanding of water use and storage in their case study [39]. Here families, rather than individuals, are the unit of analysis. Matthews et al. [32] propose *collaborative personas* to better reflect the goals and needs of working groups in the context of collaborative workplace tools. A collaborative persona, in this approach, is the description of a whole working group including group and individual goals, group tasks, members and their roles, group work style, current tools and problems, and collaboration needs. Two-level personas, which will be introduced in the next section, are suggested capturing design concerns in the context of end-user development tools.

Integration in the Design Process

The persona method has to be integrated into existing design practices to have an effect on other design representations, and finally, on the product (C4). The interview study in [34] shows successful instances of persona use, but the usage described in [34] is not suitable for all design practices. If, for example, a company prefers rapid development of new technology, a reasonable integration of personas is almost impossible [42]. In most cases, the persona approach is complemented with scenarios[2] and other user-centered design approaches. "Personas come first and drive the construction of scenarios around them" [18]. The application of personas in requirements elicitation, exploration of design ideas, decision making, usability evaluation, or even the entire design lifecycle is reported in [12, 22, 17, 23, 10]. Of course, their long-term use increases the maintenance costs (C6), and as with any other artifact, there are unintended ways of using personas. For example, Rönkkö describes in [41] how personas

[2]E.g. in [20], 'persona' encompasses both personas and scenarios. All interviewees in [34] referred to personas and scenarios as a combined method.

were used not to inform the design process, but to justify its design rationale to other project members 'after the fact.'

Involvement in Creation and Use

The degree to which personas are a shared communication tool (C5) greatly depends on how the different stakeholders are involved in their creation and use. Blomquist and Arvola in the project they studied, considered the fact that personas were not created by the developer team, but by a separate team, as the main reason why personas never became a natural part of this project [3]. Grudin and Pruitt advise against 'grass roots' persona efforts by a few project members and recommend having all groups on board to increase the acceptance of the method [19]. In another study of a telecommunication company [42], it was shown that actors and interests beyond the borders of the development organization affect the (non-)employment of personas. Furthermore, the method should neither be misused "to maintain a 'safe' distance from the people we design for" [36] nor considered as a substitute for participatory design [4]. The application of personas in design processes with stakeholder participation is discussed in some case studies [11, 47].

Skills of Persona Users

Chapman and Milham ask what happens if the designers' own observations conflicts with a persona [7]. In [36], personas are compared with reality television which helps to avoid dealing with "the inevitable messiness of real people and real life." Elastic, promotional, and 'my mother' personas are mentioned as deceptive descriptions in [22]. Skilled designers consciously apply design tools such as personas to look at a design problem from different perspectives and to overcome inappropriate preconceptions that would otherwise leave their traces in other intermediate design representations and in the final product (C4). Their skills include the ability to identify with personas that are very different from themselves [34] and to recognize a 'bad' persona more easily. Buxton says about sketching (an essential activity in interaction design) "Both the creation and reading of sketches are specialized skills that distinguish designers from nondesigners, and even experienced designers from student designers" [6]. Similarly, the creation and reading of personas can be seen as specialized skills. The results in [34] suggest, for example, that personas created in companies that are new to the method are less coherent than those created from more experienced companies. The sharing of personas (C5) can be hampered or may need additional facilitation if design team members have different skill levels, as is the case in design processes with stakeholder participation. In [46], the researchers observed that the stakeholders who were asked to check the personas sometimes disagreed with each other with respect to the persona content that depended upon the specific work context.

In our framework, the suggested dimensions are not completely independent of one another, but together with the success criteria provide a vocabulary for planning and studying persona uses and for understanding their successes and failures. They also help to more precisely describe adaptations of the method and intended improvements. Two-level personas mainly adapt the structure and content of a persona description to be more adequate for designing end-user design tools.

TWO-LEVEL PERSONAS

While "historically, the users of computers were programmers" [21] interactive systems designers today typically develop for other users, and hence the design-use gap. User-centered design approaches, such as personas, support designers to better understand the users' goals and practices. Another approach to minimize the design-use gap is end-user development, but here the aim is to produce interactive systems that enable users to act as developers again. Such systems can range from simple customizable tools to end-user design tools for domain-specific applications. Two-level personas especially address the design of end-user design tools (in short design tools). We first describe this design context with its challenges, and then explain the idea of two-level personas for nested design spaces.

Context I: End-User Development

End-user development is defined as a "set of methods, techniques, and tools that allow users of software systems, who are acting as non-professional software developers, at some point to create, modify or extend a software artefact" [27]. Ko et al. point out that end-user developers differ from their professional counterparts in their goals, and that the term describes a role rather than a state of mind or a person's skills [24]. While professional developers sell and maintain their products, and typically work in teams with specialized members and with a structured development process in order to guarantee product quality, end-user developers do not consider software development as their primary task. They want to modify, extend or create systems for situated use and for achieving their original work goals. Consequently, they have less interest in an understanding of quality criteria [24]. The end-users' real goals and work habits have to be respected in end-user development [5]. Programming by example and visual programming are two techniques which can be implemented to make design tools usable [27]. Here developers have to find an appropriate compromise between the complexity and expressiveness of the 'building blocks' they offer to end-user developers to compose their designs [21]. Also designers have to guarantee a certain level of quality in the produced applications. This can be achieved by allowing end-user programmrs to design only some aspects of an application and generating the final program code automatically [5].

End user development weakens the boundary between 'professional designers' and 'end users' and thus extends the traditional notion of system development by acknowledging that user needs and usage situations are never fully predictable [15]. Fischer et al. suggest that designers should understand themselves as meta-designers and the users, who are more familiar with the specific application context, as co-designers [15]. In the following, the term 'nested design spaces' extends the design space concept to describe the role and responsibilities of meta-designers in the context of design tools.

Context II: Nested Design Spaces

In [29] a design space is understood as an "explicit representation of alternative design options, and the reasons for choosing among those options." A design space refers to "all possible design proposals that would be regarded as meaningful to use by some people in relevant contexts" [48]. Jones et al.

state that "in a design space, a particular design artifact (e.g., a prototype) is a point or region in the space, i.e., a combination of the underlying dimensions of the space" [22]. While some design space approaches focus on a structured representation of possible design ideas and their pros and cons (e.g. [29]) other perspectives emphasize how designers generate, explore and constrain a design space (e.g. [6, 2]). Although there is no common definition for design spaces, all existing explanations support the idea that design problems typically are 'wicked' problems with no definite formulation (no fully knowable dimensions) and with no best solution [40]. Every solution has (side) effects which cannot be fully predicted, but a 'good' solution can be achieved by generating alternative solutions and reasoning about their consequences in a given context. "Design is compromise" [6] and design spaces as "abstract, conceptual spaces in which designers navigate" [2] are considered a valuable tool for understanding and guiding design processes.

As for design tools, it is especially important that designers are aware of their design space, and that they understand that their users (the designer-users) move in their own design spaces. This understanding includes the end-users' needs, goals, and tasks, which cannot be seen in isolation from the needs, goals and tasks of the designer-users. Designers are faced with two nested designer-user relationships, and the way a design tool is shaped has a profound influence on how designer-users can shape the interaction which they design into tools for their end-users. In other words, designers are faced with what we call *nested design spaces*: their own more generic design space within which various design tools lie, and the more situated design spaces of the applications of end-users, which are partly constrained by the design tool used by the designer-user.

Concept and Illustration

Two-level personas take nested design spaces into consideration by applying the persona idea twice: once in a 'classical' way to model the users of the design tool (the designer-users), and then a second time to represent 'the users of the design tool users' (the end-users). A two-level persona consists of a set of individual personas: one *first-level* and a few *second-level* personas. It serves to model a class of people who *use* a design tool in order to *design* applications for situated use. Designers have to consider the designer-users' needs and goals as well as the needs and goals of their end-users represented by the second-level personas in order to build the design tool in a responsible way.

Figure 1 contrasts the two-level persona approach with 'classical' personas to better clarify the suggested unit of analysis for end-user design tools. In contrast to common persona descriptions, a two-level persona additionally contains hints about shared practices, mutual expectations and attitudes of the first-level and the second-level personas from their individual perspectives. The designers, in their role as meta-designers, are supported by the explicit representation of designer-users and end-users. The fragmented description of the designer-user relationship between first-level and second-level personas from individual points of view prevents designers from developing an oversimplified and one-sided

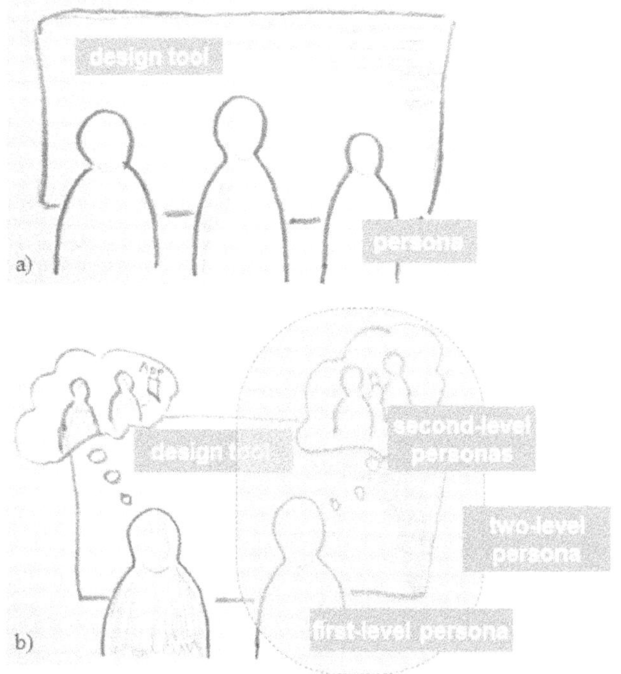

Figure 1. Sketches of a 'classical' and a two-level persona approach to design a design tool: a) individual personas representing three groups of designer-users, b) two-level personas representing two groups of designer-users, their end-users, and designer-user relationships.

picture of this relationship. This, in turn, may help them to avoid premature design decisions (whether made consciously or unconsciously) that unnecessarily constrains the design spaces of the designer-users. We come back to this point in the exploratory study presented later.

To illustrate two-level personas, we revisit the example design tool for mobile data collection (MDC) and the persona *Mary* from the introduction. The MDC design tool is intended to support designer-users such as researchers and teachers to conduct in-situ data collections. In this case, we refer to the designer-users as *questioners* and to the users of their created apps (e.g., study participants and students) as *respondents*. Figure 2 shows a two-level extension of *Mary*. *Ben* and *Paul* are both nine year old students of Mary's.

Ben's persona fragment: *Ben's parents have a small farm and he takes the bus to school. He likes to be outside and in the workshop of his father, asking him questions about what he is doing. Ben's parents have given him a simple mobile phone to call them if the bus is too late or if he gets sick at school. It doesn't bother Ben too much that he can't really compete with the other boys in his class with their smartphones and games. One of these boys is Paul.*

Paul's persona fragment: *Paul's home is not far away from school and his friends often come to his home to play computer games. He has two much older sisters. His father runs his own business and has not much time for him, but at least he buys him everything he wants. Recently, Paul let his smartphone drop into water, but within three days he had a new one. Paul finds school a bit boring. When his mother asked*

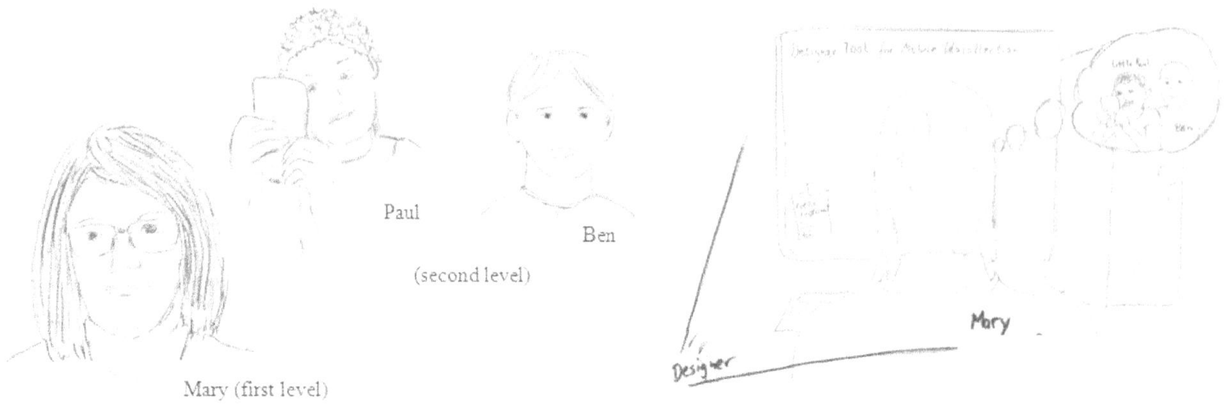

Figure 2. Portraits of the two-level persona example (left) are used to illustrate nested design spaces (right) to be explored by designers.

him after the last parent-teacher interview why he sometimes forgets to do his homework he complained about it. But today their teacher Mary told them about a two-week experiment on cress cultures they would soon conduct at home. She said that they could use mobile phones to send her their daily observations.

Collectively, all of the individual descriptions support the designers to understand how the MDC design tool should be designed to be usable by questioners, to know what the produced apps should be like to be usable by respondents, and, above all, to know how the MDC design tool could influence interactions between questioners and respondents. In the example, Paul may wonder what happens if he forgets to send a daily protocol about his cress culture. Can he do it on a later day and if so will Mary be able to detect it? The description of Paul helps the designer to think about Mary's design space more clearly. E.g., in some situations, she may want to check whether her students send their observations every day, in others she may want to enforce it or be more generous.

EXPLORATORY STUDY OF TWO-LEVEL PERSONAS

The last part of this paper presents an exploratory study. Empirical work on personas is currently dominated by ethnographic studies [3, 17], case studies [42, 12, 4], and interviews [31, 34]. A short-term comparative study is found in [23]. Our study design is similar to that of Long's study with student teams [28], which follows the suggestion made in [7]: "Assign multiple teams to design the same product, where some teams use personas and some don't. [Then ask] which teams create products that are more usable?" However, in contrast to [28], our goal was to compare effects of using 'classical' individual personas and two-level personas on the design of end-user design tools.

Method and Participants

Two teams of four and five members respectively, were tasked with developing ideas for the MDC design tool discussed in the previous section. Both teams applied personas in a comparable way, except that Team 1 used three independent individual personas and Team 2 used two first-level personas (each with two second-level personas). This situation is depicted in Figure 1. The teams did not conduct user research on their own. The need for the MDC design tool was motivated by the needs of two groups of users: researchers interested in conducting in-situ data collections of varied types [1], and teachers interested in developing similar tools for students to enhance their learning. The same usage situations for the tool were mentioned in both groups. Validation steps included a small amount of Internet research on the smartphone behaviors of younger kids and the participation of two graduate student teachers in a design meeting. The student teachers were familiar with the design task and personas.

The project's design exercises were integrated into two separate user-centred design courses in the summer semester of 2013. All participants were graduate students with a technical background (computer science, business informatics, computational engineering). They had experience in programming and software engineering from other student projects, internships, and jobs, but no prior education in user-centred design. The meetings were accompanied by lectures on personas, scenarios, sketching and prototyping. Team members were also taught about end-user development and design spaces (see previous sections) to create a common understanding of the specifics of the design task. They were not being graded nor judged on their performance. To the best of our knowledge the teams had no contact with each other. Once the teams were introduced to the design task, they each held six meetings (from May 2013 to early July 2013) with a comparable structure and content lasting 90 minutes each. At the end of this series of meetings, team members were asked to write down thoughts about their experience and their general understanding of the benefits and limitations of personas, which they did at home. Both teams developed their personas in the first two meetings[3]. The next four design meetings were organized as follows.

- *Meeting 3:* Confirmation of persona narratives, brainstorming with first sketches and scenario ideas, participation of student teacher.
- *Meeting 4:* Asking, How does the MDC design tool support the design of MDC forms (app structure)?: individual sketching, sharing of generated ideas, building consensus.

[3] The two-level persona *Mary* from the previous section is based on material from Team 2 of this experiment.

- *Meeting 5:* Asking, How does the MDC design tool support the design of MDC navigations?: discussion, scenario ideas, sketching.
- *Meeting 6:* Transition to paper-prototyping using scenarios.

Choice of the Design Task

The MDC design task was chosen for several reasons. First, the MDC design tool belongs to the considered class of design problems. Second, an early-design task was chosen because the study was conducted in an educational setting with inexperienced designers. Jones et al. point out that personas can be used to advantage in such settings to aid in the exploration of design spaces [22]. In order to compare the two persona approaches, it was important that the persona approaches worked well for both teams and the results of Jones et al. suggest this to be the case. And third, the domain of questionnaire design (a major component of the MDC tool) is well-known to a common audience and there are standardized elements. This meant it was relatively easy to find a first set of 'building blocks' for the questioners' design language and therefore team members could focus on usability aspects of the MDC design tool. But, it also meant the designers needed to overcome preconceptions and had to explore new forms of interactions between questioners and respondents using mobile devices. How could personas help?

Role of Experimenters

The experiment was conducted by both of the authors. They were familiar with the design task and had applied it before in a similar design exercise. At the beginning of each meeting, one experimenter summarized the previous meeting and set the focus of the current one. Experimenters only intervened in team discussions to make decisions or 'delay' discussed issues if they were less relevant for the agreed focus. Teams were also provided with narrative forms of personas and scenarios and with 'generic elements' for paper prototyping. This material was specifically based on each team's ideas. The 'generic elements' meant that created artifacts were comparable in its style.

Limitations

The study has an exploratory character, but employed only two small teams of novice designers. The results cannot be generalized nor can they transferred to other conditions, such as real projects which are more complex. Further research is needed here. In this study it was important to engender an active engagement of both design teams with their personas. This focus and the guidance of the experimenters have biased the results on the one hand. But, on the other hand, a comparative experiment was possible and the test design used was capable of demonstrating whether, at what points, and how two-level personas added value during the observed design meetings.

Data Collection and Analysis

Data collection included all created artifacts (notes, personas, all kinds of sketches, scenarios, paper prototypes), note-taking during all meetings, audio recordings of meeting 4 and 5, and video recordings of meeting 6. A first informal analysis was conducted in parallel to the design meetings to inform the guidance of the experimters (see the experimenters' role).

The recordings were partially transcribed and a subsequent analysis focused on whether and how the personas had been used in intra-team communications and how they influenced a team's design activities. The development or assessment of an idea was related to a team's persona use if a persona was explicitly mentioned or if a team member played the role of a persona in the direct discussion of this issue.

Results

In general both design teams actively used the personas they had developed in the first two meetings. In meeting 3, the teams discussed the complexity of the apps that could be created with the MDC design tool (see, e.g., Figure 3). We expected diverse question types for constructing MDC forms (app structure) and options for designing an MDC navigation (app navigation). Both teams developed design ideas for supporting their personas. For example, first-level persona *Mary* (Team 2) has a clear idea of the conceptual structure of her form for the cress experiment but needs help to 'translate' it into a digital version. She starts with an example design. *Mark*, the other first-level persona, explores what question types the MDC design tool offers. Similarly, Team 1 was thinking about templates for persona *Mrs. König* and a blank working area for persona *Georgios*. Team 2 used their second-level personas only in a few cases. While team 1 could not directly address the app users (respondents) using personas, they did it in an indirect way (e.g., "The student would look for the flower now.").

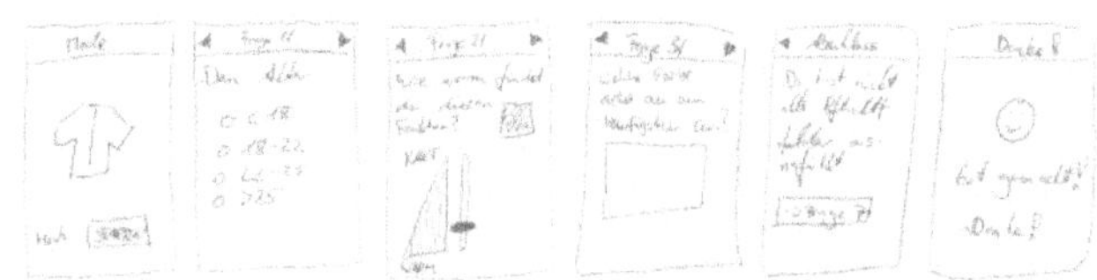

Figure 3. ***Mark*** **uses the MDC design tool: sketch of the resulting app (Team 2).**

Figure 4 indicates that both teams arrived at similar design solutions in meeting 4 where they discussed the user interface part of the MDC design tool that would allow end users to design MDC forms. Their solutions contained four main parts: (1) an overview of the app structure (MDC form), (2) a working area, (3) a toolbar with predefined elements, and (4) a preview area. Personas were used less, but they supported the discussion of different drag & drop solutions, wizards, and templates. The different persona approaches had no notable effect on discussions and sketched ideas in meetings 3 and 4.

Designing MDC Navigations

In meeting 5, the teams generated and assessed ideas on how to support the design of MDC navigations. Both groups discussed optional questions, progress bars, techniques for back and forth navigation, and issues related to submitting data. However, Team 2 used their second-level personas intensively. For example, *Paul* wants to be able to access previous forms and information about submission details, *Lisa* wants to have an overview of question groups to jump to the interesting ones, and for *Tom* it should be possible to open additional information relating to questions. In Team 1, there were statements such as "Should it be possible for [persona]

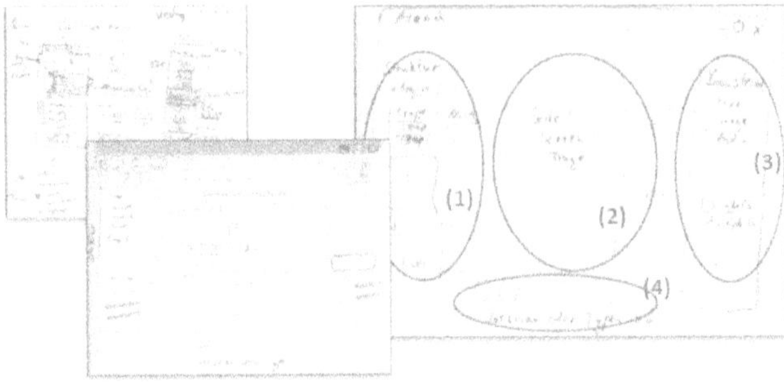

Figure 4. Left: Team 2 and Team 1 had similar ideas in meeting 4. Right: 'summary' that was presented to both teams in their meeting 5.

Figure 5. Transition to prototyping (left Team 2, right Team 1).

Sebastian Horn to say 'The students have to complete one part before answering another'?" It was more difficult for this team to directly address needs of the respondents; the 'elastic respondent' symptom was observed in their discussion.

Team 2 created richer scenarios (see next subsection) and developed a deeper understanding of designer-user relationships by reasoning about their two-level personas. The team generated significantly more design ideas concerning the design of the MDC navigations than Team 1. For example, when discussing how respondents submit their data, one member of Team 2 suggested that all responses should be immediately sent to the questioner. The advantage for the first-level persona *Mark* would be that he would have all the data, even those from respondents who later cancel his questionnaire. In addition, the questioners would not need to care about this issue because the tool could automatically add it to the apps. Other members used the second-level persona *Paul* to argue against this design choice as the only option for the first-level personas. Many on-line survey tools behave in the way suggested by the first team member. He had used such a tool himself and did not question this 'natural' behavior.

Paper Prototyping

The transition to paper prototyping in the last design meeting was informed by two narrative scenarios, which were elicited from previous meetings of each team. In contrast to the scenarios of Team 1, that of Team 2 revealed perspectives from respondents (second-level personas) that should be understood by the first-level persona while designing a MDC app. For example, second-level persona *Ben* was sick and started his cress experiment one week later. His app 'told' him after a week "Thank you for your participation" and he couldn't complete his experiment.

While going through a scenario and developing the prototype, all members of Team 2 referred, in their communication, to the first-level and second-level personas. Team 1 first assigned the persona role to one member and later all team members used the personas in their discussion. We observed that it was easier for Team 2 to find consensus and that it took less time for them go through single steps of a scenario in order to refine their prototype. Their communication also revealed that they had a more elaborated view on how the MDC design tool could influence the interaction space between questioners and respondents. For example, they used all individual descriptions of the two-level persona *Mary* (see Figure 2) to think about how the design of a data submission process should be supported by the MDC design tool. They asked themselves whether *Mary*, when using the tool, would take into consideration that a student could get sick (*Ben*) or could forget to send data (*Paul*) and decided to offer a send-button element with an attached menu, which helps questioners to explicitly think about the submission process.

Final Survey

The final survey confirmed that the participants were engaged with their personas although some were skeptical in the beginning. Some participants said that they had been thinking about user groups and their characteristics in previous projects, but had never thought about their motives or attitudes. This design exercise, though, had influenced their ideas and decisions. Two members of Team 2 referred to the usefulness of second-level personas. Others mentioned benefits and limitations that coincided with those in literature.

Discussion

The results suggest that the two-level persona approach added value to the design process. In both groups, personas aided consensus building with respect to the goals and behavior of the questioners (the designer-users in the study). However, it was more difficult for Team 1 to find a consensus about the respondents (the end-users in the study). Although they used their personas to refer to respondents (e.g., "Sebastian Horn wants that the students..."), they never viewed the behavior of an app from a respondent's point of view in their communication. Especially in the last two meetings, Team 2 used their explicit representations of the respondents to discuss the relationship between questioners and respondents and possible usage scenarios for the MDC design tool.

The results also indicate that two-level personas more powerfully support designers to uncover their own preconceptions (see, e.g., meeting 5 in the results section). Team 2 became more aware of their role as meta-designers and how they shape the interaction space between questioners and respondents. In particular, they generated more design ideas for supporting questioners when designing the navigation of their data collection apps.

Comparison with Related Approaches

'Served' personas mentioned in [9] represent people who are not users of the system under consideration, but who are directly affected by its use (e.g., patients treated by a nurse using a medical device with a complex user interface). However, served personas are treated like secondary personas and they are not related to personas representing the 'serving people'. Similar to our approach, collaborative personas [32] contain sets of individual descriptions but for a different purpose. They are typically less detailed, model roles, and are embedded in the description of a working group archetype to support the design of collaborative tools (see CPF section). Neither served nor collaborative personas explicitly consider the relationship between designer-users and end-users.

Cooper et al. recommended designers describe three types of user goals for each persona: experience goals, end goals, and life goals [9] with the latter referring to long-term desires, motivations, and self-image attributes. Still, Massanari criticizes that personas' "overemphasis on 'figuring out' the user and their immediate needs" (manifested in the term 'user research') which supports the conceptual separation between the user and designer and makes the people using technology subject to the design [30]. Personas can easily reinforce the image of users as consumers [45]. Two-level personas may help to overcome this narrow view and put people using (design) tools into a wider context with more than one voice representing the broader group. This makes the people's long-term goals more plausible and relevant for design because they describe people in relation to others. Wright and McCarthy refer to the potential of novels to express the changing and developing nature of experience with technology from multiple perspectives of different characters with different value systems [49]. Although the two-level persona approach is a much less sophisticated approach it supports this idea.

SUMMARY AND FUTURE WORK

The paper provides a discussion tool for different persona approaches (the contextualized persona framework). In the context of end-user development, we suggest using two-level personas so that designers can better understand people in their role as designer-users and also to understand their end-users. The approach mainly adapts the structure and content of a persona description to convey the different perspectives on designer-user relationships, but it also requires changes along other dimensions (e.g., an empirical basis). In future work, we would like to investigate whether and how two-level personas can be employed in participatory design processes not only to increase the understanding of the designers, but also the understanding of users in their different roles. This is particularly important in application contexts with less visible dependencies.

ACKNOWLEDGMENTS

Our thanks go to the study participants. We are very grateful to Judith Brown for her insightful comments and valuable suggestions.

REFERENCES

1. Batalas, N., and Markopoulos, P. Considerations for Computerized in Situ Data Collection Platforms. In *Proc. of EICS '12*, ACM (2012), 231–236.
2. Biskjaer, M. M., Dalsgaard, P., and Halskov, K. A constraint-based understanding of design spaces. In *Proc. of DIS '14*, ACM (2014), 453–462.
3. Blomquist, A., and Arvola, M. Personas in Action: Ethnography in an Interaction Design Team. In *Proc. of NordiCHI '02*, ACM (2002), 197–200.
4. Bødker, S., Christiansen, E., Nyvang, T., and Zander, P.-O. Personas, People and Participation: Challenges from the Trenches of Local Government. In *Proc. of PDC '12*, ACM (2012), 91–100.
5. Burnett, M. What Is End-User Software Engineering and Why Does It Matter? In *Proc. of IS-EUD'09*, IS-EUD '09, Springer-Verlag (2009), 15–28.
6. Buxton, B. *Sketching User Experiences: Getting the Design Right and the Right Design*. Morgan Kaufmann Publishers Inc., 2007.
7. Chapman, C. N., and Milham, R. P. The personas' new clothes: methodological and practical arguments against a popular method. In *The Human Factors and Ergonomics Society Annual Meeting* (2006), 634–636.
8. Cooper, A. *The Inmates Are Running the Asylum*. Macmillan Publishing Co., Inc., 1999.
9. Cooper, A., and Reimann, R. *About Face 3.0: The Essentials of Interaction Design*, 3rd revised ed. Wiley & Sons, 2007.
10. Dharwada, P., Greenstein, J. S., Gramopadhye, A. K., and Davis, S. J. A Case Study on Use of Personas in Design and Development of an Audit Management System. *Human Factors and Ergonomics Society Annual Meeting* (2007), 469–473.
11. Dotan, A., Maiden, N. A. M., Lichtner, V., and Germanovich, L. Designing with Only Four People in Mind? - A Case Study of Using Personas to Redesign a Work-Integrated Learning Support System. In *INTERACT (2)*, vol. 5727 of *LNCS*, Springer (2009), 497–509.
12. Eriksson, E., Artman, H., and Swartling, A. The Secret Life of a Persona: When the Personal Becomes Private. In *Proc. of CHI '13*, ACM (2013), 2677–2686.
13. Faily, S., and Fléchais, I. The Secret Lives of Assumptions: Developing and Refining Assumption Personas for Secure System Design. In *Proc. of HCSE'10*, Springer-Verlag (2010), 111–118.
14. Faily, S., and Fléchais, I. Persona Cases: A Technique for Grounding Personas. In *Proc. of CHI '11*, ACM (2011), 2267–2270.
15. Fischer, G., Giaccardi, E., Ye, Y., Sutcliffe, A. G., and Mehandjiev, N. Meta-design: a manifesto for end-user development. *Commun. ACM 47*, 9 (2004), 33–37.
16. Floyd, I. R., Jones, M. C., and Twidale, M. B. Resolving Incommensurable Debates: A Preliminary Identification of Persona Kinds, Attributes, and Properties. *Artifact: Journal of Virtual Design 2*, 1 (2008), 12–26.
17. Friess, E. Personas and Decision Making in the Design Process: An Ethnographic Case Study. In *Proc. of CHI '12*, ACM (2012), 1209–1218.

18. Grudin, J. Why personas work: The psychological evidence. In *The Persona Lifecycle: Keeping People in Mind Throughout Product Design* [37].

19. Grudin, J., and Pruitt, J. Personas, participatory design and product development: An infrastructure for engagement. In *Proc. of PDC'02* (2002), 144–161.

20. Gudjonsdottir, R., and Lindquist, S. Personas and scenarios: Design tool or a communication device? In *Proc. 8th Int. Conf. on the Design of Cooperative Systems* (2008).

21. Hague, R., Blackwell, A. F., and Robinson, P. End-User Programming in the Networked Home. In *Equator IRC Workshop on Ubiquitous Computing in Domestic Environments* (2001).

22. Jones, M. C., Floyd, I. R., and Twidale, M. B. Teaching Design with Personas. In *Proc. of HCIEd* (2008).

23. Judge, T., Matthews, T., and Whittaker, S. Comparing Collaboration and Individual Personas for the Design and Evaluation of Collaboration Software. In *Proc. of CHI '12*, ACM (2012), 1997–2000.

24. Ko, A. J., Abraham, R., Beckwith, L., Blackwell, A., Burnett, M., Erwig, M., Scaffidi, C., Lawrance, J., Lieberman, H., Myers, B., Rosson, M. B., Rothermel, G., Shaw, M., and Wiedenbeck, S. The state of the art in end-user software engineering. *ACM Comput. Surv. 43*, 3 (2011), 21:1–21:44.

25. Laporte, L., Slegers, K., and Grooff, D. D. Using correspondence analysis to monitor the persona segmentation process. In *NordiCHI'12* (2012), 265–274.

26. Larson, R., and Csikszentmihalyi, M. The Experience Sampling Method. *New Directions for Methodology of Social and Behavioral Science 15* (1983), 41–56.

27. Lieberman, H., Paterno, F., and Wulf, V., Eds. *End-User Development*. Kluwer/ Springer, 2006.

28. Long, F. Real or Imaginary: The effectiveness of using personas in product design. In *Proc. of the IES Conference 2009* (2009), 1–10.

29. MacLean, A., Young, R. M., Bellotti, V. M. E., and Moran, T. P. Questions, options, and criteria: elements of design space analysis. *Hum.-Comput. Interact. 6*, 3 (1991), 201–250.

30. Massanari, A. Designing for imaginary friends: information architecture, personas and the politics of user-centered design. *New Media & Society 12*, 3 (2010), 401–416.

31. Matthews, T., Judge, T., and Whittaker, S. How Do Designers and User Experience Professionals Actually Perceive and Use Personas? In *Proc. of CHI '12*, ACM (2012), 1219–1228.

32. Matthews, T., Whittaker, S., Moran, T., and Yuen, S. Collaboration Personas: A New Approach to Designing Workplace Collaboration Tools. In *Proc. of CHI '11*, ACM (2011), 2247–2256.

33. Nielsen, L. From User to Character: An Investigation into User-descriptions in Scenarios. In *Proc. of DIS '02*, ACM (2002), 99–104.

34. Nielsen, L., and Hansen, K. S. Personas is applicable: a study on the use of personas in denmark. In *CHI* (2014), 1665–1674.

35. Norman, D. Ad-Hoc Personas & Empathetic Focus. In *The Persona Lifecycle: Keeping People in Mind Throughout Product Design* [37].

36. Portigal, S. TRUE TALES: Persona Non Grata. *interactions 15*, 1 (Jan. 2008), 72–73.

37. Pruitt, J., and Adlin, T. *The Persona Lifecycle: Keeping People in Mind Throughout Product Design*. Morgan Kaufmann Publishers Inc., 2005.

38. Pruitt, J., and Grudin, J. Personas: Practice and Theory. In *Proc. of the 2003 Conference on Designing for User Experiences*, DUX '03, ACM (2003), 1–15.

39. Putnam, C., Kolko, B., and Wood, S. Communicating About Users in ICTD: Leveraging HCI Personas. In *Proc. of ICTD '12*, ACM (2012), 338–349.

40. Rittel, H. W. J., and Webber, M. M. Dilemmas in a General Theory of Planning. *Policy Sciences 4* (1973), 155–169.

41. Rönkkö, K. An Empirical Study Demonstrating How Different Design Constraints, Project Organization and Contexts Limited the Utility of Personas. In *HICSS*, IEEE Computer Society (2005).

42. Rönkkö, K., Hellman, M., Kilander, B., and Dittrich, Y. Personas is Not Applicable: Local Remedies Interpreted in a Wider Context. In *Proc. of PDC'04*, ACM (2004), 112–120.

43. Siegel, D. A. The Mystique of Numbers: Belief in Quantitative Approaches to Segmentation and Persona Development. In *Proc. of CHI '10* (2010), 4721–4732.

44. Sinha, R. Persona Development for Information-rich Domains. In *Proc. of CHI EA '03*, ACM (2003), 830–831.

45. Turner, P., and Turner, S. Is stereotyping inevitable when designing with personas? *Design Studies 32*, 1 (2011), 30–44.

46. Vincent, C. J., and Blandford, A. The challenges of delivering validated personas for medical equipment design. *Applied Ergonomics, in press* (2014).

47. Wärnestal, P., Svedberg, P., and Nygren, J. Co-constructing Child Personas for Health-promoting Services with Vulnerable Children. In *Proc. of CHI '14* (2014), 3767–3776.

48. Westerlund, B. *Design Space Exploration - co-operative creation of proposals for desired interactions with future artefacts*. Dissertation, Kungliga Tekniska högskolan, Stockholm, 2009.

49. Wright, P., and McCarthy, J. The value of the novel in designing for experience. In *Future Interaction Design*, A. Pirhonen, P. Saariluoma, H. Isomki, and C. Roast, Eds. Springer London, 2005, 9–30.

The Work of Mad Men That Makes the Methods of Math Men Work: Practically Occasioned Segment Design

Michael F Clarke
Google, Inc.
Mountain View, CA
clarkem@google.com

ABSTRACT
This study concerns the practical methods used to design segmentation models for digital advertising. I illuminate some of the collaborative activities workers rely on to create these web analytics based groupings. This work remains overlooked as the popularity of automation and statistical methods for segmenting customers continues to grow. I explain some of the ways the advertising customer is present as a background expectancy while workers make segment composition decisions. This approach is meant to complement established evaluative, technical, and statistical methods used to create segments and personas in design and marketing. This may inspire similar approaches to designing for specific groups of people while working with large data sets. Incorporating these customer-orienting practices in design and advertising processes could lead to novel approaches for both segment targeting and customer relationship management (CRM) software.

Author Keywords
Ethnomethodology; Segmentation; Personas; Ethnography; Design.

ACM Classification Keywords
H.5.3. [Information interfaces and presentation] (e.g., HCI): Group and Organization Interfaces - *Computer supported cooperative work*

INTRODUCTION

"Until now the province of nerds, the automated buying and selling of online ads is hitting the advertising industry mainstream"[10]..."Forget Mad Men, advertising now belongs to the Math Men'" [1]. These excerpts reflect new sentiment in the advertising industry. This includes stakeholder desire for an efficient path from the conception of an advertising idea to reaching a target market with a campaign. This desire is increasingly satisfied by mathematics and technology. Contemporary advertising has welcomed technocrats from mathematics and engineering with open arms. Many in the industry have substituted their faith in human sensory ability (interpretation and intuition) for algorithms, automation and programmatic execution.

CHI 2015, April 18–23, 2015, Seoul, Republic of Korea.

http://dx.doi.org/10.1145/2702123.2702493

Digital advertisements are created, launched to segments of the population, and optimized for performance. This is achieved in part through selective computer algorithms that operate with speed and scale. This phenomenon, and its impact on advertising organizations was recently described by advertising executive Jay Sears in an Adweek Magazine Interview: "It used to be that-and still, in many parts of the business, it is-that inventory was sold in gigantic blocks, and when you broke the block down, you'd find that part of it really worked for the situation you were in and part of it didn't. The magic of programmatic is that it's about de-averaging and it's about data...The automation of the buying and selling of advertising is inevitable. You only need to look at history. Look at the stock market and the evolution of trading-look where it started. It started with over-the-counter stocks, and now every blue-chip name is automated" [25]. Specialists managing these efforts are increasingly prevalent in key areas of advertising: "Well, when you look at a holding company, you're talking about tens upon tens and maybe hundreds of thousands of people around the world, and if you listen to how some of the trading desk people talk, they're organizing businesses around this march to automation" [25].

Advertising technology has enabled granular capabilities for crafting segments that are addressable and revisable. It has also provided opportunities for real-time performance feedback. These capabilities were traditionally the privilege of specialized professions such as actuaries and demographers. Professionally, these developments may be as significant as ubiquitous computing was for the workplace, when it became the catalyst for changing how we work with one another: "moving out of the control room" [11]. Here, ubiquitous computing and connectivity are combined and result in a unique form of data science applicability for everyday work.

I argue this rise of advertising technology, which in many ways flies in the face of more intuitive practices, is not a zero sum game. Despite clear changes since the days of mad men, advertising workers and the clients they serve are not simply whisked away in a technocratic ocean of automation, left to passively consume recommendations and reports from the ad technology they invest in. The relationship between the corpus of advertising specialist workplace knowledge and their collaborative activities deserves close attention. I am interested in the local practices used to build up and deploy segments of users as a feature of a digital workplace while orienting to customer issues. I argue this must not be hidden by the gloss of automation and describe how the socio-cultural constitution of segments progresses through technical workplace talk. I recommend accounting for interpretive, customer orienting practices when designing segment targeting and CRM software.

RELATED WORK

The design literature [3,4,5,17], economics literature and marketing literature [2,16,19,23,24] has dealt extensively with finding, evaluating, and constructing optimal groups of people for business performance. Frequently the latter is accomplished tactically through advertising. Common descriptions of groupings include: audiences, personas, and market segments. Highly developed topics in the space include optimal attribute or base selection frameworks and techniques (pricing, psychological, demographic, lifestyle, likelihood to purchase, product usage and consumption), the objectivity and validity of a broad swath of segmentation techniques, and segment driven meta-narratives on consumption [7,26]. However, no one has examined the practical reasoning involved in creating and deploying segments based on digital analytics for the purposes of advertising, or as in CSCW "the work that make the methods work" [9]. Nor has anyone applied those methods to design better advertiser workplace technology and practices. Much of the previous literature treats segmenting the population as a technical problem, of selecting the optimal techniques and statistical methods for product, pricing and advertising success and the best way of placing users into categories. My approach sought people working together in their everyday advertising environment to construct and deploy segments as features of an advertising workplace, and learning from this process to better design technology and organizations to support the work.

THE STUDY

The study describes how an advertising provider's workplace organizes itself to design, manage and advertise to digital segments. I looked at segments as a course of action and asked: what does someone really have to undertake to "do" segmentation successfully? I described some seen but unnoticed ways diverse teams discuss and validate segments together. This includes how they organize their knowledge and "talk" about segments in a particular way, while systematically orienting to the customer as a scenic feature. In other words, customers are referred to, and work concerns them, not for their own sake, rather their importance to the work in progress [12]. This lens enables teams with diverse skillsets and perspectives to use segment talk as a method to achieve common ground. Revealing some of the ways this work is achieved cross-functionally provides useful design direction.

To understand how workers accomplish segmentation, you need to understand the local analytic practices they employ. In the midst of algorithms and automation I considered segmentation work "as a practically occasioned form of everyday activity" [9] rather than work driven by abstract, predetermined facts and processes passively consumed by the customers and publishers creating the segments.

In short, I described some of the practical methods that typically go unnoticed when technical segmentation work is undertaken, and the mundane availability of those methods to one another in the workplace. That is, the "off script" methods of doing this work. Specifically, I showed that what professionals collectively say about the composition of a segment, while drawing on a corpus of specialized workplace knowledge, in turn contextualizes how they discursively orient to those segments.

Theory

I employed an ethnomethodologically informed ethnography to describe these practices. This method is effective for appropriating local practices for systems design direction and product development, and has been influential in HCI and CSCW [18].

Ethnomethodology turns to *how* work takes place and workers achieve social activity in concert, rather than describing *why* the work takes place [8]. This approach complements previous literature where contributors practice segmentation themselves.

The practice of constructing segments for digital advertising is as much a design issue as a research issue. Following Dourish [6] and Randall, Harper and Rouncefield [18] I produced a description of the workplace that informs design "by identifying the problems and concerns which a system has to accommodate if it is to effectively support work activities" [18]. This approach paid particular attention to the challenge of how key players in the workplace collaboratively orient to a segmentation setting and one another to produce successful advertising programs. It did not draw off of a social theory; rather it helped describe the practical reasoning happening between the workplace members *in situ*. Thus, I produced a description of local segmentation work, and the resultant organizational and technical design direction driven by that action. Here, the work *is* the design and ethnomethodology provides a description of that work.

Aligning with Dourish [6] I do not assume that designers and engineers work in a domain as deterministic, autonomous bodies. This fluid advertising setting is an example of how design need not be a separate entity. Instead, I subscribe to the notion that segment designs are "local adaptations and appropriations in particular social and cultural contexts"[6]. Thus, the direction for segment design is an outcome of the advertising setting under examination, not a constitutive nexus of advertising technology and ethnographic studies. I presume that this ethnomethodologically informed ethnography of doing segment work allows us to adapt to an organizational context and work practices that have been left unexamined.

Ethnomethodologically informed ethnography is well suited for complex work settings where the decision of who and what to study is confounded. This setting is complicated by workers' widespread reliance on technology. This includes ubicomp, connectivity, and most importantly digital analytics applications enabling employees with diverse technical aptitudes to do data science work.

Previous workplace studies literature has focused on adjacent themes with a similar methodological approach. This work includes: Sharrock and Anderson's [22] description of the taken for granted, systematic ways users are discussed, and used as a resource to create "design worlds", Martin, O'Neill, and Randall's [15] description of the artful accomplishment of creativity in design and Greiffenhagen, Mair, and Sharrock's [9] "methodography" of the working practices of statistical modeling within a group of social scientists.

The unique setting I described draws on two elements of previous work:

First, examining social science work outside of the academic and institutional domain and the undocumented practices of developing statistical models to accomplish this work: similar to Greiffenhagen et al [9] I described a cross section of (pseudo) social scientists plying their trade with previously inaccessible types, amounts and ubiquity of analytics available as a part of their everyday working world (rather than the privileged domain of demographers, actuaries or social scientists and their institutions). These workers were not officially referred to as social scientists, possessed different skills, and had different responsibilities.

Second, describing technical design work (segmentation) undertaken in light of both user and customer concerns: Martin et al [15] show how creative designers orient to the customer to accomplish their work and Sharrock and Anderson [22] describe how designers invoke the user as a scenic feature. I demonstrated how technical design work reflexively occurs between both a subject and party to design.

Method
The ethnographic observation for this study occurred over 15 hours of internal Google meetings at a regional office. The study involved 49 participants over the course of 3 months. The setting included a mix of engineers, client facing sales staff, technical analysts and marketing personnel. Typical meeting times ranged from 30 minutes to 1 hour. The topics of the meetings were either preparations for client meetings, or brainstorming sessions for developing advertising programs. Conversations were transcribed. Interviews were held for clarification purposes. Next, I conducted an ethnomethodological analysis.

Setting
I studied an organization within Google responsible for packaging and selling Internet advertising and related consulting services. The work I observed involved employees using various algorithms and related technology to deliver advertising to segments of users according to a diverse set of attributes. The work involved two functions: 1. Analysis, construction and optimization of segments and targeting and 2. Advertising client management.

In the first category, technical workers were located organizationally between client work and engineering work. Client management personnel called upon them when deeper technical product expertise was required for an advertiser project. Periodically, these analysts had direct client contact, however they most frequently worked with Product Management and Client Management teams internally. They advised on selecting and refining attributes to deliver advertising to particular groups of people and in highly technical cases would help the client management team implement solutions. Much of this work involved "translating" advertiser requirements into technical capabilities, analytical models and associated recommendations. The teams had several technologies at their disposal to reach groups of consumers with video, banner, application and search advertisements. For example, if an advertiser asked to display their brand to loyalists who use their mobile device to purchase televisions, a technical analyst could take those requirements and construct a plan to reach those users online by configuring the tools at their disposal. The analyst would select from a myriad of technical targeting options (e.g. sports lovers), advertising inventory options and format options (video advertisements in the mobile YouTube app). These were features enabled en masse by engineers; however, they require a significant amount of technical working knowledge to combine and execute. Thus, it was not uncommon for analysts hold engineering or advanced mathematics degrees. In many cases segmentation recommendations occurred prior to an advertiser request, where the technical analyst proactively constructed a model for consideration. These analytical models were prepared using various Google services and databases related to the advertiser's business:

1. *Google Adwords or Doubleclick for Advertisers:* online advertising services that allow advertisers to place and manage advertising according to a multitude of targeting options

2. *Analytical tools including Google Analytics:* a web analytics and reporting service for an advertiser's digital properties.
3. *Google Trends:* a tool for analyzing trending search queries.
4. *Other bespoke analytical and data visualization services:* developed and accessed internally to help teams demonstrate data driven opportunities for advertising partners.

When consumers visit and interact with digital properties, signals may be generated and interpreted. These allow Google to meaningfully categorize segments. Specific interactions include searching, browsing websites, watching videos and interacting with social networks. Segments range from a group of preset "Affinity Audiences" based on lifestyle interests, to customized remarketing audience segments based on specific actions taken on an advertiser's website. However, more generic audiences can be customized through filtering by criteria including (but not limited to) location, device type, campaign performance, age and gender, topic of content consumed and even time of day. All of this equips items 1 and 2 with a diverse set of digital segment capabilities and items 1-4 opportunities to analyze them.

In the second work function, advertising client management was responsible for overseeing the accounts of advertisers interested in working with Google on campaigns. Account management work concerned helping one or more advertisers grow their business, which was tied to growth of advertising revenue for Google. These workers facilitated the purchase, creation, launch and optimization of advertising and general reviews of the advertiser's business objectives in relation to that advertising. In all cases advertiser objectives included influencing a set of target segments to take a specific action. Thus, client business managers, in conjunction with analysts, strove to derive the highest value of analytics through theorizing what was represented within those analytics. In many cases Client business managers met weekly with their advertisers, including a quarterly review of advertising performance against client objectives. Given client management teams' high level of domain expertise and the general accessibility of the Google platform, in many cases the team acted as a virtually autonomous Google unit and spent most of their time working exclusively with external advertisers on their campaigns.

Beneplacitus Segment Construction Practices

Workers systematically oriented to advertisers while referring to, and acting upon segment tasks. Customers were not referred to for their own sake, rather their applicability to the work at hand. In this case, applicability was found in advertisers' receptivity to a segmentation recommendation. Decisions related to analytical segment recommendations were discursively determined separate from the technical steps required to create the model. I call these *beneplacitus segmentation construction practices*. Part of these construction practices involved attending to client desires for segment authenticity. Workers turned to new analytical options in light of this desire. These segmentation construction methods are not validated through empirical analysis, or from polling clients. Objectivity for these model decisions is realized through these discursive methods. These practical methods are not passed down as predetermined self-contained mathematical and organizing principles, Google Analytics output, or Google Adwords training instructions.

Observing the locally dependent, practical reasoning between employees in this setting reveals the socio-historical composition of a segmentation model. This occurred in a realm that often suggests analyst constructed models and the decisions behind them are an objective, singular source of self-contained truth.

In the following example, two Google technical analysts and a Google client business manager discussed a recently constructed mobile device usage segmentation model based on the consumption of categories of site content. It was built to better address smartphone behaviors with advertising. In this case, the analyst was responsible for developing mobile segmentation models from analytical tools and working with the client management teams to prepare them for presentation to clients. Here analysts, who weren't assigned to specific clients, tested the model by discussing "real world" client scenarios with a client business manager. The analysts suspected this client business manager's accounts would benefit from the model. They did not question or debate the assumption that similar types of people will respond to similar types of advertising, however, "micro-theories" were up for debate and revision. They are resolved through beneplacitus segmentation construction practices.

"We can help with their mobile audiences. [So, I decided] to compare content consumed. So, someone who lands, what percentage viewed the main categories they have on their homepage? All of the major categories will be put into pipes. I'd click through to the major categories. And basically did segments. For example give me all the visits that went to product [category a or b] to research those products. And if you look at this, here is what you find for the weekends. [X] percent of every mobile visitor does a store locate, compared to desktop and very highly correlated with the weekend. I don't know if it's worth it, but it really stood out for me. They are stereotypical, and something we can use next year. But for someone that is very online focused it could be hard." (Analyst 1)

"There is a lot of interest. They say we understand mobile is important, but have no real understanding of what it does for us. I think your info is important to some" (Client Business Manager)

"Who are you talking to?" (Analyst 1)

"A lot of people. They have a good app that works quite well, once you have the application and you're signed in, I believe that helps conversion, they do as well. It's either a mobile site or their app for actual purchasing" (Client Business Manager)

"What is the main objection?" (Analyst 2)

"The multiplier." (Client Business Manager)

"What's the [Return on Advertising Spend]? [X]:1?" (Analyst 2)

"If this is what you're tracking so be it, we'll help you get the best result" (Client Business Manager)

"But if you look at last click, the audience model will not work though. Can we figure something else out?" (Analyst 2)

"Yes, but they want to see the results they can get, and next year we can craft strategies for mobile rather than m.commerce" (Client Business Manager)

"I'm hoping the insight stretches across all the weekend stuff. I'd like a content overview, and then tell them why I think that is. You have to make concessions somewhere, but here is what is happening for a reason." (Analyst 1)

The group did not attempt to observe and extract knowledge from advertisers to construct and optimize the model. They accomplished this through discourse. The group was able to unproblematically determine if their segmentation model was a fit for a particular customer. This was a pragmatic, yet undocumented move in the process of segment configuration.

The customer was referred to for their significance in accommodating (or not) a segment solution and helped the team make decisions about the mobile segmentation model.

Specifically, the group acted on an opportunity presented using segmentation data and deliberated over model utility for the client, including the client's understanding of that utility: *"They say we understand mobile is important, but have no real understanding of what it does for us"*. They also categorized the customer in question in relation to "customers in general", and their relative receptivity to a type of technology: *"They are stereotypical"*, *"They say we understand mobile is important...I think your info is important to some"*, *"I'm hoping the insight stretches across all the weekend stuff. I'd like a content overview, and then tell them why I think that is. You have to make concessions somewhere, but here is what is happening for a reason"*. They referenced clients with varying degrees of generality when deciding whether to share a segment concept with a particular client or go back to the metaphorical drawing board and change the approach.

These deliberations do not change the statistical legitimacy of the discovery. Nor do the workers question the statistical principles or digital data collection capabilities by which segments were built. They did not determine segment viability and importance, or decide to *"figure something else out"* through empirical observation or direct conversation with *"stereotypical"* advertisers, nor *"some"* advertisers.

The analyst began with an approximate idea for an effective mobile focused segment. The group's decision focused talk concerned customer-oriented projections of model changes, future applicability of the model, and pronouncements of extensibility of the model. This talk demonstrated how a segmentation model is gradually and practically constituted through the course of the segment work. It was built up through mundane, common sense, non-empirically verifiable methods of reasoning with one another.

The members of this work group demonstrated some of the everyday collaborative methods that contributed to a segment in progress. This happened despite the perception that quantitative statistical models stand on their own, possessing intrinsic objective properties [9]. This group at Google had to see the customer sensibility in the model for to communicate that model, even if there is no discernable difference in statistical methods or efficacy.

Garfinkel [8] suggests that behavior and culture are inextricably intertwined, and you must first enter the setting of daily life before you can sufficiently articulate the social activity that comprises it. Considering Garfinkel's [8] notion of the documentary method of interpretation, we should ask how workplace data and a segment observation are treated as evidence of a structured segment issue, and how they relate to everyday practical interpretive work to accomplish segment objectives. That is, the mutual elaboration of both that fact about a segment issue, and the organizational structure it comes to represent.

In the everyday work of identifying segment strategies for serving advertising campaigns, what practical, interpretive work is employed to treat the "data" in those exercises as representative of an underlying structure? For example, when analysts are looking for patterns, or client business managers and advertisers are discussing objectives. In this case, the interpretive work is organized around a significant scenic feature: customer palatability. How did technical workers interpretively see the customer-oriented system of practices of grouping people and targeting them to generate more mobile customers in the evidence and occurrences that present themselves in that work? Accounts about segment events and observations in this everyday setting were not simply social actions responding to a static reality, they shaped this reality in return.

Here we saw that the rationality of finding and communicating a mobile segmentation model data point resides in its intelligibility to others (advertisers) as showing mobile shopping habits. They did not inhabit some static structure of meaning that existed before it. This was part of the common sense, practical work required to make the more formal statistical process of advertising using a segment work.

Further, practical everyday workplace talk and strategies between workers about the advertiser intelligibility of how to capture "mobile jeans buyers", "mobile television purchasers" or "mobile education seekers" were constitutive of how to target those segments. This was regardless of their inclusion in the set of "best practices" or technical targeting parameters set up for these purposes to begin with. The interpretive process of moving from data to data as evidence of that underlying segment order is paramount for illuminating the practice of "doing segmentation". In this case, the pattern of store locator clicks (occurring after exposure to internet advertising in a mobile buyer model) were seen to fit a particular agreed upon model for capturing those sales. This was in part through the group's orientation to the customer as a scenic feature. These everyday practical segment matters were where workers' concerns resided, not in creating stable organizational structures of interaction in the workplace or grand theory about how segments were created.

Another example of this interpretive work and "palatable" customer orientation was illustrative of Lynch's [13] notion of artifacts in scientific data. Lynch shows how natural science (neuroscience) laboratory personnel treat by-products of obtaining data as methodological realities to be remedied, or risk interpretation "as evidentiary features of purportedly natural phenomena" [13]. In rare cases Lynch [13] described brain tissue samples confirmed as "fit" for conferences and refereed journals. Here workers sorted the samples into "lookers" and "users" describing some as looking technically superior and others as more practical for their procedure. As ethnomethodologists we topicalize the relationship between formulations and activities in what are other than "truth-conditional terms" [14]. This can apply to methods for constructing segments just as easily as an "assay" in neuroscience: "that is they do not treat formulations as exclusively true or false statements; instead they investigate how they act as pragmatic moves in temporal orders of actions" [14]. All of this laboratory work was not captured in the external sociological gloss of science (or in our case pronouncements effusing magic of advertising segment automation), or by the documented textbook procedure of this particular neuroscience activity.

In this case, while these segmentation workers orient to the customer, they treated the discussion of misunderstandings, alternate conflicting business models and ad effectiveness measures as "artifacts" to remedy. These are segmentation phenomena that adversely affected the team's ability to produce and communicate a "palatable" model for the customer. That is, ad effectiveness logic in planning is analogous to scientific procedures for collecting data in the laboratory. Artifacts are imperfections resulting from this planning. The result can be changes in the model, or representation of the data set they have access to: *"But if you look at last click, the segmentation model will not work though. Can we figure something else out?"*. These "artifacts" were not treated as negative occurrences, rather routine yet critical realities of successful segmentation work, and were demonstrative of the team's orientation to the advertising customer and the palatability of the segment.

In sum, I show that segmentation models did not simply stand free or denote an objective reality in isolation. Instead, they were part of the routine, reflexive, give and take of segments that oriented to a significant contextual element of a set of advertisers. This example reveals the tacit but essential interpretive work required for internal and external working relationships with segments.

Next, we demonstrate how the specific base or lens by which these segments are considered are reflexively discussed, and programs are accomplished while orienting to the customer and vice versa.

Dividuus Scheme of Interpretation

In addition to orienting to advertising customer palatability, workers drew on practical reasoning to select bases for defining segments. These discursive methods cannot be defined formally, nor applied generally in advance of the segmentation work that occurred.

Workers decided how to define a segment, and the resources to draw upon to accomplish that definition through talk. They made choices between defining a segment by psychographics, demographics, web preferences, likelihood to purchase, their engagement with an advertiser's website, device usage, etc. This was artfully accomplished despite a consideration set that included limitless human attributes to implement in the advertising software. Teams were challenged by a lack of clear specification for segments requested. This meant they needed to make a recommendation with imperfect information. Workers were able to collaboratively and unproblematically select a "good enough" segmentation lens to be evaluated as part of an advertising purchase decision by the client. The criteria for that decision included whether the ads would further the advertiser's business interests, and consequently Google's as well. This was accomplished despite the physical absence of the customer, and the impracticality of empirically testing each decision. Past academic contributions in the area of segment base selection were practitioner efforts to find the best possible set of categories that people might reasonably fit into. Instead, I embedded myself in a setting where the work is actually taking place, and described *how* categories were reasonably constructed and deployed as a feature of the advertising workplace. I found that workers employed the customer as a seen but unnoticed scheme of interpretation when selecting these bases. In turn they reflexively considered the customer in light of successive base selections and past segment engagements. These constructions did not rely solely on worker observations: direct contact with customers and users. I call this collaborative process of drawing on interpretive customer and user resources to fit users into categories the *dividuus scheme of interpretation*.

Workers employed the customer as a non-empirically verifiable scheme of interpretation to decide upon the technical lens most appropriate for considering users. That is, when conceptualizing, constructing and deploying segments according to these bases, workers oriented to this advertiser expectancy. They referenced segment bases in light of this context with varying degrees of abstractness. They relied on typification to accomplish mutual intelligibility amongst colleagues and proceed with the segment work [21]. Typification is the notion that while two individuals cannot occupy the 'exact same' point of view at the same time, through talk they select common ground, through features, objects and know how, to achieve a common perspective that allows them to interact and collectively move on. Typifications afford a common language of sorts, and the coordination of activity across collaborative settings. Typifications allow collaborators to sustain shared understanding and accomplish order without exhaustive explication pertinent to the uniqueness of the situation (something that Garfinkel [8] would consider impossible).

Here, the impossibility of exhaustively determining the customer perspective, and empirically evaluating all permeations of segment base decisions according to those customer tastes (due to practical workplace distance) suggested to me that something else was at play in the setting. Instead, this was dealt with through the mundane availability of typificatory devices amongst the group. This orientation shaped workers' references and collective comprehension of segments, and contributed to the finished segment as a technical advertising device. Thus, these finished segments were not automated outputs that stand on their own; separate from their socio-cultural surroundings. This is a myth we should move past when designing software to support work in this setting.

Typificatory practices are essential for accomplishing segmentation work in a setting with a diverse division of labor. These practices were relied upon to facilitate communication across diverse biographies with differing technical aptitudes. Segment work proceeded unproblematically despite the impossibility of workers experiencing those segment decision points exactly as their colleagues and customers. Situational segment discourse and reasoning reflected the implicit presence of the customer, and was interpretive work that complemented the empirical, statistical categorization work used to create a mathematical model for the segment(s). Segment base decisions were validated reflexively through talk between the workers in this setting while orienting to the customer. Part of fitting the action of a segment to its context, involves Sacks, Schegloff and Jefferson's recipient design [20]: adjusting communication for the recipient in that setting. This talk cannot be determined by predefined, a priori analysis, with segment data standing alone for passive consumption by the account teams and clients.

In the next scenario, a Google team constructed a segment model in preparation for a client presentation. An analyst created an initial model to illustrate the quantitative opportunity according to an advertiser's key performance indicators. The analyst used a customizable version of Google Trends called "Google Trends for Marketers" to categorize branded keyword searches into a number of relevant categories for the advertiser (e.g. customer service, innovation etc.), and used the output to examine aggregate consumer relationship between the brand and those categories to develop advertising strategies from them. The team intended to show the advertiser opportunities within segments that would enable the latter to sell product units and associated services. The analysis was shared with the client business manager as part of an iterative editing process. The client business manager integrated the segment models into a presentation that included broader client relationship items: past performance, partnership status and opportunities, and service level discussions.

"It's tough to see" (Client Business Manager)

"Good point mark em' out. Look at share of voice" (Analyst)

"Is that [x company division]?"(Client Business Manager)

"Yes basically they are staying stagnant. We can help them grow, What I'm going to do is kill 2011. I know we like to show back there"(Analyst)

"So there is nothing happening in this market is what you're saying" (Client Business Manager)

"Nobody is gaining or losing anything. Volume is the same. Positioning moves a little bit. How can we help you grow that bubble? So the story is when you're looking of for company x you care about product [x] and [y], is that a shocker? [Product y] includes [features x and y], these are the two highest categories of interest. We looked at innovation etc. why would we show things that aren't very important? Then we look at what people are looking to but[...]This is a conversation cloud. What are some of the things people are looking for? Understanding what they are looking for will help us understand what we need to do to build that bubble for them. For [product y] how can we grow it?" (Analyst)

"For a different example. I was doing it for [company x], they're obviously smaller. I took [product category x]. Maybe I did three because that's what mattered. You can see that [company y] really owned that time frame. See quarter over quarter. What will move the needle for you is product launches. Product launches work, they matter. You have a slide like that. Say [Company x, company y], share of voice. Increased the quarter that it launched. Then you get [3rd party sales data], that shows your incremental year over year for units sold. If you're able to show company y's

share and increase in [company x]. Show share of voice and sales" (Client Business Manager)

"Who has access to [3rd party data source]?" (Analyst)

"Somebody does." (Client Business Manager)

"So for 2013 I have this. [3rd party data] shows quarter data? So for 2013 performance. This is showing their interest in the brand versus the category. Telling them to focus on people x% interested in brand and maybe x% of the way for people interested in the category. x% are choosing company y before feature x, I'm hoping the number will be more for current data. Even if it's a lower number, the message stays the same." (Analyst)

"Keep tying back to product launch."(Client Business Manager)

"Tie them back to interest in the category? When shopping for a [new product x]? Best product in the category, best customer service etc." (Analyst)

"My issue with this, is just because it's trending high, why should I care about it? So this data before makes sense to me. So maybe only show three categories instead of four. What's the user action? Maybe customer service I wouldn't use. Because if I was in the room, I would probably question that. What does that mean? If you remove it, then you have a more logical story." (Client Business Manager)

"Ensure strong messaging during product launches. And when we look at [company y], [region x] is really strong. Category interest targeting should be over [x]%, with competition rising." (Analyst)

"What's the so what here?" (Client Business Manager)

"Also, [Analyst 2] and I are putting together an [additional analytical view], and seeing what the results are." (Analyst)

"It will be good, but these guys never get interested in this. It doesn't flow. There are so many more factors." (Client Business Manager)

"Ok so basically these three points then?" (Analyst)

The analyst and client specialist decided to organize their proposal and data according to the segment's likelihood to purchase. They debated organizing it by users' interest in the brand, category and other attributes such as a customer service within this broader "likelihood to purchase" framework. These segmentation bases are a subset derived from a much larger universe of possibilities. They validated this decision/orient to perceived interest of their clients based on past experience with advertisers, and a typified customer in this space. This work reflexively shaped the constitution of the customer and the segment base decision.

They worked with large sets of information about the customer and potential user segments to understand and communicate the opportunity. They continuously oriented to the customer in order to understand how to select segment bases to fit with a typical company in that industry, and their typical advertising goals.

They did not rely exclusively on quantitative data about those segments to make this final decision. Instead, discourse and the members' scheme of interpretation in that setting were critical. They did not discuss the company as a topic for its own sake; rather they drew on it as an orienting resource for putting together the segment proposal and how they consider advertisers collectively over time. Significant utterances in this example were representative of an underlying structure, and reference past cases used to form an orientation toward *"these guys"* (a set of companies). The client business manager explains: *"If I was in the room, I would probably question that"*, asks *"what's the so what here"* and suggests *"these guys never get interested in this stuff"*. Rationale was contingently afforded to these decisions without speaking to the types of customers the employees were orienting to. Both employees entered the situation with different workplace and life experiences, yet were able to make decisions about segments collaboratively, achieved in part through this orientation.

The analyst and client business manager focused on the product behaviors of the segments. The focus allowed them to supplement, eliminate and reposition the lenses for organizing and communicating the segmentation model. The customer was referred to in a typified way with degrees of generality according to their needs. The way the segment model was discussed and considered is reflexively shaped by this orientation: *"Keep tying back to product launch"*. User actions were reconciled while projecting customer scenarios and fitting the model to those background expectancies: *"What's the user action? Maybe customer service I wouldn't use. Because if I was in the room, I would probably question that. What does that mean? If you remove it, then you have a more logical story."*

The customer was used for comparative justification and construction of the segment's specific product interest characteristics: *"for a different example. I was doing it for [company x], they're obviously smaller. I took [product category x]. Maybe I did three because that's what mattered. You can see that [company y] really owned that time frame. See quarter over quarter. What will move the needle for you is product launches. Product launches work, they matter"*. These comparisons [15], demonstrated a decision making process influenced by a distinct orientation to typified set of customers and the introduction of a customer constraint. They acted as a catalyst for the construction of a segment through a particular lens. Here that lens was grouping people by forecasted demand for a category of products during a launch in that category. The team fit the segmentation model to context discursively. This exemplified the interpretive constitution of segmentation models frequently positioned as automated, standalone mathematical entities and decisions subject to empirical verification.

The client business manager does not identify mathematical problems or discrepancies with the model or changes that would substantially modify its makeup, yet oriented to a constraint of a tacit, scenic feature [9]. This orientation to customers and related data involves an interpretation of the statistical model to fit the case at hand, and was accomplished situationally through talk. This occurred whether or not the employees consciously recognize it as a mundane process. Segments were crafted and subdivided according to the advertising customer as a scenic feature, and their identity was shaped according to that historical segment talk.

Discursively selecting perspectives to view and talk about these segments was critical for expressing and optimizing the model. Although this did not materially change the characteristics of the people available for inclusion in the model, it had important ramifications for how the advertiser and client team engaged with those segments and seemingly how they will orient to future customers in their work.

DISCUSSION AND DESIGN DIRECTION

Analogous to past approaches to creativity [15], users in design [22], and quantitative model research in the institutionalized social sciences [9] I demonstrated how language is used and workers organize themselves to design segments through talk. I highlighted the mundane and interpretive work beyond the mathematical and technical practices of segmentation [9]. This work was not determined a priori as a static corpus of organizing principles for all segmentation work. Workers did not make the choice between the "archaic" sensory world of mad men, and the modern world of statistically grounded advertising. The intelligibility of segments in light of the omni-presence of the advertiser requires practically occasioned interpretation in both of these advertising worlds. This was as critical as the statistical capabilities for workers when *doing segmentation*.

I demonstrate some of the ways that workers prepare segmentation/targeting work for clients, and the mundane ways they configure and treat the model to make it work for that context. Segmentation models are not passively consumed and automatically passed from a statistical package to advertising production. Reasoning through these findings requires unique, local knowledge and interpretive work to determine what particular statistical output is appropriate for a particular type of advertiser.

We describe some of the choices, deliberation and practical techniques relied upon to do segment work. This work is additive to following advertising and analytics software training manuals to choose the right segment for the right advertiser. These segments need to "fit" the expectations of the advertiser, and the customer must see those segments as reasonable for them to be successful. This is an alternative perspective to believing segments emerge ready-made from analytical software. Statistical output is not sufficient; workers need to see the customer in the model without having the customer in the room for every decision.

Thus, I recommend rethinking design strategies for integrating the advertiser and provider through collaborative software. When compared to consumer segmentation technology, less has been done to map disparate sources of analytics to support the B2B function and stakeholders of advertising engagements (although this is not limited to advertising). CRM systems provide a bi-directional opportunity to support some of the interpretive resources and practices observed here. I recommend building CRM and segment buying technology in a way that improves the efficiency of orienting to the customer when designing segment models. This would be a design that makes customers more "considerable" for segment decisions, and enabling subsequent segment decisions to produce signals to contribute to that "considerability". I do not suggest interpretive work will be automated, but advocate for improved mechanisms to deliver intelligence that mitigates some of the economics of information challenges that naturally prevents customer contact [22]. The system would illuminate stakeholders segment *dividuus* scheme of interpretation and segment *beneplacitus* background expectancies as segmentation design unfolds. It would help parties mutually "see" segments in light of these phenomena rather than simply acting on a segment driven request for proposal from the advertiser. Beyond software design, this principle should also influence the engagement strategy between all parties.

CRM interfaces are dominated by account tasks and revenue. I recommend incorporating mechanisms to intelligently contextualize segments by drawing on the typificatory language and their ties to local context and scenic features. For example, displaying anticipated receptivity by a "type" of customer to a segment base option (e.g. positive responses types of advertisers to mobile store locators). These "intelligibility views" should be introduced early and dynamically updated as campaigns, the relationship, and related segments are built up. In simpler terms, show the chronological evolution of customer segments and their attributes. This should be shown in light of previous sentiment. Part of this involves a segment artifact remedy system that allows the advertising provider to identify and track currently undocumented, but discursively identified customer oriented imperfections from the segment model. The system should do this on a customer-by-customer basis. This concerns the advertising provider's ability to monitor customer receptivity: model worthiness, client understanding, relative receptivity to technology, and priority bases for the purposes of both building and communicating segments.

Meaningfully integrating this work into software would facilitate the collaboration of customers and publisher alike.

This assumes that schemes of interpretation, such as how the customer is considered and referred to, are changing and dynamically updated. Who the user is, and how the client and service is typified and interpreted is expected to change, *and cannot be facilitated by statistics alone*. Part of this design work requires more attention to segments in the workplace. Focus should be diverted from statistical and technical methods, toward the underlying structures used to construct and communicate segments and the reflexive impact on the reality of client and future segments.

REFERENCES

1. Barter, P. and DeChambeau, J. *From Mad Men to Math Men*. The Intelligent Application of Technology. http://www.t4g.com/articles/from-mad-men-to-math-men/
2. Chamberlin, E.H., *The Theory of Monopolistic Competition*, Harvard University Press, Cambridge, MA, USA, 1933.
3. Chapman, C.N., Love, E., Milham, R.P., ElRif, P., and Alford, J.L., Quantitative Evaluation of Personas as Information, In *Proc of the Human Factors and Ergonomics Society 52nd Annual Meeting,* Human Factors and Ergonomics Society (2008), 1107-1111.
4. Chapman, C.N. and Milham, R.P. The Persona's New Clothes: Methodological and Practical Arguments Against a Popular Method, In *Proc of Human Factors and Ergonomics Society 50th Annual Meeting*, Human Factors and Ergonomics Society (2006), 634-636.
5. Cooper, A. *The inmates are running the asylum*. Macmillan Publishing Co, Indianapolis, IN, USA, 1999.
6. Dourish, P., Implications for design. In *Proc of CHI 2006*, ACM (2006), 541-550.
7. Firat, A.F., and Venkatesh, A, 1993, Postmodernity: the age of marketing, *International Journal of Research in Marketing 10,* 3 (1993), 227-249.
8. Garfinkel, H., *Studies in Ethnomethodology*, Englewood Cliffs, New Jersey, NJ, USA, 1967.
9. Greiffenhagen, C., Mair, M., Sharrock, W.W., From Methodology to Methodography: A Study of Qualitative and Quantitative Reasoning in Practice, *Methodological Innovations Online 6,* 2 (2011), 93-107.
10. Hof, R. *Not Just for Nerds: Automated Ad Buying Goes Mainstream*. Forbes. http://www.forbes.com/sites/roberthof/2014/03/24/not-just-for-nerds-automated-ad-buying-goes-mainstream/
11. Hughes, J., King, V., Rodden, T., and Anderson, H., Moving out of the control room: Ethnography in system design. In *Proc of CSCW 1994*, ACM (1994), 429-438.
12. Lynch, M. Preliminary Notes on Judges' Work: The Judge as a Constituent of Courtroom Hearings. In *Law in Action: Ethnomethodological & Conversation Analytic Approaches to Law*. Dartmouth Publishing, Aldershot, UK, 1997.
13. Lynch, M., *Art and Artifact in Laboratory Science: A Study of Shop Work and Shop Talk in a Research Laboratory*, Routledge Kegan & Paul, Boston, MA, USA, 1985.
14. Lynch, M., *Scientific practice and ordinary action: Ethnomethodology and social studies of science*, Cambridge University Press, Cambridge, UK, 1993.
15. Martin, D., O'Neill, J., and Randall, D., 'Talking about (my) Generation': Creativity, Practice, Technology & Talk. In *Proc of ECSCW 2009,* ACM (2009), 171-190.
16. Mitchell, A., *The Nine American Lifestyles: Who We Are and Where We're Going*, Warner Books, New York, NY, USA, 1983.
17. Pruitt, J., and Grudin, J, Personas: practice and theory. In *Proc of DUX 2003,*ACM (2003), 1-15.
18. Randall, D., Harper, R., and Rouncefield, M., *Fieldwork for Design: Theory and Practice*. Springer, London, UK, 2007.
19. Robinson, H.W., The Equilibrium Price in a Perfect Inter-Temporal Market, *Econometrica 6*, 1 (1938), 48-62.
20. Sacks, H., Schegloff, E.A., Jefferson, G., A Simplest Systematics for the Organization of Turn-Taking for Conversation, *Language 50*,4 (1974), 696-735.
21. Schutz, A., *The Phenomenology of the Social World*, Heinemann, London, UK, 1972.
22. Sharrock, W. and Anderson, B., The user as a scenic feature of the design space, *Design Studies 15*,1 (1994), 5-18.
23. Smith, W.R., Product Differentiation and Market Segmentation as Alternative Marketing Strategies, *Journal of Marketing 21*,1 (1956) 3-8.
24. Stigler, G., *The Theory of Competitive Price*, MacMillan, London, UK, 1946.
25. Thielman, S. *How Agencies Are Retooling for the Automated Ad Buy*. Adweek. http://www.adweek.com/news/advertising-branding/how-agencies-are-retooling-automated-ad-buy-153589
26. van Raaij, W.F., Postmodern consumption, *Journal of Economic Psychology 14*, 3 (1993), 541-563.

Flow of Competence in UX Design Practice

Colin M. Gray
Iowa State University
2624 Howe Hall
Ames, IA 50011 USA
cmgray@iastate.edu

Austin Toombs
Indiana University
901 E. 10th St.
Bloomington, IN 47408 USA
altoombs@indiana.edu

Shad Gross
Indiana University
901 E. 10th St.
Bloomington, IN 47408 USA
shagross@indiana.edu

ABSTRACT
UX and design culture are beginning to dominate corporate priorities, but despite the current hype there is often a disconnect between the organizational efficiencies desired by executives and the knowledge of how UX can or should address these issues. This exploratory study addresses this space by reframing the concept of competence in UX to include the flow of competence between individual designers and the companies in which they work. Our reframing resulted in a preliminary schema based on interviews conducted with six design practitioners, which allows this flow to be traced in a performative way on the part of individuals and groups over time. We then trace this flow of individual and organizational competence through three case studies of UX adoption. Opportunities for use of this preliminary schema as a generative, rhetorical tool for HCI researchers to further interrogate UX adoption are considered, including accounting for factors that affect adoption.

Author Keywords
Interaction design; practice-led research; competence.

ACM Classification Keywords
H.5.m.

INTRODUCTION
In the past decade, there has been a rapid adoption of UX in a wide range of corporations, many of which have no substantial history of a UX or design approach. This adoption is a potential issue to the research community, as the success of many of these organizational shifts relies on positive corporate acceptance in often engineering-dominated cultures. While the research community has viewed this transition more hesitantly, UX and design adoption—often occurring in tandem—is happening quickly in very large organizations. Traditionally engineering-dominated companies such as IBM, Intel, and Microsoft have invested substantial capital into creating sustainable, organization-wide design cultures, which raises many questions about the implications for UX practice and research. In this most recent adoption period, many organizations appear to desire UX talent, but individual designers frequently work in companies whose internal culture is hostile to the consideration of new perspectives on design or UX.

CHI 2015, April 18 - 23 2015, Seoul, Republic of Korea
Copyright is held by the owner/author(s). Publication rights licensed to ACM.
ACM 978-1-4503-3145-6/15/04…$15.00
http://dx.doi.org/10.1145/2702123.2702579

In addressing this adoption incongruity, we take the perspective of the individual UX designer rather than that of the organization, with special interest paid to the impact one's personal competency might have (either individually or in aggregate) in the evolution of a company's culture as it relates to UX and design. We shift from the organizational lens—which is well documented in business settings through research on change management—to the role of the individual designer, and how that designer's perception and utilization of UX competencies, an existing set which are documented by [13], in tandem with their underlying design identity, impacts how they interact with and build a UX and design culture in an organization. The literature has addressed issues of competence in a broad sense—looking across professional domains of design from an educational or licensure perspective—but has not substantially addressed this situated sense, where a designer is interacting with a culture potentially antagonistic to design or UX.

Within the framing of individual design competence in organizational change, the contributions of this paper are two-fold: 1) To understand some of the elements of competence in UX practice from successful practitioners, which has a direct impact on how we train future UX designers and how we intend to support UX practice through future research; and 2) Map the flow or movement of competence between UX practitioners and companies through several case studies, allowing us to document the UX adoption process in an exploratory way. This flow perspective allows us to look not only at competencies essential to individual success, but also competencies that allow for broader adoption of UX principles and practices in companies.

REVIEW OF LITERATURE
In focusing our attention on the competence of individual UX designers, and how this competence relates to the organization at large, we will explore a range of literature related to UX adoption in corporate environments, how this adoption has been discussed in the CHI community historically, and then how these macro-level perspectives relate to the issue of individual competence.

UX Adoption in Corporate Environments

Adoption of UX as a strategic advantage has been a significant driver in many companies in the past several years. According to a recent article in the Harvard Business Review, "The value of UX as a corporate asset is no longer in question" [7]. There are many ways of incorporating UX into existing companies, ranging from lean UX to customer-driven or R&D-based UX [7], and outside of specific implementation strategies, a renewed focus on how technology is used and felt by consumers is gaining favor [6].

Even as companies have gotten on the "bandwagon" and hired UX designers, managers, or interns, it doesn't necessarily indicate that they have a broader knowledge of what UX is, what it can do for their business, or how they expect UX designers to drive integration of these concepts in their business environment. This fundamental issue of adoption strategy raises questions about the nature of UX, and what value it might have for industry that have been left unanswered in many corporations, with numerous UX designers caught in the crossfire. Beyond a handful of case studies and panels at CHI [8,17,20,21], this is not an area that this research community has substantively explored, even while corporations and management are currently working through these issues in their quest for adoption of UX or a design culture.

A wide range of companies are shifting tentatively or radically toward a design and UX-informed approach. High profile organizations like HP or Intel have been working on their design strategies for several years, while recent advances have taken place with the creation of a company-wide design initiative at IBM [12]. So we see a range of approaches to UX and design adoption, from tentative long-scale shifts to more radical restructuring of organizations. While most visible press coverage has focused on large transitions led by executives, we will focus this paper more on the contributions of individual designers in small to medium-sized organizations to capitalize on the capabilities of individual design practitioners.

UX Adoption and CHI

There has been increased interest in the adoption of UX, moving past the arguments based on usability and efficiency grounded in the efforts of usability engineers in past decades. Research in this area began as more general work on design processes, particularly around participatory or collaborative design [3,4,5,18], but the conversation has since extended to the competencies of usability specialists [11], and the impact of 'offshoring' or non-collocated work environments [8]. In the past few years, case studies and panels at CHI have brought additional focus to the issue of UX adoption, both in situated work environments [20] and in a broader strategic sense [17,21]. The Thompson et al. panel [21] in particular brings forward a number of important provocations that have not yet been answered in detail in the HCI research community. These include issues UX designers face when working in often-hostile management or organizational structures:

> *[UX designer] roles are often misunderstood and our adjacent disciplines such as product management and development see their work as unnecessary or in some cases are threatened by them.* [...] *We find that the culture of the company we are trying to deploy UX resources into isn't ready to accept them and we find that our role becomes more that of a change manager than a user experience manager. We have a vision for what the future processes of the company can look like but we find it hard to communicate that vision....* [21]

Design Competence

As we shift our gaze to the individual UX designer, we confront the issue of what constitutes competence in interaction design or UX. A set of competencies that makes someone a good UX designer has not been fully explored in the HCI literature, but has been addressed more broadly in design theory and engineering design [15,19,23]. Gray [13] offers an initial taxonomy of UX competence, drawing on a co-construction of identity between the individual designer and their practice environment. This paper addresses this co-construction more fully, offering a way to map these relationships over time. In design theory, competence has been conflated with expertise [16], but in practical terms, explaining how a UX designer needs to be able to perform in practice, the answer is unknown and likely more complex. One broad view of competence includes "the ability to successfully meet complex demands in a particular context through the mobilization of psychosocial prerequisites" [19] with a focus on behaving in relation to a specific context. Weinert [23] defines competence in a more systemic way as "a roughly specialized system of abilities, proficiencies, or skills that are necessary or sufficient to reach a specific goal [which] can be applied to individual dispositions or to the distribution of such dispositions within a social group or an institution." In each of these broad definitions, we can see the performance of an individual actor in relation to a specific context, using cognitive skills, social skills, and situated judgments.

A set of competencies has not been explored in the context of UX beyond a preliminary set of *digital design competencies* [2] created for an education context, and focusing on a symbiosis of technical skill and communicative ability. In the corporate context, there has been an increasing focus on hiring "T-shaped" people—a term popularized by Tim Brown of IDEO [9]. According to an interview with Tim Brown: "T-shaped people are individuals with strengths in two dimensions. On the vertical axis, every member of the team needs to possess a depth of skill that allows him or her to make tangible contributions to the outcome. They also need to be able to work well in the messy environments required to solve complex problems. Design thinkers cross the 'T.'" [9]. All of these perspectives are beneficial as we discuss how UX competencies are transmitted within an organization, between individuals and groups.

Design Leadership

Another helpful concept when we discuss UX adoption in a corporate context is Nelson and Stolterman's view of design leadership [16]—the idea of being "in service" as a designer, with the goal of exceeding expectations and building communicative partnerships. There is a sense in which a design culture has to exist for design competencies to be asserted, so in places where this culture does not exist, an individual or group must take steps to create one—both for herself, and for the stakeholders and other personnel who are involved in the creation and development processes.

This leadership involves some level of individual belief that "[t]he process of design is always the most effective and efficient means of getting organizations and individuals to new places" and that "leadership is [...] an essential element of any design culture" [16]. Designers must "ask challenging questions," "never settle for the 'problem' as presented," and "expose the underlying forces of change" [16]. This is a substantial undertaking—and one promulgated by an individual through their competence and performance of their designerly identity.

RESEARCH APPROACH

This exploratory study addresses how practicing UX designers think about competence, and how these expectations of competence change over time in reaction to individual and corporate changes. The primary contribution of this work is to help the research community understand more fully how UX designers are interacting with companies that have limited UX culture—or no UX culture at all—and how the role of UX and interaction design shifts in the organization over time. This shift impacts the training UX or interaction designers should receive, as well as the potential impact UX can have on an organization over time, as bound by the individual designer's sense of identity in terms of UX, and how the organization reacts to individual competencies around UX or interaction design.

We addressed the identification of competence and changes in competence over time through an initial interview study, followed by the use of thematic analysis [10] to construct a schema to explain and discuss the flow of competence. This flow will be explored further through multiple case studies [22], drawn from an additional set of interviews.

Broad View of Designers and Competence

We interviewed six practitioners in a range of design disciplines, most including an emphasis on interaction design, in order to establish a starting point of what designers see as a working definition of competence—in both static and dynamic forms—in their profession. Interviews included discussion of how participants established their design competence, and how they maintain that competence over time.

A purposive sample of designers was created based on a selection of design colleagues from the professional network of each of the researchers. These designers represented a broad range of backgrounds, including graphic design (1), interaction design (3), instructional design (1), and craft (1). Each participant was invited to participate in an interview through videoconferencing software, and all six participants that were contacted agreed to participate. These participants were predominantly male (5), with experience in their respective design field ranging from 5-20 years.

Data Collection and Analysis

Each design practitioner participated in an approximately one-hour interview, exploring the locus or definition of competency in their specific design discipline, and what sources they draw on to increase or sustain that competency over time. Each interview was recorded, with portions transcribed for additional thematic analysis.

We then performed an emergent thematic analysis of these interviews, drawing out themes in two stages. Initially, each researcher analyzed a set of two interviews, identifying potential themes that addressed competence across both interviews, where the participant answered questions based on their own definition of competence. Following this process, we discussed the interview data and reconciled emergent themes as a group, which resulted in a formalization of the original themes. We then reconciled issues of competence in a broader theoretical sense, developing the concept of "flow" along dimensions of awareness and location in relation to the individual to explain the shifts in competence over time that were noted by the participants. The resulting semantic differential was a helpful tool to talk about how designers relate to the organizations they work with, and how these linkages may allow for generative discussion about the role of competence in UX, particularly in communicating the changes in competence and the basis of this change in regard to awareness and environment. This phase culminated in a preliminary schema of environmental or personal factors surrounding competence, and how flow between these factors might indicate more information about the competency building process from an organizational and personal perspective.

Targeted Validation of Competency Schema

We constructed an initial schema of competence that addressed flow of competence over time based on the initial interview results and formal analysis. To explore this schema further and provide some initial validation of its utility and generativity, we requested additional interviews from a new set of UX practitioners using a modified interview protocol that focused on the elements described in our schema. Participants were solicited through a social media group that included alumni working as interaction designers or user experience designers. Three practitioners agreed to participate in the study, all of whom were male. Their experience in interaction design or UX contexts ranged from two to five years, and all had previously completed a Master's degree in interaction design.

Data Collection and Case Study Analysis

Each practitioner participated in an approximately one hour interview, which included an exploration of their competency in interaction design, their design process, and what flow patterns indicated from our preliminary schema might encourage discussion of their changes in competence over time. In addition to individual competency, we also addressed broad themes of competency in interaction design, focusing on upstream and downstream flow of design competence in these practitioners' respective organizations. In particular, we attempted to identify the acceptance of UX and design in these organizations, and how the designer and organization reacted over time to this shift. Each interview was recorded, with substantial portions transcribed for additional thematic analysis.

This second phase was intended as an initial exploration of the preliminary schema, allowing for some of the flows present in the schema to be discussed in greater detail. Because of the richness of this second set of data, we will present these as three case studies, to allow for additional exploration of the individual designer and organization, and discussion of how these unique factors play out in the context of UX adoption and shifts in competence over time. These case studies show a wide amount of variation, a hallmark of a well structured multiple case study [22].

INITIAL FINDINGS AND SCHEMA CONSTRUCTION

We developed our initial findings through an analysis of the interviews with our first six participants. These participants represent a broad range of design backgrounds: one graphic designer/typographer employed as a sign painter; three interaction designers; one instructional designer/software engineer; and one knitting pattern designer/knitting teacher. Based on the responses from these interviews we developed a schema that facilitates a discussion about the competency each designer relies on in her work. This schema is meant to play a descriptive role, with both rhetorical and generative qualities to further communicate linkages between competencies, which existing literature confines to a discussion of individual or organizational competence in isolation. This schema links the two sets of competence together, and allows for a discourse to occur around how these competencies are linked, and how they might shift or evolve over time. Two main dimensions, constructed as binaries, shape this schema and address how the designers we interviewed spoke about their competence and design practices: individual v. group and espoused v. in-use.

Individual v. Group

With this dichotomy, we distinguish between the actions and beliefs of an individual practitioner, and the actions and beliefs of a group or organization as enacted through a living corporate culture. A group can refer to the company the designer works for as well as a working group of designers or other stakeholders as a subset of the organization. Each designer we interviewed differentiated the design skills and processes they personally found meaningful and those that their company or group emphasized. A productive tension that facilitates reflection on competence, skill, and practice exists between these individual beliefs and actions and the group's beliefs and actions. We discuss this tension further in the quadrants we present below.

Espoused v. In Use

Here we distinguish between internalized, tacit action—which comprises the identity and latent beliefs of the individual—and externalized, explicit action—which can be seen in concrete action, or what the individual actually does. The tension between the internally held beliefs of the individual or the group, "espoused," and the external actions of that group, "in-use," offer an insightful area for investigation that identifies how designers or groups support or fail to support their espoused beliefs with their actions. This binary was also supported by the work of Argyris and Schön [1], which includes the concept of one's theory-in-use and espoused theory, and inspired the labeling of this binary. A theory-in-use describes what one *actually* does, while one's espoused theory represents a belief about action, or the explanation that would be provided if one was asked to explain one's beliefs. The difference between these states—where action does not match up with belief—is another tension that allows us to discuss apparent contradictions between a designer or organization's externalized identity and their actions.

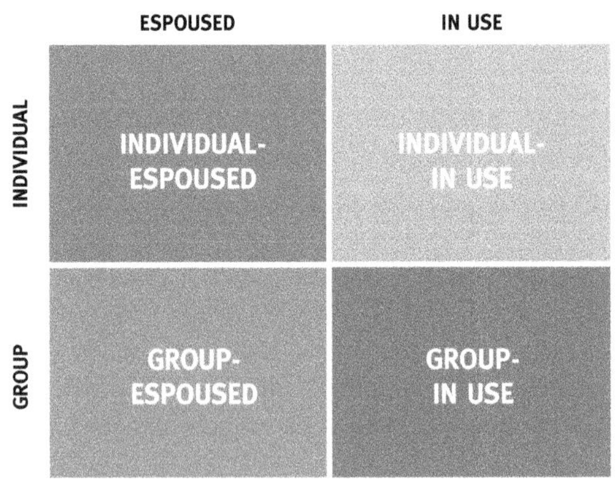

Figure 1. Schema describing quadrants of competence.

Schema Quadrants

The four quadrants of the resulting semantic differential include: individual-espoused, individual-in use, group-in use, and group-espoused. We describe each of these quadrants to build up to a discussion of the flow between quadrants, and how this flow indicates shifts between understanding and performance of competence in design action on the part of organizations and individuals.

Individual-Espoused: competence espoused by an individual
This first quadrant of the semantic differential describes the tacit understandings or beliefs that exist within an individual designer. It represents the designer's *espoused theory*—the set of beliefs by which they claim to act upon and that make up their designerly identity [1]. These decisions project who they are as a designer and what they believe it means to practice design and be competent.

Individual-In Use: competence performed by the individual
The second quadrant describes explicit activities that an individual performs to stay competent as a designer and to perform their identity and beliefs about design, as enacted in the design process. These types of activities, such as keeping up with relevant blogs in the field or purposefully consulting design exemplars, work to create an understanding of other designer's work as mediated by an individual designer and represent the designer's theory-in-use. Differences between performance and underlying belief in the individual-espoused quadrant may represent some fluidity in what a designerly identity includes and how an individual acts in a performative way [19] on their identity.

Group-Espoused: competence espoused by a group
The third quadrant describes what a company or group believes about competence building for their employees, or their beliefs about competence or design. By group we mean the entire organization, a team the designer works on, or any organizational structure in between. These groups tacitly reward certain behaviors in building competence through such actions as spending money to send employees to conferences, through the kinds of deliverables they provide to clients, by what role the organization thinks that a UX person takes on, with a codified design process, by type of project work that is done, or through anything else that looks like a tacit "corporate culture." This quadrant focuses on the underlying belief or tacit "mental model," rather than the actual enactment of the belief through performance.

Group-In use: competence performed by the group
The final quadrant describes the explicit company behaviors that reinforce competence building or assumptions about what competence includes, and in doing so perform the beliefs of the organization or group. These activities, such as attending conferences relevant to professional practice or presenting certain deliverables, represent the group's engagement with the practice community. As with the individual-in use quadrant, we may see a contradiction between tacit beliefs and actions; for instance, a company might say they believe in a particular design process, but actually perform or reinforce the design process in a different way.

Flow of Competence

The discussion of these binaries allows us to start discussing the ideas behind competence in UX in a more generative way. Rather than only addressing how competence is enacted or sustained on an individual or corporate level in a static manner, we can also see how these "states" interact with each other through discrete performances or over time. This flow of competence over time is one of our primary contributions, addressing a lack of integration in the literature. Researchers have talked about aspects of organizational and personal competency in the past [e.g., 20], but rarely do we see how these perspectives relate to one another. In particular, the relationship between an individual designer and an organization can be explored on two levels: the tacit assumptions of a designer or organization, and the external actions that conflict or concord with tacit assumptions. In this paper, we will use this flow and related schema in a rhetorical way to allow insight into how UX is adopted on a company level, the ways that an individual designer with their unique perspective affect this adoption, and the role and affect of the individual designer in this adoption.

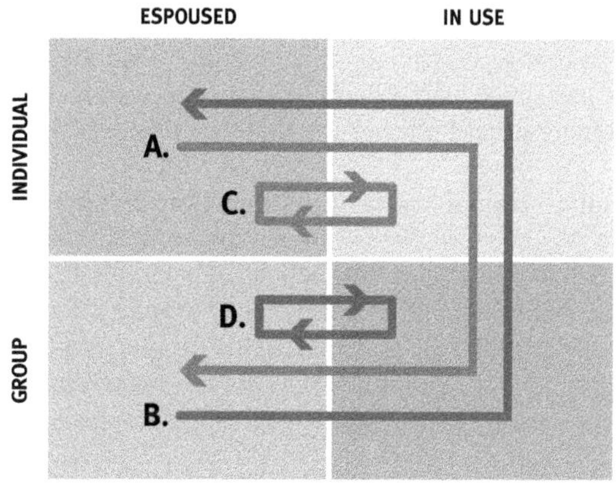

Figure 2. Schema describing the flow of competence.

A set of movements (Figure 2) will be explored in more depth through the case studies, but will briefly be described here. We propose four primary types of flow, two of which represent internal reflective actions on the part of an individual or group, reinforced through performance (C and D). Two other types of flow represent shifts in competence between an individual and group, representing how an individual designer might shift a group's way of thinking and acting (A) or how a company culture might alter an individual designer's sense of identity and practice (B). No interaction is represented directly between the individual-espoused and group-espoused quadrants, because we propose that all shifts in competence take place through performance of beliefs, as enacted through explicit action. In other words, no flow directly between an individual and group's mental state is possible; only enactment of one's espoused theory through language or action allows for change to occur.

THREE CASES OF UX ADOPTION

To facilitate a discussion of the initial competency schema, and the associated flow between quadrants, we present three different cases of competency and design leadership in UX practice. These cases demonstrate a range of UX adoption in the field from practitioners with two to five years of experience as interaction designers. A range of status of UX adoption and design culture can also be mapped, with two participants representing companies with a more design-inclusive or "design first" culture that has shifted over the past five years, and one representing a company that is just beginning the transition from an engineering dominated corporate culture.

For each case, relevant details about the individual designer and company will be presented. We will then discuss the kinds of individual competencies they bring to the company, ways they have shared competencies with others, and the ways they attempt to sustain their competence over time. Finally, we will highlight some of the flows of competence exemplified by each designer and company, demonstrating how they have impacted their corporate culture (or have been impacted) in terms of adoption of UX or design practices. This may include any ways their environment has shifted the way they practice design, and the kinds of activities that bridge or facilitate the flow of competence.

Evolution from a Nascent to Developed Design Culture

Peter has been employed by a large educational software and services company for the last five and a half years and works with a team of UX designers. He has a background in instructional design, and brings this perspective to his current work on technological systems for assignments and to-do lists used by high school students and teachers.

He has shifted from a process dominated by paper—including sketches, whiteboarding, and paper prototypes—to largely digital methods of production, using Adobe Fireworks, Adobe Ideas on the iPad, and use of the Twitter Bootstrap framework. Peter recently transitioned to a new framework, and uses a wide range of tools for collaboration, brainstorming, and other design activities.

Individual Competence

While Peter doesn't feel as competent as when he left his formal education, he thinks that beliefs of self-competence—often linked with his confidence as a designer—have been replaced by experience. "In place of that confidence has come so much experience that I can draw from, and that experience is what gives me the strength that I have to continue moving forward and progressing with my ideas." He doesn't rely on his primary job to fill his needs to sustain or build competence, but rather builds these abilities through side projects with fewer political agendas to address, "work[ing] on things in the way he thinks it is appropriate."

To stay current, he reads blogs and books, and tries to stay aware of new technologies and applications, trends in visual design, and newer methodologies for user control. Much of this awareness is accomplished through a network of fellow professionals in his home city, who hang out at a "speakeasy" which Peter describes as a "moose lodge for designers and developers." He also locates materials through Twitter, and the broader community—"the world around us"—not just relying on fellow designers to get inspiration. He tries to reflect on his changes in competence over time, engaging in outside projects to keep a balanced perspective.

Sharing of Competence

Recently, Peter's company has hired a Chief Experience Officer (CXO) to oversee design processes and create a new culture of design. Although this is currently the most dominant force in moving a design culture forward, individual efforts within the company go back to when Peter first started as an employee.

When he was hired, he was the only professionally trained designer, and had to work with others who only knew how to copy existing interaction exemplars; he wanted them to be able to not only copy existing materials, but also to understand why they worked. Since he felt an inability to directly teach these skills, he followed the path of his formal education, and asked several of his colleagues to read Don Norman's book *The Design of Everyday Things*, with an eye toward implications for design. This effort started the process toward creating a culture of design conversation in his department, and ultimately "pushed a desire in people to know more than they did previously." This grassroots work to create a design culture eventually coincided with shifts in the executive team, resulting in the hiring of a CXO, the development of cross-functional teams, and ultimately, more opportunities for collaboration.

Flow of Competence

The company Peter works for has gone through a dramatic transformation in the past five years, due in part to the design community he helped to create, in conjunction with high-level executive changes. In this way, we see a flow initiated by the company (B and D) in response to shifts brought about by individual designers like Peter (A). While this was not a fully coordinated transition to a top-down design culture, there was awareness by the incoming CXO that a design community already existed, and the CXO chose to validate that community in important ways.

Peter saw a significant link between his UX competence and his confidence as a designer, which may have reinforced this transition to a design culture. This was manifest through conversations with individuals and a willingness to engage the lack of an existing design culture, both on a personal level (C) and as an impact on the group he worked with (A). Peter reflects on the delicate balance of impacting an organization while also recognizing your own personal limitations and blind spots:

> *[Confidence and competence] quite literally go hand in hand.* [...] *when I came out of school, my realistic competence level should have been [lower], and I was way up here [higher]* [...] *and I pissed people off. I'd get into these conversations with people and really*

> *push the envelope, saying 'you know what, we aren't meeting the needs that the users have' and all of the things that you know are true. [...] competence comes in when you understand why it's not possible."*

Designing in an Engineering Culture

Martin has been employed by a large technology company for the last year as an Interactive Design Engineer. His title belies the engineering focus of the company, even as they have made substantial shifts toward implementing design practices in the last five years. Prior to joining this company, Martin worked in a research laboratory, a startup, and completed an internship with the same technology company with which he is now employed.

In his work, Martin focuses on "pure interaction design wireframes," with no substantial user research or responsibility for the implementation of design or problem scoping on a larger scale. These wireframes focus on "feature level design" including labels, error messaging, and other interaction. He works with three other designers in a non-management capacity; these other designers come from a print or visual design background, and he feels that they generally fall into the "classic pitfalls of interaction design" due to their lack of experience in more strategic design roles. He does feel that his coworkers are good visual designers, but "unfortunately, we don't do any visual design."

Individual Competence

Martin uses a variety of methods to maintain competence in his work environment, including: reading professional blogs, interviewing with other companies, and networking with designers across his company in informal contexts. He has a "set of blogs that [he] look[s] at everyday at lunchtime"—with blogs ranging from UXBooth to UX Matters to Smashing Magazine, representing a "broad pulse on different components of what I do." There are a number of pockets of designers in the company, but little organizational structure to tie them together. Because of this distance between groups, designers "are making efforts to reach out to other design groups and discuss process and find common ground" through "fireside chats" held every Friday, which are open to all designers in the company. This is a more recent phenomenon, with one of Martin's colleagues responsible for getting it started the month prior to our interview. They use this time to do "design decompression" and bring materials to critique or talk about.

Martin brings a strong competence in systems thinking to his team, which is beneficial because the company "design[s] with a lot of elements or components or attributes" which are complex and "carry a lot of embedded meaning." This competency is not share with his other team members, who are unable to "weave a golden thread through all of the components in a particular assembly." He also adds an ability to understand and communicate critique and feedback to a variety of stakeholders, using his more systemic view of design to manage the overall design of a product.

Sharing of Competence

Martin actively shares his individual competence with his group of coworkers, and is also working with local designers in an IXDA chapter that is in the process of starting up. In the department where he works, "one of the biggest challenges [...] is that [his] manager has no idea what UX is." As a result, he has taken it upon himself to share materials with his colleagues, including books and articles from blogs he reads. He has also begun to mentor one of his colleagues in a more specific way, directing her towards a MOOC on UX offered by Stanford, and through a weekly meeting to "critique her work and give her a better understanding of HCI principles." He also sends out bi-monthly "Cliff's Notes" on UX methods, "trying to get the team a better understanding of the different avenues we could employ to improve our work." His work is also evident in the formation of a local IXDA chapter, which helps Martin further his competence—promoting design activities outside of the narrow constraints of his workplace. He feels that it is "important to have a wide variety of projects [...] to keep yourself sharp and thinking appropriately," and that he is actively concerned about keeping a "contemporary process."

Flow of Competence

The company where Martin works is actively going through a transition to a more designerly culture. He notes they are "very open" to this transition—an openness to flow from individual to organizational competence (A)—but they are also unsure how to promote organizational change:

> *"Their approach is—we know we need you, but we also need you to teach us what you do and we need you to teach us how to facilitate what you do. It's a lot of education to stakeholders about what it is you do because no one here really knows about it. It's very distributed and I don't think they can look at it from the same position that someone like myself can look at it and see that all the pieces are there and everything is going on but it's just fragmented, it's a little bit disjointed."*

Even while Martin's company is open to change, he reports that he has changed his approach to design "drastically" since joining the company last year—a shift in individual competence based on the espoused and in use theory of the organization (B). Many of his colleagues have worked at the organization for 20-25 years, and "it took [him] a long time to trust them and trust the information and rationale they provided, because they were not explicitly validated or justified." Over time, he learned to "[stop] asking those questions and rely on a little bit more faith. Whether it's right or wrong really isn't in my control. I had to let go of that." This evolution has affected his individual identity as a designer, showing a flow from organizational to individual competence (B), and an iterative reshaping of process between espoused and in use competence (C).

Ultimately, this shift in company culture affects everyone—both designers and engineers. Martin explains "there are a lot of career, highly decorated engineers that now have to deal with people telling them how to design their product, and it's challenging." While this shift is happening on the individual level, there is also a lack of direction organizationally, because "a lot of employers out there don't know what they need. They have no idea how to evaluate a designer's skills in order to assess the compatibility of that designer for that position." Martin has come to the conclusion that "the responsibility is on the designer to fit themselves with the business, rather than the business trying to fit a designer, and find one that fits them," clearly privileging competence moving from the organization to the individual (B) rather than altering the organization himself (A).

Pushing Design Culture Forward

Joel works for a small software company that creates solutions for non-profit organizations, and has worked as a UX Manager for the last five and a half years. Currently, his work is primarily management focused, with design tasks including concepting, direction, and prototyping. The company has grown significantly since he joined the company, with more geographic distribution of employees, and over 100% growth in headcount. Joel works directly with six individuals in a team, including management.

Because Joel's work focuses on management and direction of tasks, he relies on ways to quickly communicate to his team members: "Sketching boxes and arrows. [...] It's meant to convey a concept so you can get that in front of users immediately." He also frequently creates quick paper prototypes or digital wireframes in Fireworks, but ultimately does research "by showing people sketches" along with more established methods like contextual inquiry.

Individual Competence

Joel uses a number of different strategies to stay competent over time, including regularly visiting professional blogs, exploring and "doing stuff," and focusing on a subset of skills within the broader context of UX. He reads a wide range of blogs, including Smashing Magazine and UX Matters, following the death or slower production of articles from powerhouses like A List Apart or Boxes and Arrows. But he is "more curious about what people are doing outside of design," looking at psychology, information architecture—things "we can learn from in UX, rather than focusing solely on UX. The UX community tends to be an echo chamber, and if you don't try to go outside of that, you're probably doing yourself a disservice in terms of education." Joel also focuses on actively exploring to learn new things: "The way they learn a prototype [...] is to have a project that forces you to learn the things you need to learn"—this is not accomplished through a lot of training or reading books but "just start doing stuff." Finally, Joel focuses on a small subset of the overall discipline of UX as he sees it. UX might have a dozen different facets, including: research, visual design, interaction design, information architecture, translation to stakeholders, strategy, etc. This diversity is "part of what makes UX an interesting field" and allows him to recognize where his interests are, so he can build those skills further. He is more focused on this holistic notion of his design identity as a UX designer rather than defining himself by specific tools or abilities: "UX designers can learn a tool like Axure in a weekend. I like to just be aware of what's out there instead of know how to use all of the tools."

Sharing of Competence

Joel has focused on sharing informal knowledge about his craft with colleagues since he began working at this company, and runs a "cultural initiative" to do education within the company, which focuses on swapping skills between those who have them and others that need them. He began this initiative around five years ago "because the design team here was terrible and we didn't have interaction designers." This education initiative was initially a move of self-preservation to "keep people from saying we don't want interaction designers," but has since grown into a design culture with rapport between colleagues. Beyond this more formal cultural initiative, Joel also created an informal blog to share interesting readings and tools—this blog was originally begun five years ago, but has been especially active as the design culture has increased in the last two and a half years. The company also provides a framework for sharing and building competence outside of the formal design environment, hosting an "off the grid" day a couple of times each year, where teams can "design and build and QA a feature of their own choosing."

Overall, Joel has led in the building of competence by example, focusing on collaboration, communication, and active reflection on process, and continually "espousing these values to [his] team." The most substantial message that he tries to communicate to his colleague as he helps them increase their competence is that you have to be "utterly confident about what you're doing while at the same time willing to admit that you're completely wrong."

Flow of Competence

While this company may have started as less design or UX-friendly, Joel has actively worked to shift the culture of the organization with a remarkable level of success. Instead of a gradual evolution toward design culture in UX, he pushed the company by redefining what UX could offer them, and "change has happened pretty quickly." In this way, the primary flow is from individual to group competence (A) with a substantial component of individual and group reflection (C and D) to bring about lasting change.

Joel accomplished this shift by initially "refus[ing] to do things [he] didn't think were interaction design," working with a team to help his colleagues understand the value of UX and his approach:

> *"I could either leave or I could make the best of it.* [...] *Looking back at it now, it seems kind of ballsy, 'cause*

> *now that I'm at this point in my career, it looks like I had a chip on my shoulder. The key to doing things like this is always to be tactful.* [...] *I'm not going to do this, but what I can offer you is this other thing that's hopefully going to get you to the same place."*

He focused on not only building UX competency within the organization and helping his colleagues understand the value he could bring to products, but also on building collegiality amongst his team—"The rapport you have with your team is one of the most unsung aspects of software development." This was a challenge, since his manager "initially [...] didn't understand what the field was about" and he had created a few enemies along the way. But in the last two years, two new vice presidents have joined the company who were sympathetic to Joel's perspective, and as a result, "our whole understanding of the discipline is so much better. [...] Having those people has really been integral to helping me push that agenda forward." In this way, Joel was able to focus on moving expectations of UX competence on several group levels (A), as well as helping to create a lasting reflective conversation within the company about the value of these new approaches (D)

Lasting change has happened in the company, and colleagues have started to approach UX in a positive manner. Joel relates an experience going out with his manager for a beer recently, where the manager said: "When you used to talk about UX, I thought you were full of shit. But now I actually believe what you do is valuable." The value to the organization was the most important factor: "results are what's important, because what they see is better products and they see customers that are happy, and they say, you know what, it wasn't just about giving them these features, it was that these features were designed well and we gave them the right things." This push results in often having to "fight to make sure your designs are implemented as you designed them" and constantly selling your approach (A). Early on, he was able to push designs through to show successes, but "lost a lot of battles" in the process (B).

DISCUSSION

As we have explored three specific implementations of UX, using our preliminary schema (Figures 1 and 2) to map the flow of competence between individuals and groups, there are a number of emergent issues relating to UX adoption that are important to discuss further.

Design Leadership in UX

As Nelson and Stolterman point out, "leadership [...] is an essential element of any design culture" [16]. In the context of UX, this design culture does not autonomously spring to life in a company. Formation of a design culture requires persistence on the part of an individual designer (or a group of designers)—an effort to promote UX practices to stakeholders and/or management. Over time, and sometimes in synchrony with changes in executive perspectives, a design or UX culture can take root, as in these case studies, but establishing this culture can be quite difficult, and can take several years and a confluence of factors to begin to thrive.

Design leadership also includes efforts to upskill designers that are already in place, and in the cases described here, this was where the process began—in creating a shared design culture among colleagues. Since many practicing UX designers were trained in other areas, or migrate into jobs that have a partial UX role, there seems to be a significant element of on-the-job training that facilitates sharing of a core set of skills. In these cases, it was less about tool knowledge (e.g., wireframing) and more about creating empathy with the user, strategically transferring that perspective into designs that could be communicated to stakeholders. Educating both colleagues and the stakeholders about the capabilities of UX, and building competencies for delivery and sustainment of UX principles appears to be key to a culture of UX taking hold.

Factors Affecting UX Adoption

There are a number of factors that stand out as important to UX adoption, based on traversing flow in our preliminary schema, exemplified through these three case studies. All participants found success through a dual strategy of actively evangelizing UX practices to stakeholders, while also teaching these practices to their colleagues. In parallel with these strategies to share competence with their team or company, there were also ways these individual designers maintained and increased their competence: reading professional blogs and books, attending conferences, finding opportunities to practice "blue sky" design and encourage creativity and innovation outside of their normal work constraints. There was also a powerful component of these designers' activities relating to communication and articulating UX practices in a form palatable and/or understandable to key stakeholders or executives. Success in translating engineering cultural norms into UX cultural norms or demonstrating the effectiveness of UX practices through successful projects seemed to be key in creating a shared conversation, and ultimately, a fledgling design culture.

Flow of Competency

Both design leadership and factors surrounding UX adoption can be framed within our preliminary schema (Figures 1 and 2) as a flow between stakeholders and an individual designer, and along a temporal dimension as well. When we are able to understand how competence shifts along these dimensions, both internally to a designer and externally to a larger group (with all of the component movements between states that are implied), we will have a greater understanding of UX competence *in situ* [14], which will lead to documentation of effective adoption strategies.

As we continue to address the development of competency, often discussed in an educational framing, and sustainment of competence, often carried out in a professional setting, looking at how these competencies are *performed* can be instructive. In particular, it is vital to address the latent states between performance and adoption, especially where beliefs and actions are incompatible or in tension. This underlines the importance of understanding an individual designer's identity, and how that development occurs in tandem with their surrounding corporate culture [13], and how this development might indicate flow of competence bidirectionally [14]. Additionally, the experiences of the participants we described promotes ongoing reflection, often on a metacognitive level, about design practice. This reflective conversation allows for beliefs (espoused theory) and performative action (theory-in-use) to become more aligned, both on the individual and group level. This framing of competence as a flow over time and between individuals and organizations opens up a wide range of future work for HCI researchers, including exploration of successful UX adoption strategies, methods for informally and formally educating practitioners, and successful approaches to articulate design concepts or issues to non-designers.

CONCLUSION

We have introduced a way of reframing the idea of UX competence within the context of corporate adoption, focusing on the experience of the individual designer, and the potential impact a sharing and shift in competence over time can have on the organization and the individual designer. Our preliminary schema allows us to trace the flow of competence between the dimensions of time, group/individual, and espoused/in use, focusing on the performative aspects of competence as a form of design leadership. The schema allows for additional discourse on these key tensions between individual and organizational competency, informing future research by enabling a better understanding of the practice community.

REFERENCES

1. Argyris, C. and Schön, D.A. *Theory in practice: Increasing professional effectiveness.* Jossey-Bass Publishers, San Francisco, 1974.
2. Arvola, M. and Artman, H. Studio life: The construction of digital design competence. *Digital Kompetanse 3,* 2 (2008), 78-96.
3. Bærentsen, K.B. and Slavensky, H. A contribution to the Design Process. *Comm. of the ACM 42,* 5 (1999), 72-77.
4. Bødker, S., Ehn, P., Sjögren, D. and Sundblad, Y. Co-operative design —Perspectives on 20 years with 'the Scandinavian IT Design Model'. *Proc. NordiCHI,* (2000), 22-24.
5. Buur, J. and Bødker, S. From usability lab to "design collaboratorium": Reframing usability practice. *Proc. DIS*, ACM (2000), 297-307.
6. Cooper, A. *The inmates are running the asylum.* Pearson Education, Indianapolis, IN, 2004.
7. Fabricant, R. Scaling your UX Strategy. Harvard Business Review, 2013, January 7. Retrieved from http://blogs.hbr.org/2013/01/scaling-your-ux-strategy/
8. Friedland, L., Innes, J., Longoria, R., Hom, W., Henry, P. and Anderson, R. Outsourcing & offshoring: Impact on the user experience. *Proc. CHI*, ACM (2005), 1170-1171.
9. Futt, Y.S. and Rasid, H. *Meta Design.* 2011, May. 156-159. Retrieved from http://www.ideo.com/images/uploads/news/pdfs/Designare.pdf
10. Glaser, B.G. and Strauss, A.L. *The discovery of grounded theory: Strategies for qualitative research.* Alpine de Gruyter, New York, 1967.
11. Gobert, D., Howlett, V., Snyder, C., Tamler, H., Tullis, T.S. and Wilson, C. What the best usability specialists are made of. *Proc. CHI*, ACM (2002), 706-707.
12. Governor, J. On The Importance of Design at IBM: Love and Margins. 2013, January 7. Retrieved from http://redmonk.com/jgovernor/2013/01/07/on-the-importance-of-design-at-ibm-love-and-margins/
13. Gray, C.M. Evolution of Design Competence in UX Practice. *Proc. CHI'14,* ACM (2014), 1645-2654.
14. Gray, C.M., Stolterman, E. and Siegel, M.A. Reprioritizing the Relationship Between HCI Research and Practice: Bubble-Up and Trickle-Down Effects. *Proc. DIS'14,* ACM (2014), 725-734.
15. Holmlid, S. and Arvola, M. 2007. Developing a thematic design curriculum as a Bologna master. *International Conference on Engineering and Product Design Education* (2007), 13-14.
16. Nelson, H.G. and Stolterman, E. *The design way: Intentional change in an unpredictable world.* MIT Press, Cambridge, 2012.
17. Nieminen, M.P., Runonen, M., Nieminen, M. and Tyllinen, M. Designer experience: Exploring ways to design in experience. *Proc. CHI*, ACM (2011), 2449-2452.
18. Olsson, E. What active users and designers contribute in the design process. *Interacting with computers 16,* 2 (2004), 377-401.
19. Rychen, D.S. and Salganik, L.H. A holistic model of competence. In *Key competencies for a successful life and a well-functioning society.* Hogrefe & Huber, Göttingen, Germany, 2003, 41-62.
20. Szóstek, A. A look into some practices behind Microsoft UX management. *Proc. CHI*, ACM (2012), 605-618.
21. Thompson, C.F., Anderson, R.I., Au, I., Ratzlaff, C. and Zada, N. Managing user experience: Managing change. *Proc. CHI*, ACM (2010), 3143-3146.
22. Yin, R.K. *Case study research: Design and methods.* Sage Publications, Los Angeles, Calif., 2009.
23. Weinert, F.E. Concept of competence: A conceptual clarification. In D.S. Rychen and L.A. Salganik, editor, *Defining and selecting key competencies.* Hogrefe & Huber, Seattle, WA, 2001, 45-66

Usees

Eric P. S. Baumer
Communication Department and Information Science Department
118 Gates Hall, Ithaca, NY 14853, USA
Cornell University
ericpsb@cornell.edu

ABSTRACT
HCI has developed a powerful vocabulary for thinking about, and methods for engaging with, users. Similarly, recent work has advanced complementary understanding of technology non-use. However, other spaces of interaction with technology may occur that sit uncomfortably between these two poles. This paper presents two case studies highlighting individuals who neither are clearly users of a system nor are clearly non-users. Based on these cases, the paper develops the concept of *usee* to help account for such situations that lie between existing analytic categories.

Author Keywords
Users; non-use; usees.

ACM Classification Keywords
H.5.m. Information interfaces and presentation (e.g., HCI): Miscellaneous. K.4.m Computers and society: Miscellaneous.

BETWEEN USE AND NON-USE
Users are the heart of HCI. A user is "an individual or group" who "uses [a] software product to perform a specific function" and "benefits from a system during its utilization" [9,10]. From user-centered design to usability testing, the user dominates both the practice and discourse of HCI, and numerous approaches have considered how (best) to engage with users [e.g., 1,13].

However, the very notion of "the user" introduces certain conceptual complexities. For instance, Cooper and Bowers [3] analyze how the user developed as a rhetorical strategy, a means of justifying the existence of HCI as a discipline while simultaneously differentiating in from related disciplines, such as computer science and cognitive psychology. Redström [15] argues that "the user" is in some senses a fiction created during the design process. In this way, user-centered design moves away from designing the object—its form, its function, its materials—and toward designing the user—defining (and at times unnecessarily constraining) the behaviors, practices, and experiences of engaging with a particular design. Woolgar [20] documents how various elements of design practice—from insistence that "real" users participate in usability trials, to warning labels exhorting users not to open a computer's case, to the documentation accompanying computer software—work to define and constrain how "proper" users (should) act. That is, these practices collectively "configure the user."

In contrast, recent work has proposed focusing specifically on technology non-use. Such work inverts the traditional focus on users, drawing attention to everything from the digital divide and technological disenfranchisement [e.g., 22] to voluntary refusal of technology [e.g., 2,17]. Doing so provides the opportunity to think more broadly about how design decisions may carry implications beyond immediate users of a technology [16].

Thus, HCI possesses well-developed vocabularies for thinking about both users and non-users of the technologies we design. However, some work on non-use suggests that a clear distinction between user and non-user belies the complex nature of the engagements in which people and technologies participate [2,16,21]. Indeed, situations may arise that fit neither in our definitions of "user" (see above) nor in established categories of non-use, such as active resistance, disinterest, or exclusion [16,21].

This paper's core contribution, then, is the provision and development of the term *usees* as an analytic means of accounting for one particular type of interaction between humans and computational systems that lies in the liminal area between use and non-use. Etymologically, the –ee suffix transforms transitive verbs into "nouns which denote a person who is the object [...] of the act specified by the verb" [23]. An "employee" is employed by someone. A "grantee" is granted something. A "fiancée" is affianced to someone. Similarly, a "usee" is, in at least some sense, used by a computational or technological system.

This paper develops this concept with two case studies. In each, it shows how some individual or group of individuals neither is well accounted for under the traditional umbrella of users nor fits cleanly into categories of non-users. It then describes how the notion of usees helps us account for these individuals in a way not previously analytically possible. Not only can this analytic approach help us escape a

CHI 2015, April 18 - 23 2015, Seoul, Republic of Korea

ACM 978-1-4503-3145-6/15/04…$15.00
http://dx.doi.org/10.1145/2702123.2702147

potentially myopic focus on "the user," it also advances our thinking about the myriad ways in which the technologies we design intersect with people's lives.

CASE STUDIES

This section presents two cases where neither definitions of user [9,10] nor definitions of non-user [16,21] account well for an observed relationship with technology. The following section synthesizes across them to draw out commonalities and articulate a definition of what constitutes a usee.

Girls Around Me

> *[G]eo-social discovery is the future of mobile web and applications, [...] sharing interests, finding new people or cool venues is a good thing.*[1]

When the iPhone app Girls Around Me loads, the user is greeted with a map-based interface. On it are shown profile photos of Foursquare users who have recently checked in near by. By default the application shows only female users, but it can also be configured to show only male users or all users. If any of those Foursquare users has linked their Facebook profile, the Girls Around Me user can click on the photo to see whatever information is publicly available on her or his Facebook profile—full name, birthdate, relationship status, high school attended, political affiliation, as well as any other publicly visible photos. Ostensibly, this functionality enables the Girls Around Me user to make a more informed choice about which venues to attend during a night out. However, media coverage depicts it as "a hook-up app [...] for potential stalkers and date rapists"[2]. This is perhaps unsurprising given the developers' own description:

> *In the mood for love, or just after a one-night stand? Girls Around Me puts you in control! [...] Browse photos of lovely local ladies.* [http://girlsaround.me]

Indeed, a wave of negative media led in part to Foursquare revoking the app's API access, effectively rendering it non-functional. As a result, i-Free, the developers of the app, subsequently pulled it from the Apple App Store.

This app and the story around it touch on such diverse concerns as privacy, surveillance, gender, personal data, responsibility (both personal and corporate), and others. Previous work has suggested that Girls Around Me exposes some of the complex interdependencies among policy, design, and practice [11]. While certainly a valuable line of inquiry, this paper instead considers the problems this story poses for the category of "user." Specifically, how do we account for the women (and men) whose information is displayed in the app? It is difficult to argue that they use Girls Around Me "to perform a specific function" [9] or that they "benefit from [the] system during its utilization" [10]. Thus, they should likely not be seen as users.

Classifying them as non-users who reject or are excluded from a technology [21] proves similarly unsatisfying. Satchell and Dourish [16] do provide for a type of non-use where individuals may be affected by, but might not come in direct contact with, a technology. Displacement involves one person indirectly making use of a technology through another person who acts as mediator. For example, rural villages may have only a single telephone, in which case one resident becomes designated as operator and relays messages to others. Indirection arguably plays a role in Girls Around Me, though not of the kind described in Satchell and Dourish's notion of displacement. Thus, prior work provides limited conceptual vocabulary for analyzing these kinds of relationships with technology.

Target-ed Advertising

Many daily purchasing decisions—soap, trashbags, toothpaste—are made based on habit, rendering advertising for those items fairly ineffective. However, marketers argue, there are particular life events around which "shopping patterns and brand loyalties are up for grabs" [5]. These events include, among others, moving to a new house, getting married, and, most notably, having a baby.

To gain a competitive edge, retailers need to know not just that a couple has *had* a baby but when they are *going to* have a baby. That is, they must detect and predict pregnancy. By analyzing shopping patterns, a team of data analysts working for the retail corporation Target were able to identify "about 25 products that, when analyzed together, allowed [them] to assign each shopper a 'pregnancy prediction' score. [Moreover, they] could also estimate her due date within a small window, so Target could send coupons timed to very specific stages of her pregnancy" [5].

> *[A] man walked into a Target outside Minneapolis and demanded to see the manager. He was clutching coupons that had been sent to his daughter, and he was angry [...]. "My daughter got this in the mail!" he said. "She's still in high school, and you're sending her coupons for baby clothes and cribs? Are you trying to encourage her to get pregnant?"*
>
> *[...] The manager apologized and then called a few days later to apologize again. On the phone, though, the father was somewhat abashed. "I had a talk with my daughter," he said. "It turns out there's been some activities in my house I haven't been completely aware of. She's due in August. I owe you an apology."* [5]

As with the previous case, numerous points could be made here about privacy, data analysis, gender, modernism, corporate strategy, etc. However, how do current conceptual

[1] http://www.cultofmac.com/158764/developers-behind-girls-around-me-stalking-app-explain-themselves-exclusive-interview/

[2] http://www.cultofmac.com/157641/this-creepy-app-isnt-just-stalking-women-without-their-knowledge-its-a-wake-up-call-about-facebook-privacy/

and theoretical frameworks account for the woman whose pregnancy was identified?

As above, she is not a user of this technology in the traditional sense. While some benefits [10] might be derived from the targeted coupons that customers receive, these customers almost certainly are not "us[ing] the software product to perform a specific function" [9]. Indeed, these customers likely remain largely if not entirely unaware of the system and its functioning.

Also as above, this woman is not a non-user. She may have availed herself of the tailored coupons sent to her. Her purchases may even become data that help shape and further refine future predictive analyses. Indeed, becoming a non-user of such corporate data-mining schemes can prove exceedingly difficult [19]. Thus, existing analytic categories prove unsatisfying at describing this relationship.

WHAT MAKES A USEE?

To fill this gap, the term *usee* designates the liminal space between use and non-use depicted in these case studies. The following definition draws inspiration from the sociology and philosophy of technology, particularly the agency of artifacts [12,14,18], power and knowledge [4,6], and the relationship between technology and human nature [4,8]. Rather than encompass every situation in which someone may be "used" by technology, the term serves a fairly specific analytic purpose: to help account for a current blind spot in our reasoning about interactions between humans and computers. Synthesizing across the two case studies, this section posits three criteria for what counts as a usee, each of which may occur in varying degrees.

Targeting

First, an individual is a usee when s/he (or information about her or him) is *explicitly targeted* by a technological system. In technical terms, this means that the system leverages some representation of the individual or her or his identity. Such individual targeting is readily apparent in the case of Target-ed advertising. "Target assigns each shopper a unique code — known internally as the Guest ID number" [5], allowing the retailer to maintain a persistent representation of each individual and her or his shopping record. Degrees of targeting may also occur. For example, Girls Around Me does not store permanent records about any person, but it still targets and aggregates information about specific individuals.

As a corollary, not anyone and everyone affected by a technology could or should be considered a usee. For example, a handrail on a staircase may influence our perceptions of safety [15], but the handrail does not explicitly target its user or maintain an internal representation of those perceptions. Thus, the targeting criterion focuses us on cases in which a technology is directed *at* an individual or a class of individuals.

(un)Awareness

Second, a usee has *limited awareness of the system* or knowledge that it is targeting her or him. In the case of Girls Around Me, the Foursquare users whose information was shown were (likely) aware that they were sharing their current location. They were similarly (likely) aware of the personal information they shared on Facebook. However, based on the reactions described in the media [see 11], most people were not aware that these data were being aggregated by this application in this particular way.

As with targeting, (un)awareness may occur in varying degrees; usees need not be completely oblivious. The young woman who was identified by Target's data mining system as being pregnant may have been aware that the corporation tracked and analyzed her purchasing patterns. However, she likely did not know that it would draw conclusions about her status as a parent-to-be, let alone make product solicitations or suggestions based on those conclusions. Indeed, "as long as a pregnant woman thinks she hasn't been spied on, she'll use the coupons. […] As long as [Target data analysts] don't spook her, it works." Compare this with someone using, e.g., a personal informatics or persuasive technology system. In those cases, the person is (usually) aware that the technology is targeting, tracking, and potentially attempting to influence, their behavior. Usees, on the other hand, do not really know the full extent of the technological systems in which they are embroiled.

(lack of) Consent

Third, to be a usee of a system, the system must do things with the individual's data to which s/he *did not knowingly consent* and to which, given the option, s/he would not likely consent. For example, a Foursquare user may not know all the details of the rules and metrics by which badges are awarded, but it seems unlikely that s/he would object to such analyses of her or his data. On the other hand, the woman in the second case study would almost certainly object to the targeted advertising of which her father became the recipient.

Unlike the other two criteria, determining (the degree of) consent with certainty may not be analytically feasible. For instance, we cannot know whether every Foursquare user *would* consent to Girls Around Me's use of their data, but we do know that such consent was neither sought nor given.

IMPLICATIONS

The groups identified above do not use the systems described to perform specific functions that benefit them [9,10]. They are neither excluded nor expelled, resistors nor rejectors [21]. They are neither lagging adopters, disenfranchised, disenchanted, nor disinterested [16]. The vocabulary proposed here helps account for these cases that sit uneasily between established poles of use and non-use.

These cases might be seen as simply technologically-mediated exercises of power. While the analysis here does not preclude such a reading, *usee* still acts as a beneficial concept for two reasons. First, viewing these as situations of technical control [cf. 6] draws attention to those acting from positions of power, providing less analytic vocabulary for the individuals on whom that power is exercised. Second, far from being exceptional, situations of this nature are likely to become more common. Algorithmically-driven systems similar to Target's advertising scheme pervade ever greater aspects of everyday life [7], not all of which carry explicitly negative moral and ethical connotations. Search engines may optimize their results based on individual browsing history. Healthcare providers may mine individual data to develop incentive mechanisms that encourage seeking preventative care. In fact, such situations suggest that users and usees may not be mutually exclusive. Future work should develop more fully how such concepts build on and extend theorizing of human-computer relationships [4,6,8,12]. This paper provides conceptual language to help begin to grapple with the nature and ramifications of these emergent sociotechnical configurations.

Furthermore, "usee" captures just one such type of interaction. A variety of other category-challenging relationships may occur between use and non-use. Current analytic approaches to such relationships can implicitly reinforce existing power dynamics [6,20], limit the disciplinary configurations possible in HCI [3], and gloss over differences between success for immediate users and secondary or tertiary repercussions of design [15]. Empirical studies giving voice to the subjective experiences of such liminal groups will prove essential in developing, and probing the limits of, these novel analytic categories. Indeed, not developing such conceptual vocabulary risks leaving us with an incomplete and inaccurate understanding of how exactly HCI technologies affect, and are affected by, the social worlds in which they are enmeshed.

ACKNOWLEDGMENTS
This material is based in part upon work supported by the NSF under Grant No. IIS-1421498. Thanks to Steve Jackson, the Interaction Design Lab, and the anonymous reviewers for constructive comments.

REFERENCES
1. Abras, C., Maloney-Krichmar, D., and Preece, J. User-Centered Design. In W. Bainbridge, ed., *Encyc. of Human-Comput. Interact*. Sage, Thousand Oaks, 2004.
2. Baumer, E.P.S., Adams, P., Khovanskaya, V., et al. Limiting, Leaving, and (re)Lapsing: A Survey of Facebook Non-use Practices and Experiences. *Proc CHI*, (2013), 3257–3266.
3. Cooper, G. and Bowers, J. Representing the User: Notes on the Disciplinary Rhetoric of HCI. In P.J. Thomas, ed., *The social and interact. dimensions of human-comput. interfaces*. Cambridge Press, Cambridge, 1995, 48–66.
4. Dreyfus, H.L. Being and Power: Heidegger and Foucault. *Int'l J of Philosophical Studies 4*, 1 (1996), 1–16.
5. Duhigg, C. How Companies Learn Your Secrets. *The New York Times Magazine*, 2012.
6. Foucault, M. *Discipline and Punish: The Birth of the Prison*. Random House, New York, 1977.
7. Gillespie, T. The Relevance of Algorithms. In T. Gillespie, P. Bockzkowski and K. Foot, eds., *Media Technologies*. MIT Press, Cambridge, MA, 2013.
8. Heidegger, M. *The Question Concerning Technology*. Harper & Row, New York, 1977.
9. ISO/IEC. 9126-1:2001 Software engineering -- Product quality -- Part 1: Quality model. 2001.
10. ISO/IEC. 15939:2007 Systems and software engineering -- Measurement process. 2007.
11. Jackson, S.J., Gillespie, T., and Payette, S. The Policy Knot: Re-integrating Policy, Practice and Design in CSCW Studies of Social Computing. *Proc CSCW*, (2014).
12. Latour, B. Where are the Missing Masses? The Sociology of a Few Mundane Artifacts. In W.E. Bijker and J. Law, eds., *Shaping Technology / Building Society*. MIT Press, Cambridge, MA, 1992, 225–258.
13. Muller, M.J. and Druin, A. Participatory Design: The Third Space in HCI. In J. Jacko, ed., *Human-Comput. Interact. Handbook*. Erlbaum, Hillsdale, NJ, 2012, 1–70.
14. Pickering, A. The Mangle of Practice: Agency and Emergence in the Sociology of Science. *Amer J of Sociology 99*, 3 (1993), 559–589.
15. Redström, J. Towards user design? On the shift from object to user as the subject of design. *Design Studies 27*, 2 (2006), 123–139.
16. Satchell, C. and Dourish, P. Beyond the user: use and non-use in HCI. *Proc OZCHI*, ACM (2009), 9–16.
17. Schoenebeck, S.Y. Giving up Twitter for Lent: How and Why We Take Breaks from Social Media. *Proc CHI*, (2014), 773–782.
18. Verbeek, P.-P. *What Things Do*. Penn State University Press, University Park, PA, 2005.
19. Vertesi, J. My Experiment Opting Out of Big Data Made Me Look Like a Criminal. *Time*, 2014.
20. Woolgar, S. Configuring the user: the case of usability trials. In J. Law, ed., *A Sociology of Monsters*. Routledge, London, 1991, 58–99.
21. Wyatt, S. Non-Users Also Matter: The Construction of Users and Non-Users of the Internet. In N. Oudshoorn and T. Pinch, eds., *How Users Matter*. MIT Press, Cambridge, MA, 2003, 67–79.
22. Wyche, S.P., Schoenebeck, S.Y., and Forte, A. "Facebook is a Luxury": An Exploratory Study of Social Media Use in Rural Kenya. *Proc CSCW*, (2013), 33–43.
23. -ee. *Dictionary.com Unabridged*.

Author Index

www.ingramcontent.com/pod-product-compliance
Ingram Content Group UK Ltd.
Pitfield, Milton Keynes, MK11 3LW, UK
UKHW051417290926
15471UKWH00009B/1654

9 781450 337762